THE ULTIMATE

Southern Living

COOKBOOK

THE ULTIMATE
Southern Living
COOKBOOK

Compiled and Edited by

Julie Fisher Gunter

Foreword by

Kaye Mabry Adams

Oxmoor House®

WE'RE HERE FOR YOU!

We at Oxmoor House are dedicated to serving you with reliable information that expands your imagination and enriches your life. We welcome your comments and suggestions. Please write us at:

Oxmoor House, Inc.
Editor, *The Ultimate Southern Living® Cookbook*
2100 Lakeshore Drive
Birmingham, AL 35209

To order additional publications, call 1-205-877-6560.

For more books to enrich your life, visit
oxmoorhouse.com

WE WANT YOUR FAVORITE RECIPES!

Southern Living cooks are the best cooks of all, and we want your secrets! Please send your favorite original recipes for main dishes, desserts, and everything in between, along with any hands-on tips and a sentence about why you like each recipe. We can't guarantee we'll print them in a cookbook, but if we do, we'll send you $20 and a free copy of the cookbook. Send each recipe on a separate page with your name, address, and daytime phone number to:

Cookbook Recipes
Oxmoor House
2100 Lakeshore Drive
Birmingham, AL 35209

Cover: *Marble Rye Braid* (page 86)
Back Cover: *Fresh Mozzarella-Tomato-Basil Salad* (page 361), *Rosemary Focaccia* (page 91), *Shrimp Scampi* (page 220), *Crème Brûlée* (page 165)

Southern Living®

Executive Editor: Kaye Mabry Adams
Foods Editors: Elle Barrett, Susan Hawthorne Nash
Associate Foods Editors: Donna Florio, Denise Gee, Andria Scott Hurst
Assistant Foods Editors: Cynthia Briscoe, Monique Hicks, Diane Hogan, Peggy Smith, Patty M. Vann
Test Kitchens Director: Vanessa Taylor Johnson
Assistant Test Kitchens Director: Judy Feagin
Test Kitchens Staff: Vanessa A. McNeil, Margaret Monroe, Jan Jacks Moon, Mary Allen Perry, Vie Warshaw
Administrative Assistant: Wanda T. Stephens
Senior Foods Photographer: Charles Walton IV
Photographers: Ralph Anderson, Tina Cornett, William Dickey, J. Savage Gibson
Senior Photo Stylist: Cindy Manning Barr
Photo Stylists: Buffy Hargett, Mary Lyn H. Jenkins

Oxmoor House, Inc.

Editor-in-Chief: Nancy Fitzpatrick Wyatt
Senior Foods Editor: Susan Carlisle Payne
Senior Editor, Editorial Services: Olivia Kindig Wells
Art Director: James Boone

The Ultimate Southern Living® Cookbook

Foods Editor: Julie Fisher Gunter
Copy Editor: Donna Baldone
Associate Copy Editor: Keri Bradford Anderson
Associate Art Director: Cynthia R. Cooper
Senior Designer: Melissa Jones Clark
Contributing Designer: Larry Hunter
Editorial Assistants: Catherine Ritter Scholl, Allison Long
Test Kitchens Director: Kathleen Royal Phillips
Assistant Test Kitchens Director: Gayle Hays Sadler
Test Kitchens Staff: Julie Christopher, Natalie E. King, Victoria Knowles, Regan C. Miller, Rebecca Mohr, Jan A. Smith, Kate M. Wheeler
Senior Photographer: Jim Bathie
Photographer: Brit Huckabay
Senior Photo Stylist: Kay E. Clarke
Photo Stylist: Virginia R. Cravens
Photo Assistant: Jan Gautro
Director, Production and Distribution: Phillip Lee
Associate Production Manager: Theresa L. Beste
Production Assistant: Faye Porter Bonner
Publishing Systems Administrator: Rick Tucker

Contributors
Editorial: Jean Wickstrom Liles
Nutrition: Caroline Grant, M.S., R.D.
Index: Mary Ann Laurens
Illustrations: Barbara Ball
Technical Assistance: Shari Wimberley

CONTENTS

FOREWORD

Each day I gather with the foods staff around a blessed and bountiful table. We sample what our grandmothers have baked, revise old favorites using today's timesaving inventiveness, and sample new dishes destined to become modern classics.

These daily taste testings bring us into your home and help us keep a finger on the pulse of what's happening in Southern kitchens. The recipes you share with us confirm how you set your table. Your letters and calls tell us what puzzles and challenges you in the kitchen.

As we listen, we note your culinary wish list. THE ULTIMATE *SOUTHERN LIVING* COOKBOOK is our offering of a definitive collection of our finest recipes, our best advice, and photography that paints pictures of these recipes and walks you step-by-step through preparing them for your family and friends.

Twelve years ago I had the privilege of testing recipes for the first volume of THE *SOUTHERN LIVING* COOKBOOK. The pages are now tattered and stained from use in my kitchen at home. This book will continue to be opened to favorite pages, but THE ULTIMATE *SOUTHERN LIVING* COOKBOOK, considered a sequel, offers even more.

The recipes reflect the same high standards—they are the very best in each food category. We include all new photographs to show you cooking techniques and images of finished recipes. Keeping in mind your time constraints and health concerns, every recipe includes prep time, cook time, and, yes, nutritional analysis. We also address food safety and food trends.

In this new volume you'll find ethnic favorites from couscous to crème brûlée, which have made their way to the Southern table. Most important, from cover to cover, this cookbook is decidedly Southern. It continues to share the South's treasured recipes and gracious entertaining ideas. We hope you enjoy it.

KAYE MABRY ADAMS
Executive Editor at Southern Living

INTRODUCTION

THE ULTIMATE *SOUTHERN LIVING* COOKBOOK explores the joy of good cooking with new attention to your busy lifestyle. The recipes and text have been fine-tuned to meet your needs and answer your cooking questions. Our mission is to arm you with fundamental food knowledge and boost your excitement about cooking.

What defines a good cook? A love of food and the desire to learn more about it. Dig into this volume and explore some timeless principles of cooking. The book begins with Cooking A to Z, a chapter that is in itself an invaluable kitchen resource. Take pointers for stocking your kitchen with essential equipment and ingredients, glance at our comprehensive cooking glossary, reap the benefits of healthy meal planning, and gain some tips for setting your table and sharing good food with family and friends. We demystify cooking terms and techniques, and often show them in illustrations and photographs.

The heart of this book, though, is the recipes. Turn to any one of the 16 food chapters for great recipes and step-by-step photographs that will entice you into the kitchen. Each chapter begins with a brief overview of equipment and pertinent information for preparing, cooking, and storing that type of food. And for your convenience we included symbols for quick recipes to indicate that they can be prepared in 30 minutes or less, along with make ahead, grilled, and vegetarian recipes, family favorites, and healthy options (see page 22 for guidelines).

You'll find pages throughout the book designed to keep you in touch with the ever-changing marketplace. These include food dictionaries paired with color photographs of fresh produce, herbs, mushrooms, cheese, and pastas. They'll help you shop for and cook with fresh ingredients, from familiar to exotic.

In the back of the book find pages of handy substitutions, metric conversions, and recommended storage times for food in the pantry, refrigerator, and freezer. And last but not least, flip through the Menu Index, which offers over three dozen easy ideas for dinner, followed by extensive Recipe and Subject indexes.

We hope you'll find lifelong inspiration in this culinary resource that's designed to give you total confidence in the kitchen. Whether you're a curious beginner who wants to learn the basics or a seasoned cook in search of new ideas, we hope these recipes and words help make cooking fun. Keep THE ULTIMATE *SOUTHERN LIVING* COOKBOOK within easy reach.

COOKING
A TO Z

*The secret to becoming a great cook begins with the basics—
using the right equipment, ingredients, and techniques. This chapter
will help you get your kitchen in order and gain you the confidence
to cook any type of food, from familiar to exotic.*

Organize Your Kitchen

You can easily reduce the time and energy you expend in the kitchen by organizing it to fit your needs. For starters, read through this chapter to get an overview of some basic recommendations and then take stock of your current inventory. Use the suggestions below to help you clean up, toss out, and reorganize.

•**Check dried herbs and spices** for freshness. We recommend storing dried herbs and other seasonings in the freezer, not in racks near the oven or cooktop where heat can cause them to deteriorate. Most herbs and spices should stay fresh up to a year if stored properly. To test for freshness, sprinkle a small amount of the seasoning in the palm of your hand; if you don't smell an immediate aroma, it's time to replace it.

•**Clean out your pantry.** Check the date on canned goods. Canned foods beyond a year old tend to lose quality as well as nutrient value. Check the date on baking goods, too, particularly baking powder and soda. If they're past their expiration dates, they won't do their job of leavening.

•**Organize your resources.** Look through food magazines, recipe files, and cooking articles, and discard any that you haven't used.

•**Plan equipment storage.** Store utensils and small appliances near the area in your kitchen where you'll be using them. Keep pot holders, kitchen towels, and baking pans near the cooktop and oven. Organize utensil drawers. Invest in drawer trays to separate small utensils and gadgets.

•**Clean out the freezer.** Bring older packages to the front and use them before using newly purchased items. Do the same with the refrigerator. Remember to stack food away from the back of the freezer and refrigerator so cold air can circulate freely.

•**Maximize efficiency.** Keep a variety of spoons, spatulas, tongs, and other well-used utensils in a canister near your work station or cooktop; then you'll always have them at your fingertips. Invest in a pot rack. Hang your favorite pots and pans overhead and within easy reach. Store knives where they'll be safe and easily accessible in a knife block or on a magnetic strip that hangs on the wall.

EQUIPMENT & INGREDIENTS

COOKWARE

Saucepans are made of clad metals, copper, aluminum, stainless steel, glass, and enameled cast-iron.

Clad metals are a combination of several metals fused and used for their best attributes. Clad metal pans are a good all-purpose choice for good heat conductivity, durability, and nonreactive and nonstick properties.

Copper cookware, which is often lined with tin, is an excellent heat conductor; it's expensive, though, and needs frequent polishing, and retinning over the years.

Aluminum cookware can react with acidic foods, altering the taste and color of food.

Stainless steel and glass pans are poor conductors of heat but are sturdy, nonreactive, and easy to clean.

Buy the best pots and pans you can afford, top-quality equipment that will be durable. Consider buying individual pieces you know you'll use rather than a whole set.

Choose pots and pans of heavy gauge (thickness) and sturdy construction—those that won't warp, dent, or scorch. Look for thick bottoms, tight-fitting lids, and heat-resistant handles that are securely attached.

Select 1-, 2-, and 3-quart saucepans; a Dutch oven; and a tall, narrow stockpot, all with lids. A double boiler (a pair of stacking saucepans) is a good investment, too.

A 12-inch heavy skillet with a lid will prove most useful, as well as a 6-inch skillet for omelets and crêpes, and 8- and 10-inch skillets. Buy nonstick for healthy cooking. A well-seasoned cast-iron skillet is an inexpensive pan for making cornbread. You can often spot this skillet for sale at antique shops and yard sales.

A grill pan is a griddle and grill in one. The ridged surface allows fat to drip away from food. For optimum results, use this heavy pan over medium-high to high heat.

BAKEWARE

Shiny aluminum bakeware and stainless steel bakeware produce the best baked goods. They conduct heat evenly and encourage a brown crust. Dark pans can cause overbrowning.

Always use the pan size specified in a recipe. The correct way to measure pans is across the inside top edges.

Baking pans and dishes: *Pans* are metal; *dishes* are glass. If a recipe calls for a pan and you have only glass in that size, reduce oven temperature by 25 degrees. You'll need 8- and 9-inch square pans and/or baking dishes, a 13-x 9-inch pan and baking dish, an 11- x 7-inch baking dish, a small and large roasting pan, and a broiler pan with a rack.

Baking sheets/cookie sheets: Purchase at least two large sturdy baking sheets as well as a 15- x 10-inch jellyroll pan.

Loafpans: Metal pans measuring 9- x 5-inches and 8½- x 4½-inches are most common.

Muffin pans: Purchase a muffin pan that holds 12 muffins rather than six; most recipes yield a dozen. Most muffin pan cups measure 2½ inches across the top. A mini-muffin pan is handy, too, and gives a petite option.

Pieplates: For pieplates, use glass, ceramic, or dull metal. The standard size is 9 inches. Deep-dish pieplates are 9½ inches.

Cakepans: We recommend owning three each of 8- and 9-inch round cakepans. Also consider a tube pan for angel food cake, Bundt pan for pound cake, and a 9-inch springform pan for cheesecakes.

Wire racks: Collect two or three wire racks if you like to bake cakes and cookies. Look for small round and oval racks as well as larger rectangular racks. Don't buy racks with large gaps between the wires.

APPLIANCES

Some appliances are more critical than others, but all of the following are handy.

Ovens: A *conventional oven* can be gas or electric; this familiar oven has been the mainstay heat source in kitchens for decades. A *convection oven* is equipped with a fan that circulates air flow evenly around food. Convection ovens heat up fast and cook food evenly and efficiently. Combination conventional/convection ovens are a good choice that offers the strengths of both types.

Grills: Outdoor grills enable you to get great smoky flavor at home. *Charcoal grills* bestow the best smoke. Choose a grill that has a lid to catch the flavor-infusing smoke. You have to preheat the charcoal and let it burn down to an ashy glow before grilling.

A *gas grill* allows you to control the heat quickly and easily, but the food's smoky flavor is less pronounced. Grilling enthusiasts often have both types of grills. Any open grill can be used for *direct grilling* (cooking food directly over the fire), including hibachis. For *indirect grilling* (cooking food over a drip pan that's surrounded by hot coals), you need a covered grill.

Smokers: Smokers are charcoal or electric grills with single or double cooking levels. They come with a cooking grill rack and a water pan. Use charcoal models to smoke, roast, grill, or steam food up to six hours using a single pan of charcoal. Electric models provide constant, even heat.

Microwave: A microwave is a handy oven alternative, noted for cooking vegetables and bacon and for heating and reheating foods efficiently. Microwave ovens vary in wattage according to specific model. The most common have been 600 to 700 watts of cooking power, although new models may exceed 1,000 watts. We tested our microwave recipes for this book with a 700-watt oven because that's what most people currently own. If your oven has higher or lower wattage, adjust cooking times accordingly.

Bread machine: A bread machine does the mixing, kneading, rising, and baking in its chamber; all you do is add the ingredients and choose the appropriate settings. It's the answer to bread baking for those too busy to cook. You can set a delayed setting and have fresh baked bread 12 hours later with no attention needed.

Electric blender: A blender is your best bet for smooth soups, sauces, and drinks. Its tall, narrow container holds more than a food processor does. Be careful not to overload it though, particularly with hot liquid; it could spew out. A blender will also chop small amounts of food for you.

Electric mixer: There are two kinds: a portable *handheld mixer* for small mixing jobs and a *heavy-duty stand mixer* for substantial baking. Lightweight portable mixers allow you to control the mixer's movement in a free-standing bowl. This mixer, however, is not made for working with large or stiff doughs. Stand mixers come with attachments like a balloon whisk, dough hook, and paddle beater. The bowl capacity is large and will handle large amounts of thick batter or knead bread for you. If you do a lot of baking, a stand mixer is for you.

Food processor: This appliance will chop, shred, and grate for you. It can also make pastry dough in a jiffy. And you can use a food processor for the same purposes as a blender. Beware though that processor bowls will leak at the base if overloaded with liquid mixture. A mini chopper is a smaller version of this appliance made for small chopping jobs.

Griddle and waffle iron: These appliances prepare those well-loved breakfast foods, pancakes and waffles. A thick, flat griddle also works great for grilled sandwiches, fried green tomatoes, and fried eggs.

Pressure cooker: This piece of equipment is made of heavy-gauge stainless steel and aluminum; it works by the steam action that builds up in a tightly sealed pot. A valve system controls the pressure, releasing excess steam through the top openings. Pressure cookers drastically cut the cooking time for foods that otherwise need lengthy simmering.

Slow cooker: An electric slow cooker allows you to safely cook a meal while you're away from home. Made of thick stoneware, the slow cooker bowl or crock is surrounded by an enclosed heating system. The low temperature gently simmers food for hours unattended. Slow cookers come in six sizes, from 1 to 6 quarts. Some models have a removable stoneware liner that's dishwasher safe.

Toaster/toaster oven: A toaster is still the simplest way to toast bread, bagels, and English muffins. A toaster oven will do the same task as well as act as a small oven. It's handy for heating small amounts of food.

Wok: Known for stir-frying, a steel wok with a rounded bottom cooks food fast and efficiently with very little fat. And when you add the cover you can use it to steam foods. With the aid of a wok ring, a steel wok fits easily on your cooktop.

STOCK YOUR KITCHEN

Whether you're planning a kitchen for the first time or adding to your current inventory, investing in good tools makes cooking easier and more fun. Buy the best-quality items you can afford. Here's a checklist for a well-equipped kitchen.

EQUIPMENT TOOLS

Mixing bowls in graduated sizes
Dry measuring cup set
Liquid measuring cups (1, 2, and 4 cup)
Measuring spoons (at least 2 sets)
Set of quality knives
Mixing spoons (plastic, metal, and wooden)
Kitchen shears
Pastry blender
Thermometers (meat, instant read, and candy)
Openers (electric, hand, bottle, and corkscrew)
Wire whisk
Vegetable peeler
Timer
Mallet
Colander
Rolling pin
Sifter
Spatulas (rubber and metal)
Wire mesh strainer
Scales (optional)
Cutting board
Grater
Brushes (pastry and basting)
Metal turner
Meat fork
Tongs
Garlic press
Ladle
Potato masher
Kitchen towels and pot holders

COOKWARE

Saucepans (1, 2, and 3 quart with lids)
Skillets (large and small)
Dutch oven with lid
Stockpot or kettle with lid
Double boiler

BAKEWARE

Pans are metal; dishes are glass.
Two or three 9-inch round cakepans
8- and 9-inch square pans
13 -x 9-inch pan
10-inch tube pan
Bundt pan
13 -x 9-inch baking dish
8- or 9-inch square baking dish
1-quart baking dish
Pair of cookie sheets
15 -x 10-inch jellyroll pan
Wire cooling racks
9 -x 5-inch loafpan
Muffin pan
9-inch glass pieplate
9-inch springform pan

KITCHEN EQUIPMENT DICTIONARY

How well a kitchen is stocked is an indication of how much the cook enjoys being in the kitchen.

Bowls: You can never have too many mixing bowls. Choose bowls in graduated sizes so that they'll be easy to stack and store. Plastic or earthenware bowls work fine for many easy mixing jobs, but a copper bowl is the ultimate for beating egg whites. Stainless steel bowls and glass bowls are best for cake batter.

Brushes: A pastry brush and basting brush are useful tools for brushing glazes and marinades on breads, meats, and other food. When selecting a brush, be sure the bristles are securely attached to the handle. The best basting brushes are made of natural boar bristles.

Grater: Invest in a sturdy upright grater that has four sizes of grating holes. Other popular graters include a two-piece metal Mouli grater, which makes tableside cheese grating easy, and porcelain graters which have sharp, fine teeth. A handheld porcelain grater grates hard cheese; a porcelain grating dish grates hard cheese as well as fresh ginger and garlic.

Coffee grinder: An electric coffee grinder not only grinds whole beans, but whole spices as well. Buy two grinders to keep for separate uses.

Crinkle cutter: This small, ridged tool gives vegetable slices an interesting edge. See this tool on pages 8 and 9.

Colander: A metal or sturdy plastic colander is essential for draining cooked pasta and vegetables, rinsing salad greens, and draining canned beans and vegetables.

Cutting board: A wooden cutting board and a plastic cutting board are standard recommendations. If you have a cutting board with a ridged edge, use it when you carve meat to catch the juices.

Garlic press: Use this tool when a recipe calls for crushed garlic, because you'll want the garlic and its juice. See a garlic press on page 9.

Juicer: A hand-juicer simplifies the process of squeezing citrus fruits.

Kitchen shears: These all-purpose scissors cut many foods more easily than a knife does. Use

them to snip fresh herbs or to chop canned tomatoes right in the can.

Ladle: This tool helps you transfer soup to serving bowls.

Mallet: Choose a stainless steel mallet for pounding meat and poultry. It will also crack ice and mash garlic.

Measuring cups: Select a nested set of metal or plastic measuring cups for dry ingredients. They come in graduated sizes of 1 cup, $\frac{1}{2}$ cup, $\frac{1}{3}$ cup, and $\frac{1}{4}$ cup. You'll also need glass or clear plastic measuring cups for liquid ingredients; they come in 1-cup, 2-cup, and 4-cup sizes.

Measuring spoons: Select a set of measuring spoons that graduate from $\frac{1}{8}$ teaspoon to 1 tablespoon.

Metal dough scraper: Use this tool to help lift and cut dough on a work surface. The sharp, straight edge can also cut fudge and bar cookies. See a dough scraper on page 9.

Mortar and pestle: These tools, a bowl and tiny bat, work together to crush and blend spices, herbs, and garlic.

Mushroom brush: Use these bristles to clean dirt from mushrooms and other vegetables.

Pastry blender: The blades of this tool make it easy to cut fat into pea-size pieces while incorporating it into a flour mixture.

Pastry wheel: A pastry wheel cuts smooth or fluted edges of pastry and cookie dough. The fluted wheel seals and crimps edges of turnovers.

Potato masher: Designs vary for this tool that does a fast job of mashing cooked potatoes and other soft foods.

Ramekins and custard cups: Use these little dishes for baking custards and soufflés.

Citrus reamer: Use this old-fashioned tool to squeeze juice from a cut lemon. See a wooden reamer on page 8.

Rolling pin: A large wooden rolling pin is necessary for rolling pastry and bread dough.

A marble rolling pin is heavier and helps keep dough cold; a tapered European rolling pin is light and easily maneuvered.

Sifter: Use this to sift cake flour and powdered sugar. Never wash a sifter; just shake out the excess powder.

Spatulas and spoons: Collect several rubber spatulas and wooden spoons; you'll use them frequently.

Strainer: Strainers have a coarse or fine wire mesh. A basic bowl strainer is used to drain or separate liquid from solid. Look for a strainer with stainless steel mesh. A strainer is called a *sieve* when it's used to separate coarse particles from fine ones.

Steamer basket: This collapsible metal insert expands to fit snugly in a saucepan for steaming vegetables or other foods.

Stripper: This single-notched tool will produce a thin strip of peel from citrus fruit.

Thermometer: We recommend three thermometers for cooking: a meat thermometer, a combination candy/deep-fry thermometer that clips onto a pan, and an all-purpose instant-read thermometer. Oven and refrigerator thermometers are optional, inexpensive investments that help regulate your appliances.

Tongs: Spring-loaded metal tongs are inexpensive and will turn meat and many other foods as they cook without piercing them and releasing their juices.

Vegetable peeler: This tool peels the skin from fruits and vegetables. Buy one with a comfortable grip.

Whisk: There are many sizes of whisks on the market. We recommend a small, medium, and large elongated stainless steel wire whisk, and a balloon whisk for whipping egg whites.

Zester: This tool has tiny holes that scrape the outer "zest" of citrus peels plus a fine mist of citrus oil. See a zester on page 9.

Knife News

A good-quality set of knives is an investment, but you'll get your money's worth with years of use. Knives come in a wide variety of shapes and sizes; each is made for a specific task. Using a sharp knife and choosing the right blade makes each cutting job easier.

Knife prices vary greatly. Select knives based on ease of use, comfort, and value. If a whole knife set isn't in your budget, just buy knives one at a time. And buy only the knives that you need and know you'll use. As a rule, the more expensive knives have nicer finishes; however, the best knives aren't necessarily the most expensive. Keeping your price range in mind, look at the knife's construction.

High-carbon stainless steel is the best value blade; often called "no stain," this blade remains sharp and is not affected by air or moisture. Carbon steel is also a good quality blade, but it may stain or rust if not dried immediately after washing.

The *tang* is the part of the knife blade that extends into the handle. Choose a knife with a full tang, which means that the blade extends throughout the length of the handle, adding balance and weight to the knife. Top-quality knives use metal rivets embedded in the handle on both sides rather than glue to hold the tang in place.

The handle should have a refined surface without crevices in which food can hide and bacteria can grow.

Before you make an investment, be sure the knife fits comfortably in your hand and is well balanced. Test the knife by supporting it with two fingers at the point where the handle joins the blade; it should stay in a horizontal position.

Take the time to care for your knives properly. Always cut on a surface that has some resilience; wood is an excellent choice. Remember to wash your knives immediately after use, and dry them thoroughly. Washing them by hand rather than in the dishwasher is critical to keeping their edges sharp. Store knives in a slotted knife block or drawer insert, or on a magnetic bar that hangs on the wall.

CUTLERY DICTIONARY

Sharpening steel: This tool, also called a *butcher's steel*, is included in many knife sets. It acts like a file on the knife's edge by realigning the edge and keeping the blade sharp.

To use a sharpening steel, draw the knife blade across the steel at a 20-degree angle, using moderate pressure. Repeat on the other side of the blade. Repeat these steps five to 10 times, always alternating the right and left side of the blade. Get into the practice of using the steel every time you use your knife.

After years of use, the steel may no longer restore the cutting edge; then it's time to have your knives professionally sharpened. Remember: A properly sharpened knife prevents accidents; cutting with a dull knife is one of the easiest ways to get hurt.

Slicing/carving knife: The blade on this knife meant for carving meats is narrower than a chef's knife. The tip can be pointed or rounded and the blade can have a smooth or serrated edge. The long, smooth-edged blade cuts thin, even slices of meats and large vegetables as well as blocks of cheese. The long scalloped edge, rounded tip knife called a *ham slicer* has a sturdy blade excellent for slicing ham and roasts. (It's shown at top of photo.)

Chef's knife: The blade of this knife is shaped like an elongated triangle and ranges from 8 to 10 inches in length. It's heavy and wide, and gradually tapers to a point. This large knife can be used for many tasks like chopping, mincing, and slicing most fruits and vegetables. Its shape lets the blade rock back and forth while the weight does the work.

Mincing and chopping is simple—grasp the handle with one hand, and hold the back of the blade near the tip between the thumb and forefinger of the other hand. Lift handle up and down in a rapid rocking motion, moving blade in an arc and pulling the food you're chopping back into a pile to make sure it's evenly chopped.

Cleaver: This wide-bladed knife chops through bone without denting or cracking. A cleaver is good for coarsely chopping meats and vegetables, but its bulky blade makes precision slicing difficult.

(Left to right) Sharpening steel, slicing knife, chef's knife, cleaver, boning knife, paring knives, tomato knife
(At top) Ham slicer, serrated bread knife

Boning knife: This knife's narrow blade is 5 to 7 inches long and is excellent for separating cooked or uncooked meat from the bone, carving a roast, or peeling fruits and vegetables.

Paring knife/utility knife: The small, lightweight paring knife has a 3- to 4-inch blade and is easy to grasp and control. It's handy for sculpting garnishes, trimming foods, and peeling and slicing small fruits and vegetables. The midsize paring knife with a 6- to 8-inch blade is called a *utility knife* or *sandwich knife*.

Serrated knives (bread knife and tomato knife): The long serrated-edged slicing knife, also called a *bread knife,* slices bread and layer cakes with ease. As you exert gentle downward pressure, drawing the knife toward you, its toothed or notched edge cuts through foods with a firm or crisp crust without tearing or crushing the soft insides. Use a back-and-forth sawing motion when cutting with a serrated knife. The shorter serrated knife called a *tomato knife* zips through tomatoes and crusty baguettes easily.

HERB DICTIONARY

Herbs are versatile and easy to use. They offer simple fresh seasoning to most any type of food, even some desserts. Once you've cooked with fresh herbs, you'll probably want to grow them. Gardeners divide herbs into two categories, *culinary* and *ornamental,* although some herbs often serve both functions.

Culinary or edible herbs like thyme, basil, and oregano add interest to many entrées, side dishes, and salads. Ornamental herbs add color, height, and fragrance to a garden or window box. You can use a few ornamental herbs like lavender, pineapple sage, and scented geranium for cooking.

Many herbs are *perennials*, meaning they die back during the winter and return in spring. Rosemary, lavender, oregano, and thyme are a few; give them a permanent spot in your garden and you can have continual clippings.

If you grow your own herbs for cooking, use them before they flower. Harvest herbs early in the morning just after the dew has dried. Wash herbs and pat dry.

If you buy fresh herbs at the grocery store, preserve them up to a week with one of two methods. Either wrap stems in a soaking wet paper towel, taking care to keep herb foliage dry; place wrapped herbs in a zip-top plastic bag, seal with air inside, and store in refrigerator. Or place stem ends in a glass with two inches of water; cover herb foliage loosely with a plastic bag, and store in refrigerator.

If a recipe doesn't specify when to add herbs, it's best to add them near the end of cooking to release their full flavor. Bay leaves are the exception; they typically simmer at length in soups.

If you want to substitute fresh herbs for dried herbs, which are more concentrated in flavor, use three times the amount of fresh herbs as dried. Rosemary is the exception; use it in equal amounts.

Experimenting with herbs is fun. When blending herbs, choose a leading flavor and combine it with a more subtle, background herb. Don't emphasize more than one strong herb in a dish. Just taste an herb to identify whether it has a pungent, spicy, fruity, or floral taste; then pair it with a compatible food.
- The strong herbs are rosemary, cilantro, thyme, oregano, and sage; go sparingly because they contribute quite a bit of flavor to a dish.

- Medium-flavored herbs are basil, dill, mint, and fennel; use them more generously.
- Use delicate herbs like parsley and chives in abundance.

Basil: One of the easiest herbs to grow, basil has a heady fragrance and a faint licorice flavor. Use it in salads, pestos, pasta dishes, pizza, and meat and poultry dishes. *Purple ruffles basil* (shown) has ruffled purple-black leaves and a mild fragrance and flavor. Cinnamon basil, Thai basil, and lemon basil are very flavorful, fragrant basils for cooking.

Bay leaves: Use fresh or dried bay leaves in soups, stews, vegetables, and bouquet garnis. Discard bay leaves before serving food.

Borage: The nodding purple flowers of borage are popular edible garnishes in green salads, on fancy cakes, or floating in a glass of wine or tea. You can use the young leaves, too. They wilt quickly, so chop and add to salads or cucumber tea sandwiches just before serving.

Chervil: A fragile herb, chervil is commonly known as *French parsley*. It has a subtle anise flavor and is best fresh or cooked only briefly. Add chervil to egg dishes, soups, and salads or use it as a substitute for parsley.

Chives: Chives are attractive, rugged herbs that are easy to grow. Snip the leaves and they'll provide a mild onion or garlic flavor to soups, salads, and vegetable dishes. In spring, chives

boast globelike lavender-colored blooms that make ideal edible garnishes for salads. The *wild (nodding) onion* shown is a type of chive in bloom.

Cilantro: Also known as *Chinese parsley*, cilantro is grown for its spicy-flavored foliage and for its seeds called *coriander*. Cilantro is the leaf; coriander is the seed or powder; the two are not interchangeable in recipes. Slightly bruise a cilantro leaf and it will give off an unmistakable pungent peppery fragrance. Use the leaves in Southwestern, Mexican, and Asian dishes. Cumin and mint are seasonings often paired with cilantro. Coriander seeds are used in Indian dishes as well as pickles and relishes.

Dill: Finely chop feathery fresh dill foliage for shrimp dishes, eggs, soups, sandwiches, potato salad, and sauces. Dill is a good salt substitute. You can harvest and dry dill seeds and use them in pickles, breads, and salad dressings.

Geranium, scented: The foliage and flowers of scented geranium are edible. Use scented leaves for flavoring pound cakes, cookies, herb butters, jellies, and iced tea. Some scented varieties are apple, lemon, orange, peppermint, rose (shown), and strawberry.

Lavender: This edible ornamental herb has purple flowers that spike in early summer. Harvest the flowers just before they're fully opened, and use them in ice cream or other desserts, marinades, and sauces. *Spanish lavender*, shown, is a gray-leafed plant with needlelike leaves that look like rosemary.

Lemon balm: This hardy, bushy member of the mint family has a mild lemony flavor. Chop the aromatic leaves to use in tea bread, scones, and salads, or use leaves whole in tea or other cold beverages.

Lemon Verbena: The strongest scented lemon herb, lemon verbena has a healthy lemony essence. Use it as you would lemon balm leaves. Pulse a handful of leaves with a cup of sugar in a food processor to make lemon sugar. Store it in a jar. Use the sugar in sweets and teas.

Mint: Add this popular herb to lamb, poultry, salads, sauces, teas, and punches. Try cooking with flavorful types of mint like peppermint, orange mint, apple mint, or chocolate mint. Shown are the common *spearmint* and variegated *pineapple mint*.

Nasturtiums: These bright red and orange edible flowers have a peppery taste. Use them in salads, sandwich spreads, or as a versatile garnish.

Oregano: These small green leaves produce strong flavor. *Greek oregano* is the most popular oregano for cooking because of its strong flavor and aromatic leaves. Add oregano to Italian dishes, meat, fish, eggs, fresh and cooked tomatoes, vegetables, beans, and marinades.

Rosemary: Unlike other herbs, rosemary has a stronger flavor when fresh than when dried. It's a hardy herb with a piney scent and flavor. To harvest rosemary, strip leaves from the stem. Use the strong-flavored leaves sparingly. Rosemary adds a wonderful accent to soups, meats, stews, breads, and vegetables.

Sage: This fuzzy gray-green hardy herb is best known for use in holiday dressings. Sage is often paired with sausage, too. And its soft texture makes it easy to tuck under the skin of poultry before roasting. *Common garden sage* and *variegated sage* are shown.

Tarragon: This tender herb plays a classic role in béarnaise sauce. It also adds flavor to soups, poultry, seafood, vegetables, and egg dishes. It's used often to make herb butter or vinegar. *French tarragon* is shown. Its leaves have a bittersweet, peppery scent with a hint of anise.

Thyme: Strip the tiny leaves from stems just before using. Use fresh thyme in marinades for basting seafood, chicken, or pork. Add thyme to mayonnaise for sandwiches or to beans, meat stews, vegetables, or rice. There are many varieties of thyme. *Lime thyme* is shown.

Rose Geranium

Basil

Lemon Balm

Cilantro

Purple ruffles basil

Lemon Verbena

Pineapple Mint

Rosemary

Wild (nodding) onion

GLOSSARY OF STAPLES

Selecting the right ingredients that a recipe specifies is a key factor in successful cooking. This glossary lists many of the basic ingredients in our recipes and describes the ways in which you can purchase them.

Breadcrumbs

You can purchase breadcrumbs in a can or you can make your own. Be sure to notice how we call for breadcrumbs in a recipe because some recipes turn out best using dry breadcrumbs and some need the soft, home-made kind.

When we call for **fine, dry bread-crumbs** (commercial), we're referring to the store-bought kind. You can purchase them plain or Italian seasoned. If we call for **soft breadcrumbs**, it refers to homemade crumbs made from leftover rolls or sandwich bread. A food processor does a quick job of making crumbs for you. Don't toast the bread; it should be soft.

Chocolate

Our recipes use **unsweetened, semi-sweet, sweet baking,** and **milk chocolate**. The first three come in 1-ounce squares or bars, so they're easy to measure. Semisweet chocolate comes in morsel form, too. You can substitute semisweet morsels for semisweet squares ounce for ounce. One cup of morsels equals six ounces. Milk chocolate comes in morsel and candy bar forms. Check the label to be sure you're using pure milk chocolate.

You can substitute **cocoa** for unsweet-ened chocolate for baking purposes. Use 3 tablespoons cocoa plus 1 tablespoon shorten-ing or oil for each 1 ounce square of unsweetened chocolate.

Chocolate-flavored candy coating is not real chocolate, but a product made to look and taste like chocolate. It's often used as a dipping chocolate in place of semisweet chocolate because it becomes firmer faster.

White chocolate is not really chocolate because it doesn't contain chocolate liquor. It's made of cocoa butter, sugar, milk solids, and flavorings. It's available in square, morsel, and bar forms. Read the label carefully to determine the real thing from a substitute. Melt white chocolate over the gentle heat of a double boiler or in the microwave.

Store all chocolate the same way—tightly wrapped and in a cool, dry place.

Cream

Whipping cream is the richest cream you can buy. It contains 30% to 40% milkfat. Heavy whipping cream has the highest per-centage of milkfat (36% to 40%). Some recipes specifically call for heavy whipping cream for its ultimate rich attributes. In our recipes that call for whipping cream we assume you'll measure the cream and whip it yourself. If a recipe calls for a carton of **frozen whipped topping**, that's the conve-nience product with a slightly different flavor.

Half-and-half, also called light cream, contains about half the amount of fat as whip-ping cream and is more like the consistency of milk than cream. It will not whip.

Sour cream is a commercially cultured product that is thick and has a slightly sour taste. Several **light sour creams** with good flavor and texture are available in the market-place. Although we don't specify using it in this cookbook, light sour cream is often a good substitute in dips and spreads.

Fats

Fats can be divided into two groups: fats and oils. Fats are solid at room temperature. They include **butter, margarine, shorten-ing,** and **lard**. Oils are liquid at room temper-ature. They include **corn oil, vegetable oil, peanut oil, sesame seed oil, olive oil, canola oil, safflower oil,** and some **nut oils.**

Butter and margarine are two fats wide-ly used in cooking and flavoring foods. While butter and margarine are often used inter-changeably, they are different products. Butter has milkfat or cream as a base, while most margarines are made from vegetable oil, with some made from a combination of vegetable oil and animal fat. Read labels to know what you're buying.

Both butter and margarine are available in salted, unsalted, and whipped form. Unsalted butter is the freshest, premium butter for bak-ing, but regular salted butter is also accept-able. Don't substitute whipped products for stick butter or margarine in baking. The whipped products have air incorporated to make them more spreadable.

Imitation margarine (often labeled light, low fat, or low calorie) is a soft mar-garine with about half the fat and more than three times the water of plain margarine. It's used primarily as a spread and isn't suitable for baking due to its high water content.

Shortening is composed of vegetable or animal fat or a combination of the two. It is solid at room temperature and has a long shelf life. It's tasteless but is commonly used for baking because it adds moisture and tenderness, particularly to piecrusts. Butter-flavored shortening is processed with a butter flavoring. Shortening is easy to measure in its stick form.

Lard is rendered pork fat. Years ago it was used almost exclusively for making pastry and biscuits. Its use has declined in this day of health-conscious lifestyles.

Olive oil is used widely in cooking, par-ticularly in vinaigrettes and other dressings where its fresh flavor is noticed. Read more about olive oil on page 361. **Vegetable oil** and **corn oil** are good all-purpose cooking oils. **Peanut oil** is excellent for frying because it has a high smoke point. This means it can withstand high heat cooking without smoking and burning.

Don't substitute oil for shortening in baked products, even when the shortening is to be melted.

Flour

Flour is milled from all kinds of grains— wheat, corn, rye, oats, and barley—each producing one or more kinds of flour. The differences lie in the particular grain used and how it's processed.

Wheat flours are divided into two basic groups: **whole grain** and **white. Whole-grain wheat flours** include whole wheat, graham, and cracked wheat. Among the **white flours** are bread, all-purpose, unbleached all-purpose, and cake flour. These are often enriched with iron and the B-vitamins to replace nutrients lost when the wheat germ is removed.

Different types of flour are not generally interchangeable in our recipes. That's because wheat flours vary in protein content, and protein affects how a flour performs during baking. When mixed with a liquid, the protein forms gluten, which gives elasticity to batters and doughs and provides the structure or framework for whatever you're baking. In addition, gluten affects the tenderness and volume of baked goods. White flours have more usable protein (gluten) than whole-grain flours.

Bread flour is a hard-wheat flour milled especially for breadmaking. It has a high protein content that produces sturdy yeast breads.

All-purpose flour is a combination of hard- and soft-wheat flour and is commonly used for all types of baked products. All-purpose flours made with more soft wheat (such as White Lily and Martha White) give good results when used for cakes, quick breads, and sweet rolls. Our recipes specify when we tested with soft-wheat flour.

Unbleached flour is an all-purpose flour that has no bleaching agents added during processing and can be used interchangeably with all-purpose. Purists like baking with unbleached flour; they claim it lends a fresher taste.

Self-rising flour is an all-purpose flour to which leavening and salt have been added. It's not meant for use in yeast breads. It's best not to substitute self-rising flour for all-purpose flour; however, you can substitute all-purpose flour for self-rising by making these adjustments: For 1 cup self-rising, use 1 cup all-purpose flour plus 1 teaspoon baking powder and ½ teaspoon salt.

Cake flour is a soft-wheat flour and has a much lower protein content than all-purpose flour. Products made with cake flour have a tender, delicate crumb. You can substitute all-purpose flour for cake flour by using 2 tablespoons less all-purpose flour per cup.

Gelatin

You can purchase gelatin either unflavored or sweetened and flavored; the two are not interchangeable. **Unflavored gelatin** is sold in packages containing slightly less than 1 tablespoon. Each package will gel 2 cups of liquid. **Flavored gelatin** is sold in 3- and 6-ounce packages and contains sugar, flavoring, and coloring. Flavored and unflavored gelatins require different softening procedures. For more details about using each type, refer to Shapely Salads on page 365.

Milk

We test recipes using **whole milk** unless otherwise stated. This milk has at least 3.25% fat content. **Fat-free milk** has the fat removed and has slightly more calcium than whole milk. **Low-fat milk** is available containing from .5% to 2% fat content. It tastes and looks more like whole milk than fat-free milk.

Evaporated milk has had 60% of the water removed. It's available in cans only. You can substitute evaporated milk for fresh milk by blending it with equal parts water.

Sweetened condensed milk has had half its water content removed and 60% sugar added. Buy it in cans. It can't be substituted for fresh milk because it's too thick and sweet.

Nonfat dry milk powder is what remains after all the water and fat have been removed from whole milk. It rehydrates easily with water or another liquid.

Buttermilk is the liquid that remains after butter is made from whole milk. Cultured buttermilk is the product left after skim milk is treated with lactic acid bacteria.

Yogurt is simply fermented milk. It's available plain or flavored. The plain can often be used as a low-calorie substitute for sour cream.

Sugar

Granulated sugar is the most common form of sugar; it's what we mean when we specify "sugar" in a recipe.

Superfine sugar is granulated sugar with smaller crystals that result from extra processing. It's used for making meringues and other desserts where quick dissolving is important. If you can't find superfine sugar in the stores, make it by processing regular granulated sugar in the food processor until it's almost powderlike.

Powdered sugar, also called confectioner's sugar, is granulated sugar that has been crushed and screened until the grains are like powder. It's used for frostings and for decorative sprinkling over plain cakes. You can tell the degree of fineness of powdered sugar by the number of x's indicated on the package. The fine powdered is 4x, the very fine powdered is 6x, and the ultrafine powdered is 10x. The 10x type is what our Test Kitchens use in recipes.

Brown sugar is less refined than granulated sugar and comes in a light and dark form. Dark brown sugar has a stronger flavor. Our recipes specify which one to use when it makes a difference; otherwise, you choose.

Brown sugar will dry out easily after opening because it's moister than granulated sugar. After a package is opened, we transfer the unused part to an airtight container; this keeps it soft and moist. You can soften hardened brown sugar by putting it in an airtight container and adding a slice of apple or bread or by brief heating in the microwave.

Caramelized sugar is not a product, but rather the result of cooking granulated sugar long enough to melt it to the golden caramel stage. This takes about 10 minutes using a cast-iron skillet and wooden spoon. We tell how to make it in the Vanilla-Poached Pears recipe on page 185.

Raw sugar or **turbinado** is a popular coarse sugar that's often stirred into espresso and other coffee drinks.

Syrup

Molasses is the syrup left after making granulated sugar from sugar cane. It is most commonly sold as light or dark molasses. **Unsulphured** and **blackstrap molasses** are less-refined forms that have a stronger flavor. Use them only when specified in a recipe.

Honey is a thick syrup made by bees from the nectar of flowers. It's sweeter than sugar and has a distinctive flavor. Clover honey is widely sold in the marketplace, but there are dozens of flavored honeys available, most of which are named for the flower that produces the honey.

Corn syrup is available in light and dark forms, the lighter being lighter in flavor as well as color. Our recipes specify which form to use.

Cane syrup comes from sugar cane that has been boiled down to the consistency of syrup.

Sorghum comes from a coarse grass by the same name. It is processed to obtain a juice, which is then boiled down to a syrup.

Maple syrup comes from the sap of the sugar maple tree. Like sugar cane, it's boiled down to the consistency of syrup.

Thickening Agents

All-purpose flour is the most common thickener. It's used for gravies, sauces, and puddings, and gives an opaque appearance. Two tablespoons of flour will thicken one cup of liquid.

Use **cornstarch** to thicken puddings and sauces when you want a more translucent look, particularly with fruit sauces. One tablespoon of cornstarch will thicken one cup of liquid.

Arrowroot is not used as often as in the past, but it will thicken fillings and sauces, leaving them sparkling clear. One tablespoon of arrowroot will thicken one cup of liquid. When old recipes call for arrowroot, you can substitute an equal measure of cornstarch.

Instant blending flour is a commercially developed mixture that will dissolve in hot liquids without lumping and can be added directly to sauces and gravies without first being dissolved in water. Don't use this kind of flour for baking.

Use **tapioca** for thickening pie fillings and puddings. It gives a characteristic granular texture to foods. Use about 1½ tablespoons tapioca per cup of liquid.

Thickening agents must be handled correctly during cooking so that they'll thicken smoothly without lumping. Refer to pages 385-386 for specific information about thickening with flour and cornstarch.

Vinegar

Vinegar gives a jolt of acidity to foods like salads, dressings, and marinades. **White vinegar** is the most common type. Use it when our recipes simply specify vinegar.

Wine vinegar, either red or white, is mild in flavor and makes a nice addition to marinades and salad dressings.

Cider vinegar, made from the juice of apples, is a strong vinegar commonly used in slaws, fruit salads, and for pickling. Whether you use cider or white vinegar for canning, make sure the label says it has 5% acidity.

Balsamic vinegar gets its dark brown color and pungent sweetness from aging in wood over a period of years. Use this luxurious vinegar sparingly. It enriches a wide range of foods from beef stew to strawberries.

Commercially available **herb vinegars** are growing in popularity. You can purchase them commercially or see our vinegar recipes on pages 414-415.

TERMS & TECHNIQUES

Barbecue: To roast meat slowly over coals on a spit or framework, or to roast in an oven, basting meat occasionally with a sauce or marinade.

Baste: To spoon or brush liquid over meats while they're cooking to keep food moist and flavorful. The liquid can be a sauce, glaze, melted butter, or pan juices.

Beat: To mix vigorously with a brisk motion using a spoon, fork, whisk, or electric mixer.

Blanch: To dip food briefly into boiling water. Blanching loosens tomato and peach skins for easy peeling.

Blend: To combine two or more ingredients together until uniformly mixed. You can use an electric mixer, blender, or spoon to blend ingredients.

Boil: To heat a liquid until bubbles break vigorously on the surface.

Braise: To cook slowly with a small amount of liquid in a tightly covered pan. (Less tender cuts of meat may be browned first on all sides in a small amount of fat; then the meat is seasoned, and water is added.)

Broil: To cook by direct dry heat under a broiler.

Bruise: To partially crush an ingredient, such as herbs, to release flavor for seasoning food.

Butterfly: To split food like shrimp or boneless leg of lamb horizontally in half, cutting almost but not all the way through food. Food is then opened flat to expose more surface area so the food cooks evenly and quickly.

Caramelize: To cook sugar in a skillet over medium heat until it forms a golden syrup. Foods like onions that contain natural sugar caramelize and turn golden during roasting.

Chop: To cut food roughly into small, irregular pieces.

GRATING & SHREDDING

Grating: When recipes specify grating an ingredient like hard cheese or chocolate, use the smallest holes of an upright grater or a small handheld grater. It will yield fine particles.

Shredding: When recipes specify shredding an ingredient like Cheddar cheese, use the largest holes of an upright grater. It will yield long shreds.

MEASURING INGREDIENTS

The correct measuring technique is critical to the success of a recipe. It's important to get in the habit of measuring ingredients with precision. Not all ingredients are measured the same way or using the same type of equipment.

These photos show different measuring equipment and techniques for specific types of food.

Measuring dry ingredients: Use stainless steel or plastic dry measuring cups. For flour, lightly spoon it into cup, letting it mound slightly. Then level top (shown at right).

Leveling dry ingredients: Level the top using the straight edge of a spatula or knife.

Measuring liquid ingredients: Measure liquids on a level surface in a glass or clear plastic measuring cup with a pouring lip. Read liquid measurements at eye level.

Measuring brown sugar: To measure accurately, use the measuring cup that holds the exact amount called for in a recipe. Pack brown sugar firmly into dry measuring cup; then level it off. The sugar will hold its shape when turned out of the cup.

Measuring syrupy ingredients: When measuring honey, molasses, corn syrup, or other sticky ingredients, first coat the measuring spoon or cup with vegetable cooking spray. Then the ingredient will slip out easily and clean up will be simple.

Core: To remove the tough or woody center of some fruits and vegetables.

Cream: To beat butter, alone or with sugar, until light and fluffy.

Crimp: To pinch dough edges to create a decorative edge on a piecrust or to seal two layers of dough together so filling doesn't seep out during baking. You can use the tines of a fork or your fingers to crimp.

Cut in: To incorporate by cutting or chopping motions, as in cutting butter or shortening into flour for pastry.

Deglaze: To create a complex, flavorful sauce by pouring liquid into a pan in which meat has been roasted or sautéed in order to absorb the essence and caramelized bits. First sauté meat in a heavy skillet; then remove food from skillet and add wine or broth. Bring to a boil over high heat, scraping up crusty bits that cling to bottom of skillet (the liquid will loosen them). Simmer briefly, and pour over food before serving. You can add cream, cheese, or herbs for richer flavor.

Devein: To remove intestinal vein of shrimp, using a small knife or shrimp deveiner.

Dice: To cut food into pieces about ⅛ to ¼ inch on each side.

Dissolve: To mix a dry substance with liquid until the dry substance becomes part of the solution.

Dot: To scatter small bits of butter over a casserole, pie, or other food before baking. The butter adds flavor and enhances a golden crust.

Dredge: To coat food lightly with a dry ingredient like flour or breadcrumbs.

Drizzle: To slowly pour liquid such as melted butter in a fine stream, back and forth, over food.

Dust: To sprinkle very lightly with a powdery ingredient like powdered sugar or flour.

Emulsify: To bind liquids such as oil and water that don't blend together naturally. Add one liquid, usually the oil, to the other liquid in a slow, steady stream while blending.

Flambé: To flame, using alcohol as the burning agent; the flame causes caramelization, enhancing flavor.

Fold: To add a whipped ingredient, such as cream or egg white, to another ingredient or mixture with a spatula by gentle over-and-under movement.

Fry: To cook food in hot fat, usually oil or melted shortening.

Grate: To obtain very small particles of food by rubbing on smallest holes of a grater.

Julienne: To cut food into thin, uniform matchsticks that are 2 to 3 inches long and ⅛ to ¼ inch wide.

Knead: To work a food (usually dough) by hand, using a folding-back-and-pressing-forward motion.

Marinate: To flavor (and sometimes tenderize) food by letting it soak in a liquid. The liquid often contains an acid like lemon juice, wine, or vinegar as well as oil and seasonings.

Mince: To chop food into very fine irregular pieces using a chef's knife.

Panbroil: To cook over direct heat in an uncovered skillet containing little or no fat.

Panfry: To cook in an uncovered skillet in small amount of fat until food is browned and cooked to proper doneness.

WORKING WITH GARLIC

Mashing/crushing garlic: Mash garlic by crushing it under the weight of your hand on a chef's knife. The skin should slip right off.

Heads or cloves? The whole bulb of garlic is the head. Remove papery skin to expose individual cloves. When buying garlic, pick firm, plump bulbs. Keep garlic in a cool, dry place up to four months.

Parboil: To partially cook in boiling water before final cooking on a grill or in the oven.

Pipe: To squeeze a smooth mixture through a decorating bag or zip-top plastic bag with a corner snipped to make a shaped dough or design.

Poach: To cook in small amount of gently simmering liquid. The surface should barely shimmer.

Pound: To flatten meats and poultry to a uniform thickness using a meat mallet or rolling pin. This promotes even thickness and tenderizes tough cuts of meat by breaking up connective tissue.

Preheat: To turn on oven so that desired temperature will be reached before food is inserted for baking. We always preheat ovens 10 minutes before baking.

WORKING WITH FRESH HERBS

Stripping woody stems: Strip the leaves from a woody stem of fresh rosemary or thyme. Then chop the leaves or use them whole.

Making a bouquet garni: Tie 3 or 4 herbs together with string or in a cheesecloth bag. Use the bundle to flavor soups and stews.

Bruising leaves: Twist a small bunch of fresh mint or basil leaves to bruise them. This releases the full flavor of the herb for use in a recipe.

Prick: To pierce food before cooking.

Proof: To test yeast for potency; the rising stage for yeast breads.

Punch down: To deflate yeast bread dough after it has risen by punching your fist into center of dough and then pulling the edges into the center.

Puree: To form a smooth mixture by blending food in a food processor or blender.

Reduce: To rapidly boil a liquid to concentrate its flavor and to reduce its amount by evaporation.

Render: To melt fat away from surrounding meat. Crispy cracklings will be left.

Roast: To cook, uncovered, in an oven by dry heat.

Sauté: To cook or brown food lightly over fairly high heat in a small amount of fat in a skillet.

Score: To cut shallow gashes on surface of food, as in scoring fat on ham before glazing.

Sear: To brown surface of meat over high heat to add depth of flavor and to caramelize the meat's exterior.

Shred: To cut, tear, or grate food into long, narrow pieces or to rub food on the large holes of a grater.

Shuck: To remove the husks of corn with your hands or the shells of oysters, mussels, or clams, using a special knife.

Simmer: To cook gently at a temperature just below the boiling point.

Skim: To remove fat from surface of liquid.

Steam: To cook with steam given off by boiling water either in a pressure cooker on a platform in a covered pan or in a special steamer.

Steep: To let food, such as tea, stand in almost boiling water until the flavor is extracted.

Stir-fry: To cook quickly in a small amount of oil over high heat, using light and constant tossing motions to preserve texture of food. A wok is the traditional pan used to stir-fry, but a skillet works, too.

Temper: To heat food gently before adding it to a hot mixture so it doesn't curdle. Temper beaten eggs by adding one-fourth of a hot mixture to eggs to raise the temperature; then stir it back into the hot mixture.

Toss: To mix together gently with light over and under motions in order not to bruise delicate food such as salad greens.

Whip: To beat rapidly to incorporate air and increase volume.

CUTTING TECHNIQUES

Slicing: Cut food into desired thickness, using a sharp chef's knife or slicing knife. Cut each slice the same thickness.

Cutting julienne strips: Cut food into thin, uniform matchsticks that are 2 to 3 inches long and ⅛ to ¼ inch wide.

Cubing and dicing: For cubes, cut food into pieces ½ inch or larger on each side. When dicing, cut food into pieces ⅛ to ¼ inch on each side. You're basically cutting small cubes.

Slicing diagonally: Hold knife at a 45° angle to the food and slice to desired thickness. This technique exposes the maximum surface area, allowing food to cook quickly.

Mincing: Chop food into very fine irregular pieces, using the knife's blade to pull pieces back into the pile until minced.

Cutting canned tomatoes: Use kitchen shears to cut tomatoes in the can when a recipe specifies "undrained and chopped."

MEAL PLANNING

Eating right can mean something different to each of us. In general, it's wise to watch portion sizes, become aware of the fat sources in your diet, and be more discerning about the foods you choose to eat. And don't forget those two words, *balance* and *moderation*. Take into consideration the points on these pages. They'll help you plan wholesome meals for family and friends.

The Food Guide Pyramid

To help Americans make nutritious food choices and plan healthful meals, the U.S. Department of Agriculture has developed the Food Guide Pyramid. Meant to update the "Basic Four" food groups, the pyramid builds on the foundation that eating right means eating a wide variety of foods in moderation every day.

The pyramid stresses that good nutrition begins with three types of food—*grains* (including breads, cereal, rice, and pasta), *vegetables*, and *fruits*. These foods supply vitamins, minerals, complex carbohydrates, and dietary fiber—important nutrients that contribute to overall health. And these foods are also inherently low in fat, sodium, and cholesterol. Foods from the *dairy* and *meat* groups are among the richest sources of protein, calcium, certain B vitamins, and minerals like iron and zinc. Recommendations for all the food groups follow and are based on the Food Guide Pyramid.

HOW WE ANALYZE RECIPES

•Each of the recipes in this book includes a nutrient analysis for calories, fat, cholesterol, and sodium.

•If a recipe ingredient has a range in amounts, we analyze with the first amount given.

•We don't include garnishes or ingredients labeled "optional" in the analyses.

•We consider a recipe healthy if it has 30% or less calories from fat and has under 800 mg sodium per serving. Look for the bright green banner at the top of these recipes.

Just remember that no one food group is more important than another—all of them are essential for good health. Plan your daily meals to include at least the minimum number of servings suggested for each food group.

The number of recommended daily servings is based on the nutrient needs of normal adults. Teenagers, men, and active adults may need more servings to meet their calorie needs.

Breads, Cereal, Rice, and Pasta Group — 6 to 11 servings daily

•These filling foods provide complex carbohydrates. You need the most servings of these foods each day.

•One serving = 1 slice of bread, ½ bagel, 7-inch tortilla, 1 ounce dinner roll, 1 ounce dry cereal, or ½ to ¾ cup cooked cereal, rice, or pasta.

Vegetable Group — 3 to 5 servings daily

•Generally high in vitamins, minerals, and fiber, fruits and vegetables contain little if any fat, no cholesterol, and are relatively low in calories.

•One serving = 1 cup raw leafy vegetables, ½ cup cooked or raw vegetables, or ¾ cup vegetable juice.

Fruit group — 2 to 4 servings daily

•Fruits and fruit juices are low in fat and sodium and provide important amounts of vitamins A and C and potassium.

•One serving = 1 medium apple, banana, or orange; ½ cup chopped cooked or canned fruit, or ¾ cup fruit juice.

•When you have a choice, eat bulkier, higher fiber foods, like an apple instead of apple juice.

Milk, Yogurt, and Cheese Group — 2 to 3 servings daily

•The Food Guide Pyramid suggests 2 servings each day for adults and 3 servings for teenagers, young adults to age 24, and women who are pregnant or breast feeding.

•One serving = 1 cup of milk or yogurt, 1½ ounces of natural/hard cheese, or 2 ounces of processed cheese.

Meats, Poultry, Fish, Dry Beans, Eggs, & Nut Group — 2 to 3 servings daily

•One serving = 3 ounces of cooked lean meat, poultry, or fish.

•For other foods in this group, count ½ cup of cooked *legumes* (dried beans and peas), 2 eggs (limit yolks to 4 per week), or 2 tablespoons of peanut butter as 1 ounce of meat (or about ⅓ of a meat serving).

Fats, Oils, and Sweets Group — use sparingly

Eat foods in this category only occasionally and in moderation. Sweet or high-fat foods such as candy, desserts, soft drinks, butter, margarine, gravy, salad dressing, and mayonnaise tend to be high in "empty calories," with little, if any, nutrients.

Planning a Great Meal

Good nutrition isn't the only factor to consider when planning a meal. Give your menus some creative attention. Select recipes and foods that look and taste great together. To put a menu together, first choose a focus and center the menu around it. Then thoughtfully plan the accompaniments.

As a rule, **let variety be your guide.** By serving a variety of foods prepared using different cooking methods, chances are you'll be providing nutritious and appealing meals for your family and friends.

Contemplate the color, flavor, texture, and size of each menu item that will go on the plate. Be sure to include contrasting colors instead of serving a monochromatic meal. Garnishes help here. Simple extras like herb sprigs or lemon twists add a splash of color to the plate. See a variety of garnish ideas on pages 26-27.

Don't repeat flavors. If you're serving a tomato appetizer, avoid serving tomato as a side dish. Be sure to introduce milder flavors before strong ones. Generally, it's a good idea to plan only one highly seasoned recipe and one starchy item in a menu.

Serve some foods hot, some cold. Cold soups, chilled fruit, and vegetable salads provide welcome contrasts to hot entrées. Always serve food at the appropriate temperature. One tip toward this goal is to chill the serving plates for cold foods and warm the serving bowls to help keep hot foods like pastas, side dishes, and many entrées hot.

Vary the shapes of food just as you would the color and texture. For instance, try not to serve several dishes of round food like meatballs, new potatoes, and brussels sprouts. And avoid serving too many mixtures (casseroles) in a meal.

Always **consider your schedule** when planning a menu. Don't overextend yourself. If time is limited, plan quick and simple recipes, use some convenience foods, and count on the neighborhood deli.

See our Menu Index on pages 478-479 for dozens of ideas to get you started.

Wine Wisdom

There are several things to ponder when pairing wines with food. First, it's important to be familiar with the qualities of wine. Once you've done some reading and experienced a wine tasting or two, then make a friend at your local wine shop. Ask questions each time you purchase wine for a meal. After that, wine selection is a matter of experimenting and personal preference.

Your sense of smell plays a major role in sampling and selecting wines. A wine's fragrance is called its *nose* or *bouquet*. The scents you detect depend on the type of grape used, where it was grown, if it was aged in oak barrels, and how long it's been in the bottle.

To swirl and taste wine, grasp the stem of the glass rather than the bowl so that you don't raise the wine's temperature. Swirl cautiously with the glass set on the table. Then bring the glass quickly to your nose, breathe deeply, and suck in a sip. Sample a variety of wines to familiarize yourself with all types.

Chardonnay is perhaps the most popular of all white-wine grapes. It's generally a deep golden color, which hints that it's been aged in oak barrels. Usually dry, chardonnay has buttery, fruity, vanilla, and toasty flavors. It pairs well with a host of entrées.

Sauvignon Blanc is a dry white wine that's lighter in color and body and more citrusy and herbaceous than Chardonnay. It's a food-friendly wine with an acidic zing. *Riesling* is a light, fruity wine with a floral fragrance. Match all three of these white wines with

most poultry, fish, and shellfish recipes, particularly from the grill.

Cabernet Sauvignon is a deep, rich ruby-red wine with peppery, berry, and vanilla qualities from oak aging. "Cab" is a big, full-bodied, and intense wine. It pairs well with beef, poultry, pasta, and game meats.

Merlot also has a deep ruby color and is a softer, more supple red wine than Cab. Its flavor can hint of berry, black cherry, plum, spice, and tobacco. It pairs well with poultry and lamb.

Pinot Noir is more delicate than the two reds listed above. Its complex flavor often hints of spicy cherries with earthy nuances. It pairs well with beef and ham.

Any wine with bubbles is a *sparkling wine*, but only sparkling wine made by a specific process in the Champagne region of France can be called *champagne*.

The wine you select will reveal its best qualities when served correctly. For example, the wine must be served at the optimum temperature, the cork should be extracted neatly, and the wine should be served in an appropriately shaped glass. Here are some pointers:

•**Temperature check:** Serve white wines just out of the refrigerator or slightly warmer; the sweeter the wine, the cooler the recommended serving temperature. Light, young red wines taste best between 55° and 60°;

full-bodied reds are typically enjoyed at 60° to 65°. You can always start with wine a little too cold; it'll warm up quickly as a meal gets under way.

•**Serving savvy:** Wine should be opened gently, using an opener that will enable you to extract the cork cleanly. Be sure to wipe off the rim of the bottle before serving or decanting the wine. If served from the bottle, twist the bottle as you pour to prevent dripping. Fill a wine glass only one-half to two-thirds full (one-third for a wine tasting). Fine table wines come in a 750-milliliter bottle; it's a little less than a quart, and it contains five to six glasses of wine. A *split* is a 375-milliliter half-bottle, meant for an intimate occasion.

•**Wine glass class:** Red wine glasses have larger bowls than white wine glasses. This allows more room for swirling so that you can enjoy the big bouquet that's the trademark of fine red wine. Ideally, a wine glass should be thin, and the rim of the glass should not be any thicker than the glass itself.

•**Order, order:** If you're serving more than one wine with a meal, serve dry before sweet, white before red, light before full-bodied, and young before aged.

•**Good to the last drop:** Store leftover wine by recorking it and storing it in the refrigerator up to two days.

ENTERTAINING

Setting the Table

When entertaining friends in your home, follow the photograph as a guide to setting your table. Add color and warmth with a linen place mat, or rest the charger (service plate) right on the table. Place a simply folded napkin on the left of the place setting or see our Fabulous Napkin Folds (opposite page) for other options. If food is served family style or filled plates are brought from the kitchen after friends are seated, you can place the napkin in the center of the service plate or place mat when setting the table.

Arrange the charger and flatware one inch from the edge of the table; position the flatware pieces beginning at the outside edge according to their order of use. Place the knife, with the blade turned toward the plate, on the right beside the plate, and spoons to the right of the knife. The soup spoon goes to the extreme right. Set the forks on the plate's left, beginning at the outside edge according to their logical sequence—salad fork, fish fork, and meat or dinner fork. The dessert fork or spoon can be brought in with dessert or you can use the European placement of this flatware at the top of the plate parallel to the edge of the table.

Place the water glass or goblet above the knife. If you're serving iced tea or wine, set this glass to the right of the water glass above the spoon. If soup or salad is served as a separate course, place the individual dish on the charger. However, salad may be served with the meal, in which case, position the salad plate or bowl on the left side by the fork.

If the entrée is served with a sauce or gravy, consider using separate small plates for bread and butter. Place each bread and butter plate above the forks. When using individual butter spreaders, rest each at the top of a bread plate parallel to the table's edge with the handle to the right. When serving coffee or tea with the meal, the cup and saucer go to the right of the spoons, but if meant to be served with dessert, bring cups and saucers in at that time.

For an informal dinner, a salt and pepper container for every two to three people is correct. On a formal table, salt and pepper containers (usually crystal) are placed directly above each place setting.

Because of busy lifestyles, it has become necessary to simplify setting the family table. Usually only a dinner plate, dessert plate, one glass, napkin, and flatware are essential. A salad plate, soup bowl, and salad fork are optional items. It's simple—use only what you need for each meal and eliminate the rest.

RULES TO REGARD

- As soon as you are seated, place your napkin in your lap.
- Wait to begin eating until the hostess takes the first bite. Also follow her lead when in doubt about which utensil to use.
- Once you pick up a piece of flatware, never place it back on the table; rest it on your plate. Leave knife at upper plate edge with blade toward plate. Leave the fork centered on the plate.
- Never butter a whole piece of bread at one time; instead, break off a bite-sized piece, butter, and eat it. Biscuits are an exception.
- Remove olive pits or any seeds from your mouth with the same utensil you used to eat the food.
- For formal service, present a served dinner plate at the left of the recipient; remove plates from the right.
- For family-style service, pass food around the table to the right.
- When passing salt and pepper, place the shakers or mills on the table rather than handing them directly to the person requesting them. And always pass both salt and pepper, even if only one is requested.
- Place your knife and fork together at the "3:15" position on your plate to signal that you've finished your meal.
- At the end of the meal as you leave the table, place your napkin on the table, not in your chair or on your plate.

FABULOUS NAPKIN FOLDS

Creative napkin folding is a simple way to add style to your table settings. With the help of the illustrations below and along with a little imagination, you can add a graceful touch to any meal. Keep in mind that solid white or ecru napkins are often used for fancy table settings, and prints and vivid colors are used for more casual tables.

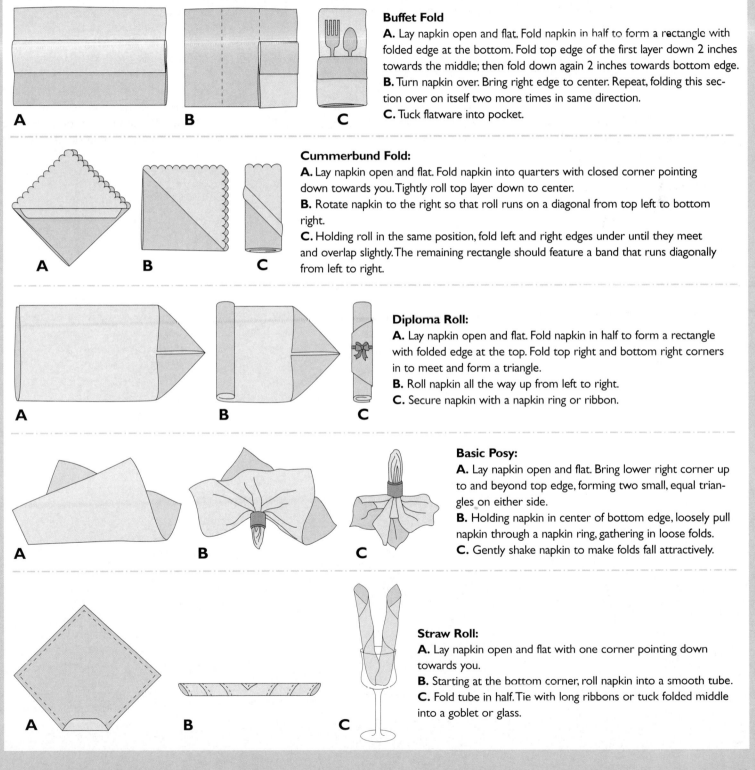

Buffet Fold
A. Lay napkin open and flat. Fold napkin in half to form a rectangle with folded edge at the bottom. Fold top edge of the first layer down 2 inches towards the middle; then fold down again 2 inches towards bottom edge.
B. Turn napkin over. Bring right edge to center. Repeat, folding this section over on itself two more times in same direction.
C. Tuck flatware into pocket.

Cummerbund Fold:
A. Lay napkin open and flat. Fold napkin into quarters with closed corner pointing down towards you. Tightly roll top layer down to center.
B. Rotate napkin to the right so that roll runs on a diagonal from top left to bottom right.
C. Holding roll in the same position, fold left and right edges under until they meet and overlap slightly. The remaining rectangle should feature a band that runs diagonally from left to right.

Diploma Roll:
A. Lay napkin open and flat. Fold napkin in half to form a rectangle with folded edge at the top. Fold top right and bottom right corners in to meet and form a triangle.
B. Roll napkin all the way up from left to right.
C. Secure napkin with a napkin ring or ribbon.

Basic Posy:
A. Lay napkin open and flat. Bring lower right corner up to and beyond top edge, forming two small, equal triangles on either side.
B. Holding napkin in center of bottom edge, loosely pull napkin through a napkin ring, gathering in loose folds.
C. Gently shake napkin to make folds fall attractively.

Straw Roll:
A. Lay napkin open and flat with one corner pointing down towards you.
B. Starting at the bottom corner, roll napkin into a smooth tube.
C. Fold tube in half. Tie with long ribbons or tuck folded middle into a goblet or glass.

GO FOR THE GARNISH

Garnishes give food a finished look and the cook an opportunity to show some artistic flair. The best garnishes are natural garnishes made from ingredients in the recipe. For example, if a recipe includes lemon juice and fresh herbs, then a lemon twist or fresh herb sprig is ideal. As a rule, keep garnishes simple. Never spend more time on the garnish than you did preparing the food. Try your hand at making the garnishes on these pages.

FROSTED GRAPES

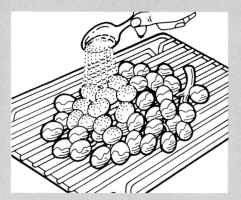

CHOCOLATE CURLS

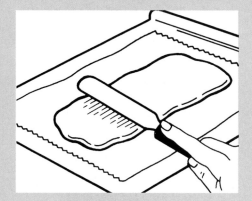

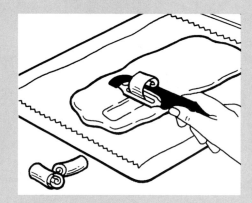

CHOCOLATE LEAVES

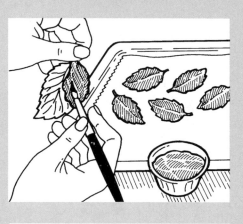

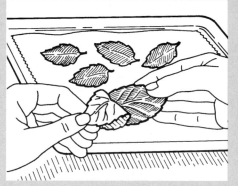

Frosted Grapes: Place grapes on a wire rack. Paint grapes lightly with thawed egg substitute, using a soft pastry brush.

While grapes are still wet, sprinkle them with granulated sugar to create a frosted look, and allow them to dry in a cool place (about 1 hour). Don't refrigerate the frosted grapes because the moisture in the refrigerator will melt the sugar.

Frosted Cranberries: Follow directions for Frosted Grapes substituting fresh cranberries.

Chocolate Curls: Melt squares or morsels of semisweet chocolate over hot water in a double boiler; cool slightly. Pour chocolate out onto a wax paper-lined baking sheet. Spread chocolate with a spatula into a 3-inch-wide strip. Smooth the top of the strip with spatula. Let stand at room temperature until chocolate cools and feels slightly tacky, but not firm. (If chocolate is too hard, curls will break; if it's too soft, chocolate won't curl.)

Gently pull a vegetable peeler across length of chocolate until curl forms, letting chocolate curl up on top of peeler. Insert wooden pick inside curl to transfer. Chill until ready to use.

Chocolate leaves: Select leaves, such as mint leaves, that are nonpoisonous. Wash leaves and dry thoroughly. Melt 1 or 2 ounces semisweet chocolate over hot water in a double boiler; cool slightly. Using a tiny brush, paint chocolate on the back of each leaf, spreading to the edges. Place leaves, chocolate side up, on wax paper-lined baking sheets. Chill until firm, at least 10 minutes. Then grasp leaf at stem end, and carefully and quickly peel leaf from chocolate. Chill chocolate leaves until ready to use.

CARROT CURLS

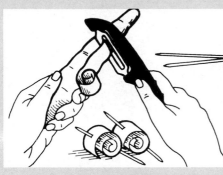

Carrot Curls: Scrape carrot. Cut off ½ inch from each end; discard. Using a vegetable peeler, cut thin lengthwise strips from carrot. Roll strips jellyroll fashion; secure with wooden picks. Drop in ice water, and refrigerate at least 1 hour for curls to set. Remove picks before serving.

CARROT FLOWERS

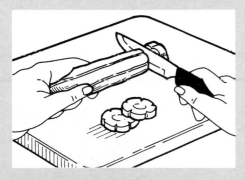

Carrot Flowers: Scrape carrot. Using a sharp paring knife, cut 4 or 5 grooves, evenly spaced, down the length of carrot; then slice the carrot to produce flowers.

RADISH ROSES

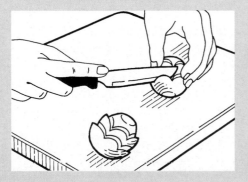

Radish Rose: Slice stem end and root tip from radish. Hold radish with root tip up, and slice 4 or 5 petals around the radish by slicing from top to, but not through, bottom. Leave a little red between each petal. Drop radish in ice water, and refrigerate at least 1 hour for rose to open.

FLUTED MUSHROOMS

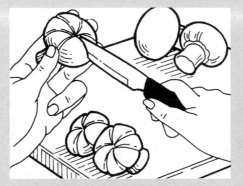

Fluted Mushrooms: Select firm, white mushrooms. Cut several slits at even intervals around each mushroom cap, cutting from the center of the cap to the edge and using a curving motion with a paring knife. Make another set of slits parallel to the first slits, allowing 1/16 inch between them. Remove and discard the thin strips of mushroom between the slits.

CELERY FANS

Celery Fans: Slice celery stalks into 3- or 4-inch lengths, and place on a cutting board. Using a sharp knife, cut several slits at one or both ends of each piece of celery, cutting almost to, but not through, the center. Place celery in ice water, and refrigerate until the fans curl.
Green Onion Fans: Follow directions for Celery Fans, but slice off root and most of onion's top portion before beginning.

TOMATO ROSES

Tomato Rose: Cut a thin slice from bottom of tomato, using a sharp paring knife; discard. Beginning at top, peel a continuous paper-thin strip (about ¾ inch wide for regular tomatoes, and about ¼ inch wide for cherry tomatoes) from entire tomato.

Beginning with first portion cut, shape the strip like a rose. With flesh side inward, coil the strip tightly at first to form the center of the rose, gradually letting it become looser to form the outer petals.

CITRUS CUPS

Citrus Cups: Cut a very thin slice from each end of the fruit so that the cups will sit level. Insert the blade of a small sharp knife at a downward angle into the middle of the fruit; remove the blade. Insert knife again at an upward angle to make a zigzag pattern. Continue cutting in this fashion all the way around fruit.

Separate halves by twisting slightly and carefully pulling them apart. Scoop out pulp if using the cups as a container for dip, sherbet, or other food.

Herbed Tomato Crostini (page 40)

APPETIZERS & BEVERAGES

We know appetizers by many names including canapés, crudités, finger food, starters, openers, first course, hors d'oeuvres, and crostini. Regardless of the name, the goal remains the same—when serving these savory bites, offer just enough to stimulate, not satisfy, the appetite.

Equipment

You probably have all the equipment you need for preparing appetizers. The most helpful tools are simply sharp knives and large baking sheets to help you cut and cook efficiently when you're planning for a crowd.

When serving appetizers, you'll want a large assortment of trays, bowls, and spreaders for setting up buffets. Select them with an eye for variation in the size, shape, and height of containers to add interest to the arrangement. Don't overlook baskets and sentimental china—they'll often double as interesting containers. And flea-market finds can be priceless conversation starters.

You may want to consider buying or borrowing warming trays and containers to keep hot appetizers at the right temperature. If you don't have a chafing dish, a fondue pot or slow cooker set on low will do the job.

Reception Appetizers

If your guest list is too large to provide each person a seat, just serve finger food. Set up one or two main appetizer buffets; then scatter a few individual hors d'oeuvres around the house. Provide plenty of napkins, and avoid serving messy foods that are apt to drip as guests eat them. Pick recipes you've prepared before, so you can serve them with confidence. Balance high-flavored items with simple, fresh options. Plan your menu so it contains both hot and cold appetizers, as well as items which guests can easily serve themselves. Limit the choices that must be spooned out, sliced, or spread to make it easy on your guests.

First Course Appetizers

Select one spectacular appetizer, such as Coconut Shrimp with Sweet Dipping Sauce (page 46), as a first course to dinner, and make servings a little more substantial than typical appetizer buffet offerings. First courses are usually served at the dining table, but you can also serve them elsewhere, such as the patio, deck, or sunroom for variety.

Freezing Appetizers

Many appetizers freeze well, especially those made with meat or bread. Avoid freezing appetizers that contain fresh vegetables, mayonnaise, or hard-cooked eggs. The secret to keeping appetizers fresh in the freezer is proper wrapping—be sure it's airtight to avoid freezer burn. Usually, you can let appetizers thaw overnight in the refrigerator (if they require refrigeration).

SNACKS

They are those tempting morsels that you'd swear you weren't eating many of—until the bowl is empty. Snacks will give you days of enjoyment when stored in an airtight container— if you can resist!

Snack recipes are generally easy to prepare. Recipes like Cheese Wafers (page 31) and Curried Party Mix (this page) yield large amounts, keep well, and make attractive gifts.

Snacks come in handy when unexpected company drops in. Keep any of the following items on hand to serve at a moment's notice: gourmet cheese and crackers, commercial picante sauce or bean dip and chips, sliced fresh fruit, and seasoned nuts. And find uses for these same items in recipes throughout this chapter.

Cinnamon-Coffee Pecans

◄ QUICK • MAKE AHEAD ►

PREP: 9 MINUTES   COOK: 25 MINUTES

These sugar-crusted nuts, accented with coffee flavor, make a great gift.

3 cups pecan halves
½ cup sugar
¼ cup water
1 tablespoon instant coffee granules
1 teaspoon ground cinnamon
Dash of salt

•Spread pecans in an ungreased roasting pan or 15- x 10-inch jellyroll pan. Bake at 350° for 10 minutes, stirring after 5 minutes.
•Combine sugar and remaining 4 ingredients in a saucepan. Cook over medium-low heat until sugar and coffee dissolve, stirring often. Add pecans, and cook 3 minutes, stirring constantly. Remove from heat.
•Spread pecans in ungreased pan. Bake at 300° for 15 minutes, stirring every 5 minutes. Cool completely; store in an airtight container. Yield: 4 cups.
Per ¼-cup serving: Calories 176 Fat 15.3g
Cholesterol 0mg Sodium 9mg

Deviled Nuts

◄ QUICK • MAKE AHEAD ►

PREP: 5 MINUTES   COOK: 20 MINUTES

Red pepper, hot sauce, and dry mustard distinguish these coated pecans as "deviled."

1 pound pecan halves
⅓ cup butter or margarine, melted
2 teaspoons hot sauce
2 teaspoons Worcestershire sauce
¾ teaspoon salt
¼ to ½ teaspoon ground red pepper
¼ teaspoon dry mustard

•Spread pecans in an ungreased roasting pan or 13- x 9-inch pan. Combine butter and remaining 5 ingredients; pour over pecans, stirring well.
•Bake at 325° for 20 minutes, stirring twice. Drain on paper towels; cool completely. Store in an airtight container. Yield: 4½ cups.
Per ¼-cup serving: Calories 199 Fat 20.5g
Cholesterol 9mg Sodium 142mg

Barbecued Cashews

◄ QUICK • MAKE AHEAD ►

PREP: 9 MINUTES   COOK: 12 MINUTES

2 tablespoons butter or margarine
1 tablespoon white wine Worcestershire sauce
1½ tablespoons soy sauce
1 teaspoon hot sauce
½ teaspoon salt
¼ teaspoon chili powder
¼ teaspoon ground red pepper
2 cups salted cashews

•Melt butter in a saucepan over medium heat. Stir in Worcestershire sauce and next 5 ingredients. Remove from heat. Add cashews, stirring to coat.
•Spread cashews in an aluminum foil-lined 15- x 10-inch jellyroll pan. Bake at 350° for 12 minutes, stirring twice. Spread cashews on paper towels; cool completely. Store in an airtight container. Yield: 2 cups.
Per ¼-cup serving: Calories 229 Fat 19g
Cholesterol 8mg Sodium 614mg

Curried Party Mix

◄ MAKE AHEAD ►

PREP: 15 MINUTES   COOK: 1 HOUR

Pull out some pantry staples to make this crispy cereal mix. The microwave instructions cut cooking time to a minimum.

¼ cup butter or margarine, melted
2 teaspoons curry powder
¾ to 1 teaspoon seasoned salt
½ teaspoon ground cumin
⅛ teaspoon ground red pepper
5 cups bite-size crispy corn squares (we tested with Corn Chex)
2 cups small pretzels (not pretzel sticks)
1½ cups whole almonds
1½ cups salted peanuts

•Combine first 5 ingredients in a small bowl. Combine cereal and remaining 3 ingredients in a large bowl. Stir butter mixture, and pour evenly over cereal mixture. Stir cereal mixture until coated.
•Spread mixture in a greased roasting pan or 15- x 10-inch jellyroll pan. Bake at 250° for 1 hour, stirring every 15 minutes. Spread mixture in a single layer on paper towels; cool completely. Store in an airtight container. Yield: 10 cups.
Per ¼-cup serving: Calories 88 Fat 6.3g
Cholesterol 3mg Sodium 168mg

Microwave Directions: Melt butter in a large microwave-safe bowl at HIGH 55 seconds; stir in seasonings. Gradually add cereal, pretzels, and nuts; stir until well coated. Microwave at HIGH 5 to 6 minutes, stirring and scraping sides and bottom of bowl with a rubber spatula every 2 minutes. Spread mixture in a single layer on paper towels; cool completely.

Cheese Wafers

◄ MAKE AHEAD ►
◄ FAMILY FAVORITE ►

PREP: 35 MINUTES

COOK: 14 MINUTES PER BATCH

A must for Southern brunches, showers, and teas, these coin-size wafers keep well in air-tight containers.

1½ cups (6 ounces) shredded sharp
    Cheddar cheese
½ cup butter or margarine, softened
1 cup all-purpose flour
Dash of salt
Dash of paprika
1½ cups corn flakes cereal, crushed
½ cup finely chopped almonds

•Process cheese and butter in a food processor until blended. Add flour, salt, and paprika; process until mixture forms a ball, stopping often to scrape down sides. Add cereal and almonds; process until blended, stopping twice to scrape down sides.
•Shape dough into 1-inch balls. Place balls about 2 inches apart on ungreased baking sheets. Flatten each ball in a crisscross pattern with a fork dipped in flour (see photo).
•Bake at 350° for 12 to 14 minutes or until lightly browned. Remove to wire racks to cool. Store in an airtight container. Yield: 4 dozen.

Per wafer: Calories 51 Fat 3.8g
Cholesterol 9mg Sodium 57mg

Easy-as-Pie Cheese Straws

◄ MAKE AHEAD ►

PREP: 15 MINUTES

COOK: 9 MINUTES PER BATCH

Only four ingredients are needed. And you choose the shape—straws or slices.

1 (11-ounce) package piecrust mix
1 (5-ounce) jar sharp process cheese
    spread
½ teaspoon ground red pepper
¼ teaspoon dry mustard

•Process all ingredients in a food processor 30 seconds or until mixture forms a ball, stopping twice to scrape down sides.

Shaping Cheese Wafers: Flatten each ball of dough in a crisscross pattern with a fork dipped in flour.

•Use a cookie press fitted with a bar-shaped disc to shape dough into 2½-inch straws, following manufacturer's instructions. Or divide dough in half, and shape each portion into a 7-inch log; wrap in plastic wrap, and chill 1 hour. Cut logs into ¼-inch slices.
•Place cheese straws on greased baking sheets. Bake at 375° for 8 minutes or until golden. Remove to wire racks to cool. Store in an airtight container. Yield: 5 dozen.

Per cheese straw: Calories 36 Fat 2.8g
Cholesterol 2mg Sodium 79mg

Granola

◄ QUICK • MAKE AHEAD ►

PREP: 4 MINUTES   COOK: 25 MINUTES

Enjoy the versatility of this granola. Alone it's a crunchy snack; with milk it's a cereal.

3 cups regular oats, uncooked
½ cup flaked coconut
½ cup sliced almonds or chopped pecans
¼ cup regular or honey-crunch wheat
    germ
¼ cup sunflower kernels
¼ cup plus 2 tablespoons honey
¼ cup vegetable oil
2½ tablespoons water
2 tablespoons brown sugar
¾ teaspoon vanilla extract
¼ teaspoon salt
¾ cup raisins

•Combine first 5 ingredients in a large bowl; stir well, and set aside.

•Combine honey and next 5 ingredients; pour over oat mixture, and stir well. Spread mixture evenly in a lightly greased 15- x 10-inch jellyroll pan.
•Bake at 350° for 25 minutes or until golden, stirring every 5 minutes. Cool. Stir in raisins. Store in an airtight container in a cool, dry place up to 1½ months. Yield: 5½ cups.

Per ½-cup serving: Calories 275 Fat 12.1g
Cholesterol 0mg Sodium 69mg

Double Nutty Granola: Stir 2 cups of mixed raw nuts (pecan halves, walnut halves, pine nuts, almonds) into the oat mixture before baking.

Fruited Granola: Stir 2 cups mixed chopped dried fruit (banana chips, dried apricots, apples, peaches, pineapple) into granola with raisins.

Candied Popcorn

◄ MAKE AHEAD ►
◄ FAMILY FAVORITE ►

PREP: 15 MINUTES   COOK: 1 HOUR

Freshly popped corn ensures crispness in this caramel-coated treat. Pop the corn with or without oil.

5 quarts freshly popped popcorn
1½ cups raw peanuts
1 cup butter or margarine
2 cups firmly packed brown
    sugar
½ cup dark corn syrup
½ teaspoon baking soda
½ teaspoon salt
½ teaspoon vanilla extract

•Place popcorn and peanuts in a lightly greased roasting pan; set aside.
•Melt butter in a large saucepan; stir in sugar and corn syrup. Bring to a boil; boil 5 minutes, stirring often. Remove from heat; stir in soda, salt, and vanilla.
•Pour sugar mixture over popcorn; stir well. Bake at 250° for 1 hour, stirring every 15 minutes. Cool; store in an airtight container. Yield: 5 quarts.

Per ½-cup serving: Calories 136 Fat 8.8g
Cholesterol 12mg Sodium 135mg

Chocolaty-Peanut Butter Horns

PREP: 24 MINUTES

Here's an easy sweet-and-salty combination for kids to make and eat.

¼ cup creamy peanut butter
2 cups corn snacks (we tested with Bugles)
3 (2-ounce) squares chocolate-flavored candy coating, melted

•Spoon peanut butter into a heavy-duty, zip-top plastic bag; seal bag, and snip a small hole in one corner of bag. Squeeze peanut butter into each corn snack (see photo); dip each into chocolate coating, and place on wax paper to dry. Store in an airtight container. Yield: 5 dozen.

Per appetizer: Calories 25 Fat 1.6g
Cholesterol 0mg Sodium 13mg

Filling corn snacks: Squeeze peanut butter to fill each corn snack. It doesn't take much.

Cracker Snackers

PREP: 1 HOUR

This favorite snack pulls double duty as a crouton when sprinkled over soup or salad. Replace the dill with your favorite herb if you'd like.

⅓ cup vegetable oil
1 clove garlic, thinly sliced
1 (11-ounce) package oyster crackers
1 (0.7-ounce) envelope Italian dressing mix (we tested with Good Seasons)
1 teaspoon dried dillweed
¼ teaspoon garlic powder

•Combine oil and garlic; let stand 30 minutes. Discard garlic.
•Place crackers in a bowl; sprinkle with oil. Combine dressing mix, dillweed, and garlic powder; sprinkle over crackers, stirring well. Let stand 30 minutes, stirring every 10 minutes. Store in an airtight container. Yield: 6 cups.

Per ½-cup serving: Calories 164 Fat 8.2g
Cholesterol 0mg Sodium 492mg

Fried Pickles

PREP: 6 MINUTES

COOK: 5 MINUTES PER BATCH

This Southern classic yields a bounty of crispy pickles to serve solo as an appetizer or alongside fried fish. Like potato chips, they'll disappear quickly.

1 large egg, lightly beaten
½ cup milk
½ cup beer
1 tablespoon all-purpose flour
¼ teaspoon hot sauce
3 cups all-purpose flour
½ teaspoon salt
¼ teaspoon garlic powder
2 teaspoons ground red pepper
1 teaspoon ground black pepper
2 (16-ounce) jars sliced dill pickles, drained
Vegetable oil

•Combine first 5 ingredients in a large bowl; stir well. Combine 3 cups flour and next 4 ingredients, stirring well. Dip pickle slices in egg mixture; dredge in flour mixture. Pour oil to depth of 2 inches into a large deep skillet; heat to 375°.
•Fry pickles, in batches, in hot oil 5 minutes or until lightly browned. Drain on paper towels, and serve immediately with Tartar Sauce (page 390), Cocktail Sauce (page 390), or Horseradish Butter (page 389). Yield: 5 cups.

Per ¼-cup serving: Calories 74 Fat 4.4g
Cholesterol 6mg Sodium 225mg

Homemade Potato Crisps

PREP: 8 MINUTES

COOK: 2 MINUTES PER BATCH

Nothing beats the taste of homemade chips. Let a food processor's very thin slicing blade or a deluxe Salad Shooter do the slicing for you. And for rustic chips, leave the peels on.

6 small baking potatoes (1½ pounds)
Vegetable oil
½ teaspoon seasoned salt or salt

•Slice potatoes thinly, and place in salted ice water (1 quart water to 1 teaspoon salt) until slicing is completed. Drain on paper towels.
•Pour oil to depth of 2 inches into a large deep skillet or Dutch oven; heat to 360°. Fry potato slices, a few at a time, 1 to 2 minutes or until golden and crisp, removing potato slices as they brown. Drain on paper towels; sprinkle with seasoned salt. Serve with ketchup. Yield: 4 cups.

Per ½-cup serving: Calories 123 Fat 6.9g
Cholesterol 0mg Sodium 299mg

THE NUTS AND BOLTS OF PLANNING

How do you know where to begin when planning appetizers for a crowd? When appetizers are going to be the entire meal, plan on 6 to 8 appetizer servings per guest. If a meal is to follow soon after appetizers, plan on 2 to 4 appetizer servings per guest. And if a meal is to follow several hours after appetizers, plan on 4 to 6 appetizer servings per guest.

DIPS & SPREADS

Dips and spreads are served often at parties because they're so easy for the host to make ahead. Just store them in the refrigerator in airtight containers; those without meat or other perishable ingredients will last several days.

Curry Dip

◀ QUICK • MAKE AHEAD ▶

PREP: 4 MINUTES

It's rich, creamy, and very thick—great for dunking broccoli and carrots.

1½ cups mayonnaise
1 teaspoon garlic powder
1 teaspoon dry mustard
¾ teaspoon curry powder
½ teaspoon celery seeds
¼ teaspoon instant minced onion
1½ teaspoons prepared horseradish
1 teaspoon white wine Worcestershire
   sauce
⅛ teaspoon hot sauce

•Combine all ingredients in a bowl; stir well. Cover and chill. Serve with assorted fresh vegetables. Yield: 1½ cups.
Per tablespoon: Calories 100 Fat 11g
Cholesterol 8mg Sodium 81mg

Sweet 'n' Spicy Mustard Dip

◀ QUICK • MAKE AHEAD ▶

PREP: 2 MINUTES

Sink chicken fingers and soft pretzels into this dip. It's good served warm or chilled.

3 tablespoons mayonnaise
3 tablespoons coarse-grained mustard
1 tablespoon prepared horseradish
2 teaspoons sugar

•Combine all ingredients in a microwave-safe bowl; microwave, uncovered, at HIGH 30 seconds, stirring once. Yield: ½ cup.
Per tablespoon: Calories 47 Fat 4.5g
Cholesterol 3mg Sodium 108mg

Antipasto Dip

Antipasto Dip

◀ MAKE AHEAD ▶

PREP: 21 MINUTES   CHILL: 8 HOURS

This colorful, high-flavor dip is just as good the second day.

1 (14-ounce) can artichoke hearts, drained
   and chopped
2 (7-ounce) cans sliced mushrooms,
   drained and chopped
1 (7-ounce) jar roasted red peppers,
   drained and chopped
1 cup pimiento-stuffed olives, drained and
   chopped
½ cup chopped green pepper
½ cup chopped celery
½ cup finely chopped onion
1 clove garlic, minced
½ cup olive oil or vegetable oil
⅔ cup white vinegar
2½ teaspoons Italian seasoning
1 teaspoon seasoned salt
1 teaspoon sugar
½ teaspoon freshly ground pepper

•Combine first 6 ingredients in a large bowl; set aside.
•Sauté onion and garlic in hot oil in a saucepan over medium heat 3 minutes or until onion is tender. Add vinegar and remaining 4 ingredients; bring to a boil. Remove from heat, and pour over vegetables; cover and chill 8 hours. Transfer to a serving dish, using a slotted spoon, if desired. Serve with crackers. Yield: 5 cups.
Per tablespoon: Calories 17 Fat 1.5g
Cholesterol 0mg Sodium 67mg

Eggplant-Mushroom Dip

◀ HEALTHY ▶

PREP: 27 MINUTES   CHILL: 2 HOURS

Pita or bagel chips complement this robust Mediterranean dip.

1 large eggplant (1½ to 2 pounds)
¼ cup olive oil
1 medium-size green pepper, chopped
1 medium onion, chopped
4 cloves garlic, minced
1 cup fresh mushrooms, chopped
1 (6-ounce) can tomato paste
½ cup water
2 tablespoons red wine vinegar
2 teaspoons sugar
½ teaspoon salt
½ teaspoon dried oregano
¼ teaspoon pepper
Lettuce leaves

•Lay eggplant on its side, cutting a thin slice from eggplant to form a flat base, if necessary. Horizontally slice off about top one-fourth of eggplant. Carefully scoop out pulp, leaving a ¼-inch shell; chop enough pulp to measure 3 cups. Reserve remaining pulp for another use. Set eggplant shell aside.
•Heat oil in a heavy saucepan over medium-low heat; add 3 cups chopped eggplant, green pepper, onion, and garlic. Cover and cook 15 minutes, stirring occasionally. Add mushrooms and next 7 ingredients. Bring to a boil; cover, reduce heat, and simmer 15 minutes or until eggplant is tender, stirring occasionally. Cool slightly; cover and chill at least 2 hours.
•Line eggplant shell with lettuce. Spoon dip into lettuce-lined shell; serve with pita chips or bagel chips. Yield: 3 cups.
Per tablespoon: Calories 18 Fat 1.2g
Cholesterol 0mg Sodium 27mg

Sauce Niçoise

◀ MAKE AHEAD ▶

PREP: 5 MINUTES   CHILL: 3 HOURS

This tangy olive dip doubles as a dressing for traditional salade niçoise ingredients—potatoes, tuna, and fresh green beans.

1 (2-ounce) can anchovies, rinsed and drained
¾ cup pitted ripe olives
1 tablespoon capers
2 cloves garlic
2 cups mayonnaise

•Process first 4 ingredients in a food processor until finely chopped, stopping once to scrape down sides. Stir in mayonnaise.
•Cover and chill at least 3 hours. Serve with fresh vegetables. Yield: 2½ cups.
Per tablespoon: Calories 84 Fat 9.1g
Cholesterol 6mg Sodium 147mg

WHAT'S A CAPER?

Capers are small, tangy green buds that resemble peppercorns. Find them on the grocery aisle near pickled items.

Tapenade

◀ QUICK ▶

PREP: 20 MINUTES

Hailing from Provence, tapenade is a thick paste of olives and capers. A crusty baguette is its ideal companion.

1 cup pitted ripe olives
¼ cup chopped fresh basil
3 canned anchovy fillets, rinsed and drained
2 tablespoons capers
1 clove garlic
1 tablespoon lemon juice
2 teaspoons coarse-grained mustard
⅛ teaspoon coarsely ground pepper
¼ cup olive oil
1 small sweet red pepper (optional)
Garnish: fresh thyme sprigs

•Process first 8 ingredients in a food processor until minced, stopping twice to scrape down sides. With processor running, slowly

pour oil through food chute; process 1 to 2 minutes or until mixture thickens, scraping down sides occasionally.
•If you'd like to serve dip in a red pepper cup, cut off stem end of red pepper; remove seeds. Cut a thin slice from the other end of red pepper, if necessary, so that pepper will stand upright, being careful not to cut through pepper. Spoon dip into pepper cup. Garnish, if desired. Serve Tapenade on baguette slices. Yield: 1 cup.
Per tablespoon: Calories 40 Fat 4g
Cholesterol 0mg Sodium 217mg

SERVING SAVVY

Be creative with serving containers—firm-textured raw fruits and vegetables make excellent dip holders. Try pineapple, cantaloupe, green pepper, tomato, or eggplant. First, cut a narrow slice from bottom so container sits flat; then carve out center, drain, and fill cavity with dip.

Layered Nacho Dip

◀ QUICK • FAMILY FAVORITE ▶

PREP: 12 MINUTES

Add a layer of shredded chicken or browned ground beef to this popular Mexican dip.

1 (16-ounce) can refried beans
½ (1¼-ounce) package taco seasoning mix (2 tablespoons)
1 (6-ounce) carton avocado dip or 1 cup Guacamole (opposite page)
1 (8-ounce) carton sour cream
1 (4¼-ounce) can chopped ripe olives, drained
2 tomatoes, diced
1 small onion, finely chopped
1 (4.5-ounce) can chopped green chiles, undrained
1½ cups (6 ounces) shredded Monterey Jack or Cheddar Jack cheese

•Combine beans and seasoning mix; spread in an 11- x 7-inch dish, a 9- or 10-inch deep-dish pieplate, or a cast-iron skillet. Layer dip and remaining ingredients in order listed. Serve with corn chips. Yield: 8 cups.
Per tablespoon: Calories 17 Fat 1.2g
Cholesterol 2mg Sodium 57mg

Black Bean Dip

◀ QUICK ▶

PREP: 3 MINUTES   COOK: 4 MINUTES

Tomato sauce, Cheddar cheese, and chili powder turn a can of beans into a south-of-the-border sensation.

1 (15-ounce) can black beans, drained
1 (8-ounce) can tomato sauce
½ cup (2 ounces) shredded Cheddar cheese
1 teaspoon chili powder
Garnish: shredded Cheddar cheese

•Combine beans and tomato sauce in a saucepan; bring to a boil over medium heat, stirring occasionally. Remove from heat.
•Mash beans with a potato masher or back of a spoon.
•Add ½ cup cheese and chili powder; cook, stirring constantly, until cheese melts. Garnish, if desired. Serve dip warm with tortilla chips or pita chips. Yield: 2 cups.
Per tablespoon: Calories 25 Fat 1g
Cholesterol 3mg Sodium 85mg

Fresh Tomato Salsa

◀ MAKE AHEAD • HEALTHY ▶

PREP: 5 MINUTES   CHILL: 3 HOURS

Garden-fresh tomatoes shine in this chunky jalapeño salsa.

2 cups peeled, chopped tomato (3 large tomatoes)
1 jalapeño pepper, seeded and finely chopped, or 1 (4.5-ounce) can chopped green chiles, drained
3 green onions, thinly sliced (½ cup)
2 tablespoons lemon or lime juice
½ teaspoon salt
½ teaspoon dried oregano
⅛ teaspoon pepper

•Combine all ingredients; stir well. Cover and chill at least 3 hours. Yield: 2 cups.
Per tablespoon: Calories 3 Fat 0g
Cholesterol 0mg Sodium 38mg

Guacamole

PREP: 12 MINUTES

Save an avocado seed to nestle in the bowl of guacamole; it helps preserve the bright green. For added pizzazz, stir in a few drops of hot sauce and four slices of crumbled cooked bacon.

3 ripe avocados
½ cup chopped tomato
¼ cup finely chopped onion
1 jalapeño pepper, chopped
1 tablespoon lemon or lime juice
1 teaspoon salt
Freshly ground black pepper

1. Hold avocado in palm of hand; stab the seed with a sharp knife. Gently twist knife and remove seed.

2. Scoop out buttery soft pulp with a spoon.

3. A few grinds from a pepper-mill add the finishing touch.

•Cut each avocado in half, and remove seed from avocado (photo 1). Scoop out avocado pulp into a large bowl (photo 2). Mash until avocado is desired consistency. Add chopped tomato and next 4 ingredients to bowl; stir until avocado mixture is blended. Top with black pepper, if desired (photo 3). Serve with tortilla chips. Yield: 2½ cups.
Per tablespoon: Calories 21 Fat 2g
Cholesterol 0mg Sodium 60mg

Roasted Tomatillo Salsa

PREP: 22 MINUTES   COOK: 15 MINUTES

To make authentic Mexican green salsa, use tomatillos—small tangy green fruit with papery husks. If they're hard to find, substitute green tomatoes.

1 pound fresh tomatillos
3 cloves garlic, unpeeled
2 large jalapeño peppers
1 medium onion, quartered
1 tablespoon vegetable oil
½ cup chopped fresh cilantro
½ teaspoon salt
½ teaspoon freshly ground pepper

•Discard tomatillo husks; rinse tomatillos.
•Toss tomatillos and next 3 ingredients in oil; spread vegetables in an ungreased roasting pan or a 13- x 9-inch pan.
•Bake at 500° for 15 minutes or until vegetables are charred; cool. Discard stems (but not seeds) from peppers. Peel garlic, discarding skin. Drain tomatillos, discarding any liquid.
•Process roasted vegetables in a food processor until coarsely chopped. Pour into a bowl; stir in cilantro, salt, and pepper. Serve with tortilla chips, fajitas, quesadillas, or grilled chicken. Cover and store in refrigerator up to 3 days. Yield: 2½ cups.
Per tablespoon: Calories 9 Fat 0.5g
Cholesterol 0mg Sodium 30mg

Southwestern Salsa with Black Beans and Corn

PREP: 10 MINUTES   COOK: 2 MINUTES

Here's a big yield for a big party. If it's more than you need, cut it in half.

1½ teaspoons cumin seeds
2 (15-ounce) cans black beans, rinsed and drained
1 (15¼ ounce) can whole kernel corn, drained
1 red pepper, minced
1 small purple onion, minced (1 cup)
½ cup chopped fresh cilantro
½ cup chopped fresh parsley
⅓ cup lime juice
¼ cup olive oil
3 cloves garlic, crushed
½ teaspoon salt
1 teaspoon dried crushed red pepper
½ teaspoon freshly ground black pepper

Southwestern Salsa with Black Beans and Corn

•Toast cumin seeds in a skillet over medium heat 1 to 2 minutes or until brown and fragrant, stirring often. Combine cumin seeds, black beans, and remaining ingredients; toss well. Cover and store in refrigerator up to 1 week. Yield: 6 cups.
Per tablespoon: Calories 18 Fat 0.7g
Cholesterol 0mg Sodium 36mg

Blending Hummus: Slowly pour oil through food chute with processor running.

Hummus

◄ QUICK • MAKE AHEAD ►

PREP: 10 MINUTES

Hummus is a Mediterranean puree of garbanzo beans, olive oil, and garlic. It's great as a dip with pita wedges, and it's also a popular sandwich spread.

3 or 4 cloves garlic
1 (19-ounce) can garbanzo beans, drained
¼ cup lemon juice
¾ teaspoon salt
½ teaspoon pepper
Dash of hot sauce
¼ cup olive oil
Garnish: fresh parsley sprigs

•Process garlic in a food processor until minced. Add beans and next 4 ingredients; process until smooth, scraping down sides occasionally. Slowly pour oil through food chute with processor running (see photo); process until smooth. Spoon into a serving bowl; cover and chill, if desired. Garnish, if desired; serve with pita bread. Yield: 2 cups.
Per tablespoon: Calories 33 Fat 1.9g
Cholesterol 0mg Sodium 76mg

Parslied Hummus: Add ¼ cup chopped fresh parsley and 3 green onions, sliced, to mixture in processor.

Nacho Fondue

◄ QUICK ►

PREP: 2 MINUTES   COOK: 13 MINUTES

If you're looking for a quick dip for a teenage crowd, this is it.

2 (11-ounce) cans fiesta nacho cheese soup, undiluted
3 cups (12 ounces) shredded 5-cheese pizza blend or Monterey Jack cheese
1 (16-ounce) jar medium salsa (1½ cups)
⅓ to ½ cup milk

•Combine all ingredients in a heavy saucepan; cook over medium heat, stirring constantly, until cheese melts and mixture is smooth. Spoon mixture into a fondue pot or chafing dish. Serve warm with tortilla chips. Yield: 6 cups.
Per tablespoon: Calories 22 Fat 1.5g
Cholesterol 4mg Sodium 74mg

Baked Artichoke Dip

◄ QUICK • FAMILY FAVORITE ►

PREP: 9 MINUTES   COOK: 20 MINUTES

Here's a familiar favorite that guests always gobble up in a hurry. Try it with hearts of palm, tender stalks similar in flavor to artichokes.

1 (14-ounce) can artichoke hearts or hearts of palm, drained and chopped
1 cup grated Parmesan cheese
¾ cup mayonnaise
1 clove garlic, minced
¼ teaspoon Worcestershire sauce
⅛ teaspoon hot sauce

•Combine all ingredients, stirring well; spoon into a lightly greased 1-quart casserole. Bake, uncovered, at 350° for 20 minutes or until bubbly. Serve with melba toast rounds. Yield: 2 cups.
Per tablespoon: Calories 52 Fat 4.9g
Cholesterol 5mg Sodium 101mg

Hot Crabmeat Dip

◄ QUICK ►

PREP: 12 MINUTES   COOK: 6 MINUTES

Serve this special-occasion appetizer with dressy crackers and a crisp white wine.

3 (8-ounce) packages cream cheese
1 small onion, grated
½ cup mayonnaise
½ teaspoon garlic powder
½ teaspoon salt
¾ teaspoon pepper
¼ cup dry white wine
1 tablespoon prepared mustard
1 to 2 tablespoons prepared horseradish
1 pound fresh lump crabmeat, drained
2 tablespoons chopped fresh chives
2 tablespoons chopped fresh parsley

•Combine first 9 ingredients in a saucepan; cook, stirring constantly, over medium heat until cream cheese melts.
•Stir in crabmeat, chives, and parsley; cook, stirring constantly, just until crabmeat is heated. Transfer to a chafing dish, and keep warm. Yield: 6 cups.
Per tablespoon: Calories 38 Fat 3.5g
Cholesterol 13mg Sodium 54mg

Vidalia Onion-Cheese Dip

PREP: 12 MINUTES   COOK: 25 MINUTES

3 large Vidalia onions or other sweet onions, coarsely chopped
2 tablespoons butter or margarine, melted
2 cups (8 ounces) shredded sharp Cheddar cheese
1 cup mayonnaise
½ teaspoon hot sauce
1 clove garlic, minced

•Sauté onion in butter in a large skillet over medium-high heat until tender.
•Combine onion, cheese, and remaining ingredients; stir well. Pour into a greased 1½-quart casserole.
•Bake, uncovered, at 375° for 20 to 25 minutes or until bubbly and golden. Serve dip with tortilla chips or assorted crackers. Yield: 4 cups.
Per tablespoon: Calories 46 Fat 4.3g
Cholesterol 7mg Sodium 46mg

Blue Cheese Spread

◄ MAKE AHEAD ►

PREP: 12 MINUTES   CHILL: 8 HOURS

Three great ingredients you probably have on hand make this spread so simple.

1 (8-ounce) package cream cheese, softened
1 (4-ounce) package blue cheese
¾ cup finely chopped pecans, toasted and divided

•Process cream cheese and blue cheese in a food processor 20 seconds or until smooth. Stir in ½ cup chopped pecans.
•Line a 1½-cup bowl with plastic wrap, and press cream cheese mixture into bowl. Cover and chill 8 hours.
•Unmold cheese; remove plastic wrap. Roll outside edge of cheese mold in remaining ¼ cup chopped pecans. Serve with apple slices and grapes. Yield: 1½ cups.
Per tablespoon: Calories 85 Fat 8.2g
Cholesterol 14mg Sodium 94mg

Garlic-Cream Cheese Spread

◄ QUICK • MAKE AHEAD ►

PREP: 5 MINUTES

This easy spread resembles Boursin, a French cream cheese.

1 or 2 cloves garlic
½ cup cottage cheese
2 (3-ounce) packages cream cheese, softened
2 teaspoons freeze-dried chives
2 teaspoons dried parsley flakes
⅛ teaspoon salt
⅛ teaspoon ground red pepper

•Process garlic in a food processor until minced. Add cottage cheese and remaining ingredients; process until smooth, stopping once to scrape down sides. Serve with toasted baguette slices or assorted fresh vegetables. Yield: 1¼ cups.
Per tablespoon: Calories 35 Fat 3.1g
Cholesterol 10mg Sodium 63mg

Shrimp and Olive Spread

◄ QUICK • MAKE AHEAD ►

PREP: 10 MINUTES

Serve this creamy shrimp spread with crackers or as a spread for tea sandwiches.

1 (8-ounce) package cream cheese, softened
1 (7-ounce) can shrimp, rinsed, drained, and chopped
6 pimiento-stuffed olives, chopped
2 tablespoons minced onion
2 tablespoons mayonnaise or salad dressing
1 teaspoon lemon juice
¼ teaspoon Worcestershire sauce
¼ teaspoon hot sauce
⅛ teaspoon garlic powder

•Combine all ingredients, stirring well. Cover and store in refrigerator. Serve with assorted crackers. Yield: 1¾ cups.
Per tablespoon: Calories 42 Fat 3.8g
Cholesterol 17mg Sodium 97mg

Smoked Whitefish Spread

◄ MAKE AHEAD ►

PREP: 15 MINUTES   CHILL: 1 HOUR

Smoked fish infuses this spread with flavor, but it's not necessary to smoke your own. Look for a ½-pound filet of smoked, flaked whitefish in the seafood department at gourmet or large grocery stores.

⅓ cup mayonnaise
⅓ cup horseradish sauce
2 tablespoons softened cream cheese
1 teaspoon lemon juice
⅛ teaspoon garlic powder
2 cups flaked smoked whitefish (about ½ pound)
¼ cup chopped green onions

•Combine first 5 ingredients; beat with a wire whisk until smooth. Stir in fish and green onions. Cover and chill at least 1 hour. Serve with assorted crackers. Yield: 2 cups.
Per tablespoon: Calories 37 Fat 3.2g
Cholesterol 4.7mg Sodium 102mg

Parmesan-Spinach Spread

PREP: 16 MINUTES   COOK: 20 MINUTES

Spinach and Parmesan cheese are a classic combination. Mix up this spread ahead, and bake it just before serving.

1 (10-ounce) package frozen chopped spinach, thawed
1 (3-ounce) package cream cheese, softened
¾ cup mayonnaise
1¼ cups freshly grated Parmesan cheese, divided
¼ cup minced onion
1 teaspoon dried Italian seasoning
1 teaspoon hot sauce
½ teaspoon garlic powder
¼ teaspoon freshly ground pepper
½ teaspoon paprika

•Drain spinach; press between paper towels to remove excess moisture.
•Combine cream cheese and mayonnaise in a bowl, stirring with a wire whisk until smooth. Add spinach, 1 cup Parmesan cheese, onion, and next 4 ingredients; stir well. Spoon into a greased 1-quart casserole.
•Bake, uncovered, at 350° for 10 minutes. Sprinkle with remaining ¼ cup Parmesan cheese and paprika; bake 10 more minutes. Serve with assorted crackers or party rye bread. Yield: 2¼ cups.
Per tablespoon: Calories 63 Fat 5.8g
Cholesterol 9mg Sodium 119mg

LAST-MINUTE PARTY OPTIONS

When you need to whip up something in a hurry, these recipes should come in handy. They contain just a few easy-to-find ingredients typically in your pantry or that you can plan to keep on hand.
•Cinnamon-Coffee Pecans (page 30)
•Deviled Nuts (page 30)
•Easy-as-Pie Cheese Straws (page 31)
•Curry Dip (page 33)
•Black Bean Dip (page 34)
•Nacho Fondue (previous page)
•Baked Artichoke Dip (previous page)
•Garlic-Cream Cheese Spread (this page)

Turkey-Mushroom Pâté in Pastry

PREP: 40 MINUTES   CHILL: 8 HOURS   COOK: 22 MINUTES

Decorate this pastry-wrapped pâté with pastry cutouts for a stunning presentation.

1 cup chopped fresh mushrooms
1 tablespoon butter or margarine, melted
2 cloves garlic
¾ pound smoked turkey, cut into 1-inch
    pieces
1½ cups chopped pecans, toasted
½ cup mayonnaise
¼ teaspoon salt
¼ teaspoon ground red pepper
½ cup finely chopped green onions
2 tablespoons soy sauce
1 (17¼-ounce) package frozen puff pastry
    sheets
1 egg yolk, beaten
Garnish: fresh parsley

•Sauté mushrooms in butter in a large skillet over medium heat until tender and liquid evaporates. Set aside.
•Process garlic in a food processor 10 seconds or until minced. Gradually add turkey and pecans; process 20 seconds after each addition or until finely ground.
•Transfer mixture to a large bowl; stir in mushroom mixture, mayonnaise, and next 4 ingredients. Spoon into a plastic wrap-lined 8½- x 4½-inch loafpan. Cover and chill 8 hours.
•Thaw puff pastry according to package directions. Unfold 1 pastry sheet, and place on a lightly floured surface; roll to a 14- x 12-inch rectangle. Unmold turkey mixture, and place in center of pastry (photo 1). Lightly moisten pastry edges with water. Fold ends and sides over mixture, pressing to seal. Place wrapped loaf, seam side down, on a lightly greased baking sheet.
•Cut decorative shapes from remaining pastry sheet freehand or with canapé cutters. Brush back of cutouts with water, and arrange cutouts on loaf (photo 2). Brush entire pastry with egg yolk. Bake at 400° for

1. Invert turkey pâté onto pastry, and remove the plastic wrap.

2. Press cutouts gently onto pastry-wrapped pâté.

3. An egg yolk "wash" helps pastry turn golden.

22 minutes or until golden (photo 3). Garnish, if desired. Slice loaf, using a serrated knife, and serve with assorted crackers, if desired. Yield: 16 appetizer servings.

Per serving: Calories 255 Fat 22g
Cholesterol 55mg Sodium 467mg

Sherry Cheese Pâté

◄ QUICK • MAKE AHEAD ►

PREP: 12 MINUTES

Cheddar cheese, chutney, and green onions blend nicely in this small, but potent, party cheese ball.

2 (3-ounce) packages cream cheese, softened
1 cup (4 ounces) shredded sharp Cheddar cheese
¼ cup dry sherry
½ teaspoon curry powder
⅓ cup chutney (we tested with Major Grey)°
2 green onions, thinly sliced

•Combine first 4 ingredients; spread into a 1-inch-thick circle on a serving plate. Cover and chill.
•Just before serving, spread chutney over cheese, and sprinkle with green onions. Serve with assorted crackers. Yield: 2 cups.
°*Find chutney on the grocery aisle with the jellies and preserves.*
Per tablespoon: Calories 40 Fat 3g
Cholesterol 10mg Sodium 44mg

Chicken Liver Pâté

◄ MAKE AHEAD ►

PREP: 15 MINUTES   CHILL: 3 HOURS

Brandy is the key ingredient that binds flavors in this traditional spread.

2 green onions, minced (¼ cup)
2 pounds chicken livers (about 4 cups)
¼ cup butter or margarine, melted
⅔ cup brandy
½ cup whipping cream
¾ teaspoon salt
¼ teaspoon ground allspice
¼ teaspoon pepper
Pinch of ground thyme
1 cup butter or margarine, melted
Green onion stems
Carrot curls
Garnish: fresh parsley sprigs

•Cook minced green onions and livers in ¼ cup butter in a large skillet over medium heat until livers are done. Process mixture in container of an electric blender or a food processor.
•Place brandy in a saucepan; simmer over medium-low heat until reduced by half. Add brandy, whipping cream, and seasonings to liver mixture; process until smooth. Add 1 cup butter to mixture; process until blended, stopping once to scrape down sides.
•Spoon pâté into a lightly oiled 5-cup mold; chill at least 3 hours. Unmold pâté. Tuck green onion stems around pâté to resemble ribbon, and place carrot curls on pâté to resemble a bow. Garnish, if desired. Serve with assorted crackers. Yield: about 5 cups.
Per tablespoon: Calories 46 Fat 3.9g
Cholesterol 60mg Sodium 61mg

Cucumber Mousse with Dill Sauce

◄ MAKE AHEAD ►

PREP: 18 MINUTES   CHILL: 2 HOURS

No time to make Dill Sauce for this refreshing mousse? A jar of mild salsa makes an ideal topper, too.

2 envelopes unflavored gelatin
3 tablespoons cold water
1 cup boiling water
2 large cucumbers
10 pimiento-stuffed olives
1 cup small-curd cottage cheese
½ cup whipping cream
1 (8-ounce) carton sour cream
3 tablespoons chopped fresh dill
2 tablespoons grated onion
1 tablespoon chopped fresh parsley
¾ teaspoon salt
¼ teaspoon ground white pepper
⅛ teaspoon hot sauce
Lettuce leaves
Dill Sauce
Thin cucumber slices
Garnish: fresh dill sprigs

•Sprinkle gelatin over cold water; stir and let stand 1 minute. Add 1 cup boiling water; stir until gelatin dissolves. Set aside.
•Thinly slice half of 1 cucumber, and set aside. Peel and seed remaining cucumbers.
•Process peeled and seeded cucumbers in a food processor 1 to 1½ minutes or until cucumber is smooth, stopping once to scrape down sides.
•Add olives, cottage cheese, and whipping cream; process 20 seconds, stopping once to scrape down sides. Pour gelatin gradually through food chute with processor running.
•Combine sour cream and next 6 ingredients in a large bowl; stir in cucumber mixture. Spoon into a lightly oiled 5-cup mold or individual molds. Cover and chill 2 hours or until firm.
•Arrange lettuce leaves on a serving plate. Unmold mousse onto prepared plate; top with Dill Sauce. Serve with cucumber slices. Garnish, if desired. Yield: 10 servings.
Per ½-cup mousse and 2 tablespoons sauce: Calories 181 Fat 15g
Cholesterol 39mg Sodium 610mg

Dill Sauce

1 (8-ounce) carton sour cream
2 tablespoons chopped fresh dill
3 tablespoons milk
1 tablespoon fresh lemon juice
½ teaspoon chopped fresh parsley
Pinch of salt

•Combine all ingredients in a small bowl. Yield: 1¼ cups.

Rosemary Date-Nut Ball

◄ QUICK • MAKE AHEAD ►

PREP: 8 MINUTES   CHILL: 30 MINUTES

This slightly sweet cheese ball can easily go on a dessert bar. It's chock-full of dates and has just a hint of rosemary.

1 (8-ounce) package cream cheese, softened
1 (10-ounce) package chopped dates
1 cup chopped pecans, toasted and divided
2 teaspoons chopped fresh rosemary (optional)

•Combine cream cheese, dates, and ½ cup pecans, and, if desired, rosemary; cover and chill 30 minutes. Shape into a ball; roll in remaining ½ cup pecans. Serve with apple wedges or gingersnaps. Yield: 2¼ cups.
Per tablespoon: Calories 71 Fat 5g
Cholesterol 7mg Sodium 19mg

Chili Cheese Balls

◀ QUICK • MAKE AHEAD ▶

PREP: 15 MINUTES CHILL: 1 HOUR

*Try a robust red wine with these spunky lit-
tle appetizers that are a twist on the standby
party cheese ball.*

3 cups (12 ounces) shredded Monterey
    Jack cheese
1 cup (4 ounces) shredded fontina cheese
1 (3-ounce) package cream cheese,
    softened
3 to 4 tablespoons prepared mustard
1 teaspoon Worcestershire sauce
½ teaspoon garlic powder
1½ tablespoons chili powder

•Combine first 6 ingredients in a bowl;
blend well. Shape into 1-inch balls. Sprinkle
chili powder in a large bowl; add cheese
balls, and toss gently to coat. Cover and chill
1 hour. Yield: 3½ dozen.
Per appetizer: Calories 50 Fat 4.1g
Cholesterol 12mg Sodium 74mg

Garlic-Cheese Logs

◀ MAKE AHEAD ▶

PREP: 15 MINUTES CHILL: 8 HOURS

*Chili-coated cheese logs make an attractive
gift. Pair them with summer sausage.*

2 (3-ounce) packages cream cheese,
    softened
1 tablespoon mayonnaise
1 tablespoon Worcestershire sauce
1 or 2 cloves garlic, crushed
1 teaspoon dry mustard
¼ teaspoon salt
¼ teaspoon hot sauce
4 cups (16 ounces) shredded sharp
    Cheddar cheese
2 teaspoons paprika
1 teaspoon chili powder

•Combine first 7 ingredients in a large mixing bowl; beat at medium speed with an
electric mixer until creamy. Gradually add
Cheddar cheese, mixing until blended.
•Divide mixture in half, and shape each portion into an 8-inch log. Combine paprika
and chili powder; roll logs in spice mixture.

•Cover and chill 8 hours. Thinly slice, and
serve with crackers. Yield: 2 (8-inch) logs.
Per ½-inch slice: Calories 80 Fat 6.9g
Cholesterol 21mg Sodium 130mg

Coating Blue Cheese-Pecan Grapes:
Wrap each grape with enough cheese mixture to cover.

Blue Cheese-Pecan Grapes

◀ MAKE AHEAD ▶

PREP: 20 MINUTES CHILL: 2 HOURS

*Tangy sweet grapes hide in the centers of
these little cheese balls.*

1 (4-ounce) package crumbled blue
    cheese
1 (3-ounce) package cream cheese,
    softened
30 seedless green or red grapes
1 cup finely chopped pecans, toasted

•Combine cheeses in a bowl. Beat at medium speed with an electric mixer until
smooth. Cover and chill at least 1 hour.
•Wash grapes; drain and pat dry with paper
towels. Wrap each grape with enough
cheese mixture to cover, about 1 teaspoon
(see photo). Roll in pecans. Cover and chill
at least 1 hour. Yield: 2½ dozen.
Per appetizer: Calories 47 Fat 4.3g
Cholesterol 6mg Sodium 61mg

APPETIZER TREE

For a festive holiday idea, skewer
coated grapes (recipe above) with wood-
en picks, and secure onto a plastic foam
cone to make an appetizer tree.

Pear-Pecan Appetizers

◀ QUICK ▶

PREP: 15 MINUTES

*Liven up a fruit tray with these nut-covered
fruit slices.*

2 ripe pears
1 quart water
2 tablespoons lemon juice
½ cup butter or margarine, softened
2 tablespoons crumbled blue cheese
1 cup finely chopped pecans, toasted

•Cut each pear into thin slices. Combine
pear slices, water, and lemon juice in a bowl.
•Beat butter and blue cheese at medium
speed with an electric mixer until smooth.
•Drain pear slices on paper towels. Dip bottom half of pear slices in butter mixture;
coat with pecans, and place on a serving
plate. Serve immediately or cover and chill
30 minutes. Yield: 2½ dozen.
Per appetizer: Calories 63 Fat 5.9g
Cholesterol 9mg Sodium 44mg

Herbed Tomato Crostini

◀ QUICK ▶

PREP: 12 MINUTES

*Use your finest olive oil and succulent yellow
and red tomatoes to dazzle friends with this
simple appetizer shown on page 28.*

2 cups seeded chopped tomato
¼ teaspoon salt
¼ teaspoon freshly ground pepper
2 tablespoons chopped fresh basil
1 tablespoon capers
1 teaspoon chopped fresh mint
1 tablespoon olive oil
1 baguette
1 clove garlic, halved
1 tablespoon olive oil

•Combine first 7 ingredients; toss well.
•Slice baguette into 16 (½-inch) slices. Toast
slices at 400° for 6 minutes, turning once.
•Rub garlic over 1 side of each slice. Spoon
tomato mixture onto slices. Drizzle with 1
tablespoon oil. Yield: 16 appetizers.
Per serving: Calories 86 Fat 2.5g
Cholesterol 1mg Sodium 212mg

Raspberry Brie in Rye

PREP: 12 MINUTES   COOK: 30 MINUTES

Gooey Brie cheese and raspberry jam await discovery in this dark loaf. Use a knife to spoon mixture onto big chunks of bread.

2 (7-inch-round) loaves rye bread
1 (15-ounce) round Brie cheese
½ cup seedless raspberry jam
¼ cup sliced almonds

•Using a large serrated knife, slice off about ½ inch from top of 1 bread loaf. Reserve top of loaf for another use.
•Place Brie on top of bread; trace around outer edge of cheese with knife (photo 1). Remove cheese, and set aside.
•Using traced mark as a guide, cut bread vertically 2 inches deep; discard bread, leaving a 5- x 2-inch cavity (photo 2). Cut second loaf into 1-inch cubes; set aside.

1. Trace around edge of cheese with a knife.

2. Cut and discard bread, leaving a cavity for the cheese.

3. Top cheese with jam and almonds.

•Slice rind from top of cheese. Place cheese in bread cavity; spread with jam, and sprinkle with almonds (photo 3). Place prepared loaf on a baking sheet.
•Bake, uncovered, at 325° for 25 minutes or until cheese is very soft. Serve immediately with reserved bread cubes. Yield: 10 appetizer servings.
Per serving: Calories 342 Fat 13.2g
Cholesterol 43mg Sodium 625mg

COLD APPETIZERS

These appetizer recipes have that convenient make-ahead quality that smart party planners look for, because they can usually be served straight from the refrigerator. Most of these cold appetizers are equally good after they come to room temperature, too, which makes them a good choice if they sit out on a buffet for a while.

Roasted Garlic

PREP: 2 MINUTES   COOK: 1 HOUR

Don't be alarmed that this recipe uses a whole head of garlic. Garlic mellows and takes on a buttery flavor as it roasts, and it softens enough to spread like butter.

1 large head garlic
1 tablespoon olive oil
¼ teaspoon salt
¼ teaspoon pepper

•Cut top off garlic, leaving head intact. Place garlic on a piece of aluminum foil, cut side up; drizzle with oil. Sprinkle with salt and pepper.
•Wrap in foil, and bake at 350° for 1 hour. Remove from oven, and cool. Discard outermost layer of papery skin from garlic. Scoop out soft garlic pulp with a small spoon or knife. Serve over French bread. Yield: 4 appetizer servings.
Per serving: Calories 54 Fat 3.5g
Cholesterol 0mg Sodium 149mg

Pickled Carrots

◄ MAKE AHEAD • HEALTHY ►

PREP: 20 MINUTES

COOK: 15 MINUTES   MARINATE: 8 HOURS

Pack several jars of these healthy pickled appetizers as gifts. They're wonderful served with a vegetable dinner.

1½ cups cider vinegar
1½ cups water
1 cup sugar
2 pounds carrots, scraped and cut into strips
2 tablespoons dillseeds
3 or 4 cloves garlic

•Combine first 3 ingredients in a large saucepan. Bring to a boil, stirring until sugar dissolves.
•Add carrot, dillseeds, and garlic; bring to a boil over medium heat. Cover, reduce heat, and simmer 6 to 8 minutes. Remove from heat; cool. Cover and chill 8 hours.
•To serve, pour mixture through a large wire-mesh strainer, discarding liquid. Discard garlic, if desired. Yield: 16 appetizer servings.
Per serving: Calories 26 Fat 0.1g
Cholesterol 0mg Sodium 16mg

GREAT GIFTS

Given in decorative jars or bottles, these recipes make ideal gifts.
•Cinnamon-Coffee Pecans (page 30)
•Garlic-Cheese Logs (previous page)
•Pickled Carrots (this page)
•Marinated Roasted Peppers (next page)
•Instant Spiced Tea Mix (page 51)
•Amaretto (page 59)
•Coffee Liqueur (page 59)

Marinated Roasted Peppers

Herb-Marinated Olives

side up, on a baking sheet; flatten with palm of hand. Broil peppers 3 inches from heat 15 minutes or until charred. Place peppers in a heavy-duty, zip-top plastic bag; seal and let stand 10 minutes to loosen skins.
•Peel peppers, and discard skins. Cut peppers into strips; place in a bowl or large heavy-duty, zip-top plastic bag.
•Combine olive oil and remaining 6 ingredients; pour over peppers. Seal bag; marinate in refrigerator 8 hours. To serve, spoon peppers into a serving dish, using a slotted spoon, if desired. Yield: 8 appetizer servings.
Per serving: Calories 48 Fat 3.7g
Cholesterol 0mg Sodium 39mg

Mexican Pinwheels

◄ MAKE AHEAD ►

PREP: 25 MINUTES
CHILL: 3 TO 24 HOURS

Green chiles, olives, and cheese dot these roll-ups with color and flavor. Wrap tightly in plastic wrap, and chill until serving time.

2 cups (8 ounces) shredded Cheddar cheese
½ cup sour cream
1 (8-ounce) package cream cheese, softened
1 (4.5-ounce) can chopped green chiles, drained
1 (2¼-ounce) can sliced ripe olives, drained
⅔ cup chopped green onions
1 clove garlic, crushed
¼ teaspoon seasoned salt
6 (9-inch) flour tortillas

•Combine first 8 ingredients. Spread about ½ cup mixture over each tortilla; roll up tortillas, jellyroll fashion. Wrap each separately in plastic wrap. Chill 3 to 24 hours.
•Unwrap each roll and, if desired, cut off and discard ends. Cut each roll into 10 slices. Secure pinwheels with wooden picks, if desired. Yield: 5 dozen.
Per appetizer: Calories 47 Fat 3.4g
Cholesterol 9mg Sodium 79mg

Note: For avocado lovers, add 1 ripe avocado, finely chopped, to cheese mixture.

Herb-Marinated Olives

◄ QUICK • MAKE AHEAD ►

PREP: 5 MINUTES   MARINATE: 8 HOURS

After eating these marinated chunky olives, serve any remaining herbed oil as a vinaigrette for greens or as a dipping oil for French bread.

½ cup olive oil
⅓ cup sherry vinegar or other flavored vinegar
1 tablespoon chopped fresh thyme or 1 teaspoon dried thyme
1 teaspoon fresh or dried rosemary
1½ teaspoons chopped fresh oregano or ½ teaspoon dried oregano
2 cloves garlic, cut into slivers
1 dried red pepper pod*
1 (8-ounce) jar kalamata olives, drained, or 1 (7.25-ounce) can colossal ripe, pitted olives, drained
1 (7-ounce) jar green pimiento-stuffed olives, drained
Fresh herb sprigs (optional)

•Combine first 7 ingredients in a bowl; stir well. Place olives in a large heavy-duty, zip-top plastic bag. Pour marinade over olives. Seal bag securely. Marinate in refrigerator 8 hours or up to 5 days, turning occasionally. Transfer to a decorative container, and add fresh herbs, if desired. To serve, spoon desired amount of olives into a serving dish. Yield: 22 appetizer servings.
*Find red pepper pods with other spices and herbs in specialty markets.
Per serving (4 olives): Calories 73 Fat 7.2g
Cholesterol 0mg Sodium 660mg

Marinated Roasted Peppers

◄ MAKE AHEAD ►

PREP: 20 MINUTES   COOK: 15 MINUTES
MARINATE: 8 HOURS

Serve these pretty pepper slivers on an antipasto tray or on bruschetta (see photo above) or other crusty bread slices.

2 large sweet red peppers
2 large green peppers
⅓ cup olive oil
2 tablespoons chopped fresh parsley
1½ tablespoons white wine vinegar
1 teaspoon dried crushed red pepper
1 clove garlic, minced
¼ teaspoon salt
¼ teaspoon pepper

•Cut peppers in half crosswise; discard seeds and membranes. Place peppers, skin

Easy Antipasto

◄ QUICK ►

PREP: 22 MINUTES   CHILL: 8 HOURS

You can lighten this hearty appetizer by using reduced-fat Italian dressing.

1 (14-ounce) can artichoke hearts, drained and quartered
1 cup cherry tomatoes, halved
½ cup pitted ripe olives
½ cup pimiento-stuffed olives
1 (10-ounce) jar pepperoncini salad peppers, drained
1 (4-ounce) jar button mushrooms, drained
1 (8-ounce) bottle zesty Italian dressing
1 (8-ounce) package mozzarella cheese
1 (6-ounce) package thinly sliced ham
Leaf lettuce

•Combine first 6 ingredients in a heavy-duty, zip-top plastic bag. Pour dressing over vegetables; seal bag. Chill 8 hours, turning bag occasionally.
•Cut mozzarella into sticks. Cut ham slices in half; roll ham into logs, and secure with wooden picks.
•Drain vegetables, reserving marinade. Arrange vegetables, cheese, and ham on a lettuce-lined tray. Drizzle reserved marinade over cheese and ham. Yield: 10 appetizer servings.
Per serving: Calories 183 Fat 13.3g
Cholesterol 24mg Sodium 1488mg

Oysters on the Half Shell

◄ QUICK ►

PREP: 10 MINUTES

Just to be on the safe side, we give you cooking directions for oysters on the half shell rather than serving them raw.

2 cups water
½ teaspoon salt
2 dozen oysters on the half shell
2 large lemons, halved
1 cup Cocktail Sauce, chilled (page 390)
Lemon wedges

•Bring water and salt to a boil in a saucepan. Loosen oysters from the shell; add oysters to boiling water. Simmer 3 to 5 minutes or until oysters are plump and opaque; drain. Return oysters to shells.
•Cut a thin slice from bottom of each lemon half so that it sits flat. Gently remove pulp, leaving shell intact. Reserve pulp for another use. Fill lemon shells with Cocktail Sauce, and place a lemon shell in center of four deep dishes filled with crushed ice.
•Arrange 6 oysters on the half shell around each bowl of sauce, and serve immediately with lemon wedges and crackers. Yield: 4 appetizer servings.
Per serving: Calories 112 Fat 2.2g
Cholesterol 46mg Sodium 669mg

Shrimp Cocktail

◄ FAMILY FAVORITE ►
◄ MAKE AHEAD ►

PREP: 45 MINUTES

Here's a simple summertime specialty.

2 cups shredded lettuce
1 pound Boiled Shrimp, peeled and chilled (page 219)
Cocktail Sauce (page 390)
Garnish: lemon wedges

•Arrange lettuce on individual serving plates or in cocktail cups or glasses. Top with chilled Boiled Shrimp; drizzle with Cocktail Sauce before serving. Garnish, if desired. Yield: 4 appetizer servings.
Per serving: Calories 125 Fat 0.9g
Cholesterol 125mg Sodium 792mg

Pickled Shrimp

◄ MAKE AHEAD ►

**PREP: 38 MINUTES   COOK: 13 MINUTES
CHILL: 8 TO 24 HOURS**

Fresh shrimp take on abundant flavor after marinating in this spicy caper vinaigrette.

4 cups water
½ cup celery leaves
¼ cup pickling spice°
1 tablespoon salt
2 pounds unpeeled medium-size fresh shrimp
2 small onions, thinly sliced
7 bay leaves
¾ cup vegetable oil
¼ cup white vinegar
3 tablespoons capers
2½ teaspoons celery seeds
1 teaspoon salt
3 or 4 drops of hot sauce
Lettuce leaves

•Bring first 4 ingredients to a boil in a Dutch oven; add shrimp, and cook 3 to 5 minutes or just until shrimp turn pink. Drain shrimp, and rinse with cold water. Peel shrimp, and devein, if desired.
•Combine shrimp, onion, and bay leaves in a large heavy-duty, zip-top plastic bag. Set bag aside.
•Combine vegetable oil and next 5 ingredients in a jar. Close tightly, and shake vigorously. Pour over shrimp. Seal bag, and chill 8 to 24 hours, turning bag occasionally.
•Drain shrimp; discard bay leaves. Serve shrimp on a lettuce-lined plate. Yield: 10 appetizer servings.
°Find pickling spice on the grocery aisle near salts and spices.
Per serving: Calories 146 Fat 11.5g
Cholesterol 88mg Sodium 396mg

HOT APPETIZERS

You'll want to cook most of these appetizers at the last minute; therefore, they'll require some planning to coordinate easy serving, particularly for large crowds.

While many of these recipes such as Coconut Shrimp with Sweet Dipping Sauce and Southern Ham 'n' Biscuits are good at room temperature, you'll want to keep some such as Quesadillas and Zucchini-Stuffed Mushrooms hot for serving. Depend on chafing dishes and warming trays to keep them at the ideal serving temperature.

Zucchini-Stuffed Mushrooms

PREP: 25 MINUTES   COOK: 23 MINUTES

Serve these stuffed mushrooms hot from the oven so they won't get soggy.

3¼ cups shredded zucchini
1 teaspoon salt
30 large fresh mushrooms (2 pounds)
¼ cup butter or margarine, melted
1 clove garlic, minced
¾ cup part-skim ricotta cheese
⅓ cup crushed saltine crackers
¼ cup grated Parmesan cheese
4 oil-packed dried tomatoes, finely
    chopped
¼ teaspoon dried oregano
⅛ teaspoon pepper

•Combine zucchini and salt in a colander; let stand 30 minutes. Press zucchini between paper towels to remove excess moisture.
•Clean mushrooms with damp paper towels. Remove stems, and reserve for another use. Brush mushroom caps with 3 tablespoons butter. Place on a rack in broiler pan.
•Sauté garlic in remaining 1 tablespoon butter in a large skillet over medium-high heat 1 minute. Add zucchini, and cook 2 more minutes. Remove from heat; cool slightly. Stir in ricotta cheese and remaining 5 ingredients. Spoon mixture evenly into mushroom caps. Bake at 375° for 20 minutes. Serve immediately. Yield: 2½ dozen.
Per mushroom: Calories 39 Fat 2.6g
Cholesterol 7mg Sodium 136mg

Fried Veggies

PREP: 5 MINUTES

COOK: 3 TO 4 MINUTES PER BATCH

Have leftover vegetables? This is a great way to use them.

1½ cups all-purpose flour, divided
½ cup yellow cornmeal
1 teaspoon baking powder
1 teaspoon salt or seasoned salt
1 tablespoon vegetable oil
1¼ cups beer
Vegetable oil
16 whole mushrooms
1½ cups sliced zucchini
1 cup baby carrots

•Combine 1 cup flour, cornmeal, and next 4 ingredients, stirring until smooth. Let stand 10 to 15 minutes.
•Pour oil to depth of 2 inches into a Dutch oven; heat to 375°.
•Dredge vegetables in remaining ½ cup flour; dip vegetables into batter twice. Fry vegetables, 8 pieces at a time, 3 to 4 minutes or until golden. Drain on paper towels. Serve with Ranch-style dressing, if desired. Yield: 8 appetizer servings.
Per serving: Calories 244 Fat 15.2g
Cholesterol 0mg Sodium 230mg

Spicy Buffalo Wings

PREP: 8 MINUTES   COOK: 45 MINUTES

Traditional chicken wings require some effort to remove wingtips and cut wings at the joint. Purchase commercially packaged drummettes, and no prep work is needed.

3 pounds chicken drummettes (about 34)
¾ cup butter or margarine
½ cup hot sauce (we tested with Tabasco)
1 (1-ounce) envelope onion soup mix
1½ tablespoons ground red pepper
1 (8-ounce) bottle blue cheese dressing

•Place chicken on a lightly greased rack of a broiler pan; set aside.
•Melt butter in a small saucepan; add hot sauce, soup mix, and red pepper. Stir well.

Brush chicken drummettes with half of butter mixture.
•Bake at 375° for 30 minutes. Remove from oven; turn chicken, and brush with remaining butter mixture. Bake 15 more minutes or until tender. Serve warm with blue cheese dressing. Yield: 34 appetizer servings.
Per serving: Calories 108 Fat 9.3g
Cholesterol 27mg Sodium 244mg

Little Pizza Snacks

◄ MAKE AHEAD ►
◄ FAMILY FAVORITE ►

PREP: 45 MINUTES   COOK: 10 MINUTES

These spicy mini pizzas make enough for a large crowd, or you can freeze them and bake a few at a time.

1 pound Italian sausage
1 pound hot ground pork sausage
1 small onion, chopped (1 cup)
½ green pepper, chopped
1 tablespoon dried oregano
1 tablespoon fennel seeds
⅛ teaspoon garlic powder
1 (16-ounce) package process American
    cheese, cut into small cubes
2 (8-ounce) packages mozzarella cheese,
    cut into small cubes
3 (8-ounce) loaves party rye bread

•Remove casings from Italian sausage; crumble into a large skillet. Add ground sausage, onion, and pepper; cook until meat is browned. Drain well on paper towels.
•Return meat mixture to skillet, and add oregano, fennel seeds, and garlic powder; heat gently over low heat. Stir in cheeses; cook until melted, and remove from heat.
•Spread a scant tablespoon of meat mixture on each bread slice. Place slices in a single layer on large baking sheets. (Freeze, if desired. When slices are frozen, place in heavy-duty, zip-top plastic bags, and keep frozen until needed. To serve, thaw and place on lightly greased baking sheets.) Bake at 425° for 8 to 10 minutes. Yield: 11 dozen.
Per appetizer: Calories 55 Fat 3.2g
Cholesterol 10mg Sodium 121mg

Quesadillas

PREP: 22 MINUTES

COOK: 10 MINUTES PER BATCH

Buttering the tortillas makes these appetizers extracrisp and flaky.

3 tablespoons butter or margarine, softened
9 (8-inch) flour tortillas
4 cups (16 ounces) shredded Monterey Jack cheese or Monterey Jack cheese with peppers
12 slices bacon, cooked and crumbled
1 tomato, seeded and chopped
4 pickled jalapeño peppers, finely chopped
1 teaspoon ground cumin
2¼ cups salsa
Garnish: pickled jalapeño peppers

•Spread butter on 1 side of each tortilla. Place tortillas, buttered side down, on ungreased baking sheets; set aside.
•Combine cheese and next 4 ingredients; spoon evenly over half of each tortilla (about ½ cup per tortilla). Fold tortillas in half, pressing lightly.
•Bake at 400° for 5 minutes; turn quesadillas, and bake 5 more minutes or until cheese melts and tortillas are lightly browned. Cut quesadillas into wedges, if desired. Spoon salsa over each quesadilla. Garnish, if desired. Serve warm. Yield: 9 servings.

Per serving: Calories 455 Fat 27.8g
Cholesterol 58mg Sodium 918mg

Egg Rolls

PREP: 25 MINUTES

COOK: 2 MINUTES PER BATCH

Peanut oil has a delicate flavor, and it fries these homemade egg rolls crisp and light.

½ pound lean boneless pork
2 tablespoons peanut oil or sesame oil
1 (8-ounce) package mushrooms, chopped
1 cup chopped bean sprouts
½ cup finely chopped water chestnuts
2 green onions, finely chopped
4 cups finely shredded cabbage
2 tablespoons soy sauce
1 tablespoon plus 1 teaspoon cornstarch
1 (16-ounce) package egg roll wrappers*
Peanut oil

•Process pork in a food processor until finely chopped. Cook pork in 2 tablespoons hot oil in a large nonstick skillet over medium-high heat 2 minutes, stirring until meat crumbles.
•Add mushrooms and next 3 ingredients; cook, stirring constantly, 4 minutes or until tender. Stir in cabbage.
•Combine soy sauce and cornstarch, stirring well; add to meat mixture. Cook 2 to 3 minutes or until thickened and bubbly.
•Spoon ⅓ cup meat mixture in center of each egg roll wrapper. Fold top corner of wrapper over filling, tucking tip of corner under filling; fold left and right corners over filling. Lightly brush remaining corner with water; tightly roll filled end toward remaining corner, and gently press to seal.

•Pour oil to depth of 2 inches into a wok or Dutch oven; heat to 375°. Fry egg rolls, a few at a time, 2 minutes or until golden, turning once; drain. Yield: 16 egg rolls.
*Find egg roll wrappers in the refrigerated produce section.

Per egg roll: Calories 196 Fat 10g
Cholesterol 11mg Sodium 305mg

Coconut-Crusted Chicken Fingers

PREP: 20 MINUTES

COOK: 2 MINUTES PER BATCH

Coat these beer-battered chicken pieces in almonds and coconut before frying. They're so good, you won't be able to stop at one serving.

½ (10-ounce) package tempura batter mix
½ (12-ounce) can beer (¾ cup)
1¾ cups flaked coconut
¾ cup sliced almonds
1 pound skinned and boned chicken breast halves, cut into 2½-inch-long strips
Vegetable oil
Honey-Poppy Seed Sauce (below) or Sweet 'n' Spicy Mustard Dip (page 33)

•Combine tempura batter mix and beer; pour into a shallow dish, and set aside. Combine coconut and almonds. Dip each chicken strip into batter mixture; then roll in coconut mixture.
•Pour oil to depth of 1½ inches into a Dutch oven; heat to 350°. Fry chicken strips, 4 at a time, 2 minutes or until golden. Drain on paper towels. Repeat procedure with remaining chicken strips.
•Serve chicken fingers with Honey-Poppy Seed Sauce (below) or Sweet 'n' Spicy Mustard Dip. Yield: 10 appetizer servings.

Per serving: Calories 487 Fat 35.4g
Cholesterol 33mg Sodium 207mg

Honey-Poppy Seed Sauce

½ cup mayonnaise
½ cup honey
1 teaspoon poppy seeds

•Combine all ingredients in a small bowl. Yield: 1 cup.

Quesadillas

Southern Ham 'n' Biscuits

◄ QUICK • FAMILY FAVORITE ►

PREP: 10 MINUTES   COOK: 12 MINUTES

2 cups all-purpose flour
1 tablespoon baking powder
½ teaspoon baking soda
⅛ teaspoon salt
⅓ cup cold butter or margarine
1 cup buttermilk
2 tablespoons butter or margarine, melted
1 (8-ounce) package cooked country ham
   or regular ham slices
Mustard Spread

•Combine first 4 ingredients; cut in cold butter with a pastry blender until mixture resembles coarse meal. Add buttermilk, stirring until dry ingredients are moistened. Turn dough out onto a floured surface, and knead 4 or 5 times. Roll dough to ½-inch thickness; cut with a 1½-inch cutter. Place biscuits on an ungreased baking sheet; bake at 450° for 10 to 12 minutes or until golden. Brush with melted butter. Serve with ham and Mustard Spread. Yield: 2 dozen.
Per ham 'n' biscuit: Calories 108 Fat 6.7g
Cholesterol 16mg Sodium 292mg

Mustard Spread

⅓ cup mayonnaise
3 tablespoons Dijon mustard
1½ tablespoons sweet pickle relish

•Combine all ingredients; stir well. Cover and chill until ready to use. Yield: ½ cup.

Appetizer Crab Casserole

PREP: 40 MINUTES   COOK: 41 MINUTES

This luscious appetizer is creamier than a dip. Serve it up on buttery toast points.

1 pound fresh lump crabmeat, drained
1 cup chopped onion
1 cup chopped celery
1 cup herb-seasoned stuffing mix
1 cup mayonnaise or salad dressing
1 cup half-and-half
1 (3-ounce) jar capers, drained
1 teaspoon Old Bay seasoning
Toast Points

•Combine first 7 ingredients in a large bowl; spoon into an 11- x 7-inch baking dish. Sprinkle with Old Bay seasoning.
•Bake, uncovered, at 350° for 35 minutes. Serve with Toast Points. Yield: 24 appetizer servings.
Per serving: Calories 152 Fat 10.6g
Cholesterol 30mg Sodium 380mg

Toast Points

12 slices day-old white bread
3 tablespoons butter or margarine, melted

•Trim crusts from bread slices. Brush 1 side of slices with butter. Cut each slice in half diagonally. Place in a single layer on a baking sheet, buttered side up.
•Bake at 400° for 6 minutes or until lightly browned. Yield: 24 servings.

Oysters Rockefeller

PREP: 25 MINUTES   COOK: 21 MINUTES

"Rockefeller" usually means the dish contains spinach, although some say that watercress was originally the key ingredient. Rock salt steadies the oyster shells in the pan so it's easy to serve this elegant appetizer at home.

Rock salt
3 green onions, finely chopped
¼ cup butter or margarine, melted
1 (10-ounce) package frozen chopped spinach, thawed and well drained
¼ teaspoon salt
⅛ teaspoon pepper
⅛ teaspoon garlic powder
3 tablespoons fine, dry breadcrumbs (commercial)
1½ dozen oysters on the half shell, drained
2 tablespoons dry sherry (optional)
Lemon juice
Hot sauce
3 slices bacon, cooked and crumbled
Garnish: 18 strips pimiento

•Sprinkle a thin layer of rock salt in a large shallow pan.
•Sauté green onions in butter in a large skillet over medium heat until tender. Stir in spinach and next 3 ingredients. Cook,

uncovered, 5 minutes, stirring occasionally. Remove from heat, and stir in breadcrumbs.
•Arrange oysters (in shells) over rock salt. Brush each oyster with sherry, if desired, and sprinkle with a few drops of lemon juice and hot sauce. Top with spinach mixture, and sprinkle with crumbled bacon.
•Bake at 350° for 15 minutes. Then broil 5 inches from heat 1 minute. Garnish, if desired. Serve immediately. Yield: 1½ dozen.
Per appetizer: Calories 36 Fat 2.7g
Cholesterol 12mg Sodium 88mg

Coconut Shrimp with Sweet Dipping Sauce

PREP: 14 MINUTES   COOK: 31 MINUTES

The mustard-marmalade dipping sauce adds a sweet touch to this crisp fried shrimp.

2 pounds unpeeled large fresh shrimp (48 shrimp)
2 cups all-purpose flour, divided
1 (12-ounce) can beer (1½ cups)
½ teaspoon baking powder
½ teaspoon paprika
½ teaspoon curry powder
¼ teaspoon salt
¼ teaspoon ground red pepper
1 (14-ounce) package flaked coconut
Vegetable oil
Sweet Dipping Sauce

•Peel shrimp, and devein, if desired, leaving tails intact. Combine 1½ cups flour, beer, and next 5 ingredients. Dredge shrimp in remaining ½ cup flour, dip in batter, and roll in coconut. Fry shrimp, in batches, in deep hot oil (350°) until golden. Serve with Sweet Dipping Sauce. Yield: 12 appetizer servings.
Per serving: Calories 429 Fat 28.5g
Cholesterol 86mg Sodium 207mg

Sweet Dipping Sauce

1 (10-ounce) jar orange marmalade
3 tablespoons Creole mustard
3 tablespoons prepared horseradish

•Combine all ingredients, stirring until smooth. Yield: 1¼ cups.

BEVERAGES

Equipment

You can make a wide variety of beverages without a lot of special equipment. Most basic of all beverage equipment might be a teapot or saucepan for steeping tea. If you make tea using loose tea leaves, you'll need a strainer or teaball to hold the leaves.

To make coffee you'll need a drip coffeepot, a vacuum coffeepot, or a percolator and paper filters to fit your coffeepot's filter basket. Some connoisseurs, however, declare that the ultimate in freshly brewed coffee comes from using a French press pot.

For the freshest coffee, grind your own beans just before brewing. Electric grinders offer the quickest and easiest way to grind fresh beans. And to clean the grinder, you need only to brush out the bowl periodically with a small soft brush. A thermal-insulated container is a good thing to keep coffee hot and fresh for an extended time period.

You'll also need an electric blender for buzzing bar drinks, milk shakes, and other ice cream beverages.

Making Beverages Ahead

You can make many beverages, especially fruit drinks and punches, a day or two ahead before you need them. Just chill them until ready to serve. But if the recipe calls for a carbonated beverage or alcohol, wait until just before serving to add it to the drink. If the recipe is served cold, make sure any last-minute additions are thoroughly chilled, so they won't warm up the previously chilled portion.

Microwaving Beverages

Few beverages actually heat faster in the microwave than they do on the cooktop, but your microwave oven can be a great tool for reheating one or two cups of a leftover beverage. Leftovers can be reheated in microwave-safe mugs or bowls. Just be sure there is no metallic rim on the mugs or other containers.

When reheating two mugs of a beverage, arrange them 2 inches apart in the center of the microwave oven. When microwaving more than two mugs, arrange them in a circular pattern. Microwave times for individual mugs of leftover beverages may vary, depending on the size of the mug, the ingredients in the beverage, and the initial temperature of the beverage. Times usually range from 1½ to 2½ minutes for one 10-ounce mug of a water-based or juice-based beverage.

COFFEE, TEA, & COCOA

There's something captivating about beverages brewed from the aromatic leaves and beans of coffee, tea, and cacao plants. They work with any meal, at any time of day. And with little adornment, they'll complement just about every type of food.

Brew the Best Coffee

There is some discrepancy on how strong coffee should be or the best way to brew it; variances depend on the type of coffee, proportion of water to coffee, brewing method, equipment, and most important—your taste. Once you arrive at a good combination, remember it.

There are two main types of coffee beans—*robusta* and *arabica*. *Robusta* is an easy-to-grow hearty coffee bean, and *arabica*, the Cadillac of coffee beans, is grown at higher elevations and develops a richer flavor and aroma. Less-expensive coffees often use mostly robusta beans, with a little arabica added for flavor. Specialty coffees generally have predominantly arabica beans. Coffee beans are roasted to different levels to optimize the mellowness, richness, and smoothness of the coffee. The longer the roasting, the darker and stronger the coffee.

Purchase coffee in small quantities because it loses its freshness quickly. Coffee will keep its flavor best stored in an airtight container at room temperature or in the freezer.

Your coffee will taste better if you clean the coffeemaker occasionally; this keeps oils and residue from building up and causing a bitter taste. Clean the coffeemaker by running a vinegar and water solution through the brew cycle.

Freshly drawn cold water makes better tasting coffee than hot tap water. And coffee is best when freshly brewed. If it must be held before serving, brew and then transfer to a thermal-insulated container or carafe. Otherwise, brew and serve within 15 minutes for optimum flavor.

Teatime

If you're a tea connoisseur, you'll know that there are literally hundreds of varieties of tea. Most tea available in the grocery store is a blend of 20 varieties, carefully teamed by producers to yield the best quality.

Black, green, and oolong are the main types of tea. All these tea leaves come from the same plant, but the processing time varies, giving each a distinct color and taste.

Black tea results from partially drying the tea leaves and then crushing them in a roller machine to release their juices. The leaves then ferment and dry in a controlled environment until they turn a brownish black. The fermentation time determines the strength of the tea. Black tea is robust and strong. Darjeeling and Ceylon are popular varieties.

Green tea is superior to other teas when it comes to its health values. It has a high concentration of cancer-fighting antioxidants that are more potent than vitamins C and E.

Green tea leaves are steamed immediately after picking, preventing them from oxidizing and changing color; then the leaves are crushed and dried for packaging. Green tea is usually a light color when brewed.

When the leaves are rolled into tiny pellets after steaming, the result is called gunpowder tea.

Oolong tea is semifermented, so it's a cross between a black and green tea. After processing, oolong leaves turn greenish brown and brew light in color.

Herb tea is not a true tea because it doesn't contain tea-shrub leaves. It resembles tea because it's made like tea by steeping, but uses various herbs, flowers, and spices.

When brewing tea, start with freshly drawn cold water; hot water has lost most of its oxygen and will make tea taste flat and stale. Bring water to a full boil; pour a little into the teapot, swirl it around and then discard it. Make your tea immediately, according to the recipe (next page), putting the lid on the pot and leaving it to brew for the correct number of minutes. If the water isn't hot enough, the tea won't fully brew. If you boil the water too long, it will become flat and lose its freshness. Brew tea only as long as the recipe directs or it will be bitter.

After brewing, remove the tea bag or tea ball immediately. If using tea bags, squeeze them just enough to remove excess water, but not enough to extract bitter tannins. And don't judge the strength of tea by its color; taste it.

On Cocoa

Cocoa powder, the most concentrated form of chocolate available, is used to make a steaming beverage (next page), as well as to flavor a host of well-known desserts.

Some cocoa powder is labeled "dutched." Dutch process cocoa is cocoa that has been treated with alkali to neutralize its natural acidity. This technique darkens the color of the cocoa and mellows its flavor. For these reasons, many people prefer dutched cocoas in their hot chocolate. Though dutched cocoas are not widely available in American supermarkets, you can find them in larger markets and gourmet shops. If your recipe lists no preference, you can use either type of cocoa. Store all types of cocoa, tightly covered, in a cool, dark place up to two years.

Café au Lait

COFFEE DICTIONARY

Café au lait: French for "coffee with milk," it consists of equal portions of brewed coffee and steamed milk poured simultaneously into a large cup.

Cappuccino: One-third espresso capped with one-third steamed milk and one-third foamed milk. The drink gets its name from the foam "cap," which is said to resemble the hooded robes of the Catholic order of Capuchin friars.

Crema: The rich and aromatic golden foam (cream) that tops a perfect cup of espresso.

Demitasse: French for "half-cup." The small cups in which espresso is traditionally served.

Espresso: Strongly brewed coffee made specifically in a steam-pressured espresso machine. When made properly, a shot of espresso will have a golden crema (foam) on top. A close substitute can be made in your own coffeemaker, using 3 to 4 tablespoons ground espresso roast coffee beans to ¾ cup water. Serve espresso in demitasse cups with lemon peel and raw sugar such as turbinado.

Latte: A popular morning coffee drink containing one-third espresso with two-thirds steamed milk and topped with little or no froth.

Macchiato: Espresso "marked" with a dollop of steamed milk foam and served in an espresso cup.

Cappuccino

Coffee

◀ QUICK ▶

PREP: 1 MINUTE   COOK: 5 MINUTES

2 tablespoons ground coffee
¾ cup cold water

•Select the particular grind of coffee that your coffeemaker requires.
Drip: Assemble drip coffeemaker according to manufacturer's directions. Place ground coffee in the coffee filter or filter basket. Add water to coffeemaker, and brew.
Percolator: Pour water into percolator; assemble stem and basket in pot. Add coffee. Replace lid. Plug in coffee pot if using an electric percolator. If using a nonelectric model, bring to a boil over high heat; reduce heat, and perk gently 5 to 7 minutes.
Vacuum: Bring water to a boil in lower bowl. Place a filter in the upper bowl, and fill with ground coffee. Reduce heat. Stir water when it rises into upper bowl. Brew 1 to 3 minutes. Remove from heat, and allow coffee to return to lower bowl.
•Serve coffee immediately with cream and sugar. Yield: ¾ cup.
Per ¾-cup serving: Calories 3 Fat 0g
Cholesterol 0mg Sodium 0mg

German Chocolate Café au Lait

◀ QUICK ▶

PREP: 10 MINUTES   COOK: 5 MINUTES

This warming concoction smells like dessert as you pour it. Use regular brewed coffee or a chocolate-flavored coffee, if desired. The "au lait" (with milk) is added directly to the coffee in the carafe.

¼ cup plus 3 tablespoons ground Swiss Mocha Almond coffee
2 cups water
2 cups hot milk
2 teaspoons coconut extract
¼ cup Frangelico or other hazelnut liqueur
¼ cup whipping cream
2 tablespoons powdered sugar
1 tablespoon plus 1 teaspoon grated sweet baking chocolate

•Prepare coffee according to manufacturer's directions, using ¼ cup plus 3 tablespoons ground coffee and 2 cups water. Stir in milk, extract, and liqueur. Pour into mugs.
•Beat whipping cream at medium speed with an electric mixer until foamy; add powdered sugar, beating until soft peaks form. Top coffee with whipped cream and grated chocolate. Yield: 4 cups.

Per 1-cup serving: Calories 243 Fat 15g
Cholesterol 57mg Sodium 81mg

Kahlúa Coffee

◀ QUICK ▶

PREP: 4 MINUTES

Sip this dark drink after dinner. It's just as good if you choose to omit the Kahlúa.

6 cups freshly brewed coffee
¾ cup chocolate syrup
¼ cup Kahlúa or other coffee-flavored
    liqueur
Unsweetened whipped cream
Ground cinnamon

•Combine first 3 ingredients in a large carafe; stir well. Top each serving with a dollop of whipped cream. Sprinkle with cinnamon. Serve immediately. Yield: 7 cups.

Per 1-cup serving: Calories 173 Fat 6.7g
Cholesterol 23mg Sodium 31mg

Irish Coffee Nog

◀ MAKE AHEAD ▶

PREP: 10 MINUTES   CHILL: 1 HOUR

This nog is so lavish, it could double as dessert. Pour individual servings into mugs, and top each with a scoop of ice cream.

3 tablespoons instant coffee granules
1 cup Irish whiskey or bourbon
2 quarts refrigerated eggnog
⅓ cup firmly packed brown sugar
½ teaspoon ground cinnamon
½ teaspoon ground nutmeg
1 quart coffee ice cream

•Dissolve coffee in whiskey in a large bowl; add eggnog and next 3 ingredients. Beat at low speed with an electric mixer until

smooth. Cover and chill at least 1 hour. Pour into a punch bowl, and top with scoops of ice cream. Yield: 13 cups.

Per ½-cup serving: Calories 229 Fat 9.9g
Cholesterol 55mg Sodium 74mg

Mocha Coffee Blend

◀ MAKE AHEAD • QUICK ▶

PREP: 10 MINUTES

Here's a homemade instant coffee blend that's not so strong on coffee flavor. You'll taste the cocoa and vanilla with each sip.

1 cup powdered nondairy coffee creamer
¾ cup sugar
½ cup instant coffee granules
3 tablespoons cocoa
1 vanilla bean

•Process first 4 ingredients in container of an electric blender until blended. Split vanilla bean lengthwise, and cut into 3 pieces. Stir vanilla bean pieces into coffee mixture. Transfer coffee blend to a jar; cover and let stand at least 24 hours before using.
•To serve, spoon 3 tablespoons coffee blend into a cup. Add ¾ cup boiling water; stir well. Yield: 2¼ cups.

Per 3-tablespoons mix: Calories 103 Fat 2.9g
Cholesterol 0mg Sodium 14mg

Vienna Blend: Reduce sugar and nondairy coffee creamer each to ⅔ cup, omit cocoa and vanilla bean, and add ¾ teaspoon ground cinnamon. Yield: 1⅔ cups.

Hot Cocoa

◀ QUICK • FAMILY FAVORITE ▶

PREP: 2 MINUTES   COOK: 5 MINUTES

Serve Hot Cocoa just as soon as it's prepared; otherwise, a skin may form on top. If it does, just spoon it off.

⅓ cup sugar
¼ cup cocoa
Pinch of salt
½ cup water
4 cups milk
¼ teaspoon vanilla extract
Marshmallows (optional)

•Combine first 3 ingredients in a heavy saucepan. Add water, and bring to a boil over medium heat, stirring constantly. Stir in milk, and heat thoroughly (do not boil). Stir in vanilla. Serve cocoa immediately with marshmallows, if desired. Yield: 4½ cups.

Per ¾-cup serving: Calories 159 Fat 5.7g
Cholesterol 22mg Sodium 106mg

Hot Cinnamon Cocoa: Prepare as above, but stir 1 teaspoon ground cinnamon into cocoa mixture before cooking. Serve cocoa with cinnamon stick stirrers, if desired.

Hot Mocha Cocoa: Prepare as above, but stir 2 tablespoons instant coffee granules into cocoa mixture before cooking.

Hot Tea

◀ QUICK ▶

PREP: 5 MINUTES

1 regular-size tea bag
¾ cup boiling water

•Warm teapot, mug, or cup by rinsing with boiling water. Place tea bag in teapot. Immediately pour ¾ cup boiling water over tea bag. Steep 5 minutes. Remove tea bag; serve with sugar and lemon, if desired. Yield: ¾ cup.

Per ¾-cup serving: Calories 2 Fat 0g
Cholesterol 0mg Sodium 5mg

Hot Fruited Tea

◄ HEALTHY ►

PREP: 5 MINUTES   COOK: 35 MINUTES

This fruit tea is perfect with scones or short-bread as a late afternoon respite.

4 (3-inch) sticks cinnamon, broken
1 teaspoon whole cloves
½ teaspoon whole allspice
1 quart hot tea
½ cup sugar
3 cups orange juice
3 cups unsweetened pineapple juice
Garnish: orange wedges

•Combine first 3 ingredients in a tea ball or cheesecloth bag; set aside.
•Combine hot tea and sugar in a large Dutch oven; stir in fruit juices. Add spice mixture, and bring to a boil. Cover, reduce heat, and simmer 30 minutes; remove spice mixture. Garnish, if desired. Serve hot. Yield: 10 cups.
Per 1-cup serving: Calories 115 Fat 0.1g
Cholesterol 0mg Sodium 4mg

Iced Tea

◄ QUICK • FAMILY FAVORITE ►

PREP: 5 MINUTES

Tea may become cloudy if you chill it after it's brewed. Add a little boiling water to the tea to clear it up.

1 tablespoon loose tea, or 3 or 4 regular-
    size tea bags, or 1 family-size tea bag
2 cups boiling water
2 cups water

•Warm teapot or glass or ceramic saucepan by rinsing with boiling water. Place loose tea in a tea ball. Place tea ball in teapot. Pour 2 cups boiling water over tea. Cover and steep 3 to 5 minutes. Remove tea ball, and stir in 2 cups water. Serve over ice. Yield: 4 cups.
Per 1-cup serving: Calories 2 Fat 0g
Cholesterol 0mg Sodium 7mg

Southern Sweetened Iced Tea: After removing tea ball, add ¼ to ½ cup sugar, stirring until sugar dissolves; then add water as directed.

Citrus Tea

◄ QUICK • HEALTHY ►

PREP: 10 MINUTES

Squeeze fresh fruit juice for maximum flavor in this refreshing tea. Serve it hot or chilled.

2 quarts water
6 whole cloves
8 regular-size tea bags
⅔ cup fresh orange juice
½ cup fresh lemon juice
1½ cups sugar

•Bring water and cloves to a boil in a large saucepan; add tea bags. Remove from heat; steep 5 minutes. Remove tea bags. Strain cloves.
•Add fruit juices and sugar, stirring until sugar dissolves. Serve tea hot or cold. Yield: 9 cups.
Per 1-cup serving: Calories 143 Fat 0g
Cholesterol 0mg Sodium 7mg

Cranberry Tea

◄ QUICK ►

PREP: 5 MINUTES

Cranberry juice cocktail turns this tea a vivid red. To make flavored ice cubes, freeze cranberry juice cocktail in ice cube trays.

2 cups boiling water
4 orange herb tea bags
3 tablespoons sugar
2 cups cranberry juice cocktail
1 cup dry white wine

•Pour boiling water over tea bags; cover and steep 5 minutes.
•Remove tea bags from water, squeezing gently. Stir in sugar; cool.
•Stir in cranberry juice cocktail and wine. Pour over flavored ice cubes, if desired. Yield: 5 cups.
Per 1-cup serving: Calories 120 Fat 0.1g
Cholesterol 0mg Sodium 6mg

Grating fresh ginger: Rub a piece of peeled ginger across porcelain teeth of a ginger grater. A regular fine-toothed grater works, too.

Ginger Tea

◄ QUICK • HEALTHY ►

PREP: 15 MINUTES

What a divine drink! To make this tea, look for knobs of fresh ginger in the produce section of the store. Peel the brown skin, and grate the fibrous pulp for this surprisingly spicy tea. It's best served over ice.

2 quarts water
⅓ to ½ cup grated fresh ginger (see photo
    above)
⅓ cup lemon juice
¼ cup honey
4 regular-size green tea bags
1½ cups sugar

•Combine first 4 ingredients in a Dutch oven; bring to a boil. Reduce heat, and simmer 5 minutes, stirring occasionally. Remove from heat.
•Add tea bags; cover and steep 5 minutes. Remove tea bags; stir in sugar, and cool.
•Pour tea through a wire-mesh strainer into a pitcher; serve over ice. Yield: 8 cups.
Per 1-cup serving: Calories 92 Fat 0.1g
Cholesterol 0mg Sodium 7mg

Mint Tea

PREP: 30 MINUTES

Dozens of mint varieties are available for growing and cooking. Try spearmint, chocolate mint, or apple mint in this tea. You'll find herbs at most garden centers.

2   quarts boiling water
10 regular-size tea bags
1½ cups sugar
18 fresh mint sprigs (1 large bunch)
3   tablespoons lemon juice

•Pour boiling water over tea bags; cover and steep 5 minutes. Remove tea bags, squeezing gently. Stir in sugar, 10 mint sprigs, and lemon juice; cover and steep 25 minutes. Strain and cool. Serve over ice. Garnish each serving with mint. Yield: 8 cups.

Per 1-cup serving: Calories 149 Fat 0g
Cholesterol 0mg Sodium 8mg

Instant Spiced Tea Mix

◀ QUICK • MAKE AHEAD ▶
◀ FAMILY FAVORITE ▶

PREP: 3 MINUTES

Keep this instant spiced tea on hand to serve when friends drop in to visit. It's an easy recipe to mix up in large quantities, so you can give jars of it as gifts.

1¼ cups instant orange-flavored breakfast
      drink (we tested with Tang)
⅔   cup instant tea with sugar and lemon
1   teaspoon ground allspice
1   teaspoon ground cloves
1   teaspoon ground cinnamon
¼   teaspoon grated lemon rind
¼   teaspoon grated orange rind

•Combine all ingredients; stir well. Store mix in an airtight container. To serve, spoon 3 to 4 teaspoons mix into a cup. Add 1 cup boiling water; stir well. Yield: about 25 servings.

Per 3 teaspoons: Calories 90 Fat 0g
Cholesterol 0mg Sodium 1mg

Orange Breakfast Drink

◀ QUICK • HEALTHY ▶

PREP: 3 MINUTES

Orange juice fans, here's a frosty breakfast smoothie for you.

1   (6-ounce) can frozen orange juice
      concentrate, thawed and undiluted
¾   cup milk
1½ cups water
¼   cup sugar
½   teaspoon vanilla extract
Ice cubes

•Combine first 5 ingredients in container of an electric blender. Add ice to 4-cup level. Process until frothy. Serve immediately. Yield: 4 cups.

Per 1-cup serving: Calories 217 Fat 1.6g
Cholesterol 6mg Sodium 24mg

Fresh Lemonade

◀ QUICK • MAKE AHEAD ▶
◀ FAMILY FAVORITE ▶

PREP: 10 MINUTES

1½ cups sugar
½   cup boiling water
1½ cups fresh lemon juice (6 to 8 large
      lemons)
5   cups cold water
Garnishes: lemon slices, fresh mint sprigs

•Combine sugar and boiling water, stirring until sugar dissolves. Add lemon juice and cold water; stir well. Cover and chill.
•Serve over ice. Garnish glasses, if desired. Yield: 8 cups.

Per 1-cup serving: Calories 157 Fat 0g
Cholesterol 0mg Sodium 1mg

Fresh Limeade: Substitute an equal amount of fresh lime juice for lemon juice.

Apple Berry Sparkler

◀ QUICK • HEALTHY ▶
◀ MAKE AHEAD ▶

PREP: 4 MINUTES

Kids will love this pretty rose-colored drink that's fit for any summer occasion.

1   (6-ounce) can frozen apple juice
      concentrate, thawed and undiluted
1   (12-ounce) can frozen cranberry juice
      concentrate, thawed and undiluted
6   cups sparkling mineral water, chilled
Garnish: lemon slices

•Combine apple juice and cranberry juice concentrates; cover and chill.
•Stir in chilled mineral water. Serve over ice, and garnish, if desired. Yield: 8 cups.

Per 1-cup serving: Calories 113 Fat 0.2g
Cholesterol 0mg Sodium 48mg

Grapefruit Blush

◀ QUICK • MAKE AHEAD ▶
◀ FAMILY FAVORITE ▶
◀ HEALTHY ▶

PREP: 13 MINUTES

Create Tipsy Grapefruit Blush by adding 1½ cups vodka or gin before serving.

¾   cup sugar
2   cups water
1   cup grapefruit juice
½   cup chopped grapefruit sections
¼   cup red maraschino cherries, halved
3   tablespoons lemon juice
2   cups sparkling mineral water, chilled
Garnish: mint sprigs

•Combine sugar and water in a saucepan; bring to a boil, stirring until sugar dissolves. Remove from heat; cool.
•Combine sugar mixture, grapefruit juice, and next 3 ingredients. Cover and chill at least 2 hours.
•Stir in mineral water just before serving. Garnish, if desired. Yield: 6 cups.

Per 1-cup serving: Calories 129 Fat 0.1g
Cholesterol 0mg Sodium 17mg

Cool ice cubes: Avoid diluting drinks served with ice by freezing a carbonated beverage, tonic, or soda water into cubes instead of using regular ice cubes. Or you can freeze a portion of the recipe itself (Citrus Cooler, right) or a fruit juice included in the recipe. This option makes colorful cubes.

Citrus Cooler

◀ QUICK • HEALTHY ▶
◀ MAKE AHEAD ▶

PREP: 10 MINUTES

CHILL: 3 HOURS   FREEZE: 4 HOURS

Ruby red grapefruit juice lends a bright pink color to this beverage and its matching ice cubes.

6½ cups ruby red or pink grapefruit juice, divided
2 cups pineapple juice
1 (6-ounce) can frozen orange juice concentrate, thawed and undiluted
2 cups lime-flavored sparkling mineral water, chilled
Garnish: lime slices

•Pour 2½ cups grapefruit juice into ice trays, filling 28 sections; freeze. Combine remaining 4 cups grapefruit juice, pineapple juice, and orange juice concentrate; stir well. Cover and chill at least 3 hours.

•Stir in mineral water just before serving. Place 3 frozen grapefruit juice cubes in each of 9 glasses (see photo); fill each with fruit juice mixture. Garnish, if desired. Serve immediately. Yield: 9 cups.
Per 1-cup serving: Calories 129 Fat 0.3g Cholesterol 0mg Sodium 14mg

Sparkling Apple Juice

◀ QUICK • HEALTHY ▶

PREP: 1 MINUTE

½ cup apple juice
½ cup ginger ale, chilled

•Combine apple juice and ginger ale. Serve over ice. Yield: 1 cup.
Per 1-cup serving: Calories 99 Fat 0.1g Cholesterol 0mg Sodium 11mg

Sparkling Grape Juice: Use grape juice instead of apple juice.

PUNCHES

Turn to these refreshing fruit beverages and punches when company is coming. When you expect a crowd, select a punch with a large yield or double or triple the recipes. Calculate how much beverage you'll need by the size of your punch cups; punch cups hold from four to eight ounces. Allow about 1½ punch cupfuls per person.

Sunshine Fizz

◀ QUICK • HEALTHY ▶
◀ FAMILY FAVORITE ▶

PREP: 4 MINUTES

Here's another great kids' drink.

1 cup pineapple juice, chilled
1 cup orange juice, chilled
1 cup orange sherbet
½ cup club soda, chilled
1 pint orange sherbet

•Process pineapple juice, orange juice, and 1 cup sherbet in container of an electric

blender until smooth, stopping once to scrape down sides. Stir in club soda, and pour into soda glasses. Add ¼ cup scoop of orange sherbet to each glass, and serve immediately. Yield: 4 cups.
Per 1-cup serving: Calories 213 Fat 2g Cholesterol 5mg Sodium 52mg

Berry Punch

◀ QUICK • HEALTHY ▶

PREP: 4 MINUTES

Looking for an extrasweet punch? This is it. And the berry flavor really comes through.

1 (10-ounce) package frozen strawberries in syrup, thawed
1 (12-ounce) can frozen cranberry juice cocktail concentrate, thawed and undiluted
1 (12-ounce) can frozen lemonade concentrate, thawed and undiluted
2 (1-liter) bottles club soda, chilled
1 (1-liter) bottle ginger ale, chilled

•Process strawberries in container of an electric blender until smooth. Pour into a punch bowl; add cranberry juice cocktail and remaining 3 ingredients. Yield: 13 cups.
Per 1-cup serving: Calories 138 Fat 0.1g Cholesterol 0mg Sodium 25mg

Slushy Citrus Punch

◀ HEALTHY • MAKE AHEAD ▶

PREP: 5 MINUTES

FREEZE: SEVERAL HOURS UNTIL FIRM

Save a half-gallon juice or milk carton for freezing this punch as a block. Use an ice pick to break it up and make it slushy enough for serving.

1¼ cups sugar
1 (46-ounce) can pineapple juice
1½ cups orange juice
¾ cup lemon juice
¼ cup lime juice
2 (2-liter) bottles ginger ale, chilled

• Rinse out a half-gallon cardboard milk or juice carton. Combine first 5 ingredients, stirring until sugar dissolves.

• Pour into milk carton, and freeze until firm. Peel carton off frozen juice block. Thaw slightly in a punch bowl. (Use an ice pick to break up frozen block, if needed.) Add ginger ale, 1 bottle at a time, stirring until slushy. Yield: 28 cups.

Per 1-cup serving: Calories 94 Fat 0g
Cholesterol 0mg Sodium 5mg

Making an ice ring: To keep fruit from floating, add just enough water to cover fruit in mold; freeze. Fill to top with water, and freeze again. (See recipe below.)

Bourbon-Citrus Punch

◄ MAKE AHEAD ►

PREP: 10 MINUTES   FREEZE: 6 HOURS

3½ cups water
1 (10-ounce) jar red maraschino cherries
1 lemon, sliced
1 small orange, sliced
1 (12-ounce) can frozen lemonade concentrate, thawed and undiluted
1 (12-ounce) can frozen orange juice concentrate, thawed and undiluted
2 (1-liter) bottles sparkling water
2 cups bourbon

• Bring water to a boil, and set aside to cool. Drain cherries, reserving juice. Arrange cherries, lemon slices, and orange slices in a 6-cup ring mold; add just enough water to cover fruit mixture (see photo). Freeze until firm (about 4 hours). Fill ring with water; refreeze.

• Combine reserved cherry juice, lemonade concentrate, and remaining 3 ingredients in

a punch bowl. Unmold ice ring, and place in punch. Yield: 14 cups.

Per 1-cup serving: Calories 184 Fat 0.1g
Cholesterol 0mg Sodium 4mg

Raspberry Sherbet Punch

◄ QUICK • HEALTHY ►

PREP: 3 MINUTES

Pink lemonade adds tang to this three-ingredient punch. It's an easy recipe to double.

1 (12-ounce) can frozen pink lemonade concentrate, thawed and undiluted
1 quart raspberry sherbet, softened
1 (2-liter) bottle raspberry ginger ale or regular ginger ale, chilled

• Combine lemonade concentrate and sherbet in a punch bowl; stir in ginger ale, breaking up sherbet. Serve immediately. Yield: 12 cups.

Per 1-cup serving: Calories 149 Fat 0.6g
Cholesterol 0mg Sodium 51mg

Christmas Nog

◄ QUICK ►

PREP: 5 MINUTES

Here's a very rich homemade nog, sized for serving a large crowd during the holidays.

3 (½-gallon) cartons vanilla ice cream, softened
1 (750-milliliter) bottle brandy
½ (750-milliliter) bottle Kahlúa or other coffee-flavored liqueur (about 1½ cups)
Ground nutmeg

• Spoon softened ice cream into a punch bowl; stir with a spoon until ice cream is smooth. Pour brandy and Kahlúa over ice cream. Stir gently just until blended. (Do not overstir; nog will be too foamy.) Sprinkle with nutmeg. Yield: 1½ gallons.

Per 1-cup serving: Calories 402 Fat 14.4g
Cholesterol 50mg Sodium 60mg

Perky Cranberry Punch

◄ QUICK • HEALTHY ►

PREP: 3 MINUTES

This great-smelling coffee alternative is a certain winter warm-up.

2 (32-ounce) bottles cranberry juice
1 (46-ounce) can pineapple juice
2 cups water
1 cup firmly packed brown sugar
2 tablespoons whole allspice
2 tablespoons whole cloves
6 (3-inch) sticks cinnamon

• Pour first 3 ingredients into a large percolator. Place brown sugar and remaining ingredients in percolator basket. Perk through complete cycle of electric percolator. Yield: 1 gallon.

Per 1-cup serving: Calories 150 Fat 0.1g
Cholesterol 0mg Sodium 9mg

Mulled Wine Punch

◄ QUICK ►

PREP: 5 MINUTES   COOK: 10 MINUTES

Some versions of mulled wine simmer for a long time to develop the flavor; this variation is speedy yet still plenty flavorful.

2 cups cranberry juice cocktail
½ cup firmly packed brown sugar
3 whole cloves
3 whole allspice
1½ cups dry red wine
Garnish: cinnamon sticks

• Combine first 4 ingredients in a saucepan; bring to a boil over medium heat, stirring until sugar dissolves.

• Reduce heat, and simmer, uncovered, 5 minutes. Remove from heat. Discard whole spices. Stir in wine. Garnish, if desired. Serve warm. Yield: 3½ cups.

Per ½-cup serving: Calories 137 Fat 0g
Cholesterol 0mg Sodium 13mg

Tying a spice bag: Tie whole spices and cinnamon sticks in a large square of cheesecloth to simmer in cider. (Ground spices would cloud the mixture.)

Quick Mulled Apple Cider

◀ QUICK • HEALTHY ▶

PREP: 5 MINUTES   COOK: 10 MINUTES

The longer you simmer this spiced cider, the more it will scent your home. Replenish the cider as it simmers, if it evaporates.

10 whole cloves
10 whole allspice
4 (3-inch) sticks cinnamon
1 (64-ounce) bottle apple cider
¼ cup firmly packed brown sugar
¼ cup lemon juice

•Tie first 3 ingredients in a cheesecloth bag (see photo above). Combine spice bag, cider, brown sugar, and lemon juice in a Dutch oven. Bring to a boil; reduce heat, and simmer 5 minutes. Discard spice bag before serving. Yield: 8 cups.
Per 1-cup serving: Calories 139 Fat 0.2g
Cholesterol 0mg Sodium 10mg

Spirited Apple Cider

PREP: 10 MINUTES   COOK: 45 MINUTES

Dark rum adds depth of flavor to this cider.

12 whole cloves
6 whole allspice
3 (3-inch) sticks cinnamon, broken
1 tablespoon grated orange rind
2 quarts apple cider
1 cup orange juice
1 cup cranberry juice cocktail
1 cup pineapple juice
½ cup dark rum
½ cup apple-flavored brandy

•Tie first 4 ingredients in a cheesecloth bag (see photo at left); combine spice bag and cider in a large saucepan or Dutch oven. Bring mixture to a boil; reduce heat to medium, and cook 35 minutes or until mixture is reduced to 4 cups.
•Discard spice bag; stir in orange juice and remaining ingredients. Simmer over medium heat until heated. Yield: 8 cups.
Per 1-cup serving: Calories 201 Fat 2.6g
Cholesterol 0mg Sodium 23mg

Wassail

PREP: 10 MINUTES   COOK: 30 MINUTES

In traditional wassail, small roasted apples float in the brew. For this version, we insert whole cloves into fresh fruit slices for a pretty presentation.

4 (3-inch) sticks cinnamon, broken
1 teaspoon whole cloves
3 quarts apple cider
1 (11.5-ounce) can apricot nectar
1 (6-ounce) can frozen lemonade
    concentrate, thawed and undiluted
1 (6-ounce) can frozen orange juice
    concentrate, thawed and undiluted
⅔ cup firmly packed brown sugar
1 teaspoon ground allspice
½ teaspoon ground ginger
½ teaspoon ground cinnamon
1 (12-ounce) bottle dark beer or ale
Garnishes: apple and orange slices or
    wedges studded with cloves

•Tie cinnamon sticks and cloves in a cheesecloth bag. Combine spice bag, cider, and next 7 ingredients in a Dutch oven.
•Bring to a boil; reduce heat, and simmer, uncovered, 20 minutes. Remove from heat, and stir in beer. Discard spice bag before serving. Garnish, if desired. Yield: 1 gallon.
Per 1-cup serving: Calories 180 Fat 0.3g
Cholesterol 0mg Sodium 12mg

Hot Buttered Rum

◀ QUICK • MAKE AHEAD ▶

PREP: 10 MINUTES

Make the sweet butter mixture ahead, and freeze it; then thaw it in serving-size portions, add boiling water, and stir with cinnamon sticks.

2 cups butter, softened
1 (16-ounce) package light brown sugar
1 (16-ounce) package powdered sugar
2 teaspoons ground cinnamon
2 teaspoons ground nutmeg
1 quart vanilla ice cream, softened
Light rum
Whipped cream
Cinnamon sticks

•Combine first 5 ingredients; beat well at medium speed with an electric mixer. Add ice cream, stirring until blended. Spoon mixture into a 2-quart freezer container; freeze.
•To serve, thaw slightly. Place 3 tablespoons butter mixture and 1 jigger rum in a large mug; fill with boiling water. Stir well. (Refreeze any unused butter mixture.) Top with whipped cream, and serve with cinnamon stick stirrers. Yield: about 25 servings.
Per 1-cup serving: Calories 428 Fat 19.8g
Cholesterol 58mg Sodium 170mg

ICE CREAM BEVERAGES

When a beverage contains ice cream, especially when it's teamed with chocolate, fruit, or a splash of spirits, it's got to be good. Just add a straw or spoon, and enjoy. Several of these beverages require an electric blender. You won't get the same slushy texture if you try to blend these beverages without one.

Rich Vanilla Milk Shake

◀ QUICK • FAMILY FAVORITE ▶

PREP: 3 MINUTES

If you have a blender, you can whip up any one of these six milk shakes at home.

3 cups premium vanilla ice cream
1 cup milk
½ teaspoon vanilla extract

•Process all ingredients in container of an electric blender until smooth. Serve immediately. Yield: 2½ cups.
Per 1¼-cup serving: Calories 497 Fat 25.2g Cholesterol 107mg Sodium 223mg

Strawberry Milk Shake: Substitute strawberry ice cream for vanilla ice cream or add 1 (10-ounce) package frozen strawberries, thawed, or 1 cup fresh strawberries to ingredients in blender.

Chocolate Milk Shake: Substitute chocolate ice cream for vanilla ice cream or add ¼ cup chocolate syrup to ingredients in blender.

Peach Milk Shake: Add 1 (16-ounce) can sliced peaches, drained, to ingredients in blender.

Banana Milk Shake: Add 1 large banana, sliced, to ingredients in blender.

Coffee Milk Shake: Substitute coffee ice cream for vanilla ice cream or add 1 tablespoon instant coffee granules to ingredients in blender.

Peanut Butter-Banana Shake

◀ QUICK ▶

PREP: 4 MINUTES

Bite-sized peanut butter sandwich cookies make this kids' shake ultrathick.

3 cups vanilla ice cream, slightly softened
⅔ cup miniature peanut butter sandwich cookies (we tested with Nutter Butter Bites)
1 ripe banana, sliced
3 tablespoons chocolate syrup

•Process first 3 ingredients in container of an electric blender just until smooth, stopping once to scrape down sides (mixture will be thick). Pour into glasses; drizzle each serving with chocolate syrup. Yield: 3 cups.
Per 1-cup serving: Calories 437 Fat 17.9g Cholesterol 60mg Sodium 191mg

Chocolate-Peanut Butter-Banana Shake: Add 3 tablespoons chocolate syrup to mixture in blender. Blend as directed.

Lemon Frappé

◀ QUICK ▶

PREP: 4 MINUTES

A frappé is a slushy dessert beverage.

1 (6-ounce) can frozen lemonade or limeade concentrate, undiluted
½ cup cold water
1 pint lemon sherbet or vanilla ice cream
1 (12-ounce) can ginger ale

•Process first 3 ingredients in container of an electric blender until smooth. Pour into a pitcher; add ginger ale. Serve immediately. Yield: 4 cups.
Per 1-cup serving: Calories 211 Fat 0.9g Cholesterol 0mg Sodium 74mg

Quick Banana-Pineapple Smoothie

◀ QUICK • HEALTHY ▶

PREP: 4 MINUTES

Smoothies are a great choice for breakfast or any time of day.

2 medium bananas, chilled
2 (8-ounce) cartons pineapple low-fat yogurt
1 (8-ounce) can crushed pineapple, undrained
Ice cubes

•Process first 3 ingredients in container of an electric blender until smooth, stopping once to scrape down sides.
•Add ice to 4-cup level, and process 1 minute or until smooth. Serve immediately. Yield: 4 cups.
Per 1-cup serving: Calories 196 Fat 1.6g Cholesterol 5mg Sodium 61mg

Kahlúa Velvet Frosty

◀ QUICK ▶

PREP: 4 MINUTES

1 cup Kahlúa
1 cup half-and-half
1 pint vanilla ice cream
⅛ teaspoon almond extract
Ice cubes

•Process all ingredients, except ice cubes, in container of an electric blender until smooth. Add ice to 5-cup level; process until smooth. Serve immediately. Yield: 5 cups.
Per 1-cup serving: Calories 322 Fat 11.4g Cholesterol 42mg Sodium 63mg

BAR FAVORITES

Blend a batch of chilled or frozen concoctions like a pro with these recipes. You'll want to whip them up and serve immediately. And don't forget the finishing touch—cut fruit garnishes are a natural with most of these spirited drinks.

Frozen Daiquiris

Mimosas

◀ QUICK ▶

PREP: 3 MINUTES

A mimosa is a morning luxury—a bubbly blend of champagne and orange juice.

1 (12-ounce) can frozen orange juice concentrate, thawed and undiluted
⅓ cup Triple Sec or other orange-flavored liqueur
1 (750-milliliter) bottle champagne, chilled

•Prepare orange juice according to can directions; stir in liqueur. Cover and chill thoroughly. Stir in champagne just before serving. Yield: 10 cups.
Per 1-cup serving: Calories 123 Fat 0.1g Cholesterol 0mg Sodium 4mg

Parson's Mimosas: You can substitute 1 (750-milliliter) bottle sparkling white grape juice for the champagne, and omit the Triple Sec. Yield: 9¼ cups.

FRUIT GARNISH FINESSE

When adding a fruit garnish to a beverage, select a fruit already in the drink or one that will complement the drink. Cut the fruit into thin slices. Then just slice the fruit from 1 edge of the slice to the center, and slip it over the rim of the glass. Some garnishes can serve double duty as stirrers, like cinnamon sticks or decorative straws. Or you can skewer fruit onto wooden picks to make stirrers that your guests can nibble on.

Frozen Daiquiris

◀ QUICK ▶

PREP: 5 MINUTES

1 (6-ounce) can frozen limeade concentrate, undiluted
1 cup light rum
Ice cubes
Garnish: lime slices

•Process frozen limeade concentrate and rum in container of an electric blender until smooth. Add ice to 4-cup level; process until smooth. Garnish, if desired. Serve immediately. Yield: 4 cups.
Per 1-cup serving: Calories 216 Fat 0g Cholesterol 0mg Sodium 2mg

Strawberry Daiquiris: Add 1½ cups frozen unsweetened whole strawberries, unthawed, and ¼ cup sifted powdered sugar. Yield: 4 cups.

Peach Daiquiris: Add 1½ cups frozen unsweetened sliced peaches, unthawed, and ¼ cup sifted powdered sugar. Yield: 4 cups.

Pineapple Daiquiris: Add 1 (15¼-ounce) can unsweetened pineapple tidbits, drained, and ¼ cup sifted powdered sugar. (For an extra slushy daiquiri, freeze drained pineapple tidbits.) Yield: 4 cups.

Icy Margaritas

◀ QUICK ▶

PREP: 5 MINUTES

Half the fun of margaritas is preparing the glasses. Spin the rims of assorted colorful glasses in salt. And prepare a Mexican appetizer such as Layered Nacho Dip (page 34) to accompany your drinks.

Lime wedge
Salt
1 (6-ounce) can frozen limeade concentrate, thawed and undiluted
¾ cup tequila
¼ cup Triple Sec or other orange-flavored liqueur
Ice cubes
Garnish: lime slices

•Rub rim of cocktail glasses with wedge of lime. Place salt in saucer; spin rim of each glass in salt. Set prepared glasses aside.
•Process limeade concentrate, tequila, and Triple Sec in container of an electric blender until smooth. Add ice to 3½-cup level; blend well. Pour into prepared glasses; garnish, if desired. Yield: 3½ cups.
Per ½-cup serving: Calories 130 Fat 0g Cholesterol 0mg Sodium 1173mg

Spicy Bloody Marys

◄ QUICK ►

PREP: 7 MINUTES

Hot sauce (we use Tabasco), horseradish, and pepper give this wake-up drink its kick.

4½ cups tomato juice or spicy vegetable juice, chilled
¼ cup lemon juice, lime juice, or clam juice
3 tablespoons Worcestershire sauce
1 tablespoon prepared horseradish
1 teaspoon celery salt
½ teaspoon freshly ground pepper
¼ teaspoon hot sauce
1 cup vodka
Garnish: celery stalks

•Combine first 7 ingredients; stir well, and chill thoroughly. Stir in vodka, and serve over ice. Garnish, if desired. Yield: 6 cups.
Per 1-cup serving: Calories 139 Fat 0.2g Cholesterol 0mg Sodium 1121mg

Virgin Marys: Omit vodka, and add 1 more cup tomato juice or spicy vegetable juice.

Thick 'n' Rich Piña Coladas

◄ QUICK ►

PREP: 9 MINUTES

Serve this fruity concoction with a straw and a spoon.

1 (8½-ounce) can cream of coconut
1 (8-ounce) can crushed pineapple, drained
⅓ cup flaked coconut
½ cup light rum
½ teaspoon banana extract
2 cups vanilla ice cream, slightly softened

•Process all ingredients in container of an electric blender until smooth. Serve immediately. Yield: 4 cups.
Per 1-cup serving: Calories 481 Fat 31.9g Cholesterol 30mg Sodium 79mg

Mock Coladas: Omit rum, and add 1 teaspoon rum extract. Yield: 3½ cups.

Apple Mint Juleps

◄ QUICK • HEALTHY ►

PREP: 15 MINUTES

If bourbon isn't your cup of tea, you can still enjoy a julep. We made this version with fruit juices, and the mint flavor is really distinct.

2 cups chopped fresh mint
8 cups apple juice
½ cup fresh lime juice
Garnish: fresh mint sprigs

•Combine mint and apple juice in a large saucepan. Bring to a boil; remove from heat. Cover and cool. Chill thoroughly.
•Pour mint mixture through a wire-mesh strainer into a 2½-quart pitcher; stir in lime juice. Serve over crushed or shaved ice. Garnish, if desired. Yield: 8 cups.
Per 1-cup serving: Calories 121 Fat 0.3g Cholesterol 0mg Sodium 8mg

Mint Julep

◄ QUICK ►

PREP: 10 MINUTES   COOK: 5 MINUTES

This mint syrup yields enough to make 48 juleps. Refrigerate any unused syrup, and use it to sweeten iced tea.

2 to 4 tablespoons bourbon
1 tablespoon Mint Syrup
Garnish: fresh mint sprig

•Combine bourbon and Mint Syrup; serve over crushed ice. Garnish, if desired. Yield: 1 serving.
Per serving: Calories 100 Fat 0g Cholesterol 0mg Sodium 0mg

Mint Julep

Mint Syrup

1½ cups coarsely chopped fresh mint
2 cups sugar
2 cups water

•Combine all ingredients in a large saucepan; bring to a boil. Cook, stirring constantly, until sugar dissolves. Remove from heat; cover and cool completely. Pour mixture through a wire-mesh strainer into a bowl; cover and chill thoroughly. Yield: 3 cups.

JULEP FAME

Meant to be sipped from a sterling silver cup, a julep is the flavor of a more genteel time. Juleps—beverages made with bourbon and a shot of sweet syrup—have been around since the late 1700s. The mint julep became the official drink of the Kentucky Derby in 1875, in part due to bourbon whiskey finding its roots in the Bluegrass state.

Guests of the derby know to grasp the bottom of the cup with a linen napkin so as not to disturb the frost, an aesthetic part of the julep experience. Fresh mint is also pertinent to the experience—and the more, the better. After a julep or two, derbygoers may proudly display a fragrant sprig behind an ear.

Red Sangría

White Sangría

Cranberry Spritzer

◄ QUICK ►

PREP: 2 MINUTES

Aromatic bitters, which are a blend of herbs, spices, and alcohol, spike this party recipe.

1 (48-ounce) bottle cranberry juice
   cocktail
2 cups pineapple juice
¼ cup Angostura bitters

•Combine all ingredients in a large pitcher, stirring well. Serve chilled or over ice. Yield: 8 cups.
Per 1-cup serving: Calories 156 Fat 0.1g
Cholesterol 0mg Sodium 8mg

Red Sangría

◄ QUICK ►

PREP: 10 MINUTES

No need to spend a lot of money on wine here. Sangría (which literally means "bleeding") is a fruit-filled acidic beverage, as good with any grocery store jug red wine as with a more expensive brand.

⅓ cup sugar
⅓ cup lemon juice
⅓ cup orange juice
1 (750-milliliter) bottle red wine, such as
   Merlot or Burgundy
1 small orange, thinly sliced
1 lemon, thinly sliced

•Combine first 3 ingredients in a large pitcher, stirring until sugar dissolves. Add wine, orange slices, and lemon slices; stir gently. Serve over crushed ice. Yield: 5 cups.
Per 1-cup serving: Calories 168 Fat 0g
Cholesterol 0mg Sodium 12mg

Parson's Sangría: Substitute 1 (25.4-ounce) bottle sparkling red grape juice, chilled, for the wine.

White Sangría

◄ QUICK ►

PREP: 14 MINUTES   CHILL: 2 HOURS

Frozen grapes help chill this white wine version of the Spanish beverage.

2 lemons, thinly sliced
2 limes, thinly sliced
1 Red Delicious apple, thinly sliced
1½ cups sugar
2 (750-milliliter) bottles Sauvignon Blanc
1 cup brandy
2 (1-liter) bottles lemon-lime sparkling water, chilled
1 cup green grapes, frozen

•Combine first 6 ingredients in a large pitcher; stir well. Chill at least 2 hours.

Gently stir in chilled sparkling water and frozen grapes before serving. Serve over ice. Yield: 9 cups.

Per 1-cup serving: Calories 148 Fat 0g
Cholesterol 0mg Sodium 4mg

Wine Spritzers

◄ QUICK ►

PREP: 3 MINUTES

Lemon and lime slices make the ideal garnish for cool summer drinks such as this spritzer, and they add a hint of fresh citrus flavor.

2 (25.4-ounce) bottles white wine
1 (1-liter) bottle club soda
Garnish: lemon or lime slices

•Combine wine and club soda; stir gently. Pour into ice-filled glasses; garnish, if desired. Yield: 10 cups.

Per 1-cup serving: Calories 105 Fat 0g
Cholesterol 0mg Sodium 33mg

Wine Cooler: Substitute 1 (1-liter) bottle lemon-lime carbonated beverage for the club soda.

YOUR OWN LIQUEUR

These homemade liqueurs taste very similar to bottled brands when splashed over ice cream or stirred into coffee. They're easier to make than you might think, and are a great gift idea.

Amaretto

◄ MAKE AHEAD ►

PREP: 20 MINUTES   COOK: 30 MINUTES

Add a dash of this homemade amaretto to a plain cheesecake filling, custard, whipped cream, or sliced fruit.

1 lemon
3 cups sugar
2 cups water
3 cups vodka
3 tablespoons brandy
2 tablespoons almond extract
2 teaspoons vanilla extract
1 teaspoon chocolate flavoring

•Peel lemon, leaving inner white skin (pith) on fruit; reserve lemon for another use. Cut lemon rind into 2- x ¼-inch strips.
•Combine lemon rind strips, sugar, and water in a saucepan. Bring to a boil; cover, reduce heat, and simmer 30 minutes.

Remove from heat; discard lemon rind strips. Cover and chill thoroughly.
•Add vodka and remaining 4 ingredients to chilled mixture; stir well. Store in an airtight container at room temperature at least 1 week before serving. Use in any recipe calling for amaretto. Yield: 6 cups.

Per tablespoon: Calories 43 Fat 0g
Cholesterol 0mg Sodium 0mg

Coffee Liqueur

◄ QUICK • MAKE AHEAD ►

PREP: 15 MINUTES

Splash this liqueur in hot coffee drinks or over ice cream.

5 cups sugar
1 (2-ounce) jar instant coffee granules
4 cups boiling water
1 (1-liter) bottle vodka
1 vanilla bean, split lengthwise

•Combine sugar and coffee granules in a large metal or glass bowl; add boiling water, stirring until sugar and coffee granules dissolve. Cool to room temperature. Stir in vodka. Pour into 3 (1-quart) jars or decorative bottles.

•Cut vanilla bean into thirds; place 1 piece in each jar or bottle. Cover and let stand at room temperature at least 12 days before serving. Use in recipes calling for coffee-flavored liqueur. Yield: 11 cups.

Per tablespoon: Calories 14 Fat 0g
Cholesterol 0mg Sodium 0mg

LUSCIOUS LIQUEUR

Collect beautiful colored glass bottles from antique shops, and fill them with your own liqueur recipes. They'll be pretty just sitting on display or great for giving as gifts.

Whole Wheat Potato Rolls (page 82),
Popovers (page 76) , Garlic-Pepper
Baguettes (page 87)

BREADS

In the extended family of breads, there are so many things to love—flaky biscuits, crispy cornbreads, gooey coffee cakes, plump muffins, crusty loaves of sourdough. And nothing quite compares to the aroma and freshness of homemade bread. It is indeed the staff of culinary life.

You can make your own bread in a matter of minutes with many quick bread recipes. They're leavened by baking powder or baking soda; they're quick to stir together, and they're baked immediately.

Yeast breads are somewhat more involved to make, but are definitely worth it. Yeast is a living organism which requires mixing with liquid at a certain temperature to activate its growth process. When making yeast breads, the kneading process is crucial to the final product. As you knead dough, its structure develops, and this ultimately leads to a perfectly textured bread.

Once you've mastered the technique of bread baking, yeast breads won't seem intimidating. Many, in fact, claim the art of yeast bread baking is therapeutic.

Equipment

If you love home-baked bread, you can never have too many baking sheets, loafpans, and specialty baking pans. Select good quality, heavy grade pans and baking sheets for long-term use. Choose shiny pans because they reflect heat best and produce baked goods with nicely browned, tender crusts.

We tested our muffin recipes in standard 2½-inch muffin pans. The loafpan we used most often is 9 x 5 inches, although some bread recipes specify pans 8½ x 4½ inches or smaller. For best results, use the size pan that the recipe calls for; otherwise, expect breads that are shallower or deeper and baking times that vary.

A popover pan, pastry blender, dough scraper, serrated bread knife, and pair of baguette pans are other valuable tools for the seasoned bread maker.

Bread machines have become a convenient solution for hassle-free homemade bread. The kneading, proofing, and baking are all done for you. Once you've become familiar with your machine through trial and error, let creativity reign when choosing the type of bread to make.

Flour for Breads

The type of flour you use and its protein content play an important role in the texture of the end product. Flour made predominantly from "hard wheat" (such as Pillsbury and Gold Medal) is higher in protein and richer in gluten than flour made predominantly from "soft wheat" (like White Lily and Martha White). Hard wheat flour absorbs liquids more readily and yields better-textured bread.

White flour is available as self-rising (with baking powder and salt added) or as all-purpose flour. Our bread recipes specify which type of flour to use; be sure to follow the recipe. Oftentimes, yeast bread recipes give a range on the amount of flour needed. It's a good idea to start with the minimum amount of flour and gradually add more until the dough will no longer easily absorb flour and the texture matches what the recipe describes.

Since most flour is sifted during the milling process, there's no need to sift before measuring. To measure flour, stir it lightly; then spoon it into a dry measuring cup (don't pack it). Level the top, using a spatula or other straight edge. Don't shake the cup level, because this packs the flour. Cake flour, however, is the one flour that does need to be sifted before use.

Storing and Freezing Breads

Bread turns stale quickly, so proper storage is important. Contrary to popular belief, bread will get stale faster in the refrigerator than at room temperature (although it will mold faster at room temperature than in the refrigerator). If you want to keep bread for several days, cover it with an airtight wrap, and store it at room temperature.

For longer storage, let bread cool completely after baking, wrap tightly in aluminum foil, place in a freezer bag, and freeze up to three months. To serve, partially unwrap and let stand at room temperature until thawed. Reheat, uncovered, at 350° until thoroughly heated.

QUICK BREADS

These breads are true to their name—they're quick and easy to make. Some quick breads start with a batter, some with a dough. The ratio of liquid to flour, the type of fat used, and the number of eggs create many variations in quick breads. And one thing's for sure, once in the oven, these breads rise quickly, leavened by steam, eggs, and the gases formed by baking powder or soda.

Double-acting baking powder is the most common type of leavening used for quick breads, and it's what we've used in testing our recipes. It contains an acid (typically cream of tartar) and an alkali (baking soda) which, when combined with a liquid, react to give off carbon dioxide. Once in a hot oven, this carbon dioxide forms tiny bubbles that expand quickly, thus giving the bread height and developing its structure. Hence the name double-acting—it reacts initially when added to liquid, and again from the heat of the oven.

That means you should bake all quick breads as soon as possible after mixing. Recipes made with double-acting baking powder will rise better than those made with other types of baking powder even if they stand at room temperature a few minutes before baking. To be sure baking powder maintains its freshness, check the date on the can, and stir before using.

Baking soda starts reacting as soon as it's combined with liquid, so recipes calling for it should be baked immediately. Baking soda is usually used only in recipes that contain an acid, such as buttermilk, lemon juice, sour cream, molasses, or chocolate, to help activate the soda.

A rule of thumb is to bake quick breads until a wooden pick inserted in the center comes out clean. The length of time, of course, will vary due to the size bread.

BISCUITS

Tender, flaky biscuits are frequently on the menu for breakfast, lunch, and dinner in the South, accounting for their broad appeal.

The most tender biscuits contain solid fat, such as shortening or cold butter. Cut the fat into the dry ingredients, using a pastry blender until the mixture is crumbly. (Two knives work almost as well if you don't own a pastry blender.) This "cutting" action distributes little lumps of fat throughout the dough that melt during baking and give biscuits their trademark flakiness. Add the liquid ingredients, and stir just until the dry ingredients are moistened. Too much mixing makes biscuits heavy.

Knead the dough on a lightly floured surface only three or four times, just until the dough feels soft and not sticky. Quickly roll, "punch" cut, and bake as the recipe directs. If you twist the cutter as you cut biscuits, they won't rise evenly.

A good biscuit has a level and golden top and straight sides. Inside the biscuit should be tender and slightly moist. For the beginner baker, drop biscuits are a great place to start. They require no kneading, rolling, or cutting.

Whipping Cream Biscuits

◄ QUICK ►

PREP: 5 MINUTES   COOK: 12 MINUTES

This recipe is so simple, you can remember it by heart. You'll probably make it often once you try it.

2 cups self-rising flour
1 cup whipping cream

•Combine ingredients, stirring with a fork until blended. (Dough will be stiff.) Turn dough out onto a lightly floured surface, and knead 10 to 12 times.
•Roll dough to ½-inch thickness; cut with a 2-inch biscuit cutter. Place on a lightly greased baking sheet. Bake at 450° for 10 to 12 minutes. Yield: 1 dozen.
Per biscuit: Calories 145 Fat 7.6g
Cholesterol 27mg Sodium 272mg

Basic Buttermilk Biscuits

◄ QUICK ►

PREP: 6 MINUTES   COOK: 14 MINUTES

Soft wheat flour and buttermilk cause these biscuits to rise and to taste ultralight. Brush them with butter while hot out of the oven.

⅓ cup butter or margarine
2 cups self-rising soft-wheat flour (we tested with Martha White)
¾ cup buttermilk
Butter or margarine, melted

•Cut ⅓ cup butter into flour with a pastry blender until mixture is crumbly. Add buttermilk, stirring until dry ingredients are moistened. Turn dough out onto a lightly floured surface, and knead 3 or 4 times.
•Roll dough to ¾-inch thickness; cut with a 2½-inch biscuit cutter. Place on a lightly greased baking sheet. Bake at 425° for 12 to 14 minutes. Brush biscuits with melted butter. Yield: 10 biscuits.
Per biscuit: Calories 174 Fat 8.9g
Cholesterol 24mg Sodium 423mg

Baking Powder Biscuits

◄ QUICK • FAMILY FAVORITE ►

PREP: 6 MINUTES   COOK: 15 MINUTES

2 cups all-purpose flour
1 tablespoon baking powder
½ teaspoon salt
⅓ cup shortening
¾ cup milk

•Combine first 3 ingredients; cut in shortening with a pastry blender until mixture is crumbly (photo 1). Add milk, stirring until dry ingredients are moistened. Turn dough out onto a floured surface, and knead lightly 3 or 4 times (photo 2).
•Roll dough to ½-inch thickness; cut with a 2½-inch biscuit cutter (photo 3). Place on a lightly greased baking sheet. Bake at 425° for 15 minutes or until golden. Yield: 1 dozen.

1. Cut shortening into dry ingredients until crumbly.

2. Knead dough lightly with heel of your hand.

3. Punch out biscuits with a 2½-inch cutter.

Per biscuit: Calories 124 Fat 5.4g
Cholesterol 2mg Sodium 206mg

Cinnamon-Raisin Biscuits

◄ FAMILY FAVORITE ►

PREP: 16 MINUTES
COOK: 15 MINUTES PER BATCH

Plump raisins and a hint of cinnamon permeate each bite of these frosted breakfast favorites.

1½ cups all-purpose flour
1½ cups sifted cake flour
1 tablespoon baking powder
1 teaspoon salt
¼ cup sugar
1½ teaspoons ground cinnamon
¾ cup butter or margarine
1 cup raisins
1 cup milk
1½ tablespoons butter or margarine, melted
1 cup sifted powdered sugar
1½ tablespoons milk

•Combine first 6 ingredients in a large bowl; cut in ¾ cup butter with a pastry blender until mixture is crumbly. Add raisins and 1 cup milk, stirring until dry ingredients are moistened. Turn dough out onto a lightly floured surface, and knead 4 or 5 times.
•Roll dough to 1-inch thickness; cut with a 2-inch biscuit cutter. Place on greased baking sheets; brush with melted butter. Bake at 400° for 15 minutes or until biscuits are lightly browned.
•Combine powdered sugar and 1½ tablespoons milk, stirring until smooth. Drizzle glaze over warm biscuits. Yield: 15 biscuits.

Per biscuit: Calories 254 Fat 11.2g
Cholesterol 30mg Sodium 352mg

Note: All-purpose flour comes presifted, but cake flour doesn't. That's why we sift one and not the other in this recipe.

Cinnamon-Raisin Biscuits

Cloud Biscuits

◄ QUICK ►

PREP: 10 MINUTES   COOK: 10 MINUTES

These large biscuits get their name from their light texture.

2¼ cups self-rising flour
1 tablespoon sugar
½ cup butter-flavored shortening or
    regular shortening
1 large egg, lightly beaten
½ cup milk
1 tablespoon butter or margarine, melted

•Combine flour and sugar in a medium bowl; stir well. Cut in shortening with a pastry blender until mixture is crumbly.
•Combine egg and milk; add to flour mixture, stirring just until dry ingredients are moistened. Turn dough out onto a lightly floured surface, and knead 3 or 4 times.
•Roll dough to ½-inch thickness; cut with a 3-inch biscuit cutter. Place on an ungreased baking sheet. Bake at 450° for 10 minutes or until golden. Remove from oven; brush melted butter over hot biscuits. Yield: 6 biscuits.
Per biscuit: Calories 345 Fat 18g
Cholesterol 43mg Sodium 635mg

Hot Cheese Drop Biscuits

◄ QUICK ►

PREP: 10 MINUTES

COOK: 9 MINUTES PER BATCH

Sharp Cheddar cheese gives these free-form biscuits extra appeal.

2 cups all-purpose flour
2 teaspoons baking powder
½ teaspoon salt
½ teaspoon ground red pepper
1 cup (4 ounces) shredded sharp Cheddar
    cheese
¼ cup shortening
1 cup buttermilk

•Combine first 4 ingredients in a large bowl; cut in cheese and shortening with a pastry blender until mixture is crumbly. Add buttermilk, stirring just until dry ingredients are moistened.
•Drop by heaping tablespoonfuls onto greased baking sheets. Bake at 450° for 9 minutes or until golden. Yield: 2 dozen.
Per biscuit: Calories 74 Fat 3.5g
Cholesterol 5mg Sodium 122mg

MEASURING UP

Remember to measure flour by lightly spooning it into a dry measuring cup and leveling it off with a straight edge. Accurate measurements keep biscuits from becoming dry.

Daisy Biscuits

PREP: 26 MINUTES

COOK: 10 MINUTES PER BATCH

These jam-filled goodies have a dainty shape that's a snap to make.

1 (3-ounce) package cream cheese
⅓ cup butter or margarine
2½ cups self-rising flour
1 cup milk
2 tablespoons orange marmalade
2 tablespoons raspberry jam

•Cut cream cheese and butter into flour with a pastry blender until mixture is crumbly. Add milk, stirring just until dry ingredients are moistened. Turn dough out onto a floured surface, and knead 3 or 4 times.
•Roll dough to ½-inch thickness; cut with a 2-inch biscuit cutter. Place on ungreased baking sheets. Make 6 slits through dough around edges of each biscuit to ¼ inch from center.
•Press thumb in center of each biscuit, leaving an indentation. Spoon ½ teaspoon marmalade or jam into each biscuit indentation. Bake at 450° for 9 to 10 minutes or until golden. Serve hot. Yield: 21 biscuits.
Per biscuit: Calories 110 Fat 4.9g
Cholesterol 14mg Sodium 238mg

Cream Cheese Biscuits: Prepare dough and cut with biscuit cutter as directed above, but don't cut and shape into daisy. Omit jam, and bake as directed.

Herbed Blue Cheese Biscuits

PREP: 20 MINUTES

COOK: 8 MINUTES PER BATCH

Wow your brunch guests with a pile of these bite-size biscuits packed with herbs and the robust flavor of blue cheese.

1 (4-ounce) package blue cheese,
    crumbled
2 tablespoons minced green onions
1 teaspoon dried oregano
1 teaspoon dried thyme
2 cups all-purpose flour
1 tablespoon baking powder
¼ teaspoon baking soda
½ teaspoon salt
⅓ cup unsalted butter, cut into pieces
¾ cup buttermilk

•Combine first 4 ingredients in a small bowl. Set aside.
•Combine flour, baking powder, soda, and salt. Cut in cheese mixture and butter with a pastry blender until mixture is crumbly. Add buttermilk, stirring until dry ingredients are moistened. Turn dough out onto a lightly floured surface, and knead 4 or 5 times.
•Roll dough to ½-inch thickness; cut with a 1½-inch biscuit cutter. Place on lightly greased baking sheets. Bake at 450° for 8 minutes or until golden. Yield: 40 biscuits.
Per biscuit: Calories 50 Fat 2.5g
Cholesterol 6mg Sodium 112mg

Herbed Parmesan Cheese Biscuits: Substitute ⅓ cup grated Parmesan cheese for blue cheese. Bake at 450° for 6 to 7 minutes or until golden.

Angel Biscuits

PREP: 18 MINUTES   RISE: 30 MINUTES

COOK: 15 MINUTES PER BATCH

Angel Biscuits are aptly named because they rise more than traditional biscuits due to the yeast in them. They're lighter and airier— more like a roll.

1 package active dry yeast
¼ cup warm water (105° to 115°)
5 cups all-purpose flour
1 tablespoon baking powder
1 teaspoon baking soda
1 teaspoon salt
¼ cup sugar
1 cup shortening
2 cups buttermilk

•Combine yeast and warm water in a 1-cup liquid measuring cup; let stand 5 minutes. Combine flour and next 4 ingredients in a large bowl; cut in shortening with a pastry blender until mixture is crumbly. Add yeast mixture and buttermilk; stir just until ingredients are moistened. Turn dough out onto a lightly floured surface, and knead 6 to 8 times.
•Roll dough to ½-inch thickness; cut with a 2½-inch biscuit cutter. Place on lightly greased baking sheets. Cover and let rise in a warm place (85°), free from drafts, 30 minutes. Bake at 400° for 15 minutes or until lightly browned. Yield: 32 biscuits.

Per biscuit: Calories 126 Fat 5.6g
Cholesterol 1mg Sodium 153mg

Sweet Potato Biscuits

◄ QUICK • HEALTHY ►

PREP: 10 MINUTES

COOK: 15 MINUTES PER BATCH

Tuck a sliver of ham, bacon, or turkey into these biscuits, and serve them warm. They make great use of leftover sweet potatoes.

2 cups self-rising flour
¼ cup sugar
3 tablespoons shortening
2 tablespoons butter or margarine
1 cup cooked, mashed sweet potatoes
    (about 1 large sweet potato)
⅓ cup milk or half-and-half

•Combine flour and sugar in a medium bowl; cut in shortening and butter with a pastry blender until mixture is crumbly. Add mashed sweet potato and milk, stirring just until dry ingredients are moistened. Turn dough out onto a lightly floured surface, and knead 4 or 5 times.
•Roll dough to ½-inch thickness; cut with a 2-inch biscuit cutter. Place on lightly greased baking sheets. Bake biscuits at 400° for 14 to 15 minutes or until lightly browned. Yield: 1½ dozen.

Per biscuit: Calories 106 Fat 3.4g
Cholesterol 4mg Sodium 194mg

THE SCOOP ON SCONES

This Scottish quick bread was originally made with oats and baked on a griddle. It's sweet, rich, and much like a biscuit, although its texture is flakier than traditional Southern biscuits.

Scones are made with cream or milk, butter, and sometimes eggs. The dough should be "shaggy" or rough; don't strive for a smooth dough here. Just as in the biscuit procedure, work quickly with cold butter, and do very little mixing for a flaky product. And pat rather than roll the dough into shape.

Scones

PREP: 16 MINUTES

COOK: 15 MINUTES PER BATCH

The secret to melt-in-your-mouth flaky scones is to use cold butter, work quickly, and handle the dough as little as possible. Then serve the scones hot with your favorite preserves.

3½ cups all-purpose flour
2¼ teaspoons baking powder
¼ cup sugar
1 cup cold butter
½ cup golden raisins
⅔ cup milk
1 large egg
1 tablespoon milk
2 teaspoons sugar
Raspberry preserves (optional)
Whipping cream, lightly whipped
    (optional)

•Combine first 3 ingredients in a large bowl; cut in butter with a pastry blender until mixture is crumbly. Stir in raisins. Combine ⅔ cup milk and egg, stirring with a wire whisk. Gradually add milk mixture to flour mixture, stirring with a fork just until dry ingredients are moistened. Turn dough out onto a lightly floured surface, and knead 3 or 4 times.
•Pat dough to 1-inch thickness; cut with a 2-inch biscuit cutter. Place scones on a lightly greased baking sheet. Brush with 1 tablespoon milk, and sprinkle with 2 teaspoons sugar.
•Bake at 400° for 15 minutes or until barely golden. Cool slightly on a wire rack. Serve warm; if desired, serve with raspberry preserves and whipped cream. Yield: 1½ dozen.

Per scone: Calories 218 Fat 11.1g
Cholesterol 41mg Sodium 164mg

Gingerbread Scones

◄ QUICK ►

PREP: 18 MINUTES   COOK: 12 MINUTES

2 cups all-purpose flour
2 teaspoons baking powder
¼ teaspoon baking soda
1 teaspoon ground ginger
1 teaspoon ground cinnamon
½ cup unsalted butter
⅓ cup molasses
⅓ cup milk

•Combine first 5 ingredients; cut in butter with a pastry blender until mixture is crumbly. Combine molasses and milk; add to flour mixture, stirring just until dry ingredients are moistened. Turn dough out onto a lightly floured surface, and knead lightly 4 or 5 times.
•Divide dough in half; shape each portion into a ball. Pat each ball into a 5-inch circle on an ungreased baking sheet. Cut each circle into 6 wedges, using a sharp knife; do not separate wedges.
•Bake at 425° for 10 to 12 minutes or until lightly browned. Serve warm. Yield: 1 dozen.

Per scone: Calories 175 Fat 8.1g
Cholesterol 22mg Sodium 116mg

MUFFINS

Muffins are a frequent choice of bread bakers because there are so many variations. Make them bite-size or big, sweet or savory. Some are meant for home-style dining, while others seem more suited for the party table. Muffin tins come in miniature, standard, and jumbo sizes. And you can even buy a shallow pan to bake just crusty muffin tops (since that's the part people love to eat first).

It's important to mix muffin batter using the right technique. Combine dry ingredients and make a well in the center by using the back of a spoon. Combine liquid ingredients, and pour them into the well; stir just until dry ingredients are moistened. Spoon batter into greased muffin pans, and bake as directed.

Remove muffins from pans as soon as they're baked to keep condensation from forming and making them soggy on the bottom.

The well-made muffin has a pebbly brown top and a rounded even shape. If overmixed, your muffins will be peaked and will have tunnels and a coarse, tough texture.

Muffins that call for beating with an electric mixer contain more sugar than the traditional muffin and have a texture more like cake. The additional mixing works well in this case; however, don't use a mixer unless the recipe specifies using one.

Blueberry Streusel Muffins

◄ FAMILY FAVORITE ►

PREP: 14 MINUTES   COOK: 18 MINUTES

A sugary streusel caps these berry-filled breakfast muffins.

1¾ cups all-purpose flour
2¾ teaspoons baking powder
¾ teaspoon salt
½ cup sugar
2 teaspoons grated lemon rind
1 large egg, lightly beaten
¾ cup milk
⅓ cup vegetable oil
1 cup fresh or frozen blueberries, thawed and drained°
1 tablespoon all-purpose flour
1 tablespoon sugar
¼ cup sugar
2½ tablespoons all-purpose flour
½ teaspoon ground cinnamon
1½ tablespoons butter or margarine

•Combine first 5 ingredients in a large bowl; make a well in center of mixture. Combine egg, milk, and oil; stir well. Add to dry ingredients, stirring just until moistened.

•Combine blueberries, 1 tablespoon flour, and 1 tablespoon sugar, tossing gently to coat. Fold blueberry mixture into batter. Spoon batter into greased muffin pans, filling two-thirds full.

•Combine ¼ cup sugar, 2½ tablespoons flour, and cinnamon; cut in butter with a pastry blender until mixture is crumbly. Sprinkle over batter. Bake at 400° for 18 minutes or until golden. Remove from pans immediately. Yield: 1 dozen.

°If using frozen blueberries, thaw and drain them, and pat dry with paper towels. This will prevent discoloration of batter.

Per muffin: Calories 219 Fat 8.9g
Cholesterol 24mg Sodium 266mg

Jumbo Blueberry Streusel Muffins:
Spoon batter into 6 (3½- x 1¾-inch) greased muffin pans, filling two-thirds full. Sprinkle with streusel mixture. Bake at 400° for 20 minutes or until golden. Yield: ½ dozen.

Poppy Seed Muffins

◄ QUICK • FAMILY FAVORITE ►

PREP: 5 MINUTES   COOK: 20 MINUTES

Butter and sour cream lend a luxurious texture to this speckled favorite.

1¾ cups all-purpose flour
¼ teaspoon baking soda
½ teaspoon salt
½ cup sugar
3 tablespoons poppy seeds
1 (8-ounce) carton sour cream
1 large egg, lightly beaten
¼ cup butter, melted
2 teaspoons vanilla extract

•Combine first 5 ingredients in a bowl; make a well in center of mixture. Combine sour cream and remaining 3 ingredients; add to dry ingredients, stirring just until moistened.
•Spoon batter into greased muffin pans, filling two-thirds full. Bake at 400° for 18 to 20 minutes or until lightly browned. Remove from pans immediately. Yield: 1 dozen.

Per muffin: Calories 195 Fat 9.6g
Cholesterol 37mg Sodium 179mg

Blueberry Streusel Muffin

Oatmeal-Bran Muffins

PREP: 9 MINUTES   COOK: 20 MINUTES

These healthy muffins taste similar to an oatmeal cookie. They're full of oats and raisins, and good-for-you bran cereal.

¾ cup shreds of wheat bran cereal (we
    tested with Bran Buds)
¾ cup regular oats, uncooked
1¼ cups milk
1 large egg
¼ cup vegetable oil
½ cup raisins
1¼ cups all-purpose flour
1 tablespoon baking powder
½ teaspoon salt
½ cup sugar

• Combine first 3 ingredients in a bowl; let stand 5 minutes. Combine egg, oil, and raisins; stir into bran mixture.
• Combine flour and remaining 3 ingredients in a large bowl, and make a well in center of mixture. Add bran mixture to dry ingredients, stirring just until moistened.
• Spoon batter into greased muffin pans, filling three-fourths full. Bake at 400° for 20 minutes or until golden. Remove from pans immediately. Yield: 1½ dozen.
Per muffin: Calories 134 Fat 4.5g
Cholesterol 15mg Sodium 173mg

Refrigerator Bran Muffins

PREP: 11 MINUTES   COOK: 24 MINUTES

Mix up this batter to keep in the refrigerator up to a week, and bake the muffins as you need them.

3 cups wheat bran flakes cereal with
    raisins (we tested with Raisin Bran)
2½ cups all-purpose flour
2½ teaspoons baking soda
½ teaspoon salt
1½ cups sugar
2 large eggs, beaten
2 cups buttermilk
½ cup shortening, melted

• Combine first 5 ingredients in a large bowl; make a well in center of mixture. Combine eggs, buttermilk, and shortening; add to dry ingredients, stirring just until moistened.
• Cover batter, and store in refrigerator up to 1 week.
• When ready to bake, spoon batter into greased muffin pans, filling two-thirds full. Bake at 350° for 22 to 24 minutes or until golden. Remove from pans immediately. Yield: 2 dozen.
Per muffin: Calories 156 Fat 4.6g
Cholesterol 19mg Sodium 494mg

Cheddar-Pepper Muffins

PREP: 12 MINUTES   COOK: 25 MINUTES

Cheddar cheese, green pepper, and pimiento dot these savory muffins.

2½ cups all-purpose flour
2 tablespoons baking powder
½ teaspoon salt
¼ cup yellow cornmeal
¼ cup sugar
¼ teaspoon ground red pepper
¾ cup (3 ounces) shredded sharp
    Cheddar cheese
¼ cup finely chopped onion
3 tablespoons finely chopped green
    pepper
1 (2-ounce) jar diced pimiento, drained
2 large eggs, beaten
1½ cups milk
¼ cup vegetable oil

• Combine first 10 ingredients in a large bowl; make a well in center of mixture. Combine eggs, milk, and oil; add to dry ingredients, stirring just until moistened.
• Spoon into greased muffin pans, filling two-thirds full. Bake at 400° for 20 to 25 minutes. Remove from pans immediately. Yield: 1½ dozen.
Per muffin: Calories 153 Fat 6.3g
Cholesterol 32mg Sodium 246mg

Bacon-and-Cheese Muffins

PREP: 12 MINUTES   COOK: 22 MINUTES

1¾ cups all-purpose flour
2½ teaspoons baking powder
½ teaspoon salt
2 tablespoons sugar
10 slices bacon, cooked and crumbled
½ cup (2 ounces) shredded sharp Cheddar
    cheese
1 large egg, lightly beaten
¾ cup milk
⅓ cup vegetable oil

• Combine first 6 ingredients in a large bowl; make a well in center of mixture. Combine egg, milk, and oil; add to dry ingredients, stirring just until moistened.
• Spoon batter into well-greased muffin pans, filling two-thirds full. Bake at 400° for 20 to 22 minutes or until golden. Remove from pans immediately. Yield: 1 dozen.
Per muffin: Calories 303 Fat 21.2g
Cholesterol 45mg Sodium 671mg

MUFFIN MAGIC

For perfectly rounded muffins, a lumpy batter is desirable. Stir gently just until dry ingredients are moistened. Don't overstir the batter.

Banana-Nut Muffins

PREP: 10 MINUTES   COOK: 20 MINUTES

1¾ cups all-purpose flour
2½ teaspoons baking powder
½ teaspoon salt
½ cup sugar
1 large egg, lightly beaten
1 cup mashed ripe banana
½ cup milk
⅓ cup vegetable oil
½ cup chopped pecans

•Combine first 4 ingredients in a large bowl; make a well in center of mixture (photo 1). Combine egg, mashed banana, milk, and oil; add mixture to dry ingredients, stirring just until moistened (photo 2). Stir in pecans.
•Spoon batter into greased muffin pans, filling three-fourths full (photo 3). Bake at 400° for 18 to 20 minutes or until golden. Remove from pans immediately. Yield: 1 dozen.

Per muffin: Calories 217 Fat 10.6g
Cholesterol 20mg Sodium 184mg

Banana-Nut Bread: Spoon batter into a greased 8½- x 4½-inch loafpan. Bake at 350° for 1 hour or until a wooden pick inserted in center comes out clean. Cool in pan 10 minutes. Yield: 1 loaf.

Mashing ripe bananas: When banana peels turn black, make banana-nut bread or muffins. The flavor and sweetness of overripe bananas are intensified, and bananas are easy to mash with a fork and blend into a batter. Two to three bananas yield 1 cup mashed fruit.

1. Make a well in center of dry ingredients; add liquids.

2. Stir just until dry ingredients are moistened.

3. Spoon batter into greased muffin pans.

Miniature Orange Tea Muffins

PREP: 13 MINUTES
COOK: 12 MINUTES PER BATCH

Here's a brunch bread for a crowd. Make these muffins ahead, and freeze them. They're delicious with chicken salad.

½ cup fresh orange juice
1 cup plus 2 tablespoons sugar
1 cup butter or margarine, softened
¾ cup sugar
2 large eggs
1 teaspoon baking soda
¾ cup buttermilk
3 cups all-purpose flour
1 tablespoon grated orange rind
¼ cup fresh orange juice
1 teaspoon lemon extract
1 cup currants

•Combine first 2 ingredients in a small saucepan; bring to a boil, stirring until sugar dissolves. Cover and chill.
•Beat butter at medium speed with an electric mixer until creamy; gradually add ¾ cup sugar, beating until light and fluffy. Add eggs, one at a time, beating after each addition.

•Combine soda and buttermilk, stirring well; add to butter mixture alternately with flour. Stir in orange rind and remaining 3 ingredients.

•Spoon batter into greased miniature (1¾-inch) muffin pans, filling three-fourths full. Bake at 400° for 10 to 12 minutes or until lightly browned. Remove from pans; dip top and sides of warm muffins in chilled sauce mixture. Place on wire racks to drain. Yield: 5 dozen.

Per muffin: Calories 89 Fat 3.6g
Cholesterol 16mg Sodium 59mg

Miniature Lemon Tea Muffins:

Substitute fresh lemon juice and rind for orange, and substitute orange extract for lemon extract.

Sour Cream Mini-Muffins

◄ QUICK ►

PREP: 6 MINUTES   COOK: 15 MINUTES

This buttery three-ingredient recipe is worth committing to memory. Serve these versatile muffins any time of day—for breakfast, with soup for lunch, or with ham for dinner.

½ cup butter, softened
1 (8-ounce) carton sour cream
2 cups biscuit and baking mix

•Beat butter at medium speed with an electric mixer until creamy; stir in sour cream. Gradually add biscuit mix, stirring just until dry ingredients are moistened. Spoon batter into lightly greased miniature (1¾-inch) muffin pans, filling full. Bake at 400° for 15 minutes or until golden. Yield: 2 dozen.

Per mini-muffin: Calories 112 Fat 8g
Cholesterol 17mg Sodium 209mg

Sour Cream Muffins:
Spoon batter into lightly greased regular muffin pans. Bake at 400° for 20 minutes or until golden. Yield: 1 dozen.

QUICK BREAD LOAVES

Many of these classic sweet and savory loaves benefit from the same quick mixing procedure as muffins. Some recipes make two loaves—perfect for eating one and freezing or sharing the other with a friend.

A small crack down the top center of a quick loaf is characteristic—so don't panic, it's supposed to be there.

Be sure to let nut breads cool completely before slicing them so they won't crumble. To cut them, use a sharp serrated-edged knife and a gentle sawing motion.

Prune-Nut Bread

PREP: 19 MINUTES   COOK: 55 MINUTES

Prunes add deep rich color and flavor to this nutty loaf.

¾ cup prune juice
¼ cup water
¾ cup coarsely chopped pitted prunes
3 tablespoons butter or margarine
1 large egg, lightly beaten
¾ teaspoon vanilla extract
1½ cups all-purpose flour
1 teaspoon baking soda
⅛ teaspoon salt
½ cup sugar
½ cup chopped pecans or walnuts

•Combine prune juice and water in a small saucepan; bring to a boil. Remove from heat, and stir in prunes and butter. Cool mixture to lukewarm. Stir in egg and vanilla.

•Combine flour and remaining 4 ingredients in a large bowl; add prune mixture, stirring just until dry ingredients are moistened.

•Spoon batter into a greased and floured 8½- x 4½-inch loafpan. Bake at 325° for 50 to 55 minutes or until a wooden pick inserted in center comes out clean. Cool in pan on a wire rack 10 minutes; remove from pan, and cool on wire rack. Yield: 1 loaf.

Per ½-inch slice: Calories 170 Fat 6.3g
Cholesterol 22mg Sodium 146mg

Date-Nut Bread: Substitute ¾ cup chopped dates for prunes.

Note: For round bread slices, divide batter, and spoon either version into two greased and floured (29-ounce) fruit cans. Bake at 350° for 55 minutes to 1 hour. Cool in cans 10 minutes; remove from cans, and cool on a wire rack.

Nutty Wheat Loaf

PREP: 14 MINUTES

COOK: 1 HOUR AND 20 MINUTES

Serve this bread alongside Boston baked beans or simply slathered with cream cheese.

1¼ cups unbleached all-purpose flour
1 cup whole wheat flour
2 teaspoons baking powder
¾ teaspoon salt
½ cup honey crunch wheat germ
1 cup firmly packed dark brown sugar
1 teaspoon ground cinnamon
½ teaspoon ground nutmeg
½ cup coarsely chopped walnuts
2 large eggs, lightly beaten
1¼ cups milk
½ cup butter or margarine, melted

•Combine first 9 ingredients in a bowl; stir well. Combine eggs, milk, and butter; add to dry ingredients, stirring just until moistened. Pour batter into a greased and floured 9- x 5-inch loafpan; bake at 325° for 1 hour and 20 minutes or until a wooden pick inserted in center comes out clean. Cool in pan on a wire rack 10 minutes; remove from pan, and cool on wire rack. Yield: 1 loaf.

Per ½-inch slice: Calories 227 Fat 9.9g
Cholesterol 46mg Sodium 242mg

Carrot Bread

PREP: 18 MINUTES COOK: 1 HOUR

Laden with grated carrot, pineapple, and nuts, this slightly sweet batter bakes into two beautiful loaves. Freeze one for a rainy day.

3 cups all-purpose flour
1 teaspoon baking soda
1 teaspoon ground cinnamon
2 cups sugar
¾ teaspoon salt
1 cup chopped pecans or walnuts
3 large eggs, lightly beaten
2 cups grated carrot
1 cup vegetable oil
1 (8-ounce) can crushed pineapple, drained
2 teaspoons vanilla extract

• Combine first 6 ingredients, stirring well.
• Combine eggs and remaining 4 ingredients; add to flour mixture, stirring just until dry ingredients are moistened.
• Spoon batter into two greased and floured 8½- x 4½-inch loafpans. Bake at 350° for 1 hour or until a wooden pick inserted in center comes out clean. Cool in pans on wire racks 10 minutes; remove from pans, and cool on wire racks. Yield: 2 loaves.
Per ½-inch slice: Calories 219 Fat 11.6g Cholesterol 24mg Sodium 117mg

Zucchini-Honey Bread

PREP: 18 MINUTES

COOK: 1 HOUR AND 10 MINUTES

Your kitchen will smell like a bakery as this honeyed loaf bakes.

3 cups all-purpose flour
1 teaspoon baking powder
1 teaspoon baking soda
1 teaspoon salt
1 tablespoon ground cinnamon
1 cup chopped pecans
2 cups shredded zucchini (about 1 large zucchini)
2 large eggs, lightly beaten
1½ cups sugar
¾ cup honey
1 cup vegetable oil
2 teaspoons vanilla extract

• Combine first 6 ingredients in a large bowl, stirring well. Combine zucchini and remaining 5 ingredients, stirring well. Add to flour mixture, stirring just until dry ingredients are moistened.
• Spoon batter into two greased and floured 8½- x 4½-inch loafpans. Bake at 350° for 1 hour and 10 minutes or until a wooden pick inserted in center comes out clean. Cool in pans on wire racks 10 minutes; remove from pans, and cool on wire racks. Yield: 2 loaves.
Per ½-inch slice: Calories 227 Fat 11.4g Cholesterol 16mg Sodium 145mg

Note: You can bake these loaves in 9- x 5-inch loafpans for 1 hour; however, they won't be quite as tall as those baked in the smaller pans.

CORNBREAD

Cornbread carries a loyal following in the South. Its crispy crust and slightly gritty texture make it a popular staple—all by itself, crumbled over chili, or smothered in butter and honey. And a well-seasoned cast-iron skillet is a must in its preparation.

You can buy cornmeal stone-ground, steel-ground, self-rising, or as a mix. It's made from either white or yellow corn, and meal made from the two types of corn can be used interchangeably. Cornbread made with yellow meal tends to be slightly coarser.

Cornbread batter should be fairly thin and pourable. If it seems too thick, add a little more liquid. Pouring the batter into a very hot skillet gives cornbread its crispy exterior.

Buttermilk Cornbread

◄ **FAMILY FAVORITE** ►

PREP: 7 MINUTES COOK: 25 MINUTES

Serve this moist cornbread warm with butter.

2 cups self-rising cornmeal
1 tablespoon sugar
1 large egg, lightly beaten
1¾ cups buttermilk
¼ cup vegetable oil

• Combine cornmeal and sugar in a large bowl; add egg, buttermilk, and oil, stirring just until dry ingredients are moistened.
• Place a well-greased 9-inch cast-iron skillet in a 450° oven for 5 minutes or until hot. Remove from oven; pour batter into hot skillet. Bake at 450° for 23 to 25 minutes or until golden. Yield: 6 servings.
Per serving: Calories 281 Fat 13.7g Cholesterol 40mg Sodium 593mg

Buttermilk Corn Muffins: Prepare batter as directed. If using cast-iron muffin pans, place well-greased pans in a 450° oven for 5 minutes or until hot. Spoon batter into hot pans, filling three-fourths full. For regular muffin pans, spoon batter into greased pans, filling three-fourths full. Bake at 450° for 15 to 18 minutes or until golden. Yield: 1 dozen.

Buttermilk Corn Sticks: Prepare batter as directed. Place a well-greased cast-iron corn stick pan in a 450° oven for 5 minutes or until hot. Spoon batter into hot pan, filling three-fourths full. Bake at 450° for 15 to 18 minutes or until golden. Yield: 1½ dozen.

Cracklin' Cornbread

PREP: 10 MINUTES   COOK: 25 MINUTES

Cracklings are crispy brown pieces of rendered pork fat. They lend a light texture and unmistakable Southern flavor to this bread. They're sold in small packages in specialty markets.

1½ cups cornmeal
¼ cup all-purpose flour
1 teaspoon baking soda
1 teaspoon salt
1 large egg, lightly beaten
2 cups buttermilk
1 cup cracklings

•Combine first 4 ingredients in a large bowl; add egg and buttermilk, stirring just until dry ingredients are moistened. Stir in cracklings.
•Place a well-greased 10-inch cast-iron skillet in a 450° oven for 4 minutes or until hot. Remove from oven; pour batter into hot skillet. Bake at 450° for 25 minutes or until golden. Yield: 10 servings.
Per serving: Calories 193 Fat 8.7g
Cholesterol 34mg Sodium 397mg

Cheesy Cornbread

PREP: 10 MINUTES   COOK: 45 MINUTES

This deluxe skillet cornbread boasts several flavor options in addition to the corn and cheese in the batter.

1 cup self-rising cornmeal
½ teaspoon baking soda
¼ teaspoon salt
1½ cups (6 ounces) shredded Cheddar cheese
½ cup chopped onion
1 cup milk
3 tablespoons bacon drippings
1 teaspoon garlic powder
3 large eggs, lightly beaten
1 (7-ounce) can whole kernel corn, drained
1 (2-ounce) jar diced pimiento, drained

•Combine first 3 ingredients in a large bowl; add Cheddar cheese and remaining 7 ingredients, stirring just until dry ingredients are

moistened. Spoon batter into a greased 10-inch cast-iron skillet. Bake at 350° for 45 minutes or until golden. Yield: 10 servings.
Per serving: Calories 210 Fat 13.3g
Cholesterol 89mg Sodium 390mg

Bacon Cornbread: Add 6 slices bacon, cooked and crumbled, with onion.

Chile Cornbread: Add 1 (4.5-ounce) can chopped green chiles, drained, with onion.

Jalapeño Cornbread: Add 3 jalapeño peppers, seeded and chopped, with onion.

Beer-Battered Hush Puppies

PREP: 11 MINUTES   COOK: 15 MINUTES

Beer adds zip to this hush puppy batter, and chopped tomato and green pepper dot it with unexpected color.

1½ cups self-rising yellow cornmeal
¼ cup self-rising flour
2 small onions, finely chopped
1 medium-size green pepper, finely chopped
1 tomato, finely chopped
1 large egg, lightly beaten
1½ teaspoons Worcestershire sauce
⅛ teaspoon hot sauce
½ cup beer
Vegetable oil

•Combine cornmeal and flour in a large bowl; stir well. Add onion, pepper, and tomato. Stir in egg, Worcestershire sauce, and hot sauce. Add beer, stirring well.
•Pour oil to depth of 2 inches into a small Dutch oven; heat to 375°. Carefully drop batter by rounded tablespoonfuls into hot oil; fry hush puppies, a few at a time, 1 to 2 minutes or until golden, turning once. Drain on paper towels. Yield: 3½ dozen.
Per hush puppy: Calories 46 Fat 2.9g
Cholesterol 5mg Sodium 68mg

Mexican Hush Puppies

PREP: 9 MINUTES   COOK: 24 MINUTES

These hush puppies won rave reviews from our Test Kitchens staff. Pair the hush puppies with fried fish (page 214), or serve them with salsa as an appetizer.

2 cups self-rising cornmeal
1 cup self-rising flour
3 tablespoons sugar
3 large eggs, lightly beaten
½ cup milk
1 (14¾-ounce) can cream-style corn
1½ cups (6 ounces) shredded sharp Cheddar cheese
2 cups chopped onion
2 jalapeño peppers, seeded and chopped
2 teaspoons chili powder
Vegetable oil

•Combine first 3 ingredients in a large bowl; make a well in center of mixture.
•Combine eggs and next 6 ingredients in a bowl; add to dry ingredients, stirring just until moistened.
•Pour oil to depth of 2 inches into a Dutch oven; heat to 375°. Drop batter by rounded tablespoonfuls into hot oil; fry hush puppies, a few at a time, 3 minutes or until golden, turning once. Drain on paper towels. Yield: 40 hush puppies.
Per hush puppy: Calories 107 Fat 6.3g
Cholesterol 21mg Sodium 180mg

Squash Fritters

PREP: 16 MINUTES   COOK: 18 MINUTES

1 (10-ounce) package frozen sliced yellow
    squash
2 large eggs, beaten
½ cup cracker crumbs
¼ teaspoon salt
¼ teaspoon pepper
1 small onion, finely chopped
Vegetable oil

•Cook squash according to package directions; drain and mash.
•Combine squash, eggs, and next 4 ingredients in a bowl.
•Pour oil to depth of 2 inches into a heavy saucepan; heat to 375°.
•Drop squash mixture by heaping tablespoonfuls into hot oil; fry until lightly browned, turning once. Drain on paper towels. Serve immediately. Yield: 13 fritters.
Per fritter: Calories 69 Fat 5.4g
Cholesterol 33mg Sodium 102mg

Old Virginia Spoonbread

PREP: 18 MINUTES   COOK: 45 MINUTES

Soufflélike spoonbread bakes up light and fluffy and is irresistible with a pat of butter melting over a serving.

4 cups milk
1 cup white cornmeal
1½ teaspoons salt
3 tablespoons butter or margarine
4 large eggs, well beaten

•Place milk in top of a double boiler; bring water to a boil. Heat milk until tiny bubbles begin to appear around edges of pan.
•Gradually add cornmeal, stirring constantly with a wire whisk. Add salt and butter. Cook, stirring constantly, 10 to 12 minutes or until butter melts and mixture is very thick. Remove from heat.
•Gradually stir about one-fourth of hot mixture into eggs; add to remaining hot mixture, stirring constantly. Spoon mixture into a lightly greased 2-quart baking dish or soufflé dish. Bake at 425° for 40 to 45 minutes or until golden. Serve with additional butter. Yield: 10 servings.
Per serving: Calories 171 Fat 8.9g
Cholesterol 108mg Sodium 460mg

THE SPOONBREAD STORY

The origin of spoonbread is unclear. Though its ingredients vary in recipes across the South, it's usually based on cornmeal and baked like a casserole. Its puddinglike texture makes it soft enough to eat with a spoon. And you can serve it as a starch with most any type of meat.

BREAKFAST BREADS & COFFEE CAKES

With just a few minutes' preparation and the right equipment, you can make pancakes and waffles from scratch. The homemade taste that comes from the fluffy batter is worth the effort, whether you're serving a few family members or a crowd.

Before you begin cooking, lightly grease the griddle or waffle iron to prevent sticking. You can tell waffles are done when steam no longer comes from the sides of the waffle iron. Most waffle irons have a signal light to tell you when they're ready.

For pancakes, as soon as the top surface is full of bubbles and the edges begin to look cooked, they're ready to turn. The second side will take only a minute or two to brown. Serve pancakes and waffles immediately after cooking or keep them warm in a single layer in a warm oven. Try not to stack them or they may get soggy.

French toast may well be the easiest of breakfast breads to prepare, especially the version that sits overnight in the refrigerator and is ready to bake whenever the oven's hot. And coffee cakes are simple to make, as well.

Whether laden with fruit or sprinkled with streusel, the batter is typically fluffy and light, yet rich but not too sweet. Some recipes use convenience products such as biscuit mix or refrigerated biscuits to speed you along during preparation. Most coffee cakes can be made a day ahead and are equally as good at room temperature as they are warm.

Cooking pancakes: When the top surface is full of bubbles, it's time to flip the pancake.

Buttermilk Pancakes with Homemade Maple Syrup

◄ **FAMILY FAVORITE** ►

PREP: 10 MINUTES
COOK: 3 MINUTES PER BATCH

Buttermilk makes these pancakes fluffy. Add 1 cup of fresh blueberries or chopped pecans to the batter, if you'd like.

2 cups all-purpose flour
2½ teaspoons baking powder
1 teaspoon baking soda
¾ teaspoon salt
2 tablespoons sugar
2 large eggs, lightly beaten
2 cups buttermilk
¼ cup vegetable oil
Homemade Maple Syrup

•Combine first 5 ingredients; stir well. Combine eggs, buttermilk, and oil in a bowl; add to flour mixture, stirring just until dry ingredients are moistened.

• For each pancake, pour about ¼ cup batter onto a hot, lightly greased griddle. Cook pancakes until tops are covered with bubbles and edges look cooked (see photo on opposite page); turn and cook other side. (Store unused batter in a tightly covered container in refrigerator up to 1 week. If refrigerated batter is too thick, add milk or water to reach desired consistency.) Serve pancakes warm with Homemade Maple Syrup. Yield: 18 (4-inch) pancakes.

Homemade Maple Syrup

1 cup water
2 cups sugar
½ teaspoon maple flavoring

• Bring water to a boil in a small saucepan; add sugar and flavoring. Boil 2 minutes, stirring constantly; remove from heat. Serve warm, chilled, or at room temperature. (Store leftover syrup in a tightly covered container in refrigerator.) Yield: about 2 cups.
Per 3 pancakes and ⅓ cup syrup: Calories 566 Fat 11.9g Cholesterol 77mg Sodium 612mg

Maple-Bacon Oven Pancake

◄ QUICK ►

PREP: 3 MINUTES   COOK: 17 MINUTES

This oven pancake is really a breakfast casserole. Maple syrup, Cheddar cheese, and bacon make a surprise combination.

2 large eggs, lightly beaten
1½ cups biscuit and baking mix
1 tablespoon sugar
¾ cup milk
¼ cup maple syrup
1½ cups (6 ounces) shredded Cheddar cheese, divided
12 slices bacon, cooked and crumbled

• Combine first 5 ingredients in a large bowl; beat at medium speed with an electric mixer until smooth. Stir in ½ cup cheese. Pour into a greased and floured 13- x 9-inch baking dish.
• Bake at 425° for 12 minutes. Sprinkle pancake with remaining 1 cup cheese and

bacon; bake 3 to 5 more minutes or until a wooden pick inserted in center comes out clean. Cut into squares, and serve with maple syrup. Yield: 8 servings.
Per serving: Calories 345 Fat 19.2g Cholesterol 93mg Sodium 710mg

German Apple Pancake

PREP: 16 MINUTES   COOK: 40 MINUTES

This sweet pancake, also called a Dutch Baby, is actually a cross between an omelet and a soufflé.

2 large eggs
½ cup all-purpose flour
¼ teaspoon salt
½ cup milk
1 tablespoon butter or margarine
¾ cup firmly packed brown sugar
1½ tablespoons cornstarch
½ cup milk
¼ cup butter or margarine, melted
4 cups peeled and sliced apple

• Heat a 10-inch ovenproof nonstick skillet at 450° for 5 minutes or until hot.
• Combine first 4 ingredients in a bowl; beat at medium speed with an electric mixer until smooth.
• Add 1 tablespoon butter to hot skillet, stirring to coat skillet; pour in batter. Bake at 450° for 10 minutes. Reduce heat to 350°, and bake 10 more minutes or until golden.
• Combine sugar and cornstarch in a saucepan; stir in ½ cup milk and ¼ cup melted butter. Cook over medium heat 5 minutes or until thickened. Add apple, and cook 10 minutes or until tender, stirring often. Spoon half of mixture onto pancake. Cut into wedges, and serve with remaining apple mixture. Yield: 4 servings.
Per serving: Calories 483 Fat 19.4g Cholesterol 153mg Sodium 371mg

Out-of-This-World Waffles

◄ FAMILY FAVORITE ►

PREP: 7 MINUTES
COOK: 8 MINUTES PER BATCH

These waffles are crisp and light. If the recipe makes more waffles than you need, you can freeze and reheat them as needed in the toaster.

2½ cups all-purpose flour
1 tablespoon plus 1 teaspoon baking powder
¾ teaspoon salt
1½ tablespoons sugar
2 large eggs, beaten
2½ cups milk
¾ cup vegetable oil

• Combine first 4 ingredients in a large bowl.
• Combine eggs, milk, and oil; add to flour mixture, stirring with a wire whisk just until dry ingredients are moistened.
• Cook in a preheated, oiled waffle iron until golden. Yield: 22 (4-inch) waffles.
Per waffle: Calories 157 Fat 10.8g Cholesterol 23mg Sodium 172mg

Pecan Waffles: Add ½ cup finely chopped or ground pecans to batter before baking.

Soft Ginger Waffles

PREP: 10 MINUTES

COOK: 8 MINUTES PER BATCH

⅓ cup butter or margarine, softened
¼ cup molasses
2 large eggs, separated
1¾ cups all-purpose flour
2¾ teaspoons baking powder
¼ teaspoon baking soda
¼ teaspoon salt
1¼ teaspoons ground ginger
¼ teaspoon ground cinnamon
¼ teaspoon ground nutmeg
½ cup plus 2 tablespoons milk
Lemon Hard Sauce (page 397)

• Beat butter at medium speed with an electric mixer until creamy; add molasses, and beat well. Add egg yolks, one at a time, beating after each addition.
• Combine flour and next 6 ingredients; add to butter mixture alternately with milk, beginning and ending with flour mixture. Mix after each addition.
• Beat egg whites at high speed until stiff peaks form; gently fold into batter. Spoon 1 cup batter onto a preheated, oiled waffle iron; spread batter to edges. Cook until lightly browned. Repeat procedure with remaining batter. Serve with Lemon Hard Sauce. Yield: 11 (4-inch) waffles.

Per waffle: Calories 181 Fat 9.6g
Cholesterol 55mg Sodium 250mg

Overnight Orange French Toast

◄ MAKE AHEAD ►

PREP: 5 MINUTES   COOK: 16 MINUTES

CHILL: 8 HOURS

8 (¾-inch-thick) slices French bread
4 large eggs
1 cup milk
2 tablespoons fresh orange juice
½ teaspoon vanilla extract
⅛ teaspoon salt
2 tablespoons butter or margarine
Powdered sugar
Orange Sauce

• Place bread in an ungreased 13- x 9-inch baking dish. Combine eggs and next 4 ingredients; beat well. Pour mixture over bread slices; turn slices over to coat evenly. Cover and chill overnight.
• Melt 1 tablespoon butter in a large skillet over medium heat; remove 4 slices bread from dish, and cook in butter 4 minutes on each side or until lightly browned. Repeat procedure with remaining butter and bread slices. Sprinkle toast with powdered sugar; serve immediately with Orange Sauce. Yield: 4 servings.

Per serving: Calories 592 Fat 13.8g
Cholesterol 238mg Sodium 537mg

Orange Sauce

1 cup firmly packed brown sugar
2 teaspoons grated orange rind
½ cup fresh orange juice

• Combine all ingredients in a saucepan, stirring well. Bring to a boil; reduce heat, and simmer until thickened (about 5 minutes), stirring often. Yield: 1¼ cups.

Marmalade Coffee Cake

PREP: 8 MINUTES   COOK: 35 MINUTES

¾ cup orange marmalade
2 tablespoons chopped walnuts
¾ cup firmly packed brown sugar
¾ teaspoon ground cinnamon
2 (10- or 11-ounce) cans refrigerated buttermilk biscuits
½ cup butter or margarine, melted

• Spread marmalade in bottom of a greased 12-cup Bundt pan; sprinkle with walnuts. Combine brown sugar and cinnamon.
• Separate biscuits; dip in melted butter, and dredge in sugar mixture. Stand biscuits on edge around pan, spacing evenly. Drizzle remaining butter over biscuits, and sprinkle with remaining sugar mixture.
• Bake at 350° for 33 to 35 minutes or until golden. Cool in pan on a wire rack 5 minutes. Invert onto a serving platter; serve immediately. Yield: 16 servings.

Per serving: Calories 260 Fat 12.8g
Cholesterol 16mg Sodium 471mg

Strawberry Jam Coffee Cake

PREP: 12 MINUTES   COOK: 35 MINUTES

A ripple of strawberry preserves flows through this cream cheese coffee cake.

1 (8-ounce) package cream cheese, softened
½ cup butter, softened
¾ cup sugar
2 large eggs, lightly beaten
¼ cup milk
1 teaspoon vanilla extract
2 cups all-purpose flour
1 teaspoon baking powder
½ teaspoon baking soda
¼ teaspoon salt
1 (18-ounce) jar strawberry preserves
1 tablespoon fresh lemon juice
½ cup chopped pecans
¼ cup firmly packed brown sugar

• Beat cream cheese and butter at medium speed with an electric mixer until creamy; gradually add ¾ cup sugar, beating well. Combine eggs, milk, and vanilla; add to cream cheese mixture. Beat well.
• Combine flour and next 3 ingredients; add to cream cheese mixture, mixing at low speed until blended. Spoon half of batter into a greased and floured 13- x 9-inch pan.
• Combine strawberry preserves and lemon juice; spread over batter in pan. Dollop remaining batter over strawberry mixture. Combine pecans and brown sugar; sprinkle over batter in pan.
• Bake at 350° for 35 minutes or until a wooden pick inserted in center comes out clean. Cool 15 minutes. Cut into squares to serve. Yield: 15 servings.

Per serving: Calories 339 Fat 15.2g
Cholesterol 62mg Sodium 200mg

Raspberry Crumb Cake

PREP: 16 MINUTES   COOK: 50 MINUTES

⅔ cup sugar
¼ cup cornstarch
¾ cup cold water
2 cups frozen raspberries
1 tablespoon fresh lemon juice
3 cups all-purpose flour
1 tablespoon baking powder
1 teaspoon salt
1 cup sugar
1 teaspoon ground cinnamon
¼ teaspoon ground mace
1 cup butter or margarine
2 large eggs, lightly beaten
1 cup milk
1 teaspoon vanilla extract
½ cup all-purpose flour
½ cup sugar
¼ cup butter or margarine
¼ cup sliced almonds

•Combine first 3 ingredients in a saucepan, stirring until smooth; add raspberries. Cook over medium heat, stirring constantly, until mixture thickens and comes to a boil. Boil 1 minute, stirring constantly. Remove from heat, and stir in lemon juice; cool.
•Combine 3 cups flour and next 5 ingredients; cut in 1 cup butter with a pastry blender until crumbly. Stir in eggs, milk, and vanilla.
•Spoon one-fourth of batter into each of two greased 8-inch round cakepans. Spread raspberry mixture over batter in pans, dividing evenly. Top evenly with remaining batter.
•Combine ½ cup flour and ½ cup sugar; stir well. Cut in ¼ cup butter with a pastry blender until crumbly. Stir in almonds. Sprinkle almond mixture over batter in pans.
•Bake at 350° for 40 minutes or until a wooden pick inserted in center comes out clean. Cool in pans on wire racks 10 minutes; remove from pans, and cool completely on wire racks. Yield: 2 (8-inch) coffee cakes, 6 servings each.
Per serving: Calories 502 Fat 22.3g
Cholesterol 91mg Sodium 513mg

Blueberry-Cream Cheese Coffee Cake

PREP: 13 MINUTES   COOK: 55 MINUTES

½ cup butter or margarine, softened
1¼ cups sugar
2 large eggs
2 cups all-purpose flour
1 teaspoon baking powder
1 teaspoon salt
¾ cup milk
¼ cup water
2 cups fresh blueberries
1 (8-ounce) package cream cheese, softened and cubed
½ cup all-purpose flour
½ cup sugar
2 tablespoons grated lemon rind
2 tablespoons butter or margarine, softened

•Beat ½ cup butter at medium speed with an electric mixer until creamy; gradually add 1¼ cups sugar, beating well. Add eggs, one at a time, beating after each addition.
•Combine 2 cups flour, baking powder, and salt; stir well. Combine milk and water; stir well. Add flour mixture to butter mixture alternately with milk mixture, beginning and ending with flour mixture. Mix at low speed after each addition until blended. Gently stir in blueberries and cream cheese. Pour batter into a greased 9-inch square pan.
•Combine ½ cup flour and remaining 3 ingredients; stir well with a fork. Sprinkle mixture over batter. Bake at 375° for 50 minutes or until golden. Serve warm or at room temperature. Yield: 12 servings.
Per serving: Calories 387 Fat 17.9g
Cholesterol 84mg Sodium 403mg

Apricot Strudel

PREP: 15 MINUTES   CHILL: 8 HOURS
COOK: 35 MINUTES

1 cup butter or margarine, softened
1 (8-ounce) package cream cheese, softened
2 tablespoons sugar
2 cups all-purpose flour
1 (12-ounce) jar apricot jam
1 cup flaked coconut
1 cup pecans, chopped
½ cup sugar
1½ teaspoons ground cinnamon
Sifted powdered sugar

•Beat first 3 ingredients in a large mixing bowl at medium speed with an electric mixer until creamy. Gradually add flour, beating at low speed just until blended. Shape pastry into 3 equal balls; cover and chill 8 hours.
•Roll 1 portion of pastry into a 10- x 8-inch rectangle. Spread ⅓ cup jam over rectangle to within ½ inch of edges. Combine coconut and next 3 ingredients; stir well. Sprinkle one-third of coconut mixture over jam.
•Roll up pastry, starting at long side, pinching and tucking under ends of pastry. Arrange pastry roll, seam side down, on a greased baking sheet. Repeat procedure twice with remaining pastry, jam, and coconut mixture.
•Bake at 350° for 30 to 35 minutes or until lightly browned. Cut each roll crosswise into fourths; cool completely on wire racks. Sprinkle with sugar. Yield: 12 servings.
Per serving: Calories 499 Fat 31.9g
Cholesterol 62mg Sodium 246mg

SPECIALTY QUICK BREADS

These quick breads, from skinny Parmesan Breadsticks to plump hollow Popovers, play a significant role in a menu. Piping hot, crusty bread is often the crowning touch to a great meal.

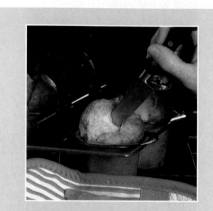

Baking crusty Popovers: Pierce popovers with a knife to let steam escape.

Popovers

PREP: 7 MINUTES   COOK: 40 MINUTES

Popovers bake into crusty, hollow shells that you can smear with butter or fill with anything from chicken salad to ice cream. It's the leavening power in eggs that causes popovers to rise high above their pans once in the oven. Resist the temptation to open the oven door as they bake, so they'll rise promptly. See photo above and on page 60.

1 cup all-purpose flour
¼ teaspoon salt
1 cup milk
2 large eggs, lightly beaten

•Combine all ingredients; beat at low speed with an electric mixer just until smooth.
•Place a well-greased popover pan (see note following recipe if you don't have a popover pan) in a 425° oven for 3 minutes or until a drop of water sizzles when dropped in it. Remove pan from oven; fill half full with batter.
•Bake at 425° for 15 minutes. Reduce heat to 350°, and bake 18 to 20 more minutes. Turn oven off. Pierce each popover with the

tip of a knife to let steam out (see photo). Return popovers to oven 5 minutes to crisp. Serve hot. Yield: 6 popovers.
Per popover: Calories 135 Fat 4.9g
Cholesterol 76mg Sodium 139mg

For popovers in muffin pans: Preheat regular muffin pans as directed in main recipe. Pour batter into hot muffin pans, filling half full. Bake at 425° for 15 minutes. Reduce heat to 350°; bake 18 to 20 more minutes. Turn oven off, and proceed as directed in main recipe. Yield: 1 dozen.

Yorkshire Pudding: Don't grease or preheat muffin pans. Spoon 1 teaspoon beef drippings (page 235) into each muffin pan; tilt to coat. Add batter; bake as for Popovers.

Herbed Popovers

PREP: 9 MINUTES   COOK: 55 MINUTES

High protein bread flour gives these popovers sturdy structure as they bake; extra egg whites make them really crisp and light.

Vegetable cooking spray
2 tablespoons grated Parmesan cheese
1 cup bread flour
1 cup milk
2 large eggs, lightly beaten
1 teaspoon dried thyme
1 teaspoon Worcestershire sauce
¾ teaspoon dried oregano
½ teaspoon salt
¼ teaspoon garlic powder
2 egg whites
1 tablespoon butter or margarine, melted

•Heavily grease a popover pan with cooking spray or shortening, and dust bottom and sides of pan with Parmesan cheese.
•Combine flour and remaining ingredients; stir with a wire whisk until blended. Fill prepared pan three-fourths full. Place in a cold oven. Turn oven to 450°; bake 15 minutes. Reduce heat to 350°; bake 35 to 40 more minutes or until popovers are crusty and brown. Serve hot. Yield: 6 popovers.
Per popover: Calories 166 Fat 6g
Cholesterol 83mg Sodium 314mg

Making crêpes: Quickly tilt hot pan in all directions so batter covers bottom before it starts to cook.

Basic Crêpes

◀ FAMILY FAVORITE ▶

**PREP: 5 MINUTES   CHILL: 1 HOUR
COOK: 1 TO 2 MINUTES PER CRÊPE**

Use this recipe for Italian Crêpes (page 250), Cherry Crêpes (page 183) or fill them with ice cream, and drizzle with chocolate sauce.

1 cup all-purpose flour
¼ teaspoon salt
1¼ cups milk
2 large eggs
2 tablespoons butter, melted
Vegetable cooking spray

•Combine first 3 ingredients; beat with a wire whisk until smooth. Add eggs; beat well. Stir in butter. Cover; chill at least 1 hour.
•Coat bottom of a 6-inch crêpe pan or heavy skillet with cooking spray; place over medium heat until hot.
•Pour 2 tablespoons batter into pan; quickly tilt pan in all directions so batter covers bottom (see photo). Cook 1 minute or until crêpe can be shaken loose. Turn crêpe over, and cook 30 seconds. Place crêpe on a cloth towel to cool. Repeat with remaining batter.
•Stack crêpes between sheets of wax paper (so they won't stick together), and place in an airtight container, if desired. Store in refrigerator up to 2 days or freeze up to 3 months. Yield: 16 (6-inch) crêpes.
Per crêpe: Calories 62 Fat 3g
Cholesterol 33mg Sodium 69mg

Skinny Parmesan Twists

PREP: 35 MINUTES

COOK: 11 MINUTES PER BATCH

Present these thin breadsticks as a center-piece for your next spaghetti dinner.

¼ cup butter or margarine, softened
1 cup grated Parmesan cheese
½ cup sour cream
1 cup all-purpose flour
½ teaspoon dried Italian seasoning
1 egg yolk, lightly beaten
1 tablespoon water
1 tablespoon caraway seeds or grated
   Parmesan cheese

•Combine butter, 1 cup cheese, and sour cream, beating well at medium speed with an electric mixer. Combine flour and Italian seasoning. Gradually add to butter mixture, beating until smooth.
•Turn dough out onto a lightly floured surface; divide in half. Roll 1 portion of dough into a 12- x 7-inch rectangle, and cut into 6- x ½-inch strips.
•Twist each strip 2 or 3 times, and place on greased baking sheets. Repeat procedure with remaining dough.
•Combine egg yolk and water. Brush strips with egg mixture; sprinkle with caraway seeds or cheese. Bake at 350° for 10 to 11 minutes or until browned. Yield: 4 dozen.

Per twist: Calories 29 Fat 1.9g
Cholesterol 8mg Sodium 38mg

Applesauce Drop Doughnuts

◄ **FAMILY FAVORITE** ►

PREP: 8 MINUTES   COOK: 35 MINUTES

¾ cup firmly packed brown sugar
2 large eggs
2 tablespoons vegetable oil
2½ cups all-purpose flour
1½ teaspoons baking powder
½ teaspoon baking soda
¼ teaspoon salt
½ teaspoon ground cinnamon
½ teaspoon ground nutmeg
¼ cup milk
1 cup applesauce
1 teaspoon vanilla extract
Vegetable oil
⅔ cup sifted powdered sugar or ½ cup
   cinnamon-sugar

•Combine first 3 ingredients in a large bowl; beat at medium speed with an electric mixer until blended.
•Combine flour and next 5 ingredients; add to sugar mixture alternately with milk, beginning and ending with flour mixture. Stir in applesauce and vanilla.
•Pour oil to depth of 2 inches in a Dutch oven; heat to 375°. Drop batter by heaping tablespoonfuls into oil; fry 4 at a time, 4 minutes, turning once. Drain doughnuts on paper towels; roll in powdered sugar or cinnamon-sugar. Yield: 2½ dozen.

Per doughnut: Calories 154 Fat 9g
Cholesterol 15mg Sodium 42mg

Note: To make your own cinnamon-sugar, combine ½ cup sugar and 1 teaspoon ground cinnamon.

YEAST BREADS

A mystique surrounds these heady leavened breads and gives them a reputation for being difficult to bake, but there's really no mystery to making beautiful yeast breads once you've learned the basics. Our series of photos on the following page will help boost a beginning bread maker's confidence.

Types of Yeast

Yeast is a living organism that produces bubbles of carbon dioxide that cause bread to rise (photo 1, next page). Yeast is available in several forms: active dry yeast, rapid-rise yeast, bread-machine yeast, and as a compressed cake. One package of active dry yeast equals a .6-ounce cake of compressed yeast.

Unless specified otherwise, we tested our recipes with active dry yeast, so you'll get the best results by using it in these recipes. If you want to substitute rapid-rise yeast, follow the package directions for necessary changes. And always remember to check the expiration date on a package of yeast before using it to be sure it's fresh.

Working with Yeast

Most of our yeast bread recipes dissolve the yeast in warm water (105° to 115°) before adding other ingredients, and the temperature of the water is critical. Water that's too hot will kill the yeast, while water that's too cool will inhibit the bread's rising.

Some of our recipes use the rapid-mix method of bread making in which the yeast is mixed with some of the dry ingredients before adding the liquids. This eliminates the need to dissolve the yeast. When using this method, the liquid should be 120° to 130° when you add it to the dry ingredients unless otherwise specified.

Kneading Dough

Turn dough out onto a smooth, lightly floured surface. With lightly floured hands, lift the edge of the dough farthest from you and fold it toward you. Using the heel of one or both hands, press down into the dough and away from you (photo 2). Give dough a quarter turn. Fold the dough toward you again, and repeat the kneading procedure until the dough begins to feel smooth and elastic—an ultimate goal that ensures good texture for all yeast breads.

Continue kneading in small amounts of flour until dough loses its stickiness; on humid days dough will absorb more flour. The kneading process can take up to 10 minutes to develop a stiff dough.

Proofing Dough

After kneading the dough, place it in a greased bowl, turning it to coat the top surface (photo 3). Cover the bowl with a barely damp kitchen towel or lightly greased plastic wrap. The ideal proofing (rising) temperature for yeast bread is 85°. An oven with a pan of very hot water placed on the rack under the dough should provide this temperature, as well as a draft-free environment (photo 4).

Rising is complete when the dough has doubled in bulk, unless the recipe specifies otherwise. To test the dough for doubled bulk, press two fingers ½ inch into the dough (photo 5). If the indentation remains, the dough has risen enough and is ready to be shaped.

You can make the dough ahead and let it rise in the refrigerator. It will take about 8 hours to rise at this cooler temperature, and it will keep there up to four days if the dough is made with water or three days if made with milk. Punch the dough down each day.

Shaping Dough

Punch the dough down in the center with your fist (photo 6), and fold edges to the center. Turn the dough over, and place it on a lightly floured surface. Divide the dough according to your recipe, and form the portion you will be using into a ball. (Dough dries out quickly, so cover and store excess in the refrigerator until needed.) Cover the dough and let it rest 5 to 10 minutes. This allows the gluten to relax, making the dough less elastic and easier to handle.

Individual recipes give specific directions for shaping the dough. After shaping, place the dough in a prepared loafpan or on a baking sheet, and allow it to rise again, according to directions. When the shaped dough is double in size, press two fingers against the edge of the loaf. If the indentation remains, the dough has risen enough.

WORKING WITH YEAST DOUGH

1. Yeast is a living organism that produces carbon dioxide bubbles when combined with warm water.

2. Use the heel of one or both hands to knead yeast dough and develop its structure.

3. Place dough in a greased bowl, and turn dough to grease top.

4. The ideal proofing temperature is 85°. (We use an oven with a pan of very hot water under the dough.)

5. Test the dough by pressing two fingers ½ inch into dough. If fingerprints remain, dough is ready to be shaped.

6. Punch dough down with your fist and fold dough into the center.

Baking Bread

Bake the bread in a preheated oven, unless the recipe specifies otherwise. Place the pan in the center of the oven to make sure your bread bakes evenly. If you're baking more than one pan in the same oven, leave some space around each pan so heat can circulate freely.

Outward appearance doesn't always indicate doneness. Tap the loaf lightly and listen for a hollow sound. Turn it on its side; it should easily fall out of the pan. If it's still soft and not hollow, return it to the oven. Remove bread from pans immediately after baking. Cool completely on a wire rack before wrapping in foil or plastic wrap. Slice bread on a cutting board, using a serrated bread knife. If slicing warm bread, turn it on its side so you don't mash the shape.

If a loaf of homemade bread is going stale, use it to make Garlic Croutons (page 352), Bread Pudding (page 168), or French toast.

VERSATILE YEAST DOUGH

Here's a basic yeast dough recipe that you can use to make any number of different breads.

The basic dough recipe is quick and easy to work with, requires little kneading, and stores in the refrigerator up to four days. First mix the dough; then cover and chill it. Next, use part or all of the dough to shape the type of bread you want from our selection of loaves, rolls, and sweet breads.

Basic Yeast Dough

PREP: 10 MINUTES

RISE: 1 HOUR TO 4 DAYS

COOK: VARIES WITH RECIPE

Use this dough for various tender breads like crescents, buns, and cloverleaf rolls.

1 package active dry yeast
1 cup warm water (105° to 115°)
3 tablespoons sugar
2 tablespoons shortening
1 large egg
½ teaspoon salt
3 to 3½ cups all-purpose flour

•Combine yeast and warm water in a 1-cup liquid measuring cup; let stand 5 minutes.
•Combine yeast mixture, sugar, shortening, egg, salt, and half of flour in a large mixing bowl; beat at low speed with an electric mixer until smooth. Gradually stir in enough remaining flour to make a soft dough.
•Place dough in a well-greased bowl, turning to grease top. Cover and let rise in a warm place (85°), free from drafts, 1 hour or until doubled in bulk or cover and store in refrigerator up to 4 days. (If chilled, let dough return to room temperature before proceeding.)
•Punch dough down; turn out onto a lightly floured surface, and knead 8 to 10 times. Shape and bake as directed in the next 5 recipes.

BREAD DICTIONARY

Baguette pans: Two long metal half-cylinder pans joined along one side, used for shaping and baking a pair of crusty French baguettes. French bread pans are similar pans, only wider.

Clay stone: A large, thick flat stone made to resemble the floor of a brick oven. When placed on the rack of a very hot oven, it will produce a bread with a superior crisp crust.

Dough hook: A hook attachment for a heavy-duty mixer that simulates the kneading process if you'd rather not knead by hand.

Dough scraper: A tool, usually square, made of stainless steel or plastic, convenient for cutting dough or scraping a work surface to lift dough and to prevent it from sticking.

Lame: A sharp curved razor for scoring the top of a loaf of bread before baking. A single-edged razor blade or a very sharp knife works just as well.

Cloverleaf Rolls

PREP: 10 MINUTES

RISE: 40 MINUTES   COOK: 12 MINUTES

1 recipe Basic Yeast Dough
¼ cup butter or margarine, melted

•Lightly grease muffin pans. Shape dough into 1-inch balls; place 3 balls in each muffin cup. Cover and let rise in a warm place (85°), free from drafts, 40 minutes or until doubled in bulk.
•Bake at 400° for 10 to 12 minutes or until golden. Brush rolls with melted butter. Yield: 2 dozen.

Per roll: Calories 90 Fat 3.4g
Cholesterol 14mg Sodium 71mg

Sesame Buns

PREP: 10 MINUTES

RISE: 30 MINUTES   COOK: 20 MINUTES

1 recipe Basic Yeast Dough
1 egg white
1 tablespoon water
1½ tablespoons sesame seeds

•Divide dough into 8 equal pieces. Roll each into a ball, and place on greased baking sheets; press down lightly with fingertips to resemble a bun.
•Cover and let rise in a warm place (85°), free from drafts, about 30 minutes or until doubled in bulk.
•Combine egg white and water, beating until frothy; brush over buns. Sprinkle buns with sesame seeds. Bake at 400° for 15 to 20 minutes or until browned. Yield: 8 buns.

Per bun: Calories 227 Fat 4.8g
Cholesterol 27mg Sodium 162mg

Cheese Crescents

PREP: 15 MINUTES   RISE: 30 MINUTES

COOK: 10 MINUTES

½ recipe Basic Yeast Dough
2 tablespoons butter or margarine, melted
¼ cup grated Parmesan cheese
Butter or margarine, melted

•Roll dough into a 12-inch circle on a lightly floured surface. Brush with 2 tablespoons melted butter, and sprinkle with Parmesan cheese. Cut into 12 wedges; roll each wedge tightly, beginning at wide end. Seal points, and place rolls on a greased baking sheet.
•Cover and let rise in a warm place (85°), free from drafts, about 30 minutes or until doubled in bulk. Bake at 400° for 8 to 10 minutes or until browned. Brush rolls with melted butter. Yield: 1 dozen.

Per crescent: Calories 116 Fat 5.7g
Cholesterol 21mg Sodium 122mg

Cinnamon Loaf

PREP: 10 MINUTES   RISE: 40 MINUTES

COOK: 35 MINUTES

½ recipe Basic Yeast Dough (previous page)
2 tablespoons butter or margarine,
   melted
1 tablespoon sugar
1 teaspoon ground cinnamon
⅓ cup raisins
1 cup sifted powdered sugar
1 to 1½ tablespoons milk
¼ cup chopped pecans

•Roll dough into a 15- x 7-inch rectangle on a lightly floured surface; brush with melted butter to within ½ inch of edges. Combine 1 tablespoon sugar and cinnamon; sprinkle over butter. Sprinkle raisins over top. Roll up, jellyroll fashion, starting at narrow edge. Pinch seams and ends together. Place loaf, seam side down, in a greased 8½- x 4½-inch loafpan.

•Cover and let rise in a warm place (85°), free from drafts, 40 minutes or until doubled in bulk. Bake at 350° for 30 to 35 minutes or until loaf sounds hollow when tapped. Remove from pan, and cool on a wire rack.
•Combine powdered sugar and milk, stirring until smooth. Drizzle over loaf, and sprinkle with pecans. Yield: 1 loaf.

Per ½-inch slice: Calories 123 Fat 3.7g
Cholesterol 11mg Sodium 54mg

Filled Coffee Ring

PREP: 20 MINUTES   RISE: 45 MINUTES

COOK: 25 MINUTES

1 recipe Basic Yeast Dough (previous page)
2 tablespoons butter or margarine, melted
½ cup raisins
½ cup chopped pecans
⅓ cup sugar
1 teaspoon ground cinnamon
1 cup sifted powdered sugar
1½ tablespoons milk

•Roll dough into a 21- x 7-inch rectangle on a lightly floured surface. Brush butter evenly over dough, leaving a 1-inch margin at sides. Combine raisins and next 3 ingredients; sprinkle evenly over dough, leaving a 1-inch margin.
•Roll up dough, jellyroll fashion, starting at long side; pinch seam to seal. Place roll, seam side down, on a large greased baking sheet; shape into a ring, and pinch ends together to seal.
•Using kitchen shears, make cuts in dough every inch around ring, cutting two-thirds of the way through roll at each cut. Gently turn each piece of dough on its side, slightly overlapping slices.
•Cover and let rise in a warm place (85°), free from drafts, 45 minutes or until doubled in bulk. Bake at 375° for 20 to 25 minutes or until golden. Transfer to a wire rack.
•Combine powdered sugar and milk; drizzle over ring while warm. Yield: 8 servings.

Per serving: Calories 413 Fat 11.9g
Cholesterol 35mg Sodium 188mg

SOURDOUGH BREAD

Sourdough bread has been around for centuries. Ancient Egyptians reportedly combined flour and water, and set the mixture outside where it captured wild yeast spores from the air. The mixture was the ideal environment for the wild yeast to grow. The mixture fermented naturally, leavening the bread and adding the characteristic tangy, sourdough flavor. This was the beginning of what we now call sourdough bread.

With commercial yeast so readily available, we no longer depend on a sourdough starter for leavening, but still love it for its distinctive flavor, chewy texture, and the novelty of its fermentation process. As sourdough starter ages, its flavor matures, imparting more sourdough flavor each time it's used.

To make this bread, follow the recipe carefully. Let the starter stand in a warm place for 72 hours, so that it will bubble up and ferment. Stir it two or three times a day; then chill it. The mixture will separate; that's okay. Just stir once a day.

Use the starter or share it with a friend within 14 days. Each time you remove a cup, replenish or "feed" it with Starter Food as directed in the recipe to follow. This maintains the volume and nourishes the yeast. If the starter sits too long without new starter food, it will become overly sour and will lose its leavening quality. If you don't use it within 14 days, pour off or give away one cup of the starter, and feed the remaining part as if you had used it.

One cup of starter is a good amount to give a friend. Provide instructions to feed it right away, and then to chill it for a couple of days before using; this allows the flavor to develop.

If properly cared for, the starter should last indefinitely. But if it becomes discolored or too sour for your taste preferences, discard it and make a new batch. See the next page for other tips for the use and care of your starter.

Sourdough Starter

PREP: 10 MINUTES   RISE: 3 DAYS

Sourdough Starter is a tangy yeast mixture used for bread making. It will last indefinitely if you keep "feeding" it with equal amounts of flour and water, as well as a tiny bit of sugar.

1 package active dry yeast
½ cup warm water (105° to 115°)
2 cups all-purpose flour
3 tablespoons sugar
1 teaspoon salt
2 cups warm water (105° to 115°)
Starter Food

•Combine yeast and ½ cup warm water in a 1-cup liquid measuring cup; let stand 5 minutes.
•Combine flour, sugar, and salt in a medium-size nonmetal bowl, and stir well. Gradually stir in 2 cups warm water. Add yeast mixture, and mix well.
•Cover starter loosely with plastic wrap or cheesecloth; let stand in a warm place (85°)

72 hours, stirring 2 or 3 times daily. Place fermented mixture in refrigerator, and stir once a day. Use within 11 days.

•To use, remove sourdough starter from refrigerator; let stand at room temperature at least 1 hour.

•Stir starter well, and measure amount of starter needed. Replenish remaining starter with Starter Food (see recipe and photo below), and return to refrigerator; use starter within 2 to 14 days, stirring daily.

•When Sourdough Starter is used again, repeat procedure for using starter and replenishing with Starter Food. Yield: 3 cups.

Per cup: Calories 334 Fat 0.9g
Cholesterol 0mg Sodium 783mg

Starter Food

1 cup all-purpose flour
1 cup water
1 teaspoon sugar

•Stir all ingredients into remaining Sourdough Starter.

Feeding Sourdough Starter: Stir Starter Food into starter each time you remove some starter for bread baking.

Country Crust Sourdough

◄ HEALTHY ►

**PREP: 25 MINUTES   RISE: 2½ HOURS
COOK: 35 MINUTES**

2 packages active dry yeast
1¼ cups warm water (105° to 115°)
1 cup Sourdough Starter (at room temperature)
¼ cup vegetable oil
¼ cup sugar
2 teaspoons salt
2 large eggs, beaten
5½ to 6 cups unbleached all-purpose flour
Vegetable oil
Butter or margarine, melted

•Combine yeast and warm water in a 2-cup liquid measuring cup; let stand 5 minutes.
•Combine yeast mixture, Sourdough Starter, ¼ cup oil, sugar, salt, eggs, and 3 cups flour in a nonmetal bowl. Gradually stir in enough remaining flour to make a soft dough.
•Turn dough out onto a floured surface, and knead until smooth and elastic (8 to 10 minutes). Place in a well-greased bowl, turning to grease top. Cover and let rise in a warm place, (85°), free from drafts, 1 to 1½ hours or until doubled in bulk.
•Punch dough down, and divide in half; place on a floured surface. Roll each half into an 18- x 9-inch rectangle. Tightly roll up dough, starting at narrow edge; pinch seam and ends together to seal. Place loaves, seam side down, in two greased 9- x 5-inch loaf-pans. Brush tops with oil. Cover and let rise in a warm place, free from drafts, about 1 hour or until doubled in bulk. Bake at 375° for 30 to 35 minutes or until loaves sound hollow when tapped. Remove loaves from pans; brush with butter. Yield: 2 loaves.

Per ½-inch slice: Calories 122 Fat 3.1g
Cholesterol 14mg Sodium 179mg

Sourdough Biscuits

PREP: 20 MINUTES   COOK: 15 MINUTES

2 cups self-rising flour
¼ teaspoon baking soda
¼ cup shortening
¾ cup Sourdough Starter (at room temperature)
½ cup buttermilk
1 tablespoon butter or margarine, melted

•Combine flour and baking soda in a nonmetal bowl; stir well. Cut in shortening with a pastry blender until mixture resembles coarse meal. Add Sourdough Starter and buttermilk, stirring until dry ingredients are moistened. Turn dough out onto a floured surface; knead lightly 10 to 12 times.
•Roll dough to ½-inch thickness; cut with a 2¾-inch biscuit cutter. Place on a lightly greased baking sheet, and brush tops with butter. Bake at 425° for 12 to 15 minutes. Yield: 10 biscuits.

Per biscuit: Calories 166 Fat 5.8g
Cholesterol 4mg Sodium 432mg

GETTING STARTED

•Mix and store the starter in glass, stoneware, or plastic. Metal can cause a chemical reaction with the starter.
•Place the starter in a bowl large enough to allow it to double in volume as it ferments.
•Never cover the container too tightly. The yeast needs air to live and the gas from the fermentation process needs to escape. Punch a small hole in a plastic wrap cover or leave the lid ajar.
•If a clear liquid forms on top of the mixture, just stir it back in.
•Allow the starter to come to room temperature before using it.

Nothing quite compares to that fresh-from-the-oven texture of home-baked rolls and the wonderful aroma as they bake, too. If you've mastered the art of making yeast breads, you'll have no problem making dinner rolls. They take a little more time to hand-shape, but they'll bake and be ready to serve faster than large loaves.

Buttery Pan Rolls

◄ FAMILY FAVORITE ►
◄ HEALTHY ►

PREP: 36 MINUTES
RISE: 2 HOURS AND 10 MINUTES
COOK: 15 MINUTES

These classic dinner rolls will match any entrée, and they're so easy to make. Just pinch off small pieces of dough, uniform in size, and shape them into balls; then dip each into melted butter before baking.

5½ cups all-purpose flour, divided
3 tablespoons sugar
2 teaspoons salt
1 package active dry yeast
1½ cups milk
½ cup water
½ cup plus 2 tablespoons butter or
    margarine, divided

•Combine 3 cups flour, sugar, salt, and yeast in a large bowl; stir well. Set aside.
•Combine milk, water, and ¼ cup butter in a saucepan; cook over medium heat until butter melts, stirring occasionally. Remove from heat, and cool to 120° to 130°.
•Gradually add liquid mixture to flour mixture, beating at low speed with an electric mixer 30 seconds. Beat at high speed 2 minutes. Gradually stir in enough remaining flour to make a soft dough.
•Turn dough out onto a lightly floured surface, and knead until smooth and elastic (8 to 10 minutes). Place dough in a well-greased bowl, turning to grease top. Cover and let rise in a warm place (85°), free from drafts, 1 hour and 15 minutes or until doubled in bulk. Punch dough down; cover and let rest 10 minutes. Melt remaining ¼ cup plus 2 tablespoons butter.

•Pinch off small pieces of dough, and shape into 40 (1½-inch) balls; dip each ball in melted butter. Place balls in two greased 9-inch square pans. Cover and let rise in a warm place, free from drafts, 45 minutes or until doubled in bulk.
•Bake at 375° for 15 minutes or until rolls are golden. Brush warm rolls with any remaining melted butter. Yield: 40 rolls.
Per roll: Calories 94 Fat 3.4g
Cholesterol 9mg Sodium 151mg

Whole Wheat Potato Rolls

◄ HEALTHY ►

PREP: 25 MINUTES
RISE: 1 HOUR AND 25 MINUTES
COOK: 20 MINUTES

See these nicely browned rolls on page 60.

2 cups whole wheat flour
1 cup instant potato flakes
¼ cup buttermilk powder°
1 package active dry yeast
3 tablespoons sugar
2 teaspoons salt
2 cups warm water (120° to 130°)
¼ cup butter or margarine, softened
2 large eggs
3 to 3½ cups all-purpose flour
1 tablespoon butter or margarine, melted

•Combine first 6 ingredients in a large mixing bowl. Add water, ¼ cup butter, and eggs; beat at low speed with an electric mixer until moistened. Beat at medium speed 2 minutes. Gradually stir in enough all-purpose flour to make a soft dough.
•Turn dough out onto a floured surface, and knead until smooth and elastic (6 to 8 minutes). Place dough in a well-greased bowl, turning to grease top. Cover and let rise in a warm place (85°), free from drafts, 55 minutes or until doubled in bulk.
•Punch dough down, and divide in half. Divide each half into 12 pieces; shape each into a ball. Place 12 balls of dough in a lightly greased 9-inch round cakepan. Repeat procedure with remaining dough.
•Cover and let rise in a warm place, free from drafts, 30 minutes or until doubled in

bulk. Bake at 375° for 20 minutes or until golden. Brush rolls with butter. Yield: 2 dozen.
°Find buttermilk powder near dry milk powder in the grocery store.
Per roll: Calories 135 Fat 3.3g
Cholesterol 25mg Sodium 235mg

Basil Batter Rolls

◄ HEALTHY ►

PREP: 23 MINUTES
RISE: 1 HOUR AND 35 MINUTES
COOK: 16 MINUTES

These pesto-flavored batter rolls couldn't be easier—no kneading!

2 packages active dry yeast
1½ cups warm water (105° to 115°)
⅓ cup shortening
4 cups unbleached flour
¼ cup sugar
1½ teaspoons salt
1 large egg
2 tablespoons pesto
2 cloves garlic, minced
Melted butter or margarine (optional)

•Combine yeast and warm water in a 2-cup liquid measuring cup; let stand 5 minutes.
•Combine yeast mixture, shortening, 2 cups flour, sugar, salt, and egg in a large mixing bowl; beat at medium speed with an electric mixer until well blended. Stir in pesto and garlic. Gradually stir in enough remaining flour to make a soft dough. (Dough will be sticky.)
•Cover and let rise in a warm place (85°), free from drafts, 50 minutes or until doubled in bulk.
•Stir dough; spoon into greased muffin pans, filling half full. Cover and let rise in a warm place, free from drafts, 45 minutes.
•Bake at 400° for 15 to 16 minutes or until golden. Brush with melted butter, if desired. Yield: 2 dozen.
Per roll: Calories 112 Fat 3.3g
Cholesterol 9mg Sodium 157mg

MAKE YOUR ROLLS SHAPELY

Find a favorite yeast roll recipe (or commercial roll dough) and create your own butter-rich and irresistible breads. As you make them, try some of these shapes, glazes, and toppings. A few twists, turns, and sprinkles will give your rolls a professionally made look—yet you'll have the aroma and goodness of home-baked bread.

Here you'll find directions and illustrations for a variety of shapes, meant for a fancy affair or your family. The shapes will be easy to adapt for most any yeast roll recipe; just make sure the recipe makes a fairly stiff dough. If the dough is too soft, the rolls won't hold their shape after rising and baking.

After the rolls are shaped and have risen, brush them very gently, but thoroughly, with one of the following glazes:
• A whole egg or egg yolk beaten with a little water. It'll make rolls shiny and give them a rich golden top.
• Egg white beaten with a little water. It can be used to hold toppings such as poppy seeds, sesame seeds, cumin or caraway seeds in place during baking. Sprinkle a combination of seeds on your next batch of rolls.
• Melted butter. It's often brushed on rolls before baking, and you can add more butter after baking for extra flavor and shine.

Cloverleaf Rolls: Lightly grease muffin pans. Shape dough into 1-inch balls; place 3 dough balls into each muffin cup. Cover and let rise until doubled in bulk. Bake.

Easy Pan Rolls: Lightly grease one or two 9-inch cakepans. Shape dough into 1½-inch balls. Place dough balls in pan, leaving ½-inch space between them. Cover and let rise until doubled in bulk. Bake.

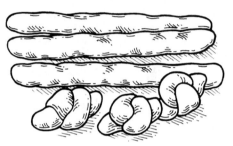

Bow Ties: Roll dough into several long ropes about ½ inch in diameter. Cut ropes into 8-inch strips. Carefully tie each dough strip into a knot. Place bow ties on a lightly greased baking sheet. Cover and let rise until doubled in bulk. Bake.

FanTans: Roll dough into a large rectangle about ¼ inch thick. Spread softened butter over dough. Cut dough lengthwise into 1-inch strips. Stack 5 or 6 strips, buttered side up, on top of one another. Cut each stack into 1-inch sections. Place each stacked section, cut side down, into lightly greased muffin pans. Cover and let rise until doubled in bulk. Bake.

Crescents: Roll dough into a 12-inch circle (about ¼ inch thick) on a lightly floured surface. (Reserve excess dough for other uses.) Spread softened butter over dough. Cut into 12 wedges; roll each wedge tightly, beginning at wide end. Seal points, and place rolls, point side down, on a greased baking sheet, curving into a half-moon shape. Cover and let rise until doubled in bulk. Bake.

Parker House Rolls: Roll dough to ¼-inch thickness; cut with a 2½-inch round cutter. Brush tops lightly with melted butter. Make an off-center crease in each round, using the dull edge of a knife. Fold each round along crease with larger half on top. Place folded rolls in rows 2 inches apart on lightly greased baking sheets. Cover and let rise until doubled in bulk. Brush again with melted butter. Bake.

Whole Grain Pan Rolls

◄ HEALTHY ►

PREP: 30 MINUTES   COOK: 20 MINUTES

1 cup water
¼ cup honey
¼ cup butter or margarine
¾ cup whole wheat flour
½ cup regular oats, uncooked
2 packages active dry yeast
1 teaspoon salt
1 large egg
2¼ to 2½ cups all-purpose flour

•Combine water, honey, and butter in a small saucepan; heat until butter melts. Remove from heat, and cool to 120°.
•Combine wheat flour, oats, yeast, and salt in a mixing bowl; stir well. Gradually add hot liquid mixture; beat at low speed with an electric mixer 1 minute. Add egg; beat 2 minutes at medium speed. Gradually add enough all-purpose flour to make a soft dough.
•Turn dough out onto a heavily floured surface; knead until smooth and elastic (about 8 minutes). Shape into 24 balls; place in a lightly greased 13- x 9-inch pan. Cover and let rise in a warm place (85°), free from drafts, 1 hour or until dough is doubled in bulk. Bake at 375° for 20 minutes or until lightly browned. Yield: 2 dozen.

Per roll: Calories 99 Fat 2.5g
Cholesterol 14mg Sodium 121mg

Sour Cream Crescent Rolls

◄ FAMILY FAVORITE ►

PREP: 31 MINUTES   CHILL: 8 HOURS
RISE: 30 MINUTES   COOK: 10 MINUTES

½ cup butter or margarine
1 (8-ounce) carton sour cream
½ cup sugar
2 packages active dry yeast
½ cup warm water (105° to 115°)
2 large eggs, beaten
4 cups all-purpose flour
1 teaspoon salt
Butter or margarine, melted

•Melt ½ cup butter in a saucepan over medium heat; stir in sour cream and sugar, and heat to 105° to 115°.

•Combine yeast and warm water in a 1-cup liquid measuring cup; let stand 5 minutes. Combine yeast mixture, sour cream mixture, and eggs in a large bowl. Combine flour and salt; gradually add to yeast mixture, stirring well. Cover and store in refrigerator at least 8 hours or up to 24 hours.
•Punch dough down; divide into 4 equal portions. Roll each portion into a 10-inch circle on a floured surface; brush with melted butter. Cut each circle into 12 wedges; roll up each wedge, beginning at wide end. Place on greased baking sheets, point side down.
•Cover and let rise in a warm place (85°), free from drafts, 30 minutes or until doubled in bulk. Bake at 375° for 10 minutes or until golden. Yield: 4 dozen.

Per roll: Calories 83 Fat 4g
Cholesterol 18mg Sodium 81mg

Broccoli-Cheddar Pinwheel Rolls

◄ HEALTHY ►

PREP: 20 MINUTES   RISE: 45 MINUTES
COOK: 20 MINUTES

Frozen bread dough gives you a head start with these cheese- and broccoli-filled roll-ups. Pair them with tomato soup.

1 (16-ounce) loaf frozen bread dough, thawed
1 (10-ounce) package frozen chopped broccoli, thawed and well drained
1 cup (4 ounces) shredded sharp Cheddar cheese
1 large egg, beaten
2 tablespoons instant minced onion
1 teaspoon onion salt
2 tablespoons butter or margarine, melted

•Roll dough into a 12-inch square on a lightly floured surface. Chop large pieces of broccoli, if desired. Combine broccoli, cheese, and next 3 ingredients; stir well. Spread mixture evenly over dough, leaving a ½-inch border. Starting on 1 side, roll up dough tightly, jellyroll fashion. Moisten seam of dough with water; press securely to seal, turning seam side down.

•Cut roll into 12 (1-inch) slices, and place on a lightly greased baking sheet. Brush with melted butter. Cover and let rise in a warm place (85°) free from drafts, 45 minutes or until doubled in bulk.
•Bake at 375° for 18 to 20 minutes or until golden. Serve immediately. Yield: 1 dozen.

Per roll: Calories 162 Fat 6.7g
Cholesterol 33mg Sodium 437mg

Cheese Buns

◄ HEALTHY ►

PREP: 24 MINUTES   RISE: 1½ HOURS
COOK: 18 MINUTES

Serve your next batch of burgers on these soft homemade buns.

1 package active dry yeast
2 cups all-purpose flour, divided
1 (5-ounce) jar sharp process cheese spread
½ cup water
¼ cup shortening
2 tablespoons sugar
½ teaspoon salt
1 large egg, beaten

•Combine yeast and 1 cup flour in a large mixing bowl, and set aside. Combine cheese spread and next 4 ingredients in a small saucepan; heat to 105° to 115°, stirring constantly.
•Add cheese mixture and egg to yeast mixture; beat 30 seconds at low speed with an electric mixer, scraping sides of bowl. Beat 3 minutes at high speed. Stir in remaining 1 cup flour.
•Turn dough out onto a lightly floured surface, and knead 1 to 2 minutes. Shape dough into 12 balls. Place in well-greased muffin pans.
•Cover and let rise in a warm place (85°), free from drafts, 1½ hours or until doubled in bulk. Bake at 350° for 15 to 18 minutes. Yield: 1 dozen.

Per bun: Calories 156 Fat 6.9g
Cholesterol 26mg Sodium 282mg

Cheesy Onion Buns: Add 2 tablespoons minced onion with egg.

YEAST BREAD LOAVES

There's a certain satisfaction that comes from baking loaves of homemade yeast bread. For some, it's even therapeutic.

If using a loafpan, be sure to use the size pan specified in the recipe; otherwise your loaf may not be shaped as pretty, and the baking time may vary.

In general, remove the loaf of bread from the pan immediately, and place it on a wire rack to cool. This is a good time to brush the hot loaf with melted butter. Once the loaf is cool, it's ready to slice. Use a bread knife (a long, slender knife with a serrated blade) and a gentle sawing motion to give a neat cut.

Basic White Bread

◄ HEALTHY ►
◄ FAMILY FAVORITE ►

PREP: 40 MINUTES

RISE: 2 HOURS   COOK: 50 MINUTES

About 7¼ cups all-purpose flour, divided
3 tablespoons sugar
2½ teaspoons salt
1 package active dry yeast
1½ cups water
½ cup milk
3 tablespoons butter or margarine

•Combine 2 cups flour, sugar, salt, and yeast in a large mixing bowl; stir well. Combine water, milk, and butter; heat until butter melts, stirring often. Cool to 120° to 130°.
•Gradually add liquid mixture to flour mixture, beating well at high speed with an electric mixer. Beat 2 more minutes at medium speed. Gradually add ¾ cup flour, beating 2 minutes at medium speed. Stir in enough remaining flour to make a soft dough.
•Turn dough out onto a floured surface; knead until smooth and elastic (10 minutes). Shape into a ball; place in a well-greased bowl, turning to grease top. Cover and let rise in a warm place (85°), free from drafts, 1 hour or until doubled in bulk.
•Punch dough down; turn out onto a lightly floured surface, and knead lightly 4 or 5 times. Divide dough in half. Roll 1 portion of dough into a 14- x 7-inch rectangle. Roll up dough, starting at narrow end, pressing

firmly to eliminate air pockets; pinch ends to seal. Place dough, seam side down, in a well-greased 9- x 5-inch loafpan. Repeat procedure with remaining portion of dough.
•Cover and let rise in a warm place, free from drafts, 1 hour or until doubled in bulk. Bake at 375° for 45 to 50 minutes or until loaves sound hollow when tapped. Remove bread from pans immediately; cool on wire racks. Yield: 2 loaves.
Per 1-inch slice: Calories 236 Fat 3.6g
Cholesterol 7mg Sodium 393mg

Cheese Bread

◄ HEALTHY ►

PREP: 37 MINUTES

RISE: 1 HOUR AND 45 MINUTES

COOK: 30 MINUTES

2 packages active dry yeast
1 cup warm water (105° to 115°)
1 cup milk
2 tablespoons sugar
2 tablespoons shortening
2 teaspoons salt
1 large egg, lightly beaten
6 to 7 cups all-purpose flour
2 cups (8 ounces) shredded Cheddar
    cheese

•Combine yeast and warm water in a 2-cup liquid measuring cup; let stand 5 minutes. Combine milk and next 3 ingredients in a saucepan; heat until shortening melts. Remove from heat, and cool to 105° to 115°.
•Combine yeast mixture, liquid mixture, egg, and 2 cups flour in a large bowl; stir until smooth. Stir in cheese; gradually stir in enough remaining flour to make a soft dough.
•Turn dough out onto a floured surface; knead dough until smooth and elastic (8 to 10 minutes). Place in a well-greased bowl, turning to grease top. Cover and let rise in a warm place (85°), free from drafts, 1 hour or until doubled in bulk.
•Punch dough down, and divide in half; cover and let rest 10 to 15 minutes. Shape each portion into a loaf. Place in two greased 9- x 5-inch loafpans. Cover and let rise in a warm place, free from drafts, 45 minutes or until doubled in bulk.

•Bake at 375° for 30 minutes or until loaves sound hollow when tapped. Remove from pans, and cool on wire racks. Yield: 2 loaves.
Per 1-inch slice: Calories 253 Fat 7.4g
Cholesterol 30mg Sodium 393mg

Honey-Oatmeal Bread

PREP: 32 MINUTES

RISE: 1 HOUR AND 40 MINUTES

COOK: 45 MINUTES

2¼ cups milk
⅓ cup honey
¼ cup shortening
2½ teaspoons salt
2 packages active dry yeast
½ cup warm water (105° to 115°)
2 cups regular oats, uncooked
6 to 6½ cups all-purpose flour
Butter or margarine, melted

•Combine first 4 ingredients in a saucepan; heat until shortening melts. Remove from heat, and cool to 105° to 115°.
•Combine yeast and warm water in a 1-cup liquid measuring cup; let stand 5 minutes. Combine yeast mixture, liquid mixture, oats, and 2 cups flour in a large mixing bowl; mix well. Stir in enough remaining flour to make a soft dough. Turn dough out onto a floured surface, and knead until smooth and elastic (8 to 10 minutes). Place in a greased bowl, turning to grease top. Cover and let rise in a warm place (85°), free from drafts, 1 hour or until doubled in bulk.
•Punch dough down; cover and let stand 10 minutes. Divide dough in half; place on a floured surface. Roll each half to a 15- x 9-inch rectangle. Roll up, jellyroll fashion, starting at narrow end; pinch seams and ends to seal. Place loaves, seam side down, in two greased 9- x 5-inch loafpans. Brush with butter.
•Cover and let rise in a warm place, free from drafts, 40 minutes or until doubled in bulk. Bake at 375° for 45 minutes or until loaves sound hollow when tapped. Cover with foil the last 15 minutes of baking to prevent excessive browning. Remove loaves from pans; cool on wire racks. Yield: 2 loaves.
Per 1-inch slice: Calories 270 Fat 5g
Cholesterol 5mg Sodium 385mg

Whole Wheat-Rye Bread

◄ HEALTHY ►

PREP: 36 MINUTES   RISE: 2 HOURS
COOK: 40 MINUTES

Whole wheat and rye flour make this bread hearty and healthy. Molasses sweetens it. See Marble Rye Braid pictured on the cover.

2 packages active dry yeast
½ cup warm water (105° to 115°)
⅓ cup molasses
1 tablespoon salt
1 tablespoon caraway seeds
¼ cup shortening
1¾ cups warm water (105° to 115°)
1½ cups rye flour
1½ cups whole wheat flour
3 to 4 cups all-purpose flour
1 egg white, lightly beaten

•Combine yeast and ½ cup warm water in a 1-cup liquid measuring cup, and let stand 5 minutes.
•Combine yeast mixture, molasses, and next 6 ingredients in a large mixing bowl. Beat at medium speed with an electric mixer until smooth. Gradually stir in enough all-purpose flour to make a soft dough.
•Turn dough out onto a floured surface, and knead until smooth and elastic (8 to 10 minutes). Place in a well-greased bowl, turning to grease top. Cover and let rise in a warm place (85°), free from drafts, 1 hour or until doubled in bulk.
•Punch dough down; roll dough into a 19- x 16-inch rectangle. Roll up dough, jellyroll fashion, starting at long side; pinch ends to seal. Place loaf, seam side down, on a greased baking sheet. Cover and let rise in a warm place, free from drafts, 1 hour or until doubled in bulk.
•Brush with egg white. Bake at 400° for 35 to 40 minutes or until loaf sounds hollow when tapped. Cool on a wire rack. Yield: 1 loaf.
Per 1-inch slice: Calories 196   Fat 3.4g
Cholesterol 0mg Sodium 447mg

Marble Rye Braid: Prepare dough for Whole Wheat-Rye Bread and Basic White Bread (previous page), letting both doughs rise the first time. Punch whole wheat-rye dough down; divide in half. Place each portion on a floured surface. Cover and let rest 15 minutes. Repeat procedure with white dough. Combine 1 portion white dough and 1 portion whole wheat-rye dough; knead 12 to 15 times.
Divide combined dough into thirds. Shape each third into an 18-inch rope. Place ropes on a greased baking sheet (do not stretch); pinch ends together at one end to seal. Braid ropes; pinch loose ends to seal. Cover and let rise in a warm place, free from drafts, 1 hour or until doubled in bulk. Repeat procedure with remaining doughs. Brush each loaf with half of a lightly beaten egg white. Bake at 400° for 35 to 40 minutes or until loaves sound hollow when tapped. Cool on wire racks. Yield: 2 loaves.

Chocolate Pinwheel Loaf

PREP: 48 MINUTES   RISE: 3 HOURS
COOK: 30 MINUTES

This pretty spiraled loaf is easy to make. Just stir melted chocolate into half the dough; then roll the doughs together, jellyroll fashion.

½ cup milk
¼ cup butter or margarine
¼ cup sugar
¾ teaspoon salt
1 package active dry yeast
¼ cup warm water (105° to 115°)
2 large eggs, beaten
3 to 3¼ cups all-purpose flour
1 (1-ounce) square unsweetened chocolate, melted and cooled
Glaze

•Combine first 4 ingredients in a saucepan; heat until butter melts. Remove from heat, and cool to 105° to 115°.
•Combine yeast and warm water in a 1-cup liquid measuring cup; let stand 5 minutes. Combine yeast mixture, liquid mixture, eggs, and 2 cups flour in a large mixing bowl; beat at medium speed with an electric mixer until smooth. Stir in enough remaining flour to make a soft dough.
•Divide dough in half, and set 1 half aside. Turn 1 portion of dough out onto a floured surface, and knead until smooth and elastic (8 to 10 minutes). Place in a well-greased bowl, turning to grease top. Cover and let rise in a warm place (85°), free from drafts, 1 hour or until doubled in bulk.
•Pour melted chocolate over remaining dough; knead until blended (8 to 10 minutes). Place in a well-greased bowl, turning to grease top. Cover and let rise in a warm place, free from drafts, 1 hour or until doubled in bulk.
•Punch each dough down, and turn out onto a floured surface; roll each into an 18- x 10-inch rectangle. Position chocolate dough on top of plain dough. Roll halves together, jellyroll fashion, starting at short end. Fold ends under, and place seam side down in a greased 9- x 5-inch loafpan. Cover and let rise in a warm place, free from drafts, 50 to 60 minutes or until doubled in bulk.
•Bake at 350° for 30 minutes or until loaf is golden. Remove from pan; cool on a wire rack. Drizzle Glaze over warm loaf. Serve warm or cool. Yield: 1 loaf.
Per ½-inch slice: Calories 175 Fat 5.1g
Cholesterol 36mg Sodium 152mg

Glaze

1 cup sifted powdered sugar
1½ tablespoons milk
½ teaspoon vanilla extract

•Combine all ingredients, stirring well. Yield: about ⅓ cup.

No-Knead French Bread

◄ HEALTHY ►

PREP: 45 MINUTES   RISE: 40 MINUTES

COOK: 25 MINUTES

Butter makes this yeast dough rich and luxurious. A series of gentle stirrings allows you to forgo kneading.

½ cup warm water (105° to 115°)
2½ teaspoons sugar
2 packages active dry yeast
1 cup boiling water
2 tablespoons butter or margarine
2 teaspoons salt
1 cup cold water
6½ to 7 cups all-purpose flour
1 large egg, beaten
2 tablespoons milk

•Combine first 3 ingredients in a 1-cup liquid measuring cup; let stand 5 minutes.
•Combine boiling water, butter, and salt in a large mixing bowl. Stir until butter melts. Add cold water; cool mixture to lukewarm (105° to 115°). Stir yeast mixture into liquid mixture. Add 2½ cups flour. Beat at medium speed with an electric mixer until blended. Gradually stir in enough remaining flour to make a soft dough.
•Let dough stand in bowl 10 minutes. Stir gently for a few seconds; cover. Repeat gentle stirring every 10 minutes for the next 40 minutes.
•Turn dough out onto a floured surface; divide into 3 equal portions. Roll each portion into a 13- x 8-inch rectangle on a floured surface. Roll up, jellyroll fashion, starting with long side; pinch ends to seal.
•Place each loaf, seam side down, on a separate greased baking sheet. Cover and let rise in a warm place (85°), free from drafts, about 40 minutes or until doubled in bulk.
•Make diagonal slits about ¼ inch deep down the length of loaves, using a sharp knife. Combine egg and milk in a small bowl, beating until blended. Brush gently over loaves after rising.
•Bake at 400° for 20 to 25 minutes or until loaves sound hollow when tapped. (This bread freezes well.) Yield: 3 loaves, 12 servings each.

Per serving: Calories 91 Fat 1.1g
Cholesterol 8mg Sodium 139mg

Garlic-Pepper Baguettes

◄ HEALTHY ►

PREP: 40 MINUTES   RISE: 2½ HOURS

CHILL: 2 HOURS   COOK: 25 MINUTES

Look for these speckled loaves on page 60.

1¾ cups water
1 tablespoon unsalted butter or margarine
3¾ to 4½ cups all-purpose flour
2 packages active dry yeast
1 tablespoon sugar
1 tablespoon garlic powder
2 teaspoons salt
1 teaspoon coarsely ground pepper
1 teaspoon dried thyme
1 tablespoon cornmeal
Vegetable cooking spray
1 egg white, lightly beaten
1 tablespoon water

•Combine 1¾ cups water and butter in a saucepan; heat until butter melts. Remove from heat, and cool to 120° to 130°.
•Combine 1½ cups flour, yeast, and next 5 ingredients in a large bowl. Gradually add liquid mixture to flour mixture, beating at medium speed with an electric mixer until blended. Beat 2 more minutes. Gradually stir in enough remaining flour to make a soft dough. (Dough will be sticky.)
•Turn dough out onto a well-floured surface, and knead until smooth and elastic (about 5 minutes). Cover and let rest 20 minutes.
•Lightly grease baguette pans or two large baking sheets; sprinkle with cornmeal.
•Divide dough in half. Roll 1 portion of dough into a 15- x 10-inch rectangle. Roll up dough, starting at long side, pressing firmly to eliminate air pockets; pinch ends to seal.
•Place dough, seam side down, on pan or baking sheet. Repeat procedure with remaining dough. Coat dough lightly with cooking spray. Cover and chill 2 hours. Uncover and let stand at room temperature 10 minutes.
•Make ¼-inch slits diagonally across baguettes. Bake at 425° for 20 minutes. Combine egg white and 1 tablespoon water; brush over loaves. Bake 5 more minutes or until golden. Cool completely on wire racks. Yield: 2 baguettes, 12 servings each.

Per serving: Calories 80 Fat 0.8g
Cholesterol 1mg Sodium 198mg

Feta Cheese Bread

PREP: 30 MINUTES   RISE: 45 MINUTES

COOK: 35 MINUTES

You'll find chunks of creamy white feta cheese buried in this bread. It's made with rapid-rise yeast, which needs only one rising in this recipe. And that rising time is half as long as when using active dry yeast.

1½ cups milk
¼ cup water
¼ cup shortening
4 to 4½ cups all-purpose flour, divided
2 teaspoons sugar
½ teaspoon salt
1 package rapid-rise yeast
¼ cup butter or margarine, softened and divided
4 ounces feta cheese, crumbled and divided
2 tablespoons butter or margarine, melted

•Combine first 3 ingredients in a saucepan; heat until shortening melts. Remove from heat, and cool to 120° to 130°.
•Combine 2 cups flour, sugar, salt, and yeast in a large mixing bowl. Add liquid mixture, beating at low speed with an electric mixer until blended. Beat 2 minutes at medium speed. Stir in enough remaining flour to make a soft dough. Turn dough out onto a floured surface; knead lightly 4 or 5 times. Divide dough in half.
•Roll 1 portion of dough into a 16- x 8-inch rectangle; spread with half of softened butter, and sprinkle with half of cheese. Roll up dough, jellyroll fashion, starting at long side; pinch ends to seal. Place dough, seam side down, in a well-greased French bread pan or on a large baking sheet.
•Repeat procedure with remaining dough, softened butter, and cheese. Brush each loaf with 1 tablespoon melted butter. Cover and let rise in a warm place (85°), free from drafts, 45 minutes or until doubled in bulk.
•Bake, uncovered, at 375° for 15 minutes. Reduce temperature to 350°, and bake 20 more minutes or until loaves sound hollow when tapped. Remove from pans immediately; cool on wire racks. Yield: 2 loaves, 12 servings each.

Per serving: Calories 137 Fat 6.4g
Cholesterol 14mg Sodium 139mg

YEAST COFFEE CAKES & DOUGHNUTS

Coffee cakes, doughnuts, and sweet rolls are the most appealing elements of a continental breakfast. Some of these recipes have a dough that can be chilled overnight. Some can be made ahead completely and taste just as good the next day. They're all at their best when enjoyed with a freshly brewed cup of coffee.

King Cake

◄ HEALTHY ►

PREP: 2 HOURS

RISE: 1 HOUR AND 20 MINUTES

COOK: 20 MINUTES PER LOAF

1 (16-ounce) carton sour cream
⅓ cup sugar
¼ cup butter or margarine, softened
1 teaspoon salt
2 packages active dry yeast
1 tablespoon sugar
½ cup warm water (105° to 115°)
2 large eggs
6 to 6½ cups all-purpose flour, divided
½ cup sugar
1½ teaspoons ground cinnamon
⅓ cup butter or margarine
Colored Frostings
Colored Sugars

• Combine first 4 ingredients in a medium saucepan. Cook over medium heat until butter melts, stirring occasionally. Remove from heat, and cool to 105° to 115°.
• Combine yeast, 1 tablespoon sugar, and warm water in a 1-cup liquid measuring cup; let stand 5 minutes. Combine yeast mixture, sour cream mixture, eggs, and 2 cups flour in a large mixing bowl; beat at medium speed with an electric mixer 2 minutes or until smooth. Gradually stir in 3 cups flour to make a soft dough.
• Turn dough out onto a floured surface, and gradually knead in remaining 1 to 1½ cups flour; knead until smooth and elastic (about 10 minutes).
• Place dough in a well-greased bowl, turning to grease top. Cover and let rise in a warm place (85°), free from drafts, 50 minutes or until doubled in bulk.

• Combine ½ cup sugar and cinnamon; set aside. Punch dough down; divide in half. Place 1 portion of dough on a floured surface; roll into a 27- x 10-inch rectangle. Spread half each of butter and cinnamon mixture on dough. Roll up dough, jellyroll fashion, starting at long side, and pinch seam to seal.
• Gently place dough roll, seam side down, on a lightly greased baking sheet. Shape into an oval ring, moistening and pinching edges together to seal. Cover and let rise in a warm place, free from drafts, 30 minutes or until doubled in bulk.
• Bake at 375° for 15 to 20 minutes or until lightly browned. Repeat procedure with remaining dough, butter, and cinnamon mixture. Decorate cakes with bands of Colored Frostings, and sprinkle with Colored Sugars. Yield: 2 cakes, 18 servings each.

Per serving: Calories 229 Fat 7.2g
Cholesterol 28mg Sodium 117mg

Colored Frostings

3 cups sifted powdered sugar
3 tablespoons butter or margarine, melted
3 to 5 tablespoons milk
¼ teaspoon vanilla extract
1 or 2 drops each of green, yellow, red, and blue liquid food coloring

• Combine powdered sugar and butter. Add milk to reach desired consistency for drizzling; stir in vanilla. Divide frosting into 3 batches, tinting one green, one yellow, and combining red and blue food coloring for purple frosting. Yield: about 1½ cups.

Colored Sugars

1½ cups sugar, divided
1 or 2 drops each of green, yellow, red, and blue liquid food coloring

• Combine ½ cup sugar and 1 drop green food coloring in a jar. Place lid on jar, and shake vigorously to evenly mix color with sugar. Repeat procedure with ½ cup sugar and yellow food coloring. For purple, combine 1 or 2 drops red food coloring and 1 drop blue food coloring before adding to ½ cup sugar. Yield: ½ cup each color.

THE KING CAKE CONNECTION

King Cake, a confection as rich in history as it is in flavor, is decorated in royal colors to honor the three kings who visited the Christ child on Epiphany. The King Cake tradition is thought to have been brought to New Orleans from France in 1870. The Creoles placed a bean or pea inside the cake before serving it, and the favor's finder was named king or queen for a day. Today a tiny plastic doll is the common prize, and the honored recipient is bound by custom to host the next party and provide the King Cake.

Cinnamon Twist Coffee Cake

PREP: 1 HOUR AND 10 MINUTES

RISE: 1 HOUR AND 45 MINUTES

COOK: 25 MINUTES

Studded with cinnamon and almonds, this spiral coffee cake needs only a pot of coffee as an accompaniment.

2 packages active dry yeast
½ cup warm water (105° to 115°)
1 cup boiling water
¾ cup instant potato flakes
1 teaspoon salt
½ cup sugar
½ cup instant nonfat dry milk powder
½ cup butter or margarine, softened
3 large eggs
5 cups all-purpose flour
½ cup butter or margarine, softened and divided
⅔ cup sugar
1½ teaspoons ground cinnamon
½ cup chopped almonds, divided
2 cups sifted powdered sugar
3 tablespoons milk
Candied cherries (optional)
Toasted slivered almonds (optional)

• Combine yeast and warm water in a 1-cup liquid measuring cup; let stand 5 minutes.
• Combine boiling water, potato flakes, and salt in a large mixing bowl; beat at medium

speed with an electric mixer. Add ½ cup sugar, dry milk powder, and ½ cup butter; beat well. Add eggs and yeast mixture, beating well. Gradually beat in 3 cups flour; add remaining flour, ½ cup at a time, beating well after each addition.

•Turn dough out onto a heavily floured surface, and knead until smooth and elastic (about 10 minutes). Place in a well-greased bowl, turning to grease top. Cover and let rise in a warm place (85°), free from drafts, 1 hour or until doubled in bulk.

•Punch dough down, and divide into 6 equal portions. Roll each portion into a 12-inch circle. Place 1 circle on a lightly greased 12-inch pizza pan. Spread 2 tablespoons butter over top of dough, leaving a ½-inch margin.

•Combine ⅔ cup sugar and cinnamon; sprinkle 2½ tablespoons cinnamon mixture and 2 tablespoons almonds over dough. Place a second circle of dough on top of first. Repeat procedure with butter, cinnamon mixture, and almonds. Top with a third circle of dough. Moisten edge of circle; seal. Repeat procedure with remaining 3 portions of dough to make a second cake.

•Place a 2½-inch round cutter in center of 1 loaf (do not cut through dough). Cut dough into 8 wedges, cutting from cutter to outside edge of dough. Gently lift each wedge, and twist several times to form a spiral pattern. Remove cutter.

•Repeat procedure with second coffee cake. Cover cakes, and let rise in a warm place, free from drafts, 45 minutes or until doubled in bulk. Bake at 350° for 20 to 25 minutes or until golden. Cool 10 minutes.

•Combine powdered sugar and milk; drizzle over bread. If desired, decorate with candied cherries and almonds. Yield: 2 (12-inch) coffee cakes, 8 servings each.

Per serving: Calories 392 Fat 12.4g
Cholesterol 64mg Sodium 272mg

Beignets

◄ FAMILY FAVORITE ►

PREP: 43 MINUTES
RISE: 1 HOUR AND 45 MINUTES
COOK: 20 MINUTES

New Orleans's best breakfast offering can happen in your very own home. These light pillowy puffs are fun to make. They're also a marvelous late-night dessert with coffee.

1 package active dry yeast
3 tablespoons warm water (105° to 115°)
¾ cup milk
¼ cup sugar
¼ cup shortening
1 teaspoon salt
3 cups all-purpose flour
1 large egg
Vegetable oil
Powdered sugar

•Combine yeast and warm water in a 1-cup liquid measuring cup, and let stand 5 minutes.

•Combine milk and next 3 ingredients in a saucepan; cook over low heat until shortening melts, stirring occasionally. Remove from heat, and cool to 105° to 115°. Combine yeast mixture, liquid mixture, 2 cups flour, and egg in a large mixing bowl; beat at medium speed with an electric mixer 2 minutes. Gradually stir in enough remaining flour to make a soft dough.

•Turn dough out onto a lightly floured surface, and knead until smooth and elastic (8 to 10 minutes). Place in a well-greased bowl, turning to grease top. Cover and let rise in a warm place (85°), free from drafts, 1 hour or until doubled in bulk.

•Punch dough down; turn out onto a floured surface. Roll dough into a 12- x 10-inch rectangle; cut into 2-inch squares. Place squares on a lightly floured surface; cover and let rise in a warm place, free from drafts, 45 minutes or until doubled in bulk.

•Pour oil to depth of 3 to 4 inches into a large heavy skillet; heat to 375°. Fry beignets, 4 at a time, in hot oil 1 minute on each side or until golden. Drain on paper towels; sprinkle with powdered sugar. Yield: 2½ dozen.

Per beignet: Calories 145 Fat 9.2g
Cholesterol 8mg Sodium 84mg

Glazed Doughnuts

◄ FAMILY FAVORITE ►

PREP: 39 MINUTES   RISE: 1½ HOURS
COOK: 12 MINUTES

Cook doughnuts, a few at a time, turn them once, and dip them, while warm, in glaze.

1 package active dry yeast
2 tablespoons warm water (105° to 115°)
¾ cup warm milk (105° to 115°)
¼ cup sugar
3 tablespoons shortening
½ teaspoon salt
½ teaspoon ground nutmeg
⅛ teaspoon ground cinnamon
1 large egg
2½ cups bread flour
Vegetable oil
Glaze

•Combine yeast and warm water in a 1-cup liquid measuring cup; let stand 5 minutes.

•Combine yeast mixture, milk, next 6 ingredients, and 1 cup flour in a large mixing bowl; beat at medium speed with an electric mixer about 2 minutes or until blended. Stir in remaining 1½ cups flour. Cover and let rise in a warm place (85°), free from drafts, 1 hour or until doubled in bulk.

•Punch dough down; turn dough out onto a well-floured surface, and knead several times. Roll dough to ½-inch thickness, and cut with a 2½-inch doughnut cutter. Place doughnuts on a lightly floured surface. Cover and let rise in a warm place, free from drafts, 30 minutes or until doubled in bulk.

•Pour oil to depth of 2 to 3 inches in a Dutch oven; heat to 375°. Cook doughnuts 4 or 5 at a time in hot oil about 1 minute or until golden on 1 side; turn and cook other side about 1 minute. Drain well on paper towels. Dip each doughnut while warm in Glaze, letting excess drip off. Cool on wire racks. Yield: 1½ dozen.

Per doughnut: Calories 219 Fat 8.9g
Cholesterol 14mg Sodium 76mg

Glaze

2 cups sifted powdered sugar
¼ cup milk

•Combine ingredients, and stir until smooth. Yield: ⅔ cup.

Sour Cream
Cinnamon Buns

Apple-Date-Nut Ring

PREP: 1 HOUR AND 10 MINUTES
CHILL: 8 HOURS **RISE:** 45 MINUTES
COOK: 25 MINUTES

Perfect for the holidays, this great Christmas recipe makes two beautiful rings, so you can freeze one or give it as a gift.

2 packages active dry yeast
½ cup warm water (105° to 115°)
¾ cup milk
½ cup sugar
½ teaspoon salt
½ cup butter or margarine
1 large egg, lightly beaten
5 cups all-purpose flour
2 tablespoons butter or margarine, melted
2 cups peeled, finely chopped apple
1 (10-ounce) package chopped dates or 1¾ cups raisins
½ cup chopped walnuts
¼ cup sugar
2 teaspoons ground cinnamon
2 cups sifted powdered sugar
3 tablespoons milk
¼ teaspoon vanilla extract

•Combine yeast and warm water in a 1-cup liquid measuring cup; let stand 5 minutes. Combine ¾ cup milk and next 3 ingredients in a saucepan; heat until butter melts, stirring occasionally. Remove from heat, and cool to 105° to 115°.

•Combine yeast mixture, liquid mixture, egg, and 2 cups flour in a large mixing bowl; beat at medium speed with an electric mixer until blended. Gradually stir in enough remaining flour to make a soft dough.

•Turn dough out onto a floured surface, and knead until smooth and elastic (about 5 minutes). Place in a well-greased bowl, turning to grease top. Cover and chill 8 hours.

•Punch dough down, and divide in half; roll each half into a 14- x 9-inch rectangle, and brush each with 1 tablespoon butter.

•Combine apple and next 4 ingredients. Spoon half of mixture evenly over each rectangle of dough, leaving a ½-inch margin.

•Roll up dough, jellyroll fashion, starting at long side; pinch seam to seal. Place each roll, seam side down, in a greased 12-inch pizza pan; shape into a ring. Pinch ends to seal. Using kitchen shears, make cuts in dough at 1-inch intervals around rings, cutting two-thirds of the way through rolls at each cut. Gently turn each piece of dough on its side, slightly overlapping slices.

•Cover and let rise in a warm place (85°), free from drafts, 45 minutes or until doubled in bulk. Bake at 350° for 20 to 25 minutes or until golden. Transfer to wire racks to cool.

•Combine powdered sugar, 3 tablespoons milk, and vanilla; stir until smooth. Drizzle over rings. Yield: 2 rings, 8 servings each.
Per serving: Calories 401 Fat 10.9g
Cholesterol 35mg Sodium 159mg

Sour Cream Cinnamon Buns

PREP: 20 MINUTES **RISE:** 35 MINUTES
COOK: 15 MINUTES

These breakfast buns rise and bake to a generous size.

1 (8-ounce) carton sour cream
2 tablespoons butter or margarine
3 tablespoons sugar
½ teaspoon salt
⅛ teaspoon baking soda
1 large egg, lightly beaten
1 package active dry yeast
3 cups all-purpose flour
2 tablespoons butter or margarine, softened
½ cup firmly packed brown sugar
2 teaspoons ground cinnamon
1½ cups sifted powdered sugar
2 tablespoons milk

•Heat sour cream in a small saucepan over medium-low heat to 105° to 115°.

•Combine warm sour cream, 2 tablespoons butter, 3 tablespoons sugar, salt, and baking soda in a large mixing bowl. Add egg and yeast; blend well. Add 1½ cups flour; beat at medium speed with an electric mixer until well blended. Gradually stir in enough remaining flour to make a soft dough.

•Turn dough out onto a lightly floured surface, and knead lightly 4 or 5 times. Cover and let rest 5 minutes.

•Roll dough into an 18- x 6-inch rectangle; spread 2 tablespoons softened butter over dough. Sprinkle brown sugar and cinnamon over dough. Roll up dough, starting at long side, pressing firmly to eliminate air pockets; pinch seam to seal.

•Slice roll into 12 (1½-inch) slices. Place slices, cut side down, in greased muffin pans. Cover and let rise in a warm place (85°), free from drafts, 30 minutes or until doubled in bulk.

•Bake at 375° for 12 to 15 minutes or until golden. Remove buns from pan immediately; let cool on a wire rack. Combine powdered sugar and milk; drizzle over buns. Yield: 1 dozen.
Per bun: Calories 302 Fat 9.2g
Cholesterol 37mg Sodium 166mg

SPECIALTY YEAST BREADS

The distinct shapes of brioche, bagels, pretzels, and focaccia define these breads as special. There's a certain artistic quality that goes into the preparation of each unique shape. Brush the various breads with melted butter, and sprinkle some with seeds or herbs as flavorful toppings.

Rosemary Focaccia

PREP: 28 MINUTES

RISE: 1 HOUR AND 45 MINUTES

COOK: 30 MINUTES

This popular Italian flatbread is great "ripping" bread. Tear off a serving-size piece, and enjoy it alone or use it to make a gourmet sandwich.

2 packages active dry yeast
2 cups warm water (105° to 115°)
6 cups all-purpose flour, divided
½ cup unsalted butter, softened
½ cup finely chopped fresh rosemary
   leaves, divided
1 teaspoon salt
½ cup olive oil, divided
8 cloves garlic, minced
2½ teaspoons kosher salt
½ teaspoon freshly ground pepper

•Combine yeast and water in a 2-cup liquid measuring cup; let stand 5 minutes.
•Place 4 cups flour in a large bowl; make a well in center. Add yeast mixture; stir until a soft dough forms.
•Cover and let rise in a warm place (85°), free from drafts, 1 hour or until doubled in bulk. (Dough will be spongy.)
•Sprinkle remaining 2 cups flour on a flat surface. Turn dough out onto floured surface, and knead until flour is incorporated to make a firm dough. Gradually knead in butter, ¼ cup rosemary, and 1 teaspoon salt.
•Knead until dough is smooth and elastic (about 5 minutes), adding additional flour, if necessary.
•Brush two 15- x 10-inch jellyroll pans with 2 tablespoons oil. Set aside. Divide dough in half. Roll each portion into a 15- x 10-inch rectangle, and place in prepared pans. Cover and let rise in a warm place, free from drafts, 30 to 45 minutes or until dough is almost doubled in bulk.
•Using fingertips, dimple the dough all over in both pans (see photo); sprinkle with minced garlic and remaining ¼ cup chopped rosemary. Drizzle with remaining 6 tablespoons olive oil, and sprinkle with kosher salt and pepper.
•Bake at 375° for 25 to 30 minutes or until golden. Cut or tear into squares. Yield: 2 flatbreads, 8 servings each.
Per serving: Calories 278 Fat 13.1g
Cholesterol 16mg Sodium 442mg

Dimpling Rosemary Focaccia dough: Using fingertips, make indentations all over surface of dough in pan.

English Muffins

PREP: 45 MINUTES
RISE: 1 HOUR AND 30 MINUTES
COOK: 30 MINUTES

1 package active dry yeast
½ cup warm water (105° to 115°)
1½ cups milk
3 tablespoons shortening
2 tablespoons sugar
1¼ teaspoons salt
6 to 7 cups all-purpose flour
¼ cup plus 2 tablespoons cornmeal

- Combine yeast and warm water in a 1-cup liquid measuring cup; let stand 5 minutes.
- Combine milk and next 3 ingredients in a small saucepan; heat until shortening melts, stirring occasionally. Remove from heat, and cool to 105° to 115°.
- Combine yeast mixture, liquid mixture, and 3 cups flour in a large mixing bowl; beat at medium speed with an electric mixer until well blended. Gradually stir in enough remaining flour to make a stiff dough.
- Turn dough out onto a floured surface, and knead until smooth and elastic (5 to 10 minutes). Place in a well-greased bowl, turning to grease top. Cover and let rise in a warm place (85°), free from drafts, 1 hour or until doubled in bulk.
- Punch dough down; turn out onto a lightly floured surface, and knead 4 or 5 times. Divide dough in half. Place half of dough on a smooth surface that has been sprinkled with ¼ cup cornmeal. Pat dough into a circle ¾ inch thick; cut dough into rounds with a 3½-inch biscuit cutter. (Cut carefully, as leftover dough should not be reused.) Repeat procedure with remaining dough.
- Sprinkle two baking sheets with remaining 2 tablespoons cornmeal. Place rounds, cornmeal side down, 2 inches apart on baking sheets (1 side should remain free of cornmeal). Cover and let rise in a warm place, free from drafts, 30 minutes or until doubled in bulk. Using a wide spatula, transfer rounds to a preheated, lightly greased electric skillet (350°), cornmeal side down. Cook 5 to 7 minutes on each side or until golden. Cool on wire racks. Yield: 8 muffins.

Per muffin: Calories 317 Fat 5.1g
Cholesterol 5mg Sodium 240mg

Cornbread-Jalapeño English Muffins

PREP: 30 MINUTES
RISE: 2 HOURS AND 15 MINUTES
COOK: 14 MINUTES

1¾ cups milk
¼ cup water
1 tablespoon butter or margarine
5½ cups all-purpose flour, divided
1 cup cornmeal
2 tablespoons sugar
2 teaspoons salt
1 package active dry yeast
6 jalapeño peppers, seeded and chopped
1 large egg

- Combine first 3 ingredients in a saucepan; heat until butter melts, stirring occasionally. Remove from heat, and cool to 120° to 130°.
- Combine 1 cup flour, cornmeal and next 3 ingredients. Gradually add milk mixture, beating at high speed with an electric mixer. Beat 2 minutes at medium speed. Add 1 cup flour, peppers, and egg; beat well. Gradually stir in enough remaining flour to make a soft dough.
- Turn dough out onto a floured surface, and knead until smooth and elastic (about 10 minutes). Place in a well-greased bowl, turning to grease top. Cover and let rise in a warm place (85°), free from drafts, 1 hour or until doubled in bulk. Punch dough down; cover and let rise in a warm place, free from drafts, 45 minutes or until doubled in bulk.
- Punch dough down; turn out onto a floured surface, and knead 5 times. Divide in half. Turn 1 portion out onto a surface sprinkled lightly with cornmeal. Roll into a ½-inch-thick circle; cut into rounds, using a 3½-inch biscuit cutter. Repeat with remaining dough.
- Sprinkle baking sheets lightly with cornmeal. Place rounds, cornmeal side down, 2 inches apart on baking sheets (1 side should remain free of cornmeal). Cover and let rise in a warm place, free from drafts, 30 minutes or until doubled. Using a wide spatula, transfer rounds to a preheated, lightly greased electric skillet (350°), cornmeal side down. Cook 5 to 7 minutes on each side or until golden. Cool on wire racks. Yield: 16 muffins.

Per muffin: Calories 221 Fat 2.9g
Cholesterol 19mg Sodium 319mg

Soft Breadsticks

PREP: 28 MINUTES   RISE: 50 MINUTES
COOK: 15 MINUTES

Serve these buttery, garlic breadsticks with spaghetti, lasagna, or other favorite tomato-sauced entrées.

2¾ to 3 cups all-purpose flour
1 package active dry yeast
1 tablespoon sugar
1 teaspoon salt
1¼ cups warm water (105° to 115°)
1 tablespoon vegetable oil
1 cup grated Parmesan cheese
1 clove garlic, minced
Butter or margarine, melted
Additional grated Parmesan cheese or sesame seeds

- Combine 1½ cups flour, yeast, sugar, and salt in a large bowl. Add water and oil; beat at medium speed with an electric mixer 3 to 4 minutes or until smooth. Stir in 1 cup Parmesan cheese, garlic, and enough remaining flour to make a stiff dough.
- Turn dough out onto a lightly floured surface, and knead until smooth and elastic (about 1 minute).
- Divide dough into fourths; shape each into a ball. Cut each ball into 10 pieces. Shape each piece into an 8-inch rope. (Cover remaining dough while working to prevent drying.) Dip rope in butter, and roll in Parmesan cheese or sesame seeds.
- Place 2 inches apart on greased baking sheets. Cover and let rise in a warm place (85°), free from drafts, 50 minutes. (Dough will not double in bulk.) Bake at 400° for 12 to 15 minutes or until lightly browned. Yield: 40 breadsticks.

Per breadstick: Calories 60 Fat 2.7g
Cholesterol 6mg Sodium 121mg

Herbed Breadsticks: Stir in 1 teaspoon dried basil and 1 teaspoon dried oregano with salt.

Bagels

PREP: 1 HOUR AND 15 MINUTES
RISE: 12 TO 18 HOURS
COOK: 22 MINUTES

Bagel means "water doughnut," as the dough is briefly boiled before it's baked. We give you several options for coating these bagels.

1 package active dry yeast
1¾ cups warm water (105° to 115°)
2 tablespoons honey
5 to 5½ cups bread flour
2 teaspoons salt
3½ quarts water
½ cup sesame seeds or any mix of poppy
    seeds, caraway seeds, sea salt, or
    dehydrated onion and garlic flakes

• Combine yeast and warm water in a 2-cup liquid measuring cup; let stand 5 minutes. Add honey, stirring well. Combine yeast mixture, 2 cups flour, and salt in a large mixing bowl; beat at low speed with a heavy-duty electric mixer 4 minutes or until smooth.
• Gradually stir in enough remaining flour to make a soft dough. Beat at medium-low speed with a dough hook 8 minutes or until smooth and elastic. Divide dough into 12 equal pieces. Roll each into a smooth ball. Cover and let rest 5 minutes.
• Shape each ball into an 11-inch rope. Bring ends of ropes together, and pinch to seal. Roll bagel around palm of hand to make a ring (photo 1). Place on greased baking sheets; cover and chill 12 to 18 hours.
• Bring water to a boil in a Dutch oven. Boil bagels, 4 at a time, 30 seconds, turning once (photo 2). Remove with a slotted spoon; place on wire racks. Dip bagels in sesame seeds (photo 3). Repeat with remaining bagels and sesame seeds.
• Place bagels on lightly greased baking sheets sprinkled with cornmeal, if desired. Bake at 450° for 13 to 14 minutes or until golden. Yield: 1 dozen.

Per bagel: Calories 255 Fat 4.2g
Cholesterol 0mg Sodium 393mg

Cinnamon-Raisin Bagels: Stir 1 cup raisins and 2 teaspoons ground cinnamon into dough before dividing dough into pieces.

1. Roll bagel on surface around palm of hand to make a ring.

2. Boil bagels briefly in a large Dutch oven to set the shape.

3. Dip bagels into sesame seeds. Place on greased baking sheets to bake.

Soft Pretzels

PREP: 35 MINUTES   RISE: 40 MINUTES

COOK: 15 MINUTES

For a great snack try these light golden pretzels. Squirt them with any type of mustard—yellow, Dijon, or coarse grained.

1 cup water
1 tablespoon butter or margarine
3 to 3½ cups all-purpose flour
2 tablespoons sugar
1 teaspoon salt
1 package active dry yeast
1 egg yolk, lightly beaten
Kosher salt

•Combine water and butter in a small saucepan; heat until butter melts, stirring occasionally. Remove from heat, and cool to 120° to 130°.
•Combine 1 cup flour, sugar, 1 teaspoon salt, and yeast in a large mixing bowl. Gradually add liquid mixture to flour mixture, beating at low speed with an electric mixer until blended. Beat 2 more minutes at medium speed. Gradually add ¾ cup flour, beating 2 minutes. Gradually stir in enough remaining flour to make a soft dough.
•Turn dough out onto a floured surface, and knead until smooth and elastic (about 5 minutes). Place in a well-greased bowl, turning to grease top. Cover and let rise in a warm place (85°), free from drafts, 40 minutes or until doubled in bulk.
•Punch dough down; divide into 12 equal portions. Roll each portion into a 20-inch rope. Twist each rope into a pretzel shape. Place about 1½ inches apart on lightly greased baking sheets. Brush dough with beaten egg yolk; sprinkle with kosher salt. Bake at 375° for 15 minutes or until golden. Serve warm or cool on wire racks. Yield: 1 dozen.
Per pretzel: Calories 143 Fat 1.9g
Cholesterol 21mg Sodium 499mg

Brioche

PREP: 30 MINUTES

RISE: 15 HOURS AND 45 MINUTES

COOK: 17 MINUTES

Brioche is an egg- and butter-enriched bread with a luxurious texture. The topknot is its signature. Use your freshest eggs and premium butter here.

1 package active dry yeast
¼ cup warm water (105° to 115°)
2 tablespoons sugar
1 teaspoon salt
3½ cups all-purpose flour
5 large eggs
1 cup butter, cut into ½-inch pieces and
   softened
1 tablespoon vegetable oil
1 large egg
1 teaspoon water

•Combine yeast and warm water in a 1-cup liquid measuring cup; let stand 5 minutes.
•Combine yeast mixture, sugar, salt, and ½ cup flour in a large mixing bowl. Beat at medium speed with a heavy-duty electric mixer with a paddle attachment 2 minutes, scraping sides of bowl occasionally.
•Add 5 eggs, one at a time, beating after each addition. Add butter, a few pieces at a time, beating just until butter is the size of small peas. Gradually add remaining 3 cups flour; beat until blended and creamy. (Dough will be very soft and batterlike.)
•Scrape dough into a well-greased bowl. Brush top of dough with oil. Cover and let rise at a cool room temperature 3 hours or until doubled in bulk.
•Punch dough down by gently folding edges into center with a rubber spatula; cover and chill 12 hours.
•Divide dough into 6 portions; divide each portion into 4 pieces. Working with half of dough at a time (keep remaining dough in refrigerator), roll each piece into a smooth ball. (Do not overhandle the dough.)
•Compress 1 side of the dough ball one-third of the way down by gently rocking the edge of your hand back and forth almost all the way through, until dough is shaped like a bowling pin.
•Hold the dough by the topknot, and gently lower it into a buttered 3½-inch brioche

pan. Tuck the topknot down into the dough with a flour-dusted finger, pressing the topknot completely down to the bottom of the pan until firmly tucked in. Repeat with remaining dough pieces.
•Combine egg and 1 teaspoon water; brush mixture over brioche. Place brioche pans at least 1 inch apart on a baking sheet. Cover and let rise at a cool room temperature until doubled in bulk (about 45 minutes). Brush again with egg mixture.
•Bake at 400° for 15 to 17 minutes or until deep golden. Remove from pans immediately; cool. Yield: 2 dozen.
Per brioche: Calories 158 Fat 9.7g
Cholesterol 74mg Sodium 192mg

Note: A cold oven is the perfect draft-free place to proof brioche. Evaporating moisture from a shallow pan of hot water placed on the shelf below the brioche keeps dough from drying, and you won't need to cover it.

BRIOCHE OPTIONS

If you don't have individual brioche pans, here are two other shaping options:
•**Two 7½-inch brioche pans**: Divide brioche dough in half, shaping each half as directed for individual rolls. Place in two 7½-inch buttered brioche pans. Cover and let rise at room temperature 2 hour or until doubled in bulk. Bake at 400° for 33 minutes or until deep golden. Remove from pans immediately; cool on wire racks.
•**Two 8½- x 4½-inch loafpans**: Divide brioche dough in half. Roll 1 portion of dough into a 12- x 8-inch rectangle. Roll up dough, starting at short side, pressing firmly; pinch seam and ends to seal. Tuck ends under, and place in a buttered 8½- x 4½-inch loafpan. Repeat procedure with remaining portion of dough. Cover and let rise at room temperature 2 hours or until doubled in bulk. Bake at 400° for 25 minutes or until loaves sound hollow when tapped. Remove from pans immediately; cool on wire racks.

Cheese-Filled Monkey Bread

◄ HEALTHY ►

PREP: 24 MINUTES RISE: 40 MINUTES
COOK: 35 MINUTES

These pull-apart rolls have a hidden surprise—melted cheese tucked in their centers.

1 (8-ounce) package sharp Cheddar or
  Monterey Jack cheese, cut into 24
  (¾-inch) cubes
1 (25-ounce) package frozen roll dough,
  thawed
2 tablespoons butter or margarine, melted

•Place 1 cheese cube in center of each roll, shaping dough into a ball around cheese cube. Pinch dough to seal. Dip in butter.
•Layer dough balls, seam side up, in a greased 12-cup Bundt pan. Cover and let rise in a warm place (85°), free from drafts, 40 minutes or until doubled in bulk. Bake at 350° for 30 to 35 minutes or until golden. Invert onto a platter, and serve warm. Yield: 2 dozen.
Per roll: Calories 125 Fat 5.2g
Cholesterol 13mg Sodium 214mg

Country White Bread

◄ HEALTHY ►

PREP: 5 MINUTES   COOK: 3½ HOURS

1 cup plus 2 tablespoons water
1¼ teaspoons salt
1½ tablespoons butter or margarine
3 cups bread flour or all-purpose flour
2 tablespoons instant dry milk powder
2 tablespoons sugar
2 teaspoons bread-machine yeast

•Combine all ingredients in bread machine according to manufacturer's instructions. Select bake cycle; start machine. Remove bread from pan, and cool on a wire rack. Yield: 1 (1½-pound) loaf, 12 servings.
Per ½-inch slice: Calories 150 Fat 2g
Cholesterol 4mg Sodium 266mg

BREAD MACHINE BASICS

•Purchase a bread machine with at least a 1½-pound capacity so you can make ample-sized loaves that will last a few days.
•Read your bread machine manual carefully. Add ingredients in the order recommended by the manufacturer of your machine.
•Make sure liquid ingredients are at room temperature before starting.
•Be precise in measuring ingredients for the bread machine. Even the slightest over measuring or under measuring can affect the results.
•When baking sweet or extra-rich breads, use the light setting.
•Don't use the delay cycle for bread recipes that contain eggs or other perishable products like dairy products or meats.
•Yeast makes the most difference in the final product. Although you can use rapid-rise yeast, we found that bread-machine yeast or active dry yeast works best. You can substitute 2¼ teaspoons of bread-machine yeast for one packet of active dry yeast.
•Occasionally, bread-machine yeast causes bread to rise so much that it touches the top of the machine and burns. If this happens, reduce the amount of yeast by a third.

Whole Wheat Toasting Bread

◄ HEALTHY ►

PREP: 9 MINUTES   COOK: 4½ HOURS

1⅔ cups bread flour
1½ cups whole wheat flour
3 tablespoons sugar
1¼ teaspoons salt
2 teaspoons bread-machine yeast
1 cup water
1 tablespoon vegetable oil

•Combine all ingredients in bread machine according to manufacturer's instructions. Select bake cycle; start machine. Remove bread from pan, and cool on a wire rack. Yield: 1 (1½-pound) loaf, 12 servings.
Per ½-inch slice: Calories 143 Fat 1.8g
Cholesterol 0mg Sodium 245mg

Red Pepper-Cheese Bread

◄ HEALTHY ►

PREP: 2 MINUTES   COOK: 3 HOURS

Extra-sharp Cheddar complements the spicy red pepper in this loaf.

1 cup warm water (105° to 115°)
1 cup (4 ounces) shredded extra-sharp
  Cheddar cheese
2 teaspoons Dijon mustard
1 tablespoon vegetable oil
3 cups bread flour
2 teaspoons sugar
½ teaspoon salt
¾ teaspoon ground red pepper
2¼ teaspoons bread-machine yeast

•Combine all ingredients in bread machine according to manufacturer's instructions. Select bake cycle; start machine. Remove bread from pan, and cool on a wire rack. Yield: 1 (1½-pound) loaf, 12 servings.
Per ½-inch slice: Calories 157 Fat 4.8g
Cholesterol 10mg Sodium 182mg

Basic Chocolate Cake (page 100)
Rich Chocolate Buttercream (page 131)

CAKES & FROSTINGS

Southerners have a knack for whipping up high and handsome cakes. These labors of love grace both elegant sideboards and kitchen tables as trademarks of a good cook and as expressions of hospitality. There's a definite skill involved in the measuring and mixing, but it's not rocket science. And the results are sure worth the effort.

Baking is no more difficult than other types of cooking, but it does require precise measuring, proper mixing, and the use of specified ingredients. A cake batter is easily thrown off balance without such attention. See our tips that follow on the next page to ensure cake baking success.

Equipment

Standard cakepans are available in 8- and 9-inch diameters. It's a good idea to stock three of each, so you can bake layers for a 3-layer cake without reusing pans. Shiny metal pans produce the lightest, most tender crust. Avoid dark metal or enamel pans; they can cause uneven and excessive browning.

Two common pans you'll want to collect for making angel food cakes and pound cakes are a 10-inch tube pan and a 13-cup Bundt pan. You can often substitute a tube pan when a recipe calls for a Bundt pan, but be careful using a Bundt pan when the recipe calls for a tube pan; most Bundt pans hold slightly less batter than tube pans.

A springform pan for baking cheesecakes is an inexpensive piece of equipment that you'll use often once you've tried it. The 9- and 10-inch sizes are most common. Springform pans are also great for baking tarts and coffee cakes.

Start accumulating different sizes of wire cooling racks. Cooling racks allow airflow underneath baked goods so the bottom doesn't get soggy. Large rectangular racks and small round racks are popular sizes. A good quality mixer and a rubber spatula are a must. And a medium-sized metal cake spatula is handy for frosting cakes.

Storing Cakes

Cool cakes completely before storing them, even the unfrosted ones. If covered while still warm, cakes may become sticky on top. Store unfrosted cakes and those with a creamy frosting under a cake dome. Covering a frosted cake well with plastic wrap will also work, but first insert wooden picks into the cake in several places to keep the wrap from touching the frosting.

Cakes with fluffy meringue frosting are best eaten the day they're made. Meringue frosting gradually disintegrates when stored several days. Cakes with a cream filling or frosting should always be stored in the refrigerator.

To Freeze or not to Freeze

Unfrosted cakes freeze best. Let cake cool completely; then wrap in aluminum foil and plastic wrap. Freeze up to five months. Partially unwrap cake; thaw at room temperature.

Frosted cakes are trickier to freeze. Those with creamy frosting freeze best. To freeze a frosted cake, place it uncovered in the freezer just until frozen. Then loosely, but thoroughly, wrap and return it to the freezer. It should keep up to three months. Unwrap frosted cake as soon as you remove it from the freezer, and let cake stand at room temperature until thawed and ready to eat.

CAKE BAKING BASICS

To grease cakepans: Use wax paper to lightly grease sides and bottoms of pans with shortening.

To flour cakepans: Dust greased pans with flour, shaking pans to coat bottoms and sides. Shake out excess flour.

To bake cakes: Place pans on center rack of preheated oven; don't let pans touch.

To test cakes for doneness: Insert wooden pick in center of cake; if it comes out clean, the cake's done.

To remove cakes: After cooling 10 minutes in pan, run a knife around edges of warm cake to loosen from sides of pan.

To cool cakes: Invert cake onto a wire rack to cool completely.

•Use shortening to grease cakepans. (Oil, butter, or margarine may cause cakes to stick or burn.) Dust greased cakepans with flour, tilting pans to coat bottoms and sides.
•All-purpose flour is presifted, so there's no need to sift it unless the recipe specifies. But always sift cake flour before measuring.
•You can substitute all-purpose flour for cake flour by using 2 tablespoons less per cup.

Measuring:
•Measure flour by spooning it lightly into a dry measuring cup, letting it mound slightly. Then level it off with a straight-edged spatula or knife.
•Measure liquids in glass or clear plastic measuring cups. Measure dry ingredients in nested metal or plastic "dry" measuring cups (those intended for dry ingredients).

Mixing:
•Beat softened butter and sugar thoroughly—5 minutes with a heavy-duty stand mixer, 6 minutes with a standard mixer, and 7 minutes with a handheld mixer.
•Add only one egg at a time to batter, and beat until blended after each addition. Do not overbeat.
•Add dry and liquid ingredients alternately to beaten mixture in about four portions. Beat after each addition just until batter is smooth. Use a rubber spatula to scrape sides of bowl often during beating.
•Unless your recipe specifies otherwise, you'll usually get favorable results if you fill cakepans half full with batter. Some recipes may vary slightly depending on what type cake you're making, but it's a good general rule of thumb that helps when you're trying to divide batter evenly.

Tips for Great Cakes
A tender and moist cake results not from luck, but from accurate measuring, mixing, and baking procedures. You'll quickly become a reputable cake baker when you follow these basics:

Ingredients and Preparation:
•For best results, let butter, milk, and eggs sit at room temperature at least 20 minutes before mixing. (Or take the chill off refrigerated eggs by running them, while still in the shell, briefly under warm water.)
•There's no substitute for real eggs, butter, or regular margarine when making a cake. Light butter, whipped butter or margarine, and egg substitute are not intended for classic baking.
•Always preheat your oven 10 minutes before baking.
•Be sure to use the correct pan size, measuring it across the top. An incorrect pan size can cause a cake to be flat and shrunken or rise to a peak and fall.

Baking and Cooling:
•Bake cake layers on the center oven rack, and stagger cakepans for even baking, being careful not to let sides of pans touch.
•Keep oven door closed until the minimum baking time has elapsed.
•Test cake for doneness before removing it from the oven. Cake is done when a wooden pick inserted in center comes out clean. (Underbaking can cause a cake to fall.)
•Let cakes cool in pans 10 minutes for layer cakes and 15 minutes for tube cakes. Then invert cakes onto wire racks to cool completely.
•Let cake layers cool completely before adding filling and frosting. Before frosting a cake, gently brush away loose crumbs.

CAKE TROUBLESHOOTING

Since cake baking requires precise measuring, as well as mixing and baking procedures, it's only natural that any number of things can go wrong along the way. Use the following chart to help diagnose and correct any problems.

If batter overflows:
•Overmixing
•Too much batter in pan

If cake falls:
•Oven not hot enough
•Undermixing
•Insufficient baking
•Opening oven door during baking
•Too much baking powder, soda, liquid, or sugar

If cake peaks in center:
•Oven too hot at start of baking
•Too much flour
•Not enough liquid

If crust is sticky:
•Insufficient baking
•Oven not hot enough
•Too much sugar

If cake sticks to pan:
•Cake cooling in pan too long
•Pan not properly greased and floured

If cake cracks and falls apart:
•Removing from pan too soon
•Too much shortening, baking powder, soda, or sugar

If texture is heavy:
•Overmixing when adding flour and liquid
•Oven temperature too low
•Too much shortening, sugar, or liquid

If texture is coarse:
•Inadequate mixing
•Oven temperature too low
•Too much baking powder or soda

If texture is dry:
•Overbaking
•Overbeating egg whites
•Too much flour, baking powder, or soda
•Not enough shortening or sugar

SHORTENING CAKES

There are two basic kinds of cakes. Most are classified as shortening or butter cakes; the others are foam (sponge-type) cakes, discussed on page 117. Shortening cakes are the most well known and typically the richer of the two. They include the basic white, yellow, and chocolate cakes, pound cakes, fruitcakes, and others that are made with solid fat. Shortening cakes usually depend on baking powder for leavening. Sometimes eggs are added whole to the batter; sometimes they're separated, the whites are beaten until soft peaks form, and then they're folded in.

Basic Yellow Cake

◀ **FAMILY FAVORITE** ▶

PREP: 12 MINUTES COOK: 23 MINUTES

These basic yellow layers go well with any flavor of frosting.

1 cup butter or margarine, softened
1½ cups sugar
4 large eggs
3 cups sifted cake flour
2½ teaspoons baking powder
½ teaspoon salt
1 cup milk
2 teaspoons vanilla extract or 1 teaspoon vanilla extract and 1 teaspoon almond extract

•Beat butter at medium speed with an electric mixer until creamy; gradually add sugar, beating well. Add eggs, one at a time, beating after each addition.
•Combine flour, baking powder, and salt; add to butter mixture alternately with milk, beginning and ending with flour mixture. Mix at low speed after each addition until blended. Stir in flavorings.
•Pour batter into three greased and floured 9-inch round cakepans. Bake at 350° for 23 minutes or until a wooden pick inserted in center comes out clean. Cool in pans on wire racks 10 minutes; remove from pans, and cool completely on wire racks. Frost as desired. Yield: 16 servings.
Per serving: Calories 277 Fat 14.1g
Cholesterol 86mg Sodium 277mg

White Cake Supreme

◀ **FAMILY FAVORITE** ▶

PREP: 20 MINUTES COOK: 30 MINUTES

This cake is white because you use egg whites and shortening rather than yolks and butter. The fluffy beaten whites yield a light airy cake.

¾ cup shortening
1½ cups sugar
2¼ cups sifted cake flour
1 tablespoon baking powder
¾ teaspoon salt
1 cup milk
1½ teaspoons vanilla extract
5 egg whites

•Beat shortening at medium speed with an electric mixer until creamy; gradually add sugar, beating well.
•Combine flour, baking powder, and salt; add to shortening mixture alternately with milk, beginning and ending with flour mixture. Mix at low speed after each addition until blended. Stir in vanilla.
•Beat egg whites at high speed until stiff peaks form. Gently fold beaten egg whites into batter.
•Pour batter into two greased and floured 9-inch round cakepans. Bake at 350° for 25 to 30 minutes or until a wooden pick inserted in center comes out clean. Cool in pans on wire racks 10 minutes; remove from pans, and cool completely on wire racks. Frost as desired. Yield: 12 servings.
Per serving: Calories 280 Fat 11.7g
Cholesterol 3mg Sodium 280mg

White Cupcakes: Spoon batter into paper-lined muffin pans, filling each cup two-thirds full. Bake at 350° for 20 minutes. Remove from pans, and cool on wire racks. Frost as desired. Yield: 26 cupcakes.

Basic Chocolate Cake

PREP: 18 MINUTES   COOK: 35 MINUTES

Slather this all-purpose rich chocolate cake in Rich Chocolate Buttercream (shown on page 96) or a whipped cream frosting.

4 (1-ounce) squares unsweetened
   chocolate
½ cup shortening
2 cups sugar
2 large eggs
2¼ cups all-purpose flour
½ teaspoon baking powder
1 teaspoon baking soda
¾ teaspoon salt
¾ cup buttermilk
¾ cup water
1 teaspoon vanilla extract

•Place chocolate in top of a double boiler; bring water to a boil. Reduce heat to low; cook until chocolate melts.
•Beat shortening at medium speed with an electric mixer until creamy; gradually add sugar, beating well. Add eggs, one at a time, beating after each addition. Add chocolate, mixing well.
•Combine flour and next 3 ingredients; add to chocolate mixture alternately with buttermilk, beginning and ending with flour mixture. Mix at low speed after each addition until blended. Add water, mixing well. Stir in vanilla.
•Pour batter into two greased and floured 9-inch round cakepans. Bake at 350° for 30 to 35 minutes or until a wooden pick inserted in center comes out clean. Cool in pans on wire racks 10 minutes; remove from pans, and cool completely on wire racks. Frost as desired. Yield: 12 servings.
Per serving: Calories 323 Fat 13.7g
Cholesterol 36mg Sodium 259mg

Chocolate Cupcakes: Spoon batter into paper-lined muffin pans, filling each cup half full. Bake at 350° for 15 to 18 minutes. Remove from pans, and cool on wire racks. Frost as desired. Yield: 3 dozen.

Chocolate Buttercream Cake

PREP: 27 MINUTES   COOK: 28 MINUTES

Transform two basic cake layers into this showstopping dessert studded with toasted almonds.

1 cup (6 ounces) semisweet chocolate
   morsels
½ cup half-and-half
1 cup butter or margarine
2½ cups sifted powdered sugar
White Cake Supreme or 2 layers of Basic
   Yellow Cake (previous page)
1 cup chopped almonds, toasted

•Combine first 3 ingredients in a saucepan; cook over medium heat, stirring until melted and smooth. Remove from heat, and stir in powdered sugar. Set saucepan in ice. Beat at medium speed with an electric mixer until frosting holds its shape, about 5 minutes.
•Spread frosting between layers and on top and sides of cake. Comb frosting on top of cake, using a metal icing comb, if desired. Gently pat chopped almonds onto sides of cake. Store in refrigerator. Yield: 12 servings.
Per serving: Calories 751 Fat 46g
Cholesterol 160mg Sodium 531mg

BAKING CUPCAKES

When you're baking cupcakes, always grease the muffin pans or line them with paper baking cups. This makes cleanup ultraeasy. Remove cupcakes from pans immediately after baking, and let cool on wire racks before frosting. Flip through our Frostings section on pages 128 to 133 to find the desired topping for your cupcakes. Spread 2 to 3 tablespoons frosting on top of each cupcake.

Old-Fashioned Gingerbread

PREP: 20 MINUTES   COOK: 40 MINUTES

Serve this family favorite spice cake with Hard Sauce (page 397), Lemon Curd (page 398), or just a dollop of whipped cream. And when the cake's warm from the oven, all you really need is a glass of milk.

½ cup butter or margarine, softened
1 cup sugar
1 cup molasses
1 large egg
2½ cups all-purpose flour
1½ teaspoons baking soda
½ teaspoon salt
1 teaspoon ground ginger
1 teaspoon ground cinnamon
1 cup hot water

•Beat butter at medium speed with an electric mixer until creamy. Gradually add sugar; beat well. Add molasses and egg; beat well.
•Combine flour and next 4 ingredients; add to butter mixture alternately with hot water, beginning and ending with flour mixture. Mix at low speed after each addition until blended.
•Pour batter into a lightly greased and floured 13- x 9-inch pan. Bake at 350° for 35 to 40 minutes or until a wooden pick inserted in center comes out clean. Cool slightly in pan on a wire rack. Yield: 15 servings.
Per serving: Calories 242 Fat 6.9g
Cholesterol 31mg Sodium 236mg

Carrot Cake Supreme

◄ FAMILY FAVORITE ►
◄ MAKE AHEAD ►

PREP: 25 MINUTES   COOK: 30 MINUTES
CHILL: 3 HOURS

Buttermilk Glaze adds extra moistness to this cake and makes it incredibly rich. Cover and chill the cake, and serve it the second day; it'll slice neater.

2 cups all-purpose flour
2 teaspoons baking soda
½ teaspoon salt
2 teaspoons ground cinnamon
3 large eggs
2 cups sugar
¾ cup vegetable oil
¾ cup buttermilk
2 teaspoons vanilla extract
2 cups grated carrot
1 (8-ounce) can crushed pineapple, drained
1 (3½-ounce) can flaked coconut
1 cup chopped pecans
Buttermilk Glaze (page 132)
Deluxe Cream Cheese Frosting (page 129)

Carrot Cake Supreme

•Grease three 9-inch round cakepans; line with wax paper. Lightly grease and flour wax paper. Set aside.
•Stir together first 4 ingredients. Beat eggs and next 4 ingredients at medium speed with an electric mixer until smooth. Add flour mixture, beating at low speed until blended. Fold in carrot and next 3 ingredients. Pour batter into prepared pans.
•Bake at 350° for 25 to 30 minutes or until a wooden pick inserted in center comes out clean.
•Drizzle warm Buttermilk Glaze evenly over warm cake layers; cool in pans on wire racks 15 minutes. Remove from pans, inverting layers. Peel off wax paper; invert again, glaze side up. Cool completely on wire racks.
•Spread Deluxe Cream Cheese Frosting between layers and on top and sides of cake. Chill cake several hours before slicing. Store in refrigerator. Yield: 16 servings.

Per serving: Calories 675 Fat 36g
Cholesterol 87mg Sodium 467mg

Carrot Sheet Cake

PREP: 22 MINUTES   COOK: 35 MINUTES

If you have only a little time for baking, here's an abbreviated version of carrot cake—almost like a snack cake.

1½ cups all-purpose flour
1 teaspoon baking powder
1 teaspoon baking soda
½ teaspoon salt
1 teaspoon ground cinnamon
1 cup sugar
1¼ cups grated carrot
⅔ cup vegetable oil
2 large eggs
1 (8-ounce) can crushed pineapple, drained
1 teaspoon vanilla extract
1 (3-ounce) package cream cheese, softened
¼ cup butter or margarine, softened
½ teaspoon vanilla extract
2¼ cups sifted powdered sugar

•Combine first 6 ingredients in a large bowl. Combine carrot and next 4 ingredients, mixing well; add to dry ingredients, and beat at medium speed with an electric mixer 2 minutes.
•Pour batter into a greased and floured 13- x 9-inch pan. Bake at 350° for 35 minutes or until a wooden pick inserted in center comes out clean. Cool in pan on a wire rack.
•Beat cream cheese and butter at medium speed until creamy; add ½ teaspoon vanilla and powdered sugar, beating until smooth. Spread on top of cake. Store in refrigerator. Yield: 15 servings.

Per serving: Calories 320 Fat 15.8g
Cholesterol 43mg Sodium 220mg

Banana Sheet Cake: Substitute 1¼ cups mashed banana for carrot, and reduce vegetable oil to ½ cup.

Peanut Butter Sheet Cake

PREP: 20 MINUTES   COOK: 50 MINUTES

Peanut butter and chocolate dominate in this easy sheet cake.

¾ cup butter, softened
¾ cup creamy peanut butter
2 cups firmly packed brown sugar
3 large eggs
2 cups all-purpose flour
1 tablespoon baking powder
½ teaspoon salt
1 cup milk
1 teaspoon vanilla extract
½ recipe Rich Chocolate Frosting (page 130)
½ cup chopped peanuts

• Beat butter and peanut butter at medium speed with an electric mixer until blended; gradually add sugar, beating well. Add eggs, one at a time, beating after each addition.
• Combine flour, baking powder, and salt; add to butter mixture alternately with milk, beginning and ending with flour mixture. Mix at low speed after each addition until blended. Stir in vanilla.
• Pour batter into a greased and floured 13- x 9-inch pan. Bake at 350° for 50 minutes or until a wooden pick inserted in center comes out clean. Cool completely on a wire rack.
• Spread Rich Chocolate Frosting on top of cake, and sprinkle with peanuts. Cut into squares. Store in refrigerator. Yield: 15 servings.
Per serving: Calories 505 Fat 28.4g
Cholesterol 87mg Sodium 456mg

Pineapple Upside-Down Cake

◀ FAMILY FAVORITE ▶

PREP: 29 MINUTES   COOK: 50 MINUTES

This old-fashioned dessert baked in a cast-iron skillet never goes out of style. And it makes great use of canned pineapple.

½ cup butter or margarine
1 cup firmly packed brown sugar
3 (8¼-ounce) cans pineapple slices, undrained
10 pecan halves
11 maraschino cherries, halved
2 large eggs, separated
1 egg yolk
1 cup sugar
1 cup all-purpose flour
1 teaspoon baking powder
½ teaspoon ground cinnamon
¼ teaspoon salt
1 teaspoon vanilla extract
¼ teaspoon cream of tartar

• Melt butter in a 10-inch cast-iron skillet over low heat. Sprinkle brown sugar in skillet. Remove from heat.
• Drain pineapple, reserving ¼ cup juice. Set juice aside. Cut pineapple slices in half, reserving 1 whole slice.
• Place whole pineapple slice in center of skillet. Arrange 10 pineapple pieces spoke fashion around whole slice in center of skillet. Place a pecan half and a cherry half between each piece of pineapple. Place a cherry half in center of whole pineapple slice.
• Arrange remaining pineapple pieces, cut side up, around sides of skillet. Place a cherry half in center of each piece of pineapple around sides of skillet.
• Beat 3 egg yolks at high speed with an electric mixer until thick and pale; gradually add 1 cup sugar; beating well. Combine flour and next 3 ingredients; stir well. Add to egg mixture alternately with reserved ¼ cup pineapple juice. Stir in vanilla.
• Beat egg whites and cream of tartar at high speed until stiff peaks form; fold beaten egg whites into batter.
• Spoon batter evenly over pineapple in skillet. Bake at 350° for 45 to 50 minutes or

until cake is set. Invert cake onto a serving plate. Scrape any remaining glaze from skillet onto cake. Cut into wedges to serve. Yield: 8 servings.
Per serving: Calories 440 Fat 15g
Cholesterol 111mg Sodium 269mg

Strawberry Shortcake

◀ FAMILY FAVORITE ▶

PREP: 40 MINUTES   COOK: 8 MINUTES
CHILL: 1 TO 2 HOURS

Sprinkling sugar on sliced strawberries draws out some of their juices and makes a sweet syrup. Spoon the berries over flaky shortcakes; top with a cloud of whipped cream.

1 quart strawberries, sliced
½ cup sugar
2 cups all-purpose flour
1 tablespoon plus 1 teaspoon baking powder
¼ teaspoon salt
¼ cup sugar
½ cup cold butter or margarine, cut into small pieces
½ cup milk
2 large eggs, separated
¼ cup sugar
1 cup whipping cream
¼ cup sifted powdered sugar
Garnish: fresh strawberries

• Combine sliced strawberries and ½ cup sugar; stir gently. Cover and chill berries 1 to 2 hours.
• Combine flour and next 3 ingredients in a large mixing bowl. Cut in butter with a pastry blender until mixture is crumbly.
• Combine milk and egg yolks; beat well. Add to flour mixture; stir with a fork until a soft dough forms. Pat dough evenly into two buttered 9-inch round cakepans. (Dough will be sticky; moisten fingers with water as necessary.)
• Beat egg whites at high speed with an electric mixer until stiff peaks form. Gently spread surface of dough with beaten egg whites; sprinkle with ¼ cup sugar.
• Bake at 450° for 8 minutes or until golden. Remove from pans, and cool completely on wire racks. (Layers will be thin.)

•Beat whipping cream at high speed until foamy; gradually add powdered sugar, beating until soft peaks form.

•Place 1 cake layer on a serving plate. Spread half of whipped cream over layer, and arrange half of sliced strawberries on top. Repeat procedure with remaining layer, whipped cream, and strawberries, reserving ½ cup whipped cream.

•Top cake with reserved whipped cream; garnish, if desired. Store in refrigerator. Yield: 10 servings.

Per serving: Calories 381 Fat 20.6g
Cholesterol 104mg Sodium 349mg

Lemon-Raspberry Cake

PREP: 30 MINUTES   COOK: 18 MINUTES

A jar of preserves jump-starts this multilayer cake that's easier to make than it looks.

1 cup shortening
2 cups sugar
4 large eggs
3½ cups sifted cake flour
2½ teaspoons baking powder
½ teaspoon salt
1 cup milk
1 teaspoon almond extract
1 teaspoon vanilla extract
1 (10-ounce) jar seedless raspberry
     preserves
Lemon Buttercream (page 131)
Garnish: lemon slices

•Grease three 9-inch round cakepans; line with wax paper. Grease and flour wax paper. Set aside.

•Beat shortening at medium speed with an electric mixer until fluffy; gradually add sugar, beating well. Add eggs, one at a time, beating after each addition.

•Combine flour, baking powder, and salt; add to shortening mixture alternately with milk, beginning and ending with flour mixture. Mix at low speed after each addition until blended. Stir in flavorings.

•Pour batter into prepared pans. Bake at 375° for 16 to 18 minutes or until a wooden pick inserted in center comes out clean. Cool in pans on wire racks 10 minutes; remove from pans, and peel off wax paper. Cool layers completely on wire racks.

•Slice cake layers in half horizontally to make 6 layers. Place 1 layer, cut side up, on a cake plate; spread with 2½ tablespoons preserves. Repeat procedure with remaining 5 layers and preserves, omitting preserves on top of last layer.

•Reserve 1 cup Lemon Buttercream; spread remaining 1¾ cups buttercream on top and sides of cake. Using a star tip, pipe reserved buttercream on top of cake. Garnish, if desired. Store in an airtight container in refrigerator. Yield: 16 servings.

Per serving: Calories 535 Fat 27.6g
Cholesterol 94mg Sodium 303mg

Caramel Cake

◀ **FAMILY FAVORITE** ▶

PREP: 25 MINUTES
COOK: 1 HOUR AND 15 MINUTES

A blonde candylike frosting makes this cake irresistible.

1 (8-ounce) carton sour cream
¼ cup milk
1 cup butter, softened
2 cups sugar
4 large eggs
2¾ cups all-purpose flour
2 teaspoons baking powder
½ teaspoon salt
1 teaspoon vanilla extract
1 teaspoon rum extract (optional)
Favorite Caramel Frosting

•Combine sour cream and milk in a small bowl; set aside.

•Beat butter at medium speed with an electric mixer until creamy; gradually add sugar, beating well. Add eggs, one at a time, beating after each addition.

•Combine flour, baking powder, and salt; add to butter mixture alternately with sour cream mixture, beginning and ending with flour mixture. Mix at low speed after each addition until blended. Stir in vanilla and, if desired, rum extract.

•Pour batter into two greased and floured 9-inch round cakepans. (Batter will be very thick.)

•Bake at 350° for 30 to 35 minutes or until a wooden pick inserted in center comes out clean. Cool in pans on wire racks 10

minutes; remove from pans, and cool completely on wire racks.

•Working quickly, spread Favorite Caramel Frosting between layers and on top and sides of cake. Yield: 12 servings.

Per serving: Calories 716 Fat 30.6g
Cholesterol 162mg Sodium 459mg

Favorite Caramel Frosting

3 cups sugar, divided
¾ cup milk
1 large egg, lightly beaten
Pinch of salt
½ cup butter or margarine, cut up

•Combine 2½ cups sugar, milk, egg, and salt in a bowl, stirring well; stir in butter.

•Sprinkle remaining ½ cup sugar in a heavy 3½-quart saucepan; place over medium-high heat. Cook, stirring constantly, until sugar melts and syrup is light golden brown (about 6 minutes). Remove from heat. Stir butter mixture into hot caramelized sugar. (The sugar will lump, becoming smooth with further cooking.)

•Cook sugar mixture over medium heat until a candy thermometer registers 235° (18 to 24 minutes), stirring often. Cool mixture 5 minutes.

•Beat frosting with a wooden spoon to almost spreading consistency (5 to 10 minutes). Immediately spread frosting on cake. Yield: 2½ cups.

Boston Cream Pie

◄ FAMILY FAVORITE ►
◄ MAKE AHEAD ►

PREP: 40 MINUTES   COOK: 36 MINUTES
CHILL: 1 HOUR

Traditionally called a pie, this is really a two-layer cake filled with thick custard and topped with a slick layer of chocolate.

½ cup butter or margarine, softened
1 cup sugar
3 large eggs
2 cups sifted cake flour
2 teaspoons baking powder
¼ teaspoon salt
½ cup milk
2 teaspoons vanilla extract
½ teaspoon butter flavoring (optional)
Cream Filling
Chocolate Glaze (page 132)

•Beat butter at medium speed with an electric mixer until creamy; gradually add sugar, beating 5 to 7 minutes. Add eggs, one at a time, beating after each addition.
•Combine flour, baking powder, and salt; add to butter mixture alternately with milk, beginning and ending with flour mixture. Mix at low speed after each addition until blended. Stir in flavorings.
•Pour batter into two greased and floured 9-inch round cakepans. Bake at 350° for 18 to 20 minutes or until a wooden pick inserted in center comes out clean. Cool in pans on wire racks 10 minutes; remove from pans, and cool completely on wire racks.
•Spread Cream Filling between cake layers. Spread Chocolate Glaze over top of cake, letting excess drip down sides. Chill at least 1 hour. Store in refrigerator. Yield: 12 servings.

Per serving: Calories 267 Fat 11.2g
Cholesterol 111mg Sodium 307mg

Cream Filling

½ cup sugar
3 tablespoons cornstarch
¼ teaspoon salt
2 cups milk
4 egg yolks, lightly beaten
1 teaspoon vanilla extract

•Combine first 3 ingredients in a heavy saucepan. Add milk and egg yolks; stir with a wire whisk until blended. Cook over medium heat, stirring constantly, until mixture comes to a boil. Boil 1 minute or until thickened, stirring constantly; remove from heat. Stir in vanilla. Cool. Yield: 2¼ cups.

Hummingbird Cake

◄ FAMILY FAVORITE ►

PREP: 25 MINUTES   COOK: 30 MINUTES

We couldn't leave out the most requested recipe in Southern Living *history. It frequents covered dish dinners all across the South.*

3 cups all-purpose flour
1 teaspoon baking soda
1 teaspoon salt
2 cups sugar
1 teaspoon ground cinnamon
3 large eggs, beaten
1 cup vegetable oil
1½ teaspoons vanilla extract
1 (8-ounce) can crushed pineapple, undrained
1 cup chopped pecans
2 cups chopped bananas
Cream Cheese Frosting (page 129)
½ cup chopped pecans

•Combine first 5 ingredients in a large bowl; add eggs and oil, stirring until dry ingredients are moistened. (Do not beat.) Stir in vanilla, pineapple, 1 cup pecans, and bananas.
•Pour batter into three greased and floured 9-inch round cakepans. Bake at 350° for 25 to 30 minutes or until a wooden pick inserted in center comes out clean. Cool in pans on wire racks 10 minutes; remove from pans, and cool completely on wire racks.
•Spread Cream Cheese Frosting between layers and on top and sides of cake; sprinkle ½ cup chopped pecans on top. Store in refrigerator. Yield: 16 servings.

Per serving: Calories 642 Fat 34.2g
Cholesterol 71mg Sodium 312mg

Light Hummingbird Cake

◄ HEALTHY ►

PREP: 15 MINUTES   COOK: 25 MINUTES

Here's a lightened version of the ever-popular Hummingbird Cake at left. Some of our staff members like it even better than the traditional version.

Vegetable cooking spray
3 cups plus 2 teaspoons all-purpose flour, divided
1 teaspoon baking soda
½ teaspoon salt
1¾ cups sugar
1 teaspoon ground cinnamon
2 large eggs, lightly beaten
½ cup unsweetened applesauce
3 tablespoons vegetable oil
1¾ cups mashed banana
1½ teaspoons vanilla extract
1 (8-ounce) can crushed pineapple in juice, undrained
Light Cream Cheese Frosting (page 129)

•Coat three 9-inch round cakepans with cooking spray; sprinkle 2 teaspoons flour into pans, and shake to coat. Set aside.
•Combine remaining 3 cups flour, soda, and next 3 ingredients in a large bowl. Combine eggs, applesauce, and oil; add to flour mixture, stirring just until dry ingredients are moistened. (Do not beat.) Stir in banana, vanilla, and pineapple.
•Pour batter into prepared pans. Bake at 350° for 23 to 25 minutes or until a wooden pick inserted in center comes out clean. Cool in pans on wire racks 10 minutes; remove from pans, and cool completely on wire racks. Spread Light Cream Cheese Frosting between layers and on top and sides of cake. Store in refrigerator. Yield: 16 servings.

Per serving: Calories 433 Fat 11.3g
Cholesterol 39mg Sodium 195mg

Italian Cream Cake

PREP: 24 MINUTES   COOK: 25 MINUTES

A light brushing of rum on these coconutty cake layers seals in moistness. It's a very rich cake, ideal for a special occasion.

1 cup butter or margarine, softened
2 cups sugar
5 large eggs, separated
2½ cups all-purpose flour
1 teaspoon baking soda
1 cup buttermilk
⅔ cup finely chopped pecans
1 (3½-ounce) can flaked coconut
1 teaspoon vanilla extract
½ teaspoon cream of tartar
3 tablespoons light rum
Deluxe Pecan-Cream Cheese Frosting
   (page 129)

•Grease three 9-inch round cakepans; line with wax paper. Grease and flour wax paper. Set aside.
•Beat butter at medium speed with an electric mixer until creamy; gradually add sugar, beating well. Add egg yolks, one at a time, beating after each addition.
•Combine flour and soda; add to butter mixture alternately with buttermilk, beginning and ending with flour mixture. Mix at low speed after each addition until blended. Stir in pecans, coconut, and vanilla.
•Beat egg whites at high speed until foamy. Add cream of tartar; beat until stiff peaks form. Gently fold egg whites into batter. Pour batter into prepared pans.
•Bake at 350° for 25 minutes or until a wooden pick inserted in center comes out clean. Cool in pans on wire racks 10 minutes; remove from pans, and peel off wax paper. Cool layers completely on wire racks.
•Sprinkle each cake layer with 1 tablespoon rum. Let stand 10 minutes. Spread Deluxe Pecan-Cream Cheese Frosting between layers and on top and sides of cake. Store in refrigerator. Yield: 16 servings.
Per serving: Calories 793 Fat 43.4g
Cholesterol 143mg Sodium 366mg

Black Walnut Cake

PREP: 22 MINUTES   COOK: 25 MINUTES

Crunchy black walnuts dot the layers and the frosting of this impressive cake.

½ cup butter or margarine, softened
½ cup shortening
2 cups sugar
5 large eggs, separated
1 cup buttermilk
1 teaspoon baking soda
2 cups all-purpose flour
1 teaspoon vanilla extract
1 cup chopped black walnuts
1 (3½-ounce) can flaked coconut
½ teaspoon cream of tartar
Deluxe Cream Cheese Frosting
   (page 129)
1 cup chopped black walnuts

•Beat butter and shortening at medium speed with an electric mixer until creamy; gradually add sugar, beating well. Add egg yolks, one at a time, beating after each addition.
•Combine buttermilk and soda; stir until soda dissolves.
•Add flour to butter mixture alternately with buttermilk mixture, beginning and ending with flour. Mix at low speed after each addition until blended. Stir in vanilla, 1 cup walnuts, and coconut.
•Beat egg whites at high speed until foamy. Add cream of tartar; beat until stiff peaks form. Gently fold egg whites into batter. Pour batter into three greased and floured 9-inch round cakepans.
•Bake at 350° for 22 to 25 minutes or until a wooden pick inserted in center comes out clean. Cool in pans on wire racks 10 minutes; remove from pans, and cool completely on wire racks.
•Spread Deluxe Cream Cheese Frosting between layers and on top and sides of cake; press remaining 1 cup walnuts onto sides of cake. Store in refrigerator. Yield: 16 servings.
Per serving: Calories 742 Fat 39.7g
Cholesterol 127mg Sodium 307mg

Stately Coconut Layer Cake

PREP: 40 MINUTES   COOK: 25 MINUTES

1 cup shortening
2 cups sugar
4 large eggs
3 cups sifted cake flour
2½ teaspoons baking powder
½ teaspoon salt
1 cup milk
1 teaspoon almond extract
1 teaspoon vanilla extract
Lemon-Orange Filling (page 132) or
   Pineapple Filling (page 132)
Boiled Frosting (page 129)
1 small fresh coconut, grated, or ½ cup
   flaked coconut

•Beat shortening at medium speed with an electric mixer until fluffy; gradually add sugar, beating well. Add eggs, one at a time, beating after each addition.
•Combine flour, baking powder, and salt; add to shortening mixture alternately with milk, beginning and ending with flour mixture. Mix at low speed after each addition until blended. Stir in flavorings.
•Pour batter into three greased and floured 9-inch round cakepans. Bake at 375° for 20 to 25 minutes or until a wooden pick inserted in center comes out clean. Cool in pans on wire racks 10 minutes; remove from pans, and cool completely on wire racks.
•Spread Lemon-Orange Filling between layers; spread Boiled Frosting on top and sides of cake, and sprinkle with coconut. Yield: 16 servings.
Per serving: Calories 460 Fat 14.9g
Cholesterol 110mg Sodium 239mg

Coconut Cream Cake

◄ MAKE AHEAD ►

PREP: 30 MINUTES   COOK: 28 MINUTES

Here's a festive dessert for the holidays.

1 cup butter, softened
2 cups sugar
3 large eggs
3 cups all-purpose flour
2 teaspoons baking powder
1 cup milk
1 teaspoon vanilla extract
½ teaspoon butter flavoring
½ cup water
1 tablespoon sugar
Coconut Frosting
3 cups flaked coconut

•Beat butter at medium speed with an electric mixer until creamy; gradually add 2 cups sugar, beating well. Add eggs, one at a time, beating after each addition.
•Combine flour and baking powder; add to butter mixture alternately with milk, beginning and ending with flour mixture. Mix at low speed after each addition until blended. Stir in flavorings. Pour batter into three greased and floured 9-inch round cakepans.
•Bake at 350° for 25 to 28 minutes or until a wooden pick inserted in center comes out clean. Cool in pans on wire racks 10 minutes; remove from pans, and cool completely on wire racks.
•Combine water and 1 tablespoon sugar in a small saucepan; bring to a boil. Reduce heat, and simmer 3 minutes. Spoon sugar mixture over cake layers.
•Stack layers, spreading about 1 cup Coconut Frosting between layers, and sprinkling ½ cup coconut on frosting between layers. Spread remaining Coconut Frosting on top and sides of cake, and sprinkle with remaining coconut. Store in refrigerator. Yield: 16 servings.
Per serving: Calories 509 Fat 30.4g
Cholesterol 114mg Sodium 240mg

Coconut Frosting

2 cups whipping cream
½ cup sifted powdered sugar
1 teaspoon vanilla extract
1 teaspoon coconut extract
2 drops of butter flavoring

•Combine all ingredients in a medium bowl; beat at medium speed with an electric mixer until soft peaks form. Yield: 4 cups.

Peppermint Candy Cake

PREP: 45 MINUTES   COOK: 45 MINUTES

Use your peppermint Christmas candy for this holiday cake. Seal candy in a zip-top plastic bag; gently crush with a rolling pin.

⅔ cup shortening
1¾ cups sugar
3 cups sifted cake flour
3½ teaspoons baking powder
½ teaspoon salt
1⅓ cups milk
1 teaspoon vanilla extract
4 egg whites
Peppermint Filling
1 cup crushed hard peppermint candy (about 36 candies), divided
½ recipe Boiled Frosting (page 129)

•Beat shortening at medium speed with an electric mixer until fluffy; gradually add sugar, beating at medium speed 5 to 7 minutes.
•Combine flour, baking powder, and salt; add to shortening mixture alternately with milk, beginning and ending with flour mixture. Mix at low speed after each addition until blended. Stir in vanilla.
•Beat egg whites at high speed until stiff peaks form. Gently fold into batter.
•Pour batter into three greased and floured 8-inch round cakepans. Bake at 350° for 25 to 27 minutes or until a wooden pick inserted in center comes out clean. Cool in pans on wire racks 10 minutes; remove from pans, and cool 10 more minutes on wire racks. While warm, prick cake layers at 1-inch intervals with a fork.
•Place 1 cake layer on a cake plate; pour one-third of Peppermint Filling over layer, and sprinkle with ¼ cup peppermint candy. Repeat with remaining layers, but don't sprinkle top layer with candy. Frost top and sides with Boiled Frosting; then sprinkle top and sides with remaining ½ cup peppermint candy. Yield: 16 servings.
Per serving: Calories 407 Fat 12.5g
Cholesterol 14mg Sodium 246mg

Peppermint Filling

⅓ cup butter or margarine
1 cup sugar
⅓ cup milk
½ teaspoon peppermint extract

•Melt butter in a small saucepan. Add sugar, milk, and peppermint extract; bring to a boil over medium heat, stirring constantly. Boil 1 minute, stirring constantly. Yield: 1⅓ cups.

Sour Cream-Spice Layer Cake

PREP: 40 MINUTES   COOK: 28 MINUTES

A white sour cream frosting drizzled with melted chocolate dresses these spiced cake layers in fine fashion.

½ cup butter or margarine, softened
1¼ cups firmly packed brown sugar
3 large eggs
1¾ cups all-purpose flour
2 teaspoons baking powder
½ teaspoon baking soda
¼ teaspoon salt
1 teaspoon ground cinnamon
½ teaspoon ground allspice
½ teaspoon ground nutmeg
¾ cup sour cream
½ cup finely chopped pecans or walnuts
1 (1-ounce) square unsweetened chocolate
1 teaspoon butter or margarine
Sour Cream Frosting (page 128)
Garnish: pecan or walnut halves

•Beat ½ cup butter at medium speed with an electric mixer until creamy; gradually add brown sugar, beating at medium speed 5 to 7 minutes. Add eggs, one at a time, beating after each addition.
•Combine flour and next 6 ingredients; add to butter mixture alternately with sour cream, beginning and ending with flour mixture. Mix at low speed after each addition until blended. Stir in ½ cup pecans. Pour batter into two greased and floured 8-inch round cakepans.
•Bake at 350° for 28 minutes or until a wooden pick inserted in center comes out clean. Cool layers in pans on wire racks 10

minutes; remove from pans, and cool completely on wire racks.

•Combine chocolate and 1 teaspoon butter in a small saucepan. Cook over low heat until chocolate and butter melt, stirring often; cool. Spread Sour Cream Frosting between layers and on top and sides of cake. Drizzle melted chocolate mixture on top of cake. Garnish, if desired. Store in refrigerator. Yield: 12 servings.

Per serving: Calories 596 Fat 29.4g
Cholesterol 111mg Sodium 318mg

Spicy Jam Cake

PREP: 1 HOUR

COOK: 1 HOUR AND 20 MINUTES

A jar of strawberry preserves is stirred into this speckled and spiced cake batter. A cooked caramel frosting is this cake's perfect complement.

1 cup shortening
2 cups sugar
3 large eggs
3 cups all-purpose flour, divided
1 teaspoon ground cloves
1 teaspoon ground cinnamon
1 teaspoon ground allspice
1 teaspoon ground nutmeg
1 teaspoon baking soda
1 cup buttermilk
1 (12-ounce) jar strawberry preserves
2 cups chopped pecans
1 cup raisins
Caramel Frosting (page 130)

•Beat shortening at medium speed with an electric mixer until creamy; gradually add sugar, beating well. Add eggs, one at a time, beating after each addition.
•Combine 2¾ cups flour and spices. Dissolve soda in buttermilk. Add flour mixture to shortening mixture alternately with buttermilk mixture, beginning and ending with flour mixture. Mix at low speed after each addition until blended. Stir in preserves.
•Combine remaining ¼ cup flour, pecans, and raisins; toss well. Stir into batter.
•Pour batter into three greased and floured 9-inch round cakepans. Bake at 350° for 30 minutes or until a wooden pick inserted in center comes out almost clean. (Pans will be

full.) Cool in pans on wire racks 10 minutes; remove from pans, and cool completely on wire racks. Spread Caramel Frosting between layers and on top and sides of cake. Yield: 16 servings.

Per serving: Calories 924 Fat 47.7g
Cholesterol 112mg Sodium 360mg

Fig Preserves Cake

PREP: 15 MINUTES

COOK: 1 HOUR AND 10 MINUTES

This is a wonderful autumn dessert. Find fig preserves on the grocery aisle with jams and jellies unless you're lucky enough to have some home-canned preserves.

1½ cups sugar
2 cups all-purpose flour
1 teaspoon baking soda
½ teaspoon salt
1 teaspoon ground nutmeg
1 teaspoon ground cinnamon
1½ teaspoons ground allspice
¼ teaspoon ground cloves
1 cup vegetable oil
3 large eggs
1 cup buttermilk
1 tablespoon vanilla extract
1 (11.5-ounce) jar fig preserves (about 1 cup)
1 cup chopped pecans
Buttermilk Glaze (page 132)

•Combine first 8 ingredients in a large mixing bowl; add oil and eggs, beating at medium speed with an electric mixer until blended. Add buttermilk and vanilla, beating well. Stir in preserves and pecans.
•Pour batter into a greased and floured 10-inch tube pan. Bake at 350° for 1 hour and 10 minutes or until a wooden pick inserted in center comes out clean. Cool in pan on a wire rack 10 minutes; remove from pan, and place on a serving plate. Pour Buttermilk Glaze over cake while both are still warm. Yield: 16 servings.

Per serving: Calories 491 Fat 26g
Cholesterol 56mg Sodium 299mg

Sweet Potato Cake

PREP: 12 MINUTES

COOK: 1 HOUR AND 30 MINUTES

⅔ cup butter or margarine, softened
2 cups sugar
4 large eggs, separated
1 cup mashed, cooked sweet potato
2 cups all-purpose flour
1 teaspoon baking soda
½ teaspoon salt
2 tablespoons cocoa
1 teaspoon ground allspice
1 teaspoon ground cinnamon
1 teaspoon ground cloves
1 teaspoon ground nutmeg
1 cup buttermilk
1 teaspoon vanilla extract
1½ cups raisins
2 cups chopped pecans
Sifted powdered sugar (optional)

•Beat butter at medium speed with an electric mixer until creamy; gradually add 2 cups sugar, beating well. Add egg yolks, one at a time, beating after each addition. Add sweet potato to mixture, mixing well.
•Combine flour and next 7 ingredients; add to butter mixture alternately with buttermilk, beginning and ending with flour mixture. Mix at low speed after each addition until blended. Stir in vanilla, raisins, and pecans.
•Beat egg whites at high speed until stiff peaks form; fold into batter. Spoon batter into a greased and floured 10-inch tube pan.
•Bake at 325° for 1 hour and 25 to 30 minutes or until a wooden pick inserted in center comes out clean. Cool in pan on a wire rack 10 minutes; remove from pan, and cool completely on wire rack. Sprinkle with powdered sugar, if desired. Yield: 16 servings.

Per serving: Calories 399 Fat 19.6g
Cholesterol 74mg Sodium 239mg

**Bourbon-Laced
Lady Baltimore Cake**

Caption: Bourbon-Laced
Lady Baltimore Cake

Bourbon-Laced
Lady Baltimore Cake

PREP: 35 MINUTES

COOK: 1 HOUR AND 8 MINUTES

This is a glorious four-layer towering cake, so have plates ready for tall slices!

1 cup butter or margarine, softened
2 cups sugar
3½ cups sifted cake flour
1 tablespoon plus ½ teaspoon baking powder
¾ teaspoon salt
1 cup milk
1 teaspoon vanilla extract
8 egg whites
Coconut-Bourbon Filling (page 133)
Boiled Frosting (page 129)

•Grease four 9-inch round cakepans; line with wax paper. Grease and flour wax paper.

•Beat butter at medium speed with an electric mixer until creamy; gradually add sugar, beating well.
•Combine flour, baking powder, and salt; add to butter mixture alternately with milk, beginning and ending with flour mixture. Mix at low speed after each addition until blended. Stir in vanilla.
•Beat egg whites at high speed until stiff peaks form. Gently fold into flour mixture. Pour batter into prepared pans.
•Bake at 375° for 20 minutes or until a wooden pick inserted in center comes out clean. Cool in pans on wire racks 10 minutes; remove from pans, and peel off wax paper. Cool layers completely on wire racks.
•Spread Coconut-Bourbon Filling between layers and on top of cake. Spread Boiled Frosting on sides of cake. Yield: 20 servings.
Per serving: Calories 662 Fat 29.3g
Cholesterol 176mg Sodium 458mg

Lord Baltimore Cake

PREP: 50 MINUTES   COOK: 40 MINUTES

Crumbled macaroons give this imperial cake added texture and an almond essence.

¾ cup shortening
2¼ cups sugar
8 egg yolks
3¾ cups sifted cake flour
1½ tablespoons baking powder
½ teaspoon salt
1¾ cups milk
½ teaspoon almond extract
½ teaspoon vanilla extract
½ teaspoon coconut extract
Boiled Frosting (page 129)
1 cup chopped mixed candied fruit
1 cup chopped pecans or walnuts
½ cup macaroon crumbs (about 3 cookies)
1 teaspoon vanilla extract
½ teaspoon almond extract

•Beat shortening at medium speed with an electric mixer until fluffy; gradually add sugar, beating at medium speed 5 to 7 minutes. Add egg yolks, one at a time, beating after each addition.

•Combine flour, baking powder, and salt; add to shortening mixture alternately with milk, beginning and ending with flour mixture. Mix at low speed after each addition until blended. Stir in ½ teaspoon almond extract and ½ teaspoon vanilla. Pour batter into three greased and floured 9-inch round cakepans.

•Bake at 350° for 22 to 25 minutes or until a wooden pick inserted in center comes out clean. Cool in pans on wire racks 10 minutes; remove from pans, and cool completely on wire racks.

•Add coconut extract to Boiled Frosting for this cake. Combine 2 cups Boiled Frosting, candied fruit, and remaining ingredients; spread between layers. Spread remaining Boiled Frosting on top and sides of cake. Yield: 16 servings.

Per serving: Calories 587 Fat 23g
Cholesterol 112mg Sodium 254mg

Black Forest Cake

◀ FAMILY FAVORITE ▶
◀ MAKE AHEAD ▶

**PREP: 25 MINUTES   COOK: 35 MINUTES
CHILL: 8 HOURS**

2 cups sifted cake flour
1¼ teaspoons baking powder
¼ teaspoon baking soda
¾ teaspoon salt
2 cups sugar
¾ cup cocoa
½ cup shortening
½ cup sour cream, divided
½ cup milk
⅓ cup kirsch or other cherry-flavored brandy
2 large eggs
2 egg yolks
4 cups whipping cream
⅓ cup sifted powdered sugar
2 tablespoons kirsch or other cherry-flavored brandy
2 (21-ounce) cans cherry pie filling

•Grease two 9-inch round cakepans; line bottoms with wax paper. Grease and flour wax paper and sides of pans. Set aside.

•Combine first 6 ingredients in a large mixing bowl; stir well. Add shortening and ¼ cup sour cream. Beat at low speed with an electric mixer 30 seconds or until blended. Add remaining ¼ cup sour cream, milk, and ⅓ cup kirsch. Beat at medium speed 1½ minutes. Add eggs and egg yolks, one at a time, beating 20 seconds after each addition. Pour batter into prepared pans.

•Bake at 350° for 30 to 35 minutes or until a wooden pick inserted in center comes out clean. Cool in pans on wire racks 10 minutes; remove from pans. Peel off wax paper, and cool layers on wire racks.

•Split cake layers in half horizontally to make 4 layers. Position knife blade in food processor bowl. Break 1 cake layer into pieces, and place in processor bowl. Pulse 5 or 6 times or until cake resembles fine crumbs. Set crumbs aside.

•Beat whipping cream until foamy; gradually add powdered sugar, beating until soft peaks form. Add 2 tablespoons kirsch, beating until stiff peaks form. Reserve 1½ cups whipped cream mixture for garnish.

•Place 1 cake layer on a cake plate, cut side up; spread with 1 cup whipped cream mixture, and top with 1 cup pie filling. Repeat procedure once, and top with remaining cake layer.

•Frost sides and top of cake with whipped cream mixture. Carefully pat cake crumbs generously around sides of frosted cake. Pipe or spoon reserved 1½ cups whipped cream mixture around top edges of cake; spoon 1 cup pie filling in center. (Reserve any remaining pie filling for another use.) Cover and chill cake 8 hours before serving. Store in refrigerator. Yield: 16 servings.

Per serving: Calories 555 Fat 31.1g
Cholesterol 140mg Sodium 196mg

Chocolate Kahlúa Cake

PREP: 40 MINUTES   COOK: 20 MINUTES

Chocolate-covered coffee beans make a tasteful garnish and hint at the coffee flavor in the cake layers.

¾ cup butter or margarine, softened
1¾ cups sugar
4 large eggs
¼ cup Kahlúa
2¼ cups all-purpose flour
1 teaspoon baking powder
½ teaspoon baking soda
¼ teaspoon salt
¾ cup milk
2 (1-ounce) squares unsweetened chocolate, melted and cooled
1 teaspoon vanilla extract
⅓ cup Kahlúa
¾ cup chopped hazelnuts or pecans, toasted and divided
Chocolate Kahlúa Frosting (page 128)
Garnish: chocolate-covered coffee beans

•Grease three 9-inch round cakepans; line with wax paper. Grease and flour wax paper. Set aside.

•Beat butter at medium speed with an electric mixer until creamy. Gradually add sugar, beating at medium speed 5 to 7 minutes. Add eggs, one at a time, beating after each addition. Add ¼ cup Kahlúa; beat until well blended.

•Combine flour and next 3 ingredients; add to butter mixture alternately with milk, beginning and ending with flour mixture. Mix at low speed after each addition until blended. Stir in chocolate and vanilla.

•Pour batter into prepared pans. Bake at 350° for 20 minutes or until a wooden pick inserted in center comes out clean. Cool in pans on wire racks 10 minutes; remove from pans. Peel off wax paper. Drizzle layers evenly with ⅓ cup Kahlúa. Cool completely on wire racks.

•Combine ½ cup hazelnuts and 1 cup Chocolate Kahlúa Frosting; spread between layers. Spread remaining frosting on top and sides of cake. Sprinkle remaining ¼ cup hazelnuts on top. Garnish, if desired. Store in refrigerator. Yield: 16 servings.

Per serving: Calories 548 Fat 27.6g
Cholesterol 101mg Sodium 270mg

Chocolate Fudge Cake

PREP: 1 HOUR   COOK: 40 MINUTES

CHILL: 30 MINUTES

Here's a light chocolate cake with a dense white filling and fudgelike frosting. It makes quite a statement when sliced.

⅓ cup half-and-half
2 (1-ounce) squares unsweetened chocolate, finely chopped
⅔ cup shortening
1¾ cups sugar
3 large eggs
2½ cups all-purpose flour
1 teaspoon baking soda
½ teaspoon salt
1 cup buttermilk
1 teaspoon vanilla extract
Fluffy White Filling
Chocolate Fudge Frosting

•Grease three 9-inch round cakepans; line with wax paper. Grease and flour wax paper. Set aside.
•Bring half-and-half to a simmer over medium heat. Remove from heat, and add chocolate. Let stand 1 minute. Stir gently until chocolate melts completely; cool.
•Beat shortening at medium speed with an electric mixer until fluffy. Gradually add sugar, beating at medium speed 5 to 7 minutes. Add eggs, one at a time, beating after each addition.
•Combine flour, soda, and salt; add to shortening mixture alternately with buttermilk, beginning and ending with flour mixture. Mix at low speed after each addition until blended. Stir in vanilla and cooled chocolate mixture.
•Pour batter into prepared pans. Bake at 350° for 20 minutes or until a wooden pick inserted in center comes out almost clean. Cool in pans on wire racks 10 minutes; remove from pans, and peel off wax paper. Cool layers completely on wire racks.
•Spread Fluffy White Filling between layers. Spread Chocolate Fudge Frosting on top and sides of cake. Store in refrigerator. Yield: 16 servings.
Per serving: Calories 606 Fat 31.5g
Cholesterol 77mg Sodium 321mg

Fluffy White Filling

¼ cup all-purpose flour
1 cup milk
½ cup butter or margarine, softened
½ cup shortening
1 cup sugar
¼ teaspoon salt
1 tablespoon vanilla extract

•Place flour in a small saucepan; gradually stir in milk. Cook over low heat, stirring constantly, until thickened. Remove from heat; cool, stirring occasionally.
•Beat butter and shortening at medium speed with an electric mixer until creamy; gradually add sugar, beating well. Add flour mixture, salt, and vanilla; beat until smooth. Cover and chill filling at least 30 minutes. Yield: 4 cups.

Chocolate Fudge Frosting

2 cups sugar
2 (1-ounce) squares unsweetened chocolate
½ cup milk
½ cup butter or margarine
1 teaspoon vanilla extract

•Combine first 4 ingredients in a heavy saucepan; cook over low heat, stirring constantly, until chocolate and butter melt. Cook over medium heat, stirring constantly, until mixture boils. Boil 1 minute, stirring constantly. Remove from heat; stir in vanilla.
•Place saucepan in a large bowl of ice. Beat chocolate mixture at high speed with an electric mixer until frosting is spreading consistency (about 15 minutes). Immediately spread on cake. Yield: 2¼ cups.

Sachertorte

PREP: 20 MINUTES   COOK: 25 MINUTES

STAND: 20 MINUTES

Frau Sacher, a famous Austrian restaurateur, gets credit for this sleek dark chocolate cake. Serve thin slivers of the cake topped with billows of whipped cream.

4 (1-ounce) squares semisweet chocolate
⅓ cup butter
4 egg yolks
½ cup sugar
5 egg whites
½ cup all-purpose flour
⅔ cup apricot preserves or jam
Bittersweet Glaze (page 132)
Unsweetened whipped cream (optional)

•Place chocolate and butter in top of a double boiler; bring water to a boil. Reduce heat to low; cook until chocolate melts. Remove from heat.
•Beat egg yolks until thick and pale. Gradually add sugar to egg yolks, beating continuously at medium speed with an electric mixer. Add chocolate mixture, beating just until blended.
•Beat egg whites at high speed until stiff peaks form; fold into chocolate mixture. Gently fold in flour. Pour batter into a greased and floured 9-inch round cakepan.
•Bake at 350° for 24 to 25 minutes or until a wooden pick inserted in center comes out clean. Cool in pan on a wire rack 10 minutes; remove from pan, and cool completely on wire rack.
•Carefully split cake in half horizontally to make 2 layers. Rub preserves through a sieve. Spread preserves between layers and on top of cake. Let stand 20 minutes. Pour Bittersweet Glaze over cake to cover completely. Serve with whipped cream, if desired. Yield: 10 servings.
Per serving: Calories 412 Fat 27.6g
Cholesterol 125mg Sodium 104mg

Petits Fours

PREP: 1 HOUR AND 20 MINUTES

COOK: 43 MINUTES

These petite cake squares are great for a wedding shower or baby shower.

1 cup shortening
2 cups sugar
3 cups all-purpose flour
2 teaspoons baking powder
¾ teaspoon salt
1 cup ice water
1½ teaspoons clear imitation butter flavor
1 teaspoon vanilla extract
¾ teaspoon almond extract
4 egg whites
½ teaspoon cream of tartar
10 cups sifted powdered sugar
1 cup water
3 tablespoons light corn syrup
1 teaspoon vanilla or almond extract
Creamy Decorator Frosting

•Beat shortening at medium speed with an electric mixer until fluffy; gradually add 2 cups sugar, beating well. Combine flour, baking powder, and salt; add to shortening mixture alternately with ice water, beginning and ending with flour mixture. Mix at low speed after each addition until blended. Stir in flavorings.

•Beat egg whites and cream of tartar at high speed until stiff peaks form. Gently fold one-third of beaten egg white into batter; fold in remaining beaten egg white. Pour batter into two greased and floured 8-inch square pans.

•Bake at 325° for 40 to 43 minutes. Cool in pans on wire racks 10 minutes; remove from pans, and cool completely on wire racks. Cover; freeze until firm.

•Trim crusts from all surfaces, making sure tops of cakes are flat. Cut each cake into 16 (1¾-inch) squares (photo 1); brush away loose crumbs. Place squares 2 inches apart on wire racks in a jellyroll pan.

•Combine powdered sugar and next 3 ingredients in a large saucepan; cook over low heat, stirring constantly, until smooth. Quickly pour warm icing over cake squares, completely covering top and sides (photo 2).

•Spoon up all excess icing; reheat until smooth. (If necessary, add a small amount of water to maintain icing's original consistency.) Continue pouring and reheating icing until all cakes have been iced twice. Let icing dry completely. Trim any excess icing from bottom of each cake square. Decorate as desired with Creamy Decorator Frosting. Yield: 32 petits fours.

Per serving: Calories 339 Fat 7.7g Cholesterol 0mg Sodium 95mg

Creamy Decorator Frosting

2 cups sifted powdered sugar
¼ cup plus 2 tablespoons shortening
2 tablespoons milk
½ teaspoon vanilla or almond extract
Dash of salt
Paste food coloring

•Combine first 5 ingredients in a small mixing bowl; beat at low speed with an electric mixer until smooth. Color frosting in small amounts with desired paste food coloring. (Keep frosting covered with a damp cloth or plastic wrap.) Yield: 1¼ cups.

1. Cut each cake into 16 squares, using a ruler for help. Brush away loose crumbs.

2. Place cake squares 2 inches apart on wire racks; quickly pour warm icing over squares, covering top and sides.

POUND CAKES

Pound cakes get their name from their original recipe—a pound each of butter, sugar, flour, and eggs. Today's pound cakes have lightened up a bit by weight, but still maintain that rich flavor and tender crumb.

To ensure the best-textured pound cake, always measure ingredients precisely and mix batter properly. A critical step is beating the butter or shortening and sugar until light and fluffy. This procedure takes about 5 minutes using an electric mixer and ingredients that have been at room temperature for 20 minutes. When adding eggs, flour, and liquid to a recipe, mix just until blended. Overbeating can cause the cake to be tough.

Old-Fashioned Pound Cake

◀ FAMILY FAVORITE ▶

PREP: 20 MINUTES

COOK: 1 HOUR AND 20 MINUTES

2 cups butter, softened
2¾ cups sugar
6 large eggs
3¾ cups all-purpose flour
⅛ teaspoon salt
¼ teaspoon ground nutmeg
½ cup milk
1 teaspoon vanilla extract

•Beat butter at medium speed with an electric mixer 2 minutes or until creamy (photo 1). Gradually add sugar, beating 5 to 7 minutes (photo 2). Add eggs, one at a time, beating just until yellow disappears (photo 3).

•Combine flour, salt, and nutmeg in a large bowl; add to butter mixture alternately with milk (photo 4), beginning and ending with flour mixture.

•Mix at low speed after each addition just until mixture is blended. Stir in vanilla. Spoon batter into a greased and floured 10-inch tube pan (photo 5).

•Bake at 325° for 1 hour and 15 to 20 minutes or until a wooden pick inserted in center comes out clean. Cool in pan on a wire rack 10 to 15 minutes; remove from pan, and cool completely on wire rack. Yield: 14 servings.

Per serving: Calories 538 Fat 29.3g Cholesterol 163mg Sodium 321mg

1. Beat butter at medium speed with an electric mixer until creamy.

2. Gradually add sugar, beating well.

3. Add eggs, one at a time, beating just until yellow disappears.

4. Add milk to butter mixture alternately with flour mixture.

5. Spoon thick batter into greased and floured tube pan, and bake.

Buttermilk Pound Cake

◄ FAMILY FAVORITE ►

PREP: 20 MINUTES   COOK: 1 HOUR

Buttermilk lends a tangy bonus to this homey cake.

½ cup butter or margarine, softened
½ cup shortening
2 cups sugar
4 large eggs
½ teaspoon baking soda
1 cup buttermilk
3 cups all-purpose flour
⅛ teaspoon salt
2 teaspoons lemon extract
1 teaspoon almond extract

•Beat butter and shortening at medium speed with an electric mixer 2 minutes or until creamy. Gradually add sugar, beating 5 to 7 minutes. Add eggs, one at a time, beating just until yellow disappears.
•Dissolve soda in buttermilk. Combine flour and salt; add to butter mixture alternately with buttermilk, beginning and ending with flour mixture. Mix at low speed after each addition just until blended. Stir in flavorings.
•Pour batter into a greased and floured 10-inch tube pan. Bake at 350° for 1 hour or until a wooden pick inserted in center comes out clean. Cool in pan on a wire rack 10 to 15 minutes; remove from pan, and cool completely on wire rack. Yield: 14 servings.
Per serving: Calories 349 Fat 14.7g
Cholesterol 79mg Sodium 154mg

Note: Cake may also be baked in two 9- x 5-inch loafpans. Bake at 350° for 45 to 50 minutes.

Chocolate Marble Pound Cake: Melt 1 tablespoon shortening and 1 (1-ounce) square unsweetened chocolate in a saucepan, stirring until smooth. Set aside. Prepare batter for Buttermilk Pound Cake, using vanilla extract in place of lemon extract. Remove 2 cups of batter; add chocolate mixture, stirring until blended. Spoon one-third of remaining plain batter into a greased and floured 10-inch tube pan; top with half of chocolate batter. Repeat layers, ending with plain batter. Swirl batter with a knife to create a marbled effect. Bake as directed above.

Chocolate Pound Cake

◄ FAMILY FAVORITE ►

PREP: 25 MINUTES
COOK: 1 HOUR AND 15 MINUTES

Cocoa gives this easy chocolate pound cake rich flavor. It's equally good with or without the glaze.

½ cup shortening
1 cup butter or margarine, softened
3 cups sugar
5 large eggs
3 cups all-purpose flour
½ teaspoon baking powder
½ teaspoon salt
½ cup cocoa
1¼ cups milk
1 teaspoon vanilla extract
Chocolate Glaze (page 132, optional)
Chopped pecans (optional)

•Beat shortening and butter at medium speed with an electric mixer 2 minutes or until creamy. Gradually add sugar, beating 5 to 7 minutes. Add eggs, one at a time, beating just until yellow disappears.
•Sift flour, baking powder, salt, and cocoa together. Add to butter mixture alternately with milk, beginning and ending with flour mixture. Mix at low speed after each addition just until blended. Stir in vanilla.
•Pour batter into a greased and floured 10-inch tube pan. Bake at 350° for 1 hour and 15 minutes or until a wooden pick inserted in center comes out clean. Cool in pan on a wire rack 10 to 15 minutes; remove from pan, and cool completely on wire rack.
•Spoon Chocolate Glaze over top of cake, if desired, allowing it to drizzle down sides. Sprinkle top of cake with chopped pecans, if desired. Yield: 14 servings.
Per serving: Calories 483 Fat 22.6g
Cholesterol 114mg Sodium 253mg

Coconut Pound Cake

PREP: 25 MINUTES
COOK: 1 HOUR AND 25 MINUTES

Flaked coconut makes this pound cake very tender. Slice the cake carefully with a serrated cake knife.

1½ cups shortening
2¼ cups sugar
5 large eggs
3 cups sifted cake flour
¼ teaspoon salt
1 cup milk
1 (7-ounce) can flaked coconut
    (2 cups)

•Beat shortening at medium speed with an electric mixer 2 minutes or until fluffy. Gradually add sugar, beating 5 to 7 minutes. Add eggs, one at a time, beating just until yellow disappears.
•Combine flour and salt; add to shortening mixture alternately with milk, beginning and ending with flour mixture. Mix at low speed after each addition just until blended. Stir in coconut. Pour batter into a greased and floured 10-inch tube pan.
•Bake at 325° for 1 hour and 25 minutes or until a wooden pick inserted in center comes out clean. Cool in pan on a wire rack 15 minutes; remove from pan, and cool completely on wire rack. Yield: 14 servings.
Per serving: Calories 471 Fat 26g
Cholesterol 78mg Sodium 111mg

QUICK-FIX DESSERT

Keep a pound cake (or half a pound cake) in your freezer, and dessert is only moments away. Just slice it, and toast or grill the slices. Then top it with sliced fresh fruit, whipped cream, or ice cream.

Bourbon-Pecan Pound Cake

PREP: 17 MINUTES

COOK: 1 HOUR AND 15 MINUTES

Here's a nutty spiked pound cake for the holiday season.

1 cup shortening
2½ cups sugar
6 large eggs
3 cups all-purpose flour
2 teaspoons baking powder
½ teaspoon salt
½ teaspoon ground nutmeg
1 (8-ounce) carton sour cream
½ cup bourbon
1 cup finely chopped pecans
Glaze

•Beat shortening at medium speed with an electric mixer about 2 minutes or until fluffy. Gradually add sugar, beating 5 to 7 minutes. Add eggs, one at a time, beating just until yellow disappears.
•Combine flour and next 3 ingredients in a bowl; stir gently.
•Combine sour cream and bourbon; add to shortening mixture alternately with flour mixture, beginning and ending with flour mixture.
•Mix at low speed after each addition just until blended. Stir in chopped pecans. Pour batter into a greased and floured 10-inch tube pan.
•Bake at 325° for 1 hour and 15 minutes or until a wooden pick inserted in center comes out clean. Cool in pan on a wire rack 10 to 15 minutes; remove from pan, and cool completely on wire rack.
•Spoon Glaze over top of cooled cake, allowing it to drizzle down sides of cake. Yield: 16 servings.
Per serving: Calories 475 Fat 21g
Cholesterol 86mg Sodium 155mg

Glaze

2¼ cups sifted powdered sugar
2 tablespoons bourbon
2 tablespoons water

•Combine all ingredients in a bowl; stir well. Yield: ⅔ cup.

FRUIT & NUT CAKES

When the holiday season rolls around, one cake in particular comes to mind—fruitcake. Its batter is dense, laden with chopped fruit and nuts. Most fruitcakes bake long and slow and can be made several weeks in advance. This allows you time to soak the cake with brandy to keep it moist and flavorful for its debut.

We offer three different fruitcakes here. Light Fruitcake is the most traditional cake and is light in color only. Japanese Fruitcake is a spiced two-toned layer cake with a translucent coconutty frosting. And The Compromise Cake will convert nonfruitcake eaters with its subtle fruitcake connection.

Japanese Fruitcake

PREP: 30 MINUTES   COOK: 20 MINUTES

A pearly white frosting thinly veils this cake.

1 cup butter or margarine, softened
2 cups sugar
4 large eggs
3¼ cups all-purpose flour
2 teaspoons baking powder
1 cup milk
1 teaspoon vanilla extract
1 teaspoon ground cinnamon
1 teaspoon ground allspice
½ teaspoon ground cloves
1 cup raisins
Lemon-Coconut Frosting

•Beat butter at medium speed with an electric mixer until creamy. Gradually add sugar, beating well. Add eggs, one at a time, beating after each addition.
•Combine flour and baking powder; add to butter mixture alternately with milk, beginning and ending with flour mixture. Mix at low speed after each addition until blended. Add vanilla, stirring to blend. Pour one-third of batter into a greased and floured 9-inch round cakepan.

•Stir cinnamon and next 3 ingredients into remaining batter; pour mixture into two greased and floured 9-inch round cakepans.
•Bake at 350° for 20 minutes or until center of cake springs back when lightly touched. (Do not overbake.) Cool in pans on wire racks 10 minutes; remove from pans, and cool completely on wire racks. Spread Lemon-Coconut Frosting between layers and on top and sides of cake, stacking white layer between spiced layers. Yield: 16 servings.
Per serving: Calories 556 Fat 22g
Cholesterol 86mg Sodium 250mg

Lemon-Coconut Frosting

2 tablespoons cornstarch
1½ cups water, divided
2 cups sugar
1 tablespoon grated lemon rind
3½ tablespoons fresh lemon juice
3½ cups frozen flaked coconut, thawed

•Combine cornstarch and ½ cup water, stirring until smooth; set aside.
•Bring remaining 1 cup water to a boil in a medium saucepan. Stir in sugar, lemon rind, and lemon juice. Return to a boil, and cook until mixture reaches soft ball stage or candy thermometer registers 236°, stirring often.

• Gradually stir in cornstarch mixture; cook, stirring constantly, over medium heat about 10 minutes or until thickened. Remove from heat; stir in coconut. Cool. Stir frosting just before spreading on cake. Yield: 2½ cups.

Light Fruitcake

◄ MAKE AHEAD ►

PREP: 1 HOUR AND 15 MINUTES
COOK: 4 HOURS

Light in color only, this fruitcake's decadent in flavor. You can make it up to three weeks in advance, dousing it with brandy each week for added flavor.

1½ cups butter, softened
1½ cups sugar
1 tablespoon vanilla extract
1 tablespoon lemon extract
7 large eggs, separated
3 cups all-purpose flour
1½ pounds diced yellow, green, and red candied pineapple (about 3 cups)
1 pound red and green candied cherries (about 2 cups)
¼ pound diced candied citron (about ½ cup)
½ pound golden raisins (about 1½ cups)
3 cups pecan halves
1 cup black walnuts, coarsely chopped
½ cup all-purpose flour
Additional candied fruit and nuts (optional)
¼ cup brandy
Additional brandy (optional)

• Draw a circle with a 10-inch diameter on a piece of brown paper or parchment paper, using a tube pan as a guide. (Do not use recycled paper.) Cut out circle; set tube pan insert in center, and draw around inside tube. Cut out smaller circle. Grease paper, and set aside. Heavily grease and flour 10-inch tube pan; set aside.
• Beat butter at medium speed with an electric mixer until creamy; gradually add sugar, beating well. Stir in flavorings. Beat egg yolks; alternately add yolks and 3 cups flour to butter mixture. Mix at low speed after each addition until blended.
• Combine candied pineapple and next 5 ingredients in a bowl; dredge with ½ cup flour, stirring to coat well. Stir mixture into batter. Beat egg whites at high speed until stiff peaks form; fold into batter.
• Spoon batter into prepared pan. Arrange additional candied fruit and nuts on top of batter, if desired. Cover pan with 10-inch brown paper or parchment paper circle, greased side down.
• Bake at 250° for 4 hours or until a wooden pick inserted in center comes out clean. Remove from oven. Take off paper cover, and slowly pour ¼ cup brandy evenly over cake; cool cake completely on a wire rack.
• Loosen cake from sides of pan, using a narrow metal spatula; invert pan, and remove cake. Invert cake again onto wire rack. Wrap cake in brandy-soaked cheesecloth. Store in an airtight container in a cool place up to 3 weeks. Pour a small amount of brandy evenly over cake each week, if desired. Yield: 24 servings.
Per serving: Calories 567 Fat 25.8g
Cholesterol 93mg Sodium 167mg

The Compromise Cake

PREP: 15 MINUTES   COOK: 1 HOUR

This isn't your traditional fruitcake. The recipe replaces the alcohol and candied fruit with dried fruit, spices, and a hint of chocolate.

1½ cups applesauce
1½ teaspoons baking soda
1 cup raisins
1 cup chopped dates
1 cup chopped pecans
½ cup shortening
1⅓ cups sugar
1 teaspoon vanilla extract
2 large eggs
2 cups sifted cake flour
2 tablespoons unsweetened cocoa
½ teaspoon salt
½ teaspoon ground cinnamon
½ teaspoon ground cloves
½ teaspoon ground nutmeg

• Grease a 10-inch tube pan; line bottom of pan with wax paper. Set aside.
• Combine applesauce and soda; let stand 10 minutes. Combine raisins, dates, and pecans; set mixture aside.

• Beat shortening at medium speed with an electric mixer until fluffy; gradually add sugar, beating well. Add vanilla and eggs, one at a time, beating after each addition.
• Combine flour and remaining 5 ingredients. Add ½ flour mixture to raisin mixture; toss gently, and set aside. Gradually add remaining flour mixture to shortening mixture, mixing well. Add applesauce mixture and raisin mixture, mixing well.
• Pour batter into prepared tube pan. Bake at 350° for 30 minutes. Reduce temperature to 325°, and bake 30 more minutes or until a wooden pick inserted in center of cake comes out clean. Cool cake in pan on a wire rack 15 minutes; remove from pan, and peel off wax paper. Cool completely on wire rack. Yield: 24 servings.
Per serving: Calories 188 Fat 7.7g
Cholesterol 18mg Sodium 107mg

THE STORY OF COMPROMISE

For years, holiday baking brought a little tension to Frances Crum's grandparents' kitchen. Her grandfather insisted on a traditional fruitcake moistened with alcohol. Her grandmother wanted no candied fruit and declared alcohol was out of the question. Wanting to keep peace in the family, they talked the situation over and created The Compromise Cake. Four generations now know the secret to the recipe as well as to a good marriage.

CAKES FROM MIXES

Keep a few packages of cake mix on hand for occasions when you're short on time and ingredients. These recipes add just a few extras to the mix, and the results will win you compliments galore. You may find yourself making these recipes even when you do have time to bake from scratch.

Study the label of the cake mix closely before you buy it. Different brands of the same flavor of cake mix can vary greatly, and this can make a difference in the end product if you use the wrong one. Be sure to choose the exact ounce size specified in the recipe, and check to see whether or not pudding is in the mix.

Key Lime Cake

PREP: 3 MINUTES   COOK: 35 MINUTES

Lemon cake mix and Key lime juice mingle in this tart yellow cake.

1 (18.25-ounce) package lemon supreme cake mix (we tested with Duncan Hines)
1 (3.4-ounce) package lemon instant pudding mix
4 large eggs
½ cup water
½ cup Key lime juice
½ cup vegetable oil
2 cups sifted powdered sugar
¼ cup Key lime juice

•Combine first 6 ingredients in a mixing bowl; beat at medium speed with an electric mixer 2 minutes. Pour batter into a greased and floured 13- x 9-inch pan. Bake at 350° for 35 minutes or until a wooden pick inserted in center comes out clean. Cool in pan on a wire rack.
•Combine powdered sugar and ¼ cup Key lime juice; drizzle over cake. Cut into squares. Yield: 15 servings.
Per serving: Calories 320 Fat 12g
Cholesterol 57mg Sodium 296mg

Honey Bun Cake

PREP: 15 MINUTES   COOK: 35 MINUTES

1 (18.25-ounce) package yellow cake mix with pudding (we tested with Pillsbury)
4 large eggs
⅔ cup vegetable oil
⅓ cup water
1 (8-ounce) carton sour cream
½ cup firmly packed brown sugar
1 teaspoon ground cinnamon
⅔ cup chopped pecans
Powdered Sugar Glaze (page 132)

•Combine first 5 ingredients in a mixing bowl; beat at medium speed with an electric mixer 2 minutes. Set aside. Combine brown sugar, cinnamon, and pecans; set aside.
•Pour half of batter into a greased and floured 13- x 9-inch pan. Sprinkle half of sugar mixture over batter. Repeat procedure with remaining batter and sugar mixture. Gently swirl batter with a knife.
•Bake at 350° for 35 minutes or until a wooden pick inserted in center comes out clean. Remove from oven. Drizzle Powdered Sugar Glaze over cake, and cool. Cut into squares. Yield: 15 servings.
Per serving: Calories 383 Fat 20.7g
Cholesterol 64mg Sodium 245mg

Chocolate-Caramel Nut Cake

PREP: 30 MINUTES   COOK: 35 MINUTES

You won't miss frosting here. Once you cut this cake, you'll see the gooey filling inside. Top servings with a scoop of ice cream.

1 (18.25-ounce) package German chocolate cake mix with pudding (we tested with Pillsbury)
1 (14-ounce) package caramels
½ cup butter or margarine
⅓ cup milk
1 cup chopped dry-roasted peanuts
¾ cup milk chocolate morsels

•Prepare cake mix according to package directions. Pour half of batter into a greased

and floured 13- x 9-inch pan. Bake at 350° for 10 minutes. (Cake will not test done.) Cool cake on a wire rack 10 minutes.
•Unwrap caramels. Combine caramels, butter, and milk in a saucepan; cook over medium heat until caramels melt, stirring often. Spread over cake.
•Sprinkle peanuts and chocolate morsels over caramel mixture. Spread remaining cake batter evenly over top. Bake at 350° for 20 to 25 minutes. Cool in pan on wire rack. Cut into squares. Yield: 15 servings.
Per serving: Calories 475 Fat 25.5g
Cholesterol 48mg Sodium 456mg

Self-Filled Cupcakes

◄ **FAMILY FAVORITE** ►

PREP: 20 MINUTES   COOK: 25 MINUTES

Kids love these, and moms do, too. There's no messy frosting on the outside, but inside hides enough rich and creamy filling to enjoy with every bite.

1 (18.25-ounce) package devil's food cake mix (we tested with Duncan Hines)
1 (8-ounce) package cream cheese, softened
⅓ cup sugar
1 large egg
1 cup (6 ounces) semisweet chocolate morsels

•Prepare cake mix according to package directions. Spoon batter into paper-lined muffin pans, filling two-thirds full.
•Beat cream cheese and sugar at medium speed with an electric mixer until fluffy. Add egg, beating well; stir in chocolate morsels. Spoon 1 heaping teaspoon cream cheese mixture into center of each cupcake.
•Bake at 350° for 25 minutes. Remove from pans, and cool on wire racks. Store in refrigerator. Yield: 2½ dozen.
Per serving: Calories 178 Fat 12.2g
Cholesterol 38mg Sodium 167mg

FOAM CAKES

Often grouped together in cookbooks, "foam" cakes include angel food, sponge, and chiffon cakes. These cakes contain an abundance of fluffy egg whites—a common element that's responsible for their similarity and characteristic lightness. But several key differences distinguish the three cakes.

Angel food cake is the purest of the foam cakes. It contains no leavening, egg yolks, or shortening. An angel food cake's structure comes from the high proportion of beaten egg white to flour. And because there's no egg yolk or other fat source, angel food cake is a great dessert for the health conscious.

In contrast, sponge cakes contain both egg whites and yolks and sometimes leavening, but never fat. And chiffon cakes are a blend of shortening cakes and foam cakes. They get their lightness from beaten egg whites, but they also contain yolks, leavening, and shortening or oil.

Foam cakes are commonly baked in an ungreased tube pan. This allows the batter to cling to the sides of the pan and rise high. Then these light cakes are cooled upside-down in the pan to prevent shrinking and falling (see photo 3 on following page).

Vanilla Sponge Cake

◄ HEALTHY ►

PREP: 20 MINUTES   COOK: 50 MINUTES

Enjoy generous slices of healthy sponge cake topped with scoops of frozen yogurt or sliced fresh strawberries for an easy and guilt-free dessert.

1 cup sifted cake flour
½ cup sugar
4 egg yolks
1 teaspoon vanilla extract
10 egg whites
1 teaspoon cream of tartar
½ teaspoon salt
¾ cup sugar

•Sift flour and ½ cup sugar together 3 times; set aside. Beat egg yolks at high speed with an electric mixer 4 minutes or until thick and pale. Add vanilla; beat at medium speed 5 more minutes or until mixture is thick. Set aside.
•Beat egg whites in a large mixing bowl at high speed until foamy. Add cream of tartar and salt; beat until soft peaks form. Add ¾ cup sugar, 2 tablespoons at a time, beating until stiff peaks form.
•Sprinkle one-fourth flour mixture over egg whites; gently fold in. Repeat procedure with remaining flour, adding one-fourth of mixture at a time.
•Gently fold beaten egg yolks into egg white mixture. Pour batter into an ungreased 10-inch tube pan.
•Bake at 350° for 45 to 50 minutes or until cake springs back when lightly touched. Invert pan carefully. Cool in pan 40 minutes. Loosen cake from sides of pan, using a narrow metal spatula; remove from pan. Yield: 14 servings.
Per serving: Calories 125 Fat 1.6g
Cholesterol 62mg Sodium 125mg

Chiffon Cake

PREP: 20 MINUTES   COOK: 1 HOUR

This airy cake is distinguished from other foam cakes by the fat it contains; in this case, oil. It lends tenderness to the cake's delicate texture.

1 cup all-purpose flour
1½ teaspoons baking powder
¼ teaspoon salt
1 cup sugar, divided
¼ cup vegetable oil
4 large eggs, separated
¼ cup water
1 teaspoon vanilla extract
½ teaspoon cream of tartar

•Sift together flour, baking powder, salt, and ½ cup sugar in a large mixing bowl. Make a well in center; add oil, egg yolks, water, and vanilla. Beat at high speed with an electric mixer about 5 minutes or until satiny smooth.
•Beat egg whites and cream of tartar in a large mixing bowl at high speed until soft peaks form. Add remaining ½ cup sugar, 2 tablespoons at a time, beating until stiff peaks form.
•Pour egg yolk mixture in a thin, steady stream over entire surface of egg whites; gently fold whites into yolk mixture.
•Pour batter into an ungreased 10-inch tube pan, spreading evenly with a spatula. Bake at 325° for 1 hour or until cake springs back when lightly touched. Invert pan; cool 40 minutes. Loosen cake from sides of pan, using a narrow metal spatula; remove from pan. Yield: 14 servings.
Per serving: Calories 142 Fat 5.4g
Cholesterol 61mg Sodium 103mg

Coffee Chiffon Cake: Dissolve 1 teaspoon instant coffee granules in ¼ cup water specified in original recipe. Frost cake with Kahlúa Cream Frosting (page 130).

Angel Food Cake

PREP: 20 MINUTES   COOK: 35 MINUTES

Try a slice of this featherlight cake toasted with butter.

12 egg whites
1½ teaspoons cream of tartar
¼ teaspoon salt
1½ cups sugar
1 cup sifted cake flour
1½ teaspoons vanilla extract

•Beat egg whites in a large mixing bowl at high speed with an electric mixer until foamy. Add cream of tartar and salt; beat until soft peaks form (photo 1). Add sugar, 2 tablespoons at a time, beating until stiff peaks form and sugar dissolves. Sprinkle flour over egg white mixture, ¼ cup at a time, folding in after each addition. Fold in vanilla.

1. Beat egg whites until soft peaks form. Add sugar; beat until stiff peaks form.

2. Cut through batter with knife to remove excess air bubbles.

3. Invert tube pan on its legs, and allow cake to cool 40 minutes in the pan.

•Pour batter into an ungreased 10-inch tube pan, spreading batter evenly in pan. Cut through batter with knife to remove air bubbles (photo 2). Bake at 375° for 30 to 35 minutes or until cake springs back when lightly touched. Invert tube pan; cool cake 40 minutes (photo 3). Gently loosen cake from sides of pan, using a narrow metal spatula; remove cake from pan. Yield: 14 servings.

Per serving: Calories 124 Fat 0.1g Cholesterol 0mg Sodium 89mg

Chocolate Angel Food Cake: For a chocolate version, sift ¼ cup cocoa in with 1 cup flour.

JELLYROLL CAKES

When baking a cake in a jellyroll pan, grease the pan well and line it with wax paper. This helps keep the thin layer from sticking to the pan and helps you invert the layer without tearing it.

Most jellyroll cake recipes start with a foam (sponge-type) cake base. Since it bakes as a very thin layer, watch cake carefully to make sure it doesn't overbake. Always check cake at the lower end of the range of baking time. If overbaked, cake will be tough.

Most jellyroll cakes are turned out onto a powdered sugared cloth towel while still warm. And then they're rolled up together to encourage the rolled shape and to prevent tearing. The rolled cake is then set aside on a wire rack to cool. The towel keeps the cake from sticking together as it cools. When cool, it's unrolled, the towel removed, and the cake is filled with a thin layer of filling. Once rerolled, a jellyroll can simply be dusted with powdered sugar, sprinkled with nuts, or covered in a lavish frosting like the French holiday cake, Bûche de Noël, on page 120.

Filling a jellyroll: Spread cake with filling, leaving border around edges so filling won't squeeze out when rolled.

Rolling a jellyroll: Tightly roll cake with filling; place, seam side down, on a plate. Cover and chill.

Chocolate Roulage

PREP: 20 MINUTES   COOK: 20 MINUTES

Roulage tastes great with or without frosting. It's also good served partially frozen.

6 large eggs, separated
½ teaspoon cream of tartar
1 cup sugar, divided
¼ teaspoon salt
1 teaspoon vanilla extract
¼ cup all-purpose flour
¼ cup cocoa
2 tablespoons powdered sugar
2 tablespoons cocoa, divided
1 cup whipping cream, whipped
Frosting (optional)

•Grease bottom and sides of a 15- x 10-inch jellyroll pan; line with wax paper, and grease wax paper. Set aside.
•Beat egg whites, cream of tartar, and ½ cup sugar at high speed with an electric mixer until stiff peaks form; set aside.
•Beat egg yolks, salt, and vanilla in a large mixing bowl until thick and pale. Stir in

remaining ½ cup sugar, flour, and ¼ cup cocoa. (Mixture will be very thick.)

•Fold one-third of egg white mixture into batter. Gently fold remaining egg white mixture into batter. Spread batter evenly in prepared pan. Bake at 325° for 20 minutes.

•Sift powdered sugar in a 15- x 10-inch rectangle on a cloth towel. When cake is done, immediately loosen from sides of pan, and turn out onto sugared towel; peel off wax paper. Dust top of cake with 1 tablespoon cocoa. Starting at narrow end, roll up cake and towel together; cool 30 minutes on a wire rack seam side down.

•Unroll cake, and remove towel. Spread cake with whipped cream, and carefully reroll. Place cake on a serving plate, seam side down. Dust cake with remaining 1 tablespoon cocoa. Frost with Frosting, if desired. Yield: 8 servings.

Per serving: Calories 477 Fat 30.3g
Cholesterol 213mg Sodium 150mg

Frosting

1 cup (6 ounces) semisweet chocolate morsels
1 (8-ounce) carton sour cream

•Melt chocolate morsels in a heavy saucepan over low heat, stirring gently. Remove from heat; cool. Combine chocolate and sour cream; beat at medium speed with an electric mixer until creamy. Yield: 2 cups.

Elegant Lemon Cake Roll

◀ MAKE AHEAD ▶

PREP: 18 MINUTES   COOK: 10 MINUTES
CHILL: 2 HOURS

A sweet lemon filling and toasted coconut dress up this easy sponge cake.

4 large eggs, separated
¼ cup sugar
1 tablespoon vegetable oil
1 teaspoon lemon extract
½ cup sugar
⅔ cup sifted cake flour
1 teaspoon baking powder
¼ teaspoon salt
1 to 2 tablespoons powdered sugar
Creamy Lemon Filling
½ cup flaked coconut, toasted

•Grease bottom and sides of a 15- x 10-inch jellyroll pan with vegetable oil; line pan with wax paper, and grease and flour wax paper.

•Beat egg yolks in a large bowl at high speed with an electric mixer until thick and pale; gradually add ¼ cup sugar, beating constantly. Stir in oil and lemon extract; set mixture aside.

•Beat egg whites at high speed until foamy; gradually add ½ cup sugar, beating until stiff but not dry. Fold beaten egg whites into yolks.

•Combine flour, baking powder, and salt; gradually fold into egg mixture. Spread batter evenly into prepared pan. Bake at 350° for 8 to 10 minutes.

•Sift powdered sugar in a 15- x 10-inch rectangle on a cloth towel. When cake is done, immediately loosen from sides of pan, and turn out onto sugared towel. Peel off wax paper. Starting at narrow end, roll up cake and towel together; cool completely on a wire rack, seam side down.

•Unroll cake, and remove towel. Spread cake with half of Creamy Lemon Filling; carefully reroll. Place on serving plate, seam side down; spread remaining filling on sides. Sprinkle cake with coconut. Chill 2 hours before serving. Store in refrigerator. Yield: 8 servings.

Per serving: Calories 401 Fat 14g
Cholesterol 123mg Sodium 230mg

Creamy Lemon Filling

1 (14-ounce) can sweetened condensed milk
1 to 2 teaspoons grated lemon rind
⅓ cup fresh lemon juice
5 drops of yellow liquid food coloring
1½ cups frozen whipped topping, thawed

•Combine first 4 ingredients in a bowl; stir well with a wire whisk. Fold in whipped topping. Yield: 3 cups.

Pumpkin Roll

PREP: 25 MINUTES   COOK: 12 MINUTES

Cream cheese makes a luxurious filling for this cinnamon-spiced pumpkin cake roll.

3 large eggs
1 cup sugar
⅔ cup mashed, cooked pumpkin
1 teaspoon fresh lemon juice
¾ cup all-purpose flour
1 teaspoon baking powder
¼ teaspoon salt
1 teaspoon ground cinnamon
1 teaspoon pumpkin pie spice
¼ teaspoon ground nutmeg
1 cup chopped pecans
1 to 2 tablespoons powdered sugar
1 (8-ounce) package cream cheese, softened
⅓ cup butter or margarine, softened
1 cup sifted powdered sugar
1 teaspoon vanilla extract
Garnishes: sweetened whipped cream or chopped pecans (optional)

•Grease and flour a 15- x 10-inch jellyroll pan; set aside.

•Beat eggs in a large bowl at high speed with an electric mixer until thick and pale; gradually add 1 cup sugar, and beat 5 minutes. Stir in pumpkin and lemon juice.

•Combine flour and next 5 ingredients; gradually stir into pumpkin mixture. Spread batter evenly in pan; sprinkle with 1 cup pecans, gently pressing into batter. Bake at 375° for 12 minutes.

•Sift 1 to 2 tablespoons powdered sugar in a 15- x 10-inch rectangle on a cloth towel. When cake is done, immediately loosen from sides of pan, and turn out onto sugared towel. Starting at narrow end, roll up cake and towel together; cool completely on a wire rack, seam side down.

•Beat cream cheese and butter in a large bowl at high speed; gradually add 1 cup powdered sugar and vanilla, beating until blended.

•Unroll cake, and remove towel. Spread with cream cheese mixture, and carefully reroll. Place cake on plate, seam side down. Garnish, if desired. Store in refrigerator. Yield: 8 servings.

Per serving: Calories 505 Fat 30.2g
Cholesterol 132mg Sodium 310mg

Bûche de Noël

Bûche de Noël

PREP: 1 HOUR AND 15 MINUTES

COOK: 10 MINUTES

This traditional French Christmas cake, shaped and decorated to look like a tree log, is filled and frosted with silky chocolate buttercream. Crunchy meringue mushrooms are the perfect contrast. Chopped pistachios scattered around resemble moss growing on the (chocolate) log.

4 large eggs, separated
⅔ cup sugar, divided
2 tablespoons water
1 teaspoon vanilla extract
½ cup ground almonds
½ cup sifted cake flour
3 tablespoons cocoa
½ teaspoon cream of tartar
Dash of salt
2 to 3 tablespoons powdered sugar
Rich Chocolate Buttercream (page 131)
½ cup chopped pistachios
Meringue Mushrooms (page 181),
   optional

•Grease bottom and sides of a 15- x 10-inch jellyroll pan; line with wax paper, and grease and flour wax paper. Set aside.
•Beat egg yolks in a large mixing bowl at high speed with an electric mixer 5 minutes or until thick and pale. Gradually add ⅓ cup sugar, beating well. Add water and vanilla. Fold in ground almonds. Gradually fold in cake flour and cocoa.
•Beat egg whites at high speed until foamy. Add cream of tartar and salt; beat until soft peaks form. Add remaining ⅓ cup sugar, 1 tablespoon at a time, beating until stiff peaks form. Gently fold into egg yolk mixture.
•Spread batter evenly into prepared pan. Bake at 375° for 10 minutes or until top springs back when touched.
•Sift powdered sugar in a 15- x 10-inch rectangle on a cloth towel. When cake is done, immediately loosen from sides of pan, and turn out onto sugared towel. Peel off wax paper. Starting at narrow end, roll up cake and towel together; cool completely on a wire rack, seam side down.
•Unroll cake, and remove towel. Spread cake with half of Rich Chocolate

Buttercream (shown on page 118); carefully reroll (shown on page 118). Cover and chill. Cut a 1-inch-thick diagonal slice from 1 end of cake roll.
•Place cake roll on a serving plate, seam side down; position cut piece against side of cake roll to resemble a knot. Spread remaining Rich Chocolate Buttercream over cake.
•Score frosting with the tines of a fork or a cake comb to resemble tree bark. Garnish with pistachios and, if desired, Meringue Mushrooms. Store cake (but not mushrooms) in refrigerator. Yield: 10 servings.

Per serving: Calories 615 Fat 33g
Cholesterol 136mg Sodium 234mg

SPECIALTY CAKES

Every cake chapter needs a few recipes to challenge the best bakers. Here are ours. Many layers make up decadent Chocolate Pecan Torte. Crispy meringue discs match with lemon filling and cake for light and layered Lemon Meringue Cake. And don't miss our simplified Almond-Butter Wedding Cake. The instructions are foolproof.

Lemon Meringue Cake

PREP: 20 MINUTES   COOK: 47 MINUTES

¼ cup butter or margarine, softened
1¾ cups sugar, divided
2 large eggs, separated
1 large egg
1⅓ cups all-purpose flour, divided
1 teaspoon baking powder
⅓ cup milk
½ teaspoon vanilla extract
2 large eggs, separated
1 cup water
½ teaspoon grated lemon rind
¼ cup fresh lemon juice
1 tablespoon butter or margarine
½ teaspoon cream of tartar

•Beat ¼ cup butter at medium speed with an electric mixer until creamy; gradually add ½ cup sugar, beating well. Add 2 egg yolks and 1 egg, beating well.
•Combine 1 cup flour and baking powder; add to butter mixture alternately with milk, beginning and ending with flour mixture. Mix at low speed after each addition until blended. Stir in vanilla. Pour batter into a greased and floured 9-inch round cakepan.
•Bake at 350° for 26 minutes or until a wooden pick inserted in center comes out clean. Cool in pan on a wire rack 10 minutes; remove from pan, and cool completely on wire rack.
•Combine 2 egg yolks and water. Combine ¾ sugar and ⅓ cup flour in a heavy saucepan; add egg yolk mixture and lemon rind. Cook over medium heat, stirring constantly, until mixture thickens and boils. Boil 2 minutes, stirring constantly. Remove from heat. Stir in lemon juice and 1 tablespoon butter. Cover with plastic wrap, and cool.
•Place cake layer on a baking sheet. Spread lemon filling over cake. Beat 4 egg whites and cream of tartar at high speed until foamy. Gradually add ½ cup sugar, 1 tablespoon at a time, beating until stiff peaks form and sugar dissolves (2 to 4 minutes). Spread meringue over lemon filling. Bake at 350° for 16 minutes. Serve warm or chill up to 2 hours. Yield: 8 servings.
Per serving: Calories 364 Fat 11.3g
Cholesterol 154mg Sodium 169mg

Chocolate Pastry Cake

◄ MAKE AHEAD ►

PREP: 21 MINUTES   COOK: 18 MINUTES
CHILL: 8 HOURS

2 (4-ounce) packages sweet baking
  chocolate
½ cup sugar
½ cup water
1½ teaspoons instant coffee granules
2 teaspoons vanilla extract
1 (11-ounce) package piecrust mix
2 cups whipping cream
Chocolate curls (optional)

•Combine first 4 ingredients in a heavy saucepan; cook over low heat, stirring constantly, until mixture is smooth. Stir in vanilla. Cool mixture to room temperature.
•Combine piecrust mix and ¾ cup chocolate mixture in a small bowl; beat at medium speed with an electric mixer until smooth. (Pastry will be stiff.)
•Divide pastry into 6 equal portions. Press each portion on bottom of an inverted 8-inch cakepan coated with cooking spray to within ½ inch of sides. Bake layers, two at a time, at 425° for 5 minutes. Trim uneven edges of circles; run a knife under pastry to loosen it from cakepans. Invert layers onto wax paper to cool.
•Beat whipping cream at medium speed until thickened but just before soft peaks form; fold in remaining chocolate mixture. Stack pastry layers on a serving plate, spreading about ⅔ cup whipped cream mixture between each layer. Spoon remaining whipped cream mixture on top of cake; sprinkle cake with chocolate curls, if desired.

•Chill at least 8 hours before serving. Store in refrigerator. Yield: 8 servings.
Per serving: Calories 617 Fat 46g
Cholesterol 82mg Sodium 323mg

Chocolate-Pecan Torte

PREP: 37 MINUTES   COOK: 18 MINUTES

4 large eggs, separated
¾ cup sugar, divided
¾ cup ground pecans
⅓ cup cocoa
⅓ cup all-purpose flour
½ teaspoon baking soda
¼ teaspoon salt
¼ cup water
1 teaspoon vanilla extract
Mocha Buttercream (page 131)
½ cup finely chopped pecans
¼ cup semisweet chocolate morsels
1 teaspoon shortening

•Grease bottoms of two 9-inch round cakepans. Line with wax paper; grease paper.
•Beat egg yolks in a large bowl at high speed with an electric mixer. Gradually add ½ cup sugar, beating until mixture is thick and pale.
•Combine ground pecans and next 4 ingredients; add to yolk mixture alternately with water, beginning and ending with pecan mixture. Mix at low speed after each addition until blended. Stir in vanilla.
•Beat egg whites at high speed until foamy. Gradually add ¼ cup sugar, beating until stiff peaks form; fold into pecan mixture. Spread batter in prepared pans. Bake at 375° for 16 to 18 minutes. Cool in pans on wire racks 10 minutes; remove from pans. Remove wax paper; cool completely on wire racks.
•Spread Mocha Buttercream between layers and on top and sides of torte. Press ½ cup chopped pecans on sides of torte.
•Combine ¼ cup chocolate morsels and shortening in a small heavy-duty zip-top bag; seal. Submerge in hot water until chocolate melts. Snip a tiny hole in one corner of bag. Pipe chocolate mixture in a decorative design over torte. Store in refrigerator. Yield: 12 servings.
Per serving: Calories 472 Fat 23.5g
Cholesterol 92mg Sodium 185mg

Almond-Butter Wedding Cake

Almond-Butter Wedding Cake

PREP: 1 HOUR AND 45 MINUTES   COOK: 2½ HOURS   ASSEMBLE AND DECORATE: 3½ HOURS

At last, a wedding cake with simple instructions and fabulous taste to make it fit for any extravagant affair. Don't let the piped frosting scare you—our design is easy, and the faster you work, the easier it is to pipe ruffly rows of buttercream. This cake will serve 85 people for an intimate wedding or anniversary. The cake uses a triple recipe of batter. The directions will divide amounts for you. To make the cake easy, we've presented the recipe as a food project, listing supplies you'll need (previous page).

3 cups butter, softened and divided
1½ cups shortening, divided
7½ cups sugar, divided
13½ cups all-purpose flour, divided
3 tablespoons baking powder, divided
1½ teaspoons salt, divided
4½ cups cold water, divided
2 tablespoons vanilla extract, divided
1 tablespoon almond extract, divided
27 egg whites, divided
Apricot Filling (recipe on following page)
Almond-Butter Frosting (recipe on
    following page)

•**To bake cake layers:** Cut two 5-inch, two 8-inch, and two 12-inch circles of wax paper.
•Grease bottoms and sides of one 5-inch, two 8-inch, and one 12-inch round cakepans with shortening. (The 5-inch and 12-inch pans will be used twice.) Line bottoms of pans with wax paper. Do not grease wax paper. Flour sides of pans; set aside.
•Beat 1 cup butter and ½ cup shortening at medium-high speed with a heavy-duty stand mixer 3 minutes. Gradually add 2½ cups sugar, beating at medium-high speed 4 minutes.
•Combine 4½ cups flour, 1 tablespoon baking powder, and ½ teaspoon salt; add to butter mixture alternately with 1½ cups cold water, beginning and ending with flour mixture, beating well after each addition. Stir in 2 teaspoons vanilla and 1 teaspoon almond extract.
•Beat 9 egg whites in a large bowl until soft peaks form (about 1½ minutes). Stir 1 cup beaten egg white into batter to lighten; fold

remaining egg white into batter. Pour 1¾ cups batter into 5-inch prepared pan; pour remaining batter (about 8 cups) into 12-inch pan. Gently drop filled cakepans on countertop twice to release air bubbles from batter.
•Bake layers together at 325° for 40 to 45 minutes or until cakes spring back when lightly touched in center and begin to pull away from sides of pans. Cool in pans on wire racks 20 minutes. Loosen edges of cakes with a knife. Remove from pans, peel off wax paper, and cool completely, rounded side up, on wire racks.
•Meanwhile, prepare a second batch of batter, using the same ingredient amounts and mixing procedure as directed; divide batter evenly into two (8-inch) prepared cakepans. Repeat baking and cooling procedures. Meanwhile, wash and dry the 5-inch and 12-inch cakepans. Grease pans; line bottoms with wax paper, and flour sides of pans.
•Prepare a third batch of batter; pour 1¾ cups batter into prepared 5-inch pan. Pour remaining batter into prepared 12-inch pan. Repeat baking and cooling procedures.
•After all 6 cake layers have cooled completely, wrap each layer tightly in heavy-duty plastic wrap, and then in aluminum foil. Store in refrigerator up to 3 days. (If possible, don't stack cake layers). You can bake cake layers up to one month ahead. Wrap tightly as directed above, and freeze. Transfer frozen layers to refrigerator to thaw the day before you plan to frost the cake.
•**To level cake layers:** Unwrap 6 cake layers, and place side by side on a flat surface (layers may vary in height). Identify the layer that's shortest in height. Adjust the cutting wire on the cake leveler to this height. Carefully cut through cake to level top of layer, using cake leveler (photo 1, next page); remove and reserve any cake trimmings. Repeat leveling procedure with remaining 5 cake layers. (If you don't have a cake leveler, use a long knife with a serrated edge and measure heights carefully with a ruler.)
•Adjust cutting wire on the cake leveler to half the height of cake layers. Cut each cake layer in half horizontally to make 2 layers. Insert two wooden picks into each layer, one

WEDDING CAKE WISDOM

•One of the most important things when building a wedding cake is to be sure your cake layers are level. (See photo 1, next page.)
•Good pans are essential. We tested with Wilton cakepans.
•Prepare all your cakepans before you begin, and then set them aside.
•Clean up as you go, so you won't get overwhelmed and make mistakes.
•Be organized. Give yourself plenty of time for each step. And while one cake is baking, prepare the next batch of batter.
•When removing top layer after splitting, mark with toothpicks on each layer so you can replace in exactly the same place.
•Cake layers can be transported with a thin layer of frosting or with vertical piping completed. But wait to assemble and pipe the border at your party location.
•Condition flowers a day in advance of cake assembly and store in refrigerator.

above the other, to indicate how the two layers should match up when going back together after filling.
•**To fill cake layers:** Beginning with a 12-inch layer, slide a cardboard round into horizontal cut. Lift top layer off, and set aside. Spread ½ cup Apricot Filling on bottom half of layer, spreading evenly over cake. Replace top layer, carefully matching wooden picks to keep layers level. Repeat filling procedure with remaining layers, using ¼ cup Apricot Filling for each 8-inch layer and 2 tablespoons filling for each 5-inch layer.
•**To frost cake layers:** Spread 2 tablespoons Almond-Butter Frosting in middle of white side of a 12-inch cardboard circle; place 1 (12-inch) filled cake layer on top of cardboard circle, pressing firmly to secure cake layer to cardboard and prevent cake layer from sliding. Spread 1½ cups frosting evenly on top of 12-inch layer, spreading to, but not over, the side; top with remaining 12-inch layer. If needed, fill in any spaces between layers with reserved cake trimmings

that remain from leveling (photo 2). Repeat procedure with 8-inch layers, using 1 cup frosting between layers, and 5-inch layers, using ½ cup frosting. When this step is completed, you'll have 3 cake layers (tiers)—5-inch, 8-inch, and 12-inch, each about 4 inches high.

•Place cake tiers, one at a time, on a turntable. Using a large metal spatula, spread top and sides of each cake with a thin layer of frosting. Hold spatula steady, and turn the turntable to create a smooth frosting on sides of each layer. At this point, you may want to transport cakes to desired location, or you can wrap layers in plastic wrap and chill until ready to complete cake.

•**To condition flowers for garnishing:** Cut flower stems the desired length at an angle, and remove excess foliage. Place stems in warm water. Mist flowers, and place in plastic bag in refrigerator overnight.

•**To prepare pastry bag for decorating:** Insert a large coupler and large metal tip into pastry bag. Spoon frosting into bag; press to remove air. Fold end of bag over, and roll toward frosting to create a good grip. Firmly squeeze bag until all air is pressed out through tip of bag. You'll hear a sound like a spatter when air escapes. Repeat each time you refill bag with more frosting.

•**To decorate cake:** Place 12-inch cake on turntable. Pipe frosting in vertical lines up sides of cake layer, beginning at bottom and frosting over top edge of cake, turning the cake as needed. Each line of frosting should just touch the previous one and overlap naturally. Pipe or spoon about 1 cup frosting on top of 12-inch tier; dip metal spatula in ice

water, and spread evenly. Repeat decorating procedure with remaining tiers.

•**To support cake layers:** Transfer 12-inch tier to a serving tray. Insert one plastic straw in center of cake, being sure to press straw to bottom of cake. Cut straw slightly above top of frosting, leaving about ¼ inch of straw visible (photo 3). Carefully remove cut straw from center of cake. Cut six more straws the same size. Insert cut straws into cake layer in a circle near edge of where the 8-inch tier will rest on the bottom tier (photo 4). The straws support the heavy cake tier and keep the tier from pressing into the bottom tier. You can use ¼-inch wooden dowels rather than straws, if desired. Remember to cut each the same length.

•Repeat procedure with 8-inch layer, beginning with the center straw. Cut five more straws the same size. Insert in cake layer in a circle near edge of where the 5-inch tier will rest on the 8-inch tier. No straws are needed for the top tier.

•**To stack cake layers:** Carefully center 8-inch tier over center of 12-inch tier. Lower the tier in place until it's resting on the straw supports. Repeat procedure with 5-inch tier, placing it on top of 8-inch tier.

•Using same pastry bag and metal tip, form stars or rosettes around the bottom edge of each tier.

•Arrange conditioned flowers on cake and serving plate. If inserting flowers directly into cake, first wrap all stem ends of flowers with florist tape or aluminum foil. Store leftovers in refrigerator. Yield: 85 servings.

Per serving: Calories 429 Fat 18.1g
Sodium 222mg Cholesterol 33mg

Apricot Filling

2 (8¾-ounce) cans apricot halves, drained
¼ cup amaretto

•Process apricot and amaretto in container of an electric blender or food processor until smooth. Yield: 1¾ cups.

Almond-Butter Frosting

1½ cups butter, softened and divided
1½ cups shortening, divided
6 (16-ounce) boxes powdered sugar, unsifted and divided
1¾ cups whipping cream, divided
1 teaspoon salt, divided
1 tablespoon almond extract, divided

•Beat ¾ cup butter and ¾ cup shortening at medium speed with a heavy-duty stand mixer 2 minutes or until creamy. Gradually add 1 box sugar, beating at medium speed 2 to 3 minutes. Add ¼ cup whipping cream, ½ teaspoon salt and 1½ teaspoons almond extract, beating well.

•Gradually add 2 more boxes sugar and ½ cup whipping cream alternately, beginning and ending with sugar, beating well after each addition. Add more cream, if necessary, to make frosting a good piping consistency. Continue beating until mixture is fluffy.

•Transfer frosting to a large bowl; cover with a damp cloth. Repeat mixing procedure with remaining ingredients. Keep frosting covered with a damp cloth while decorating cake. Yield: 14 cups.

1. Use a cake leveler to level each layer; remove cake "lid."

2. Use reserved cake trimmings to fill in gaps, if necessary, as you assemble cake.

3. Cut straw ¼ inch above top of frosted cake. Remove straw from cake; cut 6 more to match.

4. Insert cut straws into cake layer in a circle near outer edge to support weight of other layers.

CHEESECAKES

Who wouldn't love to dip a fork into a creamy bite of one of these dense sweet cheese confections? The only special equipment you'll need to make one is a springform pan. The 9- and 10-inch sizes are common.

Cheesecake is a great dessert choice because you can make it ahead and chill it until serving time. Just leave it in the springform pan until ready to unmold and serve. And the flavor variations of cheesecake crust and filling are endless.

Many cheesecakes turn out with a perfect texture if removed from the oven just as they're set. They'll continue to firm up as they cool completely and chill. Other cheesecakes require being left in the oven after baking for an hour or so with the oven turned off. Our recipes will specify when this is needed. See the chart on this page for more fail-safe cheesecake tips.

Deluxe Cheesecake

◄ **FAMILY FAVORITE** ►
◄ **MAKE AHEAD** ►

PREP: 20 MINUTES   COOK: 40 MINUTES
CHILL: 8 HOURS

If you've never made a cheesecake, this is a great basic recipe to start with. It's a rich, dense cheesecake with a white sour cream topping that hides any flaws in the cheesecake's top.

Recipe for 1 (9-inch) Graham Cracker
   Crust (page 301)
3 (8-ounce) packages cream cheese,
   softened
1 cup sugar
3 large eggs
½ teaspoon vanilla extract
1 (16-ounce) carton sour cream
3 tablespoons sugar
½ teaspoon vanilla extract

•Press Graham Cracker Crust mixture into a 10-inch springform pan; set aside.
•Beat cream cheese at high speed with an electric mixer until creamy; gradually add 1 cup sugar, beating well. Add eggs, one at a time, beating after each addition. Stir in ½ teaspoon vanilla. Pour into prepared crust.

Bake at 375° for 35 minutes or until cheesecake is set.
•Beat sour cream at medium speed 2 minutes. Add 3 tablespoons sugar and ½ teaspoon vanilla; beat 1 more minute. Spread over cheesecake. Bake at 400° for 5 minutes. Cool to room temperature on a wire rack; cover and chill 8 hours. Yield: 12 servings.
Per serving: Calories 490 Fat 35.3g
Cholesterol 146mg Sodium 337mg

Turtle Cheesecake

◄ **FAMILY FAVORITE** ►
◄ **MAKE AHEAD** ►

PREP: 30 MINUTES
COOK: 1 HOUR AND 15 MINUTES
CHILL: 10 HOURS

For those who love turtle candies, here's the cheesecake version.

2 cups chocolate wafer crumbs
¼ cup sugar
⅓ cup butter, melted
3 (8-ounce) packages cream cheese,
   softened
1¼ cups sugar
4 large eggs
1 (8-ounce) carton sour cream
1 tablespoon vanilla extract
¼ cup butter
1 cup (6 ounces) semisweet chocolate
   morsels
1 (12-ounce) jar caramel topping (we
   tested with Smucker's)
1 cup chopped pecans

•Combine first 3 ingredients; stir well. Firmly press mixture in bottom and 1 inch up sides of a lightly greased 9-inch springform pan. Bake at 325° for 10 minutes. Cool in pan on a wire rack.
•Beat cream cheese at medium speed with an electric mixer until creamy; gradually add 1¼ cups sugar, beating well. Add eggs, one at a time, beating after each addition and scraping sides and bottom as needed. Stir in sour cream and vanilla. Pour batter into prepared crust.
•Bake at 325° for 1 hour and 5 minutes. (Center will not be completely set.) Turn

oven off, and partially open oven door; leave cake in oven 1 hour. Cool completely on a wire rack; cover and chill at least 8 hours. Carefully remove sides of pan; transfer cheesecake to a serving plate.
•Melt ¼ cup butter in a small heavy saucepan; add chocolate morsels. Stir over low heat just until chocolate melts and mixture blends. Spread warm chocolate mixture over cheesecake; chill 15 minutes.
•Combine caramel topping and pecans in a small saucepan. Bring to a boil, stirring constantly, over medium heat; boil 2 minutes. Remove from heat, and cool 5 minutes. Spread over chocolate; cool completely. Serve immediately or cover and chill. Let stand at room temperature at least 30 minutes before serving. Yield: 10 servings.
Per serving: Calories 1051 Fat 70g
Cholesterol 244mg Sodium 612mg

FAIL-SAFE CHEESECAKES

Making a cheesecake is a piece of cake when you heed these tips.
•Let cream cheese soften at room temperature before you begin.
•Don't overbeat the batter when adding eggs. Beat only until blended.
•To prevent cracks, run a knife or small metal spatula around edge of cheesecake immediately after removing it from the oven. This allows the loosened sides to contract freely.
•You can freeze cheesecake up to one month. Remove pan, place cheesecake on a cardboard circle, if desired, and wrap tightly in heavy-duty aluminum foil. Thaw in the refrigerator the day before serving.

Orange Cheesecake

◄ MAKE AHEAD ►

PREP: 25 MINUTES   COOK: 58 MINUTES
CHILL: 9 HOURS

Recipe for 1 (9-inch) Graham Cracker
   Crust (page 301)
1 (11-ounce) can mandarin oranges
¼ cup Cointreau or other
   orange-flavored liqueur
4 (8-ounce) packages cream cheese,
   softened
2 tablespoons finely grated orange rind
2 teaspoons orange extract
1 teaspoon vanilla extract
1⅓ cups sugar
4 large eggs
½ cup fresh orange juice
1 tablespoon plus 1 teaspoon cornstarch

•Press Graham Cracker Crust mixture into a
10-inch springform pan. Bake at 375° for 8
minutes; cool.
•Drain mandarin oranges, reserving ½ cup
liquid. Combine mandarin oranges and
Cointreau; stir gently. Cover and chill, stirring occasionally.
•Combine cream cheese, orange rind, and
flavorings; beat at high speed with an electric mixer until creamy; gradually add sugar,
beating well. Add eggs, one at a time, beating after each addition. Pour batter into prepared crust.
•Bake at 350° for 50 minutes or until cheesecake is almost set. Turn oven off, and partially open oven door; leave cake in oven 30
minutes. Remove from oven; cool to room
temperature on a wire rack. Cover and chill
at least 8 hours.
•Drain mandarin orange mixture, reserving
Cointreau. Arrange mandarin oranges on
top of cheesecake.
•Combine reserved mandarin orange liquid,
Cointreau mixture, orange juice, and cornstarch in a saucepan; stir well. Cook over
medium heat 5 minutes or until thickened;
cool slightly. Spoon glaze over top of cheesecake; cover and chill. Yield: 12 servings.
Per serving: Calories 533 Fat 35.1g
Cholesterol 170mg Sodium 387mg

Chocolate Cheesecake with Whipped Cream Frosting

◄ MAKE AHEAD ►

PREP: 37 MINUTES
COOK: 1 HOUR AND 46 MINUTES
CHILL: 8 HOURS

*Rely on this classic recipe for a very rich,
impressive dessert for company. The lacy
chocolate garnishes can easily be made
ahead.*

1⅓ cups (8 ounces) semisweet chocolate
   morsels
3 (8-ounce) packages cream cheese,
   softened
1½ cups sugar
3 large eggs
1 tablespoon unsweetened cocoa
1½ teaspoons vanilla extract
1 (8-ounce) carton sour cream
Chocolate Wafer Crust
Whipped Cream Frosting
Lacy Chocolate Garnishes

•Place chocolate morsels in top of a double
boiler; place over hot water, and cook until
chocolate melts, stirring often.
•Beat cream cheese at high speed with an
electric mixer until creamy; gradually add
sugar, mixing well. Add eggs, one at a time,
beating after each addition. Stir in melted
chocolate, cocoa, and vanilla; beat until
blended. Stir in sour cream, blending well.
Pour into prepared Chocolate Wafer Crust.
•Bake at 300° for 1 hour and 40 minutes.
Run knife around edge of pan to release
sides. Cool to room temperature on a wire
rack; cover and chill at least 8 hours.
•To serve, spoon 2 cups Whipped Cream
Frosting into a decorating bag fitted with a
large metal star tip (such as No. 858). Set
bag aside.
•Remove cheesecake from pan, and place
on a serving plate. Spread remaining frosting
on top of cheesecake. Pipe reserved frosting
as desired on top of cheesecake. Insert 12
Lacy Chocolate Garnishes equally around
sides of cake, and place 1 in center. Store
leftovers in refrigerator. Yield: 12 servings.
Per serving: Calories 797 Fat 57.5g
Cholesterol 206mg Sodium 392mg

Chocolate Wafer Crust

1½ cups chocolate wafer crumbs
⅓ cup butter or margarine, melted

•Combine crumbs and butter, stirring well.
Firmly press crumb mixture evenly in bottom and 1 inch up sides of a 9-inch springform pan. Bake at 350° for 6 minutes. Yield:
one 9-inch crust.

Whipped Cream Frosting

1½ cups whipping cream
3 tablespoons cocoa
2 tablespoons powdered sugar
1 teaspoon vanilla extract

•Combine all ingredients in a mixing bowl;
beat at medium speed with an electric mixer
until soft peaks form. Yield: 3 cups.

Lacy Chocolate Garnishes

½ cup (3 ounces) semisweet chocolate
   morsels

•Place chocolate morsels in top of a double
boiler; place over hot water; cook until
chocolate melts, stirring often. Cool slightly,
and spoon into a decorating bag fitted with
metal tip No. 2.
•Trace pattern for lacy garnishes onto white
paper. Cover pattern with a large sheet of
wax paper. Pipe melted chocolate over wax
paper-covered pattern, moving paper to
position pattern in other places. Continue
piping over pattern and moving paper to
make 13 garnishes. Carefully transfer wax
paper to a baking sheet, and chill until
chocolate is firm. Carefully peel garnishes
from wax paper. Yield: 13 garnishes.

Chocolate Cookie Cheesecake

PREP: 38 MINUTES
COOK: 1 HOUR AND 30 MINUTES
CHILL: 8 HOURS

2 cups cream-filled chocolate sandwich
    cookie crumbs (20 cookies)
2 tablespoons butter or margarine, melted
¼ cup firmly packed brown sugar
4 (8-ounce) packages cream cheese,
    softened
1¼ cups sugar
⅓ cup whipping cream
2 tablespoons all-purpose flour
1 teaspoon vanilla extract
4 large eggs
2 cups coarsely crumbled cream-filled
    chocolate sandwich cookies
    (14 cookies)
1 (16-ounce) carton sour cream
¼ cup sugar
1 teaspoon vanilla extract
⅓ cup whipping cream
1¼ cups semisweet chocolate morsels
1 teaspoon vanilla extract
Garnish: additional cream-filled chocolate
    sandwich cookies

•Combine first 3 ingredients in a medium bowl; firmly press mixture evenly in bottom and 2 inches up sides of a lightly greased 10-inch springform pan. Bake at 325° for 12 minutes; set aside.

•Beat cream cheese at medium speed with an electric mixer until creamy. Gradually add 1¼ cups sugar, beating well. Add ⅓ cup whipping cream, flour, and 1 teaspoon vanilla; beat well. Add eggs, one at a time, beating after each addition.

•Pour 3½ cups of batter into prepared crust. Top with crumbled cookies; pour in remaining batter. Bake at 325° for 1 hour and 15 minutes.

•Combine sour cream, ¼ cup sugar, and 1 teaspoon vanilla; spread over cheesecake. Bake at 325° for 7 minutes. Turn oven off, and leave cheesecake in oven with door closed 45 minutes. Remove from oven, and cool completely on a wire rack. Cover and chill 8 hours. Remove sides of pan.

•Combine ⅓ cup whipping cream and semisweet chocolate morsels in a saucepan; stir over low heat until chocolate melts. Stir in 1 teaspoon vanilla. Remove from heat. Carefully spread mixture over cheesecake, allowing it to drip down sides. Store cheesecake in refrigerator. Garnish, if desired.
Yield: 12 servings.

Per serving: Calories 798 Fat 55.9g
Cholesterol 194mg Sodium 500mg

FROSTINGS

It's that delectably sweet swirl of frosting on cake that makes you long for a glass of cold milk. We offer over a dozen different frostings from which to choose. Although most of our cake recipes suggest one frosting to use, we separated the frostings section from the cake section to encourage you to mix and match the two. No one frosting is exclusive for any one cake, and we hope you'll create some new great-tasting combinations.

Before frosting a cake, make sure cake layers are completely cool. Brush off excess crumbs from top and sides of cake layers before you begin. You can use a pastry brush or your fingers to do this. To keep frosting off the serving plate, tuck strips of wax paper under all sides of bottom cake layer before you begin frosting.

When frosting and stacking cake layers, place first layer (or first two layers for a 3-layer cake) bottom side up on serving plate; then place top cake layer right side up. This contributes to a straight and tall cake.

Spread about one-fifth to one-fourth of frosting between each cake layer. Spread a thin layer of frosting on sides to set any remaining crumbs; this is called crumbcoating. Then spread a generous amount of frosting over the crumbcoating, making decorative swirls with spatula, if desired. Always keep the frosting just ahead of the spatula; don't backstroke until the entire area is frosted or spatula may drag up crumbs from the unfrosted area. Spread remaining frosting on top of cake, joining the frosting at the top and sides, and making decorative swirls. Then gently remove strips of wax paper from under bottom layer of frosted cake.

You'll get neater slices from your cake if you use a serrated cake knife. If crumbs and frosting adhere to the knife, wipe the blade with a damp towel before cutting another slice.

Many cakes slice better if they have a few hours to set up or chill after they've been assembled. We mention which cakes benefit from this throughout the chapter.

Preparing layers: Brush away loose crumbs from cake before frosting, using a pastry brush or your fingers.

Spreading frosting: Keep frosting just ahead of spatula as you spread. Don't backstroke or you may drag crumbs into frosting.

Crumbcoating: Spread a thin layer of frosting around sides of stacked cake layers to set any crumbs. Then spread frosting generously on sides and top.

Keeping plate free of frosting: Before frosting, place strips of wax paper under sides of cake; when cake is frosted, gently pull out strips.

Sour Cream Frosting

◄ QUICK ►

PREP: 10 MINUTES

⅔ cup butter or margarine, softened
⅓ cup sour cream
Dash of salt
4⅓ cups sifted powdered sugar
1 teaspoon vanilla extract

•Beat butter, sour cream, and salt at low speed with an electric mixer until creamy. Gradually add powdered sugar, beating until spreading consistency. Stir in vanilla. Yield: 3¼ cups.
Per tablespoon: Calories 63 Fat 2.7g
Cholesterol 7mg Sodium 28mg

Bourbon Frosting

◄ QUICK ►

PREP: 9 MINUTES

¾ cup butter or margarine, softened
6 cups sifted powdered sugar
¼ cup bourbon
¼ cup milk

•Beat butter at medium speed with an electric mixer until creamy; gradually add powdered sugar, bourbon, and milk, beating until spreading consistency. Yield: 4 cups.
Per tablespoon: Calories 66 Fat 2.2g
Cholesterol 6mg Sodium 23mg

Chocolate Kahlúa Frosting

◄ QUICK ►

PREP: 6 MINUTES

¼ cup butter, softened
1 (8-ounce) package cream cheese, softened
1 (16-ounce) package powdered sugar, sifted and divided
3 (1-ounce) squares unsweetened chocolate, melted and cooled
¼ cup Kahlúa or strongly brewed coffee

•Beat butter and cream cheese at medium speed with an electric mixer. Add 1 cup powdered sugar and chocolate; beat until smooth. Gradually add remaining powdered

sugar and Kahlúa, beating at low speed until spreading consistency. Yield: 4 cups.
Per tablespoon: Calories 56 Fat 2.7g Cholesterol 6mg Sodium 18mg

Light Cream Cheese Frosting

◀ QUICK ▶

PREP: 10 MINUTES

1 (8-ounce) package Neufchâtel cheese (do not soften)
1 tablespoon light butter (do not soften)
5 cups sifted powdered sugar
1 teaspoon vanilla extract
¾ cup chopped pecans, toasted

•Beat cream cheese and butter at high speed with an electric mixer until soft and creamy. Gradually add powdered sugar, beating at low speed just until mixture is light. Gently stir in vanilla and pecans. Chill until ready to spread. Yield: 2⅔ cups.
Per tablespoon: Calories 76 Fat 3g Cholesterol 5mg Sodium 23mg

Cream Cheese Frosting

◀ QUICK • FAMILY FAVORITE ▶

PREP: 5 MINUTES

This popular frosting complements many types of cakes. We offer several ideas for using the frosting throughout this chapter. Also, see our Deluxe Cream Cheese Frosting at right; it yields a little more, and has a pecan variation.

1 (8-ounce) package cream cheese, softened
½ cup butter or margarine, softened
1 (16-ounce) package powdered sugar, sifted
1 teaspoon vanilla extract

•Beat cream cheese and butter at medium speed with an electric mixer until smooth. Gradually add powdered sugar, beating at low speed until light and fluffy. Stir in vanilla. Yield: 3 cups.
Per tablespoon: Calories 71 Fat 3.6g Cholesterol 10mg Sodium 34mg

Deluxe Cream Cheese Frosting

◀ QUICK • FAMILY FAVORITE ▶

PREP: 7 MINUTES

This frosting is slightly softer than the traditional recipe at left. Extra cream cheese and butter enrich the frosting and give it a little more volume.

1 (8-ounce) package cream cheese, softened
1 (3-ounce) package cream cheese, softened
¾ cup butter, softened
1 (16-ounce) package powdered sugar, sifted
1½ teaspoons vanilla extract

•Beat first 3 ingredients at medium speed with an electric mixer until smooth. Gradually add powdered sugar, beating at low speed until light and fluffy. Stir in vanilla. Yield: 3½ cups.
Per tablespoon: Calories 79 Fat 4.4g Cholesterol 13mg Sodium 42mg

Deluxe Pecan-Cream Cheese Frosting: Stir 1½ cups chopped pecans into frosting along with vanilla. Yield: 5½ cups.

Boiled Frosting

◀ QUICK ▶

PREP: 5 MINUTES   COOK: 18 MINUTES

To get maximum volume with this billowy frosting, let egg whites stand at room temperature about 15 minutes before whipping them.

1½ cups sugar
½ cup water
½ teaspoon cream of tartar
⅛ teaspoon salt
4 egg whites
½ teaspoon almond extract

•Combine first 4 ingredients in a heavy saucepan. Cook over medium heat, stirring constantly, until mixture is clear. Cook, without stirring, until mixture reaches soft ball stage or candy thermometer registers 240° (photo 1).

1. Boil sugar syrup until it reaches soft ball stage on a candy thermometer.

•While syrup cooks, beat egg whites at high speed with an electric mixer until soft peaks form; continue to beat egg whites, adding the hot syrup mixture in a heavy stream (photo 2).

2. Beat egg whites at high speed while adding hot syrup in a heavy stream.

3. Beat frosting until stiff peaks form and frosting is thick enough to spread.

•Add almond extract. Beat until stiff peaks form and frosting is thick enough to spread (photo 3). Yield: 7 cups.
Per tablespoon: Calories 11 Fat 0g Cholesterol 0mg Sodium 5mg

Seven-Minute Frosting

◀ QUICK ▶

PREP: 5 MINUTES   COOK: 7 MINUTES

1½ cups sugar
¼ cup plus 1 tablespoon cold water
2 egg whites
1 tablespoon light corn syrup
Dash of salt
1 teaspoon vanilla extract

•Combine first 5 ingredients in top of a large double boiler. Beat at low speed with a handheld electric mixer 30 seconds or just until blended.
•Place over boiling water; beat constantly at high speed 7 minutes or until stiff peaks form. Remove from heat. Add vanilla; beat 2 minutes or until frosting is thick enough to spread. Yield: 4¼ cups.

Per tablespoon: Calories 19 Fat 0g
Cholesterol 0mg Sodium 4mg

Whipped Cream Frosting

◀ QUICK ▶

PREP: 5 MINUTES

2 cups whipping cream
2 to 3 tablespoons powdered sugar
1 teaspoon vanilla extract

•Beat whipping cream at medium speed with an electric mixer until foamy; gradually add powdered sugar and vanilla, beating until soft peaks form. Yield: 4 cups.

Per tablespoon: Calories 27 Fat 2.8g
Cholesterol 10mg Sodium 3mg

Kahlúa Cream Frosting: Combine 2 tablespoons Kahlúa, 1 teaspoon instant coffee powder, and 1 teaspoon water, stirring until smooth. Beat whipping cream at medium speed with an electric mixer until foamy; gradually add powdered sugar, vanilla, and coffee mixture, beating until soft peaks form. Yield: 4 cups.

Rich Chocolate Frosting

◀ QUICK ▶

PREP: 10 MINUTES

1 cup (6 ounces) semisweet or milk
   chocolate morsels
½ cup half-and-half
1 cup butter or margarine
2½ cups sifted powdered sugar

•Combine first 3 ingredients in a saucepan; cook over medium heat, stirring until melted and smooth. Remove from heat, and stir in powdered sugar. Set saucepan in ice. Beat at medium speed with an electric mixer until frosting holds its shape, about 5 minutes. Yield: 3 cups.

Per tablespoon: Calories 78 Fat 5.3g
Cholesterol 11mg Sodium 40mg

Caramel Frosting

◀ FAMILY FAVORITE ▶

PREP: 20 MINUTES   COOK: 50 MINUTES

Don't be afraid to try a cooked frosting. It's similar to making fudge. Leave mixture in saucepan, and beat with a handheld electric mixer so frosting doesn't cool too rapidly.

4 cups sugar
2 cups butter
2 cups evaporated milk
2 teaspoons vanilla extract

•Combine sugar, butter, and milk in a 4-quart saucepan or small Dutch oven; bring to a boil over medium heat. Cover and cook 2 to 3 minutes to wash down sugar crystals from sides of pan. Uncover and cook, stirring constantly, until mixture reaches soft ball stage or candy thermometer registers 234° (about 40 minutes). As frosting cooks, stir gently until it reaches 222°, and then stir more vigorously to avoid scorching. Remove from heat, and add vanilla (do not stir). Cool 10 minutes.
•Beat mixture, in saucepan, at medium speed with an electric mixer 8 to 10 minutes or until almost spreading consistency. Yield: 4½ cups.

Per tablespoon: Calories 98 Fat 5.6g
Cholesterol 16mg Sodium 60mg

Decorator Frosting

◀ QUICK ▶

PREP: 10 MINUTES

Here's a great beginner frosting for cake decorating because the shortening keeps it firm enough to pipe without melting from the heat of your hand. The frosting's soft and fluffy, and you can vary the flavor with extracts.

8 cups sifted powdered sugar
2 cups shortening
¾ cup milk
2 teaspoons vanilla extract
1 teaspoon almond extract
Paste food coloring

•Combine first 5 ingredients in a large mixing bowl; beat at low speed with an electric mixer until blended. Then beat at high speed 5 minutes or until frosting is light and fluffy. Color as desired with food coloring. Yield: 8 cups.

Per tablespoon: Calories 54 Fat 2.7g
Cholesterol 0mg Sodium 1mg

Vanilla Buttercream

◄ QUICK ►

PREP: 10 MINUTES

1½ cups butter or margarine, softened
4 cups sifted powdered sugar
2 tablespoons milk
1 teaspoon vanilla or almond extract

•Beat butter at medium speed with an electric mixer until creamy; gradually add sugar, beating until light and fluffy. Add milk; beat until spreading consistency. Stir in vanilla. Yield: 3 cups.
Per tablespoon: Calories 90 Fat 5.8g
Cholesterol 16mg Sodium 59mg

Spiced Buttercream: Substitute 2 tablespoons orange juice for milk, and stir in 1 teaspoon ground cinnamon and ¼ teaspoon ground cloves in place of 1 teaspoon vanilla extract.

Lemon Buttercream

◄ QUICK ►

PREP: 6 MINUTES

1¼ cups butter or margarine, softened
2 teaspoons grated lemon rind
3 tablespoons fresh lemon juice
3 cups sifted powdered sugar

•Beat first 3 ingredients at medium speed with an electric mixer until creamy. Gradually add powdered sugar, beating until spreading consistency. Yield: 2¾ cups.
Per tablespoon: Calories 78 Fat 5.2g
Cholesterol 14mg Sodium 53mg

Orange Buttercream: Substitute orange rind and juice for lemon rind and juice.

Mocha Buttercream

◄ QUICK ►

PREP: 17 MINUTES

1 tablespoon instant coffee granules
¼ cup hot water
½ cup butter or margarine, softened
3 tablespoons cocoa
4¼ to 4½ cups sifted powdered sugar
¾ teaspoon vanilla extract

•Dissolve coffee granules in hot water; set aside to cool.
•Beat butter and cocoa at medium speed with an electric mixer until creamy. Gradually add 4¼ cups powdered sugar to butter mixture alternately with coffee mixture, beginning and ending with powdered sugar. Beat at low speed after each addition until blended. Add additional ¼ cup powdered sugar, if necessary; beat until spreading consistency. Stir in vanilla. Yield: 2⅓ cups.
Per tablespoon: Calories 26 Fat 0.8g
Cholesterol 2mg Sodium 8mg

Rich Chocolate Buttercream

◄ QUICK • FAMILY FAVORITE ►

PREP: 10 MINUTES

2 (1-ounce) squares unsweetened chocolate
2 (1-ounce) squares semisweet chocolate
1 cup butter or margarine, softened
4 cups sifted powdered sugar
¼ cup cocoa
¼ cup milk
2 teaspoons vanilla extract

•Place chocolate in top of a double boiler; bring water to a boil. Reduce heat to low; cook until chocolate melts, stirring often. Remove from heat.
•Beat butter at medium speed with an electric mixer until creamy. Add chocolate, powdered sugar, and remaining ingredients; beat until spreading consistency. Yield: 3¾ cups.
Per tablespoon: Calories 70 Fat 4g
Cholesterol 8mg Sodium 32mg

Royal Icing

◄ QUICK ►

PREP: 5 MINUTES

Royal Icing dries to a smooth, hard finish as opposed to other frostings in this chapter. Royal Icing works well to make hard, candy-like decorations or to add a hard glaze to cookies, but it isn't a good choice for frosting entire cakes. It dries very quickly, so keep it covered with a damp cloth while working with it.

1 (16-ounce) package powdered sugar, sifted
3 tablespoons meringue powder°
6 to 8 tablespoons warm water
Paste food coloring

•Beat first 3 ingredients at low speed with an electric mixer until blended.
•Beat at high speed 4 to 5 minutes or until stiff peaks form. If icing is too stiff, add additional water, ¼ teaspoon at a time, until desired consistency.
•Color icing as desired with food coloring. Yield: 3 cups.
°*Find meringue powder at craft stores and cake decorating stores.*
Per tablespoon: Calories 57 Fat 0g
Cholesterol 0mg Sodium 5mg

Nonedible Royal Icing: For piping decorations that aren't intended to be eaten, such as gingerbread houses and other holiday items, you can use the original recipe for Royal Icing made with egg whites instead of meringue powder. The egg whites are uncooked, however, so be sure everyone understands it's not intended to be eaten.
•To make Nonedible Royal Icing, beat 3 egg whites and ½ teaspoon cream of tartar in a large mixing bowl at medium speed of an electric mixer until frothy. Add half a 16-ounce package of powdered sugar, mixing well. Add remaining sugar, and beat at high speed 5 to 7 minutes. Yield: 2 cups.

GLAZES & FILLINGS

A shimmery glaze adds just a touch of sweetness to an unfrosted cake. A glaze is at its best when simply drizzled over a cake so a little runs down the sides of the cake. Bundt cakes or cakes baked in a tube pan commonly benefit from a thin glaze.

To add moistness to a glazed cake, prick holes in top of cooled, unfrosted cake so glaze will seep down into cake.

If a glaze is too thin, add a little sifted powdered sugar; if it's too thick, stir in a tablespoon more of the liquid that's in the recipe.

Don't overlook the filling selections included here. They're fruity and gooey and taste great smoothed between tall layers of a white or yellow cake.

Buttermilk Glaze

◀ QUICK ▶

PREP: 3 MINUTES   COOK: 5 MINUTES

1 cup sugar
1½ teaspoons baking soda
½ cup buttermilk
½ cup butter or margarine
1 tablespoon light corn syrup
1 teaspoon vanilla extract

•Bring first 5 ingredients to a boil in a Dutch oven over medium heat. Boil 4 minutes, stirring constantly until glaze is golden. Remove from heat, and stir in vanilla. Cool slightly. Yield: 1½ cups.
Per tablespoon: Calories 71 Fat 3.9g
Cholesterol 11mg Sodium 97mg

Chocolate Glaze

◀ QUICK ▶

PREP: 5 MINUTES   COOK: 5 MINUTES

2 tablespoons butter or margarine
1 (1-ounce) square unsweetened chocolate
1 cup sifted powdered sugar
2 tablespoons boiling water

•Combine butter and chocolate in a small heavy saucepan. Cook over low heat until chocolate melts. Cool 3 to 4 minutes. Add

sugar and water; beat until smooth, using a wooden spoon. Yield: ¾ cup.
Per tablespoon: Calories 68 Fat 3.2g
Cholesterol 5mg Sodium 20mg

Bittersweet Glaze

PREP: 5 MINUTES   COOK: 5 MINUTES

COOL: 30 MINUTES

For this glaze known as ganache you heat whipping cream, add chopped chocolate, and stir until smooth.

⅔ cup whipping cream
2 tablespoons light corn syrup
6 ounces bittersweet chocolate, finely chopped
1 teaspoon vanilla extract

•Combine whipping cream and corn syrup in a saucepan; bring to a simmer over medium heat. Remove from heat, and add chocolate. Let stand 1 minute. Stir gently until chocolate melts completely. Stir in vanilla. Cool completely. Yield: 1 cup.
Per tablespoon: Calories 95 Fat 8.2g
Cholesterol 14mg Sodium 7mg

Powdered Sugar Glaze

◀ QUICK ▶

PREP: 3 MINUTES

You'll use this glaze often to top pound cakes, cookies, and sweet breads.

1 cup sifted powdered sugar
1 tablespoon plus 1 teaspoon milk
½ teaspoon vanilla extract

•Combine all ingredients; stir or beat at medium speed with an electric mixer until smooth. Yield: ⅓ cup.
Per tablespoon: Calories 30 Fat 0g
Cholesterol 0mg Sodium 1mg

Lemon Glaze: Substitute fresh lemon juice for milk.
Orange Glaze: Substitute fresh orange juice for milk.

Pineapple Filling

◀ QUICK • HEALTHY ▶

PREP: 10 MINUTES

3 tablespoons all-purpose flour
½ cup sugar
1 (20-ounce) can crushed pineapple, undrained
2 tablespoons butter or margarine

•Combine flour and sugar in a small saucepan; add pineapple and butter. Cook over medium heat, stirring constantly, until thickened. Cool. Yield: 2⅔ cups.
Per tablespoon: Calories 24 Fat 0.6g
Cholesterol 2mg Sodium 6mg

Lemon-Orange Filling

◀ QUICK • HEALTHY ▶

PREP: 5 MINUTES   COOK: 6 MINUTES

1 cup sugar
⅓ cup all-purpose flour
¼ teaspoon salt
¼ cup water
2 tablespoons grated orange rind
1 tablespoon grated lemon rind
1¼ cups fresh orange juice
¼ cup fresh lemon juice
4 egg yolks, well beaten

•Combine first 4 ingredients in a heavy saucepan; stir well. Stir in fruit rind and juices. Cook over medium heat, stirring constantly, until mixture thickens and boils.
•Gradually stir about one-fourth of hot mixture into egg yolks; add to remaining hot mixture, stirring constantly. Return to a boil; cook 1 to 2 minutes, stirring constantly. Remove from heat, and cool completely. (Mixture will be thick.) Yield: 2¼ cups.
Per tablespoon: Calories 36 Fat 0.6g
Cholesterol 24mg Sodium 17mg

Coconut-Bourbon Filling

◀ MAKE AHEAD ▶

PREP: 10 MINUTES   COOK: 30 MINUTES

This is a good filling for holiday layer cakes.

1½ cups raisins
1½ cups red candied cherries, halved
1½ cups pecans, coarsely chopped
1½ cups flaked coconut
12 egg yolks, lightly beaten
1¾ cups sugar
¾ cup butter
½ teaspoon salt
½ cup bourbon

•Place raisins in a small saucepan, and cover with water. Bring to a boil; cover, remove from heat, and let stand 5 minutes. Drain and pat dry.
•Combine raisins, cherries, pecans, and coconut in a large bowl; set aside.
•Combine egg yolks and next 3 ingredients in top of a double boiler; bring water to a boil. Reduce heat to medium; cook, stirring constantly, 20 minutes or until mixture is thick. Add bourbon; stir well. Pour over fruit and nut mixture, stirring well; cool completely. Yield: 6 cups.
Per tablespoon: Calories 74 Fat 7.8g
Cholesterol 31mg Sodium 32mg

Chocolate Filling

PREP: 5 MINUTES   COOK: 4 MINUTES

2 tablespoons cornstarch
½ cup sugar
½ cup water
1 tablespoon butter or margarine
2 (1-ounce) squares semisweet chocolate

•Combine cornstarch, sugar, and water in a small saucepan, stirring well; cook over medium heat, stirring constantly, until thickened. Remove from heat; add butter and chocolate, stirring until melted. Let cool. Yield: 1 cup.
Per tablespoon: Calories 52 Fat 2.6g
Cholesterol 2mg Sodium 8mg

FAST & FANCY FINISHES

If your frosted cake tastes great but needs some pizzazz, give one of these easy decorating ideas a try. They're simple to do and will win your cake rave reviews. These techniques will work on most any flavor or type of frosting.

Melted chocolate is used in most of the ideas below. We suggest melting 2 to 4 ounces of semisweet chocolate morsels or squares with 1 teaspoon of shortening in a heavy saucepan over low heat or sealed in a heavy-duty zip-top plastic bag set in simmering water.

•**Coating cake with nuts:** Jazz up a cake by pressing chopped nuts into frosting. Coat the entire cake or just the sides.

•**Adding a chocolate design:** Squeeze melted chocolate from a zip-top plastic bag in desired pattern onto frosted cake.

•**Decorating with pecans:** Place chocolate-dipped pecans in pairs around edge of frosted cake.

•**Decorating with chocolate leaves:** Arrange chocolate leaves in desired fashion on frosted cake, working quickly so the heat of your hand doesn't melt the leaves. See how to make chocolate leaves on page 26.

COOKIES & CANDIES

These bite-size sweets bring out the child in all of us. Perhaps it's a vivid memory of helping Mom decorate homemade sugar cookies or of reaching your hand deep into the cookie jar. No matter what the occasion, cookies and candies are always a fine mouthful.

Cookies are classified by the way they're shaped. You'll find drop, bars and squares, refrigerated, rolled, hand-shaped, and specially shaped cookie categories in this chapter. You'll also find hints to help you with shaping, cutting, and serving each type of cookie.

Equipment

Invest in several sturdy, shiny aluminum cookie sheets if you plan to bake a lot of cookies. When you're shopping, pick up a cookie sheet and notice how heavy it is. Weight is a good indication of quality. If it's very light-weight, it may warp in your oven.

Select cookie sheets that are at least 2 inches narrower and shorter than your oven to allow heat to circulate evenly around them. Don't use pans with high sides for baking cookies, as they deflect heat and cause cookies to bake unevenly. If you have cookie sheets with nonstick coating, watch the cookies carefully as they bake; dark-surfaced pans of this type tend to make cookies brown very quickly.

A sturdy metal spatula, one or two large wire cooling racks, and an airtight container for storage are other cookie baking essentials.

Baking Cookies

Always bake cookies in a preheated oven unless a recipe specifies otherwise. Grease the cookie sheet only if directed. Many cookie recipes contain enough fat that greasing the cookie sheet isn't necessary. If you do grease the sheet, don't worry about washing or regreasing between batches; just wipe away excess crumbs. Place dough on a cool cookie sheet; if you spoon dough onto a hot cookie sheet, the dough will spread too quickly and the cookies will be flat.

Many bakers use parchment paper to line cookie sheets before baking. It eliminates the need to grease, and promotes easy removal upon baking. Our recipes don't call for using parchment paper, but if you choose to use it, find it on the grocery aisle near aluminum foil.

For best results, bake only one pan of cookies at a time, placing the pan in the center of the oven. If you have to bake two pans at a time, position oven racks so they divide the oven into thirds, and stagger pans on the racks. If cookies begin to brown unevenly, switch the pans halfway through baking time. Don't bake cookies with one pan directly over another pan. One batch will invariably have tops that are too dark, while the other will have the opposite problem.

Cookies are often difficult to test for doneness. Since personal preference varies as to soft or crisp cookies, we give a range in our baking times. If you prefer soft and chewy cookies, take them out of the oven at the lower end of the time. Leave cookies in one or two minutes longer to make them crisper.

We often use the phrase "until lightly browned" to help in determining doneness, too. Unless the recipe states otherwise, remove cookies from cookie sheets immediately after removal from the oven. With a spatula, transfer them to a wire rack to cool, being careful not to stack cookies or let the sides touch as they cool.

Storing and Freezing Cookies

Let cookies cool completely before storing. Store soft, chewy cookies in an airtight container to help keep them from drying out.

Place crisp cookies in a jar with a loose-fitting lid. Store bar cookies directly in their baking pan and seal the pan tightly with aluminum foil. You can also stack and store unfrosted bar cookies in airtight containers with wax paper placed between the layers.

You can freeze most cookie dough and baked cookies up to six months. Thaw baked cookies at room temperature an hour before serving. Thaw cookie dough in refrigerator or at room temperature until it's the right consistency for shaping into cookies as the recipe directs. You can even slice some refrigerator cookies straight from the freezer without thawing them.

DROP COOKIES

The name literally gives you all the instruction you need—just drop cookie dough from a spoon onto cookie sheets with no further shaping necessary. Drop cookies have somewhat rounded tops and are slightly irregular in shape. For drop cookies in this chapter, we used teaspoons (not measuring spoons) for measuring. Simply pick up the desired amount of dough with one spoon, and use the back of another to push the dough onto the cookie sheet (see top photo, next page). Take care to scoop equal amounts of dough each time so cookies will be about the same size. Allow 1 to 2 inches between balls of dough on the cookie sheet so they won't run together as they bake.

Coconut Macaroons

◄ QUICK ►

PREP: 6 MINUTES   COOK: 20 MINUTES

There are just six ingredients to stir and drop for these easy coconut cookies.

1⅓ cups flaked coconut
⅓ cup sugar
2 egg whites
2 tablespoons all-purpose flour
½ teaspoon vanilla extract
⅛ teaspoon salt

•Combine all ingredients; stir well. Drop by level tablespoonfuls onto a greased cookie sheet. Bake at 350° for 20 minutes; remove to a wire rack to cool. Yield: 1 dozen.
Per macaroon: Calories 87 Fat 4.2g
Cholesterol 0mg Sodium 63mg

Oatmeal-Raisin Cookies

◄ FAMILY FAVORITE ►

PREP: 11 MINUTES
COOK: 8 MINUTES PER BATCH

1 cup butter or margarine, softened
1 cup sugar
1 cup firmly packed brown sugar
2 large eggs
1 tablespoon vanilla extract
2 cups all-purpose flour
1 teaspoon baking soda
½ teaspoon baking powder
½ teaspoon salt
1½ cups quick-cooking oats, uncooked
1 cup raisins
1½ cups chopped pecans

•Beat butter at medium speed with an electric mixer until creamy; gradually add sugars, beating well. Add eggs and vanilla; beat well.
•Combine flour and next 3 ingredients; gradually add to butter mixture, beating well. Stir in oats, raisins, and pecans.
•Drop dough by heaping teaspoonfuls onto greased cookie sheets. Bake at 375° for 8 minutes or until lightly browned. Cool slightly on cookie sheets; remove to wire racks to cool completely. Yield: 7 dozen.
Per cookie: Calories 78 Fat 4.2g
Cholesterol 11mg Sodium 51mg

Oatmeal-Chocolate Chip Cookies: Stir 2 cups (12 ounces) semisweet chocolate morsels and 3 grated (1.5-ounce) bars milk chocolate into dough before baking.

Chewy Chip Cookies

◄ FAMILY FAVORITE ►

PREP: 15 MINUTES
COOK: 10 MINUTES PER BATCH

You can freeze these chewy chocolate chippers up to three months.

½ cup shortening
½ cup butter, softened
1 cup sugar
1 cup firmly packed brown sugar
2 large eggs
1 teaspoon vanilla extract
2 cups all-purpose flour
1 teaspoon baking powder
1 teaspoon baking soda
1 cup regular oats, uncooked
1 cup corn flakes cereal
1 cup (6 ounces) semisweet chocolate morsels
½ cup chopped pecans
½ cup flaked coconut

•Beat shortening and butter at medium speed with an electric mixer until creamy; gradually add sugars, beating well. Add eggs, one at a time, beating after each addition. Add vanilla, mixing well.
•Combine flour, baking powder, and soda; gradually add to butter mixture, mixing well. Stir in oats and remaining ingredients.
•Drop dough by tablespoonfuls 2 inches apart onto ungreased cookie sheets. Bake at 350° for 10 minutes or until lightly browned. Remove to wire racks to cool. Yield: 5 dozen.
Per cookie: Calories 102 Fat 5.2g
Cholesterol 11mg Sodium 40mg

Best-Ever Chocolate Chip Cookies

◀ FAMILY FAVORITE ▶

PREP: 10 MINUTES
COOK: 11 MINUTES PER BATCH

This cookie recipe lives up to its name—you'll want to try the double chip and jumbo variations, too.

¾ cup butter or margarine, softened
¼ cup shortening
¾ cup sugar
¾ cup firmly packed brown sugar
2 large eggs
1 teaspoon vanilla extract
2¼ cups all-purpose flour
1 teaspoon baking soda
¼ teaspoon salt
2 cups (12 ounces) semisweet chocolate morsels

•Beat butter and shortening at medium speed with an electric mixer until creamy; gradually add sugars, beating well. Add eggs and vanilla, beating well.
•Combine flour, soda, and salt; add to butter mixture, mixing well. Stir in chocolate morsels.
•Drop dough by heaping teaspoonfuls onto ungreased cookie sheets.
•Bake at 375° for 9 to 11 minutes. Cool slightly on cookie sheets; remove to wire racks to cool completely. Yield: about 6½ dozen.
Per cookie: Calories 72 Fat 4g
Cholesterol 10mg Sodium 39mg

Double Chip Cookies: Prepare Best-Ever Chocolate Chip Cookies, using 1 cup peanut butter morsels or butterscotch morsels and 1 cup semisweet chocolate morsels instead of 2 cups semisweet chocolate morsels. Yield: about 6½ dozen.

Jumbo Chocolate Chip Cookies: Prepare Best-Ever Chocolate Chip Cookies, dropping them onto ungreased cookie sheets by ¼ cupfuls. Lightly press each cookie with fingertips into a 3-inch circle. Bake at 350° for 15 to 17 minutes. Yield: 1½ dozen.

Dropping dough: Use one teaspoon (not a measuring spoon) to pick up the dough and another to push dough onto the cookie sheet.

Cooling cookies: Unless otherwise directed, remove warm cookies from cookie sheet immediately to a wire rack to cool.

White Chocolate-Macadamia Nut Cookies

PREP: 10 MINUTES
COOK: 10 MINUTES PER BATCH

½ cup butter or margarine, softened
½ cup shortening
¾ cup firmly packed brown sugar
½ cup sugar
1 large egg
1½ teaspoons vanilla extract
2 cups all-purpose flour
1 teaspoon baking soda
½ teaspoon salt
1 (6-ounce) package white chocolate-flavored baking bars, cut into chunks
1 (7-ounce) jar macadamia nuts, chopped

•Beat butter and shortening at medium speed with an electric mixer until creamy; gradually add sugars, beating well. Add egg and vanilla; beat well. Combine flour, soda, and salt; gradually add to butter mixture, beating well. Stir in white chocolate and nuts.
•Drop dough by rounded teaspoonfuls 2 inches apart onto lightly greased cookie sheets. Bake at 350° for 8 to 10 minutes or until lightly browned. Cool slightly on cookie sheets; remove to wire racks to cool completely. Yield: 5 dozen.
Per cookie: Calories 100 Fat 6.7g
Cholesterol 9mg Sodium 54mg

Backpack Cookies

◀ FAMILY FAVORITE ▶

PREP: 12 MINUTES
COOK: 12 MINUTES PER BATCH

Peanuts, cereal, and chocolate candy pieces are packed into these goodies.

1 cup butter or margarine, softened
1 cup sugar
1 cup firmly packed brown sugar
2 large eggs
1 teaspoon vanilla extract
2 cups all-purpose flour
½ teaspoon baking powder
1 teaspoon baking soda
⅛ teaspoon salt
1 cup regular oats, uncooked
2 cups crisp rice cereal
2 cups candy-coated chocolate pieces
1 cup chopped unsalted roasted peanuts
½ cup flaked coconut
1 cup (6 ounces) semisweet chocolate morsels

•Beat butter at medium speed with an electric mixer until creamy; gradually add sugars, beating well. Add eggs and vanilla; beat well.
•Combine flour and next 3 ingredients; gradually add to butter mixture, mixing well. Stir in oats and remaining ingredients.
•Drop dough by rounded tablespoonfuls 2 inches apart onto ungreased cookie sheets. Bake at 350° for 10 to 12 minutes or until cookies are lightly browned. Remove to wire racks to cool. Yield: 6 dozen.
Per cookie: Calories 126 Fat 6.4g
Cholesterol 13.4mg Sodium 62mg

Monster Cookies

PREP: 18 MINUTES
COOK: 15 MINUTES PER BATCH

All your favorite cookie flavors, and primarily peanut butter, are rolled into these giant cookies. They're dropped from ¼-cup measures rather than teaspoons. Pass them out as Halloween favors or on other holiday occasions for the little ones.

½ cup butter or margarine, softened
1 cup sugar
1 cup plus 2 tablespoons firmly packed brown sugar
2 cups peanut butter
3 large eggs
1 teaspoon light corn syrup
¼ teaspoon vanilla extract
4½ cups regular oats, uncooked
2 teaspoons baking soda
¼ teaspoon salt
1 cup candy-coated chocolate pieces
1 cup (6 ounces) semisweet chocolate morsels

•Beat butter at medium speed with an electric mixer until creamy; gradually add sugars, beating well. Add peanut butter and next 3 ingredients; beat well. Add oats, soda, and salt; stir well. Stir in chocolate pieces and morsels. (Dough will be stiff.)
•Pack dough into a ¼-cup measure. Drop dough 4 inches apart onto lightly greased cookie sheets. Lightly press each cookie with fingertips into a 3½-inch circle.
•Bake at 350° for 12 to 15 minutes (centers of cookies will be slightly soft). Cool slightly on cookie sheets; remove to wire racks to cool. Yield: 2½ dozen.

Per cookie: Calories 308 Fat 16.9g
Cholesterol 30mg Sodium 207mg

Favorite Sugar Cookies

PREP: 20 MINUTES
COOK: 12 MINUTES PER BATCH

These sugar cookies don't have to be rolled and cut. They're a simplified drop-and-bake version with a great buttery flavor and sugared tops.

1 cup butter, softened
1 cup vegetable oil
1 cup sugar
1 cup sifted powdered sugar
2 large eggs
1 teaspoon vanilla extract
4 cups all-purpose flour
1 teaspoon baking soda
1 teaspoon salt
1 teaspoon cream of tartar
½ cup sugar

•Beat butter and vegetable oil at medium speed with an electric mixer until blended; gradually add 1 cup sugar and powdered sugar, beating well. Add eggs and vanilla, beating well.
•Combine flour and next 3 ingredients; add to butter mixture, beating at low speed until blended.
•Drop dough by rounded teaspoonfuls 2 inches apart on ungreased cookie sheets. Dip a flat-bottomed glass in ½ cup sugar, and flatten each mound of dough to ¼-inch thickness (about a 1½-inch circle). Bake at 350° for 10 to 12 minutes or until edges are golden. Remove to wire racks to cool. Yield: 9½ dozen.

Per cookie: Calories 61 Fat 3.6g
Cholesterol 8mg Sodium 45mg

Fruitcake Cookies

PREP: 15 MINUTES   CHILL: 1 HOUR
COOK: 10 MINUTES PER BATCH

Try these fruitcake bites from a family recipe passed down from generation to generation. The cookies just may win favor with your family, too, this holiday season.

½ cup shortening
1 cup firmly packed brown sugar
1 large egg
¼ cup buttermilk
2 cups all-purpose flour
½ teaspoon baking powder
½ teaspoon baking soda
½ teaspoon salt
1 cup chopped dates
1 cup chopped pecans
½ cup chopped red candied cherries
½ cup chopped green candied cherries
5 dozen pecan halves (optional)

•Beat shortening at medium speed with an electric mixer until fluffy; gradually add brown sugar, beating well. Add egg; beat well. Stir in buttermilk.
•Combine flour and next 3 ingredients; stir into brown sugar mixture. Stir in dates, chopped pecans, and cherries; cover and chill 1 hour.
•Drop dough by rounded teaspoonfuls 2 inches apart onto lightly greased cookie sheets. Top each cookie with a pecan half, if desired.
•Bake at 375° for 10 minutes or until lightly browned. Remove to wire racks to cool. Yield: 5 dozen.

Per cookie: Calories 81 Fat 3.7g
Cholesterol 4mg Sodium 30mg

BARS & SQUARES

If you own a 13- x 9-inch pan or a 9-inch pan, you'll use it repeatedly for these easy-to-make bar cookies. The simplest of these recipes involves minimal mixing, spreading batter in the pan, and baking; then once cool, just cut into bars or squares. Be sure to bake in the pan size indicated; otherwise, the baking time and texture of the bars may vary.

Bar cookies can have either a cakelike or a fudgelike texture, depending on the proportion of fat to flour and the number of eggs used. Brownies, the most famous of all bars and squares, leads this section. You'll find a few familiar easy brownie recipes here, as well as other scrumptious variations.

Blonde Brownies

◄ FAMILY FAVORITE ►

PREP: 11 MINUTES   COOK: 32 MINUTES

Brown sugar is what defines these brownies as blonde. Top them with vanilla ice cream and butterscotch sauce for a bonus.

1 (16-ounce) package brown sugar
¾ cup butter or margarine
3 large eggs
2¾ cups all-purpose flour
2½ teaspoons baking powder
½ teaspoon salt
1 cup chopped pecans
2 teaspoons vanilla extract

•Heat sugar and butter in a saucepan over medium heat until butter melts and mixture is smooth. Remove from heat. Cool slightly. Add eggs, one at a time, beating after each addition.
•Combine flour, baking powder, and salt; add to sugar mixture, stirring well. Stir in pecans and vanilla. Pour into a greased and floured 13- x 9-inch pan. Bake at 350° for 25 to 28 minutes. Cool in pan on a wire rack. Cut into bars. Yield: 2 dozen.
Per brownie: Calories 217 Fat 10.2g
Cholesterol 42mg Sodium 165mg

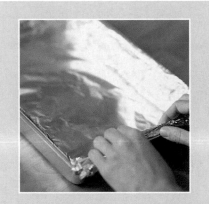

Foil lining for brownies: Line lightly greased baking pan with foil before spreading batter in pan to bake.

Easy removal and cutting: Lift foil with uncut baked brownies out of pan; then peel back foil and brownies will be easy to cut.

Candy Bar Brownies

◄ FAMILY FAVORITE ►

PREP: 15 MINUTES   COOK: 35 MINUTES

Substitute your favorite candy bar in this recipe to satisfy your sweet tooth.

¾ cup butter or margarine
2 cups sugar
2 teaspoons vanilla extract
4 large eggs
1½ cups all-purpose flour
½ teaspoon baking powder
¼ teaspoon salt
⅓ cup cocoa
4 (2.07-ounce) chocolate-coated caramel-peanut nougat bars, coarsely chopped
3 (1.5-ounce) milk chocolate bars, chopped

•Melt butter in a large saucepan over medium heat. Stir in sugar and vanilla; add eggs, and beat well.
•Combine flour and next 3 ingredients; stir into sugar mixture. Fold in chopped nougat bars. Spoon into a greased and floured 13- x 9-inch pan; sprinkle with chopped milk chocolate bars.
•Bake at 350° for 35 minutes. Cool completely, and cut into bars. Yield: 2½ dozen.
Per brownie: Calories 189 Fat 8g
Cholesterol 43mg Sodium 100mg

White Chocolate Brownies

PREP: 23 MINUTES   COOK: 35 MINUTES

⅓ cup butter or margarine
8 ounces white chocolate, chopped and divided
2 large eggs
⅔ cup sugar
1 cup all-purpose flour
½ teaspoon baking powder
¼ teaspoon salt
1 tablespoon vanilla extract
¼ cup sliced almonds

•Melt butter in a small saucepan over low heat. Add half of white chocolate, and remove from heat. (Do not stir.)
•Beat eggs at medium speed with an electric mixer until thick and pale; gradually add sugar, beating well.
•Combine flour, baking powder, and salt; add to egg mixture, mixing just until blended. Stir in melted white chocolate mixture and vanilla. Fold in remaining chopped white chocolate.
•Spoon mixture into a greased 8-inch square pan. Sprinkle with almonds. Bake at 350° for 32 to 35 minutes. Cool and cut into bars. Yield: 2 dozen.
Per brownie: Calories 128 Fat 6.6g
Cholesterol 28mg Sodium 64mg

Chewy Graham Brownies

PREP: 8 MINUTES   COOK: 24 MINUTES

You won't believe these fudgy treats have only five ingredients. The thick batter is loaded with chocolate cookie crumbs.

1 cup (6 ounces) semisweet chocolate morsels
½ cup creamy or chunky peanut butter
1 (14-ounce) can sweetened condensed milk
½ cup coarsely chopped pecans, toasted
2 cups chocolate graham cracker crumbs or chocolate wafer cookie crumbs

•Combine first 3 ingredients in a saucepan; cook over medium heat, stirring constantly, until morsels and peanut butter melt.
•Remove from heat. Stir in pecans and chocolate crumbs. (Batter will be very thick.)
•Press batter into a heavily greased 8-inch square pan. Bake at 350° for 24 minutes. Cool in pan. Cut into 2-inch squares. Yield: 16 brownies.
Per brownie: Calories 256 Fat 14.4g
Cholesterol 8mg Sodium 114mg

Choco-Mallow Brownies

PREP: 26 MINUTES   COOK: 20 MINUTES

Some folks liken these to Mississippi Mud or Rocky Road brownies.

½ cup butter or margarine, softened
1 cup sugar
2 large eggs
¾ cup all-purpose flour
½ teaspoon baking powder
Pinch of salt
3 tablespoons cocoa
1 teaspoon vanilla extract
½ cup chopped pecans
2 cups miniature marshmallows
Chocolate Frosting

•Beat butter at medium speed with an electric mixer until creamy; gradually add sugar, beating well. Add eggs, one at a time, beating after each addition.
•Combine flour and next 3 ingredients; add to butter mixture, stirring well. Stir in vanilla

and pecans. Spoon into a greased and floured 9-inch square pan.
•Bake at 350° for 18 to 20 minutes. Remove from oven; sprinkle with marshmallows. Cover with aluminum foil, and let stand 5 minutes or until marshmallows melt.
•Spread Chocolate Frosting on top of warm brownies. Cool and cut into 1½-inch squares. Yield: 3 dozen.
Per brownie: Calories 122 Fat 5.7g
Cholesterol 23mg Sodium 55mg

Chocolate Frosting

¼ cup butter or margarine, melted
2 cups sifted powdered sugar
3 tablespoons cocoa
4 to 5 tablespoons half-and-half

•Combine first 3 ingredients in a mixing bowl. Gradually add half-and-half, beating at medium speed with an electric mixer until spreading consistency. Yield: 1⅓ cups.

Note: For a shortcut, bake a commercial brownie mix that has 9-inch square pan instructions; proceed with marshmallows and frosting as directed above.

Cream Cheese Swirl Brownies

PREP: 24 MINUTES   COOK: 40 MINUTES

1 (4-ounce) package sweet baking chocolate
¼ cup plus 1 tablespoon butter or margarine, divided
½ (8-ounce) package cream cheese, softened
¼ cup sifted powdered sugar
3 large eggs
1 tablespoon all-purpose flour
½ teaspoon vanilla extract
½ cup sugar
¼ cup firmly packed brown sugar
½ cup all-purpose flour
½ teaspoon baking powder
¼ teaspoon salt
1 tablespoon Kahlúa or brewed coffee

•Melt chocolate and 3 tablespoons butter over low heat, stirring constantly. Cool.

•Beat remaining 2 tablespoons butter and cream cheese in a medium bowl at medium speed with an electric mixer until creamy. Gradually add powdered sugar, beating until light and fluffy. Stir in 1 egg, 1 tablespoon flour, and vanilla. Set aside.
•Beat remaining 2 eggs at medium speed until thick and pale. Gradually add ½ cup sugar and brown sugar, beating until thickened. Combine ½ cup flour, baking powder, and salt; add to egg mixture, mixing well. Stir in cooled chocolate mixture and liqueur.
•Spread half of chocolate batter into a greased 8-inch square pan. Spread with cream cheese mixture; top with remaining chocolate batter. Swirl batter with a knife to create a marbled effect. Bake at 350° for 35 to 40 minutes. Cool on a wire rack; cut into 2-inch squares. Yield: 16 brownies.
Per brownie: Calories 169 Fat 9.7g
Cholesterol 57mg Sodium 109mg

Frosted Fudge Brownies

PREP: 18 MINUTES   COOK: 20 MINUTES

1 cup shortening
4 (1-ounce) squares unsweetened chocolate
2 cups sugar
4 large eggs, beaten
1 teaspoon vanilla extract
1½ cups all-purpose flour
½ teaspoon salt
1 cup chopped pecans
Frosting

•Combine shortening and chocolate in top of a double boiler; bring water to a boil. Reduce heat to low; cook until chocolate melts. Add sugar, stirring well. Add eggs and vanilla; stir well.
•Stir in flour and salt. Remove chocolate mixture from heat, and stir in pecans.
•Spread batter into a well-greased 13- x 9-inch pan. Bake at 400° for 20 minutes. Cool; spread with Frosting. Cut into squares. Store in refrigerator. Yield: 2½ dozen.
Per brownie: Calories 248 Fat 13.4g
Cholesterol 31mg Sodium 62mg

Frosting

2 (1-ounce) squares unsweetened
  chocolate
2 tablespoons butter or margarine
3 cups sifted powdered sugar
⅓ cup half-and-half
1 teaspoon vanilla extract
Pinch of salt

•Combine chocolate and butter in top of a
double boiler; bring water to a boil. Reduce
heat to low; cook until chocolate and butter
melt. Remove from heat. Gradually add
powdered sugar to chocolate mixture alternately with half-and-half, beating at medium
speed with an electric mixer until smooth.
Stir in vanilla and salt. Yield: 1½ cups.

Peanut Butter and Chocolate Bars

PREP: 9 MINUTES   BAKE: 40 MINUTES

*Chocolate, peanut butter, and convenient
cake mix come together in this easy-to-make
bar cookie.*

1 (18.25-ounce) package yellow cake mix
2 large eggs
1 cup chunky peanut butter
½ cup butter or margarine, melted
1 cup (6 ounces) semisweet chocolate
  morsels
1 (14-ounce) can sweetened condensed
  milk

•Combine first 4 ingredients in a large mixing bowl; beat at medium speed with an
electric mixer 1 to 2 minutes. (Mixture will
be very thick.)
•Press half of cake mix mixture into an
ungreased 13- x 9-inch pan. Bake at 350° for
10 minutes. Remove from oven; sprinkle
with chocolate morsels, and drizzle with
condensed milk. Sprinkle with remaining
cake mix mixture. Bake at 350° for 30 minutes. Cool and cut into bars. Yield: 4 dozen.
Per bar: Calories 141 Fat 7.8g
Cholesterol 17mg Sodium 125mg

Double Peanut Butter Bars: Substitute 1
cup (6 ounces) peanut butter morsels for
chocolate morsels.

Raspberry Bars

PREP: 15 MINUTES   COOK: 20 MINUTES

*A crumbly oat mixture bakes into a pebbly
topping over raspberry preserves on a shortbread crust.*

¾ cup butter or margarine, softened
1 cup firmly packed brown sugar
1½ cups all-purpose flour
½ teaspoon baking soda
¾ teaspoon salt
1½ cups quick-cooking oats, uncooked
1 (10-ounce) jar raspberry preserves

•Beat butter at medium speed with an
electric mixer until creamy; gradually add
sugar, beating well. Combine flour and
next 3 ingredients; add to butter mixture,
mixing well.
•Press half of crumb mixture into a greased
13- x 9-inch pan. Spread raspberry preserves
over crumb mixture. Sprinkle remaining half
of crumb mixture over preserves. Bake at
400° for 20 minutes. Cool on a wire rack; cut
into bars. Yield: 32 bars.
Per bar: Calories 120 Fat 4.6g
Cholesterol 12mg Sodium 115mg

Strawberry Bars: Substitute 1 (10-ounce)
jar strawberry preserves for the raspberry
preserves.

Lemon Bars

◀ FAMILY FAVORITE ▶

PREP: 27 MINUTES   COOK: 50 MINUTES

*Here's an old-fashioned bar cookie that never
goes out of style. It's celebrated for its shortbread base and intense lemony filling.*

2½ cups all-purpose flour, divided
½ cup sifted powdered sugar
¾ cup butter or margarine
½ teaspoon baking powder
4 large eggs, lightly beaten
2 cups sugar
½ teaspoon grated lemon rind (optional)
⅓ cup fresh lemon juice
Powdered sugar

•Combine 2 cups flour and ½ cup powdered sugar; cut in butter with a pastry

blender until crumbly. Spoon mixture into a
greased 13- x 9-inch pan; press firmly and
evenly into pan, using fingertips. Bake at
350° for 20 to 25 minutes or until crust is
lightly browned.
•Combine remaining ½ cup flour and baking powder; set aside. Combine eggs, 2 cups
sugar, lemon rind, if desired, and lemon
juice; stir in flour mixture. Pour over prepared crust.
•Bake at 350° for 25 minutes or until lightly
browned and set. Cool on a wire rack. Dust
lightly with powdered sugar; cut into bars.
Yield: 2 dozen.
Per bar: Calories 183 Fat 6.7g
Cholesterol 51mg Sodium 70mg

Lime Bars: Substitute fresh lime juice and
rind for lemon juice and rind.

Pecan Pie Bars

◀ FAMILY FAVORITE ▶
◀ MAKE AHEAD ▶

PREP: 15 MINUTES   COOK: 52 MINUTES

*It's pecan pie as a bar cookie. Top with ice
cream or just enjoy a couple of bars with a
cup of coffee.*

1¾ cups all-purpose flour
⅓ cup firmly packed brown sugar
¾ cup butter or margarine
1 cup firmly packed brown sugar
4 large eggs
1 cup dark corn syrup
¼ cup butter or margarine, melted
1 teaspoon vanilla extract
⅛ teaspoon salt
1¼ cups chopped pecans

•Combine flour and ⅓ cup brown sugar;
cut in ¾ cup butter with a pastry blender
until crumbly. Press mixture evenly into a
greased 13- x 9-inch pan. Bake at 350° for
15 to 17 minutes.
•Combine 1 cup brown sugar and next 5
ingredients, stirring well. Stir in pecans.
Pour filling over prepared crust. Bake at
350° for 35 minutes or until set. Cool in pan
on a wire rack. Cut into bars. Yield: 2½
dozen.
Per bar: Calories 189 Fat 10.2g
Cholesterol 45mg Sodium 98mg

Chocolate Chess Squares

◄ MAKE AHEAD ►

PREP: 20 MINUTES COOK: 1 HOUR
CHILL: 2 HOURS

Cocoa lends a deep chocolate flavor to these gooey squares.

1 cup all-purpose flour
⅓ cup sifted powdered sugar
½ cup butter or margarine
1½ cups sugar
3 tablespoons cocoa
⅛ teaspoon salt
2 tablespoons butter or margarine, melted
2 large eggs, beaten
1 (5-ounce) can evaporated milk
1 teaspoon vanilla extract
½ cup chopped pecans

•Combine flour and powdered sugar; cut in ½ cup butter with a pastry blender until crumbly. Press mixture evenly into a 9-inch square pan. Bake at 350° for 15 minutes or until lightly browned.
•Combine sugar, cocoa, and salt. Add 2 tablespoons butter and eggs; beat 2½ minutes at medium speed with an electric mixer. Add milk and vanilla, mixing well. Stir in pecans; pour mixture over crust.
•Bake at 350° for 42 to 45 minutes or until set. Cool completely on a wire rack. Cover and chill at least 2 hours. Cut into squares. Store in refrigerator. Yield: 3 dozen.
Per square: Calories 112 Fat 5g
Cholesterol 22mg Sodium 49mg

Seven-Layer Squares

◄ FAMILY FAVORITE ►

PREP: 8 MINUTES COOK: 36 MINUTES

⅓ cup butter or margarine
1½ cups graham cracker crumbs
1 cup flaked coconut
1 cup (6 ounces) semisweet chocolate morsels
1 cup (6 ounces) butterscotch morsels
1 cup chopped pecans
1 (14-ounce) can sweetened condensed milk

•Place butter in a 9-inch square pan, and bake at 325° for 3 minutes or until melted.
•Layer graham cracker crumbs, coconut, chocolate morsels, butterscotch morsels, and pecans in pan with melted butter. (Do not stir.) Spread condensed milk evenly over top.
•Bake at 325° for 33 minutes. Cool completely in pan. Cut into 1½-inch squares. Yield: 3 dozen.
Per square: Calories 156 Fat 9.3g
Cholesterol 9mg Sodium 70mg

White Chocolate-Cinnamon Layer Squares: Stir 2 teaspoons ground cinnamon into graham cracker crumbs before layering the crumbs in pan. Substitute 1 cup chopped white chocolate for butterscotch morsels.

Pricking shortbread dough: Using a fork, prick dough in pan at 1-inch intervals.

Scottish Shortbread

◄ FAMILY FAVORITE ►

PREP: 22 MINUTES CHILL: 2 HOURS
COOK: 35 MINUTES

The secret of shortbread's buttery crumb lies in its simplicity. A basic blend of butter, sugar, and flour results in a taste far more than the sum of its parts. Good shortbread needs careful handling and precise baking.

1 pound unsalted butter, softened*
1 cup sugar
2 teaspoons vanilla extract
4 cups all-purpose flour
½ cup cornstarch
¼ teaspoon salt

•Beat butter at medium speed with an electric mixer until creamy; gradually add sugar, beating well. Stir in vanilla.
•Combine flour, cornstarch, and salt; gradually add to butter mixture, beating at low speed after each addition. (Mixture will be stiff.) Turn dough out onto a lightly floured surface; knead lightly 8 to 10 times.
•Press dough into an ungreased 15- x 10-inch jellyroll pan. Prick dough at 1-inch intervals with a fork (see photo), and score (cut) into 2½- x 1-inch bars. Cover and chill at least 2 hours.
•Bake at 325° for 35 minutes. Cool in pan on a wire rack 5 minutes; cut shortbread into bars. Cool completely before removing from pan. Store in an airtight container at room temperature up to 1 week, or freeze up to 3 months. Yield: 5 dozen.
*Use lightly salted butter and omit the salt, if desired.
Per bar: Calories 100 Fat 6.2g
Cholesterol 17mg Sodium 73mg

Coffee Toffee Bars

◄ MAKE AHEAD ►

PREP: 33 MINUTES BAKE: 32 MINUTES

The rocky tops on these luscious bar cookies come from chocolate-covered coffee beans and crushed toffee candy. See them pictured on page 134. They're great with a cup of coffee or a glass of cold milk.

¾ cup butter or margarine, softened
¾ cup firmly packed brown sugar
1 egg yolk
1½ cups all-purpose flour
¼ teaspoon salt
1 (14-ounce) can sweetened condensed milk
2 tablespoons butter or margarine
1 tablespoon Kahlúa or strongly brewed coffee
1 cup chopped walnuts
1 cup chocolate-covered coffee beans, chopped
1 cup coarsely chopped English toffee-flavored candy bars (we tested with Heath bars)

•Beat ¾ cup butter at medium speed with an electric mixer until creamy; gradually add brown sugar, beating well. Add egg yolk, beating well.

• Add flour and salt, stirring just until blended. Press dough into a lightly greased 13- x 9-inch pan. Bake at 350° for 20 minutes. Set aside.

• Combine sweetened condensed milk and 2 tablespoons butter in a medium-size heavy saucepan. Bring to a boil over medium heat; cook 5 minutes, stirring constantly. Remove from heat, and stir in Kahlúa. Pour mixture over prepared crust. Sprinkle with walnuts.

• Bake at 350° for 12 minutes. Remove from oven. Sprinkle warm bars with chopped coffee beans and toffee bars.

Gently press mixture into uncut bars. Cool completely in pan on a wire rack. Cover and chill until chocolate is firm. Let stand 5 minutes before cutting into bars. Yield: 4 dozen.

Per bar: Calories 118 Fat 7.2g Cholesterol 17mg Sodium 65mg

REFRIGERATOR COOKIES

You may know them as icebox cookies or slice 'n' bake, but the most notable thing about refrigerator cookies is their make-ahead quality.

You can roll the dough into a log, chill it up to a week, and when it's baking time, just slice the dough directly from the refrigerator, and bake only the number of cookies you want. They bake crisp and thin, make great dunkers for coffee, and are easy to stack and give as gifts.

If you don't bake all the cookies at once, you can easily return the remaining dough to the refrigerator or freezer to use at another time.

Vanilla-Pecan Icebox Cookies

◀ FAMILY FAVORITE ▶
◀ MAKE AHEAD ▶

PREP: 11 MINUTES
CHILL OR FREEZE: 4 HOURS
BAKE: 12 MINUTES PER BATCH

Roll this vanilla-scented cookie dough in wax paper, and chill until firm or freeze up to six months. Then just slice and bake the cookies when you need them. They'll be ready when you are.

1 cup butter or margarine, softened
¾ cup sugar
¼ cup firmly packed brown sugar
1 large egg
2 teaspoons vanilla extract
2¼ cups all-purpose flour
1½ teaspoons baking powder
½ teaspoon salt
1 cup finely chopped pecans

• Beat butter at medium speed with an electric mixer until creamy; gradually add sugars, beating well. Add egg and vanilla; beat mixture well.

• Combine flour, baking powder, and salt; add to butter mixture, beating well at medium speed. (Dough will be stiff.) Stir in pecans. Cover and chill dough at least 2 hours.

• Shape dough into 2 (6- x 2½-inch) rolls. Wrap rolls in wax paper, and chill or freeze until firm.

• Slice chilled dough into ¼-inch-thick slices; place on ungreased cookie sheets. Bake at 350° for 10 to 12 minutes or until lightly browned. Remove cookies to wire racks to cool. Yield: 4 dozen.

Per cookie: Calories 89 Fat 5.8g Cholesterol 15mg Sodium 78mg

Cherry Icebox Cookies

◀ MAKE AHEAD ▶

PREP: 13 MINUTES
CHILL OR FREEZE: 4 HOURS
COOK: 10 MINUTES PER BATCH

Maraschino cherries and red decorator sugar dress these icebox cookies for Christmas.

1 cup butter, softened
1 cup sugar
1 large egg
1 teaspoon vanilla extract
2¾ cups all-purpose flour
1 teaspoon baking powder
½ teaspoon salt
1 (16-ounce) jar maraschino cherries, drained and finely chopped
1 cup finely chopped pecans
¼ cup red decorator sugar crystals (optional)

• Beat butter at medium speed with an electric mixer until creamy; gradually add 1 cup sugar, beating well. Add egg and vanilla, beating well.

• Combine flour, baking powder, and salt; add to butter mixture, beating well. Pat cherries between paper towels to remove excess moisture. Stir cherries and pecans into dough; cover and chill dough at least 2 hours.

• Shape dough into 2 (8- x 1½-inch) rolls. Roll in decorator sugar crystals, if desired. Wrap rolls in wax paper, and chill or freeze until firm.

• Slice chilled dough into ¼-inch-thick slices, using a sharp knife. Place on lightly greased cookie sheets.

• Bake at 400° for 8 to 10 minutes or until golden. Cool 1 minute on cookie sheets; remove to wire racks to cool completely. Yield: 4 dozen.

Per cookie: Calories 116 Fat 6g Cholesterol 15mg Sodium 73mg

Note: If desired, substitute green candied cherries for maraschino cherries and roll in green decorator sugar crystals.

ROLLED COOKIES

Rolled cookies are prepared from dough that has been rolled to a designated thickness and cut with cookie cutters. Cut and baked plain, sprinkled with decorator candies before baking, or spread with frosting after baking, rolled cookies are particularly popular around the holidays. And they provide a good opportunity to show off your collection of cookie cutters, too.

To be rolled and shaped properly, the dough needs to be firmer than dough for most cookies. Many recipes call for chilling the dough to firm it before rolling. Large amounts of dough can be divided so you can work with one portion while the rest remains chilled. If your dough still seems too soft to roll after chilling, roll it directly onto cookie sheet, cut with cutters, and peel away the scraps. This eliminates transferring cut dough to cookie sheets, a task that can be virtually impossible when dough is soft.

Rolled Sugar Cookies

◀ FAMILY FAVORITE ▶

PREP: 27 MINUTES   CHILL: 1 HOUR
COOK: 8 MINUTES PER BATCH

Here's an easy sugar cookie to roll and cut.

½ cup butter or margarine, softened
1 cup sugar
1 large egg
1 teaspoon vanilla extract
2½ cups all-purpose flour
2 teaspoons baking powder
¼ teaspoon salt
Decorator sugar crystals

•Beat butter at medium speed with an electric mixer until creamy; gradually add 1 cup sugar, beating well. Add egg and vanilla; beat well.
•Combine flour, baking powder, and salt; gradually add to butter mixture, beating just until blended. Shape dough into a ball; cover and chill 1 hour.
•Divide dough into thirds. Work with 1 portion of dough at a time, storing remaining dough in refrigerator. Roll each portion to ⅛-inch thickness on a lightly floured surface. Cut with a 3-inch cookie cutter, and place on lightly greased cookie sheets. Sprinkle with sugar crystals. Bake at 375° for 8 minutes or until edges of cookies are lightly browned. Cool slightly on cookie sheets; remove to wire racks to cool completely. Yield: 20 cookies.
Per cookie: Calories 146 Fat 5.4g
Cholesterol 23mg Sodium 80mg

Jam Kolaches

PREP: 16 MINUTES
COOK: 15 MINUTES PER BATCH

½ cup butter or margarine, softened
1 (3-ounce) package cream cheese, softened
1¼ cups all-purpose flour
About ½ cup strawberry jam
¼ cup sifted powdered sugar

•Beat butter and cream cheese at medium speed with an electric mixer until creamy. Add flour to butter mixture, beating well.
•Roll dough to ⅛-inch thickness on a lightly floured surface; cut with a 2½-inch round cookie cutter. Place on lightly greased cookie sheets. Spoon ¼ teaspoon jam on each cookie; fold opposite sides to center, slightly overlapping edges. Bake at 375° for 15 minutes. Remove to wire racks to cool; sprinkle with powdered sugar. Yield: 3½ dozen.
Per cookie: Calories 54 Fat 3.2g
Cholesterol 8mg Sodium 30mg

Old-Fashioned Teacakes

◀ FAMILY FAVORITE ▶

PREP: 8 MINUTES   CHILL: 8 HOURS
COOK: 8 MINUTES PER BATCH

Teacakes are a cross between a cookie and a small cake. They're rolled and cut, and baked until barely browned.

1 cup butter or margarine, softened
2 cups sugar
3 large eggs
2 tablespoons buttermilk
1½ teaspoons vanilla extract
5 cups all-purpose flour
1 teaspoon baking soda
2 tablespoons sugar

•Beat butter at medium speed with an electric mixer until creamy; gradually add 2 cups sugar, beating well. Add eggs, buttermilk, and vanilla; beat well. Combine flour and soda; gradually add to butter mixture, beating well. Cover and chill at least 8 hours.
•Roll dough to ¼-inch thickness on a lightly floured surface. Cut with a 3½-inch round cookie cutter, and place 1 inch apart on lightly greased cookie sheets. Sprinkle with 2 tablespoons sugar.
•Bake at 400° for 7 to 8 minutes or until edges are lightly browned. Remove to wire racks to cool. Yield: 28 teacakes.
Per teacake: Calories 204 Fat 7.6g
Cholesterol 41mg Sodium 105mg

Gingerbread Men

◀ FAMILY FAVORITE ▶

PREP: 41 MINUTES   CHILL: 1 HOUR
COOK: 14 MINUTES PER BATCH

Use your imagination when decorating these big gingerbread men. They're edible and also fun to weave into your holiday centerpiece or mantel decor.

1 cup butter or margarine, softened
1½ cups firmly packed dark brown sugar
2 large eggs
⅔ cup molasses
⅓ cup fresh lemon juice
6½ to 7 cups all-purpose flour
2 tablespoons baking powder
½ teaspoon baking soda
⅛ teaspoon salt
2½ teaspoons ground ginger
2 teaspoons ground cinnamon
½ teaspoon ground cloves
¼ teaspoon ground nutmeg
½ cup raisins
¼ cup red cinnamon candies
White Frosting

•Beat butter at medium speed with an electric mixer until creamy; gradually add brown sugar, beating well. Add eggs, molasses, and lemon juice; beat well.
•Combine 2 cups flour, baking powder, and next 6 ingredients; stir well. Add to butter mixture, beating at low speed until blended.

Gradually add enough remaining flour to make a stiff dough, mixing well. Shape dough into 2 balls. Cover and chill at least 1 hour.

•Roll 1 portion of dough to ¼-inch thickness on a large greased cookie sheet. (Place a damp towel under cookie sheet, if necessary, to prevent cookie sheet from moving.) Cut gingerbread men with a 5½-inch cookie cutter. Remove excess dough, using the tip of a knife. Add excess dough to remaining half of dough; wrap in wax paper, and chill until needed.

•Press raisins and cinnamon candies in each gingerbread man for eyes, nose, mouth, and buttons.

•Bake at 350° for 10 to 14 minutes or until golden. Cool 1 minute on cookie sheet. Remove to wire racks to cool completely. Repeat procedure with remaining dough. Decorate Gingerbread Men with White Frosting. Yield: 2½ dozen.

Per cookie: Calories 320 Fat 10.4g
Cholesterol 32mg Sodium 179mg

White Frosting

1 (16-ounce) package powdered sugar, sifted
½ cup shortening
⅓ cup half-and-half
1 teaspoon vanilla extract

•Combine all ingredients in a large bowl; beat at medium speed with an electric mixer until mixture is spreading consistency. Use frosting to outline gingerbread and to make cuffs, collars, belts, and shoes. Yield: 2 cups.

Note: If desired, use different size cookie cutters. For an 8½-inch cookie cutter, bake 12 to 14 minutes (Yield: 11 cookies). For a 3-inch cookie cutter, bake 8 minutes; use currants instead of raisins (Yield: 8 dozen).

Speculaas

PREP: 22 MINUTES   COOK: 25 MINUTES

1 cup butter, softened
¾ cup firmly packed brown sugar
1 large egg
¼ teaspoon anise extract or ½ teaspoon anise seeds, crushed
⅛ teaspoon almond extract
3 cups all-purpose flour
1 tablespoon baking powder
Pinch of salt
2 teaspoons ground cinnamon
¾ teaspoon ground cloves
¼ teaspoon ground nutmeg
¼ teaspoon cocoa
¼ teaspoon pepper
½ teaspoon grated lemon or orange rind
¼ cup finely chopped blanched almonds
1 (6-ounce) can whole natural almonds

•Beat butter at medium speed with an electric mixer until creamy; gradually add brown sugar, beating well. Add egg, anise extract, and almond extract, beating well.

•Combine flour and next 8 ingredients; stir well. Add to butter mixture, beating at low speed until blended. Stir in chopped almonds.

•Divide dough in half. Shape 1 portion into a ball; knead 3 or 4 times until smooth. Roll dough into a 9-inch square on a lightly greased cookie sheet. Press onto floured cookie boards or cut dough into 36 (1½-inch) squares. Press a whole almond into center of each square. Repeat procedure with remaining dough.

•Bake at 325° for 25 minutes. Cool slightly on cookie sheet; remove to wire racks to cool completely. Break cookies apart, and store in airtight containers. Yield: 6 dozen.

Per cookie: Calories 69 Fat 4.4g
Cholesterol 10mg Sodium 65mg

SPECULAAS SPECTACULAR

Speculaas are heavily spiced cookies baked in wooden cookie molds. They're part of the Dutch tradition of St. Nicholas Day, celebrated December 5 in Holland. The night before, children leave carrots in their shoes for the saint's horse; in the morning, each child finds a treat in place of the carrot. Speculaas are sometimes given as the gift.

SHAPED COOKIES

For these cookies roll dough into balls with palms of your hands. Dough for this type of cookie needs to be firm so you can form it in your hands without making a mess. If dough seems too soft to shape, chill it for an hour or so until it's firm enough to shape.

When shaping the cookies, take care to roll all the balls the same size so cookies will be uniform after baking. Many of these cookies may spread as they bake, so allow 1 to 2 inches between them so they won't run together. And grease the cookie sheet only if the recipe specifies.

Many of the recipes in this section evolve from balls into other shapes or take on a coating or frosting.

Basic Butter Cookie Dough

◄ MAKE AHEAD ►

PREP: 14 MINUTES

Use this dough to make the five unique cookies that follow on the next page.

1 cup butter or margarine, softened
½ cup sugar
½ cup firmly packed brown sugar
1 large egg
3½ cups all-purpose flour
2 teaspoons baking powder
½ teaspoon salt
2 tablespoons milk
2 teaspoons vanilla extract

•Beat butter at medium speed with an electric mixer until creamy; gradually add sugars, beating well. Add egg, beating well.

•Combine flour, baking powder, and salt; add to butter mixture alternately with milk, beginning and ending with flour mixture. Mix at low speed after each addition until blended. Stir in vanilla.

•Divide dough in half; wrap each half in plastic wrap. Chill. Proceed with cookie instructions of choice. Yield: 2¼ pounds.

Almond Brickle Treats

PREP: 23 MINUTES   COOK: 12 MINUTES

1 (7½-ounce) package almond brickle chips*
½ Basic Butter Cookie Dough recipe (previous page)
2 cups (12 ounces) semisweet chocolate morsels
½ cup chopped pecans

•Stir or knead almond brickle chips into Basic Butter Cookie Dough; press dough into a lightly greased 15- x 10-inch jellyroll pan. Bake at 350° for 12 minutes or until lightly browned.
•Sprinkle chocolate morsels on top; cover with aluminum foil, and let stand 10 minutes. Spread melted morsels evenly over surface; sprinkle with pecans, and press gently into chocolate. Cool completely on a wire rack. Cut into 2- x 1-inch bars. Yield: 6 dozen.
*Find almond brickle chips on the baking aisle alongside chocolate morsels.
Per bar: Calories 74 Fat 4.7g
Cholesterol 6mg Sodium 44mg

Christmas Jammies

PREP: 20 MINUTES

COOK: 9 MINUTES PER BATCH

½ Basic Butter Cookie Dough recipe (previous page)
¼ cup seedless raspberry jam
Sifted powdered sugar

•Roll Basic Butter Cookie Dough to ⅛-inch thickness on a lightly floured surface. Cut with a 2-inch round cutter, and place on lightly greased cookie sheets.
•Cut center from half of cookies with a 1-inch star-shaped cutter. Bake at 350° for 7 to 9 minutes or until lightly browned. Remove to wire racks to cool.
•Spread raspberry jam almost to edges of solid cookies. Sprinkle cutout cookies with powdered sugar, and place over jam cookies. Yield: 20 cookies.
Per cookie: Calories 69 Fat 3g
Cholesterol 9mg Sodium 50mg

Pinwheels

PREP: 18 MINUTES   CHILL: 1 HOUR

COOK: 10 MINUTES PER BATCH

½ Basic Butter Cookie Dough recipe (previous page)
1 (1-ounce) square unsweetened chocolate, melted

•Divide chilled Basic Butter Cookie Dough in half. Knead chocolate into 1 portion until well blended.
•Roll each portion into a 12- x 9- inch rectangle on wax paper. Invert chocolate dough onto plain dough; peel off wax paper. Press chocolate dough firmly onto plain dough with a rolling pin. Roll up, jellyroll fashion, starting with long side; cover and chill 1 hour or until firm.
•Cut dough into ¼-inch slices; place on lightly greased cookie sheets. Bake at 350° for 9 to 10 minutes or until lightly browned. Remove to wire racks to cool. Yield: 3 dozen.
Per pinwheel: Calories 61 Fat 3.3g
Cholesterol 10mg Sodium 55mg

Date Bars

◄ HEALTHY ►

PREP: 16 MINUTES   COOK: 30 MINUTES

1 (10-ounce) package chopped dates
½ cup sugar
½ cup water
1 tablespoon fresh lemon juice
½ Basic Butter Cookie Dough recipe (previous page)

•Combine first 4 ingredients in a saucepan; bring to a boil over medium heat. Reduce heat, and cook 4 to 5 minutes or until thickened, stirring occasionally. Cool.
•Press two-thirds of Basic Butter Cookie Dough in a lightly greased 13- x 9-inch pan; spread date mixture over dough. Crumble remaining dough over date mixture.
•Bake at 350° for 23 to 25 minutes or until lightly browned. Cool completely in pan on a wire rack. Cut into 2- x 1-inch bars. Yield: 3 dozen.
Per bar: Calories 89 Fat 2.8g
Cholesterol 10mg Sodium 44mg

Easy Santa Cookies

PREP: 40 MINUTES

COOK: 10 MINUTES PER BATCH

½ Basic Butter Cookie Dough recipe (previous page)
¼ cup sugar
1 (4¼-ounce) tube red decorating frosting
1 (4¼-ounce) tube white decorating frosting
¼ cup (1½ ounces) semisweet chocolate morsels
¼ cup red cinnamon candies
⅔ cup flaked coconut
30 miniature marshmallows

•Shape Basic Butter Cookie Dough into 1-inch balls, and place on a lightly greased cookie sheet. Dip a flat-bottomed glass into sugar, and flatten balls to ¼-inch thickness.
•Bake at 350° for 8 to 10 minutes or until golden. Remove to wire racks to cool.
•Spread red frosting on top portion of cookie to resemble hat; spread white frosting on lower portion of cookie to resemble beard. Attach 2 chocolate morsels and 1 cinnamon candy with a small amount of frosting to resemble eyes and nose. Gently press coconut into white frosting. Press marshmallow onto red frosting to resemble tassel on hat. Yield: 2½ dozen.
Per cookie: Calories 138 Fat 5g
Cholesterol 12mg Sodium 72mg

Chocolate-Kissed Peanut Butter Cookies

◄ QUICK • FAMILY FAVORITE ►

PREP: 12 MINUTES

COOK: 10 MINUTES PER BATCH

Four ingredients become a favorite peanut butter cookie kissed with a chocolate center.

1 cup sugar
1 cup chunky peanut butter
1 large egg, lightly beaten
36 milk chocolate kisses, unwrapped

•Combine first 3 ingredients; shape into ¾-inch balls. Place on ungreased cookie sheets. Bake at 350° for 9 to 10 minutes. Immediately press a chocolate kiss in center of each cookie; remove to wire racks to cool. Yield: 3 dozen.

Per cookie: Calories 92 Fat 5.3g
Cholesterol 7mg Sodium 41mg

Old-Fashioned Peanut Butter Cookies

◄ FAMILY FAVORITE ►

PREP: 25 MINUTES   CHILL: 3 HOURS

COOK: 8 MINUTES PER BATCH

1 cup butter or margarine, softened
1 cup creamy peanut butter
1 cup sugar
1 cup firmly packed brown sugar
2 large eggs
2½ cups all-purpose flour
2 teaspoons baking soda
¼ teaspoon salt
1 teaspoon vanilla extract
Sugar

•Beat butter and peanut butter at medium speed with an electric mixer until creamy; gradually add sugars, beating well. Add eggs, beating well.
•Combine flour, soda, and salt in a medium bowl; add to butter mixture, beating well. Stir in vanilla. Cover and chill 3 hours.
•Shape into 1¼-inch balls; place 3 inches apart on ungreased cookie sheets. Dip a fork in additional sugar; flatten cookies in a criss-cross design. Bake at 375° for 7 to 8 minutes. Remove to wire racks to cool. Yield: 6 dozen.

Per cookie: Calories 83 Fat 4.6g
Cholesterol 13mg Sodium 78mg

Old-Fashioned Peanut Butter Cookies

•Process vanilla wafers in food processor until crumbs are fine. Transfer to a large bowl. Process pecans in food processor until finely chopped. Stir into vanilla wafer crumbs. Stir in honey, bourbon, and rum.
•Shape dough into 1-inch balls, and roll in ¼ cup vanilla wafer crumbs or powdered sugar. Place in an airtight container; store in refrigerator up to one week. Yield: 6 dozen.

Per ball: Calories 81 Fat 5.3g
Cholesterol 0mg Sodium 21mg

Rum Balls

◄ QUICK • MAKE AHEAD ►

PREP: 18 MINUTES

Make these sugar-coated balls ahead—they get better each day.

1 (12-ounce) package vanilla wafers
1 (16-ounce) package pecan pieces
½ cup honey
⅓ cup bourbon
⅓ cup dark rum
¼ cup vanilla wafer crumbs or ⅓ cup powdered sugar

Sugar-Coated Chocolate Cookies

PREP: 35 MINUTES   CHILL: 2 HOURS

COOK: 10 MINUTES PER BATCH

½ cup butter or margarine
3 (1-ounce) squares unsweetened chocolate
2 cups sugar
2 cups all-purpose flour
2 teaspoons baking powder
3 large eggs, lightly beaten
2 teaspoons vanilla extract
¾ cup sifted powdered sugar

•Melt butter and chocolate in a heavy saucepan over low heat.
•Combine 2 cups sugar, flour, and baking powder in a large mixing bowl. Add chocolate mixture, eggs, and vanilla; beat at medium speed with an electric mixer until blended. (Mixture will be very thin.) Cover and chill at least 2 hours.
•Shape dough into 1-inch balls, and roll balls in powdered sugar. Place 2 inches apart on lightly greased cookie sheets. Bake at 375° for 10 minutes. Remove to wire racks to cool. Yield: 6½ dozen.

Per cookie: Calories 55 Fat 2.2g
Cholesterol 11mg Sodium 24mg

Molasses-Spice Crinkles

PREP: 15 MINUTES   CHILL: 1 HOUR

COOK: 11 MINUTES PER BATCH

This old-fashioned cookie forms a crackled top as it bakes.

¾ cup shortening
1 cup sugar
1 large egg
¼ cup molasses
2 cups all-purpose flour
1 teaspoon baking powder
1 teaspoon baking soda
¼ teaspoon salt
1 teaspoon ground ginger
1 teaspoon ground cinnamon
½ teaspoon ground nutmeg
¼ teaspoon ground cloves
¼ teaspoon ground allspice
¼ cup sugar

•Beat shortening at medium speed with an electric mixer until fluffy. Gradually add 1 cup sugar, beating well. Add egg and molasses; beat well.
•Combine flour and next 8 ingredients, stirring well. Add one-fourth of flour mixture at a time to shortening mixture, beating at low speed after each addition until blended. Cover and chill 1 hour.
•Shape dough into 1-inch balls, and roll in ¼ cup sugar. Place 2 inches apart on ungreased cookie sheets.
•Bake at 375° for 9 to 11 minutes. (Tops will crack.) Remove to wire racks to cool. Yield: 3 dozen.

Per cookie: Calories 90 Fat 3.8g
Cholesterol 6mg Sodium 53mg

Brown Sugar-Pecan Cookies

PREP: 30 MINUTES   CHILL: 30 MINUTES

COOK: 12 MINUTES PER BATCH

A pale brown sugar frosting drapes these simple butter cookies. Top each with a pecan half immediately after frosting them.

1 cup butter or margarine, softened
½ cup sugar
½ cup firmly packed brown sugar
1 large egg
1 teaspoon vanilla extract
2 cups all-purpose flour
½ teaspoon baking soda
¼ teaspoon salt
½ cup finely chopped pecans
Brown Sugar Frosting
60 pecan halves (about ⅔ cup)

•Beat butter at medium speed with an electric mixer until creamy; gradually add sugars, beating well. Add egg and vanilla; beat well.
•Combine flour, soda, and salt; gradually add to butter mixture, beating well. Stir in chopped pecans. Cover and chill at least 30 minutes.
•Shape dough into 1-inch balls. Place 2 inches apart on ungreased cookie sheets.
•Bake at 350° for 10 to 12 minutes. Remove to wire racks to cool. Spread about 1 teaspoon Brown Sugar Frosting on each cookie, and top with a pecan half. Yield: 5 dozen.

Per cookie: Calories 109 Fat 5.8g
Cholesterol 13mg Sodium 54mg

Brown Sugar Frosting

1 cup firmly packed brown sugar
½ cup half-and-half
1 tablespoon butter or margarine
1¾ cups sifted powdered sugar

•Combine brown sugar and half-and-half in a saucepan. Cook over medium heat, stirring constantly, until mixture comes to a boil; boil 4 minutes. Remove from heat. Stir in butter.
•Gradually add powdered sugar, beating at medium speed with an electric mixer 2 minutes or until frosting is spreading consistency. Yield: 1½ cups.

Thumbprint Cookies

◄ **FAMILY FAVORITE** ►

PREP: 35 MINUTES   CHILL: 1 HOUR

COOK: 15 MINUTES PER BATCH

A dollop of jelly brings vibrant color to these classic cookies. This version is rolled in chopped nuts.

1 cup butter, softened
¾ cup sugar
2 large eggs, separated
1 teaspoon almond extract
2 cups all-purpose flour
¼ teaspoon salt
1¼ cups finely chopped pecans
½ cup red currant or other flavored jelly, stirred

•Beat butter at medium speed with an electric mixer until creamy; gradually add sugar, beating well. Add egg yolks and almond extract, beating until blended.
•Combine flour and salt; add to butter mixture, beating at low speed until blended. Cover and chill dough 1 hour.
•Shape dough into 1-inch balls. Lightly beat egg whites. Dip each ball in egg white; roll in pecans. Place 2 inches apart on ungreased cookie sheets. Press thumb in each cookie to make an indentation.
•Bake at 350° for 15 minutes. Cool 1 minute on cookie sheets; remove to wire racks to cool completely. Press centers again with thumb while cookies are still warm; fill center of each cookie with jelly. Yield: 3½ dozen.

Per cookie: Calories 111 Fat 7.2g
Cholesterol 22mg Sodium 63mg

Porcelain Thumbprint Cookies: Reserve egg whites for another use, and omit pecans. Bake cookies 13 to 15 minutes or until lightly browned.

Cherry Crowns

PREP: 20 MINUTES   CHILL: 1 HOUR

COOK: 15 MINUTES PER BATCH

1 cup butter or margarine, softened
1 (3-ounce) package cream cheese,
     softened
1 cup sugar
1 large egg, separated
1 teaspoon almond extract
2½ cups all-purpose flour
1 cup finely ground blanched almonds
30 red candied cherries, halved

• Beat butter and cream cheese at medium speed with an electric mixer until creamy; gradually add sugar, beating well. Add egg yolk and almond extract, mixing well; gradually stir in flour. Cover and chill 1 hour.
• Shape dough into 1-inch balls; dip tops of balls into lightly beaten egg white, and then in almonds. Place 2 inches apart on lightly greased cookie sheets. Press a cherry half in center of each ball.
• Bake at 350° for 15 minutes. Remove to wire racks to cool. Yield: 5 dozen.
Per cookie: Calories 82 Fat 4.8g
Cholesterol 13mg Sodium 37mg

Devilish Marshmallow Cookies

PREP: 25 MINUTES   CHILL: 1 HOUR

COOK: 9 MINUTES PER BATCH

½ cup shortening
1 cup sugar
2 large eggs
1¾ cups all-purpose flour
1 teaspoon baking soda
¼ teaspoon salt
½ cup cocoa
1 teaspoon vanilla extract
1 teaspoon butter flavoring
21 large marshmallows, cut in half
Frosting

• Beat shortening at medium speed with an electric mixer until fluffy. Gradually add sugar, beating well. Add eggs, one at a time, beating after each addition.
• Combine flour and next 3 ingredients; add to shortening mixture, mixing well. Stir in

vanilla and butter flavoring. (Dough will be stiff.) Cover and chill dough 1 hour.
• Shape dough into 1-inch balls; place on greased cookie sheets. Bake at 350° for 7 minutes. Place a marshmallow half on top of each cookie; bake 2 more minutes. Remove to wire racks to cool, and spread frosting over tops. Yield: 3½ dozen.
Per cookie: Calories 115 Fat 4g
Cholesterol 12mg Sodium 45mg

Frosting

½ cup (3 ounces) semisweet chocolate
     morsels
¼ cup milk
2 tablespoons butter or margarine
2 cups sifted powdered sugar

• Combine first 3 ingredients in a saucepan. Cook over low heat, stirring constantly, until chocolate melts. Add powdered sugar, and beat until smooth. Yield: 1 cup.

Peanut Butter Stacks

PREP: 18 MINUTES   CHILL: 1 HOUR

COOK: 20 MINUTES

Children will enjoy sandwiching peanut butter cup candies between classic peanut butter cookies.

½ cup butter or margarine, softened
½ cup chunky peanut butter
1 cup firmly packed brown sugar
1 large egg
1 teaspoon vanilla extract
1¼ cups all-purpose flour
½ teaspoon baking soda
½ teaspoon salt
12 (.9-ounce) peanut butter cup candies

• Beat butter and peanut butter at medium speed with an electric mixer until creamy; gradually add sugar, beating well. Add egg and vanilla; beat well.
• Combine flour, soda, and salt; add to butter mixture, beating well. Cover and chill dough at least 1 hour.
• Shape dough into 24 balls; place half of dough balls 2 inches apart on a lightly greased cookie sheet. Dip a fork in water, and flatten cookies in a crisscross pattern.
• Bake at 350° for 10 minutes. Cool slightly

on cookie sheet; remove to a wire rack to cool completely.
• Place remaining dough balls on greased cookie sheet; repeat crisscross procedure with fork. Bake at 350° for 8 minutes. Cool slightly; turn cookies over on cookie sheet, so crisscross pattern is down. Place a peanut butter cup candy on each cookie.
• Bake 2 more minutes or until candies soften. Remove from oven. Top each with a baked cookie, pressing to form sandwiches. Yield: 1 dozen.
Per sandwich cookie: Calories 378 Fat 21.9g
Cholesterol 42mg Sodium 349mg

Madeleines

PREP: 26 MINUTES

COOK: 10 MINUTES PER BATCH

2 large eggs
⅛ teaspoon salt
⅓ cup sugar
½ cup all-purpose flour
1 teaspoon grated lemon rind
½ cup butter, melted and cooled
Powdered sugar

• Beat eggs and salt at high speed with an electric mixer until foamy. Gradually add sugar; beat at high speed 15 minutes or until thick and pale. Combine flour and lemon rind; fold in 2 tablespoons at a time. Fold in butter, 1 tablespoon at a time. Spoon 1 tablespoon batter into greased and floured madeleine molds.
• Bake at 400° for 8 to 10 minutes or until lightly browned. Cool in molds about 3 minutes. Remove from molds, and cool on a wire rack, flat side down. Sprinkle with powdered sugar. Yield: 2 dozen.
Per cookie: Calories 65 Fat 4.6g
Cholesterol 28mg Sodium 57mg

THE MEANING OF MADELEINE

A madeleine is a small ridged, feather-light sponge cake eaten as a cookie. The batter is poured into a special scalloped pan that forms a shell-shaped cookie when baked.

Cocoa-Almond Biscotti

PREP: 20 MINUTES   COOK: 41 MINUTES

Biscotti are long-slivered, intensely crunchy Italian cookies, perfect for dunking into a cup of hot coffee.

½ cup butter or margarine, softened
1 cup sugar
2 large eggs
1½ tablespoons Kahlúa or other
      coffee-flavored liqueur
2½ cups all-purpose flour
1½ teaspoons baking powder
¼ teaspoon salt
3 tablespoons Dutch process cocoa or
      regular cocoa
1 (6-ounce) can whole almonds

•Beat butter and sugar in a large bowl at medium speed with an electric mixer until light and fluffy. Add eggs, beating well. Mix in liqueur.
•Combine flour and next 3 ingredients; add to butter mixture, beating at low speed until blended. Stir in almonds. Divide dough in half; using floured hands, shape each portion into a 9- x 2-inch log on a lightly greased cookie sheet (photo 1).
•Bake at 350° for 28 to 30 minutes or until firm. Cool on cookie sheet 5 minutes. Remove to a wire rack to cool.
•Cut each log diagonally into ¾-inch-thick slices with a serrated knife, using a gentle sawing motion (photo 2). Place on ungreased cookie sheets. Bake 5 minutes. Turn cookies over, and bake 5 to 6 more minutes. Remove to wire racks to cool. Yield: 2 dozen.

Per cookie: Calories 203 Fat 11.2g
Cholesterol 28mg Sodium 95mg

1. Shape chocolate biscotti dough into 9-x 2-inch logs; place several inches apart on cookie sheet.

2. Use a gentle sawing motion to cut cooled biscotti logs into diagonal slices; then bake slices again to give them their characteristic crispness.

Cocoa-Almond Biscotti

Benne Seed Wafers

PREP: 50 MINUTES   CHILL: I HOUR

COOK: 10 MINUTES PER BATCH

Benne seeds (sesame seeds) freckle these crisp, coin-sized cookies and lend a nutty, slightly sweet flavor. The recipe gives you a big yield, so you can wrap little stacks and give them as gifts. See them in the jar on page 134.

½ cup sesame seeds
½ cup butter or margarine, softened
1 cup sugar
1 large egg
½ teaspoon vanilla extract
1¾ cups all-purpose flour
2 teaspoons baking powder
½ teaspoon baking soda
½ teaspoon salt

•Toast sesame seeds in a heavy skillet over medium heat 5 minutes or until browned, stirring often. Remove from heat; set aside.
•Beat butter at medium speed with an electric mixer until creamy; gradually add sugar, beating well. Stir in sesame seeds, egg, and vanilla.
•Combine flour and remaining 3 ingredients; stir into butter mixture. Cover and chill at least 1 hour. Shape dough into ½-inch balls, and place on lightly greased cookie sheets. Flatten to ¹⁄₁₆-inch thickness with fingers or a flat-bottomed glass.
•Bake at 325° for 10 minutes or until lightly browned. Remove to wire racks to cool. Yield: 10 dozen.
Per wafer: Calories 25 Fat 1.4g Cholesterol 4mg Sodium 28mg

Swedish Heirloom Cookies

◀ FAMILY FAVORITE ▶

PREP: 30 MINUTES

COOK: 15 MINUTES PER BATCH

These wedding cookies contain ground almonds and are rolled twice in powdered sugar for a delicate finish.

½ cup shortening
½ cup butter or margarine, softened
1 cup sifted powdered sugar
½ teaspoon salt
2 cups all-purpose flour
1 tablespoon water
1 tablespoon vanilla extract
1¼ cups ground almonds
Powdered sugar

•Beat shortening and butter at medium speed with an electric mixer until creamy. Add 1 cup powdered sugar and salt, beating at low speed. Stir in flour. Add water, vanilla, and almonds, stirring well.
•Shape dough into 1-inch balls. Place on ungreased cookie sheets, and flatten.
•Bake at 325° for 12 to 15 minutes or until firm and lightly browned. Roll warm cookies in additional powdered sugar. Yield: 4 dozen.
Per cookie: Calories 86 Fat 5.4g Cholesterol 5mg Sodium 44mg

CANDIES

Follow our basic guidelines for candy making, plan to cook on a dry, sunny day, and you shouldn't have any problems with these sweets.

Equipment

You'll need several sizes of heavy saucepans. Candy mixtures usually triple in volume as they cook, so you'll need pans large enough to allow candy mixtures to boil without boiling over. For smaller candy recipes, use smaller pans. If the pan is too large for the amount of mixture you're boiling, the mixture won't be deep enough in the pan for you to insert a candy thermometer and get an accurate temperature reading.

Wooden spoons are the preferred utensil because you'll need to stir some candy mixtures while they're cooking, and wooden spoons don't heat up like metal spoons do.

While you can test for the proper candy temperature by using the cold-water test alone, a candy thermometer is almost a necessity because it allows you to cook candy to precisely the right temperature and candy stage. Always test the accuracy of your thermometer before cooking with it by letting it stand in boiling water 10 minutes. If thermometer doesn't register 212°, allow for the inaccuracy when cooking. Always read a thermometer at eye level.

Cooking Candy

In candy making, it's important to follow a few special rules. Measure ingredients precisely to keep them in proper proportions. Assemble equipment and measure ingredients before starting to cook, because you may not have time once the process begins.

The main goal of candy making is to control the formation of sugar crystals. See our photo on page 157 that shows you how we recommend buttering the sides of a saucepan as an initial way of preventing sugar crystals from clustering on the pan. Stir candy mixture gently until it comes to a boil and the sugar dissolves, still trying to prevent crystals from clustering on the pan.

The next step is to cover the pan, and cook over medium heat 2 to 3 minutes to wash down sugar crystals. Then remove the lid and continue cooking. After this point, avoid stirring unless recipe specifies. Occasional stirring of candies made with milk or cream is necessary, however, to avoid scorching. Our recipes indicate whether or not you need to stir. If so, stir gently with wooden spoon so mixture doesn't splash onto sides of pan.

Avoid doubling a candy recipe. It's safer to make a second batch. During humid or rainy weather, cook candy until thermometer registers 1 to 2 degrees higher than the recipe directions specify.

Testing for Doneness

The most accurate test for doneness is to use a candy thermometer. When using one, make sure the bulb is in the boiling mixture but not touching the bottom of the pan. Watch the thermometer carefully, because the temperature rises quickly as the candy nears doneness.

If you don't have a candy thermometer, use the cold-water test to check all candy stages except the thread stage and caramel stage. Remove the syrup from the heat while testing. Drop a small amount of syrup into a cup of very cold water; then test with your fingers to determine consistency (see chart, page 155). Use fresh, cold water each time a sample is tested. For thread stage, syrup should spin a 2-inch thread when dropped from a metal spoon. For caramel stage, syrup will be honey-colored when spooned onto a white plate.

Cooling Candy

Some recipes call for candy mixtures to cool in the pan until lukewarm (110°). Let pan sit undisturbed during this cooling period; don't stir unless instructed to do so or the candy might be grainy.

When the mixture is ready for pouring, do so quickly, and take care not to scrape the sides of the pan since this may add sugar crystals to the candy. Let candy cool completely before cutting or packaging it.

Storing Candy

Store all candies in airtight containers as soon as they're cool; this prevents them from picking up moisture from the atmosphere. Most candies will stay fresh up to a week; fudgelike candies will keep up to a week or two if properly stored.

The recipe will indicate if the candy needs refrigerating. Some chocolate-dipped candies need refrigerating to keep the coating firm. In general, candy is not a good candidate for freezing.

Microwaving Candy

Some candies are considered good for microwave cooking because they cook quickly and require minimum attention. Most suited for microwave cooking are those candies that only require melting commercial chocolates and caramels and call for only a small amount of cooking.

EASY CANDIES

These confections require either no cooking at all or just a little cooking to melt and blend ingredients. They're an excellent choice if you're a beginner, showing your youngsters how to cook, or just don't have much time to devote to candy making.

Caramel-Marshmallow-Pecan Logs

PREP: 25 MINUTES   CHILL: 11 HOURS

COOK: 24 MINUTES

These gooey candy logs resemble that old-fashioned offering from the country store. An electric knife makes easy work of slicing.

1 (16-ounce) package powdered sugar, sifted
1¾ cups marshmallow creme
1½ teaspoons vanilla extract
1 (14-ounce) package caramels
3 tablespoons water
2 cups chopped pecans

•Combine first 3 ingredients in a large bowl; stir well. Knead 10 minutes or until smooth (mixture will be dry). Shape into four 5-inch logs. Cover and chill 3 hours.
•Unwrap caramels; combine caramels and water in a large skillet. Cook over medium heat until caramels melt; reduce heat to low, and stir until smooth. Working quickly with forks, roll each log in caramel mixture. Roll in pecans, pressing firmly to coat. Cover and chill at least 8 hours. Yield: 4 (5-inch) logs.
Per ½-inch slice: Calories 128 Fat 3.6g
Cholesterol 0mg Sodium 15mg

Toasted Pecan Clusters

PREP: 10 MINUTES   COOK: 35 MINUTES

Just a few yummy ingredients are needed for these clusters. The flavor far surpasses the time it'll take you to make them.

3 tablespoons butter or margarine
3 cups pecan pieces
12 ounces chocolate-flavored candy coating

•Melt butter in a 15- x 10-inch jellyroll pan. Spread pecans evenly in pan. Bake at 300° for 30 minutes, stirring every 10 minutes.
•Place candy coating in top of a double boiler; bring water to a boil. Reduce heat to low; cook until coating melts. Cool 2 minutes; add pecans, and stir until coated. Drop by rounded teaspoonfuls onto wax paper. Cool completely. Yield: 4 dozen.
Per cluster: Calories 95 Fat 8.1g
Cholesterol 2mg Sodium 7mg

Microwave Directions: Place butter in a 1-quart glass bowl; microwave at HIGH 50 seconds or until melted. Add pecans; toss to coat with butter. Spread on a glass plate. Microwave at HIGH 6 to 8 minutes or until lightly toasted, stirring at 3-minute intervals. Place candy coating in a 1-quart glass bowl. Microwave at MEDIUM (50% power) 2 to 3 minutes or until coating is softened; stir well. Cool 2 minutes; add pecans, and stir until coated. Drop by rounded teaspoonfuls onto wax paper. Cool completely.

Cream Cheese Butter Mints

◄ QUICK ►

PREP: 32 MINUTES

These little gems are fabulous for a wedding or baby shower. They're rich and buttery, and you can subtly color them to match your party theme.

1 (3-ounce) package cream cheese, softened
2 teaspoons butter flavoring
⅛ teaspoon peppermint oil
1 (16-ounce) package powdered sugar, sifted
Paste food coloring
Cornstarch

•Combine first 4 ingredients in a large mixing bowl; beat at low speed with an electric mixer until blended. Add a small amount of food coloring; beat at medium speed until well blended (mixture will be dry). Knead mint mixture until smooth.
•Press mint mixture into rubber candy molds that have been lightly dusted with cornstarch. Yield: 4 dozen.
Per mint: Calories 50 Fat 1.2g
Cholesterol 4mg Sodium 5mg

Peppermint Christmas Candy

◄ QUICK ►

PREP: 7 MINUTES   COOK: 4 MINUTES

Two ingredients are all it takes to make this sweet holiday treat—a great Christmas gift idea when packaged in pretty tins.

1 (24-ounce) package vanilla-flavored candy coating
10 peppermint candy canes, crushed (about 4 ounces)

•Line a 15- x 10-inch jellyroll pan with wax paper; set aside.
•Place candy coating in top of a double boiler; bring water to a boil. Reduce heat to low; cook until candy coating melts, stirring occasionally. Remove from heat; stir in crushed candy canes.
•Spread mixture thinly and evenly in prepared pan. Cool completely; break into pieces. Yield: 20 servings (1½ pounds).
Per piece: Calories 204 Fat 9.6g
Cholesterol 0mg Sodium 2mg

Marzipan Fruit and Flowers

PREP: 1 HOUR

Marzipan is that fanciful almond-flavored candy that you can mold into many shapes.

1 (8-ounce) can almond paste
1½ tablespoons light corn syrup
1⅓ cups sifted powdered sugar
Yellow, red, blue, and green liquid food coloring
Glaze
2 tablespoons sugar
Whole cloves

•Knead almond paste by hand; knead in corn syrup. Gradually knead in powdered sugar. Divide dough into 6 portions.
•Tint 3 portions of dough with yellow food coloring and 2 with red food coloring, using ⅛ teaspoon food coloring for each. Add blue food coloring, 1 drop at a time, to 1 portion of red dough to make purple dough. Add red food coloring, 1 drop at a time, to 1 portion of yellow dough to make orange dough. Tint one-fourth of remaining untinted portion with 1 drop of green food coloring. Tint remaining three-fourths of portion with 2 drops of red food coloring to make pink dough. Knead each portion until food coloring is blended into dough.
•Follow directions below to shape marzipan dough, working with 1 portion of dough at a time. Wrap remaining dough in plastic wrap, and let stand at room temperature until ready to shape.

Leaves: Roll green dough to ⅛-inch thickness. Cut dough into leaf shapes. Draw leaf indentations with a wooden pick.

Roses: Shape pink dough into a log 1 inch in diameter. Cut into 1/16-inch-thick slices. Flatten slices with fingertips or a rolling pin to make petals. Shape 1 petal into a bud. Curl several petals around bud, pressing bottom of petals toward center and curling top edges outward. Pinch at bottom. Press leaves into dough at base of rose.

Strawberries: Combine 2 tablespoons sugar and 2 drops of red food coloring; stir well. Shape red dough into 3 balls. Shape a rounded point at 1 end of each ball, and slightly flatten opposite end. Indent flattened ends, using the end of a spoon handle. Brush each strawberry with Glaze; roll in red sugar. Let dry on wax paper. Press leaves into indentation in each flattened end.

Grapes: Shape purple dough into 18 small balls; brush with Glaze. Press 6 balls together to form each cluster. Press a leaf into dough at top of each cluster.

Bananas: Mold 1 portion of yellow dough into 4 banana shapes. Insert a whole clove into each banana at stem end. Brush each with Glaze.

Peaches: Shape the remaining portion of yellow dough into 4 balls. Insert a whole clove into the top of each peach. Press a groove on 1 side of each peach with a wooden pick. Combine 2 tablespoons water, 2 drops of yellow food coloring, and 2 drops of red food coloring; brush on sides of peaches to tint them.

Oranges: Shape orange dough into 4 balls. Roll balls over a small grater to obtain a rough surface. Insert a whole clove into each orange at stem end. Brush with Glaze.

•Place marzipan on wax paper to dry. Let stand overnight. Store in refrigerator in an airtight container. Yield: 1½ dozen.
Per serving: Calories 108 Fat 2.9g
Cholesterol 0mg Sodium 6mg

Glaze

2 tablespoons light corn syrup
¼ cup water

•Combine corn syrup and water; bring to a boil, stirring well. Remove from heat; cool. Yield: ⅓ cup.

CHOCOLATE CANDIES

Chocolate candies are such a universal passion that we felt it only fitting to set them apart. Perhaps the most challenging of them all are the chocolate-dipped candies. It may take a little practice and patience to achieve the same smooth and symmetrical coating as commercially dipped candies.

There are two mediums you can use for dipping—real chocolate (usually semisweet) or chocolate-flavored candy coating. Most people prefer real chocolate because it tastes like the chocolate that's most familiar; its biggest disadvantage is that after melting under home conditions, it doesn't harden back up completely and tends to be a little sticky. Many of our recipes add a little shortening to the chocolate to firm it. And some recipes call for keeping chocolates chilled so they'll be firmer.

Chocolate-flavored candy coating isn't actually real chocolate at all, but is flavored and colored to look like chocolate. It melts like real chocolate (only a little faster and easier), and when the coating cools to room temperature, there's usually not a problem with stickiness.

When dipping candies in either medium, melt the chocolate according to recipe directions. You can use two forks, a wooden pick, or a candy dipping utensil to dip and remove candy from melted chocolate. Let excess chocolate drip back into the pan; then transfer chocolates to wax paper to cool and harden.

Millionaires

PREP: 32 MINUTES   CHILL: 2 HOURS
COOK: 10 MINUTES

1 (14-ounce) package caramels
1½ tablespoons milk
2 cups coarsely chopped pecans
12 ounces chocolate-flavored candy
     coating

•Unwrap caramels; combine caramels and milk in a small heavy saucepan. Cook over low heat until melted, stirring often. Stir in chopped pecans. Drop by rounded teaspoonfuls onto buttered wax paper. Cool; cover and chill.

•Place candy coating in top of a double boiler; bring water to a boil. Reduce heat to low, and cook until coating melts. Dip caramel rounds into coating. Place on wax paper to cool. Yield: 4 dozen.
Per candy: Calories 98 Fat 5.9g
Cholesterol 0mg Sodium 23mg

Microwave Directions: Unwrap caramels; place in a 2-quart casserole. Microwave at HIGH 1 to 1¼ minutes; stir well. Add milk to caramels; microwave at HIGH 1½ to 2 minutes, stirring every 30 seconds. Stir until smooth; stir in pecans. Drop by rounded teaspoonfuls onto buttered wax paper. Cool; cover and chill. Place candy coating in a 4-cup glass measure. Microwave at MEDIUM (50% power) 2 to 3 minutes or until coating melts. Dip caramel rounds into coating. Place on wax paper to cool.

Buckeyes

PREP: 25 MINUTES

Buckeyes are a chocolate-covered peanut butter candy ball made to resemble the nut by the same name.

1¼ cups butter, softened
1 (18-ounce) jar creamy peanut
     butter
7 cups sifted powdered sugar (about
     1½ pounds)
3 cups (18 ounces) semisweet chocolate
     morsels
1½ tablespoons shortening

•Process butter and peanut butter in food processor until thoroughly blended. Add 3 cups powdered sugar, and process until smooth. Gradually add remaining powdered sugar in 2 batches, processing after each addition until mixture pulls away from sides and is no longer crumbly. Shape mixture into 1-inch balls. Cover and chill thoroughly.
•Combine chocolate morsels and shortening in top of a double boiler; bring water to a boil. Reduce heat to low; cook until chocolate melts, stirring occasionally. Remove pan from heat, leaving chocolate mixture over hot water. Use a wooden pick to dip each

ball in chocolate, coating three-fourths of ball; place on wax paper. Carefully smooth wooden pick holes. Let candies stand until chocolate hardens. Store in an airtight container in refrigerator. Yield: 8 dozen.
Per buckeye: Calories 108 Fat 6.7g
Cholesterol 6mg Sodium 51mg

Chocolate Truffles

◀ FAMILY FAVORITE ▶
◀ MAKE AHEAD ▶

PREP: 36 MINUTES   CHILL: 4 HOURS
COOK: 3½ MINUTES

Truffles provide the most intense bite of chocolate possible. You can make these ahead, and chill or freeze them.

3 (4-ounce) semisweet chocolate bars,
     finely chopped (we tested with
     Ghirardelli)
¼ cup whipping cream
3 tablespoons butter, cut up
2 tablespoons almond liqueur (or other
     favorite liqueur) or whipping cream
1 cup ground pecans, other nuts, or
     chocolate sprinkles

•Microwave chocolate and whipping cream in a 2-quart microwave-safe bowl at MEDIUM (50% power) 3½ minutes.
•Whisk until chocolate melts and mixture is smooth. (If chocolate doesn't melt completely, microwave and whisk at 15-second intervals until melted.) Whisk in butter and liqueur; place over a bowl of ice water.
•Beat at medium speed with an electric mixer 4 minutes or until mixture forms soft peaks. (Do not overbeat.) Cover and chill 4 hours or until firm.
•Shape mixture into 1-inch balls, washing hands as necessary. Roll balls in ground pecans, other nuts, or chocolate sprinkles. Cover and chill up to 1 week or freeze up to 1 month. Yield: 2 dozen.
Per truffle: Calories 120 Fat 9.8g
Cholesterol 7mg Sodium 16mg

Note: Substitute 2 cups (12 ounces) semisweet chocolate morsels for semisweet chocolate bars, if desired.

Chocolate-Dipped Strawberries

◄ QUICK • FAMILY FAVORITE ►

PREP: 16 MINUTES   COOK: 5 MINUTES

Here's a simple recipe that makes a stunning presentation at a party. Pick out your prettiest berries for dipping.

2 pints fresh strawberries
1 cup (6 ounces) semisweet chocolate
  morsels
1 tablespoon shortening

•Rinse strawberries, and dry thoroughly on paper towels. (Chocolate will not stick to wet strawberries.) Set aside.
•Place chocolate morsels and shortening in top of a double boiler; bring water to a boil. Reduce heat to low, and cook until chocolate melts. Cool chocolate to lukewarm (110°).
•Grasp strawberries by the stem, and dip in chocolate mixture; place on wax paper or a wire rack sprayed with vegetable cooking spray, and chill until firm. Serve within 8 hours. Yield: 3½ dozen.

Per strawberry: Calories 19 Fat 1.3g
Cholesterol 0mg Sodium 0mg

Chocolate-Covered Cherries

PREP: 1 HOUR   STAND: 24 HOURS

COOK: 1 HOUR

2½ cups sugar
¾ cup water
2½ tablespoons light corn syrup
2 (10-ounce) jars maraschino cherries with
  stems
2 cups (12 ounces) semisweet chocolate
  morsels
1 tablespoon shortening

•Combine first 3 ingredients in a large saucepan; cook over low heat, stirring until sugar dissolves. Bring to a boil over medium heat; cover and cook 2 to 3 minutes to wash down sugar crystals from sides of pan. Uncover and cook, without stirring, until mixture reaches soft ball stage or candy thermometer registers 236°. Pour mixture onto a marble slab that has been sprinkled with cold water. (Do not scrape pan.) Let stand 4 minutes.
•Using a dampened metal scraper, pull sides of mixture into center repeatedly to ensure mixture cools evenly. When mixture develops a yellowish tinge, continue working with dampened scraper, stirring mixture in a figure-8 motion. When mixture suddenly turns white and becomes too stiff to stir, knead with wet hands until smooth and creamy enough to form a firm ball (about 10 minutes). Place fondant in an airtight container, and let stand in a cool place at least 24 hours before using.
•Drain cherries, reserving liquid; place cherries on paper towels to drain for several hours or overnight.
•Place fondant in top of a double boiler; melt slowly over hot (not boiling) water, stirring constantly as it begins to melt. Stir in 1 tablespoon reserved cherry liquid. (Fondant should have the proper consistency for dipping when candy thermometer registers about 140°. Temperature should not rise above 140°.) If mixture seems too thick for dipping at this point, stir in 1 more tablespoon reserved cherry liquid. Remove pan from heat, leaving fondant over hot water.
•Working quickly and holding by the stem, dip each cherry into warm fondant, allowing excess to drain back into the pan. Place cherries, stem up, on wax paper; let stand 1 hour or until firm.
•Combine chocolate morsels and shortening in top of double boiler; bring water to a boil. Reduce heat to low; cook until chocolate melts, stirring occasionally. Remove pan from heat, leaving chocolate mixture over hot water.
•Holding by the stem, dip each cherry into warm chocolate mixture, allowing excess to drain back into pan. Place cherries, stem up, on wax paper; let stand 2 hours or until firm. Store cherries in an airtight container at room temperature. Yield: 5 dozen.

Per cherry: Calories 68 Fat 1.6g
Cholesterol 0mg Sodium 1mg

TESTS FOR CANDY STAGES

Thread Stage — 230° to 234°
•Syrup spins a 2-inch thread when dropped from a metal spoon.

Soft Ball Stage — 234° to 240°
•In cold water, syrup forms a soft ball that flattens when removed from water.

Firm Ball Stage — 242° to 248°
•In cold water, syrup forms a firm ball that doesn't flatten when removed from water.

Hard Ball Stage — 250° to 268°
•Syrup forms a hard, yet pliable, ball when removed from cold water.

Soft Crack Stage — 270° to 290°
•When dropped into cold water, syrup separates into threads that are hard but not brittle.

Hard Crack Stage — 300° to 310°
•When dropped into cold water, syrup separates into threads that are hard and brittle.

Caramel Stage — 310° to 340°
•Syrup will be honey-colored when spooned onto a white plate. The longer it's cooked, the darker it will be.

FUDGE

Turn your kitchen into a fudge factory with any one of these fine confections. Our selections take you far beyond the traditional chocolate variety. Fudge has good keeping quality, so you can make a multitude of it and store it easily. Seal it in an airtight container, and keep at room temperature up to two weeks.

Fast Fudge

FAMILY FAVORITE • QUICK

PREP: 18 MINUTES   COOK: 8 MINUTES

You won't find an easier fudge than this.

2 cups sugar
⅔ cup evaporated milk
½ cup butter
12 large marshmallows
Pinch of salt
1 cup (6 ounces) semisweet chocolate
   morsels
1 cup chopped pecans
1 teaspoon vanilla extract

•Combine first 5 ingredients in a large heavy saucepan. Cook over medium heat, stirring constantly, until mixture comes to a boil; boil 5 minutes, stirring constantly. Remove from heat.
•Add chocolate morsels to marshmallow mixture, stirring until chocolate melts. Add pecans and vanilla, stirring well. Spread evenly in a buttered 8- or 9-inch square pan. Cool and cut into squares. Yield: 3 dozen squares (2 pounds).
Per square: Calories 125 Fat 6.8g
Cholesterol 9mg Sodium 48mg

Mocha Fudge: Add 1 tablespoon instant coffee granules with the salt.

Sour Cream Fudge

QUICK

PREP: 2 MINUTES   COOK: 19 MINUTES

2 cups sugar
Pinch of salt
1 (8-ounce) carton sour cream
2 tablespoons butter or margarine

•Butter sides of a heavy saucepan. Combine sugar, salt, and sour cream in pan. Cook over medium heat, stirring constantly, until sugar dissolves. Cover and cook over medium heat 2 minutes to wash down sugar crystals from sides of pan. Uncover and cook, stirring constantly, until candy thermometer registers 232°. Remove from heat; stir in 2 tablespoons butter.
•Beat with a wooden spoon until mixture thickens and begins to lose its gloss (4 to 5 minutes). Spread evenly in a buttered 8-inch square pan or 9- x 5-inch loafpan. Cool and cut into squares. Yield: 25 squares (1 pound).
Per square: Calories 96 Fat 3.3g
Cholesterol 8mg Sodium 24mg

White Chocolate Fudge

MAKE AHEAD • QUICK

PREP: 20 MINUTES   COOK: 4 MINUTES

6 ounces premium white chocolate,
   chopped (we tested with Ghirardelli)
½ (8-ounce) package cream cheese,
   softened
3 cups sifted powdered sugar
½ teaspoon vanilla extract
1 cup chopped pecans
25 pecan halves

•Place white chocolate in top of a double boiler; bring water to a boil. Reduce heat to low; cook until white chocolate melts, stirring occasionally. Remove from heat.
•Beat cream cheese at high speed with an electric mixer until creamy. Gradually add sugar; beat at medium speed until smooth. Stir in melted white chocolate and vanilla; beat well. Stir in chopped pecans.
•Press mixture into a lightly buttered 8-inch square pan. Cover and chill. Cut into squares. Gently press a pecan half on each square of fudge. Store in an airtight container in the refrigerator. Yield: 25 squares (1½ pounds).
Per square: Calories 151 Fat 8g
Cholesterol 8mg Sodium 21mg

FOOLPROOF FUDGE

Our Test Kitchens staffers turn out countless pounds of candy each year. Here's their advice:

•If it's a humid day, the candy may have a more sugary texture. Best results generally occur when the weather is dry.

•Have all your ingredients chopped, measured, and ready before you begin cooking.

•Use a heavy saucepan with thick sides and bottom. It will conduct heat evenly.

•Butter the inside of saucepan before you begin. This keeps sugar from clinging to sides of pan and helps prevent fudge from becoming grainy.

•An important early step in making creamy fudge is to be sure sugar dissolves completely before boiling the candy mixture. Otherwise, fudge may be grainy and crumbly. To test this, dip a metal spoon into sugar syrup mixture and press spoon against sides of pan. If sugar's dissolved, you shouldn't feel any grains of sugar on back of spoon.

•Use a clip-on candy thermometer. Always read thermometer at eye level. Test it for accuracy by placing thermometer in boiling water 2 minutes; it should register 212°. If not, adjust temperature given in recipe by the amount that your reading deviates from 212°. For example, if your thermometer registers 210° in boiling water, it's 2° low. And you should remove candy from heat when thermometer registers 2° below what the recipe specifies.

•Adjust heat as candy cooks, if necessary, to maintain a gentle rolling boil. The candy mixture should be boiling at least halfway up sides of pan.

•Don't scrape sides of pan clean when pouring out fudge. This could lead to grainy fudge.

•Let fudge cool without any stirring before you beat it.

Preparing heavy saucepan for fudge: Butter the sides of a heavy saucepan as an initial step to prevent sugar crystals from forming.

Buttermilk Fudge

◄ QUICK ►

PREP: 10 MINUTES   COOK: 18 MINUTES

Look for this fudge to turn a rich caramel color during cooking.

2 cups sugar
1 cup buttermilk
½ cup butter
2 tablespoons light corn syrup
1 teaspoon baking soda
¾ cup chopped pecans, toasted (optional)
1 teaspoon vanilla extract

•Butter sides of a heavy 4-quart saucepan (see photo); add sugar and next 4 ingredients. Cook over medium heat, stirring constantly, 18 minutes or until candy thermometer registers 236°. Remove from heat, and cool, undisturbed, until temperature drops to 180° (about 15 minutes).
•Add pecans, if desired, and vanilla; beat with a wooden spoon until mixture thickens and just begins to lose its gloss (about 5 minutes). Quickly pour into a buttered 9- x 5-inch loafpan. Cool completely; cut into squares. Yield: 3 dozen squares (1¼ pounds).
Per square: Calories 219 Fat 11g
Cholesterol 19mg Sodium 143mg

Chocolate-Peanut Butter Fudge

◄ FAMILY FAVORITE ►

PREP: 7 MINUTES   COOK: 54 MINUTES

2½ cups sugar
¼ cup cocoa
1 cup milk
1 tablespoon light corn syrup
½ cup butter or margarine, divided
1 cup chopped peanuts
½ cup creamy peanut butter
2 teaspoons vanilla extract

•Butter sides of a heavy 3-quart saucepan. Combine sugar and cocoa in saucepan, stirring well. Stir in milk and corn syrup. Cook over medium heat, stirring constantly, until sugar dissolves. Add 2 tablespoons butter; stir until butter melts. Bring to a boil; cover and boil 2 to 3 minutes. Uncover and continue to cook, without stirring, until mixture reaches soft ball stage or candy thermometer registers 234°.
•Remove mixture from heat, and without stirring, add remaining ¼ cup plus 2 tablespoons butter, peanuts, peanut butter, and vanilla. Cool 10 minutes.
•Beat mixture with a wooden spoon just until well blended (about 3 minutes); pour immediately into a buttered 8-inch square pan. Cool; cut fudge into squares. Yield: 3 dozen squares (2 pounds).
Per square: Calories 131 Fat 6.8g
Cholesterol 8mg Sodium 82mg

Note: If you don't have peanuts or time to chop them, substitute chunky peanut butter for creamy peanut butter.

Sour Cream Fudge
Fast Fudge
Buttermilk Fudge

TRADITIONAL CANDIES

These classic candies include the crunchy and chewy sweets you remember from childhood—peanut brittle, taffy, divinity, candy apples. All are cooked to a precise candy temperature. You won't have any trouble making them if you follow the basic guidelines for minimizing sugar crystals and check for the specific end temperature as described at the beginning of the candy section. Avoid making these candies on a humid or rainy day because they can pick up moisture from the air and become sticky.

Double-Treat Toffee

◄ FAMILY FAVORITE ►

PREP: 15 MINUTES   COOK: 20 MINUTES

Covered in chocolate and sprinkled with pecans, this stick-to-your-teeth candy is irresistible. Break it into pieces, and package it for gift giving.

2 cups sugar
1 cup butter or margarine
¼ cup water
1 teaspoon vanilla extract
2½ cups (15 ounces) semisweet chocolate morsels, divided
2 cups finely chopped pecans, toasted and divided

•Combine first 3 ingredients in a heavy 3-quart saucepan. Cook over low heat until sugar dissolves, stirring gently. Cover and cook over medium heat 2 to 3 minutes to wash down sugar crystals from sides of pan. Uncover and cook to hard crack stage or until candy thermometer registers 300°. Remove from heat, and stir in vanilla. Pour into a greased 15- x 10-inch jellyroll pan, quickly spreading mixture to edges of pan.
•Sprinkle 1¼ cups chocolate morsels over hot toffee; let stand 1 minute or until chocolate begins to melt. Spread chocolate evenly over candy. Sprinkle with 1 cup chopped pecans. Let candy stand until set.
•Place remaining 1¼ cups chocolate morsels in top of a double boiler; bring water to a boil. Reduce heat to low, and cook until chocolate melts. Remove from heat. Run a sharp knife around edge of toffee in jellyroll pan. Carefully invert toffee onto a wax paper-lined cookie sheet. Spread melted chocolate over uncoated side of toffee. Sprinkle with remaining 1 cup chopped pecans. Let stand until set. Break toffee into pieces. Store in an airtight container. Yield: 20 servings (2 pounds).
Per piece: Calories 353 Fat 25.5g Cholesterol 25mg Sodium 95mg

Southern Pralines

◄ FAMILY FAVORITE ►

PREP: 10 MINUTES   COOK: 25 MINUTES

This is a candy you want to stay with as it cooks. When it's cooked, be ready to beat mixture with a wooden spoon just until it loses its gloss; then drop mounds quickly onto wax paper.

2 cups sugar
2 cups pecan halves
¾ cup buttermilk
2 tablespoons butter or margarine
⅛ teaspoon salt
¾ teaspoon baking soda

•Combine first 5 ingredients in a large heavy saucepan. Cook over low heat, stirring gently, until sugar dissolves. Cover and cook over medium heat 2 to 3 minutes to wash down sugar crystals from sides of pan.
•Uncover and cook to soft ball stage or until candy thermometer registers 234°, stirring constantly. Remove from heat, and stir in soda. Beat with a wooden spoon just until mixture begins to thicken. Working rapidly, drop by tablespoonfuls onto greased wax paper; let stand until firm. Yield: 2 dozen.
Per praline: Calories 137 Fat 7.3g Cholesterol 3mg Sodium 56mg

Microwave Directions: Combine first 5 ingredients in a 4-quart microwave-safe bowl, stirring well. Microwave at HIGH 12 minutes, stirring every 4 minutes. Stir in soda. Microwave at HIGH 1 minute. Beat with a wooden spoon just until mixture begins to thicken. Working rapidly, drop by tablespoonfuls onto greased wax paper; let stand until firm.

Peanut Brittle

◄ FAMILY FAVORITE ►

PREP: 10 MINUTES   COOK: 45 MINUTES

Hard candy can be rewarding and fun to make. Have a heavy saucepan and an accurate candy thermometer on hand.

2 cups sugar
1 cup light corn syrup
¾ cup water
2 cups raw peanuts
3 tablespoons butter or margarine
1 teaspoon vanilla extract
1 teaspoon baking soda
¼ teaspoon salt

•Combine first 3 ingredients in a heavy 3-quart saucepan. Cook over medium-low heat, stirring constantly, until sugar dissolves.
•Cover and cook over medium heat 2 to 3 minutes to wash down sugar crystals from sides of pan. Add peanuts; cook until mixture reaches hard crack stage or candy thermometer registers 300°, stirring occasionally. Remove from heat. Stir in butter and remaining ingredients. (Candy will foam as baking soda is added due to a chemical reaction. This makes the brittle porous.)
•Working quickly, pour candy mixture into a buttered 15- x 10-inch jellyroll pan; spread to edges of pan. Cool completely; break into pieces. Store in an airtight container. Yield: 15 servings (2 pounds).
Per piece: Calories 310 Fat 12.8g Cholesterol 6mg Sodium 148mg

Chocolate-Almond Brittle

PREP: 15 MINUTES   COOK: 45 MINUTES
CHILL: 1 HOUR

1 cup butter
1⅓ cups sugar
1 tablespoon light corn syrup
3 tablespoons water
1 cup coarsely chopped almonds
3 (4-ounce) bars milk chocolate
1 cup finely chopped almonds, divided

•Combine first 4 ingredients in a 3-quart saucepan. Cook over low heat, stirring gently, until sugar dissolves. Cover and cook over medium heat 2 to 3 minutes to wash down sugar crystals from sides of pan. Uncover and cook to hard crack stage (300°). Remove from heat, and stir in coarsely chopped almonds. Pour mixture into an ungreased 13- x 9-inch pan, quickly spreading to edges of pan. Cool.

•Place chocolate in top of double boiler; bring water to a boil. Reduce heat to low; cook until chocolate melts, stirring often.

•Run a sharp knife around edge of candy in pan. Spread half of melted chocolate over top of candy; sprinkle with ½ cup finely chopped almonds. Chill 30 minutes. Carefully invert candy onto a wax paper-lined baking sheet. Spread remaining melted chocolate over uncoated side of candy. Sprinkle with remaining ½ cup almonds. Chill 30 minutes. Break candy into pieces. Store in an airtight container. Yield: 25 servings (2½ pounds).

Per piece: Calories 243 Fat 17g
Cholesterol 23mg Sodium 87mg

Caramels

PREP: 10 MINUTES   COOK: 50 MINUTES

1 cup butter or margarine
2 cups sugar
2 cups light corn syrup
2 cups whipping cream, divided
2 teaspoons vanilla extract

•Combine butter, sugar, corn syrup, and 1 cup whipping cream in a large Dutch oven. Cook over low heat, stirring gently, until sugar dissolves. Cover and cook over medium heat 2 to 3 minutes to wash down sugar crystals from sides of pan. Uncover and cook until candy thermometer registers 224°, stirring occasionally.

•Stir in remaining 1 cup whipping cream. Continue to cook mixture over medium heat to firm ball stage or until candy thermometer registers 248°. Stir in vanilla.

•Pour mixture into a buttered 13- x 9-inch pan. Cool about 5 hours. Cut into squares, and wrap individually in wax paper. Yield: 10 dozen (2¾ pounds).

Per caramel: Calories 58 Fat 3.1g
Cholesterol 10mg Sodium 25mg

Old-Fashioned Taffy

PREP: 45 MINUTES   COOK: 40 MINUTES

2½ cups sugar
½ cup water
¼ cup white vinegar
1 tablespoon butter or margarine
⅛ teaspoon salt
1 teaspoon vanilla extract

•Combine first 5 ingredients in a small Dutch oven; cook over low heat until sugar dissolves, stirring gently. Cover and cook over medium heat 2 to 3 minutes to wash down sugar crystals from sides of pan. Uncover and cook over medium heat, without stirring, to soft crack stage or until candy thermometer registers 270°. Remove from heat. Stir in vanilla.

•Pour candy into a buttered 15- x 10-inch jellyroll pan or onto a slab of marble. Cool to touch; butter hands, and pull candy until light in color and difficult to pull. Divide candy in half, and pull into a rope, 1 inch in diameter. Cut into 1-inch pieces; wrap each piece in wax paper. Yield: 40 (1-inch) pieces.

Per piece: Calories 53 Fat 0.4g
Cholesterol 1mg Sodium 12mg

Candied Orange Peel

PREP: 1½ HOURS   COOK: 2 HOURS

This candied garnish makes great use of a sack of fresh citrus fruit. Try the lemon or grapefruit versions, too. The peel is a wonderful dessert to nibble on with a cup of hot tea. It makes a striking cake topper, too.

1 quart (¼-inch-wide) orange peel strips (about 15 oranges)*
½ teaspoon salt
2 cups sugar
1 cup water
1 cup sugar

•Place orange peel in water to cover in a large Dutch oven; add salt. Bring to a boil, and boil 20 minutes. Drain. Repeat boiling procedure twice without salt; drain and set orange peel aside.

•Combine 2 cups sugar and 1 cup water in a heavy saucepan; bring to a boil over medium heat, and cook until syrup spins a thread or

candy thermometer registers 234°, stirring often. Add orange peel; simmer 30 minutes, stirring often. Drain orange peel well.

•Discard syrup. Roll peel, a few pieces at a time, in 1 cup sugar. Arrange in a single layer on wire racks; dry 4 to 5 hours. Store in an airtight container. Yield: 1 pound.
Use a sharp vegetable peeler to remove peel; cut peel into ¼-inch-wide strips, using a sharp knife.

Per ¼-cup serving: Calories 40 Fat 0g
Cholesterol 0mg Sodium 13mg

Candied Lemon Peel: Substitute 1 quart lemon peel strips (about 22 large thick-skinned lemons) for orange peel. Yield: about 1 pound.

Candied Grapefruit Peel: Substitute 1 quart pink grapefruit peel strips (about 9 large thick-skinned grapefruit) for orange peel. Yield: about 1½ pounds.

CANDIED PEEL APPEAL

Use thick-skinned fruit when making these sugared strips for gifts or garnish. And use a sturdy, good quality vegetable peeler when peeling the fruit or use a sharp paring knife (we tested with a Good Grip peeler). Be careful not to peel into the white pith just under the skin. It can be bitter. As a bonus, when you're finished peeling the fruit, you'll have enough fruit left to section into a bowl, chill, and enjoy for breakfast or dessert.

Classic Divinity

◄ FAMILY FAVORITE ►

PREP: 20 MINUTES   COOK: 25 MINUTES

2½ cups sugar
½ cup water
½ cup light corn syrup
2 egg whites
1 teaspoon vanilla extract
1 cup chopped pecans, toasted

•Combine first 3 ingredients in a 3-quart saucepan, and cook over low heat, stirring constantly, until sugar dissolves. Cover and cook over medium heat 2 to 3 minutes to wash down sugar crystals from sides of pan. Uncover and cook over medium heat, without stirring, to hard ball stage or until candy thermometer registers 260°. Remove from heat.

•Beat egg whites in a large mixing bowl at high speed with an electric mixer until stiff peaks form.
•Pour hot sugar mixture in a heavy stream over beaten egg whites while beating constantly at high speed. Add vanilla, and continue beating just until mixture holds its shape (3 to 4 minutes). Stir in pecans.
•Working quickly, drop divinity by rounded teaspoonfuls onto wax paper (see photo); cool. Peel from wax paper. Yield: 3 dozen (1½ pounds).
Per piece: Calories 76 Fat 0.8g
Cholesterol 0mg Sodium 9mg

Cherry Divinity: Substitute 1 cup finely chopped red candied cherries for pecans.

Pink Divinity: Add 4 or 5 drops of red liquid food coloring with vanilla extract.

Shaping divinity: Once divinity holds its shape upon beating, quickly spoon it out by teaspoonfuls onto wax paper.

Classic Divinity

Candied Apples

PREP: 25 MINUTES COOK: 45 MINUTES

Break out this recipe in the fall when crisp apples are prime for dunking and dipping.

10 medium apples
3 cups sugar
⅔ cup water
1 teaspoon lemon juice
¼ teaspoon cream of tartar
15 whole cloves
2 or 3 drops of red liquid food coloring

•Wash and dry apples; remove stems. Insert a wooden skewer into stem end of each apple. Set aside.
•Combine sugar and remaining 5 ingredients in a heavy saucepan; stir well. Cook over low heat, stirring gently, until sugar dissolves. Cover and cook over medium heat 2 to 3 minutes to wash down sugar crystals from sides of pan. Uncover and cook over medium heat, without stirring, to hard crack stage or until candy thermometer registers 300°. Discard cloves.
•Quickly dip apples into syrup; allow excess syrup to drip off. Place on lightly buttered baking sheets to cool. Wrap tightly in plastic wrap; store in a cool place. Yield: 10 servings.
Per apple: Calories 252 Fat 0.4g
Cholesterol 0mg Sodium 0mg

Lollipops

PREP: 10 MINUTES COOK: 40 MINUTES

1 cup sugar
¼ cup water
¼ cup light corn syrup
1 to 2 drops of desired food coloring
¼ teaspoon oil of cinnamon or
   peppermint

•Brush inside surfaces of metal lollipop molds with vegetable oil; set aside.
•Combine sugar, water, and corn syrup in a medium saucepan. Cook over low heat, stirring gently, until sugar dissolves. Cover and cook mixture over medium heat 2 to 3 minutes to wash down sugar crystals from sides of pan. Uncover and cook, without stirring,

to hard crack stage (300°). Remove mixture from heat, and stir in desired food coloring and oil of cinnamon.
•Immediately pour hot mixture into prepared molds. Press sticks in indentions of molds, gently twirling sticks to embed. Cool completely; lift lollipops out of molds. Immediately wrap in plastic wrap. Store in a cool, dry place. Yield: 8 (2-inch) lollipops.
Per lollipop: Calories 127 Fat 0g
Cholesterol 0mg Sodium 13mg

Caramel Crunch Popcorn

PREP: 11 MINUTES COOK: 55 MINUTES

Take a cluster of this caramel-coated popcorn and nut mixture along to the movies or on a picnic.

6 quarts popped corn (¾ cup unpopped)
1¾ cups salted Spanish peanuts
1 cup butter or margarine
1 (16-ounce) package light brown sugar
¼ cup light corn syrup
¼ cup molasses
½ teaspoon salt
1 teaspoon vanilla extract

•Place popcorn and peanuts in a large bowl; set aside.
•Melt butter in a large heavy saucepan. Stir in brown sugar and next 3 ingredients; bring to a boil over medium heat, stirring constantly. Boil 5 minutes, stirring occasionally. Remove from heat; stir in vanilla.
•Pour mixture over popcorn mixture; stir until evenly coated. Pour into two lightly greased large roasting pans or four 13- x 9-inch pans, spreading in a thin layer.
•Bake at 250° for 45 to 50 minutes, stirring every 15 minutes. Cool in pans on wire racks. Yield: 5 quarts.
Per ½-cup serving: Calories 153 Fat 8.5g
Cholesterol 12mg Sodium 145mg

POPCORN BALL PANACHE

•Air-popped corn and corn popped in a Dutch oven with oil work equally well in this recipe.
•Remove any unpopped kernels of corn before combining the sugar mixture and the popped corn.
•We used a large roasting pan to combine the sugar mixture with the popped corn. A very large bowl works, too.
•Make sure your hands are well greased in order to keep the sticky popcorn mixture from clinging to them.

Old-Fashioned Popcorn Balls

PREP: 15 MINUTES COOK: 20 MINUTES

2 cups firmly packed dark brown sugar
¾ cup light corn syrup
¾ cup water
½ teaspoon salt
½ cup butter or margarine
1 teaspoon vanilla extract
6 quarts popped corn

•Combine first 4 ingredients in a saucepan; cook over low heat, until sugar dissolves, stirring gently. Cook over medium heat, without stirring, to hard ball stage or until candy thermometer registers 254°. Remove from heat, and stir in butter and vanilla.
•Place popped corn in a large pan. Pour hot syrup over top, stirring well with a wooden spoon. Grease hands with butter, and shape mixture into balls. Place on wax paper to dry. Wrap in plastic wrap; store in a cool, dry place. Yield: 2 dozen.
Per ball: Calories 181 Fat 6.7g
Cholesterol 11mg Sodium 111mg

Creamy Lime Sherbet (page 178),
Strawberry Ice Cream (page 175),
Blackberry Sorbet (page 178)

DESSERTS

A good dessert is hard to beat. Look through the recipe files of any serious cook, and the desserts section will no doubt be bulging with entries. It's a broad category, and whether you choose to highlight the beauty of poached fruit or a silky smooth custard, you can be as simple or as elaborate as you wish in display.

Equipment

Desserts can take on many shapes, hence our recipes make use of a variety of special molds, pans, or other baking equipment. Always read through a recipe before you begin preparation to be sure you have the equipment you need or a suitable substitute.

Rich puddings and sauces serve many purposes on these pages; therefore, a few wire whisks, large spoons, and a heavy saucepan will come in handy for creating their thick and velvety smooth texture.

Ovenproof ramekins or custard cups are ideal for making individual custards, and a large soufflé dish is a simple piece of equipment that makes a showy dessert. You'll need a large roasting pan or baking dish when making some baked custards like crème brûlée. The pan holds custard cups in a gently simmering "water bath" which insulates the custard and prevents overcooking.

And no summer cookout would be complete without the universal favorite, homemade ice cream. An ice cream freezer, whether electric or hand-crank, is easy to use when you follow the manufacturer's instructions. The key to proper freezing is using the right ratio of ice to rock salt. Be diligent about cleaning and drying your ice cream freezer well after each use to prevent it from rusting.

Storing and Freezing

Store desserts that contain fresh fruit or have a cream base in the refrigerator, both before serving if you make them ahead, and afterward if there are leftovers.

If the dessert recipe doesn't mention freezing as an option, then it's probably not a good candidate for making ahead and freezing. The low temperatures of freezing alter the texture of most fruit dishes, and pudding-based recipes have a tendency to break down. Avoid freezing a dessert that contains gelatin unless instructed to do so; some gelatin desserts freeze well, and some don't, depending on the ingredients.

One dessert component that does freeze well is crêpes. You can make extra crêpes, stack them between wax paper, and freeze up to three months sealed in a freezer bag. They'll thaw quickly and be ready for you to fill them with ice cream or fruit fillings.

CUSTARDS & PUDDINGS

In their purest form, custards and puddings are simply sweetened egg and milk mixtures. Their procedure is easy to master and virtually foolproof if you stir patiently over the proper heat. Served alone or combined with fruit and cake into trifles and parfaits, custards and puddings are a comforting treat.

Many of these recipes are thickened with flour or cornstarch; usually eggs contribute to the thickening also. Most require frequent, if not constant, stirring to ensure a smooth base. Avoid using high heat or overcooking the mixture, as this can cause the custard to curdle.

It's important to acclimate eggs slowly to a heated mixture. This procedure is called *tempering*. To temper beaten eggs into a hot mixture, stir a small amount of the heated mixture into beaten eggs, and then slowly add it all back to the original heated mixture. All the while, gently stir constantly to maintain a smooth texture.

If you end up with curdled bits of egg in your finished custard, you can always strain the custard to remove the egg or place the custard over a bowl of ice water and whisk it gently to remove the lumps.

As thickened puddings cool, they sometimes form a thin "skin" across the top. You can prevent this skin by placing a piece of plastic wrap or wax paper directly on top of a hot pudding. Once pudding has cooled, remove the covering, and spoon the pudding into dessert dishes.

Old-Fashioned Stirred Custard

◀ FAMILY FAVORITE ▶
◀ HEALTHY ▶

PREP: 5 MINUTES   COOK: 30 MINUTES

Stirred Custard is soft and fluid—similar to the consistency of a pourable sauce. Bake the same mixture in the oven, and you'll have a firmer consistency (see recipe variation below).

3 cups milk
2 large eggs
⅔ cup sugar
1½ tablespoons all-purpose flour
1 teaspoon vanilla extract

•Place milk in top of a double boiler; bring water to a boil. Cook until milk is thoroughly heated. Set aside.
•Beat eggs at medium speed with an electric mixer until frothy. Add sugar and flour, beating until thick. Gradually stir about 1 cup hot milk into egg mixture; add to remaining hot mixture, stirring constantly.
•Cook mixture in top of double boiler over low heat 30 minutes or until thickened, stirring occasionally. Stir in vanilla. Serve custard warm or cold. Yield: 6 servings.
Per serving: Calories 194   Fat 5.6g
Cholesterol 87mg   Sodium 81mg

Baked Custard: Follow procedure for first 2 paragraphs above. Pour custard mixture into six 6-ounce custard cups. Set custard cups in a 13- x 9-inch pan; add hot water to pan to depth of 1 inch. Bake at 350° for 35 to 40 minutes or until a knife inserted in center comes out clean. (Custard will still jiggle slightly, but will thicken as it cools.) Remove custard cups from water. Serve custard warm or cold.

CUSTARD CONCENTRATION

When cooking custards and puddings in a saucepan, stir with a gentle figure 8 motion. This helps to ensure a smooth sauce with no lumps. Don't stir too vigorously, though, or you might break down the thickening.

Pumpkin-Orange Custard

◀ MAKE AHEAD ▶

PREP: 15 MINUTES   COOK: 1 HOUR
CHILL: 2 HOURS

Orange rind and liqueur add subtle flavor to this pumpkin custard. It's a great fall dessert.

½ cup sugar
1 cup half-and-half
½ cup whipping cream or half-and-half
3 large eggs, lightly beaten
1 cup canned mashed pumpkin
1 tablespoon grated orange or lemon rind
2 tablespoons Grand Marnier or orange juice
¼ teaspoon ground ginger
Pinch of salt
Garnishes: sweetened whipped cream, orange rind strips

•Combine first 3 ingredients in a heavy saucepan; cook over medium heat, stirring constantly, until sugar melts and mixture comes to a simmer (do not boil). Remove from heat.
•Combine eggs and next 5 ingredients in a small bowl, stirring with a wire whisk until blended. Gradually stir about one-fourth of hot whipping cream mixture into pumpkin mixture; add to remaining hot whipping cream mixture, stirring constantly.
•Pour custard mixture evenly into six 6-ounce ramekins or custard cups. Place in a 13- x 9-inch pan; add hot water to pan to depth of 1 inch. Bake at 325° for 50 minutes or until a knife inserted in center comes out clean. Remove ramekins from water; cool slightly on wire racks. Cover and chill at least 2 hours. Garnish, if desired. Yield: 6 servings.
Per serving: Calories 288   Fat 18.3g
Cholesterol 162mg   Sodium 86mg

Crème Brûlée

PREP: 4 MINUTES   COOK: 45 MINUTES

This rich, velvety-smooth custard is capped with a shell of brown sugar which caramelizes and hardens once melted under the broiler. You can bake the custard ahead, but wait until just before serving to caramelize the sugar. The sugar crust will begin to melt if it sits more than an hour.

¾ cup sugar
3 cups whipping cream
7 egg yolks, lightly beaten
2 teaspoons vanilla extract
½ cup firmly packed brown sugar
Garnish: fresh raspberries

•Combine ¾ cup sugar and whipping cream in a heavy saucepan; cook over medium heat, stirring constantly, until sugar melts and mixture comes to a simmer (do not boil). Remove from heat.

•Combine egg yolks and vanilla in a small bowl. Gradually stir about one-fourth of hot whipping cream mixture into yolk mixture; add to remaining hot whipping cream mixture, stirring constantly (photo 1).

•Pour custard mixture evenly into eight 4-ounce ramekins. Place ramekins in a large roasting pan or two 9-inch pans; add hot water to pan to depth of 1 inch (photo 2). Bake, uncovered, at 350° for 35 minutes. Remove ramekins from water; cool slightly on wire racks. Cover and chill until ready to serve.

•Place ramekins on a baking sheet. Sprinkle brown sugar evenly over custards (photo 3). Broil 5½ inches from heat 3 minutes or until sugar melts. Cool on wire racks to allow sugar to harden. Garnish, if desired. Yield: 8 servings.

Per serving: Calories 489   Fat 37.6g
Cholesterol 313mg   Sodium 46mg

1. Add "tempered" egg yolk mixture to hot cream mixture, stirring constantly.

2. For the water bath, add hot water to roasting pan to depth of 1 inch.

3. Sprinkle brown sugar over baked custards; broil until sugar melts.

CUSTARD DICTIONARY

Baked Custard: This is the lightest and simplest of the custard desserts; it uses the highest ratio of milk to eggs. Unlike many of its rich custard cousins, this one's not unmolded before serving.

Crème Brûlée: In French, it literally means "burnt cream." Served in ramekins or custard cups and never unmolded, it's a creamy custard beneath a thin sheet of sugar crust. The sugar is caramelized (or burnt) under extremely high heat, like a broiler, just before serving. Compared to crème caramel or flan, crème brûlée is a richer custard because it usually contains heavy cream and numerous egg yolks.

Crème Caramel: This fairly light custard is typically made with milk; egg yolks are added for richness. It's baked in a metal mold lined with caramelized sugar. You unmold it for serving, and the caramel drips out of the mold and becomes a sauce.

Flan: The custard of choice in Spain, flan is similar to crème caramel in that it bakes in a caramel-lined mold and is turned out before serving. Flan, though, is richer than crème caramel because the custard is made with more eggs and yolks, as well as some half-and-half, evaporated milk, or sweetened condensed milk.

Pots de Crème: A French custard whose name means "pot of cream." This very rich, velvety custard laden with egg yolks is often flavored with chocolate and traditionally served in little lidded porcelain cups.

Flan

◄ MAKE AHEAD ►

PREP: 15 MINUTES   COOK: 50 MINUTES
CHILL: 8 HOURS

⅔ cup sugar
4 large eggs, lightly beaten
1 (14-ounce) can sweetened condensed
    milk
1¾ cups milk
2 teaspoons vanilla extract

•Sprinkle ⅔ cup sugar in a large heavy skillet. Cook over medium heat, stirring constantly with a wooden spoon, until sugar melts and turns light brown. Quickly pour hot caramel into a lightly oiled 9-inch round cakepan, tilting to coat bottom evenly; set aside. (Caramel syrup will harden and crack.)
•Combine eggs and remaining 3 ingredients; beat with a wire whisk. Pour custard mixture over syrup in cakepan. Cover cakepan, and place in a large shallow pan. Add hot water to pan to depth of 1 inch. Bake at 325° for 50 minutes or until a knife inserted near center comes out clean.
•Remove pan from water bath, and uncover; cool completely on a wire rack. Cover and chill at least 8 hours. Loosen edges of flan with a spatula, and invert onto a rimmed serving plate, letting melted caramel drizzle over the top. Yield: 8 servings.
Per serving: Calories 302   Fat 9g
Cholesterol 130mg   Sodium 121mg

Chocolate Flan: Substitute 1 (14-ounce) can chocolate-flavored sweetened condensed milk instead of regular sweetened condensed milk. Bake 1 hour or until almost set in center.

Caramel-Coffee Flan

◄ MAKE AHEAD ►

PREP: 10 MINUTES   COOK: 1½ HOURS
CHILL: 8 HOURS

Caramel and coffee flavor this flan luxuriously. It's a wonderful make-ahead dessert because it needs to chill overnight.

¾ cup sugar
1 cup half-and-half or milk
2 teaspoons instant coffee granules
2 large eggs
2 egg yolks
1 (14-ounce) can sweetened condensed
    milk
Garnish: whole coffee beans

•Sprinkle sugar in a large heavy skillet. Cook over medium heat, stirring constantly with a wooden spoon, until sugar melts and turns light brown. Quickly pour hot caramel into a lightly oiled 8-inch round cakepan, tilting cakepan to coat bottom evenly; set aside. (Caramel syrup will harden and crack.)
•Combine half-and-half and coffee granules in a large bowl; stir until coffee granules dissolve. Add eggs, egg yolks, and condensed milk; beat well with a wire whisk. Pour egg mixture over syrup in cakepan.
•Cover cakepan, and place in a large shallow pan. Add hot water to pan to depth of 1 inch. Bake at 325° for 1 hour and 10 minutes or until a knife inserted near center comes out clean.
•Remove pan from water bath, and uncover; cool completely on a wire rack. Cover and chill at least 8 hours. Loosen edges of flan with a spatula, and invert onto a rimmed serving plate, letting melted caramel drizzle over top. Garnish, if desired. Yield: 6 servings.
Per serving: Calories 408   Fat 13.7g
Cholesterol 181mg   Sodium 124mg

Vanilla Pudding

◄ QUICK ►
◄ FAMILY FAVORITE ►

PREP: 6 MINUTES   COOK: 11 MINUTES

This simple dessert recalls days gone by. Egg yolks make it extrarich and constant stirring keeps it smooth.

⅓ cup sugar
1½ tablespoons cornstarch
⅛ teaspoon salt
2 cups milk
2 egg yolks
1 tablespoon butter or margarine
1 teaspoon vanilla extract

•Combine first 3 ingredients in a large saucepan; gradually stir in milk. Cook over medium heat, stirring constantly, 6 minutes or until mixture comes to a boil. Cook 1 more minute, stirring constantly. Remove from heat.
•Beat egg yolks 2 minutes or until thick and pale. Gradually stir about one-fourth of hot mixture into yolks; add to remaining hot mixture, stirring constantly. Bring mixture to a boil over medium heat, and cook 3 minutes, stirring constantly.
•Remove from heat; stir in butter and vanilla. Pour mixture into custard cups. Cover and chill, if desired. Yield: 4 servings.
Per serving: Calories 210   Fat 9.4g
Cholesterol 133mg   Sodium 167mg

Banana Pudding

◄ FAMILY FAVORITE ►

PREP: 21 MINUTES   COOK: 35 MINUTES

Banana Pudding might just be the ultimate comfort food. Try our chocolate variation, which uses chocolate wafers.

3½ tablespoons all-purpose flour
1⅓ cups sugar
Dash of salt
3 large eggs, separated
3 cups milk
1 teaspoon vanilla extract
1 (12-ounce) package vanilla wafers
6 medium bananas
¼ cup plus 2 tablespoons sugar
1 teaspoon vanilla extract

• Combine first 3 ingredients in a heavy saucepan. Beat egg yolks; combine egg yolks and milk, stirring well. Stir into dry ingredients; cook over medium heat, stirring constantly, until smooth and thickened. Remove from heat; stir in 1 teaspoon vanilla.

• Layer one-third of wafers in a 3-quart baking dish. Slice 2 bananas, and layer over wafers. Pour one-third of custard over bananas. Repeat layers twice.

• Beat egg whites at high speed with an electric mixer until foamy. Gradually add ¼ cup plus 2 tablespoons sugar, 1 tablespoon at a time, beating until stiff peaks form. Add 1 teaspoon vanilla, and beat until blended.

• Spread meringue over custard, sealing to edge of dish. Bake at 325° for 25 to 30 minutes or until golden. Yield: 8 servings.

Per serving: Calories 559 Fat 15g
Cholesterol 92mg Sodium 271mg

Chocolate-Banana Pudding: Substitute 1 (12-ounce) package chocolate-flavored vanilla wafers for vanilla wafers.

Brown Sugar Pudding Cake

PREP: **9 MINUTES** COOK: **40 MINUTES**
STAND: AT LEAST **10 MINUTES**

When you spoon up this pudding cake, you'll find a sumptuous sauce hiding beneath the brownielike crust.

½ cup butter or margarine, softened
1½ cups firmly packed brown sugar, divided
1½ cups all-purpose flour
2 teaspoons baking powder
Pinch of salt
1 teaspoon ground nutmeg
1 teaspoon ground cinnamon
1 cup milk
½ cup raisins
1½ cups water

• Beat butter at medium speed with an electric mixer until creamy; gradually add ½ cup brown sugar, beating well.

• Combine flour and next 4 ingredients; add to butter mixture alternately with milk, beginning and ending with flour mixture.

Mix at low speed after each addition until blended. Stir in raisins. Pour batter into a greased 2-quart soufflé dish.

• Combine remaining 1 cup brown sugar and water in a medium saucepan. Bring to a boil over medium-high heat. Pour sugar mixture carefully over batter in dish. Bake at 375° for 40 minutes or until edges are golden and pull away from sides of dish. Let stand at least 10 minutes before serving. (Dessert will be very saucy at bottom of dish, but will thicken as it stands.) Yield: 6 servings.

Per serving: Calories 520 Fat 17.7g
Cholesterol 47mg Sodium 366mg

Creamy Rice Pudding

◄ FAMILY FAVORITE ►
◄ HEALTHY ►

PREP: **5 MINUTES** COOK: **43 MINUTES**

There's no need to save this dish for dessert— try it for breakfast, too. You can speed up the recipe by cooking it over medium heat rather than low, but you'll need to stir constantly.

1 quart milk
1 cup uncooked regular rice
½ teaspoon salt
1½ teaspoons vanilla extract
4 egg yolks, beaten
½ cup sugar
½ cup half-and-half
1 teaspoon ground cinnamon
1 cup raisins

• Combine first 4 ingredients in a medium saucepan. Cover and cook over low heat about 40 minutes or until rice is tender, stirring occasionally.

• Combine egg yolks and next 3 ingredients in a small bowl. Gradually stir about one-fourth of hot mixture into yolk mixture; add yolk mixture to remaining hot mixture. Cook over low heat, stirring constantly, until mixture reaches 160° and is thickened and bubbly (about 3 minutes). Stir in raisins. Serve warm or chilled. Yield: 10 servings.

Per serving: Calories 255 Fat 6.8g
Cholesterol 105mg Sodium 176mg

Chocolate Pots de Crème

Chocolate Pots de Crème

◄ MAKE AHEAD ►

PREP: **4 MINUTES** COOK: **12 MINUTES**
CHILL: **4 HOURS**

This lavish dessert is usually served in demitasse cups or dainty chocolate pots with lids.

2 cups half-and-half
2 egg yolks, lightly beaten
2 tablespoons sugar
3⅓ cups (20 ounces) semisweet chocolate morsels
3 tablespoons amaretto
2 teaspoons vanilla extract
Pinch of salt
1 cup sweetened whipped cream
Garnish: chocolate shavings

• Combine first 3 ingredients in a heavy saucepan; cook over medium heat 12 minutes or until mixture reaches 160°, stirring constantly. Add chocolate morsels and next 3 ingredients, stirring until smooth.

• Spoon into eight 4-ounce ramekins, demitasse cups, or chocolate pots; cover and chill at least 4 hours. Top each serving with whipped cream. Garnish, if desired. Yield: 8 servings.

Per serving: Calories 435 Fat 31.4g
Cholesterol 96mg Sodium 66mg

Bread Pudding with Whiskey Sauce

Here's an easy indulgence using French bread. Just tear the loaf into pieces, soak it in a custard mixture, and then bake it until set. Drizzle Whiskey Sauce over each serving.

1 (1-pound) loaf soft French bread
2 cups half-and-half
2 cups milk
3 large eggs, lightly beaten
2 cups sugar
¾ cup chopped pecans
¾ cup raisins
1 tablespoon plus 1 teaspoon vanilla
    extract
1½ teaspoons ground cinnamon
¼ cup butter or margarine, melted
Whiskey Sauce (page 397)

•Tear bread into small pieces (photo 1); place in a large bowl. Add half-and-half

1. Tear French bread into small pieces; place in a large bowl.

2. Add liquids and stir well with a wooden spoon.

3. Bake pudding, uncovered, until firm to the touch.

and milk to bowl; let mixture stand 10 minutes.
•Stir mixture well with a wooden spoon (photo 2). Add eggs and next 5 ingredients, stirring well.
•Pour butter into a 13- x 9-inch pan; tilt pan to coat evenly. Spoon pudding mixture into

pan. Bake, uncovered, at 325° for 55 to 60 minutes or until pudding is firm (photo 3). Remove from oven; cool.
•Cut into squares; spoon Whiskey Sauce over each serving. Yield: 15 servings.
Per serving: Calories 484   Fat 20.2g
Cholesterol 88mg   Sodium 344mg

Cinnamon Toast Pudding with Caramel Sauce

◀ FAMILY FAVORITE ▶

PREP: 10 MINUTES   COOK: 50 MINUTES

If you liked cinnamon toast as a child, you'll love this fabulous dish fit for breakfast or dessert. The rich-tasting caramel sauce is a bonus. Syrup and powdered sugar make fine toppings, too.

8 slices white sandwich bread or
    cinnamon-raisin bread
3 tablespoons butter or margarine,
    softened
¼ cup sugar
2 teaspoons ground cinnamon
2½ cups milk
⅔ cup sugar
Pinch of salt
4 large eggs, lightly beaten
1 tablespoon vanilla extract
Caramel Sauce

•Spread 1 side of each bread slice evenly with butter. Combine ¼ cup sugar and cinnamon; sprinkle evenly over buttered side of bread. Place bread on a baking sheet. Broil 3

inches from heat 2 minutes or until browned and bubbly. Remove from oven, and cool.
•Cut each toast slice into 4 triangles. Arrange triangles, sugared side up, on bottom and around sides of a well-buttered 9-inch quiche dish, 9-inch pieplate, or an 11- x 7-inch baking dish, overlapping slices, if necessary. Set aside.
•Place milk in a saucepan over medium heat until hot; remove from heat, and add ⅔ cup sugar and next 3 ingredients, stirring until sugar dissolves. Spoon half of custard over toast triangles in dish; let stand 5 minutes.
•Pour in remaining custard, and place dish in a large shallow pan. Add hot water to pan to depth of ¾ inch. Bake at 350° for 35 to 45 minutes or until a knife inserted in center comes out clean. Serve warm with Caramel Sauce. Yield: 8 servings.
Per serving: Calories 473   Fat 12.9g
Cholesterol 138mg   Sodium 334mg

Caramel Sauce

1 cup sugar
½ cup dark corn syrup
1 tablespoon butter or margarine
Pinch of salt
¼ cup evaporated milk
1½ teaspoons vanilla extract

•Combine first 4 ingredients in a heavy saucepan; bring to a boil over medium heat, stirring constantly. Boil 1 minute, stirring constantly. Remove from heat. Stir in evaporated milk and vanilla. Yield: 1½ cups.

Chocolate Biscuit Bread Pudding

PREP: 9 MINUTES   COOK: 40 MINUTES

Basic Buttermilk Biscuits get you off to a yummy start as the base of this bread pudding. Smother them in a chocolaty custard, and top with whipped cream.

2 cups half-and-half
½ cup butter or margarine
3 large eggs
1 cup sugar
¼ cup cocoa
1 recipe Basic Buttermilk Biscuits
    (page 62)
Sweetened whipped cream or ice cream

•Combine half-and-half and butter in a heavy saucepan; cook over medium heat until butter melts. Cool.

• Combine eggs, sugar, and cocoa; beat at medium speed with an electric mixer 1 minute. Gradually stir in half-and-half mixture; set aside.

• Crumble Basic Buttermilk Biscuits into a lightly greased 2-quart shallow baking dish; pour egg mixture over biscuits.

• Bake, uncovered, at 350° for 35 to 40 minutes or until a knife inserted in center comes out clean, covering with aluminum foil after 30 minutes to prevent overbrowning. Serve warm with whipped cream or ice cream. Yield: 8 servings.

Per serving: Calories 587   Fat 37.2g
Cholesterol 183mg   Sodium 701mg

Plum Pudding with Sherried Hard Sauce

PREP: 20 MINUTES   COOK: 3 HOURS

This specialty is so named because it originally contained plums, as well as nuts and spices. Assorted dried fruits typically replace the plums today, but the rich flavor and dense texture remain.

3 cups all-purpose flour
1 teaspoon baking soda
½ teaspoon salt
2 teaspoons ground cinnamon
½ teaspoon ground allspice
½ teaspoon ground cloves
2 cups raisins
1 medium Granny Smith apple, peeled and chopped (1 cup)
1 cup currants
1 cup light molasses
1 cup cold water
2 cups finely chopped suet*
Sherried Hard Sauce (page 397) or Hot Wine Sauce (page 397)

• Combine first 6 ingredients in a large bowl; mix well. Stir in raisins, apple, and currants.

• Combine molasses, water, and suet; add to dry ingredients, mixing well. Spoon mixture into a well-greased 2½-quart metal mold; cover tightly with lid or aluminum foil.

• Place mold on rack in a large deep kettle with enough boiling water to come halfway up mold. Cover kettle; steam pudding 3 hours in boiling water, replacing water as

needed. Uncover and let pudding stand 5 minutes before unmolding. Cut into slices, and serve with Sherried Hard Sauce or Hot Wine Sauce. Yield: 12 servings.

Suet is solid white fat rendered from beef. If it's not packaged in your supermarket's meat case, ask the butcher to cut some. It lends richness to puddings like this one.

Per serving: Calories 640   Fat 34.2g
Cholesterol 39mg   Sodium 263mg

Tiramisù

◄ **MAKE AHEAD** ►

PREP: 37 MINUTES   COOK: 8 MINUTES
CHILL: 8 HOURS

This popular Italian dessert that means "pick-me-up cake" has a coffee- and alcohol-soaked cake layer, sweetened cream cheese, and grated chocolate. For the cake, we used ladyfingers; look for them in the frozen food or bakery section of the store.

6 egg yolks
1¼ cups sugar
1¼ cups mascarpone cheese*
1¾ cups whipping cream
½ cup water
2 teaspoons instant coffee granules
¼ cup brandy
2 (3-ounce) packages ladyfingers, split
½ cup whipping cream, whipped
1 teaspoon grated unsweetened chocolate

• Combine egg yolks and sugar in top of a double boiler; beat at medium speed with a handheld electric mixer until thick and pale. Bring water to a boil; reduce heat to low, and cook, stirring constantly, 8 minutes or until mixture reaches 160°. Remove from heat. Add mascarpone, and beat until smooth.

• Beat 1¾ cups whipping cream at medium speed until soft peaks form; fold into cheese mixture.

• Combine water, coffee granules, and brandy; brush cut side of ladyfingers with ½ cup coffee mixture.

• Line sides and bottom of a 3-quart trifle bowl with 36 ladyfingers, cut side in; pour in half of filling mixture. Layer remaining ladyfingers on top; drizzle with remaining ¼ cup coffee mixture. Cover with remaining

filling. Garnish with remaining whipped cream and grated chocolate. Cover and chill 8 hours. Yield: 12 servings.

As a substitute for mascarpone cheese, combine 2 (8-ounce) packages cream cheese, ⅓ cup sour cream, and ¼ cup whipping cream; beat well. Use 1¼ cups mixture for recipe, reserving remainder for other uses.

Per serving: Calories 553   Fat 56.3g
Cholesterol 263mg   Sodium 148mg

Fruited Sabayon

◄ **QUICK** ►

PREP: 9 MINUTES   COOK: 10 MINUTES

Sabayon is a French cooked custard with a splash of Marsala, a sweet fortified wine. The custard is beautiful drizzled over a blend of fresh berries.

15 egg yolks
½ cup sugar
3 tablespoons sweet Marsala
2 cups fresh raspberries
2 cups fresh blueberries
2 cups fresh blackberries
1 cup sweetened whipped cream
Garnish: fresh mint sprigs

• Beat egg yolks in top of a double boiler at high speed with a handheld electric mixer 5 minutes; add sugar, 1 tablespoon at a time, beating until yolks are thick and pale. Gradually add Marsala, beating well.

• Bring water to a boil in bottom of double boiler. Place egg yolk mixture over water, and cook, stirring constantly with a wire whisk, 10 minutes or until mixture reaches 160°. Remove from heat, and place top of double boiler in a large bowl of ice water, stirring until mixture is cold.

• Arrange fruit in compotes or individual serving dishes; immediately spoon sauce over fruit. Dollop with whipped cream, and garnish, if desired. Yield: 10 servings.

Per serving: Calories 214   Fat 12.6g
Cholesterol 343mg   Sodium 18mg

Easy Tropical Trifle

◄ MAKE AHEAD ►

PREP: 14 MINUTES   COOK: 8 MINUTES
CHILL: 4 HOURS

This trifle uses convenience products and can be made a day ahead.

1 (4.6-ounce) package vanilla pudding mix
1 (20-ounce) can crushed pineapple, undrained
½ cup orange juice
2 medium bananas, peeled and sliced
1 (16-ounce) loaf frozen pound cake, thawed
1 (10-ounce) package frozen sliced strawberries (not in syrup), thawed and undrained
1 (12-ounce) container frozen whipped topping, thawed
¼ cup flaked coconut, toasted

•Prepare pudding mix according to package directions. Remove from heat, and cool.
•Drain pineapple, reserving ½ cup juice. Combine reserved pineapple juice and orange juice. Add banana slices and pineapple; stir gently. Drain, reserving juice mixture.
•Cut pound cake into 10 slices; cut each slice into 6 cubes. Place half of cake cubes in a 3-quart trifle bowl; sprinkle with half of juice mixture. Spoon half of berries with juice over cake cubes; top with half each of pudding, fruit mixture, and whipped topping. Repeat layers, ending with whipped topping. Sprinkle with coconut. Cover and chill at least 4 hours. Yield: 12 servings.
Per serving: Calories 383   Fat 33.9g
Cholesterol 77mg   Sodium 238mg

Peaches 'n' Cream Trifle

◄ MAKE AHEAD ►

PREP: 35 MINUTES   CHILL: 8 HOURS

This peaches 'n' cream dessert boasts a homemade cake and custard enhanced with amaretto and toasted almonds. We guarantee it's worth the effort; it received our highest rating. When you're short on time, you'll enjoy the variation that uses convenience products, too.

3 tablespoons sugar
7 fresh ripe peaches, peeled and sliced (4 cups)
1¾ cups whipping cream
¼ cup sifted powdered sugar
Crème Anglaise (page 397)
Old Fashioned Pound Cake (page 112)
½ cup amaretto
¼ cup sliced almonds, toasted

•Sprinkle sugar over peaches; toss and let stand 20 minutes or until juicy.

•Combine whipping cream and powdered sugar in a chilled mixing bowl. Beat at medium speed with an electric mixer until soft peaks form. Fold half of whipped cream into Crème Anglaise.
•Cut enough pound cake into 1-inch cubes to equal 6 cups. (Reserve remaining cake for other uses.) Place half of cake cubes in a 3-quart trifle bowl. Sprinkle ¼ cup amaretto over cubes. Top with half each of Crème Anglaise mixture and peaches. Repeat layers.
•Spread remaining whipped cream on top of trifle. Cover and chill 8 hours. Sprinkle with almonds before serving. Yield: 14 servings.
Per serving: Calories 363   Fat 16g
Cholesterol 140mg   Sodium 102mg

Quick Peaches 'n' Cream Trifle:
Substitute 1 (3-ounce) package vanilla pudding mix and 1¾ cups milk instead of Crème Anglaise; 1 (12-ounce) container frozen whipped topping, thawed, instead of whipping cream; 1 (16-ounce) frozen pound cake loaf; and ½ cup orange juice instead of amaretto.

Peaches 'n' Cream Trifle

Brownie Trifle

PREP: 18 MINUTES   COOK: 28 MINUTES
CHILL: 8 HOURS

Here's another easy and popular dessert for a supper club or potluck dinner, but the Kahlúa makes this one "for adults only." You can make it ahead and chill it up to 24 hours.

1 (19.8-ounce) package fudge brownie mix (we tested with Betty Crocker)
½ cup Kahlúa or other coffee-flavored liqueur (optional)
3 (3.9-ounce) packages chocolate instant pudding mix
1 (12-ounce) container frozen whipped topping, thawed
6 (1.4-ounce) English toffee-flavored candy bars, crushed (we tested with Heath bars)

•Prepare and bake brownie mix according to package directions in a 13- x 9-inch pan. Prick top of warm brownies at 1-inch intervals with a wooden pick, and brush with Kahlúa. Cool brownies, and crumble into small pieces.
•Prepare 3 packages pudding mix according to package directions, using a total of 4 cups milk instead of 6 cups, and omitting chilling procedure.
•Place one-third of crumbled brownies in a 3-quart trifle bowl; top with one-third each of pudding, whipped topping, and crushed candy bars.
•Repeat layers twice using remaining ingredients, ending with crushed candy bars. Cover and chill trifle at least 8 hours. Yield: 16 servings.

Per serving: Calories 440   Fat 17.6g
Cholesterol 30mg   Sodium 497mg

Peanut-Fudge Parfaits

PREP: 10 MINUTES   COOK: 8 MINUTES

10 peanut-shaped peanut butter sandwich cookies (we tested with Nutter Butter)
1 (3-ounce) package vanilla pudding mix
¼ cup creamy peanut butter
½ cup fudge sauce

•Crush 6 cookies; set aside.
•Prepare pudding mix according to package directions. Remove from heat; add peanut butter, stirring until smooth.
•Layer half of pudding evenly into four parfait glasses; add half each of crushed cookies and fudge sauce. Repeat layers with remaining pudding, crushed cookies, and fudge sauce. Arrange a whole cookie on side of each glass. Cover and chill. Yield: 4 servings.

Per serving: Calories 512   Fat 19.8g
Cholesterol 17mg   Sodium 561mg

MOUSSES, SOUFFLÉS, & GELATIN DESSERTS

Light and airy lofty desserts such as these get their lift from whipped cream or egg whites folded into them. Make one of these popular "chill until set" desserts ahead and store it in the refrigerator for a day or two until serving time. The texture of these shapely desserts is similar, but each has distinguishing characteristics.

Mousse is a French term for "froth." Any dessert that has a foamy texture can actually be called a mousse. Its consistency is light because of the air incorporated into it. Traditionally, (uncooked) beaten egg whites were the common ingredient that gave a mousse its volume, but in order to keep up with current egg safety standards, we've converted to cooked, beaten egg whites or another familiar option, whipped cream. This works as well as beaten, uncooked egg whites to fluff these sweets and adds richer flavor (and more calories) than just the whites.

Soufflés are similar in consistency, but usually lighter in texture than mousses. They always have fluffy beaten egg whites and sometimes contain whipped cream, too. Savory dinner soufflés are usually baked, whereas dessert soufflés can be baked or just chilled. When they're not baked, soufflés typically contain cooked egg whites referred to as Italian meringue and gelatin. Soufflés have a reputation as being hard to make when, in fact, if you follow directions for beating egg whites properly (page 188), they can be one of the simplest dessert offerings you can make.

Unflavored gelatin enables fancy chilled, molded desserts to hold their shape once they are removed from their containers. The key to working with gelatin is first to soften it in a liquid before completely dissolving it over heat.

Gelatin sets any number of shapely desserts, such as one known as a Charlotte Russe. It's a *Bavarian* (vanilla-flavored mousse enhanced with gelatin) wrapped in ladyfingers or sponge cake and often accompanied by a brightly colored fruit dessert sauce.

If you're looking for creative serving options, you can serve many mousse desserts in wine goblets, sherbet glasses, or champagne flutes for an attractive and easy presentation.

Butterscotch Mousse

PREP: 4 MINUTES   COOK: 10 MINUTES
CHILL: 8 HOURS

1 cup (6 ounces) butterscotch morsels
3 tablespoons butter or margarine
1 tablespoon instant coffee granules
3 tablespoons water
1 large egg, lightly beaten
¾ cup whipping cream, whipped

•Combine first 4 ingredients in a heavy saucepan; cook over low heat, stirring constantly, until morsels and butter melt. Gradually stir about one-fourth of hot mixture into egg; add to remaining hot mixture, stirring constantly.
•Cook over medium heat, stirring constantly, 1 minute or until mixture reaches 160°. Remove from heat, and cool to room temperature.
•Fold in whipped cream. Spoon into five stemmed glasses; cover and chill 8 hours. Yield: 5 servings.

Per serving: Calories 558   Fat 37.8g
Cholesterol 114mg   Sodium 148mg

Butter Pecan Mousse

◄ MAKE AHEAD ►

PREP: 15 MINUTES   COOK: 3 MINUTES
CHILL: 4 HOURS

1 tablespoon butter or margarine
¾ cup finely chopped pecans
2 (8-ounce) packages cream cheese, softened
¼ cup sugar
¼ cup firmly packed brown sugar
1 teaspoon vanilla extract
1 cup whipping cream, whipped
½ cup pecan pieces, toasted (optional)

•Melt butter in a small skillet over medium heat; add ¾ cup pecans, and cook, stirring constantly, until pecans are toasted. Remove from heat, and set aside.
•Beat cream cheese at medium speed with an electric mixer until smooth. Add sugars and vanilla, beating well. Stir in ¾ cup toasted pecans.
•Gently fold whipped cream into cream cheese mixture; spoon or pipe into serving dishes. Cover and chill thoroughly. Sprinkle each serving with 1 tablespoon toasted pecan pieces, if desired. Yield: 8 servings.
Per serving: Calories 471   Fat 44.4g
Cholesterol 111mg   Sodium 211mg

Chocolate Truffle Mousse

◄ MAKE AHEAD ►

PREP: 15 MINUTES   COOK: 10 MINUTES
CHILL: 8 HOURS

This mousse is a rich dessert with whipped cream folded in to lighten it. The chocolate mixture is so velvety smooth, it resembles a truffle in texture. Serve it in stemmed glasses for a dramatic presentation.

8 (1-ounce) squares semisweet chocolate
¼ cup light corn syrup
¼ cup butter or margarine
2 egg yolks, lightly beaten
1 cup whipping cream, divided
2 tablespoons powdered sugar
½ teaspoon vanilla extract
½ cup fresh raspberries
½ cup whipping cream, whipped
Garnish: chocolate curls

•Combine first 3 ingredients in a heavy saucepan; cook over low heat, stirring constantly, until chocolate melts.
•Combine egg yolks and ¼ cup whipping cream. Gradually stir about ½ cup chocolate mixture into yolk mixture; add to remaining chocolate mixture, stirring constantly. Cook over medium-low heat 1 minute or until mixture reaches 160°. Remove from heat; cool to room temperature.
•Beat ¾ cup whipping cream at medium speed with an electric mixer until foamy; gradually add powdered sugar, beating until soft peaks form. Stir in vanilla.
•Stir ½ cup whipped cream mixture into chocolate mixture (to lighten it); then fold in remaining cream mixture. Spoon into four stemmed glasses. Cover and chill at least 8 hours. Top each serving with fresh raspberries and a dollop of whipped cream. Garnish, if desired. Yield: 4 servings.
Per serving: Calories 792   Fat 65.4g
Cholesterol 263mg   Sodium 182mg

Vanilla Soufflé

PREP: 26 MINUTES   COOL: 20 MINUTES
COOK: 51 MINUTES

A baked soufflé is a delicate dessert with a brief moment of glory that's high and light. Be ready to dust it with powdered sugar and serve it as soon as it comes from the oven because it will deflate quickly.

1½ tablespoons butter or margarine, softened
2 tablespoons sugar
3 tablespoons butter or margarine
3 tablespoons all-purpose flour
¾ cup half-and-half
¼ cup sugar
4 large eggs, separated
2 tablespoons vanilla extract
1 egg white
2 tablespoons sugar
Sifted powdered sugar
Crème Anglaise (page 397)

•Cut a piece of aluminum foil long enough to fit around a 1½ quart soufflé dish or straight-sided casserole, allowing a 1-inch overlap; starting from one long side, fold foil into thirds. Lightly butter one side of foil and dish with 1½ tablespoons softened butter. Wrap foil around outside of dish, buttered side against dish, allowing it to extend 1½-inches above rim to form a collar; secure with string or masking tape. Add 2 tablespoons sugar, tilting prepared dish to coat sides. Set aside.
•Melt 3 tablespoons butter in a saucepan over medium heat; add flour, stirring until smooth. Cook 1 minute, stirring constantly.
•Add half-and-half, stirring constantly; stir in ¼ cup sugar. Cook over medium heat, stirring constantly, until thickened. Remove from heat; set aside.
•Beat egg yolks at medium speed with an electric mixer until thick and pale. Gradually stir about half of hot mixture into egg yolks; add to remaining hot mixture, stirring constantly. Cook over medium heat 2 minutes; stir in vanilla. Cool 15 to 20 minutes.
•Beat 5 egg whites at high speed until foamy. Gradually add 2 tablespoons sugar, beating until soft peaks form. Gradually fold egg whites into cream mixture. Spoon into prepared baking dish.
•Bake at 350° for 35 to 40 minutes or until puffed and set. Sprinkle with powdered sugar, and serve immediately with Crème Anglaise. Yield: 6 servings.
Per serving: Calories 432   Fat 22.5g
Cholesterol 369mg   Sodium 198mg

STEPS TO GREAT SOUFFLÉS

•Preheat oven and assemble your soufflé dish with a foil collar before beginning recipe preparation.
•Be sure your mixing bowl and beaters are grease free. If any fat is present, egg whites won't whip to their maximum volume.
•Separate eggs while cold (it's easiest), but for best volume, let the whites come to room temperature before beating them.
•Beat egg whites until stiff, but not dry. Overbeaten egg whites may cause a soufflé to collapse.
•Be ready to fold the rest of the ingredients together as soon as you beat the egg whites. Stir a small amount of beaten whites into soufflé mixture to lighten it; then gently and quickly fold in remaining whites, being careful not to deflate mixture.

Lemon Soufflé

◀ MAKE AHEAD ▶

**PREP: 10 MINUTES   COOK: 15 MINUTES
CHILL: 2 HOURS**

3 large eggs, separated
1 envelope unflavored gelatin
1 cup cold water
1 cup sugar, divided
⅛ teaspoon salt
2 tablespoons grated lemon rind (about 1 lemon)
3 tablespoons fresh lemon juice (about 1 lemon)
1 cup whipping cream, whipped

1. Beat egg yolks at medium speed until thick and pale.

2. Sprinkle gelatin over cold water and let soften; then stir over low heat to dissolve.

3. Fold egg white mixture and whipped cream into yolk mixture. Spoon into soufflé dish.

•Beat egg yolks at medium speed with an electric mixer until thick and pale, about 2 minutes (photo 1).
•Sprinkle gelatin over cold water in a saucepan (photo 2); let stand 1 minute. Cook over low heat, stirring until gelatin dissolves (about 2 minutes). Briskly stir in egg yolks, ½ cup sugar, and salt. Cook over medium heat, stirring constantly, until mixture begins to boil. Remove from heat; stir in lemon rind and juice. Cool.
•Combine egg whites and remaining ½ cup sugar in top of a double boiler. Place over simmering water. Cook, beating at medium speed, 5 minutes or until mixture reaches 160°. Remove from heat. Beat at high speed 2 minutes or until soft peaks form. Gently fold egg white mixture and whipped cream into yolk mixture (photo 3).
•Spoon into a 1½-quart dish or individual soufflé dishes; cover and chill until set. Yield: 6 servings.

Per serving: Calories 309   Fat 17.2g
Cholesterol 161mg   Sodium 98mg

Chilled Devonshire Soufflé

◀ MAKE AHEAD ▶

**PREP: 10 MINUTES   COOK: 5 MINUTES
CHILL: 4 HOURS**

1 envelope unflavored gelatin
½ cup cold water
5 egg yolks
¾ cup sugar
¼ cup brandy
¼ cup amaretto
2 tablespoons fresh lemon juice
3 cups whipping cream

•Sprinkle gelatin over cold water in a saucepan; let stand 1 minute. Beat egg yolks at medium speed with an electric mixer until thick and pale; stir yolks and sugar into gelatin mixture. Cook over medium heat, stirring constantly, until it begins to boil (about 5 minutes). Remove from heat; stir in brandy, amaretto, and lemon juice. Cool.
•Beat whipping cream at medium speed until soft peaks form. Fold into gelatin mixture. Spoon into a greased 2-quart soufflé dish. Cover and chill until firm. Yield: 10 servings.

Per serving: Calories 377   Fat 29.8g
Cholesterol 209mg   Sodium 40mg

Orange Chiffon Dessert

◀ MAKE AHEAD ▶

**PREP: 23 MINUTES   COOK: 5 MINUTES
CHILL: 10 HOURS**

2 (3-ounce) packages ladyfingers
3 to 4 tablespoons Grand Marnier or other orange-flavored liqueur
3 envelopes unflavored gelatin
1¾ cups cold water, divided
1¼ cups sugar
4 oranges, peeled, seeded, and sectioned
1 tablespoon grated orange rind
1¾ cups fresh orange juice
2 tablespoons fresh lemon juice
1¾ cups whipping cream
¾ cup miniature marshmallows
¼ cup chopped pecans, toasted
Garnishes: orange sections, fresh mint leaves

•Cut a 30- x 3-inch strip of wax paper; line sides of a 9-inch springform pan with strip. Split ladyfingers in half lengthwise; line sides and bottom of pan with ladyfingers, cut side in. Brush ladyfingers with liqueur. Set prepared pan aside.
•Sprinkle gelatin over ¾ cup cold water; stir and let stand 1 minute. Combine remaining 1 cup water and sugar in a large saucepan; bring to a boil, stirring until sugar dissolves. Add gelatin, stirring until it dissolves.
•Chop orange sections. Stir chopped orange, orange rind, orange juice, and lemon juice into gelatin mixture. Cover and chill 2 hours or until mixture is consistency of unbeaten egg white.
•Beat whipping cream at medium speed with an electric mixer until soft peaks form. Gently fold whipped cream and marshmallows into orange mixture. Spoon into prepared pan, and sprinkle with pecans. Cover and chill 8 hours. Remove sides of springform pan; remove wax paper. Place dessert on a serving plate; garnish, if desired. Yield: 10 servings.

Per serving: Calories 395   Fat 18.4g
Cholesterol 87mg   Sodium 143mg

Charlotte Russe

◄ MAKE AHEAD ►

**PREP: 15 MINUTES   COOK: 5 MINUTES
CHILL: 8 HOURS**

*Here's a classic dessert that takes the shape
of the mold you make it in. Once unmolded,
a Strawberry Sauce showers it with color.*

2   envelopes unflavored gelatin
¼   cup cold water
⅔   cup sugar
4   egg yolks
1⅓   cups milk
1   teaspoon vanilla extract
½   cup sour cream
⅓   cup chopped almonds, toasted
1   cup whipping cream, whipped
16   ladyfingers, split
Strawberry Sauce
Garnish: fresh raspberries or
   strawberries

•Sprinkle gelatin over cold water; let stand 1
minute. Set aside.
•Combine sugar and egg yolks in a heavy
saucepan; beat at medium speed with an
electric mixer until thick and pale. Add milk,
and cook over medium heat, stirring constantly, until mixture reaches 160° (about 5
minutes).
•Add reserved gelatin mixture, stirring until
gelatin dissolves. Stir in vanilla, sour cream,
and almonds; cool slightly. Fold in whipped
cream.
•Line a 2-quart mold with 20- x 2-inch strips
of wax paper, slightly overlapping. Line sides
and bottom of mold with ladyfingers, cut
side in.
•Spoon whipped cream mixture over
ladyfingers. Arrange remaining ladyfingers
over whipped cream mixture. Cover and
chill at least 8 hours.
•Invert mold onto a serving plate, and
remove dessert. Carefully peel off wax paper.

Serve with Strawberry Sauce; garnish, if
desired. Yield: 8 servings.
Per serving: Calories 409   Fat 21.6g
Cholesterol 187mg   Sodium 148mg

Strawberry Sauce

1   pint fresh strawberries
1   tablespoon lemon juice
½   cup sugar
2   tablespoons framboise or other
   raspberry brandy

•Wash and hull strawberries; process in a
blender until smooth.
•Add lemon juice, sugar, and framboise;
blend until smooth. Yield: 1⅓ cups.

ICE CREAMS & FROZEN DESSERTS

Making ice cream is an anticipated event
in many families—as each person hopes to
be the lucky one to remove the dasher from
the frosty cream and steal the first few bites.

In keeping with today's egg safety standards, eggs must be cooked (and then
chilled) for ice cream custards. But there are
still many easy ice cream recipes that don't
contain eggs or a cooked custard.

Before you begin, get acquainted with
your ice cream freezer. Read the manufacturer's instructions carefully. Freezers are
made of different materials, and this makes a
difference in the recommended ice-salt ratio.
Don't skimp on the ice and salt; they're
essential for proper freezing. The ice cream
freezes because its heat is absorbed by the
ice and salt. Ice alone is not cold enough to
freeze ice cream. If you use too little salt, the
brine won't get cold enough to freeze ice
cream. With too much salt, ice cream will
freeze too quickly, causing large ice crystals
to form. Rock salt is preferred over table salt
because rock salt is slower to dissolve.

Fill the freezer container only as full as
recommended by the manufacturer. Most
should be filled no more than two-thirds or

three-fourths of their capacity. When adding
ice and salt, make four fairly thick layers of
ice and four thin layers of salt, beginning
with ice and ending with salt. Add more ice
and salt as the ice melts during the freezing
process as well as after ice cream is frozen.

Most ice cream needs to "ripen" or stand
an hour or so before serving. This allows the
ice cream to harden and the flavors to blend.

To ripen ice cream, first remove the
dasher. Then cover the ice cream with foil
and replace the lid. Pack the freezer bucket
with ice and salt, using a higher ratio of salt
to ice than was used for freezing. Wrap the
top well with a towel or newspaper; let stand
in a cool place for an hour or according to
the recipe. Drain off brine; check ice and salt
often, adding more if needed. As you serve
the ice cream, take care not to let any salt
solution get into the ice cream container.
Spoon any leftover ice cream into small
freezer containers. Cover tightly, and freeze.

Aside from our ice cream recipes, you'll
find simple desserts you can make using
store-bought ice cream. And scan our dictionary for icy alternatives to ice cream. They're
easier to make, and healthier, too.

ICY DESSERTS DICTIONARY

Ice: An ice is a frozen mixture of water,
sugar, and another liquid such as coffee,
wine, or fruit juice. It's called *granité* in
France and *granita* in Italy. The proportion
is usually 4 parts liquid to 1 part sugar.
During the freezing process, the mixture is
stirred occasionally to produce a slightly
granular texture. Before serving, most ices
are scraped with the tines of a fork to fluff
up the crystals. You won't get a firm scoop
when serving an ice; just mound it in glasses and serve it right away.

Sherbet: Sherbets are made much like ice
cream, but they're not as rich and creamy.
They're made of sweetened fruit juice,
water, and sometimes added milk, cooked
and beaten egg white, or gelatin.

Sorbet: Sorbets differ from sherbets
because sorbets don't contain milk. Sorbets
are typically served as palate cleansers
between courses. A sorbet is not as granular in texture as an ice.

Freezing ice cream: Make four layers each of ice and salt, beginning with ice and ending with salt.

Removing the dasher: Lift dasher and scrape ice cream from dasher back into container. Remove dasher, and cover ice cream.

Ripening ice cream: Pack freezer bucket with ice and salt; wrap the top well with newspaper or a heavy towel. Let stand in a cool place for an hour.

Strawberry Ice Cream

◄ FAMILY FAVORITE ►

PREP: 45 MINUTES   COOK: 16 MINUTES

Summer's sweet fresh strawberries make a big difference in this ice cream. See it on page 162.

2 cups sugar, divided
¼ cup all-purpose flour
Dash of salt
3 cups milk
4 large eggs, lightly beaten
3 cups sieved or pureed fresh
   strawberries
3 cups whipping cream
1 tablespoon vanilla extract
2 teaspoons almond extract
Garnish: fresh strawberries

•Combine 1½ cups sugar, flour, and salt; set mixture aside.
•Heat milk in top of a double boiler until hot; add a small amount of milk to sugar mixture, stirring to make a smooth paste. Stir sugar mixture into remaining milk; cook over medium heat, stirring constantly, until slightly thickened. Cover and cook 10 minutes, stirring often.
•Stir about one-fourth of hot mixture into beaten eggs; add to remaining hot mixture. Cook 1 minute, stirring constantly. Cool.
•Combine strawberries, remaining ½ cup sugar, whipping cream, and flavorings; stir into custard.

•Pour into freezer container of a 1-gallon hand-turned or electric freezer. Freeze according to manufacturer's instructions. Mixture does not need ripening. Garnish each serving, if desired. Yield: 3 quarts.
Per 1-cup serving: Calories 427   Fat 25.9g
Cholesterol 161mg   Sodium 86mg

Peach Ice Cream

◄ FAMILY FAVORITE ►
◄ HEALTHY ►

PREP: 45 MINUTES

COOK: 6 MINUTES   STAND: 1 HOUR

For this ice cream, use peaches that are fragrant and ripe. They'll be easy to mash and will impart a perfumy aroma.

5 large eggs
1½ cups sugar, divided
1 (14-ounce) can sweetened condensed
   milk
1 (12-ounce) can evaporated milk
1 tablespoon vanilla extract
2 cups mashed fresh peaches
5 cups milk

•Beat eggs at medium speed with an electric mixer until frothy; add 1 cup sugar, and beat well. Add condensed milk, evaporated milk, and vanilla, mixing well. Pour mixture into a large heavy saucepan. Cook over medium heat until mixture comes to a boil, stirring constantly; boil 1 minute. Let mixture cool.

Combine peaches and remaining ½ cup sugar. Add peaches to cream mixture.
•Pour mixture into freezer container of a 5-quart hand-turned or electric freezer; add milk. Freeze according to manufacturer's instructions.
•Pack freezer with additional ice and rock salt, and let stand 1 hour before serving. Yield: 1 gallon.
Per 1-cup serving: Calories 266   Fat 7.7g
Cholesterol 93mg   Sodium 111mg

Butter-Pecan Ice Cream

PREP: 40 MINUTES   COOK: 10 MINUTES

STAND: 1 HOUR

The pecans for this ice cream are toasted in butter to bring out their full flavor. Then they're added to the rich custard just before freezing.

¼ cup butter or margarine
2 cups chopped pecans
7 cups milk, divided
1 (14-ounce) can sweetened condensed
   milk
2 cups sugar
6 large eggs, lightly beaten
1 (5.1-ounce) package vanilla instant
   pudding mix
1 teaspoon vanilla extract

•Melt butter in a large heavy saucepan over medium-high heat; add pecans, and cook, stirring constantly, 3 minutes or until lightly browned. Drain and set aside.
•Combine 1 cup milk, condensed milk, sugar, and eggs in a saucepan; cook over medium heat, stirring constantly, 5 minutes or until mixture coats back of a spoon. Cool. Stir in remaining 6 cups milk, pudding mix, and vanilla; add pecans, stirring well.
•Pour mixture into freezer container of a 5-quart hand-turned or electric freezer. Freeze according to manufacturer's instructions.
•Pack freezer with additional ice and rock salt, and let stand 1 hour before serving. Yield: 1 gallon.
Per 1-cup serving: Calories 434   Fat 20.9g
Cholesterol 110mg   Sodium 201mg

Old-Fashioned Vanilla Ice Cream

PREP: 40 MINUTES   COOK: 30 MINUTES
CHILL: 4 HOURS   STAND: 1 HOUR

Homemade vanilla ice cream is hard to beat. Be sure to try our vanilla bean variation. It's flecked with tiny seeds of the vanilla bean like the best parlor ice cream around.

6 egg yolks, lightly beaten
2⅓ cups sugar
4 cups milk
5 cups half-and-half
¼ teaspoon salt
2 tablespoons vanilla extract

•Combine first 3 ingredients in a large saucepan. Cook over low heat, stirring constantly, 25 to 30 minutes or until mixture thickens and coats a spoon; cover and chill at least 4 hours.
•Stir in half-and-half, salt, and vanilla; pour into freezer container of a 4- or 5-quart hand-turned or electric freezer. Freeze according to manufacturer's instructions.

•Pack freezer with additional ice and rock salt, and let stand 1 hour; then serve ice cream immediately or spoon into an airtight container, and freeze until firm. Yield: 3½ quarts.
Per 1-cup serving: Calories 316   Fat 14.4g Cholesterol 135mg   Sodium 115mg

Mixture coating a spoon: Custard is thickened when it coats a metal spoon; run your finger across the back of spoon, and your finger should leave a trail.

Vanilla Bean Ice Cream: Omit vanilla extract. Split 2 whole vanilla beans lengthwise (photo 1). Scrape tiny seeds into custard mixture before cooking (photo 2). Cut pods into large pieces, and add to custard mixture before cooking. Discard vanilla pods from thickened custard. Freeze as directed.

1. Split thin vanilla beans lengthwise, using a paring knife.

2. Scrape tiny seeds from split beans into custard, using knife blade.

Lightly Lemon Ice Cream

PREP: 30 MINUTES   STAND: 1 HOUR

This ice cream is a tangy and refreshing treat. Serve it with delicate sugar cookies.

3 cups sugar
4 cups milk
3 cups whipping cream
1 cup half-and-half
½ cup grated lemon rind
¾ cup fresh lemon juice

•Combine first 5 ingredients; add lemon juice, and stir well.
•Pour mixture into freezer container of a 1-gallon hand-turned or electric freezer. Freeze according to manufacturer's instructions.
•Pack freezer with additional ice and rock salt, and let stand 1 hour before serving. Yield: 2½ quarts.
Per 1-cup serving: Calories 574   Fat 32.3g Cholesterol 120mg   Sodium 86mg

Almond-Fudge Ice Cream

PREP: 20 MINUTES   COOK: 12 MINUTES
FREEZE: 2 HOURS

Toasted almonds are a crunchy addition to this chocolaty ice cream. If you'd like to vary the crunch, chop up little bits of brownies or your favorite flavor of candy bar, and stir it into the ice cream mixture instead of the almonds.

1½ cups sugar
½ cup cocoa
¼ teaspoon salt
1 quart milk, divided
2 large eggs, lightly beaten
3 cups whipping cream
¾ cup slivered almonds, toasted and chopped
½ teaspoon almond extract
Garnish: slivered almonds, toasted

•Combine first 3 ingredients in a large heavy saucepan. Combine 2 cups milk and eggs; stir into sugar mixture. Cook over medium heat, stirring constantly, until mixture thickens and coats a metal spoon (about 10 minutes). Stir in remaining 2 cups milk; cool chocolate mixture completely.
•Combine chocolate mixture, whipping cream, toasted almonds, and almond extract in freezer container of a 1-gallon hand-turned or electric freezer. Freeze according to manufacturer's instructions.
•Spoon ice cream into a 13- x 9-inch pan; cover and freeze at least 2 hours. Garnish, if desired. Yield: 2 quarts.
Per 1-cup serving: Calories 623   Fat 43.6g Cholesterol 192mg   Sodium 186mg

Chocolate Ice Cream

◄ FAMILY FAVORITE ►

**PREP: 40 MINUTES   COOK: 6 MINUTES
STAND: 1 HOUR**

3 large eggs
1 cup sugar
4 cups half-and-half
2 cups whipping cream
1 cup chocolate syrup
1 tablespoon vanilla extract
3 cups milk

•Beat eggs at medium speed with an electric mixer until frothy. Gradually add sugar, beating until thick. Add half-and-half and next 3 ingredients; mix well.
•Pour mixture into a large heavy saucepan. Cook over medium heat until mixture comes to a boil; boil 1 minute. Cool.
•Pour mixture into freezer container of a 1-gallon hand-turned or electric freezer. Stir in milk. Freeze according to manufacturer's instructions.
•Pack freezer with additional ice and rock salt, and let stand 1 hour before serving. Yield: 1 gallon.
Per 1-cup serving: Calories 323   Fat 20.6g
Cholesterol 109mg   Sodium 83mg

White Chocolate
Ice Cream

**PREP: 15 MINUTES   COOK: 12 MINUTES
FREEZE: 8 HOURS**

You don't even need an ice cream freezer to make this decadent ice cream. Your refrigerator's freezer will firm up the cream in about eight hours. Serve small scoops of it alongside a crisp cookie or fresh fruit.

1 cup water
¾ cup sugar
6 egg yolks
1½ teaspoons vanilla extract
10 ounces white chocolate, melted (we tested with Baker's)
2 cups whipping cream
Garnish: fresh strawberries

•Cook water and sugar in a heavy saucepan over low heat, stirring until sugar dissolves.

Cook over medium heat until mixture comes to a boil, stirring constantly. Boil 5 minutes.
•Beat egg yolks and vanilla at medium speed with an electric mixer 5 minutes or until thick and pale. Stir about one-fourth of hot mixture into beaten eggs; add to remaining hot mixture. Cook 1 minute, stirring constantly. Cool.
•Gradually add white chocolate; continue beating 5 minutes. Stir in whipping cream. Transfer mixture to an 8- or 9-inch metal pan. Cover and freeze 8 hours or until firm. Garnish, if desired. Yield: 5 cups.
Per 1-cup serving: Calories 829   Fat 58.8g
Cholesterol 412mg   Sodium 96mg

Note: The best way to melt (and not burn) white chocolate is to microwave it at MEDIUM (50% power) 1 minute and 30 seconds, stirring after 1 minute.

Watermelon Sherbet

PREP: 1 HOUR   COOK: 2 MINUTES

Use summer's sweetest, freshest melon, and the flavor will really come through in this unique creamy dessert.

4 cups diced seeded watermelon
1 cup sugar
3 tablespoons lemon juice
Dash of salt
1 envelope unflavored gelatin
¼ cup cold water
1 cup whipping cream

•Combine first 4 ingredients in a large bowl; cover and chill 30 minutes. Process watermelon mixture in a blender until smooth. Return to bowl.
•Sprinkle gelatin over cold water in a saucepan; let stand 1 minute. Cook over low heat, stirring until gelatin dissolves (about 2 minutes); add to watermelon mixture, stirring well. Add whipping cream; beat at medium speed with an electric mixer until fluffy.
•Pour mixture into freezer container of a 1-gallon hand-turned or electric freezer. Freeze according to manufacturer's instructions. Mixture does not need ripening. Yield: 4 cups.
Per 1-cup serving: Calories 411   Fat 22.7g
Cholesterol 82mg   Sodium 65mg

Creamy Pineapple
Sherbet

◄ HEALTHY ►

PREP: 45 MINUTES   STAND: 1 HOUR

3 cups milk
1 (15¼-ounce) can unsweetened crushed pineapple, undrained
¾ cup half-and-half
Juice of 1 lemon
1 (12-ounce) can frozen pineapple juice concentrate, thawed and undiluted
⅓ cup sugar

•Combine all ingredients in a large bowl; stir until sugar dissolves.
•Pour mixture into freezer container of a 1-gallon hand-turned or electric freezer. Freeze according to manufacturer's instructions.
•Pack freezer with additional ice and rock salt, and let stand 1 hour before serving. Yield: 9½ cups.
Per ½-cup serving: Calories 96   Fat 2.4g
Cholesterol 9mg   Sodium 24mg

Easy Orange Sherbet

◄ FAMILY FAVORITE ►
◄ HEALTHY ►

PREP: 35 MINUTES   STAND: 1 HOUR

Two ingredients make this treat easy enough to whip up while at the beach or the lake.

2 (14-ounce) cans sweetened condensed milk
6 (12-ounce) cans orange carbonated beverage (we tested with Sunkist)

•Combine condensed milk and carbonated beverage in freezer container of a 6-quart hand-turned or electric freezer, stirring well. Freeze according to manufacturer's instructions.
•Pack freezer with additional ice and rock salt, and let stand 1 hour before serving. Yield: 15 cups.
Per 1-cup serving: Calories 238   Fat 6.8g
Cholesterol 18mg   Sodium 84mg

Easy Pineapple-Orange Sherbet: Add one (8-ounce) can crushed pineapple, undrained, to mixture. Freeze as directed.

Creamy Lime Sherbet

**PREP: 40 MINUTES COOK: 3 MINUTES
STAND: 1 HOUR**

The fresh juice and grated rind from limes lend a kick to this creamy sherbet. Garnish it with tiny lime wedges as shown on page 162.

1 cup sugar
1 envelope unflavored gelatin
2 cups milk
3 cups half-and-half
1 teaspoon grated lime rind
⅔ cup fresh lime juice
Garnish: lime slices

•Combine first 3 ingredients in a large heavy saucepan; cook over medium heat until sugar and gelatin dissolve. Add half-and-half, lime rind, and juice; stir well. (Mixture will appear slightly curdled.)
•Pour mixture into freezer container of a 1-gallon hand-turned or electric freezer. Freeze according to manufacturer's instructions.
•Pack freezer with additional ice and rock salt; let stand 1 hour before serving. Garnish, if desired. Yield: ½ gallon.
Per 1-cup serving: Calories 260 Fat 12.4g
Cholesterol 42mg Sodium 69mg

MAKING SORBETS & GRANITAS

To make sorbets and granitas, keep the following in mind:
•To help develop the desired icy consistency, chill the ingredients before freezing.
•Cover sorbets and granitas while they freeze; otherwise, they may pick up flavors from other foods or moisture that can make them sticky.
•To achieve the granular texture of a granita, stir several times while it freezes.
•For the smooth but icy consistency of sorbets, process the mixture in a food processor just until fluffy after it's almost frozen. Freeze again until firm.
•Sorbets left in the freezer more than a few days can become too crystallized. If this happens, partially thaw sorbet, and process it again in food processor. Refreeze and use it within 24 hours.

Cran-Apple Spice Sorbet

**PREP: 6 MINUTES COOK: 7 MINUTES
FREEZE: 6 HOURS**

This dusty rose-colored dessert hints of cinnamon and cloves.

2 cups apple cider
2 cups cranberry juice
2 tablespoons lemon juice
½ cup sugar
½ teaspoon whole cloves
2 (3-inch) sticks cinnamon

•Combine all ingredients in a saucepan; bring to a boil, stirring constantly. Reduce heat, and simmer 5 minutes. Remove from heat. Discard cloves and cinnamon; cool.
•Pour mixture into a 9-inch square pan. Cover and freeze 3 hours or until firm, stirring occasionally.
•Break frozen mixture into chunks. Process in a food processor until smooth. Return slush mixture to pan; cover and freeze 3 hours or until firm. Spoon sorbet into individual dessert dishes. Yield: 4 cups.
Per 1-cup serving: Calories 232 Fat 0.2g
Cholesterol 0mg Sodium 9mg

Lemon Sorbet

PREP: 5 MINUTES FREEZE: 5 HOURS

This citrus sorbet makes a great palate cleanser between courses. Serve tiny scoops in sherbet glasses.

3 cups boiling water
1 cup sugar
2 teaspoons grated lemon rind
½ cup fresh lemon juice

•Combine boiling water and sugar in a large bowl, stirring until sugar dissolves; let cool. Add lemon rind and juice. Pour mixture into a 9-inch square pan; cover and freeze until firm.
•Let stand at room temperature 5 to 8 minutes before serving. Scoop into serving bowls, and serve immediately. Yield: 4 cups.
Per 1-cup serving: Calories 201 Fat 0g
Cholesterol 0mg Sodium 1mg

Grapefruit-Mint Sorbet

**PREP: 5 MINUTES COOK: 4 MINUTES
FREEZE: 10 HOURS**

Grapefruit and mint make refreshing partners in this pale pink sorbet. And chopped rosemary makes a fine substitute for mint, if preferred.

1½ cups water
⅓ cup sugar
3 tablespoons finely chopped fresh
    mint
2 cups ruby red grapefruit juice

•Combine first 3 ingredients in a heavy saucepan; bring to a boil, stirring until sugar dissolves. Cool. Add grapefruit juice. Pour into a 9-inch square pan; cover and freeze until almost firm.
•Spoon into a large mixing bowl; beat at medium speed with an electric mixer until slushy. Return to pan, and freeze 8 hours. Let stand 20 minutes before serving. Yield: 3½ cups.
Per ½-cup serving: Calories 64 Fat 0.1g
Cholesterol 0mg Sodium 1mg

Grapefruit-Rosemary Sorbet: Substitute 1 tablespoon chopped fresh rosemary for fresh mint.

Blackberry Sorbet

**PREP: 45 MINUTES COOK: 5 MINUTES
STAND: 1 HOUR**

See this deep berry-colored dessert spooned up on page 162. A fresh herb sprig or an edible flower, such as a pansy, makes a contrasting garnish.

1 cup sugar
1 cup water
2 (14-ounce) packages frozen blackberries, thawed
3 large Granny Smith apples, peeled, cored, and chopped
2 tablespoons brandy, blackberry-flavored liqueur, or orange juice
¼ cup orange juice
Garnishes: fresh mint sprigs, fresh berries

•Combine sugar and water in a saucepan; cook over medium heat until sugar dissolves. Cover and chill.

•Process blackberries and apple in a blender until smooth. Press puree through sieve to remove seeds; discard seeds. Stir puree, brandy, and orange juice into sugar mixture.

•Pour mixture into freezer container of a 1-gallon hand-turned or electric freezer. Freeze according to manufacturer's instructions. Pack freezer with additional ice and rock salt, and let stand 1 hour before serving. Garnish, if desired. Yield: 1½ quarts.

Per 1-cup serving: Calories 265 Fat 0.8g
Cholesterol 0mg Sodium 0mg

Shaving Granitas and Ices: Using a fork, scrape and shave mixture until it's fluffy. Serve immediately.

Coffee-Kahlúa Granita

PREP: 8 MINUTES FREEZE: 1 HOUR

½ cup sugar
1 cup water
1 (3-inch) stick cinnamon
2½ cups brewed coffee
½ cup Kahlúa

•Combine first 3 ingredients in a saucepan; bring to a boil, stirring until sugar dissolves. Cool to room temperature. Discard cinnamon. Combine syrup, coffee, and Kahlúa; chill.

•Pour mixture into two freezer trays or a 9-inch square pan; freeze until almost firm, stirring occasionally. Let stand at room temperature about 10 minutes before serving. Scrape and shave granita with a fork until fluffy (see photo). Serve immediately. Yield: 8 cups.

Per 1-cup serving: Calories 96 Fat 0g
Cholesterol 0mg Sodium 2mg

Merlot Ice

◄ HEALTHY ►

PREP: 3 MINUTES COOK: 6 MINUTES
FREEZE: 8 HOURS

This Merlot Ice is a deep red wine color and looks stunning served in wine goblets and garnished with fresh mint.

3 cups water
1 cup sugar
1½ cups Merlot
Garnish: fresh mint sprigs

•Combine water and sugar in a saucepan; bring to a boil, stirring until sugar dissolves. Cool. Add wine, and pour into an 8-inch square pan.

•Cover and freeze until firm, stirring occasionally. Let stand 5 minutes before serving. Scrape and shave the ice. Garnish, if desired. Yield: 5 cups.

Per 1-cup serving: Calories 203 Fat 0g
Cholesterol 0mg Sodium 7mg

Very Berry Ice

◄ HEALTHY ►

PREP: 10 MINUTES FREEZE: 8 HOURS

Pureed berries give this ice its bright red color and texture. Serve it frozen or let it stand 10 minutes, and you'll have a smoothie to enjoy.

6 cups fresh strawberries, hulled
1¾ cups sugar
1¾ cups fresh orange juice
½ cup fresh lemon juice

•Combine all ingredients in a large bowl; stir well. Process half of strawberry mixture in a food processor or blender until smooth. Pour into a 13- x 9-inch pan. Repeat procedure. Freeze until almost firm (about 4 hours), stirring occasionally.

•Spoon strawberry mixture into a large chilled mixing bowl; beat at medium speed with an electric mixer just until smooth. Return mixture to pan; freeze until firm. Let stand 5 minutes before serving. Scrape and shave the ice. Yield: 2 quarts.

Per 1-cup serving: Calories 265 Fat 0.5g
Cholesterol 0mg Sodium 40mg

Merlot Ice

Frozen Orange Dessert

◄ MAKE AHEAD ►

PREP: 10 MINUTES FREEZE: 8 HOURS

60 round buttery crackers, crushed (3 cups)
½ cup butter or margarine, melted
¼ cup sugar
1 (14-ounce) can sweetened condensed milk
1 (6-ounce) can frozen orange juice concentrate, thawed and undiluted
1 (8-ounce) container frozen whipped topping, thawed
2 (11-ounce) cans mandarin oranges, drained

•Combine first 3 ingredients; set aside ¾ cup mixture. Press remaining crumb mixture in an ungreased 13- x 9-inch baking dish; set aside.

•Combine condensed milk and orange juice concentrate; fold in whipped topping and oranges. Spoon mixture over crust, and sprinkle with reserved crumb mixture. Cover and freeze until firm. Cut into squares to serve. Yield: 12 servings.

Per serving: Calories 364 Fat 18.3g
Cholesterol 32mg Sodium 263mg

Fudge Waffles à la Mode

PREP: 14 MINUTES   COOK: 6 MINUTES

Who says waffles are just for breakfast? We dress these for dessert with ice cream and a dark Peppermint-Chocolate Sauce.

2 large eggs
1 teaspoon vanilla extract
¼ cup butter or margarine, melted
1 cup buttermilk
1 cup all-purpose flour
½ teaspoon baking powder
½ teaspoon baking soda
¼ teaspoon salt
¼ teaspoon ground nutmeg
¾ cup sugar
½ cup cocoa
½ cup chopped walnuts
¼ cup semisweet chocolate mini-morsels
Vanilla ice cream
Peppermint-Chocolate Sauce (page 396)

•Combine first 3 ingredients in a large mixing bowl; beat at medium speed with an electric mixer until foamy (about 2 minutes). Add buttermilk, mixing well. Set aside.
•Combine flour and next 6 ingredients; gradually add to egg mixture, beating at low speed just until blended. Stir in walnuts and mini-morsels.
•Bake in a preheated, oiled waffle iron until golden. Serve with vanilla ice cream and warm Peppermint-Chocolate Sauce. Yield: 12 (4-inch) waffles.
Per waffle with ¼ cup each ice cream and sauce:
Calories 470   Fat 25.3g
Cholesterol 69mg   Sodium 212mg

Coffee-Toffee Parfaits

◀ QUICK ▶

PREP: 12 MINUTES   COOK: 2 MINUTES

Serve this showy parfait for company. It has three distinct layers—rich coffee ice cream, toffee candy bits, and dollops of soft cream.

3 cups coffee ice cream
Toffee Crunch
¾ cup whipping cream, whipped

•Spoon ¼ cup ice cream into each of six parfait glasses; top each with about 2

tablespoons Toffee Crunch. Repeat layers; freeze until ready to serve. Top each parfait with a dollop of whipped cream just before serving. Yield: 6 servings.
Per serving: Calories 359   Fat 23.8g
Cholesterol 81mg   Sodium 73mg

Toffee Crunch

½ cup firmly packed dark brown sugar
¼ cup sliced almonds
1 tablespoon butter or margarine, softened

•Combine all ingredients in a food processor; pulse 10 times or until nuts are finely chopped. Press mixture into a 7-inch circle on a greased baking sheet. Broil 3 inches from heat 1 minute or until bubbly but not burned. Remove from oven, and let stand 5 minutes.
•Gently turn toffee over, using a wide spatula, and broil 1 additional minute. (Watch closely as toffee broils; let it bubble, but not burn.) Remove from oven, and cool. Break toffee mixture into ½-inch pieces. Yield: 1½ cups.

Frozen Viennese Torte

◀ MAKE AHEAD ▶

PREP: 16 MINUTES   FREEZE: 10 HOURS

Three flavors of ice cream mingle in a cinnamon-almond crust for this impressive frozen torte.

18 (2½- x 5-inch) cinnamon graham crackers
2 (2-ounce) packages slivered almonds
⅓ cup butter or margarine, cut into small pieces
1 quart chocolate ice cream, softened
1 quart coffee ice cream, softened
1 quart vanilla ice cream, softened
2½ teaspoons ground cinnamon
1 (2-ounce) package slivered almonds, toasted
Amaretto-Cinnamon Sauce

•Process graham crackers and 2 packages almonds in a food processor until crumbs are fine. Add butter, processing until blended. Firmly press mixture in bottom and 1 inch up sides of a 10-inch springform

pan. Bake at 375° for 10 minutes. Cool on a wire rack.
•Spread chocolate ice cream on bottom and 1 inch up sides of crust; freeze until firm. Spread coffee ice cream over chocolate ice cream; freeze until firm. Beat vanilla ice cream and cinnamon at low speed with an electric mixer until blended; spread over coffee ice cream, and freeze 8 hours.
•Sprinkle each serving with toasted almonds, and drizzle with Amaretto-Cinnamon Sauce. Yield: 16 servings.
Per serving: Calories 425   Fat 20.8g
Cholesterol 54mg   Sodium 218mg

Amaretto-Cinnamon Sauce

¾ cup amaretto
¾ cup honey
¼ teaspoon ground cinnamon

•Combine all ingredients in a small saucepan; cook over medium heat until mixture is thoroughly heated, stirring often. Remove from heat, and cool to room temperature. Yield: 1¼ cups.

Brownie Baked Alaska

◀ FAMILY FAVORITE ▶

PREP: 19 MINUTES   COOK: 32 MINUTES

If you think you won't have time to make Baked Alaska, see our quick version that follows the main recipe. It cuts down on time and ingredients by starting with a brownie mix.

1 quart strawberry or vanilla ice cream
½ cup butter or margarine, softened
2 cups sugar, divided
2 large eggs
1 cup all-purpose flour
½ teaspoon baking powder
¼ teaspoon salt
2 tablespoons cocoa
1 teaspoon vanilla extract
5 egg whites
½ teaspoon cream of tartar
Strawberry halves

•Line a 1-quart freezerproof bowl (about 6 inches in diameter) with wax paper, leaving an overhang around the edges. Pack ice cream into bowl, and freeze until very firm.

• Beat butter at medium speed with an electric mixer 2 minutes or until creamy; gradually add 1 cup sugar, beating well. Add eggs, one at a time, beating after each addition until blended.

• Combine flour and next 3 ingredients; gradually add to butter mixture, mixing well. Stir in vanilla.

• Pour batter into a greased and floured 8-inch round cakepan. Bake at 350° for 25 to 30 minutes or until a wooden pick inserted in center comes out clean. Cool in pan on a wire rack 10 minutes; remove from pan, and cool completely on wire rack.

• Place cake on an ovenproof wooden board or serving dish. Invert bowl of ice cream onto cake layer, leaving wax paper intact; remove bowl. Place ice cream-topped cake in freezer.

• Combine egg whites, remaining 1 cup sugar, and cream of tartar in top of a double boiler. Place over simmering water. Cook, stirring constantly with a wire whisk, 5 minutes or until mixture reaches 160°. Remove from heat. Beat at high speed 5 minutes or until soft peaks form.

• Remove ice cream-topped cake from freezer, and peel off wax paper. Quickly spread meringue over entire surface, making sure edges are sealed.

• Bake at 500° for 2 minutes or until meringue peaks are browned. Arrange strawberry halves around edges, and serve immediately. Yield: 12 servings.
Per serving: Calories 219 Fat 8.5g Cholesterol 76mg Sodium 263mg

Note: After the meringue is sealed, the dessert can be returned to the freezer and baked just before serving. Brownie Baked Alaska will keep in the freezer up to 1 week.

Quick Brownie Baked Alaska: Substitute a (10.25-ounce) package fudge brownie mix for the brownie layer. Bake in an 8-inch round cakepan according to package directions.

BAKED MERINGUES

Baked meringues grace a dessert table with high style. In contrast to soft, puffy meringues that top a multitude of pies, baked meringues produce an entirely different dessert.

The basic meringue mixture is piped or spread into freestanding shapes and then it's baked long and slowly on a low temperature setting. This method gives the shaped meringue its characteristic crisp, melt-in-your-mouth texture without browning the meringue.

For maximum volume from beaten egg whites, separate the eggs while cold, and then let whites sit at room temperature 20 minutes before whipping them. If you're fortunate enough to own a large copper bowl, it produces beaten whites with great volume due to a stabilizing chemical reaction that takes place between the egg white and copper. Otherwise, a clean, grease-free glass bowl works, too.

Don't beat egg whites for meringue until you're absolutely ready to pipe or spread and then bake once the mixture is beaten. If beaten egg whites sit too long before being baked, they'll deflate and lose their shape in the oven.

The ideal baking temperature ranges from 200° to 225°. Bake meringues until they're firm and almost dry; then turn the oven off, and leave meringues in the oven to cool several hours or overnight.

Seal baked meringues in an airtight container, and store them at room temperature up to two days. For longer storage, freeze them up to a month in an airtight freezer container.

If meringues feel soft or sticky after storage, crisp them in a 200° oven for 5 minutes. Then turn oven off and let meringues cool in the oven until dry. Fill meringues just before serving to keep them crisp.

Avoid making meringues on humid or rainy days; the extra moisture outside can make the end product soft and sticky.

Meringue Mushrooms

PREP: 16 MINUTES   COOK: 1½ HOURS
STAND: 2 HOURS

These crisp little meringues almost pass for real mushrooms—until you take a sweet, crunchy bite. See them garnishing the Bûche de Noël on page 120.

3 egg whites
¼ teaspoon cream of tartar
⅛ teaspoon salt
¼ teaspoon vanilla extract
¼ teaspoon almond extract
½ cup superfine sugar
½ cup (3 ounces) semisweet chocolate morsels, melted
2 teaspoons cocoa

• Combine first 5 ingredients; beat at high speed with an electric mixer until foamy. Add sugar, 1 tablespoon at a time, beating until stiff peaks form and sugar dissolves (2 to 4 minutes).

• Spoon mixture into a decorating bag fitted with a large round tip. Pipe 32 (1¼-inch-wide) mounds to resemble mushroom caps and 32 (1-inch-tall) columns to resemble stems onto a parchment paper-lined baking sheet.

• Bake at 200° for 1½ hours; turn oven off. Let meringues stand in closed oven 2 hours.

• Spread a thin layer of melted chocolate on flat side of caps. Trim rounded end of stems to make them flat; press stems against chocolate to attach them to caps. Sprinkle meringues lightly with cocoa. Yield: 32 mushrooms.
Per mushroom: Calories 28 Fat 1g Cholesterol 0mg Sodium 14mg

Coffee Meringues with Butterscotch Mousse

PREP: 25 MINUTES

COOK: 1 HOUR AND 15 MINUTES

STAND: 8 HOURS

Find crunchy chocolate-covered coffee beans at large supermarkets or gourmet coffee shops to garnish the tops of these mousse-filled meringues. Or you can grate a little chocolate over these meringues if you don't have the beans. It's divine either way.

3 egg whites
1 teaspoon instant coffee granules
¼ teaspoon cream of tartar
1 cup sugar
Butterscotch Mousse (page 171)
Garnish: chocolate-covered coffee beans or
    grated chocolate

• Beat first 3 ingredients at high speed with an electric mixer until foamy. Add sugar, 1 tablespoon at a time, beating until stiff peaks form.
• Line baking sheets with unglazed brown paper or parchment paper. (Do not use recycled paper.) Drop mixture by rounded teaspoonfuls onto paper. Make an indentation in center of each with back of a spoon.
• Bake at 225° for 1 hour and 15 minutes; turn oven off, and cool in oven 2 to 8 hours. Carefully remove meringues from paper; store in an airtight container up to 1 week. Just before serving, spoon Butterscotch Mousse into each meringue. Garnish, if desired. Yield: 40 meringues.
Per meringue: Calories 74 Fat 4.3g Cholesterol 14mg Sodium 19mg

Pavlova

PREP: 30 MINUTES

COOK: 45 MINUTES

1 teaspoon cornstarch
4 egg whites
1 cup superfine sugar
1 teaspoon white vinegar
1 teaspoon vanilla extract
1½ cups whipping cream
2 tablespoons strawberry jam
1 tablespoon water
1 medium banana
Lemon juice
2 kiwifruit, peeled and sliced
1 pint strawberries, sliced

• Draw an 11- x 7-inch rectangle on a piece of wax paper; place on a baking sheet. Grease wax paper, and dust with 1 teaspoon cornstarch. Set aside.
• Beat egg whites at high speed with an electric mixer until foamy. Gradually add sugar, ¼ cup at a time, beating until stiff peaks form and sugar dissolves (2 to 4 minutes). Beat in vinegar and vanilla.
• Spread meringue into an 11- x 7-inch rectangle on prepared wax paper. Bake at 275° for 45 minutes. Carefully remove meringue from baking sheet, and cool completely on wire rack. Carefully turn meringue over, and remove wax paper. Place meringue, right side up, on a serving platter.
• Beat whipping cream at medium speed until soft peaks form. Set aside 1 cup whipped cream. Spread remaining whipped cream over meringue, leaving a 1-inch border. Pipe or dollop reserved whipped cream around edges.
• Combine jam and water in a small saucepan; heat just until jam melts, stirring constantly. Strain mixture; set liquid aside to cool.
• Slice banana, and sprinkle with lemon juice. Arrange banana, kiwifruit, and strawberry slices on whipped cream. Brush strawberries with strawberry jam liquid. Yield: 10 servings.
Per serving: Calories 246 Fat 13.5g Cholesterol 49mg Sodium 37mg

PAVLOVA: A CLASSIC DESSERT

Anna Pavlova was a Russian ballerina whose delicate grace was admired the world over during the first quarter of this century. In honor of her visit to his country, an Australian chef created this special dessert—a cloudlike meringue topped with cream and assorted fruit.

FRUIT DESSERTS

Desserts made with fresh or canned fruit are often the simplest and most beautiful luxuries you can whip up. With the addition of a liqueur or some sweetened whipped cream, Sugar-Crusted Figs or Baked Pears à la Mode are just minutes away from becoming your next elegant dessert. In addition, fruit desserts may well be the most healthful dessert options available. Those without a lot of sugar or heavy sauces emphasize the freshness and flavor of the fruit without a lot of extra fat and calories. Balloon wine glasses make elegant serving dishes for these and any number of easy fruit desserts within this chapter.

Many fresh fruits are available year-round in some parts of the country. For the best buys and fullest flavor, however, buy fruit in season.

When purchasing fresh fruit, evaluate its quality by the ripeness, texture, aroma, and color. Don't buy soft or bruised fruit because it will deteriorate quickly. Whenever possible, purchase loose fruit rather than prepackaged so you can best evaluate its quality.

Frozen fruits and some canned fruits offer good alternatives to fresh fruit. Fruits frozen whole without added syrup will have flavor and texture closest to fresh.

If you choose to substitute canned fruits packed in syrup or juice, you may need to drain the fruit and pat it dry before substituting it in the fresh fruit recipes in this section.

Fresh Fruit Grand Marnier

PREP: 25 MINUTES   COOK: 43 MINUTES

CHILL: 1 HOUR

4 medium oranges
2 medium apples, peeled and diced
1 pint fresh strawberries, hulled and
   halved
1 pint fresh blueberries or blackberries
1½ cups seedless green grapes
1 cup milk
4 egg yolks
½ cup sugar
1 teaspoon cornstarch
¼ cup Grand Marnier or other
   orange-flavored liqueur
1 teaspoon vanilla extract
1 teaspoon grated orange rind
½ cup whipping cream

•Peel and section oranges. Place orange sections in a large bowl; set aside. Add apple, and next three ingredients, tossing gently to combine. Cover and chill.
•Cook milk in a small saucepan over medium heat until thoroughly heated. Process egg yolks, sugar, and cornstarch in a food processor 1 to 2 minutes or until thick and pale. Slowly pour warm milk through food chute with processor running, processing just until mixture is smooth.
•Transfer to a medium saucepan; cook over medium-low heat, stirring constantly, until mixture is thickened and coats a metal spoon (about 38 minutes). Remove from heat; stir in Grand Marnier, vanilla, and orange rind. Cover and chill thoroughly.
•Beat whipping cream at medium speed with an electric mixer until soft peaks form; gently fold whipped cream into Grand Marnier mixture. Spoon fruit mixture evenly into individual dessert dishes; top each serving with whipped cream mixture. Yield: 8 servings.
Per serving: Calories 276   Fat 9.8g
Cholesterol 133mg   Sodium 25mg

Cherry Crêpes

◄ FAMILY FAVORITE ►

PREP: 25 MINUTES   COOK: 45 MINUTES

1 recipe Basic Crêpes (page 76)
1 teaspoon vanilla extract
1¼ cups sour cream
⅓ cup firmly packed brown sugar
1½ teaspoons all-purpose flour
¼ teaspoon ground cinnamon
Cherry Sauce
Whipped cream
Toasted sliced almonds
2 cups vanilla ice cream

•Prepare Basic Crêpe batter, adding 1 teaspoon vanilla to batter. Cook as directed.
•Combine sour cream and next 3 ingredients; stir well. Spoon about 1½ tablespoons sour cream mixture on each of 12 crêpes. (Reserve remaining crêpes for another use.) Roll up crêpes, and place, seam side down, in a lightly greased 13- x 9-inch baking dish. Pour Cherry Sauce over crêpes.
•Bake at 350° for 10 to 12 minutes or until thoroughly heated. Top with whipped cream and almonds. Serve with ice cream. Yield: 6 servings.
Per serving: Calories 623   Fat 31.8g
Cholesterol 156mg   Sodium 267mg

Cherry Sauce

¼ cup sugar
1 tablespoon cornstarch
1 cup cranberry juice cocktail
1 (16-ounce) can pitted red tart cherries
   in water, drained
1 teaspoon grated orange rind
½ teaspoon almond extract

•Combine sugar and cornstarch in a medium saucepan; stir in cranberry juice and remaining ingredients. Cook, stirring constantly, over medium heat until thickened and bubbly. Yield: 2⅓ cups.

Note: To make a day ahead, prepare filled crêpes as directed, and place in baking dish; cover and store in refrigerator. Remove from refrigerator 30 minutes before serving; make Cherry Sauce, and pour over crêpes. Bake as directed.

Fruit Dessert Pizza

◄ FAMILY FAVORITE ►

PREP: 25 MINUTES   COOK: 15 MINUTES

Highlight your favorite fruit on this cookie pizza that kids of all ages will enjoy.

1 (18-ounce) package refrigerated sugar
   cookie dough
1 (8-ounce) package cream cheese,
   softened
¼ cup sifted powdered sugar
1 tablespoon whipping cream or milk
1 teaspoon vanilla extract
1 (8-ounce) can pineapple chunks, drained
1 cup sliced fresh strawberries
½ cup fresh blueberries
1 (11-ounce) can mandarin oranges,
   drained
2 kiwifruit, peeled and thinly sliced
2 tablespoons apple jelly

•Roll or pat cookie dough onto a 12-inch pizza pan coated with cooking spray, forming a rim around outer edge. Flute edges, if desired. Bake at 350° for 12 to 15 minutes or until done. Cool completely.
•Beat cream cheese at medium speed with an electric mixer until smooth. Add powdered sugar, whipping cream, and vanilla; beat well. Spread over cookie crust.
•Arrange fruit in a circular fashion over cream cheese mixture. Melt apple jelly in a small saucepan over low heat; cool slightly. Brush melted jelly lightly over fruit. Slice pizza into wedges to serve. Yield: 10 servings.
Per serving: Calories 369   Fat 19g
Cholesterol 34mg   Sodium 279mg

Note: You can use a disposable 12-inch pizza pan, if desired.

Bananas Foster

◀ FAMILY FAVORITE • QUICK ▶

PREP: 5 MINUTES   COOK: 4 MINUTES

The flavor and flames of the authentic New Orleans classic are captured in this quick and easy skillet dessert. If you don't have banana liqueur, just double the rum.

¼ cup butter or margarine
⅓ cup firmly packed dark brown sugar
½ teaspoon ground cinnamon
4 bananas, quartered
⅓ cup banana liqueur
⅓ cup dark rum
1 pint vanilla ice cream

•Melt butter in a large skillet over medium-high heat; add brown sugar and next 3 ingredients. Cook, stirring constantly, 2 minutes or until bananas are tender. Pour rum into a small long-handled saucepan; heat just until warm. Remove from heat. Ignite with a long match, and pour over bananas. Baste bananas with sauce until flames die down. Serve immediately over ice cream. Yield: 4 servings.
Per serving: Calories 455   Fat 19.2g
Cholesterol 61mg   Sodium 183mg

FLAMING DESSERTS

To flame desserts as in Bananas Foster above, heat the liquor just until warm in a small long-handled saucepan; remove from heat, and ignite with a long-stemmed fireplace match. Pour the flaming alcohol over the dessert, and serve after flames die down (usually in about a minute).

You can also flame desserts using extracts. The higher the alcohol content of the extract, the better it will flame. Extracts flame without being heated first and, because their flavor is so concentrated, you'll want to use only a scant amount (1 to 2 teaspoons). Just sprinkle an extract onto the garnish or top of dessert to soak in; then flame it.

PICK AN APPLE

Choose apples that have good color and smooth skin without bruises. For cooking or baking, select one of the following apple varieties: Granny Smith, McIntosh, Rome Beauty, Stayman, Winesap, or York Imperial.

Caramel Baked Apples

◀ FAMILY FAVORITE ▶

PREP: 35 MINUTES   COOK: 1½ HOURS

A warm caramel sauce bathes these brown sugar-baked apples.

½ cup firmly packed brown sugar
½ cup raisins or chopped dates
¼ cup chopped walnuts
3 tablespoons butter or margarine, softened
½ teaspoon ground cinnamon
6 cooking apples
1 cup water
Caramel Sauce

•Combine first 5 ingredients; stir well, and set aside.
•Core apples, cutting to, but not through, bottom; peel top third of each apple, if desired (photo 1). Stuff raisin mixture into cavities of apples (photo 2). Place apples in an 11- x 7-inch baking dish; pour water around apples.
•Cover and bake at 350° for 30 minutes. Uncover and bake 50 more minutes or until apples are tender, basting often.
•Place apples on a serving platter, using a slotted spoon. Spoon warm Caramel Sauce over apples. Yield: 6 servings.
Per serving: Calories 466   Fat 16.6g
Cholesterol 43mg   Sodium 75mg

Caramel Sauce

1 cup sugar
⅓ cup water
⅛ teaspoon cream of tartar
½ cup whipping cream
½ cup water

•Combine first 3 ingredients in a large cast-iron skillet or saucepan. Cook over medium heat, stirring constantly, until sugar melts and turns light brown. Remove from heat.
•Combine whipping cream and ½ cup water in a medium saucepan. Cook over medium heat, stirring constantly, until hot (160°). Gradually add whipping cream mixture to syrup, stirring until smooth. Bring sauce to a boil over medium heat, stirring constantly. Remove from heat. Yield: 1 cup.

1. For a fancy presentation, peel top third of each cored apple, using a vegetable peeler or paring knife.

2. Stuff raisin mixture into cavity of each apple, using a small spoon or your fingers.

Vanilla-Poached Pears

PREP: 10 MINUTES   COOK: 30 MINUTES

Poaching fruit in a flavorful liquid enhances its naturally good taste. These ripe pears drink up the vanilla-honey syrup.

4 medium-size firm, ripe pears such as
   Bosc or Bartlett
1 tablespoon lemon juice
4 cups water
3 tablespoons vanilla extract
2 tablespoons honey
½ cup sugar
2 drops of hot water
Chocolate Sauce (page 396)

•Core pears from bottom, cutting to, but not through, the stem end (photo 1). Cut a thin slice from bottoms so that pears stand upright (photo 2). Peel pears; rub lemon juice over pears.
•Combine 4 cups water, vanilla, and honey in a large saucepan; bring to a boil. Add pears (photo 3); cover, reduce heat, and simmer 15 to 20 minutes or until pears are tender. Remove pears, and cool.
•When ready to serve pears, place sugar in a heavy 1½-quart saucepan. Cook over medium heat, stirring constantly, until sugar melts and syrup is golden. Stir in 2 drops of water; let stand 1 to 2 minutes.
•To serve, spoon 2 tablespoons Chocolate Sauce on each serving plate; place pears on sauce. Working quickly, drizzle caramelized sugar from a fork, and quickly wrap threads around pears until a delicate web is formed (photo 4). Repeat with remaining pears. Serve immediately. Yield: 4 servings.
Per serving: Calories 447   Fat 21g
Cholesterol 41mg   Sodium 12mg

1. Core pears from bottom, cutting to, but not through, stem end.

2. Cut a thin slice from bottom of each pear so fruit will stand upright.

3. Gently lower pears into saucepan for poaching in vanilla syrup.

4. Working quickly, drizzle caramelized sugar from a fork in circles around each pear.

Baked Pears à la Mode

PREP: 5 MINUTES   COOK: 30 MINUTES

You can turn out this dessert in minutes with just a few simple ingredients.

2 (15¼-ounce) cans pear halves, drained
½ cup honey
½ cup butter or margarine, melted
1 cup crumbled amaretti cookies or
   almond or coconut macaroons
3 cups vanilla ice cream

•Arrange pears in an 11- x 7-inch baking dish; set aside. Combine honey and butter; pour over pears. Bake at 350° for 20 minutes. Sprinkle cookie crumbs over pears; bake 10 more minutes. Serve warm with ice cream. Yield: 6 servings.
Per serving: Calories 563   Fat 26.5g
Cholesterol 41mg   Sodium 162mg

Sugar-Crusted Figs

PREP: 15 MINUTES   COOK: 20 MINUTES

Spoon soft peaks of whipped cream over a row of these sugared figs for a lovely presentation.

¼ cup water
1 tablespoon vanilla extract
1½ pounds fresh figs, stemmed (29 figs)
1 cup superfine sugar (see box)
¾ cup whipping cream
1 teaspoon vanilla extract

•Combine water and 1 tablespoon vanilla in a 1-cup liquid measuring cup. Dip each fig in mixture; dredge in sugar, coating each thickly. Divide figs among four lightly greased individual shallow baking dishes.
•Bake at 425° for 15 to 20 minutes or until figs are very tender.

•Combine whipping cream and 1 teaspoon vanilla; beat at medium speed with an electric mixer until soft peaks form. Spoon mixture over warm figs. Yield: 4 servings.
Per serving: Calories 432   Fat 17g
Cholesterol 61mg   Sodium 19mg

SUPERFINE FINISH

Superfine sugar is a granulated sugar with the tiniest and most uniform crystals. It's also called ultrafine or castor sugar, its British name. If you can't find superfine sugar, make your own by pulsing regular granulated sugar in the food processor 30 seconds.

Herb Omelet Torte
(page 198)

EGGS & CHEESE

These universal staples make a routine appearance at most meals, and without them, we'd hardly be able to cook. Eggs and cheese fortify the flavor, texture, and color for a multitude of foods we enjoy every day.

Equipment

A few simple elements, a spatula, nonstick skillet, and whisk will ready you for just about any egg recipe in this chapter. For specialty dishes such as soufflés and quiches, consider investing in the specific cookware for the dish. Similarly shaped casserole dishes and pieplates will, however, make suitable substitutes in a pinch.

You'll find many recipes in the egg and cheese sections of this chapter include shredded or grated cheese, so buy a good quality grater. And for shaving large slivers of cheese, a sturdy vegetable peeler or cheese plane comes in handy.

Selecting Eggs

While labeling and distribution take much of the guesswork out of buying eggs, sometimes the process can still be confusing. An egg's size is determined by the average weight per dozen. The U.S. Department of Agriculture lists six size categories of eggs: jumbo, extralarge, large, medium, small, and peewee, although all markets don't carry each size. Medium, large, and extralarge are most commonly available. The size of egg you use is important for recipes that call for a specific number of beaten eggs. We test all our recipes with large eggs. If you use small eggs, your end product may be quite different. See the egg size substitution chart on page 189 for help in cooking with different sizes of eggs.

Grading has to do with the interior and exterior quality of an egg. Eggs are graded as either AA, A, or B. There is no difference in nutrients among grades of eggs. The higher quality grades are AA and A and are good for all types of egg cookery. They're especially desirable when appearance is important, such as in frying or poaching, because the white is thick and the yolk is firm and stands high. Grade B eggs are just as wholesome to eat, just not as attractive when broken. Rarely do you find grade B eggs in the retail market.

Shell color ranges from white to deep brown, depending on the breed of hen. There's no difference in the flavor, nutritive value, or cooking performance between brown and white eggs. Yolks can also vary in color, from almost orange to pale yellow. These color differences result from the hen's feed and don't affect an egg's quality or nutrients.

The nutritional content of an egg is based on its size. Flavor is not affected by an egg's size or grade or by its shell or yolk color. Most eggs have a bland flavor.

Storing Eggs

Always store eggs in the refrigerator, well away from aromatic foods, because eggs easily absorb odors. Eggs will keep three to five weeks without significant loss of quality, although some sources say to use them within a week of purchase for the best flavor and cooking quality. Most egg cartons are stamped with a "sell by" date to help you track their age.

Store eggs, large end up, preferably in the carton rather than in the refrigerator door's egg tray. This allows the yolk to stay centered, which is important when deviling eggs or slicing hard-cooked eggs for a garnish. Refrigerate hard-cooked eggs as soon after cooking as possible, and use them within a week.

If you have yolks or whites left over from recipes, refrigerate them for several days. Place leftover whites in an airtight jar, and use within four days. Need a few ideas for how to use leftover whites? They are a good clarifying agent for soup stock, provide a light coating for breaded foods, or just a good excuse to make an Angel Food Cake, page 117. Leftover yolks are more fragile. Store them in water in a tightly covered container, and use them within two days.

Working with Eggs

You'll use some techniques particular to eggs repeatedly in recipes. Following are some of the more common techniques, and how to perform them with ease.

Separating Eggs: You can buy an egg separator from a kitchen specialty shop to aid in this task, but separating eggs is not hard to do by hand. Eggs separate easiest when cold. Sharply tap the midpoint of

Separating an egg: Gently crack egg, break shell into two halves, and transfer yolk back and forth until all white has drained.

an egg against a hard surface, like a counter or rim of a mixing bowl. Hold the egg over the bowl in which you want the whites, and gently pull the two halves apart, holding one half like a cup to keep the yolk in that half, and letting the white part flow into the bowl underneath. Pass the yolk back and forth between the two shell halves until all the white has dripped into the bowl (see photo). It's safest to drop one white at a time into a small bowl and then transfer it into a larger bowl with the other separated whites. This averts the problem of getting a little yolk in the whole bowl of whites; egg whites won't beat properly with even the slightest bit of yolk in them.

Beating Egg Yolks: Some recipes call for egg yolks to be beaten until thick and pale. This means to beat the yolks at high speed with an electric mixer 3 to 5 minutes or until yolks thicken and are a pale yellow. At this stage, the yolks increase to their maximum volume.

Beating Egg Whites: Place egg whites in a copper, glass, or stainless steel bowl, and let them stand 20 minutes before beating. (Be sure no yolk is contained within the whites, as the fatty composition of the yolks will prevent the whites from expanding properly. And make sure the mixing bowl and beaters are completely grease free, too.) Beat the egg whites (and cream of tartar if recipe calls for it) until foamy (photo 1). If adding sugar to egg whites, do so at this point, adding 1 tablespoon at a time and beating until peaks form. When lightly beaten, egg whites look foamy and bubbly. At this stage, the whites easily separate back into liquid form.

For recipes that call for soft peaks, beat the whites until they are moist and shiny; the whites will mound, but no sharp tips will form

BEATING EGG WHITES

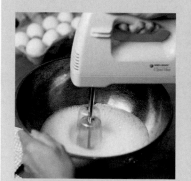

1. Foamy stage: When lightly beaten to this stage, egg whites will look bubbly and foamy.

2. Soft peak stage: When beaten to soft peak stage, egg whites will mound, but no sharp tips will form.

3. Stiff peak stage: When beaten to stiff peaks, sharp tips will form when beaters are lifted.

4. Overbeaten egg whites: When whites are overbeaten, they look curdled and dry. There's no restoring them. Better start over.

(photo 2). For stiff peaks, beat the whites until sharp peaks form when beaters are removed (photo 3); the whites will be moist and glossy. When overbeaten, the egg whites will be dry and look curdled (photo 4).

Folding in Egg Whites: Beat the egg whites at the very last minute before your recipe specifies to fold them in; otherwise, they may start to separate before you use them. Use a rubber spatula to fold, and cut straight down through the center of the bowl, across the bottom, and back up the sides. Give the bowl a quarter turn, and gently repeat the folding action just until egg whites are evenly dispersed. Be sure not to overwork the mixture or you'll lose the air incorporated into the beaten whites.

Tempering Eggs: This process prevents curdling (scrambling) the eggs when you combine uncooked eggs with a hot mixture. Beat the eggs until thick and pale. Gradually stir about one-fourth of the hot mixture into the eggs; add that slowly back to the remaining hot mixture, stirring constantly.

EGG SIZE SUBSTITUTIONS

We test our recipes with large eggs, but if you use a different size, this chart will help you figure out how many eggs to substitute.

If recipe uses this many	Substitute this many eggs, depending on size			
LARGE	JUMBO	EX-LARGE	MEDIUM	SMALL
1	1	1	1	1
2	2	2	2	3
3	2	3	3	4
4	3	4	5	5
5	4	4	6	7
6	5	5	7	8

About Freezing Eggs

If you have more eggs than you can use within four or five weeks, consider freezing them—not in the shell, though, because they'd burst.

Whether freezing just yolks or whole eggs, they require special treatment to prevent the yolk from becoming gelatinous. Add either ⅛ teaspoon salt or 1½ teaspoons sugar per 4 egg yolks or 2 whole eggs. Label the container with the date, number of eggs, and whether you've added salt (for savory dishes) or sugar (for desserts). Freeze whole eggs or egg yolks up to six months. Thaw the container of eggs 8 hours in the refrigerator or run cold water over the container until eggs are thawed.

Egg whites can be frozen without any added ingredients. Just pour into freezer containers, label with the date and the number of whites, and freeze. For convenient freezer storage of individual egg whites, place egg whites separately in ice cube trays. When frozen, remove the cubes from trays, and store them in plastic bags up to eight months. Allow one cube for each egg white called for in a recipe. Thaw egg whites 8 hours in the refrigerator or run cold water over the plastic container until eggs are thawed.

Do not freeze hard-cooked eggs, because the white part becomes leathery when frozen. Most recipes that have a high proportion of eggs to other ingredients do not freeze well.

Never Eat Raw Eggs

There was a time when Caesar Salad was prized for its unique dressing that included a coddled (partially cooked) egg. But today the USDA recommends that we avoid this salad as well as other dishes that contain raw eggs—like traditional eggnog and chilled soufflés made without cooking the eggs. Because of an increased risk of salmonella, the USDA now recommends that all eggs be cooked to an internal temperature of 160°.

When eggs are cooked to 160°, whites and yolks are firm. For recipes like scrambled eggs, this means no visible liquid remains.

All of the recipes and procedures in this book cook eggs to at least 160°. If you have old recipes containing raw eggs that you'd like to update, here are some suggestions.

• For recipes such as Caesar Salad in which the egg isn't essential, just omit the egg and adjust the recipe if needed. See our Caesar Salad offering on page 352.

• For recipes such as ice cream that contain raw eggs, cook the mixture like a custard to 160°.

• For most recipes such as uncooked soufflés that depend on beaten egg whites for their stability, cook the egg whites and sugar in the top of a double boiler to 160°; then remove from heat, and beat until soft peaks form.

• In some cases, such as casseroles and custards, you can replace raw eggs with a refrigerated or frozen product called egg substitute. It's made from real egg whites and is pasteurized, a process that heats the egg product enough to kill any salmonella that may be present. Use ¼ cup egg substitute for each egg that you replace; no further cooking of the recipe is necessary.

Microwaving Eggs

Eggs demand special treatment when cooked in a microwave oven. Unless they're scrambled or mixed with several heartier ingredients, don't use HIGH power. The yolk, which is higher in fat, cooks faster than the white. HIGH power will overcook the yolk before the white is done. All eggs should be removed from the microwave oven before they're completely set and should be allowed to stand several minutes to complete cooking.

We give microwave directions only for recipes in this section that had favorable and comparable results to conventional cooking. When cooking basic eggs in a microwave, the following tips and techniques will ensure good results.

Scrambled Eggs: Eggs scrambled in the microwave oven are fluffier than eggs cooked conventionally. It isn't necessary to use butter or oil to prevent sticking. Scrambled eggs will cook first around the edges. Stir once or twice during the microwave cycle, breaking up set portions and pushing them to the center of the dish. After microwaving, let eggs stand 1 to 2 minutes to complete cooking; stir just before serving.

Hard-Cooked Eggs: Eggs cannot be hard cooked in a microwave oven. Steam builds up inside the shell, causing the egg to burst. Refer to the hard-cooked egg discussion on the following page for a similar product.

What Went Wrong

A common problem that occurs when cooking eggs is coagulation or curdling, particularly in custards and sauces. They become lumpy when the egg curdles before it has a chance to thicken the mixture. You can avoid curdling the egg by tempering it as you add it to a hot custard or sauce (see opposite page). To try to rescue a lumpy custard or sauce, whisk it briskly with a wire whisk over a bowl of ice water or blend it in an electric blender.

Another common problem is egg whites that won't beat properly. When this happens, it probably means a little egg yolk was mixed with the whites before beating. There's no way to rescue these egg whites. For best results, make sure no yolk is mixed with the whites and use ultraclean (grease-free) beaters and bowls. Separate the eggs straight from the refrigerator, but allow whites to stand at room temperature 20 minutes before beating them.

HARD-COOKED EGGS

The simplest way to cook an egg is in its shell in hot water. When done, both the yolk and white will be firm. Hard-cooked eggs can be peeled and eaten, seasoned and stuffed, teamed with other ingredients in recipes, or used as an edible garnish.

When hard-cooking eggs, place them in a single layer in a saucepan. Add enough tap water to come at least 1 inch above eggs. Cover and bring to a boil over medium heat; then immediately remove from heat. (Never boil eggs or cook them longer than directed, because yolks may become hard and develop an unattractive gray-green ring.) Once removed from heat, let eggs stand for length of time directed in recipe; then pour off water and place eggs under cold running water until cooled. This stops the cooking process and makes eggs easier to peel. If not serving the eggs right away, keep them refrigerated.

To peel a hard-cooked egg, first crackle it by gently tapping shell all over on kitchen counter. Roll egg between hands to loosen shell; then gently peel away shell under cold running water. Usually, the fresher the egg, the harder it will be to peel; therefore, when hard-cooking a large number of eggs, buy them several days before cooking them.

Hard-Cooked Eggs

◀ QUICK • MAKE AHEAD ▶

PREP: 20 MINUTES

•Place desired number of eggs in a single layer in a saucepan. Add enough water to measure at least 1 inch above eggs. Cover and quickly bring to a boil. Remove from heat. Let stand, covered, in hot water 15 minutes for large eggs. (Adjust time up or down by about 3 minutes for each size larger or smaller.) Pour off water. Immediately run cold water over eggs or place them in ice water until completely cooled.
•To remove shell, gently tap egg all over, roll between hands to loosen egg shell; then hold egg under cold running water as you peel off shell.

Microwave Directions: Eggs cannot be hard cooked in a microwave oven. Steam builds up inside the shell, causing the egg to burst from pressure. However, a product similar to hard-cooked eggs can be achieved by microwaving.
•Break eggs into lightly greased individual custard cups or microwave-safe coffee cups; pierce each yolk with a wooden pick.
•Cover with heavy-duty plastic wrap; fold back a small edge of wrap to allow steam to escape. Microwave at MEDIUM (50% power) 1¼ to 1½ minutes for 1 egg, 1¾ to 2¼ minutes for 2 eggs, or 3¾ to 4¼ minutes for 3 eggs, or to desired doneness, turning cups halfway through cooking time. Test eggs with a wooden pick (yolks should be just firm, and whites should be almost set). Let eggs stand, covered, 1 to 2 minutes to complete cooking. (If eggs are not desired doneness after standing, cover and continue microwaving briefly.) Cool.
•While this product is not suitable for stuffing, it works well for creamed eggs, egg salad, or other dishes that use chopped eggs.

Soft-Cooked Eggs: The USDA says there is some risk involved in egg cookery in which the yolk is not firm, so if you choose to soft-cook eggs, the firmer the yolk, the better. The method the USDA currently recommends is to cook them as for hard-cooked eggs, but to cook them in boiling water 7 minutes. Immediately run cold water over eggs until cool enough to handle. To serve, slice each egg through the middle with a knife. Using a spoon, scoop egg from each shell half onto a serving plate. To serve in an egg cup, place egg in cup with the small end down. Slice off the large end of shell with a knife, and eat from shell.

Best Stuffed Eggs

◀ QUICK • FAMILY FAVORITE ▶

PREP: 10 MINUTES

Enhanced with pickle relish, these stuffed eggs are like those Grandma used to make—guaranteed to go fast at a family reunion.

6 large hard-cooked eggs
¼ cup mayonnaise
1½ tablespoons sweet pickle relish
1 teaspoon prepared mustard
⅛ teaspoon salt
Dash of pepper
Paprika
6 pimiento-stuffed olives, halved

•Slice eggs in half lengthwise, and carefully remove yolks. Mash yolks with mayonnaise. Add relish and next 3 ingredients; stir well. Spoon or pipe yolk mixture into egg whites. Sprinkle with paprika, and top each with an olive half. Yield: 6 servings.
Per serving: Calories 150 Fat 12.8g
Cholesterol 218mg Sodium 496mg

Herb-Sour Cream Stuffed Eggs

◀ QUICK ▶

PREP: 20 MINUTES

Any combination of fresh herbs adds a layer of flavor to these mild-mannered eggs laced with sour cream.

8 large hard-cooked eggs
⅓ to ½ cup sour cream
2 to 3 tablespoons finely chopped fresh chives or parsley or 2 to 3 teaspoons freeze-dried chives or parsley
1 to 2 tablespoons finely chopped fresh dill or 1 to 2 teaspoons dried dillweed
2 teaspoons white wine vinegar
¼ teaspoon salt
⅛ teaspoon pepper
3 slices bacon, cooked and crumbled
Garnish: fresh parsley sprigs

•Slice eggs in half lengthwise, and carefully remove yolks. Mash yolks; add sour cream and next 5 ingredients, stirring until smooth. Spoon or pipe mixture into egg whites. Sprinkle with bacon. Garnish, if desired. Yield: 8 servings.

Per serving: Calories 112 Fat 8.4g Cholesterol 219mg Sodium 187mg

Chile-Cheese Deviled Eggs

◄ QUICK ►

PREP: 15 MINUTES

A shake of hot sauce puts the devil in these green chile eggs.

12 large hard-cooked eggs
1 (3-ounce) package cream cheese, softened
1 (4.5-ounce) can chopped green chiles, undrained
2 tablespoons milk
¼ teaspoon salt
½ teaspoon hot sauce

•Slice eggs in half lengthwise, and carefully remove yolks. Process yolks, cream cheese, and remaining 4 ingredients in a food processor until smooth, stopping once to scrape down sides. Spoon or pipe yolk mixture into egg whites. Cover and chill until ready to serve. Yield: 12 servings.

Per serving: Calories 103 Fat 7.6g Cholesterol 221mg Sodium 184mg

Scotch Eggs

PREP: 15 MINUTES   COOK: 9 MINUTES

Find these hard-cooked eggs coated in sausage, encrusted in Italian breadcrumbs, and fried to crispy perfection. You can control the spiciness of the dish by choosing mild or hot sausage.

1 pound ground pork sausage
6 large hard-cooked eggs, peeled
1 large egg, beaten
1 cup Italian-seasoned breadcrumbs
Vegetable oil

•Divide sausage into 6 equal portions; press each portion around 1 hard-cooked egg. Dip each sausage-coated egg into beaten egg, and roll in breadcrumbs.
•Deep-fry in hot oil (350°) for 9 minutes; drain well. Cut eggs in half, and serve immediately. Yield: 6 servings.

Per serving: Calories 460 Fat 41g Cholesterol 299mg Sodium 708mg

Texas Brunch

◄ FAMILY FAVORITE ►

PREP: 20 MINUTES   COOK: 35 MINUTES

For a filling brunch, split a piece of hot crusty cornbread, and spoon this thick egg and cheese sauce over the top. Then sprinkle cornbread with crumbled bacon, green onions, and more cheese. Chop and shred the toppings ahead so you'll be ready to sprinkle them as soon as the cornbread's hot from the oven.

3 tablespoons butter or margarine
3 tablespoons all-purpose flour
2 cups milk
2 cups (8 ounces) shredded Cheddar cheese, divided
6 large hard-cooked eggs, chopped
½ cup mayonnaise
¼ teaspoon salt
¼ teaspoon hot sauce
⅛ teaspoon pepper
Buttermilk Cornbread (page 70)
8 slices bacon, cooked and crumbled
⅓ cup chopped green onions

•Melt butter in a large saucepan over low heat; add flour, stirring until smooth. Cook 1 minute, stirring constantly.
•Gradually add milk, and cook over medium heat, stirring constantly, until thickened and bubbly. Stir in ¾ cup cheese, chopped egg, and next 4 ingredients. Cook, stirring constantly, until cheese melts.
•Cut Buttermilk Cornbread into 6 wedges; remove from pan, and split each piece in half horizontally. Place 2 pieces each, cut sides up, on individual serving plates. Spoon egg mixture evenly over cornbread. Top evenly with remaining 1¼ cups cheese. Sprinkle with bacon and green onions. Yield: 6 servings.

Per serving: Calories 812 Fat 59.1g Cholesterol 336mg Sodium 1352mg

Rosy Pickled Eggs

PREP: 10 MINUTES   CHILL: 2 DAYS

Save the juice from a jar of beets for this unique recipe. The juice colors the pickling brine a pretty shade of rose.

12 large hard-cooked eggs
4 cups water
1 cup beet juice
1 cup white vinegar
1 small onion, sliced
1 clove garlic
1 bay leaf
2 teaspoons mixed pickling spices
½ teaspoon salt

•Peel eggs, and place loosely in a large jar.
•Cook water and remaining 7 ingredients in a saucepan over low heat just until thoroughly heated.
•Remove onion; pour hot vinegar mixture over eggs. Seal with an airtight lid. Store eggs in refrigerator 2 days before serving. Store in refrigerator up to 1 week. Yield: 12 servings.

Per serving: Calories 75 Fat 5g Cholesterol 212mg Sodium 78mg

PRESSED FOR A GARNISH

Press hard-cooked yolks and whites, separately or together, through a fine sieve or mash them with a pastry blender to sprinkle over other foods as a delicate garnish.

Another alternative is to garnish with slices or wedges of hard-cooked egg. Use an egg slicer or a sharp paring knife, and cut the egg gently to avoid crumbling the yolk.

Bacon and Egg Casserole

◄ MAKE AHEAD ►

PREP: 25 MINUTES   COOK: 48 MINUTES

2 large baking potatoes, unpeeled and
    cubed
¼ cup butter or margarine
¼ cup all-purpose flour
1 cup milk
1 cup half-and-half
4 cups (16 ounces) shredded sharp
    Cheddar cheese
1 teaspoon dried Italian seasoning
½ teaspoon pepper
12 large hard-cooked eggs, sliced
1 pound bacon, cooked and coarsely
    crumbled
2 cups soft whole wheat breadcrumbs
    (4 slices bread)
3 tablespoons butter or margarine, melted
Garnish: fresh herb sprigs

•Cook potato in boiling water to cover in a
large saucepan 15 minutes or just until tender. Drain and cool.
•Melt ¼ cup butter in a heavy saucepan
over medium-low heat; add flour, and stir
until smooth. Cook 1 minute, stirring
constantly. Gradually add milk and half-and-
half; cook over medium heat, stirring constantly, until thickened and bubbly. Add
cheese, Italian seasoning, and pepper, stirring constantly until cheese melts. Remove
from heat.
•Layer half each of egg slices, bacon, and
cheese sauce in a lightly greased 13- x 9-inch
baking dish. Top with potato. Top with
remaining egg slices, bacon, and cheese
sauce.

•Combine breadcrumbs and 3 tablespoons
melted butter; sprinkle over casserole. Cover
and chill overnight, if desired.
•Remove casserole from refrigerator. Let
stand at room temperature 30 minutes.
Bake, uncovered, at 350° for 30 minutes or
until thoroughly heated. Garnish, if desired.
Yield: 10 servings.
Per serving: Calories 563 Fat 40.8g
Cholesterol 350mg Sodium 765mg

Creamed Eggs in Patty Shells

PREP: 20 MINUTES   COOK: 20 MINUTES

*Serve these elegant creamy eggs for a ladies'
lunch. You can prepare everything separately
ahead; then assemble and reheat at the last
minute.*

1 (10-ounce) package frozen patty shells
¼ cup plus 2 tablespoons butter or
    margarine, divided
¼ pound fresh mushrooms, sliced
1 tablespoon finely chopped onion
3 tablespoons all-purpose flour
1½ cups milk
¾ teaspoon salt
Pinch of ground red pepper
6 large hard-cooked eggs
Fresh parsley sprigs

•Bake patty shells according to package
directions; set aside.
•Melt 2 tablespoons butter in a heavy skillet.
Add mushrooms and onion; sauté until tender. Set aside.

•Melt remaining ¼ cup butter in a heavy
saucepan over low heat; add flour, stirring
until smooth. Cook 1 minute, stirring constantly. Gradually add milk; cook over medium heat, stirring constantly, until thickened
and bubbly. Stir in salt and red pepper.
•Finely chop 5 eggs. Stir chopped eggs and
sautéed vegetables into sauce; cook, stirring
constantly, until thoroughly heated. Spoon
into patty shells. Cut remaining egg into 6
wedges. Top each serving with an egg wedge
and a parsley sprig. Yield: 6 servings.
Per serving: Calories 422 Fat 31.6g
Cholesterol 252mg Sodium 734mg

Microwave Directions: Bake patty shells
according to package directions. Place 2
tablespoons butter in a 1-quart liquid measuring cup. Microwave at HIGH 45 seconds
or until melted. Add mushrooms and onion;
microwave at HIGH 1 to 2 minutes or until
tender. Place remaining ¼ cup butter in a 1-
quart glass measure. Microwave at HIGH 55
seconds or until melted. Add flour, stirring
until smooth. Gradually add milk, stirring
well. Microwave at HIGH 4 to 5 minutes or
until thickened and bubbly, stirring after 2
minutes, and then at 1-minute intervals. Stir
in salt and red pepper. Finely chop 5 eggs.
Stir chopped eggs and sautéed vegetables
into sauce; microwave at HIGH 1 minute
or until thoroughly heated. Spoon into
patty shells. Cut remaining egg into 6
wedges. Top each serving with an egg
wedge and a parsley sprig.

Sherried Eggs in Patty Shells: Stir 1½
tablespoons dry sherry into sauce before
spooning it into shells.

FRIED EGGS

These busy days we all look for quick
cooking techniques, and frying may be the
quickest and easiest way to cook an egg.
And for such a simple cooking method,
a good bit of variety is possible in how you
can fry an egg.
  Sunny-side up (cooking the egg only on
the bottom) is a popular way to fry an egg; it
starts out in a hot skillet, but be sure to cook
it over low heat so the top of the egg gets

done before the bottom is overdone. As the
sunny-side up egg cooks, baste the top of
the egg with fat from the skillet to speed up
the time it takes for the top of the egg to
cook. Or you can flip the egg over once the
bottom is set, and cook it just until done
(*overeasy*) or until the yolk is very firm
(*overwell*). Just be sure to cook the egg long
enough for the yolk to set. Some people like
to break the yolk once the egg is flipped so

the yolk cooks quicker and distributes more
evenly over the white.
  When frying eggs, be sure your skillet is
large enough for the eggs to stay separate as
you cook them; once they join together and
cook, you'll have to cut them apart to separate them, and they won't look as pretty.

Sunny-Side-Up Eggs

PREP: 1 MINUTE   COOK: 6 MINUTES

1 tablespoon butter or margarine
2 large eggs
Salt and pepper

•Melt butter in a heavy skillet over medium-high heat, and heat until just hot enough to sizzle a drop of water. Break 1 egg into a saucer; carefully slip egg into skillet. Repeat procedure with remaining egg. Immediately reduce heat to low, and cook eggs just until whites and yolks are done (2 to 3 minutes per side); season with salt and pepper. Yield: 2 servings.

Per serving: Calories 126 Fat 10.8g
Cholesterol 228mg Sodium 415mg

Egg Foo Yong

PREP: 25 MINUTES   COOK: 10 MINUTES

Egg foo yong is a Chinese-American dish made essentially with eggs, bean sprouts, and green onions. The mixture is cooked like silver dollar pancakes on a griddle and then doused with a homemade soy sauce.

½ cup soy sauce*
½ cup water
2 tablespoons sugar
2 tablespoons white vinegar
2 cloves garlic, minced
1 tablespoon all-purpose flour
2 tablespoons water
1 (16-ounce) can bean sprouts, drained
1 (5-ounce) package frozen cooked shrimp or 1 (6-ounce) can crabmeat, drained
1 (7-ounce) can sliced mushrooms, drained
1 small onion, chopped (½ cup)
4 green onions, chopped (½ cup)
4 large eggs, beaten

•Combine first 5 ingredients in a small saucepan. Bring to a boil; reduce heat, and simmer, uncovered, 2 minutes.
•Combine flour and 2 tablespoons water in a small bowl, stirring with a wire whisk until smooth. Stir flour mixture into soy sauce mixture; cook, stirring constantly, until mixture is thickened and bubbly. Set aside, and keep warm.
•Combine bean sprouts and next 4 ingredients in a large bowl; stir beaten eggs into bean sprout mixture.
•Preheat griddle to 350° or place a large skillet over medium heat. Lightly grease griddle or skillet. For each patty, pour about ¼ cup batter onto hot griddle. Cook patties 30 seconds to 1 minute or until edges are set and golden; turn and cook other side. Serve immediately with reserved sauce. Yield: 4 servings.

*Use reduced-sodium soy sauce in this recipe if you're watching your sodium intake.

Per serving: Calories 194 Fat 5.5g
Cholesterol 282mg Sodium 2517mg

SCRAMBLED EGGS

Here's another simple skillet breakfast. The creamy curds need no adornment other than seasoning. You'll have to beat eggs to scramble them, but take care not to stir them too much while they cook. Simply draw a spatula through egg mixture as it begins to set on the bottom, forming large curds. Continue until eggs are thickened but still moist; do not stir constantly or they'll become dry and crumbly.

Scrambled Eggs

PREP: 2 MINUTES   COOK: 4 MINUTES

4 large eggs
2 tablespoons water or milk
¼ teaspoon salt
Dash of pepper
1 tablespoon butter or margarine

•Combine first 4 ingredients; stir briskly with a fork until blended. Melt butter in an 8-inch skillet over medium heat, tilting pan to coat bottom; pour in egg mixture.
•Cook, without stirring, until mixture begins to set on bottom. Draw a spatula across bottom of pan to form large curds. Continue cooking until eggs are thickened and firm throughout, but still moist. (Do not stir constantly.) Yield: 2 servings.

Per serving: Calories 200 Fat 15.8g
Cholesterol 441mg Sodium 478mg

Microwave Directions: Combine eggs, water (do not use milk), salt, and pepper; stir briskly with a fork until blended. Place butter in a shallow 1-quart casserole. Microwave at HIGH 45 seconds or until melted; rotate casserole to coat bottom of dish. Pour in egg mixture. Microwave at HIGH 1 minute. Break up set portions of egg with a fork, and push toward center of dish. Microwave at HIGH 1 to 2 minutes or until eggs are almost set (eggs will be soft and moist), stirring gently after 1 minute. Cover and let stand 2 minutes or until set.

Cheese Scrambled Eggs: Sprinkle ½ cup (2 ounces) shredded Swiss or mild Cheddar cheese over egg mixture just before scraping with a spatula.
Microwave Directions: Sprinkle cheese on eggs during standing time.
Herb Scrambled Eggs: Stir 1 tablespoon chopped fresh or 1 teaspoon dried oregano, basil, thyme, or parsley into egg mixture just before cooking.
Microwave Directions: Cut amount of herbs in half.
Bacon Scrambled Eggs: Reduce salt to ⅛ teaspoon, and stir 3 slices of bacon, cooked and crumbled, into egg mixture just before cooking.
Microwave Directions: Reduce salt to ⅛ teaspoon, and sprinkle bacon on eggs after cooking.
Ham Scrambled Eggs: Reduce salt to ⅛ teaspoon, and stir ⅓ cup diced cooked ham into egg mixture just before cooking.
Microwave Directions: Reduce salt to ⅛ teaspoon, and sprinkle ham on eggs after cooking.

Scrambling Eggs: Cook eggs, without stirring, until they begin to set on the bottom. Then repeatedly draw a spatula across bottom of skillet to form large curds until eggs are done.

Mexican Scrambled Eggs

◄ QUICK ►

PREP: 10 MINUTES   COOK: 12 MINUTES

Jalapeño, fresh cilantro, and the earthy flavor of ground cumin season these eggs with south-of-the-border flair.

8 large eggs, lightly beaten
1 large tomato, peeled, seeded, and chopped
1 tablespoon finely chopped jalapeño pepper
1 tablespoon chopped fresh cilantro or parsley
2 tablespoons milk
¼ teaspoon ground cumin
¼ teaspoon salt
⅛ teaspoon black pepper
2 to 3 tablespoons butter or margarine
½ cup chopped cooked ham

•Combine first 8 ingredients in a bowl, stirring well. Set aside.
•Melt butter in a large skillet over medium heat. Add ham, and cook 2 minutes, stirring constantly. Add egg mixture to skillet.
•Cook, without stirring, until egg mixture begins to set on bottom. Draw a spatula across bottom of pan to form large curds. Continue cooking until eggs are firm, but still moist. (Do not stir constantly.) Serve immediately. Yield: 6 servings.
Per serving: Calories 173 Fat 12.4g
Cholesterol 303mg Sodium 429mg

Creamy Egg Scramble

◄ QUICK • FAMILY FAVORITE ►

PREP: 4 MINUTES   COOK: 6 MINUTES

6 large eggs
½ cup milk
1 (3-ounce) package cream cheese, cubed
¼ teaspoon salt
⅛ teaspoon pepper
4 green onions, chopped
3 tablespoons butter or margarine

•Process first 5 ingredients in an electric blender at medium speed until frothy (7 to 10 seconds). Stir in green onions.
•Melt butter in a large nonstick skillet over medium heat, tilting pan to coat bottom; pour in egg mixture.
•Cook, without stirring, until mixture begins to set on bottom. Draw a spatula across bottom of pan to form large curds. Continue cooking until eggs are thickened, but still moist. (Do not stir constantly.) Yield: 3 servings.
Per serving: Calories 377 Fat 32.7g
Cholesterol 493mg Sodium 544mg

Microwave Directions: Process first 5 ingredients in an electric blender at medium speed until frothy (7 to 10 seconds). Stir in green onions. Place butter in a 1½-quart casserole. Microwave at HIGH 50 to 55 seconds or until melted; rotate casserole to coat bottom of dish. Pour in egg mixture. Microwave at HIGH 1 to 2 minutes. Break up set portions of egg with a fork, and push toward center of dish. Microwave at HIGH 3 to 4 minutes or until eggs are almost set (eggs will be soft and moist), stirring gently at 1-minute intervals. Stir gently again; cover and let stand 1 to 2 minutes.

Cheddar Egg Scramble

◄ QUICK • FAMILY FAVORITE ►

PREP: 6 MINUTES   COOK: 5 MINUTES

¼ cup chopped onion
¼ cup chopped green pepper
1 tablespoon butter or margarine, melted
4 large eggs, beaten
2 tablespoons milk
⅛ teaspoon seasoned salt
4 slices bacon, cooked and crumbled
¼ cup (1 ounce) shredded Cheddar cheese

•Sauté onion and green pepper in butter in a large skillet until tender. Combine eggs and next 3 ingredients; mix well. Pour egg mixture into hot skillet.
•Cook, without stirring, until egg mixture begins to set on bottom. Draw a spatula across bottom of pan to form large curds. Continue cooking until eggs are thickened, but still moist. (Do not stir constantly.)
•Remove from heat. Sprinkle with cheese; cover and let stand 1 minute. Yield: 2 servings.
Per serving: Calories 364 Fat 28.5g
Cholesterol 470mg Sodium 667mg

Garden Scramble

◄ QUICK ►

PREP: 20 MINUTES   COOK: 10 MINUTES

1 cup diced zucchini
½ cup coarsely chopped asparagus
½ cup shredded carrot
¼ cup diced sweet red pepper
2 green onions, thinly sliced
2 tablespoons butter or margarine, melted
6 large eggs
¼ cup milk
1 tablespoon fresh basil or 1 teaspoon dried basil
½ teaspoon salt
1 tablespoon butter or margarine
¼ cup (1 ounce) shredded Swiss or Gruyère cheese

•Sauté first 5 ingredients in 2 tablespoons butter in a skillet over medium heat, stirring constantly, until tender. Drain and set aside; keep warm.
•Combine eggs and next 3 ingredients in a bowl; beat with a wire whisk until blended. Melt 1 tablespoon butter in a large skillet over low heat.
•Pour egg mixture into skillet. Cook over medium-low heat, without stirring, until mixture begins to set on bottom. Draw a spatula across bottom of pan to form large curds. Continue cooking until eggs are firm, but still moist. (Do not stir constantly.) Gently stir reserved sautéed vegetables into egg mixture; sprinkle with cheese. Serve immediately. Yield: 3 servings.
Per serving: Calories 318 Fat 25g
Cholesterol 468mg Sodium 675mg

Breakfast Burritos

◀ FAMILY FAVORITE ▶

PREP: 18 MINUTES   COOK: 17 MINUTES

½ cup butter or margarine, divided
¾ cup chopped onion
½ cup chopped green pepper
1 pound ground pork sausage
12 large eggs, lightly beaten
12 (7- or 8-inch) flour tortillas
1 cup (4 ounces) shredded sharp Cheddar
    or Monterey Jack cheese
1 (8-ounce) jar picante sauce

•Melt ¼ cup butter in a large skillet over medium-high heat. Add onion and pepper; cook, stirring constantly, until vegetables are crisp-tender. Remove from skillet, and set aside.
•Brown sausage in skillet, stirring until it crumbles; drain. Wipe drippings from skillet with a paper towel.
•Melt remaining ¼ cup butter in skillet over medium heat. Add onion mixture, sausage, and eggs.
•Cook, without stirring, until egg mixture begins to set on bottom. Draw a spatula across bottom of skillet to form large curds. Continue cooking until eggs are firm, but still moist. (Do not stir constantly.) Set aside, and keep warm.
•Meanwhile, wrap tortillas tightly in aluminum foil; bake at 350° for 10 minutes or until soft and warm. Spoon about ½ cup egg mixture down center of each warm tortilla. Roll up tortillas; sprinkle evenly with cheese. Top each burrito with 1 tablespoon picante sauce. Yield: 12 servings.

Per serving: Calories 410 Fat 27.2g
Cholesterol 267mg Sodium 948mg

POACHED EGGS

Poached eggs make a simple, yet fancy, offering. For special occasions, serve them on English muffins, and top them with a rich sauce like hollandaise (page 387).

Poaching is tricky, so follow the recipe carefully. Keep the water at a gentle simmer, and make sure it's no more than 2 inches deep. You can trim away ragged edges of eggs if the shape is important to you.

To poach eggs in advance, immediately after cooking place eggs in ice water, and refrigerate until serving time. Drain eggs; place in boiling water 45 seconds, and drain again. Serve immediately.

Poached Eggs

◀ QUICK ▶

PREP: 2 MINUTES   COOK: 5 MINUTES

Serve these shapely eggs alone or as part of the recipes that follow.

•Lightly grease a large saucepan. Add water to depth of 2 inches in pan. Bring water to a boil; reduce heat, and maintain at a light simmer. Break eggs, one at a time, into a measuring cup or saucer; slip eggs, one at a time, into water, holding cup as close as possible to surface of water (see photo). Simmer 5 minutes or until done. Remove eggs with a slotted spoon. Trim edges, if desired.

Note: To cook eggs in poaching cups, grease each cup. Place poacher in a pan of simmering water so water is below the bottom of

Poaching eggs in water: Break egg into a cup; slip egg into water, holding cup as close as possible to surface of water. Simmer 5 minutes.

Using poaching cups: Break egg into a measuring cup; slip egg into poaching cup with simmering water below. Cover and simmer 5 minutes.

poacher. Break eggs into cups (see photo). Cover and cook 5 minutes or until done.

Eggs Benedict

◀ FAMILY FAVORITE ▶

PREP: 5 MINUTES   COOK: 35 MINUTES

Split and toasted, thick English muffins balance poached eggs, bacon or ham, and a smothering of hollandaise.

2 English muffins, split
2 tablespoons butter or margarine,
    softened
4 slices Canadian bacon, cooked
4 poached eggs
Hollandaise Sauce (page 387)

•Spread cut sides of muffins with butter. Broil 3 inches from heat 1 minute or until lightly browned.
•Place a slice of Canadian bacon on each muffin half; top with poached egg, and cover with Hollandaise Sauce. Yield: 2 servings.

Per serving: Calories 1016 Fat 80.8g
Cholesterol 935mg Sodium 2002mg

Tomato-Bacon 'n' Eggs Benedict: Cut 1 large tomato into 4 slices, approximately ½ inch thick. Dredge in 2 tablespoons all-purpose flour; fry in ½ cup vegetable oil about 5 minutes or until lightly browned. Sprinkle tomato slices with ½ teaspoon each of salt and pepper. Instead of Canadian bacon, cook and crumble 4 slices bacon.
•Place a fried tomato slice on each muffin half. Place poached egg on top of tomato; top with Hollandaise Sauce. Sprinkle each evenly with cooked and crumbled bacon.

Eggs Sardou

PREP: 9 MINUTES   COOK: 35 MINUTES

Meant for a special brunch, this recipe requires a bit of advance preparation; our photos walk you through the steps with ease.

2 green onions, chopped
2 teaspoons butter or margarine, melted
2 (10-ounce) packages frozen chopped
   spinach, thawed and well drained
1 (8-ounce) carton sour cream
¼ cup whipping cream
¼ cup grated Parmesan cheese
¼ teaspoon ground nutmeg
⅛ teaspoon salt
Dash of pepper
3 (14-ounce) cans artichoke bottoms,
   drained
16 poached eggs
2 recipes Hollandaise Sauce (page 387)
Paprika

• Sauté green onions in butter in a large skillet until tender; stir in spinach and next 6 ingredients (photo 1). Cook over low heat until thoroughly heated. (Do not boil.)

• Place 16 artichoke bottoms on a 15- x 10-inch jellyroll pan (photo 2), reserving any extra for another use. Bake at 350° for 10 minutes or until artichoke bottoms are heated; cover and keep warm.

• For each serving, spoon ¼ cup spinach mixture onto each individual serving plate; top with 2 artichoke bottoms. Arrange a poached egg on each artichoke bottom (photo 3). Spoon Hollandaise Sauce over each egg. Sprinkle with paprika. Serve immediately. Yield: 8 servings.

Per serving: Calories 581 Fat 47.6g
Cholesterol 678mg Sodium 816mg

1. Combine spinach, sour cream, cheese, and seasonings to make the base for Sardou.

2. Heat artichoke bottoms in the oven until ready to assemble each serving.

3. Arrange a poached egg on each artichoke bottom. Top with Hollandaise Sauce.

OMELETS

An omelet is basically the same beaten egg mixture that becomes scrambled eggs, except an omelet is left nearly undisturbed to set up in the pan where it cooks quickly over medium heat and is folded over a delectable filling. Start with our recipes, which offer various fillings, and then use your imagination to come up with your own combinations.

The most basic of all omelets is the plain omelet; the egg is beaten with a few simple ingredients and then cooked as directed. Beating the egg yolks and whites separately results in what's called a puffy omelet, the most prized type. Puffy omelets require a short baking time to cook evenly.

Whether making a plain or a puffy omelet, use a nonstick omelet pan rather

1. As omelet starts to cook, gently lift edges with a spatula, and tilt pan so uncooked portion flows underneath.

2. Place filling ingredients on 1 side of omelet. Quickly flip other half of omelet onto the filling. Slide omelet onto a serving plate.

than a regular skillet. Make sure the handle is ovenproof if making puffy omelets. If it's not, wrap the handle with aluminum foil to protect it from direct heat while baking.

Plain Omelet

◄ QUICK ►

PREP: 2 MINUTES   COOK: 3 MINUTES

2 large eggs
⅛ teaspoon salt
Dash of white pepper
1 tablespoon water
1 tablespoon butter or margarine
Omelet fillings (optional)

•Combine first 4 ingredients; whisk just until blended.
•Heat a 6- or 8-inch omelet pan or heavy skillet over medium heat until hot enough to sizzle a drop of water. Add butter; rotate pan to coat bottom. Pour egg mixture into pan. As mixture starts to cook, gently lift edges of omelet with a spatula, and tilt pan so uncooked portion flows underneath (photo 1).
•Sprinkle half of omelet with one or more of the following fillings, if desired: 2 slices bacon, cooked and crumbled; 2 tablespoons sautéed mushrooms; 2 tablespoons shredded cheese; 2 tablespoons diced cooked ham; 1 tablespoon chopped fresh or 1 teaspoon dried herbs. Fold omelet in half (photo 2), and transfer to plate. Yield: 1 serving.
Per serving: Calories 251 Fat 21.5g
Cholesterol 456mg Sodium 536mg

Puffy Omelet

PREP: 10 MINUTES   COOK: 20 MINUTES

4 large eggs, separated
2 tablespoons water
¼ teaspoon salt
1 tablespoon butter or margarine
½ recipe Cheddar Cheese Sauce (page 387)
Chopped fresh parsley

•Beat egg whites at high speed with an electric mixer until foamy; add water and salt. Beat until stiff peaks form. Beat egg yolks in

a large bowl until thick and pale. Fold whites into yolks.
•Heat an ovenproof 10-inch omelet pan or heavy skillet over medium heat until hot enough to sizzle a drop of water. Add butter, and rotate pan to coat bottom. Spread egg mixture in pan, leaving sides slightly higher. Cover, reduce heat, and cook 8 to 10 minutes or until puffed and set.
•Bake at 325° for 10 minutes or until a knife inserted in center comes out clean. Loosen omelet with a spatula; fold omelet in half. Gently slide omelet onto a serving plate; top with sauce and parsley. Yield: 2 servings.
Per serving: Calories 384 Fat 30g
Cholesterol 486mg Sodium 860mg

Spanish Omelet

PREP: 10 MINUTES   COOK: 15 MINUTES

½ cup chopped green pepper
½ cup sliced fresh mushrooms
2 tablespoons butter or margarine, melted
¾ cup diced plum tomato
6 large eggs
¼ cup water
½ teaspoon salt
Dash of black pepper
4 slices bacon, cooked and crumbled
2 tablespoons butter or margarine, divided
½ cup picante sauce

•Cook green pepper and mushrooms in 2 tablespoons melted butter over medium-high heat, stirring constantly, until crisp-tender. Add tomato, and cook 1 more minute; drain.
•Combine eggs and next 3 ingredients; stir with a wire whisk until well blended. Stir in vegetable mixture and bacon.
•Heat a 10-inch omelet pan or heavy skillet over medium heat until hot. Add 1 tablespoon butter, and rotate pan to coat bottom. Pour half of egg mixture into skillet. As mixture starts to cook, gently lift edges with a spatula, and tilt pan so uncooked portion flows underneath. Fold omelet in half, and transfer to a warm platter. Repeat procedure with remaining butter and egg mixture. Serve with picante sauce. Yield: 4 servings.
Per serving: Calories 281 Fat 23g
Cholesterol 356mg Sodium 966mg

Country French Potato Omelets

PREP: 15 MINUTES   COOK: 35 MINUTES

This recipe makes three individual omelets, piled high with crusty browned potatoes. The simple flavors are so satisfying that no toppings are needed.

¾ pound new potatoes
3 tablespoons butter or margarine, divided
¼ teaspoon salt
¼ teaspoon pepper
6 large eggs
3 tablespoons water or milk
2 tablespoons chopped fresh chives or frozen chives

•Cook potatoes in boiling salted water to cover 15 minutes or just until tender. Drain and cool slightly. Peel, if desired, and cube potatoes.
•Melt 2 tablespoons butter in an 8-inch omelet pan or heavy skillet; add cubed potato, salt, and pepper. Cook over medium-high heat until potato is browned. Remove potato with a slotted spoon.
•Whisk together eggs, water, and chives until blended. Heat omelet pan over medium heat until hot. Pour one-third of egg mixture into pan. As mixture starts to cook, gently lift edges of omelet with a spatula, and tilt pan so uncooked portion flows underneath.
•Spoon one-third of potato over half of omelet. Loosen with spatula; fold omelet in half, and transfer to a serving plate. Repeat procedure twice with remaining egg mixture and potato, using remaining butter, if needed. Yield: 3 servings.
Per serving: Calories 336 Fat 21.7g
Cholesterol 456mg Sodium 447mg

Herb Omelet Torte

PREP: 32 MINUTES   COOK: 1 HOUR

This torte's rich in flavor and quite impressive when sliced for a special lunch or brunch. A simple fruit salad provides an ideal complement. We show you the end product on page 186. An electric knife makes slicing easy.

1 (17¼-ounce) package frozen puff pastry sheets, thawed
½ pound trimmed fresh spinach
1 clove garlic, minced
2 tablespoons butter or margarine, melted and divided
1 tablespoon olive oil
¾ teaspoon salt
¼ teaspoon black pepper
2 sweet red peppers, chopped
9 large eggs
2 tablespoons chopped fresh parsley
1½ tablespoons chopped green onions or fresh chives
1 tablespoon chopped fresh dill
1 tablespoon chopped fresh tarragon
¼ teaspoon salt
¼ teaspoon black pepper
2 tablespoons butter or margarine, divided
3 cups (12 ounces) shredded Swiss cheese
½ pound thinly sliced cooked ham or turkey
1 (2¼-ounce) can sliced ripe olives, drained
1 large egg, lightly beaten
Garnish: fresh tarragon sprigs

•Unfold pastry sheets, roll lightly in opposite directions, and cut a 9-inch circle out of each sheet. Press one of the circles in bottom of an ungreased 9- x 3-inch springform pan; cover and chill remaining circle. Press enough remaining pastry scraps on sides of springform pan to form crust, leaving ¼ inch extending above pan. Seal seams by moistening with water and pressing together; cover and chill.
•Cook spinach and minced garlic in 1 tablespoon butter and oil in a Dutch oven over medium-high heat, stirring constantly, until spinach wilts and liquid evaporates. Remove from heat; stir in ¾ teaspoon salt and ¼ teaspoon pepper; cover and chill.

•Sauté red pepper in 1 tablespoon butter in a large skillet over medium-high heat, stirring constantly, until tender; set aside.
•Combine 9 eggs and next 6 ingredients in a large bowl; stir with a wire whisk until blended. Heat a 9-inch nonstick skillet over medium heat until hot enough to sizzle a drop of water. Add 1 tablespoon butter, and tilt pan to coat bottom evenly as it melts. Pour half of egg mixture into skillet. As mixture starts to cook, gently lift edges of omelet with a spatula, and tilt pan so uncooked portion flows underneath. Cook just until set. Remove omelet from pan; set aside. Repeat procedure with remaining 1 tablespoon butter and egg mixture.
•Place 1 omelet in prepared springform pan. Arrange half each of spinach mixture, cheese, and ham over omelet. Arrange red pepper and olives over ham. Repeat layers in reverse order with remaining ham, cheese, and spinach mixture. Top with remaining omelet.
•Top with remaining pastry circle; seal well, crimping edges. Brush top with beaten egg. Place pan on a baking sheet on bottom rack in oven. Bake at 400° for 20 minutes. Reduce heat to 350°, and bake 40 more minutes. Let stand 20 minutes before serving. Carefully remove sides of springform pan. Garnish torte, if desired. Yield: 8 servings.
Per serving: Calories 654 Fat 49.2g
Cholesterol 402mg Sodium 1386mg

Apple Omelet Stack

PREP: 15 MINUTES   COOK: 35 MINUTES

⅔ cup firmly packed brown sugar
⅓ cup butter or margarine
⅔ cup milk
2 tablespoons cornstarch
4 large Rome Beauty apples, peeled and coarsely chopped (5 cups)
Baked Omelets
¼ cup sour cream

•Melt brown sugar and butter in a large skillet or saucepan over medium heat. Combine milk and cornstarch; whisk into brown sugar mixture. Cook, stirring constantly, until thickened. Add chopped apple, and cook 12 to 13 minutes or until apple is tender.
•Place 1 omelet on a serving plate, browned side up; spread omelet with one-third of

apple mixture. Repeat procedure, layering remaining omelets and apple mixture. Cut into quarters; top each serving with 1 tablespoon sour cream. Yield: 4 servings.
Per serving: Calories 629 Fat 33.7g Cholesterol 191mg Sodium 495mg

Baked Omelets

2 large eggs, lightly beaten
½ cup all-purpose flour
¼ teaspoon salt
1 cup milk
3 tablespoons butter or margarine

•Whisk together first 4 ingredients until smooth.
•Heat three 9-inch round cakepans at 450° for 5 minutes or until hot. Remove pans from oven; coat with cooking spray. Add 1 tablespoon butter to each pan; rotate pan to coat bottom. Return pans to oven, if necessary, to melt butter. Pour batter evenly into pans.
•Bake, uncovered, at 450° for 7 minutes. Reduce heat to 350°, and bake 5 more minutes or until browned. (Omelets will puff as they bake and settle as they cool.) Yield: 3 (9-inch) omelets.

Italian Frittata

PREP: 20 MINUTES   COOK: 30 MINUTES

Frittatas are an easy version of omelets— there's no flipping or rolling, and you simply cut and serve wedges right from the pan.

2 medium-size red potatoes (1 pound)
½ pound mild ground Italian sausage
1 green pepper, cut into strips
1½ cups chopped purple onion
3 cloves garlic, sliced
2 tablespoons olive oil
2 tablespoons butter or margarine, melted
2 medium tomatoes, peeled and diced
2 tablespoons minced fresh parsley
1 teaspoon dried basil
1 teaspoon dried oregano
¼ teaspoon salt
¼ teaspoon black pepper
8 large eggs, beaten
3 tablespoons water
½ cup freshly grated Parmesan cheese

Eggplant and Roasted Pepper Frittata

•Peel and dice potatoes. Place in boiling water to cover; cook 7 minutes or until tender. Drain well, and set aside.
•Brown sausage over medium heat, stirring until it crumbles. Drain well, and set aside.
•Cook green pepper, onion, and garlic in oil and butter in a 12-inch ovenproof skillet over medium-high heat, stirring constantly, until tender. Add potato, sausage, tomato, and next 5 ingredients; cook 2 minutes, stirring constantly.
•Combine eggs and 3 tablespoons water; pour over mixture in skillet, stirring gently to blend. Cover, reduce heat to low, and cook 8 to 10 minutes or until eggs are set. Sprinkle with cheese.
•Place skillet under broiler; broil 5½ inches from heat 3 to 5 minutes or until golden. Cut into wedges. Serve immediately. Yield: 8 servings.
Per serving: Calories 279 Fat 18.5g Cholesterol 241mg Sodium 462mg

FRITTATA, AN OMELET?

This Italian omelet usually has chopped ingredients mixed in with the eggs rather than being folded inside. A frittata is firmer than an omelet because a frittata is cooked very slowly over low heat, and it's round because it isn't folded like a traditional omelet. Frittatas are typically finished under the broiler in the oven.

Eggplant and Roasted Pepper Frittata

PREP: 8 MINUTES   COOK: 17 MINUTES

2 cups peeled and chopped eggplant
3 tablespoons olive oil
1 (12-ounce) jar or 2 (7-ounce) jars roasted red pepper, drained and chopped
10 large eggs
½ cup milk
1 teaspoon salt
¼ teaspoon black pepper
¼ cup freshly grated Parmesan cheese

•Cook eggplant in oil in an ovenproof 10-inch nonstick skillet over medium-high heat, stirring constantly, 2 to 3 minutes or until tender. Stir in roasted red pepper.
•Beat eggs and next 3 ingredients at medium speed with an electric mixer until blended. Add egg mixture to skillet. As mixture starts to cook, gently lift edges of frittata with a spatula, and tilt pan so uncooked portion flows underneath. Cover and cook over low heat 10 to 12 minutes to allow uncooked portion on top to set.
•Uncover, sprinkle with cheese, and broil 3 inches from heat 2 minutes or until golden. Cut into wedges. Serve immediately. Yield: 6 servings.
Per serving: Calories 231 Fat 16.6g Cholesterol 359mg Sodium 653mg

BAKED EGGS

If you need to serve a lot of eggs at one time, baking is a good choice. Eggs require little attention as they bake, and they look attractive served in individual portions. Spooning milk over the eggs before cooking gives them a softer finish than fried or poached eggs. Serve baked eggs immediately.

Baked (Shirred) Eggs

◄ QUICK ►

PREP: 3 MINUTES   COOK: 15 MINUTES

4 large eggs
Salt and pepper to taste
¼ cup half-and-half or milk (optional)

•Grease four 6-ounce custard cups. Break and slip 1 egg into each custard cup. Sprinkle each egg with salt and pepper. Spoon 1 tablespoon half-and-half over each serving, if desired. Bake eggs, uncovered, at 325° for 15 minutes or until eggs reach desired doneness. Yield: 4 servings.

Per serving: Calories 94 Fat 6.8g
Cholesterol 218mg Sodium 216mg

Huevos Rancheros with Chiles

◄ FAMILY FAVORITE ►

PREP: 12 MINUTES   COOK: 35 MINUTES

6 (6-inch) corn tortillas
Vegetable oil
1 cup chopped green pepper
1 cup chopped onion
2 cloves garlic, minced
2 tablespoons olive oil
2 (16-ounce) cans diced tomatoes, drained
1 (4.5-ounce) can chopped green chiles
2 teaspoons chile powder
½ teaspoon ground cumin
¼ teaspoon salt
¼ teaspoon black pepper
6 large eggs
1 cup (4 ounces) shredded Cheddar cheese
¼ cup sliced ripe olives
Garnish: hot peppers

•Fry tortillas, one at a time, in ¼ cup hot vegetable oil in a skillet 3 to 5 seconds on each side or just until softened, adding more oil, if necessary. Drain tortillas thoroughly on paper towels. Immediately line an 11- x 7-inch baking dish with tortillas, letting tortillas extend up sides of dish. Set aside.

•Cook green pepper, onion, and garlic in olive oil over medium-high heat, stirring constantly, until tender. Add tomatoes and next 5 ingredients. Cover and simmer 3 minutes or until thickened.

•Pour tomato mixture over tortillas. Make 6 indentations in tomato mixture; break and slip 1 egg into each indentation.

•Cover and bake at 350° for 25 minutes or just until eggs are set. Sprinkle with cheese and olives. Bake, uncovered, 5 more minutes or until cheese melts. Garnish, if desired. Serve immediately. Yield: 6 servings.

Per serving: Calories 348 Fat 24.5g
Cholesterol 232mg Sodium 770mg

QUICHES & CASSEROLES

Quiche, the savory egg custard pie in a flaky crust, is a timeless brunch offering. Serve it warm from the oven or let it cool.

It's an honorable destination for leftovers, too, whether that be chopped cooked ham, crumbled bacon, or chopped vegetables.

These quiches and egg casseroles are easy to assemble. If a quiche recipe calls for a pastry crust, that's probably the most time-consuming part of the recipe—but that can be easy, too. Just use our Basic Pastry recipe in the Pies and Pastries chapter (page 299) or use ½ (15-ounce) package folded refrigerated piecrusts, instead. And if you use a frozen pastry, look for the kind labeled deep-dish; it'll be the best fit for our recipes.

If you're serving a quiche or egg casserole plus one other item, get the quiche or casserole in the oven first. There's usually plenty of time as it bakes to prepare the other dish.

Mexicana Brunch Pie

◄ FAMILY FAVORITE ►
◄ VEGETARIAN ►

PREP: 10 MINUTES   COOK: 30 MINUTES

A crustless wonder awaits here. You won't miss a flaky crust once you taste this cheese and chile pie. It's so rich and filling you can serve it as a meatless main dish for any meal of the day.

5 large eggs, beaten
2 tablespoons butter or margarine, melted
¼ cup all-purpose flour
½ teaspoon baking powder
1 cup cream-style cottage cheese
2 cups (8 ounces) shredded Monterey Jack cheese with peppers°
1 (4.5-ounce) can chopped green chiles

•Beat eggs, melted butter, flour, and baking powder in a large mixing bowl; beat at medium speed with an electric mixer until mixture is blended.

•Stir in cottage cheese, Monterey Jack cheese, and chiles; pour mixture into a well-greased 9-inch pieplate.

•Bake, uncovered, at 400° for 10 minutes; reduce heat to 350°, and bake 20 more minutes or until mixture is set. Cut into wedges. Yield: 6 servings.

°Use plain Monterey Jack cheese if you'd like; pie will not be as spicy.

Per serving: Calories 304 Fat 22g
Cholesterol 222mg Sodium 581mg

Country Breakfast Pie

◄ QUICK ►

PREP: 4 MINUTES   COOK: 20 MINUTES
STAND: 5 MINUTES

Here's a cheesy microwave breakfast pie with a hash brown crust. It's so easy that you'll come back to it again and again.

4 slices bacon, cut in half
2 cups frozen country-style hash brown potatoes with onions and green peppers (we tested with Cascadian Farm)
6 large eggs, lightly beaten
¼ cup milk
½ teaspoon salt
⅛ teaspoon black pepper
1 cup (4 ounces) shredded Cheddar cheese

• Place bacon in a 9-inch pieplate, and cover with paper towels.
• Microwave at HIGH 3½ to 4½ minutes or until bacon is crisp; remove bacon, reserving drippings in pieplate. Drain and crumble bacon, and set aside.
• Spread potato in same pieplate; microwave, uncovered, at HIGH 6 to 7 minutes.
• Combine eggs and next 3 ingredients; pour over potato mixture. Cover with heavy-duty plastic wrap; fold back a small edge of wrap to allow steam to escape. Microwave potato mixture at HIGH 6 to 7 minutes, giving dish a quarter-turn after 3 minutes.
• Sprinkle with cheese and crumbled bacon; cover and microwave at HIGH 1 to 2 minutes. Let stand 5 minutes before serving; cut into wedges. Yield: 6 servings.
Per serving: Calories 206 Fat 13.9g
Cholesterol 236mg Sodium 417mg

Note: You can substitute 2 cups frozen cubed hash brown potatoes, ¼ cup chopped green pepper, and ¼ cup chopped onion for frozen hash brown potatoes with onions and green peppers.

Cheese-Vegetable Quiche

◄ VEGETARIAN ►

PREP: 11 MINUTES   COOK: 58 MINUTES

This vegetarian entrée received our staff's best review. Substitute your choice of steamed vegetables instead of the broccoli and cauliflower, if desired.

Pastry for 9-inch pie (page 299)
1 cup chopped fresh broccoli
1 cup chopped fresh cauliflower
1½ cups (6 ounces) shredded Cheddar cheese
1½ cups (6 ounces) shredded Swiss cheese
4 egg yolks, beaten
1 cup whipping cream
1½ teaspoons seasoned salt
½ teaspoon white pepper
¼ teaspoon ground nutmeg

• Fit piecrust into a 9-inch quiche dish; trim excess pastry around edges. Prick bottom and sides of piecrust with a fork. Bake at 375° for 8 minutes; cool on a wire rack.
• Arrange broccoli and cauliflower in a steamer basket over boiling water. Cover and steam 5 minutes or until crisp-tender. Spoon into prepared crust, and top with cheeses.
• Combine egg yolks and remaining 4 ingredients, stirring well. Pour over cheese. Bake at 375° for 45 to 50 minutes or until set. Let stand 10 minutes before serving. Yield: 6 servings.
Per serving: Calories 567 Fat 44.8g
Cholesterol 262mg Sodium 997mg

Chicken-Pecan Quiche

PREP: 20 MINUTES
COOK: 1 HOUR AND 7 MINUTES

You'll love this delectable quiche with its creamy chicken-pecan filling and savory Cheddar crust.

1 cup all-purpose flour
1 cup (4 ounces) shredded sharp Cheddar cheese
¾ cup chopped pecans
½ teaspoon salt
¼ teaspoon paprika
⅓ cup vegetable oil
1 cup sour cream
½ cup chicken broth
¼ cup mayonnaise
3 large eggs, lightly beaten
2 cups finely chopped cooked chicken
½ cup (2 ounces) shredded sharp Cheddar cheese
¼ cup minced onion
3 drops of hot sauce
¼ cup pecan halves

• Combine first 5 ingredients in a medium bowl; stir well. Add oil; stir well. Firmly press mixture in bottom and up sides of a 9-inch deep-dish pieplate. Bake at 350° for 12 minutes. Cool completely.
• Combine sour cream and next 3 ingredients; stir with a wire whisk until smooth. Stir in chicken, ½ cup cheese, onion, and hot sauce. Pour chicken mixture over prepared crust. Arrange pecan halves over chicken mixture. Bake at 350° for 55 minutes or until set. Let stand 10 minutes before serving. Yield: 8 servings.
Per serving: Calories 524 Fat 41.2g
Cholesterol 152mg Sodium 434mg

Quiche Lorraine

Quiche Lorraine

PREP: 10 MINUTES   COOK: 45 MINUTES

Crisp bacon, heavy cream, Gruyère cheese, and a hint of nutmeg distinguish this classic quiche.

Pastry for 9-inch pie (page 299)
8 slices bacon, chopped
4 green onions, chopped
2 cups (8 ounces) shredded Gruyère or
   Swiss cheese, divided
6 large eggs, beaten
1 cup whipping cream
½ teaspoon salt
⅛ teaspoon ground nutmeg
Dash of ground red pepper
Dash of ground white pepper
Ground nutmeg
Garnish: green onion

•Fit piecrust into a 9-inch quiche dish; trim excess pastry around the edges. Prick bottom and sides of piecrust with a fork. Bake at 400° for 3 minutes; remove from oven, and gently prick with a fork. Bake piecrust 5 more minutes.
•Cook bacon in a skillet over medium heat until browned; add chopped green onions, and cook 1 more minute. Drain well, and sprinkle evenly in pastry shell. Top with 1 cup cheese, and set aside.
•Combine eggs and next 5 ingredients, stirring well. Pour mixture into prepared crust, and top with remaining 1 cup cheese. Sprinkle quiche lightly with additional nutmeg.
•Bake at 350° for 35 minutes or until set. Let stand 10 minutes before serving. Garnish, if desired. Yield: 6 servings.

Per serving: Calories 613 Fat 48.1g
Cholesterol 310mg Sodium 727mg

Sausage-Cheddar Quiche

PREP: 18 MINUTES   COOK: 1 HOUR

Pastry for 9-inch pie (page 299)
1 pound ground pork sausage
1½ cups (6 ounces) shredded Cheddar
    cheese
1 (4-ounce) can sliced mushrooms,
   drained
½ cup chopped onion
¼ cup chopped green pepper
½ teaspoon dried basil
⅛ teaspoon garlic powder
4 large eggs, beaten
1 cup milk
Paprika

•Fit piecrust into a 9½-inch deep-dish pieplate. Fold ends under, and crimp. Prick bottom and sides of piecrust with a fork. Bake at 400° for 8 minutes.

• Brown sausage in a large skillet, stirring until it crumbles; drain. Cool.

• Combine sausage, cheese, and next 5 ingredients; spoon into prepared crust.

• Beat eggs and milk at medium speed with an electric mixer until blended. Pour over sausage mixture; sprinkle lightly with paprika.

• Bake at 325° for 50 minutes or until set. Let stand 10 minutes before serving. Yield: 6 servings.

Per serving: Calories 571 Fat 41g
Cholesterol 231mg Sodium 1106mg

Apple-Sausage-Cheddar Quiche: Omit mushrooms, and substitute 1 cup peeled, chopped cooking apple (such as Rome Beauty).

Cream Cheese-Spinach Quiche

◄ VEGETARIAN ►

PREP: 12 MINUTES   COOK: 52 MINUTES

This spinach quiche makes a great side dish. If you'd rather enjoy it as an entrée, just cut it into six wedges.

Pastry for 9-inch pie (page 299)
1 tablespoon butter or margarine
¼ cup chopped onion
1 (8-ounce) package cream cheese, cubed
¾ cup milk
4 large eggs, lightly beaten
1 (10-ounce) package frozen chopped spinach, thawed and well drained
1 (2-ounce) jar diced pimiento, undrained
⅛ teaspoon pepper

• Fit piecrust into a 9-inch quiche dish Prick bottom and sides of piecrust with a fork. Bake at 425° for 10 to 12 minutes; set aside.

• Melt butter in a saucepan over medium-high heat; add onion, and cook until tender.

• Add cream cheese and milk to mixture in skillet; cook over low heat, whisking until cream cheese melts.

• Gradually whisk about one-fourth of hot mixture into eggs; add to remaining hot mixture, whisking constantly. Whisk in spinach, pimiento, and pepper; pour into prepared crust.

• Bake at 350° for 35 to 40 minutes or until set. Yield: 8 servings.

Per serving: Calories 295 Fat 21.7g
Cholesterol 149mg Sodium 269mg

Eggs Florentine Casserole

PREP: 30 MINUTES   COOK: 40 MINUTES

Florentine hints at spinach here. This spinach, Swiss cheese, and sausage casserole makes enough to serve a hungry crew.

1 (10-ounce) package frozen chopped spinach
1 cup (4 ounces) shredded Cheddar cheese
1 pound ground pork sausage
2 cups sliced fresh mushrooms
6 green onions, chopped (1 cup)
2 tablespoons butter or margarine, melted
12 large eggs, lightly beaten
2 cups whipping cream
1 cup (4 ounces) shredded Swiss cheese
¼ teaspoon paprika

• Cook spinach according to package directions; drain well. Sprinkle Cheddar cheese in bottom of a lightly greased 13- x 9-inch baking dish; spread spinach over cheese.

• Brown sausage in a large skillet, stirring until it crumbles; drain and sprinkle over spinach.

• Sauté mushrooms and green onions in butter in a large skillet over medium-high heat until tender. Sprinkle sautéed vegetables over sausage.

• Combine eggs and whipping cream, beating with a wire whisk until blended. Pour egg mixture over vegetable mixture. Top with Swiss cheese, and sprinkle with paprika.

• Bake, uncovered, at 350° for 40 minutes or until set. Yield: 12 servings.

Per serving: Calories 421 Fat 36.6g
Cholesterol 314mg Sodium 567mg

Farmer's Omelet Casserole

◄ FAMILY FAVORITE ►

PREP: 20 MINUTES   COOK: 53 MINUTES

This filling casserole is all you need to serve at breakfast. Full of eggs, cheese, meat, and vegetables, it's a meal in itself.

3 cups frozen cubed hash brown potatoes
1 cup chopped green pepper, divided
⅓ cup chopped onion
1 tablespoon oil
18 large eggs, beaten
2⅓ cups chopped cooked ham
1¼ cups chopped tomato, divided
½ teaspoon salt
½ teaspoon black pepper
1½ cups (6 ounces) shredded Cheddar or Monterey Jack cheese

• Cook potato, ¾ cup green pepper, and onion in oil in a large skillet over medium-high heat, stirring constantly, 8 minutes or until tender.

• Combine potato mixture, eggs, ham, 1 cup tomato, salt, and black pepper in a large bowl; stir well. Pour mixture into a lightly greased 13- x 9-inch baking dish.

• Bake, uncovered, at 325° for 40 minutes or until golden. Top with remaining ¼ cup green pepper and ¼ cup tomato. Sprinkle evenly with cheese. Bake 5 more minutes or until cheese melts. Yield: 12 servings.

Per serving: Calories 279 Fat 19.2g
Cholesterol 350mg Sodium 722mg

STRATAS & SOUFFLÉS

Stratas are egg casseroles (sometimes containing meat, vegetables, or cheese) in which beaten eggs are absorbed into sliced or torn bread and then baked. It's the large proportion of eggs that makes stratas rise.

The *soufflé*, with its brief moment of puffed glory, is perhaps an egg's ultimate use. It's the beaten egg whites folded into a soufflé that provide that extra lightness and height. Be ready to serve both dishes immediately for their optimum presentation.

A thick cream sauce typically forms the base for a soufflé; then cheese or small pieces of vegetables are added for flavor. Egg whites beaten to soft peaks are gently folded in at the last moment.

The traditional round soufflé dish is ideal to use for soufflés, but any ovenproof, straight-sided casserole dish will work, too. High-rising soufflés are aided by a removable foil collar. Directions for making a collar are given with specific recipes that need them.

Always bake soufflés in the center of the oven; remove the rack above the dish in case the soufflé puffs more than anticipated. Don't open the oven door before the end of the baking time, because the rapid loss of heat can cause the soufflé to fall. At the end of the baking time, insert a knife into the center of soufflé; it's done if the knife comes out clean. If you need to hold the soufflé a few minutes before serving it, just turn the oven off, and leave the soufflé in the oven, watching carefully to make sure it doesn't overbrown.

Ham and Broccoli Strata

◄ MAKE AHEAD ►

**PREP: 11 MINUTES   CHILL: 8 HOURS
COOK: 1 HOUR**

12 slices white bread, crusts removed
1 (10-ounce) package frozen chopped broccoli, thawed and drained
2 cups diced cooked ham
6 large eggs, lightly beaten
3¼ cups milk
1 tablespoon dried minced onion
¼ teaspoon dry mustard
3 cups (12 ounces) shredded sharp Cheddar cheese

•Cut bread into small cubes. Layer bread cubes, broccoli, and ham in a buttered 13- x 9-inch baking dish.
•Combine eggs and remaining 4 ingredients; stir well. Pour into dish; cover and chill at least 8 hours. Remove from refrigerator; let stand 30 minutes. Bake, uncovered, at 325° for 55 to 60 minutes. Yield: 8 servings.
Per serving: Calories 443 Fat 25.9g Cholesterol 238mg Sodium 947mg

Classic Cheese Soufflé

PREP: 20 MINUTES   COOK: 30 MINUTES

Light and airy, yet laden with cheese, this savory soufflé comes to the table as a main dish. Bake it in a very hot oven to encourage its initial puff; then reduce the heat to cook it through and produce its golden cap.

2 tablespoons butter or margarine
¼ cup all-purpose flour
½ teaspoon salt
¼ teaspoon pepper
¼ teaspoon dry mustard
⅛ teaspoon hot sauce
1 cup milk
1½ cups (6 ounces) shredded sharp Cheddar cheese
6 large eggs, separated

•Lightly butter a 2-quart soufflé dish. Cut a piece of aluminum foil long enough to circle the dish, allowing a 1-inch overlap. Fold foil lengthwise into thirds, and lightly butter one side. Wrap foil, buttered side against dish, so it extends 3 inches above the rim. Securely attach foil with string. Set aside.
•Melt 2 tablespoons butter in a heavy saucepan over low heat; add flour and next 4 ingredients, stirring until smooth. Cook 1 minute, stirring constantly. Gradually add milk; cook over medium heat, stirring constantly, until thickened and bubbly. Add cheese, stirring until melted. Let cool slightly.
•Beat egg yolks until thick and pale. Gradually stir about one-fourth of hot cheese mixture into yolks; add to remaining hot mixture.
•Beat egg whites at high speed with an electric mixer until stiff but not dry; fold into cheese mixture. Pour into prepared soufflé

dish. Bake at 475° for 10 minutes. Reduce heat to 400°, and bake 15 more minutes or until puffed and golden. Remove collar, and serve immediately. Yield: 6 servings.
Per serving: Calories 277 Fat 20.9g Cholesterol 262mg Sodium 507mg

Individual Cheese Soufflés: Spoon cheese mixture into six buttered 10-ounce soufflé dishes or custard cups. Bake at 350° for 15 to 20 minutes or until puffed and golden.

Note: You can freeze Individual Cheese Soufflés before baking. Use freezer-to-oven dishes. Cover with plastic wrap, and freeze. To bake, place frozen soufflés on a baking sheet; bake at 350° for 40 minutes or until golden.

Breakfast Sausage Sandwiches

◄ MAKE AHEAD ►

PREP: 15 MINUTES   COOK: 45 MINUTES

Softened butter or margarine
8 slices bread
1 pound ground pork sausage, cooked, crumbled, and drained
1 cup (4 ounces) shredded Cheddar cheese
2 large eggs, beaten
1½ cups milk
1½ teaspoons prepared mustard

•Spread butter on 1 side of each bread slice. Place 4 slices, buttered side down, in a single layer in a lightly greased 8-inch square baking dish. Top each bread slice with sausage and remaining bread slices, buttered side up. Sprinkle with cheese.
•Combine eggs, milk, and mustard; pour over sandwiches. Cover and chill at least 8 hours. Remove from refrigerator; let stand 30 minutes. Bake, uncovered, at 350° for 45 minutes. Yield: 4 servings.
Per serving: Calories 728 Fat 50.9g Cholesterol 242mg Sodium 1712mg

Breakfast Ham Sandwiches: Substitute ½ pound chopped cooked ham for sausage. Substitute Swiss cheese for Cheddar.

CHEESE

Cheese choices are virtually endless in today's market. Cheeses differ substantially in flavor, texture, and color, depending on how they're made and how long they're aged. Use the cheese photo and dictionary that follow to whet your appetite and broaden your horizons.

The Story of Cheese

The amazing range in taste and texture of individual cheeses is the result of several things: the type of milk used, the manufacturing process, and the length of time a cheese is aged. Generally speaking, the longer the aging, the sharper (stronger) the flavor, the harder the cheese, and the longer it will keep.

Ever wondered how cheese is made? Milk is typically combined with a starter such as rennet, which makes it separate into curds (solids) and whey (liquid). Whey is drained off; curds are used as fresh cheese or cured by pressing, cooking, or adding bacterial cultures.

Cheese Categories

Cheese is commonly categorized by degree of hardness, ranging from soft and semisoft, to hard (or firm), very hard, and blue-veined cheeses.

Within the soft cheese category there are soft, fresh cheeses and soft-ripened cheeses. Soft, fresh cheeses have a high moisture level, the most delicate flavor, and are the most perishable. A fresh cheese is unripened and retains much of the fresh milk flavor. (Unripened describes soft cheeses that aren't aged.) Some well-known fresh cheeses are ricotta, cottage cheese, cream cheese, feta, and mascarpone.

Soft-ripened cheeses have been allowed to mature to various degrees. They also have a high moisture content, and though mild when young, they develop a fuller flavor as they age. They ripen inside of a powdery white rind. Brie and Camembert (which look and taste almost identical) are the most popular; they have a mild, earthy flavor that blends well with a host of other flavors.

Gouda and Monterey Jack are common semisoft cheeses. Semisoft cheeses are good shredding and melting cheeses.

Hard cheeses include a broad range of textures from semifirm to firm to very firm. They contain less moisture than soft cheeses and hold their shape better. Cheddar and Swiss are common cheeses that belong in this category. These cheeses are easiest to shred when they're cold.

Very hard cheeses are exactly that—very hard; they can be easily grated. They have a granular texture that develops as they age. These cheeses have the longest keeping quality. Parmesan and Romano are the best known in this family of cheeses.

Blue-veined cheeses are sprayed with spores of special molds and aged to develop their characteristic earthy flavor.

Buying and Storing Cheese

Select cheese that looks moist, fresh, and clean. Don't buy cheese that looks dry and cracked or has shrunken from the rind. Avoid blue cheese that has any browning near the veins. Avoid cheese in a broken package or with a wet, sticky wrapper.

Keep all cheeses clean, cold, and covered. Once cut, tightly rewrap the cheese in plastic wrap. Store soft cheeses tightly wrapped in the coldest part of the refrigerator up to two weeks. If soft cheese shows signs of mold, it's time to throw away the cheese.

Wrap firm and hard cheeses in an airtight plastic bag, and store in refrigerator up to three weeks. If mold appears, simply cut it off and discard it. The rest of the cheese is still fine to eat. Just rewrap it in fresh plastic wrap, and use within a week. Very hard (grating) cheese will keep several months, wrapped, in the refrigerator. Change the wrapping weekly to prolong the life of the cheese, if desired.

Freezing is not the best method of storing cheese, but it can be done. Expect a change in texture, but the flavor and nutritional content will remain the same. You can freeze most cheeses up to six weeks. Hard cheeses freeze better than soft cheeses. To freeze, cut cheese into pieces (less than a pound), and wrap tightly in plastic wrap. Thaw cheese in refrigerator several hours, and use soon afterwards. Thawed cheese is better for cooking rather than just eating.

Cooking with Cheese

When cooking with cheese, a good rule of thumb is that most cheeses respond best to low or medium-low heat for a short time—just long enough to melt and blend with other ingredients. And if you're serving a cheese-topped casserole, add shredded cheese the last 5 or 10 minutes of baking; then heat just until cheese is melted. If overcooked, cheese tightens and becomes tough and stringy. When adding cheese to a sauce, shredding or dicing it promotes even melting. For all but very hard (grating) cheese, shredding is easiest if cheese is well chilled. Processed cheese melts and blends well if it's diced first; it's often too soft to shred.

Measure cheese by weight—4 ounces of hard cheese usually equals 1 cup shredded.

For easy cleanup when shredding, brush oil on a grater or spray vegetable cooking spray on grater before shredding cheese. Shred frequently used cheeses, such as Cheddar or Swiss, and freeze in zip-top plastic bags; then whenever you need a little cheese for cooking, just measure and use.

Serving Cheese

For cutting ease, cut cheese directly from the refrigerator while it's still cold. All cheese, with the exception of soft, fresh cheeses, tastes best if allowed to sit at room temperature (about 30 minutes) before serving. This allows its full flavor and aroma to come through.

A wooden cutting board or a marble slab makes a good serving piece for unsliced cheese. Provide a butter knife for soft cheese and a sharp knife for firmer cheeses.

A variety of crackers, bread, fruit, and wine are popular accompaniments with cheese. See our cheese-tasting discussion on page 208 for further serving suggestions.

CHEESE DICTIONARY

Common cheeses, such as Cheddar and Parmesan, are used often and are easily recognizable,
but take a look at the wide variety of other cheeses you can enjoy.

SOFT CHEESES

Boursin: A triple cream cheese with buttery texture. It's often flavored with garlic, herbs, or pepper. Good appetizer cheese; pair with dry white wine or fruity red wine.

Brie: A soft-ripened cheese that's known for its oozing, buttery interior and snow-white edible rind. Once ripe, Brie has a short shelf life and should be used within a few days. It's a popular appetizer wrapped in pastry and baked.

Crème fraîche: A specialty hailing from France, this is a very rich, thickened cream (similar to sour cream in texture) with a slightly tangy flavor. Spoon it over fresh fruit or warm cobbler for dessert.

Farmer cheese: A form of cottage cheese available fresh or very dry. A delightful country cheese. Firm; pleasantly mild. An all-purpose cheese for eating as is or for cooking; good on dark bread or with fruit and a light wine.

Feta: The classic Greek cheese. It's salty and sharp, firm and crumbly. Feta is usually sold pressed into a square cake and packed in brine. It's great crumbled over a salad or on pizza.

Goat cheese: The French call this pure white goat's milk cheese chèvre. It's sold in many shapes, though logs are most common. It has a distinct tart flavor and is sometimes coated in edible ash, herbs, or pepper. Store chèvre tightly wrapped up to two weeks in the refrigerator.

Mascarpone: A soft and fresh triple cream dessert cheese with fluffy texture. It's best known for its use in tiramisù (page 169), which combines this sweet cheese with ladyfingers soaked in espresso.

SEMISOFT CHEESES

Cream Havarti: Mild and buttery; slightly sweet with a smooth, supple texture. A favorite for snacking or for sandwiches. Excellent for slicing or melting.

Fontina: One of Italy's great cheeses with a pronounced flavor and smooth, creamy texture. A superb melting cheese. A Swedish-style fontina is also available; it's firmer and milder flavored.

Gouda: America's favorite Dutch cheese with a buttery, nutlike flavor. Enjoy it cubed as a snack or in a salad or sandwich. Its smoked version is also popular. Gouda's a good match for beer and dark bread.

Pepper Jack: A creamy, smooth and pliable version of **Monterey Jack** cheese flecked with bits of hot peppers. Slices well; melts readily. It's used often in Mexican dishes.

Port Salut: This buttery semisoft cheese was first made by Trappist monks at the Monastery of Port du Salut in France. Made from cow's milk, it has a mild flavor, satiny smooth texture, and is covered with an orange rind. It highlights fruit platters, salads, and is used in cooking.

Provolone: A firm, golden cheese with a slightly smoky tang. It's similar to mozzarella. As provolone ripens, the color becomes a richer yellow and the flavor sharpens. It's ideal for snacks and appetizers; an excellent cooking cheese, particularly in lasagna or ravioli.

String Mozzarella: A type of mozzarella shaped into ropes or sticks that "string" when pulled apart. Great pizza cheese.

HARD OR FIRM CHEESES

Asiago: A popular pale yellow Italian cheese with rich, nutty flavor. A great snack cheese when young, accompanied with beer or a full-bodied red wine; good for grating when aged over a year.

Emmentaler: Named for Switzerland's Emmental valley, this cheese is the king of Swiss cheeses. It has a distinct nutty-sweet, mellow flavor; firm texture with dime-size holes called "eyes." Traditionally used in fondue.

Gruyère: A rich, sweet, nutty-flavored Swiss that's typically aged for one year. It has a firm, pale yellow interior. A rich cooking cheese that's often used in fondue or atop French onion soup.

Jarlsberg: A buttery rich cheese from Norway with a creamy texture and mellow, nutty flavor. An all-purpose cheese, good for salads, snacking, and cooking.

Raclette: A Swiss cow's milk cheese, similar to Gruyère, it's used for fondue and in other sauces. Piquantly mild with a nutlike goodness.

Smoked Cheddar: A deep golden Cheddar with an edible brown rind; creamy, nutty flavored with a smooth, firm texture.

Vermont white Cheddar: A rich, aged, creamy Cheddar that remains undyed. It's an excellent cheese for sauce making.

VERY HARD CHEESES

Parmigiano-Reggiano: Italy's luxurious hard grating cheese that's typically aged at least 2 years. With a prized granular texture (from long aging) and complex sharp flavor, this cheese is best eaten unadorned and with fresh fruit.

Romano: A sharp and tangy, slightly salty, hard cheese. Available as pepato with black peppercorns throughout its white interior. A good cheese for grating for the same uses as Parmesan.

BLUE-VEINED CHEESES

Gorgonzola: An aged, distinctively sharp semisoft cheese with a creamy interior streaked with blue-green veins. Excellent for dessert, in salads, or tasting with a full-bodied red wine. It teams naturally with pears and walnuts. When aged over 6 months, Gorgonzola takes on a strong (some would say offensive) aroma.

Maytag blue: The best-known American blue cheese (made by the same Maytags who make washing machines). Ivory-colored blue cheese marbled with blue-gray veins. It has a tangy, slightly sweet flavor with a firm, crumbly texture.

Stilton: A blue cheese first sold in the small village of Stilton in Huntingdonshire, England. Stilton is made from whole cow's milk and is allowed to ripen four to six months. It has a creamy blue-green veined interior that's slightly crumbly. It's a rich, creamy cheese with a pungent bite. Best enjoyed with a glass of port or full-bodied red wine.

Swiss Cheese Fondue

PREP: 5 MINUTES   COOK: 15 MINUTES

Shred your cheese fresh when making authentic fondue because preshredded cheese just doesn't melt as well in this dish. And see our recommendations in the box at right for choosing a wine.

1 clove garlic, cut in half
1 cup dry white wine (we tested with
   Sauvignon Blanc)
1 tablespoon lemon juice
4 cups (16 ounces) shredded Swiss
   cheese
3 tablespoons all-purpose flour
⅛ teaspoon freshly ground pepper
⅛ teaspoon ground nutmeg
2 (16-ounce) loaves French bread, cut
   into 1-inch chunks

•Rub inside of a heavy saucepan or fondue pot with garlic; discard garlic. Add wine, and cook over medium-low heat until hot, but not boiling. Add lemon juice.
•Dredge cheese in flour. Gradually add cheese to saucepan (about ½ cup at a time), stirring constantly with a wooden spoon until melted and smooth. Stir in pepper and nutmeg. Bring almost to a boil, stirring gently, and pour into fondue pot. Keep warm over a small flame. Serve with French bread cubes or other dippers. Yield: 3 cups.
Per ¼-cup serving: Calories 370 Fat 11.9g
Cholesterol 37mg Sodium 538mg

FONDUE FACTS AND FINDS

•Crusty bread cubes, unpeeled Granny Smith apple wedges, pear slices, and steamed small red potatoes make great dippers for melted cheese. Be sure to stir the fondue as you dip into it.
•Emmentaler is the quintessential Swiss cheese often used in classic fondue, but you can use other types of Swiss like Gruyère.
•We recommend a dry Sauvignon Blanc for this classic fondue. Meridian or Napa Ridge Sauvignon Blanc are affordable choices.
•Classic fondue also has a splash of kirsch, but this cherry brandy can be hard to find. We loved the flavor without it.
•Don't overcook or overheat the fondue or it will become stringy. Add lemon juice to combat stringing.

Cheddar Fondue: Substitute 1 pound shredded sharp Cheddar cheese and 1 cup flat beer instead of Swiss cheese and white wine; omit nutmeg.

Note: To quickly make beer flat for Cheddar Fondue, pour into a 4-cup liquid measuring cup or any glass container with a large surface area; place on a flat surface covered with a folded towel. Carefully tap the measuring cup up and down on the towel for a minute or two, quickly forcing bubbles out of solution. Gently stir down the foam.

Cream-Style Cheese

PREP: 40 HOURS   CHILL: 2 DAYS

This homemade cheese tastes much like store-bought cream cheese, only fresher, and it lets you enjoy cheese making at home. It's time-consuming, but the results are worth it. Use the cheese in most recipes that use cream cheese or serve it with fruit and crackers.

3 cups half-and-half
¾ cup whipping cream
1½ tablespoons cultured buttermilk
¼ teaspoon plus ⅛ teaspoon salt

•Combine half-and-half and whipping cream in a heavy saucepan. Cook over low heat until mixture reaches 90°. Stir in buttermilk. Pour mixture into a large glass or ceramic bowl; cover with plastic wrap. Wrap a large towel around entire bowl, and place bowl in an unheated oven with light on or in a warm place, about 85°, for 28 hours or until mixture is consistency of soft yogurt.
•Cut several pieces of cheesecloth large enough to line a large colander and extend 4 inches over edges. Rinse cheesecloth, and squeeze out excess moisture; line colander with cheesecloth. Place colander in sink. Pour cream mixture into colander, and let drain 20 minutes.
•Place colander in a container to drain completely. Cover colander and container tightly with enough plastic wrap to make an airtight seal. Refrigerate 12 hours or until well

---

CHEESE-TASTING COURSE

Europeans have long celebrated cheese, and their cheese-tasting pastime has slowly made its way west. A cheese tasting can transform a casual dinner into a memorable culinary experience, and it's easy for you to do at home.
   Here are a few pointers for planning your own cheese occasion.
•Pick the highest quality cheeses you can find. Do some sampling at your local cheese shop to help narrow your decision. A few slivers of a great cheese will satisfy far more than several mediocre cheeses.

•A single superb cheese can certainly suffice; however, a standard combination for a five-cheese tasting is: an aged Cheddar, a semisoft cheese like Camembert, an aged nutty-flavored Swiss like Gruyère, a goat cheese, and a blue cheese like Stilton.
•Serve a diversity of flavors. Serve mild cheeses first; then serve stronger selections, so the stronger cheeses don't overwhelm the subtleties of their milder comrades.
•You don't need much cheese for tasting. A ½ ounce to 1 ounce serving of cheese per person per cheese is ample.

•Eat slowly. This will allow the cheeses' full flavors to settle on your tongue. The point is to linger and savor the flavors—not for you to become full.
•Some fine accompaniments with a cheese tasting are a crusty baguette or focaccia, a cluster of grapes, ripe figs, fresh peaches or pears, or toasted nuts—particularly walnuts, hazelnuts, or almonds. Be creative in the foods you pair with your favorite cheeses. You may discover a new fruit or other food that's a delicious match.
•Above all, choose cheeses you like.

drained. Spoon cheese mixture into a bowl; stir in salt. If the cheese is to be flavored and molded, do so at this point.

•If cheese is to be molded unflavored, cut four 8-inch-square pieces of cheesecloth; rinse cheesecloth, and squeeze out excess moisture. Smooth out wrinkles of cheesecloth, and stack layers on top of each other. Spoon cheese mixture in center of cloth. Wrap cheesecloth around cheese mixture, and tie ends securely. Pat cheesecloth-wrapped cheese into an oval or round shape. (Cheese can also be shaped in desired mold. Line mold with cheesecloth, and spoon in cheese mixture, pressing with back of a spoon to smoothly and firmly pack mixture.)

•Place cheesecloth-wrapped cheese (or invert mold) over a wire rack in a shallow pan. Cover pan with enough plastic wrap to make an airtight seal. Refrigerate 1 to 2 days or until firm and well drained. Unmold cheese, and remove cheesecloth. Cheese will keep in refrigerator up to 5 days. Yield: 2 cups.

Per tablespoon: Calories 49 Fat 4.7g
Cholesterol 16mg Sodium 40mg

Pimiento Cheese

◄ FAMILY FAVORITE • QUICK ►

PREP: 9 MINUTES

Sharp Cheddar and a little grated onion are key components for good pimiento cheese. For a new sandwich idea, spread pimiento cheese inside a BLT.

1 (8-ounce) package shredded sharp
   Cheddar cheese
1 (16-ounce) loaf process American
   cheese, cut into ½-inch cubes
1 tablespoon grated onion
1 (4-ounce) jar diced pimiento, drained
¾ to 1 cup mayonnaise

•Process half of cheeses in food processor until desired consistency, stopping once to scrape down sides. Transfer mixture to a bowl; set aside.

•Process remaining cheeses and onion until desired consistency, stopping to scrape down sides. Stir into cheese mixture in bowl. Stir in pimiento and mayonnaise. Yield: 4 cups.

Per ¼-cup serving: Calories 233 Fat 21.9g
Cholesterol 46mg Sodium 577mg

Chiles Rellenos

◄ FAMILY FAVORITE ►
◄ VEGETARIAN ►

PREP: 25 MINUTES   COOK: 15 MINUTES

Canned green chiles make easy work of stuffing this popular Mexican dish. Dip stuffed chiles into this thin, light coating, and then fry them immediately for crispy results.

8 ounces Monterey Jack cheese
4 (4.5-ounce) cans whole green chiles,
   drained
3 large eggs, separated
¼ cup all-purpose flour
Vegetable oil
Commercial tomato sauce or salsa

•Cut cheese into ¼-inch-thick strips; place inside chiles, trimming strips to fit chiles, if necessary. (If chiles are torn, overlap torn sides; eggs and flour will hold them.)

•Beat egg whites at high speed with an electric mixer until stiff peaks form; beat yolks until thick and pale. Fold whites into yolks.

•Dredge filled chiles in flour, coating well; dip in eggs. Pour oil to depth of 2 inches into a Dutch oven; heat to 375°. Fry chiles, 4 at a time, 3 to 5 minutes or until browned. Drain. Serve warm with tomato sauce or salsa. Yield: 4 servings.

Per serving: Calories 800 Fat 75.6g
Cholesterol 204mg Sodium 609mg

Welsh Rarebit

◄ QUICK ►

PREP: 4 MINUTES   COOK: 8 MINUTES

¾ cup milk
1½ cups (6 ounces) shredded Cheddar
   cheese
¾ teaspoon dry mustard
⅛ teaspoon ground red pepper
½ teaspoon Worcestershire sauce
1 large egg, well beaten
4 large slices French bread, toasted
4 slices bacon, cooked and crumbled

•Combine first 5 ingredients in top of a double boiler; bring water to a boil. Reduce heat to low, and cook, stirring constantly, until cheese melts. Slowly stir one-fourth of hot mixture into beaten egg; add to remaining hot mixture, stirring constantly. Cook over low heat, stirring constantly, until mixture thickens and just begins to simmer. Serve over toast; sprinkle with bacon. Yield: 4 servings.

Per serving: Calories 336 Fat 21.1g
Cholesterol 111mg Sodium 573mg

Cheese Blintzes

◄ FAMILY FAVORITE ►

PREP: 25 MINUTES   COOK: 8 MINUTES

These brunch or dessert crêpes are stuffed with a slightly sweet cheese. They're folded into plump little pillows that brown nicely in a buttered skillet.

2 (3-ounce) packages cream cheese,
   softened
1 (12-ounce) container large-curd cottage
   cheese
¼ cup egg substitute
2 tablespoons sugar
1 teaspoon grated lemon rind
12 (6-inch) Basic Crêpes (page 76)
3 tablespoons butter or margarine,
   divided
¾ cup sour cream
¾ cup strawberry preserves

•Combine cream cheese and cottage cheese; beat at medium speed with an electric mixer 2 minutes or until smooth. Add egg substitute, sugar, and lemon rind, stirring well; cover and chill 20 minutes.

•Place about 3 tablespoons cheese filling in center of each crêpe. Fold top and bottom of crêpe over filling; then fold left and right sides of crêpe over filling to form a square.

•Repeat procedure with remaining crêpes and filling. Melt 1½ tablespoons butter in a large nonstick skillet over medium heat. Place half of blintzes in skillet. Cook on both sides until lightly browned; remove from skillet, and keep warm.

•Melt remaining 1½ tablespoons butter in skillet. Repeat procedure with remaining blintzes.

•To serve, place cheese blintzes on serving plates. Top each with 1 tablespoon sour cream and 1 tablespoon strawberry preserves. Yield: 12 servings.

Per serving: Calories 251 Fat 13.9g
Cholesterol 65mg Sodium 167mg

Shrimp Scampi (page 220)

FISH & SHELLFISH

Fish and shellfish have much to offer the health-conscious cook. You can reel in fabulous flavor and nutrients when you dress fish with simple seasonings and light sauces. Enjoy our selection from flaky white fillets to spry shrimp with tails intact.

Finfish are some of the most versatile forms of animal protein available. They're generally lean, and they boast beneficial omega-3 fatty acids, as well as zinc and other nutrients. They come from saltwater and freshwater and are both wild and farmed. Fish is highly perishable, so it's important to apply some basic guidelines for buying, storing, and cooking it properly.

Selecting Fish

When shopping for fish, deal with a reputable fish and seafood market. Purchase fish from a store that has quick turnover, regularly replenishes its stock, and uses refrigerated cases to store fish. Get to know the seafood market manager, and before purchasing, ask where and when the fish was caught.

If you know the characteristics of high-quality fish, you can easily judge its freshness. The eyes of a fresh fish should be clear, clean, and full, almost bulging. The gills should be pinkish-red and not slippery. The flesh of the fish should be firm and elastic (that means it should spring back when lightly touched). The skin should have no faded markings; it should be shiny with scales firmly attached. Perhaps, though, the best indicator of freshness is odor. A fresh fish should have a clean, mild smell, not an offensive "fishy" odor.

Use some of the same pointers to judge freshness in fish that's dressed and cut. The flesh should be firm to the touch. Cut surfaces of fish steaks and fillets should be moist, not dried out. There should be no signs of yellowing or browning edges. The fish should have a mild, fresh odor.

Know What You're Buying

You can purchase fresh fish in a variety of market forms. Knowing these terms will help you pick the right type and amount of fish for your needs.

A *whole or round fish* is marketed just as it comes from the water. When cooked, a whole fish makes a dramatic presentation on the plate. Count on 1 pound per serving.

A *drawn fish* is a whole fish that has been eviscerated (internal organs removed) and scaled. Allow 1 pound per serving.

A *dressed fish* is one that has been eviscerated, scaled, and has head and fins removed. The tail may or may not be removed as well. Smaller fish that have been dressed are referred to as *pan-dressed*. Allow ½ pound per serving.

Fish steaks are crosscut slices of large dressed fish. They're usually cut about 1 inch thick. The only bone is a cross section of the backbone and ribs. Plan on about ⅓ to ½ pound per serving.

Fillets are the sides of fish cut lengthwise away from the backbone. They're often skinned and are practically boneless (though small pinbones may be present). For *butterfly fillets*, the fillets are held together by the uncut belly skin. Skinless fillets tend to dry out quickly during cooking, so watch them carefully. Allow ⅓ to ½ pound per serving for fillets.

Fat and Lean Fish

Fish are classified as *fat* or *lean*. Fat fish have an oil content of more than 5 percent and tend to be higher in calories and stronger in flavor than lean fish. The color of fat fish is usually darker due to oil distributed throughout

211

the flesh. The oil produces a pronounced flavor as well as more of a meatlike texture than in lean fish. Fat fish require less basting during cooking than lean fish to keep flesh moist and tender. Dry heat methods of cooking such as grilling, broiling, and smoking are ideal for fat fish.

Lean fish have an oil content of less than 5 percent. The oil is concentrated in the liver, which is removed when fish are cleaned. Lean fish are milder in flavor and whiter in appearance than fat fish because the oil is not distributed throughout the body of the fish. Lean fish tend to dry out during cooking because of their low fat content; therefore, moist heat methods like poaching and baking are best. Lean fish can be grilled successfully if basted often.

When substituting one fish for another in a recipe, it's best to choose a substitute from the same classification. Use the chart that follows as a guide.

FISH CLASSIFICATION

FAT FISH	LEAN FISH	
Amberjack	Cod	Scamp
Freshwater Catfish	Flounder	Scrod
Herring	Grouper	Sea Bass
Lake Trout or	Haddock	Snapper
Rainbow Trout	Halibut	Sole
Mackerel	Mahimahi	Swordfish
Mullet	Ocean Perch	Tilapia
Pompano	Orange Roughy	Tilefish
Salmon	Pike	Triggerfish
Sardines	Pollock	Turbot
Tuna	Redfish	Walleye
Whitefish	Rockfish	Whiting

Handling Fish

Fresh fish is best if cooked the day of purchase, but may be stored in the original wrapping in the coldest part of the refrigerator up to two days if the wrapping is moisture- and vapor-resistant. If it's not, wrap the fish carefully before storing. Place a damp cloth over the fish, inside the wrapping, to prevent fish from drying out. Fresh fish should be frozen within two days of purchase. Store in the freezer up to three months.

Some fish sold in the unfrozen state has been flash frozen or blast frozen to maintain quality. Once flash-frozen fish have thawed, do not refreeze. If you intend to freeze the fish, ask if it was previously frozen.

If you're not going directly home after purchasing fish, have the package placed in a plastic bag filled with ice. When you arrive home, remove fish from its wrapper, rinse in cold water, and pat dry with paper towels. Then repackage fish in wax paper and an airtight plastic bag. Place bag directly on ice in a colander set in a larger bowl.

When buying frozen fish, make sure the package is tightly wrapped and sealed. There should be little or no air within the wrapping. Be sure that there's no blood visible inside or out, that the fish is solidly frozen and free of ice crystals, which can jeopardize its texture and freshness.

Thaw frozen fish in the refrigerator. If you need to thaw it quicker than that, place the frozen fish wrapped in plastic wrap under cold running water until thawed. Drain and blot thawed fish with paper towels before cooking.

Frozen breaded fish products should not be thawed before cooking; prepare these according to package directions. Leftover cooked fish will keep two days in the refrigerator.

Cooking Fish

Choose from baking, broiling, grilling, frying, poaching, steaming, and microwaving for cooking fish. Dry heat methods are considered better for cooking fat fish, while lean fish remains more moist when cooked by moist heat methods. You can, however, cook lean fish by a dry heat method if it is basted often.

Overcooking and cooking at too high a temperature are the most common problems in cooking fish. These factors dry and toughen fish and can destroy the flavor.

Be sure to check the fish for doneness occasionally while cooking. To check for doneness, pierce the thickest part of the fish with a fork, and twist fork slightly; most fish will flake easily and come away from the bones readily when done. The flesh becomes opaque and the juices should be a milky white.

Microwaving Fish: Fish that's cooked in a microwave oven can be outstanding. With the natural tenderness and moisture of fish, the rapid cooking action of a microwave oven helps retain the delicate flavor and texture of fish.

Generally, it's best to microwave fish at HIGH power to quickly seal in juices and flavor. Arrange thicker portions to the outside of the dish so they'll get done without overcooking the thinner areas. When fish turns opaque, it's done.

The microwave oven also works well for defrosting frozen fish. Fillets can be left in their original package for defrosting. Fish defrosts rapidly, so be careful not to toughen it by overdefrosting in the microwave. Remove fish from its package while it is still slightly icy; hold fish under cold, running water to complete the defrosting process.

Grilling Fish: Fish cooked properly on the grill is a delicacy. Almost any type of fish is suitable for the grill; just remember that a lean fish will need frequent basting during grilling. And you'll want to choose a fish fillet or steak that is at least ¾ inch thick for the grill.

Prepare your grill as you would for any other type of meat. Be sure to start your fire in advance of cooking so the coals will be just right by the time you're ready to grill. One method to use when lighting a charcoal fire is to mound the briquets in a cone shape. Lightly spray briquets with lighter fluid, and let fluid soak in 1 minute before lighting.

The coals are ready for cooking when they're covered with a gray ash. At this point, spread coals evenly over an area slightly larger than the area the fish will cover.

TIMETABLE FOR COOKING FISH & SHELLFISH

COOKING METHOD	PRODUCT	MARKET FORM	APPROXIMATE WEIGHT OR THICKNESS	COOKING TEMPERATURE	APPROXIMATE TOTAL COOKING TIME BY MINUTES
Baking	Fish	Dressed	3 to 4 pounds	350°	40 to 60
		Pan-dressed	½ to 1 pound	350°	25 to 30
		Steaks	½ to 1 inch	350°	25 to 35
		Fillets	1 inch	350°	10 per inch
	Clams	Live		450°	15
	Lobster	Live	¾ to 1 pound	400°	15 to 20
			1 to 1½ pounds	400°	20 to 25
	Oysters	Live		450°	15
		Shucked		400°	10
	Scallops	Shucked		350°	25 to 30
	Shrimp	Headless		350°	20 to 25
	Spiny lobster	Headless	4 ounces	450°	20 to 25
	tails		8 ounces	450°	25 to 30
Broiling	Fish	Pan-dressed	½ to 1 pound	Broil	10 to 15
		Steaks	½ to 1 inch	Broil	10 to 15
		Fillets	1 inch	Broil	10 per inch
	Clams	Live		Broil	5 to 8
	Lobster	Live	¾ to 1 pound	Broil	10 to 12
			1 to 1½ pounds	Broil	12 to 15
	Oysters	Live		Broil	5
		Shucked		Broil	5
	Scallops	Shucked		Broil	8 to 10
	Shrimp	Headless		Broil	8 to 10
	Spiny lobster	Headless	4 ounces	Broil	8 to 10
	tails		8 ounces	Broil	10 to 12
Poaching	Fish	Pan-dressed	½ to 1 pound	Simmer	10
		Steaks	½ to 1 inch	Simmer	10
		Fillets	1 inch	Simmer	9 per inch
	Crabs	Live		Simmer	15
	Lobster	Live	¾ to 1 pound	Simmer	10 to 15
			1 to 1½ pounds	Simmer	15 to 20
	Scallops	Shucked		Simmer	4 to 5
	Shrimp	Headless		Simmer	3 to 5
	Spiny lobster	Headless	4 ounces	Simmer	10
	tails		8 ounces	Simmer	15
Frying	Fish	Pan-dressed	½ to 1 pound	375°	2 to 4
		Steaks	½ to 1 inch	375°	2 to 4
		Fillets	1 inch	375°	1 to 5
	Clams	Shucked		375°	2 to 3
	Crabs	Soft-Shell	¼ pound	375°	3 to 4
	Lobster	Live	¾ to 1 pound	375°	3 to 4
			1 to 1½ pounds	375°	4 to 5
	Oysters	Shucked		375°	2
	Scallops	Shucked		350°	3 to 4
	Shrimp	Headless		350°	2 to 3
	Spiny lobster	Headless	4 ounces	350°	3 to 4
	tails		8 ounces	350°	4 to 5

Before you put fish on the grill, be sure to grease the grill grid. Our Test Kitchens staff recommends spraying the grid with vegetable cooking spray before placing the grid over a hot fire. Of course, oil works fine, too.

A fish basket is a handy piece of equipment for grilling fish, particularly the thinner pieces. The basket holds the fish securely and keeps it from sticking to the grill. Grease the basket, arrange fish in the basket, and fasten shut. Place basket flat on the grill. To turn the fish during grilling, simply flip the basket.

You can also steam fish on the grill. Place fish (fillets work well) on a large piece of heavy-duty aluminum foil; sprinkle with your favorite seasonings or herbs. Seal foil, and cook on the grill 4 to 5 inches above the heat, approximately 15 minutes per inch of thickness. (To determine thickness, measure thickest part of fish with a ruler.)

It's easy to overcook fish, so don't leave fish unattended during grilling. Begin checking for doneness halfway through cooking time; the time will vary according to the thickness and size of the fish, the wind, the temperature of the coals, and whether or not the grill is covered.

Poaching Fish: Poaching is an excellent low-fat cooking method for fish. It preserves the delicate texture of the fish and enhances its flavor. It's important to immerse the fish completely in the poaching liquid so that an exchange of flavors between the fish and the cooking liquid will take place.

It's easy to cook large fish in a fish poacher, a long narrow piece of cookware with a removable tray. Or cut fish in half crosswise so that pieces will fit in a smaller container. Use a large skillet or saucepan to poach smaller fish, fish steaks, and fillets. Most firm-fleshed fish is suitable for poaching.

To scale a fish: Hold fish by the tail, and scrape back of knife against scales toward head. It's a messy job, so work outdoors or cover area with newspaper.

To fillet a fish: Hold knife parallel to fish and cutting board; cut lengthwise as close to the backbone as possible. Repeat on the other side.

To poach fish, have the poaching liquid simmering when fish is lowered into it; then reheat the liquid to barely simmering for cooking. Poach 10 minutes per inch of thickness, turning halfway through the cooking time.

FISH

Crispy Fried Catfish

◀ QUICK • FAMILY FAVORITE ▶

PREP: 10 MINUTES
COOK: 9 TO 12 MINUTES

A Southern favorite, for sure—this fried catfish gets a little kick from red pepper.

2   cups self-rising cornmeal
1   tablespoon garlic powder
2   tablespoons dried thyme
6   (8-ounce) farm-raised catfish fillets
1   cup buttermilk
1   tablespoon salt
2   teaspoons ground black pepper
2   teaspoons ground red pepper
Peanut oil or vegetable oil

•Combine first 3 ingredients in a shallow dish. Dip catfish fillets in buttermilk, allowing excess to drip off; sprinkle with salt and peppers, and dredge in cornmeal mixture.
•Pour oil to depth of 2 inches into an electric skillet or Dutch oven; heat to 375°. Fry fillets, two at a time, 3 to 4 minutes or until they float; drain on paper towels. Serve immediately. Yield: 6 servings.
Per serving: Calories 667 Fat 38.9g
Cholesterol 133mg Sodium 1866mg

Mexican Hush Puppies
(page 71)

Crispy Fried Catfish

Baked Fish Amandine

◄ QUICK ►

PREP: 11 MINUTES COOK: 15 MINUTES

Add zing with a squeeze of lemon over this crispy cracker- and almond-coated fish.

1 tablespoon butter or margarine, melted
2 teaspoons fresh lemon juice
1 pound fish fillets, such as flounder or
    orange roughy
¼ teaspoon salt
3 tablespoons mayonnaise
½ cup saltine cracker crumbs
3 tablespoons butter or margarine,
    melted
¼ cup slivered almonds, toasted
Lemon wedges

•Combine 1 tablespoon butter and lemon juice in a 13- x 9-inch baking dish. Arrange fillets in dish; sprinkle with salt. Spread mayonnaise on fillets.
•Combine cracker crumbs, 3 tablespoons melted butter, and almonds; sprinkle over fillets. Bake, uncovered, at 400° for 10 to 15 minutes or until fish flakes easily when tested with a fork. Serve with lemon wedges. Yield: 4 servings.
Per serving: Calories 356 Fat 25.4g
Cholesterol 95mg Sodium 574mg

Lemon Broiled Orange Roughy

◄ QUICK • HEALTHY ►

PREP: 10 MINUTES COOK: 10 MINUTES

Dijon mustard adds unexpected tang to these quick and flaky white fillets.

3 tablespoons lemon juice
1 tablespoon Dijon mustard
1 tablespoon butter or margarine, melted
¼ teaspoon pepper
1½ pounds orange roughy fillets
Freshly ground pepper
Garnish: lemon slices

•Combine first 4 ingredients; stir well.
•Place fillets on a lightly greased rack in broiler pan. Brush half of lemon juice mixture on fillets. Broil 5½ inches from heat 8 to 10 minutes or until fish flakes easily when tested with a fork.
•Transfer fillets to a serving platter. Drizzle remaining half of lemon juice mixture over fillets. Sprinkle with pepper; garnish, if desired. Yield: 4 servings.
Per serving: Calories 135 Fat 4.2g
Cholesterol 37mg Sodium 233mg

A FIRM CHOICE

When a recipe calls for firm-textured, mild fish fillets, you can always use orange roughy, flounder, or tilapia.

Smoked Fish

PREP: 20 MINUTES   MARINATE: 8 HOURS

COOK: 4 HOURS

This smoky fish makes a wonderful entrée with crisp greens and your favorite salad dressing, or enjoy it as an appetizer on baguette slices smeared with cream cheese.

5 pounds trout or mackerel, cut into
    1½-inch-thick steaks (leave skin on)
1½ cups water
⅓ cup firmly packed brown sugar
3 tablespoons salt
¼ teaspoon ground red pepper

•Soak hickory chunks in water from 1 to 24 hours.
•Place trout in a large heavy-duty, zip-top plastic bag. Combine water and remaining 3 ingredients; pour over trout. Seal bag; marinate in refrigerator 8 hours, turning bag occasionally.
•Prepare charcoal fire in smoker, and let burn 10 to 15 minutes. Cover coals with soaked hickory chunks. Place water pan in smoker; add hot water to fill pan.
•Place upper food rack on appropriate shelf in smoker. Arrange trout on food rack and discard marinade. Cover with smoker lid, and cook 3 to 4 hours or to desired doneness. Yield: 10 servings.
Per serving: Calories 193 Fat 5.1g
Cholesterol 87mg Sodium 1096mg

Catfish Meunière

◄ QUICK ►

PREP: 8 MINUTES COOK: 8 MINUTES

Meunière is a French term for fish that's lightly seasoned, dusted with flour, and pan-fried. This version's simple, yet divine.

1 large egg, lightly beaten
¼ cup milk
½ cup all-purpose flour
½ teaspoon salt
½ teaspoon ground red pepper
4 (8-ounce) farm-raised catfish fillets
½ cup butter or margarine, divided
¼ cup vegetable oil
2 tablespoons chopped fresh parsley
2 tablespoon lemon juice
½ teaspoon Worcestershire sauce
Garnishes: fresh parsley sprigs, lemon
    wedges

•Combine egg and milk in a large shallow bowl. Combine flour, salt, and pepper in a shallow dish. Dip catfish fillets in egg mixture, and dredge in flour mixture.
•Melt ¼ cup butter in a large nonstick skillet over medium heat. Add oil; increase heat to medium-high. Place fillets in skillet, and cook 4 minutes on each side or until fish flakes easily when tested with a fork. Drain on paper towels.
•Melt remaining ¼ cup butter in skillet; stir in chopped parsley, lemon juice, and Worcestershire sauce. Spoon over fillets. Garnish, if desired. Yield: 4 servings.
Per serving: Calories 646 Fat 47.7g
Cholesterol 235mg Sodium 622mg

CATFISH COMMOTION

Farm-raised catfish is growing in reputation, thanks to aquaculture, the practice of farming fish in a controlled environment. The catfish are raised in freshwater, where they eat grain and feed from the surface of the water. This controlled environment, in contrast to a natural lake, yields catfish with a mild flavor and desirable texture that are harvested year-round. As a result, chefs and home cooks alike are inspired to look at catfish with fresh ideas in mind.

Pecan Grouper

◄ QUICK ►

PREP: 8 MINUTES   COOK: 20 MINUTES

2 pounds grouper fillets
½ teaspoon salt
¼ teaspoon pepper
½ cup all-purpose flour
½ cup butter, divided
½ cup coarsely chopped pecans
¼ cup chopped fresh parsley
Lemon wedges

•Sprinkle grouper fillets with salt and pepper; dredge fillets in flour.
•Melt 3 tablespoons butter in a large skillet over medium-high heat. Add fillets, and cook 6 minutes on each side or until fish flakes easily when tested with a fork.
•Remove fillets to a serving platter; set aside, and keep warm.
•Melt remaining ¼ cup plus 1 tablespoon butter in skillet over medium heat. Add pecans, and cook, stirring constantly, 2 minutes or until butter begins to brown. Pour over fillets; sprinkle with parsley. Serve immediately with lemon wedges. Yield: 6 servings.
Per serving: Calories 362 Fat 24g
Cholesterol 97mg Sodium 432mg

Crab-Stuffed Orange Roughy

◄ FAMILY FAVORITE ►

PREP: 19 MINUTES   COOK: 30 MINUTES

1 large egg, lightly beaten
⅓ cup fine, dry breadcrumbs
     (commercial)
1 tablespoon finely chopped onion
1 tablespoon finely chopped sweet red or
     green pepper
2 teaspoons Old Bay seasoning
1 teaspoon dry mustard
2 teaspoons chopped fresh parsley
1 teaspoon hot sauce
½ pound fresh lump crabmeat, drained
8 (5- to 6-ounce) orange roughy fillets
2 tablespoons butter or margarine
2 tablespoons fresh lemon juice
¼ teaspoon paprika
Mornay Sauce (page 388)

•Combine first 8 ingredients in a bowl; stir well. Add crabmeat, and stir gently. Spoon ¼ cup crabmeat mixture onto each fillet, and roll up to enclose filling. Place rolls, seam side down, in a lightly greased 13- x 9-inch baking dish. Dot butter on each fillet; sprinkle with lemon juice and paprika.
•Bake, uncovered, at 350° for 30 minutes or until fish flakes easily when tested with a fork. Serve with Mornay Sauce. Yield: 8 servings.
Per serving: Calories 245 Fat 10.6g
Cholesterol 128mg Sodium 577mg

Savory Salmon Loaf

PREP: 22 MINUTES   COOK: 55 MINUTES

Sockeye salmon has a deep pink color which lends itself nicely to this loaf, but any type of canned salmon works fine here.

1 (14¾-ounce) can sockeye salmon
1½ cups saltine cracker crumbs, divided
¼ cup butter or margarine, melted
2 large eggs, beaten
¼ cup chopped green pepper
¼ cup grated onion
1 tablespoon butter or margarine, melted
¼ teaspoon pepper
1 tablespoon dried parsley flakes
1 tablespoon Worcestershire sauce
2 tablespoons ketchup
¼ teaspoon hot sauce
4 slices bacon, halved
Cucumber Cream Sauce (page 389)

•Drain salmon, reserving ⅓ cup liquid; set liquid aside. Remove skin and bones, if desired; flake salmon with a fork.
•Brown 1 cup cracker crumbs in ¼ cup butter in a skillet over medium heat; set aside.
•Combine salmon, reserved liquid, remaining ½ cup cracker crumbs, eggs, and next 8 ingredients. Sprinkle ½ cup browned cracker crumbs in a greased 8½- x 4½-inch loafpan.
•Spoon salmon mixture over crumbs, and shape into a loaf. Press remaining browned crumbs on top. Arrange bacon slices diagonally across loaf. Bake at 350° for 55 minutes.
•Remove from pan. Slice and serve with Cucumber Cream Sauce. Yield: 6 servings.
Per serving: Calories 470 Fat 33.8g
Cholesterol 148mg Sodium 1043mg

Poached Salmon

PREP: 9 MINUTES   COOK: 30 MINUTES

Poaching gently simmers fish (or other food) in a flavorful liquid. Here the liquid is champagne; its flavor is infused in the flesh and then met with a delicious rosemary sauce.

¼ cup sour cream
¼ cup whipping cream
1 tablespoon sugar
2 teaspoons Dijon mustard
1 teaspoon chopped fresh rosemary
⅓ cup unsalted butter, melted
3 tablespoons lemon juice
2 green onions, finely chopped
½ cup champagne
2 pounds salmon fillets (1 inch thick)

•Combine first 5 ingredients in a bowl; stir with a wire whisk until smooth. Cover and chill sauce mixture thoroughly.
•Combine butter and next 3 ingredients in a fish poacher or large skillet; bring to a boil over medium heat. Add salmon, and reduce heat to low; baste with butter mixture. Cover and poach 30 minutes or until salmon flakes easily when tested with a fork. Remove salmon from liquid; drain and place on a platter. Serve with chilled sauce. Yield: 6 servings.
Per serving: Calories 363 Fat 24g
Cholesterol 132mg Sodium 135mg

Lemony Baked Salmon

◄ QUICK ►

PREP: 4 MINUTES   COOK: 12 MINUTES

4 salmon steaks (1½ pounds)
¼ cup butter or margarine, melted
1 teaspoon lemon-pepper seasoning
1 teaspoon garlic salt
1 teaspoon paprika
Lemon wedges

•Place steaks in an 11- x 7-inch baking dish. Combine butter, lemon-pepper seasoning, and garlic salt in a small bowl; stir well. Pour over steaks, and sprinkle with paprika.
•Bake, uncovered, at 500° for 10 minutes or until fish flakes easily when tested with a fork. Serve with lemon wedges. Yield: 4 servings.
Per serving: Calories 353 Fat 21.7g
Cholesterol 97mg Sodium 1011mg

Cutting fish steaks: Remove fins, scales, and head first; then cut fish into 1-inch slices, using a hammer to tap knife through backbone, if necessary.

Grilled Swordfish Steaks

◀ GRILLED ▶

PREP: 3 MINUTES   MARINATE: 1 TO 2 HOURS
COOK: 16 MINUTES

This supple swordfish absorbs plenty of flavor while marinating; the Avocado Butter is a bonus—it's also great with beef or chicken.

8 swordfish steaks (1 inch thick)
    (3 pounds)
½ cup vegetable oil
¼ cup soy sauce
1 teaspoon grated lemon rind
¼ cup fresh lemon juice
2 cloves garlic, crushed
Avocado Butter (page 389)
Garnishes: lemon wedges, fresh parsley
    sprigs

•Place swordfish steaks in a large heavy-duty, zip-top plastic bag. Combine oil and next 4 ingredients. Pour over steaks; seal bag, and turn to coat steaks. Cover and marinate in refrigerator 1 to 2 hours, turning bag occasionally.
•Remove steaks from marinade, reserving marinade. Place marinade in a small saucepan. Bring to a boil; remove from heat.
•Grill steaks, covered with grill lid, over medium-hot coals (350° to 400°) 8 to 10 minutes on each side or until fish flakes easily when tested with a fork, basting often with marinade. Serve with Avocado Butter. Garnish, if desired. Yield: 8 servings.
Per serving: Calories 425 Fat 26.1g
Cholesterol 116mg Sodium 628mg

Red Snapper Veracruz

PREP: 15 MINUTES   COOK: 20 MINUTES

Rice is an ideal side dish to absorb the flavorful tomato broth that simmers with these snapper fillets.

¼ cup chopped green onions
2 tablespoons butter or margarine,
    melted
2 large tomatoes, seeded and chopped
1 tablespoon chopped fresh cilantro or
    parsley
3 tablespoons fresh lime juice
2 tablespoons canned chopped green
    chiles
¼ teaspoon salt
⅛ teaspoon garlic powder
Dash of pepper
2 (6- to 8-ounce) red snapper fillets
Lime wedges

•Cook green onions in butter in a large skillet, stirring constantly, until tender. Stir in tomato and next 6 ingredients. Bring to a boil; reduce heat, and simmer, 10 minutes.
•Place snapper fillets in skillet. Spoon tomato mixture evenly over fillets. Bring mixture to a boil; cover, reduce heat, and simmer 10 minutes or until fish flakes easily when tested with a fork. Serve with lime wedges. Yield: 2 servings.
Per serving: Calories 384 Fat 15.3g
Cholesterol 115mg Sodium 671mg

Greek Snapper

◀ FAMILY FAVORITE ▶

PREP: 22 MINUTES   COOK: 40 MINUTES

1 tablespoon olive oil
1 onion, chopped
1 clove garlic, minced
3 medium tomatoes, peeled, seeded, and
    chopped
¼ cup sliced ripe olives or pitted, sliced
    kalamata olives
¼ cup dry white wine
1 teaspoon dried oregano
½ teaspoon salt
¼ teaspoon pepper
1½ pounds red snapper fillets
2 ounces feta cheese, crumbled
2 tablespoons chopped fresh parsley

•Pour oil into a large skillet. Place over medium heat until hot. Add onion and garlic; cook until tender, stirring constantly. Stir in tomato and next 5 ingredients. Bring to a boil; reduce heat, and simmer, uncovered, 20 minutes.
•Place snapper fillets in a greased 13- x 9-inch baking dish. Spoon tomato mixture over fillets. Bake, uncovered, at 350° for 20 minutes or until fish flakes easily when tested with a fork. Sprinkle with cheese and parsley. Serve immediately. Yield: 6 servings.
Per serving: Calories 190 Fat 6.7g
Cholesterol 50mg Sodium 422mg

Grilled Lake Trout

◀ QUICK • GRILLED ▶

PREP: 12 MINUTES   COOK: 15 MINUTES

4 trout fillets (about 2 pounds)
1 cup dry white wine
½ cup vegetable oil
1 (4-ounce) can mushroom stems and
    pieces, drained
¼ cup chopped onion
2 tablespoons chopped fresh parsley
2 tablespoons lemon juice
2 teaspoons salt
¼ teaspoon dried thyme

•Coat four 18-inch squares of heavy-duty aluminum foil with vegetable cooking spray. Place a fillet on each square, bringing up edges of foil.
•Combine wine and remaining 7 ingredients; pour evenly over fillets. Close foil around fish, sealing tightly.
•Place packets on grill rack, and grill, covered with grill lid, over hot coals (400° to 500°) 15 minutes or until fish flakes easily when tested with a fork. Yield: 4 servings.
Per serving: Calories 596 Fat 42.8g
Cholesterol 132mg Sodium 1363mg

RESOURCEFUL FISH

When buying a whole fish, don't discard the head and tail; instead save them to make fish stock for sauces, aspics, and bouillabaisse.

Trout Amandine

PREP: 8 MINUTES   COOK: 23 MINUTES

½ cup all-purpose flour
¼ teaspoon salt
¼ teaspoon pepper
4 rainbow or brook trout, pan-dressed, or
    other pan-dressed fish (about 2 pounds)
1 large egg, beaten
¼ cup milk
¼ cup plus 3 tablespoons butter or
    margarine, divided
⅔ cup sliced or slivered almonds
3 tablespoons fresh lemon juice
2 tablespoons minced fresh parsley
Garnishes: lemon slices, fresh parsley
    sprigs

•Combine flour, salt, and pepper. Dredge trout in flour mixture. Combine egg and milk; dip trout in egg mixture, and then in flour again.
•Melt 2 tablespoons butter in a large non-stick skillet over medium-high heat; add 2 trout, and cook 6 to 8 minutes or until fish flakes easily when tested with a fork, turning once. Remove to a serving platter; keep warm. Repeat procedure with 2 tablespoons butter and remaining trout. Wipe skillet with a paper towel.
•Melt remaining 3 tablespoons butter in skillet; add almonds. Cook until golden, stirring often. Stir in lemon juice and parsley; pour over trout. Garnish, if desired. Yield: 4 servings.
Per serving: Calories 768 Fat 53.7g
Cholesterol 215mg Sodium 481mg

Lemon-Basil Grilled Tuna

**PREP: 5 MINUTES   MARINATE: 1½ HOURS
COOK: 12 MINUTES**

Fresh tuna has steaklike character, particularly after it's picked up the grill's markings and smoky flavor.

6 tuna steaks (1½ inches thick)
    (about 1½ pounds)
1 large lemon
¼ cup chopped fresh basil
¼ cup olive oil
1 teaspoon salt
½ teaspoon pepper

•Place tuna steaks in an 11- x 7-inch baking dish.
•Grate lemon rind, and squeeze juice from lemon into a bowl. Add basil and remaining 3 ingredients; pour over steaks. Cover and marinate in refrigerator 1½ hours, turning steaks once.
•Coat grill rack with vegetable cooking spray; place rack on grill over medium-hot coals (350° to 400°). Place steaks on rack, and grill, covered with grill lid, 6 minutes on each side or until fish flakes easily when tested with a fork. Yield: 6 servings.
Per serving: Calories 178 Fat 7.7g
Cholesterol 42mg Sodium 140mg

Tuna Casserole

PREP: 8 MINUTES   COOK: 40 MINUTES

A creative cracker topping transforms this tuna casserole into something special.

1 (5-ounce) package dried egg noodles
1 (10¾-ounce) can cream of mushroom
    soup, undiluted
1 (5-ounce) can evaporated milk
⅓ cup finely chopped onion
1 (6-ounce) can solid white tuna in spring
    water, drained and flaked
1 cup (4 ounces) shredded Cheddar
    cheese
1 (8.5-ounce) can English peas, drained
½ teaspoon pepper
1 cup tiny fish-shaped crackers (we tested
    with Pepperidge Farm goldfish)

•Cook noodles according to package directions; drain. Stir in soup and next 6 ingredients; pour into a lightly greased 8-inch square baking dish.
•Cover and bake at 350° for 30 minutes. Sprinkle with crackers; bake, uncovered, 5 more minutes or until thoroughly heated. Serve hot. Yield: 4 servings.
Per serving: Calories 504 Fat 21.2g
Cholesterol 92mg Sodium 1216mg

Salmon Casserole: Substitute 1 (7.5-ounce) can of salmon for tuna.

Trout Amandine

SHELLFISH

Whether fried, steamed, grilled, or broiled, shellfish are gems on menus across the South, both at home and in restaurants. Shellfish are divided into two groups: *crustaceans* and *mollusks*. Crustaceans have long bodies with soft, jointed shells and legs. These include shrimp, crabs, crawfish, and lobster. Mollusks have soft bodies with no spinal column and are covered by a shell of one or more pieces.

These include clams, mussels, oysters, and scallops, as well as squid, snails, and octopus.

Freshness is critical for shellfish because they spoil quickly out of water. Many shellfish are kept alive in water tanks or on beds of ice until time to cook them, but most are also available fresh, frozen, cooked, or frozen cooked.

SHRIMP

Shrimp are versatile little swimmers guaranteed to satisfy, whether they're boiled and eaten with cocktail sauce, breaded and fried, or basted and grilled.

Fresh raw shrimp will vary in color from light gray to pink. The color is only an indication of the type of water the shrimp came from, not quality. (All shrimp turn pale pink during cooking.) The flesh should feel firm and slippery and have a mild, almost sweet odor. An odor of ammonia indicates deterioration. Black tiger shrimp is one of the most common types of shrimp in the market these days. It has a distinct striped, gray shell.

You may see multiple sizes of shrimp to choose from at the market. Small and medium shrimp are good in salads and casseroles. Large and jumbo shrimp are ideal stuffed, grilled, or in entrées for entertaining.

Store shrimp in the refrigerator, and use within a day or two after purchasing. Shrimp may be frozen raw in the shell or cooked and peeled for longer storage.

Shrimp are usually sold headless, but if they are whole, twist off heads, being sure to remove all parts of the head region. To peel shrimp, run your thumb under the section of the shell located between the legs. The tail shell may be left on the shrimp for show, if desired. Using a small knife or deveiner, make a slit down the back of the shrimp, and remove the sand vein (see photo).

Boiled Shrimp

◀ HEALTHY • MAKE AHEAD ▶

PREP: 25 MINUTES   COOK: 5 MINUTES

Present this tender pink shrimp in the traditional manner—draped over the rims of stemmed glasses that cradle a tangy sauce.

6   cups water
2   tablespoons salt
2   bay leaves
1   lemon, halved
1   stalk celery with leaves, cut into 3-inch pieces
2   pounds unpeeled fresh shrimp
Cocktail Sauce (optional, page 390)

•Combine first 5 ingredients in a Dutch oven; bring to a boil. Add shrimp, and cook 3 to 5 minutes. Drain well; rinse with cold water. Cover and chill. Peel shrimp, and devein, if desired. Serve with Cocktail Sauce, if desired. Yield: 6 servings.
Per serving: Calories 84 Fat 0.9g
Cholesterol 166mg Sodium 1362mg

Beer-Battered Fried Shrimp

◀ FAMILY FAVORITE ▶

PREP: 30 MINUTES   COOK: 30 MINUTES

Leaving the tails intact on fried shrimp makes a dramatic presentation and provides something to hold onto when dipping the shrimp in cocktail sauce.

2   pounds unpeeled large fresh shrimp
½   cup all-purpose flour
½   cup cornstarch
½   teaspoon salt
½   cup beer
¼   cup butter or margarine, melted
2   egg yolks
Vegetable oil
Cocktail Sauce (page 390)

•Peel shrimp, leaving tails intact; devein, if desired. Combine flour, cornstarch, and salt. Add beer, butter, and egg yolks; stir until smooth.
•Pour oil to depth of 2 inches into a Dutch oven; heat to 375°. Dip shrimp into batter; fry, a few at a time, until golden. Drain. Serve with Cocktail Sauce. Yield: 6 servings.
Per serving: Calories 489 Fat 29.8g
Cholesterol 266mg Sodium 877mg

DO I NEED TO DEVEIN?

Deveining shrimp is mostly an aesthetic choice rather than a necessity. That little black line that runs down the back of a shrimp (the sand vein) is its intestinal tract.

In small shrimp, it's really not noticeable and is generally left in. But for larger shrimp, the vein is unappealing and adds a gritty, muddy taste. While there's no harm in eating cooked shrimp that haven't been deveined, most people prefer cleaned shrimp. Deveining is simple enough to do and worth the effort—see our photo at right for instruction.

To devein shrimp: Slit shrimp lengthwise down its back, using a small paring knife. Then pull vein away with tip of knife.

Barbecued Shrimp

◄ QUICK • FAMILY FAVORITE ►

PREP: 9 MINUTES   COOK: 22 MINUTES

*You'll relish the peppery bite of these shrimp;
they bake in their shells, but the robust flavor
of the seasonings still seeps in.*

¼ cup butter
½ cup Italian dressing
2 tablespoons Worcestershire sauce
2 tablespoons barbecue sauce
1 tablespoon lemon-pepper seasoning
1 tablespoon pepper
4 cloves garlic, crushed
2 bay leaves
2 lemons, sliced
1 large onion, sliced
3 pounds unpeeled medium-size fresh
  shrimp

•Melt butter in a roasting pan at 400° (1 to 2
minutes). Add Italian dressing and next 8
ingredients; stir well. Add shrimp to pan,
stirring to coat.
•Bake, uncovered, at 400° for 20 minutes or
until shrimp turn pink, stirring occasionally.
Discard bay leaves. Yield: 6 servings.
Per serving: Calories 395 Fat 23g
Cholesterol 279mg Sodium 1239mg

Shrimp Scampi

PREP: 24 MINUTES   COOK: 9 MINUTES

*Scampi is a term for large shrimp dripping
with garlic butter. Serve these succulent
shrimp in shallow pasta bowls (shown on
page 210) so you can sop up the juices.*

2 pounds unpeeled large fresh shrimp
1 (8-ounce) package dried linguine
8 cloves garlic, minced
1 cup butter or margarine, melted
1 cup dry white wine
¼ teaspoon salt
⅛ teaspoon pepper
¼ cup chopped fresh parsley

•Peel shrimp, leaving tails intact; devein, if
desired. Cook linguine according to package
directions; keep warm.
•Cook garlic in butter and wine in a large
skillet over medium heat, stirring constantly,

4 minutes or until garlic begins to brown.
Add shrimp, and cook over medium heat 3
to 5 minutes or until shrimp turn pink. Add
salt and pepper, and spoon mixture over linguine. Sprinkle with chopped parsley, and
serve immediately. Yield: 4 servings.
Per serving: Calories 810 Fat 49.9g
Cholesterol 383mg Sodium 1024mg

Shrimp Destin

PREP: 26 MINUTES   COOK: 7 MINUTES

*This is a popular recipe during the summer
months. Pair the open-faced gourmet sandwiches with a green salad or fresh tomatoes.*

2 pounds unpeeled large fresh shrimp
⅓ cup chopped green onions
1 tablespoon minced garlic
1 cup butter or margarine, melted
2 tablespoons dry white wine
1 teaspoon lemon juice
⅛ teaspoon salt
¼ teaspoon coarsely ground pepper
1 tablespoon chopped fresh dill or 1
  teaspoon dried dillweed
1 tablespoon chopped fresh parsley
2 (3¼ ounce) French rolls, split lengthwise
  and toasted

•Peel shrimp, and devein, if desired. Set
aside.
•Sauté green onions and garlic in butter in a
large skillet over medium heat 2 minutes or
until tender.
•Add shrimp, wine, and next 3 ingredients.
Cook over medium heat 5 minutes or until
shrimp turn pink, stirring occasionally. Stir in
dill and parsley.
•Place toasted roll halves on four individual
serving plates. Spoon 1 cup shrimp mixture
over each roll, and serve immediately. Yield:
4 servings.
Per serving: Calories 728 Fat 49.9g
Cholesterol 384mg Sodium 1064mg

Note: You can serve Shrimp Destin over hot
cooked rice instead of rolls, if desired.

SHRIMP COUNT

•1 pound raw unpeeled shrimp
  = 12 ounces raw, peeled, deveined shrimp
  = 8 to 9 ounces cooked, peeled, deveined
    shrimp

Spicy Shrimp Creole

◄ FAMILY FAVORITE ►

PREP: 14 MINUTES   COOK: 53 MINUTES

*Creole refers to tomato in this spicy entrée
featuring New Orleans's best ingredients.*

1½ pounds unpeeled large fresh shrimp
5 slices bacon
1 small onion, finely chopped
1 small green pepper, finely chopped
1 small sweet red pepper, finely chopped
½ cup chopped celery
¼ cup chopped green onions
3 cloves garlic, minced
2 (16-ounce) cans Cajun-style stewed
  tomatoes
2 bay leaves
2 teaspoons Creole seasoning
¼ teaspoon salt
¼ teaspoon ground red pepper
4 cups hot cooked rice

•Peel shrimp, and devein, if desired; set
aside.
•Cook bacon in a large Dutch oven until
crisp; remove bacon, reserving drippings in
pan. Crumble bacon, and set aside.
•Cook onion and next 5 ingredients in drippings over medium-high heat 3 minutes or
until tender, stirring often. Stir in tomatoes
and next 4 ingredients. Bring to a boil;
cover, reduce heat, and simmer 40 minutes,
stirring occasionally.
•Add shrimp; cook 5 minutes or until
shrimp turn pink. Discard bay leaves.
•To serve, spoon rice into individual serving
bowls. Spoon shrimp mixture evenly over
rice. Yield: 4 servings.
Per serving: Calories 657 Fat 23.4g
Cholesterol 218mg Sodium 2700mg

Sweet-and-Sour Shrimp

◄ FAMILY FAVORITE ►

PREP: 23 MINUTES   COOK: 45 MINUTES

A homemade sweet-and-sour sauce accompanies these crispy fried shrimp. If time's a concern, there are plenty of commercial sweet-and-sour sauces on the market to choose from instead.

2 pounds unpeeled jumbo fresh shrimp
½ cup all-purpose flour
¼ cup cornstarch
½ teaspoon baking powder
¼ teaspoon salt
1 large egg, beaten
½ cup water
1 teaspoon vegetable oil
Vegetable oil
Sweet-and-Sour Sauce
6 cups hot cooked rice

• Peel shrimp, and devein, if desired. Combine flour and next 6 ingredients; stir well.
• Pour oil to depth of 2 inches into a Dutch oven; heat to 375°.
• Dip shrimp into batter; fry shrimp, a few at a time, 4 minutes or until golden. Drain on paper towels. Combine shrimp and Sweet-and-Sour Sauce. Serve over rice. Yield: 6 servings.

Per serving: Calories 718 Fat 22g
Cholesterol 172mg Sodium 1460mg

Sweet-and-Sour Sauce

½ cup sliced carrot
1 medium-size green pepper, cut into pieces
1 (15¼-ounce) can pineapple chunks, undrained
½ cup sugar
⅓ cup ketchup
1 tablespoon soy sauce
¼ teaspoon salt
3½ tablespoons cornstarch
⅓ cup water
½ cup white vinegar

• Cook carrot in a small amount of boiling water 1 to 2 minutes; add green pepper, and cook 1 more minute. Drain; rinse vegetables with cold water. Drain; set aside.
• Drain pineapple, reserving juice. Combine pineapple juice, sugar, and next 3 ingredients in a saucepan; bring to a boil. Combine cornstarch and water, stirring until smooth; add cornstarch mixture and vinegar to sauce mixture. Cook over medium heat, stirring constantly, until smooth and thickened. Stir in pineapple and vegetables. Yield: 3½ cups.

Clam-Stuffed Shrimp

PREP: 30 MINUTES   COOK: 20 MINUTES

Invest in jumbo shrimp here so you'll have room to heap the garlicky clam stuffing on top. There should be 16 jumbo shrimp to a pound.

1 pound unpeeled jumbo fresh shrimp
¾ cup round buttery cracker crumbs (15 crackers)
3 tablespoons butter or margarine, melted
1 (6½-ounce) can minced clams, drained
2 tablespoons chopped fresh parsley
⅛ teaspoon garlic powder
⅛ teaspoon salt
Dash of pepper
⅓ cup dry sherry

• Peel shrimp, leaving tails intact; devein, if desired. Cut a slit almost through back of shrimp. Open shrimp, and flatten. Set aside.
• Combine cracker crumbs and butter. Stir in clams and next 4 ingredients. Top each shrimp evenly with mixture.
• Place shrimp in an ungreased 11- x 7-inch baking dish. Bake at 350° for 20 minutes, basting occasionally with sherry. Serve immediately. Yield: 4 servings.

Per serving: Calories 244 Fat 13.3g
Cholesterol 161mg Sodium 448mg

Charleston-Style Shrimp Curry

PREP: 30 MINUTES   COOK: 45 MINUTES

Here's a classic curry that comes to life when sprinkled with condiments that add flavor and crunch.

9 cups water
3 pounds unpeeled large fresh shrimp
1 large onion, finely chopped
½ cup finely chopped apple
½ cup finely chopped celery
¼ cup butter or margarine, melted
1 cup water
2 cups whipping cream
2 tablespoons curry powder
½ teaspoon salt
⅛ teaspoon pepper
6 cups hot cooked rice
Assorted condiments: flaked coconut, toasted almonds, fig preserves, chutney, crumbled bacon, sliced bananas, raisins or currants, chopped hard-cooked egg

• Bring 9 cups water to a boil; add shrimp, and cook 3 to 5 minutes. Drain well; rinse with cold water. Cover and chill. Peel shrimp, and devein, if desired.
• Sauté onion, apple, and celery in butter 5 minutes; add 1 cup water. Cook, uncovered, over low heat 30 minutes or until most of liquid is absorbed.
• Stir in whipping cream, curry powder, salt, and pepper; simmer, uncovered, 10 minutes. Add shrimp, and simmer until thoroughly heated. Serve over rice with assorted condiments. Yield: 8 servings.

Per serving: Calories 571 Fat 29.5g
Cholesterol 284mg Sodium 1037mg

SCALLOPS

A scallop is a milky white delicacy that's shucked immediately after harvest because it never closes its shells once removed from the water.

There's a vast difference in the two sizes of scallops available. *Bay scallops* are the small, tender scallops with a delicate flavor. *Sea scallops* can be as large as 2 to 3 inches in diameter. The two types can be used interchangeably in recipes, but cooking times will vary.

Fresh scallops should have little liquor around them and should have a slightly sweet odor. Rinse them well before cooking, as sand accumulates in the crevices. Scallops are highly perishable, so store them loosely covered in the coldest part of the refrigerator, and use within two days of purchase.

Bay scallops are usually only available fresh. Count on 40 to a pound. You'll find sea scallops fresh or in the frozen foods section of your market. Allow ¼ to ⅓ pound of shucked scallops per person, whether they're the smaller bay scallops or the larger sea scallops.

Oven-Fried Scallops

PREP: 20 MINUTES   MARINATE: 30 MINUTES
COOK: 20 MINUTES

A light breading and a drizzle of butter over these big scallops mimic the golden coating you get from deep-frying.

12 sea scallops (about 1 pound)
2 tablespoons vegetable oil
2 tablespoons lemon juice
1 large egg, lightly beaten
2 tablespoons water
½ cup fine, dry breadcrumbs
     (commercial)
½ teaspoon salt
Dash of pepper
Dash of paprika
¼ cup butter or margarine, melted
Lemon wedges (optional)
Tartar sauce (optional)

•Place scallops in a small heavy-duty, zip-top plastic bag. Combine oil and lemon juice; pour over scallops. Seal bag; marinate in refrigerator 30 minutes, turning occasionally.
•Remove scallops from marinade, discarding marinade. Combine egg and water; stir well. Combine breadcrumbs and next 3 ingredients. Dip each scallop in egg mixture; dredge in breadcrumb mixture.
•Place scallops in a an ungreased 8-inch square pan. Drizzle butter over scallops. Bake, uncovered, at 450° for 15 to 20 minutes or until scallops are golden. If desired, serve with lemon wedges and tartar sauce. Yield: 4 servings.
Per serving: Calories 301 Fat 17.7g
Cholesterol 122mg Sodium 716mg

Baked Gruyère Scallops

◄ QUICK ►

PREP: 15 MINUTES   COOK: 10 MINUTES

1 pound bay scallops
¼ cup butter or margarine, melted and
     divided
1 medium onion, finely chopped
1 (8-ounce) package sliced fresh
     mushrooms
1½ cups (6 ounces) shredded Gruyère or
     Swiss cheese
½ cup mayonnaise
¼ cup dry white wine
1 tablespoon lemon juice

•Sauté scallops in 2 tablespoons butter in a large skillet 2 to 3 minutes. Drain and set aside.
•Sauté onion and mushrooms in remaining 2 tablespoons butter in skillet until tender; remove from heat. Add scallops, cheese, and remaining ingredients; stir well.
•Spoon mixture evenly into four lightly greased au gratin dishes. Broil 5½ inches from heat 2 to 3 minutes or until browned. Yield: 4 servings.
Per serving: Calories 344 Fat 19.2g
Cholesterol 96mg Sodium 375mg

Coquilles St. Jacques

◄ QUICK ►

PREP: 15 MINUTES   COOK: 8 MINUTES

Coquilles is French for scallop. These pearly white nuggets from the sea are bathed in a rich wine-cream sauce. Find baking shells at most kitchen shops; they make attractive individual servings.

1 cup dry white wine
1 tablespoon minced fresh parsley
1½ teaspoons chopped fresh thyme or
     ½ teaspoon dried thyme
1 bay leaf
¼ teaspoon coarsely ground pepper
1½ pounds bay scallops
¼ cup butter or margarine
¼ cup all-purpose flour
½ cup half-and-half
1 teaspoon lemon juice
1 tablespoon chopped fresh parsley
¼ teaspoon salt
¼ cup soft breadcrumbs (homemade)
¼ cup grated Parmesan cheese

•Combine first 5 ingredients in a large saucepan; bring to a boil. Add scallops; cook 2 minutes, stirring often. Discard bay leaf. Drain scallops, reserving liquid.
•Melt butter in saucepan over low heat; add flour, stirring until smooth. Cook 1 minute, stirring constantly. Gradually add reserved scallop liquid and half-and-half; cook over medium heat, stirring constantly, until mixture is thickened and bubbly. Stir in scallops, lemon juice, 1 tablespoon parsley, and salt.
•Spoon into six lightly greased individual baking dishes or baking shells. Sprinkle each with 2 teaspoons breadcrumbs and 2 teaspoons Parmesan cheese. Broil 3 inches from heat 1 to 2 minutes or until lightly browned. Yield: 6 servings.
Per serving: Calories 234 Fat 12g
Cholesterol 68mg Sodium 442mg

Grecian Scallops

PREP: 45 MINUTES   COOK: 15 MINUTES

Here's a Mediterranean dish smothered in a medley of pepper strips and gutsy Greek olives. Served with crusty French bread, it's a one-dish meal.

3 tablespoons olive oil, divided
1½ pounds sea scallops
¼ teaspoon salt
⅛ teaspoon freshly ground black
   pepper
2 green peppers, cut into thin strips
1 sweet red pepper, cut into thin
   strips
1 small onion, sliced
2 cloves garlic, minced
5 large plum tomatoes, coarsely chopped
   (about 1½ cups)
½ cup dry white wine
16 kalamata olives, pitted
2 teaspoons chopped fresh oregano
½ teaspoon fennel seeds
¼ teaspoon salt
⅛ teaspoon freshly ground black
   pepper
⅛ teaspoon dried crushed red
   pepper
6 ounces crumbled feta cheese

Grecian Scallops

•Coat four au gratin dishes with 1 tablespoon olive oil. Arrange scallops evenly in prepared dishes; sprinkle with ¼ teaspoon salt and ⅛ teaspoon pepper.
•Cook peppers, onion, and garlic in remaining 2 tablespoons oil in a large skillet over medium-high heat, stirring constantly, until tender. Add tomato and next 7 ingredients; stir well. Bring to a boil; reduce heat, and simmer, uncovered, 5 minutes.
•Spoon tomato mixture over scallops in dishes, and sprinkle feta cheese over each serving. Bake, uncovered, at 450° for 15 minutes or until scallops are white and cheese is lightly browned. Serve hot. Yield: 4 servings.
Per serving: Calories 419 Fat 23g Cholesterol 94mg Sodium 1207mg

CRABS

Known for their succulent white meat, crabs are second only to shrimp in seafood popularity in the United States.

Crabmeat comes from several types of crabs. The most common is the *blue crab,* which weighs about ½ pound. *Dungeness crabs* are the pride of the Pacific waters, from Alaska to Mexico. These large crabs range from 2 to 3 pounds each, while the *Alaskan king crab* weighs 10 pounds plus. Usually just the legs of Alaskan king crabs are sold and eaten. The *stone crab* comes in abundance from Florida waters. Its name comes from its rocklike oval shell. Only the claw meat of a stone crab is eaten.

Blue crabs (found along the Atlantic and Gulf coasts) are commonly eaten in their *soft-shell* state. There's a period of a few days between April and September in which blue crabs shed their hard shells to grow new, larger ones. During this brief time before the new shells harden, these softshells are considered a delicacy. Whether grilled or fried to a golden crispness, the entire crab is edible.

Crabs are available live, cooked fresh or frozen in the shell, and cooked fresh or frozen out of the shell. You can get cooked *lump* crabmeat (whole pieces of the white body meat) or cooked *flaked* crabmeat (small pieces of meat from the body and claws).

Crabmeat should have very little odor when fresh. Use it within a day of purchase. For a lesson in removing meat from a whole cooked, hard-shell crab, see our photos on the next page.

HOW TO REMOVE CRABMEAT

1. To get to cooked meat, first twist off crab legs and claws intact. Crack claws, and remove meat with a small cocktail fork.

2. Invert the crab, and pry off the apron (or tail flap), and discard it. Turn crab right side up again.

3. Insert thumb under shell by apron hinge; pry off the top shell, and discard it.

4. Pull away the inedible gray gills; discard them along with internal organs. Break the body; remove meat from pockets.

Fried Soft-Shell Crabs

PREP: 40 MINUTES   COOK: 20 MINUTES

When crabs are in their molting state, they shed their hard outer shell, leaving a soft shell, which is entirely edible. You'll see this dish in many Southern restaurants.

12 fresh soft-shell crabs
3 large eggs
½ teaspoon ground black pepper
1½ cups cornmeal
1 cup all-purpose flour
2 teaspoons baking powder
¾ teaspoon salt
½ teaspoon ground black pepper
½ teaspoon garlic powder
⅛ teaspoon ground red pepper
Vegetable oil

•To clean crabs, remove spongy gills that lie under the tapering points on either side of back shell. Place crabs on back, and remove the small piece at lower part of shell that terminates in a point (the apron). Wash crabs thoroughly; drain well.
•Combine eggs and ½ teaspoon black pepper in a large shallow dish. Add crabs, turning to coat. Let stand 10 minutes.
•Combine cornmeal and next 6 ingredients. Remove crabs from egg mixture, and dredge in cornmeal mixture. Let stand 5 minutes; dredge in cornmeal mixture again.
•Pour oil to depth of ½ inch into a large heavy skillet or electric skillet; heat oil to

375°. Fry crabs 2 minutes on each side or until browned. Drain; serve immediately. Yield: 1 dozen.
Per crab: Calories 302 Fat 20.5g
Cholesterol 78mg Sodium 313mg

Steamed Blue Crabs

PREP: 10 MINUTES   COOK: 35 MINUTES

¼ cup plus 2 tablespoons Old Bay seasoning
¼ cup plus 2 tablespoons coarse salt
3 tablespoons red pepper
3 tablespoons pickling spice
2 tablespoons celery seeds
1 tablespoon crushed red pepper (optional)
White vinegar
12 live hard-shell blue crabs
Lemon Butter (page 388)

•Combine first 6 ingredients; set aside.
•Combine water and vinegar in equal amounts to a depth of 1 inch in a very large pot with a lid; bring to a boil. Place a rack in pot over boiling liquid; arrange half of crabs on rack. Sprinkle with half of seasoning mixture. Top with remaining crabs, and sprinkle with remaining seasoning mixture.
•Cover tightly, and steam 20 to 25 minutes or until crabs turn bright red. Rinse with cold water, and drain well. Serve crabs hot or cold with Lemon Butter. Yield: 1 dozen.
Per crab: Calories 37 Fat 0.8g
Cholesterol 300mg Sodium 824mg

Jumbo Crab Cakes

◄ QUICK • FAMILY FAVORITE ►

PREP: 18 MINUTES   COOK: 13 MINUTES

3 large eggs, lightly beaten
½ cup finely chopped onion
1 cup finely chopped sweet red or green pepper
3 tablespoons white wine Worcestershire sauce
1 teaspoon dry mustard
½ teaspoon ground red pepper
1 lemon, halved
1 pound fresh lump crabmeat, drained
1½ cups Italian-seasoned breadcrumbs, divided
¼ cup butter or margarine, divided
Cucumber Cream Sauce (page 389) or Tartar Sauce (page 390)
Garnish: fresh parsley sprigs

•Combine first 6 ingredients; stir in juice of one-half lemon, crabmeat, and 1 cup breadcrumbs. Shape into 8 (4-inch) patties; dredge patties in remaining breadcrumbs.
•Fry 4 patties in 2 tablespoons melted butter in a large skillet over medium heat 3 minutes on each side or until golden; drain. Melt remaining 2 tablespoons butter in skillet, and fry remaining 4 patties.
•Cut remaining lemon half into wedges. Serve crab with lemon wedges and desired sauce. Garnish, if desired. Yield: 8 servings.
Per crab cake: Calories 254 Fat 12.3g
Cholesterol 151mg Sodium 849mg

Deviled Crab

PREP: 1 HOUR AND 15 MINUTES

COOK: 20 MINUTES

¾ cup chopped celery
¾ cup chopped onion
¼ cup chopped sweet red pepper
⅓ cup butter or margarine, melted
1 pound fresh lump crabmeat, drained
1 cup saltine cracker crumbs, divided
½ cup chopped fresh parsley
¼ cup whipping cream
1 tablespoon Dijon mustard
1 teaspoon dry mustard
½ teaspoon freshly ground black pepper
½ teaspoon hot sauce
¼ teaspoon salt
1 tablespoon butter or margarine, melted
Paprika
Lemon wedges (optional)

•Cook first 3 ingredients in ⅓ cup butter in a large skillet over medium-high heat, stirring constantly, until tender. Remove from heat. Gently stir in crabmeat, ¾ cup cracker crumbs, and parsley.
•Combine whipping cream and next 5 ingredients; gently stir into crabmeat mixture. Spoon into six baking shells or individual baking dishes.

•Brown remaining ¼ cup cracker crumbs in 1 tablespoon butter in a small skillet over medium heat, stirring often. Sprinkle each serving with cracker crumbs and paprika. Bake, uncovered, at 350° for 15 to 20 minutes or until thoroughly heated. Serve with lemon wedges, if desired. Yield: 6 servings.
Per serving: Calories 274 Fat 18.7g
Cholesterol 113mg Sodium 680mg

Crab Imperial

PREP: 1 HOUR   COOK: 30 MINUTES

2 tablespoons chopped onion
2 tablespoons chopped green pepper
3 tablespoons butter or margarine
2 tablespoons all-purpose flour
½ cup milk
1 pound fresh lump crabmeat, drained
¼ cup mayonnaise
1 teaspoon Old Bay seasoning
¼ teaspoon black pepper
¼ teaspoon Worcestershire sauce
Dash of hot sauce
1 tablespoon dry sherry (optional)
Paprika

•Sauté onion and green pepper in butter in a large skillet until tender.

•Combine flour and milk, stirring well. Add to vegetable mixture; cook, stirring constantly, 1 to 2 minutes or until mixture is thickened.
•Add crabmeat and next 5 ingredients. Stir in sherry, if desired. Spoon mixture into a greased 1-quart baking dish or four individual baking shells. Sprinkle with paprika.
•Bake, uncovered, at 350° for 20 minutes or until thoroughly heated. Yield: 4 servings.
Per serving: Calories 313 Fat 22.5g
Cholesterol 135mg Sodium 606mg

WHAT IS SEAFOOD MIX?

It's often called surimi, this low-cost fish (mostly pollock) that's formed into the shape and texture of higher quality and higher priced seafood. The advantages of seafood mix are that it's generally low in fat and cholesterol, fully cooked, and ready to eat. Find it in the supermarket as fresh or frozen imitation crab-flavored flaked seafood. One drawback to this seafood mix is that during processing, the sodium often increases six to 10 times that of fresh seafood. You can substitute seafood mix for most recipes that use flaked crabmeat.

OYSTERS, MUSSELS & CLAMS

The *bivalves*—oysters, mussels, and clams—offer a stunning presentation when served from their shapely shells. And there's a simple pleasure that comes from extracting the plump meat. Please a crowd by serving fresh steamed shellfish accompanied with a simple sauce, broth, or pasta.

There are many ways to cook shellfish, and each type has its own set of rules for cleaning and cooking.

You can purchase oysters, mussels, and hard-shelled clams live in the shell. They're displayed on beds of crushed ice in the market and will keep their shells tightly closed once harvested from the water. If mussel and clam shells are broken or open and don't close when lightly tapped, discard them. If oysters are live, their shells will be tightly closed. Discard any with open shells.

Oysters and clams are available fresh shucked or shucked and canned. If they're fresh shucked and in their liquor, don't discard the liquor; it contains flavor you can add to the recipe.

Fresh shucked oysters should be plump, uniform in size, have good color, smell fresh, and be packed in clear, not cloudy, oyster liquor.

Oysters are graded by size. The smaller the oyster, the younger and more tender it will be. Fresh oysters are available year-round, but are best during the fall and winter months because oysters spawn during the summer and become soft and fatty. Allow six live oysters in the shell per person or ⅓ to ½ pint of shucked oysters per serving. The same serving sizes apply for clams and mussels.

Crusty Fried Oysters

◀ QUICK • FAMILY FAVORITE ▶

PREP: 12 MINUTES   COOK: 20 MINUTES

1 large egg, beaten
2 tablespoons cold water
1 (12-ounce) container fresh Select oysters, drained
1½ cups saltine cracker crumbs
Vegetable oil

•Combine egg and water. Dip oysters in egg mixture, and roll each in cracker crumbs.
•Deep-fry in 375° oil, a few at a time, about 2 minutes or until golden, turning to brown both sides. Drain on paper towels. Yield: 3 servings.
Per serving: Calories 591 Fat 45.3g
Cholesterol 123mg Sodium 772mg

1. To open oyster, insert oyster knife between top and bottom shells next to hinge; twist knife to pry shells apart.

2. Scrape knife between the oyster and the bottom shell to free the meat.

Easy Baked Oysters

◄ QUICK ►

PREP: 15 MINUTES   COOK: 12 MINUTES

A simple dressing of breadcrumbs, butter, and cheese transforms these oysters into a golden and delicious dinner.

⅓ cup butter or margarine, melted
1 large egg
¼ cup milk
¼ teaspoon salt
¼ teaspoon pepper
1 (12-ounce) container fresh Select oysters, drained
½ cup fine, dry breadcrumbs (commercial)
¼ cup (1 ounce) shredded Monterey Jack cheese
1 tablespoon chopped fresh parsley
⅛ teaspoon paprika

•Pour melted butter into an 11- x 7-inch baking dish.
•Combine egg and next 3 ingredients in a small bowl; beat with a wire whisk until blended. Dip each oyster in egg mixture, and dredge in breadcrumbs. Place oyster in baking dish; turn to coat with butter. Top oysters evenly with cheese, parsley, and paprika.
•Bake at 425° for 10 to 12 minutes or until lightly browned. Yield: 4 servings.
Per serving: Calories 289 Fat 21.7g Cholesterol 141mg Sodium 551mg

Low-Country Paella

PREP: 25 MINUTES   COOK: 50 MINUTES

Paella is Spain's one-dish meal; the name comes from the pan it's cooked in. If you don't have a paella pan, just use a large Dutch oven.

1 pound skinned, boned chicken breast halves, cut in half
3 tablespoons vegetable oil or olive oil
1 pound mild Italian sausage, casings removed
1 large green pepper, chopped
1 clove garlic, minced
2 large tomatoes, chopped
1 (8-ounce) bottle clam juice
2 cups water
1 large onion, chopped (about 2½ cups)
1 pound unpeeled medium-size fresh shrimp
6 cherrystone clams (about 2 pounds)
Dash of powdered saffron
1 teaspoon salt
1 teaspoon black pepper
1 cup uncooked long-grain rice
1 (10-ounce) package frozen English peas, thawed

•Brown chicken in oil in a Dutch oven over medium-high heat; remove chicken from pan, reserving drippings. Sauté sausage, green pepper, and garlic in drippings until tender; remove sausage mixture from pan with a slotted spoon. Add tomato, and cook over low heat 5 minutes, stirring occasionally.
•Add clam juice, water, and onion to tomato mixture; bring to a boil. Reduce heat, and add chicken and sausage mixture. Cook over low heat 15 minutes, stirring occasionally.

Cleaning clams: Scrub clams under cold running water with a stiff brush to remove sand and dirt. Shuck clams; release meat from bottom shells.

•Peel shrimp, and devein, if desired; scrub clams well with a brush (see photo above). Discard opened or cracked clams or any heavy ones (they're filled with sand).
•Add saffron and next 3 ingredients to chicken mixture. Cook over high heat, without stirring, 15 to 20 minutes. Add shrimp, clams, and peas; cook 5 minutes or until shrimp turn pink and clams open. Discard unopened clams.
•Remove pan from heat, and let stand, covered, until liquid is absorbed and rice is tender. Yield: 6 servings.
Per serving: Calories 656 Fat 29g Cholesterol 193mg Sodium 1376mg

Mussels Steamed in Wine

PREP: 35 MINUTES   COOK: 24 MINUTES

Inside each black shell hides a tender bite of meat, which drinks in the shallot-wine sauce.

6 dozen raw mussels in shells
½ cup butter, divided
1 large onion, chopped
2 shallots, chopped
2 cloves garlic, minced
2½ cups finely chopped fresh parsley
½ teaspoon freshly ground pepper
1½ cups dry white wine
½ cup fresh lemon juice

•Scrub mussels with a brush; remove beards (see photo next page). Discard cracked or heavy mussels (they're filled with sand), or opened mussels that won't close when tapped.
•Melt ¼ cup butter in a large Dutch oven over medium-high heat. Add mussels, onion,

and next 5 ingredients. Cover and cook 4 minutes or until mussels open, shaking pan several times.

•Transfer mussels to a serving dish with a slotted spoon, discarding any unopened mussels. Cover and keep warm.

•Pour remaining liquid in pan through a strainer into a large skillet, discarding parsley mixture. Bring to a boil. Cook 20 minutes or until thickened. Remove from heat; whisk in remaining butter. Stir in lemon juice; pour over mussels. Yield: 6 servings.

Per serving: Calories 194 Fat 16.6g Cholesterol 58mg Sodium 327mg

Evaluating opened mussels: Thump an opened shell; if it closes, mussel is still alive and fine to use. Discard any that refuse to close.

Debearding a mussel: Grasp the hairlike beard with your thumb and forefinger; pull it away from shell.

LOBSTER

There are two types of lobster found in American waters. The meatiest and most popular *American lobster* has a bluish-black shell and large claws with sharp pincers. This lobster contains a good bit of claw meat in addition to succulent tail meat. The *spiny lobster* has a reddish-brown shell and no claws. It contains meat in its tail only. Both types turn bright red when cooked. You can purchase lobsters live, fresh or frozen cooked in the shell, or cooked, shelled, and canned.

Whole lobsters should be purchased alive and kept alive until you're ready to cook them. Live lobsters should be moving and should curl their tails when they are lifted from water. Count on about one serving per 1 pound of lobster.

PREPARING LIVE LOBSTER

1. Grasp live lobster just behind the eyes with long tongs. Plunge lobster, head-first, into boiling water.

2. Place lobster on its back. Twist the body and tail shell apart. Using kitchen shears, cut the body shell open.

3. Scoop out the green tomalley (liver) and the coral roe (in female lobster only).

4. Using kitchen shears, cut down center of shell on tail underside to expose meat. Pull meat from shell in one piece.

5. Cut ¼ inch deep along outer curve of tail meat to expose intestinal vein. Discard vein.

6. Crack the claws with a seafood cracker or nut cracker, and extract the claw meat.

Boiled Lobster

PREP: 15 MINUTES   COOK: 10 MINUTES

2 (1-pound) live lobsters
3 quarts water
2 tablespoons salt
Clarified Butter (page 388)

•Plunge lobsters headfirst into boiling salted water (photo 1); return water to a boil. Cover, reduce heat, and simmer 10 minutes. Drain.

•Place lobster on its back; twist the body and tail shell apart; then cut the body shell open (photo 2). Remove liver and coral roe (photo 3). Remove meat from tail shell (photo 4). Remove intestinal vein that runs from the stomach to tip of the tail (photo 5). Crack claws, using a seafood cracker or nut cracker (photo 6). Serve with Clarified Butter. Yield: 2 servings.

Per serving: Calories 497 Fat 47.0g Cholesterol 219mg Sodium 2020mg

Lobster Thermidor

◄ QUICK ►

PREP: 4 MINUTES   COOK: 19 MINUTES

This lobster dish is sauced in a creamy béchamel that's flavored with wine, shallots, tarragon, and mustard. Before serving, spoon mixture back into shells, cap with a sprinkling of cheese, and broil until golden.

2 quarts water
3 (8- to 10-ounce) fresh or frozen lobster
     tails, thawed
2 tablespoons chopped shallot
3 tablespoons butter or margarine, melted
2 tablespoons all-purpose flour
1¼ cups half-and-half
1 tablespoon chopped fresh tarragon or
     1 teaspoon dried tarragon
2 tablespoons dry sherry
1 teaspoon dry mustard
¼ teaspoon salt
Dash of ground red pepper
⅓ cup freshly grated Parmesan cheese

•Bring water to a boil in a Dutch oven; add lobster tails. Cover, reduce heat, and simmer 12 minutes. Remove lobster tails with tongs; rinse with cold water, and drain. Split tails lengthwise. Remove meat, and cut into ½-inch pieces. Set aside. Reserve shells.
•Sauté shallot in melted butter in a large skillet until tender. Add flour, stirring until smooth. Cook 1 minute, stirring constantly. Gradually add half-and-half; cook over medium heat, stirring constantly, until mixture is thickened and bubbly. Stir in lobster meat, tarragon, and next 4 ingredients. Spoon mixture into reserved shells or three large greased baking shells or ovenproof dishes; sprinkle with Parmesan cheese. Broil 5½ inches from heat 3 to 5 minutes or until lightly browned. Yield: 3 servings.

Per serving: Calories 415 Fat 26.4g
Cholesterol 161mg Sodium 955mg

Lobster Newburg

PREP: 28 MINUTES   COOK: 25 MINUTES

1 (10-ounce) package frozen puff pastry
     shells
2 quarts water
4 (8-ounce) frozen lobster tails, thawed
1 cup sliced fresh mushrooms
¼ cup chopped green onions
¼ cup minced green pepper
2 tablespoons butter, melted
1 (2-ounce) jar diced pimiento, drained
¼ cup dry sherry
2 tablespoons butter
1 tablespoon all-purpose flour
1 cup whipping cream
½ teaspoon dry mustard
¼ teaspoon ground nutmeg
¼ teaspoon salt
⅛ teaspoon ground red pepper
Dash of paprika

•Bake puff pastry shells according to package directions. Cool on wire racks.
•Bring water to a boil in a Dutch oven; add lobster tails. Return to a boil; cook 5 to 6 minutes. Remove lobster tails with tongs; rinse with cold water, and drain. Split tails lengthwise. Remove and coarsely chop meat. Set aside.
•Cook mushrooms, green onions, and green pepper in 2 tablespoons melted butter in a large skillet over medium-high heat, stirring constantly, 2 minutes or until vegetables are tender. Stir pimiento and sherry into vegetable mixture, and cook 1 minute. Remove from heat; set aside.
•Melt 2 tablespoons butter in a heavy saucepan over low heat; add flour, stirring until smooth. Cook 1 minute, stirring constantly. Gradually add whipping cream; cook over medium heat, stirring constantly, 2 minutes or until mixture is slightly thickened and bubbly. Stir in vegetable mixture. Combine mustard and remaining 4 ingredients; add to sauce mixture. Stir lobster meat into sauce mixture; cook just until heated.
•Spoon lobster mixture evenly into pastry shells. Yield: 6 servings.

Per serving: Calories 513 Fat 36.9g
Cholesterol 121mg Sodium 574mg

Crab-Stuffed Lobster Tails

PREP: 34 MINUTES   COOK: 30 MINUTES

2 quarts water
1 tablespoon salt
2 (1½- to 1¾-pound) live lobsters
½ pound fresh lump crabmeat
1 clove garlic, minced
1 tablespoon chopped fresh parsley
2 tablespoons freshly grated Parmesan
     cheese
2 tablespoons fine, dry breadcrumbs
     (commercial)
¼ teaspoon Old Bay seasoning
¼ teaspoon pepper
2 tablespoons butter, melted
1 teaspoon lemon juice
Garlic-Butter Sauce (page 388)
Garnishes: lemon halves, fresh flat-leaf
     parsley sprigs

•Combine water and salt in a large Dutch oven; bring to a boil. Plunge lobsters head-first into boiling water; return to a boil. Cover, reduce heat, and simmer 10 minutes; drain and cool.
•Break off large claws and legs. Crack claw and leg shells, using a seafood or nut cracker; remove meat, and set aside. Break off tail. Cut top side of tail shell lengthwise, using kitchen shears. Cut through center of meat, and remove vein. Leave meat in shell or for easier serving, loosen and lift meat out of shell. Return meat to shell intact. Rinse and set aside.
•Drain crabmeat, removing any bits of shell. Combine crabmeat, garlic, and next 7 ingredients; toss gently. Spoon into lobster tails. Place on a baking sheet.
•Bake at 400° for 12 minutes or until thoroughly heated. Serve with Garlic-Butter Sauce and claw and leg meat. Garnish, if desired. Yield: 2 servings.

Per serving: Calories 843 Fat 67.1g
Cholesterol 370mg Sodium 2164mg

CRAWFISH & FROG LEGS

Crawfish, also called *crayfish* (and *craw-dads* in Louisiana), are tiny crustaceans that resemble lobsters. Louisiana has been known to claim itself "crawfish capital of the world" as much of our nation's supply is harvested from its nearby waters.

Crawfish can be prepared by most of the same methods as lobster and, like lobster, will turn bright red when cooked. Crawfish are usually eaten with your fingers, and the sweet bites of meat must be picked or sucked out of the tiny shells.

Gigging for frogs is a favorite pastime of Floridians, though the only edible part of the frog is its hind legs. The delicate white meat has been compared to that of a very young chicken. The meat is usually sold in connected pairs. You can store frog legs in the refrigerator up to two days. Frozen frog legs are available year-round. Thaw them overnight in the refrigerator before use.

Crawfish Boil

◄ QUICK • HEALTHY ►

PREP: 10 MINUTES COOK: 10 MINUTES

They're called mudbugs in Cajun country. And to capture the Louisiana flair, this recipe presents them whole, so you can peel and eat them at the table for traditional regional ambiance. A thick covering of newspaper is the tablecloth of choice.

1 onion, quartered
1 lemon, quartered
1 clove garlic, halved
1 bay leaf
6 cups water
1 tablespoon salt
2 teaspoons ground red pepper
2 pounds whole crawfish

•Tie first 4 ingredients in a cheesecloth bag. Place cheesecloth bag in a large Dutch oven, and add water, salt, and red pepper; bring to a boil, and boil 5 minutes. Add crawfish, and cook 5 minutes. Drain crawfish; peel and serve warm or chilled. Yield: 3 servings.
Per serving: Calories 65 Fat 0.8g
Cholesterol 101mg Sodium 429mg

Crawfish Étouffée

PREP: 15 MINUTES   COOK: 35 MINUTES

2 pounds crawfish tails with fat
2 teaspoons hot sauce
¼ teaspoon ground red pepper
¼ cup vegetable oil
¼ cup all-purpose flour
2 stalks celery, chopped
2 large onions, chopped
2 large green peppers, chopped
½ cup chopped green onions
¼ cup water
½ teaspoon salt
¼ teaspoon ground black pepper
¼ teaspoon ground red pepper
¼ cup chopped fresh parsley
4 cups hot cooked rice

•Remove package of fat from crawfish tails, and set aside. Sprinkle crawfish with hot sauce and ¼ teaspoon red pepper; set aside.
•Combine oil and flour in a 4-quart Dutch oven; cook over medium heat, stirring constantly, until roux is chocolate-colored (10 to 15 minutes).
•Stir in celery and next 3 ingredients; cook until vegetables are tender, stirring often. Add crawfish tails and water; cook, uncovered, over low heat 15 minutes, stirring occasionally. Stir in 2 tablespoons crawfish fat (reserve remaining fat for other uses), salt, black pepper, and red pepper; simmer 5 minutes. Stir in parsley. Serve over rice. Yield: 6 servings.
Per serving: Calories 387 Fat 14.6g
Cholesterol 50mg Sodium 763mg

CRAWFISH COUNT

• 1 pound unpeeled whole crawfish
  = 3 to 4 ounces peeled tail meat
• 1 pound unpeeled crawfish tails
  = 10 ounces (just over 1 cup) peeled tail meat
• 1 pound peeled crawfish tails
  = 1 to 2 cups meat

Crispy Fried Frog Legs

PREP: 8 MINUTES   CHILL: 3 HOURS
COOK: 15 MINUTES

Frog legs fry into a delicacy that looks and tastes much like fried chicken. Southern restaurants put frog legs on their menus, and you will, too, once you've tried them.

2½ pounds small frog legs
½ cup lemon juice or white
   vinegar
Crushed ice
⅓ cup milk
2 large eggs, separated
2 teaspoons olive oil or vegetable oil
Salt and pepper
2¼ cups all-purpose flour
Vegetable oil

•Wash frog legs thoroughly. Place in a large Dutch oven; sprinkle with lemon juice, and cover with crushed ice. Chill frog legs 1 to 3 hours.
•Combine milk, egg yolks, and 2 teaspoons oil; mix well. Beat egg whites at high speed with an electric mixer until stiff; fold into batter.
•Sprinkle frog legs with salt and pepper; dip each in batter, and dredge in flour. Pour oil to depth of 2 to 3 inches into a large Dutch oven; heat to 375°. Deep-fry frog legs, in batches, until golden. Drain on paper towels. Yield: 6 servings.
Per serving: Calories 458 Fat 22.6g
Cholesterol 136mg Sodium 294mg

Filet Mignons with Shiitake
Madeira Sauce (page 237)

MEATS

*America's appetite for meat is healthier than ever. And it's no surprise at
a time when beef and pork are showing up lean. The cook's challenge is
to keep the meat tender and juicy. These pages tell you how to achieve
optimum results every time.*

Equipment

To stock your kitchen for basic meat cookery, you'll need a small and a large roasting pan, with racks that you can use for dry heat roasting; they won't have a lid. You'll also want a few heavy skillets and a large sauté pan for panfrying and a multitude of other uses. A Dutch oven or a braising pan are all-purpose pans you'll use often.

A meat mallet is the tool to use for pounding pieces to perfect tenderness, but a rolling pin will work in a pinch. A regular meat thermometer or an instant-read thermometer will tell you when the meat's properly done. A pair of spring-loaded metal tongs will allow you to turn meat without piercing it. And it goes without saying that a set of sharp knives and a carving set will come in handy on countless occasions.

Selecting Meat

Meat inspection is not synonymous with *meat grading*. Meat inspection guarantees meat wholesomeness, safety, and accurate labeling. All meat that is sold must by law be inspected. Meat grading is a voluntary program in which beef, veal, and lamb are evaluated to help determine their palatability.

Grading is based on the amount of marbling present throughout the meat, the age of the animal, texture, color, and appearance. You'll find the meat's grade in a shield-shaped stamp indicating, in descending order of grade, Prime, Choice, Select, Standard, Commercial, Utility, Cutter, and Canner. Each grade denotes a specific level of quality as determined by the United States Department of Agriculture.

While there are eight quality grades, only three are typically found at retail—Prime, Choice, and Select. Prime meat has the most marbling and is usually sold to restaurants; however, it is available through some specialty markets. Choice is what you typically see in the marketplace. Grades below Standard are used by packers of processed meats and aren't available at retail meat counters.

Pork is not graded at the consumer level because much of it is processed into sausage and ham and carries a packer's guarantee of quality.

The color of the animal's meat is caused by the amount of a protein, myoglobin, in the animal's muscle. Myoglobin binds oxygen in the cells. Meat color is directly affected by this protein; when myoglobin is exposed to oxygen (air) it creates oxymyoglobin, which is responsible for the bright red color in fresh meat. A darker, purplish-red color is typical of vacuum-packaged meat due to the lack of oxygen. Once open and exposed to the air, meat will turn from dark red to bright red.

When shopping, choose meat last before checking out. Make sure the package is cold, without any tears. Select meat that doesn't have excessive juice in the package. Check the "sell by" date; for highest quality, buy before that date.

When buying meat, consider the cost per serving rather than the cost per pound. A substantial amount of fat and bone in cheaper cuts of meat reduces the amount of edible meat, which actually makes some more expensive cuts the better buy.

Boneless cuts, such as stew meat, ground beef, and boneless roasts and steaks, usually serve three to four people per pound. Steaks and roasts with a moderate amount of bone will serve two to three people per pound. Bone-in cuts like ribs will give 1 to 1½ servings per pound.

Storing and Freezing Meat

Place meat in the coldest part of your refrigerator as soon as possible (within 30 minutes) after purchase. Prepackaged meat can be stored unopened in its original wrapping. Use ground meat within two days, and larger roasts and steaks within two to four days. You can otherwise freeze it, without rewrapping, and use it within two weeks. For longer freezing, over wrap the original package with moisture-proof, vapor-proof freezer paper. Roasts and steaks will stay fresh in the freezer six to 12 months. Label packages with the date, cut, and weight or number of servings.

Freeze ground meat or stew meat up to three months. Leftover cooked meat will maintain good quality up to three months in the freezer. Never refreeze meat that has been frozen and thawed.

Cooking Methods for Meat

To determine the best way to cook a cut of meat, it's important to know whether the cut is classified as "tender" or "less tender."

Tenderness is determined by the location of the cut on the carcass. Tender cuts come mainly from the rib, loin, and short loin sections—the areas along the backbone. These sections include the more costly cuts, such as rib-eye steaks, rib roast, and sirloin steaks. Use *dry-heat* cooking methods, which are suitable for tender cuts. They are roasting, broiling, panbroiling, and panfrying.

The less tender cuts, usually less expensive, include the chuck, foreshank, brisket, short plate, tip, and round. These are taken from the shoulder, legs, breast, and flanks—areas that have heavy muscle development. The additional muscle or connective tissue makes the cuts from these areas tougher. By using the proper *moist-heat* cooking methods, you can easily make these cuts fork-tender. Braising and stewing in liquids make tough cuts, such as round steak, tender. Below are specifics on the various cooking methods.

Roasting: Cooking, uncovered, by dry heat in an oven without the addition of liquid. Place meat, fat side up, on a rack in a shallow roasting pan. (The fat will self-baste the meat during cooking.) Insert meat thermometer, if desired, into meaty part, not in fat or touching bone. Roast to desired doneness. Roasting is best for large tender cuts of meat such as rib roast, rolled rump roast, and tenderloin.

Broiling: Cooking by direct heat in an oven. Set the oven on broil. Place meat 3 to 5 inches from heat source (depending on thickness of meat), and broil until brown. The meat should be about half cooked. Turn, season, and broil to desired degree of doneness. Broiling is best for tender rib-eye steaks, porterhouse steaks, sirloin steaks, and ground meat patties. It's a naturally low-fat cooking method. If you choose to broil less tender cuts such as flank steak or top round steak, be sure to marinate them before broiling.

Panbroiling: Cooking by direct heat in a pan or on a griddle. Do not add fat or water to skillet unless the cut is lean and some fat is needed to prevent sticking. Cook slowly over medium-low heat, turning occasionally, making sure meat browns evenly. Don't let fat accumulate in pan as you cook, or you'll be frying instead of panbroiling. Use this method for cooking the same cuts of meat as for broiling.

Panfrying: Cooking meats in a small amount of fat in a sauté pan over medium heat. (For deep-frying, use enough oil to completely cover the meat in a deep heavy skillet or Dutch oven.) Panfrying is best for tender thin pieces of meat like cubed steaks and veal cutlets.

Braising: Cooking slowly in a small amount of liquid. The slow cooking and moist heat are vital to tenderizing tough cuts of meat.

First brown the meat in a small amount of fat; then add liquid. Cover the meat with a tight-fitting lid, and simmer until tender. Top and bottom round steaks, flank steak, eye of round, arm pot roasts, and blade roasts are all good choices for braising.

Stewing/Cooking in Liquid: Cooking in liquid that completely covers the meat. First brown the meat in a small amount of fat; then add enough liquid to cover. Cover the meat with a tight-fitting lid, and simmer gently until tender. Do not let the water boil; boiling tends to dry out meat and increase shrinkage. If vegetables are part of the recipe, add them near the end of the cooking time so they won't overcook. Corned beef, beef brisket, and stew meat are best cooked in liquid.

Grilling: You can grill over direct heat or indirect heat. Grilling imparts a marvelous smoky flavor to meats. Whether you use a charcoal grill or gas grill, the meat's fat drips down onto the hot coals and creates smoke that rises up to infuse flavor into the meat. For more information, you can read about grills and smokers on page 10.

Tenderizing Meat

There are several techniques you can use to make less tender cuts of meat more tender. Then you can consider cooking them by dry heat as well as moist heat methods.

Consider marinating meat in an acidic mixture such as wine, vinegar, or citrus juice. The acid component breaks down the connective tissue of the meat and makes it more tender. Let the meat marinate several hours in the refrigerator before cooking. Don't let it marinate longer than a recipe directs or the texture of the meat can break down too much.

Pounding meat with a meat mallet (or rolling pin) is another way of tenderizing its connective tissue. To pound meat, we recommend placing it between sheets of heavy-duty plastic wrap or in a large zip-top plastic bag; then cleanup is easy. Having the butcher run thin cuts of meat through a cubing machine serves the same function.

Commercial meat tenderizers are also available. They are derivatives of certain tropical fruits that contain papain, a natural tenderizing agent. Be sure to follow package directions, though, as meat can quickly become mushy if too much tenderizer is applied or left too long on the meat.

Using a Thermometer and Determining Doneness

There are two types of thermometers that you can use to check the internal temperature of meat for doneness. One is a *meat thermometer* that is inserted prior to cooking and left in the meat during the entire cooking process; the other is an *instant-read thermometer*, which is not oven-safe. Insert an instant-read thermometer toward the end of cooking time, leave it in 10 seconds, check temperature, and remove it.

For most meats, medium-rare doneness is 145° to 150°, medium is 160°, and well-done is 170°. Medium-rare meat will be very pink in the center. Meat cooked to medium will be light pink in the center, and the outer portion will be brown. Well-done meat will be uniformly brown throughout.

BEEF

Beef offers more variety in cuts and cooking methods than any other type of meat. And thanks to better breeding and feeding practices, beef is also leaner and healthier than ever. Roasts and steaks are being trimmed more closely before you buy them, thus offering more lean meat.

There are more than 60 beef cuts available in the meat case today, providing enough variety to satisfy all tastes and budgets. Choosing the right cut can, however, be confusing. It will benefit you to become familiar with common cuts of beef and their optimum cooking methods. Read the "Cooking Methods for Meat" section on the previous page to distinguish between tender and less tender cuts and moist and dry heat methods. Refer to the identification chart on the next page to help you locate cuts of beef in the supermarket.

Beef should have bright red meat and white fat. Vacuum-packaged beef and the interior of ground beef will look darker because the meat is not in direct contact with air. Once opened and exposed to air, the meat should turn bright red.

The meat should be fine-textured, firm to the touch, and slightly moist. Tender meat will have *marbling* throughout. Marbling is a layering of fat that's evenly distributed in meat. It makes beef tender, juicy, and flavorful. Unfortunately, the higher the amount of marbling in beef, the higher the fat and calories. Leaner cuts of beef with less marbling offer a healthier choice, but can easily be overcooked. Always consider tenderizing a lean cut or using a moist heat cooking method.

Beef cuts from the center of the animal are the *loin* and *rib* sections. They're muscles that receive very little exercise, so they're naturally tender and are best cooked by dry heat methods. Tenderloin, rib roast, and rib-eye roasts and steaks are common cuts. The *chuck* and *round* sections are cuts from the front and rear of the animal that are responsible for movement. These muscles are heavily exercised; therefore they're less tender and require moist heat cooking. Round steak, top round roast, rump roast, and chuck eye roast are common cuts.

Ground beef offers more variety in labeling than other cuts of beef. Meat labeled *ground beef* must be at least 70% lean according to federal regulations. *Ground chuck* must be at least 80% lean, while *ground round* must be 85% lean. You can see the differences in these grinds at a glance. The more fat the beef contains, the paler the meat will be. And the price will also decrease. Just because ground beef is cheaper doesn't make it a better buy. Most of the fat cooks out of the meat anyway and will be discarded. Expect more shrinkage in recipes made from ground beef. For ground beef recipes in this chapter, we call for the specific type of grind that we used in testing.

Keep in mind that ground beef is more perishable than roasts or steaks, which means it has a shorter shelf life. Immediately freeze any ground beef you don't plan to use within a few days. And remember to refrigerate leftovers promptly after serving (within 2 hours after cooking).

You can freeze beef up to two weeks in its original transparent packaging. For longer storage, rewrap beef in moisture-proof airtight material like heavy-duty aluminum foil, freezer paper, or freezer zip-top plastic bags.

TIMETABLE FOR ROASTING BEEF

CUT	APPROXIMATE WEIGHT IN POUNDS	INTERNAL TEMPERATURE	APPROXIMATE TOTAL COOKING TIMES IN HOURS AT 325°
Rib roast, bone-in	4	145° (medium-rare)	1½
		160° (medium)	1¾
		170° (well-done)	2
	6	145° (medium-rare)	2
		160° (medium)	2½
		170° (well-done)	3
Rib roast, boneless rolled	4	145° (medium-rare)	1¾
		160° (medium)	2
		170° (well-done)	2½
	6	145° (medium-rare)	2¾
		160° (medium)	3
		170° (well-done)	3½
Tenderloin, whole*	4 to 6	145° (medium-rare)	¾ to 1
half*	2 to 3	145° (medium-rare)	½ to ¾
Rolled rump	5	145° (medium-rare)	2¼
		160° (medium)	3
		170° (well-done)	3¼
Sirloin tip	3	145° (medium-rare)	1½
		160° (medium)	2
		170° (well-done)	2¼

*Roast at 425°

REFRIGERATOR/FREEZER STORAGE FOR BEEF

TYPE OF BEEF	REFRIGERATOR	FREEZER
Fresh steaks, roasts	3 to 4 days	6 to 12 months
Fresh ground beef	1 to 2 days	3 to 4 months
Leftover cooked beef (all types)	3 to 4 days	2 to 3 months

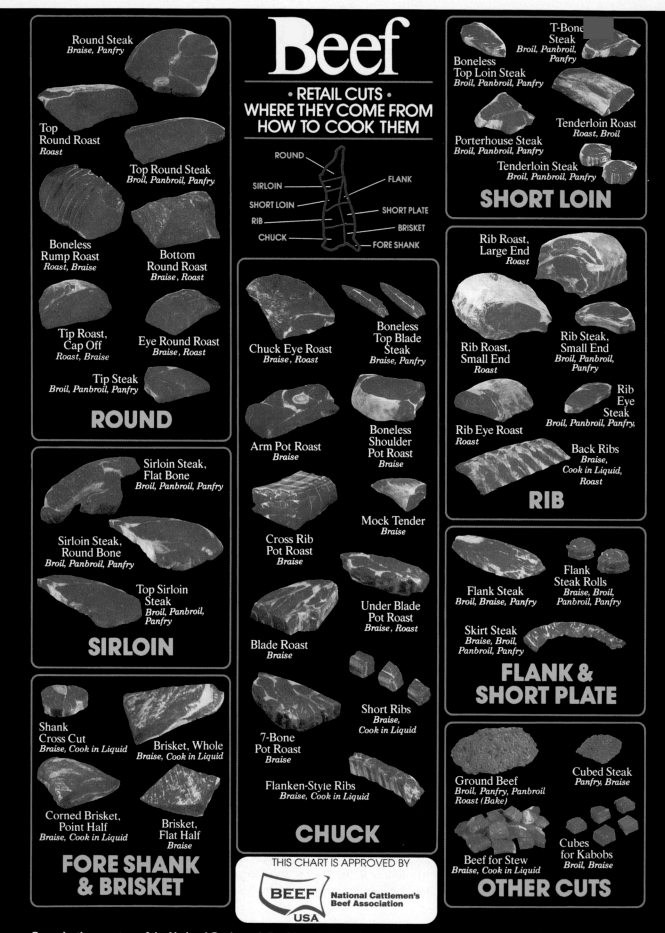

Beef

• RETAIL CUTS •
WHERE THEY COME FROM
HOW TO COOK THEM

ROUND
SIRLOIN
SHORT LOIN
RIB
CHUCK
FLANK
SHORT PLATE
BRISKET
FORE SHANK

ROUND

Round Steak
Braise, Panfry

Top Round Roast
Roast

Top Round Steak
Broil, Panbroil, Panfry

Boneless Rump Roast
Roast, Braise

Bottom Round Roast
Braise, Roast

Tip Roast, Cap Off
Roast, Braise

Eye Round Roast
Braise, Roast

Tip Steak
Broil, Panbroil, Panfry

SIRLOIN

Sirloin Steak, Flat Bone
Broil, Panbroil, Panfry

Sirloin Steak, Round Bone
Broil, Panbroil, Panfry

Top Sirloin Steak
Broil, Panbroil, Panfry

FORE SHANK & BRISKET

Shank Cross Cut
Braise, Cook in Liquid

Brisket, Whole
Braise, Cook in Liquid

Corned Brisket, Point Half
Braise, Cook in Liquid

Brisket, Flat Half
Braise

CHUCK

Chuck Eye Roast
Braise, Roast

Boneless Top Blade Steak
Braise, Panfry

Arm Pot Roast
Braise

Boneless Shoulder Pot Roast
Braise

Cross Rib Pot Roast
Braise

Mock Tender
Braise

Under Blade Pot Roast
Braise, Roast

Blade Roast
Braise

Short Ribs
Braise, Cook in Liquid

7-Bone Pot Roast
Braise

Flanken-Style Ribs
Braise, Cook in Liquid

SHORT LOIN

T-Bone Steak
Broil, Panbroil, Panfry

Boneless Top Loin Steak
Broil, Panbroil, Panfry

Porterhouse Steak
Broil, Panbroil, Panfry

Tenderloin Roast
Roast, Broil

Tenderloin Steak
Broil, Panbroil, Panfry

RIB

Rib Roast, Large End
Roast

Rib Roast, Small End
Roast

Rib Steak, Small End
Broil, Panbroil, Panfry

Rib Eye Roast
Roast

Rib Eye Steak
Broil, Panbroil, Panfry,

Back Ribs
Braise, Cook in Liquid, Roast

FLANK & SHORT PLATE

Flank Steak
Broil, Braise, Panfry

Flank Steak Rolls
Braise, Broil, Panbroil, Panfry

Skirt Steak
Braise, Broil, Panbroil, Panfry

OTHER CUTS

Ground Beef
Broil, Panfry, Panbroil Roast (Bake)

Cubed Steak
Panfry, Braise

Beef for Stew
Braise, Cook in Liquid

Cubes for Kabobs
Broil, Braise

THIS CHART IS APPROVED BY

BEEF
USA
National Cattlemen's Beef Association

There's a bit of preparation involved in readying a standing rib roast (also called prime rib and rib roast) for cooking. Most butchers will do the work for you; just be sure to call and give a few days' notice.

A full rib roast contains 7 rib bones that act as a natural roasting rack and make quite an impression upon serving. If you buy less than a full roast, request that it be cut from the loin end; it's where you'll find the largest portion of the rib "eye" meat, the most tender meat.

In trimming the roast, your butcher will *french* (trim fat and gristle) and shorten the rib bones, as well as remove the *chine bone* (back bone). He should also trim the *cap fat* to just a thin layer covering the outside of the roast. (The cap fat is a thick layer of fat that covers the top of a rib roast.)

Sources vary in serving recommendations from 2 to 4 people per rib. See the illustrations at right for the English method of carving; these are fairly thick servings. Other methods call for slicing the roast as thin as ¼ inch.

Standing Rib Roast

PREP: 5 MINUTES
COOK: 2 HOURS AND 40 MINUTES

This grand holiday roast is encrusted with coarsely ground salt and pepper. For best results, cook a large cut of meat such as this with a combination of high and low heat—first in a very hot oven to sear the outside, and then slowly roasted to keep it juicy.

1 (6-pound) fully trimmed 3-rib roast*
1½ to 2 tablespoons coarse salt
1½ teaspoons coarsely ground pepper or cracked pepper
Garnish: fresh herbs

•Place roast, rib side down, in a lightly greased shallow roasting pan. Rub salt and pepper into fat across entire top of roast, covering completely. Insert meat thermometer into roast, making sure it does not touch bone or fat.
•Roast, uncovered, at 450° for 10 minutes; reduce oven temperature to 325°, and roast

2½ hours or until thermometer registers 145° (medium-rare). Remove from oven; cover roast with aluminum foil, and let stand 20 minutes. (This allows juices to retreat back into the meat; the temperature of roast will rise slightly.) Garnish, if desired. Serve with new potatoes, carrots, and Yorkshire Pudding (page 76). Yield: 10 servings.
**Ask your butcher to cut the roast from the loin end and to french the bones for you. See* Readying a Rib Roast *in box at left for more details.*
Per serving: Calories 495 Fat 26.5g
Cholesterol 176mg Sodium 1182mg

Peppered Rib-Eye Roast

PREP: 8 MINUTES   MARINATE: 8 HOURS
COOK: 2 HOURS AND 20 MINUTES

This is the boneless version of a standing rib roast. Let the rich gravy dribble onto each slice or over some mashed potatoes.

½ cup cracked pepper or coarsely ground pepper
1 (5- to 6-pound) boneless rib-eye roast, trimmed
1 cup soy sauce
¾ cup red wine vinegar
2 tablespoons tomato paste
1 teaspoon paprika
2 cloves garlic, minced
1 tablespoon cornstarch
1 tablespoon cold water
⅛ teaspoon salt

•Lightly press pepper on top and sides of roast. Place roast in a heavy-duty, zip-top plastic bag or large shallow dish. Combine soy sauce and next 4 ingredients; pour over roast. Seal or cover, and marinate in refrigerator 8 hours, turning occasionally.
•Remove roast from marinade, discarding marinade. Place roast, fat side up, on a rack in a shallow roasting pan; insert meat thermometer into thickest part of roast, making sure it does not touch fat.
•Bake, uncovered, at 425° for 10 minutes. Reduce temperature to 325°; bake 2 hours and 10 minutes or until thermometer registers 145° (medium-rare) or 160° (medium).

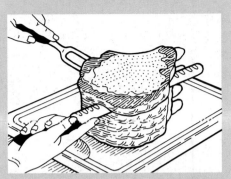

1. Place roast on cutting board with large end down. Insert carving fork just below top rib. Slice horizontally from fat side of the meat through to the rib bone.

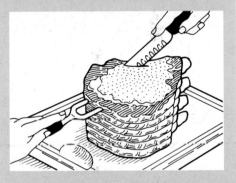

2. Slice vertically along rib bone to release each slice. Slide knife under each slice; lift and remove slice to plate.

•Remove roast to a serving platter; cover and keep warm. Add enough water (about ¾ cup) to pan drippings to make 1½ cups; return to pan. Combine cornstarch and 1 tablespoon water, stirring until smooth. Stir cornstarch mixture and salt into pan drippings. Cook over medium heat, stirring constantly, until mixture is smooth and slightly thickened. Serve roast with gravy. Yield: 12 servings.
Per serving: Calories 328 Fat 16.3g
Cholesterol 112mg Sodium 406mg

Dijon-Wine-Marinated Roast

PREP: 5 MINUTES   MARINATE: 8 HOURS
COOK: 1 HOUR AND 45 MINUTES

You can marinate this roast in just about any red wine—a Merlot or Burgundy are inexpensive options. Most important is that you choose a wine you would also enjoy serving with the meal.

1 (3- to 4-pound) boneless rib-eye roast or rump roast
½ cup red wine
2 tablespoons freshly ground pepper
2 tablespoons olive oil
1 tablespoon Dijon mustard
½ teaspoon salt
⅛ teaspoon dried tarragon
1 clove garlic, crushed

•Place roast in a heavy-duty, zip-top plastic bag or shallow dish. Combine wine and remaining 6 ingredients; stir well, and pour over roast. Seal or cover, and marinate in refrigerator 8 hours.
•Remove roast from marinade, discarding marinade. Place roast on a rack in a shallow roasting pan; insert meat thermometer into thickest part of roast, making sure it does not touch fat.
•Bake at 350° for 1 hour and 45 minutes or until thermometer registers 145° (medium-rare). Yield: 10 servings.

Per serving: Calories 243 Fat 12.9g
Cholesterol 84mg Sodium 113mg

THE GIST OF JUS

The French au jus is simple to make from the pan drippings of any roast. Here's how: Bake roast and remove to a serving platter, reserving pan drippings and crusty bits of meat. Pour drippings into a measuring cup; skim off fat. Add 1 cup of boiling water to pan; stir well to loosen crusty bits from bottom of pan. Stir in reserved drippings. Simmer over medium heat until mixture is reduced by half. Strain drippings, and season as desired. Serve jus with roast and Yorkshire Pudding (page 76) or drizzle it over mashed potatoes.

Beef Wellington

PREP: 52 MINUTES   CHILL: 2 HOURS
COOK: 1 HOUR AND 20 MINUTES

Beef Wellington sports a classic duxelles filling of finely chopped mushrooms cooked with shallots and herbs into a thick paste. This filling is spooned across the tenderloin just under a golden pastry.

1 (4-pound) beef tenderloin, trimmed
1 tablespoon freshly ground pepper
¼ cup butter or margarine, divided
1 cup sliced fresh mushrooms, finely chopped
1 shallot, finely chopped
¼ teaspoon salt
¼ teaspoon freshly ground pepper
1 tablespoon chopped fresh parsley
½ teaspoon dried basil
½ teaspoon dried tarragon
½ teaspoon dried thyme
1 (17¼-ounce) package frozen puff pastry sheets, thawed
1 large egg, lightly beaten
Garnish: fresh parsley sprigs

•Evenly shape tenderloin by tucking small end underneath; tie with string. Sprinkle tenderloin with 1 tablespoon pepper.
•Melt 2 tablespoons butter in a large skillet; add tenderloin, and cook on all sides over medium-high heat until browned. Reduce heat to medium, and cook 30 minutes, turning occasionally. Remove from skillet; cover and chill. Wipe out skillet.
•Melt remaining 2 tablespoons butter in skillet; add mushrooms and next 3 ingredients, and cook over medium-high heat 2 minutes. Stir in parsley and next 3 ingredients; cook over medium heat until all liquid evaporates.
•Place 1 sheet of pastry over the other; roll both sheets of pastry into one 16- x 14-inch rectangle. Spoon mushroom mixture down center. Remove string from tenderloin, and place tenderloin, lengthwise, in middle of pastry. Bring up sides of pastry, and overlap slightly to form a seam; trim off excess pastry. Reserve pastry trimmings. Trim ends of pastry to make even; fold over, and seal. Place tenderloin, seam side down, onto a lightly greased baking sheet; brush with beaten egg.
•Roll out pastry trimmings; cut into decorative shapes, and arrange on top of pastry as

desired. Brush pastry shapes with remaining beaten egg. Cover and chill 2 hours.
•Uncover and bake at 400° for 45 minutes or until pastry is golden and meat thermometer inserted in thickest part of tenderloin registers 145° (medium-rare) or 160° (medium). Cover with aluminum foil near end of baking if pastry overbrowns. Garnish, if desired. Yield: 10 servings.

Per serving: Calories 481 Fat 30.6g
Cholesterol 179mg Sodium 441mg

Regency Beef Tenderloin with Horseradish Butter

PREP: 10 MINUTES   MARINATE: 8 HOURS
COOK: 55 MINUTES

The perfect entrée for a special occasion or Sunday dinner, this tenderloin and flavored butter can also be served as an appetizer on party rolls.

1 cup soy sauce
⅔ cup vegetable oil
3 tablespoons brown sugar
2 tablespoons Dijon mustard
1 tablespoon white vinegar
1 teaspoon garlic powder
1 green onion, chopped
1 (5- to 6-pound) beef tenderloin, trimmed
Horseradish Butter (page 389)

•Combine first 7 ingredients; stir well.
•Place tenderloin in a large heavy-duty, zip-top plastic bag or shallow dish. Pour marinade over tenderloin; seal or cover. Marinate in refrigerator 8 hours, turning occasionally.
•Remove tenderloin from marinade, reserving marinade. Bring marinade to a boil in a small saucepan; set aside.
•Place tenderloin on a rack in a shallow roasting pan. Bake at 400° for 45 to 55 minutes or until meat thermometer inserted in thickest part registers 145° (medium-rare) or 160° (medium), basting occasionally with marinade. Let stand 10 minutes before slicing. Serve with Horseradish Butter. Yield: 12 servings.

Per serving: Calories 475 Fat 35g
Cholesterol 143mg Sodium 963mg

Beef Tenderloin with Peppercorns

PREP: 30 MINUTES COOK: 45 MINUTES

Accompany this tenderloin with green beans and roasted potatoes. A spicy red wine pairs nicely with the meal.

1 (5- to 6-pound) beef tenderloin, trimmed
3 tablespoons Dijon mustard
1 tablespoon dried sage
1½ tablespoons green peppercorns, drained
1½ tablespoons whole black peppercorns, ground and divided
1½ tablespoons whole white peppercorns, ground and divided
2 tablespoons butter, softened

•Cut tenderloin lengthwise to within ½-inch of 1 long edge, leaving edge intact.
•Open tenderloin out flat. Place heavy-duty plastic wrap on tenderloin; pound meat to flatten slightly. Remove wrap; spread meat with mustard. Sprinkle sage, green peppercorns, and ½ tablespoon each of black and white ground peppercorns over mustard.
•Fold 1 side of tenderloin back over, and tie securely at 3-inch intervals with heavy string. Spread butter over outside of tenderloin, and sprinkle with remaining ground peppercorns.
•Place tenderloin on a rack in a roasting pan; insert meat thermometer into thickest part of tenderloin.
•Bake at 425° for 45 minutes or until thermometer registers 145° (medium-rare) or 160° (medium). Let stand 10 minutes before slicing. Yield: 12 servings.
Per serving: Calories 267 Fat 13.2g
Cholesterol 104mg Sodium 206mg

BEEF'S MOST TENDER STEAKS

1. Tenderloin steak
2. Chuck top blade steak
3. Top loin steak
4. Porterhouse/T-bone steak
5. Rib-eye steak

Filet Mignons with Mustard-Caper Sauce

◄ QUICK ►

PREP: 10 MINUTES COOK: 20 MINUTES

6 (6-ounce) beef tenderloin steaks (1 inch thick)
3 tablespoons butter or margarine, melted
½ cup dry vermouth
2 green onions, chopped
½ cup whipping cream
2 tablespoons capers
2 tablespoons prepared mustard
½ teaspoon salt
½ teaspoon pepper
1 beef bouillon cube
Watercress (optional)

•Cook steaks in butter in a large skillet over medium-high heat 4 to 6 minutes on each side or to desired doneness. Remove from skillet; keep warm.
•Add vermouth; cook over high heat, deglazing skillet by scraping particles that cling to bottom. Add green onions and next 6 ingredients. Bring to a boil; reduce heat, and simmer 5 minutes or until sauce is reduced to 1 cup. Serve steaks with sauce and, if desired, on a bed of watercress. Yield: 6 servings.
Per serving: Calories 382 Fat 24.5g
Cholesterol 148mg Sodium 777mg

Steak Diane

◄ QUICK ►

PREP: 5 MINUTES COOK: 12 MINUTES

Lemon and Worcestershire are key in Steak Diane. It's a fairly quick entrée that's fit for company.

6 (4- to 6-ounce) beef tenderloin steaks (1 inch thick)
2 teaspoons lemon-pepper seasoning
2 tablespoons butter or margarine
2 tablespoons lemon juice
2 tablespoons Worcestershire sauce
1 teaspoon Dijon mustard
Garnish: lemon twists

•Sprinkle steaks with lemon-pepper seasoning. Melt butter in a large skillet over medium-high heat. Add steaks, and cook 5 minutes on each side or to desired doneness. Transfer to a platter; keep warm.
•Add lemon juice, Worcestershire sauce, and mustard to skillet; bring to a boil, stirring constantly. Pour over steaks. Garnish, if desired. Serve immediately. Yield: 6 servings.
Per serving: Calories 208 Fat 11.3g
Cholesterol 81mg Sodium 281mg

Filet Mignons with Shiitake Madeira Sauce

PREP: 7 MINUTES COOK: 27 MINUTES

See these seared filets surrounded by Madeira cream sauce on page 230. Toast points, rice, or mashed potatoes are options for soaking in the divine sauce.

½ pound fresh shiitake mushrooms
1 tablespoon olive oil
2 cloves garlic, minced
1 teaspoon dried thyme
½ teaspoon freshly ground pepper
4 (5- to 6-ounce) beef tenderloin steaks (1 to 1½ inches thick)
2 shallots, finely chopped
2 cloves garlic, minced
1 cup Madeira
½ cup condensed beef broth, undiluted
¼ cup whipping cream
Garnishes: cherry tomatoes, fresh herbs

•Remove stems from mushrooms, discarding stems. Cut mushroom caps into thin slices.
•Combine oil and next 3 ingredients; coat steaks with mixture. Place a large nonstick skillet over medium-high heat until hot; add steaks, and cook 12 minutes or to desired doneness, turning once. Remove steaks from skillet, reserving drippings in skillet. Keep steaks warm.
•Cook shallot and garlic in drippings, stirring constantly, until tender. Add Madeira; bring to a boil. Reduce heat, and simmer 10 minutes or until reduced to ½ cup.
•Add broth and mushrooms; cook 3 minutes or until tender, stirring often. Remove from heat. Stir in whipping cream; spoon some of sauce onto serving plates, and add steaks. Garnish, if desired. Serve hot. Yield: 4 servings.
Per serving: Calories 346 Fat 18.3g
Cholesterol 114mg Sodium 284mg

Steak au Poivre

PREP: 7 MINUTES CHILL: 1 HOUR

COOK: 15 MINUTES

Poivre is French for pepper; here it coats rib-eye steaks seared in a skillet and covered in a Cognac cream.

3 tablespoons cracked pepper
4 (8-ounce) rib-eye steaks
2 tablespoons butter or margarine
2 tablespoons vegetable oil
1 shallot, finely chopped
¼ cup Cognac
¼ cup whipping cream
1 tablespoon butter or margarine

•Press cracked pepper onto both sides of each steak; cover and chill 1 hour. Heat 2 tablespoons butter and oil in a skillet over medium-high heat. Cook steaks 3 minutes on each side or until browned. Remove steaks from skillet; cover and keep warm.
•Sauté shallot in skillet over medium heat until tender. Wipe out excess oil from skillet with paper towels. Pour Cognac into skillet, and ignite, using a long match.
•After flames die, stir in whipping cream. Simmer until thickened (4 to 5 minutes). Add 1 tablespoon butter, and swirl to blend. Serve over steaks. Yield: 4 servings.
Per serving: Calories 547 Fat 37.3g
Cholesterol 173mg Sodium 196mg

POT ROAST PANACHE

•Labels on beef cuts at the meat counter can be confusing. For example, chuck roast is a common cut for use in pot roast recipes and definitely should be cooked by braising. An English cut, a specific type of chuck roast, is generally one of the easiest to tenderize.
•One of the joys of cooking a tender pot roast is the many possibilities for leftovers. Of course, it makes a great sandwich. Try it on toasted sourdough with mayonnaise, pepper, and a little horseradish. Or chop some roast and use it as a burrito filling or make Old-Fashioned Beef Hash on page 241.

Deluxe Pot Roast

◄ FAMILY FAVORITE ►

PREP: 20 MINUTES

COOK: 2 HOURS AND 40 MINUTES

This pot roast recipe is a one-dish meal. The vegetables, gravy, and tender meat all simmer together, and thin slices of garlic infuse mellow flavor into the roast.

1 (4- to 5-pound) boneless chuck roast
2 large cloves garlic, sliced
½ teaspoon salt
½ teaspoon pepper
¼ cup all-purpose flour
⅓ cup olive oil
1 medium onion, sliced
1 cup dry red wine
1 (8-ounce) can tomato sauce
1 tablespoon brown sugar
1 teaspoon dried oregano
1 teaspoon prepared horseradish
1 teaspoon prepared mustard
1 bay leaf
8 small red potatoes, peeled
6 carrots, scraped and quartered
4 stalks celery, cut into 2-inch pieces
Garnish: fresh oregano sprigs

•Make small slits in top of roast. Insert a garlic slice into each slit. Rub roast with salt and pepper; dredge in flour. Brown roast on all sides in hot oil in a Dutch oven or skillet. Add onion and wine to roast in Dutch oven.
•Combine tomato sauce and next 5 ingredients; stir well. Pour over roast. Bring liquid in Dutch oven to a boil; cover, reduce heat, and simmer 1½ hours. Add potatoes, carrot, and celery; cover and simmer 1 more hour or until roast and vegetables are tender.
•Transfer roast to a serving platter; spoon vegetables around roast, using a slotted spoon. Discard bay leaf. Spoon any remaining pan drippings over roast and vegetables. Garnish, if desired. Yield: 8 servings.
Per serving: Calories 562 Fat 20.7g
Cholesterol 136mg Sodium 530mg

Italian Pot Roast

PREP: 10 MINUTES COOK: 55 MINUTES

The pressure cooker yields this tender roast in about an hour. Lots of tangy red sauce comes with it, so we recommend serving the roast on a bed of linguine.

2 tablespoons olive oil
1 (3- to 4-pound) boneless chuck roast
1 large onion, finely chopped
4 cloves garlic, minced
1 cup dry red wine
1 cup beef broth
2 (6-ounce) cans tomato paste
1 (15-ounce) can tomato sauce
1 teaspoon salt
1 teaspoon sugar
1 teaspoon dried basil
1 teaspoon hot sauce
12 ounces dried linguine
½ cup grated Parmesan cheese

•Pour oil into a 6-quart pressure cooker; place over medium-high heat until hot. Add roast; cook until browned on all sides. Remove roast, and set aside.
•Add onion and garlic to cooker, and cook, stirring constantly, until onion is tender. Add red wine and next 7 ingredients; return roast to cooker.
•Cover cooker with lid, and seal securely; place pressure control over vent and tube. Cook over high heat until pressure control rocks back and forth quickly. Reduce heat until pressure control rocks occasionally; cook 45 more minutes.
•Remove cooker from heat; run cold water over cooker to reduce pressure. Carefully remove lid so that steam escapes away from you.
•Cook linguine according to package directions, and drain. Serve roast and sauce over linguine; sprinkle with cheese. Yield: 6 servings.
Per serving: Calories 657 Fat 19.1g
Cholesterol 141mg Sodium 1129mg

Sauerbraten

PREP: 15 MINUTES MARINATE: 24 HOURS

COOK: 3 HOURS

Sauerbraten is a German-style beef roast in which gingersnap crumbs thicken and spice an accompanying gravy. Serve egg noodles or dumplings on the side to soak up the gravy.

1 (3½-pound) eye-of-round roast
1 teaspoon salt
½ teaspoon pepper
2 medium onions, sliced
1 small carrot, scraped and minced
1 stalk celery, chopped
8 whole cloves
4 bay leaves
½ teaspoon whole peppercorns
1½ cups red wine vinegar
2½ cups water
¼ cup butter or margarine
Gingersnap Gravy

•Rub roast with salt and pepper; place in a large, deep ovenproof dish. Add onion and next 5 ingredients.
•Combine vinegar and water; pour over roast. Cover and marinate in refrigerator 12 to 24 hours, turning roast occasionally. Remove roast from marinade, reserving marinade.
•Melt butter in a large Dutch oven over medium heat. Add roast; brown on all sides. Pour marinade and solids over roast.
•Cover and simmer 2½ to 3 hours or until roast is tender, turning once. Remove roast to a serving platter, reserving 1½ cups marinade for gravy. Discard solids, if desired. Serve roast with Gingersnap Gravy. Yield: 8 servings.

Per serving: Calories 403 Fat 19.9g
Cholesterol 140mg Sodium 482mg

Gingersnap Gravy

2 tablespoons brown sugar
1½ cups marinade
½ cup water
8 gingersnaps, crushed
½ cup sour cream

•Melt sugar in a medium skillet; stir in 1½ cups marinade and ½ cup water. Add gingersnap crumbs. Cook over medium heat until mixture is slightly thickened, stirring often. Stir in sour cream. Cook just until mixture is thoroughly heated. Remove from heat. Yield: 2¼ cups.

Smoked Eye of Round

PREP: 6 MINUTES

MARINATE: 12 TO 24 HOURS

COOK: 7 HOURS

½ cup Worcestershire sauce
½ cup teriyaki sauce
⅓ cup lemon juice
¼ cup white wine vinegar
2 tablespoons seasoned salt
1 (4- to 5-pound) eye-of-round roast
Hickory or mesquite chunks

•Combine first 5 ingredients; stir well. Place roast in a heavy-duty, zip-top plastic bag or large shallow dish; pour marinade over roast. Seal or cover, and marinate in refrigerator 12 to 24 hours, turning occasionally. Remove roast from marinade, discarding marinade.
•Soak hickory or mesquite chunks in water 30 minutes. Prepare charcoal fire in smoker, and let burn 10 to 15 minutes. Drain chunks and place on hot coals. Place water pan in smoker, and fill with water.
•Coat food rack with vegetable cooking spray, and place over coals. Place roast on rack; cover with smoker lid, and cook 6 to 7 hours, refilling water pan and adding charcoal as needed.
•Remove roast from food rack. Let stand 10 minutes. Slice roast thinly to serve. Yield: 12 servings.

Per serving: Calories 458 Fat 16g
Cholesterol 169mg Sodium 997mg

Pepper Steak

PREP: 18 MINUTES MARINATE: 1 HOUR

COOK: 45 MINUTES

¼ cup soy sauce
2 tablespoons dry sherry
1 teaspoon ground ginger
½ teaspoon sugar
¼ cup plus 1 tablespoon vegetable oil, divided
1 (2-pound) boneless beef chuck roast, trimmed and cut across grain into ⅛-inch-thick strips*
2 medium-size green peppers, cut into strips
2 medium onions, cut into eighths
2 stalks celery, thinly sliced
1½ teaspoons salt
¼ teaspoon pepper
2 teaspoons cornstarch
1 cup water
2 small tomatoes, cut into wedges
4 cups hot cooked rice

•Combine first 4 ingredients and 2 tablespoons oil in a bowl; stir well. Add beef strips, tossing lightly to coat well. Cover and marinate in refrigerator 1 hour.
•Pour remaining 3 tablespoons oil around top of preheated wok, coating sides; heat at medium (350°) for 1 minute. Add beef strips with marinade; stir-fry 2 to 3 minutes or until beef is browned. Reduce heat to low (200°); cover and simmer 30 minutes, stirring occasionally.
•Increase heat to medium-high (375°); add green pepper and next 4 ingredients. Stir-fry until crisp-tender (about 5 minutes).
•Combine cornstarch and water; add to vegetables and beef. Cook, stirring constantly, until slightly thickened. Stir in tomato; cook 1 more minute. Serve hot over rice. Yield: 8 servings.

Have your butcher slice the meat before you leave the store or you can easily slice meat, using a serrated knife or an electric knife.

Per serving: Calories 391 Fat 13.1g
Cholesterol 68mg Sodium 1440mg

Beef Bourguignon

PREP: 25 MINUTES

MARINATE: 2 TO 3 HOURS

COOK: 2 HOURS AND 45 MINUTES

1 (4-pound) boneless chuck roast, cut into
   2-inch cubes
2½ cups dry red wine
8 slices bacon
Bouquet garni°
2 carrots, scraped and finely chopped
3 tablespoons butter or margarine, melted
3 tablespoons all-purpose flour
1 (14½-ounce) can beef broth
1 teaspoon salt
¼ teaspoon freshly ground pepper
1 clove garlic, minced
1 (16-ounce) package frozen pearl onions,
   thawed
3 tablespoons butter or margarine, melted
1 pound small fresh mushrooms
2 tablespoons finely chopped fresh parsley
6 cups hot cooked rice or egg noodles

•Combine beef cubes and wine in a large
heavy-duty, zip-top plastic bag; seal bag.
Marinate in refrigerator 2 to 3 hours.
•Cook bacon in a large skillet over medium
heat until crisp. Drain and coarsely crumble
bacon, reserving drippings in skillet.
•Strain beef, reserving wine. Pat beef dry
with paper towels. Brown beef, in batches,
in drippings in skillet over medium heat.
Transfer beef to a greased 5-quart baking
dish. Add bouquet garni; set aside.
•Sauté carrot in 3 tablespoons butter in skillet until tender. Add flour; cook 1 minute,
stirring constantly. Gradually stir in beef
broth and reserved wine. Bring to a boil;
cook, stirring constantly, until thickened. Stir
in salt, pepper, and garlic. Pour over beef
mixture. Cover and bake at 325° for 2½
hours or until meat is tender.
•Meanwhile, brown onions in 3 tablespoons
butter in skillet over medium heat, stirring
often. Remove onions with a slotted spoon,
reserving drippings in skillet. Set onions
aside. Cook mushrooms in drippings in skillet 2 to 3 minutes, stirring often. Remove
from heat, and set aside.
•After beef has baked until tender, stir
reserved bacon, onions, mushrooms with
drippings, and parsley into beef mixture.

Bake, uncovered, 15 more minutes. Remove
bouquet garni. Serve beef mixture over rice.
Yield: 8 servings.
*A bouquet garni is a small bundle of fresh
herb sprigs such as parsley, thyme, and bay
leaves tied together with kitchen twine.*
Per serving: Calories 633 Fat 22.1g
Cholesterol 149mg Sodium 1594mg

Beef Tips on Rice

PREP: 10 MINUTES

COOK: 2 HOURS AND 15 MINUTES

*Several generations will recall this old-
fashioned recipe of tender chunks of beef
simmered in a brown gravy and spooned
over rice or egg noodles.*

3 tablespoons all-purpose flour
1 teaspoon salt
½ teaspoon pepper
½ teaspoon paprika
2 pounds boneless top sirloin roast, cut
   into 1-inch cubes°
2 tablespoons vegetable oil
2 large onions, chopped
1 beef bouillon cube
¾ cup boiling water
4½ cups hot cooked rice

•Combine first 4 ingredients in a zip-top
plastic bag; shake to mix. Add beef cubes;
seal bag, and shake until meat is coated.
Brown beef in hot oil in a Dutch oven, stirring often. Add onion, and cook until tender.
•Dissolve bouillon cube in boiling water;
add to beef mixture.
•Cover, reduce heat, and simmer 2 hours,
stirring occasionally. Serve over rice. Yield:
6 servings.
*Sometimes you can find meat labeled "beef
tips" in the grocery; if so, the work of cutting
into cubes has already been done for you.*
Per serving: Calories 475 Fat 12.7g
Cholesterol 92mg Sodium 1200mg

Hungarian Goulash

PREP: 30 MINUTES

COOK: 1 HOUR AND 40 MINUTES

*Hungarian Goulash is a stew flavored and
colored with Hungarian paprika°, which is
sweet-hot in flavor.*

2 pounds beef stew meat, cut into 1-inch
   pieces
½ cup all-purpose flour
1½ teaspoons salt
¾ teaspoon pepper
¼ cup vegetable oil
2 medium onions, coarsely chopped
1 large clove garlic, crushed
1 large green pepper, coarsely
   chopped
1½ cups tomato juice
1½ cups beef broth
1½ tablespoons Hungarian paprika°
½ teaspoon caraway seeds
4 cups hot cooked, buttered noodles
1 (8-ounce) carton sour cream

•Combine first 4 ingredients in a zip-top
plastic bag. Seal bag; shake until meat is coated. Remove meat from bag; reserve any
remaining flour mixture.
•Brown meat in hot oil in a Dutch oven over
medium-high heat. Add onion and garlic;
cook, stirring constantly, until onion is
tender.
•Add remaining flour mixture, green pepper,
and next 4 ingredients. Bring to a boil; cover,
reduce heat, and simmer 1½ hours, stirring
often.
•Uncover and simmer 10 minutes, stirring
often. Serve over noodles with a dollop of
sour cream. Yield: 6 servings.
*Hungarian paprika is considered superior in
quality to regular paprika and should be
readily available. Hungarian cuisine has long
used paprika as a mainstay flavoring rather
than just a garnish.*
Per serving: Calories 595 Fat 30.2g
Cholesterol 127mg Sodium 1388mg

Beef Stroganoff

PREP: 15 MINUTES   COOK: 20 MINUTES

Who could resist this family favorite with its chunky beef and creamy-smooth mushroom sauce?

1½ cups all-purpose flour
1½ teaspoons salt
½ teaspoon pepper
2 pounds sirloin steak, cut into 1-inch cubes
1½ cups butter or margarine, melted
3 cups sliced fresh mushrooms
1 small onion, chopped
2 cloves garlic, minced
½ cup dry white wine
3 cups beef broth
2 tablespoons tomato paste
2½ cups sour cream
7½ cups hot cooked noodles

•Combine first 3 ingredients in a large zip-top plastic bag; add steak. Seal bag, and shake until meat is coated.
•Brown meat in butter in a large skillet, stirring occasionally. Remove meat from skillet; cover and keep warm. Add mushrooms, onion, and garlic to drippings in skillet; cook, stirring constantly, until tender. Remove from pan; keep warm.
•Add wine to skillet; cook over high heat, deglazing skillet by scraping particles that cling to bottom. Cook until wine is reduced by half.
•Add beef broth and tomato paste, stirring until smooth. Cook over medium heat, stirring constantly, until thickened. Add meat and mushroom mixture; cook until thoroughly heated. Stir in sour cream; cook just until mixture is hot, stirring constantly. Serve over noodles. Yield: 10 servings.

Per serving: Calories 799 Fat 48.3g
Cholesterol 234mg Sodium 1216mg

Sirloin-Vegetable Kabobs

**PREP: 18 MINUTES   MARINATE: 2 HOURS
COOK: 12 MINUTES**

A multitude of vegetables brightly colors these skewers, and a sweet-sour sauce glazes them on the grill. Add tomatoes at the very end of cooking so they'll stay plump.

½ cup dry sherry
½ cup soy sauce
3 tablespoons sugar
3 tablespoons white vinegar
½ teaspoon garlic powder
½ teaspoon salt
½ teaspoon pepper
2 pounds sirloin steak, cut into 1-inch cubes
2 small purple onions, cut into eighths
½ pound fresh mushroom caps
2 medium-size green peppers, cut into 1-inch pieces
1 small pineapple, cut into 1-inch pieces
2 cups cherry tomatoes

•Combine first 7 ingredients in a large heavy-duty, zip-top plastic bag or shallow dish. Add beef cubes; seal or cover, and marinate in refrigerator 2 hours, turning bag occasionally. Remove beef cubes from marinade, reserving marinade. Bring marinade to a boil in a small saucepan; set aside.
•Alternately thread beef cubes, onion, mushroom caps, green pepper, and pineapple onto skewers (see photo). Grill, covered with grill lid, over medium-hot coals (350° to 400°) 10 to 12 minutes or to desired doneness, turning and basting occasionally with marinade. Add tomatoes to end of skewers during the last minute of grilling. Yield: 6 servings.

Per serving: Calories 278 Fat 7.7g
Cholesterol 85mg Sodium 734mg

Skewering kabobs: Alternately thread beef cubes and vegetable chunks onto skewers. To be sure kabobs cook evenly, don't crowd pieces on the skewers.

Old-Fashioned Beef Hash

PREP: 5 MINUTES   COOK: 15 MINUTES

Hash is the perfect way to use leftover roast beef. If you don't have leftovers, buy 6 ounces of deli roast beef. Serve the hash for breakfast or dinner, alongside toast or grits.

1 cup cubed cooked lean beef
1 cup peeled, cubed red potato
½ cup chopped onion
1 tablespoon chopped fresh parsley
¼ teaspoon salt
¼ teaspoon pepper
1 tablespoon vegetable oil
⅓ cup milk

•Combine first 6 ingredients. Cook mixture in hot oil in a large skillet over medium-high heat 10 minutes or until mixture is browned and potatoes are tender, stirring occasionally. Stir in milk; cover, reduce heat, and simmer 5 minutes. Yield: 2 servings.

Per serving: Calories 291 Fat 13g
Cholesterol 70mg Sodium 370mg

Old-Fashioned Chicken Hash: Substitute 1 cup chopped cooked chicken for beef.

Tenderizing meat: Place meat between two sheets of heavy-duty plastic wrap. Using the smooth side of a meat mallet or rolling pin, pound meat to desired thickness. Pounding breaks down muscle fibers, thus tenderizing the meat.

Grillades and Grits

PREP: 37 MINUTES   COOK: 55 MINUTES

Grillades (gree-YAHDS) and grits are an assumed pair in New Orleans. A Louisiana twist on smothered steak, grillades are thinly pounded pieces of beef in a rich brown sauce. It sounds like dinner, and sometimes it is, but brunch is the most popular menu spot for this dish.

1½ pounds top round steak
3 tablespoons all-purpose flour
1½ teaspoons salt
¾ teaspoon black pepper
½ teaspoon dried thyme
⅛ teaspoon ground red pepper
3 tablespoons butter or margarine, melted
   and divided
1 small onion, chopped
½ cup chopped celery
1 green pepper, chopped
4 cloves garlic, minced
1 (14.5-ounce) can tomatoes, undrained
   and chopped
1 cup water
4 cups hot cooked grits

•Pound steak to ¼-inch thickness with a meat mallet or rolling pin. Cut steak into 2-inch squares; set aside.
•Combine flour and next 4 ingredients in a large heavy-duty, zip-top plastic bag. Add steak; seal bag, and shake to coat.

•Brown half of steak in 1 tablespoon butter in a Dutch oven over medium-high heat about 2 minutes on each side. Remove from Dutch oven; keep warm. Repeat procedure with 1 tablespoon butter and remaining steak. Remove from Dutch oven.
•Add remaining 1 tablespoon butter, onion, and next 3 ingredients to Dutch oven. Cook over medium heat, stirring constantly, 5 minutes or until vegetables are tender. Add tomatoes and water; return steak to Dutch oven. Cover, reduce heat, and simmer 45 minutes, stirring once.
•Spoon grillades over grits, and serve hot. Yield: 4 servings.
Per serving: Calories 514 Fat 16.2g
Cholesterol 120mg Sodium 1446mg

Teriyaki Beef Broil

PREP: 20 MINUTES   MARINATE: 1 HOUR

COOK: 6 MINUTES

1¾ pounds top round steak (1 inch thick)
¼ cup soy sauce
¼ cup vegetable oil
2 tablespoons molasses
2 teaspoons ground ginger
2 teaspoons dry mustard
6 cloves garlic, minced
Strips of fresh chives (optional)

•Partially freeze steak; slice diagonally across the grain into ¼-inch-thick slices. Place steak in a heavy-duty, zip-top plastic bag or shallow dish. Combine soy sauce and next 5 ingredients; pour over steak. Seal or cover, and marinate in refrigerator 1 hour.
•Remove steak from marinade, discarding marinade. Thread steak onto eight 10-inch bamboo skewers. Place skewers on a lightly greased rack of broiler pan. Broil 5½ inches from heat 5 to 6 minutes, turning once. Serve over strips of chives, if desired. Yield: 4 servings.
Per serving: Calories 398 Fat 19.3g
Cholesterol 120mg Sodium 863mg

Thai Lemon Beef

PREP: 12 MINUTES   MARINATE: 30 MINUTES

COOK: 8 MINUTES

Lemon is common in Thai cooking. Combined with garlic and red pepper flakes, it adds intense flavor to this stir-fry.

1 (1-inch-thick) boneless top round steak
⅓ cup soy sauce
¼ cup lemon juice
¼ cup water
2 to 3 teaspoons dried crushed red pepper
4 cloves garlic, minced
1 tablespoon vegetable oil
4 green onions, cut into 2-inch pieces
2 carrots, scraped and thinly sliced
2 teaspoons cornstarch
4 cups hot cooked ramen noodles or rice

•Cut steak diagonally across grain into ⅛-inch-thick strips, and place in a bowl.
•Combine soy sauce and next 4 ingredients. Reserve half of mixture. Pour remaining mixture over steak. Cover and marinate in refrigerator 30 minutes.
•Drain steak, discarding marinade.
•Stir-fry half of steak in ½ tablespoon hot oil in a large nonstick skillet or wok over medium-high heat 1 minute or until outside of beef is no longer pink. Remove from skillet; repeat procedure with remaining steak and oil. Remove from skillet, and set aside.
•Add green onions and carrot slices to skillet; stir-fry 3 minutes or until crisp-tender.
•Whisk cornstarch into reserved soy sauce mixture; stir into vegetables, and stir-fry until thickened.
•Add steak; stir-fry until thoroughly heated. Serve over noodles or rice. Yield: 4 servings.
Per serving: Calories 488 Fat 8.7g
Cholesterol 65mg Sodium 1632mg

GOING AGAINST THE GRAIN

Use an electric knife or sharp chef's knife and place it at an angle against the grain of the meat. Slice the meat into very thin slices. The angle of the knife cutting thin slices across the meat fibers produces tender results. This slicing technique applies whether it's a partially frozen, raw piece of meat or a grilled flank steak.

Steak Fingers

◄ QUICK • FAMILY FAVORITE ►

PREP: 14 MINUTES   COOK: 8 MINUTES

Fry these tender strips of steak in batches, and serve them with a favorite dipping sauce.

1 pound boneless round steak
1 cup all-purpose flour
1 teaspoon salt
1 teaspoon pepper
2 large eggs
2 tablespoons milk
Vegetable oil

•Pound steak to ⅛-inch thickness, using a meat mallet, and cut into 4- x 1-inch strips.
•Combine flour, salt, and pepper. Combine eggs and milk; beat well. Dredge steak strips in flour mixture; dip strips in egg mixture, and dredge again in flour mixture.
•Pour oil to depth of 2 inches into a large skillet; heat to 375°. Fry steak fingers 2 minutes or until browned, turning once. Drain on paper towels. Serve immediately with Cream Gravy (page 395), steak sauce, or ketchup. Yield: 4 servings.
Per serving: Calories 632 Fat 47.8g
Cholesterol 145mg Sodium 526mg

Country-Fried Steak

PREP: 15 MINUTES   COOK: 1 HOUR

The key to these crispy steaks is not to crowd them in the skillet. Save a little coffee from your morning brew to enrich the gravy.

⅓ cup all-purpose flour
¼ teaspoon salt
¼ teaspoon pepper
1½ pounds cubed steak
¼ cup vegetable oil
2 small onions, sliced
1 cup water
¼ cup all-purpose flour
¾ cup milk
¼ cup brewed coffee
2 teaspoons Worcestershire sauce
½ teaspoon salt
½ teaspoon pepper

•Combine first 3 ingredients; cut steak into serving-size pieces. Dredge in flour mixture.
•Brown steak in hot oil in batches in a 10-inch cast-iron skillet over medium-high heat. Remove steak from skillet; set aside. Add onion to drippings in skillet; cook 5 minutes or until tender, stirring occasionally.
•Return steak to skillet; add water, and bring to a boil. Cover, reduce heat, and simmer 45 minutes or until tender. Remove steak, reserving drippings in skillet.
•Add ¼ cup flour to drippings in skillet, stirring until smooth. Gradually add milk and coffee; cook over medium heat, stirring constantly, until gravy is thickened. Stir in Worcestershire sauce, ½ teaspoon salt, and ½ teaspoon pepper. Serve steak with gravy. Yield: 4 servings.
Per serving: Calories 450 Fat 22.5g
Cholesterol 98mg Sodium 581mg

Honey-Grilled Flank Steak

◄ GRILLED ►

**PREP: 6 MINUTES   MARINATE: 8 HOURS
COOK: 16 MINUTES**

Lightly score this steak so that it will drink in the Asian flavors as it marinates.

1 (2-pound) flank steak
¾ cup vegetable oil
1 small onion, finely chopped
¼ cup soy sauce
¼ cup honey
2 tablespoons cider vinegar
1½ teaspoons garlic salt
1½ teaspoons ground ginger
½ teaspoon pepper

•Score steak diagonally across the grain at ¾-inch intervals. Place steak in a large heavy-duty, zip-top plastic bag or shallow dish. Combine oil and remaining 7 ingredients; pour over steak. Seal or cover; marinate in refrigerator 8 hours, turning occasionally.
•Remove steak from marinade, reserving marinade. Bring marinade to a boil in a small saucepan; set aside. Grill steak, uncovered, over medium-hot coals (350° to 400°) 8 to 10 minutes on each side or to desired doneness, basting with reserved marinade the last 5 minutes. To serve, slice steak diagonally across the grain. Yield: 8 servings.
Per serving: Calories 322 Fat 23g
Cholesterol 60mg Sodium 524mg

LONDON BROIL LORE

London Broil is actually the name of a recipe, not a cut of beef. However, you might find several beef cuts labeled London Broil in some markets. The recipe dates back to 1931 and takes its name from London, England, where it was first served. The recipe calls for marinating a flank steak and broiling or grilling it. Top round steak makes a fine alternative.

London Broil

**PREP: 15 MINUTES   MARINATE: 8 HOURS
COOK: 13 MINUTES**

1 (1½-pound) flank steak*
½ cup dry red wine or red wine vinegar
½ cup vegetable oil
¼ cup chopped fresh parsley
2 large cloves garlic, minced
2 green onions, minced
1 teaspoon dry mustard
2 teaspoons coarsely ground pepper
¼ teaspoon salt
Bordelaise Sauce (page 386) or Béarnaise Sauce (page 388)

•Score steak by making shallow diagonal cuts at 1-inch intervals in a diamond pattern on both sides of meat. Place steak in a large heavy-duty, zip-top plastic bag or large shallow dish.
•Combine wine and next 7 ingredients; pour over steak. Seal or cover; marinate in refrigerator 8 hours, turning occasionally.
•Drain meat, discarding marinade. Place steak on a rack in broiler pan. Broil 3 to 5 inches from heat 5 minutes; turn steak. Broil 6 to 8 more minutes or to desired doneness. Slice steak diagonally across the grain into thin slices. Serve with desired sauce. Yield: 4 servings.
*For this recipe, if your steak is 1 inch thick or less, broil it on the top rack. If it's more than 1 inch thick, broil on the second rack.
Per serving: Calories 690 Fat 59.8g
Cholesterol 315mg Sodium 570mg

Southwestern Flank Steak

◀ GRILLED ▶

PREP: 10 MINUTES MARINATE: 8 HOURS
COOK: 16 MINUTES

1 (1½-pound) flank steak
¼ cup fresh orange juice
2 tablespoons chili sauce
2 tablespoons soy sauce
2 tablespoons vegetable oil
1 teaspoon honey
2 cloves garlic, minced
1½ teaspoons grated orange rind
2 tablespoons chili powder
½ teaspoon salt
¼ teaspoon ground red pepper
1 medium-size orange, thinly sliced
Triple-Fruit Salsa (page 391)
Garnishes: orange wedges, fresh cilantro
    sprigs

•Score steak diagonally across the grain at 1-inch intervals (photo 1). Place steak in a heavy-duty, zip-top plastic bag or large shallow dish; set aside.
•Combine orange juice and next 9 ingredients; pour over steak (photo 2). Place orange slices over steak. Seal or cover, and marinate in refrigerator 8 hours, turning occasionally.
•Remove steak from marinade, discarding marinade. Grill steak, covered with grill lid, over medium-hot coals (350° to 400°) 7 to 8 minutes on each side or to desired doneness. Let stand 5 minutes. To serve, slice steak diagonally across the grain into thin slices. Serve with Triple-Fruit Salsa. Garnish, if desired. Yield: 4 servings.

Per serving: Calories 408 Fat 21.1g
Cholesterol 89mg Sodium 303mg

1. Score steak (⅛ inch deep) diagonally across the grain at 1-inch intervals, using a sharp knife.

2. Pour marinade over steak. Place orange slices over steak; seal zip-top bag and marinate in refrigerator.

Beef Fajitas

◀ GRILLED ▶

**PREP: 20 MINUTES   MARINATE: 8 HOURS
COOK: 35 MINUTES**

Fajita recipes typically call for marinating skirt steak or flank steak in a lime juice mixture, which tenderizes the meat.

2 (1-pound) skirt steaks or flank steaks
⅓ cup fresh lime juice
⅓ cup olive oil
4 large cloves garlic, minced
1½ teaspoons ground cumin
2 teaspoons cracked pepper
1 medium onion, sliced and
     separated into rings
1 tablespoon butter or margarine
Salt and pepper to taste
8 (8-inch) flour tortillas
Guacamole (page 35)
Assorted toppings (optional)

•Place steaks between two sheets of heavy-duty plastic wrap, and gently pound to an even thickness, using a meat mallet or rolling pin. Place steaks in a heavy-duty, zip-top plastic bag or large shallow dish.
•Combine lime juice and next 4 ingredients, stirring well. Pour marinade over meat. Seal or cover, and marinate in refrigerator 8 hours, turning meat occasionally.
•Remove steaks from marinade, reserving marinade. Bring marinade to a boil in a small saucepan; set aside. Grill steaks over hot mesquite coals (400° to 500°) 6 to 8 minutes on each side or to desired doneness, basting often with marinade.
•Place sliced onion and butter on a piece of heavy-duty aluminum foil; sprinkle with salt and pepper to taste. Wrap tightly. Grill over medium-hot coals (350° to 400°) 5 minutes or until tender.
•Wrap tortillas in aluminum foil, and bake at 325° for 15 minutes or until thoroughly heated.
•Slice steaks diagonally across the grain into thin slices. Divide meat and onion evenly among tortillas. Top each serving with Guacamole and, if desired, any of the following: chopped tomato, sour cream, or shredded lettuce. Roll up tortillas. Yield: 8 servings.
Per serving: Calories 438 Fat 27.5g
Cholesterol 63mg Sodium 400mg

Ropa Vieja

PREP: 13 MINUTES   COOK: 1½ HOURS

Ropa Vieja, a traditional Cuban dish, literally means "old clothes." For this dish, flank steak simmers long and slowly in a seasoned tomato sauce and is then shredded, resembling tattered clothing.

2 pounds flank steak, cut into
     1-inch strips
1 large onion, quartered
3 cups water
2 whole pimientos
2 large green peppers, cut into strips
2 large onions, cut into strips
4 cloves garlic, crushed
2 tablespoons vegetable oil
1 (10¾-ounce) can tomato puree
2 bay leaves
½ cup dry white wine
½ teaspoon salt
½ teaspoon pepper
Vegetable oil
French or Cuban bread, cut into ½-inch
     slices (8 ounces)
Garnishes: pimiento strips, English peas

•Combine steak, onion quarters, and water in a large Dutch oven; bring to a boil. Cover, reduce heat, and simmer 1 hour or until meat is tender. Drain, reserving 1½ cups liquid; cool. Shred meat mixture with two forks, and set aside.
•Place 2 whole pimientos in container of an electric blender; process until smooth.
•Cook green pepper, onion strips, and garlic in 2 tablespoons vegetable oil in a large skillet over medium-high heat 3 minutes, stirring constantly.
•Add reserved pureed pimientos, tomato puree, bay leaves, wine, salt, and pepper; cook 3 minutes.
•Stir in shredded meat and 1½ cups reserved liquid; cook 10 minutes. Discard bay leaves.
•Pour oil to depth of ¼ inch into a large skillet. Fry bread slices in hot oil over medium heat until lightly browned on each side. Place meat mixture on a platter, and surround with bread slices. Garnish, if desired. Yield: 8 servings.
Per serving: Calories 741 Fat 56.3g
Cholesterol 58mg Sodium 582mg

NEW ENGLAND BOILED DINNER

Corned beef is beef brisket that has been cured in brine for a distinct flavor. Sometimes corned beef comes with a spice packet. If not, add 1 teaspoon black peppercorns and a bay leaf to the simmering liquid.

New England Boiled Dinner

PREP: 15 MINUTES   COOK: 3½ HOURS

This one-dish meal is an East Coast classic.

1 (4-pound) corned beef brisket, trimmed
1 clove garlic, crushed
6 carrots, scraped and cut in half
3 large turnips or 1 rutabaga, peeled and
     cut into 1½-inch chunks
1 cabbage, cut into 6 wedges
1 medium onion, cut into 6 wedges
4 medium potatoes, peeled and quartered

•Place brisket and garlic in a large Dutch oven. Add spice packet. Add water to cover. Bring to a boil; cover, reduce heat, and simmer 2½ hours.
•Add carrot and next 3 ingredients. Add more water to cover, if necessary. Cover and simmer 30 minutes.
•Add potato; cover and simmer 30 more minutes or until all vegetables are tender. Transfer brisket to a serving platter. Thinly slice across the grain. Place vegetables around brisket. Serve with prepared horseradish or mustard. Yield: 8 servings.
Per serving: Calories 581 Fat 30.3g
Cholesterol 154mg Sodium 1934mg

Barbecued Beef Brisket

◄ GRILLED ►

PREP: 30 MINUTES   COOK: 4½ HOURS

Long, slow cooking makes this barbecue melt in your mouth.

1 (5- to 6-pound) boneless beef brisket
2 teaspoons paprika
½ teaspoon pepper
1 (11- x 9-inch) disposable aluminum
    roasting pan
1 cup water
Hickory chunks
Smoky Barbecue Sauce

•Sprinkle brisket with paprika and pepper; rub over surface of roast. Place roast in disposable pan; add 1 cup water, and cover with aluminum foil.
•Soak hickory chunks in water 30 minutes; drain. Wrap chunks in heavy-duty foil, and make several holes in foil.
•Light gas grill on one side; place foil-wrapped chunks directly on hot coals. Let grill preheat 10 minutes. Place pan with brisket on rack opposite hot coals; grill, covered with grill lid, 3½ to 4 hours or until tender. Turn brisket every hour, adding additional water as needed. Remove brisket from pan, reserving 1 cup pan drippings to make sauce.
•Coat grill rack with vegetable cooking spray; place rack over hot coals (400° to 500°). Place brisket on rack; grill, covered with grill lid, 10 to 15 minutes on each side. Slice brisket diagonally against the grain into thin slices. Serve with Smoky Barbecue Sauce. Yield: 12 servings.
Per serving: Calories 307 Fat 10.4g
Cholesterol 114mg Sodium 521mg

Smoky Barbecue Sauce

1 small onion, finely chopped
1 tablespoon butter or margarine,
    melted
1 cup reserved pan drippings
½ teaspoon pepper
1½ cups ketchup
1 tablespoon lemon juice
1 tablespoon Worcestershire sauce
1 teaspoon hot sauce

•Sauté onion in butter in a large skillet over medium-high heat until tender. Stir in drippings and remaining ingredients. Bring to a boil; reduce heat, and simmer 15 minutes, stirring occasionally. Yield: 3 cups.

Beer-Baked Brisket

PREP: 10 MINUTES   COOK: 4 HOURS

Beer, chili sauce, and brown sugar create a fiery sweet sauce for cooking this brisket.

1 (3- to 4-pound) beef brisket
¼ teaspoon salt
¼ teaspoon pepper
1 medium onion, sliced
1 (12-ounce) can beer
¼ cup chili sauce
3 tablespoons brown sugar
1 clove garlic, minced
½ cup water
3 tablespoons all-purpose flour

•Trim excess fat from brisket. Place brisket in a 13- x 9-inch baking dish; sprinkle with salt and pepper. Cover with onion slices.
•Combine beer and next 3 ingredients; pour over meat. Cover with aluminum foil, and bake at 350° for 3½ hours. Remove foil; bake 30 more minutes, basting occasionally with pan juices. Remove meat to a platter; keep warm.
•Skim fat from pan juices; drain, reserving 1½ cups. Combine water and flour in a saucepan, stirring until smooth. Gradually add reserved pan juices; cook over medium heat until thickened and bubbly. Slice meat across the grain into thin slices, and serve with gravy. Yield: 8 servings.
Per serving: Calories 260 Fat 12g
Cholesterol 87mg Sodium 230mg

Tangy Short Ribs and Vegetables

PREP: 12 MINUTES
SLOW COOK: 3 TO 9 HOURS

A large slow cooker is ideal for simmering several pounds of meaty little ribs. Choose the high heat setting or low heat based on how much time you need to do other things before the meal.

3 pounds lean beef short ribs
3 tablespoons vegetable oil
4 medium-size baking potatoes, unpeeled
    and quartered
4 carrots, scraped and cut into 2-inch
    pieces
1 medium onion, sliced
1 cup beef broth
2 tablespoons white vinegar
2 tablespoons ketchup
2 tablespoons prepared horseradish
1 tablespoon prepared mustard
1 teaspoon salt
½ teaspoon pepper
¼ cup all-purpose flour
3 tablespoons water

•Brown ribs in hot oil in a large skillet; drain. Place potato, carrot, and onion in a 4-quart electric slow cooker; arrange ribs over vegetables. Combine broth and next 6 ingredients; pour over ribs.
•Cover and cook on HIGH 3 to 3½ hours or on HIGH 1 hour and then reduce to LOW for 8 more hours or until ribs and vegetables are tender. Remove ribs and vegetables from slow cooker; set aside, and keep warm.
•Combine flour and water, stirring until smooth; gradually add to liquid in slow cooker. Cook, uncovered, stirring occasionally, 15 minutes or until gravy is thickened. Serve gravy with ribs and vegetables. Yield: 4 servings.
Per serving: Calories 806 Fat 36.3g
Cholesterol 158mg Sodium 1330mg

All-American Meat Loaf

PREP: 7 MINUTES   COOK: 55 MINUTES

With its sweet ketchup coating, this meat loaf may be familiar to many. For a new twist, try the Horseradish Meat Loaf variation. Your family will be pleasantly surprised by the tang.

2 pounds ground chuck
¾ cup uncooked quick-cooking oats
1 medium onion, finely chopped
½ cup ketchup
¼ cup milk
2 large eggs, lightly beaten
1 teaspoon salt
½ teaspoon pepper
½ cup ketchup
3 tablespoons brown sugar
2 teaspoons prepared mustard

•Combine first 8 ingredients in a large bowl; shape into 2 (7½- x 4-inch) loaves. Place on a lightly greased rack in broiler pan; bake at 350° for 40 minutes.
•Combine ½ cup ketchup, brown sugar, and mustard; spoon over meat loaf, and bake 15 more minutes or until meat thermometer registers 160°. Yield: 2 loaves or 8 servings.
Per serving: Calories 337 Fat 17.8g
Cholesterol 120mg Sodium 734mg

Horseradish Meat Loaf: Add 1 tablespoon prepared horseradish to beef mixture and 1 tablespoon horseradish to ketchup sauce mixture.

Blue Cheese Meat Loaf Roll

PREP: 25 MINUTES   COOK: 1 HOUR

This meat loaf has a crusty brown top and blue cheese rolled inside. Serve it with a fruit salad or just sliced apples and pears.

8 slices white bread, torn into
     small pieces
¼ cup milk
1 (4-ounce) package blue cheese,
     crumbled
1 large egg, lightly beaten
1 pound ground round
½ pound ground pork
2 cups soft breadcrumbs (homemade)
½ cup chopped onion
2 teaspoons salt
¼ teaspoon pepper
¼ cup ketchup
3 tablespoons chopped fresh parsley
1 tablespoon Worcestershire sauce
2 large eggs, lightly beaten
Garnish: fresh parsley

•Combine torn bread and milk in a bowl; stir in blue cheese and 1 egg.
•Combine ground round and next 9 ingredients; shape into a 15- x 12-inch rectangle on heavy-duty plastic wrap. Spoon blue cheese mixture on top, spreading to within 1 inch of edges. Starting at short side and using plastic wrap to lift, roll up, jellyroll fashion. Press edges and ends to seal.
•Place meat loaf roll, seam side down, on a lightly greased rack; place rack in a foil-lined broiler pan. Bake at 375° for 1 hour or until meat thermometer registers 160°. Garnish, if desired. Yield: 6 servings.
Per serving: Calories 434 Fat 15.9g
Cholesterol 189mg Sodium 1557mg

Maple-Glazed Meatballs

PREP: 25 MINUTES   COOK: 25 MINUTES

Pair these spicy-sweet meatballs with mashed potatoes or rice. Turn leftovers into a meatball sandwich.

3 slices white bread
½ cup milk
2 large eggs, lightly beaten
1 tablespoon prepared horseradish
½ teaspoon salt
½ teaspoon pepper
1½ pounds ground beef
½ cup ketchup
¼ cup water
¼ cup soy sauce
⅓ cup maple syrup
¾ teaspoon ground allspice
½ teaspoon dry mustard

•Soak bread in milk. Combine bread mixture, eggs, and next 3 ingredients in a bowl; stir well. Add beef; mix well.
•Shape beef mixture into 1 inch balls. Place on a rack in shallow broiler pan. Bake at 450° for 10 to 15 minutes or until meatballs are done.
•Combine ketchup and remaining 5 ingredients in a saucepan; cook over medium heat 5 minutes or until bubbly, stirring occasionally. Add meatballs to sauce, and cook 5 minutes or until thoroughly heated. Serve warm. Yield: 5 servings.
Per serving: Calories 445 Fat 22.1g
Cholesterol 168mg Sodium 1502mg

Sweet Sloppy Joes

◄ QUICK • FAMILY FAVORITE ►

PREP: 5 MINUTES   COOK: 23 MINUTES

Some folks like their sloppy joes sweet. Some don't. You can omit the brown sugar in this recipe, and it'll still taste great. We suggest oven-baked onion rings and sliced fruit for sides.

1½ pounds ground beef
1 small onion, chopped
1 small green pepper, chopped
1 (10¾-ounce) can tomato soup, undiluted
1 (8-ounce) can tomato sauce
1 cup ketchup
2 tablespoons brown sugar
1 tablespoon Worcestershire sauce
1 teaspoon prepared mustard
⅛ teaspoon garlic powder
4 sesame seed hamburger buns, toasted

•Cook first 3 ingredients in a large skillet until beef is browned, stirring until it crumbles; drain. Stir in soup and next 6 ingredients; simmer 10 to 15 minutes, stirring often. Serve on toasted buns. Yield: 4 servings.
Per serving: Calories 631 Fat 25.7g
Cholesterol 118mg Sodium 1814mg

Easy Tacos

◄ QUICK • FAMILY FAVORITE ►

PREP: 8 MINUTES   COOK: 5 MINUTES

A homemade seasoning blend makes these tacos unique.

12 taco shells
1 pound ground chuck
2 to 3 teaspoons Chili Seasoning Blend (page 393)
¾ cup water
¾ cup finely chopped onion
3 cups shredded lettuce
¾ cup finely chopped tomato
1½ cups (6 ounces) finely shredded Cheddar cheese
¼ cup taco sauce
¼ cup sour cream

•Heat taco shells according to package directions; keep warm. Meanwhile, brown ground chuck in a large skillet over medium heat,

stirring until it crumbles; drain. Add Chili Seasoning Blend and water, stirring well. Cook over medium heat 3 to 5 minutes or until most of liquid almost evaporates. Spoon meat mixture into shells; top with onion and remaining desired condiments. Yield: 4 servings.
Per serving: Calories 633 Fat 41.2g
Cholesterol 117mg Sodium 817mg

Beefy Chimichangas

◄ FAMILY FAVORITE ►

PREP: 30 MINUTES   COOK: 20 MINUTES

1 pound ground chuck
½ cup finely chopped onion
1 (16-ounce) can refried beans
2 teaspoons chili powder
½ teaspoon ground cumin
2 cloves garlic, minced
3 (8-ounce) cans tomato sauce
10 (10-inch) flour tortillas
1 (4.5-ounce) can chopped green chiles, drained
1 canned jalapeño pepper, seeded and chopped
Vegetable oil
1½ cups (6 ounces) shredded Cheddar or Monterey Jack cheese

•Brown ground chuck in a large skillet over medium heat, stirring until it crumbles; drain well. Stir in onion and next 4 ingredients; add ½ cup tomato sauce.
•Spoon about ⅓ cup of meat mixture off center of a tortilla. Fold edge nearest filling up and over filling, just until mixture is covered. Fold in opposite sides of tortilla to center; roll up. Secure with wooden picks. Repeat with remaining filling and tortillas.
•Combine remaining tomato sauce, green chiles, and jalapeño pepper in a saucepan; cook over medium heat just until heated.
•Pour oil to depth of 1 inch into a Dutch oven; heat to 375°.
•Fry chimichangas 2 minutes or until golden, turning once. Drain well on paper towels. Remove wooden picks. Arrange chimichangas on serving plates. Spoon hot tomato sauce over tops, and immediately sprinkle with shredded cheese. Yield: 10 servings.
Per serving: Calories 607 Fat 43.6g
Cholesterol 51mg Sodium 912mg

Moussaka

PREP: 1 HOUR AND 40 MINUTES
COOK: 46 MINUTES

Moussaka is a Greek dish of sliced eggplant and ground beef or lamb baked in a rich béchamel sauce.

1 pound ground beef or lamb
2 large onions, chopped (3 cups)
¼ cup tomato paste
1 tablespoon dried parsley flakes
¼ teaspoon salt
¼ teaspoon pepper
1 cup water
2 medium eggplants (about 2 pounds)
2 teaspoons salt
¼ cup plus 2 tablespoons olive oil
½ cup cracker crumbs, divided (about 12 saltines)
1 large egg, lightly beaten
¼ cup plus 2 tablespoons butter or margarine
¼ cup plus 2 tablespoons all-purpose flour
3 cups milk
½ teaspoon salt
¼ teaspoon pepper
⅛ teaspoon ground nutmeg
2 large eggs, lightly beaten
1 cup freshly grated Parmesan cheese

•Cook ground beef and onion in a large skillet until beef is browned, stirring until it crumbles; drain well. Stir in tomato paste and next 4 ingredients. Cover and simmer 30 minutes.
•Peel eggplants, if desired, and cut into ¼-inch-thick slices. To extract bitterness, sprinkle 1 teaspoon salt on each side of slices; let stand 30 minutes. Rinse and pat dry with a paper towel. Brush eggplant slices with olive oil; place on a lightly greased rack of broiler pan. Broil 5½ inches from heat 3 to 5 minutes. Turn, brush with olive oil, and broil 3 to 5 more minutes or until tender.
•Layer half of eggplant slices in a lightly greased 13- x 9-inch baking dish. Sprinkle ¼ cup cracker crumbs over eggplant.
•Add 1 egg and remaining ¼ cup cracker crumbs to meat sauce. Spoon half of meat sauce over eggplant. Repeat layers with remaining eggplant and meat sauce. Set aside.
•Melt butter in a large heavy saucepan over low heat; add flour, stirring until smooth.

Cook 1 minute, stirring constantly. Gradually add milk; cook over medium heat, stirring constantly, until thickened and bubbly. Stir in ½ teaspoon salt, ¼ teaspoon pepper, and nutmeg.

•Gradually stir about 1 cup white sauce into 2 eggs; return to remaining white sauce, stirring well. Pour sauce over meat. Bake, uncovered, at 350° for 40 minutes. Sprinkle with cheese; bake 6 more minutes. Yield: 8 servings.

Per serving: Calories 517 Fat 36g
Cholesterol 159mg Sodium 1239mg

Stuffed Cabbage Rolls

PREP: 30 MINUTES   COOK: 2 HOURS

1 medium-size green cabbage
    (2½ pounds)
1 large onion, chopped
2 tablespoons vegetable oil
½ cup uncooked brown rice
1 pound ground chuck
½ teaspoon salt
¼ teaspoon pepper
1 (10-ounce) can sauerkraut, drained
⅓ cup firmly packed brown sugar
3 cups tomato juice

•Remove 12 large outer leaves and 6 small leaves of cabbage; cook leaves in boiling water 5 to 8 minutes or until just tender; drain and set aside. Reserve remaining cabbage for other uses.

•Sauté onion in hot oil in a large skillet over medium-high heat until crisp-tender. Add rice, and cook 3 to 5 minutes over medium heat, stirring constantly. Cool rice mixture slightly.

•Combine rice mixture, ground chuck, salt, and pepper. Spoon about ¼ cup mixture in center of each large cabbage leaf; reserve smaller cabbage leaves. Fold left and right sides of large leaf over; roll up, beginning at bottom.

•Repeat procedure with remaining large cabbage leaves. Chill rolls overnight, if desired, or proceed immediately.

•Arrange reserved small cabbage leaves in bottom of a Dutch oven or stockpot. Spoon half each of sauerkraut and brown sugar over small cabbage leaves. Top with half of cabbage rolls, seam side down. Repeat layers

with remaining sauerkraut, brown sugar, and cabbage rolls.

•Pour tomato juice over assembled layers; bring to a boil. Cover, reduce heat, and simmer 2 hours or until rice is done. Serve immediately. Yield: 6 servings.

Per serving: Calories 424 Fat 21g
Cholesterol 57mg Sodium 963mg

Picadillo

PREP: 15 MINUTES   COOK: 35 MINUTES

This well-spiced beef mixture is laden with olives and almonds. In Cuba, it's served with black beans and rice; in Mexico, it's used as a stuffing. We recommend it over rice or rolled inside warm flour tortillas.

2 medium onions, finely chopped
2 large green peppers, chopped
2 cloves garlic, minced
1½ pounds lean ground beef or pork
½ teaspoon salt
½ teaspoon celery salt
½ teaspoon dried oregano
½ teaspoon ground cinnamon
¼ teaspoon pepper
2 tablespoons Worcestershire sauce
1 (8-ounce) can tomato sauce
1 (14.5-ounce) can whole tomatoes,
    undrained and chopped
1 (3-ounce) jar pimiento-stuffed olives,
    drained
½ cup raisins
7 cups cooked yellow rice
½ cup slivered almonds, toasted

•Cook first 4 ingredients in a large skillet over medium-high heat until beef is browned, stirring until it crumbles; drain. Add salt and next 9 ingredients; stir well. Bring to a boil; cover, reduce heat, and simmer 30 minutes, stirring occasionally. Serve over rice. Sprinkle with almonds. Yield: 7 servings.

Per serving: Calories 688 Fat 30.7g
Cholesterol 64mg Sodium 1964mg

Italian Meat Sauce

◀ FAMILY FAVORITE ▶

PREP: 10 MINUTES   COOK: 1 HOUR

Here's a basic meat sauce that's good for a multitude of uses. Freeze it in 1- or 2-cup portions so it will be quick to thaw for weeknight dinners.

1½ pounds ground chuck
1½ cups chopped onion
3 cloves garlic, minced
3 (14.5-ounce) cans plum tomatoes,
    undrained and chopped
1 medium-size green pepper, chopped
1 (6-ounce) can tomato paste
1 cup water
2 tablespoons chopped fresh parsley or
    2 teaspoons dried parsley flakes
1 tablespoon sugar
2 teaspoons salt
2 teaspoons dried oregano
2 teaspoons dried basil
½ teaspoon fennel seeds
¾ teaspoon pepper

•Cook first 3 ingredients in a Dutch oven until beef is browned, stirring until it crumbles; drain well.

•Add tomatoes and remaining ingredients; bring to a boil. Reduce heat, and simmer, uncovered, 45 minutes. Serve sauce over spaghetti or use it in lasagna or manicotti. Yield: 10 cups.

Per 1-cup serving: Calories 206 Fat 11.2g
Cholesterol 44mg Sodium 713mg

Italian Crêpes

PREP: 20 MINUTES   COOK: 2½ HOURS

You'll find these hearty Italian stuffed crêpes quite filling. Team them with a tossed salad or green beans.

2 pounds ground chuck
¼ cup diced onion
6 stalks celery, thinly sliced
½ teaspoon garlic powder
¼ teaspoon salt
½ teaspoon pepper
1 (14.5-ounce) can whole tomatoes, undrained and chopped
3 (8-ounce) cans tomato sauce
2 cups small-curd cottage cheese
2½ cups (10 ounces) shredded sharp Cheddar cheese, divided
½ cup grated Parmesan cheese
Basic Crêpes (page 76)

•Cook first 3 ingredients in a Dutch oven until beef is browned, stirring until it crumbles; drain. Stir in garlic powder and next 4 ingredients; cover, reduce heat, and simmer 1 hour, stirring often. Uncover and cook 30 minutes, stirring often.
•Combine cottage cheese, 2 cups Cheddar cheese, and Parmesan cheese; set aside.
•Spoon half of meat sauce into a lightly greased 13- x 9-inch baking dish. Layer 6 crêpes over meat mixture, and spread with half of cheese mixture. Place 6 crêpes on cheese mixture, and layer with remaining meat mixture, 4 crêpes, and cheese mixture.
•Bake at 350° for 25 minutes. Sprinkle with remaining ½ cup Cheddar cheese; bake 5 more minutes. Let stand 5 minutes before serving. Yield: 8 servings.
Per serving: Calories 608 Fat 33.8g
Cholesterol 160mg Sodium 1346mg

Note: For a quicker version, substitute 10-inch flour tortillas for crêpes. Use 1½ tortillas for each layer for a total of 4½ (10-inch) tortillas.

Salisbury Steak

◄ FAMILY FAVORITE ►

PREP: 10 MINUTES   COOK: 35 MINUTES

Serve this home-style recipe with mashed potatoes or Texas toast. It's comfort food at its finest.

1 (10¾-ounce) can golden mushroom soup, undiluted and divided
1½ pounds ground beef
½ cup finely chopped onion
¼ cup Italian-seasoned breadcrumbs
1 large egg, beaten
1½ cups sliced fresh mushrooms
⅓ cup beef broth
¼ cup Worcestershire sauce
¼ teaspoon pepper

•Combine ¼ cup soup, beef, and next 3 ingredients; stir well. Shape mixture into 6 (½-inch-thick) patties.
•Brown patties in a large skillet over medium-high heat. Remove patties, discarding half of pan drippings. Cook mushrooms in remaining drippings in skillet over medium-high heat, stirring constantly, until tender. Combine remaining soup, beef broth, Worcestershire sauce, and pepper; add to mushroom mixture.
•Return patties to skillet; bring to a boil. Cover, reduce heat, and simmer 20 minutes. Yield: 6 servings.
Per serving: Calories 386 Fat 25.8g
Cholesterol 144mg Sodium 797mg

Basic Burgers

◄ QUICK • FAMILY FAVORITE ►

PREP: 7 MINUTES   COOK: 15 MINUTES

1 pound ground chuck
1 large egg, beaten
¼ cup soft breadcrumbs (homemade)
1 tablespoon grated onion
½ teaspoon all-purpose Greek seasoning (we tested with Cavender's)
¼ teaspoon salt
¼ teaspoon pepper
2 teaspoons Worcestershire sauce
4 hamburger buns

•Combine first 8 ingredients, blending well. Shape into 4 patties. Grill, uncovered, over medium coals (300° to 350°) 15 minutes or until done, turning once. Serve on buns. Yield: 4 servings.
Per serving: Calories 395 Fat 20.4g
Cholesterol 133mg Sodium 587mg

For broiling: Place patties on broiler pan; broil 3 inches from heat about 10 minutes or until done, turning once.

For panfrying: Heat a heavy skillet until hot. Add patties, and cook over medium heat about 8 minutes or until done, turning once.

Grilled Blue Cheese Burgers

◄ GRILLED ►

**PREP: 27 MINUTES   CHILL: 1 HOUR
COOK: 24 MINUTES**

These grilled burgers deliver a punch of blue cheese with each bite. Serve the gourmet burgers with sautéed mushrooms.

4 ounces crumbled blue cheese
½ (3-ounce) package cream cheese, softened
3 pounds ground chuck
¼ cup minced onion
1 teaspoon salt
1 teaspoon pepper

•Combine cheeses in a bowl, stirring well; cover and chill.
•Combine ground chuck and remaining 3 ingredients; shape mixture into 16 thin patties. Spoon about 1 tablespoon cheese mixture onto each of 8 patties (do not spread to edges); top with remaining patties, pressing edges to seal well. Cover and chill 1 hour.
•Grill, uncovered, over medium-hot coals (350° to 400°) 12 minutes on each side or until done. Yield: 8 servings.
Per serving: Calories 413 Fat 29.3g
Cholesterol 116mg Sodium 578mg

Basil 'n' Pesto Burgers

◄ QUICK ►

PREP: 14 MINUTES   COOK: 12 MINUTES

Here's a unique burger. Fresh basil and sun-dried tomato pesto are blended into the ground beef for a sandwich that will win raves from your family.

1 pound ground chuck
½ cup chopped fresh basil
¼ cup sun-dried tomato pesto
¼ cup freshly grated Parmesan cheese
3 tablespoons minced onion
¼ teaspoon pepper
4 green leaf lettuce leaves
3 plum tomatoes, sliced
4 thin slices sweet onion
4 kaiser rolls or onion buns, split and
    toasted (optional)

•Combine first 6 ingredients; shape mixture into 4 patties.
•Place a large skillet over medium heat until hot. Add patties, and cook 5 minutes on each side or until done.
•Place a lettuce leaf, 3 slices tomato, and an onion slice on bottom half of each roll; top with patties. Top with remaining roll halves. Yield: 4 servings.
Per serving: Calories 488 Fat 24.7g
Cholesterol 88mg Sodium 571mg

Salsa Burgers

◄ GRILLED ►

PREP: 12 MINUTES   COOK: 12 MINUTES

You can minimize the heat by choosing a mild or medium salsa for this burger.

2 pounds ground round
1 onion, finely chopped
⅓ cup soft breadcrumbs (homemade)
1 large egg, beaten
2 tablespoons hot salsa
2 teaspoons brown sugar
1 teaspoon salt
1 teaspoon prepared mustard
½ teaspoon pepper
8 lettuce leaves
2 tomatoes, sliced
1 small onion, sliced
8 hamburger buns with sesame seeds
Additional salsa

•Combine first 9 ingredients in a bowl; shape into 8 patties. Cook, covered with grill lid, over medium-hot coals (350° to 400°) 5 to 6 minutes on each side or until done.
•Place lettuce, tomato, and onion on bottom half of each hamburger bun; top each with a patty. Add additional salsa. Cover with bun tops. Yield: 8 servings.
Per serving: Calories 513 Fat 33.2g
Cholesterol 123mg Sodium 713mg

Liver and Caramelized Onions

◄ QUICK ►

PREP: 6 MINUTES   COOK: 26 MINUTES

Liver smothered in caramelized onions is prized by many a Southerner.

2 medium onions, thinly sliced
3 tablespoons butter or margarine,
    melted
3 tablespoons olive oil
1 teaspoon salt
½ teaspoon pepper
1 pound thinly sliced calves' liver
¼ cup all-purpose flour

•Sauté onion in butter in a large skillet over medium heat 20 minutes or until tender and golden, stirring occasionally. Remove onion; add olive oil to skillet.
•Sprinkle salt and pepper on both sides of liver; dredge in flour. Shake off excess flour. Add liver to skillet, and cook over medium-high heat 3 minutes on each side or until browned.
•Transfer liver and onion slices to a warm serving platter; serve immediately. Yield: 4 servings.
Per serving: Calories 378 Fat 23.4g
Cholesterol 425mg Sodium 760mg

VEAL

Veal is simply very young beef. It has a mild flavor that makes it especially suitable for use in recipes that include high-flavored sauces, rich seasonings, and spicy coatings.

Because veal comes from young calves, it's usually very lean, has no marbling, and little external fat. Good veal is pale pink in color. In fact, the redder the meat, the older the veal. Bones should be porous and red. Any fat that is visible should be very pale in color.

Veal requires careful cooking because its lack of fat can cause it to become tough and dry. Veal roasts and shanks respond best to slow cooking by moist heat methods. Covering veal at least part of the time during cooking is recommended to maximize tenderness. Veal cuts such as chops, cutlets,

and scallops, however, are best when quickly pan-fried.

One rule stands true—you should never broil veal. That's because it has a high

proportion of connective tissue running through it that could make it tough. We recommend that veal be cooked to 160° (medium doneness).

TIMETABLE FOR ROASTING VEAL

CUT	APPROXIMATE WEIGHT IN POUNDS	APPROXIMATE TOTAL COOKING TIMES IN MINUTES PER POUND AT 325° (160° INTERNAL TEMPERATURE)
Rib roast	3 to 5	25 to 30
Loin	3 to 4	34 to 36
Sirloin	6 to 8	25 to 30
Boneless shoulder or rump	3 to 6	30 to 35

Veal

• RETAIL CUTS •
WHERE THEY COME FROM
HOW TO COOK THEM

LEG (ROUND)
SIRLOIN
LOIN
RIB
SHOULDER
FORESHANK & BREAST

RIB

Rib Roast
Roast

Boneless Rib Roast
Roast

Crown Roast
Roast

Boneless Rib Chop
Braise, Panfry, Broil

Rib Chop
Braise, Panfry, Broil

Short Ribs
Braise, Cook in Liquid

SHOULDER

Blade Roast
Braise, Roast

Arm Roast
Braise, Roast

Blade Steak
Braise, Panfry

Arm Steak
Braise, Panfry

Boneless Shoulder Arm Roast
Braise, Roast

Boneless Shoulder Eye Roast
Braise, Roast

LEG (ROUND)

Boneless Rump Roast
Braise, Roast

Round Steak
Braise, Panfry

Top Round Steak
Braise, Panfry

Leg Cutlet
Braise, Panfry, Broil

FORESHANK & BREAST

Breast
Braise, Roast

Boneless Breast Roast
Braise, Roast

Cross Cut Shank
Braise, Cook in Liquid

Riblet
Braise, Cook in Liquid

Shank
Braise, Cook in Liquid

LOIN

Loin Roast
Roast

Boneless Loin Roast
Roast

Loin Chop
Braise, Panfry, Broil

Kidney Chop
Braise, Panfry

Top Loin Chop
Braise, Panfry, Broil

Butterfly Chop
Braise, Panfry, Broil

SIRLOIN

Sirloin Roast
Roast

Boneless Sirloin Roast
Roast

Sirloin Steak
Braise, Panfry, Broil

Top Sirloin Steak
Braise, Panfry, Broil

OTHER CUTS

Veal for Stew
Braise, Cook in Liquid

Ground Veal
Panfry, Broil

Cubes for Kabobs
Braise

Cubed Steak
Braise, Panfry

Osso Buco

PREP: 27 MINUTES

COOK: 2 HOURS AND 25 MINUTES

This Milanese specialty of braised veal shanks is a long-simmering dish with layers of flavor. It's finished with a sprinkling of gremolata, a blend of parsley, lemon rind, and garlic.

1½ cups finely chopped onion
1 cup finely chopped carrot
½ cup finely chopped celery
2 cloves garlic, minced
¼ cup butter or margarine, melted
6 (2-inch-thick) crosscut veal shanks
   (about 6 pounds)
1 teaspoon salt
1 teaspoon pepper
½ cup all-purpose flour
½ cup olive oil
1 cup dry white wine
3 cups coarsely chopped tomato or
   1 (28-ounce) can plum tomatoes,
   undrained and chopped
2 cups chicken broth
⅓ cup chopped fresh parsley
2 bay leaves
½ teaspoon dried basil
½ teaspoon dried thyme
3 tablespoons chopped fresh parsley
1 teaspoon grated lemon rind
1 clove garlic, minced

•Sauté first 4 ingredients in butter in a Dutch oven until vegetables are tender. Set aside.
•Sprinkle veal with salt and pepper; dredge in flour. Heat oil in a large skillet; add veal, and cook until browned on both sides. Place in Dutch oven with vegetables. Discard oil.
•Add wine to skillet, and cook over medium-high heat until reduced to ½ cup (about 8 minutes). Stir in tomato and next 5 ingredients. Bring to a boil; pour over veal in Dutch oven. Cover and bake at 350° for 2 hours or until veal is tender. Discard bay leaves.
•Combine 3 tablespoons parsley, lemon rind, and 1 clove garlic; sprinkle over veal. Serve in wide-rimmed pasta bowls. Yield: 6 servings.
Per serving: Calories 607 Fat 27.4g
Cholesterol 298mg Sodium 1057mg

Note: Dip the marrow out of veal bones, using a tiny marrow scoop, if desired. It's a delicacy.

Apple Veal Chops

◀ HEALTHY ▶

PREP: 10 MINUTES   COOK: 40 MINUTES

¼ cup all-purpose flour
2 tablespoons chopped fresh marjoram or
   oregano or 2 teaspoons dried marjoram
   or oregano
½ teaspoon salt
4 (1-inch-thick) veal chops (about 2
   pounds)
2 tablespoons butter or margarine, melted
1 tablespoon olive oil
1 medium onion, thinly sliced
1 tablespoon all-purpose flour
½ cup chicken broth
¼ cup firmly packed brown sugar
¼ cup apple brandy or apple juice
2 Granny Smith apples, unpeeled and cut
   into ½-inch-thick slices

•Combine first 3 ingredients in a shallow bowl; stir well. Dredge veal chops in flour mixture.
•Brown chops in butter and oil in a large skillet over medium-high heat. Remove chops from skillet, reserving 1 teaspoon drippings in skillet.
•Add onion to drippings, and sauté 2 minutes. Add 1 tablespoon flour; cook 1 minute, stirring constantly. Combine broth, brown sugar, and apple brandy; gradually add to onion mixture.
•Return chops to skillet; top with apple slices. Cover and cook over medium-low heat 30 minutes or until chops are tender. Yield: 4 servings.
Per serving: Calories 442 Fat 14.6g
Cholesterol 161mg Sodium 611mg

Osso Buco

Veal Schnitzel

◄ QUICK ►

PREP: 7 MINUTES   COOK: 16 MINUTES

Schnitzel is German for cutlet. This skillet veal is topped with nutty Gruyère cheese.

1 pound veal cutlets
2 large eggs
1 teaspoon salt
¾ teaspoon coarsely ground pepper
½ cup all-purpose flour
1½ cups soft breadcrumbs (homemade)
¾ cup butter
5 ounces Gruyère cheese, thinly sliced
3 tablespoons chopped fresh parsley
Garnishes: lemon slices, fresh parsley sprigs

•Place veal between two sheets of heavy-duty plastic wrap; flatten to ⅛-inch thickness, using a meat mallet or rolling pin.
•Combine eggs, salt, and pepper; beat well. Dredge cutlets in flour; dip in egg mixture, and coat with breadcrumbs.
•Melt half of butter in a large skillet over medium heat; add half of cutlets, and cook 4 to 5 minutes. Turn cutlets, and top with half of cheese. Cover and cook 3 more minutes. Repeat procedure with remaining butter, veal, and cheese. Sprinkle with chopped parsley; garnish, if desired. Yield: 4 servings.
Per serving: Calories 684 Fat 52.3g
Cholesterol 333mg Sodium 1263mg

Veal Cordon Bleu

PREP: 25 MINUTES   COOK: 14 MINUTES

The key to well-made cordon bleu rolls is neatly tucking the ham and cheese inside and securing the rolls well with wooden picks. This enables the rolls to brown evenly.

4 veal cutlets (1 pound)
4 (¾-ounce) slices cooked ham
4 (¾-ounce) slices Swiss cheese
2 tablespoons all-purpose flour
¼ teaspoon pepper
¼ teaspoon ground allspice
1 large egg, beaten
½ cup fine, dry breadcrumbs (commercial)
1½ tablespoons butter, melted
1½ tablespoons olive oil

•Place veal between two sheets of plastic wrap or wax paper; flatten to ¼-inch thickness, using a meat mallet or rolling pin. Place 1 slice of ham and 1 slice of cheese in center of each veal cutlet. Fold long sides of veal over cheese; tuck ends under, and secure with wooden picks.
•Combine flour, pepper, and allspice. Dredge veal in flour mixture; dip in egg, and roll in breadcrumbs.
•Sauté veal rolls in butter and oil in a medium skillet over medium heat until fully cooked, 12 to 14 minutes, turning once. Yield: 4 servings.
Per serving: Calories 397 Fat 21.5g
Cholesterol 191mg Sodium 619mg

Veal Parmigiana

◄ FAMILY FAVORITE ►

PREP: 20 MINUTES   COOK: 48 MINUTES

We've replaced the expected eggplant with tender browned veal cutlets in this Parmigiana. You can also prepare this recipe using chicken, if desired.

2 (15-ounce) cans tomato sauce
1 tablespoon butter or margarine, melted
1 tablespoon Worcestershire sauce
1 teaspoon dried oregano
1 teaspoon dried basil
2 cloves garlic, minced
¼ teaspoon pepper
2 large eggs
¼ teaspoon pepper
2 pounds veal cutlets, cut into serving-size pieces
About 4 cups soft breadcrumbs (homemade)
½ cup olive oil
¼ cup freshly grated Parmesan cheese
1 (8-ounce) package sliced mozzarella cheese

•Combine first 7 ingredients in a saucepan; cook over medium heat 5 minutes, stirring occasionally. Set aside.
•Combine eggs and pepper; beat well. Place cutlets between two sheets of plastic wrap; flatten to ⅛-inch thickness, using a meat mallet or rolling pin.
•Dip cutlets in egg mixture, and dredge in breadcrumbs. Brown cutlets in hot oil 4 minutes over medium heat on each side. Place in a lightly greased 13- x 9-inch baking dish. Pour tomato sauce mixture over veal, and sprinkle with Parmesan cheese.
•Cover and bake at 350° for 30 minutes. Uncover and top with mozzarella cheese; bake 5 more minutes or until cheese melts. Yield: 6 servings.
Per serving: Calories 581 Fat 33.9g
Cholesterol 227mg Sodium 1392mg

Veal Marsala

◄ QUICK ►

PREP: 6 MINUTES   COOK: 13 MINUTES

Scaloppine is the thinnest piece of veal you can buy. It's so tender it saves you the time and effort of pounding meat.

1 teaspoon chopped fresh or dried rosemary
½ teaspoon salt
½ teaspoon freshly ground pepper
1 pound (¼-inch-thick) veal scaloppine
2 tablespoons olive oil
1 (8-ounce) package sliced fresh mushrooms
2 cloves garlic, minced
2 teaspoons cornstarch
1 teaspoon chicken bouillon granules
⅔ cup water
⅓ cup dry Marsala

•Rub first 3 ingredients over veal. Heat oil in a large nonstick skillet over medium heat. Add half of veal; cook 2 minutes on each side or until lightly browned. Remove veal from skillet; keep warm. Repeat with remaining veal.
•Add mushrooms and garlic to skillet; cook over medium-high heat, stirring constantly, 3 minutes or until tender.
•Combine cornstarch and remaining 3 ingredients; add to skillet. Cook, stirring constantly, 1 minute or until thick and bubbly. Serve over veal. Yield: 4 servings.
Per serving: Calories 213 Fat 10.6g
Cholesterol 94mg Sodium 599mg

Veal Piccata

PREP: 10 MINUTES   COOK: 5 MINUTES

1 pound veal cutlets
1 teaspoon salt
½ teaspoon pepper
½ cup all-purpose flour
3 tablespoons butter
2 tablespoons olive oil
3 tablespoons lemon juice
2 cloves garlic, minced
3 tablespoons dry white wine
1 tablespoon chopped fresh parsley

•Place veal between two sheets of plastic wrap or wax paper, and flatten to ¼-inch thickness, using a meat mallet or rolling pin. Cut veal into 6 serving-size pieces. Pat veal dry (photo 1). Rub salt and pepper on veal, and dredge in flour (photo 2).

•Heat butter and oil in a large skillet over medium-high heat. Add veal in 2 batches, and cook 1 to 2 minutes on each side (photo 3). Remove veal to a warm platter; cover and keep warm. Drain drippings.

•Add lemon juice, garlic, and white wine to deglaze skillet (photo 4); cook over medium heat 1 to 2 minutes. To serve, spoon juices over veal; sprinkle with parsley. Yield: 4 servings.

Per serving: Calories 294 Fat 13.5g
Cholesterol 112mg Sodium 708mg

WHAT'S A PICCATA?

Veal Piccata is a classic main dish hailing from Italy. Thin cutlets of veal are seasoned and dredged in flour and then quickly panfried until golden. Wine and lemon juice are added to deglaze the pan, and the tangy sauce is drizzled over the veal just before serving.

The piccata recipe is so simple and the results so outstanding that it's often applied to boneless chicken breasts that have been pounded to resemble thin cutlets of veal. Buttered noodles and a green vegetable pair well with this quick entrée.

1. Pat slices of veal dry with paper towels. This prevents the meat from spattering in the skillet.

2. Season veal evenly with salt and pepper. Dredge seasoned pieces of veal in flour.

3. Panfry veal, in batches, in a hot skillet, taking care not to crowd veal in skillet. This ensures proper browning.

4. Deglaze the skillet by adding lemon juice and wine. Then spoon cooked juices over veal before serving.

LAMB

Lamb is meat from sheep slaughtered when less than a year old. Mutton, meat of older sheep, is more popular in England than in the United States.

Purchase lamb with a bright pink color, pink bones, and white fat. If the meat and bones are dark red, it usually means the meat is older. Always trim excess fat. A silvery skin called *fell* usually surrounds big cuts of lamb. This skin is sometimes left on whole roasts to hold in natural juices while the lamb cooks. Trim the fell from smaller cuts before cooking or meat may curl. Most cuts of lamb are tender enough to be cooked by dry heat methods.

TIMETABLE FOR ROASTING LAMB

CUT	APPROXIMATE WEIGHT IN POUNDS	INTERNAL TEMPERATURE	APPROXIMATE TOTAL COOKING TIMES IN HOURS AT 325°
Leg			
Whole (bone-in)	6 to 7	160° (medium)	2½ to 3½
Half (bone-in)	3 to 4	160° (medium)	2 to 2¾
Shoulder (boneless)	4 to 6	160° (medium)	2½ to 3¾
Rib roast*	1½ to 2½	160° (medium)	1 to 1⅔
Crown roast (unstuffed)*	2 to 3	160° (medium)	1 to 1½

*Oven set at 375° and not preheated

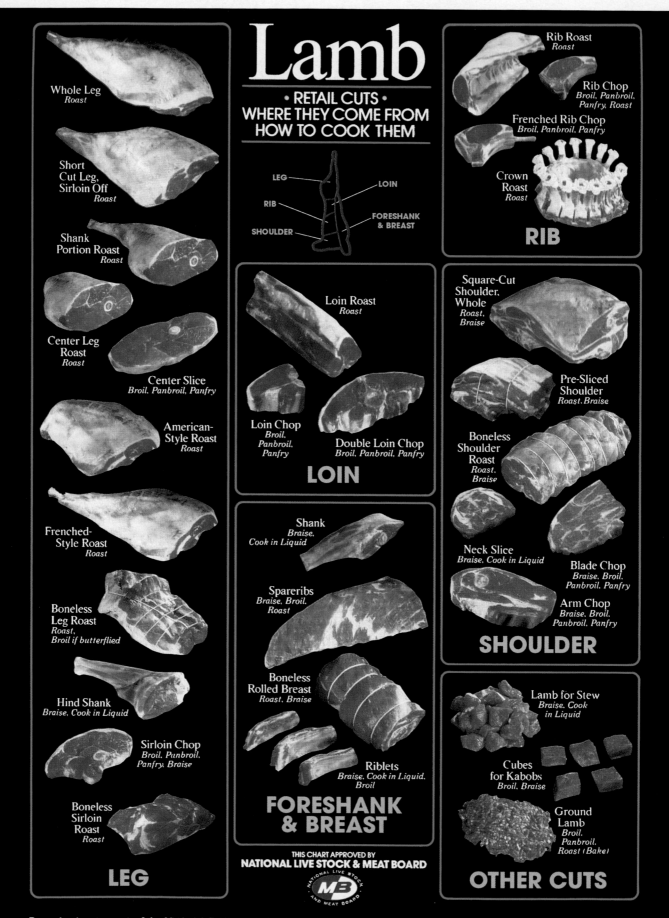

Lamb

• RETAIL CUTS •
WHERE THEY COME FROM
HOW TO COOK THEM

LEG — LOIN
RIB — FORESHANK & BREAST
SHOULDER

LEG

Whole Leg
Roast

Short Cut Leg, Sirloin Off
Roast

Shank Portion Roast
Roast

Center Leg Roast
Roast

Center Slice
Broil, Panbroil, Panfry

American-Style Roast
Roast

Frenched-Style Roast
Roast

Boneless Leg Roast
Roast, Broil if butterflied

Hind Shank
Braise, Cook in Liquid

Sirloin Chop
Broil, Panbroil, Panfry, Braise

Boneless Sirloin Roast
Roast

RIB

Rib Roast
Roast

Rib Chop
Broil, Panbroil, Panfry, Roast

Frenched Rib Chop
Broil, Panbroil, Panfry

Crown Roast
Roast

LOIN

Loin Roast
Roast

Loin Chop
Broil, Panbroil, Panfry

Double Loin Chop
Broil, Panbroil, Panfry

SHOULDER

Square-Cut Shoulder, Whole
Roast, Braise

Pre-Sliced Shoulder
Roast, Braise

Boneless Shoulder Roast
Roast, Braise

Neck Slice
Braise, Cook in Liquid

Blade Chop
Braise, Broil, Panbroil, Panfry

Arm Chop
Braise, Broil, Panbroil, Panfry

FORESHANK & BREAST

Shank
Braise, Cook in Liquid

Spareribs
Braise, Broil, Roast

Boneless Rolled Breast
Roast, Braise

Riblets
Braise, Cook in Liquid, Broil

OTHER CUTS

Lamb for Stew
Braise, Cook in Liquid

Cubes for Kabobs
Broil, Braise

Ground Lamb
Broil, Panbroil, Roast (Bake)

THIS CHART APPROVED BY
NATIONAL LIVE STOCK & MEAT BOARD

Minted Leg of Lamb

PREP: 20 MINUTES

COOK: ABOUT 2½ HOURS

Lamb and mint jelly are a classic pairing. Here the mint flavor is rubbed onto the meat before cooking.

1 teaspoon salt
1 to 1½ teaspoons dried mint flakes
½ teaspoon ground red pepper
1 (9-pound) bone-in leg of lamb
2 medium onions, chopped
3 cups dry white wine
½ cup olive oil
½ cup Dijon mustard
4 cloves garlic, chopped
2 tablespoons Worcestershire sauce

• Combine first 3 ingredients; rub into lamb. Place chopped onion in center of a lightly greased roasting pan; place lamb on top of onion.

• Combine wine and remaining 4 ingredients; pour over lamb. Insert meat thermometer into thickest part of lamb, making sure it does not touch bone or fat.

• Bake at 325° for 1 hour and 45 minutes to 2½ hours or until thermometer registers 150° (medium-rare) or 160° (medium), basting lamb every 30 minutes. Let stand 10 minutes. Yield: 12 servings.

Per serving: Calories 333 Fat 14.7g
Cholesterol 139mg Sodium 494mg

Greek-Style Leg of Lamb

◄ GRILLED ►

PREP: 10 MINUTES   MARINATE: 8 HOURS

COOK: 40 MINUTES

Butterflying a large piece of meat (splitting meat down the center, but not completely through) helps it cook quickly and evenly, especially on the grill.

1 (4-pound) boneless leg of lamb, butterflied
½ cup olive oil
½ cup lemon juice
1 tablespoon onion powder
1 tablespoon fresh oregano or 1 teaspoon dried oregano
2 tablespoons fresh or dried rosemary
6 cloves garlic, crushed

• Trim fat from lamb. Place lamb in a large heavy-duty, zip-top plastic bag or shallow dish. Combine oil and remaining 5 ingredients; pour over lamb. Seal or cover; marinate in refrigerator 8 hours, turning occasionally.

• Remove lamb from marinade, discarding marinade. Grill, uncovered, over medium coals (300° to 350°) 20 minutes; turn and grill 20 more minutes or until a meat thermometer registers 150° (medium-rare) or 160° (medium). Let stand 10 minutes. Slice diagonally across the grain. Yield: 8 servings.

Per serving: Calories 330 Fat 17.5g
Cholesterol 123mg Sodium 94mg

Shish Kabobs

◄ GRILLED ►

PREP: 42 MINUTES   MARINATE: 8 HOURS

GRILL: 20 MINUTES

Cut uniform-sized pieces of vegetables for this traditional skewered meal so they'll cook evenly on the grill.

1 cup olive oil
2 tablespoons fresh lemon juice
2 tablespoons chopped fresh mint or parsley
½ tablespoon salt
2 teaspoons dried oregano
1 teaspoon pepper
4 cloves garlic, minced
1 (3-pound) boneless leg of lamb, cut into 2-inch cubes
3 small purple onions, cut into fourths
2 green or sweet red peppers, cut into fourths
2 tomatoes, cut into fourths, or 8 whole cherry tomatoes
8 whole fresh mushrooms
3 tablespoons fresh lemon juice
3 tablespoons olive oil
Saffron Rice (page 289) or couscous (optional)

• Combine first 7 ingredients; stir well. Place lamb in a large heavy-duty, zip-top plastic bag or shallow dish. Pour marinade over lamb; seal or cover. Marinate in refrigerator 8 hours, turning occasionally.

• Remove lamb from marinade, discarding marinade.

• Alternate lamb cubes and next 4 ingredients on eight 12-inch skewers.

• Combine 3 tablespoons lemon juice and 3 tablespoons olive oil; brush on kabobs.

• Grill, covered with grill lid, over medium-hot coals (350° to 400°) 20 minutes or to desired doneness, turning once. Serve with Saffron Rice or couscous, if desired. Yield: 8 servings.

Per serving: Calories 857 Fat 61.2g
Cholesterol 163mg Sodium 530mg

CARVING A LEG OF LAMB

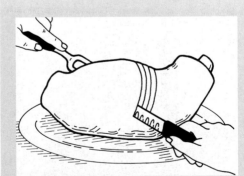

1. Place shank bone to right. Cut 3 slices from thin side parallel to leg bone. Turn leg over to rest on cut side. Steady leg with fork; cut slices to the bone (shown).

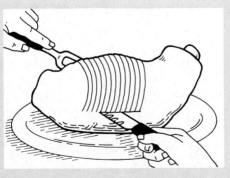

2. Steady lamb with carving fork, and cut leg horizontally along the bone to release slices. Remove slices to serving plate.

Hazelnut-Crusted Rack of Lamb with Cherry-Wine Sauce

PREP: 8 MINUTES   COOK: 45 MINUTES

Rustic yet refined, this nut-coated rack of lamb is sumptuous. Crisscrossing the racks for baking makes a fabulous presentation.

¼ cup coarse-grained Dijon mustard
2 (8-rib) lamb rib roasts (2¾ to 3 pounds each), trimmed*
¼ cup fine, dry breadcrumbs (commercial)
½ cup finely chopped hazelnuts
¼ cup finely chopped fresh parsley
1 tablespoon chopped fresh thyme or 1 teaspoon dried thyme
½ teaspoon freshly ground pepper
¼ teaspoon salt
Cherry-Wine Sauce (page 390) or mint sauce
Garnish: fresh thyme sprigs

• Spread mustard over lamb rib roasts (photo 1). Combine breadcrumbs and next 5 ingredients; pat over roasts (photo 2).
• Place roasts in a lightly greased roasting pan, fat side out and ribs crisscrossed (photo 3). Insert meat thermometer into thickest part of lamb, making sure it does not touch bone. Roast at 400° for 10 minutes. Remove from oven. Cool slightly. Cover exposed bones with strips of aluminum foil to prevent excessive browning (photo 4).

Reduce oven temperature to 375°; roast 35 more minutes or until thermometer registers 150° (medium-rare). Serve with Cherry-Wine Sauce. Garnish, if desired. Yield: 8 servings.

Ask the butcher to french (trim fat from) the chine bones for you. It's a time-saver.
Per serving: Calories 390 Fat 16.5g Cholesterol 127mg Sodium 596mg

1. Spread mustard evenly over meaty portion of lamb racks.

2. Combine breadcrumbs, hazelnuts, and seasonings; pat onto mustard-coated lamb.

3. Place racks of lamb in roasting pan, crisscrossing bones. Roast 10 minutes to brown bones.

4. After bones have browned, wrap each with aluminum foil to prevent burning. Continue roasting.

Herb-Rubbed Lamb Chops

PREP: 10 MINUTES   COOK: 26 MINUTES

Minced fresh herbs infuse much flavor into little loin chops. Count on two chops per person.

4 (4-ounce) lamb loin chops
¼ teaspoon salt
½ teaspoon freshly ground pepper
2 tablespoons minced fresh chives
2 tablespoons minced fresh parsley
2 tablespoons chopped fresh rosemary
1 tablespoon olive oil

•Trim fat from lamb chops; sprinkle chops with salt and pepper.
•Combine chives, parsley, and rosemary; press herb mixture on each side of chops (see photo).
•Heat oil in a nonstick skillet over medium-high heat. Add chops; cover and cook 13 minutes on each side or to desired doneness. Yield: 2 servings.

Per serving: Calories 303 Fat 17.6g
Cholesterol 104mg Sodium 388mg

Peppercorn-Crusted Lamb Chops

◄ GRILLED ►

PREP: 15 MINUTES   COOK: 18 MINUTES

8 (4-ounce) lamb loin chops
¼ cup coarse-grained mustard
2 tablespoons coarsely ground pepper
2 tablespoons soy sauce
2 green onions, finely chopped
2 cloves garlic, minced
Garnish: green onion fans

•Trim excess fat from lamb chops. Combine mustard and next 4 ingredients; coat both sides of each chop with mustard mixture.
•Coat grill rack with vegetable cooking spray; place on grill. Grill chops, uncovered, over medium-hot coals (350° to 400°) 7 to 9 minutes on each side or to desired doneness. Garnish, if desired. Yield: 4 servings.

Per serving: Calories 248 Fat 10.9g
Cholesterol 94mg Sodium 805mg

Applying an herb rub: Combine minced herbs, and press mixture onto both sides of lamb loin chops before cooking.

Garlic-Grilled Lamb Chops

◄ GRILLED ►

**PREP: 8 MINUTES   MARINATE: 8 HOURS
COOK: 20 MINUTES**

Be sure to purchase lamb sirloin chops, which are about twice the size of loin chops, for this savory grilled entrée.

6 (1-inch-thick) lamb sirloin chops
½ cup soy sauce
½ cup cider vinegar
3 cloves garlic, minced
3 tablespoons honey
2 teaspoons ground ginger
¼ teaspoon dry mustard
¼ teaspoon pepper

•Trim excess fat from lamb chops; place chops in a heavy-duty, zip-top plastic bag or shallow dish.
•Combine soy sauce and remaining 6 ingredients; stir well. Pour over chops. Seal or cover, and marinate in refrigerator at least 8 hours.
•Remove chops from marinade, reserving marinade. Bring marinade to a boil in a small saucepan; set aside.
•Grill chops, covered with grill lid, over medium coals (300° to 350°) 8 to 10 minutes on each side or to desired doneness, basting often with marinade. Yield: 6 servings.

Per serving: Calories 282 Fat 10.4g
Cholesterol 103mg Sodium 1453mg

Lamb Pie

PREP: 25 MINUTES   COOK: 1½ HOURS

Homemade pastry is a highlight of this Old World meat pie, but you can speed things up with a commercial crust, if needed.

2½ pounds lean boneless lamb, cut into
     ¾-inch pieces
6 cups water
1 teaspoon salt
½ teaspoon pepper
1 cup pearl onions, peeled
½ cup water
⅓ cup vegetable oil
⅓ cup all-purpose flour
½ teaspoon salt
½ teaspoon pepper
1 (10-ounce) package frozen English peas,
     thawed
1 teaspoon browning-and-seasoning sauce
Pastry for 9-inch pie (page 299)
½ teaspoon poppy seeds

•Combine first 4 ingredients in a Dutch oven. Bring to a boil; cover, reduce heat, and simmer 45 minutes or until lamb is tender. Drain, reserving 3 cups broth. Set meat and reserved broth aside.
•Combine onions and ½ cup water in a small saucepan. Bring to a boil; cover, reduce heat, and simmer 10 to 15 minutes or until onions are tender. Drain.
•Heat oil in a large heavy saucepan over medium heat; add flour, ½ teaspoon salt, and ½ teaspoon pepper. Cook 1 minute, stirring constantly. Gradually add reserved broth; cook, stirring constantly, until thickened and bubbly. Stir in lamb, onions, peas, and browning-and-seasoning sauce. Spoon mixture into a greased 2½-quart deep casserole.
•Roll pastry into a 9-inch circle; sprinkle with poppy seeds. Roll pastry until poppy seeds are pressed into pastry. Transfer pastry to top of pie; fold edges under, and crimp. Cut an X in center of pastry. Starting with 4 points in center, roll flaps of pastry toward outer edges, exposing lamb filling.
•Bake at 400° for 30 minutes or until filling is bubbly. (Cover edges of pastry with strips of aluminum foil to prevent excessive browning, if necessary.) Yield: 4 servings.

Per serving: Calories 987 Fat 55.4g
Cholesterol 187mg Sodium 1448mg

Rosemary-Skewered Lamb

◄ GRILLED ►

PREP: 15 MINUTES   MARINATE: 2 HOURS

COOK: 8 MINUTES

Sturdy, aromatic branches of rosemary double as skewers for these attractive kabobs. Thread the lamb gently onto the skewers so they don't break.

8 (8- to 10-inch) sturdy fresh rosemary branches or 8 (12-inch) wooden skewers
½ cup olive oil
3 tablespoons lemon juice
1 tablespoon chopped fresh rosemary
1 tablespoon chopped fresh oregano or 1 teaspoon dried oregano
1 tablespoon chopped fresh thyme or 1 teaspoon dried thyme
½ teaspoon salt
¼ teaspoon pepper
2 pounds boneless lean lamb, cut into 1½-inch cubes

•Soak rosemary branches or skewers in water 2 hours.
•Combine oil and next 6 ingredients; stir well. Place lamb in a large heavy-duty, zip-top plastic bag or shallow dish. Pour marinade over lamb; seal or cover. Marinate in refrigerator 2 hours, turning occasionally.
•Remove lamb from marinade, discarding marinade.
•Thread lamb onto skewers.
•Coat grill rack with vegetable cooking spray; place on grill. Grill, covered with grill lid, over medium-hot coals (350° to 400°), 8 minutes or to desired doneness, turning occasionally. Yield: 8 servings.
Per serving: Calories 245 Fat 15.1g
Cholesterol 81mg Sodium 145mg

Braised Lamb Shanks

PREP: 12 MINUTES   COOK: 1½ HOURS

Long, slow simmering in a mild barbecue sauce makes these lamb shanks fork tender. Rice makes a nice accompaniment for the saucy dish.

2 to 2½ pounds lamb shanks
1 tablespoon vegetable oil
½ cup chopped onion
½ cup chopped celery
½ cup water
½ cup catsup
2 teaspoons Worcestershire sauce
½ teaspoon salt
¼ teaspoon pepper
1 clove garlic, minced

•Cook lamb shanks in hot oil in a large skillet until browned. Drain well. Add onion and remaining ingredients to skillet.
•Cover and cook over medium heat 1 to 1½ hours or until lamb shanks are tender, stirring occasionally. Stir additional water into skillet as necessary to maintain saucy consistency. Yield: 2 servings.
Per serving: Calories 999 Fat 34.5g
Cholesterol 472mg Sodium 1710mg

Greek Meat Loaf

PREP: 15 MINUTES   COOK: 1½ HOURS

Serve leftovers in pita bread with yogurt sauce.

2½ pounds lean ground lamb
1 large onion, diced
1 medium-size green pepper, diced
1 (8-ounce) can tomato sauce
½ cup uncooked quick-cooking oats
¼ cup chopped fresh parsley
2½ teaspoons dried oregano
2 teaspoons chopped fresh mint or ½ teaspoon dried mint flakes
2 teaspoons pepper
½ teaspoon salt
2 large eggs, lightly beaten

•Combine all ingredients in a large bowl; shape into a loaf, and place in an ungreased 9- x 5-inch loafpan. Bake, uncovered, at 350° for 1½ hours or until done. Let stand 10 to 15 minutes; carefully remove meat loaf from pan to serve. Yield: 8 servings.
Per serving: Calories 244 Fat 10g
Cholesterol 149mg Sodium 433mg

Pastitsio

PREP: 20 MINUTES

COOK: 1 HOUR AND 10 MINUTES

1 (8-ounce) package elbow macaroni
1 pound ground lamb
1 large onion, chopped
2 (8-ounce) cans tomato sauce
¾ teaspoon salt
¼ teaspoon ground allspice
¼ teaspoon ground cinnamon
¼ teaspoon ground cloves
3 tablespoons butter or margarine
3 tablespoons all-purpose flour
2 cups milk
¼ teaspoon salt
2 large eggs, lightly beaten

•Cook macaroni according to package directions; drain and set aside.
•Cook ground lamb and onion in a large skillet over medium-high heat until meat is browned and onion is tender, stirring until meat crumbles. Drain.
•Stir in tomato sauce and next 4 ingredients. Bring to a boil; reduce heat, and simmer, uncovered, 5 minutes, stirring occasionally.
•Spoon half of macaroni into a lightly greased 2½-quart casserole; top macaroni with meat mixture. Spoon remaining macaroni over meat mixture.
•Melt butter in a saucepan over medium heat; add flour, stirring until smooth. Cook, stirring constantly, 1 minute. Gradually add milk; cook, stirring constantly, until thickened and bubbly. Stir in ¼ teaspoon salt.
•Gradually stir about one-fourth of hot mixture into eggs; add to remaining hot mixture, stirring constantly.
•Cook, stirring constantly, 1 minute; pour over macaroni. Bake, uncovered, at 350° for 45 minutes.
•Broil 5½ inches from heat 3 minutes or until browned. Let stand 5 minutes. Yield: 8 servings.
Per serving: Calories 316 Fat 11.6g
Cholesterol 113mg Sodium 768mg

PORK

Pork is one particular meat that has a new and improved profile. In recent years, fresh pork has seen a lean breakthrough. The hog's diet, much healthier than in days gone by, has proven successful. Besides being a leaner product that's trimmed to very little surface fat before it reaches the meat case, pork is also lower in calories and cholesterol.

There are a wide variety of fresh pork cuts to choose from today. Refer to the identification chart on the next page to help you locate certain cuts when shopping.

When selecting fresh pork, look for bright pink color. Pork takes on a gray color when it's been in the meat case too long. The bones should be pink and the fat white. Choose pork that has a high proportion of meat to fat or bone.

Store unopened pork in the refrigerator 2 to 3 days; store ground pork no longer than 2 days. To freeze, wrap and seal meat tightly in freezer wrap or heavy-duty aluminum foil. Label packages with the date, cut, and weight or number of servings. Store fresh ground pork in the freezer up to 3 months; freeze other fresh pork cuts 6 to 9 months.

Today's pork is virtually free of any trichinae (parasites), but it's still recommended that you cook all types of pork to 160°. When fresh pork has been cooked to the proper internal temperature, there should be only a trace of pink.

Almost all cuts of pork are tender and can be cooked by a dry heat method. But keep in mind that today's lean pork cooks fairly quickly, too. And overcooking can rob meat of its juiciness and tenderness, leaving a tough, dry serving. Always test pork for perfect doneness with a meat thermometer.

Pork that is smoked or grilled sometimes remains pink even when it's well-done. Rely on a meat thermometer for accurate doneness in this case.

TIMETABLE FOR ROASTING FRESH PORK

CUT	APPROXIMATE WEIGHT IN POUNDS	INTERNAL TEMPERATURE	APPROXIMATE TOTAL COOKING TIMES AT 325° IN MINUTES PER POUND
Loin			
Center	3 to 5	160°	25 to 30
Half	5 to 7	160°	30 to 35
End	3 to 4	160°	35 to 40
Roll	3 to 5	160°	30 to 35
Boneless top	2 to 4	160°	25 to 30
Crown	4 to 6	160°	25 to 30
Picnic shoulder			
Bone in	5 to 8	170°	25 to 30
Rolled	3 to 5	170°	30 to 35
Boston shoulder	4 to 6	170°	35 to 40
Leg (fresh ham)			
Whole (bone-in)	12 to 16	160°	22 to 26
Whole (boneless)	10 to 14	160°	20 to 25
Half (bone-in)	5 to 8	160°	25 to 30
Tenderloin			
Roast at 375°	½ to 1	160°	20 to 30 minutes
Back ribs		well-done	1½ to 2½ hours
Country-style ribs		well-done	1½ to 2½ hours
Spareribs		well-done	1½ to 2½ hours
Pork loaf	1½ to 2	well-done	1 to 1½ hours

Prune-Stuffed Pork Loin Roast

PREP: 15 MINUTES

COOK: ABOUT 3½ HOURS

¾ cup dry sherry
1 (12-ounce) package whole pitted prunes
2 cups apple cider
1 (8-ounce) can pineapple slices, drained
1 tablespoon grated fresh ginger
1 teaspoon seasoned salt
1 teaspoon lemon-pepper seasoning
1 (6- to 7-pound) boneless double pork loin roast, trimmed

•Heat ¾ cup sherry in a saucepan just long enough to produce fumes (do not boil); remove from heat, and ignite. Let flames die down, and set aside.

•Combine prunes and cider in a medium saucepan. Bring to a boil; reduce heat, and simmer, uncovered, 20 minutes. Remove from heat; stir in ½ cup heated sherry. Pour remaining ¼ cup sherry over pineapple; set aside.

•Combine seasonings; rub over entire surface of roast. Place 1 roast, fat side down, on a rack in a roasting pan. Reserve 4 prunes in liquid; remove remaining prunes with a slotted spoon, and place on roast.

•Place remaining roast, fat side up, atop prunes. Tie roast at 2- to 3-inch intervals with heavy string.

•Bake at 325° for 3 hours or until a meat thermometer inserted in thickest portion registers 160° (medium), basting often with reserved prune liquid.

•Remove pineapple from sherry, discarding sherry. Garnish roast with pineapple slices and reserved prunes. Serve roast with pan drippings. Yield: 16 servings.

Per serving: Calories 338 Fat 15.8g
Cholesterol 99mg Sodium 307mg

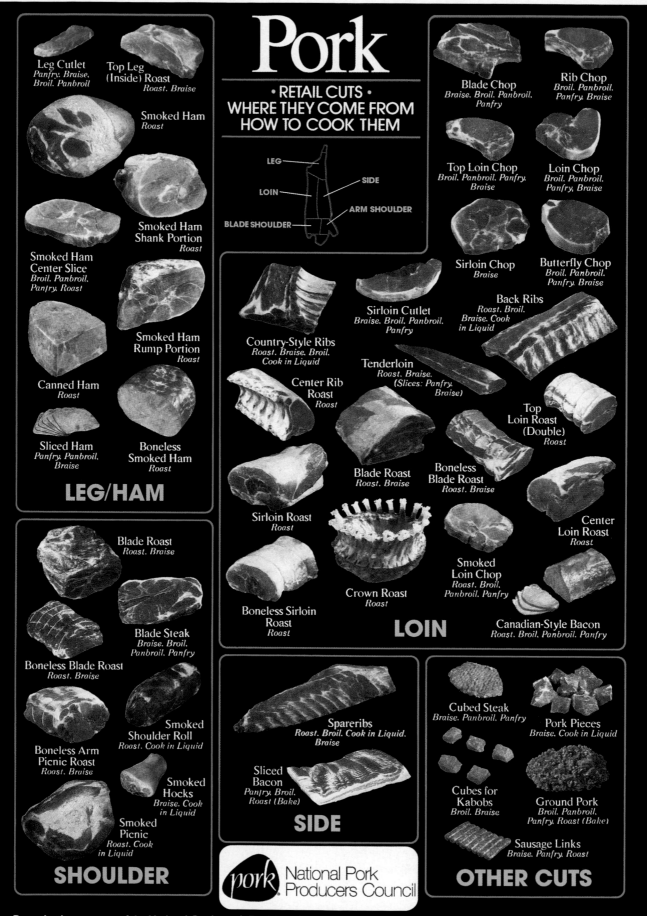

Pork

• RETAIL CUTS •
WHERE THEY COME FROM
HOW TO COOK THEM

LEG

LOIN

SIDE

ARM SHOULDER

BLADE SHOULDER

LEG/HAM

Leg Cutlet
Panfry, Braise, Broil, Panbroil

Top Leg (Inside) Roast
Roast, Braise

Smoked Ham
Roast

Smoked Ham Shank Portion
Roast

Smoked Ham Center Slice
Broil, Panbroil, Panfry, Roast

Smoked Ham Rump Portion
Roast

Canned Ham
Roast

Sliced Ham
Panfry, Panbroil, Braise

Boneless Smoked Ham
Roast

SHOULDER

Blade Roast
Roast, Braise

Blade Steak
Braise, Broil, Panbroil, Panfry

Boneless Blade Roast
Roast, Braise

Boneless Arm Picnic Roast
Roast, Braise

Smoked Shoulder Roll
Roast, Cook in Liquid

Smoked Hocks
Braise, Cook in Liquid

Smoked Picnic
Roast, Cook in Liquid

LOIN

Blade Chop
Braise, Broil, Panbroil, Panfry

Rib Chop
Broil, Panbroil, Panfry, Braise

Top Loin Chop
Broil, Panbroil, Panfry, Braise

Loin Chop
Broil, Panbroil, Panfry, Braise

Sirloin Chop
Braise

Butterfly Chop
Broil, Panbroil, Panfry, Braise

Country-Style Ribs
Roast, Braise, Broil, Cook in Liquid

Sirloin Cutlet
Braise, Broil, Panbroil, Panfry

Back Ribs
Roast, Broil, Braise, Cook in Liquid

Center Rib Roast
Roast

Tenderloin
Roast, Braise. (Slices: Panfry, Braise)

Top Loin Roast (Double)
Roast

Blade Roast
Roast, Braise

Boneless Blade Roast
Roast, Braise

Sirloin Roast
Roast

Center Loin Roast
Roast

Boneless Sirloin Roast
Roast

Crown Roast
Roast

Smoked Loin Chop
Roast, Broil, Panbroil, Panfry

Canadian-Style Bacon
Roast, Broil, Panbroil, Panfry

SIDE

Spareribs
Roast, Broil, Cook in Liquid, Braise

Sliced Bacon
Panfry, Broil, Roast (Bake)

OTHER CUTS

Cubed Steak
Braise, Panbroil, Panfry

Pork Pieces
Braise, Cook in Liquid

Cubes for Kabobs
Broil, Braise

Ground Pork
Broil, Panbroil, Panfry, Roast (Bake)

Sausage Links
Braise, Panfry, Roast

pork National Pork Producers Council

Stuffed Crown Pork Flambé

PREP: 15 MINUTES

COOK: 2 HOURS AND 10 MINUTES

Here's a showy entrée fit for holiday enter-taining. Use a long-stemmed match to flame the brandy.

1 (16-rib) crown roast of pork
½ teaspoon salt
¼ teaspoon pepper
3 green onions, sliced
¼ cup butter or margarine, melted
4 large fresh mushrooms, sliced
2 cooking apples, peeled and diced
3 cups herb-seasoned stuffing mix
1 cup applesauce
3 tablespoons brandy
1 (10- or 12-ounce) jar apricot preserves
¼ cup brandy
1 (8-ounce) jar sweet pickled kumquats, drained
¼ cup brandy

•Season roast with salt and pepper; place roast, bone ends up, on a rack in a shallow roasting pan. Insert meat thermometer, mak-ing sure it does not touch fat or bone.
•Sauté green onions in butter in a large skil-let until tender. Add mushrooms; cook, stir-ring constantly, until tender. Add apple; cook 1 minute, stirring constantly. Stir in stuffing mix, applesauce, and 3 tablespoons brandy; spoon into center of roast. Cover stuffing and exposed ends of ribs with aluminum foil.
•Heat preserves and ¼ cup brandy; set ¼ cup mixture aside for flaming. Bake roast at 325° for 2 hours or until thermometer regis-ters 160° (medium), basting with remaining preserves mixture every 10 minutes after 1 hour.
•Remove from oven, and let stand 15 min-utes; place on a serving platter. Garnish bone tips with kumquats. Heat reserved ¼ cup preserves mixture; remove from heat. Pour ¼ cup brandy over heated mixture. Ignite and pour over roast. Yield: 8 servings.
Per serving: Calories 796 Fat 31.8g
Cholesterol 216mg Sodium 786mg

Carving a crown roast: Remove any stuffing from roast. Steady roast with carv-ing fork. Slice between ribs, removing chops.

Pork with Red Plum Sauce

PREP: 15 MINUTES

COOK: 2 HOURS AND 20 MINUTES

1 (4-pound) rolled boneless pork loin roast
¼ teaspoon onion salt
¼ teaspoon garlic salt
1 cup water
¾ cup chopped onion
2 tablespoons butter or margarine, melted
1 (10-ounce) jar red plum preserves
½ cup firmly packed brown sugar
⅓ cup chili sauce
¼ cup soy sauce
2 tablespoons lemon juice
2 teaspoons prepared mustard
3 drops of hot sauce

•Remove strings from roast; trim fat. Sprinkle roast with onion and garlic salts. Reroll roast, tying with heavy string at 2-inch intervals. Place roast on a rack in a roasting pan; add water to pan. Cover with aluminum foil; bake at 325° for 2 hours. Drain; discard drippings.
•Cook onion in butter in a medium saucepan over medium-high heat, stirring constantly, until tender. Add plum preserves and remaining 6 ingredients. Cook over medium heat, uncovered, 15 minutes, stirring often.
•Pour half of sauce over roast. Bake, uncov-ered, 20 more minutes or until a meat ther-mometer inserted in thickest portion of roast registers 160° (medium), basting with half of remaining sauce. Transfer roast to a serving platter; let stand 10 minutes before slicing. Serve sauce with roast. Yield: 12 servings.
Per serving: Calories 365 Fat 13.8g
Cholesterol 82mg Sodium 643mg

Garlic Pork Loin with Sour Cream Gravy

PREP: 16 MINUTES

COOK: 1 HOUR AND 20 MINUTES

1 (3- to 4-pound) boneless pork loin roast
2 tablespoons lemon juice
1½ teaspoons salt, divided
½ teaspoon freshly ground pepper
5 cloves garlic
Sour Cream Gravy
Garnish: fresh rosemary sprigs

•Place roast, fat side up, on a rack in a shal-low roasting pan. Cut ½-inch slits at 1-inch intervals in diagonal rows on top of roast. Brush with lemon juice, and sprinkle with 1¼ teaspoons salt and ½ teaspoon pepper.
•Cut garlic into ⅛-inch slices; sprinkle garlic with remaining ¼ teaspoon salt. Insert a gar-lic slice into each ½-inch slit. Bake, uncov-ered, at 325° for 1 hour and 20 minutes or until a meat thermometer inserted in thick-est part registers 160° (medium). Let stand 10 to 15 minutes before slicing.
•Quickly chill pan drippings in freezer; dis-card solidified fat. Reserve 2 tablespoons pan drippings for Sour Cream Gravy. Serve pork roast with gravy. Garnish, if desired. Yield: 10 servings.
Per serving: Calories 275 Fat 17.6g
Cholesterol 93mg Sodium 428mg

Sour Cream Gravy

1 teaspoon cornstarch
1 tablespoon water
2 tablespoons reserved pan drippings from roast
1 (8-ounce) carton sour cream
⅛ teaspoon freshly ground pepper

•Combine cornstarch and water in a saucepan, stirring until smooth; gradually stir in reserved pan drippings, sour cream, and pepper. Cook sour cream mixture over low heat; stir constantly just until gravy is thick-ened and heated. Do not boil. Yield: 1 cup.

Barbecued Leg of Pork

◄ GRILLED ►
◄ FAMILY FAVORITE ►

PREP: 5 MINUTES
COOK: ABOUT 6 HOURS

Plan on serving this succulent pork to a big and hungry crowd. Give yourself most of the day to let it slow-cook on the grill. The Spicy Barbecue Sauce is great on grilled chicken, too.

1 (14-pound) pork leg (fresh ham)
Spicy Barbecue Sauce (page 394)

• Insert meat thermometer into leg of pork, making sure it does not touch bone or fat. Grill pork, covered with grill lid, over low coals (250° to 300°) 4½ hours; turn pork occasionally.
• Baste with barbecue sauce. Cover and grill 1 hour and 15 minutes longer or until thermometer registers 160° (medium), basting often with sauce. Let stand 10 to 15 minutes before slicing.
• Place remaining barbecue sauce in a small saucepan; bring to a boil. Serve sauce with pork. Yield: 25 servings.

Per serving: Calories 392 Fat 19.2g
Cholesterol 148mg Sodium 552mg

Note: You may need to turn off one of the gas grill burners in order to keep the temperature inside the grill low enough to cook and not burn the pork for almost 6 hours. You're not indirect cooking, just using one burner.

Maple-Baked Fresh Ham with Raisin Sauce

◄ HEALTHY ►

PREP: 8 MINUTES   COOK: 3 HOURS

1 (5- to 7-pound) pork leg half
   (fresh ham)
14 to 16 whole cloves
1 cup maple syrup
½ teaspoon ground ginger
¼ teaspoon ground nutmeg
¼ teaspoon ground allspice
Raisin Sauce (page 391)

• Score fat on ham in a diamond design, and stud ham with cloves. Place ham, fat side up, on a rack in a roasting pan. Insert meat thermometer, making sure it does not touch fat or bone.
• Combine syrup and next 3 ingredients; stir well, and pour over ham.
• Bake ham, uncovered, at 325° for 2 to 3 hours or until meat thermometer registers 160° (medium). Baste ham with drippings every 20 to 30 minutes. If ham browns too quickly, cover loosely with aluminum foil. Serve hot or cold with Raisin Sauce. Yield: 14 servings.

Per serving: Calories 446 Fat 15g
Cholesterol 129mg Sodium 125mg

CARVING A WHOLE HAM

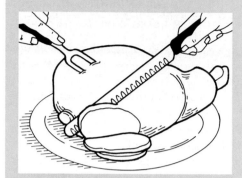

1. Place shank bone to carver's right. Cut 3 slices from thin side of ham parallel to leg bone. Turn ham over so it rests on the cut side.

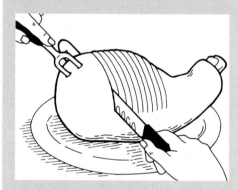

2. Steady the leg with carving fork. Make vertical slices down to the leg bone.

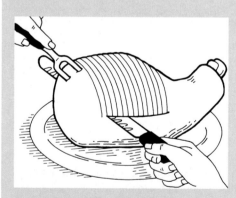

3. Cut horizontally along the bone to release slices.

Italian Pork Roast

PREP: 15 MINUTES

COOK: 1 HOUR AND 20 MINUTES

Garlic slices infuse further flavor into this roast rubbed with Italian seasoning. Serving suggestions are roasted vegetables and a full-bodied red wine.

1 (3- to 3½-pound) boneless pork loin
   roast
2 large cloves garlic, cut into 4 slices each
1 tablespoon olive oil
2 tablespoons dried Italian seasoning
1½ teaspoons coarsely ground pepper
Garnish: fresh herbs

•Place roast, fat side up, on a rack in a shallow roasting pan (photo 1). Cut 8 small slits in roast at 2-inch intervals; insert garlic deep into slits (photo 2).

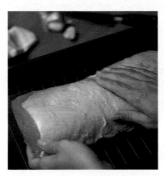

1. Place pork roast, fat side up, on a rack in a shallow roasting pan.

2. Cut 8 small slits in top of roast. Insert garlic slices deep into slits.

3. Rub seasoning mixture over entire surface of pork roast.

•Brush oil evenly over roast. Combine Italian seasoning and pepper; rub over entire surface of roast (photo 3). Bake, uncovered, at 325° for 1 hour and 20 minutes or until a meat thermometer inserted in thickest part registers 160° (medium). Let stand 10 to 15 minutes before slicing. Garnish, if desired. Yield: 10 servings.

Per serving: Calories 246 Fat 14.6g
Cholesterol 86mg Sodium 67mg

Peking Pork Tenderloin

◄ HEALTHY ►

PREP: 13 MINUTES MARINATE: 1 HOUR

COOK: 30 MINUTES

This pork recipe takes on a pronounced ginger flavor as it marinates. Two tenderloins, about the size you'll need for this recipe, typically come packaged together at the meat counter.

¼ cup soy sauce
2 cloves garlic, crushed
1 (2-inch) piece fresh ginger, peeled and
   grated
2 (¾-pound) pork tenderloins
⅓ cup honey
⅓ cup sesame seeds, toasted (about a
   2.4-ounce jar)

•Combine first 3 ingredients in a large heavy-duty, zip-top plastic bag or shallow dish; add tenderloins. Seal or cover, and marinate in refrigerator 1 hour, turning occasionally.
•Remove from marinade, discarding marinade. Pat tenderloins dry with paper towels. Coat tenderloins with honey; roll in sesame seeds.
•Place tenderloins on a lightly greased rack in broiler pan. Bake at 375° for 25 to 30

minutes or until a meat thermometer inserted in thickest part registers 160° (medium). Let stand 5 minutes before slicing. Yield: 6 servings.

Per serving: Calories 239 Fat 7g
Cholesterol 74mg Sodium 281mg

Peppery Pork Pinwheels

PREP: 25 MINUTES COOK: 1 HOUR

Finely chopped peppers make a pretty filling for these meaty spirals. And fennel seeds and lemon-pepper seasoning make a great flavored coating.

3 small sweet red or yellow peppers,
   finely chopped
¾ cup finely chopped onion
¾ cup finely chopped celery
1½ teaspoons dried thyme, crushed
¾ teaspoon garlic salt
¾ teaspoon ground red pepper
¾ teaspoon paprika
3 tablespoons vegetable oil
3 (¾-pound) pork tenderloins
1½ tablespoons fennel seeds, crushed
1½ tablespoons lemon-pepper seasoning

•Sauté first 7 ingredients in hot oil in a skillet until tender; set aside.

•Slice each pork tenderloin lengthwise down center, cutting to, but not through, bottom.
•Place each tenderloin between sheets of heavy-duty plastic wrap; pound to a 12- x 8-inch rectangle of even thickness, using a meat mallet or rolling pin.
•Spoon one-third of pepper mixture onto 1 tenderloin, spreading to within ½ inch of sides; roll up tenderloin, jellyroll fashion, starting with short side. Tie at 1½-inch intervals with heavy string. Repeat procedure with remaining tenderloins and pepper mixture. Combine fennel seeds and lemon-pepper seasoning; rub on top and sides of tenderloins.
•Place tenderloins, seam side down, on a lightly greased rack in a shallow pan. Bake, uncovered, at 325° for 1 hour or until a meat thermometer inserted in thickest part registers 160°. Let stand 10 minutes; remove strings, and slice tenderloins. Yield: 10 servings.

Per serving: Calories 164 Fat 7.7g
Cholesterol 61mg Sodium 737mg

Grilled Pork Tenderloin

◄ GRILLED ►

PREP: 10 MINUTES   MARINATE: 4 HOURS
GRILL: 16 MINUTES

½ cup peanut oil
⅓ cup soy sauce
¼ cup red wine vinegar
3 tablespoons lemon juice
2 tablespoons Worcestershire sauce
1 clove garlic, crushed
1 tablespoon chopped fresh parsley
1 tablespoon dry mustard
1½ teaspoons pepper
2 (¾-pound) pork tenderloins

•Combine first 9 ingredients; place in a heavy-duty, zip-top plastic bag or shallow container. Add tenderloins, turning to coat. Seal or cover, and marinate in refrigerator 4 hours, turning occasionally.
•Remove tenderloins from marinade, discarding marinade.
•Grill tenderloins, uncovered, over medium coals (300° to 350°) 16 minutes or until a meat thermometer inserted in thickest part registers 160° (medium), turning once. Let stand 5 to 10 minutes before slicing. Yield: 6 servings.

Per serving: Calories 208 Fat 10.5g
Cholesterol 82mg Sodium 385mg

Note: If you want to baste pork while grilling, reserve marinade, and bring to a boil in a small saucepan. Remove from heat, and baste tenderloins as desired.

Apricot-Stuffed Pork Chops

◄ GRILLED ►

PREP: 20 MINUTES   COOK: 22 MINUTES

Most butchers will cut pocket chops for you if you ask them. Otherwise, see our technique photo (page 268) if you want to do it yourself for this company-worthy entrée. The chops are easiest to slit if they're well chilled.

1 (15¼-ounce) can apricot halves, drained and chopped
1 cup unseasoned croutons
⅓ cup coarsely chopped walnuts
1 (1-ounce) envelope onion soup mix
2 tablespoons butter or margarine, melted
4 (1½-inch-thick) boneless pork loin chops (about 1¾ pounds), trimmed and cut with pockets*
½ cup apricot preserves
1 tablespoon hot water

•Combine first 5 ingredients. Stuff about ⅓ cup apricot mixture into each pocket of pork chops; secure openings with wooden picks.
•Grill chops, covered with grill lid, over medium-hot coals (350° to 400°) 16 minutes, turning once. Combine apricot preserves and hot water, stirring well; brush over chops, and grill 3 minutes. Turn chops, brush with apricot mixture, and grill 3 more minutes. Yield: 4 servings.

*These thick, meaty pork chops are sometimes labeled "America's Cut" in the grocery store.

Per serving: Calories 684 Fat 31g
Cholesterol 135mg Sodium 1073mg

Grilled Pork Tenderloin

Oven-Fried Pork Chops

PREP: 7 MINUTES   COOK: 50 MINUTES

Here's an easy dish for a busy weeknight. Just dip pork chops in an egg mixture, dredge them in seasoned crumbs, and relax while they bake.

4 (¾-inch-thick) bone-in pork loin chops (1½ pounds)
1 large egg, beaten
2 tablespoons pineapple juice
1 tablespoon soy sauce
½ cup Italian-seasoned breadcrumbs
½ teaspoon ground ginger
¼ teaspoon paprika
¼ teaspoon garlic powder
2 tablespoons butter, melted

•Trim fat from pork chops. Combine egg, pineapple juice, and soy sauce in a shallow bowl, and whisk gently. Combine breadcrumbs and next 3 ingredients. Dip chops in egg mixture, and dredge in breadcrumbs.
•Place chops on a rack in a greased roasting pan. Drizzle butter over chops. Bake at 350° for 25 minutes; turn and bake 25 more minutes or until done. Yield: 4 servings.
Per serving: Calories 309 Fat 15.5g
Cholesterol 138mg Sodium 803mg

Pork Chops and Sauerkraut

PREP: 5 MINUTES   COOK: 40 MINUTES

4 (½-inch-thick) bone-in pork chops
1 tablespoon vegetable oil
1 (14-ounce) can sauerkraut with caraway seeds
1 large tomato, peeled and cubed
½ teaspoon paprika

•Brown pork chops on both sides in hot oil in a heavy skillet.
•Top with sauerkraut and tomato; sprinkle with paprika. Cover, reduce heat, and simmer 40 minutes or until chops are tender. Yield: 4 servings.
Per serving: Calories 281 Fat 13.7g
Cholesterol 89mg Sodium 752mg

Creole Pork Chops

PREP: 20 MINUTES   COOK: 1½ HOURS

Lots of tomatoes and the trinity of chopped onions, green pepper, and celery distinguish this casserole as Creole.

¼ cup all-purpose flour
¾ teaspoon salt
¼ teaspoon black pepper
6 (¾-inch-thick) bone-in pork chops
2 tablespoons vegetable oil
¾ cup chopped onion
¾ cup chopped green pepper
2 stalks celery, thinly sliced
2 cloves garlic, minced
2 tablespoons butter or margarine, melted
2 cups beef broth
1 tablespoon chopped fresh parsley
1 (8-ounce) package small fresh mushrooms, halved
4 tomatoes, peeled and quartered
1 (6-ounce) can tomato paste
1 bay leaf
4½ cups hot cooked rice

•Combine first 3 ingredients in a shallow bowl; dredge pork chops in flour mixture. Brown chops in hot oil in a large skillet. Remove chops from skillet; drain on paper towels. Discard drippings; wipe skillet with a paper towel.
•Sauté onion and next 3 ingredients in butter in skillet over medium-high heat until vegetables are tender. Stir in broth and next 5 ingredients.
•Bring mixture to a boil; reduce heat, and simmer, uncovered, 20 minutes, stirring occasionally. Add chops; cover and cook 45 minutes, spooning tomato mixture over chops. Uncover and cook 15 minutes. Discard bay leaf. Serve chops over rice. Yield: 6 servings.
Per serving: Calories 583 Fat 17.4g
Cholesterol 115mg Sodium 1586mg

Peppered Pork Chop Casserole

PREP: 12 MINUTES
COOK: 1 HOUR AND 5 MINUTES

6 (½- to ¾-inch-thick) bone-in pork chops
¼ teaspoon salt
¼ teaspoon pepper
2 tablespoons vegetable oil
2 medium-size green peppers
1 (15-ounce) can tomato sauce
1 (14½-ounce) can Italian-style stewed tomatoes, undrained and chopped
1 cup water
½ cup chopped onion
¾ teaspoon salt
¼ teaspoon pepper
1 clove garlic, minced
1½ cups uncooked long-grain rice

•Sprinkle pork chops with ¼ teaspoon salt and ¼ teaspoon pepper. Brown chops all over in hot oil in a large skillet over medium-high heat. Remove chops from skillet; drain and set aside.
•Cut top off 1 green pepper; remove seeds. Cut 6 (¼-inch-thick) rings from green pepper; set pepper rings aside. Seed and chop remaining green pepper. Combine chopped green pepper, tomato sauce, and next 6 ingredients; stir well.
•Spread rice evenly in a lightly greased 13- x 9-inch baking dish; pour tomato mixture over rice. Arrange chops over rice mixture; top each chop with a pepper ring. Cover and bake at 350° for 1 hour or until chops and rice are tender. Yield: 6 servings.
Per serving: Calories 469 Fat 13g
Cholesterol 89mg Sodium 1091mg

Grilled Blue Cheese-Stuffed Chops

◀ GRILLED ▶

PREP: 20 MINUTES   COOK: 25 MINUTES

Rib chops are large, so it's easy to stuff this crunchy carrot-pecan mixture in their pockets.

½ cup shredded carrot
¼ cup chopped pecans
¼ cup crumbled blue cheese
1 green onion, thinly sliced
1 teaspoon Worcestershire sauce
4 (1½-inch-thick) rib pork chops, trimmed and cut with pockets (photo 1)*
1 tablespoon plus 1 teaspoon all-purpose flour
¼ cup plain low-fat yogurt
¾ cup milk
½ teaspoon chicken-flavored bouillon granules
⅛ teaspoon pepper
½ cup crumbled blue cheese

•Combine first 5 ingredients in a small bowl; stir well. Stuff carrot mixture into pockets of pork chops (photo 2); secure openings with wooden picks. Grill, covered with grill lid, over medium-hot coals (350° to 400°) 25 minutes or until done, turning once.
•Combine flour and yogurt in a small saucepan, stirring until smooth. Slowly stir in milk; add bouillon granules and pepper, and cook over medium heat, stirring constantly, until thick and bubbly. Serve chops with sauce; top with ½ cup crumbled blue cheese. Yield: 4 servings.
See photo above to cut your own pocket chops, if desired.
Per serving: Calories 616 Fat 37.1g
Cholesterol 184mg Sodium 575mg

1. Cut a pocket into pork chop by slicing deep into meaty side almost to the bone. Meat is easy to slice when well chilled.

2. Stuff carrot mixture into pocket of each pork chop. Secure each opening with a wooden pick.

Pork Chops with Caramelized Onions and Smoked Gouda

PREP: 20 MINUTES   COOK: 55 MINUTES

Hungarian paprika and smoked Gouda cheese distinguish this rich and filling special-occasion entrée. Pair it with a simple green salad, tender yeast rolls, and a robust red wine.

¾ cup all-purpose flour
1 teaspoon salt, divided
1 teaspoon pepper, divided
6 (1-inch-thick) rib pork chops (7 to 8 ounces each)
¼ cup plus 2 tablespoons vegetable oil, divided
1 tablespoon sweet Hungarian paprika, divided
2 large onions, sliced and separated into rings
½ teaspoon sugar
1½ tablespoons minced garlic (about 7 cloves)
1 (14½-ounce) can beef broth
¾ cup (3 ounces) shredded smoked Gouda cheese
2 tablespoons butter or margarine
3½ tablespoons all-purpose flour

•Combine ¾ cup flour, ½ teaspoon salt, and ½ teaspoon pepper in a large heavy-duty, zip-top plastic bag. Add pork chops; seal bag, and shake to coat.
•Heat 2 tablespoons oil in a heavy skillet over medium-high heat until hot; add 3 chops. Cook 3 minutes on each side or until browned. Transfer to a 13- x 9-inch baking dish. Repeat procedure. Sprinkle chops with 1 teaspoon paprika.
•Heat remaining 2 tablespoons oil in a Dutch oven until hot. Add onion; sprinkle with sugar. Cook 10 minutes or until caramelized, stirring often. Add garlic; cook 1 minute.
•Remove from heat; stir in remaining 2 teaspoons paprika. Spoon onion over chops. Pour broth over onion mixture. Cover and bake at 350° for 45 minutes.
•Remove from oven, and transfer chops to a serving platter. Pour onion mixture through a wire-mesh strainer into a 4-cup liquid measuring cup. Add enough water to broth mixture to measure 2 cups. Set aside. Return solids in strainer to baking dish; top with chops. Sprinkle with cheese. Bake 5 more minutes or until cheese melts. Set aside, and keep warm.
•Melt butter in a heavy saucepan over low heat; add 3½ tablespoons flour, stirring until mixture is smooth. Cook 1 minute, stirring constantly.
•Gradually add reserved broth mixture; cook over medium heat, stirring constantly, until thickened and bubbly. Stir in remaining ½ teaspoon salt and ½ teaspoon pepper. Serve chops and onion with sauce. Yield: 6 servings.
Per serving: Calories 544 Fat 29.7g
Cholesterol 139mg Sodium 1025mg

Sweet-and-Sour Pork

PREP: 25 MINUTES   COOK: 15 MINUTES

Your family will devour this tangy-sweet favorite. Use a wok or Dutch oven to fry the pork pieces in batches. To ensure crispy nuggets of pork, don't crowd the pan.

½ cup all-purpose flour
¼ cup cornstarch
½ cup cold water
1 teaspoon salt
1 large egg
2 pounds boneless pork loin roast, cut into
 ¾-inch pieces
Vegetable oil
1 (20-ounce) can unsweetened pineapple
 chunks, undrained
3 large carrots, scraped and thinly sliced
½ cup firmly packed brown sugar
½ cup white vinegar
2 teaspoons soy sauce
1 clove garlic, minced
2 tablespoons cornstarch
2 tablespoons cold water
1 green pepper, cut into ¾-inch pieces
4 cups hot cooked rice

•Combine first 5 ingredients in a medium bowl; beat with a wire whisk until well blended. Add pork, stirring well.
•Pour oil to depth of 2 inches into a Dutch oven or electric wok; heat until a deep-fat thermometer registers 375°. Fry pork in batches of 8 to 10 pieces 4 minutes or until golden, turning each piece once or twice. Fry remaining pork, letting oil return to 375° before adding each batch. Set pork aside.
•Drain pineapple, reserving juice; set pineapple aside. Add enough water to juice to make 1 cup. Combine pineapple juice, carrot, and next 4 ingredients in a Dutch oven. Bring to a boil over medium heat; cover, reduce heat, and simmer 6 minutes or until carrot is tender.
•Combine 2 tablespoons cornstarch and 2 tablespoons water, stirring well. Add to carrot mixture, stirring to blend. Stir in cooked pork, reserved pineapple chunks, and green pepper. Bring mixture to a boil, stirring constantly; reduce heat, and simmer, uncovered, 1 minute. Serve with rice. Yield: 4 servings.
Per serving: Calories 1199 Fat 46.7g
Cholesterol 189mg Sodium 1734mg

Cutting spareribs: Cut ribs apart into serving-size portions, using a sharp knife.

Oven Spareribs

PREP: 10 MINUTES   COOK: 1½ HOURS

Our staff rated these mustardy molasses ribs some of the best ribs ever. Do pay attention to details as you serve them—have some white bread ready to soak up the sauce.

4 pounds spareribs
1 cup molasses
½ cup white vinegar
½ cup prepared mustard
¼ cup Worcestershire sauce
1 teaspoon salt
1 teaspoon hot sauce

•Cut ribs into serving-size portions (see photo); place meaty side down in a large shallow pan.
•Bake, uncovered, at 450° for 30 minutes. Meanwhile, combine molasses and remaining 5 ingredients in a medium saucepan; bring mixture to a boil. Remove from heat; reserve half of sauce, and set aside.
•Reduce heat to 350°. Turn ribs over, and bake 30 more minutes. Drain excess fat.
•Bake ribs 30 more minutes, brushing often with sauce. Serve reserved sauce with ribs. Yield: 4 servings.
Per serving: Calories 1324 Fat 84.4g
Cholesterol 333mg Sodium 1303mg

Barbecued Ribs

PREP: 18 MINUTES

COOK: 1 HOUR AND 45 MINUTES

These ribs bake twice—first they're roasted to render the excess fat and to develop a rich flavor. Then they're baked again with a highly seasoned smoky sauce.

6 pounds country-style pork ribs
1 large onion, sliced
1 lemon, thinly sliced
3 cloves garlic, minced
2 tablespoons butter or margarine,
 melted
1½ cups water
1 cup ketchup
¾ cup chili sauce
¼ cup firmly packed brown sugar
1 tablespoon celery seeds
2 tablespoons Worcestershire sauce
2 tablespoons soy sauce
2 tablespoons prepared mustard
2 teaspoons chili powder
½ teaspoon salt
¼ teaspoon liquid smoke
¼ teaspoon hot sauce

•Place ribs in a large roasting pan. Cover and bake at 450° for 45 minutes; drain.
•Top ribs with onion and lemon. Sauté garlic in butter in a saucepan over medium heat until tender. Add water and remaining 11 ingredients. Bring to a boil; remove from heat, and pour over ribs. Bake, uncovered, at 350° for 1 hour, basting often. Yield: 6 servings.
Per serving: Calories 529 Fat 26.9g
Cholesterol 165mg Sodium 943mg

HAM & SAUSAGE

The leg of pork becomes ham after it's cured with seasonings and/or smoked. The label on the ham should identify the type of processing, and whether or not the ham has been cooked.

Ham labeled "fully cooked" does not require further heating and can be eaten cold, but heating it to an internal temperature of 140° brings out the full flavor of the ham.

Ham marked "cook before eating" must be cooked to 160° before serving. And if a wrapper doesn't indicate whether or not the ham has been fully cooked, assume that it needs cooking.

You'll find ham available as bone-in or boneless. Bone-in hams are sold whole, as halves, in butt or shank portions, or as center cut slices. The butt half generally has a higher proportion of meat to bone and is more expensive than the shank.

Boneless hams are easy to slice and have very little waste. They're commonly sold as halves, quarters, or steaks.

Canned hams are always boneless and fully cooked. Some hams labeled "water added" have been injected with a seasoned water solution before smoking. These hams are lower in price because part of their weight is water.

Bacon is sold in slices that vary in thickness. The flavor varies, as well, depending on the smoking and curing process that's used. You can buy bacon heavily streaked with fat or labeled lean or center cut, depending on the origination of its cut.

Pork tenderloin that is cured and smoked is known as Canadian bacon. It's typically sold thinly sliced and is quite lean. It provides a "bacon" choice to those on heart-healthy diets.

Sausage is made from seasoned ground pork. You can choose between mild, seasoned, and hot as well as sweet Italian links which are sold in casings (that are edible or just as easily removed).

Cured hams will keep in the refrigerator up to one week, cooked or uncooked. Refrigerate canned hams both before and after opening unless they are otherwise marked; unopened they'll keep up to a year unless a label states otherwise.

Freezing is not recommended for ham. Its texture and flavor will decline, but if you wrap it properly in an airtight seal, it will keep up to two months in the freezer. Don't freeze canned hams because freezing can damage the can's seal.

Cranberry-Orange Glazed Ham

◄ FAMILY FAVORITE ►

PREP: 20 MINUTES   COOK: 4½ HOURS

1 (16- to 18-pound) smoked fully cooked ham
Whole cloves
2½ cups firmly packed brown sugar, divided
1⅓ cups cranberry juice cocktail
½ cup honey
¼ cup cider vinegar
1½ tablespoons all-purpose flour
3 tablespoons prepared mustard
3 tablespoons butter or margarine
2 to 3 oranges, sliced
6 maraschino cherries, halved

•Slice skin from ham. Score fat on ham in a diamond design, and stud with cloves. Place ham, fat side up, on a rack in a shallow roasting pan. Insert meat thermometer, making sure it does not touch bone or fat. Bake at 325° for 3 to 3½ hours.
•Combine ½ cup brown sugar, juice, and next 5 ingredients in a saucepan, mixing well. Bring to a boil, and cook 1 minute.
•Coat exposed portion of ham with remaining 2 cups brown sugar. Place orange slices on ham, securing in centers with wooden picks; leave tips of picks exposed. Place cherry half on each pick.
•Pour hot cranberry mixture over ham; bake 1 more hour or until thermometer registers 140°, basting ham with pan juices twice.
Yield: 30 servings.
Per serving: Calories 353 Fat 16.9g
Cholesterol 86mg Sodium 2028mg

TIMETABLE FOR ROASTING SMOKED PORK

CUT	APPROXIMATE WEIGHT IN POUNDS	INTERNAL TEMPERATURE	APPROXIMATE TOTAL COOKING TIMES AT 325° IN MINUTES PER POUND
Ham (cook before eating)			
Whole	10 to 14	160°	18 to 20
Half	5 to 7	160°	22 to 25
Shank portion	3 to 4	160°	35 to 40
Butt portion	3 to 4	160°	35 to 40
Ham (fully cooked)			
Whole	10 to 12	140°	15 to 18
Half	5 to 7	140°	18 to 24
Loin	3 to 5	160°	25 to 30
Picnic shoulder (cook before eating)	5 to 8	170°	30 to 35
Picnic shoulder (fully cooked)	5 to 8	140°	25 to 30
Shoulder roll (butt)	2 to 4	170°	35 to 40
Canadian-style bacon	2 to 4	160°	35 to 40

Hickory-Grilled Ham

◄ GRILLED ►

PREP: 1 HOUR   COOK: 1½ HOURS

Hickory wood chunks
1 (7- to 8-pound) smoked, fully cooked
    ham half
½ cup dry mustard
½ cup firmly packed brown sugar
½ cup water
1 tablespoon whole cloves
4 slices fresh or canned pineapple
    (optional)
8 maraschino cherries

•Soak hickory chunks in water 1 to 24 hours before grilling.
•Cut ham bone loose from meat (or ask butcher to do this), but do not remove bone.
•Combine mustard and brown sugar; add ½ cup water, stirring until smooth. Brush mixture over ham.
•Prepare charcoal fire; place hickory chunks on coals around edges of grill. Place ham 8 inches from heat. Grill ham, covered with grill lid, over low coals (250° to 300°) 1 hour, turning and brushing often with mustard mixture; remove ham from grill. Cool to touch.
•Stud ham with cloves; arrange pineapple, if desired, and cherries on ham, securing with wooden picks. Return ham to grill, and grill 30 more minutes or until meat thermometer registers 140°. Remove bone before slicing ham. Yield: 16 servings.
Per serving: Calories 247 Fat 13.3g
Cholesterol 65mg Sodium 1545mg

Plantation Country Ham

PREP: 20 MINUTES   SOAK: 24 HOURS

COOK: 3 HOURS

Southerners love the salty, smoky flavor of country ham. You'll need a big bucket for soaking this ham, and a good carving set will be valuable for removing the skin and fat before studding the ham with cloves.

1 (14- to 16-pound) uncooked country
    ham
½ gallon apple juice
Whole cloves
1½ cups firmly packed brown sugar
1 tablespoon white vinegar
2 teaspoons prepared mustard
1 teaspoon ground cloves

•Place ham in a very large container; cover with water, and soak at least 24 hours. Pour off water. Scrub ham with warm water, using a stiff brush, and rinse well.
•Place ham in a large roasting pan; pour apple juice over ham. Cover and bake at 325° for 2½ hours. Carefully remove ham from pan, reserving 1 tablespoon pan juices; discard remaining juices. Let ham cool 10 minutes.
•Remove skin, and score fat in a diamond design, using a sharp knife. Return ham to pan, fat side up. Stud with whole cloves. Combine reserved pan juices, brown sugar, and remaining 3 ingredients; coat exposed portion of ham evenly with brown sugar mixture.
•Bake ham, uncovered, 20 to 30 more minutes or until a meat thermometer inserted into thickest part of meat registers 142° and brown sugar coating is crusty. To serve, slice ham across the grain into very thin slices. Yield: 26 servings.
Per serving: Calories 351 Fat 19g
Cholesterol 80mg Sodium 2058mg

Country Ham with Red-Eye Gravy

PREP: 10 MINUTES   COOK: 21 MINUTES

Serve this country fare with grits and fried eggs. Or you may rather have hot biscuits to collect the dark, peppery gravy.

6 thin slices uncooked country ham (about 1 pound)
2 teaspoons brown sugar
½ cup strongly brewed coffee
½ cup hot water
¼ teaspoon freshly ground pepper

•Cut gashes in fat to keep ham from curling. Lightly grease a 10-inch cast-iron skillet, using fat cut from ham; heat over medium-high 1 minute. Reduce heat to medium; sauté ham, in batches, in skillet 3 to 4 minutes or until browned, turning several times. Remove ham from skillet; cover and keep warm.
•Add sugar and remaining 3 ingredients to skillet; bring to a boil. Boil 3 minutes or until slightly thickened and reduced to about ½ cup. Serve gravy over ham. Yield: 8 servings.
Per serving: Calories 128 Fat 7.3g
Cholesterol 31mg Sodium 788mg

Quick Grilled Ham

**PREP: 5 MINUTES   MARINATE: 8 HOURS
COOK: 12 MINUTES**

2 (½- to 1-inch-thick) boneless, fully cooked ham slices (about 2 pounds)
½ cup ginger ale
½ cup orange juice
¼ cup firmly packed brown sugar
1½ teaspoons dry mustard
½ teaspoon ground ginger
¼ teaspoon ground cloves

•Place ham in a heavy-duty, zip-top plastic bag or large shallow dish. Combine ginger ale and remaining 5 ingredients, stirring until sugar dissolves; pour over ham. Seal or cover, and marinate in refrigerator 8 hours, turning meat occasionally.
•Drain ham, reserving marinade. (You can reuse this marinade without boiling it because ham is fully cooked.) Grill ham, uncovered, over medium-hot coals (350° to 400°) 6 minutes on each side or until a meat thermometer registers 140°, basting once with reserved marinade. Yield: 10 servings.
Per serving: Calories 233 Fat 10.4g
Cholesterol 78mg Sodium 1885mg

Ham-and-Cheese Pie

PREP: 10 MINUTES   COOK: 1 HOUR

Kids will gobble this up—it's ham and cheese in a flaky crescent roll crust.

1 (8-ounce) can refrigerated crescent rolls
1½ cups finely chopped cooked ham
1 (8-ounce) package Monterey Jack cheese, cubed
2 tablespoons grated Parmesan cheese
2 tablespoons finely chopped onion
2 large eggs, lightly beaten

•Unroll crescent rolls, and separate into 8 triangles. Fit 5 triangles into a 9-inch pie-plate, pressing edges together to seal.
•Combine ham and remaining 4 ingredients; spoon into prepared pieplate.
•Cut remaining 3 triangles into thin strips; arrange over mixture.
•Bake on lowest oven rack at 325° for 1 hour. Let stand 5 minutes before serving. Yield: 4 servings.
Per serving: Calories 566 Fat 38.8g
Cholesterol 171mg Sodium 1328mg

Grilled Bratwurst

PREP: 2 MINUTES   COOK: 15 MINUTES

2 pounds bratwurst
3 (12-ounce) cans beer or 4½ cups water

•Prick sausage with a fork. Bring beer to a boil; add sausage, and return to a boil.
•Cover, reduce heat, and simmer 5 minutes. Remove sausage, and pat dry. Grill, uncovered, over medium coals (300° to 350°) 9 to 10 minutes, turning often. Serve with coarse-grained mustard. Yield: 4 servings.
Per serving: Calories 550 Fat 45.9g
Cholesterol 102mg Sodium 1839mg

Jambalaya

PREP: 23 MINUTES   COOK: 22 MINUTES

Jambalaya gets its name from jambon, meaning ham in French. This spicy one-dish rice meal is packed with chopped ham, sausage, and chicken. We used quick-cooking rice (the boil-in-bag kind) to update this classic New Orleans dish.

1 pound andouille or other Cajun-style sausage
4 skinned and boned chicken breast halves
1½ teaspoons black pepper
2 tablespoons peanut or vegetable oil
1 large onion, finely chopped
1 medium-size green pepper, chopped
½ cup chopped celery
3 cloves garlic, minced
1 cup chopped cooked ham
2 teaspoons Cajun seasoning
1 (14½-ounce) can stewed tomatoes, undrained
½ cup chicken broth
¼ teaspoon dried thyme
¼ teaspoon ground red pepper
3 cups hot cooked rice (we tested with Success)
1 cup finely chopped green onions (1 bunch)

•Cut sausage into ½-inch slices, and cut chicken into small pieces. Sprinkle chicken with pepper.
•Cook chicken in oil in a large Dutch oven over medium-high heat 4 minutes or until browned, stirring often. Remove and set aside. Add sausage, and cook, stirring constantly, 4 minutes or until browned. Remove sausage; set aside.
•Add onion and next 3 ingredients to Dutch oven; cook, uncovered, 5 to 7 minutes or until vegetables are crisp-tender.
•Stir in chicken, sausage, ham, Cajun seasoning, and remaining ingredients; cook 7 minutes or until thoroughly heated, stirring occasionally. Yield: 5 servings.
Per serving: Calories 741 Fat 35g
Cholesterol 143mg Sodium 2882mg

Kielbasa-Vegetable Dinner

PREP: 12 MINUTES   COOK: 26 MINUTES

Serve wedges of chewy, crusty bread with this one-dish peasant meal.

4   slices bacon
1½   pounds kielbasa sausage, diagonally sliced
1½   pounds small red potatoes, thinly sliced
1   onion, chopped
3   large carrots, scraped and thinly sliced
1   teaspoon dried oregano
1½   pounds fresh broccoli, cut into flowerets (about 4 cups)
1   cup water

•Cook bacon in a large Dutch oven until crisp; remove bacon, reserving drippings in Dutch oven. Crumble bacon, and set aside. Add kielbasa to Dutch oven, and cook 3 minutes or until browned. Remove and set aside. Add potato, onion, carrot, and oregano to drippings in Dutch oven; cook over medium heat 8 minutes, stirring often.
•Add broccoli and water to vegetables in Dutch oven; bring to a boil. Cover, reduce heat, and simmer 15 minutes or until vegetables are crisp-tender, adding sausage during last 5 minutes of cooking; stir occasionally. Serve dinner in soup bowls; sprinkle with crumbled bacon. Yield: 6 servings.

Per serving: Calories 565 Fat 39.9g
Cholesterol 106mg Sodium 1027mg

Corn Dogs

◄ QUICK ►

PREP: 20 MINUTES   COOK: 10 MINUTES

1   cup yellow cornmeal
½   cup all-purpose flour
1½   teaspoons baking powder
1   teaspoon salt
2   teaspoons sugar
½   teaspoon dry mustard
¼   teaspoon pepper
½   cup diced onion
1   large egg, lightly beaten
¾   cup milk
10   hot dogs
Vegetable oil

•Combine first 8 ingredients in a medium bowl; make a well in center. Combine egg and milk; add to cornmeal mixture, stirring just until dry ingredients are moistened.
•Insert a 6- or 10-inch wooden skewer in 1 end of each hot dog, leaving a 2- to 3-inch handle. Dip each hot dog into batter, coating completely. Use a spoon to help coat hot dogs, if needed.
•Pour oil to depth of 3 to 4 inches into a large heavy saucepan; heat to 375°. Fry hot dogs in hot oil 2 to 3 minutes or until browned. Drain on paper towels; serve with mustard. Yield: 10 corn dogs.

Per corn dog: Calories 364 Fat 28.5g
Cholesterol 51mg Sodium 730mg

Sausage-and-Bean Dinner

PREP: 10 MINUTES   COOK: 38 MINUTES

If you're serving a crowd, spoon this entrée over hot cooked rice or pasta.

1   pound smoked sausage, cut into ¼-inch slices
1   large green pepper, chopped
1   medium onion, chopped
2   (14½-ounce) cans stewed tomatoes, undrained
1   (16-ounce) can pink or red beans, drained
1   (16-ounce) can pinto beans, drained
1   (15-ounce) can Great Northern beans, drained
½   teaspoon garlic powder

•Brown sausage in a Dutch oven over medium heat; remove sausage, and set aside, reserving drippings.
•Sauté green pepper and onion in reserved drippings over medium heat until tender.
•Add sausage, tomatoes, and remaining ingredients. Bring to a boil; reduce heat, and simmer over medium-low heat, uncovered, 30 minutes. Yield: 6 servings.

Per serving: Calories 482 Fat 22.4g
Cholesterol 67mg Sodium 1772mg

Sausage-and-Noodle Casserole

PREP: 7 MINUTES   COOK: 45 MINUTES

1   (8-ounce) package uncooked medium egg noodles
1   (16-ounce) package mild or hot ground pork sausage
1   (10¾-ounce) can cream of chicken soup, undiluted
1   (8-ounce) carton sour cream
½   cup crumbled blue cheese
1   (4½-ounce) jar sliced mushrooms, drained
1   (2-ounce) jar diced pimiento, drained
2   tablespoons finely chopped green pepper
1   cup soft breadcrumbs (homemade)
2   tablespoons butter or margarine, melted

•Cook noodles according to package directions; drain and set aside.
•Brown sausage in a large nonstick skillet, stirring until it crumbles; drain and set aside.
•Combine soup, sour cream, and blue cheese in a large saucepan; cook over medium heat, stirring constantly, until cheese melts. Add noodles, sausage, mushrooms, pimiento, and green pepper, tossing to coat. Spoon mixture into a lightly greased 11- x 7-inch baking dish.
•Combine breadcrumbs and butter; sprinkle over casserole. Bake, uncovered, at 350° for 30 minutes. Yield: 6 servings.

Per serving: Calories 616 Fat 39.8g
Cholesterol 125mg Sodium 1555mg

Sausage Pizza Supreme

PREP: 30 MINUTES

COOK: 1 HOUR AND 25 MINUTES

1 small green pepper, chopped
1 large onion, chopped
2 small cloves garlic, minced
3 tablespoons chopped fresh parsley
1 tablespoon vegetable oil
1 (28-ounce) can whole tomatoes, undrained
1 (6-ounce) can tomato paste
1½ teaspoons dried oregano
¼ teaspoon pepper
2 (12-inch) Thick Pizza Crusts or Thin Pizza Crusts
3 cups (12 ounces) shredded mozzarella cheese
2 cups (8 ounces) shredded Cheddar cheese
1 pound ground pork sausage
1 (3½-ounce) package sliced pepperoni
1 (2.2-ounce) can sliced ripe olives, drained
1⅓ cups sliced fresh mushrooms
¾ cup sliced green onions
2 small green peppers, sliced into rings
1 cup grated Parmesan cheese

•Sauté first 4 ingredients in hot oil in a Dutch oven until tender; set aside. Process tomatoes in an electric blender or food processor until smooth; add to onion mixture. Stir in tomato paste, oregano, and black pepper. Bring to a boil; reduce heat, and simmer 1 hour or until sauce is reduced to about 3½ cups, stirring occasionally.
•Spread sauce over each pizza crust, leaving a ½-inch border around edges. Combine mozzarella and Cheddar cheeses; sprinkle 1¼ cups over each pizza.
•Brown sausage over medium heat, stirring until it crumbles; drain. Sprinkle over pizzas.
•Layer pepperoni and next 4 ingredients on pizzas, and bake at 450° for 15 minutes. Sprinkle with remaining 2½ cups shredded cheese, and bake 5 more minutes. Top with Parmesan cheese. Yield: 16 servings.

Per serving: Calories 431 Fat 23.4g
Cholesterol 54mg Sodium 948mg

Thick Pizza Crust

1½ cups warm water (105° to 115°)
3 tablespoons vegetable oil
1 tablespoon sugar
1 teaspoon salt
2 packages active dry yeast
4½ cups all-purpose flour

•Combine first 4 ingredients in a bowl; sprinkle yeast over mixture, stirring until dissolved. Gradually add flour, mixing well after each addition.
•Turn dough out onto a lightly floured surface, and knead until smooth and elastic. Shape into a ball, and place in a greased bowl, turning to grease top. Cover and let rise in a warm place (85°), free from drafts, 1 hour or until doubled in bulk.
•Punch dough down; divide in half. Lightly grease hands, and pat dough evenly into two lightly greased 12-inch pizza pans. Cover and let rise in a warm place, free from drafts, 1 hour or until doubled in bulk. Bake at 450° for 5 minutes. Yield: 16 servings.

Thin Pizza Crust

1 cup warm water (105° to 115°)
2 tablespoons vegetable oil
2 teaspoons sugar
½ teaspoon salt
1 package active dry yeast
3 cups all-purpose flour

•Combine first 4 ingredients in a bowl; sprinkle yeast over mixture, stirring until dissolved. Gradually add flour, mixing well after each addition.
•Turn dough out onto a lightly floured surface, and knead until smooth and elastic. Shape into a ball, and place in a greased bowl, turning to grease top. Cover and let rise in a warm place (85°), free from drafts, 1 hour or until doubled in bulk.
•Punch dough down; divide in half. Lightly grease hands, and pat dough evenly into two lightly greased 12-inch pizza pans. (Do not let dough rise.) Bake at 450° for 5 minutes. Yield: 16 servings.

GAME MEATS

During hunting season, game hunters thrive in the South. And when the prize reaches the table, it's time for the hunter's feast.

Venison and other game meats have an undeserved reputation as being tough and dry. Since game is generally lean and lacks the marbling of other meat, it can be tough and dry if not cooked properly.

The key is putting the right marinade and cooking method to work to ensure tender, juicy results. Try a marinade with an acidic component such as wine, vinegar, or citrus juice to break down tough muscle fiber. And then cook by a moist heat method such as braising or stewing.

Venison Burgers

◄ QUICK • GRILLED ►

PREP: 10 MINUTES   COOK: 10 MINUTES

Tired of the same grilled burgers? Then try this venison version. It's well-seasoned and broils to perfection in a jiffy.

1 pound ground venison
1 pound ground chuck
3 tablespoons lemon-pepper seasoning
2 tablespoons Worcestershire sauce
½ teaspoon garlic powder
2 teaspoons coarse-grained mustard
Hamburger buns, toasted

•Combine first 6 ingredients in a medium bowl; mix well. Shape into 8 (¾-inch-thick) patties.
•Place patties on lightly greased broiler rack; place rack in broiler pan. Broil patties 5½ inches from heat 5 minutes on each side, turning them once. Serve burgers on toasted buns with your choice of condiments. Yield: 8 servings.

Per serving: Calories 314 Fat 11.7g
Cholesterol 96mg Sodium 681mg

Grilled Venison with Green Peppercorn Glaze

◄ GRILLED ►

PREP: 10 MINUTES
MARINATE: 8 TO 24 HOURS
COOK: 1 HOUR AND 15 MINUTES

Yes, this recipe really uses ¼ cup minced garlic in the glaze and more cloves in the marinade. Garlic mellows as it cooks and enhances the other flavoring agents in the glaze.

¼ cup olive oil
2 teaspoons chopped fresh marjoram
2 teaspoons chopped fresh rosemary
2 teaspoons chopped fresh thyme
6 cloves garlic, cut in half
1 (1½-pound) boneless venison loin
¼ cup minced garlic
½ cup minced shallots
2 tablespoons olive oil
2 cups Marsala
¼ cup balsamic vinegar
¼ cup canned green peppercorns, drained
1 (6-ounce) package dried apricot halves, cut into thin strips
1½ to 2 quarts beef broth
Salt and pepper to taste (optional)

•Combine first 5 ingredients in a large shallow dish; stir well. Add venison, turning to coat meat. Cover and marinate in refrigerator 8 to 24 hours, turning once.
•Cook ¼ cup garlic and shallot in 2 tablespoons hot oil in a large skillet over medium heat, stirring constantly, until browned. Add wine and next 3 ingredients; bring to a boil. Reduce heat, and simmer 2 minutes. Add broth; bring to a boil. Reduce heat; simmer 45 minutes or until thickened. Add salt and pepper to taste; set aside, and keep warm.
•Drain venison, discarding marinade. Grill, covered with grill lid, over medium-hot coals (350° to 400°) 25 minutes or until a meat thermometer inserted in thickest part registers 160° (medium), turning once.
•To serve, slice venison across the grain into thin slices. Serve with warm glaze. Yield: 4 servings.

Per serving: Calories 549 Fat 17.9g
Cholesterol 207mg Sodium 2672mg

SERVING GAME

Classic game accompaniments include cabbage, turnips, chestnuts, mushrooms, and onions, as well as hot buttered grits or rice. A tangy relish or chutney also pairs well with game.

Choose an appropriate bread to escort platters of game, such as hot buttered biscuits, French bread, garlic bread, cornbread or muffins, or homemade rolls.

Pepper-Crusted Venison Tenderloin

◄ HEALTHY ►

PREP: 5 MINUTES   MARINATE: 2 HOURS
COOK: 55 MINUTES

Cola as a marinade mellows the sometimes gamey taste of venison. Then this recipe brings on horseradish, cracked pepper, and coarse-grained mustard to ensure memorable flavor for the hunter's feast.

2 venison tenderloins (2 to 2½ pounds total)
1 (12-ounce) can cola-flavored beverage
¼ cup coarse-grained mustard
2 tablespoons coarsely ground or cracked pepper
½ cup red currant jelly
2 tablespoons prepared horseradish
1 tablespoon coarse-grained mustard

•Place venison and cola in a large heavy-duty, zip-top plastic bag; seal and marinate in refrigerator 2 hours. Drain venison, and discard marinade.
•Spread 2 tablespoons mustard over top and sides of each tenderloin; pat pepper over mustard. Place on a greased rack in broiler pan. Bake, uncovered, at 450° for 15 minutes; reduce heat to 350°, and bake 40 more minutes or until a meat thermometer inserted registers 160° (medium).
•Combine jelly, horseradish, and 1 tablespoon mustard; stir well. Let venison stand 10 minutes before slicing; serve with sauce. Yield: 8 servings.

Per serving: Calories 156 Fat 3.8g
Cholesterol 95mg Sodium 329mg

Spanish Rabbit Ragoût

PREP: 35 MINUTES   COOK: 1 HOUR

A rich tomato sauce tenderizes extra-lean rabbit as this stewlike dish simmers. Serve some crusty French bread for savoring the extra sauce.

¼ cup all-purpose flour
¼ teaspoon freshly ground pepper
1 (3-pound) rabbit, cleaned and cut into pieces
3 tablespoons olive oil
1 small onion, chopped
1 stalk celery, chopped
3 cloves garlic, minced
1 cup dry white wine
1 (10½-ounce) can beef broth, undiluted
4 medium tomatoes, coarsely chopped
⅓ cup ripe olives, cut in half
⅓ cup pimiento-stuffed olives, cut in half
1½ tablespoons chopped fresh oregano

•Combine flour and pepper in a large heavy-duty, zip-top plastic bag; add rabbit, shaking to coat.
•Brown rabbit in hot oil in a Dutch oven over medium-high heat; remove rabbit, reserving drippings in Dutch oven. Sauté onion, celery, and garlic in drippings over medium heat 3 minutes or until tender. Add wine, and simmer until liquid is reduced by half (about 15 minutes).
•Stir in broth; bring to a boil. Reduce heat; add tomato, olives, and oregano.
•Simmer 15 minutes, stirring occasionally. Add rabbit; simmer 30 minutes or until rabbit is tender, stirring occasionally. Yield: 4 servings.

Per serving: Calories 350 Fat 19.5g
Cholesterol 58mg Sodium 1691mg

Rigatoni with Roasted Vegetables (page 284)

PASTA, RICE & GRAINS

Move over, meat. Pasta, rice, and grains commonly share center stage on the dinner plate these days. A meal built on a base of pasta or grains is off to a quick, healthy, and satisfying start.

The passion for pasta and grains is evident and understandable in today's kitchen. Perhaps it's because they're protein- and carbohydrate-packed, high-fiber, easily affordable foods. And many of the basic recipes boil down to a few easy steps that don't require a chef's skill. The main thing to remember is that these foods are best eaten hot without delay.

Equipment

Cooking pasta, rice, and other grains such as couscous or grits doesn't require any special cookware. In fact, a sturdy set of saucepans and a large pot and colander (for preparing pasta) will get you through this chapter with ease.

A good whisk makes stirring grits easy, and a pasta machine is a big plus if you plan on making the homemade strands. The microwave doesn't gain you any time cooking pastas and grains; its best use may just be reheating many of these dishes.

Pasta Basics

Pasta comes in about as many shapes and flavors as there are ways to prepare it. And it's available in two forms—dried or refrigerated fresh.

The nutritional value of all types of pasta is about the same. Most dried pasta is made from semolina flour, a flour high in gluten-forming protein, ground from durum wheat. Dried pasta is popular because it's easy on the budget and has a long shelf life. Look for a package that has unbroken pieces.

Look for fresh pasta in the refrigerated section at the supermarket or make your own using our recipe on page 286. Fresh pasta varies in weight from dried pasta; ounce for ounce, you'll need to buy about 50 percent more fresh pasta to end up with the same amount of dried cooked pasta (see box on the following page).

Storing Pasta

Store uncooked pasta in a cool, dry place free from dust and moisture up to one year; store uncooked egg noodles up to six months. Store plain cooked pasta in the refrigerator up to four days or in the freezer for one month. You can refrigerate prepared pasta dishes one to two days (depending on any meat or seafood it contains) or freeze them as long as six months.

Measuring Pasta

Uncooked dried pasta of similar sizes and shapes can be interchanged in recipes if it's measured by weight, not volume. Cooked pasta, however, can be substituted cup for cup. When cooked, noodles swell slightly; spaghetti and macaroni double in size. In general, allow 2 ounces of uncooked dried pasta, 3 ounces of uncooked refrigerated pasta, or 1 to 1½ cups cooked pasta per person.

Cooking Pasta

Pasta needs plenty of room to roam in boiling water. Three quarts of rapidly boiling water for every 8 ounces of dried pasta provides enough water for pasta to float freely and cook evenly. Salt the water just before adding pasta. Water that tastes slightly salty will enhance the flavor of the pasta. If desired, add a small amount of vegetable oil to the boiling water to prevent sticking. Many sources, however, say no oil is needed, just occasional stirring as the pasta cooks. Gradually add pasta in small amounts to maintain a rolling boil for cooking.

When cooking long pasta shapes (spaghetti, linguine, and fettuccine), it's not necessary to break the pasta into shorter pieces. Simply hold one end of pasta by the handful, and dip the other end into boiling water, pushing pasta gently until it softens enough to submerge.

Salting pasta water: When cooking pasta, add the recommended amount of salt on the package. We account for this in each recipe analysis.

Cooking times will vary with a pasta's size, shape, and moisture content. Fresh pasta cooks in one to three minutes, while dried pasta requires five to 15 minutes. Follow the package directions.

Begin checking pasta for doneness 1 minute before its minimum cooking time. Remove a piece of pasta from the water, and cut a

HOW MUCH PASTA TO COOK

A cooked yield varies by type, shape, and size of the pasta. This chart will help you figure out how much uncooked pasta will yield 4 cups cooked.

TYPE OF PASTA	AMOUNT TO MAKE 4 CUPS COOKED
For Pasta Strands (like spaghetti, fettuccine, linguine, vermicelli, angel hair)	**Start with** •8 ounces dry strands •12 ounces refrigerated fresh strands
For Macaroni Style (tubular shapes)	**Start with** •2 cups elbow macaroni •2¾ cups medium shells •3 cups rigatoni •3⅔ cups corkscrew
For Egg Noodles	**Start with** •4 cups fine noodles •4½ cups bow ties •5 cups medium noodles

bite from it. Pasta's ready when it's al dente ("to the tooth" in Italian)—firm but tender, chewy not soggy. Slightly undercook pasta such as lasagna that will be used as part of a recipe requiring further cooking.

Sometimes it's a good idea to save a little pasta water before you drain the pasta. Then add it to the sauce before serving. The small amount of starch in pasta water encourages a light sauce to cling to pasta.

Drain pasta immediately. No rinsing is necessary unless it's specifically stated in the recipe or unless you're preparing a cold pasta salad, in which case you'll need to rinse pasta under cold water to remove excess starch. Pasta is best hot, so warm up its serving bowl, if possible, or if serving is delayed, return cooked and drained pasta to its warm cooking pot. Cover and let stand up to 10 minutes.

When cooked al dente, pasta can be reheated. Simply drop cooked pasta into boiling water that has been removed from heat, and let stand one to two minutes; then drain.

Serving Pasta

Serving long, thin pastas such as linguine or fettuccine can be tricky. Use kitchen tongs or a wooden pasta fork to transfer the pasta. This long-handled fork has pegs protruding from the flat surface that allow you to grab the pasta and easily lift it to plates.

The tremendous variety of pastas available today creates endless options for pairing pastas and sauces. Keep in mind this general rule of thumb—the bolder shaped pastas deserve chunky, robust sauces. And remember that pasta needs to be moistened with sauce, not smothered in it; you want to taste the pasta, too.

Mafalda

Radiatore
(little radiators)

Vermicelli

Long
fusilli

Gemelli

Arborio
rice

Linguine

Fettuccine

Capellini

Ravioletti

Tortellini

Orzo

Rigatoni

Fusilli
bucati

Wagon wheels
(ruote)

Rotini

Orecchiette
(little ears)

Small
shells

Farfalle
(bow ties)

Ramen
noodles

Couscous

Acini
di pepe

Mostaccioli

Angel hair
nests

Ditalini
(thimbles)

Gnocchi

Penne

Jumbo shells

Manicotti

Easy Spaghetti

PREP: 8 MINUTES   COOK: 30 MINUTES

Scores of popular entrées begin with a skillet full of ground beef and onion. Here the beef mixture is the start of a foolproof spaghetti. Simmer the sauce just long enough for the flavors to blend.

1 pound ground beef
1 small onion, chopped
1 (28-ounce) can tomatoes, undrained and chopped
2 (6-ounce) cans tomato paste
1 teaspoon dried oregano
1 teaspoon dried basil
1 large clove garlic, minced, or ½ teaspoon garlic powder
½ (16-ounce) package dried spaghetti
1 cup grated Parmesan cheese

•Cook ground beef and onion in a large skillet, stirring until meat browns and crumbles; drain well.
•Stir in tomatoes, tomato paste, and seasonings. Cook over medium heat about 20 minutes, stirring occasionally.
•Cook spaghetti according to package directions; drain. Serve sauce over spaghetti, and sprinkle with cheese. Yield: 4 main-dish servings.
Per serving: Calories 664 Fat 23.5g
Cholesterol 90mg Sodium 1047mg

Spaghetti alla Carbonara

PREP: 20 MINUTES   COOK: 12 MINUTES

Dress these strands of spaghetti with butter and cream and bits of smoky bacon. Freshly grated cheese makes a difference here.

1 (16-ounce) package dried spaghetti or fettuccine
½ cup whipping cream or half-and-half
½ cup egg substitute
1 cup freshly grated Parmesan cheese or Romano cheese, divided
¼ cup butter or margarine
8 slices bacon or pancetta*, cooked and crumbled
¼ cup chopped fresh parsley

> ### HURRY UP, H$_2$O!
>
> The most time-consuming part of cooking pasta is waiting for a big pot of water to boil. To hasten the process, put the water on to boil as soon as you come into the kitchen. Cover the pot with a lid, too; this traps the heat so the water boils faster.

•Cook spaghetti according to package directions, omitting salt. Meanwhile, heat whipping cream in a heavy saucepan. Combine egg substitute and ½ cup cheese, stirring mixture well.
•Drain spaghetti, and place in a serving bowl. Add butter; toss gently until butter melts. Add egg mixture, whipping cream mixture, bacon, and parsley; toss. Sprinkle with remaining ½ cup cheese. Serve immediately. Yield: 6 main-dish servings.
Pancetta is an Italian bacon cured with salt but not smoked.
Per serving: Calories 537 Fat 24.6g
Cholesterol 65mg Sodium 493mg

Spaghetti with Meatballs

PREP: 15 MINUTES   COOK: 40 MINUTES

Looking for spaghetti with a make-ahead step? You can shape the meatballs and freeze them in zip-top bags. Just thaw them in the refrigerator several hours when ready to proceed.

½ cup chopped onion
2 tablespoons butter or margarine, melted
1 (28-ounce) can tomatoes, undrained and chopped
1 (6-ounce) can tomato paste
1 tablespoon chopped fresh parsley
¼ teaspoon pepper
¼ teaspoon dried oregano
1 pound ground beef
2 tablespoons grated onion
½ teaspoon salt
¼ teaspoon pepper
2 tablespoons vegetable oil
½ (16-ounce) package dried spaghetti

•Sauté onion in butter in a large skillet. Add tomatoes and next 4 ingredients. Cook over medium heat 20 minutes, stirring occasionally.
•Combine ground beef and next 3 ingredients; mix well. Shape into 1½-inch meatballs. Cook in a large skillet in hot oil over medium heat until no longer pink; drain. Add meatballs to sauce; cook over low heat 15 minutes.
•Cook spaghetti according to package directions; drain. Serve sauce over spaghetti. Yield: 4 main-dish servings.
Per serving: Calories 619 Fat 28g
Cholesterol 85mg Sodium 896mg

Black Bean Spaghetti

PREP: 15 MINUTES   COOK: 20 MINUTES

You'll never miss meat in this entrée. Spoon mounds of this chunky black bean sauce over hot cooked spaghetti or your pasta of choice.

1 large onion, chopped
1 (8-ounce) package sliced fresh mushrooms
4 cloves garlic, crushed
1 sweet red pepper, cut into thin strips
2 tablespoons olive oil
2 (15-ounce) cans black beans, rinsed and drained
1 (28-ounce) can whole tomatoes, undrained and chopped
1 (2¼-ounce) can sliced ripe olives, drained
½ teaspoon dried basil
¼ teaspoon salt
½ teaspoon pepper
1 (12-ounce) package dried spaghetti or angel hair pasta
1 cup freshly grated Parmesan cheese

•Sauté first 4 ingredients in hot oil in a large saucepan over medium-high heat until tender. Add beans and next 5 ingredients. Bring to a boil; reduce heat, and simmer, uncovered, 20 minutes, stirring occasionally.
•Cook spaghetti according to package directions; drain well.
•Place spaghetti on a serving platter; top with tomato mixture. Sprinkle with cheese. Yield: 6 main-dish servings.
Per serving: Calories 501 Fat 11.2g
Cholesterol 9mg Sodium 974mg

Spaghetti-Ham Pie

PREP: 20 MINUTES   COOK: 22 MINUTES

This spaghetti entrée is easy to make and serve. Just nestle pasta, ham, and cheese into a pieplate, and bake it. The baked mixture slices neatly into wedges.

6 ounces dried spaghetti
3 or 4 cloves garlic, minced
2½ tablespoons olive oil
¼ cup all-purpose flour
¼ teaspoon salt
⅛ teaspoon freshly ground pepper
1½ cups milk
¾ cup half-and-half
¾ cup chopped cooked ham
¾ cup grated Parmesan cheese,
     divided

•Cook spaghetti according to package directions; drain and set aside.
•Sauté garlic in hot oil in a Dutch oven over medium heat 5 minutes. Stir in flour, salt, and pepper. Cook 1 minute, stirring constantly. Gradually add milk and half-and-half; cook, stirring constantly, until thickened and bubbly. Stir in spaghetti, ham, and 2 tablespoons Parmesan cheese.
•Spoon mixture into a lightly greased 9-inch pieplate; sprinkle with remaining ½ cup plus 2 tablespoons Parmesan cheese. Bake, uncovered, at 425° for 20 to 22 minutes or until lightly browned. Yield: 6 main-dish servings.
Per serving: Calories 350 Fat 17.8g
Cholesterol 42mg Sodium 766mg

PASTA AND SAUCE PAIRINGS

•Serve fresh, high-flavored sauces such as Marinara Sauce (page 390) or Pesto (page 391) with long pastas.
•Serve thick, chunky meat and vegetable sauces with tubular and shell pastas that are designed to "trap" the sauce. Thick pastas like rigatoni, ziti, and fettuccine also pair well with thick sauces.
•Rich, thick, smooth sauces blend best with flat pastas that won't trap too much sauce.

Mediterranean Shrimp and Pasta

◄ QUICK ►

PREP: 15 MINUTES   COOK: 10 MINUTES

Have some French bread ready for dipping into the flavorful tomato-wine sauce that coats this shrimp and vermicelli.

1 pound unpeeled medium-size fresh
     shrimp
8 ounces dried vermicelli
5 green onions, sliced
3 cloves garlic, minced
2 tablespoons olive oil
1 (12-ounce) jar marinated artichoke
     hearts, undrained
6 plum tomatoes, chopped
1 cup sliced fresh mushrooms
¼ cup dry white wine
2 teaspoons dried Italian seasoning
½ teaspoon fresh rosemary, minced
¼ teaspoon salt
¼ teaspoon pepper
½ cup freshly grated Parmesan cheese

•Peel shrimp, and devein, if desired; set aside.
•Cook vermicelli according to package directions; drain and keep warm.
•Sauté green onions and garlic in hot oil in a large skillet over medium-high heat until tender. Stir in artichokes and next 7 ingredients. Bring to a boil; reduce heat, and simmer 5 minutes.
•Add shrimp; cook 4 minutes or until shrimp turn pink, stirring occasionally. Serve over vermicelli; sprinkle with cheese. Yield: 4 main-dish servings.
Per serving: Calories 589 Fat 24.8g
Cholesterol 136mg Sodium 871mg

Seafood Linguine

◄ HEALTHY ►

PREP: 38 MINUTES   COOK: 40 MINUTES

Lots of rich tomato broth accompanies this dish, so consider serving it in pasta bowls. The clams in shells make a dramatic presentation. Substitute littleneck clams if they're more available in your region.

1 medium onion, chopped
3 cloves garlic, minced
½ cup chopped green pepper
     (½ medium)
⅓ cup chopped fresh parsley
¼ cup olive oil
1 (28-ounce) can tomatoes, undrained and
     chopped
1 (15-ounce) can tomato sauce
½ cup water
1 tablespoon lemon juice
1 teaspoon dried basil
1 teaspoon dried oregano
¼ teaspoon salt
¼ teaspoon black pepper
1 dozen cherrystone clams in shells
1 pound unpeeled medium-size fresh
     shrimp
1 pound fresh lump crabmeat, drained
1 (12-ounce) package dried linguine
¾ cup grated Parmesan cheese

•Sauté first 4 ingredients in hot oil in a Dutch oven; add tomatoes and next 7 ingredients. Bring to a boil; reduce heat, and simmer, uncovered, 15 minutes or until thickened, stirring occasionally.
•Meanwhile, scrub clams thoroughly, discarding any shells that are cracked or open. Peel shrimp, and devein, if desired. Add clams to sauce; cover and simmer 5 minutes.
•Add shrimp and crabmeat to clam mixture; cook 10 more minutes or until clams open and shrimp turn pink.
•Cook linguine according to package directions; drain. Place on a warm platter, and top with sauce. Sprinkle with cheese. Yield: 6 main-dish servings.
Per serving: Calories 570 Fat 16.9g
Cholesterol 175mg Sodium 1384mg

Linguine with Clam Sauce

PREP: 10 MINUTES   COOK: 28 MINUTES

8 ounces dried linguine
2 (6½-ounce) cans minced clams, undrained
½ cup chopped onion
2 cloves garlic, minced
¼ cup olive oil
¼ cup dry white wine
2 tablespoons chopped fresh parsley
⅛ teaspoon freshly ground pepper
½ cup grated Parmesan cheese

•Cook linguine according to package directions in a Dutch oven. Drain and return to pan; set aside.
•Drain clams, reserving liquid; set clams aside.
•Sauté onion and garlic in hot oil in a medium saucepan until tender. Add reserved clam liquid; reduce heat, and simmer 15 minutes. Add clams, wine, parsley, and pepper; cook until thoroughly heated.
•Add clam mixture to linguine in pan, tossing well. Cook over medium heat until thoroughly heated. Sprinkle with cheese. Serve hot. Yield: 4 main-dish servings.
Per serving: Calories 417 Fat 17g
Cholesterol 35mg Sodium 803mg

Lemon Linguine

◄ QUICK ►

PREP: 5 MINUTES   COOK: 11 MINUTES

8 ounces dried linguine
¼ cup minced onion
2 cloves garlic, crushed
1 tablespoon butter or margarine, melted
1 (8-ounce) carton sour cream
1 tablespoon milk
1½ teaspoons lemon-pepper seasoning
¼ teaspoon salt
2 tablespoons grated Parmesan cheese
2 tablespoons chopped fresh parsley
Garnish: fresh parsley sprigs

•Cook linguine according to package directions; drain and keep warm.
•Sauté onion and garlic in butter in a skillet over medium-high heat until onion is tender.

Stir in sour cream and next 3 ingredients; cook 1 minute. Remove from heat. Toss with linguine. Sprinkle with cheese and chopped parsley. Garnish, if desired. Serve hot. Yield: 4 side-dish servings.
Per serving: Calories 381 Fat 16.8g
Cholesterol 36mg Sodium 858mg

Linguine with Fresh Tomato Sauce

◄ QUICK • HEALTHY ►

PREP: 10 MINUTES   COOK: 10 MINUTES

4 large tomatoes, finely chopped
½ cup shredded fresh basil
¼ cup chopped fresh parsley
2 tablespoons olive oil
½ teaspoon salt
¼ teaspoon freshly ground pepper
2 cloves garlic, minced
1 (12-ounce) package dried linguine
½ cup pitted kalamata olives
⅓ cup freshly grated Parmesan cheese or Parmigiano-Reggiano

•Combine first 7 ingredients; toss gently.
•Cook linguine according to package directions; drain and place in a large serving bowl.
•Top linguine with tomato mixture, and sprinkle with olives and Parmesan cheese. Yield: 6 side-dish servings.
Per serving: Calories 325 Fat 9.9g
Cholesterol 3mg Sodium 757mg

Pesto and Pasta

◄ QUICK ►

PREP: 10 MINUTES   COOK: 10 MINUTES

Fresh pesto livens up this linguine. The pesto is also great tossed with any pasta. Add some shredded chicken for a more filling option.

¼ cup pine nuts or walnuts
½ cup packed fresh basil leaves
¼ cup fresh parsley sprigs
¼ cup freshly grated Parmesan cheese
1 clove garlic, halved
¼ teaspoon salt
¼ teaspoon pepper
¼ cup olive oil
6 ounces dried linguine

•Toast pine nuts in a small skillet over medium heat 1 to 2 minutes, if desired.
•Process nuts, basil, and next 5 ingredients in container of a food processor or electric blender 2 minutes or until smooth. (If using a blender, coarsely chop herbs before processing.) Gradually pour oil through food chute with processor running until a paste forms.
•Cook linguine according to package directions; drain. Spoon pesto mixture over linguine; toss gently, and serve immediately. Yield: 4 side-dish servings.
Per serving: Calories 356 Fat 21.6g
Cholesterol 3mg Sodium 384mg

Fettuccine Alfredo

◄ QUICK • FAMILY FAVORITE ►

PREP: 7 MINUTES   COOK: 11 MINUTES

8 ounces dried fettuccine
½ cup butter
½ cup whipping cream
¾ cup freshly grated Parmesan cheese
¼ teaspoon salt
¼ teaspoon pepper
2 tablespoons chopped fresh parsley
⅛ teaspoon ground nutmeg (optional)

•Cook fettuccine according to package directions; drain. Place in a serving bowl.
•Meanwhile, combine butter and whipping cream in a saucepan; cook over low heat until butter melts. Stir in cheese and next 3 ingredients; add nutmeg, if desired. Pour mixture over hot fettuccine; toss well. Serve immediately. Yield: 6 side-dish servings.
Per serving: Calories 384 Fat 25.9g
Cholesterol 75mg Sodium 570mg

PICK YOUR STYLE OF PARMESAN

You can buy Parmesan in several forms. Certain recipes really benefit from the flavor punch you get from freshly grated cheese, while others taste and work just fine with a shake from the familiar green can. When our recipes call for freshly grated Parmesan cheese, we recommend you grate a wedge of cheese. When a recipe simply calls for grated Parmesan cheese, we're referring to the canned product.

Creamy Broccoli-Parmesan Fettuccine

◄ QUICK ►

PREP: 10 MINUTES   COOK: 15 MINUTES

2 cups broccoli flowerets
8 ounces dried fettuccine
2 tablespoons butter or margarine
1 (6-ounce) package Canadian bacon, cut
    into thin strips
⅔ cup whipping cream
1½ cups freshly grated Parmesan cheese
½ teaspoon salt
½ teaspoon freshly ground pepper

•Cook broccoli in boiling water to cover 3 minutes; drain and plunge into ice water to stop the cooking process. Drain and set aside.
•Cook fettuccine according to package directions; drain and place in a serving bowl. Set aside.
•Melt butter in a large skillet over medium-high heat. Add bacon, and cook 2 minutes, stirring constantly. Stir in broccoli, and cook 1 minute or until thoroughly heated. Add broccoli mixture, whipping cream, and remaining 3 ingredients to fettuccine; toss gently. Serve immediately. Yield: 3 main-dish servings.

Per serving: Calories 791 Fat 42.8g
Cholesterol 149mg Sodium 2138mg

Noodles Romanoff

◄ QUICK ►

PREP: 6 MINUTES   COOK: 10 MINUTES

1 (8-ounce) package dried wide egg
    noodles
1 (16-ounce) carton sour cream
¼ cup butter or margarine, melted
¼ teaspoon salt
¼ teaspoon freshly ground pepper
1 small clove garlic, minced
¼ cup grated Parmesan cheese
2 tablespoons chopped fresh chives

•Cook noodles according to package directions; drain. Stir sour cream and next 4 ingredients into noodles; sprinkle with cheese and chives. Toss and serve hot. Yield: 8 side-dish servings.

Per serving: Calories 296 Fat 19.8g
Cholesterol 70mg Sodium 301mg

Pasta Primavera

◄ FAMILY FAVORITE ►

PREP: 30 MINUTES   COOK: 15 MINUTES

Primavera means spring style, referring to the crisp-tender, bright vegetables blended with this rich cream sauce and fettuccine.

8 ounces dried fettuccine or linguine
⅓ cup pine nuts
2 cups fresh broccoli flowerets
1½ cups fresh or frozen snow pea pods,
    trimmed
2 large carrots, scraped and diagonally
    sliced
¼ cup butter or margarine
10 large fresh mushrooms, sliced
2 cloves garlic, minced
1½ cups freshly grated Parmesan cheese
1 cup whipping cream
1 cup sliced green onions
12 cherry tomatoes, cut in half
¼ cup chopped fresh flat-leaf parsley
⅓ cup chopped fresh basil
½ teaspoon salt
½ teaspoon pepper
Freshly grated Parmesan cheese (optional)

•Cook fettuccine according to package directions; drain and set aside.
•Toast pine nuts at 350° in a shallow roasting pan or in a skillet over medium heat 3 to 5 minutes, stirring once; set aside.
•Cook broccoli, snow peas, and carrot in a Dutch oven in boiling water to cover 1 to 2 minutes or until crisp-tender. Drain and plunge vegetables into cold water to stop the cooking process. Drain.
•Melt butter in Dutch oven. Add mushrooms and garlic; sauté over medium heat just until tender. Add 1½ cups cheese and whipping cream, stirring until cheese melts.
•Add broccoli mixture, green onions, and next 5 ingredients to Dutch oven, stirring well. Add fettuccine, and toss until coated. Spoon onto a serving platter. Sprinkle with pine nuts, and, if desired, additional cheese. Yield: 4 main-dish servings.

Per serving: Calories 780 Fat 50.6g
Cholesterol 132mg Sodium 1082mg

Orzo with Spinach and Pine Nuts

◄ QUICK ►

PREP: 4 MINUTES   COOK: 18 MINUTES

Orzo is pasta that looks like rice. It cooks quickly and, in this dish, heat from the pasta nicely wilts the chopped fresh spinach.

2 tablespoons pine nuts
1 clove garlic, minced
1 tablespoon butter or margarine, melted
1¾ cups water
¾ cup uncooked orzo (rice-shaped pasta)
¼ teaspoon salt
1 cup tightly packed chopped fresh spinach
¼ cup grated Parmesan cheese

•Spread pine nuts in a small skillet. Cook over medium heat 1 to 2 minutes or until lightly toasted, stirring often. Set aside.
•Sauté garlic in butter in a saucepan over medium heat 1 minute. Add water, orzo, and salt, and bring to a boil. Reduce heat, and cook 12 minutes or until liquid is absorbed. Stir in spinach, cheese, and pine nuts. Serve hot. Yield: 2 side-dish servings.

Per serving: Calories 385 Fat 16.7g
Cholesterol 26mg Sodium 643mg

Baked Ziti

PREP: 4 MINUTES   COOK: 25 MINUTES

12 ounces dried ziti (3¼ cups)
6½ cups Italian Meat Sauce (page 249) or
    commercial meat sauce
1 (16-ounce) package sliced mozzarella
    cheese
½ cup grated Parmesan cheese

•Cook ziti according to package directions; drain and set aside.
•Combine Italian Meat Sauce and ziti; layer half each of ziti mixture and mozzarella cheese in a greased 13- x 9-inch baking dish. Spoon remaining ziti mixture over cheese.
•Cover and bake at 350° for 15 minutes. Uncover; add remaining mozzarella cheese, and sprinkle with Parmesan cheese. Bake 10 more minutes. Yield: 8 main-dish servings.

Per serving: Calories 514 Fat 23.9g
Cholesterol 85mg Sodium 986mg

Rigatoni with Roasted Vegetables

PREP: 25 MINUTES   COOK: 40 MINUTES

Big flavor comes from this recipe. Ridged tubes of rigatoni are tossed with roasted carrots, eggplant, and zucchini for a hearty entrée. See it pictured on page 276.

6 ounces dried rigatoni or penne
½ cup olive oil, divided
1 (1-ounce) package onion soup mix
2 tablespoons chopped fresh thyme or
   2 teaspoons dried thyme
2 large carrots, scraped and cut into
   1-inch slices
1 medium zucchini, cut into 1-inch slices
1 (1-pound) eggplant, cut into 1½-inch
   pieces
1 (8-ounce) package fresh mushrooms,
   halved
¼ cup balsamic vinegar
⅓ cup pine nuts, toasted
2 ounces fresh Parmesan cheese, shaved
Freshly ground pepper
Garnish: fresh thyme sprigs

•Cook rigatoni according to package directions; drain. Place in a large bowl, and set aside.
•Whisk ¼ cup olive oil, onion soup mix, and thyme in a bowl. Add carrot and next 3 ingredients, tossing to coat. Spread vegetables evenly in an ungreased roasting pan. Roast at 450° for 20 to 25 minutes, stirring after 15 minutes. Gently stir roasted vegetables into rigatoni.
•Whisk remaining ¼ cup oil with vinegar. Pour over pasta mixture, tossing to coat; sprinkle with pine nuts, shaved cheese, and pepper. Garnish, if desired. Serve warm. Yield: 4 main-dish servings.
Per serving: Calories 611 Fat 38.6g
Cholesterol 10mg Sodium 938mg

Macaroni and Cheese

PREP: 10 MINUTES   COOK: 35 MINUTES

Comfort food finds its definition in this traditional cheesy macaroni. Our staff recommends using the block of American cheese, not the slices. For a little extra zip, add a shake of hot sauce.

1 (8-ounce) package dried elbow macaroni
¼ cup butter or margarine
¼ cup all-purpose flour
2 cups milk
1 teaspoon salt
2 cups (8 ounces) shredded sharp Cheddar
   cheese or American cheese
Paprika (optional)

•Cook macaroni according to package directions, omitting salt. Drain and set aside.
•Melt butter in a heavy saucepan over low heat; add flour, stirring until smooth. Cook 1 minute, stirring constantly. Gradually add milk; cook over medium heat, stirring constantly, until thickened and bubbly. Stir in salt and cheese, stirring until cheese melts.
•Stir macaroni into cheese sauce, and pour into a lightly greased 2-quart baking dish or an 11- x 7-inch baking dish. Sprinkle with paprika, if desired. Bake, uncovered, at 350° for 25 to 35 minutes or until bubbly. Let stand 5 minutes before serving. Yield: 6 side-dish servings.
Per serving: Calories 427 Fat 23.4g
Cholesterol 71mg Sodium 746mg

Saucepan Macaroni and Cheese:
Prepare as directed above, reducing milk to 1½ cups. Add macaroni to cheese sauce in saucepan, and cook over medium-low heat 5 minutes; let stand 5 minutes before serving. Sprinkle with paprika, if desired.

Tortellini and Fresh Basil

PREP: 8 MINUTES   COOK: 10 MINUTES

Rounded, cup-shaped tortellini holds this fresh tomato sauce well.

1 pound ripe tomatoes, seeded and
   chopped
3 cloves garlic, minced
½ cup chopped fresh basil
¼ cup olive oil
3 tablespoons balsamic vinegar
1 teaspoon salt
½ teaspoon pepper
2 (9-ounce) packages refrigerated
   cheese-filled tortellini
½ cup crumbled feta cheese

•Combine first 7 ingredients in a serving bowl. Cook tortellini according to package directions; drain. Add tortellini to tomato mixture, and toss well. Sprinkle with cheese. Serve warm or chilled. Yield: 4 main-dish servings.
Per serving: Calories 562 Fat 22.9g
Cholesterol 73mg Sodium 1370mg

Mediterranean Ravioli

PREP: 12 MINUTES   COOK: 44 MINUTES

2 cups peeled, cubed eggplant
1 cup chopped onion
2 cloves garlic, minced
2 tablespoons olive oil
1 (15-ounce) container refrigerated
   chunky tomato sauce, pasta sauce, or
   spaghetti sauce
¼ cup sliced ripe olives
1 tablespoon balsamic vinegar
1 teaspoon dried thyme
1 (9-ounce) package refrigerated
   cheese-filled ravioli
⅔ cup freshly grated Parmesan cheese

•Sauté first 3 ingredients in hot oil in a large skillet over medium-high heat until tender. Stir in tomato sauce and next 3 ingredients. Remove from heat; set aside.
•Cook ravioli according to package directions; drain. Rinse with cold water; drain.
•Combine vegetable mixture and ravioli, tossing gently; spoon into a lightly greased

shallow 2-quart baking dish. Cover and bake at 350° for 20 minutes. Uncover and sprinkle with cheese; bake, uncovered, 10 more minutes or until thoroughly heated. Yield: 4 main-dish servings.

Per serving: Calories 444 Fat 25g
Cholesterol 53mg Sodium 1124mg

Cannelloni Florentine

◀ VEGETARIAN ▶

PREP: 32 MINUTES   COOK: 30 MINUTES

Florentine lets you know that this pasta is filled with healthy spinach. A pair of the stuffed shells makes a filling meatless meal.

8 dried cannelloni or manicotti shells
1 (10-ounce) package frozen chopped spinach, thawed
1 cup chopped fresh mushrooms
¼ cup diced onion
3 cloves garlic, minced
1 tablespoon olive oil
1 large egg, beaten
⅓ cup freshly grated Parmesan cheese
½ teaspoon dried oregano
¼ teaspoon dried basil
2 cups commercial spaghetti sauce, divided
Parmesan Sauce
2 tablespoons chopped fresh parsley

•Cook cannelloni shells according to package directions; drain and set aside.
•Place spinach between paper towels, and squeeze until barely moist; set aside.
•Sauté mushrooms, onion, and garlic in hot oil in a large skillet over medium-high heat 2 minutes. Add spinach; sauté until mushrooms are tender and liquid evaporates. Remove mixture from heat, and cool slightly.
•Stir in egg and next 3 ingredients. Stuff spinach mixture into cannelloni shells.
•Spread 1 cup spaghetti sauce in an 11- x 7-inch baking dish. Place stuffed shells on spaghetti sauce. Spread remaining spaghetti sauce over shells. Spoon Parmesan Sauce down center of dish.
•Cover and bake at 375° for 30 minutes or until thoroughly heated. Sprinkle with parsley. Yield: 4 main-dish servings.

Per serving: Calories 638 Fat 22.6g
Cholesterol 86mg Sodium 1017mg

Parmesan Sauce

2 tablespoons butter or margarine
2 tablespoons all-purpose flour
1 cup milk
⅓ cup freshly grated Parmesan cheese
¼ teaspoon ground nutmeg
¼ teaspoon white pepper

•Melt butter in a saucepan over medium heat; add flour, and cook 1 minute, stirring constantly. Gradually add milk, and cook until thickened, stirring constantly with a wire whisk. Add cheese, nutmeg, and pepper; cook, stirring constantly, until cheese melts. Yield: about 1¼ cups.

Classic Lasagna

◀ FAMILY FAVORITE ▶

PREP: 20 MINUTES   COOK: 50 MINUTES

1 pound ground beef
1 clove garlic, minced
1 teaspoon dried parsley flakes
1 teaspoon dried basil
1 (16-ounce) can tomatoes, undrained
2 (6-ounce) cans tomato paste
½ (16-ounce) package dried lasagna noodles
2 large eggs, beaten
2 (12-ounce) cartons cream-style cottage cheese or ricotta cheese
½ teaspoon pepper
½ cup grated Parmesan cheese
1 pound sliced mozzarella cheese

•Brown ground beef in a large skillet, stirring until meat crumbles; drain. Add garlic and next 4 ingredients; partially cover and simmer 15 minutes or until sauce is thick, stirring occasionally.
•Cook lasagna noodles according to package directions; drain.
•Combine eggs and next 3 ingredients, stirring well.
•Spread about ½ cup meat sauce in a greased 13- x 9-inch baking dish. Layer half each of noodles, cottage cheese mixture, mozzarella cheese, and meat sauce. Repeat layers. Cover and bake at 350° for 30 minutes; let stand 10 minutes before serving. Yield: 6 main-dish servings.

Per serving: Calories 725 Fat 33.1g
Cholesterol 192mg Sodium 1210mg

Italian Sausage Lasagna

PREP: 25 MINUTES

COOK: 1 HOUR AND 25 MINUTES

Either spicy or sweet Italian sausage is good in this well-seasoned lasagna.

1 pound Italian sausage
1 medium onion, chopped
1 clove garlic, minced
3 tablespoons dried parsley flakes, divided
1 (14½-ounce) can whole tomatoes, chopped and undrained
2 (8-ounce) cans tomato sauce
1 teaspoon sugar
1 teaspoon dried basil
¼ teaspoon salt
12 dried lasagna noodles
1 (15-ounce) carton ricotta cheese
¼ cup grated Parmesan cheese
1½ teaspoons dried oregano
2 cups (8 ounces) shredded mozzarella cheese
2 tablespoons grated Parmesan cheese

•Remove and discard casings from sausage. Cook sausage, onion, and garlic in a large skillet over medium heat, stirring until sausage crumbles; drain.
•Stir in 2 tablespoons parsley, tomatoes, and next 4 ingredients; bring to a boil. Cover, reduce heat, and simmer 30 minutes or until sauce is slightly thickened, stirring occasionally.
•Cook noodles according to package directions; drain and set aside.
•Combine remaining 1 tablespoon parsley, ricotta cheese, ¼ cup Parmesan cheese, and oregano; set aside.
•Spread 1 cup meat mixture in a lightly greased 13- x 9-inch baking dish. Top with 4 noodles, 1 cup ricotta cheese mixture, ⅔ cup mozzarella cheese, and 4 more noodles.
•Spread remaining ricotta cheese mixture over noodles, and top with 1 cup meat mixture, ⅔ cup mozzarella cheese, and remaining 4 noodles. Top with remaining meat mixture and mozzarella cheese; sprinkle with 2 tablespoons Parmesan cheese.
•Bake at 350° for 45 minutes or until bubbly. Let stand 10 minutes before serving. Yield: 6 main-dish servings.

Per serving: Calories 648 Fat 34.7g
Cholesterol 114mg Sodium 1598mg

PRODUCE YOUR OWN PASTA

Pasta purists maintain that there's a world of difference between the flavor and texture of homemade pasta versus store-bought dried pasta. But judge for yourself. When you begin a batch of pasta, you may find the following information, as well as our step-by-step photographs, helpful.

The difference between brands of flour (and how much moisture they absorb) accounts for the range in flour and water in our recipe. Start with the minimum amount of flour and water; if the dough seems too dry, add a few more drops of water. If too sticky, knead in a dusting of extra flour. The dough should be firm at the beginning, but it will soften as it's kneaded and worked through the pasta rollers.

Work with the dough and give it time to soften before you add extra water or flour. Experience is the best guide to knowing when a dough is the right consistency.

Most pasta machines have attachments for quickly cutting the dough into different widths. You can otherwise cut pasta strips with a pastry wheel, pizza cutter, or paring knife.

Gently hang the delicate strands of pasta over a wooden drying rack or clean wooden or plastic coat hangers to dry.

Seafood Manicotti

PREP: 1 HOUR

COOK: 1 HOUR AND 5 MINUTES

1 quart whipping cream
½ teaspoon salt
¼ teaspoon ground black pepper
¼ teaspoon ground red pepper
14 dried manicotti shells
2 pounds unpeeled large fresh shrimp
1 cup chopped onion
1 cup chopped green pepper
¼ cup chopped celery
1 clove garlic, minced
3 tablespoons butter or margarine, melted
1 pound fresh crabmeat, drained and flaked
1½ cups (6 ounces) shredded Monterey Jack cheese with peppers

•Combine first 4 ingredients in a large saucepan; cook over medium-high heat 30 minutes or until thickened and reduced to 2 cups. Set aside.
•Cook manicotti according to package directions; drain. Peel shrimp, and devein, if desired. Chop shrimp, and set aside.
•Sauté onion and next 3 ingredients in butter in a large Dutch oven over medium-high heat 5 minutes or until tender.
•Add shrimp and crabmeat; cook, stirring constantly, 5 minutes or until shrimp turn pink. Remove from heat. Cool 10 minutes; drain excess liquid.
•Combine seafood mixture and whipping cream mixture. Fill shells, and place in two lightly greased 11- x 7-inch baking dishes. Sprinkle with cheese.
•Cover and bake at 350° for 15 minutes. Uncover and bake 10 more minutes. Serve hot. Yield: 7 main-dish servings.
Per serving: Calories 1039 Fat 63.5g
Cholesterol 411mg Sodium 785mg

Manicotti with Meat Sauce

PREP: 25 MINUTES   COOK: 30 MINUTES

1 (8-ounce) package dried manicotti shells
2 (15-ounce) cartons ricotta cheese
1 (8-ounce) package mozzarella cheese, shredded
2 large eggs, lightly beaten
¾ teaspoon dried basil
½ teaspoon salt
2 tablespoons chopped fresh parsley
6 cups Italian Meat Sauce (page 249)
½ cup grated Parmesan cheese

•Cook manicotti shells according to package directions; drain.
•Combine ricotta cheese and next 5 ingredients. Stuff mixture into manicotti shells. Spoon half of meat sauce into a greased 13- x 9-inch baking dish. Arrange stuffed shells over sauce. Spoon remaining sauce over shells; sprinkle with Parmesan cheese.
•Bake, uncovered, at 350° for 20 minutes or until thoroughly heated. Let stand 5 minutes before serving. Yield: 6 main-dish servings.
Per serving: Calories 763 Fat 42.6g
Cholesterol 223mg Sodium 1446mg

Homemade Pasta

◀ HEALTHY ▶

PREP: 2 HOURS   COOK: 3 MINUTES

There are many benefits to making your own pasta—fresh flavor, supple texture, and quick cooking. Our photos show the Herbed Pasta variation.

3 to 4 cups all-purpose flour
3 large eggs, lightly beaten
1 tablespoon olive oil
1 teaspoon salt
4 to 6 tablespoons water
3 quarts water
1 teaspoon salt

•Place flour on work surface; make a well in center (photo 1). Combine eggs, oil, and 1 teaspoon salt; place in center of flour well. Whisk eggs with a fork, gradually stirring in flour from bottom of well (photo 2). Push some flour from sides of well into the center as mixture thickens (photo 3). Continue whisking until mixture becomes very stiff.
•Begin kneading dough by hand, and gradually work in additional flour and 4 to 6 tablespoons water (1 tablespoon at a time). Scrape up remaining flour and sift out any dried bits. Continue kneading and dusting with flour (photo 4) until dough is no longer sticky and springs back when pressed in center. Reserve any remaining flour. Cover ball of dough with plastic wrap; let rest 1 hour.
•Divide dough in half, keeping reserved dough covered to prevent drying. Working with 1 portion at a time, pass dough through smooth rollers of pasta machine on widest setting. Brush dough with flour, using a pastry brush (photo 5); fold in half, and brush both sides with flour. Repeat procedure 8 times for each portion of dough until dough becomes smooth and pliable.
•Cut each portion of dough into 3 pieces. Pass each piece once through rollers 2 through 6, brushing with flour if dough becomes sticky. Pass each dough sheet through cutting rollers of pasta machine (photo 6). Hang pasta to dry on a wooden rack no longer than 30 minutes. Repeat with remaining portion of dough.
•Combine 3 quarts water and 1 teaspoon salt in a Dutch oven, and bring to a boil. Add pasta, and cook 2 to 3 minutes or until al

1. Place flour on work surface; make a well in center, using a measuring cup.

2. Add egg mixture to the well, and whisk with a fork, stirring in flour from bottom of well.

Herbed Pasta
Marinara Sauce (page 390)

3. Knock in a little flour from the sides of the well, and blend it into the eggs.

4. Knead dough, continually dusting with flour, until dough feels smooth and resilient.

5. Use a pastry brush to brush dough sheets with flour on both sides after first pass in pasta machine.

6. Pass each dough sheet through the cutting rollers of pasta machine. Two pairs of hands are helpful here.

dente. Serve with desired sauce. Yield: 8 cups.
Per 1-cup serving: Calories 226 Fat 4.1g
Cholesterol 80mg Sodium 391mg

Spinach Pasta: Thaw, drain, and puree 1 (10-ounce) package frozen chopped spinach. Press 3 tablespoons spinach juice through a fine mesh sieve. Add spinach juice to egg mixture before blending. (Reserve spinach for another use.) Reduce amount of water added to dough to 2 to 3 tablespoons.

Herbed Pasta: Add ¼ cup finely chopped fresh "tender herbs" such as basil, parsley, oregano, or sage to egg mixture before blending in flour.

Bow Tie Pasta: Roll pasta through smooth rollers only. Cut pasta sheets into 2- x 1-inch rectangles, using a sharp knife or fluted pastry wheel. Pinch centers to form bow ties.

RICE

Rice teams readily with all types of food and can easily become any course of the meal from a sushi appetizer to a spicy side dish.

Long-grain rice is commonly preferred in the South; it cooks into distinct grains, perfect for pilafs. *Short-grain rice,* with its fat, almost round grains and high starch content, tends to stick together. As a rule, the shorter the grain, the more tender and clingy the cooked rice. This makes short-grain rice ideal for risotto and sushi.

Medium-grain rice is shorter and plumper than long grain, tends to cling like short grain, and produces a fluffy product that can be molded. It's ideal for recipes like Creamy Rice Pudding (page 167).

You can store regular-milled white, parboiled, and precooked rice indefinitely in airtight containers. Brown and wild rice are subject to rancidity due to the presence of bran, which limits shelf life to six months in an airtight container.

Each type of rice requires a different cooking time and amount of water and yields a different amount of the cooked grain. Check the package for specific cooking directions for the type of rice purchased. Cook rice, tightly covered, until all liquid is absorbed. Resist the urge to peek or stir while cooking—this causes rice to be gummy.

Cooked rice freezes well by itself or combined with other foods that are suitable for freezing. It may be frozen up to four months. Store cooked rice in the refrigerator up to one week.

Reheat cooked rice in a metal strainer or colander over steaming water. Cover strainer with aluminum foil, and steam rice 15 minutes.

Basic Rice

PREP: 2 MINUTES COOK: 22 MINUTES

2½ cups water
½ teaspoon salt
1 cup uncooked long-grain rice

•Bring water and salt to a boil in a medium saucepan; add rice. Cover, reduce heat, and simmer 20 minutes or until water is absorbed and rice is tender. Yield: 4 side-dish servings.
Per serving: Calories 169 Fat 0.3g
Cholesterol 0mg Sodium 295mg

Microwave Directions: Use very hot tap water instead of cool water when microwaving rice. Combine hot water, salt, and rice in a deep 2-quart casserole. Cover tightly with heavy-duty plastic wrap; fold back a small corner to allow steam to escape. Microwave at HIGH 5 minutes. Stir well. Cover and microwave at MEDIUM (50% power) 12 to 14 minutes or until water is absorbed and rice is tender. Let stand 2 to 4 minutes. Fluff rice with a fork.

Herbed Rice: Cook rice in chicken broth instead of water; omit salt. Stir 2 tablespoons chopped fresh parsley, basil, oregano, or thyme into cooked rice. (If substituting dried herbs, use 2 teaspoons of each, and add before cooking rice.)

Nutty Raisin Rice: Add ⅓ cup raisins with salt. Sauté ½ cup sliced almonds in 1 tablespoon melted butter or margarine until lightly browned; stir into cooked rice.

Onion Rice: Substitute onion salt for salt. Sauté ½ cup chopped white part of green onions in 2 tablespoons melted butter or margarine; stir into cooked rice. Stir 2 tablespoons raw green onion tops into cooked rice.

Orange Rice: Substitute ½ cup orange juice for ½ cup of the water. Stir in 1 tablespoon grated orange rind with salt.

Easy Oven Rice

PREP: 5 MINUTES
COOK: 1 HOUR AND 10 MINUTES

You won't find a side dish much simpler or more versatile than this. Just combine five ingredients and bake while you consider the entrée.

1 (10½-ounce) can French onion soup, undiluted
¼ cup butter or margarine, melted
1 (4½-ounce) jar sliced mushrooms
1 (8-ounce) can sliced water chestnuts
1 cup uncooked long-grain rice

•Combine soup and butter; stir well. Drain mushrooms and water chestnuts, reserving liquid. Add enough water to reserved liquid to measure 1⅓ cups.
•Add mushrooms, water chestnuts, reserved liquid, and rice to soup mixture; stir well. Pour into a lightly greased 10- x 6-inch baking dish.
•Cover and bake at 350° for 1 hour and 10 minutes or until liquid is absorbed and rice is tender. Yield: 6 side-dish servings.
Per serving: Calories 254 Fat 8.4g
Cholesterol 21mg Sodium 617mg

Microwave Directions: Combine soup and butter; stir well. Drain mushrooms and water chestnuts, reserving liquid. Add enough water to reserved liquid to measure 1⅓ cups. Add mushrooms, water chestnuts, reserved liquid, and rice to soup mixture; stir well. Pour into a lightly greased 10- x 6-inch baking dish. Cover tightly with heavy-duty plastic wrap; fold back a small corner to allow steam to escape. Microwave at HIGH 5 minutes. Give dish a quarter-turn; microwave at MEDIUM-LOW (30% power) 30 to 35 minutes or until liquid is absorbed and rice is tender, giving dish a quarter-turn every 10 minutes.

Egg Fried Rice

PREP: 5 MINUTES COOK: 5 MINUTES

Fried rice is fast and fun to make and can host any number of extra ingredients. Once you've tried it, you might want to add an extra vegetable, such as diced carrot, or meat, such as chicken or pork, the next time you make the dish. The key to this dish is to use cooked rice that's been chilled. This helps maintain its texture during stir-frying.

¼ cup chopped green onions or shallots
1 cup frozen English peas
2 tablespoons vegetable oil
3 cups cooked long-grain rice
1 egg, lightly beaten
3 tablespoons soy sauce

•Sauté green onions and peas in hot oil 2 minutes.
•Add rice, and cook until thoroughly heated. Push rice mixture to sides of skillet, forming a well in center.
•Pour egg into well, and cook until set, stirring occasionally. Stir rice mixture into egg; add soy sauce, stirring well. Yield: 6 side-dish servings.
Per serving: Calories 211 Fat 5.8g
Cholesterol 35mg Sodium 945mg

Shrimp Fried Rice: Stir 1 pound coarsely chopped cooked shrimp into Egg Fried Rice, and cook just until mixture is thoroughly heated.

Sausage Fried Rice: Cook 1 pound Italian sausage, casings removed, in a large skillet, stirring to crumble; drain. Stir sausage into Egg Fried Rice, and cook until mixture is thoroughly heated.

Baked Mushroom Rice

◄ HEALTHY ►

PREP: 10 MINUTES   COOK: 30 MINUTES

If you're looking for a colorful rice dish, this is it. And it's very easy to make, too.

2 tablespoons butter or margarine
5 green onions, sliced
3 cups chicken broth or beef broth
½ cup dry sherry
1 (4½-ounce) jar sliced mushrooms, undrained
1 (4-ounce) jar diced pimiento, drained
¾ teaspoon salt
1 teaspoon seasoned pepper
2 cups uncooked long-grain rice

•Melt butter in a large skillet; add green onions and next 6 ingredients. Bring to a boil; remove from heat, and add rice. Spoon into into a greased 13- x 9-inch baking dish.
•Cover and bake at 375° for 25 minutes or until liquid is absorbed and rice is tender. Stir before serving. Yield: 8 side-dish servings.
Per serving: Calories 219 Fat 3.8g
Cholesterol 8mg Sodium 756mg

Nutty Lemon Pilaf

PREP: 5 MINUTES   COOK: 30 MINUTES

½ cup pecan pieces
2 cups uncooked long-grain rice
2 tablespoons olive oil
2 (14½-ounce) cans chicken broth
½ teaspoon freshly ground pepper
1 tablespoon grated lemon rind
2 tablespoons fresh lemon juice
¼ cup minced fresh parsley

•Toast pecans in a heavy skillet over medium heat 4 to 5 minutes, stirring often.
•Sauté rice in hot olive oil in a heavy saucepan 5 to 6 minutes or until golden.
•Add broth and pepper; bring to a boil. Cover, reduce heat, and simmer 18 minutes; remove from heat, and let stand 5 minutes.
•Stir in pecans, lemon rind, lemon juice, and parsley. Yield: 8 side-dish servings.
Per serving: Calories 267 Fat 9.3g
Cholesterol 0mg Sodium 330mg

Hot Pepper Rice

◄ QUICK ►

PREP: 7 MINUTES   COOK: 15 MINUTES

Serve this Tex-Mex tempter alongside burritos or enchiladas. Use regular Monterey Jack cheese for milder flavor, if you'd like.

3 cups cooked long-grain rice
1 (8-ounce) carton sour cream
1 (4.5-ounce) can chopped green chiles, drained
1 (8-ounce) package Monterey Jack cheese with peppers, shredded
½ cup (2 ounces) shredded Cheddar cheese

•Combine first 3 ingredients. Layer half of rice mixture in a lightly greased 10- x 6-inch baking dish; top with half of Monterey Jack cheese. Repeat procedure; sprinkle with Cheddar cheese. Bake, uncovered, at 350° for 15 minutes. Yield: 6 side-dish servings.
Per serving: Calories 398 Fat 22.8g
Cholesterol 56mg Sodium 728mg

Saffron Rice

◄ QUICK • HEALTHY ►

PREP: 5 MINUTES   COOK: 30 MINUTES

Saffron colors this rice yellow; a little saffron goes a long way.

1 (10½-ounce) can condensed chicken broth
⅛ teaspoon ground saffron
1 cup uncooked long-grain rice
2 tablespoons olive oil
½ cup minced onion
¾ cup water
⅓ cup dry white wine

•Heat broth and saffron in a small saucepan over medium heat; keep warm.
•Cook rice in hot oil in a large heavy saucepan over medium heat until golden; add onion, and sauté 4 to 5 minutes.
•Add warm broth mixture, water, and wine; bring to a boil. Cover, reduce heat, and simmer 20 minutes or until liquid is absorbed and rice is tender. Yield: 4 side-dish servings.
Per serving: Calories 260 Fat 7.9g
Cholesterol 1mg Sodium 495mg

Island Spiced Rice

PREP: 10 MINUTES   COOK: 40 MINUTES

Curry and cinnamon spice up this aromatic basmati rice. Serve this well-seasoned side dish with grilled pork tenderloin or chicken.

1 tablespoon butter or margarine
2 cups chopped celery
1 small onion, chopped
2 cloves garlic, minced
4 cups water
2 chicken bouillon cubes
½ cup raisins
1 tablespoon brown sugar
1 teaspoon curry powder
¼ teaspoon salt
¼ teaspoon ground cinnamon
¼ teaspoon pepper
1½ cups uncooked basmati rice*
½ cup chopped pecans or walnuts, toasted
½ cup chopped apple

•Melt butter in a large saucepan; add celery, onion, and garlic. Sauté over medium heat until tender. Add water and next 7 ingredients; cover and bring to a boil.
•Stir in rice; cover, reduce heat, and simmer 20 minutes. Remove from heat, and let stand 10 minutes. Stir in pecans and apple. Yield: 6 servings.
*Basmati rice is an aromatic, fine-textured long-grain rice. Available in either brown or white, it has a distinctive buttery flavor. Find it in many Middle Eastern or Indian markets or check in the Middle Eastern or Indian departments of most supermarkets.
Per serving: Calories 320 Fat 9.5g
Cholesterol 5mg Sodium 460mg

SPICE UP YOUR RICE

For a tasty variation, try cooking rice in a flavorful liquid like chicken broth, beef broth, or fruit juice instead of water.

And just before serving, stir in a tablespoon of chopped fresh herbs or a dash of your favorite seasoning.

Hoppin' John

PREP: 15 MINUTES STAND: 1 HOUR
COOK: 2 HOURS AND 20 MINUTES

Salt pork, pepper, and hot sauce add zip to this New Year's dish of good-luck peas.

2 cups dried black-eyed peas
½ pound salt pork, quartered
2 cups chopped onion
1 cup chopped green pepper
1 bay leaf
2½ cups water
1 cup uncooked long-grain rice
1½ teaspoons salt
¼ teaspoon black pepper
¼ teaspoon ground red pepper
Few drops of hot sauce

•Sort and wash peas; place in a large Dutch oven. Add water 2 inches above peas, and bring to a boil. Boil 1 minute; cover, remove from heat, and let stand 1 hour.
•Drain peas, and return to Dutch oven; add salt pork and next 3 ingredients. Cover with water; simmer, covered, 1½ to 2 hours or until peas are tender and water has cooked very low. Remove salt pork, if desired.
•Add 2½ cups water and remaining 5 ingredients to peas. Cover and cook over low heat 20 minutes or until rice is tender. Discard bay leaf before serving. Yield: 8 side-dish servings.
Per serving: Calories 372 Fat 23.5g
Cholesterol 25mg Sodium 848mg

Spanish Rice

PREP: 11 MINUTES COOK: 31 MINUTES

3 tablespoons vegetable oil
2 cups uncooked long-grain rice
2 large green peppers, chopped
2 large stalks celery, chopped
2 medium onions, finely chopped
2 teaspoons cumin seeds, crushed
1 to 1½ teaspoons salt
1 teaspoon chili powder
½ teaspoon pepper
¼ teaspoon garlic powder
6 cups water
1 (8-ounce) can tomato sauce

•Heat oil over medium-high heat in a heavy Dutch oven; add rice and next 8 ingredients to Dutch oven, and cook until rice is browned, stirring often.
•Stir in water and tomato sauce; bring to a boil. Reduce heat to medium; cover and cook 25 minutes or until liquid is absorbed and rice is tender. Yield: 8 side-dish servings.
Per serving: Calories 266 Fat 6.1g
Cholesterol 0mg Sodium 330mg

Dirty Rice

PREP: 37 MINUTES COOK: 1½ HOURS

Chopped giblets give this rice a "dirty" look and great flavor.

2 cups uncooked long-grain rice
1 quart water
5 chicken wings (about ¾ pound)
5 chicken gizzards (about ¼ pound)
5 chicken hearts (about 1 ounce)
5 chicken livers (about ¼ pound)
1 pound ground hot pork sausage
¼ cup butter, margarine, or bacon
    drippings
1 large onion, chopped
1 cup chopped green pepper
3 stalks celery, chopped
1 tablespoon dried parsley flakes

•Cook rice according to package directions; set aside.
•Combine water and next 3 ingredients in a Dutch oven; bring to a boil. Cover, reduce heat, and simmer 20 minutes; add chicken livers, and cook 10 to 12 minutes or until tender. Drain, reserving ¾ cup liquid. Remove meat from wings; coarsely chop wing meat, gizzards, hearts, and livers. Set meat aside.
•Brown sausage in Dutch oven, stirring until it crumbles; drain and set aside.
•Melt butter in Dutch oven; add onion, green pepper, and celery. Cook over medium heat 5 minutes or until tender, stirring often. Add sausage, chopped meat, and reserved liquid. Bring to a boil; cover, reduce heat, and simmer 15 minutes. Stir in cooked rice and parsley. Serve warm. Yield: 8 main-dish servings.
Per serving: Calories 471 Fat 21.9g
Cholesterol 205mg Sodium 659mg

Cheesy Lentils and Rice

PREP: 14 MINUTES
COOK: 1 HOUR AND 5 MINUTES

Brown rice and lentils match up in this cheesy meatless dinner. Just add a green salad.

1⅔ cups water
2 tablespoons butter or margarine,
    divided
½ teaspoon salt
⅔ cup uncooked brown rice
1 cup dried lentils
1 cup chopped onion
1 cup chopped green pepper
2 cloves garlic, minced
1 (14½-ounce) can diced tomatoes,
    undrained
1 teaspoon paprika
½ teaspoon salt
½ teaspoon black pepper
¼ to ½ teaspoon ground red pepper
1½ cups (6 ounces) shredded Cheddar
    cheese

•Bring water to a boil in a heavy saucepan; add 1 tablespoon butter and ½ teaspoon salt. Stir in rice. Cover, reduce heat, and simmer 45 minutes or until rice is tender. Set aside.
•Cook lentils according to package directions; drain and set aside.
•Melt remaining 1 tablespoon butter in a large skillet over medium heat; add onion, green pepper, and garlic, and cook until tender, stirring often. Stir in lentils, tomatoes, and next 4 ingredients; cover, reduce heat, and simmer 20 minutes, stirring occasionally. Stir in brown rice. Sprinkle with cheese. Cover and let stand 5 minutes before serving. Yield: 6 main-dish servings.
Per serving: Calories 362 Fat 14.5g
Cholesterol 40mg Sodium 701mg

Risotto

PREP: 10 MINUTES   COOK: 48 MINUTES

Arborio rice, a high-starch pearly grain, captures the broth as it cooks and creates risotto's characteristic creamy finish.

1 cup uncooked Arborio rice
3 tablespoons butter or margarine, melted
½ small onion, chopped
¼ cup dry white wine
1 clove garlic, minced
3 cups chicken broth, heated
¼ teaspoon salt
2 tablespoons freshly grated Parmigiano-
   Reggiano or Parmesan cheese

1. "Toast" rice in butter in a large skillet, stirring constantly with a wooden spoon.

2. Add hot broth, 1 cup at a time, stirring until liquid is absorbed.

3. Vigorously stir in cheese just before serving; it adds the final note of flavor.

• Cook rice in butter in a large skillet over high heat 1 minute, stirring constantly (photo 1). Reduce heat to medium-high, and add onion; sauté 1 to 3 minutes until onion is tender. Stir in wine and garlic, cooking until wine is absorbed.

• Add 1 cup hot broth, stirring constantly, until liquid is absorbed (photo 2). Repeat procedure, adding remaining broth, 1 cup at a time, allowing liquid to be absorbed after each addition, stirring constantly. (This will take 30 to 45 minutes.)

• Remove from heat; add salt and cheese, stirring vigorously until blended (photo 3). Yield: 6 side-dish servings.

Per serving: Calories 202 Fat 7.1g
Cholesterol 17mg Sodium 572mg

Herbed Risotto: Stir 2 tablespoons chopped fresh herbs into risotto during last 5 minutes of cooking.

Mushroom Risotto: Before beginning risotto, place 3 ounces sliced portobello mushroom in a 9-inch cast-iron skillet. Drizzle with 2 tablespoons olive oil; sprinkle with salt and pepper. Roast at 500° for 4 minutes; turn mushroom slices over, and roast 4 more minutes (mushroom may smoke and sizzle). Chop mushrooms, and set aside; gently stir into risotto just before serving.

Herbed Risotto

Mushroom Brown Rice

PREP: 15 MINUTES   COOK: 45 MINUTES

1½ cups uncooked brown rice
¼ pound fresh mushrooms, sliced
2 small green peppers, chopped
1 large onion, chopped
1 clove garlic, minced
2 tablespoons butter or margarine, melted
2 cups peeled, chopped tomato
2 tablespoons soy sauce
1 tablespoon minced fresh cilantro or
    parsley
⅛ teaspoon pepper

•Cook brown rice according to package directions; set aside.
•Sauté mushrooms, green peppers, onion, and garlic in butter in a large skillet 5 to 7 minutes or until vegetables are tender. Stir in cooked rice and remaining ingredients; cook until thoroughly heated. Yield: 8 servings.
Per serving: Calories 181 Fat 4.2g
Cholesterol 8mg Sodium 245mg

Herbed Brown Rice

PREP: 10 MINUTES   COOK: 40 MINUTES

2 tablespoons chopped onion
1 large clove garlic, minced
2 tablespoons butter or margarine, melted
1 cup uncooked brown rice
1⅓ cups water
1 (10¾-ounce) can chicken broth, undiluted
1 tablespoon chopped fresh parsley
¼ teaspoon ground thyme
⅛ teaspoon pepper
1 bay leaf

•Sauté onion and garlic in butter until tender; add remaining ingredients. Bring to a boil; cover, reduce heat, and simmer 35 minutes or until rice is tender and liquid is absorbed. Discard bay leaf. Yield: 6 servings.
Per serving: Calories 159 Fat 5.0g
Cholesterol 10mg Sodium 203mg

Red Beans and Rice

◄ FAMILY FAVORITE ►
◄ VEGETARIAN ►

PREP: 18 MINUTES   COOK: 3 HOURS

1 pound dried red beans
1 ham hock (1 pound)
3 quarts water
1 large onion, chopped
½ cup Worcestershire sauce
1¼ teaspoons garlic salt
½ teaspoon black pepper
¼ to ½ teaspoon ground red pepper
⅛ teaspoon ground cinnamon
3 bay leaves
6 cups hot cooked rice

•Sort and wash beans. Combine beans, ham hock, and water in a large Dutch oven; bring to a boil. Cover, reduce heat, and simmer 2 hours, stirring occasionally.
•Mash about two-thirds of beans against side of Dutch oven with back of a spoon. Add onion and next 6 ingredients. Cover and bring to a boil. Reduce heat to medium-high, and cook, uncovered, 1 hour or to desired doneness, stirring often. Discard bay leaves; serve over rice. Yield: 6 main-dish servings.
Per serving: Calories 651 Fat 6.0g
Cholesterol 30mg Sodium 2181 mg

Black Beans and Yellow Rice

◄ FAMILY FAVORITE ►
◄ VEGETARIAN ►

PREP: 10 MINUTES   COOK: 1½ HOURS

1 large onion, chopped
1 medium-size green pepper, chopped
2 cloves garlic, minced
¼ cup olive oil
3 (15-ounce) cans black beans, drained
1 (14.5-ounce) can Cajun-style stewed
    tomatoes, undrained and chopped
1½ cups water
1 tablespoon red wine vinegar
1 teaspoon sugar
1 teaspoon black pepper
½ teaspoon salt
1 (8-ounce) can tomato sauce
6 cups hot cooked yellow rice
½ cup chopped green onions
Sour cream

•Sauté first 3 ingredients in hot oil in a Dutch oven over medium-high heat until vegetables are tender. Add beans and next 7 ingredients; bring mixture to a boil. Cover, reduce heat, and simmer 1 hour. Uncover and simmer 20 more minutes, stirring mixture occasionally.
•Serve black bean mixture over hot cooked rice. Top each serving with green onions and a dollop of sour cream. Yield: 6 main-dish servings.
Per serving: Calories 695 Fat 23.7g
Cholesterol 7.5mg Sodium 1707mg

GRAINS

Cereal grains include any plants from the grass family that yield an edible grain (or seed). Some of the most common grains are barley, bulgur, corn, oats, quinoa, rice, and wild rice. They provide a very affordable source of protein and carbohydrate for people worldwide.

Grains have uses that go beyond the basic side dish. They blend well into casseroles, salads, and stuffings. Grits, the small flakes of hulled, dried corn, are eaten more in the South than in other regions of the country. Hominy, whole kernels of the same corn, are a heartier option. Hominy often replaces meat in vegetarian entrées.

You'll find oatmeal and muesli on breakfast tables throughout the winter months. Serve bulgur and barley as side dishes like rice. They add nutrients and fiber to the diet.

When cooking grains and cereals, add them to boiling water in a slow, steady stream. This prevents lumping as the boiling water instantly surrounds and plumps the individual granules.

Whole grains have a short storage life because they contain an oil-rich germ that can become rancid. So it's a smart idea to buy whole grains in small quantities and keep them in airtight containers.

Barley and Vegetables

◀ QUICK ▶

PREP: 7 MINUTES   COOK: 12 MINUTES

2 (10½-ounce) cans chicken broth
1 cup uncooked quick-cooking barley
1 cup chopped onion
1 cup chopped green pepper
2 large tomatoes, chopped (2½ cups)
1 teaspoon dried oregano
1 teaspoon salt
¼ teaspoon freshly ground black pepper

•Bring broth to a boil in a saucepan. Stir in barley, onion, and green pepper; cover, reduce heat, and simmer 10 minutes or until barley is tender, stirring occasionally. Drain. Stir in tomato and remaining ingredients; cook until heated. Yield: 4 side-dish servings.

Per serving: Calories 244 Fat 2g
Cholesterol 0mg Sodium 1095mg

Full-of-Fiber Hot Cereal

◀ QUICK • HEALTHY ▶

PREP: 7 MINUTES   COOK: 20 MINUTES

4 cups water
½ cup uncooked regular oats
½ cup uncooked bulgur
¼ cup uncooked hulled buckwheat groats
¼ cup uncooked triticale flakes
2½ tablespoons uncooked regular cream of wheat
2 tablespoons regular grits
⅓ cup raisins
¼ cup chopped cashews
¼ cup sunflower kernels, toasted
¼ cup honey
1 apple, cored and chopped
1 teaspoon ground cinnamon
2 teaspoons butter or margarine
1 cup milk

•Bring water to a boil in a large saucepan; stir in oats and next 5 ingredients. Return to a boil; reduce heat, and cook 12 minutes, stirring often. Add more water, if needed, while cooking oats mixture.
•Stir in raisins and next 6 ingredients. Serve with milk. Yield: 6 servings.

Per serving: Calories 329 Fat 9.3g
Cholesterol 9mg Sodium 39mg

RICE & GRAINS DICTIONARY

Arborio rice: This Italian short-grain rice with a high-starch kernel contributes the characteristic creamy texture to risotto.

Aromatic rices: These rices have a perfumy aroma and taste like toasted nuts or popped corn. Basmati, jasmine, texmati, and wild pecan rice all qualify.

Barley: Pearl barley has the bran removed and has been steamed and polished. It's available in coarse, medium, and fine grinds and is often used in soups. Whole-grain (or hulled) barley has only the outer husk removed and is the most nutritious form of the grain.

Brown rice: This is the least processed form of rice. The outer hull is removed, but the bran layers remain on the whole unpolished grain to produce the characteristic tan color and nutlike flavor. When cooked, the inner part of the grain becomes tender, while the outer bran layers remain slightly crunchy, giving the rice a chewy texture.

Bulgur: Similar to cracked wheat, bulgur consists of wheat kernels that have been steamed, dried, and crushed. Bulgur has a tender, chewy texture and comes in coarse, medium, and fine grinds. It's used in the Middle Eastern salad tabbouleh.

Converted rice: Also called parboiled rice, this unhulled grain is soaked, pressure-steamed, and dried before milling. During this process, the grain becomes hard, translucent, and shiny. More cooking time is required for this form which, when cooked, is fluffier and drier than regular rice.

Couscous: Couscous is coarsely ground semolina wheat which can be cooked and eaten as porridge, sweetened and mixed with fruit, or served as a salad or side dish. It's a tiny grain that cooks instantly.

Instant rice: This precooked rice has been milled, cooked, and dried. This creates a porous, open grain that rehydrates quickly. The processing destroys much of the flavor.

Regular-milled white rice: Also known as polished rice, this is the least expensive and most common rice form. The husk, bran, and germ are milled away until the grain is white. Long, medium, and short grain are available.

Wild rice: Not really rice at all, wild rice is the long-grain seed of a marsh grass native to the Great Lakes area. The unpolished, dark brown, long and slender grains are high in fiber and have a nutty taste. It's often sold blended with brown or regular rice.

Wild Rice Bulgur

PREP: 7 MINUTES   COOK: 35 MINUTES

¾ cup chopped onion
¾ cup chopped celery
2 cloves garlic, minced
2 tablespoons olive oil
3 cups chicken broth
1 cup uncooked bulgur
⅓ cup uncooked instant wild rice
1 teaspoon salt
¼ teaspoon pepper

•Sauté first 3 ingredients in hot oil in a Dutch oven until crisp-tender. Add broth; bring to a boil. Stir in bulgur and remaining ingredients; cover, reduce heat, and simmer 25 minutes or until tender. Yield: 4 side-dish servings.

Per serving: Calories 305 Fat 8.6g
Cholesterol 0mg Sodium 1201mg

Pecan Wild Rice

PREP: 5 MINUTES   COOK: 30 MINUTES

Wild rice adds chewy texture, nutty flavor, and rich brown color to side dishes.

1 (4-ounce) package wild rice
1 small onion, chopped
1 cup chopped pecans
¼ cup butter or margarine, melted
1 teaspoon seasoned salt
2 to 3 tablespoons chopped fresh parsley

•Cook wild rice according to package directions, omitting salt. Sauté onion and pecans in butter; add seasoned salt. Stir in wild rice, and cook until thoroughly heated. Sprinkle with parsley. Yield: 4 side-dish servings.

Per serving: Calories 317 Fat 22.4g
Cholesterol 31mg Sodium 706mg

Curried Couscous

◄ QUICK ►

PREP: 6 MINUTES   COOK: 5 MINUTES

Couscous is favored for many reasons, one of which is how quickly it cooks. This dish cooks in about the time it takes to boil water.

1½ cups chicken broth
½ cup currants
1 teaspoon curry powder
1 cup uncooked couscous
⅓ cup vegetable oil
2 tablespoons lemon juice
½ cup sliced almonds, toasted
⅓ cup sliced green onions

•Combine first 3 ingredients in a saucepan; bring to a boil. Remove from heat, and stir in couscous. Cover and let stand 5 minutes. Fluff with a fork; let cool, uncovered.
•Combine oil and lemon juice; toss couscous with juice mixture and almonds. Sprinkle with sliced green onions. Yield: 6 side-dish servings.
Per serving: Calories 310 Fat 17.3g
Cholesterol 0mg Sodium 203mg

Mexican Hominy

PREP: 10 MINUTES   COOK: 30 MINUTES

½ cup chopped onion
1 clove garlic, minced
1 tablespoon olive oil
1 (15-ounce) can golden hominy, drained
1 cup chopped tomato
2 tablespoons canned chopped green chiles
¾ teaspoon chili powder
⅛ teaspoon salt
¼ teaspoon pepper
½ cup (2 ounces) shredded sharp Cheddar cheese

•Sauté onion and garlic in hot oil in a large skillet over medium-high heat until tender. Stir in hominy and next 5 ingredients. Spoon mixture into a greased 1-quart baking dish.
•Bake, uncovered, at 350° for 25 minutes. Sprinkle with cheese; bake 5 more minutes or until cheese melts. Yield: 4 side-dish servings.
Per serving: Calories 153 Fat 8.6g
Cholesterol 15mg Sodium 367mg

THE GRITS STORY

Grits can be very different, depending on whether they're ground at a gristmill or purchased at the supermarket. This guide will help you with the different choices.
Hominy: Dried white or yellow corn kernels from which the hull and germ have been removed. It's sold dried or ready-to-eat in cans. When dried hominy is ground, it's called **hominy grits.** Grits are available in three grinds—fine, medium, and coarse.
Instant grits: These fine-textured grits have been precooked and dehydrated. To prepare them, simply add boiling water.
Quick and regular grits: The difference between these two grits is in granulation. Quick grits are ground fine and cook in 5 minutes; regular grits are medium grind and cook in 10 minutes.
Whole-ground or stone-ground grits: These grits are a coarse grind. You'll find stone-ground grits at most gristmills and specialty food stores.

Creamy Grits

◄ QUICK ►

PREP: 4 MINUTES   COOK: 30 MINUTES

Milk makes this dish wonderfully creamy and sets it apart from basic grits cooked in water.

4 cups water
¼ cup butter or margarine
1 cup uncooked regular or stone-ground grits
2 cups milk or half-and-half, divided
½ teaspoon salt
¼ teaspoon freshly ground pepper

•Bring water and butter to a boil in a heavy saucepan. Stir in grits; return to a boil over medium heat. Reduce heat, and cook 10 minutes or until thickened, stirring occasionally. Stir in 1 cup milk; simmer 10 minutes, stirring occasionally. Add remaining milk; simmer 10 minutes, or until desired consistency, stirring occasionally. Stir in salt and pepper. Serve immediately. Yield: 4 side-dish servings.
Per serving: Calories 311 Fat 15.7g
Cholesterol 48mg Sodium 471mg

Cheese Grits Casserole

◄ FAMILY FAVORITE ►

PREP: 10 MINUTES
COOK: 1 HOUR AND 5 MINUTES

This rich and cheesy grits casserole is ideal for a weekend brunch.

4 cups water
1 teaspoon salt
1 cup uncooked quick-cooking grits
2 cups (8 ounces) shredded sharp Cheddar cheese
⅔ cup milk
⅓ cup butter or margarine
1 teaspoon Worcestershire sauce
¼ teaspoon ground red pepper
4 large eggs, lightly beaten
¼ teaspoon paprika

•Bring water and salt to a boil in a large saucepan; stir in grits. Return to a boil. Cover, reduce heat, and simmer 5 minutes, stirring occasionally. Remove from heat. Add cheese and next 4 ingredients, stirring until cheese and butter melt. Add eggs; stir well.
•Spoon mixture into a lightly greased 2-quart casserole; sprinkle with paprika. Bake, uncovered, at 350° for 1 hour or until thoroughly heated and lightly browned. Let stand 5 minutes before serving. Yield: 8 side-dish servings.
Per serving: Calories 300 Fat 20.4g
Cholesterol 159mg Sodium 595mg

Hot Grilled Grits

◄ GRILLED • VEGETARIAN ►

PREP: 20 MINUTES   CHILL: 1 HOUR
COOK: 15 MINUTES

1 (10½-ounce) can chicken broth
1 (8-ounce) jar process cheese sauce (we tested with Cheez Whiz)
½ cup water
¼ cup butter or margarine
1 tablespoon sliced pickled jalapeño peppers, minced
1 cup uncooked quick-cooking grits
1 tablespoon olive oil
2 cups commercial salsa

•Combine first 5 ingredients in a large saucepan; bring to a boil over medium heat.

Gradually stir in grits; cover, reduce heat, and simmer 5 minutes, stirring often. Pour into a lightly buttered 9-inch pieplate. Cool to room temperature; chill 1 hour.

•Unmold grits, and cut into 6 wedges; brush each side with oil.

•Coat grill rack with vegetable cooking spray; place on grill over medium coals (300° to 350°). Place wedges on rack; grill, covered with grill lid, 4 to 5 minutes on each side or until lightly browned. Serve with salsa. Yield: 3 main-dish servings.

Per serving: Calories 632 Fat 38g
Cholesterol 89mg Sodium 2034mg

Panfried Grits: Omit brushing with olive oil. Melt 2 tablespoons butter in a large skillet. Add wedges and cook 3 to 4 minutes on each side or until lightly browned.

Hot Grilled Grits

Basic Polenta

◀ QUICK • HEALTHY ▶

PREP: 2 MINUTES   COOK: 10 MINUTES

Polenta is a coarse grind of cornmeal that's famous for taking on trendy shapes and flavors in restaurants. The special cornmeal is available in most grocery stores, but regular yellow cornmeal works here, too.

3½ cups water or milk
¾ teaspoon salt
1 cup yellow cornmeal

•Bring water and salt to a boil over high heat in a heavy saucepan. Gradually add cornmeal, stirring constantly with a wire whisk. Reduce heat, and simmer 10 minutes or until thick and creamy, whisking often (photo 1). Yield: 7 side-dish servings.

Per serving: Calories 72 Fat 0.3g
Cholesterol 0mg Sodium 252mg

STIR IN FLAVOR

Choose any of these additions to add flavor to Basic Polenta.

•Sauté 1 or 2 cloves minced garlic in 2 tablespoons melted butter, and stir into polenta with 2 tablespoons whipping cream.

•Stir in ½ cup grated fresh Parmesan cheese or shredded mozzarella cheese.

•Add 1 to 1½ teaspoons dried rosemary, crushed, or dried Italian seasoning.

GET IN SHAPE

•You can serve polenta soft as you would grits. Add more liquid, if necessary, and spoon polenta onto serving plates.

•To make rectangles, spoon cooked polenta into a plastic wrap-lined 7⅜- x 4-inch loafpan, smoothing with a spatula. Cover and chill 8 hours. Remove from pan, peel off plastic wrap, and cut polenta into ½-inchthick slices (photo 2). Panfry or bake.

•For circles, squares, or triangles, spoon cooked polenta into a lightly greased 11- x 7½-inch dish. Cover and chill 8 hours. Invert dish, and tap bottom until polenta releases. Remove dish, and cut polenta into shapes with a knife or cookie cutters. Panfry or bake.

HEAT THINGS UP

•To panfry, melt butter or margarine in a large skillet; add polenta shapes, and cook 5 minutes on each side or until lightly browned. (Do not crowd skillet or polenta will be difficult to turn.)

•To bake, place shaped polenta on a lightly greased baking sheet. Bake at 425° for 7 minutes or until thoroughly heated and lightly browned.

1. Using a wire whisk, stir polenta as it simmers until very thick.

2. Cut chilled polenta into ½-inch-thick slices; then bake or panfry.

Blueberry Pie (page 303)

PIES & PASTRIES

Southerners have always had a certain affection for pecan pie, sweet potato pie, and crusty fruit cobblers. A good pie or pastry simply wraps a superb filling in a tender, flaky crust. We unfold dozens of recipe options on these pages, plus some fancy pastry tips, too.

Equipment

You can bake tender, flaky pies with just a few pieces of equipment—basically all you must have is a pieplate and rolling pin. A pastry blender is a useful tool to help cut fat into flour on its way to becoming a disc of dough. And a pastry wheel will cut straight strips of dough for a lattice-topped crust.

A cotton stockinette cover for your rolling pin and a pastry cloth for a work surface will guarantee dough doesn't stick and tear. A metal dough scraper is another tool for cutting dough and releasing it from a work surface with ease. And a wire rack is the best place to cool your pie so the bottom crust doesn't get soggy.

Nonshiny pieplates such as ovenproof glass or dull metal perform best. Avoid shiny metal pans; they reflect heat and keep pastry crusts from browning evenly. And steer clear of flimsy pans sold in the supermarket. Always use the size pieplate specified in a recipe. Standard sizes range from 9 to 10 inches in diameter and typically measure 1¼ inches deep.

Commercial Crusts

There are a variety of store-bought piecrusts available to help speed your pie making along. Frozen pastry shells and crumb crusts already in pans offer good quality but hold less filling than most homemade pastries and commercial refrigerated piecrusts. Even though their packages state they are 9-inch crusts, most are not an equivalent substitute. Piecrusts labeled "extra serving size" and "deep dish" are closer substitutes for homemade 9-inch crusts.

Freezing Pies and Pastries

You can freeze balls or flat discs of pastry dough up to six months if wrapped tightly in wax paper or plastic wrap and then in an airtight container. When ready to use, allow time to thaw the dough overnight in the refrigerator. (When thawed, pastry will be slightly more fragile than if it had not been frozen.)

You can also freeze baked or unbaked pastry directly in a pieplate. Unbaked frozen pastry can be baked without thawing; just bake frozen pastry as the recipe directs and add two or three more minutes to the baking time.

Some baked pies, particularly fruit pies, freeze well. The texture of the pastry, however, may lose crispness in the freezing and defrosting. The texture of the fruit may soften slightly, too.

To freeze baked pies, freeze them unwrapped first; then wrap them so that they're airtight, label, and return them to the freezer. Use frozen pies within two months. Thaw baked pies at room temperature 30 minutes; then reheat at 350° until warm.

It's not a good idea to freeze custard, cream, or chiffon pies that contain meringue toppings. The meringue will deteriorate in the freezing and thawing stages.

PASTRY

The key to making flaky pastry begins with measuring ingredients accurately and mixing them properly. If proportions of fat to flour to liquid are off even slightly or if you overwork the dough, your pastry can turn out tough or crumbly.

Making Basic Pastry

Cut cold fat (typically butter or shortening) into flour, using a pastry blender or two knives until the mixture is crumbly. During baking the fat particles that coat the flour will melt and leave behind pockets of air that separate layers of pastry and create a flaky crust.

Sprinkle ice water, one tablespoon at a time, over the flour mixture; stir with a fork just enough to moisten the dry ingredients. Don't overwork the dough. The more you stir and handle it, the more gluten will develop and toughen the pastry. Add the minimum amount of water to moisten the flour mixture; too much can make pastry soggy.

Gather dough into a flat disc or ball, cover tightly with plastic wrap or wax paper, and chill 30 minutes to an hour. Chilling makes the dough easier to handle and helps to achieve a flaky crust.

When ready to roll dough, let it stand briefly until it's pliable but still firm—almost like clay. Lightly dust the work surface with flour, and place chilled dough in the center; flatten dough with the heel of your hand.

Equipment Basics: These tools will be helpful in pie making: a metal dough scraper, pastry blender, glass pieplates, fluted pastry wheels, and a rolling pin with a cotton stockinette cover.

Carefully and quickly roll dough from the center out in all directions; do not roll back and forth across the dough because this stretches the dough and will cause it to shrink during baking.

Lift dough circle periodically as you roll it to make sure it's not sticking to the work surface. If it does stick, loosen underneath the dough with a dough scraper or spatula and sprinkle a little more flour under the dough onto work surface.

Roll pastry to ⅛-inch thickness and about two inches larger than the pieplate. To transfer pastry to the pieplate without tearing it, carefully and quickly fold dough in half, and then in half again. Place the point of the fold in the center of the pieplate, and unfold. Be careful not to stretch the dough as you're fitting it into the pieplate.

Trim edges of pastry dough, leaving about ½ inch overhang over rim of pieplate. Kitchen shears or a small knife make easy work of trimming. Fold the overhang dough under itself, creating a thick rim around edge of pieplate; then crimp as desired. Chill pastry right up until you're ready to bake it.

Crimping the Crust

A basic, yet impressive, pinch-edge finish for a piecrust is shown in our Pretty Pastry Edges photos on page 300. To make it, place one index finger on the outside edge of the pie, and place your other index finger and thumb on the inside of the pie, flanking your first finger; then pinch the pastry with fingers in this position to crimp the edge. Repeat the design around edge of entire pie. Try some of the other decorative finishes, too.

Single or Double Crusts

Pies that aren't topped with a top crust are known as single-crust pies. For this type of pie, crimp the pastry edge before adding filling. If the filling is unbaked, such as for Lemon Chiffon pie on page 312, you'll also need to bake the crust before adding filling.

Some of our pastry recipes offer directions for *blind baking* (baking a crust without filling). When you do this, prick the bottom and sides of the pastry dough in the pieplate to keep pastry from puffing during baking. Do not, however, prick the dough if a filling

will be baked in it from the dough state. If you do, the filling is likely to seep through the crust to the pieplate during baking and cause a mess.

Double-crust pies have both a top and bottom crust, and the filling is baked between the crusts. To make a double-crust pie, use a pastry recipe specifically for this type of pie such as our Double-Crust Pastry on page 300. You can also double a recipe for a single-crust pie. Divide the dough in half; keep one portion covered and chilled while working with the other. Line a pieplate with one portion of pastry, following directions for a single-crust pie and omitting the crimping step; then add filling. Roll remaining pastry about an inch larger than the pieplate. Moisten the edge of bottom pastry with water or beaten egg; fit the top pastry over the filling. Trim edge of pastry so ½ inch of overhang remains. Fold the overhang under the edge of the bottom pastry, pressing firmly to seal. Then crimp the thick edge. Cut a few slits in top pastry to allow steam to escape during baking.

A lattice topping makes a fine finish for a double-crust fruit pie. It allows plump berries or other fruit to peek through its woven design. A lattice-topped pie requires the same amount of pastry as a double-crust pie. Just roll and fit the bottom pastry as a single- or double-crust pie, leaving a 1-inch overhang around the edge. Then roll out remaining pastry to the same thickness and cut into ½-inch strips (10 to 14 strips is plenty for a typical lattice). Use a fluted pastry wheel for more decorative strips, if desired. If you choose to make a lattice with wider (1-inch) strips, you might need only eight to 10 strips. (See photo on page 303.)

To weave the lattice, first moisten the edge of pastry in the pieplate. Then place five or seven strips evenly across the pie going in the same direction, leaving ½ to ¾ inch between strips; fold every other strip back a little over halfway. Place one of the remaining strips across the center of the pie, perpendicular to first row of strips. Carefully fold back the flat strips and unfold the folded ones. Place another strip parallel to the center strip, leaving ½ to ¾ inch between strips. Repeat the folding and unfolding step and adding more cross strips until the lattice is completely woven. Trim edges, and press the ends of strips to seal the pastry. Then crimp the edges, if desired.

BASIC PASTRY STEPS

1. Cut fat into flour mixture, using a pastry blender, until mixture is crumbly.

2. Sprinkle ice water evenly over surface. Stir just until the dry ingredients are moistened.

3. Gather dough into a ball or flat disc. Cover and chill at least 30 minutes.

4. Roll dough with a rolling pin to ⅛-inch thickness; carefully roll dough onto pin, and then unroll into pieplate.

5. Another way to transfer dough is to fold it in half and then in half again; place point in center of pieplate. Unfold.

6. When baking pastry without a filling, prick bottom and sides with a fork. Do not prick pastry if it is to be filled before baking.

Basic Pastry for a 9-inch Pie

◄ QUICK ►

PREP: 8 MINUTES   COOK: 12 MINUTES

Use this pastry with recipes throughout the chapter. It's a blend of basic ingredients that forms a flaky base for a multitude of sweet fillings. We give you three pieplate sizes from which to choose.

1¼ cups all-purpose flour
½ teaspoon salt
⅓ cup plus 1 tablespoon shortening
3 to 4 tablespoons ice water

•Combine flour and salt; cut in shortening with a pastry blender until mixture is crumbly (photo 1). Sprinkle ice water, 1 tablespoon at a time, evenly over surface (photo 2); stir with a fork until dry ingredients are moistened. Shape into a ball (photo 3); cover and chill until ready to use.
•Roll pastry to ⅛-inch thickness on a lightly floured surface. Place in pieplate (photos 4 and 5); trim off excess pastry along edges. Fold edges under, and crimp. Chill.
•**For baked pastry shell,** prick bottom and sides of pastry shell with a fork (photo 6). Chill pastry until ready to bake. Bake at 450° for 10 to 12 minutes or until golden. Yield: 8 servings.
Per serving: Calories 142 Fat 8.6g
Cholesterol 0mg Sodium 147mg

Basic Pastry for an 8-inch Pie

1 cup all-purpose flour
½ teaspoon salt
⅓ cup shortening
2 to 3 tablespoons ice water

Follow directions at left. Yield: 6 servings.

Basic Pastry for a 10-inch Pie

1½ cups all-purpose flour
¾ teaspoon salt
½ cup shortening
4 to 5 tablespoons ice water

Follow directions at left. Yield: 10 servings.

Double-Crust Pastry

◄ QUICK ►

PREP: 5 MINUTES

2 cups all-purpose flour
1 teaspoon salt
⅔ cup plus 2 tablespoons shortening
4 to 5 tablespoons ice water

•Combine flour and salt; cut in shortening with a pastry blender until mixture is crumbly. Sprinkle ice water, 1 tablespoon at a time, evenly over surface; stir with a fork until dry ingredients are moistened. Shape into a ball; chill until ready to use. Roll and fit pastry into pieplate as pie recipe directs. Yield: 8 servings.
Per serving: Calories 253 Fat 17.1g
Cholesterol 0mg Sodium 294mg

Oil Pastry

◄ QUICK ►

PREP: 6 MINUTES

1¼ cups all-purpose flour
½ teaspoon salt
¼ cup plus 2 tablespoons vegetable oil
3 to 4 tablespoons ice water

•Combine flour and salt; add oil, stirring until mixture is crumbly. Sprinkle with ice water, 1 tablespoon at a time, stirring quickly. Gather dough into a ball.
•Roll pastry to ⅛-inch thickness on a lightly floured surface. Place in a 9-inch pieplate; trim off excess pastry along edges. Fold edges under, and crimp. Yield: 8 servings.
Per serving: Calories 158 Fat 10.4g
Cholesterol 0mg Sodium 147mg

PICK YOUR PIECRUST

We offer a variety of homemade piecrusts on these pages; however, if you're in a pinch for time, a 15-ounce package of refrigerated piecrusts works fine in all our recipes calling for Pastry for a 9-inch pie. Two piecrusts come in a package.

PRETTY PASTRY EDGES

For all designs: Fold overhanging pastry under, creating a thick edge even with pieplate rim. Be careful not to stretch the pastry.

Fork Edge: Press firmly around pastry edge with tines of fork. To prevent sticking, dip fork in flour.

Pinch Edge: Place index finger on outside of pastry rim and thumb and other index finger on inside. Pinch pastry into V shape along the edge.

Rope Edge: Place side of thumb on pastry rim at an angle. Pinch pastry by pressing knuckle of index finger into pastry toward thumb.

Braided Edge: Moisten edge of pastry, interlace two pastry strips and apply them to moistened edge. Press gently to make braid adhere.

Cutout Edge: Moisten edge of pastry, and gently press leaf cutouts or other shapes around edge, overlapping slightly.

Food Processor Pastry

PREP: 5 MINUTES   CHILL: 30 MINUTES
COOK: 12 MINUTES

The food processor is ideal for making a ball of dough in a jiffy. The key is to process ingredients just until they form a ball; if processed too long, the pastry will be tough.

1 cup all-purpose flour
¼ teaspoon salt
¼ cup shortening
¼ cup ice water

•Process flour and salt in food processor, pulsing 3 or 4 times or until combined. Add shortening, pulsing 5 or 6 times or until mixture is crumbly.
•With processor running, slowly add ice water, 1 tablespoon at a time; process just until pastry begins to form a ball and leaves sides of bowl. Chill 30 minutes.
•Roll pastry to ⅛-inch thickness on a lightly floured surface. Place in a 9-inch pieplate; trim off excess pastry along edges. Fold edges under, and crimp.
•For baked pastry shell, prick bottom and sides of pastry generously with a fork; bake at 425° for 10 to 12 minutes or until golden. Yield: 8 servings.
Per serving: Calories 101 Fat 5.4g
Cholesterol 0mg Sodium 74mg

Tart Pastry

◄ QUICK ►

PREP: 10 MINUTES COOK: 15 MINUTES

1½ cups all-purpose flour
½ teaspoon baking powder
½ teaspoon salt
¼ cup butter
¼ cup shortening
4 to 6 tablespoons milk

•Combine first 3 ingredients; cut in butter and shortening with a pastry blender until mixture is crumbly. Sprinkle milk evenly over surface; stir with a fork just until dry ingredients are moistened. Shape into a ball; cover and chill.
•Roll pastry to ⅛-inch thickness on a lightly floured surface; fit into an 11- x 7½-inch tart pan or into six 4-inch tart pans.

•For baked tart shells, prick bottom of pastry with a fork. Bake at 450° for 12 minutes or until lightly browned. Yield: 6 servings.
Per serving: Calories 255 Fat 15.5g
Cholesterol 22mg Sodium 321mg

Sweet Flaky Pastry (Pâte Sucrée)

PREP: 20 MINUTES   CHILL: 8 HOURS

Known as pâte sucrée, this is a sweet crust often used for fruit tarts, pies, and other desserts.

3 cups all-purpose flour
½ cup sugar
1 cup butter
½ cup ice water

•Combine flour and sugar in a large bowl; cut in butter with a pastry blender until mixture is crumbly. Sprinkle ice water, 1 tablespoon at a time, evenly over surface; stir with a fork just until dry ingredients are moistened.
•Divide dough into 4 equal portions; wrap each portion of dough in plastic wrap, and chill 8 hours.
•Roll each portion to ⅛-inch thickness on a lightly floured surface, and cut into 12 equal portions. Fit dough into 1- or 2-inch tartlet pans; trim excess pastry from edges. Fill and bake as filling recipe directs.
•For baked tart shells, prick bottoms of pastry with a fork. Place tins on a baking sheet. Bake at 400° for 12 to 15 minutes. Yield: enough pastry for 4 dozen tartlet shells.
Per shell: Calories 68 Fat 3.9g
Cholesterol 10mg Sodium 39mg

CRUMB CRUSTS

Crumb crusts aren't really pastries, but they're popular, easy to make, and pair well with many chilled and frozen pies. When teamed with chilled fillings, crumb crusts are usually baked briefly to set the crumbs. When used with frozen fillings like ice cream, no baking is needed. Freezing firms the crumbs sufficiently to make the crust sliceable.

In a crumb crust the crumbs should be fine and uniform in size. Make your own crumbs in the food processor or place broken crackers or cookies in a zip-top plastic bag, seal, and roll with a rolling pin until finely crushed. Then be sure you add the right proportion of melted butter to the crumbs, stir, and press firmly in a pieplate. Use the bottom of a metal measuring cup to apply pressure and make the crumb layer even.

Gingersnap Crumb Crust

◄ QUICK • FAMILY FAVORITE ►

PREP: 4 MINUTES COOK: 10 MINUTES

1½ cups gingersnap crumbs (about 26 cookies)
¼ cup sugar
⅓ cup butter or margarine, melted

•Combine all ingredients, mixing well. Firmly press crumb mixture in bottom and up sides of a 9-inch pieplate.
•For frozen pies, crust may be used without baking. For other pies, bake at 350° for 8 to 10 minutes. Cool on a wire rack. Yield: 8 servings.
Per serving: Calories 150 Fat 10.2g
Cholesterol 26mg Sodium 98mg

Chocolate Wafer Crust

◄ QUICK • FAMILY FAVORITE ►

PREP: 4 MINUTES COOK: 8 MINUTES

1¼ cups chocolate wafer crumbs (about 24 wafers)
⅓ cup butter or margarine, melted

•Combine chocolate wafer crumbs and butter, mixing well. Firmly press crumb mixture evenly in bottom and up sides of a 9-inch pieplate.
•For frozen pies, crust may be used without baking. For other pies, bake crust at 350° for 6 to 8 minutes. Cool on a wire rack. Yield: 8 servings.
Per serving: Calories 119 Fat 10.1g
Cholesterol 30mg Sodium 122mg

Graham Cracker Crust

◄ QUICK • FAMILY FAVORITE ►

PREP: 5 MINUTES COOK: 9 MINUTES

Slightly sweetened and crisp-baked, this golden crumb crust is a universal favorite for many popular pies.

1 (5⅓-ounce) packet graham crackers, crushed (about 1⅔ cups)
¼ cup sugar
¼ cup plus 2 tablespoons butter or margarine, melted

•Combine all ingredients, mixing well. Firmly press crumb mixture evenly in bottom and up sides of a 9-inch pieplate.
•For frozen pies, crust may be used without baking. For other pies, bake crust at 350° for 7 to 9 minutes. Cool on a wire rack. Yield: 8 servings.
Per serving: Calories 172 Fat 9.6g
Cholesterol 21mg Sodium 199mg

FRUIT PIES & TARTS

Fruit pies and tarts rank high on the list of favorite Southern desserts. Perhaps it's the thought of juicy berries bubbling beneath a golden crust or the aroma of all-American apple pie baked with sugar and spice. For many folks fruit pies are bound to stir up fond memories.

It goes without saying that you get the best results when you buy and use fresh fruit in season. Some frozen sliced fruit is acceptable in pie making, providing a year-round option. Just be sure to follow recipe directions when using frozen fruit. For some recipes you'll need to thaw the fruit; for others you won't. Some recipes tell you to toss fruit with a little flour to absorb any excess liquid.

You can store most fruit pies and tarts at room temperature for short periods of time, but refrigerate those that contain eggs or dairy products as soon as they cool.

Crumb-Topped Apple Pie

◀ FAMILY FAVORITE ▶

PREP: 20 MINUTES   COOK: 42 MINUTES

If you could pick only one grand apple pie to bake, consider this streusel-topped version. The thin apple slices are covered with a mound of brown sugar, oats, and pecans. After just one bite, we gave the pie our highest rating.

2 cups all-purpose flour
⅔ cup firmly packed brown sugar
½ cup uncooked regular oats
½ teaspoon salt
⅓ cup chopped pecans
¾ cup butter or margarine, melted
4 cups peeled, thinly sliced cooking apple
    (about 3 apples)
⅓ cup sugar
1½ teaspoons cornstarch
⅛ teaspoon salt
¼ cup water
½ teaspoon vanilla extract

•Combine first 5 ingredients; add butter, and stir until blended. Measure 1 cup firmly packed mixture; set aside for pie topping. Press remaining mixture in bottom and up

sides of a well-greased 9-inch pie-plate. Arrange apple slices in pieplate; set aside.
•Combine ⅓ cup sugar, cornstarch, and ⅛ teaspoon salt in a small saucepan; stir in water. Bring to a boil over medium heat; stir in vanilla. Pour hot mixture over apples; crumble reserved topping over pie.
•Bake at 350° for 42 minutes, covering with aluminum foil during last 15 minutes to prevent excessive browning, if necessary. Serve with ice cream. Yield: 8 servings.
Per serving: Calories 449 Fat 22.1g
Cholesterol 47mg Sodium 367mg

Cran-Apple Pie

PREP: 20 MINUTES   COOK: 45 MINUTES

Those glistening scarlet pearls called cranberries are tossed with apples here for a mile-high fruit pie. It's equally good served warm or cooled.

4 cups peeled, sliced cooking apple (about
    4 large)
2 cups fresh or frozen cranberries, thawed
¾ cup sugar
¼ cup all-purpose flour
¼ cup firmly packed brown sugar
½ teaspoon ground cinnamon
¼ teaspoon ground nutmeg
Pastry for 9-inch pie (page 299)
½ cup all-purpose flour
⅓ cup firmly packed brown sugar
¼ teaspoon ground cinnamon
Dash of ground nutmeg
¼ cup butter or margarine
⅓ cup chopped pecans

•Combine apple and cranberries in a large bowl. Combine ¾ cup sugar and next 4 ingredients; add to apple mixture, tossing gently. Spoon into pastry shell.
•Combine ½ cup flour and next 3 ingredients; stir mixture well. Cut in butter with a pastry blender until mixture is crumbly. Stir in pecans. Sprinkle crumb mixture over apple mixture. Bake at 375° for 45 minutes. Serve warm or at room temperature. Yield: 8 servings.
Per serving: Calories 444 Fat 18.2g
Cholesterol 18mg Sodium 357mg

Shielding a pie: To protect your pie from overbrowning, cut the center out of a square of foil. Mold foil ring around the pie's edge.

Apple Pie

◀ FAMILY FAVORITE ▶

PREP: 40 MINUTES
COOK: 1 HOUR AND 5 MINUTES

This double-crust all-American pie still draws a crowd when it's time for dessert. We like Golden Delicious apples in this version. Top with ice cream or tuck a slice of Cheddar cheese into each warm serving.

Pastry for double-crust 9-inch pie
    (page 300)
6 cups peeled, sliced cooking apple
    (about 1½ pounds)
1 tablespoon lemon juice
½ cup sugar
½ cup firmly packed brown sugar
2 tablespoons all-purpose flour
½ teaspoon ground cinnamon
¼ teaspoon ground nutmeg
2 tablespoons butter or margarine
1 egg yolk, lightly beaten
2 teaspoons sugar (optional)
⅛ teaspoon ground cinnamon (optional)

•Roll half of pastry to ⅛-inch thickness on a lightly floured surface. Place in a 9-inch pieplate; set aside.
•Combine apple and lemon juice in a large bowl. Combine ½ cup sugar and next 4 ingredients, mixing well. Spoon over apple mixture, tossing gently. Spoon filling evenly into pastry shell, and dot with butter.

- Roll remaining pastry to ⅛-inch thickness; transfer to top of pie. Trim off excess pastry along edges. Fold edges under, and crimp.
- Cut slits in top crust for steam to escape. Brush pastry lightly with beaten egg yolk. If desired, combine 2 teaspoons sugar and ⅛ teaspoon cinnamon to sprinkle on pie.
- Cover edges of pastry with aluminum foil to prevent excessive browning (see photo on previous page). Bake at 450° for 15 minutes; reduce heat to 350°, and bake 50 more minutes. Yield: 8 servings.

Per serving: Calories 447 Fat 20.9g Cholesterol 35mg Sodium 329mg

Cherry-Berry Pie

PREP: 25 MINUTES COOK: 50 MINUTES

Pastry for double-crust 9-inch pie
 (page 300)
1 (12-ounce) package frozen red
 raspberries, thawed
1 (16-ounce) can pitted tart red cherries,
 undrained
1 cup sugar
¼ cup cornstarch
¼ cup butter or margarine
¼ teaspoon almond extract
¼ teaspoon red food coloring
Garnish: fresh raspberries

- Roll half of pastry to ⅛-inch thickness on a lightly floured surface. Place in a 9-inch pieplate, leaving a 1-inch overhang around edge. Set aside.
- Drain raspberries and cherries, reserving 1 cup combined juices; set fruit aside.
- Combine sugar and cornstarch in a medium saucepan; gradually stir reserved juices into sugar mixture. Cook over medium heat, stirring constantly, until mixture begins to boil. Boil 1 minute, stirring constantly. Remove from heat; stir in butter, almond extract, and food coloring. Fold in reserved fruit; cool slightly. Spoon fruit filling into pastry shell.
- Roll remaining pastry to ⅛-inch thickness; cut 5 leaves with a 3¼-inch leaf-shaped cutter, and mark veins with a knife. Cut remaining pastry into ½-inch strips.
- Arrange strips in a lattice design over filling. Top with pastry leaves. Trim strips even with edges of bottom crust; fold edges under, and crimp.

- Bake at 375° for 45 minutes or until crust is browned. Cool on a wire rack. Garnish, if desired. Yield: 8 servings.

Per serving: Calories 513 Fat 23g Cholesterol 16mg Sodium 355mg

Weaving a lattice: Place 5 to 7 pastry strips on filling in one direction; fold back alternating strips as each crisscross strip is added.

Blueberry Pie

PREP: 15 MINUTES COOK: 35 MINUTES

Fresh berries surely make a difference in fruit pies, but you can be successful with frozen fruit, too. Look for our tip following the recipe if you want frozen fruit directions. See this fruit pie in all its splendor on page 296.

5 cups fresh blueberries°
1 tablespoon lemon juice
Pastry for double-crust 9-inch pie
 (page 300)
1 cup sugar
⅓ cup all-purpose flour
⅛ teaspoon salt
½ teaspoon ground cinnamon
2 tablespoons butter or margarine
1 large egg, lightly beaten
1 teaspoon sugar

- Sprinkle berries with lemon juice; set aside.
- Roll half of pastry to ⅛-inch thickness on a floured surface. Place in a 9-inch pieplate.
- Combine 1 cup sugar and next 3 ingredients; add to berries, stirring well. Pour into pastry shell, and dot with butter.
- Roll remaining pastry to ⅛-inch thickness. Place over filling; seal and crimp edges. Cut

slits in top of crust to allow steam to escape. Brush top of pastry with beaten egg, and sprinkle with 1 teaspoon sugar.
- Bake at 400° for 35 minutes or until golden. Cover edges with aluminum foil to prevent overbrowning, if necessary. Serve warm with vanilla ice cream, if desired. Yield: 8 servings.
°*You can substitute 2 (14-ounce) packages frozen blueberries, thawed and drained. Just increase the flour to ½ cup.*

Per serving: Calories 445 Fat 20.9g Cholesterol 34mg Sodium 372mg

Note: You can forego the solid top crust and cut the top pastry into strips and make a lattice on top of pie. (See photo at left and on page 296.)

Blackberry Pie

PREP: 26 MINUTES COOK: 1 HOUR

Similar to grandma's fruit pies, this one's juicy berries bubble up through the pastry strips during baking.

Pastry for double-crust 9-inch pie
 (page 300)
5 cups fresh or frozen blackberries,
 partially thawed
1 cup sugar
¼ cup all-purpose flour
1½ tablespoons lemon juice
¼ teaspoon salt
1 tablespoon butter or margarine

- Roll half of pastry to ⅛-inch thickness on a lightly floured surface. Place in a 9-inch pieplate; trim off excess pastry along edges. Set aside.
- Combine berries and next 4 ingredients in a bowl; toss well. Spoon berry mixture into pastry shell; dot with butter.
- Roll remaining pastry to ⅛-inch thickness; cut into ½-inch strips. Arrange strips in lattice design over blackberries. Trim strips even with edges; fold edges under, and crimp.
- Bake at 425° for 10 minutes; reduce heat to 350°, and bake 45 to 50 more minutes or until crust is browned. Yield: 8 servings.

Per serving: Calories 427 Fat 18.9g Cholesterol 4mg Sodium 382mg

Fresh Rhubarb Pie

◄ FAMILY FAVORITE ►

PREP: 25 MINUTES   COOK: 45 MINUTES

Make this simple pie in early spring when rhubarb's thin-skinned stalks are no thicker than your thumb.

Pastry for double-crust 9-inch pie
   (page 300)
1⅓ cups sugar
¼ cup cornstarch
¼ teaspoon ground nutmeg
5 cups sliced rhubarb, cut ⅛-inch thick
2 tablespoons butter or margarine
2 teaspoons sugar

•Roll half of pastry to ⅛-inch thickness on a lightly floured surface. Place in a 9-inch pieplate; trim off excess pastry along edges. Cover with plastic wrap, and chill until ready to fill.
•Combine 1⅓ cups sugar, cornstarch, and nutmeg, stirring until blended; stir in rhubarb, and let stand 15 minutes. Spoon mixture into pastry shell; dot with butter.
•Roll remaining pastry to ⅛-inch thickness; cut into ½-inch strips. Arrange strips in lattice design over filling. Trim strips even with edges; fold edges under, and crimp. Sprinkle top of pastry with 2 teaspoons sugar.
•Bake at 425° for 15 minutes; reduce heat to 350°, and bake 30 more minutes or until crust is browned. Yield: 8 servings.
Per serving: Calories 439 Fat 20.1g
Cholesterol 8mg Sodium 326mg

Strawberry-Rhubarb Pie: Follow recipe above, substituting 2½ cups thickly sliced strawberries for half of rhubarb and reducing sugar to 1 cup.

Holiday Mincemeat Pie

PREP: 10 MINUTES   COOK: 30 MINUTES

Tart apple and spicy mincemeat laced with brandy make a surprisingly festive holiday pie. Scoop a little ice cream to cap each serving.

Pastry for double-crust 9-inch pie
   (page 300)
1 (27-ounce) jar mincemeat
1½ cups diced, unpeeled Granny Smith
   apple
¼ cup brandy
2 tablespoons brown sugar

•Roll half of pastry to ⅛-inch thickness on a lightly floured surface. Place in a 9-inch pieplate; set aside. Chill remaining pastry.
•Combine mincemeat and remaining 3 ingredients in a bowl; stir well. Spoon into pastry shell.
•Roll remaining pastry to ⅛-inch thickness; cut into ½-inch strips. Twist each strip several times; arrange strips in lattice design over filling. Trim edges; seal and crimp.
•Bake at 425° for 30 minutes or until golden. Yield: 8 servings.
Per serving: Calories 469 Fat 17.7g
Cholesterol 0mg Sodium 524mg

Strawberries 'n' Cream Pie

◄ MAKE AHEAD ►

**PREP: 15 MINUTES   CHILL: 3 HOURS
COOK: 10 MINUTES**

Nestle fresh strawberries in this fluffy no-bake filling. It's cream cheese that keeps the filling so white. The top gets a gooey drizzle of chocolate, if you really want to indulge.

1 (8-ounce) package cream cheese,
   softened
⅓ cup sugar
¼ teaspoon almond extract
1 cup whipping cream, whipped
1 baked 9-inch pastry shell (page 299)
1 quart small fresh strawberries, hulled
3 (1-ounce) squares semisweet chocolate
1 tablespoon butter or margarine

•Beat cream cheese at medium speed with an electric mixer until creamy; gradually add sugar and almond extract, beating well. Stir one-fourth of whipped cream into cream cheese mixture; fold in remaining whipped cream. Spoon mixture into pastry shell. Arrange strawberries, stem side down, over whipped cream mixture. Cover and chill 3 hours.
•Melt chocolate and butter in a small heavy saucepan over low heat, stirring constantly. Remove from heat, and cool.
•Spoon melted chocolate mixture into a large heavy-duty, zip-top plastic bag or a decorating bag fitted with a No. 2 round tip; seal plastic bag. Snip a tiny hole in one corner of bag. Right before serving, pipe chocolate mixture in a decorative design over strawberries. Yield: 8 servings.
Per serving: Calories 467 Fat 34.5g
Cholesterol 79mg Sodium 403mg

Luscious Caramel-Banana Pie

◄ FAMILY FAVORITE ►

**PREP: 5 MINUTES
COOK: 1 HOUR AND 20 MINUTES
CHILL: 3 HOURS**

Cook condensed milk until it's thick and caramelized; then spoon it over sliced bananas. This combination is sinfully rich, especially after it gets a sprinkling of toffee candy.

2 (14-ounce) cans sweetened condensed
   milk
2 to 3 bananas
1 (9-ounce) graham cracker crust (extra
   serving size)
1 cup whipping cream
¼ cup sifted powdered sugar
1 or 2 (1.4-ounce) English toffee-flavored
   candy bars, crushed

•Pour condensed milk into an 11- x 7-inch baking dish; cover with aluminum foil. Place covered dish in a 13- x 9-inch pan. Add hot water to pan to depth of 1 inch.
•Bake at 425° for 1 hour and 20 minutes or until condensed milk is thick and caramel-colored (add hot water to pan as needed). Remove foil when done, and set aside.

•Cut bananas into ⅛-inch slices, and place on crust. Spread caramelized milk over bananas. Cool at least 30 minutes.
•Beat whipping cream at medium speed with an electric mixer until foamy; gradually add powdered sugar, beating until soft peaks form. Spread over caramel layer. Sprinkle with crushed candy. Chill at least 3 hours. Yield: 8 servings.

Per serving: Calories 597 Fat 26.2g Cholesterol 80mg Sodium 274mg

Fresh Peach Pie

◀ FAMILY FAVORITE ▶

PREP: 38 MINUTES COOK: 55 MINUTES

5½ cups peeled, sliced fresh peaches
    (3½ pounds)
1 cup sugar
¼ cup all-purpose flour
½ teaspoon ground cinnamon
3 tablespoons butter or margarine
1 teaspoon vanilla extract
Pastry for double-crust 9-inch pie
    (page 300)
Vanilla ice cream (optional)

•Combine first 4 ingredients in a saucepan; set aside until syrup forms. Bring mixture to a boil; reduce heat to low, and cook 10 minutes or until peaches are tender, stirring often. Remove from heat; add butter and vanilla, blending well.
•Roll half of pastry to ⅛-inch thickness on a lightly floured surface. Place pastry in a 9-inch pieplate; trim off excess pastry along edges of pieplate. Spoon filling into pastry shell.
•Roll remaining pastry to ⅛-inch thickness; cut into ½-inch strips. Arrange strips in lattice design over peaches. Trim strips even with edges; fold edges under, and crimp.
•Bake at 425° for 15 minutes; reduce heat to 350°, and bake 25 to 30 more minutes or until crust is browned. Serve warm with ice cream, if desired. Yield: 8 servings.

Per serving: Calories 458 Fat 21.5g Cholesterol 12mg Sodium 338mg

Note: Substitute 1½ (16-ounce) packages frozen unsweetened sliced peaches for fresh peaches.

PEACH POINTERS

Selection: A deep gold or yellow skin is the true sign of a ripe peach, not the rosy blush which distinguishes certain varieties. A strong, perfumy aroma is also a sign of ripeness. Don't buy peaches with wrinkles or brown spots.
Ripening: Store peaches in a loosely covered paper bag or bowl. Check them daily; peaches are ripe when they yield slightly to gentle pressure.
Storage: Peaches bruise easily, so handle them with care. Use the softest fruit first. Serve ripe peaches immediately or store in refrigerator. For the fullest flavor, serve ripe peaches at room temperature.
Preserving color: To prevent browning, sprinkle lemon juice or orange juice over sliced peaches.
Peach poundage: I pound peaches (2 large or 3 medium) yields:
    2 cups sliced peaches or
    1⅔ cups chopped peaches or
    1½ cups pureed peaches

Fried Pies

PREP: 45 MINUTES COOK: 42 MINUTES

Just like those prizewinning pies at a county fair, this recipe won't disappoint. It's a dough that you can just divide into 12 portions and fill with your choice of fruit fillings. If you have a little filling left over, try it on toast.

3 cups all-purpose flour
1 teaspoon salt
¾ cup shortening
1 large egg, lightly beaten
¼ cup water
1 teaspoon white vinegar
1 cup plus 2 tablespoons fruit filling
    (see recipes)
Vegetable oil
2 tablespoons sugar

•Combine flour and salt in a large bowl; cut in shortening with a pastry blender until crumbly.
•Combine egg and water, stirring with a fork; drizzle over flour mixture. Add vinegar, and stir with a fork just until dry ingredients are moistened.
•Divide pastry into 12 portions; roll each portion into a 5-inch circle on a lightly floured surface.
•Spoon 1½ tablespoons fruit filling onto half of each pastry circle. Moisten edges with water; fold pastry over fruit filling, pressing edges to seal. Crimp edges with a fork dipped in flour.
•Pour oil to depth of ½ inch into a large heavy skillet. Fry pies, in batches, in hot oil (375°) over medium-high heat 2 to 4 minutes or until golden, turning once. Drain well on paper towels. Sprinkle with sugar. Yield: 1 dozen.

Per pie: Calories 361 Fat 22.2g Cholesterol 18mg Sodium 213mg

Mixed Fruit Filling

1 cup chopped dried mixed fruit
¾ cup apple juice
¼ cup sugar
1 teaspoon vanilla extract
¼ cup chopped walnuts
½ teaspoon ground cinnamon

•Combine dried fruit and apple juice in a small saucepan; let stand 30 minutes. Bring to a boil over medium-high heat; reduce heat, and simmer 10 minutes or until fruit is tender and liquid evaporates, stirring often. Remove from heat; add sugar and remaining ingredients, stirring until sugar dissolves. Cool. Yield: 1½ cups.

Dried Cherry Filling

2 (3-ounce) packages dried Bing cherries,
    chopped
1 cup water
½ cup sugar
¼ teaspoon vanilla extract
¼ teaspoon almond extract
½ cup chopped almonds

•Combine cherries and water in a medium saucepan; let stand 30 minutes. Bring to a boil over medium heat; reduce heat, and simmer 20 minutes or until liquid evaporates, stirring often. Remove from heat; add sugar and remaining ingredients, stirring until sugar dissolves. Cool. Yield: 1¾ cups.

Tarte Tatin

PREP: 30 MINUTES CHILL: 1 HOUR

COOK: 55 MINUTES

Tarte Tatin is a rustic French tart named after two sisters who made their living baking this unique upside-down apple pastry. We found that Golden Delicious apples give great results.

½ cup butter
¾ cup sugar
3 pounds Golden Delicious apples, peeled, cored, and quartered
1½ tablespoons lemon juice
½ teaspoon ground cinnamon
1 teaspoon vanilla extract
Pastry

•Melt butter in a 10-inch cast-iron skillet over medium heat; sprinkle sugar evenly into skillet. Remove from heat.
•Combine apple quarters and next 3 ingredients in a large bowl; toss gently. Tightly arrange a ring of apple quarters against sides of skillet, standing apples on edge, and fitting as many as possible. Fill in center of skillet with remaining apple quarters.
•Place skillet over medium-high heat, and cook 10 minutes. Remove from heat; turn apples over, using a fork or tip of a knife. Cook 15 more minutes over medium-high heat or until juices are thick and caramel is a deep amber color.
•Slide chilled Pastry onto top of skillet. Trim excess pastry along edges (do not seal edges). Cut 2 or 3 slits in pastry for steam to escape.
•Bake at 425° for 30 minutes or until pastry is well browned. (Cover edges of Pastry with strips of aluminum foil to prevent excessive browning, if necessary.) Let stand 20 minutes; invert onto a serving platter. Serve warm with vanilla ice cream or crème fraîche (see page 207). Yield: 8 servings.
Per serving: Calories 408 Fat 22.4g
Cholesterol 52mg Sodium 342mg

Pastry

1 cup all-purpose flour
1 tablespoon sugar
½ teaspoon salt
⅓ cup cold butter, cut into pieces
2 tablespoons shortening
3 to 4 tablespoons ice water

•Combine first 3 ingredients in a medium bowl; stir well. Cut in butter and shortening with a pastry blender until mixture is crumbly. Sprinkle ice water, 1 tablespoon at a time, evenly over surface; stir with a fork until dry ingredients are moistened. Shape pastry into a flat disc; wrap in wax paper or plastic wrap, and chill at least 1 hour.
•Roll pastry into a 10-inch circle; slide onto a baking sheet, and chill until ready to use. Yield: enough pastry for one 10-inch tart.

Mixed Fruit Tart

PREP: 30 MINUTES   COOK: 15 MINUTES

CHILL: 30 MINUTES

Here's a multicolored fruit tart that's good year-round. If you can't find fresh berries in winter, use another fruit, like grapes.

1½ cups all-purpose flour
½ cup sugar
½ cup butter or margarine, softened
⅓ cup slivered almonds, ground
1 egg yolk
1 teaspoon vanilla extract
1 teaspoon almond extract
1 (8-ounce) package cream cheese, softened
3 tablespoons sugar
3 tablespoons orange juice
½ cup peach or apricot jam
1 tablespoon butter or margarine
1 tablespoon lemon juice
1 tablespoon amaretto
2 cups fresh raspberries
2 kiwifruit, peeled and sliced
1 (11-ounce) can mandarin oranges, drained
¼ cup sliced almonds, toasted

•Combine first 4 ingredients in a mixing bowl; beat at medium speed with an electric mixer 3 minutes or until blended. Add egg yolk and flavorings; mix just until dough holds together.
•Firmly press dough in bottom and up sides of an 11-inch tart pan with removable bottom. Bake at 375° for 15 minutes or until golden. Cool completely on a wire rack.
•Combine cream cheese, 3 tablespoons sugar, and orange juice; beat at medium speed 1 to 2 minutes or until smooth. Spread mixture evenly over cooled crust. Cover and chill 30 minutes or until mixture is firm.
•Combine jam and next 3 ingredients in a small saucepan. Cook over low heat, stirring constantly, 2 minutes or until jam and butter melt; set glaze aside, and cool slightly.
•Arrange raspberries, kiwifruit, and oranges over cream cheese mixture up to 2 hours before serving; brush fruit with glaze, and sprinkle with toasted almonds.
•Remove sides of tart pan before serving; serve chilled or at room temperature. Yield: 8 servings.
Per serving: Calories 494 Fat 28.2g
Cholesterol 93mg Sodium 231mg

Pear-Almond Tart

PREP: 20 MINUTES   COOK: 50 MINUTES

This fruit tart is full of pears that are sliced and fanned to put on a beautiful show.

1 recipe Tart Pastry (page 301)
¾ cup slivered almonds
½ cup sugar
1 large egg
1 tablespoon butter or margarine, melted
2 cups water
2 tablespoons lemon juice
3 large fresh pears
¼ cup sugar
3 tablespoons sliced almonds
2 tablespoons butter or margarine, melted
⅓ cup apricot preserves
¼ cup water
2 tablespoons sugar
1 tablespoon kirsch or orange juice

•Roll Tart Pastry to ⅛-inch thickness on a lightly floured surface. Fit pastry into an 11- x 7½-inch tart pan. Set aside.
•Process ¾ cup almonds in food processor 40 seconds or until finely ground. Add ½ cup sugar, egg, and 1 tablespoon melted butter; process until blended. Spread over pastry.
•Combine 2 cups water and lemon juice; stir well. Peel and core pears. Dip pears in lemon juice mixture; drain well. Cut pears in half vertically, and then cut into ⅛-inch-thick lengthwise slices, keeping slices in order as they are cut. Arrange slices over almond mixture in the shape of 6 pear halves, letting slices fan out slightly.

•Top pears with ¼ cup sugar; sprinkle with 3 tablespoons almonds, and drizzle with 2 tablespoons melted butter. Bake at 400° for 40 to 50 minutes or until golden.

•Combine preserves, ¼ cup water, and 2 tablespoons sugar; cook over low heat, stirring constantly, until sugar dissolves. Press mixture through a wire-mesh strainer, reserving syrup. Discard preserves. Stir kirsch into syrup. Carefully brush syrup over tart. Remove tart from pan before serving. Yield: 6 servings.

Per serving: Calories 629 Fat 30.2g
Cholesterol 73mg Sodium 388mg

Orange Tarts

PREP: 1 HOUR

COOK: 17 MINUTES PER BATCH

Orange curd is a luscious, superthick custard. It doesn't take much of it to fill these sweet tartlet shells.

1 recipe Sweet Flaky Pastry (page 301)
3 (1-ounce) squares semisweet chocolate, melted
1 cup Orange Curd (page 398) or commercial orange or lemon curd
Garnishes: orange curls, fresh mint

•Roll each of 4 portions of Sweet Flaky Pastry to ⅛-inch thickness on a lightly floured surface, and cut into 12 equal portions. Fit dough into 2-inch tartlet tins; trim excess pastry from edges, and prick bottoms with a fork. Place tins on a baking sheet.

•Bake at 400° for 15 to 17 minutes or until lightly browned. Cool in tins. Carefully remove from tins, and brush chocolate inside tart shells; spoon 1 teaspoon Orange Curd into each shell. Garnish, if desired. Yield: 4 dozen.

Per tart: Calories 98 Fat 6g
Cholesterol 26mg Sodium 44mg

CUSTARD & CREAM PIES

There are just a few guidelines for producing thick and smooth custard pies. The basic ingredients are not unusual and the method's easy to master. Most of these pies are thickened with eggs.

When baking custard pies, you can avoid messy spills by placing the pastry-lined pieplate on the oven rack before pouring in the filling mixture. Check for doneness with the jiggle test (see photo) and/or the knife test: When a knife inserted near center of pie comes out clean, the pie is done. The filling may still be slightly shaky (barely jiggles, thus the jiggle test), but will firm upon cooling.

Cream pies are easy to make, although their satiny-smooth texture can be intimidating. If the cream pie is thickened with flour or cornstarch, never add it directly to a hot mixture—this would cause the mixture to lump. Typically the thickening agent is blended with cold liquid before the cooking process begins.

Whether thickened with cornstarch or flour, cook the filling until it comes to a full boil; then boil 1 minute, stirring gently. If the filling also contains eggs, you'll need to boil it 3 minutes. This additional boiling kills an enzyme present in eggs that could otherwise break down their thickening ability.

If a recipe states to chill the filling before adding a topping, press plastic wrap directly on the surface of the filling to prevent a skin from forming as the filling cools (see photo on next page).

Allow custard and cream pies to cool completely before slicing and serving them. Otherwise you run the risk of a runny pie. Always refrigerate leftover custard and cream pies.

Egg Custard Pie

◄ FAMILY FAVORITE ►

PREP: 5 MINUTES

COOK: 1 HOUR AND 10 MINUTES

An old-fashioned recipe, this egg custard bakes with a sprinkling of nutmeg on top.

Pastry for 9-inch pie (page 299)
4 large eggs, lightly beaten
⅔ cup sugar
1½ teaspoons vanilla extract
¼ teaspoon salt
¼ teaspoon ground nutmeg
2 cups milk
¼ cup whipping cream
Additional ground nutmeg

•Bake pastry shell at 450° for 8 to 10 minutes or until golden.

•Meanwhile, combine eggs and next 4 ingredients; beat at medium speed with an electric mixer until blended. Gradually stir in milk and whipping cream; mix well.

•Without removing baked pastry shell from oven, pour filling into hot pastry shell; sprinkle with additional nutmeg.

Testing for doneness: Egg Custard Pie is done when it slightly jiggles 2 inches from center when you gently pull the oven rack.

•Reduce heat to 325°; bake 1 hour or until 2 inches from center is set when jiggled (see photo). Cool completely; store in refrigerator. Yield: 8 servings.

Per serving: Calories 339 Fat 18.6g
Cholesterol 138mg Sodium 432mg

Chocolate Cream Pie

Coconut Cream Pie

PREP: 32 MINUTES   COOK: 15 MINUTES

This coconut pie comes with great-tasting variations of chocolate and banana cream. It's hard to say which one's best; try them all.

¾ cup sugar
¼ cup plus 2 teaspoons cornstarch
⅛ teaspoon salt
3 egg yolks, beaten
3 cups milk
1½ tablespoons butter or margarine
1½ teaspoons vanilla extract
¾ cup flaked coconut
1 baked 9-inch pastry shell (page 299)
1 cup whipping cream
⅓ cup sifted powdered sugar
⅓ cup flaked coconut, toasted

•Combine first 3 ingredients in a heavy saucepan; stir well. Combine egg yolks and milk; gradually stir into sugar mixture. Cook over medium heat, stirring constantly, until mixture thickens and boils. Boil 3 minutes, stirring constantly. Remove from heat; stir in butter, vanilla, and ¾ cup coconut.
•Immediately pour filling into pastry shell. Cover filling with plastic wrap (see photo). Cool 30 minutes; then chill until firm.
•Beat whipping cream at medium speed with an electric mixer until foamy; gradually add powdered sugar, beating until soft peaks form. Spread whipped cream over filling; sprinkle with ⅓ cup toasted coconut. Chill. Yield: 8 servings.
Per serving: Calories 525 Fat 31.4g
Cholesterol 143mg Sodium 446mg

Chocolate Cream Pie: Omit coconut. Increase sugar to 1 cup, and stir in 3 ounces unsweetened melted chocolate with milk.

Banana Cream Pie: Omit coconut. Place 3 sliced ripe bananas in bottom of pastry before adding filling.

Protecting custard filling: Apply plastic wrap directly to surface of filling to keep a skin from forming. Remove wrap before adding a topping.

Buttermilk Chess Pie

PREP: 13 MINUTES   COOK: 45 MINUTES

A thin "crust" develops on the surface of this buttery chess filling as it bakes.

2 cups sugar
2 tablespoons cornmeal
5 large eggs, lightly beaten
⅔ cup buttermilk
½ cup butter or margarine, melted and cooled
1 teaspoon vanilla extract
2 teaspoons grated lemon rind
3 tablespoons lemon juice
Pastry for 9-inch pie (page 299)

•Combine sugar and cornmeal in a large bowl; add eggs and buttermilk, stirring until blended. Stir in butter and next 3 ingredients; pour into pastry shell.
•Bake at 350° for 45 minutes or until set. Cool on a wire rack; cover and chill. Yield: 8 servings.
Per serving: Calories 506 Fat 23.4g
Cholesterol 168mg Sodium 471mg

Chocolate Chess Pie: Add ¼ cup cocoa to filling, substitute evaporated milk for buttermilk, and omit lemon rind and juice. Bake 50 to 55 minutes or until set. Garnish with whipped cream and dust with cocoa, if desired.

French Silk Pie

PREP: 15 MINUTES   COOK: 30 MINUTES

CHILL: 2 HOURS

Traditional French Silk Pie has raw eggs that are each beaten 5 minutes, and then added to the filling to produce a velvety texture. Instead of raw eggs, this version gets its silky texture from a rich chocolaty cooked custard.

2 (1-ounce) squares unsweetened chocolate
⅓ cup butter or margarine
¾ cup sugar
⅓ cup all-purpose flour
3 cups whipping cream, divided
2 egg yolks, lightly beaten
1 baked 9-inch pastry shell (page 299)
2 tablespoons powdered sugar
Garnish: chocolate shavings

•Place chocolate and butter in top of a double boiler; bring water to a boil. Reduce heat to low; cook until chocolate and butter melt.
•Add sugar and flour; stir well. Gradually stir in 2 cups whipping cream. Cook, stirring constantly, 20 minutes or until mixture thickens. Gradually add one-fourth of hot mixture to egg yolks. Add to remaining hot mixture, stirring constantly. Cook until mixture thickens and reaches 160°. Remove from heat. Cover tightly with plastic wrap; cool to room temperature, and spoon mixture into pastry shell. Cover and chill 2 hours.
•Beat remaining 1 cup whipping cream at medium speed with an electric mixer until foamy; gradually add powdered sugar, beating until soft peaks form. Spread whipped cream on pie; garnish, if desired. Yield: 8 servings.

Per serving: Calories 668 Fat 54.2g
Cholesterol 200mg Sodium 406mg

German Chocolate Pie

◄ MAKE AHEAD ►
◄ FAMILY FAVORITE ►

PREP: 30 MINUTES   COOK: 55 MINUTES

You'll know why this pie received raves from our staff once you've tasted the crusty coconut top and chesslike fudgy filling.

Pastry for 10-inch pie (page 299)
1 (4-ounce) package sweet baking chocolate
¼ cup butter or margarine
1 (12-ounce) can evaporated milk
1½ cups sugar
3 tablespoons cornstarch
⅛ teaspoon salt
2 large eggs
1 teaspoon vanilla extract
⅔ cup flaked coconut
⅓ cup chopped pecans
1 cup sweetened whipped cream
3 tablespoons chocolate shavings

•Prepare Pastry; place in a 9½-inch deep-dish pieplate. Set aside.
•Combine baking chocolate and butter in a medium saucepan; cook over low heat, stirring until chocolate melts. Remove from heat, and gradually stir in evaporated milk; set aside.

•Combine sugar, cornstarch, and salt in a large bowl; add eggs and vanilla, mixing well. Gradually stir in chocolate mixture, using a wire whisk. Pour mixture into unbaked pastry shell, and sprinkle with coconut and chopped pecans.
•Bake at 375° for 45 minutes. (Pie may appear soft, but will become firm after cooling.) Cool at least 4 hours. Top pie with whipped cream and chocolate shavings. Yield: 8 servings.

Per serving: Calories 673 Fat 38.8g
Cholesterol 102mg Sodium 409mg

Chocolate Mocha Crunch Pie

◄ MAKE AHEAD ►

PREP: 20 MINUTES   COOK: 50 MINUTES
CHILL: 6 HOURS

The crunch in this pie comes from a wonderful crust made with piecrust mix, grated chocolate, and walnuts.

Mocha Pastry Shell
1 (1-ounce) square unsweetened chocolate, chopped
⅓ cup butter or margarine
¾ cup firmly packed brown sugar
¼ cup all-purpose flour
2 teaspoons instant coffee granules
1½ cups milk
2 egg yolks, lightly beaten
2 cups whipping cream
½ cup sifted powdered sugar
1½ tablespoons instant coffee granules
½ (1-ounce) square semisweet chocolate, grated (optional)

•Prepare Mocha Pastry Shell; set aside.
•Place 1 square chopped chocolate and butter in top of a double boiler; bring water to a boil. Reduce heat to low; stir in brown sugar, flour, and 2 teaspoons coffee granules. Gradually stir in milk, and cook 10 minutes or until mixture thickens.
•Gradually add one-fourth of hot mixture to egg yolks. Add to remaining hot mixture, stirring constantly. Cook, stirring constantly, 20 to 25 minutes or until mixture is very thick. Remove from heat. Pour filling into cooled pastry shell. Cover and chill at least 6 hours.

•About 1 or 2 hours before serving, beat whipping cream, powdered sugar, and 1½ tablespoons coffee granules in a large chilled mixing bowl at medium speed with an electric mixer until soft peaks form (do not overbeat). Spoon over chilled filling. Sprinkle with grated chocolate, if desired. Chill. Yield: 8 servings.

Per serving: Calories 700 Fat 51.6g
Cholesterol 163mg Sodium 299mg

Mocha Pastry Shell

1 piecrust stick, crumbled or ½ (11-ounce) package piecrust mix
1 (1-ounce) square unsweetened chocolate, grated
¾ cup finely chopped walnuts
¼ cup firmly packed brown sugar
1 tablespoon water
1 teaspoon vanilla extract

•Use a fork to combine crumbled piecrust stick and chocolate in a medium bowl. Stir in walnuts and brown sugar. Combine water and vanilla; sprinkle over pastry mixture. Mix with fork until mixture forms a ball.
•Line a 9-inch pieplate with aluminum foil. Press pastry mixture evenly into pieplate.
•Bake at 375° for 15 minutes; cool completely. Invert crust onto another pieplate; remove foil. Return to 9-inch pieplate. Yield: one 9-inch pastry shell.

MERINGUE PIES

Some of the most classic pies are those topped with mounds of swirling white meringue. Though the flavor of the filling can vary greatly, we've narrowed it down to three of the most popular choices—lemon, chocolate, and Key lime.

One of a pie maker's biggest fears is that her beautiful meringue will *weep* (produce tiny beads of moisture on the meringue's surface) after it's baked. Weeping can appear to be beyond the cook's control when, in fact, if you follow proper procedure, beat meringue on a dry day, and read "Making a Perfect Meringue" at right, you can master the weeping whites.

When making meringue, it's important to work with beaters and bowls that are grease-free and very clean. Even the smallest bit of grease in a bowl can keep egg whites from reaching their full volume.

When beaten enough, meringue should look glossy and have sharp peaks. At this point, quickly spread meringue onto a hot filling, anchoring meringue to the edge to seal it and to keep it from shrinking away from the crust. Bake pie immediately as recipe directs, and cool it away from drafts.

Let meringue pie cool completely before serving; if sliced in haste, the filling will most likely be runny. Therefore, it's best to make a meringue pie several hours before serving. Use a hot, wet knife to make slicing easy.

Refrigeration can cause a meringue topping to become sticky, but you do still need to refrigerate any leftovers.

Meringue

◄ HEALTHY ►

PREP: 10 MINUTES

3 egg whites
¼ teaspoon cream of tartar
⅓ cup sugar
½ teaspoon vanilla extract

•Beat egg whites and cream of tartar in a grease-free bowl at medium speed with an electric mixer until soft peaks form (tips of meringue will curl when you lift beaters). Gradually add sugar, 1 tablespoon at a time, beating at high speed until stiff peaks form

---

MAKING A PERFECT MERINGUE

•For a meringue with great volume, let the egg whites stand at room temperature for a full 30 minutes before beating.
•Be sure to use the size bowl called for in your recipe. Copper, stainless-steel, or glass bowls work best. Be sure your electric mixer beaters are clean.
•Begin to add the sugar gradually as soon as soft peaks form (tips will curl).
•After adding all the sugar, continue beating until stiff peaks form and the sugar is completely dissolved. Rub a little of the meringue between your fingers; it should feel completely smooth.

---

and sugar dissolves (2 to 4 minutes). Add vanilla, beating just until blended. Bake according to individual recipes. Yield: 2 cups.
Per ¼-cup serving: Calories 40 Fat 0g
Cholesterol 0mg Sodium 20mg

Key Lime Pie

◄ MAKE AHEAD ►
◄ FAMILY FAVORITE ►

PREP: 30 MINUTES   COOK: 30 MINUTES
CHILL: 2 HOURS

We preferred the flavor of Key lime juice in this simple pie. You can find the juice in a bottle at most grocery stores. Regular lime juice works fine in the pie, too; the flavor's just not quite as distinct.

3 egg yolks
1 (14-ounce) can sweetened condensed milk
½ cup Key lime juice or regular lime juice
⅓ cup sifted powdered sugar
1½ teaspoons grated lime rind
1 baked 9-inch pastry shell (page 299) or 1 (9-ounce) graham cracker crust (extra serving size)
Meringue (this page)

•Beat first 5 ingredients in a bowl at medium speed with an electric mixer 1 minute or until well blended. Spoon into desired crust.

•Prepare Meringue; spread Meringue over filling, sealing to edge of pastry. Bake at 325° for 30 minutes or until golden. Cool completely on a wire rack. Chill 2 hours before serving. Yield: 8 servings.
Per serving: Calories 390 Fat 14.8g
Cholesterol 101mg Sodium 378mg

Chocolate Meringue Pie

◄ FAMILY FAVORITE ►

PREP: 10 MINUTES   COOK: 28 MINUTES

1 cup sugar
3 tablespoons cornstarch
Dash of salt
2 cups milk
3 egg yolks
1 (1-ounce) square unsweetened chocolate
1 tablespoon butter or margarine
1 teaspoon vanilla extract
1 baked 9-inch pastry shell (page 299)
Meringue (this page)

•Combine first 3 ingredients in a heavy saucepan; mix well.
•Combine milk and egg yolks; beat with a wire whisk 1 to 2 minutes or until mixture is frothy. Gradually stir into sugar mixture, mixing well.
•Cook over medium heat, stirring constantly, until thickened and bubbly. Remove from heat; add chocolate, butter, and vanilla, stirring until chocolate and butter melt. Spoon into pastry shell; set aside.
•Prepare Meringue; spread Meringue over hot filling, sealing to edge of pastry. Bake at 325° for 25 minutes or until golden. Cool completely on a wire rack. Yield: 8 servings.
Per serving: Calories 384 Fat 15.7g
Cholesterol 97mg Sodium 378mg

Lemon Meringue Pie

PREP: 20 MINUTES   COOK: 38 MINUTES

This Lemon Meringue Pie is a little on the tart side—just the way we like it.

1½ cups sugar
½ cup cornstarch
¼ teaspoon salt
4 egg yolks
1¾ cups water
⅔ cup fresh lemon juice
3 tablespoons butter or margarine
1 teaspoon grated lemon rind
1 baked 9-inch pastry shell (page 299)
Meringue (previous page)
Garnish: lemon rind curls

•Combine first 3 ingredients in a large heavy saucepan.
•Combine egg yolks, water, and lemon juice; beat with a wire whisk 1 to 2 minutes or until frothy. Stir into sugar mixture.
•Cook over medium heat, stirring constantly, until mixture thickens and boils (photo 1). Boil 3 minutes, stirring constantly. Remove from heat. Stir in butter and lemon rind (photo 2). Spoon into pastry shell (photo 3).
•Prepare Meringue; spread Meringue over hot filling, sealing to edge of pastry (photo 4). Bake at 325° for 25 to 28 minutes. Cool completely. Store in refrigerator. Garnish, if desired. Yield: 8 servings.

Per serving: Calories 433 Fat 15.4g
Cholesterol 123mg Sodium 435mg

1. Cook sugar-egg yolk mixture over medium heat, stirring constantly with a whisk, until mixture thickens and boils.

2. Remove thickened filling from heat. Add butter and lemon rind, whisking gently until butter melts.

3. Spoon hot filling into baked pastry shell.

4. Spread meringue over hot filling, sealing meringue to edge of pastry. Then bake.

CHILLED & FROZEN PIES

Pies that require chilling or freezing make excellent desserts for entertaining because you can prepare them in advance and then forget about them until serving time.

Chilled pies often contain unflavored gelatin, which gives them a light texture. When making gelatin-based pies, be sure to soften and dissolve gelatin properly to ensure a smooth success.

First, soften gelatin in a small amount of cold liquid as the recipe directs. Then stir the gelatin mixture into hot liquid or over low heat until all gelatin granules dissolve and the mixture is completely smooth. Cool the mixture before folding in remaining ingredients; then chill until set.

For ice cream pies, soften ice cream 15 minutes before spooning it into a piecrust; then freeze the pie at least 8 hours. This time may vary due to the differences in freezer temperature, so it's always a good practice to prepare and freeze a pie at least a day in advance of when you plan to serve it.

Most ice cream pies need to stand at room temperature about 10 minutes before serving so they'll be sliceable. Once sliced, promptly return the rest of the pie to the freezer.

You can make a chilled pie using a baked pastry or a baked crumb crust, and a frozen pie with a baked pastry or an unbaked crumb crust.

Grasshopper Pie

◄ MAKE AHEAD ►

PREP: 18 MINUTES   FREEZE: 8 HOURS

Crème de menthe colors this cool pie green. And crushed chocolate sandwich cookies create a thick crust.

30 cream-filled chocolate sandwich cookies, divided
¼ cup butter or margarine, melted
1 (7-ounce) jar marshmallow cream
¼ cup green crème de menthe
3 drops of green food coloring (optional)
1½ cups whipping cream

•Finely crush 24 cookies. Combine cookie crumbs and butter; stir well. Firmly press

mixture in bottom and up sides of a 9-inch pieplate. Set aside.
•Combine marshmallow cream, crème de menthe, and food coloring, if desired, in a large mixing bowl; beat at medium speed with an electric mixer until smooth. Beat whipping cream at medium speed until firm peaks form. Gently fold whipped cream into marshmallow cream mixture; pour into prepared crust.
•Coarsely chop remaining 6 cookies; sprinkle on top of pie. Cover and freeze 8 hours or until firm. Let stand at room temperature 5 minutes before serving. Yield: 8 servings.
Per serving: Calories 517 Fat 31g
Cholesterol 77mg Sodium 372mg

Irish Crème Pie: Omit crème de menthe and food coloring, and substitute ⅓ cup Irish Crème liqueur.

Lemon Chiffon Pie

◄ MAKE AHEAD ►

PREP: 15 MINUTES   COOK: 15 MINUTES
CHILL: 2 HOURS

1 envelope unflavored gelatin
¼ cup cold water
4 large eggs, separated
1 cup sugar
1½ teaspoons grated lemon rind
½ cup fresh lemon juice
⅛ teaspoon salt
½ cup sugar
½ teaspoon cream of tartar
½ cup whipping cream, whipped
1 9-inch graham cracker crust (page 301) or 1 (9-ounce) graham cracker crust (extra serving size)
Garnish: lemon slices

•Soften gelatin in ¼ cup cold water; set aside.
•Beat egg yolks until thick and pale. Combine yolks, sugar, and next 3 ingredients in a saucepan; stir until smooth.
•Cook over medium heat, stirring constantly, 5 to 8 minutes or until thickened. Remove from heat; add gelatin, and stir until gelatin granules dissolve. Cool.

•Combine egg whites, ½ cup sugar, and cream of tartar in top of a double boiler. Place over simmering water. Cook, stirring constantly with a wire whisk, 7 minutes or until mixture reaches 160°. Remove mixture from heat. Beat at high speed with an electric mixer 3 minutes or until soft peaks form.
•Fold egg white mixture and whipped cream into lemon mixture, and pour into graham cracker crust. Chill at least 2 hours. Garnish, if desired. Yield: 8 servings.
Per serving: Calories 341 Fat 12.8g
Cholesterol 127mg Sodium 197mg

Black Russian Pie

◄ MAKE AHEAD ►

PREP: 5 MINUTES   COOK: 4 MINUTES
CHILL: 30 MINUTES   FREEZE: 8½ HOURS

It's a takeoff on the Kahlúa and cream nightcap, White Russian—only this pie has a "black bottom" made from dark chocolate cookies.

14 cream-filled chocolate sandwich cookies, finely crushed
2 tablespoons butter or margarine, melted
24 large marshmallows
½ cup milk
⅛ teaspoon salt
⅓ cup Kahlúa
1 cup whipping cream, whipped
Garnish: semisweet chocolate curls

•Combine cookie crumbs and butter; stir well. Firmly press mixture in bottom and up sides of an 8-inch pieplate. Freeze 30 minutes or until firm.
•Combine marshmallows, milk, and salt in top of a double boiler; bring water to a boil. Reduce heat to low; cook until marshmallows melt, stirring occasionally. Cool 1 hour. Stir in Kahlúa. Gently fold whipped cream into marshmallow mixture. Chill 30 minutes; spoon into prepared crust. Cover and freeze 8 hours or until firm. Garnish, if desired. Yield: 6 servings.
Per serving: Calories 445 Fat 24.7g
Cholesterol 67mg Sodium 299mg

Ice Cream Pie with Butterscotch Sauce

PREP: 12 MINUTES   COOK: 20 MINUTES
FREEZE: 4 HOURS

1 cup graham cracker crumbs
½ cup finely chopped walnuts
¼ cup butter or margarine, melted
1 pint coffee ice cream, softened
1 pint vanilla ice cream, softened
Butterscotch Sauce

•Combine first 3 ingredients, mixing well; press mixture firmly into a buttered 9-inch pieplate. Bake at 375° for 8 to 10 minutes, and cool.
•Spoon coffee ice cream into cooled crust, and spread evenly; freeze until ice cream is almost firm.
•Spread vanilla ice cream over coffee layer; freeze until firm.
•To serve, slice pie, and drizzle each serving with warm Butterscotch Sauce. Yield: 8 servings.

Per serving: Calories 605 Fat 39.2g
Cholesterol 65mg Sodium 241mg

Butterscotch Sauce

3 tablespoons butter or margarine
1 cup firmly packed brown sugar
½ cup half-and-half
1 cup chopped walnuts, toasted
1 teaspoon vanilla extract

•Melt butter in a heavy saucepan over low heat; add brown sugar, and cook 5 to 8 minutes, stirring constantly.
•Remove from heat, and gradually stir in half-and-half. Cook 1 minute, and remove from heat. Stir in walnuts and vanilla. Yield: about 1½ cups.

NUT & VEGETABLE PIES

Sweet potatoes, pumpkin, pecans and other toasty nuts—these are the ingredients that make pies great. Recipes with these flavors go fast at family reunions and holiday celebrations, especially in the South. These types of pies keep well, and they're just as good the next day. And they all welcome a dollop of whipped cream on top.

With many nut pies, you can interchange or mix pecans, walnuts, and almonds. Experiment and find your favorite combination. Store most nuts in the refrigerator three months or in the freezer six months to a year. Walnuts will remain fresh frozen up to a year.

NUT KNOWLEDGE

•If you buy nuts already shelled, store them in airtight containers in the freezer or in a cool, dry place.
•Unsalted nuts have a longer storage life than salted nuts. Be sure to refrigerate after opening.
•The flavor of most nuts is enhanced when you toast them before use. You can toast a small amount of nuts in a dry skillet over medium heat for just a few minutes, stirring often. Use your sense of smell to judge when they're toasted.
•To remove the skins from hazelnuts, peanuts, and pistachios, spread them on a rimmed baking sheet and roast at 350° for 10 to 15 minutes; then rub off the skins.

Favorite Pecan Pie

PREP: 5 MINUTES   COOK: 58 MINUTES

Every great cook needs a reliable pecan pie recipe in his or her repertoire. Let this be it. And if you're ready for a twist, try the dark rum variation. Chopped pecans versus pecan halves are a personal preference. We let you decide.

½ cup butter or margarine, melted
1 cup sugar
1 cup light corn syrup
4 large eggs, beaten
1 teaspoon vanilla extract
¼ teaspoon salt
Pastry for 9-inch pie (page 299)
1⅓ cups pecan halves or 1¼ cups coarsely chopped pecans

•Combine first 3 ingredients; cook over low heat, stirring constantly, until sugar dissolves. Cool slightly. Add eggs, vanilla, and salt to mixture; mix well.
•Pour filling into unbaked pastry shell, and top with pecan halves. Bake at 325° for 55 minutes or until set. Serve warm or cold. Yield: 8 servings.

Per serving: Calories 615 Fat 33.9g
Cholesterol 140mg Sodium 564mg

Rum Pecan Pie: Prepare recipe as directed above, adding 3 tablespoons dark rum with the eggs; mix well.

Pecan Tassies

PREP: 15 MINUTES   CHILL: 2 HOURS
COOK: 25 MINUTES

Fill your mini muffin pans with these pecan-packed tartlets. They make a generous gift pack.

½ cup butter or margarine, softened
1 (3-ounce) package cream cheese, softened
1 cup all-purpose flour
1½ cups firmly packed brown sugar
2 tablespoons butter or margarine, melted
2 large eggs, lightly beaten
1 teaspoon vanilla extract
⅔ cup chopped pecans

•Beat softened butter and cream cheese at medium speed with an electric mixer until creamy. Gradually add flour, beating well. Cover and chill 2 hours.
•Shape dough into 30 (1-inch) balls; press balls into lightly greased miniature (1¾-inch) muffin pans. Set aside.
•Combine brown sugar and next 3 ingredients; stir well. Stir in pecans. Spoon 1 tablespoon pecan mixture into each pastry shell. Bake at 350° for 25 minutes. Remove from pans immediately, and cool completely on wire racks. Yield: 2½ dozen.

Per tassie: Calories 125 Fat 7.3g
Cholesterol 28mg Sodium 56mg

Crustless Brownie Pie

PREP: 9 MINUTES   COOK: 45 MINUTES

This recipe has all the best attributes of a fudgy brownie, except it bakes in a pieplate! You won't miss a crust, and the pie slices easily into wedges. If you'd like a gooey pie, bake it the lesser time.

1½ cups sugar
½ cup all-purpose flour
⅓ cup cocoa
½ cup butter or margarine, softened
3 large eggs
1 teaspoon vanilla extract
Pinch of salt
1 cup chopped pecans or walnuts
Whipped cream or ice cream

•Combine first 7 ingredients; beat 4 minutes at medium speed with an electric mixer. Stir in pecans. Spread batter evenly in a buttered 9-inch pieplate.
•Bake at 325° for 40 to 45 minutes. (Pie will puff and then fall slightly.) Serve with whipped cream. Yield: 8 servings.
Per serving: Calories 457 Fat 28.3g
Cholesterol 133mg Sodium 172mg

Butternut Squash Pie

PREP: 20 MINUTES

COOK: 1 HOUR AND 37 MINUTES

Ground red pepper enhances the other flavors in this fall pie.

1 (2-pound) butternut squash
¾ cup firmly packed brown sugar
1 teaspoon ground cinnamon
½ teaspoon ground allspice
½ teaspoon ground nutmeg
¼ teaspoon ground cloves
¼ teaspoon salt
⅛ teaspoon ground red pepper
1 (12-ounce) can evaporated milk
2 large eggs, beaten
Pastry for 9-inch pie (page 299)
½ cup whipping cream, whipped
¼ teaspoon ground cinnamon

•Cut squash in half lengthwise; remove seeds. Place squash, cut side down, in a

shallow pan; add hot water to pan to depth of ¾ inch. Cover with aluminum foil, and bake at 350° for 45 minutes or until tender; drain. Scoop out pulp; mash. Discard shell. Measure 1¼ cups pulp; reserve any remaining pulp for another use.
•Combine squash, brown sugar, and next 6 ingredients in a large bowl. Gradually stir in milk and eggs. Pour into pastry shell.
•Bake at 400° for 10 minutes; reduce heat to 350°, and bake 40 more minutes or until a knife inserted in center comes out clean. Cool on a wire rack. Cover and store in refrigerator. Serve topped with whipped cream; sprinkle with cinnamon. Yield: 8 servings.
Per serving: Calories 371 Fat 18.7g
Cholesterol 89mg Sodium 444mg

Pumpkin Pie

PREP: 6 MINUTES

COOK: 1 HOUR AND 5 MINUTES

The best pumpkin pies often have several spices in the filling. If you need a shortcut, use just allspice or cinnamon in this recipe. You'll need most of two cans of pumpkin here, too.

3 cups canned pumpkin
1 cup sugar
½ teaspoon salt
½ teaspoon ground ginger
½ teaspoon ground allspice
½ teaspoon ground nutmeg
½ teaspoon ground cinnamon
3 large eggs, lightly beaten
1 (12-ounce) can evaporated milk
Pastry for 10-inch pie (page 299)
Frozen whipped topping, thawed
    (optional)

•Combine first 9 ingredients in a large bowl, stirring well. Pour filling mixture into pastry shell in a 9½- or 10-inch deep-dish pieplate.
•Bake at 425° for 15 minutes; reduce heat to 350°, and bake 50 more minutes or until knife inserted near center comes out clean. Cover and store in refrigerator. Serve with whipped topping, if desired. Yield: 8 servings.
Per serving: Calories 392 Fat 16.4g
Cholesterol 93mg Sodium 442mg

Sweet Potato Pie

PREP: 7 MINUTES   COOK: 45 MINUTES

If you want to mash your own sweet potatoes for this spiced holiday pie, use 2 large potatoes (1½ pounds). See our note following the recipe for cooking and mashing the potatoes.

1 (14½-ounce) can mashed sweet potatoes
¾ cup evaporated milk
¾ cup firmly packed brown sugar
2 large eggs
1 tablespoon butter or margarine, melted
½ teaspoon salt
½ teaspoon ground ginger
½ teaspoon ground cinnamon
Pastry for 9-inch pie (page 299)

•Process first 8 ingredients in container of an electric blender until smooth, stopping once to scrape down sides. Pour mixture into pastry shell.
•Bake at 400° for 10 minutes. Reduce heat to 350°, and bake 35 more minutes or until a knife inserted in center comes out clean, shielding edges of crust with aluminum foil after 15 minutes to prevent excessive browning. Cover and store in refrigerator. Yield: 8 servings.
Per serving: Calories 340 Fat 13.2g
Cholesterol 67mg Sodium 509mg

Note: Substitute 2 large sweet potatoes for canned. Cut potatoes in half lengthwise; cook in boiling water to cover 30 to 45 minutes or until tender. Drain; cool and mash.

PIE FROM FRESH PUMPKIN

To bake fresh pumpkin for pumpkin pie, purchase a small cooking pumpkin that weighs about 4 pounds. Wash pumpkin, and cut in half crosswise. Place halves, cut side down, in a small roasting pan or on a 15- x 10-inch jellyroll pan. Bake at 325° for 45 minutes or until fork tender; cool 10 minutes. Peel pumpkin, and discard or roast seeds. Puree pulp in a food processor or mash thoroughly. Yield: about 3½ cups.

COBBLERS & OTHER COMFORT FOODS

Fruit cobblers, crisps, and apple dumplings all fall into the comfort food category. With bumpy or flaky tops and juicy centers, they're a bit more rustic than other desserts. And they aren't complete until you've topped them with big scoops of ice cream.

Slip a baking sheet or aluminum foil under a cobbler or any juicy fruit dessert when baking to catch any bubble-over.

Peach Cobbler

PREP: 30 MINUTES   COOK: 40 MINUTES

You'll pack a lot of peach slices into this cobbler. They'll cook down beneath golden rows of pastry.

8 cups sliced fresh peaches (about 5 pounds peaches)
2 cups sugar
¼ cup all-purpose flour
½ teaspoon ground nutmeg
1 teaspoon vanilla extract
⅓ cup butter or margarine
Pastry for double-crust 9-inch pie (page 300)

•Combine first 4 ingredients in a Dutch oven; set aside until syrup forms. Bring peach mixture to a boil; reduce heat to low, and cook 10 minutes or until tender. Remove from heat; add vanilla and butter, stirring until butter melts.
•Roll half of pastry to ⅛-inch thickness on a lightly floured surface; cut into a 9-inch square. Spoon half of peaches into a lightly buttered 9-inch square pan; top with pastry square.
•Bake at 475° for 12 minutes or until lightly browned. Spoon remaining peaches over baked pastry square.
•Roll remaining pastry to ⅛-inch thickness, and cut into 1-inch strips; arrange in lattice design over peaches. Bake 15 to 18 more minutes or until browned. Spoon into serving bowls, and top each with ice cream, if desired. Yield: 8 servings.
Per serving: Calories 608 Fat 25.5g
Cholesterol 22mg Sodium 377mg

Blackberry Cobbler

PREP: 12 MINUTES   COOK: 30 MINUTES

We loved the bumpy "cobbled" top on this juicy fruit dessert. You can use fresh or frozen berries.

5 cups fresh blackberries or 2 (14-ounce) packages frozen blackberries, thawed and drained*
1 cup sugar
3 to 4 tablespoons all-purpose flour
1 tablespoon lemon juice
Crust
2 tablespoons butter or margarine, melted
1 teaspoon sugar

•Combine first 4 ingredients; toss well. Spoon into a lightly greased 8- or 9-inch square pan.
•Prepare Crust, and spoon 9 mounds over blackberries. Brush with butter, and sprinkle with 1 teaspoon sugar.
•Bake, uncovered, at 425° for 30 minutes or until browned and bubbly. Serve warm with ice cream, if desired. Yield: 9 servings.
If you use frozen berries, increase the flour to ⅓ cup.
Per serving: Calories 334 Fat 11.5g
Cholesterol 19mg Sodium 288mg

Crust

1¾ cups all-purpose flour
1½ teaspoons baking powder
¾ teaspoon salt
3 tablespoons sugar
¼ cup shortening
⅓ cup whipping cream
⅓ cup buttermilk

•Combine first 4 ingredients; cut in shortening with a pastry blender until mixture is crumbly. Stir in whipping cream and buttermilk just until blended. Yield: enough topping for 1 cobbler.

Apple Dumplings

PREP: 25 MINUTES   COOK: 40 MINUTES

Wrap this classic apple dessert in a home-made pastry square and sprinkle with cinnamon and sugar.

3 cups all-purpose flour
2 teaspoons baking powder
1 teaspoon salt
1 cup shortening
¾ cup milk
3 large Granny Smith, Winesap, or other cooking apples
2 tablespoons butter or margarine
1 tablespoon sugar
1½ teaspoons ground cinnamon
1½ cups sugar
1 cup orange juice
½ cup water
1 tablespoon butter or margarine
¼ teaspoon ground cinnamon
¼ teaspoon ground nutmeg

•Combine first 3 ingredients; cut in shortening with a pastry blender until mixture is crumbly. Gradually add milk, stirring with a fork until dry ingredients are moistened. Shape into a ball. Roll pastry to ¼-inch thickness on a lightly floured surface, shaping into a 21- x 14-inch rectangle. Cut pastry into six 7-inch squares with a fluted pastry wheel.
•Peel and core apples; cut each in half crosswise. Place 1 apple half, cut side down, on each pastry square; dot each apple half with 1 teaspoon butter. Sprinkle each with ½ teaspoon sugar and ¼ teaspoon cinnamon.
•Moisten edges of each pastry square with water; bring corners to center, pressing edges to seal. Place dumplings in a lightly greased 13- x 9-inch baking dish. Bake at 375° for 35 minutes or until apples are tender and pastry is browned.
•Combine 1½ cups sugar and remaining 5 ingredients in a saucepan. Bring to a boil; reduce heat, and simmer, uncovered, 4 minutes or until butter melts and sugar dissolves, stirring occasionally. Pour syrup over dumplings, and serve warm. Yield: 6 servings.
Per serving: Calories 808 Fat 37.1g
Cholesterol 20mg Sodium 573mg

FRUIT DESSERT DICTIONARY

Betty: A fruit dessert topped with buttered breadcrumbs and then baked until golden.

Buckle: Tender cake generally baked with fresh berries inside or on the bottom of the cake.

Cobbler: A fruit dessert made with a top crust of pastry or biscuit dough, which can be either a single layer or cut into individual biscuits, or "cobbles," thus the name.

Crisp: A fruit dessert containing a mixture of sugar, flour, butter, and sometimes nuts that's sprinkled on top of the fruit and baked until "crisp."

Crumble: The English version of a crisp. It has a crunchier texture because oats are added to the flour, sugar, and butter mixture before baking.

Pandowdy: This dessert evolved from a cobbler made with very ripe fruit. It was so juicy that the crust was pushed down into the fruit to absorb the juices. This technique is called "dowdying."

Slump: Also called a *grunt*, this dessert's similar to a fruit cobbler but is cooked in a cast-iron skillet on the cooktop. A very thick biscuit dough is spooned on top of the simmering fruit. The names probably arose because the dish "slumps" on the plate and the fruit seems to "grunt" as it cooks.

Blueberry Buckle

◄ FAMILY FAVORITE ►

PREP: 10 MINUTES   COOK: 45 MINUTES

½ cup butter or margarine, softened
1 cup sugar, divided
1 large egg
1½ cups all-purpose flour, divided
1 teaspoon baking powder
¼ teaspoon salt
½ cup milk
1 teaspoon vanilla extract
2½ cups fresh blueberries
½ teaspoon ground cinnamon
¼ cup butter or margarine

• Beat ½ cup butter at medium speed with an electric mixer until creamy; gradually add ½ cup sugar, beating mixture well. Add egg, and beat well.
• Combine 1¼ cups flour, baking powder, and salt; add to butter mixture alternately with milk, beginning and ending with flour mixture, mixing well after each addition. Stir in vanilla.
• Pour batter into a greased 8-inch square baking dish. Top with blueberries.
• Combine remaining ½ cup sugar, remaining ¼ cup flour, and cinnamon. Cut in ¼ cup butter with a pastry blender until mixture is crumbly; sprinkle crumb topping evenly over blueberries.
• Bake at 375° for 40 to 45 minutes. Yield: 6 servings.

Per serving: Calories 508 Fat 25.6g
Cholesterol 100mg Sodium 411mg

Rhubarb Crumble

◄ HEALTHY ►

PREP: 7 MINUTES   COOK: 45 MINUTES

Make sure to pile a generous portion of the sweet and crunchy oat topping onto each serving of this sweet-tart crumble. It's a fine finale—with or without ice cream.

1 cup uncooked regular oats
⅔ cup firmly packed brown sugar
⅓ cup all-purpose flour
½ teaspoon ground cinnamon
⅓ cup butter or margarine
6 cups chopped rhubarb (1½ pounds)
1 cup sugar

• Combine first 4 ingredients; cut in butter with a pastry blender until mixture is crumbly.
• Combine rhubarb and sugar; toss gently, and place in a greased 8- or 9-inch square baking dish. Top rhubarb mixture with oats mixture.
• Bake at 350° for 45 minutes or until lightly browned. Serve with ice cream, if desired. Yield: 8 servings.

Per serving: Calories 309 Fat 8.9g
Cholesterol 21mg Sodium 89mg

CREAM PUFF PASTRIES

Cream puff paste, also called pâte à choux or choux pastry, is simply a dough of butter, flour, and eggs stirred vigorously on the cooktop and baked into delicate pastries. The high proportion of eggs in the rich dough causes the pastries to "puff" to great heights. The center dough is then removed, creating a tiny pastry bowl to hold a luscious filling.

Cream puffs and éclairs start from this same pastry, but they're different in shape. Both pastries are prettiest when piped from a pastry bag fitted with a large fluted tip, but you can also just spoon the dough onto a baking sheet if you'd rather. The piped pastry will be more shapely and the other more smooth.

When piping or spooning the dough onto the baking sheet, work quickly and take care to make all the puffs the same size so they'll bake evenly. Space the puffs several inches apart on the baking sheet so they'll have room to expand during baking.

After making the dough, spoon it out, and bake immediately. The longer you wait to bake cream puffs, the less they'll rise in the oven.

You can bake cream puffs a day ahead and store them in airtight containers. Just don't fill them more than a few hours before serving or they'll become soggy.

MAKING CREAM PUFF PASTE

1. When making cream puff paste, add flour and salt to butter mixture all at once, stirring vigorously.

2. Continue to stir vigorously until mixture leaves sides of the pan and forms a smooth ball.

3. Add eggs, one at a time, beating with a wooden spoon until dough is smooth after each addition.

Cream Puff Paste

◀ QUICK ▶

PREP: 10 MINUTES   COOK: 3 MINUTES

Also called pâte à choux, this pastry is the basis for many fabulous desserts such as the four that follow.

1 cup water
½ cup butter or margarine
1 cup all-purpose flour
⅛ teaspoon salt
4 large eggs

•Combine water and butter in a medium saucepan; bring to a boil. Add flour and salt, all at once (photo 1), stirring vigorously over medium-high heat until mixture leaves sides of pan and forms a smooth ball (photo 2). Remove from heat, and cool 4 to 5 minutes.
•Add eggs, one at a time, beating thoroughly with a wooden spoon after each addition (photo 3); then beat until dough is smooth. Shape and bake pastry immediately according to recipe directions. Yield: ten 2-inch cream puffs.

Per cream puff: Calories 153 Fat 11.3g
Cholesterol 110mg Sodium 148mg

Strawberry Cream Puffs

PREP: 15 MINUTES   COOK: 35 MINUTES

1 recipe Cream Puff Paste (left)
1 cup whipping cream
⅓ cup sifted powdered sugar
3 cups fresh strawberries, sliced
Garnish: mint leaves

•Drop Cream Puff Paste into 10 equal mounds 3 inches apart on an ungreased baking sheet. Bake at 400° for 30 to 35 minutes or until golden and puffed. Cool away from drafts. Cut top off each cream puff; pull out and discard soft dough inside.
•Beat whipping cream at medium speed with an electric mixer until foamy; gradually add powdered sugar, beating until soft peaks form. Fold three-fourths of sliced strawberries into whipped cream; fill cream puffs with strawberry mixture. Arrange remaining sliced strawberries on top. Replace tops of cream puffs. Garnish, if desired. Yield: 10 servings.

Per cream puff: Calories 245 Fat 18.9g
Cholesterol 129mg Sodium 140mg

Chocolate Éclairs

◀ FAMILY FAVORITE ▶

PREP: 30 MINUTES   COOK: 44 MINUTES

Éclairs have the same origin as cream puffs, only you shape the dough into rectangles.

1 recipe Cream Puff Paste (this page)
Pudding
Chocolate Frosting

•Drop Cream Puff Paste by level one-fourth cupfuls 2 inches apart onto ungreased baking sheets, shaping each portion into a 5- x 1½-inch rectangle. Bake at 400° for 40 minutes or until golden and puffed. Cool away from drafts.
•Cut top off each éclair; pull out and discard soft dough inside. Fill bottom halves with Pudding; cover with top halves. Spread Chocolate Frosting over tops. Yield: 8 servings.

Per éclair: Calories 427 Fat 22.7g
Cholesterol 166mg Sodium 242mg

Pudding

⅓ cup sugar
1½ tablespoons cornstarch
1½ cups milk
1 large egg, beaten
1 tablespoon butter or margarine
1 teaspoon vanilla extract

•Combine sugar and cornstarch in a heavy saucepan, stirring until blended. Gradually stir in milk, egg, and butter. Cook over medium heat until thickened and bubbly, stirring often. Cook 1 more minute. Remove from heat, and stir in vanilla. Cool completely. Yield: 2 cups.

Chocolate Frosting

2 tablespoons butter or margarine
¼ cup milk
½ cup (3 ounces) semisweet chocolate
   morsels
1½ to 2 cups sifted powdered sugar

•Combine butter and milk in a heavy saucepan; cook over medium heat, stirring constantly, until butter melts. Remove from heat. Add chocolate morsels, and beat until smooth; cool.
•Gradually stir in enough powdered sugar for spreading consistency. Yield: 1 cup.

Profiteroles

•Combine egg yolks and sugar in a heavy saucepan, stirring with a wire whisk until smooth. Add flour, and stir until blended; gradually stir in milk. Cook over medium heat, stirring constantly. (Mixture will appear to curdle; continue to stir and it will become smooth.) Reduce heat to medium-low when mixture thickens and begins to bubble. Continue to cook 3 more minutes, stirring constantly. Cool to lukewarm; stir in butter and vanilla. Cover and chill 2 hours. Yield: 2½ cups.

Croquembouche

PREP: 45 MINUTES   COOK: 45 MINUTES

This tower of tiny puffs filled with pastry cream and joined with caramel is a traditional wedding cake of France. Small silver tongs will make serving elegant and easy.

1 recipe Profiteroles with Crème Pâtissière (left)
2 cups sugar
½ cup water
¼ teaspoon cream of tartar

•Prepare cream puffs for profiteroles, but do not cut tops off. Pipe Crème Pâtissière through side of each cream puff, using a pastry bag with a long, narrow star tip (we used Ateco #862).
•Combine sugar, water, and cream of tartar in a heavy saucepan; cook over medium heat, without stirring, to hard-crack stage (310°). Remove from heat; cool 6 to 8 minutes or just until syrup is slightly thickened.
•Working quickly with tongs, dip bottom of each cream puff into hot sugar mixture. (Be careful not to touch hot sugar.) Position 9 cream puffs side by side on a serving platter to form a ring. Continue adding rings of cream puffs, reducing the number on each layer so that it forms a pyramid.
•Reheat sugar mixture over low heat, if necessary; cool slightly. Dip a fork into hot sugar mixture; let excess drip back into pan. When hot mixture begins to thread, quickly spin it over the croquembouche to form a thin cage. (There will be some caramelized sugar left over.) Yield: 4 dozen.

Per profiterole: Calories 94 Fat 4g
Cholesterol 70mg Sodium 40mg

FILLING PROFITEROLES

1. Cut top off each small puff; pull out and discard soft dough inside.

2. Spoon about 1 tablespoon of thick Crème Pâtissière into bottom half of each puff. Replace tops to serve.

Profiteroles

PREP: 55 MINUTES   COOK: 35 MINUTES
CHILL: 2 HOURS

Profiteroles are miniature cream puffs filled with a sweet or savory mixture. Three small puffs make a gracious dessert serving.

1 recipe Cream Puff Paste (previous page)
Crème Pâtissière
Chocolate Sauce (page 396)

•Drop Cream Puff Paste by rounded teaspoonfuls 2 inches apart on ungreased baking sheets. Bake at 400° for 25 minutes or until golden and puffed. Cool away from drafts.
•Cut top off each cream puff; pull out and discard soft dough inside (photo 1). Fill bottom halves with about 1 tablespoon Crème Pâtissière (photo 2), and cover with top halves. Arrange cream puffs on a serving platter, and drizzle with Chocolate Sauce. Serve immediately or cover and chill. Yield: 4 dozen.

Per profiterole: Calories 87 Fat 5.5g
Cholesterol 71mg Sodium 37mg

Crème Pâtissière

5 egg yolks
¾ cup sugar
½ cup all-purpose flour
2 cups milk
1 tablespoon butter or margarine, softened
2 teaspoons vanilla extract

PHYLLO

The paper-thin pastry called phyllo is best known for its use in the popular nut-filled and syrup-soaked dessert, baklava. Here the pastry sheets are layered, baked, and then sliced into diamonds that show off the characteristic flaky quality.

These days you don't have to venture very far to get a phyllo fix. The exotic tissue-thin layers of dough are showing up regularly in appetizers, entrées, and desserts in restaurants across the country. And packaged frozen phyllo dough has become increasingly easy to find in supermarkets. You can also find shredded phyllo called *kataifi* in some Greek markets. It bakes into a crispy nest, which you can fill with sweet or savory mixtures.

Because phyllo is so thin and fragile, it's important to handle it with proper care. Thaw phyllo in its package as the label directs, typically overnight. If used before completely thawed, the thin sheets may tear. Once opened, use phyllo within three days.

Work with only one sheet at a time; keep the remaining sheets covered with a damp towel. If phyllo is left uncovered, it will become brittle. Brush each sheet generously with melted butter; this makes the layers crisp upon baking.

You can keep frozen phyllo up to a year. If you refreeze thawed phyllo, wrap it well and know that the next time you use it, it will become drier and more brittle. Handle it with care.

Baklava

**PREP: 45 MINUTES   COOK: 50 MINUTES
STAND: 24 HOURS**

Use any combination of nuts listed in this recipe or use all of one kind for layering between the flaky pastry sheets.

1 (16-ounce) package frozen phyllo pastry, thawed
1 cup butter, melted
3 cups finely chopped or ground pecans, walnuts, pistachios, or almonds
¼ cup sugar
1½ teaspoons ground cinnamon
½ teaspoon ground nutmeg
Syrup

•Butter a 13- x 9-inch pan. Set aside.
•Cut phyllo in half crosswise, and cut each half to fit prepared pan; discard trimmings. Cover phyllo with a slightly damp towel.
•Layer 10 sheets of phyllo in pan, brushing each sheet with melted butter. Set aside.
•Combine nuts and next 3 ingredients; stir well. Sprinkle one-third of nut mixture over phyllo in pan; lightly drizzle with melted butter.
•Top nut mixture with 11 sheets of phyllo, brushing each sheet with melted butter. Repeat procedure twice with remaining nut mixture, phyllo, and butter, ending with buttered phyllo.
•Cut stack into diamond shapes, using a sharp knife. Bake at 350° for 45 minutes or until golden. Cool completely. Drizzle Syrup over Baklava. Cover and let stand at room temperature 24 hours. Yield: 3 dozen.
Per piece: Calories 185 Fat 13.1g
Cholesterol 14mg Sodium 110mg

Syrup

1 cup sugar
½ cup water
¼ cup honey

•Combine all ingredients in a medium saucepan, and bring to a boil. Reduce heat, and simmer, uncovered, 4 minutes. Yield: 1¼ cups.

Caramelized Onion, Fig, and Goat Cheese Strudel

**PREP: 8 MINUTES   STAND: 30 MINUTES
COOK: 33 MINUTES**

Put this savory strudel on a brunch buffet. It's slightly sweet and can double as a dessert or appetizer.

1 (8-ounce) package dried figs, diced
½ cup raisins
½ cup apricot nectar
⅓ cup honey
½ cup chopped purple onion
1 tablespoon butter or margarine, melted
1 tablespoon balsamic vinegar
1 (4-ounce) package goat cheese, crumbled
8 sheets frozen phyllo pastry, thawed
¼ cup butter, melted, or butter-flavored cooking spray
2 teaspoons powdered sugar

•Combine first 4 ingredients in a small saucepan; bring to a boil, and boil 5 minutes, stirring occasionally. Remove from heat; cover and let stand 30 minutes.
•Sauté onion in 1 tablespoon butter and vinegar 6 minutes or until onion is deep golden. Remove from heat; stir in fig mixture and cheese. Set aside.
•Place 1 sheet of phyllo on a damp towel (keep remaining phyllo covered). Brush phyllo with melted butter or cooking spray. Layer remaining phyllo sheets on top, brushing each sheet with butter or cooking spray.
•Spoon onion mixture lengthwise down half of phyllo stack, leaving a 2-inch border. Fold in short edges 2 inches. Roll up, starting at long edge nearest onion mixture, and place, seam side down, on a lightly greased baking sheet. Cut ¼-inch-deep diagonal slits, 1 inch apart, across top. Coat strudel with butter or cooking spray.
•Bake at 350° for 30 minutes or until lightly browned. Sprinkle lightly with powdered sugar. Let stand 10 minutes before slicing; serve warm. Yield: 8 servings.
Per serving: Calories 331 Fat 13g
Cholesterol 31mg Sodium 592mg

PUFF PASTRY

There's a definite technique and time frame involved in making puff pastry, but the results are well worth the time invested. Some of the most fabulous desserts are built on a billowy base of puff pastry.

Puff pastry may appear difficult to make, but it's not. The repetition of a simple rolling, folding, and chilling process creates alternating layers of dough and butter and ultimately gives the pastry dough its characteristic lightness when baked. Two hours of chilling are essential between each rolling and folding stage. Chilling keeps the butter firm and helps the layers rise evenly.

As you roll and fold the dough, dust it lightly with flour to prevent sticking. Add as little flour as possible. Excess flour toughens the pastry. After the rolling, folding, and chilling is completed, refrigerate the dough for a couple of days before shaping it. If storing it longer, wrap it in plastic wrap and freeze it in an airtight container up to two months. Thaw it in the refrigerator at least eight hours before using it.

Keep the dough smooth and level when rolling it out for final shaping; this will ensure even rising during baking. Baking sheets used for puff pastry are generally not greased. Just before baking, brush the pastry with beaten egg yolk to give it a golden shine; then freeze the pastry, uncovered, for 10 minutes to firm up the butter in the dough. Bake it immediately after removing from the freezer for the puffiest results.

Basic Puff Pastry

◄ MAKE AHEAD ►

PREP: 30 MINUTES

CHILL: 6 HOURS AND 20 MINUTES

¼ cup butter
1¾ cups all-purpose flour, chilled
½ cup cold water
¾ cup butter, softened
¼ cup all-purpose flour, chilled

•Cut ¼ cup butter into 1¾ cup flour with a pastry blender until mixture is crumbly. Sprinkle cold water, 1 tablespoon at a time, evenly over surface; stir with a fork until dry ingredients are moistened. Shape into a ball, and wrap in wax paper. Chill 15 minutes.
•Combine ¾ cup butter and ¼ cup flour; stir until smooth. Shape mixture into a 6-inch square on wax paper. Chill 5 minutes.
•Roll pastry into a 15-inch circle on a lightly floured surface; place chilled butter mixture in center of pastry. Fold left side of pastry over butter mixture; fold right side of pastry over left. Fold upper and lower edges of pastry over butter, making a thick square.
•Working quickly, place pastry, folded side down, on a lightly floured surface; roll pastry into a 20- x 8-inch rectangle. Fold rectangle into thirds, beginning with short side. Roll pastry into another 20- x 8-inch rectangle; again fold rectangle into thirds.
•Wrap pastry in wax paper, and chill about 2 hours.
•Repeat rolling, folding, and chilling process 2 times. Chill 2 hours. Yield: 8 servings.
Per serving: Calories 313 Fat 23.3g
Cholesterol 62mg Sodium 235mg

Puff Pastry Patty Shells

PREP: 10 MINUTES   COOK: 25 MINUTES

½ recipe Basic Puff Pastry (above)
1 large egg, beaten

•Roll Basic Puff Pastry to ⅜-inch thickness on a lightly floured surface. Cut pastry with a 3-inch cutter, cutting rounds as close together as possible to reduce scraps.

•Place rounds on an ungreased baking sheet. Using a 2-inch cutter, make an indentation about ¼ inch through center of pastry rounds, and lightly brush tops with beaten egg. Freeze 10 minutes.
•Preheat oven to 450°; place pastry in oven. Reduce heat to 400°, and bake 20 to 25 minutes or until puffed and golden. Remove to wire rack to cool. Remove centers of patty shells. Yield: 4 shells.
Per shell: Calories 331 Fat 24.6g
Cholesterol 115mg Sodium 251mg

Napoleons

◄ FAMILY FAVORITE ►

PREP: 40 MINUTES   COOK: 28 MINUTES

1 recipe Basic Puff Pastry (at left)
Napoleon Cream (next page)
1 cup sifted powdered sugar
1 teaspoon vanilla extract
1 tablespoon hot water
½ cup (3 ounces) semisweet chocolate morsels
1 teaspoon shortening

•Divide Basic Puff Pastry in half lengthwise. Roll each half into a 15- x 6-inch rectangle. Sprinkle two baking sheets with water; shake off excess water. Carefully transfer pastry to baking sheets.
•Prick pastry well with a fork. Trim sides with a sharp knife, if necessary, to make edges even. Freeze 10 minutes.
•Bake at 425° for 15 minutes or until pastry is puffed and golden. Gently remove pastry from baking sheets with spatulas, and cool on wire racks.
•Trim sides of pastry again, if necessary, to make edges even. Carefully split each layer in half horizontally, using a long serrated knife. Set aside the prettiest bottom layer for top of Napoleon.
•Place 1 pastry strip on serving platter, browned side down; spread evenly with one-third of Napoleon Cream. Repeat layering twice. Top with reserved bottom layer, browned side up.
•Combine powdered sugar, vanilla, and water; spoon glaze over top pastry layer, spreading evenly.

- Combine chocolate and shortening in top of a double boiler; bring water to a boil. Reduce heat to low; cook until chocolate melts. Cool slightly.
- Spoon chocolate into a decorating bag fitted with metal No. 2. Pipe 5 lengthwise strips of chocolate evenly across top of glaze. Pull a wooden pick crosswise through chocolate at ¾-inch intervals, reversing the pulling direction each time.
- Refrigerate 30 minutes before serving. To serve, cut into 1½-inch crosswise slices, using a serrated knife. Yield: 10 servings.

Per serving: Calories 472 Fat 27.3g
Cholesterol 152mg Sodium 219mg

Napoleon Cream

¾ cup sugar
¼ cup cornstarch
⅛ teaspoon salt
1½ cups milk
4 egg yolks
1½ teaspoons vanilla extract
½ cup whipping cream, whipped

- Combine first 3 ingredients in a heavy saucepan, stirring until blended. Stir in milk. Cook over low heat, stirring constantly, until mixture is thickened.
- Beat egg yolks until thick and pale. Gradually stir about one-fourth of hot mixture into yolks; add to remaining hot mixture, stirring mixture constantly. Cook, stirring constantly, until mixture thickens. Remove from heat, and stir in vanilla.
- Cover filling with a sheet of wax paper, and chill thoroughly. Gently fold whipped cream into chilled filling. Yield: 2½ cups.

PUFF PASTRY OPTION

You don't have to use our Basic Puff Pastry recipe for successful results with the recipes on these pages. You can substitute a 17¼-ounce package of frozen puff pastry for one recipe of our homemade pastry. Just thaw pastry according to package directions. Two sheets come in a package.

Strawberry Tart

PREP: 20 MINUTES   COOK: 15 MINUTES
CHILL: 10 MINUTES

This rectangular tart houses rows of fresh berries and has a flaky puff pastry bottom.

½ (17¼-ounce) package frozen puff pastry, thawed
1 egg yolk
1 teaspoon water
⅔ cup sugar
2½ tablespoons cornstarch
¾ cup lemon-lime soft drink
Few drops of red food coloring
1½ pints whole strawberries
Garnish: fresh mint sprigs

- Roll pastry into a 14½- x 7½-inch rectangle. Sprinkle a baking sheet with water, and shake off excess water. Place pastry on baking sheet.
- Cut a ¾-inch-wide strip from each long side of pastry. Brush strips with water, and place them, moist side down, on top of each long side of pastry rectangle, edges flush together. Repeat procedure on short sides of rectangle, trimming away excess pastry at corners. Prick pastry generously with a fork, excluding the border.
- Combine egg yolk and 1 teaspoon water; brush border of pastry with egg mixture. Freeze 10 minutes. Bake at 425° for 10 to 12 minutes or until puffed and golden. Gently remove pastry from baking sheet, and cool completely on a wire rack.
- Meanwhile, combine sugar and cornstarch in a saucepan; gradually stir in soft drink. Cook over medium heat, stirring constantly, 15 minutes or until smooth and thickened. Stir in food coloring.
- Transfer pastry shell to a serving platter. Wash strawberries; remove stems. Arrange strawberries in pastry shell, stem end down. Brush glaze over berries. Cover and chill. Garnish, if desired. Yield: 8 servings.

Per serving: Calories 240 Fat 11.3g
Cholesterol 62mg Sodium 168mg

Cream Horns

PREP: 40 MINUTES   COOK: 22 MINUTES

½ recipe Basic Puff Pastry (previous page)
1 egg yolk
1 teaspoon water
¾ cup whipping cream
3 tablespoons powdered sugar
1 teaspoon grated chocolate

- Roll Basic Puff Pastry into a 15- x 9-inch rectangle. Cut into 9 (15- x 1-inch) strips. Starting at tip of mold, wrap 1 strip around an ungreased 4-inch metal cream horn mold, winding strip, spiral fashion, and overlapping edges about ¼ inch. Place on a lightly greased baking sheet, end of strip down. Repeat with remaining strips. Combine egg yolk and water; brush over entire pastry. Freeze 10 minutes.
- Bake at 425° for 10 to 12 minutes or until puffed and golden. Remove from oven, and gently slide molds from pastry. Turn oven off. Return pastry to oven 10 minutes. Remove from oven, and cool completely on a wire rack.
- Beat whipping cream and powdered sugar at medium speed with an electric mixer until soft peaks form. Spoon whipped cream into a decorating bag fitted with metal tip No. 4B. Pipe whipped cream into pastry horns. Sprinkle grated chocolate over tops of cream horns. Cover and chill until ready to serve. Yield: 9 servings.

Per serving: Calories 229 Fat 18.8g
Cholesterol 79mg Sodium 113mg

Roast Turkey with Herbs (page 343)

POULTRY

Poultry is a popular pick for the dinner table, and for many, this means several times a week. Americans celebrate chicken's high-protein and low-fat content as well as its versatility in cooking. Go beyond crispy Southern fried chicken and the Thanksgiving turkey; expand your poultry panache with grilled Cornish hens, panbraised dove, and sage-smoked quail for starters.

Equipment

A good sharp boning knife, poultry shears, and a large cutting board will serve you well if you plan to cut up whole chickens. A roasting pan and meat thermometer are essential when roasting a bird. Vertical roasting racks are popular as a naturally low-fat cooking rack. They're inexpensive and are sold at most kitchen shops. A wok is another economical piece of equipment that can produce a one-dish dinner in mere minutes. Use nonmetal utensils to protect the wok's surface.

Poultry Primer

White meat of poultry has less fat than dark meat; dark meat has less fat than many cuts of red meat. Small chickens such as broiler-fryers are leaner than roasters, and roasters are leaner than hens and capons. Most of the fat in poultry comes from the skin and pockets of fat under the skin. You can remove the skin and cut away excess fat before or after cooking. With fat, however, comes flavor. Some fat will naturally be rendered during cooking if you leave the skin intact. It's up to the personal preferences of each cook as well as a recipe's instructions.

The neck and giblets (liver, heart, and gizzard) are usually packaged separately and placed in the bird's body and neck cavities. They're also sold individually. When cooking a whole bird, remove the packages from cavities before cooking.

Determine the type of poultry you buy by how you want to cook it. If your recipe calls for cut-up chicken or assorted pieces, you can cut up a broiler-fryer yourself, buy it precut, or take advantage of packaged chicken "parts," buying all legs or thighs if dark meat is your preference, or all breasts if white meat is your choice.

Aside from chicken pieces, you can buy whole birds to serve two or 20. The average-size Cornish game hen weighs 1½ pounds; a plump turkey can weigh 20 pounds or more. Choose the size bird and recipe which best suits your needs.

Domesticated birds commonly found at the meat counter of most supermarkets are as follows:

Cornish hens are one of the smallest members of the poultry family, weighing from 1 to 2 pounds. They're often split when cooked on the grill. One bird typically serves one, but larger or stuffed hens can be split to serve two people.

Petit Poussin is French for a very young, small chicken weighing no more than 1½ pounds. It's best grilled or broiled.

The *broiler-fryer* is the most commonly purchased whole bird, ranging from 2 to 4 pounds. This economical all-purpose bird can be cooked by just about any method, from roasting or grilling to stewing. A 3-pound broiler-fryer yields four to six servings or about 3 cups chopped cooked chicken.

Roasters are slightly larger than broiler-fryers; they weigh from 4 to 6 pounds. They are higher in fat than fryers, too, which makes them ideal for ovenroasting and rotisserie cooking. The cooked chicken is flavorful in salads, soups, and casseroles.

Hens or stewing chickens range from 3 to 8 pounds. They're flavorful mature birds, but less tender. Moist-heat cooking such as stewing or braising suits these tougher birds.

A *capon* is a rooster that has been castrated while very young. It weighs from 4 to 10 pounds and is full-breasted with flavorful meat particularly suited to roasting.

Free-range or *free-roaming* chickens are not necessarily organic chickens, but they are chickens that have been allowed access to the outside. They're fed a special vegetarian diet, and they have more freedom of movement than chickens that are mass produced. These added amenities can cause free-range birds to cost more. They weigh 4 to 5 pounds typically.

Ducklings have a lower proportion of meat to bone than most poultry. They weigh from 3 to 6 pounds. Plan on 1 pound per serving. Ducklings are commonly available in the frozen meat section.

TIMETABLE FOR ROASTING POULTRY

KIND OF POULTRY	READY TO COOK WEIGHT IN POUNDS	OVEN TEMPERATURE	INTERNAL TEMPERATURE (IN THIGH)	APPROXIMATE TOTAL ROASTING TIME IN HOURS
Chicken (unstuffed)*	2 to 2½	375°	180°	¾ to 1
	2½ to 3	375°	180°	1 to 1¼
	3 to 4	375°	180°	1¼ to 1¾
	4 to 5	375°	180°	1¾ to 2
Capon (unstuffed)	4 to 7	325°	180°	1¾ to 2½
Cornish hen (stuffed)	1 to 1½	375°	180°	1 to 1¼
Duckling (unstuffed)	3½ to 5½	325°	180°	2 to 2¾
Goose (unstuffed)	7 to 9	350°	180°	2 to 2½
	9 to 11	350°	180°	2½ to 3
	11 to 13	350°	180°	3 to 3½
Turkey (unstuffed)*	8 to 12	325°	180°	2¾ to 3
	12 to 14	325°	180°	3 to 3¾
	14 to 18	325°	180°	3¾ to 4¼
	18 to 20	325°	180°	4¼ to 4½
	20 to 24	325°	180°	4½ to 5

* Stuffed chickens and turkeys require about 5 additional minutes per pound.

Geese range from 6 to 15 pounds, and they, too, have a lower proportion of meat to bone. Look for them in the frozen meat section.

Turkeys, the largest domestic birds, range from 5 to 30 pounds. Count on one serving per pound of turkey. So if you buy a 12-pound turkey, it will serve 12 people. Turkeys are available year-round in the frozen meat section and fresh during the holiday season.

Buying and Storing Poultry

Fresh poultry is highly perishable. When shopping, check the "sell by" date and choose the freshest product available. It should look and smell fresh. Never purchase poultry with an off odor or skin that looks dry. Poultry skin should be smooth and soft. Chicken with yellow skin is no more or less nutritious than chicken with cream-colored skin. Skin color is due to the type of feed the chicken is given.

Pick up poultry items last, and make sure they're bagged separately from other food at the checkout counter. Juices from raw poultry should not touch other foods. As soon as possible, store poultry well-wrapped in plastic wrap in the coldest part of your refrigerator. It will keep up to two days. Most cooked chicken or turkey can be refrigerated up to four days after preparation; however, cooked ground chicken and chicken in gravy should be used within two days.

Freezing Poultry

You can freeze properly packaged poultry parts up to nine months and a whole bird up to a year. Freeze giblets and ground chicken up to four months. For best results, remove poultry from its packaging, rinse, and pat dry. Wrap poultry tightly in heavy-duty plastic wrap or freezer paper. Label and date the package before freezing.

Freeze cooked poultry dishes four to six months. First cool the dish in the refrigerator and then wrap securely and freeze. Avoid freezing poultry dishes that contain mayonnaise or hard-cooked egg; these items will suffer a loss of quality in the freezing process. And never refreeze chicken that has been thawed.

Safe Poultry Pointers

Always rinse chicken before cooking, and use a clean knife and cutting board. Wash your hands, knife, and cutting board with hot, soapy water immediately after use to prevent cross-contamination with other foods.

The safest place to thaw poultry is in the refrigerator. To safely thaw frozen poultry more quickly, place the wrapped package in a large bowl of cold water and allow it to stand at room temperature 30 minutes. Change the water and repeat the process until the poultry is thawed. Never leave a package of poultry sitting on the counter to thaw—bacteria thrive at room temperature.

Cook thawed chicken or turkey immediately or refrigerate it until cooking time. Cooked chicken should always be well done, never medium or rare. The most accurate way to determine doneness is to use a meat thermometer. When inserted into meaty part of poultry thigh, thermometer should register 180°. If you're cooking a turkey or chicken breast, the thermometer should register 170°. Juices from cooked poultry should run clear when the meat is pierced with a fork.

Never place cooked chicken or other poultry on the same platter that held the uncooked meat. And don't leave cooked poultry at room temperature more than 1 hour. Chicken salad is safe to take on a picnic as long as it's packed on ice in a cooler.

Never refrigerate a raw or cooked whole bird with stuffing inside the body or neck cavities because of the risk of increased bacterial growth. Instead, store the bird and stuffing separately. Read more on stuffing versus dressing on page 341.

BROILER-FRYERS

A broiler-fryer is perhaps the most economical form of chicken you can buy. These pages offer dozens of recipes using whole fryers as well as assorted pieces. When buying whole chickens, always choose a meaty, full-breasted bird with plump short legs.

For many chicken recipes you can substitute one cut for another. Just remember that bone-in chicken pieces require longer cooking times than boneless pieces. See our detailed definitions below for help in the supermarket.

A *cut-up chicken* is a broiler-fryer conveniently cut into pieces; two breast halves, two thighs, two drumsticks, and two wings. Some producers offer a popular combination package of three breast halves, three thighs, and three drumsticks.

A package of *chicken halves* or *splits* contains two halves of a broiler-fryer. These are ideal for outdoor grilling.

Chicken *breast quarters* and *leg quarters* are often packaged separately. A breast quarter is all white meat and includes the wing, breast, and back portion. The leg quarter is all dark meat and includes a drumstick, thigh, and back portion. Each chicken quarter usually yields one serving.

The chicken *breast half* or *split breast* is the leanest cut of chicken. Purchase four chicken breast halves with bone and skin or four skinned, boned chicken breast halves for four servings. Two chicken breast halves will yield about 1 cup chopped cooked chicken.

The *chicken leg* is all dark meat and includes the whole leg with unseparated drumstick and thigh. One chicken leg is considered a serving. It's sometimes called a *chicken leg quarter.*

The *drumstick* is the lower portion of the chicken leg. Two drumsticks make a serving.

The *thigh* is that portion of the leg above the knee joint. It's usually packaged with skin and bone intact. Skinned, boned thighs are also available and can typically be substituted for skinned, boned chicken breast halves. You may have to cook thighs a little longer, though. Plan on one or two thighs for each serving.

The *wing* contains three sections and is all white meat. A *drummette* is the meaty first section of the wing and is often used as an hors d'oeuvre.

Ground chicken is typically made from skinned, boned chicken thighs. It's a great alternative to ground beef in meat loaf, soups, or sandwiches. You can also ask your butcher to grind skinned, boned chicken breasts for a leaner white meat grind. One pound of ground chicken yields four servings.

In addition to these choices, you can also purchase *chicken tenders, nuggets, patties* and other semi-prepared (marinated) and frozen chicken products. *Canned* chicken is another option for busy cooks. Just keep in mind that it tends to be high in sodium.

Roasted Lemon-Herb Chicken

PREP: 7 MINUTES   COOK: 45 MINUTES

Let this simple roasted chicken be the centerpiece for an easy dinner. Just squeeze lemon over the bird and rub with seasonings; then baste once or twice while it's in the oven. Add some chunks of vegetables to roast alongside the chicken during the last 30 minutes.

1 large lemon
1 (3- to 3½-pound) broiler-fryer
Several sprigs fresh thyme*
1 tablespoon olive oil
1 tablespoon lemon-pepper seasoning
1 tablespoon chopped fresh thyme*

•Cut lemon in half, and squeeze juice over chicken. Put lemon halves and thyme sprigs in body cavity of chicken. Brush chicken with olive oil; rub chicken with seasoning and chopped thyme. Place chicken, breast side up, on a greased rack in broiler pan or on a vertical roasting rack.
•Roast at 400° for 45 minutes or until a meat thermometer inserted in thigh registers 180°, basting occasionally with pan drippings. Yield: 4 servings.
If you don't have fresh thyme, use rosemary or oregano.
Per serving: Calories 402 Fat 24.7g
Cholesterol 132mg Sodium 1003mg

Citrus-Glazed Chicken

PREP: 23 MINUTES   MARINATE: 8 HOURS
COOK: 1½ HOURS

This chicken acquires a dark brown glaze during baking. Fresh fruit really makes a flavor difference in this marinade as well as an easy, colorful garnish.

1 medium onion, sliced
8 cloves garlic, minced
¼ cup olive oil
½ cup fresh orange juice
⅓ cup fresh lime juice
3 tablespoons dry white wine or chicken broth
1 teaspoon sugar
1 teaspoon salt
¼ teaspoon pepper
1 teaspoon white vinegar
1 (3- to 3½-pound) broiler-fryer
Garnishes: lime slices, orange slices, fresh cilantro sprigs

•Sauté onion and garlic in hot oil in a saucepan over medium-high heat 2 minutes. Add orange juice and next 6 ingredients to pan. Bring mixture to a boil. Remove from heat, and cool. Reserve ¼ cup marinade in refrigerator.
•Place chicken in a heavy-duty, zip-top plastic bag or shallow dish. Pour remaining marinade over chicken. Seal or cover, and marinate in refrigerator 8 hours, turning chicken occasionally.
•Remove chicken from marinade, discarding marinade. Pat chicken dry with paper towels. Place chicken on a lightly greased rack in broiler pan.
•Bake at 400° for 15 minutes; reduce heat to 350°, and bake 1 hour and 15 minutes or until a meat thermometer inserted in thigh registers 180°, basting with reserved ¼ cup marinade. Cover chicken with aluminum foil after 1 hour to prevent excessive browning. Place chicken on a serving platter. Garnish, if desired. Yield: 4 servings.
Per serving: Calories 435 Fat 26.8g
Cholesterol 132mg Sodium 360mg

Crispy Herbed Chicken

PREP: 25 MINUTES

COOK: 1 HOUR AND 5 MINUTES

The key to this crispy-skinned chicken is to baste it well with a butter mixture before it goes in the oven but not at all during roasting.

⅓ cup chopped onion
⅓ cup scraped, diced carrot
⅓ cup diced celery
1 tablespoon chopped fresh parsley
3 tablespoons dry white wine
1 (3- to 3½-pound) broiler-fryer
¼ cup butter or margarine, melted
2 teaspoons chopped fresh basil
2 teaspoons chopped fresh oregano
2 teaspoons chopped fresh thyme
½ teaspoon salt
¼ teaspoon pepper
Garnishes: fresh basil, oregano, and thyme sprigs

•Combine first 5 ingredients; toss gently. Set aside. Remove giblets and neck from chicken; reserve for another use. Rinse chicken; pat dry with paper towels. Lightly stuff body cavity with reserved vegetable mixture. If desired, tie ends of legs together with heavy string. Lift wingtips up and over back of chicken, tucking wingtips under chicken.
•Place chicken, breast side up, on a rack in a shallow roasting pan. Combine butter and next 5 ingredients. Brush chicken with butter mixture. Roast at 375° for 1 hour or until a meat thermometer inserted in thigh registers 180°. Place chicken on a serving platter. Garnish, if desired. Yield: 4 servings.
Per serving: Calories 438 Fat 29.1g
Cholesterol 156mg Sodium 434mg

Crispy Herbed Chicken with Garlic: Cut 2 heads of garlic in half; drizzle with 1 tablespoon olive oil. Place on rack next to chicken to roast. To serve, spread soft roasted garlic onto bread that accompanies meal.

Chicken Tetrazzini

PREP: 30 MINUTES

COOK: 1 HOUR AND 50 MINUTES

Tetrazzini is said to have been named for an opera singer. A wine and Parmesan cheese sauce adds the top note to this chicken spaghetti.

1 (3- to 3½-pound) broiler-fryer*
1 teaspoon salt
1 teaspoon pepper
1 (8-ounce) package dried spaghetti or linguine
1 cup sliced fresh mushrooms
1 large green pepper, chopped
1 small onion, chopped
¼ cup butter or margarine, melted
¼ cup all-purpose flour
½ teaspoon salt
½ teaspoon garlic powder
½ teaspoon poultry seasoning
½ teaspoon pepper
1 cup half-and-half
2 cups (8 ounces) shredded sharp Cheddar cheese, divided
1 (10¾-ounce) can cream of mushroom soup, undiluted
¾ cup grated Parmesan cheese, divided
¼ cup dry sherry
1 (4-ounce) jar sliced pimiento, drained
1 teaspoon paprika
¾ cup sliced almonds, toasted

•Place broiler-fryer in a Dutch oven; add water to cover. Add 1 teaspoon salt and 1 teaspoon pepper, and bring to a boil. Cover, reduce heat, and simmer 1 hour or until chicken is tender. Remove chicken from broth, reserving broth. Let chicken cool to touch. Bone and shred chicken.
•Add enough water to reserved broth to measure 3 quarts. Bring to a boil. Cook spaghetti in broth according to package directions. Drain.
•Sauté sliced mushrooms, green pepper, and onion in butter in a Dutch oven over medium heat until tender. Add flour and next 4 ingredients; stir until smooth. Cook 1 minute, stirring constantly. Gradually stir in half-and-half, and cook until mixture is thickened, stirring gently. Add ¾ cup Cheddar cheese, stirring until cheese melts. Add shredded

Crispy Herbed Chicken with Garlic

chicken, mushroom soup, ½ cup Parmesan cheese, sherry, and pimiento; stir well.

•Combine chicken mixture and spaghetti, tossing until combined. Spread mixture in a greased 13- x 9-inch baking dish.

•Bake, uncovered, at 350° for 20 to 25 minutes or until thoroughly heated. Combine remaining ¼ cup Parmesan cheese and 1 teaspoon paprika; stir well. Sprinkle remaining 1¼ cups Cheddar cheese in diagonal rows across top of casserole. Repeat procedure with almonds and Parmesan-paprika mixture. Bake 5 more minutes or until Cheddar cheese melts. Yield: 6 servings.

If you'd like to use leftover chopped cooked chicken, you'll need 3 to 3¼ cups. You'll need 3 quarts of chicken broth (or boiling salted water) to cook the spaghetti.

Per serving: Calories 822 Fat 47.2g
Cholesterol 170mg Sodium 1462mg

Country-Style Chicken and Dumplings

PREP: 30 MINUTES   COOK: 2 HOURS

This old-style recipe features rolled (or slick) dumplings.

1 (3- to 3½-pound) broiler-fryer
2 quarts water
1 carrot, halved
1 stalk celery, halved
1 medium onion, quartered
¾ teaspoon salt
½ teaspoon pepper
2 cups all-purpose flour
2 teaspoons baking powder
1 teaspoon salt
⅓ cup shortening

•Combine first 7 ingredients in a Dutch oven. Bring to a boil; cover, reduce heat, and simmer 1 hour or until chicken is tender. Remove chicken and vegetables from broth, discarding vegetables and reserving broth in Dutch oven. Skim fat from broth, if desired. Reserve and set aside ⅔ cup broth. Let chicken cool. Skin, bone, and coarsely chop chicken; return to broth in Dutch oven.

•Combine flour, baking powder, and 1 teaspoon salt; cut in shortening with a pastry blender until mixture is crumbly. Add reserved ⅔ cup broth, stirring with a fork just until dry ingredients are moistened. Turn dough out onto a lightly floured surface, and knead lightly 1 to 2 minutes. Roll dough to ⅛-inch thickness; cut dough into 2-inch squares or 2- x ¾-inch strips.

•Bring broth mixture in Dutch oven to a boil; drop dumplings, one at a time, into boiling broth. Cover, reduce heat, and simmer 25 to 30 minutes. Yield: 6 servings.

Per serving: Calories 395 Fat 16.2g
Cholesterol 79mg Sodium 857mg

Note: You can substitute a 5-pound hen for the broiler-fryer, if desired, simmering 1½ hours or until meat is tender.

Creamy Chicken Casserole

PREP: 9 MINUTES

COOK: 1 HOUR AND 35 MINUTES

1 (3½-pound) broiler-fryer*
1 quart water
1 teaspoon salt
1 teaspoon pepper
1 bay leaf
1 (10¾-ounce) can cream of chicken soup with herbs, undiluted
1 (10¾-ounce) can cream of celery soup, undiluted
1 (8-ounce) carton sour cream
½ teaspoon pepper
½ (16-ounce) package oval-shaped buttery crackers, crushed (2 stacks) (3 cups)
¼ cup butter or margarine, melted

•Combine first 5 ingredients in a large Dutch oven; bring to a boil. Reduce heat, and simmer, uncovered, 1 hour or until tender. Remove chicken, and cool slightly. (Reserve broth for another use.)

•Skin and bone chicken; cut chicken into bite-size pieces. Combine chicken, chicken soup, and next 3 ingredients, stirring well.

•Place half of crushed crackers in a lightly greased 11- x 7-inch baking dish; spoon chicken mixture over crackers. Top chicken mixture with remaining crackers, and drizzle with butter.

•Bake, uncovered, at 325° for 35 minutes or until lightly browned. Yield: 6 servings.

If you'd rather use leftover chopped cooked chicken, you'll need 3¼ cups.

Per serving: Calories 619 Fat 37.8g
Cholesterol 136mg Sodium 1371mg

No-Bake Chicken Spaghetti

PREP: 30 MINUTES

COOK: 2 HOURS AND 5 MINUTES

1 (6- to 6½-pound) hen or 2 (3-pound) broiler-fryers*
3 quarts water
1 (12-ounce) package dried spaghetti, broken in half
1½ cups chopped onion
1 cup chopped green pepper
1 cup chopped celery
1 (16-ounce) loaf process American cheese, shredded
1 (6-ounce) jar sliced mushrooms, drained
1 (4-ounce) jar diced pimiento, drained
½ teaspoon salt
½ teaspoon pepper

•Combine hen and water in a large Dutch oven. Bring to a boil; cover, reduce heat, and simmer 1½ hours or until hen is tender. (If cooking 2 broiler-fryers instead of hen, reduce cooking time to 1 hour.) Remove hen from broth, reserving broth. Let hen cool.

•Skin, bone, and chop chicken. Skim fat from broth. Reserve 6 cups broth. Reserve remaining broth for another use, if desired.

•Bring 5 cups reserved broth to a boil in Dutch oven; add spaghetti and next 3 ingredients. Cook, uncovered, 10 minutes or until spaghetti is tender; drain.

•Combine chopped chicken, remaining 1 cup reserved broth, spaghetti mixture, cheese, and remaining ingredients in Dutch oven; cook, stirring constantly, over low heat until cheese melts and mixture is thoroughly heated. Yield: 8 servings.

If you'd rather use leftover chopped cooked chicken, you'll need 4 to 5 cups. You'll also need 6 cups chicken broth.

Per serving: Calories 690 Fat 30.9g
Cholesterol 195mg Sodium 1250mg

Oven-Fried Chicken

PREP: 14 MINUTES   COOK: 45 MINUTES

You might enjoy this alternative to fried chicken more than you think. The crispiness comes from a corn flake coating and a high oven temperature.

3 cups corn flakes cereal, crushed (about 1 cup)
⅓ cup grated Parmesan cheese
1 teaspoon salt
¼ teaspoon garlic powder
¼ teaspoon pepper
1 (2½- to 3-pound) package assorted chicken pieces, skinned
½ cup butter or margarine, melted

•Combine first 5 ingredients in a large heavy-duty, zip-top plastic bag; seal and shake well.
•Dip chicken pieces in butter, 2 at a time, and place in bag. Seal and shake to coat chicken completely. Remove chicken, and repeat with remaining chicken pieces.
•Place chicken on a lightly greased 15- x 10-inch jellyroll pan; sprinkle remaining corn flake crumbs over chicken pieces. Bake, uncovered, at 400° for 45 minutes or until done. Serve hot. Yield: 4 servings.

Per serving: Calories 439 Fat 20.2g
Cholesterol 173mg Sodium 1227mg

Dixie Fried Chicken

PREP: 10 MINUTES   COOK: 20 MINUTES

1 (2½- to 3-pound) broiler-fryer, cut up, or 2½ pounds assorted chicken pieces
½ teaspoon salt
⅛ teaspoon black pepper
2 cups all-purpose flour
1 teaspoon ground red pepper
1 large egg, lightly beaten
½ cup milk
Vegetable oil
Cream Gravy (page 395)

•Season chicken with salt and black pepper. Combine flour and red pepper; set aside. Combine egg and milk; dip chicken in egg mixture, and dredge in flour mixture, coating chicken well.

CUTTING UP A WHOLE CHICKEN

1. Remove leg-thigh portion by cutting between thigh and body. Twist thigh to break hip joint. Cut through joint.

2. Separate drumstick and thigh by cutting through meat at knee joint; break joint, and cut two pieces apart.

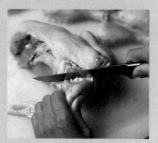

3. Remove wings by cutting through skin and joint on inside of wings.

4. Using kitchen or poultry shears, cut through ribcage along backbone. Reserve bony back portion for broth.

5. Split breast into two breast halves by cutting along breastbone.

6. Cutting up your own chicken gives you these 8 pieces—2 breasts, 2 thighs, 2 drumsticks, and 2 wings.

•Pour oil to depth of 1 inch in a heavy 10- to 12-inch skillet; heat to 350°. Fry chicken in hot oil over medium heat 15 to 20 minutes or until golden, turning occasionally. (Remove small pieces earlier, if necessary, to prevent overbrowning.) Drain chicken on paper towels. Serve with Cream Gravy. Yield: 4 servings.

Per serving: Calories 924 Fat 54.1g
Cholesterol 199mg Sodium 835mg

BRINING

Brining a chicken (soaking it in a salt-water solution) produces crispy skin and tender meat. Use this procedure on any whole bird or chicken pieces to be fried as the first step of preparation. To brine a bird, dissolve ¾ cup salt in 3 quarts water in a large pot. Soak chicken in solution 2 hours in refrigerator. Remove chicken, rinse and pat dry. Then proceed as recipe directs.

Spicy Fried Chicken

PREP: 13 MINUTES   MARINATE: 8 HOURS
COOK: 20 MINUTES

Red pepper and hot sauce kick up the heat in the coating for this crispy chicken.

2 cups buttermilk
1 teaspoon salt
1 teaspoon ground red pepper
1 teaspoon freshly ground black pepper
1 to 2 teaspoons hot sauce
1 (2½- to 3-pound) broiler-fryer, cut up, or 2½ pounds assorted chicken pieces
Vegetable oil
1½ cups all-purpose flour
1 teaspoon garlic powder
1 teaspoon salt
2 teaspoons ground red pepper
2 teaspoons freshly ground black pepper

•Combine first 5 ingredients in a heavy-duty, zip-top plastic bag. Add chicken; seal bag,

and squeeze to coat chicken pieces. Marinate in refrigerator at least 8 hours.
•Pour oil to depth of 1 inch in a 10- to 12-inch cast-iron skillet or electric skillet; heat to 350°.
•Meanwhile, drain chicken, discarding buttermilk mixture. Combine flour and remaining 4 ingredients in a shallow dish. Dredge chicken in flour mixture, pressing gently to coat chicken.
•Carefully place chicken in oil, skin side down. Cook, uncovered, 15 to 20 minutes or until golden, turning occasionally. (Remove small pieces earlier, if necessary, to prevent overbrowning.) Drain chicken on paper towels. Yield: 4 servings.

Per serving: Calories 566 Fat 33.8g
Cholesterol 136mg Sodium 625mg

Oven-Barbecued Chicken

PREP: 12 MINUTES   COOK: 1 HOUR

If it's too cold to grill outdoors—or even if it isn't—consider this version of oven-barbecued chicken.

½ cup all-purpose flour
1 teaspoon paprika
½ teaspoon salt
⅛ teaspoon pepper
1 (2½- to 3-pound) broiler-fryer, cut up
¼ cup butter or margarine, melted
½ cup ketchup
½ medium onion, chopped
2 tablespoons water
1 tablespoon white vinegar
1 tablespoon Worcestershire sauce
½ teaspoon salt
½ teaspoon chili powder
¼ teaspoon pepper

•Combine first 4 ingredients; stir well. Dredge chicken in flour mixture.
•Pour butter into a 13- x 9-inch pan. Arrange chicken in pan, skin side down. Bake, uncovered, at 350° for 30 minutes.
•Combine ketchup and remaining 7 ingredients, stirring well.
•Remove chicken from oven, and turn; spoon sauce over chicken. Bake 30 more minutes. Yield: 4 servings.

Per serving: Calories 618 Fat 40.9g
Cholesterol 176mg Sodium 1235mg

Mushroom-Chicken Bake

◄ **FAMILY FAVORITE** ►

PREP: 6 MINUTES   COOK: 1 HOUR

A simple dish using just a handful of pantry ingredients, this recipe makes an easy supper.

1 (2½- to 3-pound) broiler-fryer, cut up and skinned
½ cup zesty Italian dressing
½ teaspoon paprika, divided
¼ teaspoon pepper
1 (4-ounce) can sliced mushrooms, drained
⅓ cup grated Parmesan cheese

•Place chicken in a greased 13- x 9-inch baking dish. Drizzle dressing over chicken; sprinkle with ¼ teaspoon paprika and pepper.
•Bake, uncovered, at 350° for 30 minutes, basting occasionally. Turn chicken, and add mushrooms; sprinkle with Parmesan cheese and remaining ¼ teaspoon paprika. Bake 30 more minutes or until chicken is tender. Yield: 4 servings.

Per serving: Calories 454 Fat 27.9g
Cholesterol 142mg Sodium 764mg

Roasted Chicken with Lemon, Garlic, and Rosemary

PREP: 30 MINUTES

MARINATE: 8 HOURS   COOK: 1 HOUR

The aroma's wonderful as this big recipe bakes. Buy ingredients in bulk for it—a bag of lemons, bunches of rosemary, and a few heads of garlic. Use a mini chopper, if you have one, to mince the garlic.

2 heads garlic, minced (½ cup)
1 cup fresh lemon juice (6 lemons)
⅔ cup fresh rosemary sprigs, coarsely chopped
1 tablespoon salt
1½ teaspoons freshly ground pepper
2 cups olive oil
3 (2½- to 3-pound) broiler-fryers, cut up
3 lemons, sliced
Garnish: fresh rosemary sprigs

•Combine first 5 ingredients, stirring until blended; gradually add oil, stirring with a wire whisk. Pour mixture evenly into three large heavy-duty, zip-top plastic bags; add chicken pieces and lemon slices. Seal bags, and marinate in refrigerator at least 8 hours, turning bags occasionally.
•Grease two roasting pans. Remove chicken from marinade, reserving marinade. Arrange chicken in pans; drizzle with marinade, and top with lemon slices.
•Bake, uncovered, at 425° for 1 hour or until done, basting with pan juices every 20 minutes. Garnish, if desired. Yield: 12 servings.

Per serving: Calories 477 Fat 35.8g
Cholesterol 110mg Sodium 202mg

Picnic Barbecued Chicken

◄ **GRILLED • FAMILY FAVORITE** ►

PREP: 10 MINUTES   COOK: 55 MINUTES

The sauce colors this chicken a rich red and sweetens the meat with a bit of brown sugar. This recipe won rave reviews from our staff.

2 cloves garlic, crushed
2 teaspoons butter or margarine, melted
1 cup ketchup
¾ cup chili sauce
¼ cup firmly packed brown sugar
1 tablespoon celery seeds
1 tablespoon prepared mustard
2 tablespoons Worcestershire sauce
2 dashes of hot sauce
½ teaspoon salt
2 (2½- to 3-pound) broiler-fryers, quartered

•Sauté garlic in butter in a saucepan until tender. Stir in ketchup and next 7 ingredients, and bring to a boil. Remove from heat; reserve 1 cup sauce for basting, and set remaining sauce aside.
•Grill chicken, covered with grill lid, over medium-hot coals (350° to 400°) 15 minutes; baste with reserved barbecue sauce. Grill 30 to 40 more minutes or until a meat thermometer inserted in thickest part of breast registers 170°, basting every 10 minutes with reserved barbecue sauce. Serve with remaining sauce. Yield: 8 servings.

Per serving: Calories 393 Fat 18.4g
Cholesterol 113mg Sodium 908mg

Sesame-Pecan Chicken

PREP: 21 MINUTES   COOK: 1½ HOURS

1 cup buttermilk
1 large egg
1 cup all-purpose flour
1 tablespoon salt
1 tablespoon paprika
⅛ teaspoon pepper
1 cup ground pecans
¼ cup sesame seeds
6 pounds assorted chicken pieces
½ cup corn oil
¼ cup finely chopped pecans

•Combine buttermilk and egg in a small bowl, stirring until blended.
•Combine flour and next 5 ingredients in a small bowl.
•Dip chicken pieces in buttermilk mixture, and dredge in flour mixture. Quickly dip in oil, and drain.
•Place chicken, skin side up, in a large roasting pan; sprinkle with chopped pecans.
•Bake, uncovered, at 350° for 1½ hours. Yield: 8 servings.

Per serving: Calories 505 Fat 36.7g
Cholesterol 134mg Sodium 795mg

Chicken Marengo

PREP: 30 MINUTES   COOK: 30 MINUTES

Take a break from rice; try this tomato- and wine-braised chicken over couscous.

1 (8-ounce) package sliced fresh mushrooms
1 tablespoon butter or margarine, melted
2½ to 3 pounds assorted chicken pieces
2 tablespoons olive oil or vegetable oil
2 green onions, sliced
1 clove garlic, minced
½ cup dry white wine
2 tomatoes, peeled and cut into wedges
¾ teaspoon salt
¼ teaspoon pepper
1 teaspoon chopped fresh thyme or ¼ teaspoon dried thyme
2 tablespoons minced fresh parsley

•Sauté mushrooms in butter 2 minutes; set aside.

•Cook chicken in hot oil in a large skillet over medium-high heat until browned. Remove chicken from skillet, and set aside, reserving pan drippings in skillet.
•Sauté green onions and garlic in reserved drippings until onion is tender. Stir in wine and next 4 ingredients, scraping bottom of skillet. Add chicken, stirring well; cover, reduce heat, and simmer 30 minutes or until chicken is tender. Stir in mushrooms, and sprinkle with parsley. Serve over couscous or rice, if desired. Yield: 4 servings.

Per serving: Calories 535 Fat 39.2g
Cholesterol 152mg Sodium 618mg

Jerk Chicken

◄ GRILLED ►

**PREP: 30 MINUTES   CHILL: 2 HOURS
COOK: 1 HOUR AND 45 MINUTES**

Jerk recipes have a highly seasoned paste that includes habaneros, the hottest peppers in town. You can use jalapeños and still get great results; they're not quite as hot.

8 medium habanero or jalapeño peppers, seeded and coarsely chopped
3 green onions, chopped
2 tablespoons mustard seeds
1 tablespoon dried rosemary
3 tablespoons dried thyme
2 tablespoons dried basil
1 tablespoon whole allspice
1 teaspoon salt
1 teaspoon pepper
¼ cup fresh lime juice
¼ cup prepared mustard
2 tablespoons white vinegar
2 tablespoons orange juice
6 chicken leg quarters

•Process all ingredients except chicken in container of food processor 2 to 3 minutes or until smooth. Cover and chill at least 2 hours for flavors to blend; then spread pepper mixture generously on both sides of chicken quarters.
•Prepare charcoal fire in one end of grill; let burn 15 to 20 minutes. Place chicken on grill opposite the hot coals. Grill, covered with grill lid, 1 hour and 30 to 45 minutes or until chicken is done. Yield: 6 servings.

Per serving: Calories 285 Fat 15.5g
Cholesterol 92mg Sodium 613mg

Coq au Vin

**PREP: 5 MINUTES
COOK: 1 HOUR AND 45 MINUTES**

This French-inspired chicken in wine simmers in the oven. If you have a 14-inch skillet, you can simmer the chicken on the cooktop, which is more traditional.

4 slices bacon
1 cup all-purpose flour
1½ teaspoons salt
1 teaspoon pepper
3½ pounds assorted chicken pieces
2 tablespoons olive oil
3 large carrots, scraped and thinly sliced
1 small onion, chopped (about 1 cup)
1 small green pepper, chopped
2 cloves garlic, minced
1 (10½-ounce) can beef consommé
1 cup dry red wine
4 cups hot cooked rice

•Cook bacon in a large skillet over medium heat until crisp; drain on paper towels, reserving drippings in skillet. Coarsely crumble bacon, and set aside.
•Meanwhile, combine flour, salt, and pepper in a large heavy-duty, zip-top plastic bag. Add chicken pieces; seal and shake well to coat.
•Add olive oil to drippings in skillet. Brown chicken on all sides in skillet over medium-high heat.
•Place chicken in a lightly greased 13- x 9-inch baking dish. Top with carrot and next 3 ingredients. Pour consommé over vegetables and chicken.
•Cover and bake at 350° for 1 hour. Uncover and pour wine over vegetables and chicken. Sprinkle with bacon. Cover and bake 20 more minutes or until chicken is done. Serve over rice. Yield: 4 servings.

Per serving: Calories 1135 Fat 53.2g
Cholesterol 223mg Sodium 2484mg

Chicken Cacciatore

PREP: 20 MINUTES

COOK: 1 HOUR AND 5 MINUTES

Polenta is a traditional companion for this hunter-style stewed chicken. We think it's good over spaghetti, too.

¼ cup all-purpose flour
1 teaspoon salt
1 teaspoon pepper
2½ to 3 pounds assorted chicken pieces, skinned
¼ cup olive oil
1 large onion, chopped
3 cloves garlic, minced
½ cup dry red wine or white wine
1 (8-ounce) package sliced fresh mushrooms
1 (14.5-ounce) can whole tomatoes, undrained and quartered
1 (6-ounce) can tomato paste
3 bay leaves
1 teaspoon dried thyme
1 teaspoon dried oregano
¾ teaspoon salt
¼ teaspoon pepper
1 (2.25-ounce) can sliced ripe olives
2 medium-size green peppers, cut into strips
Polenta or hot cooked spaghetti

•Combine first 3 ingredients in a shallow dish; dredge chicken in flour mixture. Brown chicken, in batches, in hot oil in a 12-inch skillet over medium-high heat. Remove chicken, reserving drippings; drain chicken on paper towels.

•Cook onion and garlic in drippings in skillet over medium heat 5 minutes. Add wine, and cook over medium-high heat until wine evaporates. Stir in mushrooms and next 9 ingredients; add chicken to skillet. Bring to a boil; cover, reduce heat, and simmer 40 minutes or until chicken is tender. Discard bay leaves. Serve with polenta or hot cooked spaghetti. Yield: 6 servings.

Per serving: Calories 506 Fat 15.2g
Cholesterol 74mg Sodium 1094mg

Chicken Cacciatore

Arroz con Pollo

PREP: 7 MINUTES   COOK: 42 MINUTES

The colorful Latin American dish of chicken with rice is ready in less than an hour.

3 to 3½ pounds assorted chicken pieces
¾ cup olive oil or vegetable oil
1 onion, chopped
1 green pepper, chopped
2 cloves garlic, minced
1 cup uncooked long-grain rice
2½ cups chicken broth
½ cup tomato sauce
½ teaspoon salt
½ teaspoon curry powder
¼ teaspoon pepper
⅛ teaspoon ground saffron
1 cup frozen English peas
¼ cup sliced pimiento-stuffed olives

•Brown chicken in hot oil in a Dutch oven over medium-high heat. Drain chicken on paper towels. Reserve 1 tablespoon drippings in Dutch oven. Sauté onion, green pepper, and garlic in drippings until tender. Stir in rice and next 6 ingredients.

•Place chicken over rice mixture. Bring to a boil; cover, reduce heat, and simmer 25 minutes. Add peas and olives. Cover and cook 5 to 10 more minutes or until rice and chicken are tender. Yield: 4 servings.

Per serving: Calories 732 Fat 38.6g
Cholesterol 131mg Sodium 1209mg

Country Captain

◄ FAMILY FAVORITE ►

PREP: 13 MINUTES   COOK: 55 MINUTES

This subtly sweet chicken curry received our highest rating. The toasted almonds on top are a bonus.

½ cup all-purpose flour
1 teaspoon salt
½ teaspoon pepper
2½ to 3 pounds assorted chicken pieces
Vegetable oil
2 medium onions, chopped
2 medium-size green peppers, chopped
1 clove garlic, minced
2 (16-ounce) cans tomatoes, undrained and chopped
½ cup currants or raisins
2 to 3 teaspoons curry powder
1 tablespoon brown sugar
1 teaspoon ground ginger
½ teaspoon ground cinnamon
¾ teaspoon salt
¼ teaspoon pepper
½ teaspoon dried thyme
3 cups hot cooked rice
½ cup slivered almonds, toasted

•Combine first 3 ingredients in a shallow dish. Skin chicken, if desired. Dredge chicken in flour mixture. Pour oil to depth of ½ inch in a large heavy skillet; heat to 350°. Fry chicken, in batches, in hot oil 3 to 4 minutes on each side or until browned. Drain well, and arrange in a 13- x 9-inch baking dish. Reserve 2 tablespoons drippings in skillet.
•Sauté onion, green pepper, and garlic in reserved pan drippings in skillet until tender. Add tomatoes and next 8 ingredients; stir well, and spoon over chicken. Cover and bake at 350° for 40 minutes or until chicken is done.
•Remove chicken to a large serving platter, and spoon rice around chicken. Spoon sauce over rice, and sprinkle with almonds. Yield: 4 servings.
Per serving: Calories 924 Fat 38.7g
Cholesterol 120mg Sodium 2099mg

Chicken-Eggplant Parmigiana

PREP: 25 MINUTES   CHILL: 10 MINUTES

COOK: 30 MINUTES

Add a little spaghetti on the side and some extra sauce, and you'll have a meal. You don't even have to peel the eggplant.

4 skinned, boned chicken breast halves
¾ cup Italian-seasoned breadcrumbs
½ teaspoon salt
¼ teaspoon pepper
1 large egg, lightly beaten
1 small eggplant
¼ cup vegetable oil or olive oil
1 tablespoon vegetable oil or olive oil
1 (14-ounce) jar meatless spaghetti sauce
2 tablespoons grated Parmesan cheese
1 cup (4 ounces) shredded mozzarella cheese
¼ cup chopped fresh parsley

•Place chicken between two sheets of heavy-duty plastic wrap; flatten to ¼-inch thickness, using a meat mallet or rolling pin.
•Combine breadcrumbs, salt, and pepper. Dip chicken in egg, and coat with breadcrumbs. Place chicken on an ungreased baking sheet; cover and chill 10 minutes.
•Peel eggplant, if desired; cut lengthwise into 4 slices.
•Brown chicken in ¼ cup hot oil in a large skillet over medium heat, turning once. Remove chicken from skillet, and place in a 13- x 9-inch baking dish.
•Add 1 tablespoon oil to skillet, and cook eggplant over medium heat until browned on both sides; drain on paper towels.
•Place 1 slice eggplant on each chicken breast half. Spoon spaghetti sauce over eggplant; sprinkle with Parmesan cheese. Bake at 375° for 15 minutes. Top each eggplant slice with mozzarella cheese, and bake 5 more minutes or until cheese melts and sauce is bubbly. Sprinkle with parsley. Yield: 4 servings.
Per serving: Calories 565 Fat 28.1g
Cholesterol 152mg Sodium 1262mg

Chicken Parmigiana: Omit eggplant from recipe.

HOW TO BONE A CHICKEN BREAST

If you're in a hurry, boned, skinned chicken breast halves make cooking quick and easy. If you have time, however, you may appreciate the economy of boning the breasts at home.

First, remove the skin from the chicken, and discard skin. Split the breast in half lengthwise. Then starting at the breastbone side of the chicken, slice meat away from the bone, using a thin, sharp knife, cutting as close to the bone as possible.

Chicken Amandine

PREP: 4 MINUTES   COOK: 30 MINUTES

1 (2.25-ounce) package sliced almonds (⅓ cup)
2 tablespoons butter or margarine, melted
4 skinned, boned chicken breast halves
3 tablespoons all-purpose flour
1 teaspoon salt
1 teaspoon freshly ground pepper
½ cup dry white wine

•Sauté almonds in butter in a large skillet over medium heat 4 minutes or until lightly browned. Remove almonds, using a slotted spoon, reserving butter in skillet. Set almonds aside.
•Place chicken between two sheets of heavy-duty plastic wrap; flatten to ¼-inch thickness, using a meat mallet or rolling pin.
•Combine flour, salt, and pepper. Dredge chicken in flour mixture. Brown chicken in reserved butter over medium-high heat. Stir in wine; cover, reduce heat, and simmer 15 minutes or until chicken is done.
•Remove chicken to a serving platter, reserving juices in skillet. Bring juices to a boil; stir in reserved almonds. Spoon almond mixture over chicken. Yield: 4 servings.
Per serving: Calories 248 Fat 11.1g
Cholesterol 91mg Sodium 440mg

Chicken Fricassee

PREP: 13 MINUTES   COOK: 20 MINUTES

Fricassee is a thick, chunky, stewlike dinner of browned chicken simmered with assorted vegetables.

¼ cup butter or margarine, divided
6 skinned, boned chicken breast halves
¼ cup all-purpose flour
2 cups sliced fresh mushrooms
3 carrots, scraped and sliced
1 (1.1-ounce) envelope herb-with-lemon
    soup mix
1 cup half-and-half
½ cup water or white wine
2 teaspoons chicken bouillon granules

•Melt 2 tablespoons butter in a large skillet over medium heat. Dredge chicken in flour; brown in butter. Remove from skillet; set aside.
•Melt remaining 2 tablespoons butter in skillet; add mushrooms and carrot, and cook over medium heat, stirring constantly, 4 minutes or until tender.
•Combine soup mix and remaining 3 ingredients; pour over mushroom mixture. Bring to a boil, stirring constantly. Add chicken; reduce heat, and simmer 10 minutes or until chicken is done. Yield: 6 servings.
Per serving: Calories 344 Fat 15g
Cholesterol 111mg Sodium 977mg

Chicken 'n' Chile Casserole

◄ HEALTHY ►

PREP: 6 MINUTES   COOK: 45 MINUTES

8 skinned, boned chicken breast halves
½ teaspoon salt
½ teaspoon pepper
1 (8-ounce) package shredded mozzarella
    cheese
1 (4-ounce) can sliced mushrooms,
    drained
1 (10¾-ounce) can cream of chicken soup,
    undiluted
2 tomatoes, peeled and diced
1 (4.5-ounce) can chopped green chiles
6 cups hot cooked rice

•Sprinkle chicken with salt and pepper; place in a lightly greased 11- x 7-inch baking dish.

•Combine cheese and next 3 ingredients; pour over chicken. Sprinkle with chiles. Bake, uncovered, at 350° for 35 to 45 minutes. Serve over rice. Yield: 8 servings.
Per serving: Calories 266 Fat 8.5g
Cholesterol 95mg Sodium 767mg

Grilled Basil Chicken

◄ GRILLED ►

PREP: 15 MINUTES   MARINATE: 30 MINUTES
COOK: 30 MINUTES

This short ingredient list is no indication of how flavorful the grilled results are. Use bone-in chicken breasts or meaty thighs.

3 tablespoons lemon juice
2 tablespoons chopped fresh basil or
    2 teaspoons dried basil
1 clove garlic, minced
¼ cup olive oil
4 skinned, bone-in chicken breast halves
    or 8 skinned chicken thighs

•Process first 3 ingredients in container of an electric blender 30 seconds. With blender running, gradually add oil in a slow, steady stream, processing until blended. Reserve ¼ cup basil mixture.
•Brush chicken with remaining basil mixture; cover and marinate in refrigerator 30 minutes. Grill chicken, covered with grill lid, over medium coals (300° to 350°) 30 minutes or until done, basting twice with reserved basil mixture. Yield: 4 servings.
Per serving: Calories 244 Fat 16.1g
Cholesterol 62mg Sodium 54mg

Honey-Glazed Chicken

◄ GRILLED • HEALTHY ►

PREP: 4 MINUTES   COOK: 40 MINUTES

¼ cup soy sauce
¼ cup honey
½ teaspoon garlic powder
1½ teaspoons dry mustard
½ teaspoon grated lemon rind
1 tablespoon lemon juice
¼ teaspoon ground ginger
¼ teaspoon seasoned pepper
6 bone-in chicken breast halves, skinned,
    if desired

•Combine first 8 ingredients in a small bowl, stirring well; set aside.
•Coat grill rack with vegetable cooking spray; place on grill over medium coals (300° to 350°). Place chicken on rack, and grill, uncovered, 10 minutes on each side. Baste with sauce. Grill 20 more minutes, basting occasionally and turning often, until done. Yield: 6 servings.
Per serving: Calories 199 Fat 6g
Cholesterol 62mg Sodium 739mg

Grilled Jalapeño Chicken

◄ GRILLED • HEALTHY ►

PREP: 15 MINUTES
MARINATE: 8 HOURS   COOK: 1 HOUR

This recipe has a good smoky flavor. Don't open the grill during smoke-cooking. It slows the cooking process.

6 skinned, bone-in chicken breast halves
⅓ cup fresh lime juice (2 large limes)
2 tablespoons fresh cilantro leaves
3 jalapeño peppers, sliced
3 cloves garlic, chopped
¼ teaspoon salt
¼ teaspoon pepper
¼ cup honey
2 tablespoons soy sauce

•Place chicken in a large heavy-duty, zip-top plastic bag or shallow dish; set aside.
•Process lime juice and remaining 7 ingredients in container of an electric blender until smooth, stopping once to scrape down sides. Reserve ¼ cup marinade, and pour remaining marinade over chicken, turning to coat. Seal or cover, and marinate in refrigerator 1 to 8 hours.
•Prepare a fire by piling charcoal or lava rocks on each side of grill, leaving center empty. Place a water pan between coals. Coat grill rack with vegetable cooking spray; place on grill. Drain chicken, and arrange, breast side down, on rack over water pan.
•Grill, covered with grill lid, 30 minutes. Turn chicken, and brush with reserved marinade. Grill, covered, 25 to 30 more minutes or until meat thermometer registers 170°. Yield: 6 servings.
Per serving: Calories 159 Fat 2.6g
Cholesterol 62mg Sodium 345mg

Chicken with White Barbecue Sauce

◀ GRILLED ▶

PREP: 10 MINUTES   MARINATE: 8 HOURS
COOK: 45 MINUTES

White barbecue sauce is a pleasant tangy change from the ol' red sauce. Some connoisseurs call this recipe chicken blonde.

3 pounds skinned, bone-in chicken breast halves
1 recipe White Barbecue Sauce (page 394)

•Arrange chicken in a shallow dish. Pour 1 cup White Barbecue Sauce over chicken, turning to coat. Cover and marinate in refrigerator 8 hours, turning chicken once.
•Remove chicken from sauce, discarding sauce. Grill chicken, covered with grill lid, over medium coals (300° to 350°) 35 to 45 minutes or until a meat thermometer inserted in thickest part of breast registers 170°, turning every 15 minutes. Heat remaining sauce; serve with chicken. Yield: 6 servings.
Per serving: Calories 537 Fat 37.5g
Cholesterol 137mg Sodium 370mg

Chicken Cordon Bleu

◀ FAMILY FAVORITE ▶

PREP: 25 MINUTES   COOK: 50 MINUTES

We've enhanced this classic with a creamy mushroom sauce.

4 large bone-in chicken breast halves
4 (1-ounce) slices cooked ham or prosciutto
4 (1-ounce) slices Swiss cheese such as Gruyère
Salt and pepper
2 tablespoons butter or margarine, melted
1 (10¾-ounce) can mushroom soup, undiluted
1 (4-ounce) can sliced mushrooms, drained
¼ teaspoon garlic powder
⅛ teaspoon curry powder
¼ cup dry white wine
½ cup sour cream
Whole wheat toast points (optional)

•Loosen skin from chicken, forming a pocket without detaching skin. Arrange 1 slice each of ham and cheese under skin of each breast half; secure skin with wooden picks. Sprinkle chicken with salt and pepper; place in an ungreased baking dish.

•Bake, uncovered, at 375° for 30 to 40 minutes or until chicken is done, basting with melted butter after 20 minutes.
•Remove chicken from drippings; set chicken aside, and keep warm. Pour pan drippings into a large skillet, and cook over high heat until liquid is reduced to about ¼ cup. Add soup and next 3 ingredients; stir well. Cook over medium heat until thoroughly heated. Stir in wine and sour cream. Remove from heat.
•Remove wooden picks from chicken. Serve mushroom sauce with chicken. Serve with whole wheat toast points, if desired. Yield: 4 servings.
Per serving: Calories 602 Fat 41g
Cholesterol 171mg Sodium 1653mg

Chicken Breasts Lombardy

PREP: 20 MINUTES   COOK: 45 MINUTES

2 cups sliced fresh mushrooms
2 tablespoons butter or margarine, melted
12 skinned, boned chicken breast halves
½ cup all-purpose flour
⅓ cup butter or margarine, melted and divided
¾ cup Marsala*
½ cup chicken broth
½ teaspoon salt
⅛ teaspoon pepper
½ cup (2 ounces) shredded mozzarella cheese
½ cup grated Parmesan cheese
2 green onions, chopped

•Cook mushrooms in 2 tablespoons butter in a large skillet, stirring constantly, just until tender. Remove from heat; set aside.
•Cut each chicken breast half in half lengthwise. Place chicken between two sheets of heavy-duty plastic wrap; flatten to ⅛-inch thickness, using a meat mallet or rolling pin.
•Dredge chicken pieces in flour. Place 5 or 6 pieces of chicken in 1 to 2 tablespoons butter in a large skillet; cook over medium heat 3 to 4 minutes on each side or until golden. Place chicken in a lightly greased 13-x 9-inch baking dish or other large casserole, overlapping edges. Repeat procedure with remaining chicken and butter. Reserve pan

Chicken with White Barbecue Sauce

drippings in skillet. Sprinkle reserved mushrooms over chicken.

•Add wine and broth to skillet. Bring to a boil; reduce heat, and simmer, uncovered, 10 minutes, stirring occasionally. Stir in salt and pepper. Pour sauce over chicken. Combine cheeses and green onions; sprinkle over chicken.

•Bake, uncovered, at 450° for 12 to 14 minutes. Broil 5½ inches from heat 1 to 2 minutes or until browned. Yield: 6 servings.

Instead of ¾ cup Marsala, you can use ⅔ cup dry white wine plus 2 tablespoons brandy.

Per serving: Calories 527 Fat 21.9g
Cholesterol 203mg Sodium 789mg

Chicken Kiev

◄ FAMILY FAVORITE ►

PREP: 45 MINUTES   FREEZE: 45 MINUTES

CHILL: 1 TO 8 HOURS   COOK: 24 MINUTES

The key to Kiev is to seal and bread the chicken packets tightly so the pats of butter don't seep out during cooking. Then when served and sliced, the melted butter spurts out onto the plate.

¼ cup plus 2 tablespoons butter,
   softened
1 tablespoon chopped fresh parsley
1 clove garlic, minced
¼ teaspoon dried tarragon or other
   desired herb
¼ teaspoon salt
⅛ teaspoon pepper
6 skinned, boned chicken breast halves
¼ teaspoon salt
⅛ teaspoon pepper
1 large egg, beaten
1 tablespoon water
½ cup all-purpose flour
1½ to 2 cups soft breadcrumbs
   (homemade)
½ cup vegetable oil

•Combine first 6 ingredients in a small bowl; stir until blended. Shape butter mixture into a 3-inch stick; cover and freeze 45 minutes or until firm.

•Place chicken between two sheets of heavy-duty plastic wrap; flatten to ¼-inch thickness, using a meat mallet or rolling pin.

Season chicken with ¼ teaspoon salt and ⅛ teaspoon pepper.

•Cut butter stick into 6 pats; place 1 pat in center of each chicken breast half; fold long sides of chicken over butter, fold ends over, and secure with wooden picks.

•Combine egg and water, stirring well. Dredge each chicken roll in flour, dip in egg mixture, and dredge in breadcrumbs. Cover and chill rolls 1 to 8 hours.

•Heat ½ cup oil to 350° in a large skillet; fry chicken in hot oil 3 minutes or until browned, turning to brown rolls evenly. Transfer chicken to a baking sheet; bake at 350° for 16 to 18 minutes. Yield: 6 servings.

Per serving: Calories 379 Fat 23.4g
Cholesterol 143mg Sodium 458mg

Swiss Chicken and Artichokes with Dressing

PREP: 18 MINUTES

COOK: 1 HOUR AND 10 MINUTES

A dish of tender chicken with dressing underneath, this entrée breaks from classic turkey and dressing.

6 skinned, boned chicken breast halves
2 tablespoons butter or margarine,
   melted
1 (8-ounce) package cornbread stuffing
   mix
3 slices bread, crumbled
2 large eggs, lightly beaten
¾ cup chopped onion
½ cup chopped celery
1 (14½-ounce) can ready-to-serve chicken
   broth
1 (14-ounce) can artichoke hearts, drained
   and quartered
1 (10¾-ounce) can cream of celery soup,
   undiluted
¾ cup dry white wine
½ teaspoon dried basil
1 cup sliced fresh mushrooms
1 (6-ounce) package Swiss cheese slices,
   cut in half
¼ cup grated Parmesan cheese
2 tablespoons minced fresh parsley

•Brown chicken in butter in a large skillet over medium heat. Drain; set aside.

•Combine stuffing mix and next 5 ingredients; spoon into a greased 13- x 9-inch baking dish. Arrange artichoke quarters over dressing mixture; top with chicken.

•Combine soup, wine, and basil; pour over chicken. Top with mushrooms. Cover and bake at 350° for 50 minutes.

•Uncover and arrange cheese slices over casserole; sprinkle evenly with Parmesan cheese and parsley. Bake, uncovered, 10 more minutes. Yield: 6 servings.

Per serving: Calories 566 Fat 21.9g
Cholesterol 173mg Sodium 1798mg

Chicken and Snow Pea Stir-Fry

◄ QUICK ►

PREP: 15 MINUTES   COOK: 11 MINUTES

¾ cup chicken broth
¼ cup soy sauce
2 tablespoons cornstarch
1 tablespoon peanut oil or vegetable oil
2 skinned, boned chicken breast halves,
   cut into thin strips
1½ cups sliced celery
¼ pound fresh snow pea pods,
   trimmed
4 large mushrooms, sliced
3 green onions, sliced
½ cup slivered almonds, toasted
2 cups hot cooked rice

•Combine first 3 ingredients in a small bowl; set aside.

•Pour oil into a wok preheated to 375° or large skillet over medium-high heat. Add chicken; cook, stirring constantly, 3 to 4 minutes or until chicken is browned.

•Add celery and next 3 ingredients; cook, stirring constantly, 3 to 4 minutes or until vegetables are tender and chicken is done.

•Stir in broth mixture, and cook, stirring constantly, until mixture thickens and boils. Boil 1 minute, stirring constantly. Stir in almonds. Serve over rice. Yield: 2 servings.

Per serving: Calories 697 Fat 22g
Cholesterol 62mg Sodium 3293mg

Note: For a spicier stir-fry, stir ¼ teaspoon dried crushed red pepper into the broth mixture.

Sesame Chicken Kabobs

◄ GRILLED ►

PREP: 8 MINUTES   MARINATE: 3 HOURS
COOK: 10 MINUTES

Serve these pretty kabobs with couscous. Teriyaki sauce and dark sesame oil give the dish an Asian accent.

6 skinned, boned chicken breast halves (about 1½ pounds)
⅓ cup teriyaki sauce
¼ cup soy sauce
2 tablespoons sesame seeds
3 tablespoons vegetable oil
2 tablespoons dark sesame oil
2 medium-size sweet red peppers, cut into pieces
2 medium-size sweet yellow peppers, cut into pieces
2 small purple onions, cut into wedges

•Cut chicken into 1-inch pieces; place in a heavy duty, zip-top plastic bag or a shallow dish. Combine teriyaki sauce and next 4 ingredients, stirring well. Pour over chicken. Seal or cover, and marinate in refrigerator 3 hours, turning occasionally.
•Remove chicken from marinade, reserving marinade. Bring marinade to a boil in a small saucepan; set aside. Thread chicken alternately with peppers and onion onto skewers.
•Grill kabobs, covered with grill lid, over medium-hot coals (350° to 400°) 3 to 5 minutes on each side or until chicken is done, basting twice with reserved marinade. Yield: 4 servings.
Per serving: Calories 446 Fat 20.2g
Cholesterol 121mg Sodium 1513mg

Chicken Chow Mein

PREP: 19 MINUTES   COOK: 19 MINUTES

A wok is the perfect cooking vessel for health-conscious cooks. Foods stir-fried quickly in a wok retain nutrients, color, and crisp texture. Serve this dish over rice instead of fried noodles for a healthy one-dish meal.

3 tablespoons cornstarch
3 cups chicken broth, divided
¼ cup dry sherry
¼ cup soy sauce
¼ teaspoon pepper
2 tablespoons vegetable oil
4 skinned, boned chicken breast halves, cut into thin strips
3 stalks celery, diagonally sliced
1 green pepper, chopped
1 (8-ounce) package sliced fresh mushrooms
1 bunch green onions, sliced
1 (16-ounce) can bean sprouts, drained
1 (8-ounce) can bamboo shoots, drained
½ cup sliced water chestnuts
6 cups chow mein noodles

•Combine cornstarch and ¼ cup broth; stir until smooth. Combine cornstarch mixture, remaining 2¾ cups broth, sherry, soy sauce, and pepper in a medium bowl; stir well, and set aside.
•Pour oil around top of a preheated wok or large skillet; heat at medium-high (375°) for 30 seconds. Add chicken, and stir-fry 4 to 6 minutes or until lightly browned. Remove chicken from wok; drain.
•Add celery and green pepper to wok; stir-fry 2 minutes. Add mushrooms and green onions; stir-fry 2 to 3 minutes or until vegetables are crisp-tender. Add cornstarch mixture, chicken, bean sprouts, bamboo shoots, and water chestnuts; cover and cook 6 to 8 minutes or until mixture is thickened and thoroughly heated. Serve immediately over chow mein noodles. Yield: 6 servings.
Per serving: Calories 455 Fat 19.5g
Cholesterol 56mg Sodium 1211mg

Chicken Curry

PREP: 21 MINUTES
COOK: 1 HOUR AND 10 MINUTES

Some condiments to adorn this dish are flaked coconut, chopped peanuts, raisins, chopped green onion, and crumbled bacon.

6 skinned, bone-in chicken breast halves
4 black peppercorns
2 bay leaves
2 cloves garlic
1 teaspoon salt
3 tablespoons butter or margarine
1 apple, peeled, cored, and chopped
1 medium onion, chopped
1 large carrot, scraped and sliced
½ cup chopped celery
1½ tablespoons curry powder
½ teaspoon ground cumin
1 tablespoon all-purpose flour
½ teaspoon salt
¼ teaspoon ground cinnamon
¼ teaspoon ground cloves
3 cups hot cooked rice
2 tablespoons chopped fresh cilantro
Chutney (optional)

•Combine first 5 ingredients in a Dutch oven; add water to cover. Bring to a boil; cover, reduce heat, and simmer 35 minutes or until tender. Remove chicken from broth, reserving broth. Discard peppercorns, bay leaves, and garlic cloves. Let chicken cool. Bone chicken; cut into bite-size pieces. Skim fat from broth; set aside 1¾ cups broth.
•Melt butter in Dutch oven; cook apple and next 3 ingredients in butter 20 minutes or until tender. Add curry powder and cumin; cook 5 minutes, stirring occasionally. Stir in ¾ cup broth. Cool slightly.
•Process apple mixture in electric blender until smooth, stopping once to scrape down sides. Add flour, and process until blended. Return mixture to Dutch oven; add remaining 1 cup reserved broth. Cook over medium heat 5 minutes, stirring constantly.
•Add chicken, ½ teaspoon salt, cinnamon, and cloves; cook, stirring constantly, until mixture is thoroughly heated. Serve over rice; sprinkle with cilantro, and serve with chutney, if desired. Yield: 4 servings.
Per serving: Calories 474 Fat 13.5g
Cholesterol 117mg Sodium 1525mg

Cashew Chicken

PREP: 15 MINUTES   COOK: 11 MINUTES

2 teaspoons chicken bouillon granules
1 cup hot water
1 pound skinned, boned chicken breast
   halves, cut into 1-inch pieces
1 tablespoon vegetable oil
1 tablespoon cornstarch
2 tablespoons soy sauce
½ cup sliced green onions
2 teaspoons brown sugar
½ teaspoon ground ginger
1 (8-ounce) package sliced fresh
   mushrooms
1 small green pepper, cut into 1-inch
   pieces
1 (8-ounce) can sliced water chestnuts,
   drained
½ cup cashews, toasted
3 cups hot cooked rice

•Dissolve bouillon granules in hot water; set
aside.
•Brown chicken in hot oil in a large skillet
over medium-high heat. Remove chicken,
reserving drippings in skillet; set chicken
aside.
•Combine cornstarch and soy sauce; stir
until smooth. Stir in bouillon mixture, green
onions, brown sugar, and ginger. Set aside.
•Cook mushrooms, green pepper, and water
chestnuts in drippings over medium-high
heat, stirring constantly, until tender.
•Add chicken and bouillon mixture to vegetable mixture; cook over medium heat, stirring constantly, 2 minutes or until thickened.
Stir in cashews. Serve over rice. Yield: 3
servings.
Per serving: Calories 685 Fat 18.7g
Cholesterol 88mg Sodium 2268mg

Chicken Divan

◄ **FAMILY FAVORITE** ►

PREP: 35 MINUTES

COOK: 1 HOUR AND 15 MINUTES

*A sprig of fresh rosemary livens up the
poaching broth for this traditional chicken
casserole.*

4 skinned, bone-in chicken breast
   halves*
1 large sprig fresh rosemary
½ teaspoon salt
¼ teaspoon pepper
2 tablespoons butter or margarine
¼ cup all-purpose flour
1 cup milk
1 egg yolk, lightly beaten
1 (8-ounce) carton sour cream
½ cup mayonnaise
½ teaspoon grated lemon rind
1½ tablespoons lemon juice
½ teaspoon salt
½ to ¾ teaspoon curry powder
2 (10-ounce) packages frozen broccoli
   spears, thawed and drained
⅓ cup grated Parmesan cheese
Paprika

•Combine first 4 ingredients in a large
saucepan; add water to cover. Bring to a boil;
cover, reduce heat, and simmer 35 to 40
minutes or until chicken is tender. Remove
chicken from broth, reserving ½ cup broth;
reserve remaining broth for another use, if
desired. Discard rosemary sprig. Let chicken
cool; bone and chop chicken. Set aside.
•Melt butter in a heavy saucepan over low
heat; add flour, stirring until smooth. Cook 1
minute, stirring constantly.
•Gradually add reserved ½ cup chicken
broth and milk; cook over medium heat, stirring constantly, until mixture is thickened
and bubbly.
•Gradually stir about one-fourth of hot
mixture into beaten egg yolk; add to remaining hot mixture, stirring constantly. Cook 1
minute, stirring constantly. Remove from
heat; add sour cream and next 5 ingredients,
stirring well.
•Layer half each of broccoli, chopped
chicken, and sauce in a lightly greased
2-quart casserole. Repeat layers; sprinkle
with cheese.

•Bake, uncovered, at 350° for 35 minutes or
until bubbly. Sprinkle with paprika. Yield: 6
servings.
*If you'd like to use leftover chopped cooked
chicken, you'll need 4 cups. You'll also need
½ cup chicken broth.
Per serving: Calories 571 Fat 33.8g
Cholesterol 193mg Sodium 878mg

Kung Pao Chicken

PREP: 25 MINUTES   COOK: 13 MINUTES

*Spicy flavor and a peanut topping are part of
the Kung Pao tradition.*

¼ cup dry sherry
¼ cup soy sauce
1½ tablespoons sugar
1 tablespoon cornstarch
½ teaspoon pepper
2 teaspoons white vinegar
1 teaspoon peanut oil or vegetable oil
½ teaspoon hot sauce
3 tablespoons peanut oil or vegetable oil
4 small dried red chile pepper pods
1 pound skinned, boned chicken breast
   halves, cut into 1-inch pieces
1 green pepper, coarsely chopped
6 green onions, sliced
3 stalks celery, sliced
½ cup sliced fresh mushrooms
1 clove garlic, minced
1 cup salted roasted peanuts or cashews
3 cups hot cooked rice

•Combine first 8 ingredients in a 1-cup
liquid measuring cup; stir well. Set aside.
•Pour 3 tablespoons oil around top of a preheated wok, coating sides; heat at medium-
high (375°) for 30 seconds. Add chile pepper
pods, and stir-fry 1 minute. Remove chile
pepper pods from wok; set aside.
•Add chicken, and stir-fry 5 to 6 minutes or
until done. Remove chicken from wok; set
aside.
•Add green pepper and next 4 ingredients;
stir-fry 4 minutes or until crisp-tender. Stir in
reserved chicken, chile pepper pods, and
peanuts. Add reserved soy sauce mixture,
and stir-fry until thickened. Serve over rice.
Yield: 4 servings.
Per serving: Calories 679 Fat 29.3g
Cholesterol 66mg Sodium 1435mg

Double-Crust Chicken Pot Pie

◄ FAMILY FAVORITE ►

PREP: 20 MINUTES   COOK: 1 HOUR

6 skinned, boned chicken breast halves,
    cut into 1-inch pieces
1 medium onion, chopped
2 tablespoons butter or margarine,
    melted
1 stalk celery, chopped
1½ cups frozen English peas and carrots,
    thawed and drained
1 cup sliced fresh mushrooms
1 cup peeled, chopped potato
1 cup chicken broth
¼ cup dry white wine
½ teaspoon dried parsley flakes
¼ teaspoon pepper
1 bay leaf
2 tablespoons cornstarch
2 tablespoons water
1 (10¾-ounce) can cream of mushroom
    soup, undiluted
1 cup (4 ounces) shredded Cheddar
    cheese
¼ cup sour cream
Pot Pie Pastry
1 egg yolk, lightly beaten
1 tablespoon milk

•Cook chicken and onion in butter in a large
skillet over medium-high heat, stirring constantly, until chicken is browned and onion is
tender. Stir in celery and next 8 ingredients.
Bring to a boil; cover, reduce heat, and simmer 15 minutes or until vegetables are tender. Discard bay leaf.
•Combine cornstarch and 2 tablespoons
water, stirring until smooth; add to chicken
mixture. Bring to a boil over medium heat,
stirring constantly. Remove from heat; stir in
soup, cheese, and sour cream.
•Roll half of Pot Pie Pastry to ⅛-inch thickness on a lightly floured surface; fit pastry
into an ungreased 2-quart casserole. Spoon
chicken mixture into casserole. Roll remaining pastry to ⅛-inch thickness, and place
over chicken mixture; trim, seal, and crimp
edges. Cut slits in pastry. Combine egg yolk
and milk; brush over pastry.
•Bake at 400° for 35 minutes or until gold-
en, shielding pastry with aluminum foil

during last 5 minutes to prevent excessive
browning, if necessary. Yield: 6 servings.
Per serving: Calories 816 Fat 44.7g
Cholesterol 133mg Sodium 1174mg

Pot Pie Pastry

3 cups all-purpose flour
1 teaspoon salt
1 cup shortening
6 to 8 tablespoons cold water

•Combine flour and salt; cut in shortening
with a pastry blender until mixture is
crumbly. Sprinkle cold water, 1 tablespoon at
a time, evenly over surface; stir with a fork
until dry ingredients are moistened. Shape
into a ball; chill. Yield: pastry for 1 double-
crust pie.

Chicken Crêpes

PREP: 22 MINUTES   COOK: 37 MINUTES

3 cups finely chopped cooked chicken
1½ cups freshly grated Parmesan cheese,
    divided
⅓ cup butter or margarine
⅓ cup all-purpose flour
3 cups milk
1 cup whipping cream
¼ pound finely chopped fresh mushrooms
    (1½ cups)
1 tablespoon butter or margarine,
    melted
¾ teaspoon salt
¼ teaspoon pepper
¼ teaspoon ground nutmeg
12 Basic Crêpes (page 76)
⅓ cup sliced almonds, toasted

•Combine chicken and 1 cup cheese; set
aside.
•Melt ⅓ cup butter in a heavy saucepan
over low heat; add flour, stirring until
smooth. Cook 1 minute, stirring constantly.
Gradually add milk; cook over medium heat,
stirring constantly, until thickened and bubbly. Remove from heat, and stir in whipping
cream. Cool slightly; reserve ⅔ cup sauce.
•Meanwhile, sauté mushrooms in 1 tablespoon butter until tender; stir in salt, pepper,
and nutmeg. Add mushroom mixture and
reserved ⅔ cup sauce to chicken mixture,
stirring well. Spoon ⅓ cup mixture into

center of each crêpe, and roll up tightly.
Place crêpes, seam side down, in a lightly
greased 13- x 9-inch baking dish.
•Pour remaining sauce over crêpes, and
bake at 350° for 25 minutes. Sprinkle with
remaining ½ cup Parmesan cheese and
sliced almonds, and bake 5 more minutes.
Yield: 6 servings.
Per serving: Calories 760 Fat 52.1g
Cholesterol 265mg Sodium 1025mg

Spicy Chicken Enchiladas

PREP: 12 MINUTES   COOK: 45 MINUTES

2 canned jalapeño peppers, seeded and
    chopped
1 large tomato, finely chopped
½ cup finely chopped onion
¼ cup tomato juice
½ teaspoon salt
½ teaspoon ground cumin*
¼ cup butter or margarine
¼ cup all-purpose flour
2 cups chicken broth
1 (8-ounce) carton sour cream
2 canned jalapeño peppers, seeded and
    chopped
12 (6-inch) corn tortillas
2 cups chopped cooked chicken
2 cups (8 ounces) shredded Monterey Jack
    cheese with peppers, divided
¾ cup chopped onion

•Combine first 6 ingredients; stir well. Cover
and chill.
•Melt butter in a saucepan over medium
heat; add flour, stirring until smooth. Cook 1
minute, stirring constantly. Gradually add
broth; cook, stirring constantly, until thickened and bubbly. Remove from heat; stir in
sour cream and 2 jalapeño peppers.
•Pour half of sour cream mixture into a
lightly greased 13- x 9-inch baking dish; set
dish and remaining sour cream mixture
aside.
•Wrap tortillas tightly in aluminum foil; bake
at 350° for 15 minutes.
•Spoon 2 heaping tablespoons chicken, 1
tablespoon cheese, and 1 tablespoon onion
down center of each tortilla. Roll up tortillas;
place tortillas, seam side down, in prepared
dish. Pour remaining sour cream mixture
over enchiladas.

•Bake at 400° for 25 minutes or until thoroughly heated. Sprinkle with remaining 1¼ cups cheese; bake 3 to 5 minutes or until cheese melts. Serve with chilled tomato mixture. Yield: 6 servings.

Bring out the flavor of cumin by toasting it in a dry skillet over medium heat for about 30 seconds; then stir into tomato mixture.

Per serving: Calories 598 Fat 34.4g
Cholesterol 121mg Sodium 1043mg

Chicken and Bean Tacos

PREP: 15 MINUTES   COOK: 20 MINUTES

This recipe sandwiches a crisp taco shell within a soft flour tortilla for a unique play on textures.

8 (6½-inch) "soft taco" flour tortillas (we tested with Azteca)
⅔ cup chopped onion
⅓ cup chopped green pepper
2 tablespoons vegetable oil or olive oil
2 cups shredded cooked chicken
1 (16-ounce) jar taco sauce
1 teaspoon sugar
1½ teaspoons chili powder
1 (15-ounce) can refried beans
1 (4.5-ounce) can chopped green chiles
8 crisp taco shells
2 cups shredded lettuce
1 cup chopped tomato
1 cup (4 ounces) shredded Cheddar cheese

•Heat tortillas according to package directions; set aside.

•Sauté onion and green pepper in hot oil in a heavy saucepan over medium heat until tender. Stir in chicken and next 3 ingredients; cook until thoroughly heated.

•Cook refried beans and green chiles in a small saucepan over medium-low heat until thoroughly heated. Place about 2 tablespoons refried bean mixture on each tortilla, spreading mixture to within ½ inch of edge. Place a taco shell in center of each tortilla, pressing tortilla up and onto sides of taco shell.

•Fill each taco shell with about ⅓ cup chicken mixture, ¼ cup shredded lettuce, 2 tablespoons tomato, and 2 tablespoons shredded cheese. Serve immediately. Yield: 8 tacos.

Per taco: Calories 486 Fat 17.2g
Cholesterol 61mg Sodium 995mg

Easy Chicken à la King

◄ QUICK ►

PREP: 5 MINUTES   COOK: 20 MINUTES

Serve this creamy chicken on cornbread, toast points, or croissants if you don't have puff pastry shells.

2 frozen puff pastry shells
1½ cups coarsely chopped cooked chicken
1 (10¾-ounce) can cream of chicken soup, undiluted
¼ cup milk or half-and-half
1 (2-ounce) jar diced pimiento, drained
1 (4-ounce) can whole mushrooms, drained
¼ teaspoon pepper

•Bake puff pastry shells according to package directions. Meanwhile, combine chicken and remaining 5 ingredients in a heavy saucepan; cook over low heat 10 minutes, stirring often. Spoon into puff pastry shells. Yield: 2 servings.

Per serving: Calories 690 Fat 35.7g
Cholesterol 139mg Sodium 1635mg

Chicken Lasagna Florentine

PREP: 1 HOUR   COOK: 1 HOUR

Try this fabulous lasagna with its creamy white sauce, bright green ribbon of spinach, and chunks of chicken.

6 dried lasagna noodles
1 (10-ounce) package frozen chopped spinach, thawed
2 cups chopped cooked chicken
2 cups (8 ounces) shredded Cheddar cheese
⅓ cup finely chopped onion
¼ teaspoon ground nutmeg
1 tablespoon cornstarch
½ teaspoon salt
¼ teaspoon pepper
1 tablespoon soy sauce
1 (10¾-ounce) can cream of mushroom soup, undiluted
1 (8-ounce) carton sour cream
1 (4.5-ounce) jar sliced mushrooms, drained
⅓ cup mayonnaise
1 cup (4 ounces) freshly grated Parmesan cheese
Butter-Pecan Topping

•Cook noodles according to package directions; drain and set aside.

•Drain spinach well, pressing between layers of paper towels. Combine spinach, chopped chicken, and next 11 ingredients in a large bowl; stir well.

•Arrange 3 noodles in a greased 11- x 7-inch baking dish. Spread half of chicken mixture over noodles. Repeat with remaining noodles and chicken mixture. Sprinkle with Parmesan cheese and Butter-Pecan Topping.

•Cover and bake at 350° for 55 to 60 minutes or until hot and bubbly. Let stand 15 minutes before cutting. Yield: 6 servings.

Per serving: Calories 746 Fat 53.2g
Cholesterol 131mg Sodium 1690mg

Butter-Pecan Topping

1 tablespoon butter or margarine
⅔ cup chopped pecans

Melt butter in a skillet over medium heat; add pecans, and cook 3 minutes. Cool completely. Yield: ⅔ cup.

Creamed Chicken

PREP: 15 MINUTES   COOK: 20 MINUTES

1 (8-ounce) package sliced mushrooms
⅓ cup chopped green pepper
1 medium onion, chopped
¼ cup butter or margarine, melted
⅓ cup all-purpose flour
1 (14½-ounce) can chicken broth
1 cup half-and-half
2½ cups chopped cooked chicken
½ teaspoon poultry seasoning
Dash of pepper
3 tablespoons dry sherry
1 (2-ounce) jar diced pimiento, drained
½ cup sliced almonds, toasted (optional)
Buttermilk Cornbread (page 70) or commercial cornbread

•Sauté first 3 ingredients in butter until tender. Add flour, stirring until smooth; cook 1 minute, stirring constantly. Gradually add broth and half-and-half; cook over medium heat, stirring constantly, until thickened. Stir in chicken and next 5 ingredients; cook 5 minutes. Serve over cornbread. Yield: 6 servings.

Per serving: Calories 508 Fat 26.5g
Cholesterol 108mg Sodium 800mg

Caribbean Grilled Chicken Thighs

◄ GRILLED ►

**PREP: 10 MINUTES MARINATE: 8 HOURS
COOK: 16 MINUTES**

This marinade also tastes great on chicken breasts and pork tenderloin.

8 large chicken thighs, skinned
½ cup soy sauce
¼ cup chopped green onions
¼ cup lime juice
2 tablespoons dark brown sugar
1 tablespoon honey
1 teaspoon dried crushed red pepper
1 large clove garlic, crushed
Lime wedges (optional)
Fresh parsley sprigs (optional)

•Place chicken in an 11- x 7-inch baking dish. Combine soy sauce and next 6 ingredients; stir well. Pour over chicken. Cover and marinate in refrigerator 8 hours, turning occasionally.
•Drain chicken, reserving marinade. Place marinade in a small saucepan; bring to a boil. Grill chicken, covered with grill lid, over medium coals (300° to 350°) 8 minutes on each side or until done, basting often with marinade. If desired, garnish with lime wedges and parsley. Yield: 4 servings.
Per serving: Calories 396 Fat 18.3g
Cholesterol 160mg Sodium 1696mg

Tangy Dijon Drumsticks

**PREP: 9 MINUTES MARINATE: 2 HOURS
COOK: 45 MINUTES**

⅓ cup Dijon mustard
1 tablespoon vegetable oil or olive oil
1 tablespoon Worcestershire sauce
2 cloves garlic, crushed
1 teaspoon paprika
1½ teaspoons hot sauce
8 chicken drumsticks

•Combine first 6 ingredients in a large heavy-duty, zip-top plastic bag; seal and squeeze to blend. Add chicken; seal and marinate in refrigerator 2 hours, turning bag occasionally.

•Remove chicken from marinade, discarding marinade. Place chicken on a lightly greased rack in broiler pan. Bake, uncovered, at 375° for 45 minutes or until chicken is done. Yield: 4 servings.
Per serving: Calories 171 Fat 10.4g
Cholesterol 52mg Sodium 474mg

FOR LIVER LOVERS ONLY

Chicken liver is the mildest flavored, most tender liver compared to beef and other livers used in cooking. Chicken livers are sold whole fresh as well as frozen. Purchase liver that has a bright color and slightly moist surface. A quick cooking method like sautéing is recommended because liver easily can be overcooked to disappointingly tough results.

Chicken Livers over Rice

◄ QUICK ►

PREP: 5 MINUTES COOK: 22 MINUTES

Chicken livers are a good source of protein, iron, and vitamin A. These livers simmer in wine and herbs; catch the juices with rice.

1 pound chicken livers
3 tablespoons butter or margarine, melted
1 (8-ounce) package sliced fresh mushrooms
1 large onion, chopped
1 clove garlic, minced
1 tablespoon all-purpose flour
½ cup dry white wine
1 (14½-ounce) can whole tomatoes, drained and chopped
¼ cup chopped fresh parsley
½ teaspoon dried thyme
½ teaspoon salt
3 cups hot cooked rice

•Cook livers in butter in a large skillet over medium-high heat 7 to 9 minutes, stirring constantly. Remove livers, reserving drippings in skillet. Set livers aside; keep warm.
•Add mushrooms, onion, and garlic to drippings in skillet; cook, stirring constantly, 5 minutes or until tender. Reduce heat to low.
•Combine flour and wine, stirring until smooth; add flour mixture, tomatoes, and

next 3 ingredients to mushroom mixture. Bring to a boil; reduce heat, and simmer, uncovered, 5 minutes. Stir in livers; cook until heated, stirring occasionally. Serve over rice. Yield: 4 servings.
Per serving: Calories 474 Fat 13.8g
Cholesterol 521mg Sodium 1302mg

Chicken Liver Sauté

◄ QUICK ►

PREP: 3 MINUTES COOK: 19 MINUTES

These chicken livers are smothered in peppers, onions, and olives, and then sprinkled with bacon. Think twice before you say you don't like livers.

8 slices bacon
1 medium onion, thinly sliced
1 medium-size green pepper, cut into ¼-inch strips
1 pound chicken livers
⅓ cup sliced pimiento-stuffed olives
⅓ cup sliced ripe olives
3 tablespoons dry sherry

•Cook bacon in a large skillet over medium heat until crisp; remove bacon, reserving drippings in skillet. Crumble bacon, and set aside.
•Sauté onion and green pepper in drippings 5 minutes or until tender. Remove vegetables, reserving drippings in skillet.
•Sauté livers in drippings 6 to 8 minutes or until done. Stir in sautéed vegetables, olives, and sherry. Cook over medium heat just until thoroughly heated. Serve over rice or toasted English muffins. Sprinkle with bacon. Yield: 4 servings.
Per serving: Calories 502 Fat 38.9g
Cholesterol 536mg Sodium 1073mg

TURKEY & OTHER BIRDS

Turkey stands out in the South around the holiday season along with its welcomed companions, cornbread dressing and Giblet Gravy (page 395). A typical-sized roast turkey offers a plentiful amount of both white and dark meat as well as the coveted crispy skin.

Although some tom turkeys can weigh well over 50 pounds, turkeys you commonly see in the marketplace range in size from 5 to 20 pounds. And the larger 15- to 20-pound birds have a higher ratio of meat per pound. So a larger bird will offer more meat for the money.

If it's just the white meat you desire, you can find bone-in and boneless turkey breasts readily available these days. They cook quicker than the whole bird, but stuffing them is not an option. And for dark meat fans, you can find turkey drumsticks and wings sold separately, too.

You'll find turkey in other forms in most supermarkets around the South. When shopping, look for these labels: tenderloins, cutlets, ground turkey, and sausages.

Tenderloins are fillets of turkey cut from the breast; they are especially good for baking, broiling, or grilling. *Cutlets* are ⅛- to ¾-inch-thick slices of turkey also cut from the breast. They take only about 3 minutes to cook on each side because they're so thin. Some supermarkets mistakenly label turkey cutlets as steaks, although the term *"steak"* refers to slices of turkey that are ½ to 1 inch thick.

Ground turkey, a blend of white and dark turkey meat, substitutes well for ground beef in many recipes. The fat content of ground turkey can vary, depending on how much dark meat (higher in fat) is used.

Turkey sausage is available in the form of links and patties in many markets. And just like other types of sausage, turkey sausage can be panfried or broiled.

The goose and duckling are other fine offerings for a holiday meal or casual dinner. Both contain a higher fat percentage than other birds, so be sure to prick the skin all over before cooking to render much of the fat during cooking. And don't baste these birds with added fat (butter or oil) during roasting as you might a turkey.

Thawing the Bird

If you purchase a frozen turkey, it's important to thaw it properly before cooking. The best way to let a turkey thaw is in the refrigerator—and this may take several days depending on the weight of the bird. Thawing in the refrigerator instead of at room temperature is the safest method to use because it reduces the risk of bacterial growth.

Leave the turkey in its original wrapper, place it in a pan to catch any juices, and refrigerate until it's thawed. Allow two to four days for thawing. A 4- to 12-pound bird will take one to two days to thaw; a 12- to 20-pound bird will take two to three days; and a 20- to 24-pound turkey will take up to four days to thaw. Once thawed, a turkey should be cooked immediately.

Stuffing the Turkey

Remove the giblets and neck from a whole turkey, and then rinse and cook them within 12 hours. Use them to make gravy.

Rinse turkey thoroughly, and pat dry. Don't salt the body cavity if you plan to stuff the bird. Stuff turkey just before roasting; never stuff it the night before. And likewise, a cooked stuffed turkey should never be refrigerated with stuffing intact. The stuffing should be thoroughly removed and refrigerated in a separate container.

Lightly spoon stuffing into body and neck cavities of turkey, if desired. Don't pack stuffing too tightly, because it needs room to expand during roasting.

If you choose not to stuff your turkey, another option is to place a few pieces of onion, celery, fruit, or fresh herb sprigs in the body cavity before roasting. This infuses subtle flavor into the bird as it cooks. Then discard the ingredients before serving.

Stuffing versus Dressing

When talking stuffing, everyone wants it "like Mom used to make." For some it's a crispy, crumbly cornbread mixture; for others it means moist bread dressing. The main difference is in the moistness. Many recipes offer a range in the amount of broth or other liquid, so if you like yours moister than most, add all the liquid recommended. And if you prefer it on the dry side, add the lesser amount of liquid.

Oh, and by the way, we call it *stuffing* if it's inside the bird and *dressing* if it's baked separately in a pan.

When you make stuffing, spoon it lightly into the bird's cavities just before roasting. When you test the turkey for doneness, check the stuffing, too. The stuffing needs to register 165° on an instant-read thermometer. Promptly remove the stuffing from the turkey before serving.

Cooking the Turkey

To roast a turkey, first place it, breast side up, on a rack in a shallow roasting pan or simply in a greased roasting pan. Brush turkey with vegetable oil or melted butter. Roast, uncovered, at 325° without adding any liquid to the pan. Then baste the turkey with pan drippings or melted butter occasionally during roasting. Differing recipes will instruct you to tent the turkey with aluminum foil at different times during roasting to prevent overbrowning.

The most accurate way to determine doneness of the turkey is to use a meat thermometer. Insert thermometer into the meaty part of thigh, making sure thermometer doesn't touch the bone. When it registers 180°, the turkey is done. At this point, juices should run clear, and drumsticks should move up and down easily.

Storing Leftovers

Always chill leftover turkey meat, stuffing or dressing, and gravy separately. You can keep cooked turkey in the refrigerator up to two days.

Extend the storage life of your turkey leftovers by freezing them. Slice, chop, or shred the meat, and then package it in meal-size portions.

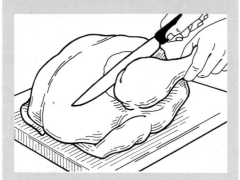

1. To remove turkey leg, cut between thigh and body and through joint. To serve dark meat, slice thigh meat and drumstick meat with knife parallel to the bone.

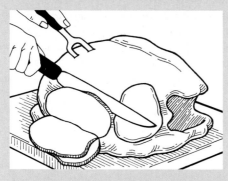

2. To carve breast meat, make a deep horizontal cut just above wing. Cut thin slices down to the horizontal cut (shown).

Carving the Turkey

Let the turkey "rest," covered with aluminum foil, 15 minutes before carving. Make sure you have the proper carving utensils on hand, mainly a sharp knife so you can produce pretty slices. Carve the bird, breast side up, on a cutting board in the kitchen or on a serving platter at the table.

Uncover turkey, and remove stuffing to a serving bowl. Grasp the end of a drumstick, and pull it away from the body. Cut through the skin and meat between the thigh and body (illustration 1); bend the leg away from the bird to expose the leg joint. Slice through the joint, and remove the leg.

Cut through the joint that separates the thigh and drumstick. Slice the dark meat from the bones of the leg and thigh rather than placing them whole on the serving platter.

To carve the breast meat, steady the bird with a carving fork and make a deep horizontal cut into the breast just above the wing. (Use this cut to mark the end of each slice of breast meat.) Beginning at the outer top edge of breast, cut thin slices from the top down to the horizontal cut (illustration 2). Carve from one side of the turkey at a time, carving only as much meat as needed for serving.

If wingtips were twisted under turkey before roasting, you should be able to carve the whole turkey without removing them. Otherwise, remove wings by cutting through the joints where the wing bones and backbone meet.

Save the turkey carcass to make a rich broth for homemade soup. You can store the broth in the freezer up to four months.

Bread Dressing

PREP: 15 MINUTES   COOK: 25 MINUTES

If you need dressing for only a few folks, try this simple and very moist version for the holiday table.

1 (1-pound) loaf day-old bread, cubed
1½ teaspoons poultry seasoning
½ teaspoon pepper
1 cup chicken broth
2 large eggs, lightly beaten
¾ cup chopped onion
¾ cup chopped celery
½ cup butter or margarine, melted

• Combine first 5 ingredients in a large bowl; set aside.
• Sauté onion and celery in butter until tender. Add to bread mixture, stirring well. Spoon into a lightly greased 2-quart casserole. Cover and bake at 325° for 20 minutes. Yield: 6 servings.
Per serving: Calories 387 Fat 20.3g
Cholesterol 115mg Sodium 706mg

Note: This dressing is too moist to bake in a turkey.

Old-Fashioned Cornbread Dressing

◀ **FAMILY FAVORITE** ▶

PREP: 25 MINUTES
COOK: 1 HOUR AND 10 MINUTES

2 cups cornmeal
2 teaspoons baking powder
1 teaspoon baking soda
½ teaspoon salt
2 large eggs, beaten
2 cups buttermilk
2 tablespoons bacon drippings, melted
3 stalks celery, chopped
1 medium onion, chopped
⅓ cup butter or margarine, melted
12 slices day-old bread, crumbled
2 to 2½ cups turkey or chicken broth
1 cup milk
2 large eggs, beaten
¼ teaspoon salt
1 teaspoon poultry seasoning
½ teaspoon rubbed sage
¼ teaspoon pepper

• Combine first 4 ingredients in a large bowl; add 2 eggs, buttermilk, and melted bacon drippings, stirring well.
• Place a well-greased 10-inch cast-iron skillet in a 450° oven for 4 minutes or until hot. Remove skillet from oven; spoon batter into skillet. Bake at 450° for 35 minutes or until cornbread is lightly browned. Cool; crumble cornbread into a large bowl.
• Sauté celery and onion in butter until tender. Add sautéed vegetables, bread, and remaining 7 ingredients to crumbled cornbread, stirring well. Spoon dressing into a lightly greased 13- x 9-inch pan. Bake at 350° for 25 to 30 minutes. Yield: 8 servings.
Per serving: Calories 436 Fat 18.4g
Cholesterol 138mg Sodium 990mg

Note: Substitute 1 (10¾-ounce) can chicken broth and 1 cup water for homemade chicken broth.
To stuff a turkey: Spoon dressing into turkey cavities just before roasting. Spoon any remaining dressing into a lightly greased 2-quart casserole; bake at 350° for 25 to 30 minutes. Remove stuffing, and refrigerate it separately from turkey if any stuffing is left over.

Roast Turkey with Herbs

PREP: 20 MINUTES   COOK: 3 TO 4 HOURS

See this beautifully browned bird on page 322. The aromatic herbs just under a crispy skin produce the most flavorful herb-infused slices of meat, especially the top slice.

1   (12 to 14-pound) turkey
1   bunch fresh rosemary sprigs
6   fresh large sage leaves
1   cooking apple, cut into quarters
1   stalk celery, cut in half
1   onion, cut in half
½   cup butter or margarine, melted
Garnishes: apple wedges, kumquats,
        rosemary sprigs, sage leaves

1. Lift wingtips up and over back, and tuck under bird.

2. Loosen skin from turkey breast without detaching or tearing skin.

3. Carefully place herb leaves and sprigs under skin; replace skin.

•Remove giblets and neck from turkey; reserve for another use such as making broth. Rinse turkey with cold water; pat dry. Drain body cavity well. Place turkey in a greased broiler pan or roasting pan.
•Lift wingtips up and over back, and tuck under bird (photo 1).
•Loosen skin from turkey breast without totally detaching skin (photo 2); carefully place several rosemary sprigs and sage leaves under skin (photo 3). Replace skin.
•Place apple quarters, celery, and onion into body cavity of turkey. Place remaining rosemary and sage into neck cavity. Brush entire bird with melted butter. Loosely cover turkey with heavy-duty aluminum foil.
•Bake at 325° for 3 to 4 hours or until a meat thermometer inserted in meaty part of thigh registers 180°, basting often with pan drippings. Uncover turkey during the last hour of cooking. (To prevent overcooking, begin checking turkey for doneness after 3 hours.) Remove turkey from roasting pan; cover and let stand 15 minutes before carving. Reserve drippings for gravy. (See sauces chapter beginning on page 385.) Garnish, if desired. Yield: 12 servings.
Per serving: Calories 692 Fat 36.8g
Cholesterol 267mg Sodium 282mg

Roast Turkey

◀ FAMILY FAVORITE ▶

PREP: 15 MINUTES   COOK: 3 TO 4 HOURS

1   (12- to 14-pound) turkey
Salt and pepper (optional)
Vegetable oil or melted butter or
        margarine

•Remove giblets and neck from turkey; reserve for other uses. Rinse turkey thoroughly with cold water; pat dry. Sprinkle body cavity with salt and pepper if you are not going to stuff turkey. If stuffing is desired, lightly spoon stuffing into body and neck cavities of turkey. If excess skin around tail has been cut away, tuck legs under flap of skin around tail. If excess skin is intact, close cavity with skewers, and truss. Tie ends of legs to tail with heavy string. Lift wingtips up and over back, and tuck under bird.
•Place turkey on a roasting rack, breast side up; brush entire bird with vegetable oil.
•Bake at 325° for 3 to 4 hours or until a meat thermometer inserted in meaty part of thigh registers 180°. If turkey starts to brown too much during cooking, cover loosely with aluminum foil.
•When turkey is two-thirds done, cut the string or band of skin holding the drumstick ends to the tail; this will ensure that the thighs are cooked internally. Turkey is done when drumsticks are easy to move up and down. Let stand 15 minutes before carving. Yield: 12 servings.
Per serving: Calories 664 Fat 33.7g
Cholesterol 246mg Sodium 399mg

Herbed Turkey Breast

PREP: 12 MINUTES   COOK: 2 HOURS

¼   cup olive oil
3   cloves garlic, minced
1   teaspoon fresh or dried rosemary
1   (5- to 5½-pound) bone-in turkey breast
1   teaspoon salt
1   teaspoon pepper

•Combine first 3 ingredients. Loosen skin from turkey breast without totally detaching skin; brush about one-third of olive oil mixture under skin. Replace skin. Sprinkle breast with salt and pepper; place in a lightly greased 11- x 7-inch baking dish. Cover loosely with aluminum foil.
•Bake at 325° for 1 hour. Uncover and bake 1 more hour or until a meat thermometer registers 170°, basting with remaining oil mixture every 15 minutes. Yield: 12 servings.
Per serving: Calories 247 Fat 12.8g
Cholesterol 80mg Sodium 263mg

PREFER WHITE MEAT?

Serving a turkey breast rather than a whole turkey eliminates waste and is a smart choice if your family prefers just white meat.

Deep-Fried Cajun Turkey

PREP: 20 MINUTES   MARINATE: 12 HOURS

COOK: 45 MINUTES

Fried turkey is all the rage now. You'll know why once you've tasted the tender, juicy meat under an ultracrispy skin. We liked this recipe using the whole can of seasoning, but go sparingly if you want the turkey less salty.

1 (12-pound) fresh or frozen turkey, thawed
1 (8-ounce) can Cajun seasoning (we tested with Tony Chachere's)
3 gallons peanut oil

•Remove giblets and neck from turkey; reserve for other uses. Rinse turkey thoroughly with cold water; pat dry. Drain body cavity well. Remove plastic pop-up timer from turkey, if necessary. Place turkey in a large shallow dish or roasting pan. Rub outside of turkey with half of seasoning mixture. Cover and refrigerate 12 hours.

•Drain body cavity well, and rub turkey with remaining seasoning mixture, sprinkling some into body cavity.

•Pour oil into a deep propane turkey fryer or 26-quart stockpot, and heat to 325°. (If unsure about fryer size or how much oil to use, place turkey in pot prior to seasoning, and fill pot with water just until turkey is covered. Remove turkey; this is the amount of oil needed.)

•Place turkey on fryer rod. Wearing heavy-duty work gloves or an oven mitt, carefully lower turkey into hot oil with rod attachment. Slowly increase heat so oil temperature returns to 325° to 350° (this may take some time). Fry turkey 45 minutes or until a meat thermometer inserted in meaty part of thigh registers 180°. Remove from oil; drain and cool slightly before slicing. Yield: 14 servings.

Per serving: Calories 536 Fat 28g
Cholesterol 200mg Sodium 5241mg

Note: Set turkey fryer up outside in an open area. Use a long-stemmed deep-fry thermometer that clips onto the rim of the turkey fryer to monitor oil temperature.

Stuffed Turkey Roll

PREP: 45 MINUTES   COOK: 50 MINUTES

12 ounces ground pork
1 (10-ounce) package frozen chopped spinach, thawed and well drained
1 large egg, beaten
½ cup soft breadcrumbs (homemade)
⅓ cup minced onion
2 cloves garlic, minced
¾ teaspoon dried thyme
¾ teaspoon dried rosemary, crushed
½ teaspoon salt
½ teaspoon freshly ground pepper
1 (3-pound) boneless turkey breast
¼ cup butter or margarine, melted

•Combine first 10 ingredients; set aside.
•Lay turkey breast flat on wax paper, skin side down. Remove tendons, and trim fat, keeping skin intact. From center, slice horizontally (parallel with skin) through thickest part of each side of breast almost to outer edge; flip cut piece and breast fillets over to enlarge breast. Pound breast to flatten and to form a more even thickness.

•Spoon stuffing mixture in center of width of turkey breast, leaving a 2-inch border at sides. Fold in sides of turkey breast over filling; roll up turkey breast over filling, starting from bottom. (Roll should be 12 to 14 inches long.)
•Tie turkey breast roll securely in several places with heavy string; place, seam side down, on a rack in a roasting pan. Insert meat thermometer, making sure bulb rests in meat of turkey. Pour butter evenly over roll.
•Bake at 425° for 30 minutes, basting often with pan drippings. Reduce heat to 350°, and bake 20 more minutes or until thermometer registers 170°, basting often. Let stand 10 minutes before slicing. Yield: 10 servings.

Per serving: Calories 315 Fat 15.6g
Cholesterol 137mg Sodium 285mg

Parmesan-Walnut Crusted Turkey

◄ QUICK ►

PREP: 7 MINUTES   COOK: 8 MINUTES

½ cup grated Parmesan cheese
½ cup all-purpose flour
⅓ cup walnut pieces
1¼ pounds turkey tenderloins
½ teaspoon salt
¼ teaspoon pepper
½ cup milk
2 tablespoons olive oil
¼ cup finely chopped fresh parsley

•Process first 3 ingredients in container of food processor until walnuts are finely chopped. Set aside.
•Cut each turkey tenderloin in half lengthwise along tendon; remove tendons. Cut tenderloins in half crosswise.
•Place turkey between two sheets of heavy-duty plastic wrap; flatten to ¼-inch thickness, using a meat mallet or rolling pin.
•Sprinkle with salt and pepper. Dredge turkey in cheese mixture. Dip in milk, and dredge in cheese mixture again, coating well.
•Heat oil in a large nonstick skillet over medium-high heat until hot; add turkey, and cook 8 minutes or until lightly browned, turning occasionally. Sprinkle with parsley. Yield: 4 servings.

Per serving: Calories 437 Fat 22.3g
Cholesterol 98mg Sodium 644mg

Braised Goose

PREP: 45 MINUTES

COOK: 2 HOURS AND 10 MINUTES

Garnish this holiday goose with apples, shallots, and herbs. Use the drippings to make a golden gravy.

1 (8- to 10-pound) dressed goose
1 Rome apple, sliced
1 medium onion, sliced
1 (14½-ounce) can ready-to-serve chicken broth
2 carrots, scraped and sliced
2 to 3 shallots, chopped
1 tablespoon lemon juice
1 tablespoon Worcestershire sauce
½ teaspoon ground cloves
½ teaspoon dried marjoram
½ teaspoon dried rosemary
⅛ teaspoon ground red pepper
¾ cup port or other sweet red wine or orange juice
2 tablespoons butter or margarine
1 tablespoon all-purpose flour

•Remove giblets and neck from goose; set aside. Rinse goose thoroughly with cold water; pat dry. Stuff cavity with apple and onion; close cavity with skewers. Tie ends of legs together with heavy string. Lift wingtips up and over back, and tuck under bird.
•Combine reserved giblets, neck, chicken broth, and next 9 ingredients in a large saucepan. Bring to a boil; reduce heat, and simmer, uncovered, 10 minutes. Remove from heat, and set aside.
•Place goose, breast side up, on a rack in a roasting pan. Insert meat thermometer into thigh, making sure it does not touch bone.
•Bake goose, uncovered, at 400° for 15 minutes. Pour reserved broth mixture into roasting pan.
•Cover and bake 1 hour and 45 minutes or until meat thermometer registers 180° in the thigh. Transfer goose to a serving platter. Let stand 15 minutes before carving.
•Strain drippings from roasting pan through a sieve. Skim and discard fat; set drippings aside.
•Melt butter in a heavy saucepan over low heat; add flour, stirring until smooth. Cook 1 minute, stirring constantly. Gradually add reserved drippings; cook over medium heat, stirring constantly, until mixture is thickened and bubbly. Serve goose with gravy. Yield: 8 servings.

Per serving: Calories 729 Fat 52.6g
Cholesterol 213mg Sodium 378mg

Citrus Grilled Cornish Hens

◄ GRILLED ►

PREP: 9 MINUTES   MARINATE: 8 HOURS

COOK: 1 HOUR AND 15 MINUTES

Use indirect heat to grill these birds. Splitting them helps speed the cooking.

4 (1¼-pound) Cornish hens, split
2 teaspoons dried thyme
½ teaspoon salt
1 teaspoon pepper
1 tablespoon ground cumin
2 tablespoons olive oil
¼ cup lime juice
¼ cup orange juice
1 teaspoon hot sauce
1 tablespoon Worcestershire sauce

•Remove giblets from hens; reserve for another use. Rinse hens with cold water, and pat dry. Place hens in a large heavy-duty, zip-top plastic bag or shallow dish; set aside.
•Combine thyme and remaining 8 ingredients, stirring well; pour over hens, coating thoroughly. Seal or cover, and marinate in refrigerator 8 hours, turning occasionally.
•For a charcoal grill, prepare fire by piling charcoal or lava rocks on each side of grill, leaving center empty. Place a drip pan between coals. For a gas grill, light one burner, placing drip pan on opposite side.
•Remove hens from marinade, reserving marinade. Bring marinade to a boil in a small saucepan; set aside. Coat food rack with vegetable cooking spray, and place rack on grill. Arrange hens, breast side up, on food rack over drip pan.
•Grill, covered with grill lid, over medium-hot coals (350° to 400°) 35 minutes. Brush with marinade; cook 40 more minutes or until meat thermometer inserted into meaty part of thigh registers 180°. Yield: 4 servings.

Per serving: Calories 641 Fat 37.7g
Cholesterol 221mg Sodium 376mg

Note: You can partially cook hens in the microwave prior to grilling. Place hens, breast side down, on a microwave-safe rack placed inside a 13- x 9-inch baking dish. Cover hens with a tent of wax paper. Microwave at HIGH 10 minutes. Turn hens over, and rotate dish; brush with marinade. Cover and microwave at HIGH 7 minutes. Drain hens.
•Grill hens, breast side down and covered with grill lid, over medium coals (300° to 350°) 10 minutes, basting occasionally. Turn hens, and grill 10 more minutes or until meat thermometer inserted into meaty part of thigh registers 180°.

Lime and Sesame Roasted Cornish Hens

PREP: 15 MINUTES   MARINATE: 8 HOURS

COOK: 45 MINUTES

2 (1½-pound) Cornish hens, split
⅓ cup soy sauce
¼ cup vegetable oil or olive oil
3 cloves garlic, sliced
2 tablespoons sesame seeds, lightly toasted in a dry skillet
1 tablespoon brown sugar
2 teaspoons ground ginger
3 tablespoons lime juice
Garnish: lime wedges

•Place hens, breast side down, in a heavy-duty, zip-top plastic bag or large shallow dish; set aside.
•Process soy sauce and next 6 ingredients in container of an electric blender until smooth, stopping once to scrape down sides. Pour marinade over hens. Seal or cover, and marinate in refrigerator 8 hours, turning occasionally.
•Remove hens from marinade. Bring marinade to a boil in a small saucepan, and set aside.
•Place hens, breast side up, in a lightly greased 13- x 9-inch pan or on a rack of a roasting pan. Bake, uncovered, at 400° for 45 minutes or until done, basting occasionally with marinade after 20 minutes. Garnish, if desired. Yield: 4 servings.

Per serving: Calories 366 Fat 23.3g
Cholesterol 110mg Sodium 567mg

GAME BIRDS: WILD & DOMESTIC

The term "game" has come to include birds once caught in the wild that are now also raised domestically. Quail is a popular example. Game birds tend to be leaner than common domestic birds, which means they can easily become tough when slightly overcooked. Moist-heat cooking methods are often recommended for this reason. And when roasting game birds, remember to baste them frequently. Some recipes will wrap birds with bacon or other fat to keep them tender and juicy as they cook. This is called *barding*.

With younger wild birds, serve only the breasts as an entrée; save the other parts for stock.

Pheasant is available both domestic and wild. The domestic bird tastes mild and has a texture much like chicken. The wild version has a pronounced gamey flavor. Whole pheasants weigh between 2 and 3 pounds. They can be substituted in most chicken recipes, if desired, with a reduction in cooking time since pheasant is leaner than chicken.

You won't find dove, as Southerners know it, in the retail market. You have to be the lucky recipient of a hunter's catch. We've included a dove recipe that applies moist-heat cooking with a flavorful braising liquid. When cooking dove, remember the key is not to overcook the dark meat or it will taste too livery.

Quail are lean game birds. They're the smallest game birds commonly eaten in this country. The domestic birds are mild flavored, and the wild ones have a subtle gamey taste. When serving quail as an entrée, allow two birds per person. Look for quail in the frozen meats section at the supermarket.

Duck Breasts with Raspberry Sauce

**PREP: 25 MINUTES   MARINATE: 2 HOURS
COOK: 20 MINUTES**

The Raspberry Sauce for these duck breasts is out of this world. This entrée makes a stunning presentation when sliced and served with the deep purple sauce.

½ cup dry red wine
¼ cup soy sauce
2 tablespoons vegetable oil
1 clove garlic, minced
¼ teaspoon freshly ground pepper
4 skinned, boned wild duck breasts
Raspberry Sauce
Garnish: fresh blackberries, lime slices

•Combine first 5 ingredients in a bowl, stirring well. Place duck breasts in a heavy-duty, zip-top plastic bag or shallow dish; add marinade. Seal or cover, and marinate in refrigerator 2 hours, turning meat occasionally.
•Remove duck breasts from marinade, discarding marinade; place duck breasts on a rack in broiler pan. Broil 5½ inches from heat 15 to 20 minutes or until meat thermometer registers 180°, turning once. Thinly slice breast, and serve with Raspberry Sauce. Garnish, if desired. Yield: 4 servings.
Per serving: Calories 549 Fat 18.1g
Cholesterol 246mg Sodium 1193mg

Raspberry Sauce

¼ cup seedless black raspberry preserves
¼ cup dry red wine or water
1½ tablespoons Dijon mustard
1 tablespoon soy sauce
1 teaspoon lime juice
½ teaspoon salt
¼ to ½ teaspoon freshly ground pepper

•Combine all ingredients in a small saucepan; cook over low heat until thoroughly heated. Yield: ¾ cup.

Pan-Braised Dove

PREP: 9 MINUTES   COOK: 25 MINUTES

If you have hunters in your family who share their bounty, consider this dove recipe. The whole breasts simmer in a rich wine gravy.

¼ cup all-purpose flour
1 teaspoon salt
2 teaspoons freshly ground pepper
16 skinless whole bone-in dove breasts
2 tablespoons butter or margarine, melted
2 tablespoons olive oil
1 cup dry red wine, divided
1 (10½-ounce) can chicken broth, divided
¼ cup red currant jelly
2 tablespoons all-purpose flour

•Combine first 3 ingredients; dredge dove breasts in flour mixture. Brown dove all over in butter and olive oil in a large skillet over medium-high heat. Gradually add ½ cup wine, ½ cup broth, and jelly; cover and cook over low heat 20 minutes.
•Remove dove from skillet; cover and keep warm. Combine 2 tablespoons flour, remaining ½ cup red wine, and remaining broth, stirring until smooth. Gradually add flour mixture to mixture in skillet; cook over medium heat, stirring constantly, until mixture thickens.
•Return dove to skillet to reheat. Serve dove and gravy over hot cooked rice or egg noodles. Yield: 4 servings.
Per serving: Calories 376 Fat 16.9g
Cholesterol 27mg Sodium 974mg

Pheasant à l'Orange

PREP: 30 MINUTES   COOK: 2½ HOURS

Use an inexpensive dry Muscat wine to flavor this pheasant. The wine's musky taste and aroma go well with the golden raisins and zesty orange rind. The pecan rice is well worth preparing to accompany the pheasant.

4 (2-pound) pheasants, dressed
½ lemon
½ teaspoon salt
½ teaspoon pepper
⅓ cup butter or margarine, softened
1 (14½-ounce) can chicken broth
½ cup Muscat wine or chicken broth
1 cup golden raisins
1 teaspoon grated orange rind (optional)
¾ cup orange juice
¼ cup all-purpose flour
Pecan Rice

•Rinse pheasants with cold water; pat dry. Rub with lemon, and sprinkle with salt and pepper. Place pheasants, breast side up, in a roasting pan; rub with butter.
•Combine broth, wine, raisins, and, if desired, orange rind; pour mixture over pheasants.
•Bake, uncovered, at 350° for 1 hour and 45 minutes or until a meat thermometer inserted in meaty part of thigh registers 180°, basting pheasants every 15 minutes. Transfer pheasants to a serving platter; keep warm.
•Pour pan drippings into a gravy strainer; reserve drippings, and discard fat. Set drippings aside.
•Combine orange juice and flour in a saucepan; stir until blended. Add drippings, and cook over medium heat, stirring constantly, until mixture is thickened. Serve pheasant with sauce and Pecan Rice. Yield: 8 servings.

Per serving: Calories 920 Fat 46.8g
Cholesterol 209mg Sodium 838mg

Pecan Rice

3 cups chicken broth
1½ cups uncooked long-grain rice
⅔ cup chopped pecans, toasted
3 tablespoons butter or margarine
2 tablespoons minced fresh parsley or
    2 teaspoons dried parsley
⅛ teaspoon ground white pepper

•Combine broth and rice in a large saucepan; bring to a boil. Cover, reduce heat, and simmer 20 minutes or until liquid is absorbed and rice is tender. Remove from heat; stir in pecans and remaining ingredients. Yield: 6 cups.

Sage-Smoked Maple Quail

PREP: 1 HOUR AND 20 MINUTES

CHILL: 30 MINUTES   COOK: 2 HOURS

The combination of ingredients that are stuffed in, wrapped around, and brushed on these quail is flavor-blending at its best. Needless to say, our staff gave this entrée high marks.

4 sweet yellow apples, diced
½ cup chopped pecans
½ teaspoon salt
1 (0.4-ounce) jar dried sage, divided
12 quail, dressed
12 pepper-cured bacon slices
Hickory chunks
1 quart apple cider
⅓ cup pure maple syrup

•Combine apple, pecans, salt, and 2 teaspoons sage; stuff each quail with apple mixture, and wrap a bacon slice around each quail, securing ends with a wooden pick. Cover and chill 30 minutes.
•Soak chunks in water 1 hour; moisten remaining sage with water.
•Prepare charcoal fire in smoker; let burn 15 to 20 minutes. Drain chunks; place chunks and one-third of remaining sage on hot coals. Place water pan in smoker; add 1 quart cider.
•Place quail, breast side up, on grill rack; brush quail with maple syrup. Cook, covered with smoker lid, 2 hours or until done, adding remaining sage at 30-minute intervals. Yield: 6 servings.

Per serving: Calories 860 Fat 58.8g
Cholesterol 138mg Sodium 621mg

Smothered Quail with Vegetables

PREP: 20 MINUTES

COOK: 1 HOUR AND 20 MINUTES

Serve this skillet full of seasoned quail with mashed potatoes or rice.

12 quail, dressed
1 teaspoon salt
½ teaspoon pepper
⅔ cup all-purpose flour
Vegetable oil
2½ cups chicken broth
¼ cup molasses
2 tablespoons Worcestershire sauce
1 tablespoon lemon juice
1 teaspoon poultry seasoning
1 clove garlic, crushed
1 (8-ounce) package fresh mushrooms, halved
4 stalks celery, cut into 2-inch pieces
3 large carrots, scraped and sliced
½ cup dry white wine
4 green onions, chopped

•Sprinkle quail with salt and pepper; dredge in flour. Pour oil to depth of ½ inch in a large heavy skillet. Brown quail in hot oil. Remove quail; discard oil. Return quail to skillet.
•Combine chicken broth and next 5 ingredients; add to skillet. Bring to a boil; cover, reduce heat, and simmer 30 minutes. Add mushrooms and next 3 ingredients. Cover and simmer 30 minutes. Add green onions just before serving. Yield: 6 servings.

Per serving: Calories 603 Fat 37.7g
Cholesterol 100mg Sodium 899mg

Grilled Asian Chicken Salad (page 368)

SALADS & DRESSINGS

Salad is such a multipurpose menu item. You can toss tender, young greens with a light dressing for its traditional role, add chunks of grilled chicken for an impressive entrée, or mold a fruit salad for a refreshing dessert. Salad is indeed gaining ground as the meal's main attraction.

Equipment

Not much equipment is needed to produce a pretty salad. In fact, the essentials may amount to a wooden salad bowl, salad tongs, and a cruet for serving your favorite dressing. A chef's knife and a cutting board are other basics for chopping fresh vegetables for salad. Of course, a food processor does this job, and swiftly too. A salad spinner can be useful for drying lettuce once you've washed it, and a Mouli grater will twirl shreds of cheese atop fresh-dressed greens. An egg slicer comes in handy for neatly slicing ingredients such as mushrooms and strawberries that commonly top salads.

Everyone needs a culinary collection of some type. Consider copper or aluminum molds for both individual and multicup salads. You'll find the molds useful on countless occasions for brunch. And the molds are quite decorative, too.

Chill, Don't Freeze

Most salads enhanced with chopped fruits and vegetables don't make good candidates for the freezer. The texture of these ingredients will deteriorate upon freezing. And mayonnaise, a common binding ingredient for creamy-type salads, tends to break down upon freezing. Never freeze a gelatin salad that contains fruits or vegetables. The fruits and vegetables may leach liquid during freezing and cause the salad to become watery.

So when you're in the market for a make-ahead type of salad, stick with chilled options only. Consider one of our gelatin salads that can be refrigerated overnight. And you can make potato salads, bean salads, and coleslaws and chill them a day in advance as well. Their flavor improves overnight.

Chop raw vegetables for salads and package them separately in zip-top plastic bags. You can chill them for a day or two, and then toss with greens and add dressing just before serving.

You can also make salad dressings in advance and chill them several days. Just whisk before serving. Remember to give oil and vinegar dressings time to return to room temperature before serving. Shake vigorously to blend ingredients.

SALAD GREENS DICTIONARY

Today there are so many types of greens in the produce department that salad making should be one endless adventure. Let the photograph inspire you to pick some new greens the next time you shop.

Arugula: Also called *rocket*, arugula is a slightly bitter green with an assertive peppery mustard flavor. It's sold in small bunches with roots attached. Arugula leaves tend to hold a lot of grit so be sure to rinse the bunch well just before using. Look for a bunch with fresh, bright green leaves.

Belgian endive: These small, torpedo-shaped tight heads of white leaves have a slightly bitter flavor. The sturdy leaves are often used individually to hold an appetizer serving. Only the leaf tips have pale color (typically yellow-green), because Belgian endive is grown in total darkness. Once exposed to light, the leaves turn too green and the bitterness intensifies. Buy crisp, firmly packed pale heads.

Bibb: Bibb lettuce forms a small round head with loosely packed soft leaves. The leaves are usually pale green and have a delicate sweet flavor. Since Bibb is in the butterhead family, it's often called just *butterhead* or *butter* lettuce.

Boston: Similar to Bibb lettuce in flavor, texture, and appearance, Boston lettuce is slightly larger.

Butterhead: Boston and Bibb are two well-known lettuces in this family. They have small, round, loosely formed heads. The leaves are quite tender and require gentle care when handling.

Curly endive: This endive grows in loose heads with lacy green leaves that curl at the tips. Curly endive leaves have a prickly texture and a slightly bitter taste. These sharp greens blend well with other milder greens.

Dandelion greens: These jagged-edged greens grow wild and are also farmed. The leaves have a tangy, bitter flavor. Dandelion greens are at their prime in early spring. Wash the bright green, tender leaves well and refrigerate them up to five days. Enjoy them fresh in a salad or sautéed like spinach.

Endive: There are three main varieties of endive—Belgian endive, curly endive, and escarole. See individual entries for the distinctions.

Escarole: The mildest member of the endive family, escarole has broad, slightly curved green leaves. It's available year-round and will keep several days in the refrigerator. Choose a fresh head with healthy-looking leaves.

Green and red leaf lettuce: These leaf lettuces have large flaring leaves that grow in loose bunches rather than tight heads. The green leaf variety is a vivid green; the red leaf variety is green with red tips. Leaf lettuce is crisp when cold, but wilts rather quickly. Plan to store it only a few days in the refrigerator.

Iceberg: Probably the most common lettuce around, iceberg is crisp, mild in flavor, readily available, and keeps up to a week in the refrigerator. It's a good background lettuce when making a mixed green salad.

Kale and ornamental kale: A member of the cabbage family, kale is easily identifiable by its frilly edges. It has dark green leaves and a mild cabbage flavor. Fresh kale is at its peak from fall through spring. The center stalk is tough so be sure to remove it before cooking. Kale is actually a highly nutritious vegetable. It's a rich source of vitamin C and calcium. Use kale within three days of purchase. Ornamental varieties are quite beautiful; they can be lavender, deep purple, yellow-green, and white. Ornamental kale has a slightly bitter taste and fairly crisp texture. It's commonly used as a garnish.

Mesclun: Also called *gourmet salad mix* in some markets, mesclun is simply a mixture of tender, young salad greens. It can include greens like arugula, dandelion, sorrel, and oakleaf. Wash the tender mix with care and blot dry before using.

Napa cabbage: This Chinese cabbage has tall and crinkly, thick-veined leaves that are a pale yellow-green color. Unlike the strongly flavored waxy leaves of a common round head of cabbage, napa cabbage has a delicate, clean taste and crisp bite. It's available year-round and is good when eaten raw, sautéed, or braised.

Oakleaf: This is a popular small, tender leaf lettuce with red-tipped leaves and a nutty, mild flavor.

Radicchio: A tight head of radicchio is easy to identify. With its wine-red, cup-shaped leaves, radicchio makes a beautiful salad when blended with other greens. Radicchio has a slightly tangy flavor. Store it up to a week in the refrigerator. You'll find it in the supermarket all year long.

Romaine: Romaine is an elongated bunch of greens with coarse, crisp leaves and heavy ribs. Cut out and discard tough ribs before serving. Romaine adds crunch to tossed salads and is famous for its presence in Caesar Salad (page 352).

Sorrel: Resembling fresh spinach, sorrel leaves are bright green with sturdy stems. Sorrel ranges in length from 2 to 12 inches and is at its peak in the spring. Use it raw in salads or briefly sautéed like fresh spinach. Trim or tear tough stems.

Spinach: Spinach has vivid green leaves that are curly or smooth. Fresh spinach is available year-round. Its leaves tend to be gritty, so rinse spinach well and blot dry before using. Trim or tear off tough stems. Find fresh spinach commonly packaged in 10-ounce bags. You might still want to rinse this spinach and tear off stems. Use spinach raw or cooked.

Watercress: Watercress has a pungent, peppery bite to it and is sold in small bundles. Its dark green leaves are small and crisp. Wash and shake watercress dry just before serving. Use it raw in salads, on sandwiches, as a garnish, or briefly cooked in soups.

Some of the simplest, yet best-dressed, food comes from the salad bowl. A well-made salad can be a work of art. Let the shape of the food speak for itself—ruffly leaf lettuce or jagged dandelion greens may need only a light dressing and tiny tomatoes to please both the palate and the eye.

When buying bunches of greens, choose those with fresh-looking, brightly colored, healthy leaves with no sign of wilting. Avoid any that are spotted, limp, or yellowing; these greens are past their prime.

A brown core is a sign of oxidation and doesn't necessarily indicate poor quality. After lettuce is cut at harvest, the core naturally browns as the cut surface seals to keep the head fresh and to hold in nutrients.

To store, gently rinse the leaves, and shake off excess moisture. Store in your refrigerator crisper drawer in zip-top plastic bags with a paper towel to absorb moisture, squeezing out as much air as possible before sealing. Use within a day or two. Crisp lettuces like iceberg hold up longer (sometimes up to a week) than more fragile greens like oakleaf.

In most markets, you can find an abundance of packaged trimmed, torn greens that are ready to use. These packages proclaim that the greens are cleaned, but you might want to rinse them lightly to freshen the greens.

The taste, shape, and texture of greens vary, particularly between bunches and heads. Refer to our salad greens photograph and our dictionary of greens on the previous two pages to familiarize yourself with new salad options.

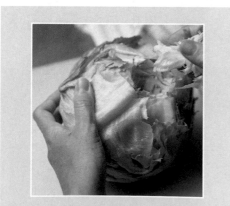

To core a head of lettuce: Tap core end on the counter; then twist and remove the core.

Caesar Salad

◀ **FAMILY FAVORITE** ▶

PREP: 25 MINUTES   CHILL: 2 HOURS
BAKE: 15 MINUTES

This famous salad was created by accident. The story goes that a Mexican restaurateur named Caesar was overwhelmed by guests one day and had to prepare a salad from the few simple ingredients on hand—romaine lettuce, coddled eggs, Parmesan cheese, lemons, and dry bread. The guests were delighted—and lucky. Caesar didn't know as we do today that it's not safe to eat uncooked eggs. Our version omits the traditional coddled egg.

1 large head romaine lettuce
¾ cup olive oil
¼ cup red wine vinegar
1 teaspoon Worcestershire sauce
½ teaspoon salt
¼ teaspoon dry mustard
1 large clove garlic, crushed
1 lemon, halved
Freshly ground pepper
¼ cup freshly grated Parmesan cheese
Garlic Croutons
1 (2-ounce) can anchovy fillets, drained (optional)

•Wash romaine under cold running water. Trim core, and separate stalk into leaves; discard wilted or discolored portions. Shake leaves to remove moisture. Place romaine in a large zip-top plastic bag; chill at least 2 hours.
•Combine olive oil and next 5 ingredients in a jar. Cover tightly, and shake vigorously. Set aside.
•Cut coarse ribs from large leaves of romaine (see photo at right); tear leaves into bite-size pieces, and place in a large salad bowl. Pour dressing over romaine; toss gently until coated.
•Squeeze juice from lemon halves over salad. Grind a generous amount of pepper over salad; sprinkle with cheese. Toss salad. Top with Garlic Croutons and, if desired, anchovies. Serve salad immediately. Yield: 4 servings.
Per serving: Calories 530 Fat 52.5g
Cholesterol 44mg Sodium 963mg

Garlic Croutons

3 tablespoons butter or margarine, softened
3 (¾-inch-thick) slices French bread
¼ teaspoon garlic powder

•Spread butter over both sides of bread slices; sprinkle with garlic powder. Cut slices into ¾-inch cubes. Place on a baking sheet, and bake at 350° for 15 minutes or until croutons are crisp and dry. Cool; store in an airtight container. Yield: about 1½ cups.

To remove tough ribs: Cut fibrous ribs from larger romaine leaves; then tear leaves for salad.

Chef's Garden Salad

PREP: 38 MINUTES

1 large head iceberg lettuce, torn
1 large tomato, cut into thin wedges
1 small cucumber, sliced
1 small green pepper, chopped
½ cup sliced celery
5 ounces cooked deli ham, cut into strips
5 ounces cooked deli chicken, cut into strips
½ (8-ounce) block Cheddar cheese, cut into strips
2 large hard-cooked eggs, sliced
Thousand Island Dressing (page 370)

•Combine first 5 ingredients in a salad bowl; toss well. Arrange ham and next 3 ingredients on salad. Serve with Thousand Island Dressing. Yield: 6 servings.
Per serving: Calories 504 Fat 40.8g
Cholesterol 148mg Sodium 1483mg

Greek Salad

PREP: 15 MINUTES

Feta cheese, tangy olives, and pepperoncini are common components of a Greek salad. Try using one of the flavored fetas available for variety.

1 medium head iceberg lettuce, torn or shredded (see photo below)
1 small purple onion, thinly sliced
1 cucumber, peeled, seeded, and chopped
½ cup pepperoncini salad peppers
½ cup kalamata olives
4 ounces crumbled feta cheese
½ cup red wine vinaigrette or Basil Vinaigrette (page 372)
Garnish: tomato wedges

• Combine first 7 ingredients in a salad bowl; toss gently, and garnish, if desired. Serve immediately. Yield: 4 servings.
Per serving: Calories 450 Fat 44.6g
Cholesterol 25mg Sodium 1131mg

Shredding lettuce: Cut a head of iceberg lettuce into quarters; then thinly slice lettuce, using a sharp chef's knife.

Spinach-Apple Salad

PREP: 23 MINUTES   STAND: 2 HOURS

An interesting mix of peanuts, raisins, apples, and curry toss great flavor into this spinach salad. Leave the peel on the pretty red apples for maximum color.

¼ cup vegetable oil
¼ cup white vinegar
1½ teaspoons chutney
½ teaspoon salt
½ teaspoon curry powder
½ teaspoon dry mustard
1 (10-ounce) package fresh spinach, torn
2 large Red Delicious apples, chopped
⅔ cup salted dry-roasted peanuts
½ cup raisins
3 green onions, sliced
2 tablespoons sesame seeds, toasted

• Combine first 6 ingredients in a small bowl; stir well with a wire whisk. Cover and let dressing stand at room temperature 2 hours for flavors to blend.
• Combine spinach and remaining 5 ingredients in a salad bowl; toss well. Pour dressing over spinach mixture, and toss gently. Serve immediately. Yield: 6 servings.
Per serving: Calories 291 Fat 19.2g
Cholesterol 0mg Sodium 382mg

Salad Greens with Apple and Brie

PREP: 15 MINUTES   COOK: 21 MINUTES

Crisp apples and walnut-coated Brie top this salad and make it marvelous. In fact, you can just serve the warm Brie and apples as an appetizer.

2 large Red Delicious apples, cut into thin wedges
½ cup apple cider, divided
4 slices bacon
¼ cup balsamic vinegar
1 tablespoon brown sugar
6 cups mixed salad greens, torn
Walnut-Baked Brie

• Dip apple wedges in ¼ cup cider to prevent browning; set aside.

• Cook bacon in a skillet over medium heat until crisp; remove bacon, reserving 1 tablespoon drippings in skillet. Crumble bacon, and set aside. Add remaining ¼ cup cider, balsamic vinegar, and brown sugar to drippings; cook dressing over medium heat, stirring constantly, until sugar dissolves.
• Just before serving, arrange greens, apple slices, and warm Walnut-Baked Brie on plates. Drizzle with dressing, and sprinkle with crumbled bacon. Yield: 6 servings.
Per serving: Calories 347 Fat 25g
Cholesterol 48mg Sodium 385mg

Walnut-Baked Brie

1 (8-ounce) round Brie
2 tablespoons brown sugar
¼ cup walnuts, toasted and coarsely chopped

• Remove top rind from Brie. Cut cheese into 6 wedges; place on a lightly greased baking sheet. Sprinkle cheese with brown sugar and walnuts. Bake at 450° for 2 to 3 minutes or just until soft. Serve immediately on salad greens. Yield: 6 servings.

Orange-Walnut Salad

PREP: 20 MINUTES

2 heads Bibb lettuce, torn into bite-size pieces
1 (10-ounce) package fresh spinach, torn
2 oranges, peeled, seeded, and sectioned
½ medium onion, sliced and separated into rings
½ cup coarsely chopped walnuts
2 teaspoons butter or margarine, melted
Sweet-and-Sour Dressing (page 373)

• Place first 4 ingredients in a large salad bowl. Sauté walnuts in butter in a small skillet over medium heat until toasted; add to salad. Toss with Sweet-and-Sour Dressing. Yield: 6 servings.
Per serving: Calories 538 Fat 46.3g
Cholesterol 3mg Sodium 469mg

Seven-Layer Salad

PREP: 35 MINUTES

Show off the many layers of this hefty salad by stacking them in a trifle bowl, if you have one, or any large glass bowl.

4 cups torn iceberg lettuce
1 cup chopped celery
1 cup chopped green pepper
1 cup chopped purple onion
1 (10-ounce) package frozen English peas, thawed
3 cups torn fresh spinach
3 cups chopped smoked turkey
¾ cup mayonnaise
¾ cup sour cream
½ cup sliced pimiento-stuffed olives
½ cup (2 ounces) finely shredded Cheddar cheese
6 slices bacon, cooked and crumbled

•Layer first 7 ingredients in a 3-quart bowl.
•Combine mayonnaise and sour cream, stirring well; spread mixture over turkey. Sprinkle olives around outer edge of salad. Sprinkle cheese and bacon in center of salad. Cover and chill salad before serving. Yield: 10 servings.

Per serving: Calories 294 Fat 22.3g
Cholesterol 49mg Sodium 627mg

Turkish Salad

PREP: 30 MINUTES

Try the unusual blend of flavors in this colorful salad sprinkled with almonds and capers.

6 cups thinly sliced spinach
3 cups shredded red cabbage
½ cup large pimiento-stuffed olives, sliced
½ cup small pitted ripe olives, sliced
½ cup currants
½ cup finely chopped gherkins
½ cup capers, drained
½ cup sliced almonds, toasted
2 tablespoons fresh lemon juice
3 oranges, sectioned
Balsamic Vinaigrette (page 373)

•Place half of spinach in a large glass bowl; top with cabbage and next 4 ingredients.
•Reserve 1 tablespoon each of capers and almonds; sprinkle remaining capers and almonds over cabbage mixture. Top with remaining spinach, and sprinkle with lemon juice.
•Arrange orange sections on top; sprinkle with reserved capers and almonds. Cover and chill, if desired. Serve with Balsamic Vinaigrette. Yield: 8 servings.

Per serving: Calories 287 Fat 25.1g
Cholesterol 0mg Sodium 1045mg

Peppery Greens with Raspberry Dressing

PREP: 5 MINUTES

The raspberry taste really comes through in this slightly sweet dressing that coats these peppery greens. If you can't find watercress, you can still make the salad using 4½ cups of arugula or fresh spinach.

¼ cup cranberry-raspberry juice drink
¼ cup seedless raspberry jam
3 tablespoons raspberry vinegar
2 tablespoons olive oil
½ teaspoon salt
⅛ teaspoon freshly ground pepper
3 cups watercress leaves
1½ cups arugula or spinach
¼ cup freshly shaved Parmesan cheese

•Combine first 6 ingredients in a jar; cover tightly, and shake vigorously.
•Combine watercress and arugula in a salad bowl; drizzle with raspberry dressing, tossing to coat. Sprinkle with cheese; serve immediately. Yield: 4 servings.

Per serving: Calories 144 Fat 8.1g
Cholesterol 3mg Sodium 399mg

WHAT ABOUT WATERCRESS?

It's peppery in flavor with tender, gangly stems. Be sure to remove stems before using watercress. It makes a nice shapely garnish, too. Try it next time instead of parsley.

HEARTS OF PALM

Tender ivory stalks of hearts of palm are harvested from the core of the cabbage palm tree. Hearts of palm are slender, pale, delicately flavored stalks. They're firm and smooth and taste like artichokes. They're wonderful sliced and served in salads. The canned variety packed in water that we enjoy in this country usually comes from Costa Rica or Brazil.

Hearts of Palm Salad

PREP: 10 MINUTES   CHILL: 4 HOURS

Slices of tender hearts of palm adorn these greens. Mixed baby greens are called mesclun; see them pictured among other greens on page 351.

1 clove garlic, minced
⅓ cup olive oil
2 tablespoons white wine vinegar
1 tablespoon Dijon mustard
¼ teaspoon salt
½ teaspoon pepper
6 cups mesclun*
2 (14.8-ounce) jars hearts of palm, drained and sliced into ½-inch rings
1 medium tomato, cut into thin wedges

•Combine first 6 ingredients in a small bowl; stir with a wire whisk until blended. Cover and chill 4 hours for flavors to blend.
•Combine salad greens, hearts of palm, and tomato in a large salad bowl. Pour dressing over salad; toss gently. Serve immediately. Yield: 6 servings.

Find mesclun in the produce section of most large grocery stores. It's described on page 350 in our Salad Greens Dictionary.

Per serving: Calories 148 Fat 12.7g
Cholesterol 0mg Sodium 543mg

Greens and Tuna Salad

◄ QUICK ►

PREP: 25 MINUTES

½ head romaine lettuce, torn
½ head Bibb lettuce, torn
4 Belgian endive leaves
½ head iceberg lettuce, torn
1 head Boston lettuce, torn
1 medium cucumber, chopped
1 small onion, thinly sliced
2 (7-ounce) cans tuna, drained and flaked
4 large hard-cooked eggs
½ cup olive oil
¼ cup lemon juice
1 teaspoon mayonnaise
½ teaspoon dry mustard
½ teaspoon salt
Dash of pepper

•Combine first 8 ingredients in a large salad bowl. Toss. Cut 3 hard-cooked eggs into wedges; add to salad greens and tuna.
•Press remaining hard-cooked egg through a sieve; add oil and remaining 5 ingredients just before serving, stirring well. Pour dressing over salad; toss gently. Yield: 6 servings.
Per serving: Calories 299 Fat 22.9g
Cholesterol 156mg Sodium 406mg

Salmon on Mixed Greens with Creamy Dill Dressing

◄ QUICK ►

PREP: 10 MINUTES COOK: 15 MINUTES

2½ pounds salmon fillet, cut into 6 pieces
2 tablespoons olive oil, divided
½ teaspoon salt
½ teaspoon pepper
¼ cup red wine vinegar
¼ cup olive oil or vegetable oil
2 teaspoons Dijon mustard
1 large clove garlic, minced
1 teaspoon dried dillweed
Dash of salt
Dash of pepper
1 cup whipping cream
12 cups mixed salad greens

•Brush salmon with 1 tablespoon olive oil; sprinkle with ½ teaspoon salt and ½ teaspoon pepper. Cook salmon, skin side down,

in remaining 1 tablespoon olive oil in a large skillet over medium-high heat 5 minutes. Turn salmon, and reduce heat to medium; cook 5 more minutes or until done. Remove skin, if desired.
•Combine vinegar and next 6 ingredients in a medium bowl; slowly add whipping cream, stirring with a wire whisk until blended. Arrange salad greens on a serving platter; drizzle half of dressing over greens, and top with warm salmon. Serve with remaining dressing. Yield: 6 servings.
Per serving: Calories 566 Fat 43.5g
Cholesterol 174mg Sodium 388mg

Grilled Fennel and Radicchio Salad

◄ GRILLED ►

PREP: 35 MINUTES COOK: 17 MINUTES

Serve this impressive and unique grilled salad with chicken or fish. The radicchio leaves and ridged fennel bulbs gain delicious-looking grill marks as they cook. Be ready to eat as soon as the salad greens come off the grill.

4 bulbs fennel
1 head radicchio, separated into leaves
½ cup orange juice
¼ cup orange marmalade
2 tablespoons olive oil
1 tablespoon white wine vinegar
2 cloves garlic, minced
½ teaspoon salt
¼ teaspoon freshly ground pepper
Garnish: fennel sprigs

•Cut fennel bulbs vertically into ½-inch slices. Blanch fennel in boiling water 3 minutes or just until crisp-tender; drain. Combine fennel and radicchio in a large bowl; set aside.
•Combine orange juice and next 6 ingredients in a jar. Cover tightly, and shake vigorously. Chill ¼ cup vinaigrette; pour remaining vinaigrette over fennel and radicchio, tossing gently to coat. Let fennel mixture stand 15 minutes; drain.
•Grill fennel, covered with grill lid, over medium-hot coals (350° to 400°) 15 minutes, turning once. Remove fennel from grill, and set aside. Grill radicchio, covered with grill

lid, 2 minutes or until crisp-tender. Toss fennel and radicchio with reserved vinaigrette; garnish, if desired. Serve immediately. Yield: 5 servings.
Per serving: Calories 118 Fat 4.2g
Cholesterol 0mg Sodium 145mg

Note: Don't core fennel before grilling. The core will hold the slices of fennel together so they won't fall through the grill rack.

Tabbouleh

STAND: 1 HOUR PREP: 20 MINUTES

CHILL: 1 HOUR

Tabbouleh is a Middle Eastern salad of bulgur wheat tossed with lots of fresh parsley, mint, and lemon juice. It makes a great sandwich filling, too. Just spoon it into pita pockets with mayonnaise and tomato slices.

½ cup bulgur
1 cup water
3 cups finely shredded lettuce
2 cups tightly packed, chopped fresh parsley (about 1½ large bunches)
2 large tomatoes, seeded and finely chopped
1 small onion, minced
¼ cup chopped fresh mint
1 clove garlic, minced
¼ cup lemon juice
2 tablespoons olive oil
1 teaspoon salt
½ teaspoon pepper

•Combine bulgur and water in a bowl; cover and let stand 1 hour or until water is absorbed. Drain well in a strainer or small colander. Press excess water from bulgur, using a fork. (This will prevent the salad from being soggy.)
•Press lettuce and parsley between paper towels to remove excess moisture; toss together in a large salad bowl. Add bulgur, tomato, and next 3 ingredients; toss gently.
•Combine lemon juice and remaining 3 ingredients in a small bowl. Stir with a wire whisk, and pour dressing over salad; toss gently. Cover and chill 1 hour. Toss again just before serving. Yield: 6 servings.
Per serving: Calories 107 Fat 5g
Cholesterol 0mg Sodium 404mg

VEGETABLE SALADS

Salads made with vegetables are an important part of a healthy eating plan. Vegetables boost the nutritional impact of a simple green salad and add a depth of flavor and texture, too.

Crisp vegetable salads add a splash of color to menus, and many of them are quick to make. Some are as simple as opening cans of beans and vegetables and adding a briefly boiled marinade. You can keep most marinated salads in the refrigerator for several days.

Fresh vegetable salads can take a few extra minutes to prepare since you'll need to clean and trim the vegetables, but their unmatched fresh flavor makes up for the time spent. Put the food processor to work for you when you can.

Green Bean Salad with Feta

Asparagus Salad

◄ QUICK ►

PREP: 13 MINUTES   COOK: 8 MINUTES

A tall, slender asparagus steamer makes easy work of steaming the long green spears for this simple salad.

1 pound fresh asparagus spears
¼ cup lemon juice
2 tablespoons honey
1 tablespoon vegetable oil
¼ teaspoon salt
¼ teaspoon pepper
8 green leaf lettuce leaves
1 (2-ounce) jar diced pimiento, drained

•Snap off tough ends of asparagus. Arrange asparagus in a steamer basket; place over boiling water. Cover and steam 5 to 6 minutes or until crisp-tender.
•Plunge asparagus into ice water to stop the cooking process. Drain and chill.
•Whisk together lemon juice and next 4 ingredients in a small bowl. Cover and chill, if desired.
•Arrange lettuce leaves on salad plates; top with asparagus, and drizzle with dressing. Sprinkle with pimiento. Yield: 4 servings.
Per serving: Calories 95 Fat 3.8g
Cholesterol 0mg Sodium 162mg

Green Bean Salad with Feta

◄ MAKE AHEAD ►

PREP: 42 MINUTES   COOK: 12 MINUTES
CHILL: 1 HOUR

Leave these slender beans whole for a pretty presentation. And grind a little pepper over them just before serving.

¾ cup olive oil
¼ cup white wine vinegar
1 clove garlic, minced
½ teaspoon salt
¼ teaspoon pepper
2 pounds green beans
1 small purple onion, thinly sliced
1 (4-ounce) package feta cheese, crumbled
1 cup coarsely chopped walnuts, toasted

•Combine first 5 ingredients; whisk until blended.
•Trim stem end of green beans; cut or snap beans into thirds, if desired, and arrange in a steamer basket over boiling water. Cover and steam 10 to 12 minutes or until crisp-tender. Immediately plunge beans into cold water to stop the cooking process; drain and pat dry.
•Combine beans, onion, and cheese in a large bowl; toss well. Cover and chill, if desired.

•Pour oil mixture over bean mixture; cover and chill 1 hour. Add walnuts, and toss just before serving. Yield: 8 servings.
Per serving: Calories 385 Fat 35.4g
Cholesterol 13mg Sodium 312mg

Zesty Double-Bean Salad

◄ HEALTHY • QUICK ►
◄ MAKE AHEAD ►

PREP: 21 MINUTES   CHILL: 3 HOURS

1 (15-ounce) can Great Northern beans, rinsed and drained
1 (15-ounce) can black beans, rinsed and drained
4 plum tomatoes, chopped
1 medium-size green pepper, chopped
6 green onions, chopped
½ cup salsa
¼ cup red wine vinegar
2 tablespoons chopped fresh cilantro
½ teaspoon salt
½ teaspoon black pepper

•Combine all ingredients; serve immediately or cover and chill. Toss gently before serving. Yield: 6 servings.
Per serving: Calories 129 Fat 0.8g
Cholesterol 0mg Sodium 484mg

Four-Bean Marinated Salad

◄ FAMILY FAVORITE ►
◄ MAKE AHEAD ►

PREP: 12 MINUTES   CHILL: 4 HOURS

This familiar bean salad shows up often at potluck suppers and family reunions. It's a faithful make-ahead salad that tastes better the second day, and it never goes out of style.

1 (17-ounce) can lima beans, drained
1 (16-ounce) can cut green beans, drained
1 (16-ounce) can cut wax beans, drained
1 (16-ounce) can kidney beans, rinsed and drained
1 small green pepper, chopped
1 small onion, chopped
1 (2-ounce) jar diced pimiento, drained
¾ cup sugar
½ cup vegetable oil
½ cup white vinegar
½ teaspoon salt
½ teaspoon pepper

•Combine first 7 ingredients in a large bowl; toss. Combine sugar and remaining 4 ingredients in a small saucepan; bring to a boil over low heat, stirring until sugar dissolves. Pour hot vinegar mixture over bean mixture; stir gently. Cover and chill at least 4 hours. Serve with a slotted spoon. Yield: 10 servings.
Per serving: Calories 240 Fat 11.2g
Cholesterol 0mg Sodium 438mg

Chilled Corn Salad

◄ MAKE AHEAD ►

PREP: 5 MINUTES   CHILL: 4 HOURS

1 (12-ounce) can whole kernel corn, drained
1 small onion, chopped
½ cup chopped green pepper
2 tablespoons minced fresh parsley
2 tablespoons cider vinegar
1 tablespoon vegetable oil
¼ teaspoon salt
¼ teaspoon pepper

•Combine all ingredients. Cover and chill at least 4 hours. Yield: 4 servings.
Per serving: Calories 105 Fat 3.9g
Cholesterol 0mg Sodium 351mg

Barley-Vegetable Salad

◄ MAKE AHEAD ►

**PREP: 5 MINUTES   COOK: 15 MINUTES
CHILL: 8 HOURS**

3 cups water
1 teaspoon salt
1 cup quick-cooking barley, uncooked
1 small green pepper, chopped
1 small sweet red pepper, chopped
1 (16-ounce) can whole kernel corn, drained
¼ cup chopped fresh parsley
¼ cup white wine vinegar
⅓ cup olive oil
½ teaspoon salt
¼ teaspoon pepper
⅛ teaspoon paprika

•Combine water and 1 teaspoon salt in a saucepan; bring to a boil. Stir in barley; return to a boil. Cover, reduce heat, and simmer 15 to 16 minutes or until barley is tender, stirring occasionally; drain.
•Combine barley, green pepper, and next 3 ingredients; set aside. Combine vinegar and remaining 4 ingredients; pour over barley mixture, and toss. Cover and chill 8 hours. Yield: 6 servings.
Per serving: Calories 272 Fat 12.8g
Cholesterol 0mg Sodium 516mg

Broccoli-Cauliflower Salad

◄ QUICK ►

PREP: 22 MINUTES

Take this big salad on a picnic along with fried chicken. The crisp raw vegetables are covered with a sweet creamy dressing.

1½ pounds fresh broccoli, cut into flowerets
1 medium cauliflower, cut into flowerets
½ red onion, vertically sliced
½ cup sliced celery
1 (2-ounce) jar diced pimiento, drained
1 cup mayonnaise
2 tablespoons sugar
1 teaspoon dry mustard
¼ teaspoon salt
⅛ teaspoon pepper
2 tablespoons vegetable oil

◄ BARLEY ►

BARLEY

Barley looks like a round form of oats, but is a different grain altogether. Before it reaches the market, it has a tough husk that is "polished" away and the bran removed, so it's often labeled "pearl" barley. Like oats, barley is available in both regular and quick-cooking varieties.

•Combine first 5 ingredients in a large bowl.
•Combine mayonnaise and remaining 5 ingredients; spoon over vegetables, tossing to coat. Cover and chill until ready to serve. Yield: 8 servings.
Per serving: Calories 279 Fat 25.7g
Cholesterol 16mg Sodium 265mg

Marinated Vegetable Salad

◄ FAMILY FAVORITE ►
◄ MAKE AHEAD ►

**PREP: 10 MINUTES   COOK: 4 MINUTES
CHILL: 8 HOURS**

This salad is easy and portable, too. Take it to a gathering, and we guarantee someone will ask for the recipe.

½ cup sugar
⅓ cup white vinegar
¼ cup vegetable oil
½ teaspoon pepper
¼ teaspoon salt
1 (16-ounce) can French-style green beans, drained
1 (17-ounce) can English peas, drained
1 (12-ounce) can shoepeg whole kernel corn, drained
1 (2-ounce) jar diced pimiento, drained
1 cup chopped celery
1 green pepper, finely chopped
1 bunch green onions, chopped

•Combine first 5 ingredients in a medium saucepan, and bring to a boil, stirring to dissolve sugar. Cool.
•Combine beans and remaining 6 ingredients; stir in vinegar mixture. Cover and chill at least 8 hours, stirring occasionally. Serve with a slotted spoon. Yield: 10 servings.
Per serving: Calories 145 Fat 5.8g
Cholesterol 0mg Sodium 288mg

Dilled Cucumber Salad

◀ MAKE AHEAD ▶

PREP: 20 MINUTES   CHILL: 3 HOURS

2 large cucumbers, unpeeled and thinly
    sliced
⅓ cup thinly sliced onion
1 tablespoon fresh dill or 1 teaspoon dried
    dillweed
1 tablespoon white vinegar
½ teaspoon salt
⅛ teaspoon ground white pepper
⅛ teaspoon sugar
¾ cup sour cream
Lettuce leaves

•Pat cucumber slices between paper towels.
Combine cucumber, onion, and next 5 ingredients in a bowl; toss gently. Fold in sour
cream; cover and chill up to 3 hours. Serve
on lettuce leaves. Yield: 6 servings.
Per serving: Calories 77 Fat 6.1g
Cholesterol 13mg Sodium 214mg

Crispy Coleslaw

◀ FAMILY FAVORITE ▶
◀ MAKE AHEAD ▶

PREP: 15 MINUTES   CHILL: 2 HOURS

1 small cabbage, shredded (1½ pounds)
1 medium onion, chopped
1 carrot, scraped and shredded
1 small green pepper, chopped
1 small sweet red pepper, chopped
1 small sweet yellow pepper, chopped
1 cup sugar
⅔ cup white vinegar
½ cup vegetable oil
1 teaspoon salt
¼ teaspoon ground white pepper
1 teaspoon celery seeds
¼ teaspoon mustard seeds

•Combine first 6 ingredients in a bowl; stir.
•Combine sugar and remaining 6 ingredients
in a saucepan; bring to a boil, stirring until
sugar dissolves. Pour vinegar mixture over
cabbage mixture; toss gently. Cover and chill
at least 2 hours. Serve with a slotted spoon.
(Coleslaw will keep in the refrigerator several
days.) Yield: 8 servings.
Per serving: Calories 141 Fat 7.1g
Cholesterol 0mg Sodium 161mg

Sweet-and-Sour Hot Slaw

◀ FAMILY FAVORITE • QUICK ▶
◀ MAKE AHEAD • HEALTHY ▶

PREP: 25 MINUTES

*This is great slaw for topping barbecue sand-
wiches. Traditionally, cabbage is finely shredded for this type of marinated slaw—let your
food processor do the work.*

1 medium cabbage, shredded (about 3
    pounds)
¾ cup chopped onion
1 small green pepper, chopped
1 cup sugar
1 cup white vinegar
1½ teaspoons salt
1 teaspoon celery seeds
1 teaspoon paprika
¾ teaspoon black pepper
½ teaspoon ground red pepper

•Combine first 3 ingredients in a large bowl;
set aside. Combine sugar and remaining 6
ingredients; stir until blended. Pour over cabbage mixture; cover and chill until ready to
serve. Serve with a slotted spoon. Yield: 16
servings.
Per serving: Calories 41 Fat 0.1g
Cholesterol 0mg Sodium 119mg

Creamy Coleslaw

◀ FAMILY FAVORITE • QUICK ▶

PREP: 20 MINUTES

*Use a food processor to quickly prepare the
vegetables for this coleslaw; just be careful
not to overprocess them.*

1 small cabbage, finely shredded (about
    1½ pounds)
1 small carrot, scraped and shredded
½ cup diced green pepper
½ cup diced celery
¼ cup diced onion
½ cup mayonnaise
½ cup sour cream
2 tablespoons sugar
2 tablespoons white vinegar
1 tablespoon prepared mustard
½ teaspoon salt
½ teaspoon paprika
¼ teaspoon pepper

•Combine first 5 ingredients; toss well, and
set aside. Combine mayonnaise and remaining 7 ingredients; stir well. Pour dressing over
vegetables; toss gently. Yield: 8 servings.
Per serving: Calories 167 Fat 14.2g
Cholesterol 14mg Sodium 277mg

Summer Garden Salad With Pita Crisps

◀ MAKE AHEAD ▶

PREP: 25 MINUTES   COOK: 10 MINUTES
CHILL: 1 HOUR

*This is a takeoff on the Middle Eastern bread
salad called* fattoush, *in which pieces of pita
bread are tossed with chopped ingredients.
Here the pita is toasted and served alongside
the salad, like croutons.*

4 (6-inch) pita bread rounds
1 bunch fresh parsley, finely chopped
4 medium tomatoes, finely chopped
1 large green pepper, finely chopped
1 bunch green onions, finely chopped
1 medium cucumber, peeled, seeded, and
    finely chopped
3 cloves garlic, minced
⅓ cup fresh lemon juice (about 2 large
    lemons)
⅓ cup olive oil
¼ cup finely chopped fresh mint
¼ teaspoon salt
¼ teaspoon pepper
2 cups shredded romaine lettuce
4 ounces feta cheese, crumbled

•Cut each pita round into 6 wedges, and separate each wedge into 2 triangles. Place triangles in a single layer on a baking sheet. Bake
at 400° for 10 minutes or until crisp and
brown. Cool completely; place pita triangles
in a zip-top plastic bag, and set aside.
•Combine parsley and next 10 ingredients;
toss gently. Cover and chill 1 hour.
•Toss parsley mixture with shredded
romaine; sprinkle with feta cheese. Serve
with toasted pita triangles. Yield: 8 servings.
Per serving: Calories 234 Fat 13.1g
Cholesterol 13mg Sodium 432mg

Southwestern Pasta Salad

PREP: 33 MINUTES   COOK: 10 MINUTES

CHILL: 1½ HOURS

Toss in a little shredded smoked chicken to make this salad a main dish.

1 (16-ounce) package dried penne or
   wagon wheel pasta
Creamy Southwestern Dressing
1 (15-ounce) can black beans, drained
1 (8¾-ounce) can whole kernel corn,
   drained
1 sweet red pepper, chopped
3 green onions, sliced
¼ cup chopped fresh cilantro
Garnish: fresh cilantro sprigs

•Cook pasta according to package directions; drain. Rinse with cold water, and drain again.
•Combine pasta and 1¾ cups Creamy Southwestern Dressing; toss gently. Cover and chill up to 1½ hours.
•Spoon pasta mixture onto a serving platter. Top with black beans and next 4 ingredients. Garnish, if desired. Serve with remaining dressing. Yield: 8 servings.

Per serving: Calories 350 Fat 7.4g
Cholesterol 12mg Sodium 536mg

Creamy Southwestern Dressing

1 teaspoon ground cumin
1 (8-ounce) carton sour cream
1 (16-ounce) jar mild thick and chunky
   salsa
2 cloves garlic, minced

•Toast cumin in a small skillet over low heat until fragrant; cool. Combine cumin, sour cream, salsa, and garlic, stirring well; cover and chill. Yield: 2¾ cups.

Dill and Sour Cream Potato Salad

Dill and Sour Cream Potato Salad

◀ FAMILY FAVORITE ▶

PREP: 12 MINUTES   CHILL: 8 HOURS

3 pounds unpeeled new potatoes
⅔ cup mayonnaise
1 (8-ounce) carton sour cream
2 tablespoons chopped fresh dill
2 tablespoons grated onion
2 tablespoons chopped fresh parsley
1 teaspoon salt
½ teaspoon pepper
Garnish: fresh dill

•Cook potatoes in boiling, salted water to cover 14 to 15 minutes or until tender; drain potatoes, and cool to touch.
•Cut potatoes into quarters or eighths, leaving skins on; place in a large bowl.
•Combine mayonnaise and next 6 ingredients in a small bowl. Add to potato, and toss gently. Serve immediately or cover and chill up to 8 hours. Garnish, if desired. Yield: 8 servings.

Per serving: Calories 320 Fat 20.7g
Cholesterol 23mg Sodium 425mg

SALAD SPUDS

When you're selecting potatoes for potato salad, it's important to pick a variety that keeps its shape when cooked. *Waxy* potatoes such as long whites and round reds have a smooth texture and waxy, moist flesh that performs well for this purpose. (*Starchy* potatoes such as Idaho are best for baking purposes that desire fluffy results.) New potatoes are not a type of potato but are just young, small potatoes; they're often the round red variety.

New potatoes are a fine choice for potato salads. Yukon gold and yellow Finn potatoes are good choices as well. They're thin-skinned potatoes with a wonderful buttery flavor.

Classic Potato Salad

PREP: 35 MINUTES   COOK: 30 MINUTES
CHILL: 2½ HOURS

2½ pounds red potatoes or yellow Finn
      potatoes
1 stalk celery, diced
⅓ cup sweet pickle relish or ½ cup
      chopped sweet pickles
2 large hard-cooked eggs, sliced
2 green onions, chopped
1 cup mayonnaise
2 tablespoons lemon juice
1 teaspoon salt
¼ teaspoon pepper
½ teaspoon dry mustard (optional)

•Cook potatoes in boiling water to cover 25
minutes or just until potatoes are tender.
•Drain well, and cool slightly. Peel and cube
potatoes. Combine potato, celery, and next 3
ingredients in a large bowl; toss gently.
•Combine mayonnaise, next 3 ingredients,
and, if desired, dry mustard in a small bowl.
Spoon mayonnaise mixture over potato mixture, tossing gently to combine. Serve warm
or chilled. Yield: 7 servings.
Per serving: Calories 385 Fat 26.7g
Cholesterol 79mg Sodium 639mg

German Potato Salad

PREP: 15 MINUTES   COOK: 30 MINUTES

16 new potatoes (1½ pounds)
6 slices bacon
½ cup chopped celery
1 tablespoon all-purpose flour
1 tablespoon sugar
2 teaspoons Dijon mustard
½ teaspoon salt
½ teaspoon celery seeds
Dash of ground white pepper
⅓ cup water
¼ cup white vinegar
½ cup chopped green onions
1 (2-ounce) jar sliced pimiento, drained

•Cook potatoes in boiling, salted water to
cover 15 minutes or until potatoes are tender. Drain, cool, and quarter potatoes.

•Cook bacon in a large skillet over medium
heat until crisp. Remove bacon, reserving 3
tablespoons drippings in skillet. Discard
remaining drippings. Crumble bacon, and
set aside.
•Cook celery in bacon drippings over
medium-high heat, stirring constantly, until
tender. Add flour and next 5 ingredients, stirring until smooth. Cook 1 minute, stirring
constantly. Gradually add water and vinegar;
cook over medium heat, stirring constantly,
until mixture is slightly thickened. Stir in
potato, green onions, and pimiento. Cook
just until thoroughly heated, stirring gently to
coat. Transfer to a serving bowl. Sprinkle
with bacon. Yield: 6 servings.
Per serving: Calories 264 Fat 16.6g
Cholesterol 19mg Sodium 557mg

Panzanella

PREP: 25 MINUTES

*Succulent tomatoes and fragrant fresh herbs
highlight this Italian bread salad that's a vegetarian main dish. Use only the freshest summer produce and a chewy, stale bread for
this salad.*

½ (1-pound) loaf day-old Italian bread or
      any chewy rustic loaf (such as
      sourdough), torn into bite-size pieces
1 (8-ounce) package mozzarella cheese,
      cut into cubes
3 large tomatoes, chopped
1 small cucumber, chopped
1 cup chopped purple onion
½ cup chopped fresh basil leaves
½ cup kalamata olives, pitted and halved,
      or pitted whole black olives
½ cup olive oil
¼ cup red wine vinegar or balsamic
      vinegar
3 cloves garlic, minced
½ to 1 teaspoon freshly ground pepper
¾ teaspoon salt

•Combine first 7 ingredients in a large salad
bowl; toss gently. (Drain tomato and cucumber on paper towels first if they're extra
juicy.)
•Combine oil and remaining 4 ingredients;
whisk until blended. Pour over salad; toss
well. Let stand 10 to 15 minutes for bread to

absorb flavor. Serve at room temperature.
Yield: 7 servings.
Per serving: Calories 356 Fat 23.5g
Cholesterol 19mg Sodium 775mg

To make a chiffonade: Tightly roll
leaves of basil or salad greens, and slice
thinly to make long shreds.

Marinated Tomato and Brie Salad

PREP: 50 MINUTES   STAND: 1 HOUR

*Basil abounds in this fresh mix meant for
summertime. It fares well with just about any
meat hot off the grill. A hot and moist knife
aids in cutting the Brie—just run the knife
under hot tap water as you begin.*

1 (15-ounce) round Brie
5 medium or 4 large tomatoes, seeded and
      cut into ½-inch cubes
1 cup fresh basil, cut into thin shreds (see
      photo)
3 or 4 cloves garlic, crushed
⅓ cup olive oil
¼ teaspoon salt
½ teaspoon freshly ground pepper
Garnish: fresh basil sprigs

•Remove rind from Brie with a sharp knife,
if desired. Dip knife in hot water, pat dry,
and cut Brie into ½-inch cubes. (Continue
dipping procedure as needed.)
•Combine Brie, tomato, and next 5 ingredients in a serving bowl; cover and let stand at
room temperature 1 hour. Garnish, if
desired. Yield: 5 servings.
Per serving: Calories 389 Fat 34.3g
Cholesterol 70mg Sodium 570mg

Fresh Mozzarella-Tomato-Basil Salad

◄ MAKE AHEAD ►

PREP: 10 MINUTES CHILL: 4 HOURS

For an extra sprinkling of color, use multi-colored peppercorns and grind them over the salad just before serving.

½ pound fresh mozzarella cheese°
2 large red tomatoes, sliced
1 large yellow tomato, sliced
½ teaspoon salt
3 tablespoons extra-virgin olive oil
Freshly ground pepper
½ cup shredded or chopped fresh basil

•Remove cheese from brine, and cut into 12 slices; sprinkle tomato slices evenly with salt. Alternate tomato and cheese slices on a platter; drizzle with olive oil. Cover and chill 4 hours. Just before serving, sprinkle with freshly ground pepper and basil. Yield: 6 servings.

Fresh mozzarella is a soft white cheese available at gourmet grocery stores or cheese shops. Sometimes it's packed in brine, a strong solution of water and salt used for pickling or preserving foods.

Per serving: Calories 282 Fat 22.7g
Cholesterol 40mg Sodium 767mg

EXTRA, EXTRA

Ever wonder what the difference is between olive oil and extra-virgin olive oil? Extra-virgin olive oil is from the olive's first pressing. It has the deepest color, richest flavor, is the least acidic tasting, and the most expensive. Thus you don't really want to cook with it. The more the olives are pressed, the lighter the color, the greater the acidity, and the less you pay for the oil. It's best to use the most expensive oil where you'll taste it—in vinaigrettes or drizzled over fresh ingredients just before serving.

Fresh Mozzarella-Tomato-Basil Salad

Summer Zucchini Salad

◄ MAKE AHEAD • QUICK ►

PREP: 20 MINUTES COOK: 3 MINUTES

A sprinkling of toasted pecans is the ideal flavor balance for fresh herbs and summer zucchini. Partner any type of fish with this simple dish.

8 medium zucchini, cut into thin strips (3 pounds)
1 tablespoon minced garlic
¼ cup olive oil
2 tablespoons finely chopped fresh basil
2 tablespoons finely chopped fresh mint
¾ teaspoon salt
¼ cup chopped pecans, toasted

•Cook zucchini and garlic in hot oil in a large skillet over medium-high heat, stirring constantly, 3 minutes or until tender. Remove from skillet; cool.
•Combine zucchini mixture, basil, and remaining ingredients in a large bowl, stirring gently. Serve at room temperature or chill, if desired. Stir before serving. Yield: 8 servings.

Per serving: Calories 111 Fat 9.6g
Cholesterol 0mg Sodium 225mg

FRUITS DICTIONARY

Fruit selection has never been so broad and bountiful.
Familiarize yourself with some refreshingly juicy options on these pages.

Apricot: Related to the peach, an apricot is smaller and has a smooth, oval pit that is easily removed when the fruit is halved. Apricots are highly perishable and seasonal; they're at their peak during June and July. Dried apricots are pitted, unpeeled apricot halves that have had most of their moisture removed.

Avocado: Yes, it's a fruit. The avocado is known for its buttery texture and mild nutlike flavor. The two most available varieties are *Haas*, with an almost black skin, and the green skinned *Fuerte*. Once you cut an avocado, prepare and eat it right away or rub its surface with lemon juice to prevent browning.

Bananas: Bananas are picked and shipped green. They develop flavor when ripened after picking. The yellow Cavendish variety is most common in U.S. supermarkets. *Red bananas* are short, chunky bananas that are sweeter than the common yellow type. The *plantain* is a very large, firm, mild cooking banana. Plantains are popular in Latin American cuisine and are used much like we use potatoes.

Cantaloupe: This melon is juicy and sweet and particularly fragrant when it's ripe. Choose cantaloupes that are heavy for their size. Store unripe cantaloupes at room temperature, ripe ones in the refrigerator. Slice the melon and remove seeds before serving.

Cucumber: This cylindrical green-skinned fruit is a member of the gourd family. Its seeds are edible; peeling the thin skin is a personal preference. The small, stubby cucumbers are used for pickling; the longer, more expensive *English cucumber* can grow up to 2 feet long and is virtually seedless. Store whole cucumbers in the refrigerator up to 10 days.

Feijoa: Also called *pineapple guava,* this small egg-shaped fruit has a thin skin and fragrant cream flesh that encases a jellylike center. Remove the peel before serving this mildly sweet fruit that hints at pineapple. Use feijoas in fruit salads and desserts.

Honeydew: This heavy melon is distinguished by its pastel green flesh and pale yellow rind. Like cantaloupe, honeydew is sweet and juicy and fragrant when ripe. Choose one that's heavy for its size—typically 4 to 8 pounds. Honeydew, a good source of vitamin C, is available year-round but is at its sweetest in late summer.

Kiwifruit: Its fuzzy brown exterior hides a black-seed speckled brilliant green flesh. Kiwifruit, hailing from New Zealand, is available year-round, can be stored in the refrigerator up to three weeks, and is a good source of vitamin C. Use it in salads, salsas, or desserts.

Kumquat: A tiny member of the citrus family, the whole kumquat, skin and flesh, is edible. Kumquats are available November to March and are often pickled or preserved in marmalade.

Lemon: Some lemons have thin skins and some have very thick rinds, which can be bitter. The flesh is juicy and acidic. Lemons are always available, but peak in the summer months. Pick lemons that are firm, plump, and heavy. You can keep vitamin C-packed lemons 10 days in the refrigerator.

Mango: A mango has a spicy peach flavor and perfumelike aroma. In its center is a big seed that clings to the flesh. Cut fruit in half, cutting around the seed, and score the flesh into squares for easy eating (see photo).

Nectarine: When ripe, a nectarine's smooth skin is deep gold with a red blush. Nectarines are slightly sweeter and have a firmer flesh than peaches. Nectarines peak in late summer, and you can store them in the refrigerator five days.

Orange: There are three basic types of oranges—sweet, loose-skinned, and bitter. Sweet oranges are prized for their juice and for eating fresh out of hand. Most common are the seedless *navel, Valencia*, and the red-fleshed *blood orange*. Loose-skinned oranges are prized for their plump segments, easily sectioned once the skin is removed. Mandarin varieties are loose skinned. Among the most common mandarin

oranges are *tangerines, clementines,* and *satsumas.* All of them are small oranges; some of them have seeds, and some don't. *Seville* is the best known bitter orange and is valued for its peel, which can be used to make marmalade.

Papaya: When ripe, this golden yellow-skinned fruit is best eaten raw. Its center is full of black seeds, which are edible, but are generally discarded. Shop for richly colored papaya that yield slightly to gentle pressure. If you buy a green one, it will ripen quickly at room temperature.

Passion fruit: This deep purple, egg-shaped fruit is wrinkled when it's ripe. Passion fruit has a soft golden flesh and edible tiny black seeds. It has a sweet-tart flavor that's popular in desserts. You can store passion fruit up to five days in the refrigerator.

Pear: There are hundreds of varieties of pears available. Some of the more common are shown in our photograph: *Bosc, Anjou, comice, Bartlett,* and the not-so-common *Asian pear.* Pears don't ripen well on a tree; they're picked when mature, but not ripe. So buy pears that are firm and still unripe. You'll know when a pear is ripe by applying gentle pressure at the base of the stem. If it yields slightly to pressure, it's ripe. Color is not always a good indicator of ripeness as far as pears are concerned—Bartlett pears turn color when ripe, but Anjou and Bosc pears do not.

Rhubarb: These pink, tart, celerylike stalks are best in early spring and are sliced and eaten as fruit, often in desserts. Rhubarb is highly perishable; you can keep it in the refrigerator up to three days.

Strawberry: This beautiful green-capped berry peaks April through June, but is available year-round. Avoid shriveled, soft, or moldy berries. Look for plump berries with bright green tops. Wash these berries right before you're going to eat or cook them. They are a great source of vitamin C.

Honeydew

Bosc pear

Anjou pear

Comice pear

English cucumber

Asian pear

Apricots

Plantain

Nectarine

Papaya

Feijoa
(pineapple guava)

Bartlett pear

Red bananas

Mango

Avocado

Passion fruit

Kiwifruit

Rhubarb

Kumquats

FRUIT SALADS

It's hard to find a salad more refreshing than one made of succulent fresh fruit with the scent of citrus wafting through the air. Many fruit salads are just sweet enough to double as dessert if that's your pleasure. Ever-popular Ambrosia (this page) and All-Season Fruit Salad (next page) are two such options.

When preparing fruit salads, don't slice and blend the fruit too far in advance unless the recipe recommends it. Some fruit salads will become soggy and limp if made ahead.

Consider serving fruit salad to guests in your favorite wine goblets or compotes. If it's a large fruit salad, serve it from a glass trifle bowl or other footed dish. Sometimes a sprinkling of coconut or a sprig of fresh mint can provide the perfect finishing touch.

Waldorf Salad

◄ FAMILY FAVORITE ►
◄ MAKE AHEAD ►

PREP: 20 MINUTES   CHILL: 2 HOURS

1 large Granny Smith apple, unpeeled and diced
1 large Red Delicious apple, unpeeled and diced
1 large Golden Delicious apple, unpeeled and diced
½ cup seedless green grapes, halved
½ cup coarsely chopped walnuts
½ cup diced celery
⅓ cup raisins
¼ cup mayonnaise
1½ teaspoons sugar
½ teaspoon lemon juice
¼ cup whipping cream, whipped
Lettuce leaves

•Place first 7 ingredients in a medium bowl; toss gently to combine.
•Combine mayonnaise, sugar, and lemon juice in a small bowl; stir well. Gently fold whipped cream into mayonnaise mixture. Spoon whipped cream mixture over fruit mixture, stirring gently to combine. Cover and chill 2 hours. Serve on lettuce-lined salad plates. Yield: 8 servings.
Per serving: Calories 208 Fat 14.6g
Cholesterol 14mg Sodium 52mg

Ambrosia

◄ FAMILY FAVORITE ►
◄ HEALTHY ►

PREP: 15 MINUTES   CHILL: 8 HOURS

9 oranges, peeled, seeded, and sectioned
2 (20-ounce) cans crushed pineapple, drained
1 cup honey
1 to 2 teaspoons almond extract
1 cup flaked coconut

•Combine all ingredients in a large bowl, and stir gently; cover and chill at least 8 hours. Yield: 8 servings.
Per serving: Calories 316 Fat 4.7g
Cholesterol 0mg Sodium 35mg

Cantaloupe Cooler Salad

◄ QUICK ►

PREP: 15 MINUTES

1 large or 2 small cantaloupes
Lettuce leaves
1 large onion, thinly sliced and separated into rings
½ pound (about 12 slices) bacon, cooked and crumbled
Poppy Seed Dressing (page 373)

•Peel cantaloupe, and cut into bite-size pieces; arrange on lettuce leaves on individual salad plates. Top cantaloupe with onion rings and crumbled bacon. Drizzle Poppy Seed Dressing over salad. Yield: 8 servings.
Per serving: Calories 393 Fat 33.7g
Cholesterol 10mg Sodium 484mg

Melon and Prosciutto Salad

◄ QUICK ►

PREP: 20 MINUTES

½ ripe honeydew melon, seeded
8 slices prosciutto
2 tablespoons vegetable oil
1 tablespoon lime juice
1 tablespoon honey
½ teaspoon poppy seeds

SECTIONING CITRUS

1. To section an orange, first peel it with a paring knife, and be sure to remove the white pith.

2. Holding fruit over a bowl to catch juices, slice between membrane and 1 side of 1 segment of fruit; then lift the segment out with the knife blade.

•Cut honeydew half into 8 lengthwise slices. Remove rind from each slice, using a sharp knife. Wrap 1 slice of prosciutto around each melon wedge. Set aside.
•Combine oil and remaining 3 ingredients; stir until smooth.
•To serve, place 2 melon slices on each serving plate; drizzle melon slices with honey mixture. Yield: 4 servings.
Per serving: Calories 189 Fat 9.7g
Cholesterol 17mg Sodium 443mg

Fruited Wild Rice Salad

◄ MAKE AHEAD • HEALTHY ►

PREP: 11 MINUTES   COOK: 5 MINUTES

CHILL: 8 HOURS

This is good picnic food fit for a crowd.

2 (2.75-ounce) packages quick-cooking
   wild rice
1 teaspoon salt
2 cups golden raisins
⅓ cup dry sherry
1 tablespoon grated orange rind
½ cup fresh orange juice
½ cup commercial Caesar dressing
¼ teaspoon freshly ground pepper
2 Granny Smith apples, chopped
4 green onions, sliced (about ⅔ cup)
1 cup sunflower kernels

•Cook wild rice according to package direc-
tions, using 1 teaspoon salt; set aside.
•Combine raisins and sherry; set aside.
Combine orange rind and next 3 ingredients.
Combine rice, raisin mixture, apple, green
onions, and sunflower kernels; stir. Add juice
mixture; toss gently. Cover and chill 8 hours.
Stir before serving. Yield: 10 servings.
Per serving: Calories 347 Fat 11g
Cholesterol 4mg Sodium 297mg

Four-Fruit Salad

◄ MAKE AHEAD • HEALTHY ►

PREP: 30 MINUTES   CHILL: 1 HOUR

1 fresh pineapple, cut into chunks, or 1
   (20-ounce) can pineapple chunks in
   juice, drained
3 pink grapefruit, peeled and sectioned
1 pint fresh strawberries, hulled and sliced
1 mango, peeled and sliced
Citrus-Cilantro Dressing (page 373)

•Combine first 4 ingredients in a large bowl;
toss with Citrus-Cilantro Dressing. Cover
and chill 1 hour; serve with a slotted spoon.
Yield: 8 servings.
Per serving: Calories 98 Fat 0.5g
Cholesterol 0mg Sodium 2mg

All-Season Fruit Salad

◄ MAKE AHEAD • HEALTHY ►
◄ FAMILY FAVORITE ►

PREP: 15 MINUTES   CHILL: 2 HOURS

1 pint fresh strawberries, sliced
1½ cups seedless green grapes
1 cup honeydew melon balls
2 oranges, peeled, seeded, and
   sectioned
2 kiwifruit, peeled and sliced
1 apple, unpeeled, cored, and sliced
¼ cup orange juice
2 tablespoons honey
1 tablespoon lime juice
2 bananas, sliced

•Combine first 6 ingredients in a
large bowl.
•Combine orange juice, honey, and lime
juice; pour over fruit in bowl, tossing gently.
Cover and chill 2 hours. Add banana just
before serving. Yield: 12 servings.
Per serving: Calories 85 Fat 0.5g
Cholesterol 0mg Sodium 3mg

SHAPELY SALADS

Gelatin makes a molded salad of any size keep its shape. Before you embark on a molded mixture, it's important to know the basics of using the little packet of powder. There are two types of gelatin available, and they're not interchangeable.

Types of Gelatin

Flavored gelatin comes in a wide assortment of fruit flavors and colors and has sugar added. All recipes that specify flavored gelatin will make sweet salads. For flavored gelatin, stir boiling water into gelatin until granules dissolve; then stir in cold liquid and other ingredients. Follow the label for exact cup amounts of solids that flavored gelatin will suspend.

Unflavored gelatin is colorless, flavorless, and has no added sugar. It comes packaged in envelopes that contain enough gelatin to gel 2 cups of liquid. When working with unflavored gelatin, first soften the gelatin in cold water 1 to 5 minutes to allow the granules to swell. Then dissolve it by adding hot water and cooking and stirring over low heat until it's clear and no granules remain.

With both types of gelatin, it's crucial that you properly soften and dissolve the granules before adding other ingredients; otherwise the end product will not gel enough to hold its shape when cut or unmolded.

Salad Additions

You can freely add fruits and vegetables to a salad in amounts specified on the gelatin package. Just don't add more than directions recommend or the salad won't gel. In general, finely chop all the ingredients you add; pieces that are too large may cause the salad to fall apart upon serving.

Lemon juice, vinegar, wine, and other acids will make a molded salad softer and more fragile. One to two tablespoons of an acid per cup of liquid is probably the most you'll want to add to a shapely dish. Never use fresh pineapple pulp or juice, kiwifruit, or papaya in a gelatin salad. This fresh fruit contains an enzyme that prevents gelatin

from setting up; canned pineapple and juice, however, is fine to use because the canning process destroys this enzyme.

If you plan to serve a molded salad outdoors in warm weather, place the unmolded salad on its serving plate on a bed of crushed ice rather than add extra gelatin to the mixture when cooking. Too much gelatin will make the salad rubbery.

Selecting a Mold

Always use the size mold recommended in the recipe. If the mold is too small, you'll have mixture left over. If the mold is too large, the ingredients won't completely fill the mold, and you'll lose the effect of the shape. For ease in unmolding, lightly oil the mold with vegetable oil or vegetable cooking spray before adding the gelatin mixture.

Chill to the Proper Consistency

Chilling a gelatin mixture to the consistency of unbeaten egg white means to refrigerate the mixture until it's slightly thick—and looks like an egg white from a just-broken egg. This chilling takes from 30 minutes to several hours, depending on the amount of mixture. Check the mixture periodically. Don't let the mixture congeal too much or it will be difficult to fold in remaining ingredients. If the gelatin gets too firm, set the container of gelatin in a bowl of warm water and stir until the mixture softens enough to add other ingredients.

Unmolding and Serving the Salad

After your salad has completely congealed, carefully unmold it. To break the suction, run a knife around the edge of the mold to release the salad. If the mold has fluted sides, press the edge of the salad lightly with your finger and gently pull away from sides (see photo 3, next page). Unmold salad, using warm water bath (see photo 2, next page) or the hot towel method. Wet a dish towel with hot water, and wring it out. Wrap the towel around the bottom and sides of mold and let it stand for 1 to 2 minutes. Then place a serving platter on top of the mold and flip it over. If it doesn't unmold, repeat the process.

Many salads of this nature benefit from a soft dollop of whipped topping or sour cream on each serving. It provides a nice contrast in color and flavor and finishes the dish.

Pineapple-Peach Salad

◄ MAKE AHEAD • HEALTHY ►

PREP: 5 MINUTES   COOK: 10 MINUTES

CHILL: 1 HOUR

You can chill or freeze this peachy salad that's ideal for a ladies' luncheon.

2 (3-ounce) packages peach-flavored
   gelatin
½ cup cold water
1 (8-ounce) can crushed pineapple,
   undrained
1½ cups buttermilk
1 (8-ounce) container frozen whipped
   topping, thawed
Lettuce leaves
Garnish: frozen whipped topping, thawed,
   and fresh mint leaves

•Soften gelatin in cold water in a small saucepan 1 minute. Add pineapple, and

cook 5 to 10 minutes or until gelatin dissolves, stirring often. Remove from heat, and stir in buttermilk and container of whipped topping.
•Pour mixture into a lightly greased 7-cup ring mold. Cover and chill 1 hour or until mixture is firm.
•Unmold salad onto a lettuce-lined serving tray. Garnish, if desired. Yield: 8 servings.
Per serving: Calories 207 Fat 5.8g
Cholesterol 2mg Sodium 130mg

Ambrosia Cream Cheese Mold

◄ MAKE AHEAD ►

PREP: 20 MINUTES   CHILL: SEVERAL HOURS

1 envelope unflavored gelatin
½ cup cold water
1 (15½-ounce) can pineapple chunks,
   undrained
⅓ cup sugar
Juice of 1 lemon
2 (3-ounce) packages cream cheese,
   softened
1 orange, peeled, sectioned, and diced
½ cup chopped pecans
½ cup flaked coconut
Lettuce leaves (optional)

•Sprinkle gelatin over cold water; let stand 1 minute.
•Drain pineapple, and reserve juice; set pineapple chunks aside. Add enough water to juice to make 1 cup.
•Place juice in a 2-quart saucepan; heat to boiling; add gelatin mixture, and stir until gelatin dissolves. Remove from heat.
•Stir in sugar, lemon juice, and cream cheese, using a wire whisk to blend. Chill until consistency of unbeaten egg white; fold in pineapple chunks, orange, pecans, and coconut.
•Spoon mixture into a lightly oiled 1-quart mold; cover and chill until firm. Unmold on lettuce, if desired. Yield: 6 servings.
Per serving: Calories 308 Fat 19.9g
Cholesterol 31mg Sodium 108mg

Frosty Cranberry Salad

◄ FAMILY FAVORITE ►
◄ MAKE AHEAD ►

PREP: 5 MINUTES   FREEZE: SEVERAL HOURS

1 (16-ounce) can whole-berry cranberry
   sauce
1 (8-ounce) can crushed pineapple,
   drained
1 teaspoon lemon juice
1 (8-ounce) carton sour cream
Lettuce leaves (optional)

•Combine first 4 ingredients in a bowl; stir until blended. Pour mixture into an 8½- x 4½-inch loafpan; cover and freeze until firm. Cut into 1-inch slices. Serve on lettuce leaves, if desired. Yield: 8 servings.
Per serving: Calories 158 Fat 6g
Cholesterol 12mg Sodium 32mg

Note: You can pour this cranberry mixture into paper-lined muffin cups and freeze. Just peel away paper before serving.

Mincemeat Salad

◄ MAKE AHEAD ►

PREP: 7 MINUTES   CHILL: 8 HOURS

Here's a grand alternative to the expected holiday cranberry salad.

2 (3-ounce) packages orange-flavored
   gelatin
1½ cups boiling water
2 cups mincemeat
½ cup chopped walnuts or pecans
Lettuce leaves
Garnishes: orange slices, chopped walnuts
   or pecans

•Combine gelatin and boiling water in a large bowl; stir 2 minutes or until gelatin dissolves. Chill 20 minutes or until consistency of unbeaten egg white.
•Gently fold mincemeat and ½ cup walnuts into gelatin mixture. Spoon into eight lightly oiled individual molds; cover and chill at least 8 hours.
•Unmold onto lettuce-lined plates; garnish, if desired. Yield: 8 servings.
Per serving: Calories 293 Fat 19.8g
Cholesterol 0mg Sodium 255mg

Tomato Aspic

PREP: 30 MINUTES   CHILL: SEVERAL HOURS

3 envelopes unflavored gelatin
4 cups tomato juice, divided
1 tablespoon prepared horseradish
2 teaspoons Worcestershire sauce
1 teaspoon hot sauce
½ teaspoon celery salt
⅔ cup finely chopped green pepper
⅔ cup finely chopped celery
1 tablespoon plus 1 teaspoon grated onion
1 medium cucumber
Curly leaf lettuce

•Sprinkle gelatin over 1 cup tomato juice in a medium saucepan; let stand 1 minute. Cook over medium heat, stirring constantly, 3 to 5 minutes or until gelatin dissolves. Remove from heat; transfer mixture to a large bowl.
•Stir in remaining 3 cups tomato juice, horseradish, and next 3 ingredients. Chill mixture to the consistency of unbeaten egg white

1. Chill tomato juice mixture until it's the consistency of unbeaten egg white.

2. One way to unmold a salad is to briefly dip it into a bowl of warm water to loosen the seal; then invert.

3. Another way to unmold a salad is to gently pull the salad away from the edge of the mold to break the seal.

(photo 1). Fold in green pepper, celery, and onion. Spoon tomato mixture into eight lightly oiled individual ½-cup molds. Cover and chill several hours until firm.
•Score cucumber with tines of a fork. Slice cucumber into paper-thin slices. Place lettuce leaves on individual salad plates, and arrange cucumber slices in a circle over lettuce leaves.
•Unmold salads onto prepared plates (photos 2 and 3). Yield: 8 servings.
Per serving: Calories 44 Fat 0.2g Cholesterol 0mg Sodium 605mg

ENTRÉE SALADS

Most meat and seafood salads are hearty enough to be the meal's main attraction. They include adequate amounts of protein to meet main-dish requirements, and the serving size is typically larger than other salads.

Just about every one of the salads in this section contains some type of meat or seafood that you'll need to cook before using. So remember to allow enough time for this in the preparation. And don't forget to give the salad time to chill for the flavors to mingle and blend.

Bacon and Egg Salad

PREP: 10 MINUTES   COOK: 23 MINUTES

6 large hard-cooked eggs, chopped
1 cup chopped celery
3 green onions, chopped
7 slices bacon, cooked and crumbled
½ cup mayonnaise
1 tablespoon prepared horseradish
⅛ teaspoon salt
¼ teaspoon pepper
2 tablespoons chopped fresh parsley

•Combine first 4 ingredients in a large bowl; set aside.
•Combine mayonnaise and next 3 ingredients; fold into egg mixture. Sprinkle with parsley. Salad can be chilled up to 24 hours, if desired; bacon will soften slightly. Serve as a salad or sandwich filling. Yield: 3 servings.
Per 1-cup serving: Calories 536 Fat 48.5g Cholesterol 462mg Sodium 759mg

Yolkless Egg Salad

PREP: 10 MINUTES   COOK: 30 MINUTES

6 large hard-cooked eggs
3 tablespoons sweet pickle relish
2 green onions, finely chopped
1 tablespoon diced pimiento, undrained
½ cup cooked mashed potato
3 tablespoons mayonnaise
1 teaspoon Dijon mustard
½ teaspoon salt
⅛ to ¼ teaspoon pepper
2 teaspoons curry powder

•Remove yolks from eggs, and discard or reserve for another use; chop egg whites. Combine egg white, pickle relish, green onions, and pimiento in a medium bowl; set aside.
•Combine mashed potato and remaining 5 ingredients; gently fold into egg white mixture. Serve as a salad, sandwich filling, or stuffing for fresh vegetables. Yield: 4 servings.
Per ½-cup serving: Calories 147 Fat 9.4g Cholesterol 9mg Sodium 569mg

Chicken Salad

PREP: 16 MINUTES   COOK: 15 MINUTES

Dress up this basic chicken salad by stirring in ½ cup toasted pecans and chopped artichoke hearts.

4 cups chopped cooked chicken
2 cups thinly sliced celery
¼ cup sweet pickle relish
2 tablespoons minced onion
¾ cup mayonnaise
1 tablespoon lemon juice
½ teaspoon salt

•Combine first 4 ingredients in a large bowl, stirring well. Combine mayonnaise, lemon juice, and salt, stirring until blended; add to chicken mixture, and toss well. Cover and chill. Serve salad on lettuce leaves, in tomato cups, or on sandwiches. Yield: 6 servings.
Per 1-cup serving: Calories 395 Fat 25.7g Cholesterol 107mg Sodium 529mg

Mandarin Chicken Salad

PREP: 20 MINUTES   CHILL: 1 HOUR

3 cups chopped cooked chicken
1 cup diced celery
2 tablespoons lemon juice
1 tablespoon minced onion
⅓ cup mayonnaise
½ teaspoon salt
1 cup seedless green grapes
1 (2-ounce) package slivered almonds, toasted
1 (11-ounce) can mandarin oranges, drained
Leaf lettuce

•Combine first 4 ingredients; cover and chill at least 1 hour.
•Combine mayonnaise and salt. Add mayonnaise mixture, grapes, and almonds to chilled chicken mixture; toss gently. Stir in oranges. Serve chicken mixture on lettuce. Yield: 6 servings.
Per serving: Calories 311 Fat 19.6g Cholesterol 64mg Sodium 347mg

Grilled Asian Chicken Salad

**PREP: 20 MINUTES   COOK: 15 MINUTES
CHILL: 1 HOUR**

This glorious salad shown on page 348 is a clever use of crunchy ramen noodles.

4 skinned, boned chicken breast halves
1 tablespoon dark sesame oil
¼ teaspoon salt
¼ teaspoon pepper
1 (3-ounce) package ramen noodles
1 tablespoon sesame seeds
½ cup white wine vinegar
⅓ cup honey
2 tablespoons hoisin sauce
1½ tablespoons dark sesame oil, divided
1 medium-size yellow tomato
1 medium tomato
6 cups mixed salad greens
½ head napa cabbage, shredded
½ bunch fresh cilantro, chopped

•Brush both sides of chicken with 1 tablespoon sesame oil, and sprinkle with salt and pepper. Grill chicken, covered with grill lid, over medium-hot coals (350°to 400°) 6 to 8 minutes on each side or until done; cool. Cut into thin slices; set aside.
•Coarsely crumble noodles into a 9-inch round cakepan, discarding seasoning packet; add sesame seeds. Bake at 350° for 5 minutes or until lightly browned, stirring once. Cool and set aside.
•Combine vinegar, honey, hoisin sauce, and 1 tablespoon sesame oil, stirring well; reserve ⅓ cup dressing. Combine remaining dressing with chicken in a large bowl. Cover and chill at least 1 hour.
•Peel, seed, and chop tomatoes. Combine tomato, salad greens, cabbage, and cilantro; drizzle with reserved ⅓ cup dressing and remaining 1½ teaspoons sesame oil, tossing to coat. Arrange salad and chicken on individual serving plates, and sprinkle with noodles. Yield: 6 servings.
Per serving: Calories 392 Fat 13.2g Cholesterol 87mg Sodium 357mg

Grilled Chicken Salad With Mango Salsa

**PREP: 50 MINUTES   MARINATE: 1 HOUR
COOK: 16 MINUTES**

Caribbean flavors tie this salad together.

1 tablespoon olive oil
1 tablespoon soy sauce
1 tablespoon balsamic vinegar
1 tablespoon rice wine vinegar
1 tablespoon dry sherry
1 tablespoon grated fresh ginger
1 teaspoon ground cinnamon
¼ teaspoon ground red pepper
4 skinned, boned chicken breast halves
⅓ cup rice wine vinegar
2 tablespoons sugar
8 cups tightly packed mixed salad greens
Mango Salsa

•Combine first 8 ingredients in a heavy-duty, zip-top plastic bag or shallow dish; add chicken. Seal or cover; marinate in refrigerator 1 hour, turning chicken occasionally.
•Remove chicken from marinade, discarding marinade. Grill chicken, uncovered, over medium-hot coals (350° to 400°) 6 to 8 minutes on each side or until no longer pink.
•Combine ⅓ cup vinegar and sugar; stir until sugar dissolves. Place salad greens on individual serving plates; drizzle with vinegar mixture. Slice and fan chicken, if desired, over salad greens. Top each serving with ½ cup Mango Salsa. Yield: 4 servings.
Per serving: Calories 376 Fat 11.3g Cholesterol 129mg Sodium 305mg

Mango Salsa

1 large mango, finely chopped
1 large cucumber, peeled, seeded, and finely chopped
1 jalapeño pepper, seeded and minced
¼ cup chopped purple onion
1 teaspoon grated fresh ginger
1 tablespoon chopped fresh basil
1 tablespoon rice wine vinegar
1 tablespoon balsamic vinegar
1 tablespoon olive oil

•Combine all ingredients, stirring well. Yield: 2 cups.

Smoked Turkey Primavera Salad

PREP: 21 MINUTES   CHILL: 2 HOURS

½ pound broccoli
8 ounces dried bow tie pasta
Versatile Vinaigrette (page 373)
½ (10-ounce) package fresh spinach
½ pound smoked turkey breast, cut into thin strips
½ pint cherry tomatoes, halved
½ cup chopped fresh basil
¼ cup chopped fresh parsley
⅓ cup pine nuts, toasted

• Remove broccoli leaves and tough ends of stalks; discard. Wash broccoli thoroughly, and coarsely chop. Cook in boiling water to cover 1 minute; drain and immediately plunge into ice water. Drain and pat dry with paper towels; chill.
• Cook pasta according to package directions; drain. Rinse with cold water, and drain. Toss pasta with Versatile Vinaigrette. Place in a large heavy-duty, zip-top plastic bag. Chill at least 2 hours.
• Remove spinach stems; wash leaves thoroughly, and pat dry. Arrange spinach on serving plates. Combine broccoli, pasta, turkey, and remaining 4 ingredients, tossing gently; serve on spinach leaves. Yield: 8 servings.
Per serving: Calories 344 Fat 22.4g
Cholesterol 16mg Sodium 573mg

Taco Salad

◀ FAMILY FAVORITE • QUICK ▶

PREP: 15 MINUTES   COOK: 10 MINUTES

1 pound ground beef
1¾ cups commercial taco sauce, divided
2 cloves garlic, minced
1 (1¼-ounce) envelope taco seasoning mix
1 (15¼-ounce) can Mexican-style whole kernel corn, drained
1 (15-ounce) can red kidney beans, drained
½ (9-ounce) package tortilla chips, coarsely crushed
1 medium head iceberg lettuce, shredded
2 cups (8 ounces) shredded Longhorn cheese
2 medium tomatoes, chopped
¾ cup sour cream

• Brown beef in a large skillet, stirring until it crumbles; drain. Stir in 1 cup taco sauce, garlic, and next 3 ingredients. Remove from heat, and cool slightly.
• Layer half each of tortilla chips, meat mixture, lettuce, cheese, and tomato in a large serving bowl; repeat layers. Serve immediately with remaining ¾ cup taco sauce and sour cream. Yield: 6 servings.
Per serving: Calories 684 Fat 30.3g
Cholesterol 82mg Sodium 1459mg

Shrimp and Black Bean Salad

◀ MAKE AHEAD ▶

PREP: 20 MINUTES   CHILL: 8 HOURS

6 cups water
2 pounds unpeeled large fresh shrimp
1 (15-ounce) can black beans, drained
1 small green pepper, finely chopped
½ cup sliced celery
½ cup sliced purple onion, separated into rings
2 tablespoons chopped fresh cilantro
⅔ cup picante sauce
¼ cup lime juice
2 tablespoons vegetable oil
2 tablespoons honey
¼ teaspoon salt
Lettuce leaves

• Bring water to a boil; add shrimp, and cook 3 to 5 minutes or until shrimp turn pink. Drain well; rinse with cold water. Chill.
• Peel shrimp, and devein, if desired. Combine shrimp, beans, and next 4 ingredients in a large bowl, tossing gently. Combine picante sauce and next 4 ingredients in a small bowl; stir with a wire whisk until well blended. Pour picante sauce mixture over shrimp mixture; toss gently to combine. Cover and chill 8 hours.
• Arrange shrimp around edge of a lettuce-lined serving platter; spoon bean mixture into center of platter. Yield: 4 servings.
Per serving: Calories 332 Fat 8.8g
Cholesterol 249mg Sodium 1067mg

Seafood Louis Salad

◀ QUICK ▶
◀ MAKE AHEAD ▶

PREP: 30 MINUTES

What a refreshing supper this salad makes after a busy day. You can prepare everything the day before and simply assemble it at suppertime.

1 cup mayonnaise
¼ cup chili sauce
3 green onions, chopped
1 teaspoon lemon juice
¼ teaspoon salt
3 tablespoons whipping cream
1 head iceberg lettuce, shredded
1 pound fresh crabmeat, drained and flaked
1 pound peeled cooked shrimp*
2 large tomatoes, cut into thin wedges
4 large hard-cooked eggs, cut into wedges

• Combine first 6 ingredients in a large bowl, whisking until well blended; set aside.
• Place shredded lettuce on a platter; arrange crabmeat, shrimp, tomato wedges, and egg wedges on lettuce. Serve with dressing. Yield: 8 servings.
If you cook and peel your own shrimp, start with 2 pounds unpeeled raw shrimp.
Per serving: Calories 380 Fat 28.2g
Cholesterol 283mg Sodium 631mg

Note: Substitute 2 pounds imitation crabmeat or 2 pounds peeled cooked shrimp for fresh crabmeat and shrimp.

Tuna Niçoise

PREP: 30 MINUTES   COOK: 20 MINUTES

CHILL: 30 MINUTES

2 (12½-ounce) cans solid white tuna,
    drained and flaked
2 tablespoons lemon juice
1 tablespoon capers
¼ teaspoon salt
¼ teaspoon coarsely ground pepper
1 pound fresh baby green beans, trimmed
1 pound small new potatoes, unpeeled
2 small purple onions, sliced and
    separated into rings
1 pound plum tomatoes, quartered
¾ cup Niçoise olives or other small black
    olives
1 head curly leaf lettuce
Garlic Vinaigrette
2 hard-cooked eggs, sliced

•Place tuna in a medium bowl. Combine
lemon juice and next 3 ingredients; drizzle
over tuna. Cover and chill at least 30 minutes for flavors to blend.
•Cook green beans in a small amount of
boiling water 5 minutes or just until crisp-
tender. Drain beans and immediately plunge
into ice water to stop the cooking process.
Drain again.
•Cook potatoes in boiling water 15 minutes
or until tender. Drain and cool. Quarter
potatoes.
•Arrange onion, beans, potato, tomato, and
olives on a large serving platter lined with
lettuce leaves. Mound tuna in center of the
platter. Drizzle Garlic Vinaigrette over salad.
Garnish with hard-cooked egg slices. Yield: 6
servings.
Per serving: Calories 459 Fat 25.9g
Cholesterol 105mg Sodium 1055mg

Garlic Vinaigrette

½ cup olive oil or vegetable oil
¼ cup red wine vinegar
2 tablespoons lemon juice
4 large cloves garlic, crushed
1 tablespoon minced fresh oregano or
    1 teaspoon dried oregano
½ teaspoon salt
½ teaspoon sugar

•Combine all ingredients in a jar; cover
tightly, and shake vigorously.
•Chill, if desired, until ready to serve. Shake
again just before serving. Yield: ¾ cup.

DRESSINGS

The dressing is a salad's most crucial
component. It can tie together a blend of
tender greens and fresh vegetables. Or if the
dressing is too salty, too oily, or too spicy, it
can ruin the salad. The amount of dressing
is critical, too. Too much wilts the greens
and they'll be swimming in the salad bowl.
When adding dressing, remember the drier
the leaves, the better the dressing will cling.

Dressings can be broken down into four
types: vinaigrettes, mayonnaise-based dressings, cooked dressings, and creamy dressings. A true vinaigrette is three parts oil to
one part vinegar with added seasonings.
Many vinaigrette recipes tend to stray from
these basic proportions and still provide
great flavor. Dressings and sauces such as
Rémoulade (page 390) use mayonnaise as
their base. And cooked dressings appear in
recipes like German Potato Salad (page
360) or meat and pasta salads. Creamy
dressings often have yogurt, buttermilk, or
sour cream as a base.

The best way to dress a salad is to drizzle
dressing over greens just before serving,
adding only a portion of the dressing. Then
toss lightly to coat the greens and other
ingredients, and serve the remaining

dressing at the table. This way each person
can add the desired amount of dressing.

Dressings need to be stored in the
refrigerator. Most will keep from three to
five days.

Thousand Island Dressing

◄ MAKE AHEAD ►
◄ FAMILY FAVORITE ►

PREP: 15 MINUTES

*Thousand Island Dressing is one of the most
popular dressings around. It comes from
common ingredients that you probably have
on hand. Aside from salads, it's also good on
sandwiches and some vegetables.*

1 cup mayonnaise or salad dressing
½ cup chili sauce
3 tablespoons chopped pimiento-stuffed
    olives
1 tablespoon chopped fresh parsley
1 tablespoon diced pimiento
1 tablespoon honey
½ teaspoon lemon juice
¼ teaspoon onion powder
12 capers

•Combine mayonnaise and chili sauce; stir in
olives and remaining ingredients. Cover and
chill. Serve over salad greens. Yield:1¾ cups.
Per tablespoon: Calories 65 Fat 6.3g
Cholesterol 5mg Sodium 182mg

Russian Dressing: Omit olives and capers;
add 1 teaspoon each prepared horseradish
and paprika, and 1 tablespoon sugar.

Blue Cheese Dressing

◄ MAKE AHEAD • QUICK ►

PREP: 12 MINUTES

*Blue cheese fans, here's a dressing you'll love.
It's full of bits of the gutsy cheese. And don't
miss the two variations.*

1 tablespoon dried Italian seasoning
1 tablespoon dried parsley flakes
1 cup mayonnaise
¾ cup buttermilk
1½ (4-ounce) packages blue cheese,
    crumbled
7 drops of hot sauce
1 teaspoon steak sauce
1 clove garlic, crushed

•Combine all ingredients, and stir well. Cover and chill. Serve over salad greens. Yield: 2¼ cups.

Per tablespoon: Calories 58 Fat 5.8g Cholesterol 6mg Sodium 87mg

Buttermilk Dressing: Omit blue cheese. Yield: 1¾ cups.

Buttermilk-Parmesan Dressing: Omit blue cheese. Add ½ cup grated Parmesan cheese. Yield: 2¼ cups.

Creamy Roquefort Dressing

◄ MAKE AHEAD • QUICK ►

PREP: 7 MINUTES

1 (8-ounce) carton sour cream
4 ounces Roquefort cheese, crumbled
2 teaspoons lemon juice
¼ teaspoon dry mustard
⅛ teaspoon pepper
4 drops of hot sauce

•Combine all ingredients in a small bowl, stirring with a wire whisk until blended. Cover and chill thoroughly. Serve over salad greens. Yield: 1½ cups.

Per tablespoon: Calories 38 Fat 3.4g Cholesterol 8mg Sodium 91mg

Peppercorn-Parmesan Dressing

◄ MAKE AHEAD • QUICK ►

PREP: 10 MINUTES

¾ cup mayonnaise
½ cup grated Parmesan cheese
½ teaspoon sugar
1½ teaspoons coarsely ground pepper or cracked pepper
¼ cup milk

•Combine all ingredients in a small bowl, stirring with a wire whisk until smooth. Cover and chill. Yield: 1 cup.

Per tablespoon: Calories 93 Fat 9.3g Cholesterol 9mg Sodium 123mg

Honey-Mustard Dressing

Tangy French Dressing

Creamy Roquefort Dressing

Peppercorn-Parmesan Dressing

Tangy French Dressing

◄ MAKE AHEAD ►
◄ FAMILY FAVORITE ►

PREP: 15 MINUTES

This dressing is tartly sweet and red-orange in color. Enjoy it on cabbage.

¼ cup white vinegar or cider vinegar
¼ cup ketchup
1 tablespoon dried minced onion
1 teaspoon salt
¼ cup sugar
1 teaspoon dry mustard
1 teaspoon celery seeds (optional)
1 cup vegetable oil

•Process vinegar and ketchup in a blender or food processor until blended. Add onion and next 3 ingredients, and, if desired, celery seeds; process until smooth, stopping once to scrape down sides. With blender on high, gradually add oil in a slow, steady stream; blend until thickened. Cover and chill. Stir before serving. Yield: 1½ cups.

Per tablespoon: Calories 93 Fat 9.1g Cholesterol 0mg Sodium 128mg

Honey-Mustard Dressing

◄ MAKE AHEAD • QUICK ►
◄ FAMILY FAVORITE ►

PREP: 10 MINUTES

Dip a batch of crispy hot chicken fingers in this creamy thick dressing. It's very easy and very good.

¾ cup plain yogurt
¼ cup mayonnaise
2 tablespoons Dijon mustard
2 tablespoons coarse-grained mustard
¼ cup honey
1 tablespoon cider vinegar
⅛ teaspoon ground red pepper

•Combine all ingredients in a small bowl, stirring with a wire whisk until smooth. Cover and chill, if desired. Serve over salad greens or fruit. Yield: 1½ cups.

Per tablespoon: Calories 34 Fat 2.1g Cholesterol 2mg Sodium 72mg

Fresh Ginger Dressing

PREP: 15 MINUTES

⅓ cup olive oil
1 teaspoon grated lime rind
¼ cup fresh lime juice
1½ tablespoons grated fresh ginger
1 teaspoon sugar
¾ teaspoon salt
¾ teaspoon garlic salt
1½ teaspoons chopped fresh basil
1½ teaspoons soy sauce
1½ teaspoons red wine vinegar

•Combine all ingredients in a jar; cover tightly, and shake vigorously. Serve over salad greens. Yield: ¾ cup.
Per tablespoon: Calories 57 Fat 6g Cholesterol 0mg Sodium 320mg

Homemade Mayonnaise

◄ MAKE AHEAD ►
◄ FAMILY FAVORITE ►

PREP: 5 MINUTES   COOK: 20 MINUTES

Homemade Mayonnaise is a novelty to make and it's preservative free, unlike some brands of commercial mayonnaise. Use it on sandwiches, to bind salads, or as a base to make other dressings like Thousand Island.

3 egg yolks
¼ cup water
2 cups vegetable oil
2 tablespoons lemon juice
¾ teaspoon dry mustard
½ teaspoon salt
Dash of paprika
3 drops of hot sauce

•Beat egg yolks in a deep, narrow bowl at high speed with an electric mixer until thick and pale. Stir in water, and pour mixture into top of a double boiler. Cook over hot, not boiling, water, stirring constantly with a wire whisk, 8 minutes or until thermometer registers 160°. Return mixture to bowl. Add oil, 1 tablespoon at a time; beat until mixture begins to thicken. Gradually add lemon juice, beating until thickened. Add dry mustard and remaining ingredients, stirring well.

•Spoon mayonnaise into a glass or plastic container; cover and chill. Do not store mayonnaise in a metal container. Yield: 2½ cups.
Per tablespoon: Calories 101 Fat 11.3g Cholesterol 16mg Sodium 30mg

Herbed Mayonnaise: Stir 2 to 3 tablespoons chopped fresh herbs into prepared mayonnaise before chilling.

Italian Dressing

◄ MAKE AHEAD • QUICK ►
◄ FAMILY FAVORITE ►

PREP: 10 MINUTES

The creamy and zesty versions of this household favorite are even better than the main recipe.

½ cup vegetable oil
2 tablespoons white vinegar
2 tablespoons lemon juice
1 teaspoon sugar
½ teaspoon dry mustard
¼ teaspoon salt
¼ teaspoon seasoned salt
¼ teaspoon dried Italian seasoning
⅛ teaspoon pepper

•Combine all ingredients in a jar. Cover tightly, and shake vigorously; chill thoroughly. Shake before serving. Serve over salad greens. Yield: ¾ cup.
Per tablespoon: Calories 83 Fat 9.1g Cholesterol 0mg Sodium 98mg

Creamy Italian: Combine ½ cup Italian Dressing (above) and ½ cup mayonnaise in a small bowl, stirring with a wire whisk until smooth. Add 1 to 2 tablespoons milk, if needed. Yield: 1 cup.

Zesty Italian: Add ¼ teaspoon dried red pepper flakes and 2 cloves garlic, minced, to Italian Dressing. Yield: ¾ cup.

Hot Bacon Dressing

◄ FAMILY FAVORITE • QUICK ►

PREP: 5 MINUTES   COOK: 5 MINUTES

You can forego the bacon drippings in this dressing and use 2 tablespoons vegetable oil.

4 slices bacon
¼ cup cider vinegar
2 tablespoons water
1 tablespoon sugar
1 teaspoon grated onion
⅛ teaspoon dry mustard

•Cook bacon in a large skillet over medium-high heat until crisp; remove bacon, reserving 2 tablespoons drippings in skillet. Crumble bacon, and set aside.
•Add cider vinegar and remaining 4 ingredients to skillet; bring just to a boil. Add bacon. Whisk dressing just before serving. Serve warm over spinach or other salad greens. Yield: ½ cup.
Per tablespoon: Calories 86 Fat 8.2g Cholesterol 9mg Sodium 97mg

Basil Vinaigrette

◄ MAKE AHEAD • QUICK ►

PREP: 6 MINUTES

This vinaigrette is highly flavored, so a little goes a long way on salad greens. And if you have fresh tomatoes on hand, slice them, and drizzle with this vinaigrette for a simple summer salad.

⅔ cup olive oil
⅓ cup red wine vinegar
1 teaspoon sugar
¾ teaspoon salt
2 tablespoons chopped fresh basil or 2 teaspoons dried basil
¼ to ½ teaspoon freshly ground pepper

•Combine all ingredients in a jar; cover tightly, and shake vigorously. Store in refrigerator. Yield: 1 cup.
Per tablespoon: Calories 81 Fat 9g Cholesterol 0mg Sodium 110mg

Balsamic Vinaigrette

◄ MAKE AHEAD • QUICK ►

PREP: 5 MINUTES

A basic vinaigrette is three parts oil to one part vinegar. Pungent balsamic vinegar takes this vinaigrette to its maximum tang.

¾ cup olive oil
¼ cup balsamic vinegar
1 shallot, minced
¼ teaspoon salt
¼ teaspoon freshly ground pepper

•Combine all ingredients in a jar; cover tightly, and shake vigorously. Store in refrigerator. Yield: 1 cup.
Per tablespoon: Calories 90 Fat 10.1g
Cholesterol 0mg Sodium 37mg

Versatile Vinaigrette

◄ MAKE AHEAD • QUICK ►

PREP: 5 MINUTES

¾ cup vegetable oil
¼ cup white wine vinegar
1 teaspoon salt
½ to 1 teaspoon freshly ground pepper
1 clove garlic, crushed

•Combine all ingredients in a jar. Cover tightly, and shake vigorously. Store in refrigerator. Yield: 1⅓ cups.
Per tablespoon: Calories 70 Fat 7.8g
Cholesterol 0mg Sodium 112mg

Citrus-Cilantro Dressing

◄ HEALTHY • QUICK ►

PREP: 5 MINUTES

⅓ cup orange juice
⅓ cup fresh lime juice
3 tablespoons finely chopped fresh
   cilantro
2 tablespoons honey

•Combine all ingredients in a small bowl; stir well with a wire whisk. Serve over salad greens or fresh fruit. Yield: ¾ cup.
Per tablespoon: Calories 16 Fat 0.0g
Cholesterol 0mg Sodium 1mg

Poppy Seed Dressing

◄ FAMILY FAVORITE • QUICK ►

PREP: 10 MINUTES

½ cup white vinegar or red wine vinegar
⅓ cup sugar
1 teaspoon salt
1 teaspoon dry mustard
1 teaspoon grated onion
1 cup vegetable oil
1 tablespoon poppy seeds

•Process first 5 ingredients in a blender 20 seconds. With blender on high, gradually add oil in a slow, steady stream. Stir in poppy seeds. Serve over fresh spinach or fruit. Yield: 1⅔ cups.
Per teaspoon: Calories 28 Fat 2.8g
Cholesterol 0mg Sodium 29mg

Sweet-and-Sour Dressing

PREP: 2 MINUTES

1 cup vegetable oil
½ cup white vinegar
½ cup sugar
1 teaspoon salt
1 teaspoon dry mustard
1 teaspoon paprika
1 teaspoon grated onion
1 teaspoon celery seeds

•Process first 7 ingredients in a blender until smooth. Stir in celery seeds. Cover and chill. Stir again just before serving. Serve over salad greens or fruit. Yield: 1¾ cups.
Per tablespoon: Calories 84 Fat 7.8g
Cholesterol 0mg Sodium 84mg

Papaya Dressing

◄ MAKE AHEAD • QUICK ►

PREP: 10 MINUTES

1 ripe papaya, peeled and seeded
3 cloves garlic
2 tablespoons sugar
2 tablespoons chopped onion
½ teaspoon salt
¼ teaspoon pepper
½ cup white wine vinegar
½ cup club soda
½ cup olive oil

•Process first 8 ingredients in a food processor until smooth, stopping once to scrape down sides. Pour olive oil gradually through food chute with processor running; process until smooth. Serve over fresh fruit. Store in refrigerator. Yield: 2½ cups.
Per tablespoon: Calories 33 Fat 2.7g
Cholesterol 0mg Sodium 48mg

Infused Oils

◄ MAKE AHEAD ►

COOK: 20 MINUTES   COOL: 8 HOURS

Try any number of herb or spice oils listed below. They're all attractive and will keep up to two weeks in the refrigerator.

Basic Recipe: Place herb or spice in a heavy saucepan; add 1 cup canola oil. Warm over low heat 20 minutes, stirring occasionally; cool at least 8 hours. Pour oil through a wire-mesh strainer into a bowl, discarding solids. Cover and store oil in refrigerator up to 2 weeks; then discard any unused portion of oil. Yield: 1 cup.
Per tablespoon: Calories 120 Fat 13.6g
Cholesterol 0mg Sodium 0mg

Basil Oil: Use 1 cup chopped fresh basil.

Black Pepper Oil: Use ½ cup coarsely ground black pepper.

Chile Pepper Oil: Crumble 2 dried red chile peppers, and place in a heat-proof container. Heat oil, and pour over chiles.

Chive Oil: Use 1 cup chopped fresh chives; reduce oil to ¾ cup.

Ginger Oil: Place ⅓ cup chopped fresh ginger in a heat-proof container. Heat oil, and pour over ginger.

Mint Oil: Use 1 cup chopped fresh mint.

Rosemary Oil: Use ½ cup chopped fresh rosemary.

Sage Oil: Use ½ cup chopped fresh sage leaves.

Thyme Oil: Use 1 cup fresh thyme leaves.

Fried Oyster Po' Boy (page 381)

SANDWICHES

*Some of its names like panini and pita wrap may be new, but a
sandwich is still simple and straightforward food. It's an opportunity
to stack favorite ingredients on wonderfully fresh bread. And the better
the ingredients you build with, the more delicious the results.*

History tells us that an eighteenth century card-playing English diplomat named John Montague—the fourth Earl of Sandwich—gets credit for naming the sandwich. He couldn't bear to be called away from a card game just to eat lunch, so he summoned his servants to deliver something to eat out of hand. And thus, our beloved midday food gained its name.

Though he may have named the sandwich, the earl certainly wasn't its originator. The sandwich idea has been around for centuries in just about every culture known to man. Perhaps the greatest variety of sandwiches is found in the United States where we've borrowed breads and fillings from many cuisines to create some modern mouthfuls. Among these pages we celebrate a great assortment of sandwiches from Chili Dogs to Calzones.

Build the Best Sandwich

A sandwich is very versatile. You can serve it hot, cold, grilled, fried, rolled, open face, or with knife and fork. Don't be shy when it comes to experimenting with types of bread and fillings. Here are some tips for stacking a great sandwich.
•Use only the freshest ingredients—meat, produce, bread, and condiments. And trim ingredients to fit the bread—eye appeal matters.
•Generally speaking, firm-textured breads work best in sandwich making. Their heartiness helps hold the filling in place and makes eating easy.
•Toast the bread for sandwiches that will hold soft or saucy fillings.

•Consider the texture of breads and fillings when putting the two together. A moist chunky filling like chicken salad will burst out of soft bread, and dry layers of filling will fall out of a hard, crusty roll.
•Spread softened butter or whipped spread to the edges of bread on the side that will hold the filling. This seals the bread and prevents a soggy sandwich.
•You can make sturdy sandwiches like subs and heroes ahead. Just wrap them in heavy-duty plastic wrap, zip-top plastic bags, or aluminum foil, and refrigerate 3 to 4 hours.
•Don't make sandwiches with moist fillings like egg salad in advance; they'll get soggy.
•Use a very sharp knife to cut a sandwich neatly. This will prevent rough edges and squashed layers.
•Avoid freezing sandwiches that contain hard-cooked eggs, sour cream, mayonnaise, and lettuce and tomato. These ingredients don't freeze well; wait to add them just before serving. Otherwise, you can wrap and freeze sandwiches up to a month in moisture-proof wrap. Most sandwiches thaw at room temperature within three hours. That means they'll still be chilled at noon if you brown bag them on the way out the door in the morning.

Tea Anyone?

Always use thinly sliced bread for tea sandwiches; trimming the crust is a personal preference. Go light on the filling for this type of sandwich. Once assembled, cut these dainty sandwiches into triangles or circles (using a biscuit cutter) for serving.

Egg Salad BLTs

PREP: 40 MINUTES

It's not just a BLT; this toasted sandwich has egg salad between the layers, too.

4 large hard-cooked eggs, chopped
½ cup finely chopped celery
⅓ cup mayonnaise
1 to 2 tablespoons sweet pickle relish
¼ teaspoon salt
⅛ teaspoon pepper
12 slices buttered toast
6 lettuce leaves
2 medium tomatoes, thinly sliced
12 slices bacon, cooked and drained

•Combine first 6 ingredients, stirring well. Spread egg mixture on 6 slices of toast; arrange lettuce, tomato, and bacon on top, and top with remaining toast. Cut each sandwich in half, using wooden picks to secure each half. Yield: 6 servings.

Per serving: Calories 406 Fat 25.7g
Cholesterol 173mg Sodium 774mg

Tuna Salad Sandwiches: Substitute 1 (9-ounce) can tuna, drained, for eggs. Add 1 teaspoon lemon juice, and omit bacon.

Ham Salad Sandwiches: Substitute 1½ cups finely chopped or ground smoked ham for eggs; omit bacon.

Triple-Cheese Club Sandwiches

PREP: 25 MINUTES   COOK: 8 MINUTES

1 (3-ounce) package cream cheese, softened
1 (2-ounce) package blue cheese, crumbled
1 teaspoon dried minced onion
Dash of Worcestershire sauce
12 slices sandwich bread, toasted
8 slices tomato
8 slices cooked turkey (about 8 ounces)
4 slices Swiss cheese (about 6 ounces)
8 slices bacon, cooked and drained
4 green leaf lettuce leaves
¼ cup mayonnaise

•Combine first 4 ingredients in a small bowl; stir well.
•Spread cheese mixture on 4 slices of toast. Top each with 2 slices tomato, 2 slices turkey, and 1 slice Swiss cheese. Add second slice of toast; top each with 2 slices bacon and lettuce.
•Spread remaining toast evenly with mayonnaise, and place over lettuce leaves. Secure each sandwich with wooden picks. To serve, cut each sandwich into 4 triangles. Yield: 4 servings.

Per serving: Calories 751 Fat 45g
Cholesterol 143mg Sodium 1527mg

Cucumber Sandwiches

PREP: 30 MINUTES

Teatime isn't complete without a plateful of petite cucumber sandwiches. They're light in flavor, and you can use the leftover bread trimmings to make fresh breadcrumbs to top a casserole.

1 (8-ounce) package cream cheese, softened
⅓ cup mayonnaise
20 very thinly sliced white sandwich bread slices (we tested with Pepperidge Farm)
20 very thinly sliced wheat bread slices (we tested with Pepperidge Farm)
1 large cucumber, finely shredded and patted dry
2 teaspoons grated onion
¼ teaspoon garlic salt
½ to 1 teaspoon chopped fresh dill (optional)

•Process cream cheese and mayonnaise in container of an electric blender or food processor until smooth, stopping once to scrape down sides.
•Cut crusts from bread. Combine cheese mixture, cucumber, onion, garlic salt, and, if desired, dill. Thinly spread cucumber mixture onto white bread slices, and top with wheat bread.
•Cut sandwiches in half diagonally. Store in an airtight container up to 1 hour before serving. Yield: 40 sandwiches.

Per serving: Calories 52 Fat 3.7g
Cholesterol 7mg Sodium 76mg

Big Veggie Sandwiches

PREP: 23 MINUTES

1 (1-pound) loaf unsliced whole wheat bread
1 (8-ounce) container chives-and-onion-flavored cream cheese
6 green leaf lettuce leaves
1 small green pepper, thinly sliced
1 large tomato, thinly sliced
2 ripe avocados, peeled and sliced
1 small cucumber, thinly sliced
¾ cup alfalfa sprouts
¼ to ⅓ cup Italian dressing

•Cut bread into 12 slices. Spread a thin layer of cream cheese on 1 side of each slice. Arrange lettuce and next 5 ingredients on 6 slices. Drizzle dressing over vegetables, and top with remaining 6 bread slices. Yield: 6 servings.

Per serving: Calories 493 Fat 28g
Cholesterol 37mg Sodium 682mg

Veggie Burgers

PREP: 10 MINUTES   COOK: 45 MINUTES

CHILL: 1 HOUR

Even beef lovers will enjoy this meatless burger. It's made from cooked lentils that are well seasoned and mixed with good garden ingredients.

1 cup dried lentils, sorted and washed
2½ cups water
¼ cup ketchup
¼ teaspoon garlic powder
1 small onion, finely chopped
½ cup shredded carrot
1 cup uncooked quick-cooking oats
1 large egg
1 teaspoon salt
¼ teaspoon pepper
1 tablespoon whole wheat flour
2 tablespoons vegetable oil
8 hamburger buns
8 slices tomato
8 green leaf lettuce leaves
16 dill pickle slices

- Combine lentils and water in a saucepan; bring to a boil over medium-high heat. Cover, reduce heat, and simmer 25 minutes. Cook, uncovered, 10 minutes or until water is absorbed and lentils are tender.
- Stir ketchup and next 7 ingredients into lentils. Shape into 8 patties; sprinkle with flour. Cover and chill 1 hour.
- Pour 1 tablespoon oil into a large skillet. Fry 4 patties over medium-high heat 1 to 2 minutes on each side or until golden. Repeat procedure with remaining 1 tablespoon oil and 4 patties.
- Place a patty on bottom half of each bun; top with tomato, lettuce, and pickles; add top half of bun. Serve with mayonnaise or Thousand Island Dressing (page 370). Yield: 8 servings.

Per serving: Calories 324 Fat 8.6g
Cholesterol 40mg Sodium 625mg

Grilled Fish Sandwiches

◀ GRILLED • FAMILY FAVORITE ▶

PREP: 20 MINUTES   MARINATE: 1 HOUR

COOK: 20 MINUTES

Turn the fresh catch of the day into this gourmet grilled specialty.

4 green onions, minced
2 cloves garlic, minced
¼ cup olive oil
¼ cup dry white wine
2 tablespoons lemon juice
½ teaspoon salt
1 teaspoon cracked black pepper
1 pound amberjack fillets, grouper fillets, or other firm white fish (½ inch thick)
4 kaiser rolls, split
4 green leaf lettuce leaves
1 large tomato, sliced
4 thin slices purple onion
¼ cup tartar sauce

- Sauté green onions and garlic in hot olive oil in a small skillet over medium-high heat until tender. Stir in wine and next 3 ingredients; simmer 1 minute. Remove from heat, and cool completely.
- Cut fish into 4 pieces; place in a heavy-duty, zip-top plastic bag or shallow dish. Pour wine mixture over fish. Seal or cover, and marinate in refrigerator 1 hour, turning once.

- Remove fillets from marinade, discarding marinade. Grill fillets, covered with grill lid, over medium coals (300° to 350°) 6 to 8 minutes on each side or until fish flakes easily when tested with a fork. To serve, butter and toast rolls, if desired. Top bottom half of each roll with lettuce, tomato, onion, tartar sauce, and a grilled fillet. Cover with tops of rolls. Yield: 4 servings.

Per serving: Calories 546 Fat 28.6g
Cholesterol 66mg Sodium 866mg

Note: For a gourmet fish sandwich, substitute mixed baby lettuces for green leaf lettuce, Caramelized Onions (page 458) for thin slices of purple onion, and Rémoulade (page 390) for tartar sauce.

Tuna Burgers

◀ QUICK • HEALTHY ▶

PREP: 15 MINUTES   COOK: 4 MINUTES

Here's a healthy and flavorful alternative to hamburger. Tartar sauce makes a tasty bread spread.

1 large egg, lightly beaten
1 (9-ounce) can tuna in spring water, drained and flaked
½ cup coarsely crushed saltine crackers (11 crackers)
¼ cup finely chopped green pepper
2 tablespoons finely chopped celery
2 tablespoons finely chopped onion
¼ teaspoon pepper
1 teaspoon vegetable oil
8 hamburger buns, toasted

- Combine first 7 ingredients in a large bowl; shape into 4 patties.
- Coat a large nonstick skillet with vegetable cooking spray. Add oil; place skillet over medium-high heat until hot. Add tuna patties. Cook 2 minutes or until browned and crusty. Turn patties and cook 2 more minutes or until browned.
- Serve patties on buns with tomato, lettuce, onion, and tartar sauce. Yield: 4 servings.

Per serving: Calories 409 Fat 11.1g
Cholesterol 95mg Sodium 572mg

Salmon Burgers: Substitute 1 (7.5-ounce) can salmon, drained, for tuna.

Fried Grouper Sandwiches

◀ QUICK ▶

PREP: 18 MINUTES   COOK: 5 MINUTES

This tall, crispy sandwich is guaranteed to please.

1 cup all-purpose flour
¼ cup cornstarch
1 tablespoon garlic powder
½ teaspoon pepper
4 (4-ounce) grouper fillets
½ teaspoon salt
¼ teaspoon pepper
½ cup buttermilk
Canola oil
Herb Mayonnaise
4 onion sandwich buns, toasted
4 lettuce leaves
2 large tomatoes, sliced

- Combine first 4 ingredients in a shallow dish. Season grouper with salt and ¼ teaspoon pepper. Dredge grouper in flour mixture; dip in buttermilk, and dredge in flour mixture again.
- Pour oil to depth of 3 inches into a Dutch oven; heat to 350°. Fry fillets in hot oil 5 minutes or until golden; drain on paper towels.
- Spread Herb Mayonnaise on bottom half of each bun. Place a fillet on bottom half of each bun, and top with lettuce and tomato; add top half of bun. Serve immediately. Yield: 4 servings.

Per serving: Calories 727 Fat 39.5g
Cholesterol 59mg Sodium 782mg

Herb Mayonnaise

½ cup mayonnaise
1 tablespoon chopped fresh basil
1 tablespoon chopped fresh thyme
1 tablespoon lemon juice
1 teaspoon chopped fresh oregano
1 teaspoon capers
1 clove garlic, crushed

- Combine all ingredients in a bowl, stirring well; cover and chill. Yield: ⅔ cup.

Spicy Southwestern Chicken Sandwiches

◄ QUICK ►

PREP: 20 MINUTES   COOK: 8 MINUTES

We gave this sandwich rave reviews. Thin pieces of chicken are coated with a spicy fajita seasoning, browned in a skillet, and topped with a jalapeño mayonnaise.

⅓ cup mayonnaise
2 tablespoons chopped fresh cilantro
1½ teaspoons grated lime rind
1½ tablespoons fresh lime juice
1 jalapeño pepper, seeded and minced
4 skinned, boned chicken breast halves
1 to 2 tablespoons fajita seasoning (we tested with Spice Hunter)
1 tablespoon vegetable oil
4 hamburger buns, toasted
1 red or green tomato, sliced
4 slices purple onion

•Combine first 5 ingredients in a small bowl; stir well, and set aside.
•Place chicken between two sheets of heavy-duty plastic wrap; flatten to ¼-inch thickness, using a meat mallet or rolling pin. Sprinkle chicken with fajita seasoning.
•Cook chicken in hot oil in a large skillet over medium-high heat about 4 minutes on each side.
•Spread 1 tablespoon mayonnaise mixture evenly on bottom half of each bun. Top each with chicken, tomato, onion, 1 more tablespoon mayonnaise mixture, and top half of bun. Yield: 4 servings.
Per serving: Calories 503 Fat 25.5g
Cholesterol 118mg Sodium 512mg

DRESSED UP DOGS

Give your next batch of hotdogs a new twist. Add any of the following options to our Chili Cheese Dogs.
•**Slaw Dogs:** Top with a heaping spoonful of coleslaw.
•**Junkyard Dogs:** Top with sauerkraut, coleslaw, and bacon bits.
•**Kids' Dogs:** Slice the franks before putting them on buns.

Chili Cheese Dogs

◄ QUICK • FAMILY FAVORITE ►

PREP: 7 MINUTES   COOK: 10 MINUTES

12 frankfurters
3 (15-ounce) cans chili without beans or 5 cups Beef and Bean Chili (page 436)
12 hot dog buns
1 (6-ounce) jar prepared mustard
1 (10-ounce) jar sweet pickle relish
1½ cups chopped onion
2 cups (8 ounces) shredded sharp Cheddar cheese

•Cook frankfurters according to package directions; drain. Meanwhile, heat chili in a saucepan over low heat 6 to 8 minutes or until thoroughly heated.
•Place frankfurters in buns. Top evenly with warm chili, mustard, and remaining 3 ingredients. Yield: 12 servings.
Per serving: Calories 536 Fat 28.5g
Cholesterol 83mg Sodium 1535mg

Steak Sandwiches

PREP: 10 MINUTES   COOK: 26 MINUTES

3 large onions, thinly sliced
3 tablespoons butter, melted
1 tablespoon garlic oil or vegetable oil
1 (1¼-pound) round tip steak, cut into wafer-thin slices*
6 steak sandwich rolls or unsliced hoagie rolls (we tested with Cobblestone Mill)
½ cup picante sauce

•Sauté onion in butter in a large skillet over medium-high heat until tender and browned. Remove onion from skillet, and set aside.
•Pour garlic oil into skillet; place over medium-high heat until hot. Add steak slices, and cook, stirring constantly, 5 minutes or until meat is browned. Drain.
•Cut unsliced rolls horizontally to, but not through, other side. Toast rolls lightly.
•Combine steak and onion in skillet; cook over medium-high heat 1 minute, stirring constantly, or just until thoroughly heated. Arrange steak and onion on bottoms of rolls. Top with picante sauce, if desired, and roll tops. Yield: 6 servings.
*This cut of meat is labeled "wafer-thin breakfast steak" in the meat department.
Per serving: Calories 362 Fat 14g
Cholesterol 68mg Sodium 666mg

Grilled Reubens

◄ QUICK ►

PREP: 12 MINUTES   COOK: 5 MINUTES

2 cups canned sauerkraut, drained
¾ teaspoon caraway seeds
Thousand Island Dressing (page 370)
12 slices rye bread without caraway seeds, divided
6 slices pumpernickel bread
12 (1-ounce) slices Swiss cheese
1 pound corned beef, thinly sliced
Butter or margarine, softened
6 pimiento-stuffed olives (optional)

•Combine sauerkraut and caraway seeds. Spread 1⅓ cups Thousand Island Dressing over 1 side of 6 slices rye and 6 slices pumpernickel bread. Place 1 slice cheese over dressing on each bread slice. Layer sauerkraut mixture and corned beef evenly over cheese slices. Stack to make 6 (2-layer) sandwiches. Spread remaining 6 rye bread slices with remaining dressing; invert onto tops of sandwiches.
•Spread butter on tops of sandwiches; invert sandwiches onto a hot, nonstick griddle or skillet. Cook until bread is golden. Spread butter on ungrilled sides of sandwiches; turn carefully, and cook until bread is golden and cheese is slightly melted. Secure sandwiches with wooden picks; top with olives, if desired. Serve warm. Yield: 6 servings.
Per serving: Calories 976 Fat 61g
Cholesterol 169mg Sodium 2743mg

Hot Brown

PREP: 35 MINUTES   COOK: 17 MINUTES

Hot Brown is a famous open-faced sandwich that was created at the Brown Hotel in Louisville, Kentucky.

¼ cup butter or margarine
¼ cup all-purpose flour
1 cup milk
1 cup chicken broth
1 cup (4 ounces) shredded Cheddar cheese
¼ teaspoon salt
8 slices bread, toasted
1 pound sliced cooked turkey or chicken breast
8 slices bacon, cooked and drained
4 slices tomato
½ cup grated Parmesan cheese

•Melt butter in a saucepan over low heat; add flour, stirring until smooth. Cook 1 minute, stirring constantly. Gradually add milk and broth; cook over medium heat, stirring constantly, until thick and bubbly. Stir in Cheddar cheese and salt, and continue stirring until cheese melts. Remove from heat.
•Cut 4 slices of toast in half diagonally. Place 2 halves, cut side in, with 1 whole slice in center, on an ovenproof plate or 15- x 10-inch jellyroll pan. Repeat with remaining toast. Top each with turkey, cheese sauce, 2 slices bacon crisscrossed, tomato slice, and 2 tablespoons Parmesan cheese. Broil 3 inches from heat 2 to 3 minutes or just until bubbly. Serve hot. Yield: 4 servings.

Per serving: Calories 708 Fat 38.5g
Cholesterol 187mg Sodium 2321mg

Roast Beef 'n' Horseradish Sandwiches

PREP: 11 MINUTES

Dress up roast beef sandwiches with this horseradish cream. You'll find hoagie rolls with or without seeds in the store. You choose.

4 (2-ounce) hoagie rolls, split
1 (3-ounce) package cream cheese, softened
2 tablespoons mayonnaise
2 tablespoons chutney
2 to 3 teaspoons prepared horseradish
4 lettuce leaves
12 ounces thinly sliced roast beef
2 medium tomatoes, sliced
4 ounces mozzarella cheese, thinly sliced
Freshly ground pepper
1 or 2 slices purple onion, separated into rings

•Toast rolls, if desired. Combine cream cheese and next 3 ingredients; spread on bottoms of rolls. Place lettuce leaves on cream cheese mixture; top evenly with roast beef, tomato slices, and cheese. Sprinkle with pepper. Add onion; cover with roll tops. Serve immediately or wrap each sandwich tightly in heavy-duty plastic wrap, and chill up to 4 hours. Yield: 4 servings.

Per serving: Calories 536 Fat 25.4g
Cholesterol 116mg Sodium 1180mg

Italian Sausage Sandwiches

PREP: 7 MINUTES   COOK: 31 MINUTES

1½ pounds Italian link sausage
½ Spanish onion, sliced and separated into rings
1 medium-size green pepper, cut into thin strips
1 medium-size sweet red pepper, cut into thin strips
1 teaspoon dried oregano
6 large French rolls
1½ cups (6 ounces) shredded mozzarella or provolone cheese

•Cut sausage links lengthwise to, but not through, skin. Brown sausage, cut sides down, in a large skillet over medium heat; drain well, and set aside. Add onion, green pepper, and red pepper to skillet. Cook over medium heat, stirring constantly, until tender. Remove from heat; stir in oregano.
•Heat rolls according to package directions; split rolls in half.
•Place 1 sausage link on bottom half of each roll. Spoon vegetable mixture over sausage, and sprinkle with cheese; cover with top half of rolls. Place on a baking sheet; bake at 400° for 2 minutes or until cheese melts. Yield: 6 servings.

Per serving: Calories 675 Fat 28.8g
Cholesterol 86mg Sodium 1527mg

Grilled Pizza-Pesto Sandwiches

PREP: 8 MINUTES   COOK: 5 MINUTES

1 (6-ounce) package sliced mozzarella cheese, cut into thirds
8 (1-inch-thick) slices Italian bread
¼ cup pizza sauce
¼ cup pesto sauce
20 slices pepperoni
2 tablespoons butter or margarine, softened

•Arrange 1 cheese slice on each of 4 slices of bread; spread evenly with pizza sauce. Top each with another cheese slice, and spread evenly with pesto sauce. Arrange 20 pepperoni slices over pesto sauce; top with remaining cheese slices and remaining bread slices.
•Spread half of butter on tops of sandwiches. Invert sandwiches onto a hot, nonstick griddle or skillet, and cook over medium heat until browned. Spread remaining butter on ungrilled sides of sandwiches; turn and cook until browned. Serve immediately. Yield: 4 servings.

Per serving: Calories 508 Fat 29.2g
Cholesterol 63mg Sodium 1293mg

Vegetable Pita Sandwiches

◄ VEGETARIAN ►

PREP: 37 MINUTES

1 (3-ounce) package cream cheese, softened
1 cup buttermilk
1 cup mayonnaise
1 (8-ounce) carton sour cream
1 (1-ounce) envelope Ranch-style dressing mix
2 tablespoons chopped fresh or frozen chives
2 small tomatoes
1 small cucumber, chopped
1 small onion, chopped
2 carrots, scraped and shredded
2 pita rounds, cut in half
4 lettuce leaves
½ cup alfalfa sprouts

• Beat cream cheese at medium speed with an electric mixer until fluffy; beat in buttermilk and next 4 ingredients. Set dressing aside.
• Seed and chop tomatoes; pat dry with paper towels. Combine tomato, cucumber, onion, and carrot in a bowl; toss with ½ cup dressing.
• Line pita halves with lettuce leaves. Fill each pita half evenly with vegetable mixture. Top with alfalfa sprouts. Serve immediately with remaining dressing. Yield: 4 servings.

Per serving: Calories 463 Fat 33g
Cholesterol 42mg Sodium 596mg

WRAPPIN' IT UP

The sky's the limit when it comes to creative sandwich wraps. Besides pita bread, try wontons, tortillas, crêpes, several sheets of phyllo, refrigerated bread or pizza dough, or a sushi wrap called a handroll.

Peppery Chicken Pita Wrap

Peppery Chicken Pita Wraps

PREP: 20 MINUTES   MARINATE: 2 HOURS
COOK: 15 MINUTES

Wraps are all the rage. This one folds teriyaki-marinated chicken inside a pita with a horseradish mayonnaise.

6 skinned, boned chicken breast halves (1½ pounds)
¼ cup teriyaki sauce
1 teaspoon dried thyme
1 teaspoon ground white pepper
1 teaspoon black pepper
½ teaspoon garlic powder
½ teaspoon ground red pepper
2 tablespoons olive oil
6 (8-inch) pita bread rounds
⅔ cup mayonnaise
2 tablespoons prepared horseradish
3 cups shredded iceberg lettuce or red leaf lettuce

• Slice chicken lengthwise into ½-inch strips, and place in a shallow dish. Pour teriyaki sauce over chicken; cover and marinate in refrigerator 2 hours.
• Remove chicken from marinade, discarding marinade. Combine thyme and next 4 ingredients in a small bowl; sprinkle evenly over chicken.
• Heat 1 tablespoon olive oil in a large skillet over medium-high heat. Cook half of chicken 5 to 7 minutes, turning once; drain on paper towels. Repeat procedure with remaining oil and chicken.
• Wrap pita rounds, two at a time, in heavy-duty plastic wrap, and microwave at HIGH 30 seconds or until thoroughly heated. Meanwhile, combine mayonnaise and horseradish. Spread each pita round with about 2 tablespoons mayonnaise mixture; sprinkle evenly with lettuce, and top with chicken. Fold 2 sides over chicken, and secure with a wooden pick. Yield: 6 servings.

Per serving: Calories 560 Fat 28.5g
Cholesterol 87mg Sodium 579mg

Falafel

PREP: 25 MINUTES   COOK: 5 MINUTES

Falafel (feh-LAH-fehl) are small deep-fried chick-pea patties that are Middle Eastern in origin. Tahini, a thick paste of ground sesame seeds, is their common sauce companion.

2 (15 ounce) cans chick-peas (garbanzo beans), rinsed and drained
½ cup fine, dry breadcrumbs (commercial)
4 cloves garlic, crushed
½ cup chopped fresh parsley
2 tablespoons ground cumin
1 teaspoon salt
½ teaspoon ground red pepper
2 large eggs
Vegetable oil
5 (8-inch) pita bread rounds
Tahini Sauce
Cucumber Relish

•Process first 8 ingredients in food processor until smooth, stopping once to scrape down sides of bowl. Shape mixture into 10 (½-inch-thick) patties.
•Pour oil to depth of ½ inch into a large heavy skillet; place over medium heat until hot. Fry patties in hot oil 3 to 5 minutes or until golden, turning once. Drain on paper towels.
•Cut pita bread rounds in half, and place 1 patty into each pita half. Top with Tahini Sauce and Cucumber Relish, and serve immediately. Yield: 5 servings.
Per serving: Calories 700 Fat 29.8g
Cholesterol 85mg Sodium 1463mg

Tahini Sauce

⅓ cup tahini
¼ cup lemon juice
3 tablespoons olive oil
2 teaspoons water
½ teaspoon salt
2 cloves garlic, minced

•Combine all ingredients in a small bowl, stirring well; cover and chill. Yield: ½ cup.

Cucumber Relish

2 large cucumbers, peeled, seeded, and chopped
8 plum tomatoes, chopped
4 cloves garlic, crushed
½ cup chopped fresh parsley
¼ cup lemon juice
½ teaspoon salt
½ teaspoon pepper

•Combine all ingredients; cover and chill. Yield: 4 cups.

Giant Meatball Sandwich

PREP: 8 MINUTES   COOK: 27 MINUTES

This sandwich is a hungry man's dream. It's a row of meatballs smothered in spaghetti sauce and cheese.

1 pound ground chuck
½ pound ground pork sausage
2 cups spaghetti sauce with peppers and mushrooms
1 clove garlic, minced
1 (1-pound) loaf unsliced Italian bread
1 (6-ounce) package sliced provolone cheese

•Combine ground chuck and sausage; shape into 1-inch balls. Cook meatballs in a large skillet over medium-high heat 8 to 10 minutes or until browned. Drain meatballs on paper towels. Discard drippings.
•Combine meatballs, spaghetti sauce, and garlic in skillet; bring to a boil. Reduce heat, and simmer, uncovered, 12 to 15 minutes or until meatballs are done, stirring mixture occasionally.
•While sauce simmers, slice bread in half horizontally. Place bread, cut side up, on a baking sheet. Broil 5½ inches from heat 1 to 2 minutes or until bread is lightly toasted.
•Spoon meatball mixture over bottom half of toasted bread; arrange cheese on top of meatballs, overlapping as needed. Cover with top of bread. Cut sandwich into 6 pieces; serve immediately. Yield: 6 servings.
Per serving: Calories 615 Fat 29.5g
Cholesterol 90mg Sodium 1452mg

Fried Oyster Po' Boys

PREP: 30 MINUTES   COOK: 23 MINUTES

A Po' Boy is picnic food at its best. Serve this long, crusty sandwich shown on page 374 with coleslaw and chips. Need a shortcut? Use ½ cup tartar sauce from a jar instead of making it.

1 (1-pound) loaf unsliced French bread
¼ cup butter or margarine, melted
2 (12-ounce) containers Standard oysters, drained
1⅓ cups cornmeal mix
6 cups vegetable oil
⅓ cup mayonnaise
2½ tablespoons sweet pickle relish
1 tablespoon lemon juice
⅛ teaspoon hot sauce
1 cup shredded lettuce
1 large tomato, thinly sliced

•Slice off top third of loaf; hollow out bottom section, reserving crumbs for another use. Spread inside surfaces of bread with butter. Place bread on a baking sheet, and bake at 400° for 8 minutes. Set aside.
•Dredge oysters in cornmeal mix. Fry oysters, in batches, in deep hot oil (375°) 2 minutes or until oysters float to the top and are golden. Drain oysters well on paper towels; keep warm.
•Combine mayonnaise and next 3 ingredients; stir well. Stir in lettuce. Spread lettuce mixture in hollowed bread. Top with tomato slices, oysters, and top of loaf. Cut loaf into 4 portions. Yield: 4 servings.
Per serving: Calories 1013 Fat 60.7g
Cholesterol 138mg Sodium 1423mg

Shrimp Po' Boys: Substitute 2 pounds unpeeled large fresh shrimp for oysters. Peel shrimp, and devein, if desired, before dredging and frying.

Muffulettas

PREP: 20 MINUTES   COOK: 20 MINUTES

A finely chopped "olive salad" makes a muffuletta unique. The sandwich, native to New Orleans, is stuffed with salami, pastrami, and mild cheese, and then capped off with the tangy olive condiment.

2 (12-ounce) jars mixed pickled vegetables
½ cup pimiento-stuffed olive slices, coarsely chopped
3 tablespoons olive oil or vegetable oil
1 tablespoon minced garlic
1 (1-pound) round loaf Italian bread with sesame seeds
2 tablespoons olive oil
¼ pound thinly sliced salami
¼ pound thinly sliced pastrami
4 ounces thinly sliced mozzarella, provolone, or Swiss cheese

• Drain mixed vegetables, reserving 1 tablespoon liquid. Finely chop vegetables. Combine vegetables, reserved liquid, olives, 3 tablespoons oil, and garlic; stir well.
• Slice bread in half horizontally. Drizzle 2 tablespoons olive oil over cut sides of loaf. Layer half each of olive mixture, meats, and cheese alternately on bottom of loaf. Repeat with remaining ingredients. Top with remaining bread layer.
• Slice sandwich into 4 wedges. Wrap sandwich in aluminum foil, and place on a baking sheet. Bake at 375° for 15 to 20 minutes or until cheese melts and sandwich is thoroughly heated. Yield: 4 servings.
Per serving: Calories 751 Fat 37.5g Cholesterol 62mg Sodium 2287mg

Mini Muffulettas: Substitute 4 (6-inch) French rolls for 1 round loaf. Slice rolls in half horizontally. Drizzle each roll with 1 tablespoon olive oil. Layer half each of olive mixture, meats, and cheese alternately on roll bottoms. Repeat with remaining ingredients. Cover with tops of rolls. Wrap each roll in aluminum foil; place on a baking sheet. Bake at 375° for 10 to 15 minutes or until sandwiches are thoroughly heated.

Note: You can omit the baking step and serve muffulettas at room temperature.

Prosciutto and Fontina Panini

Prosciutto and Fontina Panini

◄ QUICK ►

PREP: 10 MINUTES   COOK: 15 MINUTES

In Italy the word panini (pah-NEE-nee) is synonymous with sandwiches. This recipe uses Boboli, but any bakery flatbread such as focaccia would taste great, too.

1 (8-ounce) package Boboli (two 6-inch rounds) or other flatbread
6 ounces very thinly sliced prosciutto, salami, ham, or other cold cuts
4 ounces thinly sliced fontina cheese
2 cups trimmed arugula
2 thin slices purple onion, separated into rings
2 tablespoons balsamic vinegar
⅛ to ¼ teaspoon freshly ground pepper
Additional balsamic vinegar (optional)

• Slice each Boboli round in half horizontally. Divide prosciutto between bottom halves of bread; top evenly with cheese, arugula, and onion slices.
• Drizzle ingredients with 2 tablespoons vinegar, and sprinkle with pepper; cover with top halves of bread.
• Wrap sandwiches tightly in aluminum foil, and bake at 300° for 15 minutes. Cut each sandwich in half to serve. Serve with additional balsamic vinegar, if desired. Yield: 4 servings.
Per serving: Calories 492 Fat 18.8g Cholesterol 59mg Sodium 1391mg

PANINI PANACHE

Panini are putting a savvy new spin on the art of sandwich making. Rustic panini are usually simple sandwiches that feature fresh and healthy ingredients commonly associated with Italian cooking. Good chewy bakery bread is crucial to their success.

Calzones

PREP: 25 MINUTES   RISE: 1½ HOURS
COOK: 35 MINUTES

A calzone is a hefty Italian turnover filled with pizza toppings. Smother it with marinara sauce or pizza sauce.

1 package active dry yeast
1 cup warm water (105° to 115°)
3 to 3½ cups all-purpose flour, divided
¼ cup vegetable oil
1 teaspoon salt
1 pound bulk pork sausage
½ cup chopped onion
2½ cups (10 ounces) shredded mozzarella
   cheese
1 teaspoon dried basil
1 teaspoon dried oregano
1 (6-ounce) can tomato paste
Olive oil
Marinara Sauce (page 390)
Garnish: grated Parmesan cheese

•Dissolve yeast in warm water in a large bowl; let stand 5 minutes. Add 2 cups flour, vegetable oil, and salt; beat at medium speed with an electric mixer until blended. Stir in enough remaining flour to make a stiff dough.
•Turn dough out onto a lightly floured surface, and knead until smooth and elastic (about 5 minutes). Place dough in a well-greased bowl, turning to grease top. Cover and let rise in a warm place (85°), free from drafts, 1 hour or until doubled in bulk.
•Cook sausage and onion in a skillet over medium heat until sausage is browned, stirring until meat crumbles; drain well.
•Combine sausage mixture, shredded cheese, and next 3 ingredients in a medium bowl; stir well.
•Punch dough down; divide dough into 6 equal portions. Roll each portion into a 7-inch circle.
•Spoon ½ cup sausage mixture onto each circle; moisten edges with water. Fold circles in half; press edges together with a fork dipped in flour. Transfer to a lightly greased baking sheet. Crimp edges, if desired.
•Brush dough gently with olive oil. Cover and let rise in a warm place, free from drafts, 30 minutes.
•Make slits in top of dough to allow steam to escape. Bake at 400° for 25 minutes or until golden. Serve with Marinara Sauce. Garnish, if desired. Yield: 6 servings.
Per serving: Calories 832 Fat 48.2g
Cholesterol 74mg Sodium 1798mg

Mediterranean Torta

PREP: 25 MINUTES   COOK: 1 HOUR

You'll have your hands full with a wedge of this colorful sandwich in a crust. It's hearty enough to be lunch or dinner.

1 (32-ounce) package frozen bread dough,
   thawed
2 (10-ounce) packages frozen chopped
   spinach, thawed
1 (14-ounce) can artichoke heart quarters
1 (12-ounce) jar roasted red peppers
1 (6-ounce) can pitted ripe olives
1 pound small fresh mushrooms
1 tablespoon olive oil
8 ounces thinly sliced salami
8 ounces thinly sliced provolone cheese
8 ounces thinly sliced cooked ham
1 large egg
1 tablespoon water

•Cut 1 loaf of bread dough in half crosswise. Roll out 1 half on a lightly floured surface into a 10-inch circle. Cover dough, and set aside.
•Press together remaining 1½ dough loaves, and roll out onto a lightly floured surface into a 12-inch circle. Fit dough into a lightly greased 9-inch springform pan, allowing edges to overhang.
•Drain spinach and next 3 ingredients. Press spinach and red pepper strips between layers of paper towels; set aside.
•Sauté mushrooms in oil in a large nonstick skillet over medium heat 8 minutes; drain.
•Place half of salami in dough-lined pan; top with mushrooms, olives, half of cheese, and half of ham. Top with spinach, pepper strips, remaining salami, remaining ham, artichokes, and remaining cheese.
•Stir together egg and water; brush on overhanging pastry edges. Fold edges over cheese; top with remaining pastry round. Tuck edges into pan; press to seal. Brush top with remaining egg mixture.
•Bake at 350° on bottom oven rack 30 to 35 minutes. Remove from oven, and cover with aluminum foil, if necessary, to prevent excessive browning.
•Bake 15 to 20 more minutes. Cool in pan on a wire rack. Remove sides of pan, and cut torta into wedges. Yield: 8 servings.
Per serving: Calories 626 Fat 23.9g
Cholesterol 80mg Sodium 1856mg

Goat Cheese-Roasted Pepper French Loaf

PREP: 15 MINUTES

This sandwich keeps with European tradition. Simple, fresh flavors are packed in a crusty loaf.

½ (16-ounce) package twin French breads
   (we tested with Pepperidge Farm Hot
   and Crusty)
2 to 3 ounces goat cheese, softened
1 (7-ounce) jar roasted red peppers,
   drained and sliced
6 large basil leaves
1 teaspoon capers
1 tablespoon olive oil
⅛ teaspoon salt
⅛ teaspoon freshly ground pepper

•Slice bread horizontally in half lengthwise. Toast according to package directions, if desired.
•Spread cheese over cut side of bottom half of loaf. Arrange peppers, basil leaves, and capers on top. Drizzle with oil. Sprinkle with salt and pepper. Top with top half of loaf. Cut sandwich crosswise in half. Yield: 2 servings.
Per serving: Calories 513 Fat 19.2g
Cholesterol 20mg Sodium 1246mg

Tart Cranberry Sauce
(page 398)

SAUCES & CONDIMENTS

*Sauces are often more intensely flavored than the foods they cover.
For this reason, it's ever important to prepare sauces with accuracy, using
fresh, quality ingredients. This chapter's first half is devoted to classic sauces
like hollandaise, marinara, and rémoulade. The second half is given to
condiments you can enjoy through food preservation. Savor summer's bounty
all year long once you grasp how to preserve fresh produce.*

Equipment

Sauce and condiment recipes often have short ingredient lists, but they require a few key tools to produce proper results. A top-quality 1½- to 3-quart heavy saucepan is a worthwhile lifelong investment. For many basic sauces you'll need a straight-sided or sloping-sided saucepan. Consider investing in one made of heavy copper or copper-bottomed stainless steel with iron handles, not brass; brass handles get too hot too fast. Saucepans with sloping sides are excellent for reducing or cooking down sauces to concentrate their flavor; they allow sauces to boil down quickly, and the slanted sides facilitate whisking and stirring. Avoid aluminum saucepans which may react with some ingredients and cause an off flavor or color.

Many sauces such as Hollandaise Sauce (page 387) are egg-based and require a double boiler to prevent curdling.

One utensil that you'll use repeatedly in sauce making is an elongated wire whisk. A whisk is vital for making emulsified sauces like hollandaise. There are several sizes of whisks to choose from in kitchen shops. A medium-size stainless steel whisk is a good all-purpose choice. Serious cooks will collect small, medium, and large whisks, as well as a balloon whisk, which is used mainly for beating egg whites.

You'll often need spatulas and wooden spoons, and occasionally a ladle, strainer, or sieve. A fat separator will come in handy for gravy making. It's a glass or plastic pitcher with a tubular spout attached to the base. Fat floats to the top of the pitcher and liquid is then poured off from the bottom.

You'll find that a food processor is your best help in chopping ingredients for condiments like Chowchow (page 409), a blend of eight vegetables.

Sauce Basics

The base of many sauces is a fat and flour mixture called a *roux*. A roux has several color stages which are each used for different types of sauces and soups. A *white roux* cooks about 1 minute and is the beginning of the versatile White Sauce (page 387). This brief cooking time is just long enough to release the starch from the flour and eliminate a raw flour taste. This type sauce takes approximately 2 tablespoons flour to thicken 1 cup liquid. (See page 432 for more discussion on the rich brown roux which cooks 20 to 30 minutes and develops a nutty flavor that's the trademark of a good gumbo.)

Sauces made with a roux need constant stirring as they cook to prevent lumping. If you must leave a sauce unattended for a moment, take it off the heat.

Cornstarch is a thickening agent commonly used for sauces. It has twice the thickening power of flour; 1 tablespoon cornstarch will thicken 1 cup liquid. Sauces thickened with cornstarch have a transparent look; that's why this thickening agent is often used for fruit dessert sauces.

Never add cornstarch (or flour) directly to a hot mixture because it will lump. Instead, combine it with about twice as much cold liquid, and stir until smooth. Then gradually stir the cold mixture into the hot mixture. Cook, stirring gently, until it comes to a full boil. Boil for at least 1 minute. It takes only a short time for the starch granules to swell, absorb some of the liquid, and then thicken the sauce.

Don't think that the longer you cook a cornstarch mixture, the thicker it will become. Overcooking can cause the sauce to break down and be runny. Remember that some sauces may look thin while they're cooking, but will thicken as they cool.

If you're making a sauce with an acidic ingredient like lemon juice, first cook the cornstarch mixture until thickened. Then remove it from heat and gently stir in the acid component. If you cook an acid in with a sauce, it negates the thickening power and results in a runny sauce.

Eggs are another thickening agent for sauces. They lend luscious consistency to classic French sauces like hollandaise and béarnaise. Keep in mind that thickening with eggs can be touchy. Handle eggs carefully over heat to prevent curdling. Don't overcook eggs or use heat that is too high. The gentle heat of a double boiler keeps this from happening. Always heat egg mixtures slowly and stir constantly.

When a recipe requires adding eggs to a hot mixture, use a technique called *tempering* to prevent curdling or lumping. First, beat eggs slightly; then warm them by gradually stirring in one-fourth of the hot mixture. Next, stir the tempered egg mixture into the remaining hot mixture. Cook, stirring constantly, until sauce is thickened.

A *reduction* is a technique of simmering a meat or poultry sauce to concentrate its flavor and reduce its yield. And in so doing, the sauce naturally becomes thick and syrupy. This happens quickest when you use a large skillet rather than a saucepan, because a skillet has more surface area.

Freezing Sauces

Many sauces have such small yields that they're eaten entirely at one meal. When you do have a little left over, remember that flour-based and tomato-based sauces freeze best. Pack them in rigid plastic containers, leaving ½ inch headspace. Thaw sauces in the refrigerator or over low heat in a heavy saucepan, stirring often.

Microwaving Sauces

Making sauces is one of the best uses of a microwave oven. Microwave sauces are quick to make and usually don't incur the problems of lumping, scorching, and constant stirring.

A glass measuring cup is ideal for microwaving sauces. Just be sure it's large enough to prevent the sauce from boiling over as it cooks. For instance, a sauce that yields 1 cup should be cooked in a 2-cup measuring cup.

Microwaved sauces need to be stirred occasionally (typically at 1- to 2-minute intervals) during cooking for smooth results. The microwave is excellent for reheating leftover sauces and heating commercially prepared sauces. You can reheat sauces packaged in glass jars directly in the jar; remember to remove the lids first. Sauces that aren't delicate can be heated at HIGH, stirring at 1-minute intervals.

What Went Wrong

You can often rectify a lumpy sauce by vigorously whisking or by pouring the sauce through a fine wire-mesh sieve. Thin the consistency of an overly thick sauce by gradually adding milk, 1 tablespoon at a time, as the sauce cooks. If too thin, blend additional flour and milk or water together and add to the sauce, cooking and stirring until thickened.

To rescue a curdled hollandaise or béarnaise sauce, combine a teaspoon of lemon juice and a tablespoon of curdled sauce. Beat with a wire whisk until mixture is thick and creamy. Gradually beat in remaining sauce, 1 tablespoon at a time, making sure each addition has thickened before adding the next.

VEGETABLE & MEAT SAUCES

Basic Brown Sauce, White Sauce, and Hollandaise Sauce are three of the classic "mother sauces." White Sauce on its own is mild in flavor, but offers endless possibilities for variation and is the basis for many creamy casseroles and soups as well.

Rich emulsions of hollandaise and béarnaise are close cousins of mayonnaise, except they are served hot. These luxurious egg-enriched sauces pair particularly well with brunch egg dishes and beef entrées. Use a double boiler for gentle simmering and never let water in the bottom of the boiler touch the insert. Basic Brown Sauce easily becomes bordelaise which dresses up a good steak. Conquer these basic sauces, and you'll gain confidence for pesto, marinara, and a host of other options.

Basic Brown Sauce

◄ QUICK ►

PREP: 4 MINUTES   COOK: 5 MINUTES

4 thin slices onion
1½ tablespoons butter or margarine, melted
1½ tablespoons all-purpose flour
1 teaspoon beef bouillon granules
1 cup water
⅛ teaspoon pepper

•Sauté onion in butter in a heavy skillet until onion is tender; discard onion. Cook butter over low heat until it begins to brown. Add flour, stirring until smooth. Cook 1 minute, stirring constantly. Add bouillon granules, and gradually stir in water. Cook over medium heat, stirring constantly, until thickened and bubbly. Stir in pepper. Serve sauce with beef or pork. Yield: 1 cup.
Per tablespoon: Calories 13 Fat 1.1g
Cholesterol 3mg Sodium 74mg

Bordelaise Sauce: Substitute ⅓ cup dry red wine for ⅓ cup of the water, and stir in ¾ teaspoon dried parsley flakes and ¼ teaspoon dried thyme; increase pepper to ¼ teaspoon. Serve with beef or pork.

Mushroom Brown Sauce: Sauté ½ cup sliced mushrooms in 2 tablespoons butter; drain and stir into Basic Brown Sauce. Serve with beef.

White Sauce

◄ QUICK ►

PREP: 2 MINUTES   COOK: 4 MINUTES

Probably the most basic of all sauces, White Sauce can take on many flavors. Our photos capture a thick white sauce in process.

Thin White Sauce

1 tablespoon butter or margarine
1 tablespoon all-purpose flour
1 cup milk
¼ teaspoon salt
Dash of ground white pepper

Medium White Sauce

2 tablespoons butter or margarine
2 tablespoons all-purpose flour
1 cup milk
¼ teaspoon salt
Dash of ground white pepper

Thick White Sauce

3 tablespoons butter or margarine
3 tablespoons all-purpose flour
1 cup milk
¼ teaspoon salt
Dash of ground white pepper

1. Melt butter in a heavy saucepan over low heat; add flour, and stir until smooth.

2. Gradually add milk to "white roux," stirring constantly.

3. Cook, stirring constantly, until thickened and bubbly. Add salt and pepper.

• Melt butter in a heavy saucepan over low heat; add flour, stirring until smooth (photo 1). Cook 1 minute, stirring constantly.
• Gradually add milk (photo 2); cook over medium heat, stirring constantly, until thickened (photo 3). Stir in salt and pepper.
• Serve over poached eggs, poultry, seafood, or vegetables. Yield: 1 cup.
Per tablespoon Medium White Sauce:
Calories 25 Fat 1.9g
Cholesterol 6mg Sodium 59mg

Microwave Directions: Place butter in a 1-quart liquid measuring cup. Microwave at HIGH 45 seconds or until melted. Add flour, stirring until smooth. Gradually add milk, and stir well. Microwave at HIGH 3 to 4 minutes or until thickened and bubbly, stirring after 2 minutes, and then at 1-minute intervals. Stir in salt and pepper.

Velouté Sauce: Substitute 1 cup chicken, beef, or fish broth for milk. Omit salt if broth is salted.

Cheddar Cheese Sauce: Stir in 1 cup (4 ounces) shredded Cheddar cheese and ¼ teaspoon dry mustard with salt and pepper.

Hollandaise Sauce

◄ QUICK • FAMILY FAVORITE ►

PREP: 2 MINUTES   COOK: 10 MINUTES

3 egg yolks
⅛ teaspoon salt
⅛ teaspoon ground red pepper
2 tablespoons lemon juice
½ cup butter or margarine, cut into pieces

• Whisk first 3 ingredients in top of a double boiler (photo 1); gradually add lemon juice, stirring constantly. Add about one-third of butter to egg mixture; cook over hot, not boiling, water, stirring constantly with a wire whisk until butter melts (photo 2). Add another third of butter, stirring constantly.

As sauce thickens, stir in remaining butter (photo 3). Cook until temperature reaches 160°, stirring constantly (photo 4).
• Remove sauce from double boiler; serve immediately. Yield: ¾ cup.
Per tablespoon: Calories 84 Fat 9.0g
Cholesterol 75mg Sodium 104mg

1. Whisk egg yolks, salt, and red pepper in top of a double boiler. Gradually add lemon juice.

2. Add about one-third of butter to egg mixture, whisking until butter melts.

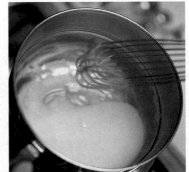

3. As sauce begins to thicken, keep adding pieces of butter, whisking constantly until smooth.

4. Cook until sauce temperature reaches 160°; remove from heat, and serve immediately.

Béarnaise Sauce

◄ QUICK ►

PREP: 8 MINUTES   COOK: 2 MINUTES

Swirl this tarragon-vinegar reduction into Hollandaise Sauce (previous page), and serve it over fish or beef, particularly the well-known London Broil (page 243).

3 tablespoons white wine vinegar
1 teaspoon minced green onion
¼ teaspoon coarsely ground pepper
½ teaspoon dried tarragon
Hollandaise Sauce (previous page)

•Combine first 3 ingredients in a small saucepan; bring to a boil over medium heat.
•Reduce heat to low, and simmer until half the liquid evaporates. Pour mixture through a strainer, reserving liquid; discard solids. Cool vinegar mixture slightly; stir in tarragon.
•Add to thickened Hollandaise Sauce just before removing from heat. Serve sauce with vegetables, fish, or beef. Yield: ¾ cup.
Per tablespoon: Calories 85 Fat 8.9g
Cholesterol 75mg Sodium 105mg

Mornay Sauce

PREP: 15 MINUTES

Mornay sauce is a basic white sauce enriched with egg and cheese. It's particularly delicious when spooned over fancy brunch egg dishes.

1 tablespoon butter or margarine
1 tablespoon all-purpose flour
1 cup milk
½ teaspoon salt
⅛ teaspoon ground white pepper
1 egg yolk, beaten
2 tablespoons whipping cream
2 tablespoons (½ ounce) shredded Swiss cheese
2 tablespoons freshly grated Parmesan cheese

•Melt butter in a heavy saucepan over low heat; add flour, stirring until smooth. Cook 1 minute, stirring constantly.
•Gradually add milk; cook over medium heat, stirring constantly, until mixture is thickened and bubbly. Stir in salt and pepper.

•Combine egg yolk and whipping cream. Gradually stir about one-fourth of hot mixture into yolk mixture; add to remaining hot mixture, and cook, stirring constantly, until thickened (2 to 3 minutes). Add cheeses, stirring until melted. Remove from heat. Yield: 1¼ cups.
Per tablespoon: Calories 27 Fat 2.1g
Cholesterol 17mg Sodium 82mg

Clarified Butter

◄ QUICK • MAKE AHEAD ►

PREP: 4 MINUTES

Also called drawn butter, Clarified Butter and its lemon variation are great for dipping succulent bites of seafood like lobster and crabmeat.

1 cup butter

•Melt butter over low heat; fat will rise to the top, and milk solids will sink to the bottom. Skim off white froth that appears on top (photo 1). Then strain off the clear, yellow butter (photo 2), keeping back the sediment of milk solids.
•Chill clarified butter until ready to serve; then reheat. Yield: about ¾ cup.
Per tablespoon: Calories 136 Fat 15.3g
Cholesterol 41mg Sodium 156mg

Lemon Butter: Add ½ cup lemon juice to clarified butter, stirring well. Yield: 1¼ cups.

Garlic-Butter Sauce

◄ QUICK ►

PREP: 1 MINUTE   COOK: 3 MINUTES

½ cup butter
2 tablespoons whipping cream
1 clove garlic, minced
2 tablespoons lemon juice

•Melt butter in a small saucepan over low heat; add whipping cream and garlic, and cook 1 minute, stirring constantly with a wire whisk.
•Stir in lemon juice. Remove from heat. Yield: ⅔ cup.
Per tablespoon: Calories 87 Fat 9.6g
Cholesterol 27mg Sodium 90mg

CLARIFYING BUTTER

1. Melt butter in a skillet or saucepan over low heat. Skim white foam off top; then strain off clear yellow butter, leaving behind the milk solids.

2. To clarify is to clear a cloudy liquid by removing sediment. Clarified butter has a higher smoke point than regular butter, can be cooked at higher temperatures, and will keep longer.

White Butter Sauce

◄ QUICK ►

PREP: 3 MINUTES COOK: 11 MINUTES

The French call this pearly butter sauce beurre blanc. *It enhances poultry, fish, and vegetables.*

¼ cup dry white wine
¼ cup white wine vinegar
1 shallot, minced
1 cup butter, cut into pieces

•Combine first 3 ingredients in a saucepan; bring to a boil. Reduce heat, and simmer 3 minutes or until mixture is reduced to ¼ cup.

Add butter, 1 tablespoon at a time, stirring constantly with a wire whisk until butter melts and sauce is thickened. Strain, if desired. Serve immediately. Yield: 1⅓ cups.

Per tablespoon: Calories 80 Fat 8.7g
Cholesterol 24mg Sodium 90mg

Avocado Butter

◄ QUICK • MAKE AHEAD ►

PREP: 6 MINUTES

This butter has double appeal, as the avocado takes on a buttery quality of its own when ripe. A little salt and lime juice balance the flavors.

½ cup butter, softened
½ cup mashed ripe avocado
3 tablespoons fresh lime juice
2 tablespoons minced fresh flat-leaf parsley
2 cloves garlic, minced
½ teaspoon salt

•Combine butter and avocado in a small bowl; mash with a potato masher until smooth. Add lime juice and remaining ingredients; stir well. Cover and chill until firm. If desired, shape butter mixture into small balls before serving. Yield: 1 cup.

Per tablespoon: Calories 64 Fat 6.8g
Cholesterol 16mg Sodium 133mg

Horseradish Butter

◄ QUICK • MAKE AHEAD ►

PREP: 2 MINUTES

This horseradish blend is a great complement to fancy tenderloin (page 236). It's also good on savory biscuits, rolls, or baked potatoes.

½ cup butter, softened
1 (8-ounce) package cream cheese, softened
¼ cup mayonnaise
¼ cup prepared horseradish, drained

•Combine all ingredients in a mixing bowl; beat at medium speed with an electric mixer until blended. Serve at room temperature. Yield: 2 cups.

Per tablespoon: Calories 63 Fat 6.7g
Cholesterol 17mg Sodium 62mg

Chinese Hot Mustard

◄ MAKE AHEAD ►

PREP: 2 MINUTES   STAND: 8 HOURS

Similar to the sauce served in Chinese restaurants, a dab of this hot mustard goes a long way. Egg rolls remain its best pairing.

¼ cup dry mustard
1 teaspoon sugar
¼ cup boiling water
2 teaspoons vegetable oil

•Combine mustard and sugar; stir in water and oil. Cover and let stand 8 hours before serving. Store in refrigerator. Yield: ⅓ cup.

Per teaspoon: Calories 13 Fat 1.0g
Cholesterol 0mg Sodium 0mg

Bourbon Mustard

◄ MAKE AHEAD ►

PREP: 3 MINUTES   CHILL: 2 HOURS

½ cup stone-ground or Dijon mustard
3 tablespoons bourbon

•Combine mustard and bourbon in a small bowl, stirring well; cover and chill at least 2 hours. Serve with pork or beef. Yield: ½ cup.

Per tablespoon: Calories 31 Fat 1.0g
Cholesterol 0mg Sodium 445mg

Lemon Mayonnaise

◄ QUICK • MAKE AHEAD ►

PREP: 10 MINUTES

Try this lemony mayonnaise on a fish sand-wich, steamed green beans, or broccoli.

⅓ cup fat-free egg substitute
1 tablespoon grated lemon rind
½ teaspoon sugar
½ teaspoon dry mustard
¼ teaspoon salt
Dash of paprika
2 tablespoons fresh lemon juice
3 drops of hot sauce
1 cup vegetable oil

•Process first 8 ingredients in a food processor 20 seconds. Slowly pour oil in a thin stream through food chute with processor

running. Process 30 seconds or until thick-ened. Yield: 1½ cups.

Per tablespoon: Calories 83 Fat 9.1g
Cholesterol 0mg Sodium 30mg

Herbed Yogurt Sauce

◄ MAKE AHEAD ►

PREP: 4 MINUTES   CHILL: 1 HOUR

1 (8-ounce) carton plain low-fat yogurt
⅓ cup mayonnaise
¾ teaspoon dried thyme
¾ teaspoon dry mustard
½ teaspoon dried oregano
¼ teaspoon dried marjoram
1½ tablespoons tarragon vinegar
1 teaspoon soy sauce
1 clove garlic, minced

•Combine all ingredients, stirring well. Cover and chill at least 1 hour. Serve over cooked, chilled vegetables or seafood. Yield: 1¼ cups.

Per tablespoon: Calories 34 Fat 3.1g
Cholesterol 3mg Sodium 46mg

Cucumber Cream Sauce

◄ QUICK ►

PREP: 10 MINUTES

Cucumber's crisp quality lends freshness and texture to this creamy sauce that's wonderful with crab cakes.

1 medium cucumber
½ cup sour cream
1 tablespoon lemon juice
1 teaspoon grated onion
¼ teaspoon pepper

•Peel and seed cucumber. Grate enough cucumber to measure ½ cup. Combine grated cucumber, sour cream, and remain-ing ingredients, stirring well. Cover and chill. Yield: 1 cup.

Per tablespoon: Calories 17 Fat 1.5g
Cholesterol 3mg Sodium 4mg

Tartar Sauce

◄ FAMILY FAVORITE ►
◄ MAKE AHEAD ►

PREP: 4 MINUTES

⅔ cup mayonnaise
2 tablespoons sweet pickle relish
1 tablespoon minced fresh parsley or
   1 teaspoon dried parsley flakes
1 tablespoon capers
1 tablespoon grated onion
1 tablespoon lemon juice
Dash of hot sauce

•Combine all ingredients, stirring well. Cover and chill. Yield: 1 cup.
Per tablespoon: Calories 69 Fat 7.3g
Cholesterol 5mg Sodium 110mg

Rémoulade Sauce

◄ QUICK • MAKE AHEAD ►

PREP: 5 MINUTES   CHILL: 30 MINUTES

Rémoulade is a classic French sauce that's easy to stir together and has a tangy flavor that complements fish particularly well.

1 cup mayonnaise
1 to 2 tablespoons lemon juice
1½ tablespoons Dijon mustard
1 tablespoon chopped gherkin pickle
1 tablespoon capers
1 teaspoon dried tarragon
1 teaspoon dried chervil
½ teaspoon anchovy paste

•Combine all ingredients, stirring well. Cover and chill at least 30 minutes. Serve with hot or cold meat, fish, or shellfish. Yield: 1 cup.
Per tablespoon: Calories 102 Fat 11.0g
Cholesterol 8mg Sodium 191mg

Cocktail Sauce

◄ HEALTHY • MAKE AHEAD ►
◄ FAMILY FAVORITE ►

PREP: 3 MINUTES   CHILL: 2 HOURS

⅔ cup chili sauce
¼ cup lemon juice
3 tablespoons prepared horseradish
2 teaspoons Worcestershire sauce
¼ teaspoon hot sauce

•Combine all ingredients, stirring until smooth. Cover and chill at least 2 hours. Yield: 1 cup.
Per tablespoon: Calories 13 Fat 0g
Cholesterol 0mg Sodium 144mg

Marinara Sauce

◄ FAMILY FAVORITE ►

PREP: 10 MINUTES   COOK: 35 MINUTES

Marinara is a richly seasoned Italian tomato sauce. Simmer it just long enough for it to thicken; then spoon it over your pasta of choice.

1 small onion, chopped
5 cloves garlic, minced
¼ cup olive oil
2 (28-ounce) cans diced tomatoes, undrained, or 2 (28-ounce) cans whole tomatoes, undrained and chopped
½ cup chopped fresh parsley or basil or ¼ cup each
2 tablespoons lemon juice
½ teaspoon sugar

•Sauté onion and garlic in hot oil in a large saucepan or Dutch oven, stirring constantly, over medium heat until tender. Add tomatoes and remaining ingredients; bring mixture to a boil. Reduce heat to medium, and cook, uncovered, 30 minutes or until mixture thickens and liquid evaporates, stirring often. Yield: 6 cups.
Per tablespoon: Calories 9 Fat 0.6g
Cholesterol 0mg Sodium 61mg

Sweet-and-Sour Sauce

◄ QUICK • MAKE AHEAD ►
◄ FAMILY FAVORITE ►

PREP: 2 MINUTES   COOK: 5 MINUTES

½ cup sugar
¼ cup white wine vinegar
2 tablespoons prepared mustard
1 teaspoon ground ginger
½ cup crushed pineapple, undrained
1 tablespoon cornstarch
½ cup pineapple juice

•Combine sugar and vinegar in a small saucepan; cook over medium heat, stirring constantly, until sugar dissolves. Remove from heat; stir in mustard, ginger, and pineapple.
•Combine cornstarch and juice, stirring until blended. Gradually stir about one-fourth of hot mixture into cornstarch mixture; add to remaining hot mixture, stirring constantly. Cook over medium heat, stirring constantly, until smooth and thickened. Yield: 1½ cups.
Per tablespoon: Calories 30 Fat 0.1g
Cholesterol 0mg Sodium 20mg

Jezebel Sauce

◄ QUICK • MAKE AHEAD ►
◄ HEALTHY ►

PREP: 4 MINUTES

Try this thick dipping sauce with fried shrimp or onion rings, or use the suggestions below.

1 (18-ounce) jar pineapple preserves
1 (18-ounce) jar apple jelly
1 (1.12-ounce) can dry mustard
1 (5-ounce) jar prepared horseradish
1 tablespoon cracked peppercorns

•Combine all ingredients; stir well. Pour sauce into airtight containers; store in refrigerator. Serve sauce over cream cheese with crackers as an appetizer spread or with pork or beef. Yield: 3⅔ cups.
Per teaspoon: Calories 16 Fat 0.1g
Cholesterol 0mg Sodium 3mg

Cherry-Wine Sauce

◄ QUICK • HEALTHY ►

PREP: 5 MINUTES   COOK: 7 MINUTES

This regal dark cherry sauce received our highest recipe rating. See it served with rustic rack of lamb on page 258.

⅔ cup dry red wine
⅓ cup beef broth
3 tablespoons honey
½ teaspoon dried thyme or 1½ teaspoons chopped fresh thyme
¼ teaspoon salt
¼ teaspoon dry mustard
2 teaspoons cornstarch
2 tablespoons balsamic vinegar
1 (16½-ounce) can pitted dark cherries, drained

•Combine first 6 ingredients in a heavy saucepan; bring to a boil, and boil 5 minutes.
•Combine cornstarch and vinegar, stirring well; add to wine mixture. Bring to a boil over medium-high heat; boil 1 minute. Stir in cherries. Yield: 1½ cups.

Per tablespoon: Calories 17 Fat 0g
Cholesterol 1mg Sodium 48mg

Raisin Sauce

PREP: 4 MINUTES   COOK: 16 MINUTES

1 cup firmly packed brown sugar
1½ tablespoons cornstarch
¾ cup raisins
½ cup water
2 tablespoons orange juice
2 tablespoons white vinegar
1 tablespoon butter or margarine
⅛ teaspoon salt

•Combine brown sugar and cornstarch in a small saucepan, stirring well; add raisins and remaining ingredients. Cook, uncovered, over low heat 15 minutes, stirring often. Serve warm with ham. Yield: 1 cup.

Per tablespoon: Calories 82 Fat 0.8g
Cholesterol 2mg Sodium 32mg

Microwave Directions: Combine brown sugar and cornstarch in a 1-quart liquid measuring cup, stirring well; add remaining ingredients. Microwave at HIGH 5 to 6 minutes or until thickened, stirring after 2 minutes, and then at 1-minute intervals. Serve warm with ham.

Pesto

PREP: 6 MINUTES

Pesto makes great use of just-harvested fresh herbs. Blend leftovers with a little olive oil; freeze it in ice cube containers for later use.

2 cups fresh basil leaves (1 large bunch)
¼ cup chopped walnuts or pine nuts
¼ cup olive oil
2 teaspoons lemon juice
2 cloves garlic
1 teaspoon salt
¼ cup freshly grated Parmesan cheese
2 tablespoons freshly grated Romano cheese

•Process first 6 ingredients in a food processor or blender 2 minutes or until smooth, stopping twice to scrape down sides. Stir in cheeses.
•Toss desired amount of pesto with hot cooked pasta or spoon 2 tablespoons pesto into six sections of an ice cube tray; cover and freeze up to 3 months. Thaw and reheat slowly before serving. Yield: ⅔ cup.

Per tablespoon: Calories 75 Fat 7.9g
Cholesterol 3mg Sodium 282mg

Triple-Fruit Salsa

PREP: 15 MINUTES   CHILL: 8 HOURS

The peppery spice of cilantro enhances this slightly sweet three-fruit salsa. It's a versatile condiment; serve it over any grilled meat, fish, or poultry.

1 cup diced fresh pineapple or canned pineapple tidbits, undrained
1 cup chopped fresh papaya or mango
1 kiwifruit, peeled and chopped
¾ cup diced sweet red pepper
3 tablespoons minced fresh cilantro
1½ tablespoons sugar
2½ tablespoons white wine vinegar
¼ to ½ teaspoon dried crushed red pepper

•Combine all ingredients in a small bowl, tossing gently. Cover and chill up to 8 hours.
•Let stand at room temperature before serving. Serve with a slotted spoon. Yield: 2 cups.

Per tablespoon: Calories 10 Fat 0.1g
Cholesterol 0mg Sodium 1mg

Pesto

MARINADES, RUBS & BARBECUE SAUCES

A *marinade* is a seasoned liquid added to uncooked food for flavor and sometimes tenderizing. Marinades can be cooked or uncooked; most contain an acid such as wine, citrus juice, or vinegar that helps tenderize meat.

Marinate food in nonmetal containers like glass dishes, plastic bowls, or heavy-duty plastic bags that won't react with acidic components in the marinade. Allow ½ cup marinade for every pound of meat, poultry, or seafood. Always marinate food, covered, in the refrigerator, turning occasionally.

To simply add flavor, marinate most foods 30 minutes to 2 hours. To tenderize meat, marinating 8 hours is ideal, but you can marinate large cuts of meat up to 24 hours with good results. Meat that marinates longer than that can become mushy.

Never reuse a marinade in which raw meat, fish, or poultry has soaked until you first bring it to a boil. This will kill any bacteria that may have been transferred from the raw food.

A *rub* is a blend of dry seasonings, usually spices and dried herbs, applied to meat, seafood, or poultry before cooking. A rub is often left on the food for a while before cooking to allow flavors to penetrate.

When a small amount of liquid like olive oil or crushed garlic with its juice is added to a rub, it becomes a *paste*. A paste is easy to apply to meat, because it clings to the food well. You can apply a rub or paste to food up to 24 hours before cooking for maximum flavor.

Barbecue sauces can be sweet or spicy; most are tomato-based. A form of glaze, barbecue sauce should be applied to food during the last 15 to 45 minutes of cooking, depending on how sweet the sauce is. If the sauce has much sugar in it, wait until the last 15 minutes to apply it; this keeps the meat or poultry from burning on the grill. A nonsweet sauce, however, can be brushed on at any point during cooking. Always be sure to save a little sauce for passing at the table.

Buttery Basting Sauce

◄ QUICK ►

PREP: 2 MINUTES   COOK: 5 MINUTES

½ cup butter or margarine, melted
¼ cup lemon juice
3 tablespoons finely chopped onion
1 tablespoon Worcestershire sauce
1 teaspoon Dijon mustard
½ teaspoon salt
⅛ teaspoon pepper

•Combine all ingredients in a saucepan. Bring to a boil; cover, reduce heat, and simmer 5 minutes. Use to baste chicken, pork chops, ribs, or kabobs. Yield: ¾ cup.
Per tablespoon: Calories 71 Fat 7.7g
Cholesterol 21mg Sodium 201mg

Oriental Marinade

◄ QUICK • MAKE AHEAD ►
◄ HEALTHY ►

PREP: 6 MINUTES

Soy sauce darkens this marinade and ginger provides the predominant flavoring. Use a portion of it in your next stir-fry.

1½ cups fresh orange juice
⅓ cup dry sherry
⅓ cup soy sauce
3 tablespoons dark brown sugar
2 tablespoons peeled, finely chopped fresh
   ginger
1 tablespoon grated orange rind
2 cloves garlic, minced
1½ teaspoons coriander seeds, crushed
1½ teaspoons freshly ground pepper
¼ teaspoon salt

•Combine all ingredients; stir well. Use to marinate flank steak or chicken before cooking. After marinating, bring marinade to a boil before using it to baste during cooking. Yield: 2⅓ cups.
Per tablespoon: Calories 9 Fat 0g
Cholesterol 0mg Sodium 165mg

Sweet-and-Sour Marinade

◄ QUICK • MAKE AHEAD ►

PREP: 2 MINUTES

½ cup soy sauce
¼ cup pineapple juice
¼ cup white vinegar
¼ cup firmly packed brown sugar
⅛ teaspoon garlic powder

•Combine all ingredients; stir well. Use to marinate beef or pork before cooking. After marinating, bring marinade to a boil before using it to baste during cooking. Yield: 1 cup.
Per tablespoon: Calories 20 Fat 0g
Cholesterol 0mg Sodium 516mg

Oil and Vinegar Marinade

◄ QUICK • MAKE AHEAD ►

PREP: 2 MINUTES

¼ cup vegetable oil
¼ cup red wine vinegar
¼ cup lemon juice
½ teaspoon sugar
½ teaspoon salt
½ teaspoon dried thyme
½ teaspoon pepper

•Combine all ingredients; stir well. Use to marinate beef, pork, or poultry before cooking. After marinating, bring marinade to a boil before using it to baste during cooking. Yield: ¾ cup.
Per tablespoon: Calories 43 Fat 4.5g
Cholesterol 0mg Sodium 98mg

Southwestern Marinade

◄ QUICK • MAKE AHEAD ►

PREP: 5 MINUTES

The flavors of the Southwest—lime juice, cilantro, jalapeño—prevail in this lively marinade for chicken, fish, and grilled foods.

⅓ cup fresh lime juice
⅓ cup olive oil
2 tablespoons chopped fresh cilantro
2 tablespoons tequila
1 jalapeño pepper, seeded and chopped
1 clove garlic, minced
¼ teaspoon salt
¼ teaspoon pepper

•Combine all ingredients, stirring well. Use to marinate peeled and deveined shrimp, soft-shell crab, or chicken before cooking. After marinating, bring marinade to a boil before using it to baste during cooking. Yield: 1 cup.
Per tablespoon: Calories 42 Fat 4.5g
Cholesterol 0mg Sodium 37mg

Jerk Rub

◄ QUICK • MAKE AHEAD ►

PREP: 3 MINUTES

A dry seasoning blend that comes from Jamaica, this mixture usually contains a blend of peppers, thyme, and spices. Rub it directly on the surface of meat before grilling.

1½ tablespoons sugar
1 tablespoon onion powder
1 tablespoon dried thyme
2 teaspoons ground allspice
2 teaspoons freshly ground black pepper
2 teaspoons ground red pepper
1 teaspoon salt
¾ teaspoon ground nutmeg
¼ teaspoon ground cloves

•Combine all ingredients; store in an airtight container. Rub on chicken or seafood before grilling. Yield: ⅓ cup.
Per tablespoon: Calories 27 Fat 0.3g
Cholesterol 0mg Sodium 447mg

Herb Rub

◄ QUICK • MAKE AHEAD ►
◄ HEALTHY ►

PREP: 3 MINUTES

1 tablespoon dried thyme
1 tablespoon dried oregano
1½ teaspoons poultry seasoning
1 teaspoon dried rosemary
1 teaspoon dried marjoram
1 teaspoon dried basil
1 teaspoon dried parsley flakes
½ teaspoon salt
⅛ teaspoon pepper

•Combine all ingredients; store in an airtight container. Rub on fish, poultry, or pork before grilling. Yield: ¼ cup.
Per tablespoon: Calories 10 Fat 0.3g
Cholesterol 0mg Sodium 295mg

Seafood Seasoning Rub

◄ QUICK • MAKE AHEAD ►

PREP: 3 MINUTES

1½ teaspoons ground bay leaves
1½ teaspoons dry mustard
1½ teaspoons black pepper
1 teaspoon salt
¾ teaspoon ground nutmeg
½ teaspoon ground celery seeds
½ teaspoon ground cloves
½ teaspoon ground ginger
½ teaspoon paprika
½ teaspoon ground red pepper

•Combine all ingredients; store in an airtight container. Rub on seafood or chicken before grilling. Yield: ¼ cup.
Per tablespoon: Calories 14 Fat 0.7g
Cholesterol 0mg Sodium 588mg

Mexican Rub

◄ QUICK • MAKE AHEAD ►

PREP: 3 MINUTES

All the earthy south-of-the-border flavors are blended in this Mexican mix. Use it as recommended in the recipe or to season ground beef.

¼ cup chili powder
1 tablespoon onion powder
1 tablespoon ground cumin
2 teaspoons salt
1½ teaspoons dried oregano
1 teaspoon garlic powder
1 teaspoon ground red pepper

•Combine all ingredients; store in an airtight container. Rub on chicken, ribs, or fish before grilling. Yield: ½ cup.
Per tablespoon: Calories 20 Fat 0.9g
Cholesterol 0mg Sodium 626mg

Chili Seasoning Blend

◄ QUICK • MAKE AHEAD ►

PREP: 3 MINUTES

Shake this simple seasoning on ground beef for Easy Tacos (page 248). It's also nice sprinkled on a baked potato or oven-baked fries.

3 tablespoons chili powder
1 tablespoon salt
1 tablespoon garlic powder
1½ teaspoons black pepper
¾ teaspoon ground red pepper

•Combine all ingredients; store in an airtight container up to 1 month. Use with beef, chicken, or pork. Yield: ⅓ cup.
Per tablespoon: Calories 21 Fat 0.9g
Cholesterol 0mg Sodium 1362mg

White Barbecue Sauce

PREP: 5 MINUTES

Mayonnaise provides the "white" in this North Carolina-style sauce that's tangy with vinegar and pumped up with pepper.

1½ cups mayonnaise
⅓ cup cider vinegar
¼ cup lemon juice
2 tablespoons sugar
2 tablespoons cracked pepper
2 tablespoons white wine Worcestershire sauce

•Combine all ingredients in a small bowl; stir with a wire whisk. Cover and chill. Use to baste chicken during grilling. Yield: 2¼ cups.
Per tablespoon: Calories 53 Fat 5.5g
Cholesterol 4mg Sodium 45mg

Easy Barbecue Sauce

◄ QUICK • MAKE AHEAD ►
◄ HEALTHY ►

PREP: 4 MINUTES

1 (10-ounce) jar orange marmalade
1 (12-ounce) bottle chili sauce
¼ cup white vinegar
1 tablespoon Worcestershire sauce
1½ teaspoons celery seeds

•Combine all ingredients; stir well. Use to baste spareribs and other meats during cooking. Yield: 2 cups.
Per tablespoon: Calories 34 Fat 0.1g
Cholesterol 0mg Sodium 152mg

Spicy Barbecue Sauce

◄ QUICK • MAKE AHEAD ►
◄ FAMILY FAVORITE ►

PREP: 5 MINUTES   COOK: 8 MINUTES

1 cup water
¾ cup firmly packed brown sugar
¾ cup ketchup
½ cup white vinegar
½ cup Worcestershire sauce
½ cup butter or margarine
¼ cup lemon juice
1 tablespoon salt
1½ tablespoons dry mustard
1½ tablespoons chili powder
1½ tablespoons paprika
2 teaspoons ground red pepper

•Combine all ingredients in a large saucepan; stir well. Cook, uncovered, over medium heat 8 minutes or until butter melts and sugar dissolves, stirring often. Use to baste chicken, beef, or pork during grilling. Yield: 4 cups.
Per tablespoon: Calories 30 Fat 1.6g
Cholesterol 4mg Sodium 179mg

Southern Barbecue Sauce

◄ QUICK • FAMILY FAVORITE ►
◄ HEALTHY ►

PREP: 3 MINUTES   COOK: 6 MINUTES

2 cloves garlic, crushed
2 tablespoons butter or margarine, melted
1 cup ketchup
1 cup water
¾ cup chili sauce
¼ cup firmly packed brown sugar
2 tablespoons prepared mustard
2 tablespoons Worcestershire sauce
1½ teaspoons celery seeds
½ teaspoon salt
2 dashes of hot sauce

•Sauté garlic in butter 4 to 5 minutes in a saucepan. Add ketchup and remaining ingredients; bring to a boil. Use to baste pork or chicken during cooking. Yield: 3½ cups.
Per tablespoon: Calories 18 Fat 0.5g
Cholesterol 1mg Sodium 138mg

Microwave Directions: Combine garlic and butter in a deep 1½-quart casserole; cover with lid. Microwave at HIGH 1 minute. Add ketchup and remaining ingredients; cover and microwave at HIGH 8 to 10 minutes or until thoroughly heated. Use to baste pork or chicken during cooking.

GRAVIES

A gravy is a "jus," the natural juice from a cooked roast, that has been thickened with flour. Gravies made from meat pan drippings are some of the richest flavored and easiest sauces to make. It's really just a matter of properly adding the flour to get a thickened smooth sauce. Half of these recipes add an equal amount of flour to fat already in the pan; the others make a *slurry* of water and flour and add it to the gravy. Try one of these six easy gravies for starters.

Pan Gravy

◄ QUICK ►
◄ FAMILY FAVORITE ►

PREP: 2 MINUTES   COOK: 4 MINUTES

Make Pan Gravy from the natural drippings left in the roasting pan from roasts, steaks, chops, and other meats.

2 tablespoons pan drippings (fat and juice)
2 tablespoons all-purpose flour
1 cup meat juices, broth, or water
¼ teaspoon salt
⅛ teaspoon pepper

•Pour off all except 2 tablespoons drippings from pan in which meat was cooked. Add flour, stirring until smooth. Cook 1 minute, stirring constantly.
•Gradually stir in meat juices; cook over medium heat, stirring constantly, until mixture is thickened and bubbly. Stir in salt and pepper.
•Serve hot with roast and mashed potatoes. Yield: 1 cup.
Per tablespoon: Calories 22 Fat 1.6g
Cholesterol 4mg Sodium 136mg

Cream Gravy

PREP: 2 MINUTES   COOK: 5 MINUTES

Cream Gravy is the expected sauce for Southern fried chicken. Bake up some biscuits to soak up any extra gravy.

¼ cup pan drippings
¼ cup all-purpose flour
2½ to 3 cups hot milk
½ teaspoon salt
⅛ to ¼ teaspoon pepper

• Pour off all except ¼ cup drippings from skillet in which chicken was fried; place skillet over medium heat. Add flour; stir until browned. Gradually add hot milk; cook, stirring constantly, until thickened and bubbly. Add salt and pepper. Serve hot. Yield: 2¾ cups.
Per tablespoon: Calories 21 Fat 1.6g
Cholesterol 3mg Sodium 33mg

Giblet Gravy

PREP: 10 MINUTES
COOK: 1 HOUR AND 10 MINUTES

Thanksgiving is not complete without Giblet Gravy. It's meant to be served not only over turkey, but dressing and mashed potatoes, too.

Giblets and neck from 1 turkey or chicken
1 small onion, chopped
2 stalks celery, chopped
½ teaspoon salt
Pan drippings from 1 roasted turkey or chicken
3 tablespoons all-purpose flour
¼ cup water
1 hard-cooked egg, chopped
¼ teaspoon pepper

• Combine giblets (except liver), neck, onion, celery, and salt in a saucepan. (Set liver aside.) Cover with water. Bring to a boil; cover, reduce heat, and simmer 45 minutes or until giblets are fork-tender. Add liver, and simmer 10 more minutes. Drain, reserving broth. Remove meat from neck; coarsely chop neck meat and giblets. Discard onion and celery.

• Skim fat from pan drippings of roasted poultry, and discard fat. Add reserved broth to pan drippings; stir until bits are loosened from bottom of roaster. Measure broth mixture; add water to equal 1½ cups, if necessary.
• Combine flour and ¼ cup water in a medium saucepan; stir until smooth. Add broth mixture; cook over medium heat, stirring constantly, until thickened and bubbly. Stir in reserved neck meat, giblets, egg, and pepper. Serve hot with roasted poultry. Yield: 2 cups.
Per tablespoon: Calories 10 Fat 0.3g
Cholesterol 14mg Sodium 55mg

Pot Roast Gravy

PREP: 2 MINUTES   COOK: 4 MINUTES

Make Pot Roast Gravy from the liquid in which the roast has simmered. Once the gravy has thickened, taste it before you correct the seasonings. It may not need any.

¼ cup cold water
2 tablespoons all-purpose flour
1 cup broth from pot roast
¼ teaspoon salt
⅛ teaspoon pepper

• Combine water and flour in a jar; cover tightly, and shake until thoroughly blended. Stir flour mixture slowly into broth in a saucepan. Cook over medium heat until thickened, stirring constantly. Add salt and pepper. Yield: 1¼ cups.
Per tablespoon: Calories 6 Fat 0g
Cholesterol 2mg Sodium 109mg

Microwave Directions: Combine water and flour in a jar; cover tightly, and shake until thoroughly blended. Stir flour mixture slowly into broth in a 2-cup liquid measuring cup. Microwave at HIGH 2½ to 3 minutes or until thickened, stirring at 1-minute intervals. Add salt and pepper.

Note: If pot roast broth is salty, you may want to reduce or omit salt in gravy recipe.

Sausage Gravy

PREP: 4 MINUTES   COOK: 12 MINUTES

For an added flavor boost, try sage-seasoned pork sausage in this cream gravy.

¾ pound ground pork sausage
¼ cup all-purpose flour
2 cups half-and-half or milk
1 teaspoon salt
½ teaspoon freshly ground pepper

• Brown sausage in a large heavy skillet, stirring until it crumbles. Drain sausage on paper towels, reserving ½ cup drippings in skillet.
• Whisk flour into sausage drippings until smooth. Cook over medium-high heat, whisking constantly, 3 minutes or until browned.
• Stir in sausage. Gradually add half-and-half, and cook over medium heat, stirring constantly, until thickened and bubbly. Stir in salt and pepper. Serve gravy with biscuits and grits. Yield: 3 cups.
Per tablespoon: Calories 45 Fat 4.0g
Cholesterol 9mg Sodium 100mg

Tasso Gravy

PREP: 3 MINUTES   COOK: 30 MINUTES

Tasso is cured pork or beef that's highly seasoned and smoked. Mashed potatoes, grits, or biscuits are the best "serve-with" suggestions.

2 tablespoons butter or margarine
½ pound tasso, diced
3½ tablespoons all-purpose flour
1 cup brewed coffee
2 cups chicken broth
1 fresh thyme sprig, minced
¼ teaspoon pepper

• Melt butter in a large skillet; add tasso, and cook over medium-high heat 5 minutes or until browned, stirring often. Add flour, stirring constantly with a wire whisk until lightly browned.
• Add coffee and broth, stirring with a wire whisk; simmer 20 minutes, stirring occasionally. Add thyme and pepper, stirring well. Yield: 3 cups.
Per tablespoon: Calories 14 Fat 0.7g
Cholesterol 4mg Sodium 74mg

DESSERT SAUCES

Whether it's fudge sauce, caramel, or crème anglaise, a dessert sauce is an easy and impressive way to dress up store-bought cake, pie, or ice cream. Typically quick to make, most dessert sauces store for several days in the refrigerator.

There's a variety of flavors from which to choose—from fudge and chocolate sauces to please the chocoholics to tangy lemon curd for filling tarts.

Hot Fudge Sauce

◄ QUICK • FAMILY FAVORITE ►

PREP: 4 MINUTES   COOK: 4 MINUTES

As long as there's ice cream in the freezer, you might want to keep a cup of this thick hot fudge sauce on hand as well. It's a family favorite that never goes out of style.

¼ cup plus 2 tablespoons sugar
1 (5-ounce) can evaporated milk
¾ cup (4½ ounces) semisweet chocolate
   morsels
1½ teaspoons butter or margarine
½ teaspoon vanilla extract

•Combine first 3 ingredients in a small saucepan. Cook over medium heat, stirring until chocolate melts and mixture boils. Remove from heat; stir in butter and vanilla. Serve hot over ice cream. Yield: 1 cup.
Per tablespoon: Calories 75 Fat 3.9g
Cholesterol 4mg Sodium 14mg

Microwave Directions: Combine first 3 ingredients in a 1-quart glass bowl. Microwave at MEDIUM HIGH (70% power) 4 to 5 minutes or until chocolate melts and mixture is very hot, stirring after 1 minute and then at 30-second intervals. Stir in butter and vanilla. Serve hot over ice cream.

Chocolate Sauce

◄ QUICK • MAKE AHEAD ►
◄ FAMILY FAVORITE ►

PREP: 3 MINUTES   COOK: 7 MINUTES

Even when pinched for time, you can whip up this velvety rich sauce in minutes. Drizzle it over ice cream, pound cake, pastries, or in your coffee.

½ cup whipping cream
1 (4-ounce) package sweet baking
   chocolate, chopped
¼ teaspoon vanilla extract

•Heat whipping cream in a heavy saucepan over medium heat until hot (do not boil); remove from heat. Add chocolate; stir until melted. Stir in vanilla. Yield: ¾ cup.
Per tablespoon: Calories 82 Fat 6.8g
Cholesterol 14mg Sodium 4mg

Peppermint-Chocolate Sauce

◄ QUICK • MAKE AHEAD ►

PREP: 4 MINUTES   COOK: 12 MINUTES

Crushed candy melts readily to lend a cool hit of peppermint to this simple dessert sauce.

2 cups (12 ounces) semisweet chocolate
   morsels
1¼ to 1½ cups half-and-half, divided
½ cup finely crushed hard peppermint
   candy

•Combine chocolate morsels, 1 cup half-and-half, and candy in a small saucepan; cook over medium-low heat about 12 minutes or until candy melts, stirring often.
•Stir in enough remaining half-and-half for desired consistency. Serve over waffles, pound cake, or ice cream. Store sauce in refrigerator up to 2 weeks. Yield: 2½ cups.
Per tablespoon: Calories 60 Fat 3.8g
Cholesterol 2.5mg Sodium 3mg

Butterscotch Sauce

◄ QUICK • FAMILY FAVORITE ►

PREP: 4 MINUTES   COOK: 4 MINUTES

2 cups firmly packed brown sugar
¾ cup plus 2 tablespoons light corn syrup
¼ cup butter or margarine
⅛ teaspoon salt
1 (5-ounce) can evaporated milk

•Combine first 3 ingredients in a saucepan; bring to a boil over medium-low heat, stirring constantly. Remove from heat. Stir in salt and evaporated milk. Serve sauce warm over ice cream. Yield: 2½ cups.
Per tablespoon: Calories 78 Fat 1.4g
Cholesterol 4.2mg Sodium 36mg

Microwave Directions: Combine first 3 ingredients in a 1-quart liquid measuring cup; stir well. Microwave at HIGH 3 to 4 minutes, stirring once. Stir in salt and evaporated milk. Serve warm over ice cream.

Praline Sauce

◄ QUICK • FAMILY FAVORITE ►

PREP: 4 MINUTES   COOK: 20 MINUTES

1½ cups chopped pecans
¼ cup butter or margarine
1¼ cups firmly packed light brown sugar
¾ cup light corn syrup
3 tablespoons all-purpose flour
1 (5-ounce) can evaporated milk

•Toast pecans in a shallow pan at 300° for 15 minutes, stirring occasionally. Set aside.
•Melt butter in a saucepan; add brown sugar, corn syrup, and flour, stirring well. Bring mixture to a boil; reduce heat and simmer 5 minutes, stirring constantly. Remove from heat; cool to lukewarm. Gradually stir in evaporated milk and toasted pecans. Serve sauce warm over ice cream. Yield: 3 cups.
Per tablespoon: Calories 77 Fat 3.8g
Cholesterol 4mg Sodium 22mg

Microwave Directions: Spread pecans on a large glass pieplate. Microwave at HIGH 5 to 6 minutes or until lightly toasted, stirring at 2-minute intervals.

Place butter in a 1-quart glass bowl; microwave at HIGH 55 seconds or until melted. Add brown sugar, corn syrup, and flour, stirring well. Microwave at HIGH 3 to 4 minutes or until mixture is very hot, stirring at 2-minute intervals. Gradually stir in milk and pecans. Serve warm over ice cream.

Caramel Sauce

◄ FAMILY FAVORITE ►

PREP: 2 MINUTES   COOK: 25 MINUTES

Making caramelized sugar for this luscious sauce is really not hard. You'll need a cast-iron skillet, a wooden spoon, and some patience while the sugar slowly melts into a golden syrup.

1 cup sugar
½ cup butter
½ cup half-and-half

•Sprinkle sugar into a large cast-iron skillet. Cook over medium heat, stirring constantly with a wooden spoon, until sugar melts and turns light brown. Remove from heat; add butter, and stir until blended.
•Return mixture to low heat; gradually add half-and-half to hot mixture, 1 tablespoon at a time, stirring constantly. Continue to cook mixture over low heat, stirring constantly, 10 minutes or until mixture is thickened and creamy. Serve sauce warm over ice cream or pound cake. Yield: 1 cup.
Per tablespoon: Calories 109 Fat 6.6g Cholesterol 18mg Sodium 62mg

Crème Anglaise

◄ MAKE AHEAD ►

PREP: 4 MINUTES   COOK: 14 MINUTES

Crème Anglaise is a thin, pourable custard sauce. You'll need to stir it constantly and gently as it cooks. Dribble the delicate sauce around a poached pear, sweet soufflé, cream puff, or slice of pie.

2 cups milk or 1 cup milk and 1 cup
   half-and-half
½ cup sugar
5 egg yolks
1 teaspoon vanilla extract

•Bring milk to a simmer over medium heat. Beat sugar and egg yolks at high speed with an electric mixer until pale and mixture forms a ribbon.
•Gradually add hot milk to egg yolk mixture, whisking until blended; return to saucepan. Cook over low heat, stirring constantly, until custard thickens and coats a spoon. Remove from heat; pour through a wire-mesh strainer into a bowl, and cool 10 minutes. Stir in vanilla. Cover and chill. Yield: 2 cups.
Per tablespoon: Calories 31 Fat 1.3g Cholesterol 36mg Sodium 9mg

Coffee Crème Anglaise: Add 2 teaspoons instant coffee to ¾ cup boiling water, stirring until coffee dissolves. Prepare above sauce, using ¾ cup strong coffee and 1 cup half-and-half in place of 2 cups milk.

Whiskey Sauce

◄ QUICK ►

PREP: 5 MINUTES   COOK: 8 MINUTES

Bread pudding's best friend is found in this buttery bourbon sauce.

½ cup butter
1 cup sugar
½ cup half-and-half
2 tablespoons whiskey

•Combine first 3 ingredients in a heavy saucepan; cook over medium heat until sugar dissolves. Bring to a boil; reduce heat, and simmer 5 minutes. Remove from heat; cool. Add whiskey. Yield: 1½ cups.
Per tablespoon: Calories 75 Fat 4.4g Cholesterol 12mg Sodium 41mg

Hot Wine Sauce

◄ QUICK • HEALTHY ►

PREP: 2 MINUTES   COOK: 3 MINUTES

1 cup dry white wine
1 cup orange juice
½ cup sugar

•Combine all ingredients in a small saucepan. Cook, stirring constantly, over medium heat until sugar dissolves. Serve warm sauce with Plum Pudding (page 169)

or Old-Fashioned Gingerbread (page 100). Yield: 2¼ cups.
Per tablespoon: Calories 14 Fat 0g Cholesterol 0mg Sodium 1mg

Lemon Hard Sauce

◄ QUICK • MAKE AHEAD ►

PREP: 5 MINUTES

Hard sauce is an old-fashioned butter and sugar topping that's chilled, but quickly melts into a sauce when spooned over a serving of piping hot fruit cobbler or gingerbread.

½ cup butter, softened
1 teaspoon grated lemon rind
¼ cup sifted powdered sugar
1 tablespoon fresh lemon juice

•Beat butter and lemon rind in a small mixing bowl at medium speed with an electric mixer. Gradually add powdered sugar and lemon juice, beating until light and fluffy. Cover and chill until ready to serve. Serve at room temperature. Yield: ½ cup.
Per tablespoon: Calories 117 Fat 11.5g Cholesterol 31mg Sodium 117mg

Sherried Hard Sauce

◄ QUICK • MAKE AHEAD ►

PREP: 5 MINUTES

Leave the sherry out and enjoy a basic hard sauce, if you wish. Both versions are tasty atop warm Plum Pudding (page 169).

½ cup butter, softened
1 cup sifted powdered sugar
2 tablespoons sherry

•Beat butter at medium speed with an electric mixer until creamy. Gradually add sugar and sherry, beating until fluffy. Cover and chill. Serve sauce over warm Plum Pudding. Yield: 1 cup.
Per tablespoon: Calories 82 Fat 5.8g Cholesterol 16mg Sodium 59mg

Brandied Hard Sauce: Substitute brandy for sherry.

Tart Cranberry Sauce

◄ QUICK • MAKE AHEAD ►
◄ HEALTHY ►

PREP: 1 MINUTE COOK: 8 MINUTES

This sauce can swing sweet or savory. See it pictured on page 384 over ice cream. We also recommend it on ham.

2 cups fresh cranberries or frozen
    cranberries, partially thawed
½ cup sugar
2 tablespoons water
1 to 2 tablespoons grated orange rind
½ teaspoon ground cinnamon
¼ teaspoon ground ginger
⅛ teaspoon ground cloves

•Combine all ingredients in a saucepan; cook over medium heat 6 to 8 minutes or until cranberry skins pop and sauce thickens, stirring occasionally. Serve warm or cold over ice cream or with turkey or ham. Yield: 1¾ cups.
Per tablespoon: Calories 17 Fat 0g
Cholesterol 0mg Sodium 0mg

Fresh Strawberry Sauce

◄ QUICK • MAKE AHEAD ►
◄ HEALTHY ►

PREP: 5 MINUTES

1 pint fresh strawberries
1 tablespoon lemon juice
½ cup sugar
2 tablespoons framboise or other raspberry
    brandy

•Wash and hull strawberries; process in a blender until smooth.
•Add lemon juice, sugar, and framboise; blend until smooth. Yield: 1⅓ cups.
Per tablespoon: Calories 27 Fat 0g
Cholesterol 0mg Sodium 0mg

Raspberry Sauce

◄ QUICK • MAKE AHEAD ►
◄ HEALTHY ►

PREP: 2 MINUTES

This sauce is as simple as pureeing a package of fruit and then adding a little sugar and lemon.

1 (10-ounce) package frozen raspberries in
    syrup, thawed and undrained
1 tablespoon lemon juice
1 to 3 tablespoons sugar

•Process thawed raspberries with syrup in a blender or food processor 10 seconds or until pureed. Pour mixture through a wire-mesh strainer into a bowl; press with back of a spoon against sides of strainer to squeeze out juice, discarding solids. Add lemon juice and sugar to puree, stirring until sugar dissolves. Yield: 1¼ cups.
Per tablespoon: Calories 20 Fat 0g
Cholesterol 0mg Sodium 0mg

Orange Curd

◄ QUICK • MAKE AHEAD ►

PREP: 10 MINUTES COOK: 15 MINUTES

5 large eggs
3 egg yolks
½ cup sugar
5 tablespoons frozen orange juice
    concentrate, thawed and undiluted
2 tablespoons finely chopped orange rind
⅛ teaspoon salt
1 cup unsalted butter, cut into small pieces
2 tablespoons Triple Sec
2 tablespoons orange extract

•Combine first 6 ingredients in top of a double boiler; bring water to a boil. Reduce heat to low; cook, stirring constantly with a wire whisk, until thickened. Add butter, a few pieces at at time, stirring constantly. Stir in liqueur and extract. Spoon into a glass container, and cool completely.
•Serve over pound cake or use as a filling for a layer cake. Store curd in a tightly covered glass container in refrigerator up to 2 weeks. Yield: 3 cups.
Per tablespoon: Calories 61 Fat 4.7g
Cholesterol 46mg Sodium 14mg

Fresh Orange Syrup

◄ HEALTHY • MAKE AHEAD ►

PREP: 8 MINUTES COOK: 25 MINUTES

Serve this syrup over pancakes or as a dessert sauce over angel food cake. For the secret to sectioning citrus, see page 364.

1 cup sugar
1⅓ cups unsweetened orange juice
1⅓ cups fresh orange sections (about 4
    medium oranges)

•Combine sugar and orange juice in a large nonaluminum saucepan. Bring to a boil over medium heat; cook 20 to 25 minutes or until reduced to 1 cup, stirring occasionally. Remove from heat; stir in orange sections.
•Serve warm or chilled with pancakes or over angel food cake. Store in an airtight container in the refrigerator. Yield: 2 cups.
Per tablespoon: Calories 33 Fat 0g
Cholesterol 0mg Sodium 0mg

Lemon Curd

◄ QUICK • MAKE AHEAD ►

PREP: 5 MINUTES COOK: 18 MINUTES

This deep yellow curd is an ideal filling for tarts.

2 cups sugar
1 cup butter or margarine
3 tablespoons grated lemon rind
⅔ cup fresh lemon juice
2 teaspoons cornstarch
4 large eggs, lightly beaten

•Combine first 5 ingredients in top of a double boiler. Cook over simmering water, stirring constantly, until butter melts. Gradually stir about one-fourth of hot mixture into eggs; add to remaining hot mixture, stirring constantly. Cook over simmering water, stirring constantly, until mixture thickens and coats a spoon (about 15 minutes). Remove from heat; cool. Cover and chill.
•Serve Lemon Curd over pound cake or gingerbread, or use it as a filling for tarts. Store in a tightly covered glass container in refrigerator up to 2 weeks. Yield: 3½ cups.
Per tablespoon: Calories 63 Fat 3.6g
Cholesterol 24mg Sodium 38mg

CONDIMENTS

One of the blessings of summer in the South is the bounty of fruits and vegetables that comes from the garden. **Food Preservation** makes it possible to capture seasonal produce to enjoy in homemade condiments and other canned goods throughout the year. The preservation process is well worth the time investment; the rewards are juicy and long lasting. In this section we cover the basics of canning, pickling, preserving, and freezing so that you can reap the fruits of your summer labor year-round.

Canning Basics

Canning is a way of preserving food by heating jars of food hot enough and long enough to keep food from spoiling. Use the freshest ingredients picked at the peak of their season—this is prime time for canning.

There are two basic methods of home canning, and the type of food you want to can determines the method to use. The *boiling water method* is used for *high acid* foods such as fruits, fruit spreads, tomatoes, pickles, and relishes, and it processes the food in a water-bath canner (at 212°). The *steam pressure method* is used for *low acid* foods like most vegetables, meats, poultry, and seafood. It processes food in a pressure canner at a higher temperature (240°).

Canning food that is heated before being packed into the jars is called *hot pack;* canning food that's still raw is called *raw pack.* The food is raw, but the liquid is hot. Raw pack is often recommended for soft foods that may not hold their shape through lengthy cooking. Some recipes offer you a choice of methods; others specify only the preferable method.

Equipment

Before you begin canning, be sure you have the proper equipment. For high acid foods you'll need a water-bath canner with a round kick rack that fits inside or you can use a large kettle. Just make sure it has a tight-fitting lid and that the jars fit easily inside. For low acid foods you'll need a pressure canner. For both methods of canning you'll need a jar lifter, a funnel or filler, a narrow nonmetal spatula, and a kitchen timer.

Use only standard canning jars and lids; old-style or antique canning jars and recycled commercial jelly jars are not safe for home canning. Check jars for cracks, scratches, and chips before you begin. Today's jars are reusable, as are the metal bands as long as they aren't dented or rusty. Lids are not reusable because the sealing compounds on them work only once. Always buy new jar lids with each use. Most canning supplies are available at grocery stores, kitchen-supply stores, department stores, and through mail-order catalogs.

The Preparation

As with any recipe, prepare your work area and collect all the equipment you'll need before you get started. And read the recipe through more than once.

Select produce that is in season, firm, ripe, and has no bruises or bad spots. Wash produce well, and prepare as recipe directs.

Canning jars should be as clean as possible. Wash them in the dishwasher or in hot, soapy water; rinse well, and keep hot. If the processing time in a water-bath canning recipe is less than 10 minutes, you'll need to sterilize the jars.

To sterilize jars, place jars, right side up, on the rack in a boiling-water canner or pressure canner; fill canner with enough hot water so that the water level is 1 inch above the jar tops. Bring water to a boil; boil 10 minutes. Carefully remove the hot jars with a jar lifter, and drain, saving the hot water for processing the filled jars. Follow manufacturer's instructions to sterilize lids. For some brands you bring water to a boil and leave lids in hot water; others need boiling for a certain amount of time. Do not use the dishwasher for sterilizing jars or lids.

Place fruits or vegetables in hot jars using a funnel and following recipe directions for raw- or hot-pack methods. It's important to be accurate in filling jars to the recommended *headspace.* Headspace is the space between the inside of the lid and the top of the food in the jar. Headspace is critical for expansion of food as it's processed and for forming a vacuum seal in the cooled jars. Too much headspace occurs when air bubbles trapped inside the jar rise to the top during processing; this can prevent proper sealing.

Once jars are filled, remove air bubbles by running a nonmetal spatula around the edge of the jar, gently shifting the food so that any trapped air escapes. Don't use anything metallic to remove air bubbles because metal might scratch the glass and cause it to break during processing. After removing air bubbles you may need to adjust headspace.

Wipe each jar rim with a clean, damp cloth to help ensure a tight seal. Then place the lid on the jar rim and screw on the metal band with your fingertips just until you feel resistance. If the band is too loose, liquid can escape during processing, and the seal can fail. If the band is too tight during processing, air can't vent, and this can cause food to discolor during storage.

When processing in a water-bath canner, use a jar lifter and position filled jars on rack in the canner, leaving space for water to flow evenly around them. If necessary, add more hot water so that the water level is 2 to 3 inches above capped jars. Bring water to a boil; cover and reduce heat to maintain a gentle boil throughout the specified processing time. Set your timer for processing when water returns to a boil. If you use the raw pack method, add jars while water is warm to prevent jar breakage.

Low acid foods such as vegetables must be processed in a pressure canner to make them safe. The 240° temperature obtained in a pressure canner is necessary to kill bacteria that thrive in low-acid conditions. Check the dial gauge on the canner for accuracy before each canning season.

When using a pressure canner, be sure to allow steam to escape from the vent for 10 minutes after attaching the lid. Then close the dial gauge vent or set the weight in place and regulate the heat source to maintain 10 pounds pressure. The weight should jiggle or rock gently about three or four times a minute. Begin to count processing time after the canner reaches 10 pounds pressure.

After processing, remove the canner from heat and allow pressure to drop to 0. This will take 30 minutes to an hour. Don't rush this cooling process. Then raise the lid away from yourself to avoid a blast of steam.

Once jars have been processed by either method, carefully remove each jar with a jar lifter and place right side up on a cloth towel or wire rack to cool. Let jars cool naturally 12 to 24 hours. When removing jars from the boiling water, don't be tempted to retighten the bands; you could interfere with the seal that's forming. As the jars cool you might hear loud pops indicating the vacuum seal has occurred.

When jars are completely cooled, remove bands (not lids) and check each jar for a proper seal. The center of the lid should dip downward. Press down on the center of the lid; it should not spring back when released.

Wipe off the processed jars; label, date, and replace bands. Store jars in a cool, dry place. Most home-canned fruits and vegetables will maintain good quality for at least a year.

If a lid fails to seal, the food should be repacked and reprocessed in hot jars within 24 hours with new, properly prepared lids. Or, if you don't have time to reprocess, store food in the refrigerator. Length of storage will vary, depending on the type of food.

FRUIT

SYRUPS FOR CANNING FRUIT

TYPE OF SYRUP	CUPS OF SUGAR	CUPS OF LIQUID	CUP YIELD
Very light	½	4	4½
Light	1	4	4¾
Medium	1¾	4	5
Heavy	2¾	4	5⅓
Very heavy	4	4	6

Directions: Combine sugar and water or fruit juice. Heat, stirring constantly, until sugar dissolves. Keep syrup hot. Use just enough hot syrup to cover the fruit—usually ½ to ¾ cup per pint.

Apples

•Peel apples; cut into halves or quarters, and remove cores. Cut into slices, if desired. To prevent apples from darkening during preparation, use commercial ascorbic-acid powder (we tested with Fruit Fresh) according to manufacturer's directions or immerse peeled apples in a sugar-syrup or lemon juice solution (¾ cup lemon juice to 1 gallon water). Prepare a very light, light, or medium syrup. (See chart above.) Use hot-pack method only.
Hot Pack: Simmer apples in hot syrup 5 minutes. Pack hot apples into hot jars, filling to ½ inch from top. Cover apples with boiling syrup, filling to ½ inch from top. Remove air bubbles; wipe jar rims.
•Cover at once with metal lids, and screw on bands. Process in boiling water bath 20 minutes for pints and quarts.

Berries

(EXCEPT STRAWBERRIES AND RASPBERRIES)

•Use for blackberries and other berries that hold their shape well. Select fully ripened berries. Handle as little as possible. Wash and, if necessary, cap and stem berries; drain well.
Hot Pack: Add ½ cup sugar to each 4 cups berries; cook until sugar dissolves and mixture comes to a boil, stirring gently to keep berries from sticking.
•Pack hot berries into hot jars, filling to ½ inch from top. (If there is not enough syrup to cover berries, add boiling water, filling to ½ inch from top.) Remove air bubbles; wipe jar rims.
•Cover at once with metal lids, and screw on bands. Process in boiling water bath 15 minutes for pints; process 20 minutes for quarts.

Peaches and Pears

•Peel fruit; cut into halves or quarters, and remove cores or pits. Cut into slices, if desired. To prevent fruit from darkening during preparation, use commercial ascorbic-acid powder (we tested with Fruit Fresh) according to manufacturer's directions, or immerse the peeled fruit in a sugar-syrup or lemon-juice solution (¾ cup lemon juice to 1 gallon water). Prepare a very light, light, or medium syrup. (See chart at left.)
Hot Pack: Simmer peaches or pears in hot syrup 3 to 5 minutes. Pack hot fruit into hot jars, filling to ½ inch from top. Cover fruit with boiling syrup, filling to ½ inch from top. Remove air bubbles; wipe jar rims.

•Cover at once with metal lids, and screw on bands. Process in boiling water bath 20 minutes for pints; process 25 minutes for quarts.
Raw Pack: Pack raw peaches or pears into hot jars, filling to ½ inch from top. Cover fruit with boiling syrup, filling to ½ inch from top. Remove air bubbles; wipe jar rims.
•Cover at once with metal lids, and screw on bands. Process in boiling water bath 25 minutes for pints; process 30 minutes for quarts.

Plums

•Peel plums, if desired. Prick plums in several places with a fork if not peeled. (This keeps plums from splitting.) Prepare a very light, light, or medium syrup. (See chart at left.)
Hot Pack: Simmer plums in hot syrup 2 minutes. Cover, remove from heat, and let stand 20 minutes. Pack hot plums into hot jars, filling to ½ inch from top. Cover fruit with boiling syrup, filling to ½ inch from top. Remove air bubbles; wipe jar rims.
•Cover at once with metal lids, and screw on bands. Process in boiling water bath 20 minutes for pints; process 25 minutes for quarts.
Raw Pack: Pack raw plums into hot jars, filling to ½ inch from top. Cover plums with boiling syrup, filling to ½ inch from top. Remove air bubbles; wipe jar rims.
•Cover at once with metal lids, and screw on bands. Process in boiling water bath 20 minutes for pints; process 25 minutes for quarts.

Applesauce

PREP: 12 MINUTES   COOK: 30 MINUTES
PROCESS: 15 MINUTES

Select apples that are sweet, juicy, and crisp.

20 large apples, quartered (about 7 pounds)
3 cups water
2 cups sugar

• Combine apples and water in a large stockpot; cook over medium heat until tender. Pour off liquid. Put apple mixture through a sieve or colander. Add sugar to apple pulp, and bring to a boil.
• Pack hot applesauce into hot jars, filling to ½ inch from top. Remove air bubbles; wipe jar rims.
• Cover at once with metal lids, and screw on bands. Process in boiling water bath 15 minutes. Yield: 5 pints.

Per tablespoon: Calories 19 Fat 0.1g
Cholesterol 0mg Sodium 0mg

Cinnamon-Apple Rings

PREP: 12 MINUTES   COOK: 35 MINUTES
PROCESS: 15 TO 20 MINUTES

Pick 6 pounds firm, tart apples for this recipe.

Ascorbic-acid powder (Fruit Fresh)
14 medium-size cooking apples, unpeeled
4 cups sugar
1 quart water
1½ teaspoons ground cinnamon
10 to 12 drops of red food coloring

• Prepare ascorbic-acid solution according to manufacturer's directions; set aside.
• Core apples; slice into ¼-inch rings. Drop rings into ascorbic-acid solution. (Allow to stand in solution only 20 minutes.)
• Combine sugar and remaining 3 ingredients in a Dutch oven, and bring to a boil; boil 5 minutes. Remove syrup from heat. Drain apple rings, and add to syrup; let stand 10 minutes. Return apple mixture to heat, and bring to a rolling boil; reduce heat, and simmer, uncovered, 20 minutes, stirring occasionally. Remove from heat, and cool slightly.

• Drain apples, reserving syrup. Bring syrup to a boil. Pack hot apple rings into hot jars, filling to ½ inch from top. Cover with boiling syrup, filling to ½ inch from top. Remove air bubbles; wipe jar rims.
• Cover at once with metal lids, and screw on bands. Process in boiling water bath 15 minutes for pints; process 20 minutes for quarts. Yield: 6 pints or 3 quarts (28 servings).

Per serving: Calories 164 Fat 0.3g
Cholesterol 0mg Sodium 0mg

Whole Cranberry Sauce

PREP: 2 MINUTES   COOK: 14 MINUTES
PROCESS: 15 MINUTES

A holiday table's not complete without a dish of glistening cranberry sauce. It's great with turkey, ham, and all the trimmings.

4 cups sugar
4 cups water
8 cups fresh cranberries (2 pounds)

• Combine sugar and water in a Dutch oven; bring to a boil, and boil 5 minutes. Add cranberries; boil, without stirring, 6 to 8 minutes or until cranberry skins pop. Spoon quickly into hot jars, filling to ½ inch from top. Remove air bubbles; wipe jar rims.
• Cover at once with metal lids, and screw on bands. Process in boiling water bath 15 minutes. Yield: 4 pints.

Per tablespoon: Calories 28 Fat 0g
Cholesterol 0mg Sodium 0mg

Brandy-Spiced Peaches

PREP: 30 MINUTES   COOK: 10 MINUTES
STAND: 28 HOURS   PROCESS: 20 MINUTES

1 (1-inch) piece fresh ginger, sliced
2 (4-inch) sticks cinnamon
1 tablespoon whole allspice
1 tablespoon whole cloves
5 cups sugar, divided
3 cups white vinegar (5% acidity)
1¼ cups peach brandy*
¾ cup water
24 small firm, ripe peaches, peeled

• Place first 4 ingredients on a piece of cheesecloth; tie ends. Combine spice bag, 2 cups sugar, vinegar, brandy, and water in a Dutch oven; bring to a boil. Add peaches; simmer 2 minutes or until thoroughly heated. Remove from heat; let stand 3 to 4 hours.
• Remove peaches from syrup; set peaches aside. Add 2 cups sugar to syrup, and bring to a boil. Remove from heat, and add peaches; cover and let stand 24 hours.
• Heat peaches thoroughly in hot syrup. Pack hot peaches into hot jars, filling to ½ inch from top. Add remaining 1 cup sugar to syrup; bring to a boil. Cover peaches with boiling syrup, filling to ½ inch from top. Remove air bubbles; wipe jar rims.
• Cover at once with metal lids, and screw on bands. Process in boiling water bath 20 minutes. Yield: 6 pints (24 servings).
*Substitute 3 tablespoons pure brandy flavor for peach brandy, if desired. If using brandy flavor, increase water to 2 cups.

Per serving: Calories 219 Fat 0.1g
Cholesterol 0mg Sodium 1mg

Pear-Apple Mincemeat

PREP: 45 MINUTES   COOK: 5 MINUTES
PROCESS: 25 MINUTES

15 pears, peeled and ground (7 pounds)
12 apples, peeled and chopped (about 4½ pounds)
2¾ cups raisins, ground
2¼ cups firmly packed brown sugar
1 cup sugar
1 unpeeled orange, seeded and ground
½ cup white vinegar (5% acidity)
1 tablespoon salt
2 teaspoons ground cinnamon
1 teaspoon ground nutmeg
1 teaspoon ground cloves
½ teaspoon ground ginger

• Combine all ingredients in a Dutch oven; bring to a boil, stirring constantly. Spoon hot mixture into hot jars, filling to 1 inch from top. Remove air bubbles; wipe jar rims.
• Cover at once with metal lids, and screw on bands. Process in boiling water bath 25 minutes. Yield: 8 pints.

Per ¼-cup serving: Calories 102 Fat 0.3g
Cholesterol 0mg Sodium 114mg

VEGETABLES

Green, Snap, or Wax Beans

•Wash beans, trim ends, and remove strings, if necessary; cut into 1- to 2-inch lengths or leave whole.

Hot Pack: Cover beans with boiling water, and boil 5 minutes. Pack hot beans loosely into hot jars, filling to 1 inch from top. Add ½ teaspoon salt to pints and 1 teaspoon to quarts, if desired. Cover with boiling liquid, filling to 1 inch from top. Remove air bubbles; wipe jar rims.

•Cover at once with metal lids, and screw on bands. Process in pressure canner at 10 pounds pressure (240°). Process pints 20 minutes and quarts 25 minutes.

Raw Pack: Pack beans tightly into hot jars, filling to 1 inch from top. Add ½ teaspoon salt to pints and 1 teaspoon to quarts, if desired. Cover with boiling water, filling to 1 inch from top. Remove air bubbles; wipe jar rims.

•Cover at once with metal lids, and screw on bands. Process in pressure canner at 10 pounds pressure (240°). Process pints 20 minutes and quarts 25 minutes.

Lima Beans

•Shell and wash young tender beans.

Hot Pack: Cover beans with boiling water, and boil 3 minutes. Pack hot beans loosely into hot jars, filling to 1 inch from top. Add ½ teaspoon salt to pints and 1 teaspoon to quarts, if desired. Cover with boiling liquid, filling to 1 inch from top. Remove air bubbles; wipe jar rims.

•Cover at once with metal lids, and screw on bands. Process in pressure canner at 10 pounds pressure (240°). Process pints 40 minutes and quarts 50 minutes.

Raw Pack: Pack beans loosely in hot jars, filling to 1 inch from top. (Do not shake or press beans down.) Add ½ teaspoon salt to pints and 1 teaspoon to quarts, if desired. Cover with boiling water, filling to 1 inch from top. Remove air bubbles; wipe jar rims.

•Cover at once with metal lids, and screw on bands. Process in pressure canner at 10 pounds pressure (240°). Process pints 40 minutes and quarts 50 minutes.

Beets

•Select small, uniform beets (1 to 2 inches). Wash beets carefully; remove tops, leaving 1 inch of stem. Leave taproot. Use hot-pack method only.

Hot Pack: Place beets in a saucepan; cover with boiling water, and boil about 15 minutes or until skins slip easily. Remove skins, and trim beets. Leave baby beets whole; cut large beets into quarters or slices.

•Pack hot beets into hot jars, filling to 1 inch from top. Add ½ teaspoon salt to pints and 1 teaspoon to quarts, if desired. Cover with boiling water, filling to 1 inch from top. Remove air bubbles; wipe jar rims.

•Cover at once with metal lids, and screw on bands. Process in pressure canner at 10 pounds pressure (240°). Process pints 30 minutes and quarts 35 minutes.

Corn

•Husk corn, and remove silks; wash corn. Cut corn from cob at about two-thirds the depth of kernels; do not scrape cob.

Hot Pack: Add 1 cup boiling water to 4 cups cut corn; simmer 5 minutes. Pack hot corn into hot jars, filling to 1 inch from top. Add ½ teaspoon salt to pints and 1 teaspoon to quarts, if desired. Cover with boiling water, filling to 1 inch from top. Remove air bubbles; wipe jar rims. Cover at once with metal lids, and screw on bands. Process in pressure canner at 10 pounds pressure (240°). Process pints 55 minutes and quarts 1 hour and 25 minutes.

Raw Pack: Pack corn in hot jars, filling to 1 inch from top. Do not pack down. Add ½ teaspoon salt to pints and 1 teaspoon to quarts, if desired. Cover with boiling water, filling to 1 inch from top. Remove air bubbles; wipe jar rims.

•Cover at once with metal lids, and screw on bands. Process in pressure canner at 10 pounds pressure (240°). Process pints 55 minutes and quarts 1 hour and 25 minutes.

Okra

•Select young, tender pods of okra. Wash okra; trim stem ends. Use hot-pack method only.

Hot Pack: Cook okra 2 minutes in boiling water; drain. Leave whole or cut 1-inch slices.

•Pack hot okra into hot jars, filling to 1 inch from top. Add ½ teaspoon salt to pints and 1 teaspoon to quarts, if desired. Cover with boiling water, filling to 1 inch from top. Remove air bubbles, and wipe jar rims.

•Cover at once with metal lids, and screw on bands. Process in pressure canner at 10 pounds pressure (240°). Process pints 25 minutes and quarts 40 minutes.

Summer Squash

•Wash and trim ends from squash; do not peel. Cut squash into ½-inch slices; then cut slices into uniform pieces.

Hot Pack: Add just enough water to cover squash; bring to a boil. Pack hot squash loosely into hot jars, filling to 1 inch from top. Add ½ teaspoon salt to pints and 1 teaspoon to quarts, if desired. Cover with boiling liquid, filling to 1 inch from top. Remove air bubbles; wipe jar rims.

•Cover at once with metal lids, and screw on bands. Process in pressure canner at 10 pounds pressure (240°). Process pints 30 minutes and quarts 40 minutes.

Raw Pack: Pack squash tightly into hot jars filling to 1 inch from top. Add ½ teaspoon salt to pints and 1 teaspoon to quarts, if desired. Cover with boiling water, filling to 1 inch from top. Remove air bubbles; wipe jar rims.

•Cover at once with metal lids, and screw on bands. Process in pressure canner at 10 pounds pressure (240°). Process pints 30 minutes and quarts 40 minutes.

Tomatoes

•Use just-ripe tomatoes. Peel tomatoes; remove stem and blossom ends. Leave whole or cut into quarters. Use raw-pack method only.

Raw Pack: Add 1 tablespoon bottled lemon juice or ¼ teaspoon ascorbic-acid powder to hot pint jars; add 2 tablespoons bottled lemon

juice or ½ teaspoon ascorbic-acid powder to hot quart jars. Add ½ teaspoon salt to pints and 1 teaspoon salt to quarts, if desired.
•Fill jars with raw tomatoes ½ inch from top, pressing until spaces between them fill with juice. Remove air bubbles; wipe jar rims.
•Cover at once with metal lids, and screw on bands. Process pints or quarts in boiling water 1 hour and 25 minutes or in pressure canner at 10 pounds pressure (240°) 25 minutes.

Succotash

PREP: 30 MINUTES   COOK: 10 MINUTES
PROCESS: 1 HOUR

10 ears fresh corn
1½ quarts shelled fresh lima beans
3½ teaspoons salt (optional)
Boiling water

•Place corn in a Dutch oven, and cover with water. Bring to a boil, and cook 5 minutes. Remove from heat, and cool.
•Cook beans, uncovered, in boiling water to cover 5 minutes. Drain, reserving liquid.
•Cut corn from cob as for whole kernel corn; combine corn and beans. Pack into hot jars, filling to 1 inch from top. Pour in boiling bean liquid, filling to 1 inch from top. (Supplement with boiling water if you don't have enough bean liquid.) Add ½ teaspoon salt to pints and 1 teaspoon salt to quarts, if desired. Remove air bubbles; wipe jar rims.
•Cover at once with metal lids, and screw on bands. Process in pressure canner at 10 pounds pressure (240°). Process pints for 1 hour and quarts for 1 hour and 25 minutes. Yield: 7 pints or 3½ quarts.
Per ¼-cup serving: Calories 30 Fat 0.0g
Cholesterol 0mg Sodium 150mg

Note: When reheating Succotash, sprinkle in additional seasonings as desired.

HIGH ALTITUDE ADDITIONS

If you live in a high altitude area of over 1,000 feet above sea level, processing times will increase. Check canning guide books for times specific to your area.

Chili Sauce

PREP: 30 MINUTES   COOK: 1 HOUR
PROCESS: 15 MINUTES

Stir this Chili Sauce into chopped barbecue meat or sloppy joes.

4 quarts peeled, chopped fresh tomatoes (about 7½ pounds)
2 cups chopped onion
3 green peppers, chopped
2 cups white vinegar (5% acidity)
½ cup firmly packed brown sugar
2 tablespoons salt
1½ teaspoons dry mustard
1½ teaspoons ground cloves
1½ teaspoons ground allspice
1½ teaspoons pepper

•Combine all ingredients in a Dutch oven; bring to a boil. Cover, reduce heat, and simmer 1 hour, stirring occasionally.
•Pour hot mixture quickly into hot jars, filling to ½ inch from top. Remove air bubbles; wipe jar rims.
•Cover at once with metal lids, and screw on bands. Process in boiling water bath 15 minutes. Yield: 11 half-pints.
Per tablespoon: Calories 8 Fat 0.1g
Cholesterol 0mg Sodium 82mg

Tomato Sauce

PREP: 20 MINUTES
COOK: 2 HOURS AND 35 MINUTES
PROCESS: 35 MINUTES

24 medium tomatoes (about 12½ pounds), peeled and chopped
3 cups chopped onion
2 cups chopped celery
1½ cups chopped green pepper
1 tablespoon salt
¼ cup plus 1½ teaspoons lemon juice or 1½ teaspoons ascorbic-acid powder

•Combine all ingredients in a large kettle. Bring to a boil; reduce heat, and simmer, uncovered, 30 minutes, stirring often. Remove from heat; put through a food mill or sieve, reserving tomato juice.

•Bring juice to a boil; reduce heat, and simmer, uncovered, 2 hours or until thick, stirring often.
•Pour hot mixture quickly into hot jars, filling to ½ inch from top. Remove air bubbles; wipe jar rims.
•Cover at once with metal lids, and screw on bands. Process in boiling water bath 35 minutes or in pressure canner at 10 pounds pressure (240°) 15 minutes. Yield: 9 half-pints.
Per tablespoon: Calories 2 Fat 0g
Cholesterol 0mg Sodium 51mg

Homemade Ketchup

PREP: 15 MINUTES   COOK: 4 HOURS
PROCESS: 15 MINUTES

46 medium tomatoes (24 pounds), sliced
3 medium onions, coarsely chopped
3 cups white vinegar (5% acidity)
3 (3-inch) sticks cinnamon
1 tablespoon whole cloves
3 cloves garlic, chopped
1½ cups sugar
1 tablespoon salt
1 tablespoon paprika
⅛ teaspoon ground red pepper

•Combine tomato and onion in two large kettles. Bring to a boil; reduce heat, and simmer, uncovered, 45 minutes, stirring often. Remove from heat; put through a food mill or sieve, reserving tomato juice. Set aside.
•Pour vinegar into a saucepan. Tie cinnamon sticks, cloves, and garlic in a cheesecloth bag; add to vinegar in saucepan. Bring to a boil; reduce heat, and simmer, uncovered, 30 minutes. Remove bag; set spiced vinegar aside.
•Cook reserved tomato juice, uncovered, in kettle over medium-high heat 2 hours or until volume is reduced by half, stirring often. Add spiced vinegar, sugar, and remaining ingredients. Cook tomato mixture, uncovered, 30 to 40 minutes or until thickened.
•Pour hot mixture quickly into hot jars, filling to ⅛ inch from top. Remove air bubbles; wipe jar rims.
•Cover at once with metal lids, and screw on bands. Process in boiling water bath 15 minutes. Yield: 6 pints.
Per tablespoon: Calories 18 Fat 0.2g
Cholesterol 0mg Sodium 41mg

Beef Stew Base With Vegetables

PREP: 30 MINUTES   COOK: 20 MINUTES

PROCESS: 1 HOUR

4 to 4½ pounds lean beef for stewing, cut into 1-inch cubes
3 tablespoons vegetable oil
3 quarts peeled and cubed potatoes (½-inch cubes)
2 quarts thinly sliced carrots
3 cups chopped celery
3 cups chopped onion
1½ tablespoons salt
1 teaspoon dried thyme
½ teaspoon pepper

•Brown beef cubes in batches in hot oil in a large kettle; drain well. Add cubed potato and remaining ingredients; stir well. Add boiling water just until mixture is covered. Spoon hot mixture into hot jars, filling to 1 inch from top. Remove air bubbles; wipe jar rims.
•Cover jars at once with metal lids, and screw on bands. Process in pressure canner at 10 pounds pressure (240°). Process pints 1 hour and quarts 1 hour and 15 minutes. Yield: 18 pints or 9 quarts.
Per cup: Calories 135 Fat 3.3g
Cholesterol 29mg Sodium 340mg

Note: When reheating beef stew, add seasonings as desired.

Vegetable Soup Base

PREP: 1 HOUR   COOK: 10 MINUTES

PROCESS: 1 HOUR

2 quarts peeled, chopped tomatoes
1½ quarts peeled, cubed potatoes (½-inch cubes)
1½ quarts thinly sliced carrots
1 quart fresh shelled lima beans
1 cup fresh cut corn
2 cups sliced celery
2 cups chopped onion
1½ quarts water
Salt

•Combine first 8 ingredients in a large kettle; bring to a boil over medium heat, stirring often. Boil 5 minutes.

•Spoon mixture into hot jars, filling to 1 inch from top; add ¼ teaspoon salt to each pint jar, and ½ teaspoon salt to each quart jar. Remove air bubbles; wipe jar rims.
•Cover at once with metal lids, and screw on bands. Process in pressure canner at 10 pounds pressure (240°). Process pints 1 hour and quarts 1 hour and 15 minutes. Yield: 14 pints or 7 quarts.
Per cup: Calories 82 Fat 0.5g
Cholesterol 0mg Sodium 318mg

Note: When reheating soup base, add seasonings as desired.

Chicken and Rice Soup Stock

PREP: 20 MINUTES   COOK: 1 HOUR

PROCESS: 1½ HOURS

1 (3- to 4-pound) broiler-fryer
1 large onion, sliced
2 stalks celery, cut into 1-inch pieces
3 cups hot cooked rice (cooked without fat)

•Place chicken, onion, and celery in a Dutch oven; cover with water, and bring to a boil.
•Cover, reduce heat, and simmer 1 hour or until tender. Remove chicken, reserving broth; let cool. Bone chicken, and chop meat; set aside.
•Strain broth mixture; skim fat from surface. Add chopped chicken to broth; return to a boil. Spoon ¾ cup hot rice into each of four hot jars. Add hot broth mixture, filling to 1 inch from top. Remove air bubbles; wipe jar rims. •Cover at once with metal lids, and screw on bands. Process in pressure canner at 10 pounds pressure (240°). Process quarts 1½ hours. Yield: 4 quarts.
Per cup: Calories 130 Fat 4.5g
Cholesterol 27mg Sodium 656mg

Note: When reheating soup stock, add seasonings as desired.

Tomato Soup Base

PREP: 1 HOUR   COOK: 30 MINUTES

PROCESS: 1 HOUR AND 15 MINUTES

14 quarts tomatoes, peeled and chopped (about 20 pounds)
7 medium onions, chopped (about 3¼ pounds)
1 stalk celery, chopped
1 cup chopped fresh parsley
3 bay leaves
¾ cup plus 2 tablespoons butter or margarine
¾ cup plus 2 tablespoons all-purpose flour
½ cup sugar
3 tablespoons salt
2 teaspoons ground white pepper

•Combine tomato, onion, celery, parsley, and bay leaves in a large kettle; bring to a boil over medium heat. Reduce heat to low, and simmer 15 to 20 minutes or until celery is tender. Put vegetable mixture through a food mill, reserving juice; discard solids.
•Melt butter in a large Dutch oven over low heat; add flour, stirring until smooth. Cook 1 minute, stirring constantly.
•Gradually add reserved juice; cook over medium heat, stirring constantly, until mixture is thickened and bubbly. Stir in sugar, salt, and pepper. (If a smoother consistency of soup base is desired, pour through a sieve and discard any solids.)
•Pour hot tomato soup into hot jars, filling to 1 inch from top. Remove air bubbles; wipe jar rims.
•Cover at once with metal lids, and screw on bands. Process in pressure canner at 10 pounds pressure (240°). Process pints 1 hour and quarts 1 hour and 15 minutes. Yield: 12½ pints.
Per cup: Calories 191 Fat 7.8g
Cholesterol 17mg Sodium 952mg

Note: When reheating Tomato Soup Base, add seasonings as desired.

PICKLING

Summer is prime time for pickling fresh garden produce. It's the best and safest way to reap fruit and vegetable rewards all year long. With your efforts, the pantry becomes a canvas painted with jar after jar of vibrant-colored vegetables and verdant pickles.

Equipment

You'll need much the same utensils for processing pickles as you do for high-acid canned goods—a water-bath canner with a kick rack, standard canning jars, new metal lids, metal bands, a jar filler or funnel, jar lifter, nonmetal spatula, kitchen timer, and slotted spoon.

For brining pickles (soaking in a salt solution) use only glass, plastic, or stoneware bowls or containers. Don't use other materials such as copper, brass, galvanized steel, or iron; these materials might react with the acidity in the pickles.

The Pickling Process

Always start with just-ripe produce that is free from deformities, bruises, or bad spots. It's best to begin pickling within 24 hours after picking fruits or vegetables. If it's not possible for you to start pickling right away, refrigerate the produce, unwashed, or spread it in a cool, ventilated area. Remember that cucumbers deteriorate quickly at room temperature.

Be sure to select a pickling variety of cucumber. They're typically 4 to 5 inches long. If you plan to pickle them whole, choose unwaxed cucumbers since pickling solutions won't penetrate the wax.

Wash cucumbers well, especially around the stem end since it can harbor undesirable bacteria, which affect the pickles. Be sure to remove the blossom end before pickling since enzymes that are stored there cause pickles to soften.

Vinegar and salt are essential for making pickles, and amounts should never be reduced or diluted. Vinegar provides the acidity necessary for preservation of fresh-pack pickles. Always use vinegar of at least 5% acidity (it's marked on the label). White vinegar is the common choice. You can use cider vinegar, but it can darken light-colored vegetables and fruits.

Be sure to use granulated uniodized pickling or canning salt. Table salt may leave white sediment on the pickles or cloud the brine.

Most pickling recipes call for some sugar, since it helps crisp and plump the pickles. Unless the recipe specifies brown sugar, use white sugar.

Spices give pickles their distinctive flavor. Dill, garlic, cinnamon, mustard seeds, and cloves are just a few typically used. It's best to start with fresh, whole spices; powdered spices can darken and cloud the pickled product.

Packing the Pickles

When pickles are ready, place them firmly in hot canning jars without packing the jars too tightly. Cover with boiling syrup or brine, leaving the recommended headspace.

After adding boiling liquid to pickles, run a nonmetal spatula around the inside edge of jars to remove air bubbles. Don't use a metal utensil such as a kitchen knife, since it could scratch the glass and cause the jar to break.

Wipe jar rims clean before putting the metal lids in place. Then screw on metal bands.

Processing the Pickles

Water-bath processing destroys yeast, mold, and bacteria that cause spoilage. It also inactivates enzymes that can change color, flavor, and texture.

To process pickles in a water bath, put the jars on a rack in the canner filled with simmering water. The water should cover the jar tops by 2 to 3 inches. Start to count processing time when water reaches a boil. Some relishes and pickles made from vegetables other than cucumbers and cabbage may require longer processing times.

For pickles, especially Kosher Dills (page 407) and Bread and Butter Pickles (page 408), you'll enjoy the best flavor if you store the processed jars four to five weeks before opening.

IN A PICKLE?

Problems and Possible Causes

Soft or slippery pickles:
- Blossom ends not removed
- Vinegar of too low acidity used
- Not enough salt in brine
- Cucumbers not completely submerged in brine
- Improper processing

Hollow pickles:
- Cucumbers too large
- Too much time between picking and brining
- Improper brining process

Shriveled pickles:
- Brine or vinegar too strong
- Syrup too heavy
- Overcooking or overprocessing
- Too much time between picking and brining
- Dry weather during vegetable growth

Dark or discolored pickles:
- Hard water used
- Spices left in pickles
- Iodized salt used
- Ground spices used

Spoilage:
- Processing time too short
- Canning jars and/or new lids not used
- Ingredients not measured accurately
- Vinegar that has lost strength used

Mixed Vegetable Pickles

◄ **HEALTHY • MAKE AHEAD** ►

PREP: 25 MINUTES   COOK: 5 MINUTES

CHILL: 18 HOURS   PROCESS: 15 MINUTES

1 cup pickling salt
4 quarts cold water
1 quart sliced small pickling cucumbers
  (1-inch slices)
2 cups sliced carrot (1½-inch slices)
2 cups sliced celery (1½-inch slices)
2 cups small boiling onions
2 sweet red peppers, cut into ½-inch
  strips
1 small cauliflower, broken into flowerets
6½ cups white vinegar (5% acidity)
2 cups sugar
1 fresh hot red pepper, sliced crosswise
¼ cup mustard seeds
2 tablespoons celery seeds

•Dissolve salt in water; pour over cucumbers
and next 5 ingredients in a large crock or
plastic container. Cover and refrigerate 12 to
18 hours. Drain well.
•Combine vinegar and remaining 4 ingredients in a 10-quart Dutch oven; bring to a boil,
and boil 3 minutes. Add vegetables; reduce
heat, and simmer until thoroughly heated.
•Pack hot vegetables into hot jars, filling to ½
inch from top (photo 1). Cover with hot liquid, filling to ½ inch from top (photo 2).
Remove air bubbles; wipe jar rims (photo 3).
•Cover at once with metal lids, and screw on
bands. Process in boiling water bath 15
minutes (photos 4 and 5). Yield: 6 pints (48
servings).
Per ¼-cup serving: Calories 13 Fat 0.1g
Cholesterol 0mg Sodium 303mg

1. Pack hot vegetable mixture into hot jars, filling to
½ inch from the top.

2. Cover vegetables with
hot liquid, filling to within
½ inch from the top.

3. Wipe each jar rim with
a clean, damp towel. This
helps ensure a tight seal.

4. Cover jars with metal
lids and bands. Process in
boiling-water bath canner.

5. After processing, lift
rack and remove jars,
using a jar lifter.

Okra Pickles

PREP: 15 MINUTES   PROCESS: 10 MINUTES

Okra Pickles belong on a Southern vegetable plate. These are subtly seasoned with dill.

3½ pounds small okra pods
7 cloves garlic
7 small fresh hot peppers
1 quart water
2 cups white vinegar (5% acidity)
⅓ cup pickling salt
2 teaspoons dill seeds

•Pack okra tightly into hot jars, filling to ½ inch from top; place a garlic clove and a hot pepper in each.
•Combine water and remaining 3 ingredients in a saucepan; bring to a boil.
•Pour boiling vinegar mixture over okra, filling to ½ inch from top. Remove air bubbles; wipe jar rims.
•Cover at once with metal lids, and screw on bands. Process in boiling water bath 10 minutes. Yield: 7 pints (75 servings).
Per 3 okra pickles: Calories 8 Fat 0g
Cholesterol 0mg Sodium 95mg

Watermelon Rind Pickles

**PREP: 20 MINUTES   STAND: 16 HOURS
COOK: 1 HOUR AND 15 MINUTES
PROCESS: 10 MINUTES**

Watermelon rind pickles are a favorite condiment for a fried chicken and biscuit dinner. This recipe is packed with spices; it makes a great gift jar.

1 large watermelon, quartered
¾ cup salt
3 quarts water
2 quarts ice cubes
1 tablespoon whole cloves
1 tablespoon whole allspice
9 cups sugar
3 cups white vinegar (5% acidity)
3 cups water
1 lemon, thinly sliced
5 (3-inch) cinnamon sticks

•Peel watermelon; remove pulp, and reserve for another use. Cut rind into 1-inch cubes; reserve 12 cups rind cubes in a container.
•Stir together salt and 3 quarts water; pour over rind. Add ice; cover and let stand 8 hours. Rinse well, and drain.
•Cook rind and water to cover in a Dutch oven over high heat 10 minutes or until tender. Drain.
•Place cloves and allspice on a 3-inch square of cheesecloth; tie with a string.
•Stir together sugar, vinegar, and 3 cups water; add spice bag, and bring to a boil. Boil 5 minutes, and pour over rind. Stir in lemon slices. Cover and let stand 8 hours.
•Bring rind and syrup mixture to a boil; reduce heat, and simmer 1 hour, stirring occasionally. Discard spice bag.
•Pack rind mixture into hot jars, filling to ½ inch from top. Add 1 cinnamon stick to each jar. Remove air bubbles; wipe jar rims.
•Cover at once with metal lids, and screw on bands. Process in boiling water bath 10 minutes. Yield: 5 (12-ounce) jars (30 servings).
Per ¼-cup serving: Calories 275 Fat 0g
Cholesterol 0mg Sodium 157mg

Kosher Dills

PREP: 23 MINUTES   PROCESS: 10 MINUTES

These pickles will shrivel after processing. They'll plump later in sealed jars.

4 pounds (4-inch) pickling cucumbers
14 cloves garlic, halved
¼ cup pickling salt
3 cups water
2¾ cups white vinegar (5% acidity)
14 fresh dill sprigs
28 peppercorns

•Wash cucumbers; cut in half lengthwise.
•Combine garlic and next 3 ingredients in a saucepan; bring to a boil. Remove garlic, and place 4 halves into each hot jar. Pack jars with cucumber to ½ inch from top, adding 2 dill sprigs and 4 peppercorns to each jar.
•Pour boiling vinegar mixture over cucumbers, filling to ½ inch from top. Remove air bubbles; wipe jar rims.
•Cover at once with metal lids, and screw on bands. Process in boiling water bath 10 minutes. Yield: 7 pints (42 servings).
Per serving: Calories 6 Fat 0.1g
Cholesterol 0mg Sodium 168mg

Cucumber Chips

**PREP: 30 MINUTES   STAND: 15 HOURS
COOK: 25 MINUTES   PROCESS: 10 MINUTES**

24 small (4- to 5-inch) pickling cucumbers, sliced ¼ inch thick
½ cup pickling salt
3 cups white vinegar (5% acidity)
1 quart water
1 tablespoon ground turmeric
1 quart white vinegar (5% acidity)
1 cup water
2 cups sugar
2 (3-inch) sticks cinnamon
1 (1-inch) piece fresh ginger
1 tablespoon mustard seeds
1 teaspoon whole cloves
2 cups firmly packed brown sugar

•Place cucumber in a large bowl, and sprinkle with salt. Cover and let stand 3 hours. Drain well.
•Combine 3 cups vinegar, 1 quart water, and turmeric in a large Dutch oven; bring to a boil, and pour over cucumber. Cover and let stand until cooled to room temperature; drain. Rinse cucumber, and drain again.
•Combine 1 quart vinegar, 1 cup water, and 2 cups sugar in Dutch oven. Tie spices in a cheesecloth bag, and add to vinegar mixture. Bring vinegar mixture to a boil; reduce heat, and simmer, uncovered, 15 minutes. Pour mixture over cucumbers. Let stand at least 12 hours in a cool place.
•Drain syrup from cucumber into Dutch oven. Add brown sugar, and bring to a boil.
•Pack cucumber into hot jars, filling to ½ inch from top. Pour boiling syrup over cucumbers, filling to ½ inch from top. Remove air bubbles; wipe jar rims.
•Cover at once with metal lids, and screw on bands. Process in boiling water bath 10 minutes. Yield: 4 pints (48 servings).
Per serving: Calories 21 Fat 0.1g
Cholesterol 0mg Sodium 149mg

Bread and Butter Pickles

PREP: 1 HOUR AND 45 MINUTES

CHILL: 3 HOURS   PROCESS: 10 MINUTES

Bread and Butter Pickles enhance just about any sandwich. These are wonderfully crisp and slightly sweet.

6 pounds pickling cucumbers (about 25 cucumbers)
6 medium onions, sliced
2 medium-size green peppers, chopped
3 cloves garlic
⅓ cup pickling salt
Crushed ice
5 cups sugar
3 cups cider vinegar (5% acidity)
2 tablespoons mustard seeds
1½ teaspoons ground turmeric
1½ teaspoons celery seeds

•Wash cucumbers, and thinly slice. Combine cucumber, onion, and next 3 ingredients in a large Dutch oven. Cover with ice; mix thoroughly, and refrigerate 3 hours. Drain.
•Combine sugar and remaining 4 ingredients; pour over cucumber mixture. Heat just until boiling.
•Pack hot mixture into hot jars, filling to ½ inch from top. Remove air bubbles; wipe jar rims. Cover at once with metal lids, and screw on bands. Process jars in boiling water bath 10 minutes. Yield: 9 pints (90 servings).

Bread and Butter Pickles

Per serving: Calories 12 Fat 0.1g
Cholesterol 0mg Sodium 196mg

RELISHES

Pickle relishes are the fruition of chopped, seasoned, and pickled fruits and vegetables. The pickling process for relishes is similar to that of most pickles, but more time is required in preparation because the ingredients must be chopped. If you have a food processor, use it here. Just be careful not to overprocess ingredients because they can quickly go from chopped to mushy with a few pulses in the food processor.

Sweet Pickle Relish

PREP: 30 MINUTES   STAND: 2 HOURS

COOK: 15 MINUTES   PROCESS: 10 MINUTES

4 cups chopped cucumber
2 cups chopped onion
1 green pepper, chopped
1 sweet red pepper, chopped
¼ cup pickling salt
1¾ cups sugar
1 cup cider vinegar or white vinegar (5% acidity)
1½ teaspoons celery seeds
1½ teaspoons mustard seeds

•Combine first 4 ingredients in a large bowl; sprinkle evenly with pickling salt, and cover vegetables with cold water. Let stand 2 hours. Drain.
•Combine sugar, vinegar, and spices in a Dutch oven; bring to a boil, and add vegetables. Return to a boil; reduce heat, and simmer 10 minutes.
•Pack hot mixture into hot jars, filling to ½ inch from top. Remove air bubbles; wipe jar rims.
•Cover at once with metal lids, and screw on bands. Process in boiling water bath 10 minutes. Yield: 4 half-pints.

Per tablespoon: Calories 55 Fat 0.3g
Cholesterol 0mg Sodium 444mg

Pepper Relish

PREP: 30 MINUTES   COOK: 35 MINUTES
PROCESS: 10 MINUTES

6 green peppers, minced
6 sweet red peppers, minced
6 medium onions, minced
1 hot pepper
2 cups white vinegar (5% acidity)
1½ cups sugar
2 tablespoons plus 1 teaspoon mustard
   seeds

•Combine all ingredients in a Dutch oven,
and bring to a boil. Reduce heat to medium;
cook, uncovered, 30 minutes, stirring occasionally. Discard hot pepper.
•Spoon hot relish quickly into hot jars, filling
to ½ inch from top. Remove air bubbles;
wipe jar rims.
•Cover at once with metal lids, and screw on
bands. Process in boiling water bath 10 minutes. Yield: 10 half-pints (40 servings).
Per ¼-cup serving: Calories 49 Fat 0.4g
Cholesterol 0mg Sodium 2mg

Corn Relish

PREP: 30 MINUTES   COOK: 22 MINUTES
PROCESS: 15 MINUTES

*Make this relish in the summertime when
corn is abundantly fresh and naturally sweet.*

4 cups fresh cut corn
3 medium-size green peppers, chopped
1 cup chopped onion
1 cup chopped cucumber
¼ cup chopped celery
1 (28-ounce) can whole tomatoes,
   undrained and chopped
1 cup sugar
2 teaspoons salt
1 teaspoon whole mustard seeds
¾ teaspoon ground turmeric
¼ teaspoon dry mustard
1½ cups white vinegar (5% acidity)

•Combine all ingredients in a Dutch oven;
simmer over low heat 20 minutes. Bring mixture to a boil.

•Pack hot mixture into hot jars, filling to ½
inch from top. Remove air bubbles; wipe jar
rims. Cover at once with metal lids, and
screw on bands. Process in boiling water
bath 15 minutes. Yield: 4 pints (32 servings).
Per ¼-cup serving: Calories 52 Fat 0.4g
Cholesterol 0mg Sodium 192mg

Green Tomato Sweet Relish

PREP: 20 MINUTES   STAND: 4 HOURS
COOK: 20 MINUTES   PROCESS: 15 MINUTES

12 large green tomatoes, quartered
6 green peppers, quartered
2 sweet red peppers, quartered
3 large onions, quartered
2 teaspoons pickling salt
4 cups sugar
3 cups cider vinegar (5% acidity)
2 teaspoons ground turmeric
1 (6-ounce) jar prepared mustard

•Process vegetables, a few at a time, in a
food processor until ground. Transfer to a
large nonaluminum bowl; sprinkle with pickling salt, and let stand 3 to 4 hours. Drain.
•Combine sugar, vinegar, and turmeric in a
Dutch oven; cook over medium heat, stirring constantly, until sugar dissolves. Add
vegetables, and bring to a boil. Stir in mustard, and cook, stirring constantly, until
thickened.
•Pack hot mixture into hot jars, filling to ½
inch from top. Remove air bubbles; wipe
jar rims.
•Cover at once with metal lids, and screw on
bands. Process in boiling water bath 15 minutes. Yield: 7 (12-ounce) jars.
Per tablespoon: Calories 25 Fat 0.1g
Cholesterol 0mg Sodium 21mg

Chowchow

PREP: 30 MINUTES   STAND: 8 HOURS
COOK: 25 MINUTES   PROCESS: 15 MINUTES

*Chowchow is a pickled blend of sweet sum-
mer vegetables and legumes.*

2 cups chopped cabbage
2 cups peeled, chopped cucumber
2 cups chopped onion
2 cups peeled, chopped green tomato
1 cup chopped green pepper
1 cup chopped sweet red pepper
1½ cups salt
2 quarts water
2 cups scraped, thinly sliced carrot
2 cups fresh green beans, cut into ½-inch
   pieces (about ¾ pound)
2 cups frozen baby lima beans, thawed
3 cups sugar
3 cups white vinegar (5% acidity)
1½ cups water
3 tablespoons mustard seeds
1½ tablespoons celery seeds
1 tablespoon ground turmeric

•Combine first 6 ingredients in a large nonmetal container. Dissolve salt in 2 quarts
water; pour over cabbage mixture. Cover
and let stand 8 hours. Drain and rinse well.
Place cabbage mixture in a Dutch oven; set
aside.
•Cook carrot, green beans, and lima beans
separately in small amounts of boiling water
until crisp-tender; drain. Add cooked vegetables to cabbage mixture in Dutch oven. Add
sugar and remaining ingredients, stirring
gently to combine. Bring to a boil; reduce
heat to medium, and cook 10 minutes.
•Pack vegetables and liquid into hot jars, filling to ½ inch from top. Remove air bubbles;
wipe jar rims.
•Cover at once with metal lids, and screw on
bands. Process in boiling water bath 15 minutes. Yield: 8 pints (64 servings).
Per ¼-cup serving: Calories 55 Fat 0.3g
Cholesterol 0mg Sodium 444mg

Pear Relish

PREP: 1 HOUR   COOK: 35 MINUTES
PROCESS: 20 MINUTES

We recommend the brown Bosc pear in this relish. Try it on toast or English muffins.

12½ pounds pears (1 peck), peeled and
    cored
8 jalapeño peppers, seeded
6 sweet red peppers, quartered
6 green peppers, quartered
6 medium onions, quartered
1 tablespoon salt
1 tablespoon celery seeds
5 cups sugar
5 cups white vinegar (5% acidity)

• Process pears, a few at a time, in a food processor until pears are chopped, pulsing processor 2 or 3 times.
• Transfer chopped pear to a large Dutch oven. Repeat procedure to chop all pears, peppers, and onions.
• Add salt and remaining 3 ingredients to vegetables in Dutch oven, stirring well. Bring mixture to a boil over medium heat; reduce heat, and simmer mixture 30 minutes, stirring occasionally.
• Spoon hot relish into hot jars, filling to ½ inch from top. Remove air bubbles; wipe jar rims.
• Cover at once with metal lids, and screw on bands. Process in boiling water bath 20 minutes. Yield: 14 pints.

Per tablespoon: Calories 17 Fat 0.1g
Cholesterol 0mg Sodium 16mg

BENEFITS OF BOSC

Bosc pears are highly aromatic, flavorful pears with a firm, dense flesh that makes them ideal for canning, cooking, and baking. Bosc pears are also excellent eaten fresh, out of hand, or sliced in salads. Unlike some more common pears, the brown skin of a Bosc does not change color as it ripens.

JAMS, JELLIES & PRESERVES

Fruit spreads look so brilliant and beautiful in their jars. During the summer months you'll find Southern cooks busily putting up multicolored jars of jams, jellies, and preserves ultimately destined for slathering on some wonderful fresh bread.

Equipment

Before you begin the process of jelly making, be sure you have all the necessary equipment: an 8- to 10-quart deep, heavy, flat-bottom kettle; cheesecloth or a jelly bag; a candy or deep-fat thermometer; a kitchen timer; a jar filler or funnel; a jar lifter; a boiling water-bath canner with a rack and tight-fitting lid; and standard jelly jars with metal bands and new lids.

In jelly making, jars need to be sterilized 10 minutes in boiling water before filling. This is necessary for all jellied products that are processed in a water bath for less than 10 minutes.

The Ingredients

The ingredients are simple for these summer-fresh spreads. Only fruit, sugar, acid, and fruit pectin are needed. Three-fourths of the fruit should be just ripe and the remaining one-fourth slightly underripe for the best gelled product.

The proper amount of sugar is important for achieving a good gel, so never reduce the recommended amount. Sugar contributes to the taste of the product and acts as a preservative, preventing the growth of microorganisms.

You can substitute honey or light corn syrup for some of the sugar, but adjustments are sometimes necessary in other ingredient amounts. If you choose to use another sweetener, be sure to check with a local Extension agent for advice.

Acid and pectin, contained in the fruit itself, are necessary for gel formation as well. Fruit contains varying amounts of both, depending on the type of fruit and the degree of ripeness. Pectin is at its highest quality in just-ripe fruit, and acid content is higher in underripe fruit. If the fruit is naturally low in acid, lemon juice can be added.

Some of the guesswork as to acidity level and doneness of the cooked mixture can be eliminated with the use of store-bought pectin. A disadvantage of using added pectin is that the natural fruit flavor may be masked to some extent since more sugar is needed with this product.

Jelly Making

Be sure to follow recipe directions exactly, and never double a recipe. Each batch

should start with no more than 4 to 6 cups of juice. When a recipe calls for juice extracted from fresh fruit, prepare fruit as the recipe directs first. Then pour fruit into a damp jelly bag or four layers of cheesecloth, and allow juice to drip into a bowl. Jelly is clearer when allowed to drip rather than being squeezed or pressed from a bag. If using a fruit press, strain the juice again.

When making jelly without added pectin, it's tricky to tell when the hot fruit mixture has reached the proper consistency since it will thicken as it cools.

To test for doneness, dip a cool metal spoon into boiling jelly and lift spoon out of steam so syrup runs off side of spoon. When two drops of the syrup come together and "sheet" off the spoon, the jellying point has been reached.

When jelly is done, remove from heat, skim off foam, and pour into hot sterilized jars, filling to ¼ inch from the top. Wipe jar rims, cover at once with metal lids, and screw on metal bands. Then process as directed.

Processing Fruit Spreads

Processing in a boiling water bath is recommended for all jellies and fruit spreads with the exception of freezer fruit spreads.

Place filled jars on a rack in a water-bath canner with water gently boiling. Add water to a level of 2 to 3 inches above the jar tops. Cover and begin to count processing time when water returns to a boil.

Sealed jellied products should keep well at least one year if stored in a cool, dark, dry place. However, they should be used as soon as possible since flavor and quality begin to decrease within a few months. Mold on jellied products is the result of improper sealing or underprocessing. Discard the jar if mold is present.

Apple Jelly

◀ HEALTHY • MAKE AHEAD ▶
◀ FAMILY FAVORITE ▶

PREP: **2 MINUTES**   COOK: **5 MINUTES**
PROCESS: **5 MINUTES**

4 cups apple juice
1 (1¾-ounce) package powdered pectin
5 cups sugar

•Combine apple juice and pectin in a Dutch oven; bring to a boil, stirring occasionally. Add sugar, and bring mixture to a full, rolling boil. Boil 1 minute, stirring constantly. Remove from heat, and skim off foam with a metal spoon.
•Pour hot jelly quickly into hot sterilized jars, filling to ¼ inch from top; wipe jar rims.
•Cover at once with metal lids, and screw on bands. Process in boiling water bath 5 minutes. Yield: 7 half-pints.
Per tablespoon: Calories 40 Fat 0g
Cholesterol 0mg Sodium 0mg

Quick Grape Jelly

◀ HEALTHY • MAKE AHEAD ▶
◀ FAMILY FAVORITE ▶

PREP: **2 MINUTES**   COOK: **5 MINUTES**
PROCESS: **5 MINUTES**

2 cups bottled unsweetened grape juice
3½ cups sugar
1 (3-ounce) package liquid pectin

•Combine grape juice and sugar in a Dutch oven; bring to a boil, stirring constantly. Stir in pectin; boil 1 minute, stirring constantly.

Remove from heat, and skim off foam with a metal spoon.
•Pour hot jelly quickly into hot sterilized jars, filling to ¼ inch from top; wipe jar rims.
•Cover at once with metal lids, and screw on bands. Process in boiling water bath 5 minutes. Yield: 4 half-pints.
Per tablespoon: Calories 52 Fat 0g
Cholesterol 0mg Sodium 1mg

Vidalia Onion Jelly

◀ QUICK • MAKE AHEAD ▶
◀ HEALTHY ▶

PREP: **12 MINUTES**   COOK: **8 MINUTES**
PROCESS: **5 MINUTES**

Serve this sweet onion jelly with slivers of roast beef or ham.

2 pounds Vidalia onions or other sweet onions, thinly sliced (about 9 cups)
2 cups water
1 (1¾-ounce) package powdered pectin
¾ cup white vinegar (5% acidity)
5½ cups sugar

•Combine onion and water in a Dutch oven; bring to a boil. Remove from heat, and cool. Press onion through a jelly bag or cheesecloth to extract juice. If necessary, add water to juice to measure 3 cups. Discard onion pulp.
•Combine onion liquid, pectin, and vinegar in a large saucepan; stir well. Bring to a boil, stirring constantly. Stir in sugar, and return to a boil. Remove from heat; skim off foam with a metal spoon.
•Pour hot jelly quickly through a sieve into hot sterilized jars, filling to ¼ inch from top; wipe jar rims.
•Cover at once with metal lids, and screw on bands. Process in boiling water bath 5 minutes. Yield: 6 half-pints.
Per tablespoon: Calories 48 Fat 0g
Cholesterol 0mg Sodium 0mg

JELLY DICTIONARY

Butters: Fruit is pureed for butters instead of chopped, and the amount of sugar is usually lower than in other fruit spreads.
Conserves: Conserves start with a jamlike base but have chopped nuts added.
Jams: Jams are less firm than jellies and are made with crushed or finely chopped fruit rather than juice.
Jellies: Jellies are sparkling clear gelatin-like spreads that are the result of cooking sugar and fruit juice or other liquid together.
Marmalades: Marmalades offer a tangy twist to basic jams; they contain citrus peel and fruit pieces.
Preserves: Preserves are very similar to jams, but they utilize larger pieces of fruit than jams. They are often made with whole fruits, such as strawberries and other berries.

Blackberry Jelly

◀ HEALTHY • MAKE AHEAD ▶
◀ FAMILY FAVORITE ▶

PREP: **10 MINUTES**   COOK: **5 MINUTES**
PROCESS: **5 MINUTES**

About 3 quarts ripe blackberries
7½ cups sugar
2 (3-ounce) packages liquid pectin

•Sort and wash berries; remove stems and caps. Crush enough berries and press through a jelly bag or cheesecloth to extract 4 cups juice. Combine juice and sugar in a Dutch oven, and stir well. Cook over high heat, stirring constantly, until mixture comes to a rapid boil. Boil hard 1 minute, stirring constantly. Add pectin, and bring to a full rolling boil; boil 1 minute, stirring constantly. Remove from heat, and skim off foam with a metal spoon.
•Pour hot jelly quickly into hot sterilized jars, filling to ¼ inch from top; wipe jar rims.
•Cover at once with metal lids, and screw on bands. Process in boiling water bath 5 minutes. Yield: 8 half-pints.
Per tablespoon: Calories 55 Fat 0g
Cholesterol 0mg Sodium 1mg

Herb Jelly

PREP: 2 MINUTES   COOK: 6 MINUTES
PROCESS: 5 MINUTES

1½ cups white grape juice
½ cup water
3½ cups sugar
Prepared herbs (variations follow)
Food coloring (optional)
1 (3-ounce) package liquid pectin

•Combine first 4 ingredients and, if desired, food coloring in a Dutch oven. Bring to a rolling boil; cook 1 minute, stirring constantly. Add pectin, and bring to a full rolling boil. Boil 1 minute, stirring often. Remove from heat, and skim off foam with a metal spoon.
•Pour hot jelly quickly through a sieve into hot sterilized jars, filling to ¼ inch from top; wipe jar rims.
•Cover at once with metal lids, and screw on bands. Process in boiling water bath 5 minutes. Yield: 4 half-pints.
Per tablespoon: Calories 50 Fat 0g
Cholesterol 0mg Sodium 0mg

Rosemary Jelly: Add 3 tablespoons chopped fresh rosemary leaves before boiling.

Thyme Jelly: Add 3 tablespoons crushed fresh thyme leaves before boiling.

Basil Jelly: Add 3 tablespoons chopped fresh basil leaves and, if desired, 4 drops of yellow food coloring before boiling.

Mint Jelly: Add ¾ cup crushed fresh mint leaves and, if desired, 2 drops of green food coloring before boiling.

Note: Serve jelly with biscuits or scones, or over cream cheese with crackers as an appetizer. You can also brush on chicken before broiling or grilling.

Jalapeño Jelly

PREP: 10 MINUTES   COOK: 9 MINUTES

We skipped the canning process to make an easy, keep-in-the-fridge jelly.

4 fresh jalapeño peppers, seeded and coarsely chopped
½ green pepper, coarsely chopped
3 cups sugar
½ cup cider vinegar (5% acidity)
½ (3-ounce) package liquid pectin
2 tablespoons fresh lime juice

•Process jalapeño pepper and green pepper in food processor until smooth, stopping several times to scrape down sides.
•Combine pepper puree, sugar, and cider vinegar in a large nonaluminum saucepan. Bring to a boil over medium-high heat, stirring constantly. Boil 3 minutes; stir in pectin and lime juice. Boil 1 minute, stirring constantly. Remove from heat, and skim off foam with a metal spoon.
•Pour into hot sterilized jars, filling to ¼ inch from top; wipe jar rims. Cover at once with metal lids, and screw on bands; cool.
•Store in refrigerator. Serve over cream cheese with crackers or toast as an appetizer or with meats as a relish. Yield: 3 half-pints.
Per tablespoon: Calories 55 Fat 0g
Cholesterol 0mg Sodium 0mg

Blueberry Jam

PREP: 20 MINUTES   COOK: 4 MINUTES
PROCESS: 5 MINUTES

Find a blueberry patch and pick your own bucketful to use in this homemade jam.

1½ quarts stemmed blueberries, crushed
¼ cup lemon juice
1 (1-inch) stick cinnamon
7 cups sugar
2 (3-ounce) packages liquid pectin

•Combine first 4 ingredients in a Dutch oven; bring to a boil until sugar dissolves, stirring often. Boil 2 minutes, stirring often; remove from heat. Discard cinnamon stick.

Add pectin, and stir 5 minutes. Skim off foam with a metal spoon.
•Pour hot jam quickly into hot sterilized jars, filling to ¼ inch from top. Remove air bubbles; wipe jar rims.
•Cover at once with metal lids, and screw on bands. Process in boiling water bath 5 minutes. Yield: 5 half-pints.
Per tablespoon: Calories 81 Fat 0g
Cholesterol 0mg Sodium 1mg

Strawberry Preserves

PREP: 15 MINUTES   COOK: 28 MINUTES
STAND: 28 HOURS   PROCESS: 5 MINUTES

1½ quarts small strawberries
5 cups sugar
⅓ cup lemon juice

•Wash and hull strawberries. Combine strawberries and sugar in a Dutch oven; stir well, and let stand 3 to 4 hours.
•Slowly bring strawberry mixture to a boil until sugar dissolves, stirring occasionally. Stir in lemon juice. Boil about 12 minutes or until berries are clear, stirring occasionally. Remove from heat, and skim off foam with a metal spoon.
•Carefully remove fruit from syrup with a slotted spoon, and place in a shallow pan. Bring syrup to a boil; cook about 10 minutes or until syrup has thickened to desired consistency. Pour syrup over fruit.
•Cover loosely with paper towels, and let stand 12 to 24 hours in a cool place. Shake pan occasionally (do not stir) so berries will absorb syrup and remain plump. Skim off foam with a metal spoon.
•Heat mixture in Dutch oven, and ladle hot preserves into hot jars, filling to ¼ inch from top. Remove air bubbles; wipe jar rims.
•Cover at once with metal lids, and screw on bands. Process in boiling water bath 5 minutes. Yield: 4 half-pints.
Per tablespoon: Calories 65 Fat 0.1g
Cholesterol 0mg Sodium 0mg

Fig Preserves

◄ MAKE AHEAD ►

PREP: 20 MINUTES

COOK: 1 HOUR AND 35 MINUTES

PROCESS: 5 MINUTES

We recommend brown Turkey figs or black Mission figs in this recipe.

4½ pounds fresh figs, stemmed
7 cups sugar
¼ cup lemon juice
6 cups water
2 lemons, thinly sliced

• Coarsely chop figs, if desired. Place figs in a Dutch oven; add water to cover. Bring to a boil; reduce heat, and cook, uncovered, 20 minutes. Drain figs, and set aside.
• Combine sugar, lemon juice, and 6 cups water in Dutch oven; cook over medium heat, stirring constantly, until sugar dissolves (about 15 minutes). Add figs; return to a boil, and cook 10 minutes, stirring occasionally. Add lemon slices, and boil 30 minutes or until figs are tender and clear.
• Carefully remove figs with a slotted spoon; boil syrup 15 minutes or until desired thickness; remove from heat, and skim off foam with a metal spoon. Return figs to syrup.
• Pack figs in hot sterilized jars, filling to ¼ inch from top. Cover fruit with hot syrup, filling to ¼ inch from top. Remove air bubbles; wipe jar rims.
• Cover at once with metal lids, and screw on bands. Process in boiling water bath 5 minutes. Yield: 8 half-pints (16 servings).
Per serving: Calories 433 Fat 0.4g
Cholesterol 0mg Sodium 2mg

Pear Butter

◄ HEALTHY • MAKE AHEAD ►

PREP: 20 MINUTES   COOK: 55 MINUTES

PROCESS: 5 MINUTES

10 large ripe pears (5 pounds), quartered and cored
1 cup water
2 cups sugar
½ teaspoon grated orange rind
3 tablespoons fresh orange juice
¼ teaspoon ground nutmeg

• Combine pears and water in a large Dutch oven. Cover and cook over medium-low heat 40 minutes or until pears are soft, stirring occasionally. Drain.
• Press pears through a sieve or food mill; measure 1 quart of puree. Combine 1 quart puree, sugar, and remaining ingredients in Dutch oven. Cook over medium heat 15 minutes or until mixture thickens, stirring often. Remove from heat; skim off foam with a metal spoon.
• Pour hot mixture into hot sterilized jars, filling ¼ inch from top. Remove air bubbles; wipe jar rims.
• Cover at once with metal lids, and screw on bands. Process in boiling water bath 5 minutes. Yield: 2 pints.
Per tablespoon: Calories 30 Fat 0.03g
Cholesterol 0mg Sodium 1mg

Apple Butter

◄ HEALTHY • MAKE AHEAD ►
◄ FAMILY FAVORITE ►

PREP: 45 MINUTES   COOK: 50 MINUTES

PROCESS: 5 MINUTES

Apple butter takes most people back to their childhood. It's a beloved breakfast spread.

5 pounds Granny Smith apples, peeled, cored, and sliced
3 cups water
3 cups sugar
3 cups firmly packed brown sugar
1 (1.75-ounce) package powdered pectin
1 tablespoon ground cinnamon
1 teaspoon ground allspice
¼ teaspoon ground cloves
¼ teaspoon ground nutmeg

• Combine apple and water in a large Dutch oven; bring to a boil. Reduce heat, and cook 25 minutes or until tender. Mash until smooth. Stir in sugars and remaining ingredients. Bring to a boil; cook 2 minutes, stirring constantly.
• Pour mixture quickly into hot sterilized jars, filling to ¼ inch from top; wipe jar rims.
• Cover at once with metal lids, and screw on bands. Process in boiling water bath 5 minutes. Yield: 6 pints.
Per tablespoon: Calories 31 Fat 0g
Cholesterol 0mg Sodium 1mg

Peach Chutney

◄ HEALTHY • MAKE AHEAD ►

PREP: 40 MINUTES   COOK: 38 MINUTES

PROCESS: 10 MINUTES

Try this Peach Chutney on grilled pork or ham.

1 large lemon
5 pounds firm peaches, peeled and chopped
1⅔ cups golden raisins
1 (8-ounce) package chopped dates
2 cups white vinegar (5% acidity)
3 cups sugar
½ cup chopped pecans
1 (2.7-ounce) jar crystallized ginger (½ cup)
1 teaspoon ground ginger
½ teaspoon ground allspice
½ teaspoon ground cinnamon
½ teaspoon ground cloves

• Cut lemon into fourths, and thinly slice.
• Combine lemon, peaches, and next 3 ingredients in a nonaluminum Dutch oven; bring to a boil over medium heat. Reduce heat, and simmer 5 minutes or until peaches are soft, stirring occasionally.
• Add sugar; return to a boil. Reduce heat; simmer 18 to 25 minutes or until mixture thickens and liquid evaporates, stirring occasionally. Add pecans and remaining ingredients; cook 5 minutes, stirring occasionally.
• Pack into hot jars, filling to ½ inch from top. Remove air bubbles; wipe jar rims.
• Cover at once with metal lids, and screw on bands. Process in boiling water bath 10 minutes. Serve chutney with chicken or pork. Store in refrigerator after opening. Yield: 13 half-pints.
Per tablespoon: Calories 25 Fat 0.2g
Cholesterol 0mg Sodium 1mg

Orange-Pineapple Marmalade

PREP: 20 MINUTES   COOK: 35 MINUTES
PROCESS: 5 MINUTES

Serve this marmalade over ice cream or pound cake, or brush it over fruit tarts.

3 medium oranges
1 medium lemon
1 (20-ounce) can crushed unsweetened
    pineapple, drained
6¾ cups sugar
½ cup hot water
1 (6-ounce) jar maraschino cherries,
    drained and chopped

• Wash oranges and lemon; cut into quarters.
• Remove seeds and membrane from each piece. Grind unpeeled fruit in a meat grinder or food processor.
• Combine ground fruit, pineapple, sugar, and water in a Dutch oven; bring to a boil over high heat. Reduce heat; simmer 30 minutes, uncovered, stirring often. Remove from heat; stir in cherries.
• Pour hot mixture into hot sterilized jars, filling to ¼ inch from top. Remove air bubbles; wipe jar rims. Cover at once with metal lids, and screw on bands. Process in boiling water bath 5 minutes. Yield: 8 half-pints.
Per tablespoon: Calories 11 Fat 0g
Cholesterol 0mg Sodium 0mg

Cranberry Conserve

PREP: 15 MINUTES   COOK: 40 MINUTES
PROCESS: 5 MINUTES

4 cups fresh cranberries°
¾ cup water
3 cups sugar
¾ cup water
1 medium orange, peeled and finely
    chopped
½ cup chopped pecans or walnuts
⅓ cup raisins

• Combine cranberries and ¾ cup water in a Dutch oven; bring to a boil. Cover, reduce heat, and simmer 6 to 8 minutes or until skins pop.
• Drain cranberries, and put through a food mill. Add sugar and remaining ingredients; bring to a boil, stirring often. Reduce heat, and simmer, uncovered, 30 minutes.
• Spoon hot conserve quickly into hot sterilized jars, filling to ¼ inch from top. Remove air bubbles; wipe jar rims.
• Cover at once with metal lids, and screw on bands. Process in boiling water bath 5 minutes. Yield: 4 half-pints.
°A 12-ounce bag of fresh cranberries holds about 3 cups, so you'll need to buy 2 bags for this recipe.
Per tablespoon: Calories 49 Fat 0.7g
Cholesterol 0mg Sodium 0mg

VINEGARS

Flavored vinegars are very popular these days in the marketplace. They're made with fresh berries, herbs, and spices and are then poured into a wide array of decorative bottles. Part of their charm is their brilliant color display.

Making your own vinegar isn't hard. For flavor and color variations, just pour cider vinegar, red or white wine vinegar, or champagne vinegar over the solids. Bring vinegar almost to a boil (190°) before pouring over herbs.

There are endless uses for flavored vinegars. Use them in homemade vinaigrettes for salads, add a spoonful to black bean soup or beef stew, or splash some over steaming hot roasted vegetables.

Basil Vinegar

PREP: 5 MINUTES   COOK: 4 MINUTES

⅔ cup loosely packed fresh basil leaves
1 (17-ounce) bottle champagne wine
    vinegar or white wine vinegar
Fresh basil sprig (optional)

• Slightly crush basil with back of a spoon, and place in a 1-quart jar. Bring vinegar almost to a boil, and pour over basil. Cover and let stand at room temperature 1 to 2 weeks.
• Pour through a wire-mesh strainer into a 2-cup liquid measuring cup, discarding basil. Transfer to a hot sterilized decorative bottle or jar; add a fresh basil sprig, if desired. Seal bottle with a cork or other airtight lid. Store in refrigerator. Yield: 2 cups.
Per tablespoon: Calories 2 Fat 0g
Cholesterol 0mg Sodium 2mg

Tarragon Vinegar: Substitute 2 large fresh tarragon sprigs for basil leaves. Twist tarragon gently instead of crushing it, and place in a 1-quart glass jar. Proceed as directed.

Raspberry Wine Vinegar

PREP: 5 MINUTES   COOK: 10 MINUTES

3 cups fresh or frozen raspberries
2 (17-ounce) bottles white wine vinegar
1 cup sugar

• Combine all ingredients in a saucepan; bring to a boil. Cover, reduce heat, and simmer 10 minutes. Pour through a wire-mesh strainer into hot sterilized decorative bottles; discard pulp. Cover and store in refrigerator. Yield: 5 cups.
Per tablespoon: Calories 13 Fat 0g
Cholesterol 0mg Sodium 1mg

Tomato-Herb Vinegar

◄ MAKE AHEAD ►
◄ HEALTHY ►

PREP: 10 MINUTES   COOK: 5 MINUTES
STAND: 2 WEEKS

Splash this rosy herbed vinegar on fresh salad greens or use it to stir up a homemade vinaigrette. See our salad dressings section for a wealth of ideas.

10 large sprigs fresh rosemary
6 large sprigs fresh basil
4 large sprigs fresh oregano
12 small cloves garlic, peeled and halved
10 dried tomato halves
1 teaspoon black peppercorns
3 (32-ounce) bottles red wine vinegar
Fresh rosemary sprigs (optional)

• Clean and wash herbs. Twist stems of herbs gently to bruise leaves, and press garlic with back of a spoon to crush it. Place herbs and garlic in a large glass container. Add tomato and peppercorns. Set aside.
• Bring vinegar just to a boil, and pour over herb mixture. Cover and let stand at room temperature 2 weeks.
• Pour vinegar mixture through a large wire-mesh strainer into hot sterilized decorative bottles, discarding solids. Add additional cleaned and washed rosemary sprigs, if desired. Seal bottles, and store in refrigerator. Yield: 11 cups.

Per tablespoon: Calories 2 Fat 0g
Cholesterol 0mg Sodium 0mg

MAKING VINEGARS

• Use four large fresh herb sprigs or 10 spice berries or hot peppers for each pint of vinegar.
• If you harvest herbs from your garden, pick the leaves before the plant blooms. And clip healthiest herbs early in the morning. Wash leaves, and pat dry.
• Put herb leaves, berries, or peppers into sterilized glass bottles. Find bottles at kitchen and home stores or recycle your own bottles. Always wash and sterilize the bottles in boiling water 10 minutes before filling.
• Bring vinegar just to a boil; pour into bottles, making sure leaves and peppers are completely covered.
• Cover bottles tightly with nonmetallic caps; contact with metal spoils the vinegar.
• Flavored vinegar tastes best when allowed to age a few weeks at room temperature. At this point, strain vinegar, and pour into sterilized bottles again with fresh herb sprigs that have been washed. Store vinegar in the refrigerator.

FRESH FROM THE FREEZER

Freezing is no doubt the easiest method of food preservation if you have the space for it. It's a quick and reliable way to put up fresh produce without much fuss.

The key is to select the best quality produce, and freeze it as soon as possible after harvest in the proper containers. The quicker the produce is prepared and frozen, the better the flavor will be. Salt is added for flavor only and is not necessary to prevent spoilage.

Equipment

Whether you're freezing fruits or vegetables, you'll need the following items to help prepare the produce: a sharp knife, cutting board, colander, kitchen scales, measuring cups, and sturdy plastic freezer containers. To freeze vegetables, you'll also need equipment for blanching, such as a blancher or a large Dutch oven or saucepan with a wire-mesh basket, and a kitchen timer. It's also a good idea to have a large bowl on hand to fill with ice water for cooling the blanched vegetables.

Freezer containers come in many forms. Packaging materials must be moisture- and vapor-resistant, as well as durable and leakproof. They should be easy to seal and to mark. Good freezer containers include aluminum, glass, plastic, tin, and heavy-duty aluminum foil. Heavy-duty foil, however, is mainly recommended as an overwrap since it can be easily punctured. Wax paper is not a recommended freezer wrap because it's not moisture-resistant.

Rigid containers made of plastic or glass are recommended for foods packed in liquid. Select freezer containers with straight sides and flat tops for easy stacking. Lids for rigid containers should be tight fitting and can be reinforced with freezer tape. Wide-mouth containers are convenient for easy removal of partially thawed food.

Plastic freezer bags are the best flexible packaging for dry-pack vegetables and fruits. You can also use them for liquid packs. See the chart on the following page to determine the recommended headspace for each type of freezer container.

Freezing Vegetables

Start with just-harvested vegetables at their peak and prepare amounts to fill only a few containers at a time. Discard any damaged produce. Wash and drain the vegetables before peeling or shelling, and prepare them according to chart directions on page 418.

For the best quality frozen product, most vegetables should be *blanched* before canning. Blanching is heating or scalding vegetables in boiling water for a short period of time to inactivate natural enzymes that cause loss of flavor, color, and texture. Blanching also heightens and sets vegetables' color and flavor, helps retain nutrients, and destroys surface microorganisms.

Be sure to follow the recommended blanching time for each vegetable. Overblanching causes a loss of color, flavor, and nutrients, while underblanching stimulates rather than inactivates damaging enzymes.

Cooling vegetables immediately and thoroughly after blanching is essential to halt the cooking process. Have a large bowl of ice water handy to plunge hot vegetables into to "shock" them and stop further cooking. Then drain vegetables well before packing to eliminate extra moisture which can cause a noticeable loss of quality during freezing.

For blanching, bring 1 gallon of water to a boil for every pound of prepared vegetables. (Use 2 gallons of water per pound of *leafy green* vegetables.) Place vegetables in a blanching basket, and submerge in boiling water. Cover and begin timing as chart on page 418 directs when water returns to a boil. Then remove basket from boiling water and immediately plunge into ice water for the same number of minutes recommended for blanching. Drain well.

After blanching, freeze vegetables in a *dry pack* or a *tray pack*. For a dry pack, place cooled vegetables in freezer containers, leaving the recommended headspace, and freeze.

In a tray pack, freeze vegetables individually so they remain loose in the frozen package. Simply spread vegetables in a single layer on a shallow tray or baking sheet, and freeze until firm. Begin checking vegetables every 10 minutes after 1 hour.

Package the individually frozen vegetables, leaving no headspace; seal, and freeze. See the Freezing Vegetables chart on page 418 for preparation and blanching times.

When cooking frozen vegetables, you get the best tasting results if you cook them in their frozen state. Leafy greens and corn on the cob are two exceptions which cook more evenly if allowed to partially thaw.

Freezing Fruit

Wash and drain fruit before peeling, pitting, or capping; do not soak the fruit.

Avoid copper or iron utensils in preparation of naturally acidic fruit. These materials can react with the acid in the fruit.

Enzymes in some fruit such as apples, peaches, pears, plums, figs, and persimmons can cause browning and loss of vitamin C when the peeled fruit is exposed to air. You can prevent this from happening by adding ascorbic-acid powder (we tested with Fruit Fresh).

Ascorbic-acid powder is most effective in controlling browning. Use ascorbic-acid powder according to instructions for each type of fruit pack listed. For crushed and pureed fruit, stir dissolved ascorbic-acid powder directly into fruit.

You can freeze fruit in one of three ways: unsweetened, with sugar, or in sugar syrup. Sugar is not added as a preservative, yet it does help fruit retain the best texture, color, and flavor.

Berries, blanched apples, rhubarb, and figs freeze quite well unsweetened. Directions for each type of pack are included in the following text. Preparation instructions and recommended packs for individual fruits are listed in the Freezing Fruits chart on page 419.

Syrup pack: While a 40% sugar syrup is recommended for most fruit, a lighter syrup can be used for mild-flavored fruit to keep from masking its flavor. A heavier, sweet syrup may be needed for tart fruit like sour cherries. Use the Sugar Syrups chart on this page for directions on making the different syrup concentrations.

Use just enough cold syrup to cover the fruit—usually ½ to ⅔ cup for each pint. Stir dissolved ascorbic-acid powder into syrup just before using to prevent fruit from darkening, if necessary.

When using rigid containers, place crumpled wax paper between the fruit and

lid to submerge fruit with syrup. Seal, label, and freeze.

Sugar pack: Spread fruit in a shallow tray, and sprinkle with ascorbic-acid powder dissolved in water to prevent darkening, if necessary. Sprinkle fruit with recommended amount of sugar, and let stand 10 to 15 minutes to draw out the juices and allow sugar to dissolve. Stir gently to coat fruit, and package with the juices. Seal, label, and freeze.

Unsweetened pack: For a *liquid* pack, you can freeze unsweetened fruit in water containing ascorbic-acid powder, if needed, or in unsweetened juice. Package as for syrup pack, using chilled liquid.

For unsweetened *dry pack*, place fruit in containers, leaving the recommended headspace, and freeze. Sprinkle ascorbic-acid powder dissolved in water over fruit before packing, if necessary.

You can also freeze fruit pieces separately in a *tray pack*; this makes it easy to measure frozen fruit for a recipe without thawing it. This is a good process to use, especially for fresh berries, if you're an avid pie baker. When you're ready to bake a fruit

---

HEADSPACE FOR FILLED FREEZER CONTAINERS

Liquid pack for vegetables or fruit packed in juice, sugar, syrup, or water

WIDE-MOUTH CONTAINERS

Pint	Quart
½ inch	1 inch

NARROW-MOUTH CONTAINERS

Pint	Quart
¾ inch	1½ inches

Dry pack for vegetables or fruit packed without added sugar or liquid

WIDE-MOUTH CONTAINERS

Pint	Quart
½ inch	½ inch

NARROW-MOUTH CONTAINERS

Pint	Quart
½ inch	½ inch

SUGAR SYRUPS FOR FREEZING FRUIT

TYPE OF SYRUP	PERCENT SYRUP	CUPS OF SUGAR	CUPS OF WATER	CUP YIELD
Very Light	10%	½	4	4½
Light	20%	1	4	4¾
Medium	30%	1¾	4	5
Heavy	40%	2¾	4	5⅓
Very Heavy	50%	4	4	6

Directions: Combine sugar and warm water, stirring until sugar dissolves. Chill. Use just enough cold syrup to cover fruit—usually ½ to ⅔ cup per pint.

pie, just pull out the frozen packs and the berries will be easy to measure.

To prepare a tray pack, spread fruit in a single layer on a tray; sprinkle with dissolved ascorbic-acid powder, if necessary. Place tray in freezer, and freeze just until fruit is firm; then package, leaving no headspace. Seal, label, and freeze.

Packaging the Fruit

Fruits will be most convenient to use if packed in small amounts to be used for a single meal or recipe. Don't use freezer containers larger than ½ gallon capacity. Food packed in larger containers than this freeze

too slowly to maintain a quality product. Have all the food cooled before packing to help speed freezing. Chill syrup or juice for liquid packs before using. Pack food tightly in containers to leave as little air as possible, but leave recommended headspace to allow for expansion during freezing.

With freezer bags, press all air from the bag, and seal securely.

When sealing food in rigid freezer containers, keep the edge free from food or moisture to ensure a good seal. Lids should be tight fitting and can be reinforced with freezer tape.

Freezing Tips

Survey available freezer space. Freeze only the amount of food that will freeze within 24 hours. Food is best frozen quickly; overloading your freezer slows the freezing rate. Check your freezer temperature to be sure it's set at 0° or below.

Vegetables and most fruits retain good quality in the freezer for eight to 12 months, citrus fruits for four to six months. Freeze food as soon as it is packaged, sealed, and

labeled. Leave some space between packages for air circulation. After 24 hours you can stack and move packages closer together.

FREEZING PROBLEMS AND SOLUTIONS

PROBLEM	CAUSE	PREVENTION
Freezer burn	•Torn or unsealed packages	•Be sure all packages are sealed tightly so no air can seep in.
	•Packaging not moisture- and vapor-resistant	•Use only packaging appropriate for freezing (see page 415).
	•Too much air in package	•Press out all air in wrapped foods. With containers use just the right size for the amount of food that will leave the proper headspace.
Gummy liquid in fruits	•Fruits frozen too slowly	•Freeze foods at 0°F or below immediately after packaging. Don't overload your freezer.
	•Freezer temperature too warm	•Always keep the temperature set at 0°F or below.
	•Fluctuating temperature	•Maintain a constant temperature of 0°F or below. Open door as infrequently as possible.
Grassy flavors in vegetables	•Not blanching vegetables before freezing	•Blanch all vegetables for the recommended times before freezing.
Green vegetables turn olive-brown	•Not blanching vegetables before freezing	•Blanch all vegetables as directed.
Mushy food	•Large ice crystals form on food, damaging the cell structure	•Freeze foods at 0°F or below immediately after packaging and maintain that temperature throughout storage.

FREEZING VEGETABLES

VEGETABLE	PREPARATION	BLANCHING TIME
Beans (butter, lima, and pinto)	Choose tender beans with well-filled pods. Shell and wash; sort according to size.	Small beans, 2 minutes; medium beans, 3 minutes; large beans, 4 minutes
Beans (green, snap, and wax)	Select tender young pods. Wash beans, and cut off tips. Cut lengthwise or into 1- or 2-inch lengths.	3 minutes
Corn (on the cob)	Husk corn, and remove silks; trim and wash.	Small ears, 7 minutes; medium ears, 9 minutes; large ears, 11 minutes
Corn (whole kernel)	Blanch ears first; then cut kernels from cob about ⅔ depth of kernels.	4 minutes
Corn (cream-style)	Blanch ears first. Cut off tips of kernels. Scrape cobs with back of a knife to remove juice and hearts of kernels.	4 minutes
Greens (beet, chard, collard, mustard, spinach, turnip)	Select tender, green leaves. Wash thoroughly, and remove woody stems.	Collards, 3 minutes; other greens, 2 minutes
Okra	Select tender green pods. Wash and sort according to size. Remove stems at end of seed cells. After blanching, leave pods whole or slice crosswise.	Small pods, 3 minutes; large pods, 4 minutes
Peas (black-eyed and field)	Select pods with tender, barely mature peas. Shell and wash peas; discard hard, immature, and overly mature ones.	2 minutes
Peas (green)	Select tender young peas. Shell and wash.	2 minutes
Peppers (green and sweet red)	Select crisp, tender, green or red pods. Wash peppers. Cut off tops; remove seeds and membrane. Dice peppers; cut into halves or cut into ½-inch strips or rings. Pack raw, or blanch, if desired.	(Blanching is optional.) Pepper halves, 3 minutes; strips or rings, 2 minutes
Peppers (hot)	Wash peppers; remove stems. Place in containers leaving no headspace.	Not required
Squash (summer)	Select young squash with small seeds and tender rind. Wash and cut into ½-inch slices.	2 minutes
Tomatoes	Raw: Dip tomatoes in boiling water 30 seconds to loosen skins. Core and peel. Chop or quarter tomatoes, or leave whole.	Stewed: Remove stem end and core from tomatoes; peel and quarter tomatoes. Cover and cook until tender (10 to 20 minutes). Place pan containing cooked tomatoes in cold water to cool.

FREEZING FRUITS

FRUIT	PREPARATION	TYPE OF PACK (SYRUP, SUGAR, UNSWEETENED, PUREE)	REMARKS
Apples	Wash, peel, and core. For sugar pack, apples may be steam-blanched 1½ to 2 minutes to retain shape and color.	Syrup: 40% Sugar: Use ½ cup sugar to 1 quart apples.	To prevent browning, use ½ teaspoon ascorbic-acid powder per quart of syrup for syrup pack. Sprinkle ¼ teaspoon ascorbic-acid powder mixed with ¼ cup water over each quart for sugar pack.
Blackberries, Dewberries, Raspberries	Select fully ripe berries. Wash quickly; remove caps, and drain.	Syrup: 40% or 50% Sugar: Use ¾ cup sugar to 1 quart berries. Unsweetened: dry pack or tray pack Puree: Use 1 cup sugar to 1 quart pureed berries.	Freezes especially well in unsweetened tray pack.
Blueberries, Huckleberries	Select fully ripe berries. For unsweetened pack, do not wash.	Unsweetened: dry pack Puree: Use 1 cup sugar to 1 quart pureed berries.	Wash berries frozen in unsweetened pack before using.
Figs	Select soft-ripe figs. Sort, wash, and cut off stems; do not peel. Halve or leave whole.	Syrup: 40% Unsweetened: dry or liquid pack	To prevent browning, use ¾ teaspoon ascorbic-acid powder per quart of syrup for syrup pack or per 1 quart water for unsweetened liquid pack. May use ½ cup lemon juice per quart syrup instead of ascorbic-acid powder.
Peaches, Nectarines	Select firm, ripe peaches. Peel; halve or slice.	Syrup: 40% Sugar: Use ⅔ cup sugar to 1 quart peaches. Unsweetened: liquid pack Puree: Use 1 cup sugar to 1 quart pureed peaches.	To prevent browning, use ½ teaspoon ascorbic-acid powder per quart of syrup for syrup pack or 1 teaspoon ascorbic-acid powder per quart of water for unsweetened pack. Sprinkle ¼ teaspoon ascorbic-acid powder mixed with ¼ cup water over each quart for sugar pack. Use ⅛ teaspoon ascorbic-acid powder per quart of puree.
Pears	Peel pears; cut in halves or quarters, and remove cores. Heat pears in boiling syrup 1 to 2 minutes. Drain and cool. Chill the syrup.	Syrup: 40%	To prevent browning, use ¾ teaspoon ascorbic-acid powder per quart of cold syrup.
Persimmons	Select orange-colored, soft-ripe persimmons. Peel, cut into quarters, and remove seeds. Press pulp through a sieve to puree.	Sugar: Use 1 cup sugar to 1 quart puree. Unsweetened: dry pack	To prevent browning, use ⅛ teaspoon ascorbic-acid powder per quart of puree.
Plums	Select firm, ripe plums. Sort and wash. Leave whole or cut into halves or quarters; remove pits.	Syrup: 40% to 50%	To prevent browning, use 1 teaspoon ascorbic-acid powder per quart of syrup.
Strawberries	Select fully ripe, firm, deep-red berries. Wash a few at a time; drain and remove caps.	Syrup: 50% Sugar: Use ¾ cup sugar to 1 quart whole berries.	Strawberries may be crushed or sliced for sugar pack.

White Bean Chili (page 437)

S O U P S
& S T E W S

Soup has soulful benefits. The aroma of a simmering soup or stew can restore your spirits. And soups and stews are great when made ahead because their flavor improves overnight. The secret to flavorful soups begins with the broth. Let our broth and stock basics inspire you toward the cooktop.

Equipment

Most soups need only a Dutch oven or stockpot to simmer. To begin you'll need the basics—an 8- or 10-quart stockpot for making stock and large-yield soups and a 3- or 4-quart heavy-bottomed pot for other soups. For making a rich brown stock, you'll need a roasting pan for one of its essential steps.

Sometimes an electric blender or food processor comes in handy for pureeing a soup's ingredients to a smooth texture. A large strainer and sieve (or the conical chinois) are needed for broth and stock. A fat separator is also recommended. A wooden spoon and a ladle are essential for stirring and serving soup. And a set of double-handled soup bowls and ovenproof bowls should cover your bases for serving soup, chowder, and chili.

Soup Servings

Our soup yields are given in cup amounts rather than numbers of servings so you can decide how much soup makes a serving. This will depend on which course of the meal the soup will be—appetizer, entrée, or even dessert. Allow ¾ to 1 cup soup when the soup is to be an appetizer or dessert. For an entrée, 2 cups is often satisfying.

Soups served as the main course tend to be chunkier, meatier recipes like chilies, gumbos, and gutsy stews. On the contrary, choose lighter, more delicate soups to serve as an appetizer. An appetizer soup should offer just enough to stimulate the appetite. And when spooning up a slightly sweet fruit soup, consider serving the soup in a variety of glass compotes or balloon wine glasses, especially when they're to be dessert.

Broth Options

Many recipes in this chapter call for broth. We leave it to you to choose between commercially canned broth, our homemade recipe on the next page, or bouillon cubes or granules. Dilute and dissolve granules and cubes according to directions. Some brands of soup are condensed and need to be diluted for use, while others are ready to serve. Be sure to use the exact size can that a recipe specifies. Keep in mind that commercial broth is saltier than homemade; always taste soup before adding seasoning.

Storing and Freezing Soup

Many soups take on a richer taste if refrigerated for a day to give the flavors time to blend and develop. This makes them a natural make-ahead suggestion for entertaining friends or simply feeding your family.

Most soups freeze well, particularly thick gumbos, chilies, and stews, which tend to have large yields and the need for storing leftovers. Package soups and stews in pint or quart plastic freezer containers or heavy-duty zip-top freezer bags. Be sure to label them with the recipe name, date, and amount. You can freeze soup up to three months. Thaw in refrigerator and then slowly reheat in a saucepan over low heat, stirring often. Dense soups tend to get thicker during storage. Add a little broth, milk, or water when reheating until you reach desired consistency.

We've included microwave directions for some of our simpler soups that have only a few steps and small yields. Using the microwave to make soups with large yields and more steps won't save you much time. Of course, the microwave's great for reheating small amounts of any soup.

BROTH & STOCK

Broth is one of the simplest soups to make, has universal appeal, and forms the flavor base for a variety of sauces and gravies. *Broth* is a thin, clear liquid resulting from simmering meat, poultry, vegetables, herbs, or seafood in water. A big difference between broth and stock is that broth counts on flavor from meat, while *stock* is made using more bones than meat. The bones contribute gelatin, which adds richness and body to stock. So when you're choosing meat or bones for making soup, keep in mind that meat adds flavor and bones contribute body.

Broth simmers less than stock and has a fresher, lighter flavor. Broth preparation is simple. Just wash and cut vegetables; there's no need to scrape or trim them since they'll be removed after cooking. Vegetables and herbs add depth of flavor; carrots and onions deepen the color and add sweetness. If you want to be healthy, trim fat from meat before adding meat to the pot.

After bringing ingredients to a boil, reduce the heat, and let the mixture simmer gently. If the liquid is allowed to boil, the broth will be cloudy. As the broth simmers, remove any scum that collects on the surface.

After broth has cooked, strain it through several thicknesses of cheesecloth to remove meat, vegetables, and herbs. Allow broth to cool completely so the fat can rise to the surface and solidify. Chilling the broth is a quick way to solidify the fat. Then just spoon hardened fat off the top of the broth with a large spoon. The same principal applies to stock; see photo 4 on opposite page to show you how easily it's done.

You can refrigerate fresh broth up to three days or freeze it up to three months in containers of various sizes—anything from pint or quart containers to freezer bags to ice cube trays. Once cubes are frozen, you can easily transfer them to a plastic bag and refreeze. Fish stock is the exception; it needs to be used within two months of being frozen. Degrease broth and stock before freezing because frozen fat can turn rancid.

The characteristics of a good stock are flavor, body, and clarity. The best stock is made from mature vegetables cooked slowly to extract every bit of flavor. Stock provides richer taste and more body than broth.

A classic stock begins with bones, simmers for hours, and is then strained and reduced for rich results. If a stock tastes weak after you've strained it, just discard the fat, and simmer stock briskly again to reduce the water content and to make the flavor more concentrated.

Chicken Broth

◄ HEALTHY • MAKE AHEAD ►

PREP: 10 MINUTES   COOK: 1½ HOURS

Chicken broth is the basic component for a host of soups, sauces, and entrées. You can always buy it in a can or as granules, but it's also simple to make. This recipe makes a large quantity so you can freeze it for three months and thaw as needed.

6 pounds chicken pieces
2½ quarts water
3 stalks celery with leaves, quartered
2 medium onions, quartered
2 fresh thyme sprigs or ½ teaspoon dried thyme
1 bay leaf
1½ teaspoons salt
¾ teaspoon pepper

•Combine all ingredients in a large Dutch oven. Bring to a boil; cover, reduce heat, and simmer 1½ hours. Line a large wire-mesh strainer with a double layer of cheesecloth; place in a large bowl. Pour broth through strainer, discarding chicken pieces, vegetables, and herbs. Cover broth, and chill thoroughly. Skim and discard solidified fat from top of broth.
•Store broth in a tightly covered container in the refrigerator up to 3 days or freeze up to 3 months. Thaw and use as directed in recipes that call for chicken broth. Yield: 10 cups.
Per cup: Calories 22 Fat 0.0g
Cholesterol 0mg Sodium 356mg

Lemon-Egg Drop Soup

◄ QUICK ►

PREP: 5 MINUTES   COOK: 20 MINUTES

Discover how easy it is to make Egg Drop Soup just like you'd order in a restaurant. The key is to slowly stir beaten eggs into a simmering seasoned broth.

5 cups Chicken Broth (at left) or 3 (14½-ounce) cans chicken broth
1 cup sliced fresh mushrooms
¼ cup fresh lemon juice
2 cloves garlic, halved
1 tablespoon soy sauce
⅛ teaspoon ground white pepper
2 large eggs, lightly beaten
Garnishes: lemon slices, chopped green onions

•Combine first 5 ingredients in a large saucepan, and bring to a boil. Cover, reduce heat, and simmer 15 minutes. Stir in white pepper.
•Slowly pour in beaten eggs, stirring constantly, until eggs form lacy strands. Immediately remove from heat; discard garlic. Ladle soup into bowls, and garnish, if desired. Yield: 6 cups.
Per 1-cup serving: Calories 66 Fat 2.9g
Cholesterol 71mg Sodium 876g

SOUP & STEW TIPS

•Be sure to save celery leaves from a bunch. The leaves add great flavor to a simmering soup.
•Use a bulb baster to remove fat from the surface of broth, soup, or stew.
•For another fat-skimming option, wrap an ice cube in damp cheesecloth and skim it over the surface of a soup. The fat will congeal on contact with the ice; then fat is easily removed.
•If you've added too much salt to a soup, simply drop in a peeled, raw potato and cook a few minutes. Then remove the potato before serving the soup.
•A few slices of bacon will add a meaty depth of flavor to soups.

Beef Stock

PREP: 19 MINUTES   COOK: 7 HOURS

Some things in life you just can't rush—homemade soup stock is one of them. A good, rich stock begins by roasting bones and vegetables to draw out a natural caramelized flavor. The roasted essence then simmers in the dark stock for several hours to develop its characteristic flavor.

5 pounds beef bones
2 large carrots, quartered
3 large onions, quartered
2 stalks celery, quartered
4 quarts cold water, divided
¼ cup tomato paste
8 fresh parsley sprigs
4 fresh thyme sprigs
½ teaspoon black peppercorns
2 bay leaves
3 cloves garlic, crushed

•Place first 4 ingredients in a large roasting pan (photo 1); roast, uncovered, at 500° for 45 minutes to 1 hour or until well browned, turning occasionally (photo 2).
•Transfer bones and vegetables to a stockpot. Add 2 cups water to roasting pan; bring to a boil over medium-high heat, stirring to loosen bits that cling to bottom of pan (photo 3); pour into stockpot. Add remaining 3½ quarts water and tomato paste to stockpot. Tie parsley, thyme, and remaining ingredients in a bundle. Add to stockpot.
•Bring to a simmer; simmer, partially covered, 6 hours. Skim fat and foam off top of stock after first 10 minutes of simmering.
•Line a large wire-mesh strainer with a double layer of cheesecloth; place over a large bowl. Use a ladle to strain stock. Discard solids. (Using a ladle and avoiding sediment in bottom of pot prevents cloudiness.) Cool stock slightly.

STOCK BASICS

•Use a narrow and high stockpot to prevent excessive evaporation during cooking.
•Start with cold water to cover ingredients. Bring stock slowly just to a boil; cook at a gentle simmer.
•Never rush a stock by boiling it.
•Simmer stock partially covered.
•Never add salt to stock as it's simmering. The long simmering time would concentrate the salt and ruin the resulting stock.

•Cover and chill; discard solidified fat from top of stock (photo 4). Store stock in a tightly covered container in refrigerator up to 3 days or freeze up to 3 months. Yield: 8 cups.
Per cup: Calories 72 Fat 0.4g
Cholesterol 0mg Sodium 28mg

1. Spread beef bones and vegetable pieces in a roasting pan.

2. Roast at 500° for 45 minutes or until well browned. Remove bones and vegetables to stockpot.

3. Add water to pan; bring to a boil, stirring to loosen bits that cling to pan. Then add to stockpot.

4. Cool and chill stock; discard solidified fat from top, using a large spoon.

CREAMS & PUREES

A cream or pureed soup is ideal to serve as an appetizer or as a light supper along with a green salad. You'll need a food processor or electric blender to obtain that luxuriously smooth texture known to this family of rich soups. Be careful not to overload the equipment though, because the hot liquid can overflow and leak out. It's always safer to puree soups in batches, filling the blender or processor about half full each time.

The smooth texture of these soups suggests that they can be "sipping soups," rather than necessarily being served from a soup bowl. Depending on the formality of the meal, options range from hefty mugs to delicate wine glasses.

Cream soups and purees usually benefit from a garnish on top, whether it's a dollop of sour cream, a sprinkling of cheese, or a sprig of fresh herb. Simple is best so that the garnish doesn't overpower the soup.

Some of these soups are served hot; some are best served cold. And some can be served at either temperature, depending on your menu and the time of year. A loose rule of thumb says to serve cold soups in the summer, warm soups during winter.

Cream of Broccoli Soup

PREP: 15 MINUTES

COOK: 1 HOUR AND 10 MINUTES

3 (10¾-ounce) cans chicken broth,
   undiluted
1 large carrot, scraped and chopped
1 stalk celery, chopped
1 medium onion, chopped
1 medium-size baking potato, peeled and
   finely chopped
1 bay leaf
1½ pounds fresh broccoli, broken into
   flowerets, or 1 pound broccoli flowerets
2 cups half-and-half
½ teaspoon salt
⅛ teaspoon ground white pepper
¼ teaspoon curry powder (optional)

•Combine first 6 ingredients in a Dutch
oven; bring to a boil. Cover, reduce heat,
and simmer 25 minutes or until vegetables
are tender. Discard bay leaf.
•Chop broccoli; add to broth mixture. Bring
to a boil; cover, reduce heat, and simmer 20
minutes or until broccoli is tender.
•Remove from heat; pour half of broccoli
mixture into a large container, and set aside.
Process remaining broccoli mixture in an
electric blender or food processor until
smooth.
•Heat half-and-half in a small saucepan over
medium-low heat until hot. (Do not boil.)
Add 1 cup half-and-half to mixture in
blender. Process until smooth. Return
pureed mixture to Dutch oven. Repeat procedure with reserved broccoli mixture and
remaining half-and-half. Heat soup thoroughly. Add salt, pepper, and curry powder,
if desired. Yield: 9 cups.
Per 1-cup serving: Calories 124 Fat 7.0g
Cholesterol 20mg Sodium 509mg

Creamy Cucumber Soup

◄ QUICK • MAKE AHEAD ►
◄ FAMILY FAVORITE ►

PREP: 15 MINUTES

*If you enjoy the crisp, fresh qualities of a
cucumber, this creamy light soup is just your
style. It's quick to make and tastes better the
longer you let it chill.*

2 cucumbers, peeled, seeded, and coarsely
   chopped
1 green onion, coarsely chopped
1 tablespoon lemon juice
1 cup half-and-half
1 (16-ounce) carton sour cream
1 tablespoon minced fresh dill or 1
   teaspoon dried dillweed
½ teaspoon salt
¼ teaspoon ground white pepper
Dash of hot sauce
Fresh dill sprigs (optional)

•Process first 3 ingredients in a food processor 2 minutes or until smooth, stopping once
to scrape down sides. Transfer pureed mixture to a serving bowl; gently stir in half-and-
half and next 5 ingredients. Cover and chill.
Stir before serving; garnish, if desired. Yield:
4½ cups.
Per ¾-cup serving: Calories 224 Fat 20.6g
Cholesterol 48mg Sodium 254mg

Cream of Peanut Soup

PREP: 10 MINUTES   COOK: 42 MINUTES

4 stalks celery, chopped
1 large onion, chopped
½ cup butter or margarine, melted
¼ cup all-purpose flour
2 (14½-ounce) cans ready-to-serve
   chicken broth
1½ cups creamy peanut butter
¼ to ½ teaspoon pepper
½ teaspoon paprika
¼ teaspoon salt
2 cups milk
2 cups half-and-half

•Sauté celery and onion in butter in a large
saucepan over medium heat 5 minutes or
until tender. Add flour, stirring until smooth;
cook 1 minute, stirring constantly. Gradually
add chicken broth; cook over low heat 30
minutes, stirring occasionally.
•Remove from heat; pour mixture through a
large wire-mesh strainer into a bowl, discarding vegetables. Return to saucepan; stir in
peanut butter and next 3 ingredients.
Gradually add milk and half-and-half, stirring constantly; cook over low heat 5 minutes
or until thoroughly heated (do not boil).
Yield: 7 cups.
Per 1-cup serving: Calories 611 Fat 52.3g
Cholesterol 71mg Sodium 941mg

Cream of Mushroom Soup

PREP: 3 MINUTES   COOK: 35 MINUTES

*The "meaty" attribute of mushrooms is
evident in this rich appetizer soup enhanced
with cream and a little wine. The soup pairs
particularly well with a beef entrée.*

3 (8-ounce) packages sliced fresh
   mushrooms
1 medium onion, finely chopped
3 tablespoons butter, melted
½ cup all-purpose flour
2 (14½-ounce) cans ready-to-serve
   chicken broth
3 cups whipping cream
¼ cup dry white wine
1½ teaspoons salt
1 teaspoon dried tarragon
1 teaspoon Worcestershire sauce
¼ teaspoon freshly ground pepper

•Coarsely chop mushrooms, if desired. Sauté
mushrooms and onion in butter in a large
Dutch oven over medium heat 10 minutes
or until tender. Add flour, stirring until
smooth. Cook 1 minute, stirring constantly.
•Stir in broth and remaining ingredients.
Bring to a boil; reduce heat to medium-high.
Cook 20 minutes or until thickened, stirring
often. Yield: 10 cups.
Per 1-cup serving: Calories 338 Fat 30.7g
Cholesterol 107mg Sodium 696mg

Cream of Roasted Garlic Soup

PREP: 28 MINUTES

COOK: 1 HOUR AND 20 MINUTES

Roasted garlic gives a subtle sweet flavor to this superb soup thickened with potato. The rustic croutons add a welcome crunch, but the soup's fine solo, too.

2 large heads garlic
1 tablespoon olive oil
½ cup finely chopped shallots
2 tablespoons butter or margarine, melted
1½ cups buttermilk
1 cup whipping cream
½ cup cubed cooked red potato
½ teaspoon salt
½ teaspoon minced fresh thyme
Freshly ground pepper
Homemade Croutons (page 428)
Garnish: fresh thyme sprigs

•Cut off top one-fourth of each garlic head, and discard. Place garlic heads, cut side up, on aluminum foil, and drizzle with olive oil. Wrap foil around garlic heads, sealing foil at top. Bake at 350° for 1 hour. Remove from oven, and cool. Remove papery skin, and squeeze out soft garlic into a small bowl. Set garlic aside.

•Sauté shallots in butter in a saucepan over medium heat until tender. Stir in buttermilk and whipping cream. Bring just to a boil; reduce heat, and simmer, uncovered, 5 minutes. Remove from heat; set aside, and cool.

•Process garlic, buttermilk mixture, and potato in a food processor 1 minute or until smooth. Return pureed mixture to saucepan; stir in salt and minced thyme. Cook over medium heat until thoroughly heated, stirring often.

•To serve, ladle soup into individual soup bowls. Sprinkle with freshly ground pepper and Homemade Croutons. Garnish, if desired. Yield: 3 cups.

Per 1-cup serving: Calories 670 Fat 50.4g Cholesterol 134mg Sodium 988mg

Cream of Roasted Garlic Soup

Tomato Soup with Herbed Croutons

PREP:10 MINUTES   COOK: 50 MINUTES

½ cup chopped onion
3 tablespoons butter or margarine, melted
3 tablespoons all-purpose flour
1 cup chicken broth
1 (28-ounce) can Italian-style tomatoes, undrained
3 tablespoons tomato paste
1 tablespoon minced fresh parsley
1 tablespoon sugar
1 teaspoon salt
½ teaspoon dried basil
¼ teaspoon pepper
1 bay leaf
Herbed Croutons
Garnish: fresh basil sprigs

•Sauté onion in butter in a Dutch oven over medium-high heat 3 minutes or until tender. Reduce heat to low; add flour, stirring until smooth. Cook 1 minute, stirring constantly. Gradually add broth; cook over medium heat, stirring constantly, until thickened and bubbly.

•Add tomatoes and next 7 ingredients; stir well. Bring to a boil; cover, reduce heat, and simmer 30 minutes. Discard bay leaf.

•Process half of tomato mixture in an electric blender until smooth. Repeat procedure with remaining tomato mixture. To serve, ladle soup into individual serving bowls. Top each serving with Herbed Croutons, and garnish, if desired. Yield: 3½ cups.

Per ½ cup soup and 2 croutons: Calories 149 Fat 7.6g Cholesterol 18mg Sodium 859mg

Herbed Croutons

2 slices white bread
1 tablespoon butter or margarine, melted
1 tablespoon grated Parmesan cheese
½ teaspoon dried basil

•Trim and discard crusts from bread slices. Brush melted butter over bread; sprinkle with cheese and basil. Cut each slice into 4 squares; cut each square into 2 triangles. Place on an ungreased baking sheet; bake at 350° for 12 minutes or until croutons are dry and browned. Yield: 16 croutons.

Beer Cheese Soup

PREP: 1 MINUTE   COOK: 25 MINUTES

Enjoy the tang of beer and the smooth texture of melted cheese in the same bowl. This time-honored soup is wonderful with a sandwich.

¼ cup butter or margarine
¼ cup all-purpose flour
2 cups half-and-half
1 (12-ounce) can beer
1 (16-ounce) loaf process cheese spread, cubed
1 tablespoon Worcestershire sauce
¼ teaspoon ground red pepper
¼ teaspoon hot sauce
⅛ teaspoon salt
Ground red pepper

•Melt butter in a Dutch oven or large saucepan over medium-low heat; add flour, stirring until smooth. Cook 1 minute, stirring constantly. Gradually add half-and-half and beer; cook over medium heat, stirring constantly with a wire whisk, until thickened.
•Add cheese; cook over medium heat until cheese melts. Stir in Worcestershire sauce, ¼ teaspoon red pepper, hot sauce, and salt. Ladle into bowls. Sprinkle with additional red pepper before serving. Yield: 5 cups.

Per 1-cup serving: Calories 508 Fat 39.6g
Cholesterol 121mg Sodium 1599mg

Vichyssoise

PREP: 20 MINUTES   COOK: 42 MINUTES

1 large leek
½ cup chopped onion
2 tablespoons butter or margarine, melted
3 medium potatoes, peeled and sliced
2 cups chicken broth
1½ cups milk
¼ teaspoon salt
¼ teaspoon ground white pepper
1 cup whipping cream
Garnish: chopped fresh chives

•Remove and discard root, tough outer leaves, and green top from leek. Thinly slice remaining white portion of leek. Sauté leek and onion in butter in a large saucepan over low heat until tender. Stir in potato and broth; bring to a boil. Cover, reduce heat, and simmer 35 minutes or until potato is tender.
•Process half of mixture in a food processor or blender until smooth. Repeat procedure with remaining half of potato mixture.
•Return pureed mixture to saucepan; stir in milk, salt, and pepper. Cook over medium heat until thoroughly heated, stirring often. Cool; stir in whipping cream. Cover and chill. Ladle chilled soup into individual bowls or cover and store in refrigerator up to 24 hours. Garnish, if desired. Yield: 6 cups.

Per 1-cup serving: Calories 249 Fat 21.0g
Cholesterol 73mg Sodium 447mg

Rich Wild Rice Soup

PREP: 15 MINUTES   COOK: 25 MINUTES

¾ cup butter or margarine, divided
1 large onion, finely chopped
3 cups finely chopped celery with leaves
1 (8-ounce) package sliced fresh mushrooms
¼ cup all-purpose flour
1 teaspoon salt
½ teaspoon pepper
2½ cups milk
1½ cups half-and-half
1¾ cups cooked long-grain-and-wild rice mix
Garnish: celery leaves

•Melt ½ cup butter in a skillet over medium heat; add onion, and cook, stirring constantly, until tender. Add chopped celery and mushrooms; cook until tender. Set aside.
•Melt remaining ¼ cup butter in a Dutch oven. Add flour, salt, and pepper; stir until smooth. Cook 1 minute, stirring constantly. Gradually add milk and half-and-half; cook over medium heat, stirring constantly, until thickened. Stir in vegetables and rice; reduce heat to low, and simmer 15 minutes. Garnish, if desired. Yield: 8 cups.

Per 1-cup serving: Calories 341 Fat 25.8g
Cholesterol 75mg Sodium 713mg

FRUIT SOUPS

Fruit soups make a delicate appetizer or a light dessert idea. They're commonly served well chilled. Serve them in glass dishes or compotes to show off the beautiful pale color that hints at the soup's fruit. A simple fresh mint sprig or a drizzle of cream can be the finishing touch. And if the soup's dessert, add a crisp cookie on the side.

Chilled Rosy Berry Soup

PREP: 12 MINUTES   COOK: 20 MINUTES
CHILL: 8 HOURS

2 (10-ounce) packages frozen raspberries or strawberries, thawed
2 cups dry red wine
2½ cups water
1 (3-inch) stick cinnamon
¼ cup sugar
2 tablespoons cornstarch
⅓ cup whipping cream

•Combine first 5 ingredients in a stainless steel saucepan (mixture will discolor aluminum). Bring to a boil; reduce heat, and simmer 15 minutes. Press raspberry mixture through a wire-mesh strainer into a bowl, discarding seeds; return to saucepan.
•Combine cornstarch and ¼ cup raspberry liquid; stir until smooth. Bring remaining liquid to a boil. Reduce heat to low; stir in cornstarch mixture. Cook, stirring constantly, until slightly thickened. Pour into a large bowl. Cover and chill 8 hours. Ladle into bowls. Drizzle cream in soup; swirl. Yield: 5 cups.

Per 1-cup serving: Calories 151 Fat 6.0g
Cholesterol 22mg Sodium 16mg

Cold Peach Soup

◄ MAKE AHEAD ►

PREP: 30 MINUTES   CHILL: 2 HOURS

1½ pounds peeled, sliced fresh peaches
1 (8-ounce) carton sour cream
1 (8-ounce) carton peach yogurt
1½ cups fresh orange juice
1 cup pineapple juice
1 tablespoon fresh lemon juice
2 tablespoons sugar
Garnish: fresh mint sprigs

•Process peaches in a food processor until smooth. Add sour cream and next 4 ingredients; process until mixture is smooth and blended.
•Press peach mixture through a wire-mesh strainer or several layers of cheesecloth into a large bowl. Add sugar, stirring well. Cover and chill 2 hours. Ladle soup into individual serving bowls; garnish, if desired. Yield: 8 cups.

Per 1-cup serving: Calories 176 Fat 6.4g Cholesterol 14mg Sodium 31mg

JUST PEACHY

Wait until peaches are in season in the summer to whip up this delightful and easy fruit soup. It's tangy and slightly sweet. Serve it as an appetizer or dessert at a ladies' luncheon.

VEGETABLE & BEAN SOUPS

These hearty soups have many benefits. They can be cooked ahead and easily reheated. They're made from pantry ingredients, dried peas and beans, and often leftovers. And they provide plenty of protein and other nutrients depending on the vegetables included.

When you add vegetables to soup, remember that they don't all cook in the same amount of time. First add the thickest vegetables that take the longest to cook. Then add remaining vegetables as the recipe directs. Be careful to cut like vegetables the same size so they'll cook evenly. Add frozen vegetables after fresh (no need to thaw them). Add canned vegetables last, and cook just until heated.

French Onion Soup

PREP: 15 MINUTES   COOK: 37 MINUTES

French Onion Soup has a double dose of cheese—a slice of Swiss and a sprinkle of Parmesan.

4 large onions, thinly sliced and separated into rings
½ cup butter or margarine, melted
2¾ cups Beef Stock (page 423) or 2 (10½-ounce) cans ready-to-serve beef broth, undiluted
2 cups water
¼ cup dry white wine
¼ teaspoon pepper
8 (¾-inch-thick) slices French bread, toasted
8 slices Swiss cheese
½ cup grated Parmesan cheese

•Sauté onion in butter in a Dutch oven over medium heat 20 minutes or until tender. Gradually add beef broth and next 3 ingredients. Bring to a boil; reduce heat, and simmer, uncovered, 15 minutes.
•Place eight ovenproof serving bowls on a baking sheet. Place 1 bread slice in each bowl; ladle soup over bread. Top with 1 cheese slice; sprinkle with Parmesan cheese. Broil 5½ inches from heat until cheese melts. Yield: 8 cups.

Per 1-cup serving: Calories 317 Fat 18.8g Cholesterol 51mg Sodium 837mg

Gazpacho

◄ HEALTHY • FAMILY FAVORITE ►
◄ MAKE AHEAD ►

PREP: 15 MINUTES   CHILL: 6 HOURS

Gazpacho is a refreshing Spanish soup that contains all the best things your garden has to offer.

1 (10¾-ounce) can tomato soup, undiluted
1½ cups tomato juice
1¼ cups water
½ to 1 cup chopped cucumber
½ to 1 cup chopped tomato
½ cup chopped green pepper
½ cup chopped onion
3 tablespoons wine vinegar or Italian dressing
1 tablespoon lemon or lime juice
1 clove garlic, minced
¼ teaspoon pepper
¼ teaspoon hot sauce

•Combine all ingredients; cover and chill at least 6 hours. Yield: 6 cups.

Per 1-cup serving: Calories 60 Fat 0.9g Cholesterol 0mg Sodium 578mg

Quick Vegetable Soup

◄ QUICK • FAMILY FAVORITE ►

PREP: 4 MINUTES   COOK: 25 MINUTES

This version of vegetable soup may fast become one of your favorites because it tastes great. It's easy, too. You probably have the ingredients on hand to get started. Don't miss the beefy variation. You can add leftover chopped cooked roast beef, too.

1 (14½-ounce) can stewed tomatoes, undrained
1 (8-ounce) can tomato sauce
1 (10-ounce) package frozen mixed vegetables
2 cups water
1½ teaspoons beef bouillon granules
⅛ teaspoon freshly ground pepper

•Combine all ingredients in a Dutch oven. Bring to a boil; cover, reduce heat, and simmer 20 minutes, stirring occasionally. Yield: 7 cups.

Per 1-cup serving: Calories 59 Fat 0.6g Cholesterol 0mg Sodium 650mg

Quick Vegetable-Beef Soup: Brown 1 pound ground chuck in a large skillet, stirring until it crumbles. Drain. Add to soup, and bring to a simmer.

Fresh Vegetable Soup

PREP: 20 MINUTES   CHILL: 8 HOURS

COOK: 2 HOURS

1 (1-pound) meaty beef shank bone
2½ quarts water
1 (16-ounce) can stewed tomatoes,
      undrained and coarsely chopped
1½ cups fresh or frozen lima beans
1 cup cut corn
½ cup chopped onion
1 large potato, peeled and cubed
1 large carrot, scraped and sliced
1 tablespoon brown sugar (optional)
1 teaspoon salt
1 teaspoon dried Italian seasoning
½ teaspoon pepper
½ teaspoon hot sauce
1 bay leaf
1½ tablespoons all-purpose flour
1½ tablespoons water

•Bring shank bone and 2½ quarts water in a large Dutch oven to a boil. Cover, reduce heat, and simmer 1 hour. Cover and chill 8 hours.
•Discard solidified fat on top of broth. Strain broth; return to Dutch oven. Bring to a boil; add tomatoes and next 11 ingredients. Reduce heat, and simmer, uncovered, 1 hour.
•Combine flour and water, stirring to make a paste; add to soup, stirring until blended. Cook, stirring constantly, until soup thickens. Discard bay leaf. Yield: 10 cups.
Per 1-cup serving: Calories 109 Fat 0.6g
Cholesterol 0mg Sodium 368 mg

Split Pea Soup

PREP: 15 MINUTES   COOK: 3 HOURS

1 (16-ounce) package dried green split peas
2 quarts water
1 medium onion, chopped
1 medium potato, peeled and diced
1 cup chopped celery
1 large meaty ham bone
1 clove garlic, minced
1 teaspoon salt
¼ teaspoon pepper
1 bay leaf
2 cups chopped carrot
Homemade Croutons

•Sort and rinse peas; place in a Dutch oven. Cover with water 2 inches above peas; let soak overnight. Drain; add 2 quarts water and next 9 ingredients. Bring to a boil; cover, reduce heat, and simmer 2½ hours, stirring occasionally. Remove ham bone; cut off meat, and dice. Discard bone and bay leaf. Let soup cool slightly.
•Process mixture in batches in an electric blender until smooth. Return mixture and meat to Dutch oven; cover and simmer 5 minutes or until thoroughly heated. Sprinkle each serving with Homemade Croutons. Yield: 1 gallon.
Per 1 cup soup and ¼ cup croutons: Calories 188
Fat 4.8g Cholesterol 9mg Sodium 497mg

Homemade Croutons

3 to 4 tablespoons olive oil
1 clove garlic, minced
½ teaspoon salt
½ teaspoon pepper
6 (1-inch) slices French bread, cubed

•Combine all ingredients in a large zip-top plastic bag; seal and shake well. Spread cubes on a 15- x 10-inch jellyroll pan; bake at 425° for 10 minutes, stirring after 5 minutes. Yield: 4 cups.

Baked Potato Soup

PREP: 15 MINUTES

COOK: 1 HOUR AND 12 MINUTES

You might think you're eating a loaded baked potato when you first spoon into this Baked Potato Soup. It's a unique recipe you'll want to make for friends on many a wintry evening.

4 large baking potatoes
⅔ cup butter or margarine
⅔ cup all-purpose flour
6 cups milk
¾ teaspoon salt
½ teaspoon pepper
1½ cups (6 ounces) shredded Cheddar cheese, divided
12 slices bacon, cooked, crumbled, and divided
4 green onions, chopped and divided
1 (8-ounce) carton sour cream

•Wash potatoes; prick several times with a fork. Bake at 400° for 1 hour or until done; cool. Cut potatoes in half lengthwise; scoop out pulp, and reserve. Discard shells.
•Melt butter in a Dutch oven over low heat; add flour, stirring until smooth. Cook 1 minute, stirring constantly. Gradually add milk; cook over medium heat, stirring constantly, until thickened and bubbly.
•Stir in potato, salt, pepper, 1 cup cheese, ½ cup bacon, and 2 tablespoons green onions; cook until heated (do not boil). Stir in sour cream; cook just until heated (do not boil). Sprinkle servings with remaining cheese, bacon, and green onions. Yield: 10 cups.
Per 1-cup serving: Calories 407 Fat 31.6g
Cholesterol 88mg Sodium 629mg

Hearty Lentil Soup

PREP: 20 MINUTES   COOK: 55 MINUTES

A splash of balsamic vinegar enhances this soup packed with brown rice and lentils.

8 cups Beef Stock (page 423) or canned beef broth
3 large carrots, scraped and diced
1 (28-ounce) can tomatoes, undrained and chopped
1½ cups dried lentils, rinsed and sorted
1 cup uncooked brown rice
1 onion, chopped (about 1 cup)
1 stalk celery, chopped (about ½ cup)
3 cloves garlic, minced
2 bay leaves
½ teaspoon dried basil
½ teaspoon dried oregano
¼ teaspoon dried thyme
½ cup chopped fresh parsley
2 tablespoons balsamic vinegar
1 teaspoon salt
½ teaspoon pepper
Garnish: grated Parmesan cheese

•Bring broth to a boil in a large Dutch oven. Add carrot and next 10 ingredients; stir well. Bring to a boil; cover, reduce heat, and simmer 45 minutes. Stir in parsley and next 3 ingredients. Discard bay leaves before serving. Garnish, if desired. Yield: 12 cups.
Per 1-cup serving: Calories 153 Fat 0.6g
Cholesterol 0mg Sodium 1299mg

Adding egg white to soup: Slowly pour egg white into Hot-and-Sour Soup, gently stirring the soup.

Hot-and-Sour Soup

PREP: 10 MINUTES   COOK: 23 MINUTES

1 (0.5-ounce) package dried wood ear mushrooms
1 cup sliced fresh mushrooms
3 (14½-ounce) cans ready-to-serve chicken broth
2 teaspoons minced fresh ginger
1 (8-ounce) can bamboo shoots, drained and cut into thin strips
3 tablespoons rice vinegar
3 tablespoons soy sauce
¼ teaspoon hot sauce
¼ teaspoon pepper
1 egg white, lightly beaten
3 green onions, sliced
½ (16-ounce) package firm tofu, drained well and cut into cubes
1 tablespoon cornstarch
¼ cup water

•Rehydrate wood ear mushrooms according to package directions; coarsely chop.
•Combine mushrooms, broth, and ginger in a Dutch oven; bring to a boil. Add bamboo shoots; reduce heat, and simmer 5 minutes.
•Add rice vinegar and next 3 ingredients; return to a boil. Slowly pour egg white into soup, stirring constantly (see photo). (The egg white forms lacy strands as it cooks.) Stir in green onions and tofu.
•Combine cornstarch and water, stirring until smooth. Add to soup, and return to a boil; boil 1 minute, stirring gently. Yield: 7 cups.
Per 1-cup serving: Calories 104 Fat 4.3g
Cholesterol 0mg Sodium 1043mg

Minestrone

PREP: 15 MINUTES   COOK: 35 MINUTES

Minestrone is a traditional Italian soup that contains enough protein from pasta, beans, and cheese to be a complete meal.

1 cup thinly sliced carrot
1 cup thinly sliced celery
1 cup chopped onion
1 clove garlic, crushed
2 tablespoons butter or margarine, melted
9 medium tomatoes, peeled and chopped
2 teaspoons salt
1 teaspoon dried oregano
1 teaspoon dried basil
½ teaspoon pepper
2 (14½-ounce) cans ready-to-serve beef broth
1 (16-ounce) can navy beans, undrained
1 (15-ounce) can kidney beans, undrained
1 large zucchini, cut in half lengthwise and sliced
1 cup uncooked elbow macaroni
¼ cup chopped fresh parsley
Freshly grated Parmesan cheese (optional)

•Sauté first 4 ingredients in butter in a Dutch oven over medium-high heat until crisp-tender. Add tomato and next 4 ingredients. Bring to a boil; cover, reduce heat, and simmer 15 minutes, stirring occasionally.
•Stir in beef broth and next 5 ingredients. Bring to a boil; cover, reduce heat, and simmer 15 minutes or until macaroni is tender. Sprinkle each serving with Parmesan cheese, if desired. Yield: 14 cups.
Per 1-cup serving: Calories 137 Fat 2.3g
Cholesterol 4mg Sodium 943mg

Cassoulet

**PREP: 15 MINUTES   STAND: 1 HOUR
COOK: 3 HOURS**

Meats and white beans baked together in a stewlike casserole define the classic French cassoulet (ka-soo-LAY). It's peasant food meant to be eaten with gusto, using crusty bread to mop up the broth.

2 cups dried Great Northern beans
8 cups water
2 tablespoons olive oil
1 pound boneless center-cut pork chops
8 slices thick-cut smoked bacon, chopped
2 medium onions, chopped
8 cloves garlic, halved
1 tablespoon chopped fresh thyme
¼ cup tomato paste
8 cups chicken broth
1 cup dry white wine
1 cup fresh French breadcrumbs (homemade)
1 tablespoon butter or margarine, melted

•Sort and rinse beans; combine beans and 8 cups water in a Dutch oven. Bring to a boil; cover, reduce heat, and simmer 2 minutes. Remove from heat. Let stand 1 hour; drain.
•Heat oil in a Dutch oven over medium-high heat; add pork chops. Cook 4 minutes on each side or until browned. Remove pork from Dutch oven, reserving drippings in pan. Cool pork slightly, and chop. Cover and refrigerate.
•Cook bacon in reserved pork drippings in Dutch oven until crisp. Add onion, and cook 5 minutes or until tender. Add beans, garlic, and next 3 ingredients. Bring to a boil; cover, reduce heat, and simmer 1 hour or until beans are almost tender. Drain; reserve bean mixture and 3 cups broth separately.
•Return bean mixture to Dutch oven or other ovenproof cookware; add reserved pork, 3 cups reserved broth, and wine. Cover and bake at 350° for 1 hour and 15 minutes or until most of liquid has been absorbed.
•Combine breadcrumbs and butter; toss. Sprinkle over bean mixture; bake, uncovered, 20 minutes or until crumbs are golden. Yield: 8 cups.
Per 1-cup serving: Calories 504 Fat 23.3g
Cholesterol 54mg Sodium 1193mg

Black Bean Soup

PREP: 1 HOUR AND 5 MINUTES
COOK: 3 HOURS AND 10 MINUTES

1 pound dried black beans
3 (14½-ounce) cans ready-to-serve chicken broth
2 cups chopped onion
1 tablespoon minced garlic
2 tablespoons vegetable oil
1 (10-ounce) can diced tomatoes and green chiles, undrained
½ cup lemon juice
½ teaspoon pepper
1 teaspoon hot sauce
1 (8-ounce) carton sour cream

• Sort and rinse beans; place in a Dutch oven. Cover with water 2 inches above beans.
• Bring beans to a boil; cover, remove from heat, and let stand 1 hour. Drain beans, and return to Dutch oven.
• Add chicken broth to beans in Dutch oven. Partially cover, and cook over medium-low heat 3 hours or until beans are tender, stirring occasionally.
• Sauté chopped onion and garlic in hot oil in a large skillet over medium-high heat until tender.
• Reduce heat to medium; stir in tomatoes and next 3 ingredients. Cook 5 more minutes.
• Process tomato mixture and 2 cups beans in a food processor, pulsing 3 times or until mixture is blended. Stir into remaining beans in Dutch oven. Ladle into soup bowls, and top each serving with sour cream. Yield: 7 cups.
Per 1-cup serving: Calories 386 Fat 12.7g Cholesterol 14mg Sodium 782mg

MEAT & SEAFOOD SOUPS & GUMBOS

These are hearty soups packed full of chunks of meat and seafood swimming in rich stock or broth. Serve these soups hot with crusty bread.

Use fresh crab and shrimp for optimum flavor in the seafood soups. Seafood soups are stunning when served in shallow, broad-rimmed bowls.

Let our series of photos on page 432 walk you through the steps of making a rich brown roux, the necessary beginning for a great gumbo. A roux, which is a mixture of equal parts fat and flour, is the thickening agent of choice for traditional gumbo. Cook a roux long and slowly to its dark brown stage; this gives gumbo its characteristic color and nutty flavor. When you cook a roux to this stage, it loses some of its thickening power, so you'll often see gumbo filé (a powdered thickener) served at the table. (Filé is added after cooking is complete because filé becomes stringy if it's heated.) Many gumbo recipes contain okra, which is a natural thickener as well.

Chunky Chicken-Noodle Soup

PREP: 15 MINUTES
COOK: 1 HOUR AND 10 MINUTES

1 (3-pound) broiler-fryer, skinned, or 2½ pounds chicken pieces
6 cups water
3 fresh celery leaves
¼ teaspoon dried thyme
⅓ cup sliced green onions
½ cup sliced celery
½ cup sliced carrot
2 tablespoons minced fresh parsley
½ teaspoon salt
¼ teaspoon coarsely ground pepper
1 teaspoon chicken bouillon granules or 1 chicken bouillon cube
1 cup uncooked fine egg noodles
1 bay leaf
Coarsely ground pepper (optional)

• Combine first 4 ingredients in a Dutch oven; bring to a boil. Cover, reduce heat, and simmer 45 minutes. Remove chicken from broth, and cool.
• Strain broth; discard celery leaves and solidified fat. Return broth to Dutch oven; add green onions and next 8 ingredients. Cover and simmer 20 minutes.
• Bone and chop chicken; add to broth. Cook 5 more minutes. Discard bay leaf. Sprinkle soup with pepper, if desired. Yield: 7 cups.
Per 1-cup serving: Calories 173 Fat 5.7g Cholesterol 70mg Sodium 360mg

Mulligatawny Soup

PREP: 21 MINUTES   COOK: 39 MINUTES

Mulligatawny Soup has roots in India. It's a broth-based soup highly seasoned with curry and flavored further with chicken, coconut, and light cream.

½ cup diced onion
1 cup diced celery
1 cup diced carrot
3 tablespoons vegetable oil
1½ tablespoons all-purpose flour
1 tablespoon curry powder
1 (32-ounce) carton ready-to-serve chicken broth
1½ cups diced cooked chicken
1 bay leaf
1 teaspoon salt
¼ teaspoon pepper
⅛ teaspoon dried thyme
½ teaspoon grated lemon rind
½ cup half-and-half, warmed
1¼ cups hot cooked rice
¼ cup flaked coconut

- Sauté first 3 ingredients in hot oil in a Dutch oven over medium-high heat until tender. Stir in flour and curry powder; cook over medium heat 3 minutes, stirring constantly. Gradually add broth; bring to a boil. Reduce heat, and simmer, uncovered, 15 minutes.
- Add chicken and next 5 ingredients; simmer, uncovered, 15 minutes. Discard bay leaf. Stir in warm half-and-half.
- Ladle soup over rice in individual soup bowls. Top with coconut. Yield: 5 cups.

Per 1-cup serving: Calories 348 Fat 17.6g
Cholesterol 49mg Sodium 1362mg

Spicy Thai Shrimp Soup

PREP: 25 MINUTES   COOK: 28 MINUTES

Tart lime, coconut broth, and sweet-hot ginger give this soup Thai undertones.

¾ pound unpeeled medium-size fresh shrimp
2 tablespoons minced fresh ginger
½ to ¾ teaspoon dried crushed red pepper
2 tablespoons peanut oil
3 (14½-ounce) cans ready-to-serve chicken broth
1 tablespoon lime rind strips, cut into 1-inch pieces
⅓ cup uncooked long-grain rice
6 large mushrooms, sliced
1 (13½-ounce) can coconut milk
½ cup chopped onion
2 tablespoons fresh lime juice
Garnish: chopped green onions

- Peel shrimp, and devein, if desired. Set aside.
- Sauté ginger and red pepper in hot oil in a large Dutch oven over medium-high heat 1 minute. Add broth and lime strips. Bring to a boil; stir in rice. Cover, reduce heat, and simmer 20 minutes.
- Add reserved shrimp, mushrooms, coconut milk, and onion to Dutch oven. Cook, uncovered, 3 to 5 minutes or until shrimp turn pink. Remove from heat. Add lime juice, and stir well. Garnish, if desired. Yield: 10 cups.

Per 1-cup serving: Calories 180 Fat 12.5g
Cholesterol 39mg Sodium 454mg

Crab Soup

PREP: 20 MINUTES   COOK: 24 MINUTES

This recipe's from the Low Country of South Carolina where succulent crabs are trapped and cooked in great abundance.

3 stalks celery, cut into 1-inch pieces
1 medium onion, quartered
1 medium leek (white portion only), quartered
1 carrot, scraped and cut into 1-inch pieces
1 shallot, halved
3 tablespoons butter, divided
1 clove garlic, minced
¼ cup all-purpose flour
2 cups chicken broth
2 cups milk
2 bay leaves
1 tablespoon Old Bay seasoning
Pinch of powdered saffron
1 teaspoon Worcestershire sauce
½ teaspoon salt
¼ teaspoon ground mace
¼ teaspoon ground red pepper
1 pound fresh lump crabmeat
¼ cup brandy
1 cup half-and-half
1 tablespoon chopped fresh parsley

- Process first 5 ingredients in a food processor until finely chopped. Melt 2 tablespoons butter in a Dutch oven over medium heat. Add finely chopped vegetables and garlic to Dutch oven; cover and cook 8 minutes, stirring occasionally.
- Uncover and stir in flour; cook 1 minute, stirring constantly. Gradually stir in broth and milk. Bring to a simmer; add bay leaves and next 6 ingredients, and cook 10 minutes, stirring occasionally.
- Drain crabmeat, removing any bits of shell. Melt remaining 1 tablespoon butter in a small skillet; add crabmeat. Toss gently, and cook over medium heat until thoroughly heated; add brandy. Stir crabmeat mixture, half-and-half, and parsley into mixture in Dutch oven. Discard bay leaves. Yield: 8 cups.

Per 1-cup serving: Calories 213 Fat 11.1g
Cholesterol 81mg Sodium 592mg

Southern Seafood Gumbo

◄ **FAMILY FAVORITE** ►

PREP: 1 HOUR
COOK: 3 HOURS AND 45 MINUTES

½ cup vegetable oil
½ cup all-purpose flour
4 stalks celery, chopped
2 medium onions, chopped
1 green pepper, chopped
2 cloves garlic, minced
1 pound okra, sliced
2 tablespoons vegetable oil
1 quart chicken broth
1 quart water
¼ cup Worcestershire sauce
1 teaspoon hot sauce
1 teaspoon salt
2 slices bacon or 1 small ham slice, chopped
1 bay leaf
¾ teaspoon dried thyme
¼ teaspoon sweet red pepper flakes
2 pounds unpeeled medium-size fresh shrimp
1 pound fresh lump crabmeat
1 (12-ounce) container Standard oysters, undrained (optional)
Gumbo filé (optional)
7 cups hot cooked rice

- Combine ½ cup oil and flour in a Dutch oven; cook over medium heat, stirring constantly, until roux is caramel-colored (about 20 minutes). Stir in celery and next 3 ingredients; cook 45 minutes, stirring occasionally.
- Fry okra in 2 tablespoons hot oil until browned. Add to gumbo, reduce heat to low, and stir well. (At this stage, the mixture may be cooled, packaged, and frozen or refrigerated for later use.)
- Add broth and next 8 ingredients; bring to a boil. Reduce heat, and simmer, uncovered, 2 to 2½ hours, stirring occasionally.
- Peel shrimp, and devein, if desired. Add shrimp, crabmeat, and oysters, if desired, to vegetable mixture during last 10 minutes of cooking; cook just until shrimp turn pink and oyster edges curl. Remove from heat, and stir in gumbo filé, if desired. Discard bay leaf. Serve over rice. Yield: 14 cups.

Per 1-cup serving: Calories 376 Fat 12.7g
Cholesterol 117mg Sodium 1028mg

Chicken and Sausage Gumbo

◄ FAMILY FAVORITE ►

PREP: 25 MINUTES
COOK: 2 HOURS AND 45 MINUTES

Gumbo's great flavor begins with a rich brown roux. See our series of photos below to guide you through the steps.

1 pound hot smoked link sausage such as andouille, cut into ¼-inch slices
4 skinned chicken breast halves
¼ to ⅓ cup vegetable oil
½ cup all-purpose flour
1 cup chopped onion
1 green pepper, chopped
½ cup sliced celery
3 cloves garlic, minced
7 cups hot water
2 teaspoons Creole seasoning
1 tablespoon Worcestershire sauce
½ teaspoon dried thyme
1 teaspoon hot sauce
2 bay leaves
½ cup sliced green onions
6 cups hot cooked rice
Gumbo filé (optional)

•Cook sausage in a Dutch oven over medium heat until browned. Remove sausage, reserving drippings. Set sausage aside. Cook chicken in drippings until browned. Remove chicken, reserving drippings.
•Measure drippings, adding enough oil to measure ½ cup. Add oil mixture to Dutch oven; place over medium heat until hot. Add flour, and cook, stirring constantly, until roux is chocolate-colored, 20 to 30 minutes. (See photos 1, 2, and 3.)
•Add chopped onion and next 3 ingredients to roux (photo 4); cook until vegetables are tender, stirring often. Remove from heat; slowly add hot water, stirring constantly. Bring mixture to a boil. Add chicken, Creole seasoning, and next 4 ingredients to Dutch oven; reduce heat, and simmer, uncovered, 1 hour, stirring occasionally.
•Remove chicken from Dutch oven; set aside to cool. Add sausage to Dutch oven; cook, uncovered, 30 more minutes. Stir in green onions; cook, uncovered, 30 more minutes.
•Bone chicken; coarsely shred. Add chicken to gumbo; cook until mixture is thoroughly heated. Discard bay leaves. Serve gumbo over hot rice with gumbo filé, if desired. Yield: 9 cups.

Per 1-cup serving: Calories 513 Fat 23g
Cholesterol 70mg Sodium 1570mg

1. Add flour to oil in Dutch oven, and cook, stirring constantly. This is the first stage of a roux.

2. The roux is beginning to brown. Keep cooking and stirring constantly.

3. This is a rich brown roux at the end of its cooking time. You'll detect a nutty smell at this stage.

4. Add chopped onion, pepper, celery, and garlic to roux. It'll sizzle and give off a great aroma.

CHOWDERS, STEWS & CHILIES

They all have *chunky* in common, these chowders, stews, and chilies that are especially appropriate for the cold winter months. Each is thick with vegetables, meat, or seafood, yet each has a different flavor base. Chowder has milk or cream added for richness as well as crackers crumbled on top. And starchy potato often enhances the thickness, too.

Stews and chilies typically have a tomato base and lots of meat. The pieces of meat and vegetables in a stew are generally larger than in a soup and the mixture is considerably thicker. There's one important guideline to remember about stews. Don't cheat on the simmering time—the long, slow simmer helps extract maximum flavor and ensure fork-tender results.

Fresh Corn Chowder

◀ FAMILY FAVORITE ▶

PREP: 18 MINUTES   COOK: 37 MINUTES

You don't have to add much to fresh sweet corn to get a great-tasting soup. Whether you use white or yellow corn is your choice— white corn will be a little sweeter; yellow corn will give a prettier color.

8 ears fresh corn
6 slices bacon
½ cup chopped onion
½ cup peeled, cubed baking potato
1 cup water
2 cups milk, divided
1 teaspoon sugar
½ teaspoon dried thyme
½ teaspoon salt
¼ teaspoon pepper
1 tablespoon cornstarch

•Cut off tips of corn kernels into a large bowl, scraping cobs well to remove all milk.
•Cook bacon in a Dutch oven over medium heat until crisp; remove bacon, reserving drippings in pan. Crumble bacon, and set aside.
•Cook onion in drippings over medium-high heat, stirring constantly, 4 minutes or until tender. Stir in corn, potato, and water. Bring to a boil; cover, reduce heat, and simmer 10 minutes, stirring occasionally. Stir in 1½ cups milk, sugar, and next 3 ingredients.

•Combine cornstarch and remaining ½ cup milk, stirring until smooth; gradually add to corn mixture, stirring constantly. Cook, uncovered, 15 minutes, stirring often, until thickened. Top each serving with crumbled bacon. Yield: 6 cups.
Per 1-cup serving: Calories 265 Fat 14.5g Cholesterol 24mg Sodium 381mg

New England Clam Chowder

◀ FAMILY FAVORITE ▶

PREP: 20 MINUTES   COOK: 20 MINUTES

Chowder comes from the French chaudière, a large kettle that fishermen used when making their soups or stews. Oyster crackers are a must with chowder.

3 cups water
2 chicken bouillon cubes
4 medium-size round red potatoes, diced
2 (6½-ounce) cans minced clams, undrained
4 slices bacon, cut into 1-inch pieces
¾ cup chopped onion
3 tablespoons butter or margarine
¼ cup plus 2 tablespoons all-purpose flour
4 cups milk
¾ teaspoon salt
¼ teaspoon pepper

•Combine water and bouillon cubes in a Dutch oven; bring to a boil. Add diced potato; cover and simmer 10 minutes or until tender. Drain potato, and set aside. Drain clams, reserving juice. Set clams and juice aside.
•Cook bacon and onion in a medium skillet over medium-high heat, stirring constantly, until bacon is crisp and onion is tender. Remove bacon and onion, reserving 2 tablespoons drippings. Set bacon and onion aside.
•Combine reserved drippings and butter in Dutch oven; cook over low heat until butter melts. Add flour, stirring until smooth. Cook 1 minute, stirring constantly. Gradually add reserved clam juice and milk; cook over medium heat, stirring constantly, until thickened and bubbly. Remove from heat;

stir in potato, clams, bacon mixture, salt, and pepper. Cook, stirring constantly, until thoroughly heated (do not boil). Serve with oyster crackers. Yield: 8 cups.
Per 1-cup serving: Calories 290 Fat 12.8g Cholesterol 48mg Sodium 699mg

Manhattan-Style Seafood Chowder

PREP: 20 MINUTES   COOK: 42 MINUTES

4 medium onions, chopped
1 large green pepper, chopped
¼ cup vegetable oil
2 tablespoons all-purpose flour
3 (14½-ounce) cans stewed tomatoes, undrained
1 tablespoon celery salt
1 teaspoon garlic powder
1 teaspoon hot sauce
½ teaspoon pepper
2 pounds unpeeled medium-size fresh shrimp
½ pound fresh lump crabmeat
½ pound firm white fish fillets, cut into bite-size pieces
1 (12-ounce) container Standard oysters, drained

•Sauté onion and green pepper in hot oil in a Dutch oven over medium-high heat until tender. Add flour; cook 1 minute, stirring constantly.
•Stir in tomatoes and next 4 ingredients. Bring to a boil; cover, reduce heat, and simmer 15 minutes.
•Peel shrimp, and devein, if desired. Add shrimp, crabmeat, fish, and oysters to Dutch oven; cover and simmer 15 minutes. Yield: 12 cups.
Per 1-cup serving: Calories 213 Fat 7.3g Cholesterol 126mg Sodium 958mg

CHOWDER CHOICES

There are two main types of chowders—Manhattan style, which is tomato based, and New England style, which is milk or cream based.

Vegetable Cheddar Chowder

PREP: 18 MINUTES   COOK: 20 MINUTES

3 cups water
3 chicken bouillon cubes
4 medium potatoes, peeled and diced
1 medium onion, sliced
1 cup thinly sliced carrot
½ cup diced green pepper
⅓ cup butter or margarine
⅓ cup all-purpose flour
3½ cups milk
4 cups (16 ounces) shredded sharp
   Cheddar cheese
1 (2-ounce) jar diced pimiento, drained
¼ teaspoon hot sauce
Garnish: fresh parsley sprigs

•Combine water and bouillon cubes in a Dutch oven; bring to a boil. Add diced potato and next 3 ingredients; cover and simmer 12 minutes or until vegetables are tender.
•Melt butter in a heavy saucepan over low heat; add flour, stirring until smooth. Cook 1 minute, stirring constantly. Gradually add milk; cook over medium heat, stirring constantly, until thickened and bubbly. Add cheese, stirring until melted.
•Stir cheese sauce, pimiento, and hot sauce into vegetable mixture. Cook over low heat until thoroughly heated (do not boil). Garnish, if desired. Yield: 10 cups.

Per 1-cup serving: Calories 331 Fat 24.4g
Cholesterol 76mg Sodium 667mg

Beef Stew

PREP: 32 MINUTES
SLOW COOK: 4 TO 10 HOURS

Let the slow cooker simmer this hearty mix of chunks of beef and assorted vegetables.

3 pounds beef stew meat, cut into 1-inch
   pieces
2 tablespoons vegetable oil
2 stalks celery, chopped
2 cloves garlic, minced
1 medium onion, chopped
2 teaspoons salt, divided
½ teaspoon pepper
¾ cup all-purpose flour
2 cups water, divided
1 cup dry red wine
1 cup chopped fresh tomato
1 tablespoon chopped fresh parsley
¼ teaspoon dried thyme
2 bay leaves
5 small onions, quartered
5 carrots, scraped and cut into 2-inch pieces
12 small round red potatoes, halved, or
   5 medium potatoes, quartered

•Brown meat in hot oil in a large Dutch oven; drain, if necessary. Add celery, garlic, chopped onion, 1 teaspoon salt, and pepper. Cook over medium heat, stirring constantly, until vegetables are tender.
•Combine flour and 1 cup water, stirring until smooth; add to meat mixture, stirring well. Spoon meat mixture into a 4-quart electric slow cooker.
•Combine remaining 1 teaspoon salt, remaining 1 cup water, wine, and next 4 ingredients; pour over meat mixture. Place onion quarters, carrot, and potato over meat mixture (do not stir). Cover and cook on HIGH 4 to 4½ hours, or on HIGH 1 hour and reduce to LOW 8½ hours or until meat and vegetables are tender. Discard bay leaves. Yield: 12 cups.

Per 1-cup serving: Calories 269 Fat 7.2g
Cholesterol 65mg Sodium 473mg

Cooktop Beef Stew: Brown meat in hot oil in a large Dutch oven; drain. Add celery and remaining ingredients. Bring to a boil; reduce heat, and simmer, covered, 2½ hours or until meat and vegetables are tender. Add additional water, if necessary.

Brunswick Stew

PREP: 30 MINUTES
COOK: 2 HOURS AND 45 MINUTES

Brunswick Stew has endless variations, though this pork and chicken version seems to be typical. While a bowl of Brunswick Stew can easily stand alone, it's not uncommon to serve it with barbecue.

1 (4½-pound) pork roast
1 (4½-pound) hen
3 (16-ounce) cans whole tomatoes,
   undrained and chopped
1 (8-ounce) can tomato sauce
3 large onions, chopped
2 small green peppers, chopped
¾ cup white vinegar
¼ cup sugar
¼ cup all-purpose flour
1 cup water
1 teaspoon salt
½ teaspoon pepper
½ teaspoon ground turmeric
2 tablespoons hot sauce
1 (16-ounce) package frozen shoepeg corn

•Place pork roast, fat side up, on a rack of a roasting pan. Insert meat thermometer, being careful not to touch bone or fat. Bake at 325° for 2 hours or until thermometer registers 160°. Cool. Trim and discard fat; cut pork into 2-inch pieces.
•Meanwhile, place hen in a Dutch oven, and cover with water. Bring to a boil; cover, reduce heat, and simmer 2 hours or until tender. Remove hen from broth, and cool. (Reserve broth for another use.) Bone hen, and cut meat into 2-inch pieces.
•Coarsely grind pork and chicken in food processor or with meat grinder. Combine ground meat, tomatoes, and next 5 ingredients in a large Dutch oven.
•Combine flour and water, stirring until smooth; stir into meat mixture. Stir in salt and next 3 ingredients. Cook over medium heat 30 minutes, stirring occasionally. Add water, if needed, to reach desired consistency. Stir in corn, and cook 10 more minutes. This stew freezes well. Yield: 22 cups.

Per 1-cup serving: Calories 207 Fat 7.9g
Cholesterol 61mg Sodium 332mg

Oyster Stew

◄ QUICK ►

PREP: 8 MINUTES   COOK: 12 MINUTES

2 green onions, chopped
2 tablespoons butter or margarine, melted
1 (12-ounce) container Standard oysters, undrained
1 quart half-and-half or milk
¼ teaspoon salt
¼ teaspoon ground white pepper
⅛ teaspoon ground red pepper

•Sauté green onions in butter in a Dutch oven until tender. Add oysters and remaining ingredients. Cook over low heat until oyster edges begin to curl and mixture is hot, but not boiling. Serve with crackers. Yield: 6 cups.
Per 1-cup serving: Calories 285 Fat 23.8g
Cholesterol 101mg Sodium 267mg

Lamb Ragoût

PREP: 25 MINUTES   COOK: 2 HOURS

2 pounds boneless lamb, cut into 1½-inch cubes
¼ cup plus 1 tablespoon all-purpose flour
2 tablespoons vegetable oil
3 cups water
1 (10½-ounce) can ready-to-serve beef broth, undiluted
¼ cup tomato puree
1 teaspoon salt
1 teaspoon dried thyme
1 teaspoon dried parsley flakes
1 clove garlic, crushed
1 bay leaf
4 medium potatoes, peeled and cubed
12 baby carrots
1 cup frozen English peas

•Dredge meat in flour; cook in hot oil in a large Dutch oven until meat is browned. Stir in water and next 7 ingredients; cover, reduce heat, and simmer 1 hour. Cool. Chill.
•Discard fat from top of beef mixture. Cook beef mixture over medium heat until simmering, stirring often. Add potato, carrots, and peas; cover and cook over medium-low heat 45 minutes or until vegetables are tender, stirring often. Discard bay leaf. Yield: 13 cups.
Per 1-cup serving: Calories 166 Fat 7.1g
Cholesterol 48mg Sodium 381mg

Kentucky Burgoo

◄ FAMILY FAVORITE ►

**PREP: 45 MINUTES   CHILL: 8 HOURS
COOK: 4 HOURS**

Kentucky Burgoo is a stew of Southern origin. It usually includes at least two types of meat and a garden's worth of fresh vegetables. This recipe serves a crowd or you can easily freeze it.

1 (4- to 5-pound) hen
2 pounds beef or veal stew meat
1½ to 2 pounds beef or veal bones
1 stalk celery with leaves, cut into 1-inch pieces
1 carrot, scraped and cut into 1-inch pieces
1 small onion, quartered
1 (6-ounce) can tomato paste
3 quarts water
1 red pepper pod
1 to 1½ tablespoons salt
1½ to 2 teaspoons black pepper
½ teaspoon ground red pepper
2 tablespoons lemon juice
1 tablespoon Worcestershire sauce
6 onions, finely chopped
8 to 10 tomatoes, peeled and chopped
1 turnip, peeled and finely chopped
2 green peppers, finely chopped
2 cups fresh butterbeans
2 cups thinly sliced celery
2 cups finely chopped cabbage
2 cups sliced fresh okra
2 cups fresh cut corn

•Combine first 14 ingredients in a large Dutch oven. Bring to a boil; cover, reduce heat, and simmer 1 hour. Cool. Strain meat mixture, reserving meat and liquid; discard vegetables. Remove skin, gristle, and meat from bone; finely chop meat. Return meat to liquid; cover and chill 8 hours.
•Discard fat layer on mixture; add onion and remaining ingredients. Bring mixture to a boil; reduce heat, and simmer, uncovered, 3 hours or to desired consistency, stirring mixture often to prevent sticking. Yield: 30 cups.
Per 1-cup serving: Calories 175 Fat 6.5g
Cholesterol 47mg Sodium 299mg

Note: Kentucky Burgoo freezes well. To serve, thaw and cook until stew is thoroughly heated.

Gulf Coast Cioppino

PREP: 40 MINUTES   COOK: 1 HOUR

When Italian immigrants settled in San Francisco, they brought with them the recipe for cioppino, a tomato-based fish and shellfish stew.

20 fresh mussels
20 fresh clams
2 cups chopped celery
2 cups chopped green pepper
1 cup chopped green onions
2 cloves garlic, crushed
¼ cup butter or margarine, melted
1 tablespoon olive oil
1 (16-ounce) can crushed tomatoes
1 (15-ounce) can tomato sauce
1 to 1½ tablespoons dried Italian seasoning
1½ teaspoons paprika
1 teaspoon sugar
1 teaspoon salt
1 teaspoon ground red pepper
½ teaspoon black pepper
2 (14½-ounce) cans ready-to-serve chicken broth
1 pound grouper, amberjack, or sea bass fillets, cut into bite-size pieces

•Scrub mussels with a brush, removing beards. Wash clams. Discard any opened or cracked mussels and clams. Set aside.
•Sauté celery and next 3 ingredients in butter and hot oil in a Dutch oven over medium-high heat until vegetables are tender. Stir in crushed tomatoes and next 7 ingredients; cook 3 minutes, stirring occasionally. Add chicken broth. Bring to a boil; reduce heat, and simmer, uncovered, 45 minutes, stirring occasionally.
•Stir in mussels, clams, and fish; cook 4 minutes, stirring occasionally. (Mussels and clams should open during cooking.) Discard any unopened mussels and clams. Serve immediately. Yield: 12 cups.
Per 1-cup serving: Calories 146 Fat 6.5g
Cholesterol 33mg Sodium 802mg

SOUP DICTIONARY

Bouillabaisse: Seafood stew that contains a variety of fresh fish and shellfish, as well as onions, tomato, white wine, garlic, and herbs. It's typically ladled over French bread in bowls.

Broth: An all-purpose flavorful liquid that results from simmering vegetables, herbs, meat, poultry, or seafood in water.

Cassoulet: A rustic French country dish of white beans and a variety of meats stewed very slowly to develop a complex flavor. Cassoulet bakes in the oven with a golden breadcrumb crust.

Chowder: A general term used to describe any thick, rich soup containing chunky food. Also a specific chunky seafood soup; see page 433 for the difference between New England and Manhattan-style chowders.

Cioppino: A robust tomato-based stew brimming with fish and shellfish.

Consommé: The consummate clear broth, enriched with meat and vegetables and clarified with egg white.

Gumbo: A thick soup that can contain chicken, sausage, ham, shrimp, or oysters. Gumbo gets its flavor base from a rich brown roux that cooks slowly to develop a nutty taste. Gumbo's often thickened with okra or gumbo filé powder, which is added at the table.

Ragoût: A very thick, well-seasoned stew of meat, poultry, fish, and sometimes vegetables.

Stew: Simmered slowly for several hours in a tightly covered pot, stew is known for yielding melt-in-your-mouth tender meat.

Stock: The strained liquid from vegetables, meat, or fish simmered with seasonings. When making stock, bones are added to extract flavor and gelatin for body. For a rich brown stock, first roast bones and vegetables to develop a rich flavor base before adding water.

Bouillabaisse

◄ HEALTHY ►

PREP: 25 MINUTES   COOK: 40 MINUTES

Bouillabaisse brings to us the best ingredients of Provence, France—tomatoes, onions, wine, olive oil, garlic, herbs, and, of course, local fish and shellfish. We've adapted this recipe to use fish from our own Southern waters. Ladle this Old World stew over thick slices of French bread.

1 large onion, coarsely chopped
2 cloves garlic, minced
¼ cup butter, melted, or olive oil
2 tablespoons all-purpose flour
2 cups water
1 cup coarsely chopped fresh tomato
1 (8-ounce) can tomato sauce
½ cup white wine
1 bay leaf
1 teaspoon salt
¼ teaspoon ground red pepper
¼ teaspoon dried thyme
⅛ teaspoon ground allspice
Pinch of ground saffron
1 pound unpeeled medium-size fresh shrimp
2 pounds red snapper, skinned and cut into large pieces
1 (12-ounce) container Standard oysters, undrained
Toasted French bread slices

•Sauté onion and garlic in butter or oil in a large Dutch oven until tender. Add flour, stirring until smooth. Cook 1 minute, stirring constantly. Gradually stir in water.
•Add tomato and next 8 ingredients. Bring to a boil; reduce heat, and simmer, uncovered, 30 minutes.
•Peel shrimp, and devein, if desired. Add shrimp, fish, and oysters; simmer 5 minutes or until shrimp turn pink and fish flakes easily when tested with a fork. Discard bay leaf. Serve each portion over a 1-inch-thick slice of toasted French bread. Yield: 10 cups.
Per 1-cup serving: Calories 283 Fat 8.1g
Cholesterol 116mg Sodium 714mg

Venison Chili

PREP: 20 MINUTES

COOK: 1 HOUR AND 25 MINUTES

This robust chili is enriched with red wine. Serve it with crusty sourdough or cornbread.

¼ pound salt pork, cut into 4 pieces
2 pounds ground venison
2 medium onions, chopped
1 (14½-ounce) can diced tomatoes, undrained
1 cup water
¾ cup red wine
2 to 3 large green chiles, diced (we tested with Anaheim)
1 clove garlic, minced
3 tablespoons chili powder
¾ teaspoon dried oregano
½ teaspoon cumin seeds, crushed

•Brown salt pork in a Dutch oven over medium heat. Add venison and onion; cook over medium-high heat until venison is browned and crumbled, stirring often.
•Stir in tomatoes and remaining ingredients. Reduce heat, and simmer, uncovered, 1 hour, stirring occasionally. Remove salt pork before serving. Yield: 7 cups.
Per 1-cup serving: Calories 331 Fat 31.4g
Cholesterol 124mg Sodium 428mg

Beef and Bean Chili

◄ FAMILY FAVORITE ►

PREP: 14 MINUTES   COOK: 1 HOUR

4 stalks celery, chopped
3 green onions, chopped
2 cloves garlic, minced
1 large onion, chopped
1 green pepper, chopped
1 tablespoon vegetable oil
2 pounds ground beef
1 (15-ounce) can tomato sauce
1 (6-ounce) can tomato paste
2 cups water
6 tablespoons chili powder
1 teaspoon salt
Dash of pepper
1 (16-ounce) can kidney beans, undrained
Condiments: shredded lettuce, shredded Cheddar cheese, diced onion, tortilla chips (optional)

• Sauté first 5 ingredients in hot oil in a large Dutch oven over medium-high heat 5 minutes or until tender. Add ground beef and brown, stirring until meat crumbles. Drain meat well.

• Add tomato sauce and next 5 ingredients to beef mixture; stir well. Bring to a boil; reduce heat, and simmer, uncovered, 30 minutes or to desired consistency. Add beans during the last 15 minutes. Serve with condiments, if desired. Yield: 10 cups.

Per 1-cup serving: Calories 274 Fat 13.6g
Cholesterol 56mg Sodium 761mg

Four-Way Cincinnati Chili

◄ HEALTHY ►

PREP: 15 MINUTES   COOK: 35 MINUTES

Next time you serve chili, go beyond the bowl. Spoon spiced up Cincinnati Chili over a bed of pasta, and top it with cheese, onions, and oyster crackers. This recipe makes eating chili a whole new experience.

1 pound ground round
2 cloves garlic, minced
2 cups chopped onion
1 cup chopped green pepper
2 teaspoons ground cinnamon
2 teaspoons paprika
1 teaspoon ground cumin
1 teaspoon chili powder
¾ teaspoon salt
½ teaspoon ground allspice
½ teaspoon dried marjoram
¼ teaspoon ground nutmeg
¼ teaspoon pepper
2 (14½-ounce) cans whole tomatoes, undrained and chopped
8 ounces uncooked dried spaghetti
Condiments: shredded Cheddar cheese, chopped onion, oyster crackers (optional)

• Combine first 4 ingredients in a large non-stick skillet; cook over medium heat, stirring until meat crumbles and vegetables are tender.

• Stir in cinnamon and next 9 ingredients; bring to a boil. Reduce heat, and simmer, uncovered, 20 minutes, stirring occasionally.

• While beef mixture simmers, cook spaghetti according to package directions; drain and return to pan to keep warm.

• To serve, place pasta on individual serving plates; spoon beef mixture over spaghetti. If desired, top with cheese, chopped onion, and oyster crackers. Yield: 4 servings.

Per serving: Calories 568 Fat 12.6g
Cholesterol 80mg Sodium 1079mg

White Bean Chili

◄ FAMILY FAVORITE ►

PREP: 30 MINUTES   SOAK: OVERNIGHT
COOK: 2 HOURS AND 20 MINUTES

Once you try this cheesy white bean chili, you may never go back to the red stuff.

1 pound dried Great Northern beans
2 medium onions, chopped
1 tablespoon olive oil
3 (4.5-ounce) cans chopped green chiles, undrained
4 cloves garlic, minced
2 teaspoons ground cumin
2 teaspoons dried oregano
6 cups chicken broth
5 cups chopped cooked chicken breast
3 cups (12 ounces) shredded Monterey Jack cheese with jalapeño peppers
½ teaspoon salt
¼ teaspoon pepper
¼ cup chopped fresh cilantro (optional)

• Sort and rinse beans; place in a large Dutch oven. Cover with water 2 inches above beans; let soak overnight. Drain; set beans aside.

• Sauté onion in hot oil in Dutch oven over medium-high heat until tender. Add green chiles and next 3 ingredients; cook 2 minutes, stirring constantly. Add beans and chicken broth. Bring to a boil; cover, reduce heat, and simmer 2 hours or until beans are tender, stirring occasionally.

• Add chicken, 1 cup cheese, salt, and pepper. Bring to a boil; reduce heat, and simmer, uncovered, 10 minutes, stirring often. Stir in cilantro, if desired.

• To serve, ladle chili into individual soup bowls. Top each serving with remaining 2 cups cheese. Yield: 13 cups.

Per 1-cup serving: Calories 359 Fat 12.3g
Cholesterol 71mg Sodium 984mg

Vegetarian Chili

◄ FAMILY FAVORITE ►
◄ VEGETARIAN ►

PREP: 7 MINUTES   COOK: 55 MINUTES

1 large onion, coarsely chopped
1 tablespoon vegetable oil
1 (28-ounce) can whole tomatoes, undrained and coarsely chopped
⅔ cup picante sauce
1½ teaspoons ground cumin
1 teaspoon salt
½ teaspoon dried oregano
2 (15-ounce) cans black beans, rinsed and drained
1 large green pepper, cut into ¾-inch pieces
1 large sweet red pepper, cut into ¾-inch pieces
2 large carrots, scraped and sliced
4 cups hot cooked rice
1½ cups (6 ounces) shredded Cheddar cheese
1 (8-ounce) carton sour cream

• Sauté onion in hot oil in a Dutch oven over medium-high heat until tender. Add tomatoes and next 4 ingredients; stir well. Bring to a boil; cover, reduce heat, and simmer 5 minutes.

• Stir in beans, peppers, and carrot. Cover and cook over medium-low heat 25 minutes or until vegetables are tender, stirring mixture occasionally.

• Spoon rice into individual soup bowls; ladle chili over rice. Top evenly with cheese and sour cream. Yield: 6 cups.

Per 1-cup serving: Calories 598 Fat 21.3g
Cholesterol 46mg Sodium 1900mg

Corn Pudding (page 451)
Fried Corn (page 450)

VEGETABLE & FRUIT SIDE DISHES

The Southern vegetable plate is enjoying a revival. These days you'll find farmers market produce in simple abundance, meant to be enjoyed at the peak of its season, and enhanced by only brief cooking.

The way Southerners approach vegetables has evolved over the years. Current cooking methods are a far cry from vegetables stewed to excess with fatback for flavor. The legacy of long cooked vegetables still lingers, however, and we pay tribute to it with recipes like Southern-Style Collards and Turnip Greens (both on page 453).

Flip through these pages and see simple recipes such as Roasted Vegetables (page 455), Sautéed Spinach (page 454), and Grilled Vegetable Skewers (page 463). Quicker, smarter cooking procedures leave you with fuller flavor, better texture, and more nutrients.

Equipment

If you like steamed vegetables, you'll benefit from a selection of saucepans with snug-fitting lids, as well as a collapsible metal steamer basket. A large skillet or an electric wok will serve you well for sautéing and stir-frying vegetables.

Both fresh and frozen vegetables will put your microwave oven to its best use. And if you want to put some produce on the grill next to a thick steak, start a collection of metal skewers.

A sharp paring knife, chef's knife, and sturdy vegetable peeler will be needed for trimming, peeling, and slicing vegetables. A couple of cutting boards will supply the stable surface to complete the task.

Always Buy in Season

Purchase vegetables that are in season. Not only will they yield the highest quality and flavor, but they'll be reasonably priced. When you buy produce out of season you often pay a premium for it.

When selecting fresh produce, look for bright color and crisp appearance. Small vegetables tend to be sweeter and more tender than larger ones in the same family. Generally speaking, buy firm vegetables rather than soft. Avoid any vegetables that are bruised. If vegetables are limp when you buy them, chances are they won't improve when you get them home. The best use for mature vegetables is to add them to a simmering stock.

When buying frozen vegetables, look for well-frozen packages. Damp packages or packages that are a solid block have probably defrosted once. When vegetables thaw and refreeze, quality declines.

VEGETABLE DICTIONARY

Farmers markets offer an abundance of fresh and exotic vegetables every day, piled right next to some familiar favorites. Peek at our peak selections that will inspire you to cook— and maybe even grow—some vegetables of your own.

Acorn squash: This dark green, deeply ridged small winter squash has an orange flesh. This squash is typically split, stuffed with a savory or sweet filling, and baked.

Artichoke: Artichokes are buds from a large thistle plant. The globe artichoke is most common. Choose heavy artichokes with tightly closed, deep green leaves. A very fresh artichoke will squeak when you squeeze the head. Store unwashed artichokes in the refrigerator up to four days.

Bok choy: This mild vegetable is available year round. Cook its crunchy white stalks and tender green leaves as a side dish or use in stir-fries.

Broccoli raab: This leafy green vegetable has clusters of tiny broccoli-like buds. Its flavor is pleasantly bitter. Enjoy broccoli raab steamed, braised, or sautéed.

Brussels sprouts: Select firm, compact, tight heads with healthy, bright green leaves. Small sprouts are more tender; large sprouts can be bitter. To facilitate even cooking, cut an X in the stem end of each sprout.

Butternut squash: This large, smooth, tan-skinned winter squash has an orange flesh that's often chopped and used in soups. Butternut, like other winter squash, bakes best in its own skin.

Chayote squash: Also called *mirliton* and the *vegetable pear* due to its pearlike shape and color, this squash has a pale green flesh and a mild taste comparable to both zucchini and cucumber. Chayote squash should always be peeled and seeded before cooking. And it should never be eaten raw. It's excellent stuffed and baked with a savory filling.

Corn: For optimum flavor, cook corn within a day of purchase—before the sugar converts to starch and the natural sweetness is reduced. Look for healthy green husks that cling tightly to the cob and tight rows of kernels plump with milk.

Eggplant: Varieties abound, ranging in color from deep purple to white, and from oblong to round in shape. Peeling is optional for this vegetable; the skin is edible and adds color to many dishes. Eggplant do, however have a spongelike capacity to absorb oil, so keep this in mind when cooking. Choose eggplant that are heavy, but not

hard, with smooth, glossy skin. Eggplant are highly perishable; store in a cool, dry place, and use within two days of purchase.

Fennel: Fennel has a firm, white bulb, straight stalks, and feathery green leaves. All parts of the vegetable are edible. Cooking accentuates fennel's anise flavor. Select fennel with fresh-looking green tops and plump, firm 3- to 4-inch bulbs. Trim off stalks to within 1 inch of bulb, discarding any tough stalks and reserving feathery leaves for garnish. Braised or roasted fennel makes a tasty side dish.

Haricots verts: Pronounced *ah-ree-koh-VEHR,* these slender, tender, stringless French green beans are considered a delicacy.

Jerusalem artichoke: This small, pale brown tuber, also called a *sunchoke,* is a member of the sunflower family. It has an ivory flesh that's extremely crisp like a water chestnut. The flavor is similar to a common artichoke heart. Scrub with a stiff vegetable brush to remove dirt before cooking. Peel this small knobby tuber and enjoy it raw as a crudité or sliced in a salad. Or cook it; then slice and serve as a potato alternative. Store these tubers in plastic zip-top bags in the refrigerator up to a week.

Jícama: Pronounced *hee-ka-ma,* this fleshy tuber has a crunchy, sweet taste and texture similar to water chestnuts. Simply peel away the light brown skin and enjoy jícama raw or cooked.

Kohlrabi: Sometimes called a *cabbage turnip,* kohlrabi resembles a turnip but tastes like mild cabbage. It's a plump, pale green bulbous vegetable that grows above ground. Look for 3-inch bulbs with crisp leaves. Kohlrabi is excellent steamed or stir-fried.

Okra: These small, bright green pods become a natural thickener when sliced and cooked. Gumbo benefits from this. The smaller pods have the best flavor. Large pods can be tough and fibrous. Store okra in refrigerator and use within two to three days. Okra can be cooked any number of ways, but is particularly enjoyed lightly battered and fried.

Parsnip: This root vegetable looks like a white carrot. You can store parsnips in the refrigerator for several weeks. After peeling parsnips, soak

them in a lemon-water solution to prevent discoloration. Shop for well-shaped, small- to medium-size parsnips.

Rutabaga: Rutabagas have a yellow-orange flesh and a thin coating of wax applied to their skin during processing to prevent moisture loss and improve storing quality. You can easily remove it by peeling. Rutabagas and turnips can be used interchangeably in recipes; however, rutabagas have a stronger flavor. Select smooth, firm, and unblemished rutabagas.

Shallot: Shallots have a delicate onion flavor. Peel and treat them just like other onions. Store in a cool, dry place. Substitute 3 to 4 shallots for 1 medium onion.

Spaghetti squash: This large, watermelon-shaped winter squash has a golden flesh that separates into spaghetti-like strands upon cooking.

Summer squash: Zucchini and yellow squash fall into this category. You'll find the curved *crookneck* and *straight neck* yellow squash. And zucchini squash is long and typically deep green in color. Enjoy the light, fresh flavor of summer squash raw or cooked.

Swiss chard: Chard is part of the beet family. It's two vegetables in one—use the stems like celery; cook the ruffly large leaves like spinach.

Tomatillo: We think of this small green fruit as a vegetable. It has a papery husk and citric edge akin to lemon. It's popular in salsa and other southwestern dishes. Remove the husks, rinse fruit, and use tomatillos raw in salsas or cooked in sauces and other recipes. Cooking enhances the flavor of the tomatillo and softens the skin.

Tomato: It's technically a fruit, but we think of it as a vegetable. Tomato varieties vary in sweetness and acidity. Shown are the yellow teardrop tomato, Roma (plum) tomato, and tomatillo. Roma tomatoes are thick-skinned and not as juicy as other varieties; they hold up in sauces and recipes where you don't want added moisture. In general, select firm, heavy, deeply colored tomatoes. Store tomatoes at room temperature out of direct sunlight. *Never* store tomatoes in the refrigerator—unless they're overripe.

Turnips: This mild vegetable is available year-round. See page 466 for more information.

Bok choy

Swiss chard

Leek

Rutabaga

Fennel

Haricots verts

Acorn squash

Butternut
squash

Kohlrabi

Eggplant

Chayote squash

Roma tomato

Artichoke

Jícama

Tomatillos

Parsnips

Jerusalem
artichokes

Broccoli raab

Yellow teardrop
tomatoes

Shallots

Storing Vegetables

For maximum flavor and nutritive value, use fresh vegetables within one to two days of purchase. Store most vegetables dry and unwashed. Wash most vegetables just before using. Too much moisture causes vegetables to deteriorate rapidly.

To prevent flavor and odor penetration and to minimize water loss, store different types of produce (except potatoes, tomatoes, and onions) in closed plastic bags in the refrigerator.

Store potatoes and onions in a cool, dry, well-ventilated place such as a pantry out of direct sunlight. Don't, however, store potatoes and onions together as they tend to hasten spoilage of each other. Store tomatoes at room temperature in a basket or on a windowsill out of direct sunlight.

To prevent wilting and flavor change, rinse leafy green vegetables under cool water, and drain thoroughly. Wrap in paper towels, place in zip-top plastic bags, and refrigerate.

Corn, beans, and peas lose sweetness as their natural sugar turns to starch during storage. Store these vegetables dry and unwashed in plastic bags in the refrigerator and use as soon as possible.

It's a good idea to check vegetables daily for spoilage no matter where they're stored (pantry, refrigerator, or simply at room temperature). If one piece shows signs of spoilage like mold, oozing, or sliminess, it can quickly ruin the whole lot. So if you detect spoilage, promptly discard those vegetable pieces.

Once cut, all vegetables should be stored in the refrigerator in plastic bags.

Freezing Vegetables

Most vegetables require blanching before freezing in order to maintain good quality. Blanching is a brief boiling that arrests maturation of food. Refer to the detailed discussion of freezing fresh vegetables on page 415 in the Sauces & Condiments chapter.

Leftover cooked vegetables and vegetable casseroles freeze fairly well, although when reheated their texture won't be as crisp.

Preparing Vegetables

Brush off loose dirt before washing vegetables. Use a stiff vegetable brush to remove dirt from the more durable vegetables like sunchokes that tend to harbor dirt in their nooks. A sinkful of lukewarm water is recommended for removing sand and grit from vegetables like artichokes, zucchini, spinach, and leeks.

Peel vegetables when a recipe specifies. Many vegetables such as small eggplant, summer squash, and potatoes don't have to be peeled. Leaving the skin on is optional and can help retain nutrients.

Some vegetables discolor quickly once they're peeled or sliced. To prevent discoloration, briefly dip vegetables in acidulated water, a solution of 1 tablespoon lemon juice to 1 cup water.

Cooking Vegetables

Cook most vegetables as briefly as possibly in as little liquid as possible to retain nutrients, color, and texture. The microwave oven is perfect for cooking fresh vegetables, because you need only a scant amount of water. In turn, the vegetables cook quickly, retaining good color and nutrients. Steaming fresh vegetables in a steamer basket over boiling water preserves more vitamins than cooking in boiling water. Be sure the boiling water level does not touch the basket.

There are some vegetables such as artichokes, large green beans, cabbage, and some greens that you'll want to cook uncovered in a large pot of boiling water. The boiling activity will soften tough vegetable fibers.

Sautéing and stir-frying are quick and easy, and ideal for many vegetables. Stirring vegetables in a small amount of hot fat over medium to medium-high heat preserves color, texture, and nutrients. When stir-frying, it's often recommended that you cut vegetables on the diagonal; this is to expose the most surface area for quick cooking. See our cutting techniques on page 21 for details.

Braising (cooking slowly, covered, in a flavorful liquid) is a recommended cooking method for many root vegetables as well as cabbage and brussels sprouts. These vegetables will absorb the flavor of the braising liquid during long, slow cooking.

Roasting enhances the natural sweetness of many vegetables. This dry heat cooking with no added liquid preserves nutrients and concentrates flavor. You can roast any number of vegetables by this simple method: Cut similarly textured vegetables to the same size pieces. Prepare to roast only enough vegetable pieces to create a single layer in a roasting pan. Drizzle vegetables with one to two tablespoons of olive oil, and sprinkle with salt and pepper. Roast at 450° or 500° for 6 to 8 minutes, stirring once. Some vegetables such as potatoes will take much longer to cook. See individual recipes for recommended times. Roasted vegetables are so simple to prepare and are quite versatile. You can match them with many entrées and casseroles.

For some vegetables, the degree of doneness is a matter of personal preference. We give a range in cooking time for recipes such as asparagus, green beans, snow peas, and peppers, because some folks like crisp-tender and some like very tender results. Some vegetables such as onions and cabbage benefit from long cooking times. They gain a natural sweetness that can't be rushed.

If you're cooking vegetables to serve crisp-tender and cold, a recipe may instruct you to plunge the cooked vegetable into ice water immediately after cooking. This sudden change in temperature "shocks" the vegetable and stops the cooking process.

VEGETABLES

Whole Cooked Artichokes

◄ HEALTHY ►

PREP: 15 MINUTES   COOK: 35 MINUTES

4 large artichokes
Lemon wedge
3 tablespoons lemon juice

•Wash artichokes by plunging up and down in
cold water. Cut off stem ends, and trim about
½ inch from top of each artichoke. Remove
any loose bottom leaves. With scissors, trim
one-fourth off top of each outer leaf, and
rub cut edges with lemon wedge to prevent
discoloration.
•Place artichokes in a stainless steel Dutch
oven; cover with water, and add lemon juice.
•Bring to a boil; cover, reduce heat, and simmer 35 minutes or until lower leaves pull out
easily. Drain artichokes. Serve with Clarified
Butter (page 388), White Butter Sauce (page
388), or Hollandaise Sauce (page 387). Yield:
4 servings.
Per serving: Calories 78 Fat 0.3g
Cholesterol 0 mg Sodium 120mg

Microwave Directions: Stand artichokes in
an 11- x 7-inch baking dish, and add 1 cup
water to dish. Cover dish with heavy-duty
plastic wrap.Microwave at HIGH 15 to 20
minutes, giving dish a quarter-turn halfway
through cooking time. Let stand 5 minutes.
(When done, the petal near the center will
pull out easily.) Yield: 4 servings.

HOW TO EAT AN ARTICHOKE

With just a little more work than
required for other vegetables, artichokes
offer great rewards. Pluck leaves from a hot
cooked artichoke, one at a time, beginning
at the base; dip the meaty end of each leaf
into Clarified Butter (page 388). Draw each
leaf between your teeth, scraping off the
meat. Discard leaves on a plate or in a
large bowl.

After leaves are removed, a fuzzy choke
remains. Remove choke with a spoon.

Just under the choke is the prized heart.
Quarter it and dip it into Clarified Butter.

Sun-Dried Tomato-Stuffed Artichokes

PREP: 25 MINUTES   COOK: 40 MINUTES

*Fill these artichokes to overflowing with a
tangy sun-dried tomato and herb breadcrumb mixture. Then bake them briefly for
a dish worthy of company.*

4 large artichokes
2 tablespoons lemon juice
1 tablespoon olive oil
¾ cup sliced fresh mushrooms, chopped,
   or 1 (4-ounce) jar sliced mushrooms,
   drained and chopped
4 cloves garlic, chopped
1 cup chopped onion
1 cup soft whole wheat breadcrumbs
   (homemade)
4 sun-dried tomatoes (packed without oil),
   chopped
1 teaspoon dried basil
¼ cup chopped fresh parsley
¼ cup grated Parmesan cheese

•Wash artichokes by plunging up and down
in cold water. Cut off stem ends; trim about
½ inch from top of each artichoke. Remove
any loose bottom leaves. With scissors, trim
one-fourth off top of each outer leaf.
•Place artichokes in a stainless steel Dutch
oven; add water to depth of 1 inch. Add
lemon juice. Bring to a boil; cover, reduce
heat, and simmer 25 minutes or until almost
tender. Drain; cool. Spread leaves apart;
scrape out fuzzy choke with a spoon.
•Place a large skillet over medium-high heat
until hot; add oil. Add mushrooms, garlic,
and onion; cook, stirring constantly, until
onion is tender. Add breadcrumbs; stir well.
Remove from heat, and add tomato and
remaining 3 ingredients; stir well.
•Spoon mixture evenly into center and
between leaves of artichokes. Place stuffed
artichokes in a 13- x 9-inch baking dish.
Bake, uncovered, at 350° for 15 minutes.
Serve immediately. Yield: 4 servings.
Per serving: Calories 171 Fat 4.4g
Cholesterol 6mg Sodium 459mg

Preparing asparagus: Hold asparagus
spear with both hands, and snap off tough
end where it seems to break naturally.

Marinated Asparagus

PREP: 10 MINUTES   COOK: 8 MINUTES
CHILL: 4 HOURS

*A sweet and tangy marinade turns simple
asparagus spears into an all-purpose
side dish.*

1½ pounds fresh asparagus spears*
1 green pepper, chopped
1 small bunch green onions, chopped
1 stalk celery, finely chopped
¾ cup vegetable oil
½ cup red wine vinegar
½ cup sugar
1 small clove garlic, minced
¼ teaspoon paprika
Pimiento strips

•Snap off tough ends of asparagus. Cover
and cook asparagus in boiling water 6 to 8
minutes or until crisp-tender. Drain.
•Place asparagus in a 13- x 9-inch dish.
Combine green pepper and next 7 ingredi-
ents; stir well, and pour over asparagus.
Cover and chill at least 4 hours. Drain before
serving; garnish with pimiento strips. Yield: 6
servings.
*You can use 2 (14½-ounce) cans asparagus
spears, drained, instead of fresh, if desired.
Just omit the cooking step.*
Per serving: Calories 188 Fat 14.0g
Cholesterol 0mg Sodium 11mg

Asparagus Custard

PREP: 6 MINUTES   COOK: 38 MINUTES

This savory custard laden with cheese and tender asparagus pieces resembles a quiche, although it's too tender to slice into wedges. Instead spoon up individual servings to accompany most any entrée.

1 pound fresh asparagus
1 cup (4 ounces) shredded Cheddar
    cheese
1 cup milk
¾ cup saltine cracker crumbs
3 large eggs, lightly beaten
1 tablespoon diced pimiento
½ teaspoon salt
¼ teaspoon pepper
2 tablespoons butter or margarine,
    melted

•Snap off tough ends of asparagus. Arrange asparagus in a steamer basket over boiling water; cover and steam 5 to 6 minutes or until crisp-tender. Cut into 1-inch pieces.
•Combine asparagus, cheese, and next 6 ingredients; stir well. Pour into a greased 1½-quart casserole. Drizzle with melted butter. Bake, uncovered, at 350° for 25 to 30 minutes or just until set. Yield: 6 servings.
Per serving: Calories 234 Fat 15.8g
Cholesterol 142mg Sodium 566mg

Ginger Asparagus

PREP: 4 MINUTES   COOK: 12 MINUTES

CHILL: 1 HOUR

It doesn't take long to infuse the flavor of this Asian ginger dressing into fresh asparagus spears—just an hour or so.

¾ cup rice vinegar
1½ tablespoons minced fresh ginger
2 tablespoons sugar
1 pound fresh asparagus
3 tablespoons vegetable oil
2 tablespoons dark sesame oil
1 clove garlic, minced
1 teaspoon soy sauce
½ teaspoon salt

•Combine vinegar and ginger in a small saucepan; bring to a boil. Boil 7 minutes or

until liquid is reduced by half. Remove from heat, and stir in sugar. Set aside.
•Snap off tough ends of asparagus. Place asparagus in a large skillet; add cold water to cover. Bring to a boil; remove from heat. Plunge asparagus into cold water to stop the cooking process; drain. Arrange asparagus on a serving platter.
•Combine vegetable oil and remaining 4 ingredients, stirring well; drizzle over asparagus. Drizzle vinegar mixture over asparagus; cover and chill 1 hour. Yield: 4 servings.
Per serving: Calories 207 Fat 17.3g
Cholesterol 0mg Sodium 386mg

Sweet-and-Sour Green Beans

◄ QUICK • HEALTHY ►

PREP: 11 MINUTES   COOK: 12 MINUTES

1 pound fresh green beans*
1 small onion, thinly sliced
1 tablespoon vegetable oil
1 (4-ounce) jar sliced pimiento,
    undrained
¼ cup cider vinegar
¼ cup vegetable oil
2 tablespoons sugar
1 teaspoon salt

•Wash beans; trim stem ends. Cook in boiling water to cover 6 minutes or until crisp-tender; drain. Plunge into ice water to stop the cooking process; drain and set aside.
•Sauté onion in 1 tablespoon hot oil in a large skillet over medium heat until tender. Drain; set aside.
•Drain pimiento, reserving 2 tablespoons liquid. Set pimiento aside. Combine reserved pimiento liquid, vinegar, and remaining 3 ingredients, whisking until blended. Set dressing aside.
•Combine beans, onion, and pimiento; add dressing, tossing to coat. Cover and chill 2 hours, if desired. Serve with a slotted spoon. Yield: 4 servings.
*You can substitute 2 (9-ounce) packages frozen whole green beans cooked according to package directions for fresh green beans, if desired.
Per serving: Calories 143 Fat 9.3g
Cholesterol 0mg Sodium 304mg

Pecan Green Beans

◄ QUICK ►

PREP: 17 MINUTES   COOK: 8 MINUTES

Tiny and tender haricots verts, French green beans (pictured on page 441), are ideal for this dish. Just a light sprinkling of buttered pecans enhances their delicate flavor. You can use larger green beans in this recipe; just increase the cooking time by 2 to 4 minutes.

2 pounds small fresh green beans (haricots
    verts)
½ teaspoon salt
½ cup chopped pecans
¼ cup butter or margarine, melted
1 teaspoon salt
¼ teaspoon pepper

•Wash beans; trim stem ends. Cook beans and ½ teaspoon salt in a small amount of boiling water in a Dutch oven 4 to 5 minutes or until crisp-tender; drain beans, and return to pan.
•Meanwhile, sauté pecans in butter in a medium skillet until butter is lightly browned and pecans are toasted.
•Pour butter-pecan mixture over beans; sprinkle with 1 teaspoon salt and pepper, tossing gently to coat. Yield: 8 servings.
Per serving: Calories 137 Fat 11.1g
Cholesterol 16mg Sodium 431mg

Green Beans Amandine

◄ FAMILY FAVORITE ►

PREP: 15 MINUTES   COOK: 20 MINUTES

Amandine refers to the sautéed slivered almonds that top these beans.

2 pounds fresh green beans
1 small ham hock
1 cup water
⅔ cup slivered almonds
⅓ cup minced onion
3 tablespoons butter or margarine, melted
1 teaspoon salt

•Wash beans; trim stem ends. Cut beans into 1½-inch pieces. Place in a Dutch oven; add ham hock and water. Bring to a boil; cover, reduce heat, and simmer 12 to 15 minutes or until crisp-tender. Drain.

•Sauté almonds and onion in butter in Dutch oven until onion is tender. Add beans along with salt; toss lightly. Yield: 8 servings.

Per serving: Calories 132 Fat 10.2g Cholesterol 13mg Sodium 490mg

Home-Cooked Pole Beans

◀ FAMILY FAVORITE ▶

PREP: 26 MINUTES   COOK: 19 MINUTES

Here's an easy bean recipe flavored with bacon drippings. Be sure to remove the strings from the beans before snapping them.

2 pounds fresh pole beans
3 slices bacon
1 cup water
1 teaspoon salt
¼ teaspoon sugar
¼ teaspoon pepper

•Wash beans; trim stem ends. Cut beans into 1½-inch pieces, and set aside.
•Cook bacon in a large saucepan until crisp; remove bacon, reserving drippings in pan. Crumble bacon, and set aside.
•Add water and remaining 3 ingredients to saucepan; bring to a boil over high heat. Add beans; cover, reduce heat to medium, and cook 15 minutes or to desired doneness. Sprinkle with crumbled bacon. Serve with a slotted spoon. Yield: 8 servings.

Per serving: Calories 73 Fat 4.2g Cholesterol 5mg Sodium 348mg

Chuckwagon Beans

◀ HEALTHY ▶
◀ FAMILY FAVORITE ▶

PREP: 25 MINUTES   COOK: 45 MINUTES

This is kids' food guaranteed, especially the beans and franks version.

2 medium onions, finely chopped
1 medium-size green pepper, finely
   chopped
2 (16-ounce) cans pork and beans
¾ cup ketchup
½ cup firmly packed brown sugar
½ cup molasses
1 teaspoon liquid smoke
Dash of hot sauce

•Combine all ingredients, stirring well. Spoon into a lightly greased shallow 2-quart baking dish. Bake, uncovered, at 425° for 30 to 45 minutes or until bubbly. Yield: 6 servings.

Per serving: Calories 362 Fat 2.5g Cholesterol 11mg Sodium 1041mg

Chuckwagon Beans and Franks: Add 1 (16-ounce) package frankfurters, cut into ¾-inch pieces, to bean mixture. Spoon into a lightly greased 13- x 9-inch baking dish. Bake as directed above. Yield: 6 servings.

Hearty Baked Beans

◀ HEALTHY ▶
◀ FAMILY FAVORITE ▶

**PREP: 20 MINUTES   SOAK: 8 HOURS
COOK: 4 HOURS**

These rustic, stick-to-your-ribs beans bake with ground beef, ham, and a little molasses. Bake the beans long and slowly, and take to a picnic.

1 pound dried navy beans
2 quarts water
1 small ham hock
1 bay leaf
¾ pound ground beef, cooked
1 large onion, chopped
1 small green pepper, chopped
2 cups ketchup
1 (8-ounce) can tomato sauce
1 cup firmly packed brown sugar
3 tablespoons Worcestershire sauce
2 tablespoons molasses
1 tablespoon dry mustard
½ teaspoon ground ginger

•Sort and rinse beans; place in a Dutch oven. Cover with water 2 inches above beans; let soak overnight. Drain.
•Add 2 quarts water, ham hock, and bay leaf. Bring to a boil; cover, reduce heat, and simmer 2 hours. Drain; reserve 1 cup liquid. Discard bay leaf.
•Remove ham from bone; chop. Add ham, beef, and remaining 9 ingredients to beans. Transfer to a greased 5-quart casserole; add reserved liquid. Cover and bake at 350° for 2 hours; stir occasionally. Yield: 10 servings.

Per serving: Calories 436 Fat 8.3g Cholesterol 34mg Sodium 934mg

Baked Beans Quintet

◀ HEALTHY ▶
◀ FAMILY FAVORITE ▶

**PREP: 37 MINUTES
COOK: 1 HOUR AND 25 MINUTES**

Five types of beans make this just about the best-looking and best-tasting bean dish around.

6 slices bacon
1 cup chopped onion
1 clove garlic, minced
1 (16-ounce) can butter beans, drained
1 (15¼-ounce) can lima beans, drained
1 (15-ounce) can pork and beans
1 (15¼-ounce) can red kidney beans,
   drained
1 (19-ounce) can garbanzo beans, drained
¾ cup ketchup
½ cup molasses
⅓ cup firmly packed brown sugar
1½ tablespoons Worcestershire sauce
1 tablespoon prepared mustard
½ teaspoon pepper

•Cook bacon in a large skillet until crisp; remove bacon, reserving drippings in skillet. Crumble bacon, and set aside.
•Cook onion and garlic in bacon drippings, stirring constantly, until tender; drain.
•Combine bacon, onion mixture, butter beans, and remaining ingredients in a large bowl.
•Spoon mixture into a lightly greased 2½-quart bean pot or baking dish. Cover and bake at 375° for 1 hour or until beans are tender. Yield: 8 servings.

Per serving: Calories 451 Fat 14.8g Cholesterol 14mg Sodium 1062mg

Butterbeans with Bacon and Green Onions

PREP: 5 MINUTES   COOK: 37 MINUTES

Splash these tender limas with balsamic vinegar and top with bacon just before serving.

2 (10-ounce) packages frozen butter beans
6 slices lean bacon
4 green onions, chopped
2 cloves garlic, minced
½ cup chopped fresh parsley
½ teaspoon salt
½ teaspoon pepper
1 tablespoon balsamic vinegar (optional)

•Cook butter beans according to package directions, and set aside.
•Cook bacon in a large skillet over medium-high heat until crisp; remove bacon, reserving drippings in skillet. Crumble bacon, and set aside.
•Cook green onions and garlic in bacon drippings until tender, stirring often. Stir in beans, parsley, salt, pepper, and, if desired, vinegar. Cook just until heated. Sprinkle with crumbled bacon. Yield: 6 servings.
Per serving: Calories 237 Fat 11.3g
Cholesterol 13mg Sodium 355mg

Butterbeans with Bacon and Green Onions

Roasted Beets with Warm Dijon Vinaigrette

PREP: 35 MINUTES

COOK: 1 HOUR AND 45 MINUTES

Beets have the highest sugar content of any vegetable. Roasting beets caramelizes the sugar, adding a depth of flavor. Slice these roasted beets and nestle them beside the tender beet greens. Then drizzle with dressing.

3 pounds medium beets with greens
1 tablespoon olive oil
⅓ cup sliced green onions
2 tablespoons balsamic vinegar
2 tablespoons Dijon mustard
⅓ cup olive oil
1 teaspoon salt, divided
½ teaspoon freshly ground pepper
1 tablespoon minced fresh dill

•Leave root and 1-inch stem on beets; reserve greens. Scrub beets with a vegetable brush. Drizzle beets with 1 tablespoon olive oil. Roast beets in a small roasting pan at 400° for 1 to 1½ hours or until tender.
•Meanwhile, process green onions, vinegar, and mustard in a food processor until smooth, stopping once to scrape down sides. Pour ⅓ cup olive oil through food chute with processor running, processing until smooth. Place vinegar mixture in a small saucepan; cook over low heat until thoroughly heated, stirring occasionally.
•Wash beet greens thoroughly; pat dry with paper towels. Cut greens into thin strips.

Place beet greens in a medium saucepan; cover with water, and add ½ teaspoon salt. Bring to a boil; reduce heat, and simmer, uncovered 10 minutes. Drain well. Set aside; keep warm.
•Cool roasted beets. Trim off roots and stems, and rub off skins. Cut beets into ¼-inch slices.
•Place greens and beets on individual serving plates; top evenly with vinegar mixture. Sprinkle with remaining ½ teaspoon salt, pepper, and dill. Serve immediately. Yield: 6 servings.
Per serving: Calories 167 Fat 12.6g
Cholesterol 0mg Sodium 560mg

Broccoli with Garlic Butter and Cashews

◄ QUICK ►

PREP: 4 MINUTES   COOK: 15 MINUTES

1½ pounds fresh broccoli
⅓ cup butter or margarine
1 tablespoon brown sugar
3 tablespoons soy sauce
2 teaspoons white vinegar
¼ teaspoon pepper
2 cloves garlic, minced
⅓ cup salted roasted cashews

•Remove and discard broccoli leaves and tough ends of stalks; cut broccoli into spears. Cook in a small amount of boiling water 8 minutes or until crisp-tender. Drain well. Arrange broccoli on a serving platter. Set aside, and keep warm.
•Melt butter in a small skillet over medium heat; add brown sugar and next 4 ingredients. Bring to a boil; remove from heat. Stir in cashews. Pour sauce over broccoli, and serve immediately. Yield: 6 servings.
Per serving: Calories 168 Fat 13.8g
Cholesterol 28mg Sodium 688mg

Sesame Broccoli

◄ QUICK ►

PREP: 11 MINUTES   COOK: 16 MINUTES

You can count on wok cooking to be quick and fresh tasting. Serve this broccoli side dish with chicken or beef.

1½ pounds fresh broccoli
2 tablespoons sesame seeds
3 tablespoons peanut oil or vegetable oil
3 tablespoons dry white wine
3 tablespoons soy sauce
⅛ teaspoon salt
2 teaspoons minced garlic
1 (8-ounce) can sliced water chestnuts, drained

•Remove and discard broccoli leaves and tough ends of lower stalks. Cut away tops, and set aside. Cut stalks into ¼-inch slices; set aside.
•Toast sesame seeds in a wok or nonstick skillet, stirring often; remove and set aside.

Heat oil in wok over medium-high heat 1 minute. Add broccoli stalks, and stir-fry 5 minutes.
•Combine wine, soy sauce, and salt; add wine mixture, broccoli tops, garlic, and water chestnuts to wok, stirring well. Cover and cook 5 minutes; sprinkle with sesame seeds before serving. Yield: 6 servings.
Per serving: Calories 120 Fat 8.6g
Cholesterol 0mg Sodium 590mg

Olive-Nut Broccoli

◄ QUICK ►

PREP: 12 MINUTES   COOK: 8 MINUTES

Broccoli needs to steam only about 5 minutes for crisp-tender status here. Then top it with the black-olive butter.

3 pounds fresh broccoli
2 teaspoons lemon-pepper seasoning
1 (2¼-ounce) can sliced ripe olives, drained
2 cloves garlic, crushed
3 tablespoons lemon juice
½ cup butter or margarine, melted
½ cup slivered almonds, toasted

•Remove and discard broccoli leaves and tough ends of stalks; cut into flowerets. Arrange broccoli in a steamer basket over boiling water. Cover and steam 5 minutes or until crisp-tender. Arrange broccoli on a serving platter; sprinkle with lemon-pepper seasoning. Set aside, and keep warm.
•Cook olives, garlic, and lemon juice in butter in a small skillet over medium-high heat 3 minutes, stirring constantly. Stir in almonds. Spoon sauce over broccoli. Serve immediately. Yield: 8 servings.
Per serving: Calories 180 Fat 15.8g
Cholesterol 31mg Sodium 431mg

Creamy Broccoli Casserole

◄ FAMILY FAVORITE ►

PREP: 5 MINUTES   COOK: 35 MINUTES

This is that familiar five-ingredient broccoli casserole seen at many covered dish dinners. It goes with just about any entrée.

2 (10-ounce) packages frozen chopped broccoli
1 (10¾-ounce) can cream of mushroom soup, undiluted
1 (8-ounce) can sliced water chestnuts, drained
1 (2.8-ounce) can French fried onions
¾ cup (3 ounces) shredded Cheddar cheese

•Cook broccoli according to package directions; drain.
•Combine broccoli, soup, water chestnuts, and onions in a bowl; stir well. Spoon into a lightly greased 1½-quart baking dish.
•Cover and bake at 350° for 20 to 25 minutes. Uncover and sprinkle with cheese; bake 2 to 3 more minutes or until cheese melts. Yield: 8 servings.
Per serving: Calories 171 Fat 11.7g
Cholesterol 12mg Sodium 441mg

Brussels Sprouts With Walnuts

PREP: 15 MINUTES   COOK: 12 MINUTES

A tangy vinaigrette elevates these brussels sprouts to a dish befitting the holiday table. The smaller sprouts are the most tender.

1½ pounds fresh brussels sprouts°
½ cup olive oil
3 tablespoons red wine vinegar
2 tablespoons white wine Worcestershire
    sauce
1 tablespoon Dijon mustard
2 teaspoons sugar
½ teaspoon salt
½ teaspoon pepper
⅔ cup chopped walnuts, toasted
½ cup mandarin orange segments

•Wash brussels sprouts; remove discolored leaves. Cut off stem ends, and cut a shallow X in the bottom of each sprout. Place brussels sprouts in a saucepan; add water to cover. Bring to a boil; cover, reduce heat, and simmer 8 minutes or until tender. Drain. Transfer brussels sprouts to a serving bowl; keep warm.
•Combine olive oil and next 6 ingredients in a saucepan. Cook over medium heat until thoroughly heated. Pour over brussels sprouts. Add walnuts and orange segments; toss gently. Serve warm. Yield: 6 servings.
°You can substitute 3 (10-ounce) packages frozen brussels sprouts for 1½ pounds fresh brussels sprouts.
Per serving: Calories 308 Fat 26.4g
Cholesterol 0mg Sodium 345mg

Brussels Sprouts Medley

PREP: 20 MINUTES   COOK: 20 MINUTES

1½ pounds fresh brussels sprouts°
3 cups water
2 chicken bouillon cubes
1½ cups thinly sliced carrot
1½ cups sliced celery
⅓ cup butter or margarine
¾ cup dry-roasted cashew nuts
¼ teaspoon salt
¼ teaspoon dried thyme
⅛ teaspoon pepper

•Wash brussels sprouts thoroughly, and remove discolored leaves. Cut off stem ends, and slash bottom of each sprout with a shallow X.
•Place water and bouillon cubes in a medium saucepan; bring to a boil. Add brussels sprouts, carrot, and celery; return to a boil. Cover, reduce heat, and simmer 12 to 15 minutes or until vegetables are tender. Drain; place vegetables in a serving bowl.
•Melt butter in a small skillet; add cashews and seasonings. Cook over low heat 3 to 4 minutes or until cashews are lightly toasted; pour over vegetables. Yield: 8 servings.
°You can substitute 3 (10-ounce) packages frozen brussels sprouts for 1½ pounds fresh brussels sprouts.
Per serving: Calories 194 Fat 14.2g
Cholesterol 21mg Sodium 491mg

Cabbage Casserole

PREP: 12 MINUTES   COOK: 55 MINUTES

Cooked cabbage wedges get doused with Cheddar cheese sauce. Even half-hearted cabbage fans will find this tasty.

1 medium cabbage, cut into thin wedges
½ cup water
¼ cup butter or margarine
¼ cup all-purpose flour
2 cups milk
½ teaspoon salt
½ teaspoon pepper
⅔ cup (2.6 ounces) shredded Cheddar
    cheese
½ cup chopped green pepper
½ cup chopped onion
½ cup mayonnaise
1 tablespoon chili sauce

•Combine cabbage wedges and water in a Dutch oven; bring to a boil. Cover, reduce heat, and simmer 15 minutes. Drain well; place cabbage wedges in an ungreased 13- x 9-inch baking dish.
•Melt butter in a heavy saucepan over low heat; add flour, stirring until smooth. Cook 1 minute, stirring constantly. Gradually add milk; cook over medium heat, stirring constantly, until thickened and bubbly. Stir in salt and pepper; pour over cabbage. Bake, uncovered, at 375° for 15 minutes.

•Combine cheese and remaining 4 ingredients in a small bowl; stir well. Spread over cabbage. Bake 10 more minutes. Serve hot. Yield: 8 servings.
Per serving: Calories 279 Fat 22.0g
Cholesterol 42mg Sodium 425mg

Braised Red Cabbage

PREP: 18 MINUTES   COOK: 32 MINUTES

Nutty caraway seeds hint at the German roots of this robust cabbage dish. We recommend serving it with pork or game.

1 small onion, chopped
1 clove garlic, minced
½ teaspoon dried thyme
¼ teaspoon caraway seeds
2 bay leaves
½ teaspoon grated lemon rind
½ teaspoon salt
¼ teaspoon ground white pepper
2 tablespoons olive oil
1½ quarts water
1 cup red wine vinegar
¼ cup salt°
1 small head red cabbage, thinly sliced
    (8 cups)
2 tablespoons red wine vinegar
¼ cup chicken broth

•Cook first 8 ingredients in hot oil in a large skillet over medium-high heat, stirring constantly, until onion is tender.
•Combine water, 1 cup vinegar, and ¼ cup salt in a large Dutch oven; bring to a boil. Add cabbage, and cook 10 seconds, stirring constantly; drain.
•Add cabbage, 2 tablespoons vinegar, and chicken broth to onion mixture; bring to a boil. Cover, reduce heat, and simmer 15 to 20 minutes or until cabbage is crisp-tender. Discard bay leaves. Yield: 4 servings.
°One-fourth cup salt is correct for this dish. Most of the salt is drained away after cooking.
Per serving: Calories 119 Fat 7.3g
Cholesterol 0mg Sodium 944mg

Honey-Kissed Carrots

PREP: 17 MINUTES   COOK: 43 MINUTES

Honey plumps the raisins and sweetens the carrots in this simple side dish.

1 pound carrots, scraped and diagonally
   sliced
¼ cup golden raisins
¼ cup butter or margarine, melted
3 tablespoons honey
1 tablespoon lemon juice
¼ teaspoon ground ginger
¼ cup sliced almonds, toasted

•Cook carrot in a small amount of boiling water 8 minutes; drain. Combine carrot, raisins, and next 4 ingredients. Spoon into an ungreased 1-quart baking dish. Bake, uncovered, at 375° for 30 to 35 minutes or until carrot is tender, stirring occasionally. Sprinkle with almonds. Yield: 4 servings.
Per serving: Calories 261 Fat 14.8g
Cholesterol 31mg Sodium 155mg

Cheese Scalloped Carrots

PREP: 14 MINUTES   COOK: 40 MINUTES

A light-colored cheese sauce covers crisp-tender carrots beneath buttery breadcrumbs. This recipe's sure to be well received.

2 pounds carrots, scraped and sliced
½ cup finely chopped celery
¼ cup finely chopped onion
2 tablespoons butter or margarine,
   melted
2 tablespoons all-purpose flour
½ teaspoon salt
¼ teaspoon dry mustard
Dash of pepper
1½ cups milk
1 cup (4 ounces) shredded Cheddar
   cheese
1 cup soft breadcrumbs (homemade)
2 tablespoons butter or margarine, melted
2 tablespoons chopped fresh parsley

•Cover and cook carrot in a small amount of boiling salted water 8 to 10 minutes or until tender; drain and set aside.
•Sauté celery and onion in 2 tablespoons butter in a heavy saucepan until tender. Add flour and next 3 ingredients, stirring until blended. Cook 1 minute, stirring constantly.
•Gradually add milk; cook over medium heat, stirring constantly, until thickened and bubbly. Stir in cheese and carrot; spoon into a lightly greased 1½-quart casserole.
•Combine breadcrumbs, 2 tablespoons butter, and parsley; sprinkle over carrot mixture. Bake, uncovered, at 350° for 25 minutes. Yield: 6 servings.
Per serving: Calories 284 Fat 17.1g
Cholesterol 49mg Sodium 528mg

Carrot and Turnip Puree

◄ **HEALTHY** ►

PREP: 15 MINUTES   COOK: 20 MINUTES

Root vegetable purees like this one make an impressive mashed potato rival. Cooked carrots and turnips are whipped together for a colorful dish that pairs nicely with turkey or roast chicken.

1½ pounds carrots, scraped and cut into
   chunks
2 small fresh turnips, peeled and
   quartered*
¼ cup firmly packed brown sugar
¼ cup frozen orange juice concentrate,
   undiluted
2 tablespoons butter or margarine, melted
⅛ teaspoon ground nutmeg
Garnish: chopped fresh parsley

•Cook carrot and turnip in boiling salted water 20 minutes or until tender; drain and mash together.
•Stir in brown sugar and next 3 ingredients. Garnish, if desired. Serve immediately. Yield: 6 servings.
You can substitute 1 (1¾-pound) rutabaga for turnips.
Per serving: Calories 140 Fat 4.1g
Cholesterol 10mg Sodium 105mg

Festive Cauliflower

PREP: 6 MINUTES   COOK: 30 MINUTES

1 large cauliflower
2 cups water
½ teaspoon salt
1 tablespoon minced onion
1 tablespoon minced green pepper
1 tablespoon minced sweet red pepper
1 tablespoon butter or margarine, melted
3 tablespoons butter or margarine
3 tablespoons all-purpose flour
1 cup milk
1 cup (4 ounces) shredded Cheddar
   cheese
¼ teaspoon dry mustard
Dash of ground white pepper
2 slices bacon, cooked and crumbled
1 tablespoon sliced natural almonds,
   toasted

•Remove and discard outer leaves and stalk of cauliflower, leaving head whole.
•Place cauliflower in a large saucepan; add water and salt. Bring to a boil; cover, reduce heat to medium, and cook 10 to 12 minutes or until tender. Drain well. Cut cauliflower into 8 portions; place on a serving platter, and keep warm.
•Sauté onion, green pepper, and red pepper in 1 tablespoon melted butter in a skillet until tender; drain well, and set aside.
•Melt 3 tablespoons butter in skillet over low heat; add flour, stirring until smooth. Cook 1 minute, stirring constantly. Gradually add milk; cook over medium heat, stirring constantly, until thickened and bubbly. Add cheese, dry mustard, and white pepper, stirring until cheese melts. Remove from heat; stir in reserved onion mixture.
•Spoon sauce over cauliflower. Sprinkle with crumbled bacon and toasted almonds. Serve immediately. Yield: 8 servings.
Per serving: Calories 168 Fat 11.7g
Cholesterol 33mg Sodium 266mg

Cauliflower with Herb Butter

◀ QUICK ▶

PREP: 10 MINUTES · COOK: 10 MINUTES

1 large cauliflower
Juice of 1 lemon
⅓ cup butter or margarine, melted
1 tablespoon chopped fresh parsley
1 tablespoon chopped fresh basil or
  ¼ teaspoon dried basil
¼ teaspoon salt
1 clove garlic, crushed
Garnish: lemon twists, fresh parsley sprigs

•Remove large outer leaves of cauliflower. Break cauliflower into flowerets. Cover and cook in a small amount of boiling water 8 to 10 minutes or until tender; drain. Arrange flowerets in a serving dish, and sprinkle with lemon juice.
•Combine butter and next 4 ingredients; pour herb butter over flowerets. Garnish, if desired. Yield: 6 servings.
Per serving: Calories 115 Fat 10.4g
Cholesterol 28mg Sodium 229mg

Microwave Directions: Remove large outer leaves of cauliflower. Break cauliflower into flowerets. Place flowerets in a shallow 2-quart casserole; add ¼ cup water. Cover with lid, and microwave at HIGH 8 to 10 minutes or until tender, stirring once. Drain cauliflower; arrange flowerets in a serving dish, and sprinkle with lemon juice. Combine butter and next 4 ingredients; pour herb butter over flowerets. Garnish, if desired. Yield: 6 servings.

Celery and Corn Sauté

◀ QUICK ▶

PREP: 6 MINUTES COOK: 6 MINUTES

2 cups diagonally sliced celery
3 tablespoons butter or margarine, melted
1 (10-ounce) package frozen whole kernel corn
1 (2-ounce) jar sliced pimiento, drained
½ teaspoon salt
¼ teaspoon pepper

•Sauté celery in butter in a large skillet over medium heat 5 minutes.
•Cook corn according to package directions; drain. Add to celery in skillet. Stir in pimiento, salt, and pepper. Cook until thoroughly heated. Yield: 4 servings.
Per serving: Calories 150 Fat 8.9g
Cholesterol 23mg Sodium 449mg

Vegetable Burritos

◀ VEGETARIAN ▶

PREP: 25 MINUTES COOK: 10 MINUTES

Wrap a medley of vegetables in these warm soft tortillas. The recipe requires a few minutes of prep work, but assembly's easy.

⅔ cup chopped onion
½ cup shredded carrot
1 clove garlic, crushed
1 tablespoon olive oil
1 (15-ounce) can black beans, rinsed and drained
1 (10-ounce) package frozen chopped broccoli, thawed and drained
1 (10-ounce) package frozen whole kernel corn, thawed and drained
1 (8-ounce) can tomato sauce
1 tablespoon chili powder
½ teaspoon salt
¼ teaspoon ground cumin
Dash of hot sauce
8 (9-inch) flour tortillas
2 cups (8 ounces) shredded Cheddar cheese
Commercial salsa
Commercial guacamole or Guacamole (page 35)

•Sauté first 3 ingredients in hot oil in a large skillet over medium-high heat 2 minutes. Add beans and next 7 ingredients; bring to a boil. Reduce heat, and simmer 5 minutes.
•Heat tortillas according to package directions.
•Spoon about ½ cup vegetable mixture down center of each tortilla; top each with ¼ cup cheese. Fold bottom third of each tortilla over filling. Fold 1 side of tortilla in toward center, and fold top over. Serve with salsa and guacamole. Yield: 4 servings.
Per serving: Calories 895 Fat 41.7g
Cholesterol 60mg Sodium 2281mg

Grilled Corn on the Cob

◀ QUICK · GRILLED ▶

PREP: 12 MINUTES COOK: 20 MINUTES

The flavor of fresh corn is really enhanced on the grill. If you purchase young tender ears, be sure to cook the shorter time.

6 ears fresh corn
¼ cup butter or margarine, melted
1 teaspoon salt
1 teaspoon pepper

•Remove and discard husks and silks from corn. Brush corn with butter; sprinkle with salt and pepper. Wrap each ear tightly in aluminum foil. Grill, covered with grill lid, over medium coals (300° to 350°) 15 to 20 minutes, turning often. Yield: 6 servings.
Per serving: Calories 134 Fat 8.4g
Cholesterol 21mg Sodium 479mg

Microwave Directions: Break husked ears in half; arrange corn in a circle on a round microwave-safe platter or pizza dish with thicker ends of cobs toward center of circle. Brush with melted butter, and sprinkle with salt and pepper. Cover corn loosely with wax paper. Microwave at HIGH 12 to 15 minutes, rotating dish one-half turn after 6 minutes. Yield: 6 servings.

Fried Corn

◀ FAMILY FAVORITE ▶

PREP: 15 MINUTES COOK: 27 MINUTES

Fried corn tastes best when cooked in a cast-iron skillet, but other skillets work fine, too. See this dish on page 438.

12 ears fresh corn
8 slices bacon, uncooked
¼ cup butter or margarine
2 to 4 tablespoons sugar
1 teaspoon salt
½ teaspoon pepper

•Slice whole kernels from cob; set aside. Cook bacon in a large skillet until crisp; remove bacon, reserving 3 tablespoons drippings in skillet. Crumble bacon; set aside.
•Cook corn, butter, and remaining 3 ingredients in bacon drippings over medium heat

20 minutes or until corn is lightly browned, stirring often. Spoon corn mixture into a serving dish, and sprinkle with crumbled bacon. Yield: 12 servings.

Per serving: Calories 177 Fat 11.8g Cholesterol 19mg Sodium 330mg

Corn Pudding

◄ FAMILY FAVORITE ►

PREP: 18 MINUTES   COOK: 47 MINUTES

Creamed corn baked into a slightly sweet custard is a Southern tradition worth preserving. See it on page 438.

9 ears fresh corn
4 large eggs, beaten
½ cup half-and-half
1½ teaspoons baking powder
⅓ cup butter or margarine
2 tablespoons sugar
2 tablespoons all-purpose flour
1 tablespoon butter or margarine, melted
⅛ teaspoon freshly ground pepper

•Remove and discard husks and silks from corn. Cut off tips of corn kernels into a bowl; scrape milk and remaining pulp from cob with a paring knife to measure 3 cups. Set corn aside.
•Combine eggs, half-and-half, and baking powder, stirring well with a wire whisk.
•Melt ⅓ cup butter in a large saucepan over low heat; add sugar and flour, stirring until smooth. Remove from heat; gradually add egg mixture, stirring constantly with a wire whisk until smooth. Stir in corn.
•Pour corn mixture into a greased 1½-quart casserole. Bake, uncovered, at 350° for 40 to 45 minutes or until pudding is set. Drizzle casserole with 1 tablespoon butter; sprinkle with pepper.
•Broil 5½ inches from heat 2 minutes or until golden. Let stand 5 minutes before serving. Yield: 6 servings.

Per serving: Calories 311 Fat 19.5g Cholesterol 182mg Sodium 269mg

CUTTING CORN FOR CREAMING

1. To prepare corn for creaming, first cut tips from an ear of corn, using a paring knife.

2. Then scrape milk and pulp from the cob, using a sturdy vegetable peeler or paring knife.

Southern-Style Creamed Corn

◄ QUICK • FAMILY FAVORITE ►

PREP: 15 MINUTES   COOK: 15 MINUTES

Creamed corn is one of the South's best offerings. Be sure to buy very fresh ears for this recipe; they'll yield the most milk from scraping the cobs.

8 ears fresh white corn
¼ cup butter or margarine
¼ cup water
½ cup half-and-half or milk
2 teaspoons cornstarch
½ teaspoon salt

•Cut off tips of corn kernels into a large bowl, scraping cobs well with a paring knife to remove all milk.
•Combine corn, butter, and water in a heavy saucepan. Cover and cook over medium heat 10 minutes or until corn is done, stirring occasionally.
•Combine half-and-half, cornstarch, and salt, beating with a wire whisk until cornstarch is blended; add to corn mixture, stirring well. Cover and cook 3 minutes or until thickened and bubbly, stirring often. Yield: 4 servings.

Per serving: Calories 276 Fat 16.5g Cholesterol 42mg Sodium 443mg

Macque Choux

PREP: 19 MINUTES   COOK: 25 MINUTES

Macque Choux is a Native American dish meaning "smothered corn." The recipe makes an abundant yield.

12 ears fresh corn
2 tablespoons vegetable oil
1 tablespoon butter or margarine
2 tomatoes, peeled and chopped
1 large onion, chopped
1 medium-size green pepper, chopped
1 clove garlic, minced
1 tablespoon sugar
1 teaspoon salt
¼ teaspoon pepper

•Cut off tips of corn kernels into a bowl, scraping cobs well with a paring knife or vegetable peeler to remove all milk; set aside.
•Combine oil and butter in a large skillet; heat until butter melts. Add corn, tomato, and remaining ingredients; cook 5 minutes, stirring constantly. Cover, reduce heat, and simmer 20 minutes, stirring often. Yield: 12 servings.

Per serving: Calories 114 Fat 4.2g Cholesterol 3mg Sodium 219mg

Ratatouille

PREP: 20 MINUTES   COOK: 31 MINUTES

Ratatouille is a Provençal vegetable dish of stewed eggplant, squash, peppers, and tomatoes. You can serve it hot or cold.

1 eggplant, cubed
1 large zucchini, cubed
2 medium yellow squash, cubed
¼ cup olive oil
1 small green pepper, coarsely chopped
1 small sweet yellow pepper, coarsely chopped
1 small sweet red pepper, coarsely chopped
1 medium onion, chopped
2 cloves garlic, minced
2 (14½-ounce) cans fancy tomato wedges, undrained
½ cup dry white wine
⅓ cup small pitted ripe olives
1 teaspoon salt
2 teaspoons dried Italian seasoning
1 bay leaf
¾ cup freshly grated Parmesan cheese (optional)

•Sauté first 3 ingredients in hot oil in a large Dutch oven over medium-high heat 6 to 8 minutes. Add peppers, onion, and garlic; sauté 8 minutes, stirring occasionally. Add tomatoes and next 5 ingredients; cover, reduce heat to medium, and simmer 15 minutes or until tender. Discard bay leaf.
•Transfer ratatouille to a large serving dish. Sprinkle with cheese, if desired. Serve with a slotted spoon. Yield: 10 servings.
Per serving: Calories 131 Fat 8.0g
Cholesterol 4mg Sodium 514mg

Ratatouille

Eggplant Parmigiana

◄ FAMILY FAVORITE ►
◄ VEGETARIAN ►

PREP: 22 MINUTES   COOK: 1 HOUR

2 large eggs, lightly beaten
½ cup grated Parmesan cheese, divided
¼ cup milk
1 tablespoon chopped fresh parsley or 1 teaspoon dried parsley
½ teaspoon garlic powder
¼ teaspoon salt
¼ teaspoon pepper
1 cup all-purpose flour
1 (1½-pound) eggplant, peeled and cut into ½-inch slices
½ cup vegetable oil
1 (14-ounce) jar spaghetti sauce
2 cups (8 ounces) shredded mozzarella cheese
6 cups hot cooked spaghetti (optional)

•Combine eggs, 2 tablespoons Parmesan cheese, milk, and next 4 ingredients in a shallow bowl, stirring well; set aside.
•Place flour in a shallow dish. Dredge eggplant slices in flour, shaking off excess; dip in egg mixture.
•Pour oil into a large skillet; place over medium-high heat until hot. Fry eggplant slices in hot oil until golden on each side. Drain on paper towels.
•Arrange half of eggplant slices in a lightly greased 11- x 7-inch baking dish. Pour half of spaghetti sauce over eggplant, and sprinkle with half of remaining Parmesan cheese. Repeat procedure with remaining eggplant, sauce, and Parmesan cheese.
•Bake, uncovered, at 350° for 25 minutes. Sprinkle with mozzarella cheese; bake 5 to 10 more minutes or until cheese melts. Serve over spaghetti, if desired. Yield: 6 main-dish servings.
Per serving: Calories 666 Fat 33.4g
Cholesterol 101mg Sodium 701mg

Steamed Fennel with Garlic Butter

◄ QUICK ►

PREP: 10 MINUTES   COOK: 12 MINUTES

Fennel tastes a bit like licorice. See photos that show how to slice this ribbed vegetable.

2 cloves garlic, minced
¼ cup butter or margarine, melted
2 pounds fennel (2 to 3 bulbs)
¼ teaspoon pepper
Lemon wedges

•Sauté garlic in butter in a small skillet over medium-high heat 1 minute. Set aside.
•Rinse fennel thoroughly. Trim stalks to within 1 inch of bulb. Discard hard outside stalks; reserve leaves for another use. Cut a slice off bottom of bulb (photo 1). Cut out tough core from bottom of bulb. Starting at 1 side, cut bulbs lengthwise into ¼-inch-thick slices.
•Arrange fennel in a steamer basket over boiling water. Cover and steam 10 minutes; transfer to a serving dish.
•Pour butter mixture over fennel, and sprinkle with pepper; toss gently. Serve immediately with lemon wedges. Chop feathery fennel tops for garnish, if desired (photo 2). Yield: 4 servings.
Per serving: Calories 136 Fat 12.0g
Cholesterol 31mg Sodium 128mg

Southern-Style Collards

PREP: 20 MINUTES
COOK: 1 HOUR AND 35 MINUTES

1 bunch collard greens (about 3 pounds)
1 pound cured smoked pork shoulder or ham hock
1½ quarts water
¼ teaspoon salt
Pickapepper sauce or vinegar (optional)

•Check leaves of collards carefully; remove pulpy stems and discolored spots on leaves. Wash leaves thoroughly; drain and chop.
•Combine pork shoulder and water in a Dutch oven; bring to a boil. Reduce heat, and simmer, partially covered, 45 minutes or until meat is tender. Remove pork; add salt to water. Add greens to pan.

PREPARING FENNEL

1. To prepare fennel bulb, trim stalks to within 1 inch of bulb; cut a slice off bottom of bulb. Slice bulb as recipe directs.

2. Chop feathery tops (that resemble fresh dill) for garnish, if desired.

•Simmer, uncovered, 45 minutes or until greens are tender, adding more water, if necessary. Serve greens with pickapepper sauce or vinegar, if desired. Yield: 6 servings.
Per serving: Calories 66 Fat 4.5g
Cholesterol 4mg Sodium 409mg

Turnip Greens

◄ HEALTHY ►

PREP: 20 MINUTES   COOK: 1 HOUR

These greens will add a Southern accent to your Thanksgiving table.

2 quarts water
2 teaspoons salt
1 ham hock
6 pounds fresh turnip greens, trimmed and rinsed*
½ cup sugar
1 tablespoon hot sauce

•Combine first 3 ingredients in a stockpot; bring to a boil. Cover, reduce heat, and simmer 20 minutes.
•Add greens, a few at a time, to stockpot; add sugar and hot sauce. Cover and cook over medium heat 40 minutes or to desired doneness; discard ham hock. Yield: 8 servings.
*You can substitute 3 (10-ounce) packages frozen chopped turnip greens, thawed, for fresh.
Per serving: Calories 145 Fat 2.5g
Cholesterol 2mg Sodium 867mg

Creamed Swiss Chard

◄ QUICK ►

PREP: 4 MINUTES   COOK: 16 MINUTES

3 pounds fresh Swiss chard
2 tablespoons butter or margarine
1½ tablespoons all-purpose flour
1 cup half-and-half or milk
½ teaspoon salt
¼ teaspoon pepper
¼ teaspoon ground nutmeg

•Wash chard leaves thoroughly; remove and discard ribs from larger leaves. Coarsely chop chard leaves.
•Place chard in a large Dutch oven (do not add water). Cover and cook over medium heat 10 minutes or until tender. Drain chard well; squeeze between paper towels until barely moist. Return chard to Dutch oven.
•Melt butter in a heavy saucepan over low heat; add flour, stirring until smooth. Cook 1 minute, stirring constantly. Gradually add half-and-half; cook over medium heat, stirring constantly, until thickened and bubbly.
•Stir in salt, pepper, and nutmeg. Stir creamed mixture into chard. Yield: 6 servings.
Per serving: Calories 122 Fat 8.8g
Cholesterol 25mg Sodium 573mg

RUFFLY SWISS CHARD

Swiss chard has broad green leaves and big ribs. The ribs can be white, ruby red, or golden; see them pictured on page 441. Swiss chard is a good source of vitamins A and C. Cook it as you would spinach.

Sautéed Spinach

◄ QUICK ►

PREP: 10 MINUTES   COOK: 6 MINUTES

1 (10-ounce) package fresh spinach
2 green onions, chopped
2 tablespoons butter or margarine, melted
¼ teaspoon sugar
¼ teaspoon salt
¼ teaspoon pepper
Lemon wedges (optional)

•Remove stems from spinach; rinse leaves, and pat dry. Set spinach aside.
•Sauté green onions in butter in a large skillet over medium heat until tender. Add spinach, sugar, salt, and pepper. Sauté 3 to 5 minutes until spinach is wilted and tender; drain. Serve immediately with lemon wedges, if desired. Yield: 3 servings.
Per serving: Calories 91 Fat 8.0g
Cholesterol 21mg Sodium 343mg

Spinach Parmesan

◄ QUICK ►

PREP: 14 MINUTES   COOK: 18 MINUTES

2 (10-ounce) packages fresh spinach
¼ cup water
½ cup freshly grated Parmesan cheese
¼ cup whipping cream
2½ tablespoons butter or margarine, melted
2½ tablespoons finely chopped onion
⅛ teaspoon pepper
½ cup fresh whole wheat breadcrumbs (homemade)

•Remove stems from spinach; rinse leaves. Combine spinach and water in a Dutch oven; cover and cook over medium heat 8 minutes or until tender. Drain well in a colander, pressing with paper towels to remove excess moisture.
•Combine spinach, Parmesan cheese, and next 4 ingredients; spoon into a lightly greased 1-quart baking dish. Top with breadcrumbs. Bake, uncovered, at 450° for 10 minutes or until thoroughly heated. Yield: 4 servings.
Per serving: Calories 206 Fat 16.9g
Cholesterol 47mg Sodium 366mg

Creamed Spinach

◄ QUICK • FAMILY FAVORITE ►

PREP: 10 MINUTES   COOK: 10 MINUTES

1 pound fresh spinach
1 medium onion, chopped
1 clove garlic, crushed
¼ cup butter or margarine, melted
½ cup sour cream
Dash of salt
¼ teaspoon pepper
Pinch of ground nutmeg
Paprika

•Remove stems from spinach; wash leaves thoroughly, and tear into large pieces. Cook spinach in a small amount of boiling water 5 to 8 minutes or until tender. Drain; place on paper towels, and squeeze until barely moist.
•Sauté onion and garlic in butter in a large skillet until tender. Stir in sour cream and next 3 ingredients. Add spinach, and cook over low heat until thoroughly heated; sprinkle with paprika. Yield: 4 servings.
Per serving: Calories 201 Fat 18.0g
Cholesterol 44mg Sodium 251mg

Spinach-Artichoke Bake

PREP: 20 MINUTES   COOK: 30 MINUTES

2 (10-ounce) packages frozen chopped spinach
1 (14½-ounce) can artichoke hearts, undrained
½ cup finely chopped onion
¼ cup butter or margarine, melted
1 (8-ounce) carton sour cream
¼ teaspoon salt
¼ teaspoon pepper
½ cup freshly grated Parmesan cheese, divided

•Cook spinach according to package directions. Drain well, pressing between layers of paper towels to remove excess moisture; set aside.
•Drain artichoke hearts, reserving ¼ cup liquid. Chop artichoke hearts.
•Sauté onion in butter in a large skillet over medium heat until tender. Gently stir in spinach, artichoke hearts, reserved liquid, sour cream, salt, pepper, and ¼ cup Parmesan cheese.

•Spoon into a lightly greased 1½-quart casserole; sprinkle with remaining ¼ cup Parmesan cheese. Bake, uncovered, at 350° for 25 to 30 minutes. Yield: 6 servings.
Per serving: Calories 235 Fat 18.9g
Cholesterol 43mg Sodium 495mg

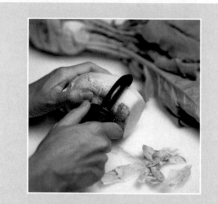

Preparing kohlrabi: Trim kohlrabi roots and tops. Peel woody fibers from bulb, using a vegetable peeler or sharp knife.

Sautéed Kohlrabi

◄ QUICK ►

PREP: 15 MINUTES   COOK: 16 MINUTES

Kohlrabi may be a new vegetable to some folks. The bulb tastes like a mild cabbage. It's a firm vegetable that's easy to peel and slice for sautéing or steaming.

1½ pounds kohlrabi
½ teaspoon salt
1 small onion, sliced and separated into rings
1 clove garlic, minced
¼ cup butter or margarine, melted
½ teaspoon dried basil
⅛ teaspoon freshly ground pepper

•Trim kohlrabi roots and tops; peel kohlrabi bulb (see photo), and cut into julienne strips. Combine kohlrabi and salt in a Dutch oven; cover with water, and bring to a boil. Cover, reduce heat, and simmer 10 minutes or until almost tender. Drain.
•Sauté kohlrabi, onion, and garlic in butter in a large skillet 5 to 6 minutes or until vegetables are tender. Toss with basil and pepper. Yield: 5 servings.
Per serving: Calories 118 Fat 9.4g
Cholesterol 25mg Sodium 231mg

Braised Leeks

PREP: 10 MINUTES   COOK: 35 MINUTES

Leeks are related to garlic and onion, and they're the mildest of the bunch. Leeks can trap a good bit of dirt, so wash them well.

6 medium leeks
2 tablespoons butter or margarine
¾ cup water
¼ cup freshly grated Parmesan cheese
¼ teaspoon salt
¼ teaspoon freshly ground pepper

•Remove root, tough outer leaves, and tops from leeks, leaving 2 inches of dark leaves. Wash thoroughly; cut into 2-inch pieces.
•Melt butter in a large skillet; add leeks, tossing to coat with butter. Cover and cook over medium heat 10 minutes. Add water, and bring to a boil; cover, reduce heat, and simmer 20 minutes or until tender. Drain.
•Combine Parmesan cheese, salt, and pepper; sprinkle over leeks. Yield: 4 servings.
Per serving: Calories 186 Fat 7.7g
Cholesterol 19mg Sodium 328mg

Roasted Vegetables

PREP: 10 MINUTES   COOK: 45 MINUTES

Roasting encourages flavorful caramelization as these vegetables cook and brown.

3 medium leeks (about 2 pounds)
1 pound large carrots, scraped and cut into 2-inch pieces
2 pounds new potatoes, quartered
¼ cup olive oil
1 clove garlic, crushed
½ teaspoon salt
½ teaspoon pepper

•Remove roots, tough outer leaves, and tops from leeks, leaving 4 inches of dark leaves. Wash leeks thoroughly. Cut into 1-inch slices.
•Place leeks, carrot, and potato in a greased roasting pan. Combine oil and remaining 3 ingredients; drizzle over vegetables, stir gently.
•Roast at 450° on bottom rack of oven 45 minutes or until vegetables are tender, stirring occasionally. Yield: 8 servings.
Per serving: Calories 200 Fat 7.5g
Cholesterol 0mg Sodium 183mg

MUSHROOM MANIA

The mushroom market goes far beyond the white button variety we all know so well. Exotic options like shiitake and portobello with their big, meaty taste are quickly becoming mainstream. Generally speaking, the darker the mushroom, the stronger the flavor.

The mushrooms pictured on the following page all have a more intense flavor than the button mushroom. Most of them are available in fresh and dried forms.

Whenever you rehydrate dried mushrooms, consider saving the liquid. It has a rich flavor that can enhance a soup, sauce, or rice dish.

To rehydrate, soak dried mushrooms in warm water 30 minutes; drain well, reserving liquid, and remove tough stems. Then toss the plumped mushrooms into pasta, soup, or a sauce for meats like Shiitake Madeira Sauce on page 237.

Buy fresh mushrooms that are plump, firm, and unblemished. To store fresh mushrooms, place them in a loosely closed paper bag (rather than a plastic grocery bag) in the refrigerator. Plastic produce bags hold moisture and can cause mushrooms to become slimy. Store dried mushrooms in their original package in the pantry.

Clean fresh mushrooms with a mushroom brush or damp paper towels just before using. Never soak fresh mushrooms in water. Mushrooms are like sponges; they'll absorb the water.

Garlic-Stuffed Mushrooms

◄ QUICK ►

PREP: 16 MINUTES   COOK: 13 MINUTES

A threesome of these cheese and garlic stuffed mushroom caps makes a satisfying side dish.

12 large fresh mushrooms
1 tablespoon butter or margarine, melted
1 (4-ounce) package goat cheese, softened
2 cloves garlic, crushed
2 tablespoons chopped fresh parsley
½ teaspoon dried rosemary
¼ teaspoon salt
¼ teaspoon dried basil or thyme
⅛ teaspoon pepper
1 tablespoon butter or margarine, melted
2 tablespoons dry white wine

•Clean mushrooms with damp paper towels. Remove and chop stems; set caps aside. Sauté stems in 1 tablespoon butter in a medium skillet until tender; set aside. Add caps to skillet, and sauté 2 minutes on each side; drain caps on paper towels.
•Combine goat cheese and remaining 8 ingredients in a small bowl; stir with a fork until blended. Stir in chopped mushroom stems. Spoon mixture evenly into reserved mushroom caps. Place mushrooms on an ungreased baking sheet; broil 5½ inches from heat 5 minutes or until lightly browned. Serve hot. Yield: 4 servings.
Per serving: Calories 145 Fat 12.1g
Cholesterol 46mg Sodium 345mg

Burgundy Mushrooms

◄ QUICK ►

PREP: 10 MINUTES   COOK: 10 MINUTES

Serve these wine-enhanced mushrooms with grilled steak or burgers.

1 pound fresh mushrooms, cut in half
½ cup coarsely chopped onion
2 tablespoons butter or margarine, melted
½ cup Burgundy or other dry red wine or beef broth
1 tablespoon Worcestershire sauce
¼ teaspoon salt
⅛ teaspoon pepper

•Clean mushrooms with damp paper towels. Sauté mushrooms and onion in butter in a large skillet over medium-high heat 3 minutes.
•Combine Burgundy and remaining 3 ingredients; add to skillet. Cook over medium-high heat 4 minutes or until most of liquid evaporates. Serve hot. Yield: 4 servings.
Per serving: Calories 89 Fat 6.2g
Cholesterol 16mg Sodium 249mg

Chanterelle · Crimini · Oyster · Shiitake · Enoki · Fresh Wood ear · Dried Wood ear · Portobello · Porcini/cèpe · Portobello · Dried morels · Fresh morels

MUSHROOM DICTIONARY

Chanterelle: This trumpet-shaped mushroom has a chewy texture and ranges in color from golden to yellow-orange. Unlike many exotic mushrooms, the chanterelle has a delicate flavor.

Crimini: Crimini is the brown variety of the button mushroom.

Enoki: This oriental mushroom grows in clumps. It's easily identified by its long, slender stems and tiny caps. Cut away and discard the mass at the base of the clump of mushrooms before using. This mushroom is particularly good eaten raw in salads.

Morel: Available dried and fresh, this mushroom with its elongated honeycomb cap has a rich, smoky flavor. Its shape deliciously traps sauce well.

Oyster: This oriental gray mushroom has a short stem and a ruffled cap resembling an oyster shell. It's mild in flavor.

Porcini: Also called cèpe, you can find this mushroom fresh or dried. It's brown with a strong woodsy, nutty taste. Dried porcini are most commonly found in the U.S. market.

Portobello: This popular mushroom is prized for its huge cap that carries a meaty flavor and texture. Under its cap are exposed gills and somewhat woody stems that aren't always used in cooking. A portobello is actually just a mature brown mushroom.

Shiitake: You can buy this oriental mushroom in fresh or dried form. It has a floppy, flat cap and rich, meaty flavor. Typically only the cap is eaten.

Wood ear: Also called *cloud ear* or *tree ear*, this oriental mushroom is available fresh or dried. Fresh, it resembles large, floppy dark brown "ears." The dried form looks like tiny black chips, but when rehydrated increases five to six times in size. Wood ear mushrooms are popular in oriental soups and stir-fries.

Sautéed Portobello Mushrooms

◄ QUICK ►

PREP: 6 MINUTES   COOK: 4 MINUTES

3 fresh portobello mushrooms
4 cloves garlic, minced
¼ cup olive oil
3 tablespoons chopped fresh Italian parsley
¼ teaspoon salt
¼ teaspoon pepper

•Cut mushrooms into ¼-inch-thick slices. Sauté garlic in hot oil in a large skillet over medium-high heat 1 minute. Add mushrooms to skillet; reduce heat to medium, and sauté 2 to 3 minutes or until mushrooms are tender. Add parsley. Sprinkle with salt and pepper. Serve hot. Yield: 3 servings.

Per serving: Calories 176 Fat 18.2g Cholesterol 0mg Sodium 198mg

Mushroom Casserole

◄ MAKE AHEAD ►

PREP: 20 MINUTES   CHILL: 8 HOURS
COOK: 1 HOUR AND 10 MINUTES

Sautéed mushrooms give this casserole great meaty flavor. Make it a day ahead, and chill it overnight.

¼ cup butter or margarine
1½ pounds fresh mushrooms, sliced*
1 large onion, chopped
½ cup chopped celery
½ cup chopped green pepper
½ cup mayonnaise
8 slices white bread, cut into
   1-inch pieces
2 large eggs, lightly beaten
1½ cups milk
1 (10¾-ounce) can cream of mushroom
   soup, undiluted
1 cup freshly grated Romano cheese

•Melt butter in a large skillet or Dutch oven. Add mushrooms and next 3 ingredients, and cook over medium heat, stirring constantly, until tender; drain well. Stir in mayonnaise.
•Place half of bread evenly into a lightly greased 13- x 9-inch baking dish. Spoon mushroom mixture evenly over bread. Top with remaining bread.
•Combine eggs and milk; pour over bread pieces. Cover and chill at least 8 hours.
•Pour soup over casserole; top with cheese. Cover and bake at 350° for 1 hour or until thoroughly heated and bubbly. Yield: 6 servings.

You can substitute gourmet mushrooms like shiitake, crimini, and portobello for fresh mushrooms. Be sure to chop the portobello mushrooms.

Per serving: Calories 499 Fat 35.7g
Cholesterol 127mg Sodium 999mg

Fresh Okra and Tomatoes

◄ FAMILY FAVORITE ►

PREP: 15 MINUTES   COOK: 25 MINUTES

8 slices bacon
3 tablespoons all-purpose flour
4 cups sliced okra (1 pound)
¾ cup chopped onion
2 cloves garlic, minced
3 cups chopped tomato
½ teaspoon salt
½ teaspoon black pepper
¼ teaspoon ground red pepper

•Cook bacon in a large skillet over medium heat until crisp. Remove bacon, reserving 3 tablespoons drippings in skillet; discard remaining drippings. Crumble bacon, and set aside.
•Stir flour into reserved bacon drippings, and cook over medium heat, stirring constantly, until roux is caramel-colored (10 to 15 minutes).
•Add okra, onion, and garlic; cook 2 minutes, stirring constantly. Stir in tomato and remaining 3 ingredients. Cover and simmer 15 to 20 minutes or until okra is tender, stirring occasionally. Sprinkle with reserved crumbled bacon. Yield: 4 servings.

Per serving: Calories 307 Fat 22.3g
Cholesterol 25mg Sodium 572mg

Fresh Okra and Tomatoes

Fried Okra

◄ QUICK • FAMILY FAVORITE ►

PREP: 6 MINUTES

COOK: 4 MINUTES PER BATCH

This is old-fashioned fried okra without the heavy batter sometimes used in restaurants. For best results, start with good quality fresh okra, and leave a little moisture on the okra so the cornmeal will cling.

1¼ pounds fresh okra
Vegetable oil
¼ to ½ cup cornmeal
¼ teaspoon salt

•Wash okra well; drain. Cut off tips and stem ends; cut okra crosswise into ½-inch slices.
•Pour oil to depth of 2 inches into a Dutch oven; heat to 350°.
•Dredge okra in cornmeal (okra should be very damp for cornmeal to adhere). Fry okra, in batches, 4 minutes or until golden. Drain well on paper towels. Sprinkle with salt. Serve hot. Yield: 4 servings.

Per serving: Calories 306 Fat 27.6g
Cholesterol 0mg Sodium 157mg

Beer-Battered Onion Rings

◄ FAMILY FAVORITE ►

PREP: 40 MINUTES   STAND: 30 MINUTES

COOK: 20 MINUTES

These crisp, puffed golden rings garnered our staff's highest rating.

3 large Vidalia, Spanish, or Bermuda onions
2¼ cups all-purpose flour
2 teaspoons baking powder
1 teaspoon salt
¼ cup yellow cornmeal
2 cups beer
1 large egg, lightly beaten
Vegetable oil

•Peel onions; cut into ½-inch-thick slices, and separate into rings. Place rings in a large bowl of ice water; let stand 30 minutes. Drain on paper towels.
•Combine flour and next 3 ingredients; stir well. Add beer and egg, stirring until thoroughly blended and smooth. Chill batter 15 minutes.

•Dip onion rings into batter, coating both sides well. Pour oil to a depth of 2 to 3 inches in a Dutch oven; heat to 375°. Fry onion rings, a few at a time, 3 to 5 minutes or until golden on both sides. Drain well on paper towels. Serve immediately. Yield: 8 servings.

Per serving: Calories 325 Fat 21.4g
Cholesterol 20mg Sodium 292mg

Caramelized Onions

PREP: 25 MINUTES   COOK: 25 MINUTES

Caramelized Onions are great solo or on burgers, grilled fish, or steaks.

4 medium onions (2 pounds)
1 tablespoon chopped fresh parsley
1 tablespoon chopped fresh chives
1 tablespoon chopped fresh thyme
1 teaspoon salt
½ teaspoon pepper
1 tablespoon butter or margarine
1 tablespoon olive oil

•Cut onions into ¼-inch-thick slices, and separate into rings. Combine onion rings, parsley, and next 4 ingredients in a large bowl, tossing to coat.
•Melt butter in a large heavy skillet or Dutch oven over medium heat; add oil and onion mixture, and cook 25 minutes or until onion is browned and tender, stirring often. Yield: 5 servings.

Per ⅓-cup serving: Calories 103 Fat 5.3g
Cholesterol 6mg Sodium 497mg

Roasted Onions with Pecans

PREP: 15 MINUTES   COOK: 1 HOUR

In this recipe, the onions' natural sugar caramelizes during the long, slow roasting. Top these dark onions with a sprinkling of sugared pecans.

1 cup balsamic vinegar
2 large purple onions, peeled and cut in half crosswise (about 1½ pounds)
½ cup chopped pecans
¼ cup sugar
1 teaspoon pepper

•Bring vinegar to a boil in a 10-inch cast-iron skillet over medium-high heat. Remove from heat; place onions, cut side down, in skillet.
•Roast, uncovered, at 400° for 50 minutes or until onions are tender and browned.
•Meanwhile, combine pecans and sugar in a small skillet. Cook over low heat, stirring constantly, 10 minutes or until sugar melts and coats pecans. Stir in pepper. Spoon pecan mixture onto wax paper; cool. Break into small chunks.
•Place an onion half, cut side up, on each plate. Reserve vinegar in skillet. Sprinkle pecan mixture evenly around onions; drizzle each with vinegar. Yield: 4 servings.

Per serving: Calories 233 Fat 12.3g
Cholesterol 0mg Sodium 7mg

Glazed Parsnips

◄ QUICK ►

PREP: 10 MINUTES   COOK: 10 MINUTES

Parsnips are easy to prepare and adapt to just about any cooking method. Treat them like carrots—with some quick peeling and slicing you can whip out this easy dish in minutes.

1 pound parsnips, scraped and diagonally sliced
3 tablespoons butter or margarine, melted
¼ cup firmly packed brown sugar
1 tablespoon lemon juice
¼ teaspoon salt
⅛ teaspoon freshly ground pepper
1 tablespoon chopped fresh parsley or fresh mint

•Cook parsnips in butter in a large skillet over medium heat 5 minutes, stirring occasionally. Cover and cook over low heat 3 to 4 minutes or until parsnips are crisp-tender.
•Uncover and add brown sugar and next 3 ingredients, stirring about 1 minute to coat parsnips. Remove from heat; stir in parsley. Yield: 4 servings.

Per serving: Calories 205 Fat 8.9g
Cholesterol 23mg Sodium 250mg

Minty Orange Peas

◄ QUICK • HEALTHY ►

PREP: 5 MINUTES   COOK: 6 MINUTES

2 (10-ounce) packages frozen English peas
2 tablespoons butter or margarine
1 tablespoon grated orange rind
2 tablespoons mint jelly
¼ teaspoon salt
1 (8-ounce) can sliced water chestnuts, drained

•Cook peas according to package directions.
•Melt butter in a small saucepan; add orange rind, jelly, and salt. Heat, stirring constantly, until jelly melts. Stir water chestnuts and jelly mixture into peas; stir well, and heat thoroughly. Yield: 6 servings.

Per serving: Calories 135 Fat 4.2g
Cholesterol 10mg Sodium 247mg

Green Peas and Pearl Onions

◄ HEALTHY ►

PREP: 35 MINUTES   COOK: 24 MINUTES

3 pounds fresh English peas in shells (3 cups shelled peas)
½ pound frozen pearl onions
2 tablespoons butter or margarine
2 tablespoons all-purpose flour
1 cup milk
¾ teaspoon salt
⅛ teaspoon pepper
Pinch of ground nutmeg

•Shell and wash peas; cover peas and onions with water in a large saucepan, and bring to a boil. Cover, reduce heat, and simmer 12 to 15 minutes or until peas are tender; drain.

•Melt butter in a heavy saucepan over low heat; add flour, stirring until smooth. Cook 1 minute, stirring constantly. Gradually add milk; cook over medium heat, stirring constantly, 3 minutes or until thickened and bubbly. Stir in salt, pepper, and nutmeg. Spoon sauce over vegetables; toss gently. Yield: 6 servings.

Per serving: Calories 205 Fat 5.8g
Cholesterol 16mg Sodium 361mg

Skillet Snow Peas

◄ QUICK ►

PREP: 6 MINUTES   COOK: 4 MINUTES

Snow peas are best briefly cooked or eaten raw in salads. Their bright green pods are tender and crisp, and the tiny seeds inside are naturally sweet.

1 pound fresh snow pea pods or 2 (6-ounce) packages frozen snow pea pods, thawed
2 green onions, chopped
1 clove garlic, minced
2 tablespoons soy sauce
⅛ teaspoon freshly ground pepper
2 tablespoons olive oil or vegetable oil

•Wash snow peas; trim ends, and remove any tough strings. Sauté snow peas, green onions, and next 3 ingredients in hot oil just until crisp-tender. Yield: 4 servings.

Per serving: Calories 110 Fat 7.0g
Cholesterol 0mg Sodium 520mg

Sugar Snaps and Peppers

◄ QUICK • HEALTHY ►

PREP: 10 MINUTES   COOK: 6 MINUTES

Sugar Snap peas are a cross between snow peas and English peas. They're best eaten raw or just barely cooked to retain their fresh, crisp attributes.

1 clove garlic, minced
1 tablespoon olive oil
½ cup chopped sweet red pepper
½ cup chopped sweet yellow pepper
1 pound fresh Sugar Snap peas, trimmed
¼ teaspoon salt
¼ teaspoon pepper

•Sauté garlic in hot oil in a large skillet over medium-high heat. Add chopped peppers; cook, stirring constantly, 3 minutes or until peppers are crisp-tender. Add peas, and cook 2 more minutes. Sprinkle with salt and pepper. Yield: 4 servings.

Per serving: Calories 89 Fat 3.8g
Cholesterol 0mg Sodium 152mg

Spicy Hot Black-Eyed Peas

PREP: 15 MINUTES   COOK: 35 MINUTES

1 pound shelled fresh black-eyed peas°
½ cup water
3 slices bacon
1 (16-ounce) can whole tomatoes, undrained and chopped
1 cup chopped onion
1 large green pepper, chopped
1 clove garlic, minced
1 teaspoon salt
1 teaspoon ground cumin
1 teaspoon dry mustard
½ teaspoon curry powder
½ teaspoon chili powder
½ teaspoon pepper
Chopped fresh parsley

•Combine peas and water. Bring to a boil; cover, reduce heat, and simmer 10 minutes or until peas are almost tender. Drain and set aside.
•Cook bacon in a large skillet until crisp. Remove bacon, reserving drippings in skillet; crumble bacon, and set aside.
•Stir peas, tomatoes, and next 9 ingredients into bacon drippings in skillet. Bring to a boil; reduce heat, and simmer 20 minutes, stirring occasionally. Pour mixture into a serving dish; sprinkle with bacon and parsley. Yield: 6 servings.

*You can substitute 1 (17-ounce) can or 1 (16-ounce) package of frozen black-eyed peas, drained, for fresh. Do not cook canned or frozen peas before adding them to the recipe.

Per serving: Calories 179 Fat 6.5g
Cholesterol 6mg Sodium 586mg

Sautéed Red and Green Peppers

◄ QUICK ►

PREP: 5 MINUTES   COOK: 6 MINUTES

Red and green peppers provide a colorful side dish and a flavor that complements any kind of meat.

2 sweet red peppers, cut into ¼-inch strips
2 green peppers, cut into ¼-inch strips
1 small onion, sliced and separated into rings
1 clove garlic, minced
3 tablespoons olive oil or vegetable oil
½ teaspoon salt
½ teaspoon dried basil
¼ teaspoon freshly ground pepper

•Sauté first 4 ingredients in hot oil in a large skillet just until tender. Stir in salt, basil, and pepper. Yield: 4 servings.
Per serving: Calories 125 Fat 10.6g
Cholesterol 0mg Sodium 297mg

Hash Brown Potatoes

◄ FAMILY FAVORITE ►

PREP: 25 MINUTES   COOK: 31 MINUTES

2 pounds round red potatoes, halved
2 tablespoons bacon drippings
2 tablespoons butter or margarine
1 small onion, chopped
2 tablespoons minced fresh parsley
½ teaspoon dried oregano
2 cloves garlic, minced
¼ teaspoon salt
⅛ teaspoon pepper

•Place potatoes in a Dutch oven with water to cover; bring to a boil. Cook, uncovered, 8 minutes; drain and chill at least 20 minutes. Dice potatoes, and set aside.
•Melt bacon drippings and butter in a 9-inch cast-iron skillet over medium-high heat. Add diced potato, stirring until coated. Cook potato 10 minutes, turning occasionally. Add onion and remaining ingredients, stirring gently; cook 10 minutes or until potato is browned on all sides. Yield: 4 servings.
Per serving: Calories 290 Fat 12.5g
Cholesterol 22mg Sodium 222mg

Basic Mashed Potatoes

◄ QUICK • FAMILY FAVORITE ►

PREP: 5 MINUTES   COOK: 15 MINUTES

4 medium-size baking potatoes, peeled and cut into eighths (1½ to 2 pounds)
3 tablespoons butter or margarine, cut up
½ cup milk or half-and-half
¾ teaspoon salt
¼ teaspoon pepper

•Cook potatoes in boiling water to cover 15 minutes or until tender; drain well. Return potatoes to pan (photo 1). Add butter, and mash with a potato masher. Stir in milk, salt, and pepper. Mash again to desired consistency (photo 2). Serve hot. Yield: 4 servings.
Per serving: Calories 194 Fat 9.8g
Cholesterol 27mg Sodium 559mg

Roasted Garlic Mashed Potatoes

◄ FAMILY FAVORITE ►

PREP: 10 MINUTES
COOK: 1 HOUR AND 20 MINUTES

2 heads garlic, unpeeled°
Olive oil
2 pounds red potatoes, peeled and quartered
2 teaspoons salt, divided
¼ cup milk
¼ cup refrigerated shredded Parmesan cheese
3 tablespoons butter or margarine
⅓ cup chopped fresh parsley
½ teaspoon pepper

•Cut top off garlic, leaving heads intact. Place garlic heads on a piece of aluminum foil, and drizzle with olive oil. Fold foil to seal.
•Bake at 350° for 1 hour; cool 10 minutes. Remove outermost layers of papery skin from garlic. Squeeze out soft garlic pulp, and set aside.
•Bring potatoes, 1 teaspoon salt, and water to cover to a boil in a Dutch oven; boil 15 to 20 minutes or until potatoes are tender. Drain well. Return potatoes to pan. Mash potatoes; stir in garlic, remaining 1 teaspoon salt, milk,

MASHING POTATOES

1. Cook potatoes in boiling water until tender; drain well. Return potatoes to warm pan.

2. Add butter and mash. Then add milk and seasonings, and mash until desired texture.

and remaining ingredients. Mash until mixture is smooth. Yield: 8 servings.
°For an easy shortcut, substitute 2 tablespoons commercial roasted garlic in a jar for roasted garlic.
Per serving: Calories 159 Fat 7.1g
Cholesterol 14mg Sodium 535mg

POTATO "A-PEEL"

There's no rule that says you have to peel potatoes for mashing, although most people do. Scrub the skins well, and do not peel potatoes to compare the difference sometime. Potatoes mashed with skins on have a rustic look and a wonderful earthy flavor. Leaving the skins on saves time, too.

Fried Potato Patties

◄ QUICK • FAMILY FAVORITE ►

PREP: 11 MINUTES   COOK: 12 MINUTES

2 cups cooked, mashed potato (2 medium-
   size baking potatoes)
1 cup (4 ounces) shredded mozzarella
   cheese
1 large egg, lightly beaten
½ teaspoon salt
½ teaspoon garlic powder
½ teaspoon onion powder
¼ teaspoon pepper
1 large egg, lightly beaten
1 cup soft breadcrumbs (homemade)
¼ to ½ cup vegetable oil

•Combine first 7 ingredients; shape into 6
(¾-inch-thick) patties. Dip each pattie in
egg, and coat lightly with breadcrumbs.
•Fry patties in hot oil in a large skillet over
medium heat 12 minutes or until lightly
browned, turning once. Drain on paper
towels. Yield: 6 servings.
Per serving: Calories 233 Fat 14.1g
Cholesterol 82mg Sodium 358mg

Oven Fries

◄ HEALTHY ►
◄ FAMILY FAVORITE ►

PREP: 5 MINUTES   COOK: 30 MINUTES

*These fries are crisp and lean, and they come
with a pair of great-tasting variations, too.*

1½ pounds baking potatoes, cut into thin
   strips
1 tablespoon vegetable oil
1 teaspoon salt

•Pat potatoes dry with paper towels, and
place in a large heavy-duty, zip-top plastic
bag. Add oil, and turn bag to coat potatoes.
Sprinkle potatoes with salt, turning bag
to coat.
•Arrange potatoes in a single layer on a large
greased baking sheet or jellyroll pan. Bake at
450° for 15 minutes. Turn potatoes with a
spatula, and cook 15 more minutes or until
golden, turning every 5 minutes. Serve hot.
Yield: 4 servings.
Per serving: Calories 158 Fat 3.7g
Cholesterol 0mg Sodium 598mg

Chili Fries: Combine 1 teaspoon salt, 2 teaspoons chili powder, ½ teaspoon dried
oregano, ¼ teaspoon garlic powder, and ¼
teaspoon ground cumin, stirring well.
Sprinkle chili mixture over oiled potatoes in
bag, turning to coat. Yield: 4 servings.

Cheese Fries: Reduce salt to ½ teaspoon,
and combine with 2 to 3 tablespoons grated
Parmesan cheese, ¼ teaspoon garlic powder,
¼ teaspoon paprika, and ¼ teaspoon pepper
in a small bowl, stirring well. Sprinkle over
oiled potatoes in bag, turning to coat. Yield:
4 servings.

Duchess Potatoes

PREP: 18 MINUTES   COOK: 30 MINUTES

2½ pounds baking potatoes, peeled and
   quartered
¼ cup butter or margarine
¼ cup milk
1 teaspoon salt
¼ teaspoon pepper
2 egg yolks
2 tablespoons butter or margarine, melted
¼ teaspoon paprika

•Cook potatoes in boiling water to cover 15
minutes or until very tender; drain and mash
well. Stir in butter and next 3 ingredients;
cool 10 minutes. Stir in egg yolks.
•Spoon mixture into a large decorating bag
fitted with a large star tip. Pipe 14 (2-inch)
rosettes onto a lightly greased baking sheet.
Drizzle with melted butter, and sprinkle with
paprika.
•Bake at 400° for 15 minutes or until lightly
browned around the edges. Yield: 7 servings.
Per serving: Calories 228 Fat 16.0g
Cholesterol 102mg Sodium 460mg

Note: To make ahead, pipe potato mixture
into rosettes; cover and chill up to 3 hours.
Let stand at room temperature 30 minutes;
bake as directed.

Easy Stuffed Potatoes

◄ QUICK • FAMILY FAVORITE ►

PREP: 15 MINUTES   COOK: 16 MINUTES

*Turn these sour cream-stuffed potatoes out in
just half an hour. The recipe makes optimum
use of the microwave.*

4 slices bacon
2 medium-size baking potatoes (about 1
   pound)
¾ cup (3 ounces) shredded Cheddar
   cheese
½ cup sour cream
¼ teaspoon salt
¼ teaspoon pepper
2 green onions, chopped

•Place bacon on a rack in an 11- x 7-inch
baking dish; cover with paper towels.
•Microwave at HIGH 3 to 4 minutes or until
bacon is crisp. Drain bacon, crumble, and set
aside.
•Scrub potatoes, and prick several times with
a fork. Place potatoes, 1 inch apart, on a
microwave-safe rack or on paper towels.
Microwave at HIGH 7 to 8 minutes; let
stand 5 minutes.
•Cut a 1-inch lengthwise strip from top of
each potato. Carefully scoop out pulp, leaving shells intact. Mash potato pulp; stir in
cheese, sour cream, salt, pepper, and green
onions.
•Spoon potato mixture into shells. Top with
crumbled bacon. Place on a microwave-safe
plate, and microwave at HIGH 1 minute or
until potatoes are thoroughly heated. Yield: 2
servings.
Per serving: Calories 618 Fat 33.3g
Cholesterol 82mg Sodium 829mg

Balsamic Roasted New Potatoes

◄ HEALTHY ►

PREP: 12 MINUTES   COOK: 37 MINUTES

2 tablespoons olive oil or butter
2 pounds new potatoes, unpeeled and
   quartered
1 tablespoon minced garlic
1 teaspoon chopped fresh thyme
1 teaspoon chopped fresh rosemary
⅛ teaspoon ground nutmeg
3 tablespoons balsamic vinegar
½ teaspoon salt
¼ teaspoon pepper

•Heat oil in a large cast-iron skillet over medium-high heat. Add potatoes and next 4 ingredients. Toss. Remove skillet from heat; place in oven.
•Roast potatoes, uncovered, at 425° for 30 minutes or until potatoes are tender, stirring occasionally. Add vinegar, and toss well. Sprinkle with salt and pepper. Roast, uncovered, 6 more minutes. Serve immediately. Yield: 5 servings.
Per serving: Calories 193 Fat 5.6g
Cholesterol 0mg Sodium 248mg

Sweet Potato Casserole

PREP: 42 MINUTES

COOK: 1 HOUR AND 20 MINUTES

This traditional sweet potato casserole has a crunchy brown sugar top. You can make it ahead and chill it overnight; just add 5 minutes to the baking time.

6 medium-size sweet potatoes
½ cup firmly packed brown
   sugar
2 large eggs
1 teaspoon vanilla extract
⅓ cup half-and-half or milk
½ cup butter or margarine,
   melted
1 cup firmly packed brown
   sugar
2 tablespoons all-purpose flour
¼ cup butter or margarine
1 cup coarsely chopped pecans
½ cup flaked coconut (optional)

MICRO-BAKED POTATOES

Rinse potatoes and pat dry; prick several times with a fork. Arrange potatoes in microwave oven, leaving 1 inch between each. (If microwaving more than 2 potatoes, arrange them in a circle.)

Microwave at HIGH according to the times at right, turning and rearranging potatoes once. Let potatoes stand 5 minutes before serving. (If potatoes are not done after standing, microwave briefly and let stand 2 minutes.)

NUMBER OF POTATOES	MINUTES AT HIGH POWER
1	4 to 6
2	7 to 8
3	9 to 11
4	12 to 14
6	16 to 18

Note: These times are for cooking medium-size potatoes (6 to 7 ounces). If potatoes are larger, allow more time.

•Cook sweet potatoes in boiling water to cover 30 to 45 minutes or until tender. Let cool to touch; peel and mash potatoes.
•Combine sweet potato, ½ cup sugar, and next 4 ingredients; beat at medium speed with an electric mixer until smooth. Spoon into a greased 13- x 9-inch baking dish.
•Combine 1 cup brown sugar and flour; cut in ¼ cup butter with a pastry blender until mixture is crumbly. Stir in pecans and, if desired, coconut; sprinkle over casserole. Bake, uncovered, at 350° for 30 to 35 minutes or until lightly browned and bubbly around edges. Yield: 8 servings.
Per serving: Calories 644 Fat 32.1g
Cholesterol 103mg Sodium 247mg

Candied Sweet Potatoes

◄ HEALTHY ►

PREP: 25 MINUTES   STAND: 1 HOUR

COOK: 1½ HOURS

6 large sweet potatoes (about 4
   pounds)
1 lemon, unpeeled
1 orange, unpeeled
¾ cup butter or margarine, melted
2 cups sugar
½ cup orange juice
2 teaspoons ground cinnamon
1 teaspoon vanilla extract

•Peel potatoes; cut potatoes, lemon, and orange into ¼-inch-thick slices.
•Place potato slices in a lightly greased 13- x 9-inch baking dish; arrange lemon and orange slices over potato.

•Combine melted butter and remaining 4 ingredients; pour over potato mixture. Cover and let stand 1 hour.
•Bake, uncovered, at 350° for 1½ hours or until potatoes are tender, basting often with pan juices. Serve with a slotted spoon. Yield: 10 servings.
Per serving: Calories 220 Fat 5.3g
Cholesterol 12mg Sodium 62mg

Simple Steamed Rutabagas

◄ HEALTHY ►

PREP: 20 MINUTES   COOK: 35 MINUTES

Rutabagas resemble large turnips and have a slightly sweet, firm flesh. Here they're steamed and tossed with a hint of honey.

4 cups peeled, cubed rutabaga
3 tablespoons butter or margarine, melted
1 tablespoon lemon juice
1 tablespoon honey
⅛ teaspoon hot sauce
1 tablespoon chopped fresh parsley
½ teaspoon salt
Dash of pepper

•Arrange rutabaga in a steamer basket over boiling water. Cover and steam 30 to 35 minutes or until tender. Drain.
•Place rutabaga in a bowl. Add butter and next 3 ingredients; toss. Sprinkle with parsley, salt, and pepper; toss gently. Yield: 6 servings.
Per serving: Calories 96 Fat 6.0g
Cholesterol 16mg Sodium 274mg

Zucchini-Parmesan Toss

◄ QUICK ►

PREP: 3 MINUTES   COOK: 5 MINUTES

1 pound fresh zucchini, cut into ¼-inch
  slices
1 tablespoon olive oil
3 tablespoons freshly grated Parmesan
  cheese
¼ teaspoon grated lemon rind
¼ teaspoon salt
¼ teaspoon pepper

•Sauté zucchini in hot oil in a large skillet
over medium-high heat 5 minutes or until
crisp-tender. Spoon into a serving dish.
•Combine cheese and remaining 3 ingredients. Sprinkle over squash; toss gently. Serve
immediately. Yield: 2 servings.
Per serving: Calories 383 Fat 26.3g
Cholesterol 51mg Sodium 1492mg

Yellow Squash Casserole

◄ FAMILY FAVORITE ►

PREP: 25 MINUTES   COOK: 55 MINUTES

*We tested several versions of this favorite
Southern vegetable casserole, and then gave
this cheese and bacon rendition our seal of
approval.*

2 pounds yellow squash, sliced
1 cup minced onion
2 tablespoons butter or margarine,
  melted
1¼ cups round buttery cracker crumbs (18
  crackers), divided
1½ cups (6 ounces) shredded sharp
  Cheddar cheese
2 large eggs, beaten
4 slices bacon, cooked and crumbled
1 (2-ounce) jar diced pimiento,
  drained
¼ teaspoon salt
¼ teaspoon pepper

•Combine squash and water to cover in a
medium saucepan; bring to a boil. Cover,
reduce heat, and simmer 10 minutes or until
squash is tender. Drain well, and mash; set
aside.
•Sauté onion in butter until tender. Combine
onion, squash, ¾ cup cracker crumbs, cheese,

and remaining 5 ingredients. Spoon into a
lightly greased 2-quart casserole or an 11- x 7-
inch baking dish. Sprinkle with remaining ½
cup cracker crumbs. Bake, uncovered, at 350°
for 45 minutes. Yield: 6 servings.
Per serving: Calories 294 Fat 20.6g
Cholesterol 115mg Sodium 497mg

Squash and Tomato Bake

◄ FAMILY FAVORITE ►

PREP: 28 MINUTES   COOK: 45 MINUTES

2 pounds yellow squash, sliced
1 cup water
2 (14½-ounce) cans stewed tomatoes
1 tablespoon all-purpose flour
2 teaspoons sugar
1 teaspoon salt
1 teaspoon paprika
½ teaspoon garlic powder
¼ teaspoon pepper
2 cups (8 ounces) shredded mozzarella
  cheese
½ cup grated Parmesan cheese

•Combine squash and water in a large
saucepan. Bring to a boil; cover, reduce heat,
and simmer 10 minutes or until squash is
tender, stirring occasionally. Remove from
heat; drain.
•Drain tomatoes, reserving ¼ cup liquid.
Combine tomatoes, reserved liquid, flour,
and next 5 ingredients in a saucepan. Bring to
a boil; reduce heat, and simmer 5 minutes.
Remove from heat. Place half of squash in a
lightly greased shallow 2-quart casserole;
pour one-fourth of tomato mixture over
squash. Top with 1 cup shredded mozzarella
cheese and one-fourth of tomato mixture.
•Repeat layers with remaining squash, tomato mixture, and mozzarella cheese. Sprinkle
with Parmesan cheese. Bake at 350° for 30
minutes. Let stand 10 minutes before serving. Yield: 8 servings.
Per serving: Calories 166 Fat 7.3g
Cholesterol 21mg Sodium 808mg

Grilled Vegetable Skewers

◄ GRILLED ►

**PREP: 20 MINUTES   STAND: 1 HOUR
COOK: 12 MINUTES**

2 large yellow squash, cut into ¾-inch-
  thick slices
1 large zucchini, cut into ¾-inch-thick
  slices
1 large green pepper, cut into 1-inch
  squares
1 large sweet yellow pepper, cut into
  1-inch squares
1 large sweet red pepper, cut into 1-inch
  squares
¼ cup olive oil
2 tablespoons tarragon vinegar
1 clove garlic, crushed
¼ teaspoon dried thyme
¼ teaspoon salt
¼ teaspoon pepper
¾ pound medium-size fresh mushrooms

•Combine first 5 ingredients in a Dutch
oven. Cook in boiling water to cover 2 minutes; drain. Plunge into ice water to stop the
cooking process; drain and set aside.
•Combine oil and next 5 ingredients in a
large bowl, stirring with a wire whisk. Add
cooked vegetables and mushrooms; toss gently. Cover and let stand 1 hour, tossing
occasionally.
•Drain vegetables, and thread alternately on
skewers. Grill, covered with grill lid, over
medium-hot coals (350° to 400°) 10 minutes
or until tender, turning once. Yield: 10
servings.
Per serving: Calories 52 Fat 3.1g
Cholesterol 0mg Sodium 33mg

YELLOW SQUASH STANDARDS

When you're selecting yellow squash,
be sure to look at the stem; it can indicate
the quality of the squash. If the stem is
hard, dry, shriveled, or dark, the squash is
not fresh.

Apple-Spiced Acorn Squash

PREP: 13 MINUTES   COOK: 50 MINUTES

Acorn squash has beautiful golden flesh. Here it's paired with apple, sausage, and spices, and then returned to bake in its own sturdy green shell. Pair this squash with pork tenderloin or turkey.

1 large acorn squash (about 2 pounds)
¼ pound ground pork sausage
1 large Granny Smith apple, cored and chopped
1 tablespoon brown sugar
¼ teaspoon ground nutmeg
¼ teaspoon ground cinnamon
½ teaspoon salt
Butter or margarine

•Cut squash in half horizontally, and remove seeds. Cut a small slice from both ends of squash so halves sit upright, like a shell.
•Cover and cook squash shells in boiling water 10 minutes or just until tender; remove from water, and cool 5 minutes. Scoop pulp from shells.
•Brown sausage in a skillet, stirring until it crumbles; stir in apple and squash pulp. Cook over medium heat 10 minutes, stirring often. Add brown sugar and next 3 ingredients; stir well.
•Spoon mixture into squash shells; dot with butter. Place shells in a 9-inch square pan; bake, uncovered, at 350° for 30 minutes. Serve immediately. Yield: 2 servings.
Per serving: Calories 391 Fat 16.5g
Cholesterol 65mg Sodium 751mg

Spaghetti Squash Italiano

PREP: 25 MINUTES   COOK: 37 MINUTES

Inside each large yellow shell hides a mound of spaghetti-like strands. Once the squash is cooked, remove the strands, and add them to the herbed vegetable filling.

1 (4-pound) spaghetti squash
⅓ cup water
2 cloves garlic, minced
1 small onion, chopped
1 tablespoon olive oil
2 large yellow squash, halved lengthwise and sliced
½ cup chopped sweet yellow pepper
1 medium tomato, seeded and chopped
1 (7-ounce) jar sun-dried tomatoes in oil, drained and cut into strips
1 tablespoon minced fresh basil or 1 teaspoon dried basil
1 tablespoon minced fresh parsley
2 teaspoons minced fresh oregano or ½ teaspoon dried oregano
½ teaspoon salt
⅛ teaspoon pepper
¼ cup grated Parmesan cheese, divided
Garnish: fresh basil sprigs

•Pierce spaghetti squash several times with a fork; place in a 13- x 9-inch baking dish. Microwave, uncovered, at HIGH 10 minutes. Cut in half lengthwise; discard seeds.
•Place spaghetti squash, cut side up, in baking dish; add water. Cover tightly with heavy-duty plastic wrap, turning back one corner to allow steam to escape. Microwave at HIGH 12 to 14 minutes or until tender, turning squash every 5 minutes. Let stand 5 minutes. Drain and cool.
•Using a fork, remove spaghetti-like strands to yield 4 cups, leaving 2 (¼-inch-thick) shells. Place strands in a large bowl; set aside. Drain shells, cut side down, on paper towels.
•Sauté garlic and onion in hot oil in a large skillet 3 minutes or until onion is tender. Add yellow squash and yellow pepper; cook 3 to 4 minutes or until crisp-tender. Add onion mixture to squash strands. Stir in chopped tomato and next 6 ingredients. Add 2 tablespoons Parmesan cheese; toss gently.
•Spoon squash mixture into reserved squash shells. Place stuffed shells in baking dish, and microwave, uncovered, at HIGH 5 to 6

minutes or until thoroughly heated. (Or place baking dish in oven, and bake at 400° for 5 minutes.) Sprinkle with remaining 2 tablespoons Parmesan cheese. Garnish, if desired. Scoop out to serve. Yield: 6 servings.
Per serving: Calories 155 Fat 6.4g
Cholesterol 4mg Sodium 356mg

Stuffed Chayote Squash

PREP: 45 MINUTES   COOK: 1 HOUR

These small, green, pear-shaped squash are called mirlitons *in Louisiana. They're mild in flavor and sometimes split, stuffed, and baked like acorn squash.*

4 chayote squash, cut in half
3 slices bacon, chopped
1 small onion, chopped
1 clove garlic, minced
½ teaspoon salt
¼ teaspoon pepper
¼ teaspoon dried thyme
¼ teaspoon dried marjoram
¼ cup (1 ounce) shredded Cheddar cheese
2 tablespoons soft breadcrumbs (homemade)
2 tablespoons chopped fresh parsley
2 tablespoons grated Parmesan cheese

•Cook squash in boiling water to cover 10 minutes; drain and cool. Using a melon baller or spoon, carefully scoop out pulp, leaving shells intact. Chop pulp, and set aside with shells.
•Cook bacon in a large skillet over medium-high heat until crisp; remove bacon, reserving drippings in skillet. Add onion and next 5 ingredients to skillet; cook until onion is tender.
•Combine bacon, onion mixture, squash pulp, Cheddar cheese, breadcrumbs, and parsley; stir well. Spoon into reserved shells, and sprinkle with Parmesan cheese.
•Bake, uncovered, at 350° for 45 minutes to 1 hour or until tender. Yield: 8 servings.
Per serving: Calories 82 Fat 5.9g
Cholesterol 9mg Sodium 248mg

Praline-Topped Winter Squash

PREP: 20 MINUTES

COOK: 1 HOUR AND 10 MINUTES

5 pounds butternut or hubbard squash
2 tablespoons butter or margarine
2 tablespoons brown sugar
⅓ cup golden raisins
½ teaspoon salt
¼ teaspoon ground nutmeg
⅛ teaspoon pepper
2 tablespoons finely chopped pecans
1 tablespoon brown sugar
1 tablespoon light corn syrup
1 tablespoon butter or margarine

• Cut squash in half lengthwise, and remove seeds. Place squash, cut side down, in shallow pans; add water to depth of ½ inch. Cover and bake at 400° for 1 hour or until tender. Drain. Scoop out pulp, and discard shell.
• Combine squash pulp, 2 tablespoons butter, and 2 tablespoons brown sugar in a large saucepan; blend with a potato masher until smooth. Add raisins, salt, nutmeg, and pepper; cook over medium heat 10 minutes, stirring often.
• Combine pecans and remaining 3 ingredients in a small saucepan; cook over medium heat until sugar dissolves, stirring constantly.
• Spoon squash into a serving dish. Drizzle praline topping over squash. Yield: 8 servings.

Per serving: Calories 155 Fat 5.8g
Cholesterol 12mg Sodium 202mg

Stuffed Seasoned Tomatoes

◀ FAMILY FAVORITE ▶

PREP: 27 MINUTES COOK: 10 MINUTES

8 medium-size firm ripe tomatoes*
1 cup Italian-seasoned breadcrumbs
⅓ cup chopped green onions
¼ cup grated Parmesan cheese
1 tablespoon chopped fresh thyme
2 cloves garlic, minced
½ teaspoon salt
¼ teaspoon pepper
¼ cup olive oil

• Cut a ¼-inch-thick slice from top of each tomato; scoop out pulp into a bowl, leaving shells intact. Place shells upside down on paper towels to drain. Drain and chop pulp, discarding liquid.
• Add breadcrumbs and remaining 7 ingredients to chopped pulp, stirring well; spoon mixture into tomato shells, and place in a lightly greased 13- x 9-inch baking dish.
• Bake at 450° for 10 minutes. Yield: 8 servings.
*You can substitute 12 plum tomatoes, cut in half lengthwise, for 8 medium-size tomatoes.

Per serving: Calories 178 Fat 9.0g
Cholesterol 3mg Sodium 618mg

Stewed Tomato Bake

◀ QUICK • HEALTHY ▶

PREP: 10 MINUTES COOK: 20 MINUTES

2 (14½-ounce) cans stewed tomatoes, undrained
1½ tablespoons cornstarch
1¼ teaspoons dried basil
½ teaspoon dried marjoram
½ teaspoon freshly ground pepper
10 round buttery crackers, crushed
3 tablespoons grated Parmesan cheese

• Drain tomatoes, reserving juice. Add cornstarch to reserved juice, stirring until blended. Pour juice into a lightly greased 1-quart baking dish. Add tomatoes, and sprinkle with basil, marjoram, and pepper. Bake at 450° for 15 minutes. Remove from oven, and stir gently. Combine cracker crumbs and cheese; sprinkle evenly over tomatoes. Bake 5 more minutes or until crumbs are browned. Yield: 4 servings.

Per serving: Calories 141 Fat 4.5g
Cholesterol 3mg Sodium 664mg

Microwave Directions: Drain tomatoes, reserving juice. Add cornstarch to reserved juice, stirring until blended. Pour juice into a lightly greased 1-quart baking dish. Add tomatoes, and sprinkle with basil, marjoram, and pepper. Cover loosely with a paper towel, and microwave at HIGH 5 to 7 minutes or until bubbly. Remove from oven; stir gently. Combine cracker crumbs and cheese; sprinkle evenly over tomatoes. Microwave at HIGH 2 minutes.

A QUICK PEEL FOR TOMATOES

1. To peel a tomato, first blanch it in boiling water 30 seconds.

2. Remove tomato from water, and pull skin away, using a sharp paring knife.

Southern Fried Green Tomatoes

◄ QUICK • FAMILY FAVORITE ►

PREP: 12 MINUTES   COOK: 15 MINUTES

We prefer breading tangy green tomato slices in fine white cornmeal for this Southern favorite. Or you can coat them in cracker crumbs or breadcrumbs. Be ready to eat as soon as these fried slices come off the heat to enjoy at their crispy best.

⅔ cup white cornmeal
¼ teaspoon salt
¼ teaspoon pepper
3 large green tomatoes, sliced
1 large egg, lightly beaten
¼ cup plus 2 tablespoons vegetable oil or olive oil

• Combine first 3 ingredients in a small bowl; stir well. Dip tomato slices in beaten egg; dredge in cornmeal mixture, coating well on both sides.
• Heat 2 tablespoons oil in a large skillet over medium-high heat until hot. Add 1 layer of coated tomato slices, and fry 3 to 5 minutes or until browned, turning once. Remove tomato slices from skillet. Drain; set fried tomato slices aside, and keep warm. Repeat procedure twice with remaining oil and tomato slices. Serve immediately. Yield: 6 servings.

Per serving: Calories 204 Fat 15.0g
Cholesterol 35mg Sodium 117mg

Fresh Tomato Tart

◄ HEALTHY ►
◄ FAMILY FAVORITE ►

PREP: 20 MINUTES   COOK: 45 MINUTES

Enjoy this attractive tart not only as a side dish, but also as an appetizer or meatless entrée. Be sure to use plum tomatoes; they give the prettiest slices for topping the tart, and they're not as juicy as some other varieties.

½ (15-ounce) package refrigerated piecrusts
2 cups (8 ounces) shredded mozzarella cheese
3 tablespoons chopped fresh basil, divided
1 large clove garlic, sliced into 8 slivers
6 to 8 plum tomatoes, cut lengthwise into ½-inch slices
1½ tablespoons olive oil
¼ teaspoon salt
¼ teaspoon pepper

• Place piecrust in a 10-inch tart pan according to package directions; trim off excess pastry along edges. Generously prick bottom and sides of pastry with a fork; bake at 400° for 5 minutes.
• Sprinkle cheese into pastry shell, and top with 2 tablespoons basil; sprinkle garlic over cheese and basil. Arrange tomato slices on top; brush with oil, and sprinkle with salt and pepper. Place on a baking sheet; place baking sheet on lower rack of oven.
• Bake at 400° for 35 to 40 minutes. Remove from oven; sprinkle with remaining 1 tablespoon basil. Let stand 5 minutes before serving. Yield: 8 servings.

Per serving: Calories 228 Fat 14.2g
Cholesterol 22mg Sodium 311mg

TANGY TURNIPS

Turnips are round with whitish skin and a purple band. When turnips are eaten raw, the crunchy mild flavor hints of radishes. Fresh turnips are available year-round. Look for roots that are smooth, firm, and heavy for their size. Store roots in a cool, moist area or in a plastic bag in the refrigerator crisper drawer.

Tangy Turnips

PREP: 5 MINUTES   COOK: 30 MINUTES

3 medium turnips, peeled and sliced
1 teaspoon salt
4 slices bacon, chopped
¼ cup sugar
1 teaspoon all-purpose flour
¼ cup white vinegar

• Place sliced turnips in a saucepan; cover with water. Add salt; bring to a boil. Cover, reduce heat, and simmer 15 to 20 minutes or until turnips are tender. Drain and arrange turnip in a serving dish.
• Meanwhile, cook bacon in a skillet over medium heat until crisp. Combine sugar, flour, and vinegar, stirring well; stir into bacon and drippings. Cook over medium heat, stirring constantly, until slightly thickened. Pour mixture over turnip, and toss gently. Yield: 4 servings.

Per serving: Calories 189 Fat 10.7g
Cholesterol 12mg Sodium 797mg

Microwave Directions: Place turnips in a shallow 1½-quart casserole. Add ¼ cup water and salt; cover and microwave at HIGH 6 to 8 minutes or until turnips are tender, stirring twice. Let stand, covered, 2 minutes. Drain and set aside. Place bacon in a shallow 1-quart casserole; cover with paper towels. Microwave at HIGH 3½ to 4½ minutes or until bacon is crisp. Combine sugar, flour, and vinegar, stirring well; stir into bacon and drippings. Microwave at HIGH 1 to 2 minutes or until slightly thickened, stirring twice. Pour mixture over turnip, and toss gently. Yield: 4 servings.

FRUIT SIDE DISHES

Side dishes don't always mean vegetables. Some of the most surprising flavor combinations of entrées and accompaniments happen when you use fruit in the pairing. To enjoy a fruit side dish at its best, use fruit that's in season, fragrant, and perfectly ripe.

Some of the same rules for preparing and storing vegetables apply to fruits, too. Choose healthy, plump, bright-colored fruit. Wash fruit just before cooking. Leave the peel on fruit when you can (if it hasn't been waxed).

Check daily for spoilage, and promptly discard any bad pieces. Use fresh fruit within a few days of purchase. (Or see our Freezing Fruits chart on page 419.)

For meal planning, fruit offers fresh flavor fast. Apply a quick cooking method such as broiling, brief baking, or simmering in very little liquid. Dried fruits are also a good option for side dishes. Plump dried fruit by soaking it in warm fruit juice or other liquid before adding to a recipe.

Warm Curried Fruit

◄ HEALTHY ►

PREP: 15 MINUTES   COOK: 33 MINUTES

We recommend a late harvest sweet wine such as a Riesling or Gewürztraminer to cook and blend best with this fruit.

1 (29-ounce) can pear halves
1 (29-ounce) can peach halves
1 (20-ounce) can pineapple chunks
1 (16½-ounce) can pitted Royal Anne cherries
1 (15¼-ounce) can apricot halves
1 (11-ounce) can mandarin oranges
¼ cup sugar
3 tablespoons all-purpose flour
3 tablespoons butter or margarine
½ cup golden raisins
1 teaspoon curry powder
½ cup white wine such as Riesling or Gewürztraminer or apple juice

•Drain fruit, reserving all juice. Combine juices; stir well, and set aside ¾ cup. (Reserve remaining juice for another use.)

•Combine sugar and flour in a saucepan, stirring well. Gradually stir in reserved ¾ cup fruit juice. Add butter and raisins, and cook over medium heat, stirring constantly, until mixture comes to a boil. Boil 1 minute, stirring constantly; remove from heat.
•Gradually stir in curry powder and wine. Stir sauce into fruit, and spoon mixture into a 3-quart baking dish. Bake at 350° for 30 minutes. Yield: 10 servings.
Per serving: Calories 231 Fat 3.7g
Cholesterol 9mg Sodium 47mg

Buttery Baked Apples

◄ HEALTHY ►

PREP: 19 MINUTES   COOK: 27 MINUTES

Even if you're not a curry fan, you'll enjoy the subtle flavor of these buttery apple slices. If you omit the curry, you'll still have delicious cinnamon apples.

2½ pounds cooking apples such as Granny Smith, peeled, cored, and cut into ½-inch slices
2 tablespoons butter or margarine
⅓ cup orange marmalade
⅓ cup chutney (we tested with Major Grey)
1 teaspoon ground cinnamon
½ teaspoon curry powder

•Arrange apple slices in a lightly greased 11- x 7-inch baking dish; set aside.
•Melt butter in a small saucepan; add marmalade and remaining 3 ingredients. Bring to a boil over medium heat, stirring constantly; pour over apple slices.
•Bake at 400° for 25 minutes or to desired doneness. Serve with ham or pork. Yield: 8 servings.
Per serving: Calories 139 Fat 3.1g
Cholesterol 8mg Sodium 150mg

Baked Pears with Walnuts and Gorgonzola

PREP: 10 MINUTES   COOK: 31 MINUTES

These pears are baked and broiled with a sweet, toasty pungent cheese topping.

2 large ripe pears, such as Bartlett, Bosc, or Anjou
1½ tablespoons butter or margarine, softened
¼ teaspoon salt
¼ teaspoon white pepper
Dash of ground nutmeg
1 (2.25-ounce) package walnut pieces (about ½ cup), chopped and toasted
2 tablespoons brown sugar
1 tablespoon butter or margarine, melted
¼ cup crumbled Gorgonzola cheese

•Peel pears, if desired; cut in half, and core. If needed, slice about ¼ inch from rounded sides to make pears sit flat. Brush pears with softened butter, and place, cored side down, in a buttered 9-inch pan.
•Bake at 450° for 15 minutes. Remove from oven, turn pears over, and sprinkle with salt, white pepper, and nutmeg. Bake 10 to 15 more minutes or until soft and lightly browned.
•Meanwhile, combine walnuts, brown sugar, and melted butter in a small bowl, stirring to coat nuts. Top pear halves with walnuts and cheese. Broil pears 5½ inches from heat until cheese melts. Yield: 4 servings.
Per serving: Calories 283 Fat 21.6g
Cholesterol 33mg Sodium 429mg

Spiced Fruit Cup

◄ MAKE AHEAD • HEALTHY ►

PREP: 29 MINUTES   CHILL: 8 HOURS

Here's a simple multifruit make-ahead side dish. Orange juice and honey add flavor and help plump the dried fruit.

1 (11-ounce) can mandarin oranges, drained
2 Red Delicious apples, unpeeled and cut into bite-size pieces
1 cup raisins
⅔ cup pitted prunes (14 prunes), cut into quarters
½ cup dried apricot halves (14 halves), cut into quarters
½ cup orange juice
¼ cup honey
2 tablespoons lemon juice
¼ teaspoon ground cinnamon

•Combine first 5 ingredients in a medium bowl; set aside.
•Combine orange juice and remaining 3 ingredients; pour over fruit. Cover and chill 8 hours. Yield: 9 servings.
Per ½-cup serving: Calories 178 Fat 0.7g Cholesterol 0mg Sodium 16mg

Spiced Pink Grapefruit

◄ HEALTHY ►

**PREP: 12 MINUTES   COOK: 5 MINUTES
CHILL: 4 HOURS**

2 large pink grapefruit
1 large lemon
⅔ cup water
¼ cup sugar
1 (3-inch) stick cinnamon, broken
4 whole cloves

•Cut 2 (3- x 1-inch) strips of rind from each grapefruit and lemon; set aside.
•Peel grapefruit, and cut into ½-inch-thick slices. Discard seeds, and place slices in an 8-inch square dish; set aside.
•Squeeze 2 tablespoons juice from lemon, and set juice aside.
•Scrape white pith from rind strips. Combine rind strips, water, and remaining 3 ingredients in a small saucepan. Bring to a boil; reduce heat, and simmer 3 minutes.
•Stir in lemon juice; pour mixture over grapefruit in dish. Cover and chill at least 4 hours. Remove cinnamon sticks, cloves, and rind strips. Yield: 2 servings.
Per serving: Calories 197 Fat 0.3g Cholesterol 0mg Sodium 0mg

Pineapple Casserole

◄ FAMILY FAVORITE ►

PREP: 12 MINUTES   COOK: 30 MINUTES

Cheddar cheese and buttery crackers transform a can of pineapple chunks into this wonderful old-fashioned casserole.

1 (20-ounce) can pineapple chunks in juice, undrained
½ cup sugar
3 tablespoons all-purpose flour
1 cup (4 ounces) shredded Cheddar cheese
1 cup buttery cracker crumbs (we tested with Ritz)
3 tablespoons butter or margarine, melted

•Drain pineapple, reserving 3 tablespoons juice. Combine sugar and flour; stir in reserved pineapple juice. Stir in cheese and pineapple chunks. Spoon mixture into a greased 1-quart casserole.
•Combine cracker crumbs and butter, stirring well; sprinkle over pineapple mixture. Bake, uncovered, at 350° for 20 to 30 minutes or until browned. Serve hot. Yield: 4 servings.
Per serving: Calories 454 Fat 23.0g Cholesterol 53mg Sodium 426mg

COOKING VEGETABLES

VEGETABLE	SERVINGS	PREPARATION	COOKING INSTRUCTIONS (ADD SALT, IF DESIRED)	COMPATIBLE SEASONINGS AND SAUCES
Artichoke, globe	2 per pound (2 medium artichokes)	Wash; cut off stem and ½ inch of top. Remove loose bottom leaves. Cut off thorny tips with scissors. Rub cut surfaces with lemon.	Cook, covered, in small amount of boiling water 25 to 35 minutes.	Garlic butter, hollandaise sauce, vinaigrette
Artichoke, Jerusalem	3 per pound	Wash; peel. Leave whole or slice.	Cook, covered, in small amount of boiling water 15 minutes (slices) to 30 minutes (whole).	Butter, lemon juice, cream sauce, hollandaise sauce
Asparagus	3 to 4 per pound	Snap off tough ends. Remove scales, if desired.	To boil: Cook, covered, in small amount of boiling water 6 to 8 minutes or until crisp-tender. To steam: Cook, covered, on a rack above boiling water 8 to 10 minutes.	Cheese sauce, hollandaise sauce, orange sauce, vinaigrette, lemon juice, mustard seeds, tarragon, dill

COOKING VEGETABLES

VEGETABLE	SERVINGS	PREPARATION	COOKING INSTRUCTIONS (ADD SALT, IF DESIRED)	COMPATIBLE SEASONINGS AND SAUCES
Beans, dried	6 to 8 per pound	Sort and wash. Cover with water 2 inches above beans; soak overnight. Drain.	Cover soaked beans with water. Bring to a boil; cover, reduce heat, and simmer 1½ to 2 hours or until tender.	Garlic, cumin, chili powder, bacon, onion
Beans, green	4 per pound	Wash; trim ends, and remove strings. Cut into 1½-inch pieces.	Cook, covered, in small amount of boiling water 12 to 15 minutes.	Almonds, butter, bacon, basil, dill, savory, thyme, nuts
Beans, lima	2 per pound unshelled, 4 per pound shelled	Shell and wash.	Cook, covered, in small amount of boiling water 20 minutes.	Butter, cream sauce, oregano, sage, savory, tarragon, thyme
Beets	3 to 4 per pound	Leave root and 1 inch of stem; scrub with vegetable brush.	Cook, covered, in boiling water 35 to 40 minutes. Remove peel.	Butter, lemon juice, orange juice, wine vinegar, allspice, ginger
Broccoli	3 to 4 per pound	Remove outer leaves and tough ends of lower stalks. Wash; cut into spears.	To boil: Cook, covered, in small amount of boiling water 8 to 10 minutes. To steam: Cook, covered, on a rack above boiling water 10 to 15 minutes.	Cheese or hollandaise sauce, lemon-butter sauce, vinaigrette, dill, mustard seeds, tarragon
Brussels sprouts	4 per pound	Wash; remove discolored leaves. Cut off stem ends; slash bottom with an X.	Cook, covered, in small amount of boiling water 8 to 10 minutes.	Cheese sauce, butter, caraway seeds, basil, dill, mustard seeds, sage, thyme
Cabbage	4 per pound	Remove outer leaves; wash. Shred or cut into wedges.	Cook, covered, in small amount of boiling water 5 to 7 minutes (shredded) or 10 to 15 minutes (wedges).	Cream or cheese sauce, butter, caraway seeds, dill, savory, tarragon
Carrots	4 per pound	Scrape; remove ends, and rinse. Leave tiny carrots whole; slice large carrots, or cut into strips.	Cook, covered, in small amount of boiling water 8 to 10 minutes (slices) or 12 to 15 minutes (strips).	Butter, brown sugar glaze, vinaigrette, dill, chives, ginger, mace, mint, nutmeg
Cauliflower	4 per medium head	Remove outer leaves and stalk. Wash. Leave whole, or break into flowerets.	Cook, covered, in small amount of boiling water 10 to 12 minutes (whole) or 8 to 10 minutes (flowerets).	Cream or cheese sauce, herb butter, basil, caraway seeds, mace, tarragon
Celery	4 per medium bunch	Separate stalks; trim off leaves and base. Rinse. Slice diagonally.	Cook, covered, in small amount of boiling water 10 to 15 minutes.	Butter, cream or cheese sauce, grated Parmesan cheese, mustard, thyme, tarragon
Corn	4 per 4 large ears	Remove husks and silks. Leave corn on cob, or cut off tips of kernels, and scrape cob with dull edge of knife.	Cook, covered, in boiling water 10 minutes (on cob) or in small amount of boiling water 8 to 10 minutes (cut).	Cream sauce, herb butter, garlic, chili powder, red pepper, basil
Cucumbers	2 per large cucumber	Peel, if desired; slice or cut into strips.	Generally served raw.	Sour cream, dill, basil, mint, tarragon
Eggplant	2 to 3 per pound	Wash and peel, if desired. Cut into cubes, or cut crosswise into slices.	To boil: Cook, covered, in small amount of boiling water 8 to 10 minutes. To sauté: Cook in small amount of butter or vegetable oil 5 to 8 minutes.	Grated Parmesan cheese, basil, curry, oregano, marjoram

COOKING VEGETABLES

VEGETABLE	SERVINGS	PREPARATION	COOKING INSTRUCTIONS (ADD SALT, IF DESIRED)	COMPATIBLE SEASONINGS AND SAUCES
Greens	3 to 4 per pound	Remove stems; wash thoroughly. Tear into bite-size pieces.	Cook, covered, in 1 to 1½ inches boiling water 5 to 8 minutes (spinach); 10 to 20 minutes (Swiss chard); 30 to 45 minutes (collards, turnip greens, mustard, kale).	Cream sauce, butter, onion, mushroom, wine vinegar, lemon juice, horseradish, bacon, dill, marjoram, rosemary, nutmeg
Kohlrabi	3 to 4 per pound	Remove leaves; wash. Peel; dice, slice, or cut into strips.	Cook, covered, in small amount of boiling water 15 to 20 minutes.	Butter, cheese sauce, lemon juice, sour cream, chives, garlic, basil
Leeks	3 per pound	Remove root, tough outer leaves, and tops, leaving 2 inches of dark leaves. Wash thoroughly. Slice, if desired.	Cook, covered, in small amount of boiling water 12 to 15 minutes (whole) or 10 to 12 minutes (sliced).	Flavored butters, crumbled bacon, cream sauce, grated Parmesan cheese, mushroom sauce, dill, basil, thyme, rosemary
Mushrooms	4 per pound	Wipe with damp paper towels or wash gently and pat dry. Cut off tips of stems. Slice, if desired.	Sauté in butter 5 minutes.	Cream sauce, vinaigrette, marjoram, oregano, rosemary, savory, tarragon
Okra	4 per pound	Wash and pat dry. Trim ends.	Cook, covered, in small amount of boiling water 5 to 10 minutes.	Butter, cream sauce, garlic, lemon juice, tomatoes, chives, basil, nutmeg
Onions	4 per pound	Peel; cut large onions into quarters or slices, or leave small onions whole.	Cook, covered, in small amount of boiling water 15 minutes or until tender. Or sauté slices in butter 3 to 5 minutes.	Cream or cheese sauce, brown sugar glaze, butter, basil, ginger, oregano, parsley, thyme
Parsnips	4 per pound	Scrape; cut off ends. Slice or cut into strips.	Cook, covered, in small amount of boiling water 15 to 20 minutes.	Cream sauce, brown sugar glaze, butter, Worcestershire, honey, parsley, nutmeg
Peas, black-eyed	2 per pound unshelled, 4 per pound shelled	Shell and wash.	Cook, covered, in small amount of boiling water 15 to 20 minutes or until tender.	Bacon, butter, garlic, red pepper, cumin, chili powder, basil
Peas, dried	6 to 8 per pound	Sort and wash. Cover with water 2 inches above peas; soak overnight. Drain.	Cover soaked peas with water. Bring to a boil; cover, reduce heat, and simmer 1½ to 2 hours.	Butter, garlic, red pepper, bacon, cumin, chili powder
Peas, green	2 per pound unshelled, 4 per pound shelled	Shell and wash.	Cook, covered, in a small amount of boiling water 12 to 15 minutes.	Cream or cheese sauce, butter, garlic, marjoram, nutmeg, chervil, mint, rosemary, tarragon
Peas, snow	4 per pound	Wash; trim ends, and remove tough strings.	Cook, covered, in small amount of boiling water 3 to 5 minutes, or sauté in vegetable oil or butter 3 to 5 minutes.	Onion, garlic, soy sauce, basil
Peppers, green	1 per medium pepper	Cut off top, and remove seeds. Leave whole to stuff and bake; cut into thin slices or strips to sauté.	To bake: Cook, covered, in boiling water 5 minutes; stuff and bake at 350° for 15 to 25 minutes. To sauté: Cook in butter or vegetable oil 3 to 5 minutes.	Meat, vegetable, or rice stuffing; garlic, basil, oregano, fennel

COOKING VEGETABLES

VEGETABLE	SERVINGS	PREPARATION	COOKING INSTRUCTIONS (ADD SALT, IF DESIRED)	COMPATIBLE SEASONINGS AND SAUCES
Potatoes, all-purpose	3 to 4 per pound	Scrub potatoes; peel, if desired. Leave whole or slice or cut into chunks.	Cook, covered, in small amount of boiling water 30 to 40 minutes (whole) or 15 to 20 minutes (slices or chunks).	Cream or cheese sauce, butter, bacon, sour cream, basil, chives, garlic, dill, oregano
Potatoes, baking	2 to 3 per pound	Scrub potatoes; rub skins with vegetable oil.	Bake at 400° for 1 hour or until done.	Butter, sour cream, cheese, chives, garlic, oregano, thyme, green onion
new	3 to 4 per pound	Scrub potatoes; peel, if desired.	Cook, covered, in boiling water to cover 15 minutes or until tender.	Cream or cheese sauce, butter, onion, lemon juice, vinaigrette, parsley
Potatoes, sweet	2 to 3 per pound	Scrub potatoes; leave whole to bake or slice or cut into chunks to boil.	Bake at 375° for 1 hour or until done. To boil: Cook in boiling water to cover 20 to 30 minutes.	Butter, brown sugar glaze, marmalade, honey, maple syrup, allspice, cinnamon, nutmeg
Pumpkin	4½ to 5 cups cooked, mashed pumpkin per one 5-pound pumpkin	Slice in half crosswise. Remove seeds.	Place cut side down on baking pan. Bake at 325° for 45 minutes or until tender. Cool; peel and mash.	Butter, brown sugar or maple syrup glaze, cinnamon, nutmeg, mace, ginger
Rutabagas	2 to 3 per pound	Wash; peel and slice or cube.	Cook, covered, in boiling water 15 to 20 minutes. Mash, if desired.	Butter, maple syrup, brown sugar, lemon, cinnamon, nutmeg
Squash, spaghetti	2 per pound	Rinse; cut in half lengthwise, and discard seeds.	Place squash, cut side down, in Dutch oven; add 2 inches water. Bring to a boil; cover, reduce heat, and cook 20 minutes or until tender. Drain and separate strands with a fork.	Butter, onions, tomato sauce, basil, garlic, oregano
Squash, summer	3 to 4 per pound	Wash; trim ends. Slice or dice.	To boil: Cook, covered, in small amount of boiling water 8 to 10 minutes (slices) or 15 minutes (whole). To steam: Cook, covered, on a rack over boiling water 10 to 12 minutes (sliced or diced).	Butter, cheese, onion, garlic, cinnamon, marjoram, dill, ginger, allspice, rosemary
Squash, winter (acorn, butternut, hubbard)	2 per pound	Rinse; cut in half, and remove seeds.	To boil: Cook, covered, in boiling water 20 to 25 minutes. To bake: Place cut side down in shallow baking dish; add ½ inch water. Bake, uncovered, at 375° for 30 minutes. Turn and season or fill; bake 20 to 30 minutes or until tender.	Brown sugar glaze, orange juice, apple filling, butter, crumbled bacon, candied ginger, cinnamon, nutmeg
Tomatoes	4 per pound (2 large tomatoes)	Wash; peel, if desired. Slice or cut into quarters.	Generally served raw or used as ingredient in cooked dishes.	Vinaigrette, grated Parmesan cheese, onion, chives, marjoram, oregano, sage, tarragon, basil
Turnips	3 per pound	Wash; peel and slice or cube.	Cook, covered, in boiling water to cover 15 to 20 minutes or until tender.	Sweet-and-sour sauce, butter, soy sauce, onion, bacon, chives, dill, thyme

APPENDICES

FOOD	WEIGHT OR COUNT	YIELD
Apples	1 pound (3 medium)	3 cups sliced
Bacon	8 slices cooked	½ cup crumbled
Bananas	1 pound (3 medium)	2½ cups sliced or about 2 cups mashed
Bread	1 pound / 1½ slices	12 to 16 slices / 1 cup soft crumbs
Butter or margarine	1 pound / ¼-pound stick	2 cups (4 sticks) / ½ cup (1 stick)
Cabbage	1 pound head	4½ cups shredded
Candied fruit or peels ½ pound		1¼ cups chopped
Carrots	1 pound	3 cups shredded
Cheese		
American or Cheddar 1 pound		about 4 cups shredded
cottage	1 pound	2 cups
cream	3-ounce package	6 tablespoons
Chocolate morsels	6-ounce package	1 cup
Cocoa	16-ounce can	5 cups
Coconut, flaked or shredded	1 pound	5 cups
Coffee	1 pound	80 tablespoons (40 cups brewed)
Corn	2 medium ears	1 cup kernels
Cornmeal	1 pound	3 cups
Crab, in shell	1 pound	¾ to 1 cup flaked
Crackers		
chocolate wafers	19 wafers	1 cup crumbs
graham crackers	14 squares	1 cup fine crumbs
saltine crackers	28 crackers	1 cup finely crushed
vanilla wafers	22 wafers	1 cup finely crushed
Cream, whipping	1 cup (½ pint)	2 cups whipped
Dates, pitted	1 pound / 8-ounce package	3 cups chopped / 1½ cups chopped
Eggs	5 large	1 cup
whites	8 to 11	1 cup
yolks	12 to 14	1 cup
Flour, all-purpose	1 pound	3½ cups unsifted
cake	1 pound	4¾ to 5 cups sifted
whole wheat	1 pound	3½ cups unsifted
Green pepper	1 large	1 cup diced
Lemon	1 medium	2 to 3 tablespoons juice; 2 teaspoons grated rind

FOOD	WEIGHT OR COUNT	YIELD
Lettuce	1-pound head	6¼ cups torn
Lime	1 medium	1½ to 2 tablespoons juice; 1½ teaspoons grated rind
Macaroni	4 ounces dry (1 cup)	2 cups cooked
Marshmallows		
large	10	1 cup
miniature	10	1 large marshmallow
	½ pound	4½ cups
Milk		
evaporated	5-ounce can	½ cup
	12-ounce can	1½ cups
sweetened condensed	14-ounce can	1¼ cups
Mushrooms	3 cups raw (8 ounces)	1 cup sliced, cooked
Nuts		
almonds	1 pound	1¾ cups nutmeats
	1 pound shelled	3½ cups
peanuts	1 pound	2¼ cups nutmeats
	1 pound shelled	3 cups
pecans	1 pound	2¼ cups nutmeats
	1 pound shelled	4 cups
walnuts	1 pound	1⅔ cups nutmeats
	1 pound shelled	4 cups
Oats, quick cooking	1 cup	1¾ cups cooked
Onion	1 medium	½ cup chopped
Orange	1 medium	½ cup juice; 2 tablespoons grated rind
Peaches	2 medium	1 cup sliced
Pears	2 medium	1 cup sliced
Potatoes		
white	3 medium	2 cups cubed cooked or 1¾ cups mashed
sweet	3 medium	3 cups sliced
Raisins, seedless	1 pound	3 cups
Rice		
long grain	1 cup	3 to 4 cups cooked
precooked	1 cup	2 cups cooked
Shrimp, raw, unpeeled	1 pound	8 to 9 ounces cooked, peeled, deveined
Spaghetti	7 ounces	about 4 cups cooked
Strawberries	1 quart	4 cups sliced
Sugar		
brown	1 pound	2⅓ cups firmly packed
powdered	1 pound	3½ cups unsifted
granulated white	1 pound	2 cups

EQUIVALENT MEASURES

3 teaspoons	1 tablespoon	2 tablespoons (liquid)	1 ounce	1/8 cup	2 tablespoons
4 tablespoons	1/4 cup	1 cup	8 fluid ounces	1/3 cup	5 tablespoons plus 1 teaspoon
5 1/3 tablespoons	1/3 cup	2 cups	1 pint (16 fluid ounces)		
8 tablespoons	1/2 cup	4 cups	1 quart	2/3 cup	10 tablespoons plus 2 teaspoons
16 tablespoons	1 cup	4 quarts	1 gallon	3/4 cup	12 tablespoons

HANDY SUBSTITUTIONS

INGREDIENT	SUBSTITUTION
BAKING PRODUCTS	
Arrowroot, 1 teaspoon	• 1 tablespoon all-purpose flour • 1 1/2 teaspoons cornstarch
Baking powder, 1 teaspoon	• 1/2 teaspoon cream of tartar plus 1/4 teaspoon baking soda

Chocolate
  semisweet, 1 ounce
  unsweetened, 1 ounce or square
  chips, semisweet, 1 ounce
  chips, semisweet, 6-ounce package, melted
	
	• 1 ounce unsweetened chocolate plus 1 tablespoon sugar
	• 3 tablespoons cocoa plus 1 tablespoon fat
	• 1 ounce square semisweet chocolate
	• 2 ounces unsweetened chocolate, 2 tablespoons shortening plus 1/2 cup sugar

Cocoa, 1/4 cup	• 1 ounce unsweetened chocolate (decrease fat in recipe by 1/2 tablespoon)

Coconut
  flaked, 1 tablespoon
  cream, 1 cup
  milk, 1 cup
	
	• 1 1/2 tablespoons grated fresh coconut
	• 1 cup whipping cream
	• 1 cup whole or reduced-fat milk

Corn syrup, light, 1 cup	• 1 cup sugar plus 1/4 cup water • 1 cup honey
Cornstarch, 1 tablespoon	• 2 tablespoons all-purpose flour or granular tapioca

Flour
  all-purpose, 1 tablespoon
 	
  all-purpose, 1 cup sifted
    Note: Specialty flours added to
    yeast bread will result in a reduced
    volume and a heavier product.
 	
  cake, 1 cup sifted
  self-rising, 1 cup
	
	• 1 1/2 teaspoons cornstarch, potato starch, or rice starch
	• 1 tablespoon rice flour or corn flour
	• 1 1/2 tablespoons whole wheat flour
	• 1/2 tablespoon whole wheat flour plus 1/2 tablespoon all-purpose flour
	• 1 cup plus 2 tablespoons sifted cake flour
	• 1 cup minus 2 tablespoons all-purpose flour (unsifted)
	• 1 1/2 cups breadcrumbs
	• 1 cup rolled oats
	• 1/3 cup cornmeal or soybean flour plus 2/3 cup all-purpose flour
	• 3/4 cup whole wheat flour or bran flour plus 1/4 cup all-purpose flour
	• 1 cup rye or rice flour
	• 1/4 cup soybean flour plus 3/4 cup all-purpose flour
	• 1 cup minus 2 tablespoons all-purpose flour
	• 1 cup all-purpose flour, 1 teaspoon baking powder plus 1/2 teaspoon salt

Marshmallows
  cream, 7-ounce jar
  miniature, 1 cup
	
	• 16-ounce package marshmallows, melted, plus 3 1/2 tablespoons light corn syrup
	• 10 large

Pecans, chopped, 1 cup	• 1 cup regular oats, toasted (in baked products)

HANDY SUBSTITUTIONS (CONTINUED)

INGREDIENT	SUBSTITUTION
Shortening	
melted, I cup	• I cup cooking oil (do not use cooking oil if recipe does not call for melted shortening)
solid, I cup (used in baking)	• I cup minus 2 tablespoons lard
	• I 1/8 cups butter or margarine (decrease salt called for in recipe by 1/2 teaspoon)
Sugar	
brown, I cup firmly packed	• I cup granulated white sugar
maple, 1/2 cup	• I cup maple syrup
powdered, I cup	• I cup sugar plus I tablespoon cornstarch (processed in food processor)
granulated white, I teaspoon	• 1/8 teaspoon noncaloric sweetener solution or follow manufacturer's directions
granulated white, I cup	• I cup corn syrup (decrease liquid called for in recipe by 1/4 cup)
	• I cup firmly packed brown sugar
	• I cup honey (decrease liquid called for in recipe by 1/4 cup)
Tapioca, granular, I tablespoon	• I 1/2 teaspoons cornstarch
	• I tablespoon all-purpose flour
Yeast, active dry, I (1/4-ounce) package	• I tablespoon active dry yeast

DAIRY PRODUCTS

Butter, I cup	• 7/8 to I cup shortening or lard plus 1/2 teaspoon salt
	• I cup margarine (2 sticks; do not substitute whipped or low-fat margarine)
Cream	
heavy (30% to 40% fat), I cup	• 3/4 cup milk plus 1/3 cup butter or margarine (for cooking and baking; will not whip)
light (15% to 20% fat), I cup	• 3/4 cup milk plus 3 tablespoons butter or margarine (for cooking and baking)
	• I cup evaporated milk, undiluted
half-and-half, I cup	• 7/8 cup milk plus 1/2 tablespoon butter or margarine (for cooking and baking)
	• I cup evaporated milk, undiluted
whipped	• I (13-ounce) can of evaporated milk (chilled 12 hours). Add I teaspoon lemon juice. Whip until stiff.
Egg	
I large	• 2 egg yolks (for custard and cream fillings)
	• 2 egg yolks plus I tablespoon water (for cookies)
2 large	• 3 small eggs
I egg white (2 tablespoons)	• 2 tablespoons egg substitute
	• 2 teaspoons sifted, dry egg white powder plus 2 tablespoons warm water
I egg yolk (1 1/2 tablespoons)	• 2 tablespoons sifted dry egg yolk powder plus 2 teaspoons water
	• I 1/2 tablespoons thawed frozen egg yolk
Milk	
buttermilk, I cup	• I tablespoon vinegar or lemon juice plus whole milk to make I cup (let stand 10 minutes)
	• I cup plain yogurt
	• I cup whole milk plus 1 3/4 teaspoons cream of tartar
fat free, I cup	• 4 to 5 tablespoons nonfat dry milk powder plus enough water to make I cup
	• 1/2 cup evaporated skim milk plus 1/2 cup water
whole, I cup	• 4 to 5 tablespoons nonfat dry milk powder plus enough water to make I cup
	• 1/2 cup evaporated milk plus 1/2 cup water
	• I cup fruit juice or potato water (for use in baking)
sweetened condensed, I (14-ounce) can (about 1 1/4 cups)	• Heat the following ingredients until sugar and butter dissolve: 1/3 cup plus 2 tablespoons evaporated milk, I cup sugar, 3 tablespoons butter or margarine
sweetened condensed, I cup	• Heat the following ingredients until sugar and butter dissolve: 1/3 cup evaporated milk, 3/4 cup sugar, 2 tablespoons butter or margarine
	• Add I cup plus 2 tablespoons nonfat dry milk powder to 1/2 cup warm water. Mix well. Add 3/4 cup sugar, and stir until smooth.
Sour cream, I cup	• I cup plain yogurt plus 3 tablespoons melted butter
	• I cup plain yogurt plus I tablespoon cornstarch
	• I tablespoon lemon juice plus evaporated milk to equal I cup
Yogurt, I cup (plain)	• I cup buttermilk

HANDY SUBSTITUTIONS (CONTINUED)

INGREDIENT	SUBSTITUTION

FRUIT AND VEGETABLE PRODUCTS

Lemon
  1 medium
  juice, 1 teaspoon
  peel, dried, 1 teaspoon

- 2 to 3 tablespoons juice plus 2 teaspoons grated rind
- 1/2 teaspoon vinegar
- 2 teaspoons freshly grated lemon rind
- 1/2 teaspoon lemon extract

Orange
  1 medium
  peel, dried, 1 tablespoon

- 1/2 cup juice plus 2 tablespoons grated rind
- 1 1/2 teaspoons orange extract

Mushrooms, 1 pound fresh

- 1 (8-ounce) can sliced mushrooms, drained
- 3 ounces dried mushrooms, rehydrated

Onion, chopped, 1 medium

- 1 tablespoon dried minced onion
- 1 teaspoon onion powder

Pepper
  sweet red or green, chopped,
    3 tablespoons
  sweet red, chopped, 3 tablespoons

- 1 tablespoon dried sweet red or green pepper flakes

- 2 tablespoons chopped pimiento

Shallots, chopped, 3 tablespoons

- 2 tablespoons chopped onion plus 1 tablespoon chopped garlic

Tomatoes
  fresh, chopped, 2 cups
  juice, 1 cup

- 1 (16-ounce) can (may need to drain)
- 1/2 cup tomato sauce plus 1/2 cup water

Tomato sauce, 2 cups

- 3/4 cup tomato paste plus 1 cup water

MISCELLANEOUS

Broth, beef or chicken
  canned broth, 1 cup

  powdered broth base, 1 teaspoon
  powdered broth base, 1 teaspoon
    dissolved in 1 cup water

- 1 bouillon cube dissolved in 1 cup boiling water
- 1 teaspoon powdered broth base dissolved in 1 cup boiling water
- 1 bouillon cube
- 1 cup canned or homemade broth
- 1 bouillon cube dissolved in 1 cup boiling water

Chili sauce, 1 cup

- 1 cup tomato sauce, 1/4 cup brown sugar, 2 tablespoons vinegar, 1/4 teaspoon cinnamon, dash of ground cloves plus dash of ground allspice

Gelatin, flavored, 3-ounce package

- 1 tablespoon unflavored gelatin plus 2 cups fruit juice

Honey, 1 cup

- 1 1/4 cups sugar plus 1/4 cup water

Ketchup, 1 cup

- 1 cup tomato sauce, 1/2 cup sugar, plus 2 tablespoons vinegar (for cooking)

Macaroni, uncooked, 2 cups (4 cups cooked)

- 8 ounces spaghetti, uncooked
- 4 cups fine egg noodles, uncooked

Mayonnaise, 1 cup (for salads and dressings)

- 1/2 cup plain yogurt plus 1/2 cup mayonnaise
- 1 cup sour cream
- 1 cup cottage cheese pureed in a blender

Rice, uncooked, 1 cup regular (3 cups cooked)

- 1 cup uncooked converted rice
- 1 cup uncooked brown rice or wild rice

Vinegar, balsamic, 1/2 cup

- 1/2 cup red wine vinegar (some flavor difference)

SEASONING PRODUCTS

Allspice, ground, 1 teaspoon

- 1/2 teaspoon ground cinnamon plus 1/2 teaspoon ground cloves

Apple pie spice, 1 teaspoon

- 1/2 teaspoon ground cinnamon, 1/4 teaspoon ground nutmeg plus 1/8 teaspoon ground cardamom

HANDY SUBSTITUTIONS (CONTINUED)

INGREDIENT	SUBSTITUTION
Bay leaf, 1 whole	• $\frac{1}{4}$ teaspoon crushed bay leaf
Beau Monde seasoning, 1 teaspoon	• 1 teaspoon seasoning salt or seasoned salt • $\frac{1}{2}$ teaspoon salt
Chives, chopped, 1 tablespoon	• 1 tablespoon chopped green onion tops
Dillweed, fresh or dried, 3 heads	• 1 tablespoon dill seed

Garlic
  1 small clove
  garlic salt, 1 teaspoon
	
	• $\frac{1}{8}$ teaspoon garlic powder or minced dried garlic
	• $\frac{1}{8}$ teaspoon garlic powder plus $\frac{7}{8}$ teaspoon salt

Ginger
  crystallized, 1 tablespoon
  fresh, grated, 1 tablespoon
  ground, $\frac{1}{8}$ teaspoon
	
	• $\frac{1}{8}$ teaspoon ground ginger
	• $\frac{1}{8}$ teaspoon ground ginger
	• 1 tablespoon crystallized ginger rinsed in water to remove sugar, and finely cut
	• 1 tablespoon grated fresh ginger

Herbs, fresh, chopped, 1 tablespoon	• 1 teaspoon dried herbs or $\frac{1}{4}$ teaspoon ground herbs
Horseradish, fresh, grated, 1 tablespoon	• 2 tablespoons prepared horseradish
Mustard, dried, 1 teaspoon	• 1 tablespoon prepared mustard
Onion powder, 1 tablespoon	• 1 medium onion, chopped • 1 tablespoon dried minced onion
Parsley, dried, 1 teaspoon	• 1 tablespoon fresh parsley, chopped
Pimiento, chopped, 2 tablespoons	• rehydrate 1 tablespoon dried sweet red pepper • 2 to 3 tablespoons chopped fresh sweet red pepper
Pumpkin pie spice, 1 teaspoon	• $\frac{1}{2}$ teaspoon ground cinnamon, $\frac{1}{4}$ teaspoon ground ginger, $\frac{1}{8}$ teaspoon ground allspice plus $\frac{1}{8}$ teaspoon ground nutmeg
Spearmint or peppermint, dried, 1 tablespoon	• 3 tablespoons chopped fresh mint
Vanilla bean, 1 (1 inch)	• 1 teaspoon vanilla extract
Worcestershire sauce, 1 teaspoon	• 1 teaspoon bottled steak sauce

ALCOHOL SUBSTITUTIONS

ALCOHOL	SUBSTITUTION
Amaretto, 2 tablespoons	$\frac{1}{4}$ to $\frac{1}{2}$ teaspoon almond extract*
Bourbon or **Sherry,** 2 tablespoons	1 to 2 teaspoons vanilla extract*
Brandy, fruit-flavored liqueur, port wine, rum, or **sweet sherry:** $\frac{1}{4}$ cup or more	Equal amount of unsweetened orange or apple juice plus 1 teaspoon vanilla extract or corresponding flavor
Brandy or **rum,** 2 tablespoons	$\frac{1}{2}$ to 1 teaspoon brandy or rum extract*
Grand Marnier or other orange-flavored liqueur, 2 tablespoons	2 tablespoons unsweetened orange juice concentrate or 2 tablespoons orange juice and $\frac{1}{2}$ teaspoon orange extract
Kahlúa or other coffee- or chocolate-flavored liqueur, 2 tablespoons	$\frac{1}{2}$ to 1 teaspoon chocolate extract plus $\frac{1}{2}$ to 1 teaspoon instant coffee dissolved in 2 tablespoons water
Marsala, $\frac{1}{4}$ cup	$\frac{1}{4}$ cup white grape juice, or $\frac{1}{4}$ cup dry white wine plus 1 teaspoon brandy

Wine
  red, $\frac{1}{4}$ cup or more
  white, $\frac{1}{4}$ cup or more
	
	Equal measure of red grape juice or cranberry juice
	Equal measure of white grape juice or apple juice

*Add water, white grape juice, or apple juice to get the specified amount of liquid (when the liquid amount is crucial).

BAKING PAN SUBSTITUTIONS

If a recipe calls for a pan you don't have, try substituting one of a similar capacity. You may need to adjust the baking time.

SHAPE	DIMENSIONS	CAPACITY	SUBSTITUTIONS
Rectangular	11- x 7- x 1½-inch	8 cups	8- x 8- x 2-inch
	13- x 9- x 2-inch	12 to 15 cups	two 9-inch round or three 8-inch round
Square	8- x 8- x 2-inch	8 cups	11- x 7- x 1½-inch
	9- x 9- x 2-inch	10 cups	9- x 5- x 3-inch loafpan or two 8-inch round
Round	8- x 1½-inch	5 cups	10- x 6- x 2-inch
	8- x 2-inch	6 cups	8½- x 4½- x 2½-inch loafpan
	9- x 1½-inch	6 cups	8- x 2-inch round
Tube	10- x 4-inch	16 cups	10-inch ring mold or cake mold
Loaf	8½- x 4½- x 2½-inch	6 cups	two or three 6- x 3- x 2-inch loafpans
	9- x 5- x 3-inch	8 cups	three or four 6- x 3- x 2-inch loafpans
Pieplate	9- x 1½-inch	5 cups	No substitution unless tart pans are used
	10- x 1½-inch	6 cups	
Jellyroll pan	15- x 10- x 1-inch	10 cups	Do not substitute baking sheet for jellyroll pan

RECOMMENDED STORAGE GUIDE

IN THE PANTRY

Baking powder and soda	1 year
Flour, all-purpose	10 to 15 months
Milk, evaporated and sweetened condensed	1 year
Mixes	
cake	1 year
pancake	6 months
Peanut butter	6 months
Salt and Pepper	18 months
Shortening	8 months
Spices (discard if aroma fades)	
ground	6 months
whole	1 year
Sugar	18 months

IN THE REFRIGERATOR

Butter and margarine	1 month
Buttermilk	1 to 2 weeks
Eggs (fresh in shell)	3 to 5 weeks
Half-and-half	7 to 10 days

Meat	
casseroles, cooked	3 to 4 days
steaks, chops,	
roasts, uncooked	3 to 5 days
Milk, whole and skimmed	1 week
Poultry, uncooked	1 to 2 days
Sour cream	3 to 4 weeks
Whipping cream	10 days

IN THE FREEZER

Breads	
quick	2 to 3 months
yeast	3 to 6 months
Butter	6 months
Cakes	
cheesecakes and pound cakes	2 to 3 months
unfrosted	2 to 5 months
with cooked frosting	not recommended
with creamy-type frosting	3 months
Candy and fudge	6 months
Casseroles	1 to 2 months
Cheese	4 months

Cookies	
baked, unfrosted	8 to 12 months
dough	1 month
Eggs (not in shell)	
whites	1 year
yolks	8 months
Ice cream	1 to 3 months
Meat	
cooked	2 to 3 months
ground, uncooked	3 to 4 months
roasts, uncooked	9 months
steaks or chops, uncooked	4 to 6 months
Nuts	8 months
Pies	
pastry shell	2 to 3 months
fruit	1 to 2 months
pumpkin	2 to 4 months
custard, cream, meringue	not recommended
Poultry	
cooked	3 to 4 months
parts, uncooked	9 months
whole, uncooked	12 months
Soups and Stews	2 to 3 months

MENU INDEX

SOUTHWESTERN SUMMIT
Serves 6
Quesadillas (p. 45)   Icy Margaritas° (p. 56)
Southwestern Flank Steak° (p. 244)
Triple-Fruit Salsa (p. 391)
Hot Pepper Rice (p. 289)
Chile Cornbread (p. 71)
Caramel-Coffee Flan (p. 166)

CASUAL ITALIAN
Serves 6
Osso Buco (p. 253)
Saffron Rice (store-bought mix)
Hearts of Palm Salad (p. 354) or Green Salad
Commercial Italian Bread
Tiramisù (p. 169)

PUTTING ON THE RITZ
Serves 8
French Onion Soup (p. 427)
Lemon Sorbet (p. 178)
Filet Mignons with Shiitake Madeira Sauce° (p. 237) or
Hazelnut-Crusted Rack of Lamb with
Cherry-Wine Sauce (p. 258)
Roasted Garlic Mashed Potatoes (p. 460)
Minty Orange Peas° (p. 459)
Sour Cream Crescent Rolls (p. 84)
Turtle Cheesecake (p. 125)

COOKING CAJUN
Serves 6
Caesar Salad° (p. 352)
Crawfish Étouffée (p. 229) or Jambalaya (p. 272)
No-Knead French Bread (p. 87 or store-bought)
Bread Pudding with Whisky Sauce (p. 168)

APPETIZER BUFFET
Serves 12
Peking Pork Tenderloin (p. 265)
Store-bought Chutney   Party Rolls
Pear-Pecan Appetizers (p. 40)
Eggplant-Mushroom Dip (p. 33)   Bagel Chips
Garlic-Cream Cheese Spread° (p. 37)   Crackers
Curried Party Mix (p. 30)
Slushy Citrus Punch (p. 52) or
Bourbon-Citrus Punch (p. 53)
Lemon Bars (p. 141)
White Chocolate-Macadamia Nut Cookies (p. 137)

BRUNCH FOR A BUNCH
Serves 8 to 12
Herb Omelet Torte (p. 198) or
Eggs Florentine Casserole (p. 203)
Spiced Fruit Cup (p. 468)
Cinnamon-Raisin Biscuits (p. 63) or
Refrigerator Bran Muffins (p. 67)
Spicy Bloody Marys or Virgin Marys° (p. 57)

MEDITERRANEAN INSPIRATION
Serves 4 to 6
Tomato Soup with Herbed Croutons (p. 425)
Grecian Scallops (p. 223) or
Greek Snapper (p. 217)
Orzo with Spinach and Pine Nuts°° (p. 283)
Crusty Loaf Bread
Baklava (p. 319)

MOSTLY COOKING WITHOUT LOOKING
Serves 8
Beer-Baked Brisket (p. 246)
Baked Potatoes
Hearty Baked Beans (p. 445)
Green Salad
French Bread
Ice Cream   Praline Sauce (p. 396)

COOKING FOR A CROWD
Serves 30
Cranberry-Orange Glazed Ham (p. 270)
Baked Beans Quintet°°° (p. 445)
Sweet-and-Sour Hot Slaw° (p. 358)
Dinner Rolls
Peaches 'n' Cream Trifle° (p. 170)

SPECIAL OCCASIONS

LUNCH FOR THE NEW YEAR
Serves 6
Grilled Pork Tenderloin (p. 266) or
Barbecued Ribs (p. 269)
Spicy Hot Black-Eyed Peas (p. 459) or
Hoppin' John (p. 290)
Southern-Style Collards (p. 453)
Cheesy Cornbread (p. 71)
Banana Pudding (p. 166)

VALENTINE DINNER FOR TWO
Serves 2
Cream of Roasted Garlic Soup (p. 425)
Steak au Poivre (p. 238, halve recipe)
Easy Stuffed Potatoes (p. 461)
Ginger Asparagus (p. 444, halve recipe)
Garlic Bread
Chocolate Truffle Mousse (p. 172)

MARDI GRAS BRUNCH
Serves 4
Easy-as-Pie Cheese Straws (p. 31)
Spicy Bloody Marys (p. 57)
Grillades and Grits (p. 242)
Cloud Biscuits (p. 64)
King Cake (p. 88)

REHEARSAL DINNER
Serves 24
Shrimp and Olive Spread (p. 37)   Crackers
Champagne
Chicken Tetrazzini°°° (p. 326) or
Chicken Lasagna Florentine°°° (p. 339)
Green Beans Amandine°° (p. 444-445)
Buttery Pan Rolls (p. 82)
Chocolate Cheesecake with
Whipped Cream Frosting (p. 126), or
Turtle Cheesecake (p. 125)

FOURTH OF JULY EXTRAVAGANZA
Serves 6
Layered Nacho Dip (p. 34)   Tortilla Chips
Picnic Barbecued Chicken (p. 329)
Grilled Corn on the Cob (p. 450)
Chuckwagon Beans (p. 445)
Creamy Coleslaw (p. 358)
Nutty Wheat Loaf (p. 69)
Peach Ice Cream (p. 175)
Fresh Lemonade (p. 51)

THANKSGIVING FEAST
Serves 8 to 10
Deep-Fried Cajun Turkey (p. 344) or
Roast Turkey with Herbs (p. 343)
Old-Fashioned Cornbread Dressing (p. 342)
Giblet Gravy (p. 395)
Tart Cranberry Sauce (p. 398)
Candied Sweet Potatoes (p. 462)
Creamy Broccoli Casserole (p. 447)
Whole Grain Pan Rolls (p. 84)
Carrot Cake Supreme (p. 101)
Rum Pecan Pie (p. 313)

CHRISTMAS DINNER
Serves 8
Stuffed Crown Pork Flambé (p. 263) and/or
Beef Tenderloin with Peppercorns (p. 237)
Roasted Garlic Mashed Potatoes (p. 460)
Green Peas and Pearl Onions° (p. 459)
Ambrosia (p. 364)
Sour Cream Crescent Rolls (p. 84)
Peppermint Candy Cake (p. 106) or
Bûche de Noël (p. 120)
Pear-Almond Tart (p. 306)

HOLIDAY APPETIZER BUFFET
Serves 24
Blue Cheese Spread° (p. 37)   Crackers
Regency Beef Tenderloin with
Horseradish Butter (p. 236)   Party Rolls
Antipasto Dip (p. 33) or
Parmesan-Spinach Spread° (p. 37)   Crackers
Peanut Brittle (p. 158)   Fruitcake Cookies (p. 138)
Rosemary Date-Nut Ball (p. 39)   Gingersnaps
Quick Mulled Apple Cider°° (p. 54) or
Christmas Nog (p. 53)

RECIPE KEY: °*Double recipe*   °°*Triple recipe*   °°°*Quadruple recipe*

METRIC EQUIVALENTS

The recipes that appear in this cookbook use the standard United States method for measuring liquid and dry or solid ingredients (teaspoons, tablespoons, and cups). The information in the following charts is provided to help cooks outside the U.S. successfully use these recipes. All equivalents are approximate.

METRIC EQUIVALENTS FOR DIFFERENT TYPES OF INGREDIENTS

A standard cup measure of a dry or solid ingredient will vary in weight depending on the type of ingredient. A standard cup of liquid is the same volume for any type of liquid. Use the following chart when converting standard cup measures to grams (weight) or milliliters (volume).

STANDARD CUP	FINE POWDER (ex. flour)	GRAIN (ex. rice)	GRANULAR (ex. sugar)	LIQUID SOLIDS (ex. butter)	LIQUID (ex. milk)
1	140 g	150 g	190 g	200 g	240 ml
3/4	105 g	113 g	143 g	150 g	180 ml
2/3	93 g	100 g	125 g	133 g	160 ml
1/2	70 g	75 g	95 g	100 g	120 ml
1/3	47 g	50 g	63 g	67 g	80 ml
1/4	35 g	38 g	48 g	50 g	60 ml
1/8	18 g	19 g	24 g	25 g	30 ml

USEFUL EQUIVALENTS FOR LIQUID INGREDIENTS BY VOLUME

1/4 tsp					=	1 ml		
1/2 tsp					=	2 ml		
1 tsp					=	5 ml		
3 tsp	=	1 tbls		=	1/2 fl oz	=	15 ml	
		2 tbls	= 1/8 cup	=	1 fl oz	=	30 ml	
		4 tbls	= 1/4 cup	=	2 fl oz	=	60 ml	
		5 1/3 tbls	= 1/3 cup	=	3 fl oz	=	80 ml	
		8 tbls	= 1/2 cup	=	4 fl oz	=	120 ml	
		10 2/3 tbls	= 2/3 cup	=	5 fl oz	=	160 ml	
		12 tbls	= 3/4 cup	=	6 fl oz	=	180 ml	
		16 tbls	= 1 cup	=	8 fl oz	=	240 ml	
		1 pt	= 2 cups	=	16 fl oz	=	480 ml	
		1 qt	= 4 cups	=	32 fl oz	=	960 ml	
					33 fl oz	=	1000 ml	= 1 l

USEFUL EQUIVALENTS FOR DRY INGREDIENTS BY WEIGHT

(To convert ounces to grams, multiply the number of ounces by 30.)

1 oz	=	1/16 lb	=	30 g
4 oz	=	1/4 lb	=	120 g
8 oz	=	1/2 lb	=	240 g
12 oz	=	3/4 lb	=	360 g
16 oz	=	1 lb	=	480 g

USEFUL EQUIVALENTS FOR LENGTH

(To convert inches to centimeters, multiply the number of inches by 2.5.)

1 in				=	2.5 cm	
6 in	=	1/2 ft		=	15 cm	
12 in	=	1 ft		=	30 cm	
36 in	=	3 ft	= 1 yd	=	90 cm	
40 in				=	100 cm	= 1 m

USEFUL EQUIVALENTS FOR COOKING/OVEN TEMPERATURES

	FAHRENHEIT	CELSIUS	GAS MARK
Freeze Water	32° F	0° C	
Room Temperature	68° F	20° C	
Boil Water	212° F	100° C	
Bake	325° F	160° C	3
	350° F	180° C	4
	375° F	190° C	5
	400° F	200° C	6
	425° F	220° C	7
	450° F	230° C	8
Broil			Grill

RECIPE INDEX

SUBJECT INDEX

ACKNOWLEDGMENTS

Aletha Soulé, The Loom Co., New York, NY

Annieglass, Watsonville, CA

Barbara Eigen Arts, Inc., Jersey City, NJ

Bridges Antiques, Birmingham, AL

Bromberg's, Birmingham, AL

Calmac Nursery, Cullman, AL

Carolyn Rice, Marietta, GA

Gorham, Mount Kisco, NY

Henhouse Antiques, Birmingham, AL

Jill Rosenwald, Boston, MA

Judy Jackson Pottery, New York, NY

Le Jacquard Francais, Charlottesville, VA

Mariposa, Manchester, MA

Mark's Outdoors, Birmingham, AL

National Cattlemen's Beef Association

National Pork Producers Council

Pastis & Company, New York, NY

Potluck, Accord, NY

Stonefish Pottery, Hartford, CT

The Garden Shop on 280, Birmingham, AL

Union Street Glass, San Francisco, CA

Vietri, Hillsborough, NC

V. Richards Market, Birmingham, AL

Wedgwood, Wall, NJ

Williams-Sonoma, San Francisco, CA